12/02

DATE DUE

			PRINTED IN U.S.A.

12/02

DRAMA
CRITICISM

Guide to Gale Literary Criticism Series

When you need to review criticism of literary works, these are the Gale series to use:

If the author's death date is:	You should turn to:

After Dec. 31, 1959 (or author is still living)

CONTEMPORARY LITERARY CRITICISM

for example: Jorge Luis Borges, Anthony Burgess, William Faulkner, Mary Gordon, Ernest Hemingway, Iris Murdoch

1900 through 1959

TWENTIETH-CENTURY LITERARY CRITICISM

for example: Willa Cather, F. Scott Fitzgerald, Henry James, Mark Twain, Virginia Woolf

1800 through 1899

NINETEENTH-CENTURY LITERATURE CRITICISM

for example: Fyodor Dostoevsky, Nathaniel Hawthorne, George Sand, William Wordsworth

1400 through 1799

LITERATURE CRITICISM FROM 1400 TO 1800 (excluding Shakespeare)

for example: Anne Bradstreet, Daniel Defoe, Alexander Pope, François Rabelais, Jonathan Swift, Phillis Wheatley

SHAKESPEAREAN CRITICISM

Shakespeare's plays and poetry

Antiquity through 1399

CLASSICAL AND MEDIEVAL LITERATURE CRITICISM

for example: Dante, Homer, Plato, Sophocles, Vergil, the Beowulf Poet

---

Gale also publishes related criticism series:

CHILDREN'S LITERATURE REVIEW

This series covers authors of all eras who have written for the preschool through high school audience.

SHORT STORY CRITICISM

This series covers the major short fiction writers of all nationalities and periods of literary history.

POETRY CRITICISM

This series covers poets of all nationalities and periods of literary history.

DRAMA CRITICISM

This series covers dramatists of all nationalities and periods of literary history.

ISSN 1056-4349

DRAMA
CRITICISM

Criticism of the Most Significant and Widely Studied
Dramatic Works from All the World's Literatures

VOLUME 1

Lawrence J. Trudeau, Editor

Linda M. Ross, Assistant Editor

 Gale Research Inc. · *DETROIT* · *LONDON*

STAFF

Lawrence J. Trudeau, *Editor*
Linda M. Ross, *Assistant Editor, DC*

Mary L. Onis, Zoran Minderović, Sean R. Pollock, Joann Prosyniuk,
Joseph C. Tardiff, Bridget Travers, *Associate Editors*

Stephen B. Barnard, John P. Daniel, Andrea Gacki, Tina N. Grant,
Eric Priehs, Allyson J. Wylie, *Assistant Editors*

Jeanne A. Gough, *Permissions & Production Manager*
Linda M. Pugliese, *Production Supervisor*
Maureen Puhl, Jennifer VanSickle, *Editorial Associates*
Donna Craft, Paul Lewon, Lorna Mabunda, Camille Robinson,
Sheila Walencewicz, *Editorial Assistants*

Maureen Richards, *Research Supervisor*
Paula Cutcher-Jackson, Judy L. Gale, *Editorial Associates*
Jennifer Brostrom, Robin Lupa, Mary Beth McElmeel,
Editorial Assistants

Sandra C. Davis, *Permissions Supervisor (Text)*
Josephine M. Keene, Denise M. Singleton, Kimberly F. Smilay,
Permissions Associates
Maria L. Franklin, Michele Lonoconus, Shelly Rakoczy, Shalice Shah,
Nancy K. Sheridan, Rebecca A. Stanko, *Permissions Assistants*

Patricia A. Seefelt, *Permissions Supervisor (Pictures)*
Margaret A. Chamberlain, *Permissions Associate*
Pamela A. Hayes, Keith Reed, *Permissions Assistants*

Mary Beth Trimper, *Production Manager*
Evi Seoud, *Assistant Production Manager*

Arthur Chartow, *Art Director*
Kathleen A. Mouzakis, *Graphic Designer*
C. J. Jonik, Yolanda Y. Latham, *Keyliners*

Contents

Preface

Drama Criticism (*DC*) is principally intended for beginning students of literature and theater as well as the average playgoer. The series is therefore designed to introduce readers to the most frequently studied playwrights of all time periods and nationalities and to present discerning commentary on dramatic works of enduring popular appeal. Furthermore, *DC* seeks to acquaint the reader with the uses and functions of criticism itself. Selected from a diverse and often bewildering body of commentary, the essays in *DC* offer insights into the authors and their works but do not assume that the reader possesses a wide background in literary studies. Where appropriate, reviews of important productions of the plays discussed are also included to give students a heightened awareness of drama as a dynamic art form, one that many claim is fully realized only in performance.

DC was created in response to suggestions by the staffs of high school, college, and public libraries. These librarians observed a need for a series that assembles critical commentary on the world's most renowned dramatists in the same manner as Gale's *Short Story Criticism* (*SSC*) and *Poetry Criticism* (*PC*), which present material on writers of short fiction and poetry. Although playwrights are covered in such Gale literary criticism series as *Contemporary Literary Criticism* (*CLC*), *Twentieth-Century Literary Criticism* (*TCLC*), *Nineteenth-Century Literature Criticism* (*NCLC*), *Literature Criticism from 1400 to 1800* (*LC*), and *Classical and Medieval Literature Criticism* (*CMLC*), *Drama Criticism* directs more concentrated attention on individual dramatists than is possible in the broader, survey-oriented entries in these Gale series.

Scope of the Series

By collecting and organizing commentary on dramatists, *DC* assists students in their efforts to gain insight into literary history, achieve better understanding of the texts, and formulate ideas for papers and assignments. A variety of interpretations and assessments is offered, allowing students to pursue their own interests and promoting awareness that literature is dynamic and responsive to many different opinions.

Each volume of *DC* presents:

- 12-15 entries per volume

- authors and works representing a wide range of nationalities and time periods

- a diversity of viewpoints and critical opinions.

Organization of an Author Entry

Each author entry consists of some or all of the following elements, depending on the scope and complexity of the criticism:

- The **author heading** consists of the playwright's most commonly used name, followed by birth and death dates. If an author consistently wrote under a pseudonym, the pseudonym is listed in the author heading and the real name given in parentheses on the first line of the introduction. Also located at the beginning of the introduction are any name variations under which the dramatist wrote, including transliterated forms of the names of authors whose languages use nonroman alphabets.

- A **portrait** of the author is included when available. Most entries also feature illustrations of people, places, and events pertinent to a study of the playwright and his or her works. When appropriate, photographs of the plays in performance are also presented.

- The **biographical and critical introduction** contains background information that familiarizes the reader with the author and the critical debates surrounding his or her works. When applicable, the introduction is followed by references to other Gale series that contain entries on the playwright.

- The list of **principal works** is divided into two sections, each of which is organized chronologically by date of first publication. If a play was written a significantly long time before it was published (a work by a writer of antiquity, for example), the composition date is used. The first section of the principal works list contains the author's dramatic pieces. The second section provides information on the author's major works in other genres.

- Whenever available, **author commentary** is provided. This section consists of essays or interviews in which the dramatist discusses his or her own work or the art of playwriting in general.

- Essays offering **overviews and general studies of the dramatist's entire literary career** give the student broad perspectives on the writer's artistic development, themes and concerns that recur in several of his or her works, the author's place in literary history, and other wide-ranging topics.

- **Criticism of individual plays** offers the reader in-depth discussions of a select number of the author's most important works. In some cases, the criticism is divided into two sections, each arranged chronologically. When a significant performance of a play can be identified (typically, the premiere of a twentieth-century work), the first section of criticism will feature **production reviews** of this staging. All entries include sections devoted to **critical commentary** that assesses the literary merit of the selected plays. When necessary, essays are carefully excerpted to focus on the work under consideration; often, however, essays and reviews are reprinted in their entirety.

- As an additional aid to students, the critical essays and excerpts are prefaced by **explanatory annotations.** These notes provide several types of useful information, including the critic's reputation and approach to literary studies as well as the scope and significance of the criticism that follows.

- A complete **bibliographic citation,** designed to help the interested reader locate the original essay or book, follows each piece of criticism.

- The **further reading** list at the end of each entry comprises additional studies of the dramatist. It is divided into sections that reflect the organization of the overall author entry and will help students quickly locate the specific information they need.

Other Features

- A **cumulative author index** lists all the authors who have appeared in *DC, CLC, TCLC, NCLC, LC, CMLC, SSC,* and *PC,* as well as cross-references to related titles published by Gale, including *Contemporary Authors* and *Dictionary of Literary Biography.* A complete listing of the series included appears at the beginning of the index.

- A **cumulative nationality index** includes each author featured in *DC* by nationality, followed by the number of the *DC* volume in which the author appears.

- A **cumulative title index** lists in alphabetical order the individual plays discussed in the criticism contained in *DC.* Each title is followed by the author's name and the corresponding volume and page number(s) where commentary on the work may be located. Translations and variant titles are cross-referenced to the title of the play in its original language so that all references to the work are combined in one listing.

A Note to the Reader

When writing papers, students who quote directly from any volume in the Literary Criticism Series may use the following general formats to footnote reprinted criticism. The first example pertains to material drawn from periodicals, the second to materials reprinted from books.

[1]Susan Sontag, "Going to the Theater, Etc.," *Partisan Review* XXXI, No. 3 (Summer 1964), 389-94; excerpted and reprinted in *Drama Criticism,* Vol. 1, ed. Lawrence J. Trudeau (Detroit: Gale Research, 1991), pp. 17-20.

[2]Eugene M. Waith, *The Herculean Hero in Marlowe, Chapman, Shakespeare and Dryden* (Chatto & Windus, 1962); excerpted and reprinted in *Drama Criticism,* Vol. 1, ed. Lawrence J. Trudeau (Detroit: Gale Research, 1991), pp. 237-247.

Suggestions are Welcome

Readers who wish to suggest authors to appear in future volumes of *DC,* or who have other suggestions, are cordially invited to contact the editor.

Acknowledgments

The editors wish to thank the copyright holders of the excerpted criticism included in this volume, the permissions managers of many book and magazine publishing companies for assisting us in securing reprint rights, and Anthony Bogucki for assistance with copyright research. We are also grateful to the staffs of the Detroit Public Library, Wayne State University Purdy/Kresge Library Complex, and the University of Michigan Libraries for making their resources available to us. Following is a list of the copyright holders who have granted us permission to reprint material in this volume of *DC.* Every effort has been made to trace copyright, but if omissions have been made, please let us know.

COPYRIGHTED EXCERPTS IN *DC,* VOLUME 1, WERE REPRINTED FROM THE FOLLOWING PERIODICALS:

Amistad, v. I, 1970 for "A Fiery Baptism" by Calvin C. Hernton. Copyright © 1970 by Calvin Hernton. All rights reserved. Reprinted by permission of Calvin Hernton.—*The Atlantic Monthly,* v. 171, March, 1943. Copyright 1943, renewed 1971 by The Atlantic Monthly Company, Boston, MA./ v. 197, April, 1956 for "The Family in Modern Drama" by Arthur Miller. Copyright 1956 by The Atlantic Monthly Company, Boston, MA. Renewed 1984 by Arthur Miller. Reprinted by permission of the author.—*Black American Literature Forum,* v. 17, Summer, 1983 for "The Descent of Charlie Fuller into Pulitzerland and the Need for African-American Institutions" by Amiri Baraka. Copyright © 1983 Indiana State University. Reprinted by permission of Sterling Lord Literistic, Inc.—*Black World,* v. XXI, April, 1972. © 1972 Johnson Publishing Company, Inc. Reprinted by permission of *Black World.*—*College English,* v. 26, November, 1964 for "Arthur Miller's 'The Crucible'," by Henry Popkin. Copyright © 1964 by the National Council of Teachers of English. Reprinted by permission of the publisher and the author.—*The Commonweal,* v. LVII, February 20, 1953. Copyright © 1953, renewed 1981 by Commonweal Publishing Co., Inc./ v. LXVII, December 27, 1957. Copyright © 1957, renewed 1985 by Commonweal Publishing Co., Inc. Both reprinted by permission of Commonweal Foundation.—*Educational Theatre Journal,* v. XX, October, 1968; v. XXII, December, 1970; v. 25, December, 1973. © 1968, 1970, 1973 University College Theatre Association of the American Theatre Association. All reprinted by permission of the publisher.—*English Studies,* Netherlands, v. 63, February, 1982. © 1982 by Swets & Zeitlinger B.V. Reprinted by permission of the publisher.—*The Hudson Review,* v. XXXV, Autumn, 1982. Copyright © 1982 by The Hudson Review, Inc. Reprinted by permission of the publisher.—*Modern Drama,* v. VII, February, 1965; v. X, December, 1967; v. X, February, 1968; v. XVIII, March, 1975; v. XX, September, 1977. Copyright 1965, 1967, 1968, 1975, 1977 *Modern Drama,* University of Toronto. All reprinted by permission of the publisher.—*Monumenta Nipponica,* v. XXXVII, Spring, 1982. Copyright in Japan, 1982 by *Monumenta Nipponica.* Reprinted by permission of the publisher.—*The Nation,* New York, v. 200, May 10, 1965; v. 234, January 23, 1982. Copyright 1965, 1982 *The Nation* magazine/The Nation Company, Inc. Both reprinted by permission of the publisher.—*The New Leader,* v. LXV, July 12-26, 1982. © 1982 by The American Labor Conference on International Affairs, Inc. Reprinted by permission of the publisher.—*The New Republic,* v. 150, May 16, 1964 for "Everybody's Protest Play" by Robert Brustein. © 1964 The New Republic, Inc. Reprinted by permission of the author.—*The New York Review of Books,* v. IX, December 21, 1967. Copyright © 1967 Nyrev, Inc. Reprinted with permission from *The New York Review of Books.*—*The New York Times,* January 22, 1926; November 21, 1934; February 16, 1939. Copyright 1926, 1934, 1939 by The New York Times Company. All reprinted by permission of the publisher./February 25, 1970. Copyright © 1970 The New York Times Company. Reprinted by permission of the publisher./ February 11, 1949; February 27, 1949; January 23, 1953. Copyright 1949, renewed 1977; copyright 1953, renewed 1981 by The New York Times Company. All reprinted by permission of the publisher./ Section II, November 12, 1944. Copyright 1944 by The New York Times Company. Reprinted by permission of the publisher./ March 8, 1970. Copyright © 1970 by The New York Times Company. Reprinted by permission of the publisher.—*The New Yorker,* v. XXIII, July 26, 1947. Copyright 1947 by The New Yorker Magazine, Inc. Reprinted by permission of the publisher.—*Partisan Review,* v. XXXI, Summer, 1964 for "Going to the Theater, Etc." by Susan Sontag. Copyright © 1964 by *Partisan Review.* Reprinted by permission of the publisher and the author.—*Plays and Players,* v. 22, June, 1975. © 1975 Plusloop. Reprinted with permission of the publisher.—*Renaissance and Modern Studies,* v. 28, 1984. Reprinted by permission of the publisher.—*The Russian Review,* v. 39, April, 1980 for "Laughing Through the Apocalypse: The Comic Structure of Gogol's 'Government Inspector' " by Milton Ehre. Copyright 1980 by The Russian Review, Inc. Reprinted by permission of the author.—*Saturday Review,* v. XLVIII, May 1, 1965. © 1965 *Saturday Review* magazine. Reprinted by permission of the publisher.—*The Saturday Review of Literature,* v. XXV, December 19, 1942; v. XXVII, December 30, 1944; v. XXXII, February 26, 1949. Copyright 1942, 1944, 1949 *Saturday Review* magazine. All reprinted by permission

1951, renewed 1979 by the President and Fellows of Harvard College. Excerpted by permission of the publisher.—Wilder, Thornton. From *Three Plays.* Harper & Row, 1957. Copyright © 1957 by Thornton Wilder. Renewed 1985 by Union Trust Company. All rights reserved. Reprinted by permission of HarperCollins Publishers, Inc. Woodard, Thomas. From "The Electra of Sophocles," in *Sophocles: A Collection of Critical Essays.* Edited by Thomas Woodard. Prentice-Hall, 1966. Copyright © 1966 by Prentice-Hall, Inc. All rights reserved. Used by permission of Prentice-Hall, Inc., Englewood Cliffs, NJ.—Yourcenar, Marguerite. From *Mishima: A Vision of the Void.* Translated by Alberto Manguel and Marguerite Yourcenar. Farrar, Straus and Giroux, 1986. Translation copyright © 1986 by Alberto Manguel. All rights reserved. Reprinted by permission of Farrar, Straus and Giroux, Inc.

PHOTOGRAPHS AND ILLUSTRATIONS APPEARING IN *DC,* VOLUME 1, WERE RECEIVED FROM THE FOLLOWING SOURCES:

James Baldwin

1924-1987

A dramatist, novelist, essayist, poet, juvenile fiction writer and critic, Baldwin is considered one of the most prestigious writers in contemporary American literature. Although he is best known for his novels and essays, his plays, particularly *Blues for Mister Charlie,* had an important influence on American protest theater of the 1960s. Baldwin was considered by many during that period to be the leading literary spokesman for the civil rights movement. Through his works, he exposed the racial and sexual polarization of American society and consistently challenged his audience to confront and resolve these differences. His writings attest to his premise that the African American, as an object of suffering and abuse, represents a universal symbol of human conflict.

Much of Baldwin's work is loosely based on his childhood and adolescence. He was born into poverty in Harlem and raised in a strict religious household headed by his stepfather, a storefront preacher who had migrated from New Orleans. As a junior high school student, Baldwin participated in his school's literary club. The club's academic advisor was Countee Cullen, a renowned poet of the Harlem Renaissance, a major literary and artistic movement of black Americans during the 1920s. In 1938, Baldwin began to preach at the Fireside Pentecostal Church in Harlem, where his sermons emphasized the vision of the apocalypse described in the Book of Revelation. After graduating from high school in 1942, Baldwin renounced the ministry. Moving to New Jersey, he worked at several defense factories and witnessed violent confrontations between urban blacks and whites who had moved from the South in search of employment opportunities spawned by military-related industries. Baldwin returned to Harlem following his stepfather's death in 1943. Over the next five years, he held a succession of menial jobs and began to write book reviews for such periodicals as the *Nation* and the *New Leader.* In 1948, shortly after the publication of his first essay, "The Harlem Ghetto," in *Commentary,* Baldwin moved to Paris. His first and best known novel, *Go Tell It on the Mountain,* was published in 1953. The author received nearly unanimous praise for his skillful evocation of the characters' squalid lives and for his powerful language, which some critics likened to a fire and brimstone oratory.

Despite this success, Baldwin decided to shift from writing novels to composing drama in what he would later call a "desperate and even irresponsible act." The desperation, he maintained, stemmed from the sudden realization that he was being trapped by the expectations of white American society into the position of a "Negro writer" who would not be allowed to progress beyond his initial work. To avoid this snare he wrote *The Amen Corner,* a play that drew on his recollections of the dilemma faced by his parents as they attempted to survive in a society that was bent on their destruction.

Although the drama was written in 1955 and performed by small theater companies throughout the United States, it was not published until its Broadway debut ten years later. Critics have argued that *The Amen Corner* is the more theatrically effective of Baldwin's two dramatic works because of the smooth flow of action and the degree to which it engages the audience in the plot. Yet the second play, *Blues for Mister Charlie,* has received significantly more critical attention. Darwin Turner contended that the reason for this discrepancy is that *Blues for Mister Charlie* is written for a white audience—the segment of society that exercises control over the theater. Carolyn Wedin Sylvander, however, argued that the difference in critical response occurs because *Blues for Mister Charlie* raises universal questions which continue to address the social concerns of successive generations.

Blues for Mister Charlie was first produced on Broadway in 1964. The play was based on the murder of a young black man, Emmett Till. The accused murderer was a white man who was tried and acquitted of the charges but later proudly admitted to performing the deed. The drama received harshly negative reviews from most critics, many of whom agreed with Susan Sontag's assessment of

Baldwin's construction of the play; *Blues,* she claimed, "gets bogged down in repetitions, incoherence, and in all sorts of loose ends of plot and motive." Others attacked Baldwin for perpetuating racial misunderstanding through the use of stereotypes. In contrast to the castigation given by most critics, Tom Driver presented a systematic defense of the play. He asserted that Baldwin was misunderstood because, rather than depicting the racial struggle in the economic and political terms to which most white Americans were accustomed, he chose instead to define "racial strife as *racial* strife, warfare between the black people and white people that is rooted in their separate ways of experiencing life." As a result of this viewpoint, the periodical for which Driver was working refused to publish the review. The critic resigned from his position and published the article elsewhere. The play had a short run which, according to Calvin Hernton, was due not to the artistic failure of the play itself, but to Baldwin's "straightforward, realistic and secular" portrayal of racial issues, which made these problems difficult for whites to confront.

Baldwin's plays were written during the beginning of his participation in the civil rights movement. Throughout the 1960s, he became increasingly prominent in his role as a literary spokesperson for the movement. At the end of the decade, after the assassinations of Martin Luther King, Jr. and Robert Kennedy, Baldwin returned to Paris fearing that his own life was in danger. He continued to write novels, essays, and poetry at his home in France until his death in 1987.

(For further information on Baldwin's life and career, see *Contemporary Literary Criticism,* Vols. 2, 3, 4, 5, 8, 15, 17, 42, 50; *Contemporary Authors,* Vols. 1-4, rev. ed; *Contemporary Authors New Revision Series,* Vol. 3; *Contemporary Authors Biographical Series,* Vol. 1; *Something about the Author,* Vol. 9; *Dictionary of Literary Biography,* Vols. 2, 7, 33; and *Concise Dictionary of American Literary Biography,* 1941-1968.)

PRINCIPAL WORKS

PLAYS

*The Amen Corner 1955
Blues for Mister Charlie 1964

OTHER MAJOR WORKS

Go Tell It on the Mountain (novel) 1953
Notes of a Native Son (essays) 1955
Giovanni's Room (novel) 1956
Nobody Knows My Name: More Notes of a Native Son (essays) 1961
Another Country (novel) 1962
The Fire Next Time (essays) 1963
Going to Meet the Man (short stories) 1965

Tell Me How Long the Train's Been Gone (novel) 1968
If Beale Street Could Talk (novel) 1974
The Devil Finds Work (criticism) 1976
Just above My Head (novel) 1979 .
The Evidence of Things Not Seen (nonfiction) 1985
Jimmy's Blues: Selected Poems (poetry) 1985
The Price of the Ticket: Collected Nonfiction, 1948-1985 (essays) 1985

**This work was written and first produced in 1955 but was not published until its production on Broadway in 1965.

AUTHOR COMMENTARY

Notes for *Blues* (1964)

[*In the following essay, Baldwin elucidates the conflicts surrounding the writing of* Blues for Mister Charlie. *He particularly concentrates on the difficulty in developing the murderer Lyle Britten as a sympathetic character. Baldwin observes that although he himself finds such a figure repellent, he wished to show in Lyle the belief that "no man is a villain in his own eyes."*]

This play [**Blues for Mister Charlie**] has been on my mind—has been bugging me—for several years. It is unlike anything else I've ever attempted in that I remember vividly the first time it occurred to me; for in fact, it did not occur to me, but to Elia Kazan. Kazan asked me at the end of 1958 if I would be interested in working in the Theatre. It was a generous offer, but I did not react with great enthusiasm because I did not then, and don't now, have much respect for what goes on in the American Theatre. I am not convinced that it *is* a Theatre; it seems to me a series, merely, of commercial speculations, stale, repetitious, and timid. I certainly didn't see much future for me in that frame-work, and I was profoundly unwilling to risk my morale and my talent—my life—in endeavors which could only increase a level of frustration already dangerously high.

Nevertheless, the germ of the play persisted. It is based, very distantly indeed, on the case of Emmett Till—the Negro youth who was murdered in Mississippi in 1955. The murderer in this case was acquitted. (His brother, who helped him do the deed, is now a deputy sheriff in Rulesville, Mississippi.) After his acquittal, he recounted the facts of the murder—for one cannot refer to his performance as a confession—to William Bradford Huie, who wrote it all down in an article called "Wolf Whistle." I do not know why the case pressed on my mind so hard—but it would not let me go. I absolutely dreaded committing myself to writing a play—there were enough people around already telling me that I couldn't write novels— but I began to see that my fear of the form masked a much deeper fear. That fear was that I would never be able to draw a valid portrait of the murderer. In life, obviously, such people baffle and terrify me and, with one part of my mind at least, I hate them and would be willing to kill them. Yet, with another part of my mind, I am aware that no man is a villain in his own eyes. Something in the man knows—*must* know—that what he is doing is evil; but in order to accept the knowledge the man would have to change. What is ghastly and really almost hopeless in our racial situation now is that the crimes we have committed are so great and so unspeakable that the acceptance of this knowledge would lead, literally, to madness. The human being, then, in order to protect himself, closes his eyes, compulsively repeats his crimes, and enters a spiritual darkness which no one can describe.

But if it is true, and I believe it is, that all men are brothers, then we have the duty to try to understand this wretched man; and while we probably cannot hope to liberate him, begin working toward the liberation of his children. For we, the American people, have created him, he is our servant; it is we who put the cattleprodder in his hands, and we are responsible for the crimes that he commits. It is we who have locked him in the prison of his color. It is we who have persuaded him that Negroes are worthless human beings, and that it is his sacred duty, as a white man, to protect the honor and purity of his tribe. It is we who have forbidden him, on pain of exclusion from the tribe, to accept his beginnings, when he and black people loved each other, and rejoice in them, and use them; it is we who have made it mandatory—honorable—that white father should deny black son. These are grave crimes indeed, and we have committed them and continue to commit them in order to make money.

The play then, for me, takes place in Plaguetown, U. S. A., now. The plague is race, the plague is our concept of Christianity: and this raging plague has the power to destroy every human relationship. I once took a short trip with Medgar Evers to the back-woods of Mississippi. He was investigating the murder of a Negro man by a white storekeeper which had taken place months before. Many people talked to Medgar that night, in dark cabins, with their lights out, in whispers; and we had been followed for many miles out of Jackson, Mississippi, not by a lunatic with a gun, but by state troopers. I will never forget that night, as I will never forget Medgar—who took me to the plane the next day. We promised to see each other soon. When he died, something entered into me which I cannot describe, but it was then that I resolved that nothing under heaven would prevent me from getting this play done. We are walking in terrible darkness here, and this is one man's attempt to bear witness to the reality and the power of light. (pp. xiii-xv)

> *James Baldwin, "Notes for Blues," in his* Blues for Mister Charlie, *Dial Press, 1964, pp. xiii-xv.*

Notes for *The Amen Corner* (1968)

[*In the excerpt below, Baldwin relates the circumstances that precipitated his shift from writing novels to composing drama, noting in particular his desire to break away from what he felt were societal boundaries that trapped him as a "Negro writer." He also likens the relationship between playwright and audience to that of preacher and* congregation, *in which the evangelist attempts to "involve the people, even against their will, to shake them up, and, hopefully, to change them."*]

Writing **The Amen Corner** I remember as a desperate and even rather irresponsible act—it was certainly considered irresponsible by my agent at that time. She did not wish to discourage me, but it was her duty to let me know that the American theatre was not exactly clamoring for plays on obscure aspects of Negro life, especially one written by a virtually unknown author whose principal effort until that time had been one novel [*Go Tell It on the Mountain*]. She may sincerely have believed that I had gotten my signals mixed and earnestly explained to me that, with one novel under my belt, it was the *magazine* world that was open to me, *not* the world of the theatre; I sensibly ought to be pursuing the avenue that was open, especially since I had no money at all. I couldn't explain to her or to myself why I wasted so much time on a play. I knew, for one thing, that very few novelists are able to write plays and I really had no reason to suppose that I could be an exception to this age-old, iron rule. I was perfectly aware that it would probably never be produced, and, furthermore, I didn't even have any ambition to conquer the theatre. To this last point we shall return, for I was being very dishonest, or perhaps merely very cunning, with myself concerning the extent of my ambition. (p. xi)

I had no idea whether or not I could write a play, but I was absolutely determined that I would not, not at that moment in my career, not at that moment in my life, attempt another novel. I did not trust myself to do it. I was really terrified that I would, without even knowing that I was doing it, try to repeat my first success and begin to imitate myself. I knew that I had more to say and much, much more to discover than I had been able to indicate in *Mountain.* . . . [So I] began what I told myself was a "writing exercise": by which I meant I'm still a young man, my family now knows that I really am a writer—that was very important to me—let us now see if I am equipped to go the distance, and let's try something we've never tried before. The first line written in **The Amen Corner** is now Margaret's line in the Third Act: "It's a awful thing to think about, the way love never dies!" That line, of course, says a great deal about me—the play says a great deal about me—but I was thinking not only, not merely, about the terrifying desolation of my private life but about the great burdens carried by my father. I was old enough by now, at last, to recognize the nature of the dues he had paid, old enough to wonder if I could possibly have paid them, old enough, at last, at last, to know that I had loved him and had wanted him to love me. I could see that the nature of the battle we had fought had been dictated by the fact that our temperaments were so fatally the same: neither of us could bend. And when I began to think about what had happened to him, I began to see why he was so terrified of what was surely going to happen to me.

The Amen Corner comes somewhere out of that. For to think about my father meant that I had also to think about my mother and the stratagems she was forced to use to save her children from the destruction awaiting them just outside her door. It is because I know what Sister Margaret goes through, and what her male child is menaced by, that I become so unmanageable when people ask me to confirm their hope that there has been *progress*—what a word!—in white-black relations. There has certainly not been enough progress to solve Sister Margaret's dilemma: how to treat her husband and her son as men and at the same time to protect them from the bloody consequences of trying to be a man in this society. No one yet knows, or is in the least prepared to speculate on, how high a bill we will yet have to pay for what we have done to Negro men and women. She is in the church because her society has left her no other place to go. Her sense of reality is dictated by the society's assumption, which also becomes her own, of her inferiority. Her need for human affirmation, and also for vengeance, expresses itself in her merciless piety; and her love, which is real but which is also at the mercy of her genuine and absolutely justifiable terror, turns her into a tyrannical matriarch. In all of this, of course, she loses her old self—the fiery, fast-talking little black woman whom Luke loved. Her triumph, which is also, if I may say so, the historical triumph of the Negro people in this country, is that she sees this finally and accepts it, and, although she has lost everything, also gains the keys to the kingdom. The kingdom is love, and love is selfless, although only the self can lead one there. She gains herself.

One last thing: concerning my theatrical ambitions, and my cunning or dishonesty—I was armed, I knew, in attempting to write the play, by the fact that I was born in the church. I knew that out of the ritual of the church, historically speaking, comes the act of the theatre, the *communion* which is the theatre. And I knew that what I wanted to do in the theatre was to recreate moments I remembered as a boy preacher, to involve the people, even against their will, to shake them up, and, hopefully, to change them. I knew that an unknown black writer could not possibly hope to achieve this forum. I did not want to enter the theatre on the theatre's terms, but on mine. And so I waited. And the fact that **The Amen Corner** took ten years to reach the professional stage says a great deal more about the American theatre than it says about this author. The American Negro really is a part of this country, and on the day we face this fact, and not before that day, we will become a nation and possibly a great one. (pp. xv-xvii)

> *James Baldwin, "Notes for 'The Amen Corner'," in* The Amen Corner, *Dial Press, 1968, pp. xi-xvii.*

OVERVIEWS AND GENERAL STUDIES

Carlton W. Molette   (essay date 1977)

[*In the following essay, Molette assesses Baldwin's plays based on theatrical rather than literary criteria. He concludes that the smooth flow of action and audience engagement with the events on stage make* The Amen Corner *more effective theatrically than* Blues for Mister Charlie.]

At first glance, the whole subject of Baldwin as a playwright seems destined to be rather uncomplicated. After all, he has had only two plays professionally produced, and subsequently published. But the depth of Baldwin's characters simply does not permit uncomplicated answers to questions of some substance. Baldwin's characters—those in his plays—have the same kind of depth and complexity with which the characters in his novels are endowed. After all, he is a novelist; and novelists—the good ones—are supposed to be able to do that: create characters of great depth and complexity. But novels provide ways of delving into character that plays do not have at their disposal. And the concern here is with plays.

I will leave it to the literary critics to examine Baldwin's literature—to examine Baldwin as a writer. I am a theater worker, and I will confine my concern to Baldwin as a playwright, and to the plays that he has wrought. I would further like to emphasize that plays are *wrought,* not written. This is an important concept to reckon with. Writers work wherever and whenever they will. Playwrights must work with and for the other theater workers, or theaterwrights. Plays are events that occur, not words that are written. So, to examine James Baldwin as a playwright is to examine something that only seldom, and quite inadvertently, has to do with things literary. My concerns with any script have largely to do with such questions as: Does it come alive on the stage? Does the action of the play flow smoothly and continuously? Will it hold the attention of the audience? Will it have meaning and worth for the audience? There have been many great writers throughout history who have not been able to *wright* a play that is successful, according to the above criteria.

Remarkably enough, James Baldwin's very first play, **The Amen Corner,** is one of the most successful Afro-American plays that I have seen. The play was first presented at Howard University, and directed by Owen Dodson. At its best, the collaboration of playwright and director causes the work of both to be better than it would have been otherwise. Baldwin's influence upon Dodson and Dodson's influence upon Baldwin have, undoubtedly, made a better theatrical event than either would have been able to produce without the collaborative interchange that took place while the premiere production of **The Amen Corner** was in rehearsal. **The Amen Corner** is built upon the rhythms of the Afro-American church. The action of the play flows smoothly and effortlessly to the rhythms of the language and of the music of the play. This flow of the action includes the transitions back and forth between the three locales of the play. The dominant force in the play is the rhythm. The congregation is swept up in this rhythm. The congregation is compelled to participate. I say "the congregation" because this play is more of a black church ritual than it is a play in the sense that modern Western culture defines a play. So one of the major goals in this particular collaborative effort between playwright and director must be to affect the congregation in a way very similar to that of the black church ritual. This effect might be called a purgation of the emotions. Two of the most important means of creating this purgation of the emotions have already been suggested. First, there is the rhythmic response from the congregation to the events on stage. Secondly, the very response of those who are gathered together reinforces the rhythm and the sense of belonging, of community, of togetherness within the congregation. Both of these are important elements in the traditional black church ritual.

The Amen Corner is also more a black church ritual because of its content. *The Amen Corner* is about love—about the enduring strength that love gives—about the love between (not among) four people who comprise a particular black family. In addition to family love, there is an extended-family love that surrounds the congregation on the stage (the actors) and the congregation in the auditorium (the audience). There is a love that transcends all the petty bickering, the jealousies, the family fights. And this love is made to come alive in the theater via the same ritual techniques that the black church uses. As a black ritual event, *The Amen Corner* works. The first professional production was moving as theater ought to be but seldom is. But was it moving because of something contained in James Baldwin's script? The professional premiere was produced and directed by Frank Silvera, designed by Vantile Whitfield, and performed by a phenomenally impressive cast, headed by Bea Richards. The cast also included Maidie Norman, Juanita Moore, Robert DeCoy, Isabelle Sanford, Whitman Mays, and Gloria Foster. It is highly doubtful that such a cast could have been put together—even by Frank Silvera—if there had been some other meaningful work available to black actors in Los Angeles at the time. But, the point I want to make is this: With a cast like that one, one might be moved by a play that is only mediocre to fairly good. It has happened before. But there have been other productions of this play. The range in production quality has been rather wide. I have seen audiences moved by this play even when it was not particularly well produced. Now, that is something special.

On the other hand, the play is not perfect. And people do expect critics to find fault with things. Ironically enough, *The Amen Corner* is at its worst as a play precisely when it is at its best as literature. There are several two-character scenes between the members of the Alexander family that are true literary gems. They are also the scenes of greatest character revelation. They actually tell us too much about the characters. Now, all that is told needs to be told; but some of it ought to be told through means other than words. That is what actors are supposed to use their "instruments" to do. The emotional tonality of these scenes makes it mandatory that the tempo be slowed; thus, the rhythm becomes less pronounced. On these few occasions, in act two of a three-act play, the action slows down, and the word becomes far more important than the deed. In the theater, that usually means trouble. This is especially a problem with the scenes that involve the father (Luke), because he is confined to his sickbed, making visual interest through movement very difficult to achieve, as well.

Of course, the Frank Silvera production was able to mask this flaw in play construction quite effectively. As the mother (Margaret), Bea Richards was capable of maintaining interest with her voice alone. And the language in these scenes is beautiful and powerful in and of itself. On the other hand, we are frequently told essentially the same thing for several speeches in a row. The use of repetition can work very well when the goal is to create a rhythmic response from the congregation. But in these quiet, introspective, two-character scenes, repetition primarily serves to increase the playing time of the scene. Having pointed out what I consider to be the major flaw of the play, I must add that, when I directed a production of *The Amen Corner,* I was not willing to cut a single one of those words.

I have never directed Baldwin's other play, but I think I would have virtually the same reaction to the words in *Blues for Mister Charlie* if I were placed in a position of deciding on some specific words that could just as well be omitted. I seriously doubt that there are any. One of the most illuminating moments that I have spent in a theater was spent in watching a particular scene in *Blues for Mister Charlie.* This particular scene is a soliloquy. I am sure that, if I had read the scene prior to seeing it performed, I would have said, "It will not work on the stage. It is too long. And besides, soliloquies are no longer acceptable as a principal means of character revelation." Fortunately, I was privileged to witness a truly gifted actress, Miss Diana Sands, perform the soliloquy before I had an opportunity to say all of those incorrect things. But again the question arises, Is it the play? Or did Miss Sands make it work in spite of the script rather than because of it? After all Diana Sands could transform even *The Owl and the Pussycat* into an arresting evening of theater. I am afraid that, in the hands of a lesser artist than Miss Sands, that soliloquy could be transformed from the highpoint to the lowpoint of the play. On the other hand, this soliloquy does not stand out as a readily perceived flaw. The play is too complex, really, for anything to stand out as a readily perceived anything. Again Baldwin has wrought a play in which its worst theatrical characteristics are its best literary characteristics. As a piece of literature, the complexity of *Blues for Mister Charlie* is an admirable trait; as a theatrical event, that same complexity is its major flaw.

But, before we get into the details of the above assertion, let us look for a moment at both of these plays, and the times out of which they grew. *The Amen Corner* is a play of the 1950s. It tells a story of love and hope for a better tomorrow. The story is told in an uncomplicated, straightforward manner. It grew out of the years just before college students were marching, arm in arm, to the strains of "We Shall Overcome." On the other hand, *Blues for Mister Charlie* grew out of the years just before Watts, and the others, burned. *Blues for Mister Charlie* is a "protest" play. It is a complicated, angry play. It is a play that is self-consciously black. When blacks do protest plays, to whom do they protest? To whites, of course. So *Blues for Mister Charlie* is largely aimed at a white audience. This is not intended to imply that the play says nothing to blacks. On the other hand, *The Amen Corner* does not protest to whites; it informs, educates, illuminates blacks. The play was first staged on the campus of a black university. It is not self-consciously black. The play assumes that there are some elementary aspects of black culture that do not require explanation within the body of the play. It assumes, in effect, a black audience. It is not an anti-white play, it is an a-white play.

Blues for Mister Charlie tries to be all things to all people. It tries to explain whites to blacks and blacks to whites. That probably requires two different plays. That is certainly one major reason for the complexity of the play. And, since plays must be absorbed in the span of time it takes to perform them, complexity can be a liability. Conversations among average white audience members in the theater lobby during intermission and following ***Blues for Mister Charlie*** all seemed to revolve around the fact that there was content that the blacks understood that the whites did not. "What are *they* laughing at?"—meaning the blacks in the audience—the whites kept asking each other. But the reverse situation applied as well. The white characters were frequently not understood, or not accepted as valid, by the black audience members. Actually, blacks did not want to face an essential truth in the character of Lyle Britten. That truth is that Lyle is not some kind of a demonic redneck character. Lyle is *not* a bad guy— just ask Lyle, he'll tell you. Baldwin says, "No man is a villain in his own eyes." [see Author Commentary dated 1964]. So most blacks in the audience were presented with a character that they either refused to admit was there, or refused to admit was true. What they wanted was some kind of wild-eyed, nigger-hating, stereotyped redneck villain. Instead they got a real man who was backed into a corner, not by Richard Henry but by the system.

But that is only one of a number of paradoxes. Richard Henry thinks he must destroy "Mr. Charlie" in order to achieve his own salvation. On the other hand, he knows that the system is programmed to destroy him if he attempts to destroy the man. He knows that he cannot realistically expect to beat the whole system singlehandedly. So he knows that his act of destruction perpetrated against "Mr. Charlie" will inevitably result in his own destruction. Yet he wants to live. He is not suicidal. Still a third paradox. And this one clearly marks this as a statement of 1960s point of view. The leader of the white community and the leader of the black community get together to tell each other how much progress they are making within the system. But even they know that it is a lie.

In addition to these, and other, paradoxes, ***Blues for Mister Charlie*** is made even more complicated by a number of fluctuations. There are fluctuations in at least three major aspects of the production: time, locale, and acting style. Time fluctuates between time present and time past. The locale of the play also fluctuates between two distinctly different atmospheres. There are black locales and white locales. There is a fluctuation between two distinct acting styles. Most of the performance requires an illusionistic, representational style of acting—one in which the action of the play revolves around relationships between the actors. But there is some fluctuation into the realm of soliloquy that requires quite a different approach, or style, for the actors. When the play moves into the realm of soliloquy, a less illusionistic style is necessitated—one that requires the actor to relate more inwardly to his own character; and at the same time, more outwardly to the audience, but not to the other characters.

Blues for Mister Charlie fluctuates among eight different combinations of these six elements: black atmosphere,

white atmosphere, time present, time past, representational style, soliloquy style. If the play is to have its optimum effect upon the audience, the audience must be able to keep up with these fluctuations. Further, the audience must manage this without devoting a great deal of concentration to the effort. After all, primary attention must be devoted to receiving the message, not to determining the where, the when, and the how of the transmission of the message. In spite of all these complexities, the play can work as a play. The inherent complexities do create production problems. Actually, the script would work better as a film than it does as a play. But Baldwin has achieved one very important requisite for *wrighting* a play. Further, this achievement is undoubtedly why the play works, despite its complexity. Baldwin has not attempted to provide complete verbal transitions for all of these fluctuations and paradoxes.

I am sure that such restraint must be difficult for a novelist to achieve. Such restraint must be particularly difficult for a novelist to achieve because it requires that one artist turn his creative efforts over to someone else before it can be completed. So the transitions are achieved through the use of music, lighting, scenery, costume, and, of course, acting. That requires from the playwright a trust of and a reliance upon many other artists. The ability to accomplish that collaborative working relationship may very well be the reason for Baldwin's success as a playwright where so many other novelists have failed.

Certainly, Baldwin would be an even better playwright if he would gain more experience in the theater. But who can blame him for not doing so? After all, his first obligation is the physical and artistic survival of James Baldwin. Given the present system of producing plays professionally in the United States, we are lucky indeed to get one play per decade from the likes of James Baldwin. (pp. 183-88)

> *Carlton W. Molette, "James Baldwin as a Playwright," in* James Baldwin: A Critical Evaluation, *edited by Therman B. O'Daniel, Howard University Press, 1977, pp. 183-88.*

Darwin T. Turner   (essay date 1977)

[In the essay below, Turner argues that although The Amen Corner *is the better of Baldwin's two plays,* Blues for Mister Charlie *has met with greater public success because it is written for a white audience. Turner further contends that this is an indication of the difficulty encountered by the black artist who desires to address his own culture through a medium over which white society exercises complete control.]*

In his two dramas—***Blues for Mister Charlie*** (1964) and ***The Amen Corner,*** produced professionally in 1965 but written during the 1950s—James Baldwin reflects two divergent positions of contemporary black dramatists. Ironically, in the earlier of the two—***The Amen Corner***—he more closely resembles Afro-American dramatists of the 1970s than in ***Blues for Mister Charlie,*** even though the latter play not only aroused sensation among theatergoers in general but also evoked admiration from many blacks.

The issue that distinguishes one group of contemporary

black playwrights from another is whether the black writer should direct himself to a white audience—to entertain them, or to educate them about black people—or should direct himself to a black audience—to educate them to awareness of their needs. Many people fail to appreciate the dilemma. They argue that a writer should not concern himself with the cultural or racial identity of his audience. Such an attitude, however, is naive and academic in a society in which blacks and whites cling to differing visions of the realities of black life. What white Americans have learned of black life through Joel Chandler Harris, Thomas Dixon, Margaret Mitchell, and William Faulkner is often their only vision of the reality of that life. Black people know, however, that the white literary view frequently ignores or contradicts the facts of black life. One group's reality is the other group's stereotype.

Traditionally, black writers have directed their works to the white population, either to achieve personal rewards or to serve black people by winning support from whites. This habit has governed black playwrights even more because they have known that they must win box-office support from white patrons. Consequently, Langston Hughes (*Mulatto*, 1935) appealed for sympathy for a mulatto who wants to be identified publicly as his white father's son. Lorraine Hansberry (*A Raisin in the Sun*, 1959) taught that, despite their lack of money, urban blacks possess and practice such revered American virtues as pride, decency, and hard work, and define "the good life" in ways identical to those of American whites. LeRoi Jones (*Dutchman*, 1963) denounced whites who, stereotyping blacks as dull-witted and imitative sexual studs, destroy any blacks who refuse to conform to the stereotype. All these sought to educate white audiences.

In contrast, since 1965 a group of black playwrights, following the lead of Imamu Amiri Baraka (LeRoi Jones), has consciously directed its work toward black audiences in what is called Black Arts drama. Such playwrights propose to educate blacks to awareness of their needs for liberation, either by teaching them to know their enemies or by making them aware of the internal problems of black communities.

In his dramas, James Baldwin has followed both paths of contemporary black playwrights—most consciously writing for white spectators when he seems to be denouncing them (*Blues for Mister Charlie*), most effectively creating for black audiences when he seems unaware of any audience (*The Amen Corner*). Yet the varying reactions to the two plays clearly illustrate the problem of the black playwright. Sensational, melodramatic, and written for whites, *Blues for Mister Charlie* provoked controversy that increased the attention accorded to it. The more thoughtful, more realistic, more credible *The Amen Corner* waited a decade for professional production, then appeared almost without comment. The question that arises is, Can a black be respected simultaneously as an artist and as a faithful portrayer of black life if his reputation depends upon an audience that neither knows nor cares about the world depicted by that black, but is concerned only with the effect of that world on the lives of white Americans?

Blues for Mister Charlie tells the story of Richard Henry, a black youth, who temporarily found success in the entertainment world in the North before drug addiction ended his career. When he returns to his home in the South, he discovers love, which gives him a new strength. But, unwilling to relapse to the subordinate position required for blacks in his community, he provokes a confrontation with Lyle Britten, a white store-owner, whose murder of a black man has been overlooked by white keepers of law and order. Because Richard Henry insults the white store-owner by asserting his own economic and sexual superiority, Richard is killed. The white murderer is acquitted, however, because his wife claims that Henry tried to assault her. The traditional lie succeeds because another witness, Parnell, who considers himself a friend of black people, cannot force himself to deny publicly the words of a respected Southern white woman. As the play ends, the Reverend Meridian Henry, Richard's father, has begun to understand that he cannot depend upon white men of good will to effect improvements in interracial relationships. Instead, blacks themselves must effect the change, and must arm themselves for protection against whites.

When Baldwin wrote the play, protest marches were timely and popular subject matter. Still fresh in the minds of black people was the torture-murder of young Emmett Till in Mississippi by white men subsequently acquitted by a white jury. Furthermore, the play appealed to many young blacks because Richard Henry was the first black stage character in their lifetime to attack white society boldly.

Nevertheless, *Blues for Mister Charlie* is written for a white audience. It is patterned on the protest tradition, modified only slightly—perhaps because Baldwin remembered that, in earlier years, he had denounced that tradition. Lyle Britten, the antagonist, is treated so gently that, whereas blacks despise him, whites can find sympathy. To blacks he is an arrogant and vulgar brute, characterized by the very lust and coarseness with which racists stereotype blacks. An adulterer, he raped a black woman whom he regarded merely as an exploitable sex object. He murdered her husband when the husband objected to the illicit relationship. Recalling the sexual pleasure he found in the woman, he arrogantly presumes that she found equal pleasure in him. He murders Richard because he cannot hold his own in a verbal duel. Yet he sees himself—and undoubtedly many whites see him—as a good-natured white American who loves his child, works hard at his business, and professes to have no ill will toward blacks.

The wife, whose lie results in her husband's acquittal, is handled less gently; nevertheless, Baldwin carefully provides white spectators with an excuse for her behavior. Conscious of aging into a weak position in the marriage race, she considered herself lucky to find Britten. Now, fearful of losing her husband, she will do anything necessary to protect him.

Other characters familiar to white audiences through literature at least are Parnell, an ineffectual liberal supported by the wealth of his dead father and motivated by the memory of his love for a black girl; Meridian Henry, a minister whose dignity recalls the temper that James Weldon Johnson ascribed to the creators of the spirituals;

Richard Henry, a rebellious and arrogant black youth who boasts of the white women he has known; and Juanita, who attracts and inspires Parnell and the Henrys.

Because of his own belief in the necessity of integration, Baldwin suggests the interrelationship of blacks and whites by stage directions for shadowy images of whites appearing in the background during the black scenes and the sounds of black church services as a background for the white scenes. Less obviously, he suggests the similarity of blacks and whites by ascribing to whites the moral weaknesses stereotypically identified with blacks and by ascribing to blacks the virtues traditionally identified with whites. For example, as I noted earlier, Lyle Britten exhibits the carnality that white society has projected as a dominant characteristic of black men. In contrast, the Reverend Meridian Henry displays the courage identified with whites. Baldwin even draws comparison between Henry's proposal to take a gun to church and the manner in which American pioneers armed themselves for protection against "savages."

Despite the interest of blacks in the boldness of Richard Henry, the play seems to speak more directly to whites than to blacks. *Blues for Mister Charlie,* like works by some white Americans of the 1960s, calls upon the Parnells of America to defend their convictions even if such action pits them against their neighbors. Otherwise, black men of peace and goodwill, like Meridian Henry, must use weapons to defend themselves.

In contrast, although it was written in the 1950s, when many black writers were promoting integration, *The Amen Corner* seems more clearly designed as a drama written about black experience for a black audience. In this respect, it resembles Black Arts drama, in which the dramatist presumes that he must write without concern for the white spectator, who exists outside the black experience and without comprehension of it. I do not wish to imply that Baldwin consciously designed the play for the education of a black audience. Instead, I am suggesting that he found strength in writing meaningfully about an experience he knew while assuming that his audience would be equally familiar with that experience.

The Amen Corner is the story of the lesson in godliness learned by Sister Margaret, a minister who demands moral perfection from her congregation. She disapproves of a parishioner's driving a liquor truck; she wishes her son to have no life outside the church. She even suggests that a young wife consider leaving her husband in order to discover purity in God. Although Margaret considers herself so flawless as a leader that she volunteers to guide a Philadelphia congregation to the path to God, her power is challenged by her son and by members of her own congregation, who envy her position and resent her autocratic rule. Her situation is further complicated by the return of her musician-husband who, she has said, deserted her. Dismayed by discovery of this allegation, Luke, the husband, little by little forces Margaret to recall the past and to perceive the truth that her venture into religion was not a response to a call from God but a flight motivated by her own fear of life. When Margaret lost a child because she was too undernourished to give it life-strength, she blamed

her husband. Knowing her need for someone to protect her and finding no such strength in Luke, she fled into a fanatic abjuration of the flesh, into the worship of a merciless God. Simultaneously, because Luke needed comfort, which he could not find in Margaret, he turned to drinking. After her desertion, he tried to forget love by involving himself totally in his musical career, but he knew that a career could not be an adequate substitute for the human love he needed. Despite her efforts to abjure her need for love, Margaret finally admits that her greatest wish always has been to be a woman and a wife. Her discovery comes too late. She loses both husband and career. After Luke dies, her new sense of herself as a human being in love incapacitates her to preach the authoritarian, wrathful message that has enslaved her congregation. Ironically, then, at the very moment at which a new understanding of and compassion for human beings makes her most fit to be a minister, she loses her position. However, hope remains for her son, David. Enlightened, educated by the experience of his parents, he leaves the church, not to flee into music as a refuge (as his mother had fled to a merciless God) but to seek in music a means of expressing his people and their needs.

Freeing himself from the need to create characters familiar to white spectators, Baldwin projected individuals who are known within the black culture: a hypocritical churchgoer who professes to support her minister while she simultaneously agitates and leads a rebellion against the minister; a male gossip who resents female authority. Such freedom of portrayal extends to the major characters. Although Luke, like Meridian Henry, may be somewhat idealized as a man who blends emotion with wisdom derived from experience, Margaret appears vividly as an excessively arrogant, compassionless minister who must learn her humanity and her need for human love.

Baldwin's theme in *The Amen Corner* is not restricted to black people. The need for love and understanding is propounded as emphatically in *Another Country,* where Baldwin shows that white, middle-class people must learn to love each other. This theme, in fact, dominates Baldwin's work: human beings must learn to give themselves totally to other human beings if humankind is to survive. Nevertheless, he seems to develop this recurrent thesis more credibly within the traditionally religious context and church setting of *The Amen Corner* than in the topical, political situation of *Blues for Mister Charlie.*

In short, in *The Amen Corner* Baldwin achieved a success in theme and characterization surpassing his effort in *Blues for Mister Charlie.* His success, I feel, did not result solely from his re-creation of a church setting that was familiar to him but from his presumption that his audience required no interpretation, no modification, because it already knew the cultural setting. Thus Baldwin achieved an artistic freedom rarely granted a black dramatist except when he works within the theater of a black community.

The question raised earlier in this essay, however, remains to challenge the black artist and students of black culture. If the black artist, like artists of any group, writes most effectively about his own culture, how severely is his growth restricted by publishing houses which will promote his work only when it appeals widely to audiences of a different culture? *Blues for Mister Charlie* appeared as a separate volume within a year after its production on the professional stage. *The Amen Corner,* artistically superior, was produced first at a black college, then remained unpublished for many years, until it finally appeared in the Dial Press edition of 1968.

Given such conditions, is it any wonder that most supporters of Black Arts literature disdain efforts to secure production through the established and white-controlled publishing companies? Black artists will remain forever in an untenable position if they must modify their knowledge of black life to conform to the visions of reality maintained by those who have remained aloof from that black life. Yet fame and fortune in America require publication by white-controlled companies and production before white audiences. *The Amen Corner* is art; *Blues for Mister Charlie* earned sensation and money for Baldwin. (pp. 189-94)

> *Darwin T. Turner, "James Baldwin in the Dilemma of the Black Dramatist," in* James Baldwin: A Critical Evaluation, *edited by Therman B. O'Daniel, Howard University Press, 1977, pp. 189-94.*

Carolyn Wedin Sylvander   (essay date 1980)

[In the following essay, Sylvander examines Baldwin's stagecraft and finds that although The Amen Corner *is*

Baldwin in New York.

more theatrically effective, Blues for Mister Charlie *is of more lasting significance because the issues it raises continue to be current.]*

In "Notes for *The Amen Corner*," which preface the published play [see Author Commentary dated 1968], James Baldwin speaks of his intent in writing for the theater, a difficult undertaking for any essayist and novelist.

"I knew that out of the ritual of the church, historically speaking, comes the act of the theatre, the *communion* which is the theatre. And I knew that what I wanted to do in the theatre was to recreate moments I remembered as a boy preacher, to involve the people, even against their will, to shake them up, and, hopefully, to change them."

In a 1961 essay [published in *Negro Digest,* April 1966], Baldwin stated the "real aims" of the theater are "to instruct through terror and pity and delight and love. The only thing we can do now for the tired businessman is to scare the living daylights out of him."

The active, physical community of the theatrical experience involves, educates, and changes an audience more readily and more noticeably than do the essay and novel forms. Such a simple (and not so simple) element as music, threading its way through the novels and short stories, reaching a kind of climax in his latest novel, *Just Above My Head,* can be used to hold the theatrical experience together, and to reach and involve even an audience which has not previously *heard* that music. Such involvement is much less predictable with the novel or short story, where evoking sound depends entirely upon the reader's previous sound experience.

Carlton W. Molette, playwright, drama scholar, and director of play production at Spelman College, Atlanta, has written from the theatrical rather than literary point of view about Baldwin's two published plays: *The Amen Corner,* written in the 1950s, first professionally produced in 1965, and published in 1968; and *Blues for Mister Charlie,* written, produced, and published in 1964 [see overview dated 1977]. He poses the following questions about the effectiveness of a play from a theater worker's view: "Does it come alive on the stage? Does the action of the play flow smoothly and continuously? Will it hold the attention of the audience? Will it have meaning and worth for the audience?" Dr. Molette concludes that, indeed, his experience with Baldwin's two plays enables him to answer yes to these questions. And he credits Baldwin's success in moving from novel to play form, while other novelists have failed, to his "trust of and . . . reliance upon many other artists." The theater demands that the individual artist turn his creation over to others before it is totally complete.

Considering Baldwin's stated intent and Molette's standards for evaluating, this chapter will look at each of Baldwin's two plays with the following questions in mind. First, how do the plot and the form of the play recreate experience? Second, what techniques are used to make the play "come alive," to involve the audience (or the reader)? Third, beyond involving the audience, what in form and content are designed to shake up the viewer or reader? Finally, what are the meaning and worth of the play; how is the viewing or reading likely to change or affect the audience? (pp. 89-90)

The Amen Corner is a better play than its production history or critical attention would seem to indicate. Molette calls it "one of the most successful Afro-American plays that I have seen." Here, Baldwin is directly trying to recreate the ritual of the black church, as he knew it, in the ritual of the theater, while teaching a lesson antithetical to the lesson emanating from the church. The play is powerful. The lesson is somewhat less so.

Baldwin's set is ideally suited to the play's action and message. The "church and home of Margaret Alexander," pastor, are at stage right and stage left respectively. The church, with its "camp chairs" for the congregation, is "dominated by the pulpit" and by an "immense, open Bible," and a "thronelike" chair, both on a platform placed in such a way that a speaker from the pulpit is speaking simultaneously to the congregation on stage and the audience in the theater. Pastor Margaret's apartment, which she shares with her older sister, Odessa, her eighteen-year-old son, David, and later with her returned husband, Luke, is placed on a level below the church, at stage left. The church, Baldwin writes in the stage directions, "should give the impression of dominating the family's living quarters."

Action throughout the play moves from the church to the apartment and back to the church. The opening scene takes place in the church; the closing scene has Margaret and Odessa leaving the church and returning to the apartment. At key points in the plot, action in the upper, church, level occurs while stage lights also illuminate characters in the apartment. Both church and apartment have doors to the outside world which are used symbolically and literally for entering and exiting.

The plot of the story is relatively simple and is developed in a straightforward, realistic, Ibsenesque form, with no flashbacks or expressionistic revelations. All events that took place before the opening time of the play are revealed through simple exposition.

Margaret Alexander has been pastor of the church for several years. Her son, David, has been, until the time of the play, a well-behaved boy who plays the piano for Sunday school and church. On the particular Sunday morning of Act I, Margaret preaches the sermon upstairs and goes down to her apartment to finish packing for a trip to a Philadelphia church. She wants to take David with her; David tries to avoid going.

Elders of the congregation enter the apartment and are subtly critical of Margaret—of the expense of her trip, of her new Frigidaire, and of her son's behavior. Through their conversation, we discover that David's father is in town, working at a jazz club. With that preparation, Luke, the father, arrives, very ill. We discover, with David, that Margaret took her son and left Luke ten years earlier after the death of their baby daughter. Despite Luke's obviously terminal illness, Margaret ends Act I by leaving for Philadelphia, without David. As she says, "In this home, the Lord comes first. The Lord made me leave that man in there a long time ago because he was a sinner. And the Lord ain't told me to stop doing my work just because he's come the way all sinners come."

Act II occurs late the following Saturday. The critical murmurings of the church elders are growing louder, fed by the revelation of Margaret's past life and the current behavior of her son. "How come she think she can rule a church when she can't rule her own house," says Brother Boxer, who is peeved with Margaret largely because she has ruled that it would be a sin for him to drive a beer truck.

David and Luke have their only conversation in this act, about their past as a family, about music, and about pain. Broken-down Luke is given a key speech of the play in his advice to David. "Son—don't try to get away from the things that hurt you—sometimes that's all you got. You got to learn to live with those things—and—use them. I've seen people—put themselves through terrible torture—and die—because they was afraid of getting hurt." Later Luke explains his imminent demise as due to lack of love at the crucial time when Margaret left him. "A man can lose a whole lot . . . but he can keep on—he can even die with his head up, hell, as long as he got that one thing. That one thing is *him,* David, who he is inside—and, son, I don't believe no man ever got to that without somebody loved him."

When Margaret returns from Philadelphia to face the restless elders, the wayward son, and the dying husband, she is full of "God-given" justification for her own behavior. In dialogue with Luke, she explains her conversion and her leaving him as "finding a hiding place." Luke sees hiding indeed. "Then that other woman—that funny, fast-talking, fiery little thing I used to hold in my arms—[God] done away with her?" And about their son, he avers, "I ain't going to let you make him safe." To Margaret's attempts to make Luke repent to save his soul, he responds, "I guess I could have told you—it weren't *my* soul we been trying to save." Act II ends with the elders gathering up in the church for a business meeting to consider her dismissal, while Margaret, below in her kitchen, weeps and prays "Lord, help us to stand. . . . Lord, give me strength!"

Act III opens with Margaret mounting to the church early the following morning. There she converses with a minor character, but an important alter ego, Mrs. Jackson, who has come from the hospital where her baby has died in great pain. In the church service of Act I, Mrs. Jackson had come forward to ask for prayers for her sick child. At that time, Margaret, questioning the young woman as to why her husband wasn't with her, said, "Maybe the Lord wants you to leave that man." Now Margaret's view has begun to change. To the woman's fear of having more babies, the fear of going through more pain, Margaret says, "That ain't right. That ain't right." And, finally, Margaret advises her to "get on home to your husband. Go on home to your man."

Margaret returns downstairs, while the elders meet above to clinch her ouster. In conversation with David, who comes home drunk, she reveals her protective motivation for seeking his "salvation." "I remember boys like you down home, David, many years ago—fine young men, proud as horses, and I seen what happened to them. I seen them go down, David. . . ." But David refuses further protection. "Mamma, I want to be a man. It's time you let me be a man. You got to let me go."

In the pain of David's leaving and the remembering of her past love for Luke, Margaret says to Odessa:

> I tried to put my treasure in heaven where couldn't nothing get at it and take it away from me and leave me alone. . . . I didn't expect that none of this would ever rise to hurt me no more. . . . And there it stand, my whole life, just like I hadn't never gone nowhere. It's an awful thing to think about, the way love never dies!

(This last line, Baldwin says, is the first line he wrote for the play.) Finally, Margaret goes to Luke and they embrace, with the congregation singing above. "I never stopped loving you, Luke. I tried. But I never stopped loving you," she says. And Luke dies.

Margaret ascends to the church and begins a standard sermon, but breaks off in confusion when she realizes she is holding Luke's trombone mouthpiece in her hand, picked up from where he dropped it in death. As the backbiting Sister Moore cries, "Look at her! the gift of God has left her," Margaret speaks with what Baldwin certainly intends to be God's true message:

> Children. I'm just now finding out what it means to love the Lord. It ain't all in the singing and the shouting. It ain't all in the reading of the Bible. . . . It ain't even . . . in running all over everybody trying to get to heaven. To love the Lord is to love all His children—all of them, everyone!—and suffer with them and rejoice with them and never count the cost!

Margaret leaves the church. The lights dim on the church and come up on Margaret, below, falling beside Luke's bed.

Baldwin tells us in his notes to *The Amen Corner* that he wrote the play after publishing *Go Tell It on the Mountain,* and wrote it over the protests of his literary agent. "I remember [it] as a desperate and even rather irresponsible act." As *Go Tell It on the Mountain* in many respects came out of his relationship to his father, *The Amen Corner* grew from consideration of what motivated his mother, consideration of "the strategems she was forced to use to save her children from the destruction awaiting them just outside her door" [see Author Commentary dated 1968]. When we ask how this personal but infinitely duplicated experience is recreated in dramatic form in *The Amen Corner,* we will have to say that the tensions of pain and refuge, acceptance of the physical and seeking of the spiritual are certainly the core of the play, expressed in everything from the Luke-Margaret dichotomy to the jazz-spiritual dichotomy.

But the church, even as protection from the streets, is not given any positive characteristics here; its depiction is much less balanced than it was in *Go Tell It on the Mountain.* The scales of judgement are heavily loaded in favor of worldly love and family rather than congregational communion. No member of the congregation is admirable for any reason. Most are despicable—sex-starved, ambitious, jealous, cruel. This unbalanced view of the church is the greatest weakness in the play. A realistic treatment of any church would likely find at least as much virtue or kindness or love or fellowship there as in other human institutions.

As in other weighted attacks on the church after *Go Tell It on the Mountain*—in *Tell Me How Long the Train's Been Gone* and *If Beale Street Could Talk,* for example—the very vehemence of Baldwin's assaults undercuts his criticism. When one asks how the play recreates experience, one is led to think that it recreates external experience less than it tries to exorcise the power of Baldwin's early religious training.

Despite this lack of balance in the forces set against each other, however, the play is certainly constructed in such a way as to truly "come alive" on the stage. Much of that liveliness and power to involve is transmitted through the music. Group singing, individual singing, instrumental accompaniment, jazz (Luke on record), all provide choral commentary on character and conflict. The rhythms of the Bible readings, the sermons, and the antiphonal phrases—"Praise the Lord!" "Amen!"—are bound to arouse audience reaction.

As to elements of the play designed to "shake up" a viewer or reader, that will largely depend upon the audience. Darwin Turner in "James Baldwin in the Dilemma of the Black Dramatist" [see commentary dated 1977] concludes that *The Amen Corner* is unselfconsciously written for a black audience, much as later "Black Arts literature" is written consciously for a black audience. Baldwin's "presumption that his audience required no interpretation, no modification, because it already knew the cultural setting," gave him "an artistic freedom rarely granted a black dramatist except when he works within the theater of a black community," Turner says.

If this is so, and it certainly seems to be, the shock to a 1950s black audience would have been the attack on the black church, for even those unaccustomed to believing in it at that time were not accustomed to seeing its conventions so directly contradicted. Shock to later black audiences, in the 1960s, when it was professionally produced, or the 1970s was likely much less. As to most white audiences, were they to have seen the play in the 1950s or were they to see it in the 1980s, they would probably be startled chiefly by the liveliness of the black church service.

What are the meaning and worth of *The Amen Corner,* and how is viewing or reading it likely to change or affect the audience? The meaning is clear in Luke's advice not to avoid pain, but to use it, in Margaret's realization that love never dies, and in her choosing to comfort a dying man she loves down below rather than fight for her job as superior, more-holy pastor above. Such insight is likely to influence a viewer or reader only if he or she is a member of an organized church. If so, the member of the audience could question the form and content of belief, the motive and impact of action. The nonchurch member is less likely to change in word or deed and is more likely to be confirmed in the suspicion that the organized church is the refuge of the self-righteous and the frigid and the cowardly.

Turning to the later play, *Blues for Mister Charlie,* and comparing it to *The Amen Corner,* one finds a series of differences in form and content and similarity largely in the use of music, again, to involve the audience. *Blues for Mister Charlie* is expressionistic rather than realistic, and it is much more a protest play, with a white audience in the author's mind. It is designed to shock and change the audience, particularly by warning. The period in which it was written, and the American historical events it makes use of, date it to a certain extent. Nevertheless, it remains a powerful educational device, particularly for readers and viewers who are not familiar with the 1960s.

Expressionism in dramatic form may differ from realism in what appears on the stage. A realistic play like *The Amen Corner* has a solid set with an actual Frigidaire, table, chairs, pulpit present on the stage, giving the viewers the feeling that they are looking at actual rooms with the fourth wall removed. The expressionistic set which Baldwin uses in his second play, on the other hand, exists much more by suggestion.

In *Blues for Mister Charlie,* Baldwin describes the stage set as multiple, with the "skeleton being the Negro church in the first two acts and the courthouse in the third." The powerful symbols of the cross and the flag are continuously visible.

> The church and the courthouse are on opposite sides of a southern street; the audience should always be aware, during the first two acts, of the dome of the courthouse and the American flag. During the final act, the audience should always be aware of the steeple of the church, and the cross.
>
> [Act I].

Props on stage serve dual function to fit the change of set from church to courthouse. The pulpit of the first two acts, placed downstage at an angle, "so that the minister is simultaneously addressing the congregation and the audience," becomes in the third act the witness stand of the courthouse.

The aisle of the church "also functions as the division between WHITETOWN and BLACKTOWN." Other scenes such as Richard's room, Lyle's store, Papa D.'s jukebox joint, Jo's kitchen "are to exist principally by suggestion," and appear on the black or the white side of town according to whether the characters are black or white. Additionally, Baldwin says:

> for the murder scene, the aisle functions as a gulf. The stage should be built out, so that the audience reacts to the enormity of this gulf, and so that RICHARD, when he falls, falls out of sight of the audience, like a stone, into the pit.

Blues for Mister Charlie does not follow a straight chronology of events. It opens frighteningly, in the dark of the theater, with a gunshot. As lights come up on stage, Lyle Britten, a Southern, white store owner, is seen disposing

of a body of a young black man. "And may every nigger like this nigger end like this nigger—face down in the weeds!" he cries.

The rest of the play goes both backward and forward from this opening scene. It goes backward to show the dead, young black man, Richard Henry, returning home from up North, where he has been both a successful singer and a drug addict. It shows his inability to adjust to the racial realities of the Southern town of his birth. He is not humble, soft-spoken, or discreet, and he inevitably gets into trouble with Lyle Britten and his wife, Jo, who are representative of white townspeople who can't imagine what has gone wrong with all the "good niggers" they grew up with.

For the town has been in the throes of typical, early-1960s demonstrations, in support of integration of public facilities. Students from the local college have for months met in the black church run by Reverend Meridian Henry, Richard's father, and have gone out from their training in nonviolence to demonstrate peacefully, to get spat on, to get beaten up, to be jailed, to be released, and to go out again. Blacktown and Whitetown are exceedingly tense as a result, with rumors of sabotage and fear of sounds in the dark.

Love interest in the plot is provided by one of the demonstrating students, Juanita, who was a childhood friend of Richard Henry. She has been pursued unsuccessfully by another student, Pete; by Reverend Henry, who lost his wife years earlier; and by Parnell James, the wealthy, white, liberal, newspaper editor. When Richard returns, Juanita and Richard realize and consummate their love, and Richard is on the path to a new life and new goals when he is shot by Britten.

Throughout the rest of the play the events leading up to the opening murder scene are interspersed with events following the murder. Parnell James, although a good friend of Lyle Britten, succeeds in gaining Lyle's arrest for the murder of Richard Henry. Lyle is put on trial and is ultimately, predictably, acquitted. On the witness stand, black and white witnesses alike lie, and, in nonrealistic fashion, the thoughts and reactions of Blacktown and Whitetown are expressed in chorus. As witnesses testify, the audience sees not only their lies but glimpses, through their expressed memories, the histories which explain their testimonies.

The overriding question of *Blues for Mister Charlie,* perhaps more relevant for the black liberation movement in 1964 than in 1980, is the individual and communal debate over nonviolent protest versus "freedom by any means necessary." The dominant symbol for "any means necessary" is the gun. Much is made by the state prosecutor, when Parnell James is on the witness stand, of the fact that Parnell has hunted frequently with white Lyle Britten, his avowed friend, but has never hunted with black Meridian Henry, also his avowed friend. "Is it not true, Mr. James," he is questioned, "that it is impossible for any two people to go on a hunting trip together if either of them has any reason at all to distrust the other?"

Whitetown is of course armed; Blacktown is not. Richard

Henry brings a gun with him when he returns home from the North, but he turns it over to his father when he begins to see a new life ahead with Juanita. After the murder of Richard and the acquittal of his murderer, Reverend Meridian Henry (the very name suggests a moderate, or middle, view), changes his mind. In Act I, as Meridian begins to question events, Parnell admonishes him, "Meridian, you can't be the man who gives the signal for the holocaust." Meridian asks in response: "Must I be the man who watches while his people are beaten, chained, starved, clubbed, butchered?" At the end of the play, Meridian says, "You know, for us, it all began with the Bible and the gun. Maybe it will end with the Bible and the gun." "What did you do with the gun, Meridian?" asks Juanita. It is "in the pulpit," Meridian replies, "under the Bible. Like the pilgrims of old."

Within this overriding question of appropriate or moral means to desired ends, other issues are explored. For example, what is the role of the white liberal in racial struggle? Parnell is the only character who communicates with both sides, the only character who even wishes to do so. Yet he is not totally heroic. On the witness stand, he cannot bring himself to expose white woman Jo Britten's lie that Richard Henry tried to rape her, even though he knows it is a lie.

At the end of the play, as Blacktown gathers to march once again, Parnell asks Juanita, "Can I join you on the march, Juanita? Can I walk with you?" Juanita replies "Well, we can walk in the same direction; work toward the same goals; but work in your own community" [Act III]. This advice to the white liberal in 1964 predates by a year or two the Black Power movement, which sought to remove whites from powerful positions in civil rights organizations. Racism is not essentially a black problem; it is a white problem. As Malcolm X advised, so suggests Baldwin: walk in the same direction; work in your own community.

Another issue explored, the one, Baldwin says, which forced him to write the play, is trying to understand how a man like Lyle Britten can do what he does—kill. The "germ of the play" for Baldwin was in the murder of fifteen-year-old Emmett Till in 1955 in Mississippi. Till was a young, Northern black who whistled at a white woman and consequently was killed. His murderer was acquitted. "I do not know *why* the case pressed on my mind so hard," Baldwin says in his prefatory "Notes for *Blues for Mister Charlie* [see Author Commentary dated 1964]." "In life, obviously, such people baffle and terrify me and, with one part of my mind at least, I hate them and would be willing to kill them."

But Baldwin goes on, in a statement that forms the key to the depiction of the white characters in the play,

> Yet, with another part of my mind, I am aware that no man is a villain in his own eyes. Something in the man knows—*must* know—that what he is doing is evil; but in order to accept the knowledge the man would have to change. What is ghastly and really almost hopeless in our racial situation now is that the crimes we have committed are so great and so unspeakable

that the acceptance of this knowledge would lead, literally, to madness. The human being, then, in order to protect himself, closes his eyes, compulsively repeats his crimes, and enters a spiritual darkness which no one can describe. . . . [But] we have the duty to try to understand this wretched man; and while we probably cannot hope to liberate him, begin working toward the liberation of his children. For we, the American people, have created him, he is our servant. . . . It is we who have locked him in the prison of his color.

In order to help the reader and viewer understand Lyle Britten as he appears to himself rather than simply as a villain, Baldwin shows us the man with his family, with his baby son ("old pisser," as he calls him), and gives us a great deal of Lyle's sexual and racial history. As one would expect in Baldwin, sex and race are closely related in Lyle's history. Lyle's wife, Jo, is given a sympathetic portrayal within the racial and sexual limits of her upbringing. Her lying on the witness stand becomes understandable from her viewpoint.

Let us summarize to this point what we have said about *Blues for Mister Charlie* and answer more directly the question, "How do the plot and the form of the play recreate experience?" The expressionistic form of the play recreates experience very well, for the race attitudes Baldwin is depicting exist in confused, dreamlike form, he is saying, in every American, black or white. The outcomes of the confusion, the prejudices, the fears are historically accurate—marches, beatings, jailings, rapes, killings. Inner and outer experience of a particular time and particular place are powerfully and accurately recreated.

How, then, does the play come alive? Much is done here, as in *The Amen Corner,* with music and with other sounds. The first sound is the terrifying shot in the dark. The next sounds are from the training sessions of withstanding taunts that the demonstrators go through before facing the streets. "Hey, boy, where's your mother? I bet she's lying up in bed, just a-pumping away. . . . You get your ass off these streets from around here, boy, or we going to do us some cutting—we're going to cut that big black thing off of you, you hear?" [Act I].

Later sounds include Richard singing; Meridian, Juanita, and Peter singing Richard's songs, one about freedom and one about prison; jukebox music and dancing in Papa D.'s joint; menacing car sounds and telephone sounds; Richard's guitar; white folks singing "For He's a Jolly Good Fellow" at Lyle's and Jo's anniversary, while the sounds of Blacktown singing are heard in the background; Jo singing the baby to sleep; the singing at Richard's funeral; Jo's and Lyle's baby crying as Jo takes the witness stand; student demonstrators singing in the jail; journalists' reports in many tongues at Lyle's trial; and again, near the end of the play, as the full story of the killing is replayed, gunshots.

Blues for Mister Charlie is designed to shock the audience, though here, as with *The Amen Corner,* the shock for a white audience and a black audience will be very different. Darwin Turner has said, in "James Baldwin in the

Dilemma of the Black Dramatist" [see overview dated 1977], that *Blues for Mister Charlie* is written for a white audience," is "patterned on the protest tradition," and "calls upon the Parnells of America to defend their convictions even if such action pits them against their neighbors." Carlton Molette agrees that it is written for a white audience, but explains some of the play's unwieldy complexity as the result of trying "to be all things to all people. It tries to explain whites to blacks and blacks to whites" [see overview dated 1977].

Interestingly, Molette describes conversations among blacks and among whites in the theater lobby during intermissions and following *Blues for Mister Charlie.* Whites were mystified by portions of the play blacks understood, and blacks were unable to adjust to Lyle Britten's *not* being portrayed as what they expected or wanted to see— "some kind of wild-eyed, nigger-hating, stereotyped redneck villain." From such reaction it is apparent that Baldwin succeeds in shocking both audiences.

The worth of *Blues for Mister Charlie* lies particularly in raising, recreating, and struggling with questions that have not been resolved in the sixteen years since its writing. Names and datelines and groups change; the questions reoccur. In liberation movements that have followed on the black struggle, which itself has by no means ended, the same positions, the same arguments, the same questions arise. In the women's, Native American, Chicano, immigrant, gay, handicapped liberation movements, at what point are violent action and violent defense necessary? At what point are they inevitable? At what point are they justified? Moral? Productive?

It is easy to forget, when one has lived through a period of history noted for events and debates, that the schools and the courts and the hospitals and the voting booths are continually being repopulated by people who have not lived through the events or the debates. If there is to be learning from the past, the past must be recreated repeatedly. *Blues for Mister Charlie* does a masterful job of recreating. It deserves being produced, viewed and read now, as it did in 1964. (pp. 91-105)

> *Carolyn Wedin Sylvander, in her* James Baldwin, *Frederick Ungar Publishing Co., 1980, 181 p.*

BLUES FOR MISTER CHARLIE

PRODUCTION REVIEWS

Michael Smith   (review date 30 April 1964)

> [*In the following review, Smith castigates Baldwin for subordinating in* Blues for Mister Charlie *"his instincts as an artist"* to his *"obligations as a participating spokesman"* for Negro America.]

Unfortunately James Baldwin has become a spokesman

for American Negroes. He has cast himself in this role, and at least by whites he has been accepted in it. All Negro artists are in this situation to some extent, and it may account for the achievement. But Baldwin, as the outstanding Negro writer, is outstandingly afflicted by his obligations. The situation is unfortunate because it nearly prevents him from functioning as an artist.

In his play, *Blues For Mister Charlie* (at the ANTA), the drama is constantly being deflected and deflated by the issues it stems from and reflects. Baldwin again and again seems to subordinate his instincts as an artist to his obligations as a participating spokesman. The kind of truth that Baldwin seems most deeply drawn toward, except when he is distracted by sentiment, is the modern truth, unformulated and senseless, the kind of truth that comes only in an intuitive plunge and has nothing to do with sociology.

It seems to me that the theatre can do two things: it can make us forget how disturbed we are by the senselessness of life; or it can, by tuning us in (or turning us on), enable us to distinguish the features of our distress more exactly. The artist in Baldwin knows this, but the Negro spokesman in Baldwin forces him to submerge it. And his play, except in the remarkable performances of Diana Sands and Al Freeman, Jr., contains little of it.

Baldwin's alternate instincts are betrayed by the fact that the play is a poor polemic. If his intentions were simply to propagandize, to detail further the tension between Negroes and whites in this country, he would have done better to write a conventional drama. If his intention were purely to editorialize, to preach, he would have written a simpler story. In terms of direct impact, in terms of showing complacent Northern whites the extent of the outrage we continue to permit within our nation, he would have done better to make a documentary. In this case, fiction is pale by comparison with reality. When one Negro character had a nightmare about "prods," the woman next to me turned to her companion and asked, "What? What's a prod?" Of course she could not get an answer, and nothing as outrageous as putting electric cattle prods to human beings entered that theatre or reached that audience.

Baldwin knows this, but the audience doesn't. And they react to the play as if it were in both senses a black-and-white contest being waged on the stage. Of course everybody—or at least everybody who would go see a Baldwin play—is now in favor of the Negroes, the persecuted, misconceived, misrepresented historical underdogs, and so it is no real contest. Negroes in the audience see themselves morally vindicated; whites have the choice of wallowing in self-contempt, swearing righteous oaths for the future, or disassociating themselves from any responsibility. (The fourth possibility—being moved to action—is unlikely among Broadway theatregoers.) In short, the play falls into the traps of all propagandistic art: those who already believe feel complacent, and those who don't stay away. In so far as the play "speaks for" Negroes, the white Broadway audience goes to it out of moral masochism.

As drama and as message, the play stumbles over itself too many times to be effective. Baldwin tells of a young Negro, the son of a minister, who has come from a small Southern town to New York, slept with a number of white girls, become a drug addict, gone to Lexington, and who now returns to a tense home town and is murdered. This hero, Richard, is mean and tormented and looking for trouble, and in a town wracked with racial tension he finds it easily. He is murdered by Lyle, a poor white man who has already murdered one Negro. Richard provokes Lyle as much as he can, and Lyle shoots him. The town breaks sharply into factions, black and white, and Lyle is acquitted of the crime, which he then confesses.

The polemical fault in this story is that Lyle kills Richard not so much because he is a Negro as because he asks for it. Richard picks out Lyle's tender spots and is as nasty as possible about poking into them. He makes fun of Lyle's poverty, for one thing; but more important, he repeatedly, graphically slurs Lyle's masculinity. Richard seeks out Lyle to insult him; Lyle is a weak and defensive man; Richard provokes him as much as he can. Finally Lyle, more in defense of his sexual self-respect than of his race, murders Richard.

In that final confrontation before the murder, which Baldwin makes the final scene of the play, there is a serious cop-out. Into the mouth of Richard, the super-provoker, Baldwin puts this line: "Why don't you go home? And let me go home? Do we need all this shit? Can't we live without it?" [Act III]. If I maintain that Richard is the one who started this particular shit—which is the truth—I will seem to be opposed to change. And yet Baldwin is presenting a false case.

As the climax of Act II, and the play's prime policy speech, Baldwin has written a sermon for Richard's father to speak at the funeral; its climax reads: " . . . give me a sign! A sign that in the terrible Sahara of our time a fountain may spring, the fountain of a true morality, and bring us closer, oh, my Lord, to that peace on earth desired by so few throughout so many ages. Let not our suffering endure forever. Teach us to trust the great gift of life and learn to love one another and dare to walk the earth like men. Amen." This is the sermon; but plays like men exist primarily in their actions, not their self-descriptions. In **Blues for Mister Charlie** Baldwin very clearly presents this sermon and Lyle's plea as representative Negro actions, and murder and murder's acceptance as representative white actions.

Baldwin has made an effort to show Lyle in the round, to make him a complete man rather than a stark symbol. Although his devices include the cute cliche of showing him loving his baby, the trick works to a certain extent, and the focus of the play simply moves off him. It moves onto the white community, which is revealed in some clever but loaded racist dialogue. And then the Negro minister becomes the spokesman for everybody's guilt and pain. He cannot understand how these people can claim to be Christians, and he wrestles with the contradiction between Christian belief and the dreadful reality around him. But this again is a false problem: we have repeatedly seen that on a simplistic level the Negroes are in a position similar to that of the Jews who invented Christianity; but on a more sophisticated level, Baldwin's certainly, the world

has changed and men have thought for a long time since then. The fact that the events in the South won't fit the terms of primitive Christian morality cannot be blamed on the white man and is in fact irrelevant, and making a minister the spokesman for good in the play is a corny fallacy.

Similarly, I can't think of any motive but psychic sadism for Baldwin's harping on the traditional theme of Negro sexual prowess versus the white man's limited potency. It simply seems unfair. Segregation is a tough problem but not an impossible one: action gets results. But if Negroes are genetically better in bed, I wonder where we whites should sit-in to catch up.

Baldwin has said that his play was written at Elia Kazan's suggestion, and in a way it betrays much the same confusion that has marred Kazan's recent work. Baldwin seems to be writing a '30s play, a play which uses the theatre as a social weapon in the same way that Odets did in '*Waiting for Lefty*,' for an obvious example. I honor the impulse, but the available means have changed. [Rolf Hochhuth's] *The Deputy* and [Arthur Miller's] *After the Fall* fit into the same category of false documentary in a time when consciousness can penetrate beyond the "meaning" of events. In this kind of play the ultimate possibility is for the meaning to become clear. What did it "mean" that Quentin in *After the Fall* allowed Maggie to destroy herself? What did it "mean" that the Pope failed to denounce the Nazi atrocities? In the terms of moral philosophy the questions may still be significant, but in art they are not. Art—even the theatre—is finding the possibility of penetrating past meaning into the act itself. Baldwin is capable of this as Miller probably is not. Baldwin is capable of realizing that the self-deception of those whites who actively condone segregation is not the most important or most urgent agony facing the world. For the moment he is trapped in his role and has written a bad play, but its very badness is a sign that he may be breaking free.

Diana Sands and Al Freeman, Jr., give brilliant performances as Richard and his girl friend, Juanita. Miss Sands has the courage and resources to play at full emotional pitch, and she is one of the strongest and best actresses in the theatre today. Mr. Freeman is more complex, more in taut restraint, with a jittery energy and fervent concentration and an exact sense of transitions. His work is beautiful and better in every role. Rip Torn's mannerisms threaten always to get out of hand, but his portrayal of Lyle seems to me most effective. Pat Hingle is precise and touching as a torn, sympathetic newspaper editor, and Ann Wedgeworth makes the most of Lyle's cliche-ridden wife. Burgess Meredith's direction manages all the movements so smoothly that it seems to locate the play somewhere in dreamland. As in the writing, its attempt to generalize too often leads to vagueness, and vagueness leads to error. This is a play and production that everyone, Negro and white alike, should approach with a careful awareness that it is not gospel. (pp. 12, 18)

Michael Smith, "Thoughts on Baldwin," in The Village Voice, *Vol. IX, No. 28, April 30, 1964, pp. 12, 18.*

Robert Brustein   (review date 16 May 1964)

[*Brustein is an American essayist, educator, and critic. He has directed drama programs at both Yale and Harvard Universities and has been a panel member of the National Endowment for the Arts. His writings include* The Theatre of Revolt: An Approach to the Modern Drama *(1964),* Cultural Watch: Essays on the Theatre and Society, 1969-1974 *(1975), and* Critical Moments: Reflections on Theatre and Society: 1973-1979 *(1980). In the following review, Brustein deplores the "moral and intellectual deficiency" of* Blues for Mister Charlie *and Baldwin's use of stereotypes. He particularly censures Baldwin's "curious insistence on the superiority of negro sexuality" and concludes that* Blues for Mister Charlie *is "more a work of provocation than conviction."*]

> Let us say, then, that truth, as used here, is meant to imply a devotion to the human being, his freedom and fulfillment; freedom which cannot be legislated, fulfillment which cannot be charted. This is the prime concern, the fame of reference; it is not to be confused with a devotion to Humanity which is too easily equated with a devotion to a Cause; and Causes, as we know, are notoriously bloodthirsty.
>
> —*Everybody's Protest Novel*

James Baldwin wrote these words 15 years ago in an essay which still stands as the *locus classicus* on the subject of protest fiction; I imagine they sometimes return to haunt him in his dreams. **Blues for Mr. Charlie,** certainly, is the embodiment of everything he once professed to deplore, being "notoriously bloodthirsty" propaganda of the crudest sort, with little existence either as truth, literature, or life. Uncontrolled, hysterical, self-indulgent, employing a clumsy flashback technique and proceeding by means of a surprisingly flabby rhetoric, it is a play of thumbs—fashioned, I would guess, to gouge the eyes of the audience.

It is well known that Baldwin has radically changed his conception of himself over the past few years, suppressing the private side of his character to become an Official Spokesman for a Cause. I have not been among those who admired him in this new role, but I never assumed the decision was easy—or even wholly avoidable, for it may be, as Irving Howe suggests, that the Negro writer cannot find "freedom and fulfillment" until he achieves his Cause. On the other hand, Baldwin's rage, formerly authentic and precise, has begun to seem increasingly mechanical, trumped-up, and free-floating, while his self-righteousness has been expressed at the cost of complexity and scruples. In this play, for example, he is—despite a usually delicate awareness of the deadening effect of racial abstractions—dedicated to perpetuating stereotypes, and doing so in a manner which can only create confusion or dissension. The characters have no life apart from narrow racial categories, and the categories themselves are based on prejudice and prejudgment.

No doubt, Baldwin's material is partly to blame. Any work inspired by the Emmett Till case is almost automatically destined to be a melodrama. **Blues for Mr. Charlie,** however, simplifies the historical events even further—the stage is given over literally to a conflict between black and white, or Blacktown versus Whitetown. It is the author's apparent conviction now that all white men are Mr. Charlie, the oppressor, for they are characterized either as sadists and supremacists, burning with hatred for Negro men and lust for Negro women, or as vacillating liberals who befriend the Negroes only to betray them when the chips are down. As for the Negro characters, they enjoy more noble racial stereotypes: the Uncle Tom who redeems himself by fingering the murderer after a lifetime of subservience to him; the integrationist minister who finally determines to keep a gun under his Bible, and fight the white man with his own weapons; the strongminded, white-haired grandmammy of the past generation who believes in pious passiveness; the angry hero who has returned from the North, furious at all the white women who have seduced him, to goad a Southern peckerwood into shooting him; the childhood sweetheart who is rather quixotically persuaded of the necessity for love ("I'm going to learn from Richard how to love! I won't let him die for nothing!" [Act II]) by the hero's angry life and violent death. Since many of these characters are also fixtures of the Broadway stage (Baldwin already manipulates theatrical clichés with the weariness of an experienced commercial dramatist), few of the actors are able to transcend the oppressive conventionality of their roles—though Al Freeman, Jr., is a handsome, vigorous actor, and Diana Sands has an affecting moment of grief—while Burgess Meredith, who directed the Actors Studio production, has been forced to give it the form of a mass meeting in a Union Hall, especially in the courtroom scene, where Black confronts White in angry turmoil, and witnesses detach themselves to deliver impassioned soliloquies downstage.

The most disappointing thing about the play, however, is not its aesthetic flatness but rather its moral and intellectual deficiency. Particularly depressing is Baldwin's curious insistence on the superiority of Negro sexuality, especially since this is a myth which the author himself once took pains to explode. You would never learn from **Blues for Mr. Charlie** that segregation has social, political, or economic roots; like Tennessee Williams, whose *Sweet Bird of Youth* his play occasionally resembles, Baldwin has determined that the major cause of anti-Negro feeling is sexual envy. This suggests something of the incredible chauvinism which permeates the work—a strain as virulent here as anything to be found in White Citizens' Councils, and even less honest, since Baldwin attempts to vindicate his own feelings by victimizing his characters. (One finds the same desire to make hatred look virtuous in Leroi Jones' *Dutchman* where the chauvinism and violence of the Negro protagonist are forced from him by a white woman who needles, provokes, and finally kills him—but the rage belongs to the author.) Here, for example, is Baldwin ventriloquizing through his hero, when he is crawling on the ground with three bullets in his belly: "White man! I don't want nothing from you. You ain't got nothing to give me! You can't eat because none of your sad-assed chicks can cook. You can't talk because won't nobody talk to you. You can't dance because you've got nobody to dance with. . . . Okay. Okay. Okay. Keep your old lady home, you hear? Don't let her near no nig-

ger. She might get to like it. You might get to like it, too"
[Act III]. In contrast with the "dried-up white women"
and the "faggoty white boys," however, Baldwin's Negroes are all extraordinarily virile, courageous, passionate,
and alive, even to the point of displaying, during a dance
hall sequence, a natural sense of rhythm.

At this point, the healthiest thing for spectators of both
races would be to rise up and repudiate these romantic
fabrications, and loudly too; but since the theater audience
is far from healthy, the play merely sinks the white spectator deeper into an impotent, self-defeating guilt. (An index
of this is the cowardly way in which the play was received
by the daily reviewers—to praise inferior art, simply because it is produced by a Negro, is to let guilt turn into
an inverted form of prejudice.) Worse than this, the play
attempts to lacerate an ugly rage in the heart of the colored spectator; *Blues for Mr. Charlie,* for all its conventional gestures towards love, emerges finally as an inflam-
matory broadside of race hatred which will profit nobody
but the author. If we are locked in the stereotypes that
Baldwin conceives, and Negro and White can confront
each other only in mutual distrust and anger, then we will
have to assume that the Negro "problem" is still too crude
for the stage; but such a work as Atholl Fugard's *Blood
Knot,* with its more controlled form and deeper understanding, proves there is nothing inevitable about these
oppostions at all.

The fault, I am afraid, lies not in the "problem" but in the
author. The very terms we use to criticize Baldwin were
learned in his school, since it is he, along with Ralph Ellison, who did most to make the Negro visible as a complicated human being. But considering all that Baldwin once
knew and wrote, it is difficult not to conclude that *Blues
for Mr. Charlie* is more a work of provocation than conviction—the author has tasted power and is rolling that
taste around on his tongue. The ultimate difficulty, then,
is not a racial difficulty at all; it is the difficulty of the modern intellectual, torn between the way of influence and the
way of truth. This conflict has driven more than one gifted
individual of our time to a sorry abuse of his talents, as
well as to that almost pathological frustration that often
accompanies it; and I suspect that much of the exasperation in this play stems from Baldwin's inability to reconcile the private and public aspects of his character. Until
he does, however, he has ceased to illuminate our consciousness. Early in his career, James Baldwin declared it
his ambition to be "an honest man and a good writer." In
Blues for Mr. Charlie he is neither. There, the complex
man of sensibility has been totally absorbed by the simplistic man of power—and that constitutes what Baldwin
himself once called "his corruption and our loss." (pp.
35-7)

> Robert Brustein, "Everybody's Protest Play,"
> in The New Republic, Vol. 150, No. 20, May
> 16, 1964, pp. 35-7.

Susan Sontag   (review date Summer 1964)

[*Sontag is an influential American critic, essayist, and
educator best known for her collections* Against Inter-

Portrait of Baldwin.

pretation and Other Essays *(1966) and* Styles of Radical Will *(1969). In the following excerpt, Sontag excori-
ates* Blues for Mister Charlie *as "a long, over-long, rambling work" that "gets bogged down in repetitions, incoherence, and in all sorts of loose ends of plot and motive." The critic suggests that the play is not about racial
conflict, but rather sexual conflict, for which, Sontag
claims, the racial issue serves as a metaphor. This review
was later collected in Sontag's* Against Interpretation
(1966).]

The currency of exchange for most social and moral attitudes is that ancient device of the drama: personifications,
masks. Both for play and for edification, the mind sets up
these figures, simple and definite, whose identity is easily
stated, who arouse quick loves and hates. Masks are a peculiarly effective, shorthand way of defining virtue and
vice.

Once a grotesque, a figure of folly—childlike, lawless, lascivious—"the Negro" is fast becoming the American theatre's leading mask of virtue. For definiteness of outline,
being black, he even surpasses "the Jew," who has an ambiguous physical identity. (It was part of the lore of the
advanced position on Jewishness that Jews didn't have to
look like "Jews." But Negroes always look like "Negroes," unless, of course, they are inauthentic.) And for
sheer pain and victimage, the Negro is far ahead of any
other contender in America. In just a few short years, the
old liberalism, whose archetypal figure was the Jew, has
been challenged by the new militancy, whose hero is the
Negro. But while the temper which gives rise to the new

militancy—and to "the Negro" as hero—may indeed scorn the ideas of liberalism, one feature of the liberal sensibility hangs on. We still tend to choose our images of virtue from among our victims.

In the theatre, as among educated Americans generally, liberalism has suffered an ambiguous rout. The American theatre has always had a large streak of moralism, of preachiness. And we would all, I suppose, blush to have to reexperience plays like *Waiting for Lefty, Watch on the Rhine, Tomorrow the World, Deep Are the Roots, The Crucible*—the classics of Broadway liberalism. But what was wrong with these plays, from the most contemporary point of view, is not that they aimed to convert their audiences, rather than simply entertaining them. It was, rather, that they were too optimistic. They thought problems could be solved. James Baldwin's **Blues for Mister Charlie** is a sermon, too. To make it official, Baldwin has said that the play is loosely inspired by the Emmett Till case, and one may read, on the theatre program under the director's name, that the play is "Dedicated to the memory of Medgar Evers, and his widow and his children, and to the memory of the dead children of Birmingham." But it is a sermon of a new type. In **Blues for Mister Charlie,** Broadway liberalism has been vanquished by Broadway racism. Liberalism preached politics, that is, solutions. Racism regards politics as superficial (and seeks some deeper level); it emphasizes what is unalterable. Across a virtually impassable gulf, the new mask of "the Negro," manly, toughened, but ever vulnerable, faces his antipode, another new mask, "the white" (sub-genus: "the white liberal")—who is pasty-faced, graceless, lying, sexually dull, murderous.

No one in his right mind would wish the old masks back. But this does not make the new masks wholly convincing. And whoever accepts them should notice that the new masks of "the Negro" has become visible only at the price of emphasizing the fatality of racial antagonisms. If D. W. Griffith could call his famous white supremacist film about the origins of the Ku Klux Klan *Birth of a Nation,* then James Baldwin could, with more justice to the overt political message of his **Blues for Mister Charlie** ("Mister Charlie" is Negro slang for "white man"), have as well called his play "Death of a Nation." Baldwin's play, which takes place in a small Southern town, opens with the death of its brash tormented Negro jazz musician hero, Richard, and ends with the acquittal of his white murderer, a resentful inarticulate young buck named Lyle, and the moral collapse of the local liberal, Parnell. There is the same insistence on the painful ending, even more starkly presented, in LeRoi Jones's one act play *Dutchman,* now running off-Broadway. In *Dutchman,* a young Negro sitting on the subway reading and minding his own business is first accosted, then elaborately teased and taunted to the point of rage, then suddenly knifed by a twitchy young hustler; while his body is being disposed of by the other passengers, whites, the girl turns her attention to a new young Negro who has just boarded the train. In the new post-liberal morality plays, it is essential that virtue be defeated. Both **Blues for Mister Charlie** and *Dutchman* turn on a shocking murder—even though, in the case of *Dutchman,* the murder is simply not credible in terms of the more or less realistic action that has gone before,

and seems crude (dramatically), tacked on, willed. Only murder releases one from the mandate to be moderate. It is essential, dramatically, that the white man win. Murder justifies the author's rage, and disarms the white audience, who have to learn what's coming to *them.*

For it is indeed an extraordinary sermon that is being preached. Baldwin is not interested in dramatizing the incontestable fact that white Americans have brutally mistreated Negro Americans. What is being demonstrated is not the social guilt of the whites, but their inferiority as human beings. This means, above all, their sexual inferiority. While Richard jeers about his unsatisfying experiences with white women up North, it turns out that the only passions—in one instance carnal, in the other romantic—ever felt by the two white men who figure importantly in the play, Lyle and Parnell, have been with Negro women. Thus, the oppression by whites of Negroes becomes a classic case of *ressentiment* as described by Nietzsche. It is eerie to sit in the ANTA Theatre on 52nd Street and hear that audience—sizably Negro, but still preponderantly white—cheer and laugh and break into applause at every line cursing white America. After all, it's not some exotic Other from across the seas who is being abused—like the rapacious Jew or the treacherous Italian of the Elizabethan drama. It is the majority of the members of the audience themselves. Social guilt would not be enough to explain this remarkable acquiescence of the majority in their own condemnation. Baldwin's plays, like his essays and novels, have undoubtedly touched a nerve other than political. Only by tapping the sexual insecurity that grips most educated white Americans could Baldwin's virulent rhetoric have seemed so reasonable.

But after applause and cheers, what? The masks which the Elizabethan theatre proposed were exotic, fantastic, playful. Shakespeare's audience did not come streaming out of the Globe Theatre to butcher a Jew or string up a Florentine. The morality of *The Merchant of Venice* is not incendiary, but merely simplifying. But the masks which **Blues for Mister Charlie** holds up for our scorn are our reality. And Baldwin's rhetoric *is* incendiary, though let loose in a carefully fireproofed situation. The result is not any idea of action—but the vicarious pleasure in the rage vented on the stage, with no doubt an undertow of anxiety.

Considered as art, **Blues for Mister Charlie** runs aground for some of the same reasons it stalls as propaganda. Baldwin might have done something much better with the agitprop scheme of his play (noble, handsome Negro student youth pitted against stupid, vicious town whites), for to that in itself I have no objection. Some of the greatest art comes out of moral simplification. But this play gets bogged down in repetitions, incoherence, and in all sorts of loose ends of plot and motive. For example: it is hard to believe that in a town beset by civil rights agitation and with a race murder on its hands, the white liberal, Parnell, could move so freely, with so little recrimination, from one community to another. Again: it is not credible that Lyle, who is Parnell's close friend, and his wife aren't bewildered and irate when Parnell secures Lyle's arraignment on the charge of murder. Perhaps this remarkable equanimity owes to the place of love in Baldwin's rhetoric.

Love is always on the horizon, a universal solvent almost in the manner of Paddy Chayefsky. Again: from what we are shown of the romance struck up between Richard and Juanita—which begins only a few days before Richard is killed—it is unconvincing that Juanita should proclaim that what she has learned from Richard is how to love. (The truth seems rather that Richard was just beginning to learn to love, for the first time, from her.) More important: the whole confrontation between Richard and Lyle, with its explicit tones of masculine sexual rivalry, seems inadequately motivated. Richard simply has not enough reason, except that the author wants to say these things, to introduce the theme of sexual envy on all the occasions that he does. And quite apart from any consideration of the sentiments expressed, it is grotesque, humanly and dramatically, for Richard's dying words, as he crawls at Lyle's feet with three bullets in his gut, to be: "White man! I don't want nothing from you. You ain't got nothing to give me! You can't talk because nobody won't talk to you. You can't dance because you've got nobody to dance with . . . Okay. Okay. Okay. Keep your old lady home, you hear? Don't let her near no nigger. She might get to like it. You might get to like it, too" [Act III].

Perhaps the origin of what seems forced, hysterical, unconvincing in **Blues for Mister Charlie**—and in *Dutchman*—is a rather complex displacement of the play's true subject. Race conflict is what the plays are supposed to be about. Yet also, in both plays, the racial problem is drawn mainly in terms of sexual attitudes. Baldwin has been very plain about the reason for this. White America, he charges, has robbed the Negro of his masculinity. What whites withhold from Negroes, and what Negroes aspire to, is sexual recognition. The withholding of this recognition—and its converse, treating the Negro as a mere object of lust—is the heart of the Negro's pain. As stated in Baldwin's essays, I am persuaded. (This account doesn't hinder me from considering other consequences, political and economic, of the Negro's oppression). But what one reads in Baldwin's last novel, or sees on the stage in **Blues for Mister Charlie,** is considerably less persuasive. In Baldwin's novel and play, it seems to me, the racial situation has become a kind of code, a metaphor for sexual conflict. But a sexual problem cannot be wholly masked as a racial problem. Different tonalities, different specifics of emotion are involved.

The truth is that **Blues for Mister Charlie** isn't really about what it claims to be about. It is supposed to be about racial strife. But it is really about the anguish of tabooed sexual longings, about the crisis of identity which comes from confronting these longings, and about the rage and destructiveness (often, self-destructiveness) by which one tries to surmount this crisis. It has, in short, a psychological subject. The surface may be Odets, but the interior is pure Tennessee Williams. What Baldwin has done is to take the leading theme of the serious theater of the 'fifties—sexual anguish—and work it up as a political play. Buried in **Blues for Mister Charlie** is the plot of several successes of the last decade: the gruesome murder of a handsome virile young man by those who envy him his virility.

The plot of *Dutchman* is similar, except that here there is an added fillip of anxiety. In place of the veiled homoerotic hang-ups of **Blues for Mister Charlie,** there is class anxiety. As his contribution to the mystique of Negro sexuality, Jones brings up the question—which is never raised in **Blues for Mister Charlie**—of being authentically Negro. (Baldwin's play takes place in the South; perhaps one can only have such a problem up North.) Clay, the hero of *Dutchman,* is a middle-class Negro from New Jersey, who has gone to college and wanted to write poetry like Baudelaire, and has Negro friends who speak with English accents. In the early part of the play, he is in limbo. But in the end, poked and prodded by Lula, Clay strips down to his true self; he stops being nice, well-spoken, reasonable, and assumes his full Negro identity: that is, he announced the homicidal rage toward whites that Negroes bear in their hearts, whether they act on it or not. He will not kill, he says. Whereupon, he is killed.

Dutchman is, of course, a smaller work than **Blues for Mister Charlie.** In only one act and with only two speaking characters, it is a descendant of the sexual duels to the death dramatized by Strindberg. At its best, in some of the early exchanges between Lula and Clay, it is neat and powerful. But as a whole—and one does look back on the play in the light of the astonishing fantasy revealed at the end—it is altogether too frantic, too overstated. Robert Hooks played Clay with some subtlety, but I found the spasmic sexual contortions and raucousness in Jennifer West's performance as Lula almost unbearable. There is a smell of a new, rather verbose style of emotinal savagery in *Dutchman* that, for want of a better name, I should have to call Albeesque. Undoubtedly, we shall see more of it. . . . In contrast, **Blues for Mister Charlie** is a long, over-long, rambling work which is virtually an anthology, a summa of the trends of serious big American plays of the last thirty years. It has lots of moral uplift. It carries on the good fight to talk dirty on the legitimate stage to new, splendid victories. And it adopts a complex, pretentious form of narration—the story is told in clumsy flashbacks, with the ornament of a non-functioning chorus, some kind of world-historical disk jockey ensconced stage right, wearing earphones and fiddling with his apparatus all evening. The production itself, directed by Burgess Meredith, wobbles through several different styles. The realistic parts come off best. In roughly the last third of the play, which takes place in the courtroom, the play founders completely; all pretense at verisimilitude is dropped, there being no fidelity to courtroom rituals observed even in darkest Mississippi, and the play crumbles into bits of internal monologue, whose subjects have little bearing on the present action, which is Lyle's trial. In the last part of **Blues for Mister Charlie,** Baldwin seems bent on dissipating the play's dramatic power; the director needed only to follow. Despite the flabbiness of the direction, though, there are a number of affecting performances. Rip Torn, a sexy rough-trade Lyle, rather upstaged the other actors; he was fun to watch. Al Freeman, Jr. was appealing as Richard, though he was saddled with some remarkably maudlin lines, especially in the Moment of Truth With Father scene, which has been obligatory in the serious Broadway theatre for the last decade. Diana Sands, one of the loveliest actresses around, did well with the under-realized role of Juanita except in what has been the most praised part of her performance, her downstage-center-and-face-the-audience aria of lament for Richard, which I thought terribly forced. As Parnell, Pat Hingle, an actor spectacularly embalmed in his own mannerisms, is still the very same indecisive lumbering old dear that he was last year as Nina Leeds's husband in the Actor's Studio production of *Strange Interlude*. (pp. 389-94)

Susan Sontag, "Going to Theater, Etc.," in Partisan Review, *Vol. XXXI, No. 3, Summer, 1964, pp. 389-94.*

Tom F. Driver (review date 4 June 1964)

[*Driver is an American educator, critic, essayist, and lecturer who has written and contributed to numerous books on drama. His career as a drama critic has included positions with* motive *(1953-1955),* Christian Century *(1956-1963),* New Republic *(1958-1959) and the* Reporter *(1963-1964). In the following essay, Driver addresses the critical reaction to* Blues for Mister Charlie, *claiming that the play was misunderstood by many reviewers because Baldwin stepped outside the economic and political contexts in which most white Americans see the racial struggle and chose to depict "racial strife as* racial *strife, warfare between the black people and white people that is rooted in their separate ways of experiencing life." This essay proved controversial, as Driver's editors refused to print it. As a result, he resigned from his position as a critic for the* Reporter *and the essay was later published by several other periodicals.*]

The closing notice is up, and I am left to sing the blues for *Blues for Mister Charlie.* During its brief career I went twice to see James Baldwin's play on Broadway. For one thing I wanted more of the performance by Diana Sands, the best any American actress has given all season. For another I wanted to make sure whether the play's faults were really enough to force its closing, as some critics seem to think, or whether, as I suspected, its virtues did it in. I am now ready to maintain the latter and to see in this a phenomenon of some social importance, but before arguing the point let me pay homage to the lady.

Diana Sands first came among us some years ago in *Raisin in the Sun,* a soap opera for dark skins and light consciences not much to my liking. It required Miss Sands merely to be pert, which she was, and nothing more. My joy at seeing her unfold in the Baldwin play was great.

In the third act she had a long soliloquy, a lament for her dead lover, in which she poured over the theater a libation of anger, love and blasphemy. The sexual language of this speech is direct. It demands to be uttered without shame. Miss Sands did it with such conviction that her dignity increased with each revealing line. Furthermore, she played it at the top of the emotional register, shouting, weeping and pounding the air with her fists, an indulgence few performers could risk without disaster.

Here was acting in the grand manner. After putting it to the test of a second viewing, I can report that it lost nothing in the repetition. Honor to Miss Sands for bringing it off, to Burgess Meredith, her director, for letting her do

it, and to James Baldwin for writing words to make it possible.

The play itself is based—"very distantly," as Baldwin has said—on the case of Emmett Till, murdered in 1955 by a white man who was acquitted but who later confessed. In the play the murderer's guilt is clear from the start, and so is the acquittal the jury will give. A Negro youth (Al Freeman Jr.), rebellious and unstable to the point of courting death, runs afoul of a poor white (Rip Torn) with enough pride of race and insecurity of personality to pull the trigger. Baldwin is interested in these two men only as types. His portrayal of them is therefore in sketch but with absolute mastery of detail.

From these sketches our eyes are led to watch the town's reaction to the murder. The whites form an almost solid front, that abstraction called justice being less real to them than their fear. The front is broken—at any rate cracked—by Parnell, a newspaper owner (in which role Pat Hingle gave the best performance he has ever brought us). A confidant of both the victim's father and the murderer, he tries to remain friends with both while seeing that justice is done. This, of course, is impossible; and when, on the witness stand, he has to choose, it is the truth he lets go.

Among the blacks, the most important reaction we watch is that of the boy's clergyman father (Percy Rodriguez). He has long been a spokesman and a bargainer for civil rights. He becomes an agitator ready to take up arms.

The play is about the breakdown of "moderation" in the face of antagonisms that are by nature irrational and immoderate.

James Baldwin's *forte* has never been the making of plots, the structuring of fiction, nor the psychological delineation of character. He is first and last a preacher. But preaching in the theater is by no means always a fault, let alone something bad for the box office. In [Rolf Hochhuth's] *The Deputy* Broadway has a sermon that is a solid hit, and the Lincoln Center Repertory has another in *After the Fall.* Neither is written half as well as *Blues for Mister Charlie.* The only trouble with sermons is that the more they are needed the less they are liked.

The terms in which James Baldwin chose to address his audience are not the terms in which they have wanted to listen. On the one hand, he alienated a large part of the liberal intelligentsia by paying scant attention to the political and economic roots of segregation. Marxist and socialist theory have not detained him. Absent also is any concern with the structure of American law and the elective process.

In other words, Baldwin stepped right outside the context in which most Americans now see the racial struggle. To them, it is a question of "civil rights," a constitutional question coupled, perhaps, with problems of unemployment, job training and other economic factors.

Instead of talking about all this, Baldwin has taken what will seem to many a reactionary step: he has described racial strife as *racial* strife, warfare between the black people and white people that is rooted in their separate ways of experiencing life, the difference symbolized in their sexuality. Baldwin thus opened himself to two attacks that critics were not slow to make: that he had swallowed "the myth of Negro sexual superiority," and that his characters were caricatures.

That is how it happened that Robert Brustein of the *New Republic* [see review dated 16 May 1964] saw eye to eye with Howard Taubman of the *New York Times,* with whom he had intended strongly to disagree. They both uttered the damning judgment that the characters were stereotyped. As a matter of fact, no play about the Negro has ever been seen in America that represented small-town Southern white people more accurately than does *Blues for Mister Charlie.* (I will not judge its representation of Negroes in such a town, not having lived among them.) What the play sins against is not the reality down South but the social (hence aesthetic) myths up North.

On the other hand, Baldwin alienated the middle-class paying audience by presenting a view of the racial conflict that it fears is true. Unlike Lorraine Hansberry, who wrote the box office success *Raisin in the Sun,* he did not flatter the audience by telling it what it wanted to believe—namely, that Negroes have the same ambitions, aches and pains as other people. The moral of *that* message is that there is nothing to fear.

James Baldwin, by contrast, has been saying for some years, notably in *The Fire Next Time,* that there is plenty to fear. He tells us in *Blues for Mister Charlie* that Negroes do *not* feel and think as white people and that the assumption they do is simply a manifestation of the white's innate sense that his own values and experience are normative.

The shape of the play is not a comic one of movement from problem to solution, which would be a kind of civic reassurance. It is a movement, in the Negroes themselves, from "liberality" to warfare. As this movement is not comic, neither is it tragic. There is no catharsis in it.

Though Baldwin is not Brecht, the temper of his play is Brechtian but not Marxist. It is Brechtian in avoiding both comedy and tragedy. It is Brechtian in that it is a call to action rather than an imitation of action. It is Brechtian in that it uses what people will think are stereotypes for the deliberate purpose of challenging received ideas. It asks us to reconsider whether the "stereotypes" may not be nearer the truth than the theory that explains them away. Far from being, as some have charged, a "commercial" sort of play, this one has failed on Broadway for the same reason Brecht fails there: it frightens people by challenging the *status quo,* while at the same time it challenges their way of *seeing* the *status quo.*

The social significance of *Blues for Mister Charlie* lies in what it reveals about our fear of fear. It should be looked at side by side with the reaction many people made to the threatened "stall-in" at the World's Fair, the threat of water wastage proposed by Brooklyn CORE, and other demonstrations that go beyond attack on specific injustices in a spirit of generalized protest.

There is indeed something illogical in these actions. The public, including many white liberals, seems to see in them a threat of anarchy, and many Negro leaders have warned that riots and the temporary breakdown of law enforcement can be expected. The North is discovering its kinship with the South, and its reaction is beginning to show itself as fear. At this point some of our fixed notions display their inadequacy, and the Baldwin play becomes relevant.

Dogma has it that nothing stands in the way of racial harmony but the ill will of benighted Southerners and other reactionaries who deny civil rights to Negroes. Ill will can be cured in due time by education, preaching and better laws. This view is so utterly rational and progressivist in character that it cannot accommodate into its understanding irrational antagonisms between racial groups. Hence it declares, contrary to much evidence, that sexual envy, which no doubt is irrational, has nothing to do with the problem. When a Baldwin says that it does, for Negro as well as white, he is said to be a purveyor of "myth."

The dogma, being designed to rule out fear, breaks down when fear becomes unavoidable. That is just where we are now. Southern "moderates" have been there a long time. Having no adequate resources to help them face that fear, having been told it was unrealistic, they became paralyzed by it and were notoriously ineffective in Southern politics. Power was exercised by the Faubuses, Barnetts and Wallaces who, however unprincipled, were realistic enough to see that fear existed, that it was inevitable and action must be predicated on it.

On the other side, Negroes became a political force in the South by virtue of the fact that they, who had lived long in fear, ceased to be afraid of it. They did not eliminate it, could not and did not try it. But they ceased to try to avoid it, and in that moment their ineffectiveness ended. I do not deny that an awakened class or racial consciousness had its importance, but class consciousness without the courage to face fear is impotent.

Impotence born of the fear of fear is what has been overcome by Negroes in the past 15 years, and it is what Baldwin is talking about in the Rev. Meridian Henry, who puts down his brief case and takes up his gun and his Bible. The message is not very sophisticated, but it is true enough; and it could hardly be more to the point at a time when the paralysis of the Southern "moderate" is creeping all over the country.

The sober citizens of the North, Midwest and West, if they do not want to be swept onto the sidelines in the next five or ten years, will have to learn that some (we don't know how much) violence is unavoidable. They will have to learn that violence itself is far from the worst of evils, even in a peaceable democracy. The repression of violence by a force that perpetuates injustice is worse. The violence of terrified people is worse than the violence of brave men.

Moderates will have to know that fear is their lot. Those who cannot risk when they are afraid, who cannot cope with anything but rational progress, will be made impotent by their fear; and their impotence will bring anarchy and violence all the closer. If Baldwin's play is offensive, or even just unrealistic, to them, they will find their moment of truth arrived too late. (pp. 16-17)

Tom F. Driver, "Barking Off Cue, or Mr. Charlie's Dilemma," in The Village Voice, *Vol. IX, No. 33, 4 June 1964, pp. 16-17.*

CRITICAL COMMENTARY

Calvin C. Hernton   (essay date 1970)

[*In the following excerpt from an essay that was first published in* Amistad I *(1970), Hernton surveys the criticism of* Blues for Mister Charlie. *He concludes that the play caused white Americans' "vicarious and pornographic romance" with Baldwin to come to an end, not because the play was an artistic failure but because it was "so straightforward, realistic and secular that whites found it difficult to face."*]

In "Blood of the Lamb," I made several analytical predictions. One was that Baldwin's writing would undergo a fiery baptism; I also asserted that when this happened the vicarious and pornographic romance that white Americans were carrying on with him would quietly cease.

The truth of this assertion was confirmed when James Baldwin wrote his play, **Blues for Mister Charlie,** and by the manner in which the white world reacted to its production. The play was brute, crude, violent, and bold, more in the fashion of Richard Wright (or LeRoi Jones . . .) than of the usual suffering, pleading, metaphysical Baldwin of *The Fire Next Time* and prior works.

Unlike most plays written by Negroes, **Blues for Mister Charlie** is not about civil rights or any of the other "acceptable" subjects on Negro-white relations. The play is based on the Emmett Till murder case of 1955, and it deals with the sexual variable, which is perhaps the most hushed-up and yet the most explosive factor involved in racism in the United States. And Baldwin's treatment of it is so straightforward, realistic and secular that whites found it difficult to face what they have been hiding and gliding over for centuries. Moreover, this Baldwin—the **Blues for Mister Charlie** Baldwin—is an aggressive, a masculine Baldwin. Add to this the fact that the sexuality of the Negroes in the play is earthy, rich, full of power and human animalism—all of which Baldwin does not apologize for, but affirms with dignity and prowess. It was simply too much for the majority of whites to accept or seriously consider.

For instance, both times I saw the play there were as many, if not more, whites in the audience than there were Negroes. One could not help but feel the negative vibrations radiating from the whites during the major portion of the evening. They seemed to squirm throughout the play and grow little in their seats; many tried to hold a straight face (face of chalk), but one could see and feel the hot charge boiling beneath their white masks. Upon two occasions—(a) when Richard (the Negro hero), back down South telling his friends how many white girls he has slept with up North, is showing a photograph of a girl with long hair and remarks, "Man, you know where all that hair's been"; and (b) when Richard tells Lyle, (the Southern bigot) who has been threatening him, "Man, are

you scared I'm going to get in your wife's drawers?"—I thought half of the white audience might jump up and storm out of the theater. But they held onto their seats. Again, after Richard has been murdered by Lyle, and Juanita (Richard's sweetheart, played by Diana Sands) in lamentation delivers her speech on how Richard made love to her, describing it in plain but powerful language, telling how she took Richard into her womb and how she "grind" him and how meaningful the act was—again, I saw the theater faces of white people twist and contort in agony and revulsion. In fact, the white ladies sitting next to me began gossiping very rapidly about the careers of Rip Torn (Lyle) and Pat Hingle (Parnell, the Southern liberal) as if nothing was happening on stage at all. And the applause of the whites—one got the impression that it was as much out of nervous reaction to cover up embarrassment as it was an expression of honest enthusiasm.

On the other hand, Negroes seemed to be enthralled with delight and moral vindication to see for the first time the true nature of their lives, and their plight, played back to them with dignity and no beating around the bush. Many Negroes were there with white companions. I recall one tall dark Negro who is a famous man. He came in with his white girl and sat down as if he was out for the usual "highbrow" theater evening. Before the play was half through, the Negro had unbuttoned his collar, had reared back in his seat, and was looking around as if he himself had written **Blues for Mister Charlie.** Pride was bursting on his face and chest.

Not only did whites in general recoil from the play, but the press, in most cases, reviewed something other than what the play was. The majority of reviewers said the play failed as a "civil rights" play. Those few who admitted what the play was about found ways of debunking it as far-fetched, saying that Richard got lynched because he "asked for it" [see Michael Smith's review dated 30 April 1964]. Only one reviewer wrote a favorable piece about the play. His name is Tom Driver and he has since resigned mysteriously from *The Reporter.* His favorable review was not printed in the magazine.

What Tom Driver said in his review (which was eventually published in the *Negro Digest, The Village Voice,* and *Christianity and Crisis*) was that the *virtues* of the play killed it [see review dated September 1964]. He praised the language of the play, which was raw, earthy, and full of four-letter words (and caused whites to shiver in their seats). After lauding Diana Sands' portrayal as the "best performance any American actress has given this year," Driver went on to affirm the essential reality of the play: that the white man (and woman) in America has a sexual hang-up about himself vis-à-vis the Negro, and it is this hang-up that terrifies the white man whenever he encounters the Negro, and that causes so much violence and bloodshed. Most of all, Driver viewed favorably Baldwin's stereotyped projection of Southern Negroes and whites; that is, the "sterile and sexually insecure" white male who places his "lily-white" wife upon a pedestal while he slips around at night with Negro women, and the "virile and lusty" Negro who enjoys the sex act to the fullest without guilt or reservations. Parnell, the Southern liberal, confesses his deep sexual involvement with a Negro woman. Lyle, the Southern bigot who is so afraid that Richard is after his wife, brags about how he has taken the bodies of many Negro girls. In fact, Lyle is really interested in Richard's sweetheart Juanita, rather than the other way around. And Jo (Lyle's wife, brilliantly played by Ann Wedgeworth), the typical fragile and neglected Southern "lady" who usually knows about her husband's clandestine behavior with black women and who herself has come to accept all the stereotyped notions and emotions about and toward the Negro, leaps (almost gladly!) to comply with her husband's accusation that Richard has "attacked" her when the latter came to Lyle's store to buy a Coke. In reality Richard never touched the woman and she knows it; yet in court she testifies to the contrary, and Lyle is set free *for* murdering Richard. After which Lyle brags again, "Hell yes, I killed that nigger," and is glad of it.

We "liberals" in America always want justice to win out in the end. Well, in the South there is no justice when it comes to the Negro. And Baldwin wrote it as it really is. The murderers of countless Emmett Tills are still running amuck throughout the entire South.

As I have indicated, many of the reviewers accused Baldwin of not writing a play, "technically" speaking. Well now, several of the plays of Arthur Miller, Eugene O'Neill, Clifford Odets, and others (*The Deputy,* by Rolf Hochhuth, for instance) are not plays, "technically" speaking. Yet such plays enjoy successful runs on as well as off Broadway. Any art form, I say art *form,* that deals with man's inhumanity to man and does not end with "justice winning out" or "crime does not pay" is viewed and reviewed in America as "controversial." Let's come closer to home. In regard to the Negro, when the white man is portrayed as a barbarous, unmitigated bigot, we not only label the art form as "controversial," we also cry out that it is not "art"; we call it "propaganda." Specifically, *Blues for Mister Charlie* hits white America between the eyes, and does not apologize for doing so. Evidently to talk about the white man's sexual fears and guilts is to strike him in the most vulnerable corners of his ego. And he loses all rationality, all objectivity. He either goes blank or he tries to absolve his guilt by simpleminded rationalizations. For instance, Michael Smith (*The Village Voice,* April 30, 1964) claims, " . . . Lyle kills Richard not so much because he is a Negro as because he asks for it." Later Smith asserts, "Lyle, more in defense of his sex-self-respect than of his race, murders Richard."

Unfortunately (or is it fortunately?) these remarks reveal more about Mr. Smith than they do about *Blues for Mister Charlie.* First of all, Richard does not behave around whites (Lyle and his wife) according to the "bowing-and-scraping" pattern that bigoted whites demand in the South. No, Richard walks and talks like a man who is aware of his dignity and inherent equality as a human being. To the psychotic white in the South this takes on a sexual meaning; it is perceived as a sexual assault. Secondly, the only sexual self-respect Lyle has is a false one, a guilty one shot through with and based on white male supremacy! Doesn't Mr. Smith know that sexual guilt and

paranoia are intricate aspects of racism in America? James Baldwin does! And thirdly, if Richard is "mean and tormented and looking for trouble," why is he mean, by what is he tormented? But most of all, Mr. Smith, like his Southern counterpart, seems to interpret Richard's "talking back" and standing up to Lyle and his wife as "looking for trouble."

I suppose that great numbers of Negroes in the South today are standing up and talking back and demanding human respect and in the process are "looking for trouble." I suppose that their endeavoring to secure their God-given rights and make America a better place in which ALL Americans can live means, with reference to their lynching, that Medgar Evers and James Chaney and countless others "asked for it." And finally, while throughout the decades the sexuality as well as the general behavior traits of Negroes has been thought of and portrayed as vulgar, subhuman and derogative, it is a telling thing that only when these same traits are portrayed with prowess and dignity against the barbarity, both sexual and otherwise, of whites, that only then (only now!) white men rise up to shout down intrusions. My grandmother used to say, "The ones who yell the loudest is the culprits with the mostest to hide."

In fact, there seemed to have been, at one time or another, an inside move to kill *Blues for Mister Charlie* before it came to its natural end, if indeed its end was natural. One day, an editor of a New York magazine called the box office for ticket reservations and was told by someone that all seats were sold out. The same editor waited several hours and called again, for he had been told such would happen and, behold, he was informed this time by another person that there were plenty of tickets available. I also understand that someone significantly connected with the play was quoted as having said, "Before I will have the things said about white men that are being said upon that stage, I'd as soon go broke."

Now, what does all this mean in terms of Baldwin's development as a writer and as a Negro? First, as a writer he is no longer addressing a predominantly white audience, at least no longer in the guilt-soothing terms that characterized most of his previous essays. In *Blues for Mister Charlie* he was no longer dealing exclusively with the subjective or moral coefficients of the white world's inhumanity toward the Negro. Rather, Baldwin was dealing with the raw, brute, objective facts of the white man's barbarity toward black people in America. Along with the terrible facts, there are the white man's fears, anxieties, and most of all, his guilt! *Blues for Mister Charlie* plowed deep into the very psyche of white America; with justified animosity and vindictiveness it hurled all of his atrocious deeds and horrible guilts solidly back into the white man's face! And seemingly it was too much for whites to bear. But Negroes loved it.

Which means that Baldwin, as a Negro, is writing less to soothe white folks' guilt and more to enlighten, dignify and anger American Negroes. With *Blues for Mister Charlie,* Baldwin plunged into the position of being a true spokesman not just for the middle class but for the masses of his people. Michael Smith of *The Village Voice* made this observation and added that it was "unfortunate," claiming that being a spokesman for the Negro nearly prevented Baldwin from being an "artist." Why is it that after the production of **Blues for Mister Charlie** appeared the very same whites who used to praise Baldwin now rise up to put him down!

Baldwin is not merely a writer. He is a Negro writer, and we Americans—especially white Americans—have seen to that and no doubt will continue to see to it for a long time hence. The question of whether **Blues for Mister Charlie** was artistically a bad play is about as relevant to the real issue as saying that *Crime and Punishment* is artistically a bulky, sloppy novel, which it certainly is. To wit, *Another Country* is so bad artistically that I am relatively sure its publication had little to do with art. But the critics "raved." They did not talk about the artistry of the book, but about how "bold" it was. With drooling mouths the public consumed it to the ticker tape of the best-seller lists. I saw them on subways, on buses, at lunch counters and midtown Madison Avenue restaurants—especially the young, up-and-coming, clean-shaven, no-mustached, gray-flanneled. Coming and going, I saw them reading about the country of A-not-her! Talk about art vs. propaganda. *Another Country* was almost nothing but propaganda; propaganda for homosexuality. I am definitely not making a moral judgment about homosexuality as artistic subject matter, or about James Baldwin. I *am* making a moral analysis of the character of white Americans in regard to their good faith when it comes to facing up to the social, political, economic and sexual horrors, in artistic presentations as well as in reality, that have been and are being heaped upon the American Negro. It seems—and this is the real issue—that whites in *this* country, despite an abundance of liberalism, are not yet morally capable of accepting any open presentation, on the one hand, of their sexual feelings regarding black men, and on the other hand, of the sexual depravity that white men (especially Southerners) have historically inflicted upon Negro women, the guilt stemming from it. This is what killed **Blues for Mister Charlie** and, in my opinion, severed the romantic involvement between James Baldwin and white America, forever.

Although James Baldwin may not sell as many books and will not be so affectionately discussed in white circles, or for that matter in lily-nice, middle-class Negro circles, the cessation of the romance represents a step forward rather than a stumble backward. Characteristically, Baldwin has written of the race problem, or of Negro-white relations, with a deep burning love (submission) that was rooted in the religion of the long-suffering. Repeatedly, incessantly, James Baldwin has pleaded with passion for forgiveness and love between whites and blacks as the solution for the nightmare that makes havoc of our lives. But, I believe, it has become apparent to Baldwin that the probability of a cleansing love and forgiveness between Negroes and whites is long in forthcoming. America is one of the most spiritually bankrupt countries in a world where it is, as Baldwin must know by now, terribly difficult to create and maintain a personal love, let alone love of mankind. But this is not to say that we will no longer see in Baldwin's work the influence of a deeply religious man. Emile

Capouya, a former editor at Macmillan who once shared an apartment with Baldwin, pointed out in 1963 in a lecture at the New School for Social Research that James Baldwin is not really a deep thinker in the sense of an academic or even a rugged intellectual; rather, he is a provincial preacher with a grand intelligence for literary style and eloquence—and he is at his best, as can be seen by comparing his essays with his fiction, when he is writing out of the depths of his spiritual background. And this background will continue to echo in his labor—no matter how charged otherwise with secular rage—until he lays his pen down and saunters into elemental peace. (pp. 109-15)

> *Calvin C. Hernton, "A Fiery Baptism," in* James Baldwin: A Collection of Critical Essays, *edited by Keneth Kinnamon, Prentice-Hall, Inc., 1974, pp. 109-19.*

THE AMEN CORNER

PRODUCTION REVIEWS

Henry Hewes   (review date 1 May 1965)

[Hewes is an American drama critic who wrote for the Saturday Review *from 1951-77. In the following review, Hewes admires "the compassion of Baldwin's writing" and the universality of the conflicts presented in* The Amen Corner.]

Novelist James Baldwin's 1954 play, **The Amen Corner,** has come here following a one-year run in Los Angeles. While its Harlem characters, its locale of the storefront gospel-singing church, and its juxtaposition of jivey talk and religious sanctimony is peculiar to Negroes, the play deals with racial discrimination not at all, and the deeper problems of its three central characters are universal.

At the beginning of the piece we see Sister Margaret, a woman who has rejected her husband and dominated her now eighteen-year-old son in order to answer what she believes to be the call of the Lord. We hear her preach with quiet confidence to her flock, and her interpretation of the gospel is as amusing in its way as are Tevye's misquotes from "the good book" in *Fiddler on the Roof.* Particularly droll is her explanation of why the king calls on Isaiah when in trouble but never invites him to his parties. Why should the best people be so treated? "Well, amen," she says. "They just holy" [Act I].

But Mr. Baldwin is out to demonstrate that Sister Margaret's holiness is not so all-sufficient and noble as it seems. We soon see that her son, David, is being torn by the desire to live his own life and yet to live up to his mother's vision of puritanical virtue. And when his estranged father, Luke, a jazz trombonist dying of tuberculosis, shows up, the untruth of her life begins to descend upon her. David learns that his father did not desert them, but that she walked out on him when she interpreted the death of her baby as a sign from God.

The horror of her act is beautifully revealed when Luke tells David that the most terrible time in a man's life is when everything that had held him together is suddenly gone and he can't find it. He laments, "Then that man start going down. If don't no hand reach out to help him that man goes under" [Act II].

Luke explains how a man can survive the most drastic losses if he has one thing. "That one thing is *him,* who he is inside—and I don't believe no man never got to that without somebody loved him, somebody *looked* at him, looked way down *in* him, spied him way down there and showed him to himself, and then started a-pulling, a-pulling him up so he could live."

When David asks his father why the wonderful jazz music he has created didn't give him enough satisfaction to keep him proud and happy, Luke sadly replies, "Music ain't kissing. Kissing's what you want to do. Music's what you got to do, *if* you got to do it. Question is how long can you keep on with the music when you ain't got nobody to kiss. Music don't come out of the air, baby!"

In the remainder of the play we watch Sister Margaret lose everything, too. Her church rejects her, her son tells her that he cannot stand lying to her any more and leaves to live his own life, and Luke dies. Margaret is now faced with harsh alternatives. One parishioner tells her, "I hope you make it to Heaven, because you is too late to catch any other train." And, looking back at her mistakes, she first defends her behavior toward her husband by saying, "Every time a woman's heart is grieved, a man is sleeping somewhere sound." Then she bewails what she did by exclaiming, "A woman's life is nothing but one long fight with a man, and Lord, you looks the most impossible man there is."

The scene in which she faces her catastrophe is remarkable. Bea Richards, who has appeared deceptively assured for two acts, explodes into agonized desperation and tears, but suddenly, in the middle of it all, the grotesque disproportion of her life's farcical pretense strikes her and she laughs violently. It is one of the most effective and daring moments in our current theater. At the end of the play she is left disillusioned but joyously fortified.

Director Frank Silvera's staging of the play in a unit setting that places important scenes far left front and far right front without completely blacking out the rest of the stage is awkward, and we frequently find ourselves tuning out on the kind of detail that is more appropriate to a novel than to a play. Similarly, the director's "theater of being" approach has led to performances that are often more convincing than dramatic. Miss Richards is unnecessarily complacent until her last-act eruption into high emotion. Frank Silvera appears a little too inspiredly wise as the wreckage of a returning ex-husband, and Art Evans overly cowed as David. One is apt to be more impressed with Isabell Sanford and Josie Dotson, who shine in briefer moments, and with the compassion of Mr. Baldwin's writing. For without compromising his convictions, he has in *The Amen Corner* told what appears to be a more timelessly

true story than he did in his more temporal and more categorically unforgiving *Blues for Mister Charlie.*

Henry Hewes, "The Gospel Untruth," in Saturday Review, *Vol. XLVIII, No. 18, May 1, 1965, p. 49.*

Harold Clurman   (review date 10 May 1965)

[*A celebrated director and theater critic, Clurman founded, in association with Lee Strasberg and Cheryl Crawford, the Group Theatre in 1931. For the next ten years, as its managing director, he helped create many notable productions, particularly of American plays. He served the* Nation, *the* New Republic, *and the* Observer *as drama critic from 1949 to 1963. His publications include* The Fervent Years: The Story of the Group Theatre *(1945),* Lies Like the Truth: Theatre Essays and Reviews *(1958), and* The Divine Pastime: Theatre Essays *(1974). In the review below, Clurman praises the "genuineness" of* The Amen Corner, *noting that Baldwin's "sure feeling for race, place and universality of sentiment" overshadows the drama's occasional "crudities" and "banalities" and thus makes watching the play a gratifying experience.*]

James Baldwin's *The Amen Corner* (Ethel Barrymore Theatre) provides one of the very few evenings which afforded me true pleasure this season. And how surprising. For if I wished to be "real critical" (which means a little foolish) I could easily point out the play's crudities, banalities, *longueurs,* etc. Text and production are marred by many blemishes but the total effect is touching and valuable. Drama does not live by technique alone, nor is art all a matter of "mastery."

What makes *The Amen Corner* gratifying is its genuineness. I don't mean "realism." The play's locale is a "storefront church"—the kind of Harlem church which has no exact denomination or theology except for its own blasted blessedness; and I am not in the least familiar with such an establishment. The sense of genuineness the play creates comes from its sure feeling for race, place and universality of sentiment. It is folk material unadorned and undoctored. It is the stuff which has made the best in Baldwin. It has heart and reaches the heart.

Its crucial passages are beautifully written, wrought of living speech from the mouths of the people whose very clichés somehow transform themselves into poetry. A woman is described as being "full of nature." A man dies and his wife says without emphasis, "My baby. You done joined hands with the darkness" [Act III]. But quotations out of context offer only the barest hint of the sudden poignancy of some of the play's phrases and idioms which are uttered as commonplaces.

The weakest moments are the conventionally comic and the factually "satiric" ones. The play is not "propaganda": it does not insist that religiosity turns the sorry creatures of the community away from reality. There is no glib anticlericalism here. "This way of holiness ain't no joke," says the unhappy and presumably bigoted woman minister who is the play's central character. "To love the Lord," she learns, "is to love all His children—all of them, everyone! and suffer with them and rejoice with them and never count the cost!" [Act III]. One believes this as one believes a spiritual. In a much simpler, a less probing way, Baldwin has used the material of his past somewhat as O'Neill used his own early youth in *Long Day's Journey Into Night.*

The Amen Corner was written before *Blues for Mister Charlie,* which is Baldwin in an angrier, more sophisticated, less appealing but perhaps more immediately "useful" vein. But nothing in the later play is as moving as the confrontation of the derelict father and his neglected son, or the minister's "reconversion" (a reconversion to a profounder humanity) in *The Amen Corner.*

It is possible that a great part of my enthusiasm for this production is due to its acting. The play is not well staged or designed. Some of the actors are awkward, insufficiently trained. Yet nearly everything "works" because there is an organic relation between the play's essence and the company. There is little art but much "nature."

Still, Frank Silvera's Luke (the father: a moribund jazz trombonist) strikes home. He may be a trifle soft in his interpretation but there is in him a will to contact the very core of his partners' (his son's, his wife's) being which overrides every other consideration and which moves one inescapably.

Bea Richards' Sister Margaret (the minister) is glorious. Hers is certainly the outstanding achievement in acting of this past season. Again, qualifications which might be damaging in other instances—a rather thin voice and a delivery that threatens to become monotonous, an interpretation that tends to subtract some of the iron and soul-smashing drive of the character—dissolve in the truth of Miss Richards' pathos, the overwhelming fullness of her womanliness in which the sorrow of bitter experience and the abiding humor and tenderness of a total cycle of life manifest themselves effortlessly and yet with electrifying surprise. (pp. 514-15)

> Harold Clurman, "The Amen Corner," in The Nation, *New York, Vol. 200, No. 19, May 10, 1965, pp. 514-15.*

CRITICAL COMMENTARY

Louis H. Pratt   (essay date 1978)

[*In the following excerpt, Pratt argues that* The Amen Corner *is not merely a "religious drama" but a complex exploration of the themes of illusion, self-deception, perversion of humanitarianism, and the search for identity.*]

I *The Common Chord*

There has always been a need for the unrestrained expression of black culture in American literature—the hope and despair, courage and fear, satisfaction and frustration, joy and sorrow felt by black people with concern neither for the values of white society nor for the restrictions that it seeks to impose upon the black artist. Indeed, there is no reason why the black artist should espouse white val-

ues, nor should he desire to incorporate those values in his writings.

As the artist exercises this unlimited freedom to explore the black soul, the mosaic pattern of a black world view emerges. We would not, of course, expect this view to coincide with the white world view anymore than it would be reasonable to assume that Orientalism would duplicate the world view of the Occident. Yet, in any world view—black, white, Oriental, or Occidental—in a very basic sense, we can recognize certain *inherent* values of a universal nature. Listed among these yearnings and striving are freedom from oppression, the discovery of self-identity, a profound pride in one's racial origins, a deep and abiding respect for one's culture, and a fervent belief in posterity as a means of propagating the heritage of the past and pointing toward new directions for the future.

In a real sense, then, the major problem of the black dramatist is identical to that of the black novelist: He must be able to effect the transmutation of his experience into the complex embodiment of a work of literary art. He must never *deny* the experiences of his culture, but he must be able to *interpret* his own cultural background in terms of universality, in terms of those experiences that strike a common chord of understanding and appreciation among humankind. He must present a work that radiates a certain limitlessness through the presentation of ideas, issues, and conflicts which are not bound by the ethnic, social, or even cultural milieu out of which they have come.

The term "universality," then, refers to those overlapping cultural elements that are recognizable and meaningful to peoples of differing ethnic, social, and cultural backgrounds. The black dramatist (or novelist, for that matter) must never abandon or underestimate the legitimacy of his own experiences. Instead, he must reaffirm those experiences within the broader context of human worth and values. He must accept the role of luminary which, according to Baldwin, is the *raison d'etre* of the artist in society: ". . . the conquest of the physical world is not man's only duty. He is also enjoined to conquer the great wilderness of himself. The precise role of the artist, then, is to illuminate that darkness, blaze roads through that vast forest, so that we will not, in all our doing, lose sight of its purpose, which is, after all, to make the world a more human dwelling place" [*Saturday Review,* 8 February 1964].

Let us consider Baldwin's plays from this perspective. The questions for which we shall seek answers are these: How do Baldwin's dramas, in fact, project beyond the world of protest and racism into the sanctuary of art? What are the dramatic techniques that he uses in his painstaking efforts to depict black life and culture and reveal the inherent universal values which emerge from the portraits he has drawn? What is there of human value in the ideas of these dramas? What illumination is shed on the "great wilderness of self" as man gropes amid the darkness in quest of self-identity and fulfillment?

II *Confusion and Conflict*

Sometimes the phrase "religious drama" is applied by Baldwin's critics to his first dramatic effort, *The Amen Corner.* This meaningless and inappropriate epithet re-

Scene from a performance of The Amen Corner *at the 1979 Black Theatre Festival U.S.A. in New York.*

flects a superficial grasp of the more significant aspects of the drama. It is a categorization which precisely points up the reason many critics are unable to analyze the broader philosophical aspects that dominate the play. They cannot view the *whole* drama of conflict because religion, the *part,* has obscured their view. Perhaps also, the critics have fallen victim to the idea that the black man's world is a sphere of religious and racial consciousness, and therefore it is expected that the theme of religion should dominate his writings in the instances where race has failed to prevail. I suggest that **Amen** is not a "religious drama" but rather a drama of interpersonal conflict, set against the background of a storefront Holy Roller church in Harlem. Only if we view the drama from this perspective can we discover the deeper human emotions and involvements with which the playwright is concerned.

Near the opening of **The Amen Corner** it becomes obvious that Margaret Alexander, the church's pastor, has fled the world of reality to take refuge—not in religion—but in illusion and self-deception. We find her in the midst of a homiletic rejoinder to the congregation's concepts of religion: "Some of you say, 'Ain't no harm in reading the funny papers.' But children, *yes,* there's harm in it. While you reading them funny papers, your mind ain't on the Lord. And if your mind ain't stayed on Him, every hour

of the day, Satan's going to cause you to fall. Amen! Some of you say, 'Ain't no harm in me working for a liquor company. I ain't going to be drinking the liquor, I'm just going to be driving the truck!' But a saint ain't got no business delivering liquor to folks all day . . . " [Act I].

This admonition raises the ancient, yet valid question of whether or not some objects can be considered intrinsically good or evil apart from their social context. Obviously, Margaret's response would be affirmative. But illusion suggests confusion, and even Margaret is not always consistent in her attitude. When she is questioned about the "worldliness" of the drums and trumpets that the Philadelphia church members plan to bring to New York, she tells Sister Rice that "the evil is in what folks do [with the drum or trumpet] and what it leads them to. Ain't no harm in praising the Lord with anything you get in your hands" [Act II].

But that "anything" does not include a liquor truck. Sister Boxer recognizes this incongruity and continues her challenge: "Well, ain't a truck a *thing?* And if it's all right to blow a trumpet in church, why ain't it all right for Joel to drive that truck, so he can contribute a little more to the house of God?" Margaret replies simply that there is "all the difference in the world." She can clearly see that a musical instrument has no intrinsic moral significance, but she fails to regard the liquor truck in that same light.

Another theme in the play concerns the perversion of one of the basic concepts of Christianity: humanitarianism. The foundation of Christian doctrine rests on the compassion and sympathy of one human being for another—the saved and the unsaved—and we would expect that one as holy as Margaret would practice what she preaches. Yet we are struck by a merciless, hypocritical piety which becomes apparent when Luke returns home and collapses. In spite of her husband's need, Margaret refuses to postpone her trip to Philadelphia because "the Lord made me leave that man in there a long time ago because he was a sinner. And the Lord ain't told me to stop my work . . . " [Act I]. Here we have the curious parodox of the woman of God who refuses to help an unsaved brother—her husband—precisely because he is a "sinner." Margaret has other souls to save.

When we consider the allusions to fancy cars and good times which the Philadelphia congregation seems to enjoy, the ostensible purpose for her visit lies open to question. This is particularly true in light of the apparent neglect of her own congregation, as seen when Sister Moore raises the question of Margaret's visit to Sister Rice's mother while Sister Boxer listens. The two women begin to empathize with Margaret because the Philadelphia visits have left her with her "hands full," but Sister Boxer recognizes the hypocrisy inherent in their pastor's priorities and counters, "She got her hands full right down there in her own house. Reckon she couldn't get over to pray for your mother, Sister Rice, she couldn't stay here to pray for her own husband" [Act II].

III *"A Fatal Weakness"*

The social significance of the play, as I have suggested, is paramount. On this level the familiar Baldwin theme of the search for identity becomes apparent. Fred L. Standley's succinct analysis [in *South Atlantic Quarterly,* 65 (Summer 1966)] of the significance of this quest in Baldwin's writings provides a context for my consideration here:

> This search or quest for identity is indispensable in Baldwin's opinion, and the failure to experience such is indicative of a fatal weakness in human life. . . .
>
> The quest for identity always involves a man with other men—there can be no self-perception apart from our outside the context of interpersonal relationships. Only within the dynamic interplay of personalities can men become profoundly aware of the significance of being a man. Baldwin sees the lack of interpersonal relations as explicitly related to the breakdown of communication between persons—specifically 'the breakdown of communication between the sexes'. . . .

Luke appears in Act I, and we soon discover that David believes his father had abandoned him. But it is Margaret who is guilty of desertion. She had interpreted the death of their second baby as a sign from the Lord to leave her husband and find a "hiding place." She finds sanctuary in

the church because all other doors are closed to her, and she begins her quest for self as a minister of God. But, as Standley's comments indicate, Margaret has made a tragic mistake which is revealed when Mrs. Jackson comes forward to have Margaret pray for her ailing baby:

> MARGARET: Maybe the Lord wants you to leave that man.
>
> MRS. JACKSON: No! He don't want that!
> [Act I]

Mrs. Jackson refuses Margaret's advice because she has already discovered that her identity can only be achieved through an open line of communication with her husband. Margaret has yet to realize this.

The parallel story of the two women becomes even more significant when we consider the sharp contrast which Baldwin makes. In Act III, after her baby has died, Mrs. Jackson tells Margaret, "I ain't like you, Sister Margaret. I don't want all this, all these people looking to me. I'm just a young woman, I just want my man and my home and my children." Margaret, too, had lost a child when she was a young woman but instead of standing by Luke, she nagged him to drink because she felt that he was responsible for the baby's death. She deprived Luke and David of the family relationship which each needed so badly, though no more than she herself required. And as Mrs. Jackson stands alone in the church—a young woman who has just lost her second child—she is bewildered and perplexed. Margaret, however, begins to see her own mistake from the past. Realizing that she has taken the wrong road, Margaret reverses the advice that she had given to Mrs. Jackson prior to the baby's death. "Go on home to your husband," she advises compassionately. "Go on home to your man."

In all probability, Luke is the most sensitive and perceptive character in the play. In one of the most memorable scenes, he describes his suffering, and we are moved to empathy and pity. He tells David that he has failed in his quest for identity—not because of his music—but because he has been denied the most basic human quality—love: "I don't believe no man ever got to . . . [who he is inside] without somebody loved him. Somebody *looked* at him, looked *way* down there and showed him to himself—and then started pulling, a-pulling of him up—so he could live" [Act II]. Luke realizes that Margaret's distorted sense of reality has precluded the extension of her love and understanding, thereby denying David the pursuit of his manhood. He knows that any efforts either to prescribe the terms of that quest or to protect him from its consequences can only result in the pain and misery of failure which he himself knows only too well. Luke has learned that a man must strike out, against the odds, if necessary, to discover the meaning of his own life. And he encourages David to take the first step toward reaching that goal.

Baldwin skillfully uses the contrasting qualities of vision and blindness to symbolize Margaret's lack of inner sight as compared to that possessed by Luke. This juxtaposition becomes particularly significant near the end of the drama, as the two parents discuss the boy—Margaret as if he were dead, Luke affirming that he is alive:

MARGARET: He's gone.

LUKE: He's gone into the world. He's gone into the world!

MARGARET: Luke, you won't never see your son no more.

LUKE: But I seen him one last time. He's in the world, he's living.

MARGARET: He's gone. Away from you and away from me.

LUKE: He's living. He's living. Is you got to see your God to know he's living?

[Act III]

The references to "dark" and "white" further serve to draw our attention to the contrasting moods and heighten our awareness of these two different reactions to the boy's departure:

MARGARET: Everything—is dark this morning.

LUKE: You all in white . . .

[Act III]

Luke's subsequent death occasions Margaret's remorse and enhances the cognizance of her own identity. She is forced into a reexamination of those values that have precipitated her misfortune, and she emerges in the final scene with a fuller understanding of the error of her ways: "Her triumph . . . is that . . . although she has lost everything, [she] also gains the keys to the kingdom. The kingdom is love, and love is selfless, although only the self can lead one there. She gains herself." (pp. 82-7)

Louis H. Pratt, in his James Baldwin, *Twayne Publishers, 1978, 157 p.*

FURTHER READING

THE AMEN CORNER

"Amen." *Newsweek* LXV, No. 17 (26 April 1965): 90.
Brief review which condemns *The Amen Corner* as "inept and tedious, making earnestness do the work of imagination."

Sheed, Wilfrid, "Amen, Amen." *Commonweal* LXXXII, No. 7 (7 May 1965): 221-22.
Unfavorable review in which the critic argues that *The Amen Corner* is ineffective because it is dated.

BLUES FOR MISTER CHARLIE

Bigsby, C. W. E. "The Committed Writer: James Baldwin as Dramatist." *Twentieth Century Literature* 13, No. 1 (April 1967): 39-48.
Examines *Blues for Mister Charlie* in light of Baldwin's other writings, specifically the essay "Everybody's Protest Novel." Bigsby concludes that throughout the play, Baldwin "demonstrates his failure to abide by his own strictures" and that the work "matches with disturbing precision his own definition of sterile protest literature."

"Blues for Mr. Charlie." *Ebony* XIX, No. 8 (June 1964): 188-93.
Photo-essay containing brief commentary on *Blues for Mister Charlie.*

Lewis, Theophilus. Review of *Blues for Mr. Charlie. America* 110, No. 22 (30 May 1964): 776-77.
Praises *Blues for Mister Charlie* as exciting, "intrinsically charged with conflict" and "the most challenging play of the season."

Rogoff, Gordon. "Muddy Blues." *The Commonweal* LXXX, No. 10 (29 May 1964): 299-300.
Unfavorable review of *Blues for Mister Charlie* in which the critic censures Baldwin for a lack of depth in the arguments presented. Rogoff finds that the assertions of the play "take us toward the fringe areas of truth while leaving the depths unplumbed."

Tedesco, John L. "*Blues for Mister Charlie*: The Rhetorical Dimension." *Players* 50, No. 1-2 (Fall-Winter 1975): 20-3.
Isolates and examines Baldwin's "rhetorical strategies as they emerge from the form and context" of *Blues for Mister Charlie* and places these strategies in their historical context.

Turpin, Walter E. "The Contemporary American Negro Playwright." *CLA Journal* IX, No. 1 (September 1965): 12-24.
Affirmative interpretation of *Blues for Mister Charlie* which defends Baldwin's plot structure as appropriate to his subject matter.

Williams, Sherley Anne. "The Black Musician: The Black Hero as Light Bearer." In *James Baldwin: A Collection of Critical Essays,* edited by Keneth Kinnamon, pp. 147-54. Englewood Cliffs, N. J.: Prentice-Hall Inc., 1974.
Explores Baldwin's use of the musician in *Blues for Mister Charlie* as a representative of the black American male experience.

William Wells Brown

1816?-1884

William Wells Brown was the author of *The Escape; or, a Leap for Freedom,* the first drama published by an African American writer. Similarly, his *Clotel; or, the President's Daughter; A Narrative of Slave Life in the United States* was the first novel published by a black American. In addition, Brown was an internationally recognized historian and lecturer.

Brown was born and lived the first twenty years of his life on a plantation near Lexington, Kentucky, the son of a slave mother and a white slaveholding father. As a bondman, young William was often "hired out" by a succession of masters, a practice which gave him the opportunity to expand the limited horizons normally imposed upon a victim of the "peculiar institution" of slavery. In 1830, after several years laboring in hotels and on steamboats, he began working for Elijah P. Lovejoy, an abolitionist newspaperman who was later murdered by a proslavery mob. Under Lovejoy's direction, William acquired a rudimentary education, though he remained functionally illiterate for some time. After six months with Lovejoy, the young man was again hired out as a steward on a steamboat. It was from this ship, the *Chester,* while it was docked at a small town on the Ohio River, that William made his escape to freedom on New Year's Day, 1834. While a fugitive, William was befriended by an Ohio Quaker named Wells Brown. The young man was so grateful for the assistance he received that he honored his benefactor by taking his name. From then on the ex-slave was known as William Wells Brown.

Brown first settled in Cleveland, where he met and married Elizabeth Schooner, a free Negro. (Elizabeth died in 1851; nine years later he married his second wife Annie Elizabeth Gray.) In Cleveland, Brown worked as a handyman while continuing to teach himself reading and writing. He then moved to Monroe, Michigan, where he set up his own barbershop and established a small bank, both of which were profitable. Despite these successes, he decided to hire on as a steward on a Lake Erie steamboat. During this period, Brown became an important link in the Underground Railroad, helping other escaped slaves reach freedom in Canada. He eventually moved to Buffalo, New York, where he established a temperance society, and where he met the abolitionist William Lloyd Garrison, who enlisted him as a lecturer in the antislavery cause. Brown became a tireless speaker on behalf of reform, temperance, and antislavery, delivering literally thousands of lectures both in the United States and abroad.

Brown's first publication, *Narrative of William W. Brown, a Fugitive Slave, Written by Himself* was the author's vivid account of his life, trials, and escape to freedom. It was a great success, going through four printings in two years, and establishing Brown as an important social reformer.

The success of the *Narrative* encouraged him, and in 1848 he collected a group of antislavery songs and published them under the title *The Anti-Slavery Harp: A Collection of Songs for Anti-Slavery Meetings.*

Because of his ability as a speaker, Brown was chosen by the American Peace Society as its representative to the Paris Peace Congress of 1849. He was to remain in Europe for the next five years. Warmly received in European intellectual circles, Brown became friends with the English statesman Richard Cobden, the French writers Victor Hugo and Alexis de Tocqueville, and other notable figures of the day. These activities, as well as his extensive travels as an abolitionist lecturer, are chronicled in his next publication, *Three Years in Europe; or, Places I Have Seen and People I Have Met.* Brown was at this time still a fugitive slave, and it was not until several English friends raised the money to pay his indenture that he became a legally free man.

While in England, Brown released the novel *Clotel; or, the President's Daughter: A Narrative of Slave Life in the United States,* a work that proved to be a popular success and something of a scandal. Drawing on the legend that Thomas Jefferson had fathered many children by his slave mistress, Brown cast his heroine, Clotel, as the slave daughter of the former president. This version was never published in the United States; instead, Brown issued a revised version titled *Miralda; or, The Beautiful Quadroon; a Romance of American Slavery, Founded on Fact.* This was printed in New York as a newspaper serial in 1860-1861. Three years later he published another version with the title *Clotelle: A Tale of the Southern States.* It was again reissued in 1867 as *Clotelle; or, The Colored Heroine: A Tale of the Southern States.*

For these American versions Brown chose not to suggest presidential parentage for his heroine, concentrating instead on the heroism of his black characters in their fight for freedom.

By 1856 Brown had also written a drama, *Experience; or, How to Give a Northern Man a Backbone.* This work was never published and is now lost. Numerous synopses and reports of Brown's readings of it do survive, however. These accounts indicate that audiences were warm in their regard for the play. Within a year, Brown had composed a second play, *The Escape; or, a Leap for Freedom.* Just as *Clotel* was the first novel published by an African American, this work holds that distinction in drama. Though *The Escape* was never performed on stage, Brown gave many readings of the play, largely to antislavery gatherings in the North. Again Brown's recitals were enthusiastically received. Researchers have discovered references to a play called *Doughface* (or *Doe-face*) written sometime in the 1850s by a "Mr. Brown." Some scholars have argued that this was a third dramatic work by William Wells Brown; others have maintained that *Doughface* was an alternative title for *Experience.* Recently, however, scholars have concluded that *Doughface* was not composed by William Wells Brown but by an otherwise unknown writer, James Brown.

It is perhaps as a historian of the African American experience that Brown is best remembered. In such works as *The Black Man: His Antecedents, His Genius, and His Achievements, The Negro in the American Rebellion: His Heroism and His Fidelity,* and *The Rising Son; or The Antecedents and Advancement of the Colored Race,* Brown illustrates the importance of blacks to American culture. In his last work, *My Southern Home; or, The South and Its People,* Brown presents essays of a nostalgic nature, combining his political and social concerns in a reminiscence of the South.

The Escape tells the story of Glen and Melinda, slaves who must suffer the whims and passions of their masters. The two secretly marry, despite having been expressly forbidden to do so. When Melinda's master Dr. Gaines learns of the marriage, he arranges to have Glen imprisoned and whipped. Glen overpowers his jailer, however, and escapes. The lovers meet in a woods and set out together for freedom in Canada. They are chased by Dr. Gaines and professional slave catchers. This story is interspersed with numerous comic scenes and subplots featuring minor characters. One such sequence concerns Cato, a clownish figure who is also a slave to Dr. Gaines. When the doctor goes out after Glen and Melinda, he takes Cato with him, not knowing that the slave longs for freedom. Cato es-

capes, eventually joining Glen and Melinda in their flight. The play's climax occurs when the three fugitives are confronted by their pursuers just as they are about to board a ferry that will take them across the Niagara river to Canada. A fight ensues, which is won by the former slaves, who then make good their escape.

Critics of *The Escape* have consistently recognized the significance of the play in the history of African American literature and have acknowledged its usefulness as one of Brown's many tools in the fight against slavery. Critical response to the play as a work of art, however, has varied greatly since it was first written and presented. As already suggested, accounts of Brown's own readings of the play are universally favorable. These reports of "large and appreciative" audiences that listened "with deepest interest" testify to the high regard in which it was originally held. At the end of the published text of *The Escape* are reprinted extracts from several admiring reviews. Among them is a notice from the *Philadelphia Evening Bulletin* claiming that a reading by Brown of *The Escape* was "highly entertaining, and gave the greatest satisfaction to an intelligent and appreciative audience. The Drama is instructive, as well as very laughable." Similarly, the *Philadelphia Morning Times* observed that it "is well executed, and was finely delivered." The Auburn, New York *Daily Advertiser* judged the drama "a masterly refutation of all apologies for slavery" and praised its abundance of "wit, satire, philosophy, argument and facts, all ingeniously interwoven into one of the most interesting dramatic compositions of modern times." The reviewer for the *Seneca Falls Courier* stated that "Mr. Brown exhibits a dramatic talent possessed by few who have, under the best instructions, made themselves famous on the stage. He evinces a talent for tragic and comic representation rarely combined. If you want a good laugh, go and hear him. If you want instruction or information upon the most interesting question of the day, go and hear him. You cannot fail to be pleased." Clearly, Brown's initial audiences delighted in the play's unique mixture of comedy and pathos, fact and fiction, entertainment and education.

Early twentieth-century scholars and historians, however, were much less admiring. Basing their judgments of *The Escape* on the printed text rather than on reports of Brown's masterful oral presentation of the drama, they routinely condemned it as disorganized and melodramatic. The editors of *The Negro Caravan,* Sterling A. Brown, Arthur P. Davis, and Ulysses Lee, dismissed it as simply "a bad play" and found fault with precisely what the earlier audiences had admired: its variety of styles and moods. These critics considered it a flaw in the play that "comic skits are interspersed among the lugubrious and elegant passages." Similarly, J. Saunders Redding found *The Escape* "loosely constructed according to the formula of the day and marred by didacticism and heroic sentimentality." More serious was the charge common among such critics that Brown often reduced his characters to stereotypes and mere blackface minstrel figures.

Since the 1960s, *The Escape* has increasingly been the subject of serious study, and it has significantly risen in critics' estimation. Rather than censuring the drama as formulaic, as Redding had done, Doris Abramson defended the drama as "a well-made play by standards of the period." These nineteenth-century standards embraced melodrama, "variety of characterization," and "spine-chilling scenes of seduction and revenge," all of which *The Escape* has in abundance, she observed. James V. Hatch and Ted Shine likewise regarded Brown as a skillful author who "knew what his audience liked—melodrama!" and therefore gave them "plays that moved in a succession of short scenes arranged for maximum variety of emotions—from the lover's tryst, to dialect comedy, to a fight, to a song." Thus, they concluded, "as a piece of theatre, Mr. Brown's play deserves our attention." Although William Edward Farrison was less favorably disposed toward *The Escape,* finding it forced and artificial in both characters and dialogue, he nevertheless judged it "an authentic and vivid portrayal of slavery."

Brown was a passionate, committed writer and speaker who was, as he himself seemed to suggest, more concerned with the content than the form of his works. Nevertheless, critics agree, in such pieces as *The Escape,* Brown strove to offer more than merely an informational lecture. By exploring serious issues through humorous or thrilling action in *The Escape,* he sought to move his listeners as well as persuade them, to entertain as well as inform. Whether or not he was successful remains the subject of critical debate. What is certain is that Brown was a dedicated fighter for the abolitionist cause who devoted his life and his work to the freedom and dignity of his people. Self-educated and strong-willed, he defied the barriers of racial prejudice to contribute the first play, the first novel, and some of the first notable works of history by an African American, enriching the lives of all Americans through an explication of the black experience.

(For further information on Brown's life and career, see *Nineteenth-Century Literature Criticism,* Vol. 2; and *Dictionary of Literary Biography,* Vols. 3 and 50.)

PRINCIPAL WORKS

PLAYS

Experience; or, How to Give a Northern Man a Backbone [unpublished] 1856?
**The Escape; or, a Leap for Freedom* 1858

OTHER MAJOR WORKS

Narrative of William W. Brown, A Fugitive Slave, Written by Himself (autobiography) 1847; enlarged 1848
The Anti-Slavery Harp: A Collection of Songs for Anti-Slavery Meetings [editor] (songs) 1848
Three Years in Europe; or, Places I Have Seen and People I Have Met (travel essays) 1852; expanded as *The American Fugitive in Europe. Sketches of Places and People Abroad* 1855

***Clotel; or The President's Daughter: A Narrative of Slave Life in the United States* (novel) 1853
The Black Man; His Antecedents, His Genius, and His Achievements (history) 1863
The Negro in the American Rebellion: His Heroism and His Fidelity (history) 1867
The Rising Son; or, The Antecedents and Advancement of the Colored Race (history) 1873
My Southern Home; or, The South and Its People (narrative essays) 1880

*This is the date of first publication rather than first performance.

**This novel was revised as *Miralda; or, The Beautiful Quadroon; a Romance of American Slavery, Founded on Fact,* 1860-1861; also revised as *Clotelle; A Tale of the Southern States,* 1864; also revised as *Clotelle: or, The Colored Heroine; A Tale of the Southern States,* 1867

AUTHOR COMMENTARY

Author's Preface to *The Escape* (1858)

[*The following essay is Brown's introduction to the printed version of* The Escape. *He admits that the play may have defects but claims that it was "written for my own amusement" and was not meant to be made public.*]

This play was written for my own amusement, and not with the remotest thought that it would ever be seen by the public eye. I read it privately, however, to a circle of my friends, and through them was invited to read it before a Literary Society. Since then, the Drama has been given in various parts of the country. By the earnest solicitation of some in whose judgment I have the greatest confidence, I now present it in a printed form to the public. As I never aspired to be a dramatist, I ask no favor for it, and have little or no solicitude for its fate. If it is not readable, no word of mine can make it so; if it is, to ask favor for it would be needless.

The main features in the Drama are true. GLEN and MELINDA are actual characters, and still reside in Canada. Many of the incidents were drawn from my own experience of eighteen years at the South. The marriage ceremony, as performed in the second act, is still adhered to in many of the Southern States, especially in the farming districts.

The ignorance of the slave, as seen in the case of "BIG SALLY," is common wherever chattel slavery exists. The difficulties created in the domestic circle by the presence of beautiful slave women, as found in DR. GAINES's family, is well understood by all who have ever visited the valley of the Mississippi.

The play, no doubt, abounds in defects, but as I was born in slavery, and never had a day's schooling in my life, I owe the public no apology for errors.

W. W. B.
(pp. 3-4)

William Wells Brown, in a preface to his The
Escape; or, A Leap for Freedom: A Drama in
Five Acts, *1858. Reprint by Rhistoric Publica-
tions, 1969, pp. 3-4.*

OVERVIEWS AND GENERAL STUDIES

Benjamin Brawley   (essay date 1935)

[*One of the most prolific writers of all African American
educators, Brawley is best known for his works in literary and social history. Several of his books are considered standard texts in college and university curricu-
lums. Among these are* The Negro in Literature and Art
in the United States *(1918),* The Negro Genius: A New
Appraisal of the Achievement of the American Negro
in Literature and the Fine Arts *(1937), and* Negro
Builders and Heroes *(1937). In the following excerpt
from his 1935 work* Early Negro American Writers,
*Brawley provides a summary of Brown's life and career.
Regarding* The Escape, *the critic states that "the language is stilted and there is an excess of moralizing" in
the play, "but occasionally there are flashes of genuine
drama."*]

In his day William Wells Brown attempted more different
things than any other writer connected with the Negro
race, and he won success; but his importance is now almost wholly historical. He was born in Lexington, Ky.,
about 1815. His father was a slaveholder, and his mother,
a mulatto, a slave. As a child he was taken to St. Louis and
when ten years of age was hired to the captain of a steamboat on the Mississippi River. At twelve he was employed
as office boy by Elijah P. Lovejoy, then editor of the *St.
Louis Times,* but in little more than a year was again on
a steamboat. In 1834, at Cincinnati, he escaped, and in
making his way farther North was assisted by a Quaker,
Wells Brown, whose name he adopted. Having found employment on a boat on Lake Erie, he later became a steward, and in this capacity helped many fugitives to get to
Canada. The number thus assisted amounted each year to
hardly less than sixty-five; and at Buffalo, where he made
his home, Brown organized a vigilance committee to help
any slave who might be making his way to freedom. Meanwhile he strove in every way to advance in education. In
1843 he was employed as an agent by the Western New
York Anti-Slavery Society, in 1847 he transferred to the
Massachusetts Anti-Slavery Society, and in 1849 went to
England, with strong letters of introduction. He was received as a distinguished representative of the anti-slavery
cause, and a speech that he made at the Peace Congress
in Paris won the warm approval of Victor Hugo, the president. As the Fugitive Slave Law of 1850 made it dangerous for him to return, Brown remained in England for five
years, until 1854, when he was formally manumitted. He
supported himself by lectures and writing; and, having
studied medicine, he settled in Cambridge, Mass., as a
physician, later residing in Chelsea. Much of his time,
however, was given to his books, and he was also interest-

ed in the temperance movement, woman suffrage, and
prison reform. He died November 6, 1884.

Brown was a voluminous author. He contributed freely to
the anti-slavery press, and was also the first American
Negro to write a novel, a play, and a book of travel. He
had, however, neither a sound education nor a sure sense
of form, and he depended unduly on the sensational. In
1847 appeared in its first form *Narrative of William W.
Brown,* and other editions followed rapidly. It was said
that the first three editions, amounting to eight thousand
copies, were sold in eight months. The book succeeded by
its use of the concrete, many stories of slavery being included. The next year Brown edited *The Anti-Slavery
Harp,* a small collection of song poems, including "Jefferson's Daughter," which was based on a statement that a
daughter of Thomas Jefferson had been sold in New Orleans for $1,000—a theme that became the basis of the novel
Clotel. Three Years in Europe (London, 1852) was assisted
to wide circulation by the excitement over *Uncle Tom's
Cabin. Clotel, or The President's Daughter* (London, 1853)
was the story of an efficient colored woman, represented
as the housekeeper of Jefferson, who had two beautiful
daughters. The young women at first lived in comfort, but
later they were called to pass through many harrowing situations until at last the heroine, pursued by slave-catchers,
drowned herself in the Potomac in sight of the Capitol.
The scene shifts rapidly, and the crowded story includes
several episodes that, like the Nat Turner insurrection,
have no generic connection with the main theme. There
were American editions in 1864 and 1867, but for these
the the title was *Clotelle: A Tale of the Southern States,* and
any reference to Jefferson was deleted. **The Escape, or A
Leap for Freedom** (Boston, 1858) was a drama in five acts.
In this the language is stilted and there is an excess of moralizing, but occasionally there are flashes of genuine
drama, as when a mistress reveals her jealousy of a favorite
slave. One finds references to another novel and another
play that Brown is said to have written, but neither of
these works is now accessible. *The Black Man: His Antecedents, His Genius, and His Achievements* (New York and
Boston, 1863) appeared just after the issuing of the Eman-
cipation Proclamation and within a year was in the third
edition. It was followed by the *The Negro in the American
Rebellion: His Heroism and His Fidelity* (Boston, 1867).
In this work Brown showed that he had not the capacity
for research or the accuracy and perspective of the trained
historian, but by gossip and human interest stories he succeeded in producing a readable book. Both works contributed to and were superseded by *The Rising Son* (Boston,
1874). This book was not as scholarly as William C. Nell's
Colored Patriots of the American Revolution (1855), to say
nothing of George W. Williams' *History of the Negro Race
in America* (1883), but, like most of Brown's efforts, it was
a success, ten thousand copies being sold within a year. *My
Southern Home, or The South and Its People* (Boston,
1880), is a series of narrative essays, sketchy, but often
bright, and sometimes valuable for the information they
give. (pp. 168-70)

*Benjamin Brawley, "William Wells Brown,"
in his* Early Negro American Writers: Selections with Biographical and Critical Intro-

ductions, *1935. Reprint by Books for Libraries Press, 1968, pp. 168-70.*

J. Saunders Redding   (essay date 1939)

[*Redding was an American educator, critic, historian, and author. His 1939 work* To Make a Poet Black, *from which the following excerpt is taken, has been highly praised as a landmark study of African American literature. His other writings include* Stranger and Alone: A Novel *(1950),* On Being a Negro in America *(1951), and* The Negro *(1967). Redding here surveys Brown's life and writings.* The Escape, *he charges, "shows clearly that Brown knew nothing of the stage."*]

The most unusual figure in the literary history of the American Negro is William Wells Brown. A great deal of the interest which attaches to him is, perhaps, artificial, growing out of the confusion and variety of the stories he told about himself. At one time or another he put forward at least three versions of his parentage and early childhood. In what seems to be the first autobiographical account, he tells us that he was born in Kentucky of slave parents, and that as a child he learned to work in the field and in the house. In the second account he sheds no further light on his ancestry, but tells us that he was stolen by a slave trader shortly after birth. Finally, in the second revised edition of his *Narrative,* he divulges that he was born on an undetermined date in Lexington, Kentucky, of a white father (scion of the family to which his mother was slave) and a mother whose father, "it was said, was the noted Daniel Boone." All accounts agree on two circumstances: that he was born in Kentucky, and that later, while still a boy, he escaped into Ohio.

The discrepancies in the stories of Brown's birth and his early life may be due to one of three things: Brown himself may have been untruthful; unscrupulous publishers, seeking to dress an old tale in more attractive colors, may have been responsible; and last, the white-father, Daniel Boone-grandfather version may have been invented by abolitionist editors in an effort further to stigmatize slavery. White (and generally aristocratic) paternity was certainly a favorite propagandic device in the fictional stories of slaves. It was used to show the demoralizing effect of slavery upon the master class. Many so-called biographies and autobiographies of "escaped slaves" were pure inventions of white writers of the period.

When Brown escaped into Ohio he was befriended by a Quaker, Wells Brown, from whom he took his name. Later he seems to have been recaptured, and through various changes in his ownership he became a cabin boy on the Mississippi, a confidential assistant to a slave trader, and finally a printer's devil in (and this is his own unestablished story) the news office of Elijah P. Lovejoy, an abolitionist journalist in St. Louis who was later killed for his liberal views. Brown tells us that it was in his capacity as printer's devil that he learned to read. Later he went into Canada.

Brown earned his living as he could and spent most of his spare time in study. Certainly in western New York State, to which he eventually made his way, there was abroad

enough of the spirit of freedom and democracy to encourage him. An impressionable man all his life, he was touched by nearly everything he heard and saw, absorbing much that was odd and valueless along with that that was solid and worthwhile. His autobiographies are full of his early impressions as an escaped slave. Finally, "impressed with the importance of spreading anti-slavery truth, as a means of abolishing slavery, I commenced lecturing as an agent of the western New York Anti-Slavery Society, and have ever since devoted my time to the cause of my enslaved countrymen." Though this work engaged him for fifteen years, and though it has been estimated that he delivered in England alone a thousand speeches during a stay of five years from 1849 to 1854, Brown's speeches are lost for the most part. This apparently studied neglect of his own speeches seems to indicate that he was interested chiefly in writing.

William Wells Brown was the first serious creative prose writer of the Negro race in America. Three editions of the *Narrative of William Wells Brown,* his first considerable work, appeared under the sponsorship of the Massachusetts Anti-Slavery Society between 1847 and 1849. *The Black Man, St. Domingo,* and *Three Years In Europe* were published before the close of the Civil War, and though the first two of these were attempts at objective historical writing and the third was a travel account, Brown was so dominated by "the cause of my countrymen" that his facts are garbled to serve the ends of propaganda.

When the slavery controversy had settled into well-defined patterns and the cause for which he had begun his career was no longer so pressing, Brown launched his purely imaginative efforts. This period from about 1850 to 1865 was productive of two novels, *Clotel; or The President's Daughter* (1853) and *Miralda; or The Beautiful Quadroon* (1867) and a play, ***The Escape*** (1858). These are the first pieces of fiction and the first play by an American Negro. After the war Brown did his more reasonable and most ambitious works, two histories and a group of narrative essays. *The Negro in the American Rebellion* was published in 1868, *The Rising Son* in 1874, and *My Southern Home* in 1880.

In facility of expression, in artistic discrimination, and in narrative skill Brown advanced steadily from the *Narrative* to the essays which comprise his last work. Historically more important in the development of Negro literature than any of his contemporaries, he was also the most representative Negro of the age, for he was simply a man of slightly more than ordinary talents doing his best in a cause that was his religion. Frederick Douglass was too exceptional; [Charles] Remond too selfish. Almost without forethought, like an inspired prophet, Brown gave expression to the hope and despair, the thoughts and yearnings of thousands of what he was pleased to call his "countrymen."

Brown had the vital energy that is part of the equipment of all artists. He wrote with force, with clarity, and at times with beauty. There is in his work, however, a repetitious amplification that is not altogether accountable to a desire for perfection. His autobiography, first published in 1847, had been spun out to twice its original length by the time of its publication in London two years later. *St. Domingo,* originally a speech and later a pamphlet, finally became the basis for several chapters on the West Indies in *The Rising Son.* Certain episodes from his *Narrative* were used as starting points for pieces in *My Southern Home. Three Years in Europe* came to America as *Sketches of Places and People Abroad. Clotel* was attenuated (by deleting the unseen antagonist, Thomas Jefferson, and by making various lengthening changes) into *Clotelle; a Tale of the Southern States.* If Brown's play, *Doughface,* mentioned by William Simmons [in his *Men of Mark*], ever comes to light, it is likely that it will be found to be merely an earlier sketch of the drama, ***The Escape, or A Leap for Freedom,*** published in 1858 and read in many parts of the country prior to that. Even *Miralda* got mixed up with *Clotel,* but this time it was *Clotelle, The Colored Heroine.*

Brown was driven by the necessity for turning out propaganda in a cause that was too close to him for emotional objectivity and reasonable perspective. He had power without the artist's control, but in spite of this his successes are considerable and of great importance to the history of Negro creative literature. First novelist, first playwright, first historian: the list argues his place. It is doubtful that in the writing of his novels, plays, and histories he saw beyond "the cause." Even in the later years of his life, when it seems he would have been free to focus artistically, he did not change too appreciably. *The Rising Son,* done with an eye to fact, to cause and effect, and to arriving at logical conclusions, is undoubtedly an advance over *The Black Man,* but it is also a deliberate plea in behalf of the Negro race. *My Southern Home* is a vastly better book than the *Narrative,* but less in the sense of artistic objectivity than in craftsmanship. All his days Brown was first a Negro and then a writer.

At its best Brown's language is cursive and strong, adapted to the treatment he gives his material. When he held his bitterness in check, he was inclined to lay on a heavy coating of sentimental morality. Often his lack of control did hurt to an otherwise good passage. A slave-auction scene in *Clotel* illustrates his fault. After a racy and realistic description of a Richmond slave market in which a beautiful quadroon girl was struck off to the highest bidder, Brown ends thus:

> This was a Virginia slave-auction, at which the bones, sinews, blood and nerves of a young girl of eighteen were sold for $500: her moral character for $200; her superior intellect for $100; the benefits supposed to accrue from her having been sprinkled and immersed, together with a warranty of her devoted christianity, for $300; her ability to make a good prayer for $200; and her chastity for $700 more. This, too, in a city thronged with churches, whose tall spires look like so many signals pointing to heaven, but whose ministers preach that slavery is a God-ordained institution.

Though it is possible that Brown was true to fact in the following passage, there is nevertheless a loss of force. This loss is due to his failure to see *truth* beyond mere fact. It may be that his mother did talk and act as he has her

talk and act in the following passage of the *Narrative,* but she is not real to us either as an individual or a type.

> At about ten o'clock in the morning I went on board the boat and found her there in company with fifty or sixty other slaves. She was chained to another woman. On seeing me, she immediately dropped her head on her heaving bosom. She moved not, neither did she weep. Her emotions were too deep for tears. I approached, threw my arms around her neck, kissed her, and fell upon my knees, begging her forgiveness, for I thought myself to blame for her sad condition. . . .
>
> She finally raised her head, looked me in the face, (and such a look none but an angel can give!) and said, "My dear son, you are not to blame for my being here. You have done nothing more nor less than your duty. Do not, I pray you, weep for me. I cannot last long upon a cotton plantation. I feel that my heavenly master will soon call me home, and then I shall be out of the hands of the slaveholders!"

Like many of Brown's shortcomings, the fault of sacrificing truth to fact is the result of the necessity of yielding to the demands of propaganda. He never entirely rid himself of this fault, but in *My Southern Home,* his last book, he does have southern field Negroes talk and act like southern field Negroes.

The play ***The Escape,*** in five acts and seventeen scenes, shows clearly that Brown knew nothing of the stage. Loosely constructed according to the formula of the day and marred by didacticism and heroic sentimentality, its chief characters are but pawns in the hands of Purpose. The heroine Melinda is the identical twin of Miralda; and Clotel might have been their mother. Except the pronounced black type, all Brown's women conform to the character pattern set by Charles Brockden Brown and the ancestral pattern established by Fenimore Cooper's Cora Munro [in *The Last of the Mohicans*]. William Brown's women are all octoroons, quadroons, or, at the very least, mulattoes. The unconscious irony in creating such characters is very sharp, whispering his unmentionable doubt of the racial equality he preached. His characters are no more representative of the Negroes he was supposed to depict than are Eliza and Uncle Tom. His women are beautiful and charming, finely mannered, appealing. What did the women of the master class have that Melinda or Cynthia lacked?

> Poor Cynthia! I knew her well. She was a quadroon, and one of the most beautiful women I ever saw. She was a native of St. Louis, and had there an irreproachable character for virtue and propriety of conduct. Mr. Walker bought her for the New Orleans market, and took her down with him on one of the trips I made with him. Never shall I forget the circumstances of that voyage! On the first night that we were on board the steamboat, he directed me to put her in a stateroom that he had provided for her, apart from the other slaves. I had seen too much of the workings of slavery not to know what this meant. I accordingly watched him into the state-

room, and listened to hear what passed between them. I heard him make his base offers and her reject them. . . . Neither threats nor bribes prevailed, however, and he retired disappointed of his prey.

[*Narrative of William Wells Brown*]

Brown's work as historian and commentator is far more substantial than his work in the purely creative field. Two of his earlier historical works, *The Black Man* and *The Negro in the American Rebellion,* were but as notes for *The Rising Son,* a work comprehending not only the ancient history of the Negro race in Africa, but treating successively the great epochs in the racial career down to Brown's own day. Using key episodes and men as the basis for historical narratives of more than ordinary interest, *The Rising Son* is an outline of history rather than a detailed relation of it. In this work Brown's blunt prejudices are shown softened into calmer rationalism: the swords he usually ground are here beaten into crude ploughshares. It should not be expected that after fifty years he could change precipitantly and wholly, but there is no doubt that in the end the artistic core of him rose up to assert itself.

Even more evident of the victory of his artistic consciousness over his social consciousness is his last work, *My Southern Home.* He came at last to the recognition of permanent literary values over the ephemeral sensational. He is a composed Brown in *My Southern Home,* writing charmingly and interestingly of experiences close to him and of people who are *people.* Humor and pathos, sense and nonsense are skillfully blended in pieces that show his narrative skill at its best. He does not avoid propaganda altogether, but he administers it sparingly and in sugar-coated doses. The warmth and sunshine of the South glows over his pages. It is completely right that *My Southern Home,* his last book, should be also his best.

Brown died in 1884 in Cambridge, Massachusetts, after a full life of devotion to the cause of freedom. His prose adds ballast to the whole mass of antislavery writing. His place in the social history of America and in the literary history of the American Negro is assured. The first Negro writer of the drama and the novel, he was also the first American man of color to earn his living by his pen. Undoubtedly Brown stands high in the impressive list of Americans of Negro blood. (pp. 23-30)

J. Saunders Redding, "Let Freedom Ring," in his To Make a Poet Black, *1939. Reprint by Cornell University Press, 1988, pp. 19-48.*

THE ESCAPE

PRODUCTION REVIEWS

The Liberator   (letter date 5 March 1858)

[The Escape *was Brown's second play. His first was Ex-*

THE

ESCAPE;

OR,

A LEAP FOR FREEDOM.

A Drama,

IN FIVE ACTS.

BY WILLIAM WELLS BROWN,

AUTHOR OF " CLOTEL," " SKETCHES OF PLACES AND PEOPLE ABROAD," ETC.

" Look on this picture, and on this." — HAMLET.

BOSTON:

R. F. WALLCUT, 21 CORNHILL.

1858.

Title page of the first edition of The Escape.

perience; or, How to Give a Northern Man a Back-bone, a work that was never published and is now lost. Although neither drama was ever performed on stage, Brown frequently gave readings from them at antislavery rallies and meetings. The following letter was published in the influential abolitionist newspaper the Liberator *and is addressed to the editor, William Lloyd Garrison. The writer, who signs the letter with the initials "W. H. F.," provides a report of readings by Brown in Cortland, New York before a "large and appreciative audience."*]

DEAR MR. GARRISON:

WENDELL PHILLIPS has just made us his annual visit, and laid the friends of Freedom and Progress, in this place, under new obligations to him for the very eloquent and efficient 'labors of love' described in the article which I forward you from the Cortland Co. *Republican.* 'Œ.,' it is no more than justice to say, is Mr. Alvin Sturtevant, a young man who not only holds the pen of a ready writer, but of a promising one also. The report reflects much credit upon him, not only for its ability, but for its accuracy, particularly as he took no notes, and wrote solely from memory. Mr. Phillips's audiences varied from three hundred to five hundred persons, gradually increasing to the last—a large collection of people for a country and sectarian village like ours. Of course, he made again a deep impression upon the public sentiment in favor of himself and his views.

CHARLES C. BURLEIGH and WM. WELLS BROWN have also been with us, and done good service, each in his own way, for the Anti-Slavery movement. Mr. Burleigh's lectures were, of course, admired for their logical, rhetorical and critical ability; and Mr. Brown's Dramas have compared favorably with the most attractive Lyceum entertainments of the season. Had I the leisure, I should like to speak, at length, of the labors of each, but I have not, and must pass them over with this slight notice. Mr. Brown is still hereabouts, working industriously, and, I think, profitably, both for himself and the cause of the slave. I saw him yesterday at the Academic Exhibition of Central College, McGrawville, which was, by the way, a fine affair, and very creditable to the students and institution—nearly a thousand persons being present as spectators. Mr. Brown gave one of his Dramas, in the evening, to a large and appreciative audience in the College Hall.
                                                        W. H. P.

W. H. P., in a letter to the editor, in The Liberator, *Boston, Vol. XXVIII, No. 10, March 5, 1858, p. 39.*

Henry C. Wright   (letter date 8 October 1858)

[An author, reformer, and orator, Wright was active in the anti-slavery movement and was known as an eloquent and moving speaker for the cause of abolition. His published works include Man-Killing by Individuals and Nations Wrong *(1841),* Human Life Illustrated *(1849), and* The Living Present and the Dead Past *(1865). The following excerpt is taken from a "Letter to the Editor" of the* Liberator, *William Lloyd Garrison. Wright gives an account of one of Brown's readings in Utica, New York.* The Escape, *he asserts, "is written with much power, and Mr. Brown reads it with a most happy dramatic effect."]*

                                        UTICA, Sept. 29, 1858.

DEAR GARRISON:

A few evenings since, I attended a meeting to hear Wm. Wells Brown read his Drama—delineating the effects of labor on the family relations of masters and slaves, and the efforts of slaves to gain their freedom by escaping to Canada. Admission fee, 10 cents.

Nobody could write such a drama but one who, himself, had been a slave, and had been born and trained in the mysteries of that 'sum of all villanies,' American slavery. The Drama is written with much power, and Mr. Brown reads it with a most happy dramatic effect. The audience listened to his reading—or, rather, *reciting*— with deepest interest, and the only regret seemed to be, that it was too short, though the delivery of it occupied an hour and a quarter.

The wretched condition of the white wives of the South, by reason of the universal and *licensed* licentiousness of their husbands with their slave women, and the universal corruption of the household, sons and brothers, of the South, in subjecting to their brutal passions the female victims of slavery, are portrayed with great power. The full story of the effects of slavery on the family relations of slaveholders can never be told. Fathers, themselves, prostituting their daughters to their own lusts, and training them and selling them on purpose to prostitute them to the lusts of others, and brothers prostituting their sisters, and living with them as wives, cover the entire slave States with revolting *incest.* Nearly two thirds of all the women of South Carolina, and over one third of the women of Virginia, Maryland, Kentucky, and of all the fifteen slave States are, by *law,* handed over to the lusts of the white men of the State, and subjected to the penalty of death if they make the least resistance! Such is the condition of the entire South as to the chastity of women and men. It is a reeking Sodom of pollution. The Five Points of New York is a place of purity compared to the entire South. And this condition of the family state in the South is sanctioned by law and religion, and by the customs of society.

The jealous wife and incontinent husband are drawn with great power—as necessary elements of slaveholding life, and in a way that can offend none, except to arouse to greater activity to do away a system that sanctions such abominations.

Slaveholding priests, religion and revivals, and marriage among slaves, are drawn with great power. Then the escape by the underground railway, the settlement in Canada, and the condition of the freed slave under the protection of Victoria, where no American kidnapper can ever set his foot, are all vividly presented to the mind by Mr. Brown.

I wish all in every city and town could hear Mr. Brown's Drama, as read and recited by him. They could not but feel a deeper interest to deliver the country and the world from the curse of slavery. No one who hears him read these Dramas will regret the expense and trouble. All would feel that it pays well to hear them. Mr. Brown, in delivering them, is doing an anti-slavery work which he could not do so effectually in any other way.

                                        Yours, truly,

                                        HENRY C. WRIGHT.

Henry C. Wright, "William Wells Brown— His Dramas—Their Power for Good," in The Liberator, *Boston, Vol. XXVIII, No. 41, October 8, 1858, p. 163.*

CRITICAL COMMENTARY

Vernon Loggins   (essay date 1931)

[Loggins was an American educator, author, and critic. His works include The Negro Author: His Development in America to 1900 *(1931) and* The Hawthornes: The Story of Seven Generations of an American Family *(1951). In the following excerpt from* The Negro Author, *Loggins gives a brief assessment of* The Escape. *Although the play is "feeble" as a work of art, he contends,*

as "a pioneer venture of the American Negro into the field of the drama, it is a landmark in his literature."]

From 1854 to 1863 Brown is regularly referred to in the antislavery papers as engaged for lectures. During this most active period of his career as an abolition agent, he possibly took the time to make a trip to the West Indies, and he is credited with having written during this period a second novel, *Miralda, or, The Beautiful Quadroon*. But if such a work was ever printed, it seems to be no longer in existence. This is likewise true of *Doughface*, a drama, which has been attributed to Brown and which might possibly have been written before 1858. But since we cannot prove that *Doughface* ever existed, we must take Brown's **The Escape; or, A Leap for Freedom,** published in 1858, as the American Negro's first definitely known attempt to write a play.

Brown claimed that he wrote **The Escape** for his "own amusement" [see Author Commentary]. He said:

> I read it privately, however, to a circle of friends, and through them was invited to read it before a Literary Society. Since then the Drama has been given in various parts of the country.

He meant, of course, that he had given it as a reading; and it seems that the public for a time preferred it to his lectures. The play is made up of five acts, each divided into many scenes. Some of the farcical episodes are diverting, but the attempts at seriousness are unpardonably forced. The slave heroine, Melinda, pours out freely such sentiments as the following, which she speaks to her amorous master after he has lured her to a hut on one of his remote plantations:

> Sir, I am your slave; you can do as you please with the avails of my labor, but you shall never tempt me to swerve from the path of virtue.
> [Act III, Scene iv]

Her husband, Glen, also a slave, indulges in endless anti-slavery heroics. One does not wonder that it is good luck rather than the initiative of the two which in the end lands them safe in Canada. **The Escape** as a play is far more feeble than *Clotel* is as a novel. However, since **The Escape** is a pioneer venture of the American Negro into the field of the drama, it is a landmark in his literature. (pp. 168-69)

> Vernon Loggins, "Writings of the Leading Negro Antislavery Agents, 1840-1865," in his The Negro Author: His Development in America to 1900, *1931. Reprint by Kennikat Press, Inc., 1964, pp. 127-75.*

Sterling A. Brown, Arthur P. Davis, and Ulysses Lee (essay date 1941)

[*Brown is an influential scholar, critic, and poet, who was named Poet Laureate of the District of Columbia in 1984. Although his* Negro Poetry and Drama *(1937) and* The Negro in American Fiction *(1937) were largely ignored when they were first published, they were hailed as important pioneering critical works when they were reissued together in 1969. Davis is a journalist, critic, and educator. Lee was a historian and educator.*

These three collaborated on The Negro Caravan, *a work that is considered one of the most significant collections of writings by African Americans yet compiled. In the following excerpt from this work, the critics dismiss* The Escape *as simply "a bad play." When Brown attempts comedy, they charge, he falls "right into the prevailing minstrel tradition."]*

William Wells Brown, who ventured into almost all of the literary fields, was the first Negro to write a play, **The Escape, or a Leap for Freedom** (1858). This was probably never staged, but Brown gave numerous readings from it. Even for nineteenth-century drama **The Escape** is a bad play. The central plot, based on the old triangle, involves a beautiful and innocent slave heroine, a lustful master, and a heroic slave lover. For *deus ex machina* there is an abolitionist who aids the two lovers to escape across the river into Canada in the last scene. The language is drawn out of the old stock:

> Sir, I am your slave, you can do as you please with the avails of my labor, but you shall never tempt me to swerve from the path of virtue.
> [Act III, Scene iv]

There is also consciously intended humor in the play. Comic skits are interspersed among the lugubrious and elegant passages. It is interesting that Brown fell right into the prevailing minstrel tradition when he attempted comedy. His letters as antislavery worker show that Brown could be humorous in an unforced and untraditional way, but when he attempted playwriting, it seems that he had to imitate blackface minstrelsy. (p. 497)

> Sterling A. Brown, Arthur P. Davis, and Ulysses Lee, in an introduction to "Drama," in The Negro Caravan: Writings by American Negroes, Sterling A. Brown, Arthur P. Davis, Ulysses Lee, eds., 1941. Reprint by Arno Press and The New York Times, 1970, pp. 494-505.

Doris Abramson (essay date 1968)

[*A critic and educator specializing in theater studies, Abramson is the author of* Negro Playwrights in the American Theatre *(1969). The following essay was first published in 1968 in the* Educational Theatre Journal *and later included in* Negro Playwrights. *This study is among the first critical assessments to treat* The Escape *as a serious work of art. Abramson defends the drama as "a well-made play by standards of the period" and argues that Brown's readings of the piece were universally praised.]*

In J. Saunders Redding's book, *On Being a Negro in America*, published in 1951 and reissued with "no updating needed" in 1962, that distinguished Negro scholar and teacher observed:

> Negro scholars have written thousands of dissertations, theses, monographs, articles, essays and books in a gigantic effort to correct the multiple injuries done the race by white writers. Five great collections—at Howard, Hampton, Fisk, Yale, and the Harlem Branch of the New York Public Library—house thousands of volumes

and hundreds of magazine and newspaper files, but few except Negroes bother to disturb their dust. Whites show little interest in this Negroana. They seem to feel that they do not need to know about the Negro; they seem to feel that the basic truths about him were established long ago.

Whether or not Redding would revise these statements in view of recent scholarship and changing social attitudes is not the issue here. The fact remains that too much dust has been gathering on the manuscripts and scrapbooks and volumes housed in the great collections he mentions and in less likely ones where Negro materials have managed to land by chance or whim—the Theatre Collection of the New York Public Library at Lincoln Center or the Harvard Theatre Collection or even the Boston Athenaeum, all of which contain some Negroana.

As a preface to an analysis of the earliest extant play written by an American Negro, and in order to suggest the difficulty as well as the satisfaction that comes with finding such a document, I want to detail briefly my search for William Wells Brown's *The Escape.* Having read that William Wells Brown was the first American Negro to write a novel and also the first to write a play, I looked for his works among the many old and rare volumes at the Schomburg Collection, the Harlem branch of the New York Public Library. His novels were there but not his plays, although there were references to the latter in several secondary sources. I then went to Yale University's James Weldon Johnson Collection and, finding no William Wells Brown plays there, moved on to Boston. There was nothing of his in the Harvard Theatre Collection, but I happened to go to the Boston Athenaeum, an old library near the State House, at the top of Beacon Hill, and there I found *The Escape; Or, A Leap for Freedom: A Drama, In Five Acts* by William Wells Brown, published in Boston in 1858, probably the first play of Negro authorship published in America. It turned out to be a fascinating literary and social document.

William Wells Brown was born a slave and later, after his escape from bondage, became a professional lecturer. He was also the author of novels, plays, travel accounts, and of a history of the Negro's contribution to the Civil War. In all these literary forms he was a pioneer as a Negro writer. Between roughly 1830 and 1865, Negro leaders worked closely with Northern abolitionists; Brown, along with Frederick Douglass, lectured for New York and Massachusetts anti-slavery societies. The lectures were occasions for the reading of his dramas, which were probably never performed on stage but only on platforms.

A review in William Lloyd Garrison's abolitionist paper, *The Liberator* [1 August 1856], praised an anti-slavery play by William Wells Brown that was probably *Experience, or How to Give a Northern Man a Backbone* (1856):

> On Tuesday evening Mr. Brown read his Drama, written by himself. The scene is played in a Boston parsonage, the pastor is a Northern man with Southern partialities. The author takes him South on a pleasure tour, and by a strange turn of events, the pastor is sold into slavery, and undergoes the frightful "breaking-in" process

applied by planters to refractory slaves. He is kept there long enough to convince him that his views of slavery were taken from a wrong standpoint, and he is brought back by his friends with opinions thoroughly changed on the subject. The Drama closes by introducing to the pastor a fugitive slave seeking aid to escape to Canada. There are many vivid, graphic and thrilling passages in the course of the reading, and they are brought out by Mr. Brown with telling power.

The Escape; Or, A Leap for Freedom has been characterized [by Sterling A. Brown in his *Negro Poetry and Drama*] as "a hodge-podge with some humor and satire and much melodrama." It would be difficult to defend the play against these charges, but it is fair to say that such charges could be brought against most plays by white playwrights of the period. And *The Escape* did carry a message of importance to abolitionist audiences. In his preface the author stated that many incidents in the play came from his experience of eighteen years "at the South"; the characters were based on real persons then residing in Canada. There is something admirable in the concluding sentence of the preface: "The play, no doubt, abounds in defects, but as I was born in slavery, and never had a day's schooling in my life, I owe the public no apologies for errors" [see Author Commentary].

The Escape, a drama in five acts, is set in the Mississippi valley, a clearing in the forest, a Quaker home in a free state, and finally at the Canadian border. Clearly it is autobiographical. Just as clearly it is nineteenth-century melodrama. [Dion] Boucicault, with all his education in the theatre of England and France, would have been pleased with the plot and might have written some of the dialogue.

The chief antagonists are a white couple, Dr. and Mrs. Gaines, who mouth Christian sentiments while threatening to whip their slaves. When a clergyman, Reverend John Pinchen, visits Mrs. Gaines, he recounts a dream he has had of Paradise and of old friends he visited there. The slave Hannah asks him, "Massa Pinchen, did you see my ole man Ben up dar in hebben?" The ensuing dialogue may be rather blatant in its humor; it is, nevertheless, telling:

> Mr. P.: No, Hannah; I didn't go amongst the niggers.
>
> Mrs. G.: No, of course Brother Pinchen didn't go among the Blacks, what are you asking questions for? Never mind, my lady, I'll whip you well when I am done here. I'll skin you from head to foot. (*Aside*) Do go on with your heavenly discourse, Brother Pinchen; it does my very soul good, this is indeed a precious moment for me. I do love to hear of Christ and Him crucified.
>
> [Act I, Scene iv]

Hero and heroine of the piece are Glen and Melinda, two young slaves. Their dialogue is not the "darky" dialect used by the other slaves. Presumably they have had a chance for some education. We know that their creator, William Wells Brown, was chosen to be the playmate of his master's son and thereby gained some advantages early in life. Slaves who were chosen to work in the household rather than in the fields had a chance to acquire literacy and perhaps to learn a craft. Often their light skins moved slaves from field to parlor. Since Melinda is described by Dr. Gaines as a "yellow wench," lightness no doubt helped her to gain refinement of speech as well as of sentiment.

A speech from Act I, scene 3, reveals Glen's special quality of language in contrast to that of other slaves. Notice, too, the comments on marriage among slaves and the Negro woman's special position in a slaveocracy.

> GLEN: How slowly the time passes away. I've been waiting here two hours, and Melinda has not yet come. What keeps her, I cannot tell. I waited long and late for her last night, and when she approached, I sprang to my feet, caught her in my arms, pressed her to my heart, and kissed away the tears from her moistened cheeks. She placed her trembling hand in mine, and said, "Glen, I am yours; I will never be the wife of another." I clasped her to my bosom, and called God to witness that I would ever regard her as my wife. Old Uncle Joseph joined us in Holy Wedlock by moonlight; that was the only marriage ceremony. I look upon the vow as ever binding on me, for I am sure that a just God will sanction our union in Heaven. Still, this man, who claims Melinda as his property, is unwilling for me to marry the woman of my choice, because he wants her for himself. But he shall not have her. What he will say when he finds that we are married, I cannot tell; but I am determined to protect my wife or die.

Marriage among slaves, except by the kind of pledge exchanged by Glen and Melinda, was unknown. William Wells Brown's mother gave birth to seven children, no two of them having the same father. Frederick Douglass saw his own mother only a few times during his lifetime, for they were separated during his infancy; nor did he know who his father was. Psychologists Kardiner and Ovesey have observed [in their *Mark of Oppression: A Psychosocial Study of the American Negro*] that, since a slave was no more to his master than a horse, something to be exploited for his "utility value," all cultural practices which might harm that value had to be suppressed. Slaves were allowed sexual activity, even entertainment after working hours, but *not* family organization. "Neither paternity nor permanent marriage could be recognized, for this would interfere with the free mobility of the slave for sale purposes."

Melinda's position in the household of Dr. Gaines is the special one that could be attained by sexual attractiveness, something that "can never be contained within the limits of utility." It is common knowledge that the white plantation owners took attractive Negro women as concubines. It is also true that the white master or his son often discriminated in favor of the Negro mistress' offspring, even to the point of freeing some of them. This sort of situation has provided many a playwright with a plot. In *The Escape,* Mrs. Gaines tries to sell Melinda because her husband is overly fond of the slave.

Another of the Gaines's slaves, Cato, speaks so-called "darky" dialect. He has been trusted by Dr. Gaines to "doctor" other slaves.

> CATO: I allers knowed I was a doctor, an' now de ole boss has put me at it. I muss change my coat. Ef any niggers comes in, I wants to look suspectable. Dis jacket don't suit a doctor; I'll change it. (*exit Cato—immediately returning in a long coat.*) Ah! now I looks like a doctor. Now I can bleed, pull teef, or cut off a leg. Oh! well, well, ef I ain't put de pills stuff an' the intment stuff togedder, by golly, dat ole cuss will be mad when he finds it out, won't he? . . . Ah! yonder comes Mr. Campbell's Pete an' Ned; dems de ones massa said was coming. I'll see ef I looks right. (*goes to the looking glass and views himself.*) I em some punkins, ain't I?
>
> [Act I, Scene ii]

His comic speeches are the stuff of minstrelsy and, like Topsy in *Uncle Tom's Cabin,* he even has songs to sing. (One song, a long list of wrongs done to Negro slaves on Southern plantations, must have been very popular with abolitionist audiences.) Cato, like so many other "happy slaves," has a longing to go to Canada. One critic has wondered, in view of how many carefree blacks are described in literature and pictured in art, "why Frederick Douglass fled Maryland to the North, or why the Underground did not go bankrupt like a modern railroad" [Sidney Kaplan, in his *Portrayal of the Negro in American Painting*].

The Escape is a message play from beginning to end. Sometimes the action stops for a soliloquy, sometimes for a song. This soliloquy by Glen is particularly moving, especially when one remembers that William Wells Brown declaimed it from abolitionist platforms:

> Oh, God! thou who gavest me life, and implanted in my bosom the love of liberty, and gave me a heart to love, Oh pity the poor outraged slave! . . . Oh, speak, and put a stop to this persecution! What is death compared to slavery? Oh, heavy curse, to have thoughts, reason, taste, judgment, conscience and passions like another man, and not have equal liberty to use them! Why was I born with a wish to be free, and still be a slave? Why should I call another man master?
>
> [Act III, Scene iv]

A Quaker who helps the escaping slave, sings "The Underground Wagon" to the tune of "Wait for the Wagon."

> Oh, where is the invention
>   of this growing age,
> Claiming the attention,
>   Of statesman, priest, or sage,
> In the many railways
>   Through the nation found,
> Equal to the Yankees'
>   Railway underground?
>
> *Chorus* No one hears the whistle,
>   Or rolling of the cars,
>   While Negroes ride to freedom
>   Beyond the stripes and stars.
>
> [Act V, Scene iv]

Glen and Melinda, as well as the good Cato who knew

how to please while despising his master, escape to Canada with the help of Northern abolitionists. When Mr. White, a citizen of Massachusetts, tells the men in a Mississippi bar that he thanks God that he is from a free state and thinks slavery the worst act a man can commit, he is accused of talking treason. The answer Mr. White receives from a barkeeper when he claims that the Constitution gives him the right to speak his sentiments is one we sometimes hear even today—from Congressmen as well as barkeepers: "We don't care for Constitutions nor nothin' else. We made the Constitution, and we'll break it" [Act V, Scene i].

This crude yet effective play ends with a rousing fight in which Mr. White of Massachusetts fends off the Mississippi villains—with his umbrella. Glen, Melinda, and Cato, leaping into the boat just as it pulls away from the shore, are shouting loudly for freedom as the curtain falls or, more exactly, as the reading ends.

Opinions of the press in Philadelphia and in various New York towns are quoted at the end of the published version of the play. A critic from the Philadelphia *Morning Times* was of the opinion that "the Drama is instructive, as well as very laughable." One can agree with him on both points and add that the play is a remarkable statement of the evils of slavery by a man who learned in bondage how to please and lived to be a free man who could instruct other free men.

When he was in England on a lecture tour, delivering over a thousand abolitionist lectures between 1849 and 1854, William Wells Brown may very well have seen plays by Dion Boucicault and other melodramatists of the period. In London nothing would have prevented a black man from attending the theatre, and Boucicault's plays were being presented in many London theatres at the time. Many of the stage effects suggested in Brown's plays are similar to those employed in Boucicault's.

Although reviews of Mr. Brown's play readings praised his message and fervor rather than his skill as a playwright, it is true that *The Escape* is a well-made play by standards of the period. Written in five acts, the play has variety of characterization, careful exposition, a well-designed if obvious plot, and spine-chilling scenes of seduction and revenge. The last-minute escape in the boat is not the only stage effect familiar to readers and viewers of English and American plays of the period. A striking example of melodrama occurs in Act III, scene 5. Dr. Gaines, having imprisoned the lovely slave, Melinda, tries to force his attentions on her. She protests that the doctor would be committing a double crime: outraging a woman and forcing her to be false to her husband. The doctor is enraged at the idea of her being married. He goes off to find Glen "and roast him at the stake." On the heels of the doctor's departure, Mrs. Gaines arrives with a proposition that could be anticipated by any audience familiar with nineteenth-century melodrama.

> MRS. G.: I know that your master loves you, and I intend to put a stop to it. Here, drink the contents of this vial—drink it!

MELINDA: Oh, you will not take my life,—you will not!

MRS. G.: Drink the poison this moment!

MELINDA.: I cannot drink it!

MRS. G.: I tell you to drink this poison at once . . . or I will thrust this knife to your heart! The poison or the dagger this instant!

William Wells Brown turned the drama of his own experience into the melodrama acceptable in the theatre of his day. That his plays were not produced may have been due to his being a Negro. On the other hand, as a militant reformer he may have chosen the platform over the stage. The combination of his overwhelming anti-slavery bias and what he learned of dramaturgy from playwrights of his time make *The Escape; Or, A Leap For Freedom* an interesting document both from a social and a theatrical point of view. (pp. 370-75)

> *Doris Abramson, "William Wells Brown: America's First Negro Playwright," in* Educational Theatre Journal, *Vol. XX, No. 3, October, 1968, pp. 370-75.*

William Edward Farrison   (essay date 1969)

[*Farrison was perhaps the foremost scholar and critic of William Wells Brown, having produced numerous essays on the writer, editions of* Clotel *(1969) and* The Negro in the American Rebellion *(1971), and a full-length biography,* William Wells Brown: Author and Reformer *(1969). The following excerpt is taken from the chapter in the last-named work that examines* The Escape. *Farrison provides a detailed analysis of the play and concludes that "The Escape* is indeed distinctive as an authentic and vivid portrayal of slavery."]

If Brown returned to Boston before the end of 1857, he either went away again soon after the beginning of the new year or remained inactive in the city for a month or more. For a short time he was expected to participate in the annual meeting of the Massachusetts Anti-Slavery Society on January 28-29, 1858, but the *Liberator*'s report of the meeting [5 February 1858] does not refer to his being present.

Late in February a resident of Cortland, New York, informed Garrison concerning the antislavery lecturers who had recently visited that town. He said that in addition to Wendell Phillips,

> Charles C. Burleigh and Wm. Wells Brown have also been with us, and done good service, each in his own way, for the Anti-Slavery movement. Mr. Burleigh's lectures were, of course, admired for their logical, rhetorical and critical ability; and Mr. Brown's Dramas have compared favorably with the most attractive Lyceum entertainments of the season. . . . Mr. Brown is still hereabouts, working industriously, and, I think, profitably, both for himself and the cause of the slave. I saw him yesterday at the Academic Exhibition of Central College, McGrawville, which was, by the way, a fine affair, and very creditable to the students and institution—nearly a thou-

sand persons being present as spectators. Mr. Brown gave one of his Dramas, in the evening, to a large and appreciative audience in the College Hall [see review dated 5 March 1858].

The statement concerning Brown's working industriously and profitably for himself as well as for the cause of the slave probably implied that he was then working, not as an agent for any antislavery society, but independently as a lecturer and dramatic reader.

During most of the following spring, Brown was more or less active in Boston and its vicinity. He had an engagement to lecture in the Joy Street Baptist Church on Sunday evening, April 11, on "The Great Men of the St. Domingo Revolution." Obviously this was to be his old lecture on Haiti somewhat remodeled. The next day he wrote to William Lloyd Garrison, Jr., who was then in Lynn, saying, "You will see by the hand bill I send you, that I am reading my new drama, which I consider far superior to the one I gave in Lynn." The new drama was **The Escape,** and Brown inquired about the possibility of reading it in Lynn. Garrison, Jr. must have replied favorably as well as promptly, for on April 17 Brown wrote him another letter, along with which he sent three hundred handbills for distribution. It appears from this letter that Brown was to read the drama in Sagamore Hall in Lynn on the evening of the nineteenth. In the letter he requested Garrison, Jr. to make some of the final arrangements for the reading, explaining that he would not get to Lynn "till six or seven o'clock," and that "I shall drive back the same night, as I shall have a lady with me that must be returned." The lady Brown had in mind was probably Annie Elizabeth Gray of Cambridgeport, who became his second wife two years later.

Late in the spring, the public having been apprised that it was forthcoming, Brown's new play entitled **The Escape; or, A Leap for Freedom: A Drama in Five Acts** was published by Robert F. Wallcut of Boston. This, of course, was not Brown's first play and was not, therefore, the first play written by an American Negro, as it has been frequently said to have been. Until evidence to the contrary is discovered, however, it may still be considered the first play by an American Negro author to be published.

The Escape is an octavo pamphlet of fifty-two pages. Brown said in his preface that he wrote the play "for my own amusement and not with the remotest thought that it would ever be seen by the public eye," that he read it "privately, however, to a circle of my friends, and through them was invited to read it before a Literary Society. Since then," he continued, "the Drama has been given [presented as a dramatic reading by himself] in various parts of the country. By the earnest solicitation of some in whose judgment I have the greatest confidence, I now present it in a printed form to the public." With unnecessary bluntness he explained that never having aspired to be a dramatist, he had "little or no solicitude" for the fate of the work, but was content to let it stand on whatever merits it might have. He also attested that "The main features in the Drama are true," that his hero and heroine—Glen and Melinda—were still living in Canada, and that "Many of the incidents were drawn from my own experi-

ence of eighteen years at the South." With something less than good grace, he ended his preface with the assertion that he owed the public no apology for the defects in the drama, because as he had reminded his audiences on many occasions, "I was born in slavery, and never had a day's schooling in my life" [see Author Commentary].

Apparently Brown was prone to forget that not everyone who had been formally educated either spoke or wrote well, and that some of the celebrated authors he had read and admired had had but little formal education. Otherwise he might have recognized the fact that there was not necessarily any direct causal connection between his want of formal schooling and the imperfections in his works.

Whatever might have been his original purpose in writing **The Escape,** Brown made it primarily an antislavery argument. The subject matter of the drama belonged to the same department of the "peculiar institution" as did much of the subject matter of *Clotel*—the department of romances between masters and beautiful slave women, usually mixed breeds. The course reviewed in the drama, however, was successful only in reverse. The master-professor flunked, and the unwilling slave-student passed, but without the usual grade—a mulatto or quadroon offspring.

The time of the action in the drama might have been any time after the 1830's—after the Underground Railroad began doing a remarkably large amount of business. In addition to being a physician and politician, Dr. Gaines of Muddy Creek and Poplar Farm, Missouri, was a connoisseur of beautiful slave women. In the opinion of Mrs. Gaines, his wife, he had long ago succeeded embarrassingly well in at least one master-slave romance. For on his first visit to the Gaineses' home, a certain Major Moore noticed the striking resemblance between Dr. Gaines and Sampey, a mulatto house slave in his teens. Moore assumed that the boy was the son of both Mrs. Gaines and the physician and complimented him accordingly to Mrs. Gaines, very much to her annoyance.

Dr. Gaines was now enamored of Melinda, one of his mulatto slaves—not without being suspected by Mrs. Gaines. Melinda, nevertheless, had bravely withstood his blandishments. For some time she had been in love with Glen, the property of the physician's brother-in-law, and had recently been secretly married to him in a moonlight ceremony conducted by "Old Uncle Joseph," the plantation slave preacher.

Meanwhile, when Walker, a slave trader, visited Muddy Creek, Mrs. Gaines insisted that her husband sell Melinda, as Wildmarsh, a neighbor who happened to be present, admitted to Dr. Gaines that he had sold his own mulatto daughter a week earlier because of his wife's jealousy of him. Instead of selling Melinda, however, as he led his wife to believe he had done, Dr. Gaines hid her in a cottage on Poplar Farm. A night later he went to the cottage and again importuned Melinda to become his mistress. The frigid style with which her replies were invested, of which the following is representative, must have been as devastating as their content:

> Sir, I am your slave; you can do as you please
> with the avails of my labor, but you shall never
> tempt me to swerve from the path of virtue
>   [Act III, Scene v.]

In less artificial language Melinda finally told the physician about her marriage to Glen four weeks earlier, whereupon he went away determined to get even with both her and Glen—with the young woman for spurning him and with the young man for successfully rivaling him. The means by which he chose to get even was to have Glen imprisoned and whipped.

Dr. Gaines left the cottage just in time to avoid being caught there by Mrs. Gaines, who, like a horsewoman of the Apocalypse, descended upon the place bent on destruction. She had decided to terminate her husband's pursuit of Melinda by putting the young woman beyond pursuit forever. In soap opera fashion—whether intentional on Brown's part or not—she tried in vain to compel Melinda to commit suicide by drinking poison. Then in a frenzy of anger she attempted to stab Melinda with a dagger. The soap opera now reduced itself to slapstick comedy. In the ensuing battle far from royal between the two women, Melinda's weapon of both defense and offense was a broom with which, according to Brown's stage directions, she "sweeps off Mrs. Gaines—cap, combs and curls" as the scene ends.

A day or two later, while Glen was in prison soliloquizing about the wrongs he had suffered at the hands of Dr. Gaines, Sampey came and informed him of Melinda's whereabouts. When soon after Sampey's visit, Scragg, the overseer, arrived to flog Glen as Dr. Gaines had requested him to do, Glen overpowered him and escaped. The following night, while he and Melinda were searching for each other, they fortuitously met in a forest (act 4, scene 3) and immediately set out together for Canada. In telling Melinda about his escape from prison, Glen said in English more colloquial and more natural than he ordinarily used, "I pounded his [Scragg's] skillet well for him, and then jumped out of the window. It was a leap for freedom. Yes, Melinda, it was a leap for freedom. I've said 'master' for the last time."

Brown did not develop his plot involving Dr. Gaines, Melinda, and Glen as rapidly as the synopsis of it thus far may lead one to suppose. From the beginning he introduced a variety of characters and incidents which he did not fuse into subplots, but which he obviously intended to exemplify the brutalities and grotesqueries of slavery. There was Cato, the clownish slave who assisted Dr. Gaines in his office and practiced medicine on fellow slaves. There was the occasion on which Mrs. Gaines entertained the Reverend Mr. Pinchen in her dining room and pretended to saintly piety while planning to whip the slave Hannah for no good reason. There was the appallingly ignorant Big Sally, whom Dr. Gaines sold to Walker. At the same time the doctor sold Hannah's husband to the slave trader, thus separating the husband from his wife forever. There was Tapioca, whom Cato described as a "mulatter gal," and who was a refinement of Topsy in *Uncle Tom's Cabin*.

Near the beginning of a kitchen scene [Act III, Scene i], Cato, who was indeed no less knave than fool, belied the belief that he was a contented, happy-go-lucky slave by soliloquizing about his wish to escape to Canada. He ended his soliloquy with a part of "A Song of Freedom," one of the selections in all of the editions of Brown's *Anti-Slavery Harp*.

Ignorant of Cato's real attitude towards his situation, as Price [Brown's master] was of Brown's in December, 1833, Dr. Gaines took Cato along with himself and Scragg in pursuit of Glen and Melinda. One night in a hotel in a town in Ohio, while Dr. Gaines and Scragg were asleep, Cato dressed himself in the doctor's clothes and escaped. Cato's scheme was not new in Brown's writing. Brown had already told in *Clotel* about a fugitive slave who escaped from his captors in southeastern Ohio by the same scheme. Cato joined Glen and Melinda, apparently by chance, in the home of a Quaker in northern Ohio, whence after being refreshed, all three of the fugitives were sped on their way to freedom. But they were not yet completely out of danger. Their pursuers caught up with them at noon one day just as they were about to be ferried across the Niagara River to Ontario. At the ferry there was a fight between Dr. Gaines and his official slave catchers on the one hand and the fugitives and their friends, including two comical peddlers, on the other. The latter group won, and amid cheers the fugitives were ferried across the river to a haven in Canada.

One of the contributions to *The Liberty Bell* for 1858, which was actually published by the middle of December, 1857, was Mrs. Lydia Maria Child's *The Stars and Stripes*, an antislavery melodrama in eight scenes. There are obvious similarities between Brown's drama and Mrs. Child's in characterizations and plots, though in neither setting nor style. Dr. Gaines, Melinda, Glen, and Cato have their counterparts respectively in Mr. Masters, Ellen, William, and Jim in *The Stars and Stripes*. The action in Mrs. Child's drama began on Mr. Masters' plantation in South Carolina and ended at a ferry at Detroit. The time of the action was fixed by Mr. Masters' reference in scene one to how "our brave Brooks served that miserable traitor Sumner."

With regard to the similarities in the dramas; if Mrs. Child was not indebted to Brown, it is not likely that Brown was indebted to her. By the end of 1856 *The Escape* existed in a more or less complete version, and early in 1857 Brown began presenting it in dramatic readings, some of which Mrs. Child might have witnessed. On the contrary, even if Mrs. Child's drama already existed in manuscript when Brown began reading his publicly, it is hardly any more probable that Brown had seen her manuscript than it is that she had seen his. The similarities between the dramas could have resulted, of course, from the writers' drawing upon a common stock of antislavery literature, as Mrs. Child seems to have drawn upon the story of William and Ellen Craft not only in choosing names for her hero and heroine but also in having them escape from slavery disguised as a servant and his master. Brown himself had contributed much from his own experience to the stock of antislavery literature and was familiar with it, therefore, from personal experience as well as from reading.

The similarity between the last scenes of the dramas is

traceable to the kind of incident which had become a part of the stock of antislavery literature. This was the vain attempt of slave catchers to recapture slaves at an American-Canadian ferry. One such incident had been related by Alvan Stewart of Utica, New York, at the annual meeting of the American Anti-Slavery Society in New York City in May, 1836. A similar incident, it should be remembered, had been related by Brown himself in the fourth American edition of his *Narrative.* The last scene in Mrs. Child's drama is obviously an adaptation of the incident related by Stewart. The last scene in *The Escape* was doubtless based on the incident related by Brown himself.

By the time Brown wrote *The Escape,* the subject matter of which he composed it had become so familiar and indeed so stereotyped that it needed a newer and more original treatment than he gave it. All of the principal characters in the drama are stock characters. Their being such is not a fault in itself, but it is a fault that there is little or no character development as the action proceeds except in one instance. That is the one involving Mrs. Gaines, who at first tried to appear as the very soul of piety, but who appeared more and more as the termagant she really was. Among the numerous dramatic situations in the play, those most effectively realized are the farcical ones—the kind most easily portrayed. Much of the dialogue in the comical scenes consists of the speech of illiterate slaves, which Brown represented by what has traditionally become known as dialect writing. His representations are more or less typical of that kind of writing; this is to say, they are as much mutilated English as anything else.

By far the worst defect in the drama is the artificial dialogue in which it abounds. In many places in this work, as in many places especially in the latter half of *Clotel,* Brown seems to have made special efforts to write beautifully instead of simply and effectively; and like others who have indulged in such misdirected efforts, he succeeded in writing much worse than he otherwise might have written. In act 1, scene 3, for example, and again in act 3, scene 4, he seems to have tried, although vainly, to model Glen's soliloquizing after Hamlet's first two soliloquies; and in act 3, scene 5, he tried to make Melinda soliloquize about sleep somewhat as Macbeth talked about it. In all of these instances he doubtless would have written less artificially and more convincingly had he tried to make his hero and heroine talk like themselves rather than like Shakespearean characters. In spite of its defects, however, *The Escape* is indeed distinctive as an authentic and vivid portrayal of slavery because of its human-interest appeal, and as a pioneering effort among Negro authors in the writing of dramas. (pp. 295-304)

> *William Edward Farrison, in his* William Wells Brown: Author and Reformer, *The University of Chicago Press, 1969, 482 p.*

Thomas D. Pawley   (essay date 1972)

[*Pawley is an educator, critic, poet, playwright, and author (with William Reardon) of* The Black Teacher and the Dramatic Arts *(1970). His plays have appeared in various anthologies, including Sterling A. Brown, Ar-*

Portrait of Brown at age thirty-six.

thur P. Davis, and Ulysses Lee's Negro Caravan *(1941) and James V. Hatch and Ted Shine's* Black Theater, USA *(1974). In the essay from which the following excerpt is taken, Pawley examines the careers of four nineteenth-century writers—a "Mr. Brown," the noted actor Ira Aldridge, the American-born French dramatist Victor Sejour, and William Wells Brown—and assesses the claims each has to being considered the first African American playwright. In his discussion of William Wells Brown, reprinted below, Pawley stresses the author's use of* The Escape *in his campaign against slavery and argues that it should be judged by its success as a political piece rather than as a work of art.*]

Of all the candidates for the first Black American playwright, William Wells Brown alone was unproduced. He is singular also in that he was not a man of the theater; rather he was seeking novel ways of presenting the horrors of slavery and promoting the anti-slavery cause. An ex-slave himself, he knew well the conditions about which he wrote; thus, he had two of the ingredients of successful playwriting—knowledge of his material and sincerity of purpose. But these alone cannot make a play. His works were closet dramas belonging in the same *genre* as Seneca's tragedies, Byron's *Manfred* and Shelley's *Las Cenci.*

Although Brown's plays were unproduced, this does not mean that he was unfamiliar with the theater. On the contrary. We have it on the authority of Dr. W. E. Farrison, who has spent a lifetime studying him, that Brown had read a considerable number of dramas, including many of

Shakespeare's, and that he had seen many plays on stage in both America and Great Britain. Brown himself records at length his evaluation of [Ira] Aldridge's *Hamlet* in 1863 during a visit to England. He also refers to Aldridge's *Othello,* which he had seen on the previous evening, and to [Charles] Kean's *Hamlet,* which he had seen at the Princess Theatre.

Why did he turn to writing plays? The answer is not hard to find. "Brown had learned by experience that in order to win and hold the attention of converts to the anti-slavery cause he must vary from time to time the form in which he presented his anti-slavery arguments" [W. E. Farrison, in his *William Wells Brown: Author and Reformer*].

He had tried direct argument, songs, prose fiction, and history. "But there was still another literary form which remained to be tried. He tried it and became a pioneer among Negro authors in . . . drama."

William Wells Brown is not the first writer to recognize the powerful influence of drama in changing social attitudes. Although he was himself a persuasive speaker, when a colleague named Robinson objected to his giving dramatic readings of his plays instead of lecturing, he complained that Robinson seemed not to understand " . . . that there were places in which these (readings) were far more effective than lectures. 'People will pay to hear the drama (presumably *The Escape*) that would not give a cent in an anti-slavery meeting.' "

In 1856, he wrote his first play, a satire on Rev. Dr. Nehemiah Adams and his *A Southside View of Slavery.* The drama, which he read publicly for the first time on April 9, was eventually entitled *Experience, or, How to Give a Northern Man Backbone.* Dr. Farrison speculates that Brown may at first have given the play another title since he was credited with writing a play, *Doughface,* by one Alonzo D. Moore and *Doe Face,* by a William Simmons, the latter obviously a corruption of the former. However, the title is more or less applicable to the protagonist of the play since that kind of Northern preacher was known in the slang of the time as a "doughface." Apparently the play was never published but records indicate that Brown presented it frequently as a dramatic reading.

The play concerns a Northern preacher with Southern sympathies. Inadvertently, he is sold into slavery himself. When he is finally freed his attitude has changed drastically. We can only guess at the effectiveness of Brown's first effort but apparently his audiences loved it. How much of its impact was due to Brown's reading and how much to his *playrighting* is also a matter for speculation, as the following comments indicate.

A report in the Liberator for June 13, 1856, noted that Brown's audience in Boston on May 27 was "highly appreciative and delighted" and his drama "first rate." The same issue contained a letter which stated in part: "The drama is not only extremely *amusing* (italics mine) but is really a very effective plea for the cause of anti-slavery." The humor was probably induced by the minister's predicament. In July of 1856, the Vergennes (Vermont) Citizen commented: "There are many vivid, graphic, and thrilling

passages in the course of the reading and they are brought out by Mr. B. with telling power. It was no surprise to us in the last act when the trembling fugitive burst forth into a peroration towering and noble in language and sentiment in favor of freedom as it should be, that scarcely a dry eye was to be seen in the room." From this we can conclude that Brown was an excellent dramatic reader.

The success of his first effort was such that within the same year, in October of 1856, he had written another play later published under the title *The Escape, or, A Leap for Freedom;* and again it was the cause to which he had dedicated his life which motivated the writing. "Whatever might have been his original purpose in writing *The Escape,* Brown made it primarily an anti-slavery argument. The subject matter of the drama belonged to the same department of the 'peculiar institution' as did much of the subject matter of *Clotel* (his novel), the department of romances between masters and beautiful slave women, usually mixed breeds" [see commentary by William Edward Farrison, dated 1969].

The first recorded public reading of the play was made on a lecture tour in Ohio, on February 4, 1857, in Salem. It was published in the spring of 1858 by Robert F. Wallcut of Boston, " . . . the first play by an American Negro author to be published." Unless we exclude the French language plays of [Victor] Sejour, this credit would have to be modified.

Escape concerns the trials and tribulations of Mellisa and Glen in their efforts to reach Canada and freedom. They were joined during the course of the escape by a self-serving slave who today would be described as an Uncle Tom but who has nothing of the nobility of George Aiken's character.

Critical opinions of the play vary. Brown himself wrote William Lloyd Garrison on April 11, 1857, prior to the play's publication: "You will see by the handbill I send you that I am reading my new drama, which I consider far superior to the one I gave at Lynn." "A hodge podge with some humor, satire and much melodrama," state the editors of *Negro Caravan*" [see commentary by Brown, Davis, and Lee, dated 1941]. But Doris Abramson counters, " . . . it is no more a . . . hodge podge than most of the plays by white playwrights of the period and however crude the container, it carries an honest message" [see commentary dated 1968]. Going even further, she argues it is a well made play by the standards of the period. [Fannin Belcher in his *The Place of the Negro in the Evaluation of the American Theatre, 1767 to 1940*] condemns the play with these words: "As it will frequently happen, the Negro writer proves as susceptible to minstrel humor as his white colleagues. But all the farce of minstrels and the sententiousness of the moral tract cannot conceal the fact that, in playwriting, William Wells Brown's reach exceeded his grasp."

Perhaps the most comprehensive evaluation is that of Dr. Farrison, who points out that the subject matter was stereotyped, the principal characters stock ones, and that there is little character development. The dialogue between slaves is traditional "dialect writing," *i.e.,* "as much mutilated English as anything else." In his judgment the artificial language is the worst defect. "Brown seems to have made special effort to write beautifully instead of simply and effectively." On the positive side Dr. Farrison credits him with humor and an authentic and vivid portrayal of slavery.

My own judgment after a careful reading of the play is that, as drama, it leaves much to be desired, but as a message play in its own day, it undoubtedly made its point. Brown never intended—so far as we know—to stage the play. Therefore, it is perhaps unfair to judge it as theater. The question to be asked is whether he achieved the goal which he set for himself in using the dramatic form in the anti-slavery cause. The answer is yes, possibly because an excellent reader can overcome defects in a script. Brown faced the problem which all writers who seek to effect social change through their writings face—that of making the message an inherent part of the story. It takes a Bernard Shaw, Amiri Baraka, or James Baldwin to stop a play, lecture the audience and make them like it. (pp. 21-4)

> *Thomas D. Pawley, "The First Black Playwrights," in* Black World, *Vol. XXI, No. 6, April, 1972, pp. 16-24.*

James V. Hatch and Ted Shine   (essay date 1974)

[Hatch and Shine are both award-winning playwrights. Hatch is also a poet, critic, and educator specializing in drama and theater. His published works include Poems for Niggers and Crackers *(with Ibrahim Ibn Ismail; 1965),* The Black Image on the American Stage: A Bibliography *(1970), and* Black Playwrights, 1823-1977 *(with Oanii Abdullah; 1977). Shine's plays include* Morning, Noon, and Night *(1964);* Contributions: Three Short Plays *(1972);* Herbert III *(1974); and* Going Berserk *(1984). The two writers also co-edited* Black Theater, USA, *an anthology of dramatic works that includes* The Escape. *The following essay is their introduction to Brown's play, which they judge "an insightful study of the white institution of slavery."]*

In 1857, the United States Supreme Court held that a man once defined as property could not shed the title of property merely by walking about in "free territory", but had to be returned to his original owner. The Dred Scott decision reaffirmed the sanctity of property.

In 1859, John Brown, angered and impatient with federal law and order, attacked Harper's Ferry in what he hoped would be the beginning of protracted guerilla warfare—protracted until the conscience of America could distinguish men from property.

Taking his plot from man-as-property and his viewpoint from abolitionism, William Wells Brown published *The Escape* in 1858. This play was based on personal experience, an experience as bizarre as it was common: birth into slavery.

> I was born in Lexington, Ky. The man who stole me as soon as I was born recorded the birth of all the infants which he claimed to be born his property. . . . My father's name as I learned from my mother, was George Higgins. He was

a white man, a relative of my master, and connected with some of the first families in Kentucky.

With these sentences Mr. Brown begins his autobiography, *Narrative of William Wells Brown, a Fugitive Slave* (1847), a story that traces his life from his unhappy childhood to his escape in 1834 at the age of twenty. Mr. Brown's rage against the humiliations of slavery began early:

> my master, Dr. Young, had no children of his own, but had a nephew, the son of his brother. When this boy was brought to Dr. Young, his name being William, the same as mine, my mother was ordered to change mine to something else. This, at the time, I thought to be one of the most cruel acts that could be committed upon my rights; and I received several very severe whippings for telling people that my name was William.

Later the author not only reassumed his given name, but chose his own surname, Wells Brown, after the Ohio Quaker who befriended him on his last flight for freedom.

His two previous attempts to escape had failed. His first recapture resulted in "Virginia play," a punishment in which the slave was tied in the smokehouse, flogged, then smoked by setting piles of tobacco stems afire. After the slave had coughed his lungs out, he was untied and sent back to work.

The Escape parallels the author's autobiography in a number of incidents. The "melodramatic" ending, where Glen and Melinda fight off their pursuers to "jump into the boat as it leaves the shore" for Canada [Act V, Scene v], is more than a great theatrical climax; it is a rendering of a real battle near Buffalo in which Brown, with black and white friends, fought off the sheriff and a posse to save slaves from recapture.

Relentlessly, through humor and pathos, Mr. Brown records "rottened" virtue. The master, his wife, the clergyman, the overseer ("the Yankees were the most cruel"), and the slave speculator claim virtue but demonstrate that they do not have it. *The Escape* is a documentation of the thesis that *power corrupts.*

The play deserves to be read for more reasons than the gratuity that "William Wells Brown was the first Negro to . . . ". *The Escape* is an insightful study of the white institution of slavery. Our bookshelves groan under white studies of the Negro "problem." Mr. Brown provides us with a firsthand empirical black study of the white "problem." The script is a refutation of the southern romantic tradition of antebellum chivalry and *noblesse oblige.* It reveals the South as a corrupt society.

The play was written for the abolitionists of the North. Mr. Brown read the play aloud to these white liberals, hoping—one must assume—to outrage their consciences. The author employed the devices that made his audience feel comfortable; for example, he created Cato, the darkey dialect comic. But Cato, when he sees his opportunity, makes his leap for freedom—an action that no white playwright of that period ever considered for a low comedy character. By this leap for freedom, Cato becomes a human being.

"The [Negro] stereotype," writes Sterling Brown, "is very flattering to a [white] race which for all its self-assurance seems to stand in great need of flattery." This great need, which spun a thousand stories and plays, oozed up from the festering conscience of the New World where God—if not the framers of the Constitution—recognized all men as equal.

To possess the riches of the virgin continent, to make it possible for future politicians to boast of an economy that provided greater material gifts than those of any other place in the world, the land had to be seized from the red man—justified by the "cowboy'n'indian" myths. The land had to be worked by the black man—justified by "nigger" myths. This need to justify began an unbroken chain of American stereotypes. From *The Candidates* (1770) to the present, each stereotype helped to smother the American conscience.

But for all the constant reassurance the New World democrat took from his playwrights, the truth that he was a racist killer burst out into his everyday encounters. If the slaves were happy, why did the plantation's overseer need dogs?

As a piece of theater, Mr. Brown's play deserves our attention. The author knew what his audience liked—melodrama! *Uncle Tom's Cabin,* already six years old in 1858, clearly demonstrated what the public would listen to: plays that moved in a succession of short scenes arranged for maximum variety of emotions—from the lover's tryst, to dialect comedy, to a fight, to a song. The "box" set had not yet made its appearance: painted scenic drops, dioramas, and sliding wings mounted on tracks enabled these epics to lurch forward at a cinematic pace.

Evaluations of Mr. Brown's play have varied over the years, perhaps reflecting the individual critic's own time as much as an objective appraisal of the play. The abolitionists liked it when the author gave dramatic readings in the late 1850's.

> Mr. Brown's Drama is, in itself, a masterly refutation of all apologies for slavery, and abounds in wit, satire, philosophy, arguments and facts, all ingeniously interwoven into one of the most interesting dramatic compositions of modern times.
>
> [Auburn N. Y., *Daily Advertiser*]

Or again,

> Mr. Brown exhibits a dramatic talent possessed by few who have under the best instructions, made themselves famous on the stage.
>
> [*Seneca Falls Courier*]

After the Civil War the play was neglected—as *Uncle Tom's Cabin* was not. In 1937, Sterling Brown noted in his book *Negro Poetry and Drama* that the play was a "hodgepodge with some humor and satire and much melodrama." Playwright Loften Mitchell, in his history, *Black Drama* (1967), writes, "[Brown's] scenes, unfortunately, are close to blackface minstrelsy, much more so than the

author's personal slave experiences should have permitted." In her study *Negro Playwrights in the American Theater, 1925-1959* (1969), Doris Abramson, who is to be thanked for uncovering a copy of the play in the Boston Athenaeum Library, summarizes her evaluation by calling it "an interesting document both from a social and theatrical point of view" [see commentary dated 1969], Louis Phillips, in a preface to a published edition of *The Escape* (1969), praises the script: "As a play it can certainly hold its own with *Uncle Tom's Cabin*." Yet, as James Weldon Johnson states in *Black Manhattan* (1930) Brown's career was "in no degree a direct factor in the Negro's theatrical development". The North's victories in battle did not admit black playwrights onto the American stage. (pp. 34-5)

> *James V. Hatch and Ted Shine, "Those Who Left and Those Who Stayed," in* Black Theater, USA: Forty-five Plays by Black Americans, 1847-1974, *edited by James V. Hatch, The Free Press, 1974, pp. 34-58.*

FURTHER READING

Bontemps, Arna. "The Negro Contribution to American Letters." In *The American Negro Reference Book,* edited by John P. Davis, pp. 850-78. Englewood Cliffs, N.J.: Prentice-Hall, Inc., 1966.
> Valuable survey of African American literature that regards Brown as "the first creative prose writer of importance produced by the Negro race in America."

Farrison, W. Edward. "Phylon Profile XVI: William Wells Brown." *Phylon* IX, No. 1 (First Quarter 1948): 13-23.
> Biographical portrait of the writer by the foremost Brown scholar.

———. "Brown's First Drama." *College Language Association Journal* II, No. 2 (December 1958): 104-10.
> Assembles the information known of Brown's first play, *Experience; or How to Give a Northern Man a Backbone,* a work now lost.

———. *William Wells Brown: Author and Reformer.* Chicago: University of Chicago Press, 1969, 482 p.
> Definitive, full-length study of Brown and his works.

Moore, Alonzo D. "Memoir of the Author." In *The Rising Son; or, The Antecedents and Advancement of the Colored Race* by William Wells Brown, pp. 9-35. 1874. Reprint. New York: Negro Universities Press, 1970.
> Appreciation of Brown by one of his contemporaries.

Sekora, John. "William Wells Brown." In *Fifty Southern Writers Before 1900: A Bio-Bibliographical Sourcebook,* edited by Robert Bain and Joseph M. Flora, pp. 44-54. New York: Greenwood Press, 1987.
> Includes a brief biography of Brown, a discussion of the major themes of his writing, a survey of the criticism of his works, and a bibliography of works by and about him.

Trent, Toni. "Stratification Among Black by Black Authors." *Negro History Bulletin* 34, No. 8 (December 1971): 179-81.

> Examines the role African American writers played in establishing and maintaining "Blacks' own acceptance of color distinctions as bases for judging each other's value." Brown was, Trent states, "obsessed with the obvious distinctions between dark and light Blacks."

Yellin, Jean Fagan. "William Wells Brown." In *The Intricate Knot: Black Figures in American Literature, 1776-1863,* pp. 154-81. New York: New York University Press, 1972.

> Biographical and critical study of Brown that focuses particularly on the relations of his works to the social and political events of his time.

Karel Čapek

1890-1938

A Czechoslovakian dramatist, novelist, short story writer, journalist, and essayist, Čapek is best known for antiutopian works such as *R. U. R.* and *And So Ad Infinitum* (*The Life of the Insects*) (*Ze života hmyzu*) in which he warns against the dehumanizing aspects of modern civilization and satirizes a number of social, economic, and political theories. These innovative and well-crafted fantasies are credited with changing the direction of science-fiction and with bringing the genre of science-fiction drama into its own.

Čapek was born in northeastern Bohemia, a region that has become part of modern-day Czechoslovakia. A frail and sickly child, he formed a particularly close relationship with his older brother Josef, with whom he later collaborated on numerous plays and short stories. In 1917, Čapek embarked on a career in journalism that would last the rest of his life. In his essays and articles he consistently championed the causes of Czech nationalism and liberalism. Čapek enthusiastically greeted the post-World War I independence of Czechoslovakia, and his intense involvement in the development of the infant nation together with his zeal for the new democratic government led to a personal friendship with Thomas Masaryk, the country's first president. Čapek later wrote a biography of the politician. As World War II approached, the Čapek brothers, whose bitter denunciations of fascism were widely known, were advised to leave Prague for their own safety; they chose instead to stay and continue their fight. Čapek died in December 1938, three months before the Nazi invasion of Prague. Shortly after entering the city, the German secret police, unaware of Čapek's death, arrived at his home seeking to arrest him for his association with the democratic government.

Čapek was a prolific writer who expressed himself in many genres, but it was through the plays *R. U. R.* and *And So Ad Infinitum* (the latter written in collaboration with his brother) that he achieved international acclaim. *R. U. R.* (the initials stand for Rossum's Universal Robots, a company that manufactures artificial human laborers) introduced the word "robot" into the English language. The work, with its futuristic science-fiction setting, was an immediate success upon its debut in Prague and received 184 performances in its initial New York run. Čapek liked it least of all his dramas, however, and critics noted numerous flaws. Ludwig Lewisohn, for example, in his review of the New York premiere called it a "strange mixture of wavering brilliance and mere confusion." *The Spectator* reviewer, covering the London debut, considered it an "exciting and thrilling play," but faulted several instances of what he judged absurdities in the plot. Nevertheless, audiences were both fascinated and terrified by the play's vision of a technically advanced society unable to control its

ultimate labor-saving creation, the robot. Playgoers were untroubled by perceived gaps in structure and argument and focused instead on the drama's theatrical effectiveness and originality.

And So Ad Infinitum and *The Makropoulos Secret* (*Věc Makropoulos*) were also well received by audiences. The former, a parable in which the insect world is used to examine human weaknesses and vices, was deemed ingenious. John Gassner, writing on a 1948 New York revival, characterized it as a "Slavic tour de force" and compared it favorably with *Gulliver's Travels*. *The Makropoulos Secret* questions the value of immortality by presenting the struggles of a woman who has obtained and used a formula for eternal youth but has become disillusioned with life after 342 years of endlessly repeating the same experiences. The piece aroused debate when critics suggested that it was written in answer to Bernard Shaw's *Back to Methuselah*. Unlike Shaw's play, which argued that extended life would result in great spiritual growth, Čapek's work suggested that it would only lead to boredom and stagnation. Critics were thus often puzzled by the dramatist's insistence that *The Makropoulos Secret* was an optimistic play. In writing his next play *Adam the Creator* (*Adam stvořitel*), Čapek once again collaborated with his brother Josef. The drama centers around Adam who has been assigned the task of creating a world which is free from imperfection. Adam fails, as did the play.

After a ten-year hiatus from writing for the theater, Čapek returned to compose his last two dramatic works, *Power and Glory* (*Bílá nemoc*) and *The Mother* (*Matka*). These plays, both written within one year of the Nazi invasion of Czechoslovakia, are concerned with the subject of war. Through these two works, Čapek attempted to refute the notion put forth by various critics that he was a pacifist. He also sought to convince his countrymen of the imminent political danger posed by the German military build-up. *Power and Glory* (also called *The White Plague* and *The White Scourge*) is about a country whose power-hungry, irresponsible leaders have brought it to the brink of a war which must be fought not by those who wield power, but by the nation's young men. Ironically, these rulers find themselves subject to forces beyond their control as a leprosy-like disease breaks out among only those people who are over forty. Dr. Galen, the one man who has the cure, uses his precious information to blackmail the dictator who has been stricken with the disease. Just as the secret is about to be revealed, the doctor is killed by a frenzied crowd. Given Hitler's strong influence in Prague in 1937, Čapek had difficulty getting the play produced because of its anti-Nazi bias. *The Mother,* which was the more widely performed of his last two plays, presents the struggle of a woman who has lost her husband and three of her four sons to the ravages of war and disease. The ghosts of these men return to converse with the mother, who must eventually decide to send her youngest son to battle. The relevance of the play to contemporary world events was not fully recognized during its initial run, but shortly thereafter, as German tanks rolled across the Czechoslovakian border and into the Sudetenland, Čapek's words resounded in the ears of his compatriots.

Čapek's work has been favorably compared to the utopian and antiutopian writings of G. K. Chesterton and H. G. Wells. Some critics, however, have suggested that the themes and ideas in his plays often supersede the development of plot and characterization. The vivid depictions of such creatures as the robots, these critics also charge, are obtained at the expense of the human figures. Others, including Čapek himself, have contended that the dramatist's objectives were to examine general human traits and to expose the dangers of technological advancement, endeavors best facilitated from a distance and involving little individual character development. Regardless of critical dispute, Čapek remains one of his country's foremost writers and is considered the father of Czechoslovakian drama. Employing the inherently public and social medium of theater, Čapek successfully brought about a marriage between two important forms of human expression, literature and politics.

(For further information on Čapek's life and career, see *Twentieth-Century Literary Criticism,* Vol. 6 and *Contemporary Authors,* Vol. 104.)

PRINCIPAL WORKS

PLAYS

R. U. R., 1920
  [*R. U. R.,* 1923]
*Ze života hmyzu [with Joseph Capek] 1921
  [*And So Ad Infinitum* (*The Life of the Insects*), 1923]
Věc Makropoulos 1923
  [*The Makropoulos Secret,* 1925]
Adam stvořitel [with Joseph Capek] 1927
  [*Adam the Creator,* 1929]
†*Bílá nemoc* 1937
  [*Power and Glory,* 1938]
Matka 1938
  [*The Mother,* 1940]

OTHER MAJOR WORKS

Zářivé hlubiny ["The Luminous Depths"; with Josef Capek] (short stories) 1916
Trapné provídky ["Painful Tales"] (short stories) 1921
  [*Money and Other Stories,* 1929]
Továrna na Absolutno ["Factory for the Absolute"] (novel) 1922
  [*The Absolute at Large,* 1927]
Krakatit (novel) 1924
  [*Krakatit,* 1925]
Povídky z jedné kapsy; Povídky z druhé kapsy (short stories) 1929
  [Selections published in *Tales from Two Pockets,* 1932]
Hordubal (novel) 1932-33
  [*Hordubal,* 1934]
Povětroň (novel) 1933-34
  [*Meteor,* 1935]
Obyčejný život (novel) 1933-34
  [*An Ordinary Life,* 1936]
Válka s mloky (novel) 1936
  [*The War with the Newts,* 1937]
Život a dílo skladatele Foltýna ["The Life and Work of Composer Foltýna"] (unfinished novel) 1939
  [*The Cheat,* 1941]

*This work is also known as *From the Insect World, The World We Live In, The Insect Comedy,* and *The Insect Play.*

†This work is also known as *The White Plague* and *The White Scourge.*

AUTHOR COMMENTARY

The Meaning of *R. U. R.* (1923)

[*In the following essay, Čapek offers a rebuttal to a public discussion that was held in London in June, 1923. The participants, including the noted writers Bernard Shaw and G. K. Chesterton, expounded various inter-*

pretations of R. U. R., which for the most part focused on the robots. Čapek here disputes this emphasis, claiming that he himself was "much more interested in men than in the Robots." R. U. R. is, he maintains, a "comedy of truth," in which all of the opposing human characters are right "in the plain and moral sense of the word."]

I have just learnt of the discussion about the meaning of a play [**R. U. R.**] which, for certain serious reasons, I lay claim to as my own. Authors are reputed to be childishly vain, and as one of them I claim the privilege of saying a few words on behalf of my work.

Mr. Chesterton, in the course of the discussion, said rightly that nobody can say what is the tendency of a work of art. I cannot tell it myself. But the discussion was by no means useless, in that it gave an opportunity to the distinguished participators to express their personal opinions, creeds and ideals. I enjoyed very much the creeds and ideals of Mr. Chesterton, as well as those of Mr. Shaw and Commander Kenworthy. But it seems to me that, so far as my play was concerned, their chief interest was centred upon Robots. For myself, I confess that as the author I was much more interested in men than in Robots.

There are some fathers who are, shall we say, more interested in education in general than in that of their own children in particular. Allow me to take the opposite view, of a father who speaks of his own child rather than of the principles of education. I am not altogether sure of what I have written, but I know very well what I wished to write. I wished to write a comedy, partly of science, partly of truth. The old inventor, Mr. Rossum (whose name in English signifies Mr. Intellect or Mr. Brain), is no more or less than a typical representative of the scientific materialism of the last century. His desire to create an artificial man—in the chemical and biological, not the mechanical sense—is inspired by a foolish and obstinate wish to prove God to be unnecessary and absurd. Young Rossum is the modern scientist, untroubled by metaphysical ideas; scientific experiment is to him the road to industrial production, he is not concerned to prove, but to manufacture. To create a Homonculus is a mediaeval idea; to bring it in line with the present century this creation must be undertaken on the principle of mass-production. Immediately we are in the grip of industrialism; this terrible machinery must not stop, for if it does it would destroy the lives of thousands. It must, on the contrary, go on faster and faster, although it destroy in the process thousands and thousands of other existences. Those who think to master the industry are themselves mastered by it; Robots must be produced although they are, or rather *because* they are, a war industry. The conception of the human brain has at last escaped from the control of human hands. This is the comedy of science.

Now for my other idea, the comedy of truth. The General Manager Domin, in the play, proves that technical progress emancipates man from hard manual labour, and he is quite right. The Tolstoyan Alquist, on the contrary, believes that technical progress demoralizes him, and I think he is right, too. Bussman thinks that industrialism alone is capable of supplying modern needs; he is right. Ellen is

instinctively afraid of all this inhuman machinery, and she is profoundly right. Finally, the Robots themselves revolt against all these idealists, and, as it appears, they are right, too.

We need not look for actual names for these various and controverted idealisms. Be these people either Conservatives or Socialists, Yellows or Reds, the most important thing is—and this is the point I wish particularly to stress—that all of them are right in the plain and moral sense of the word. Each and every one of them has the deepest reasons, material and mental, for his beliefs, and according to his lights seeks the greatest happiness for the greatest possible number of his fellow-men. I ask whether it is not possible to see in the present social conflict of the world an analogous struggle between two, three, five, equally serious verities and equally generous idealisms? I think it is possible, and this is the most dramatic element in modern civilization, that a human truth is opposed to another truth no less human, ideal against ideal, positive worth against worth no less positive, instead of the struggle being, as we are so often told it is, one between noble truth and vile selfish error.

These are the things I should like to have said in my comedy of truth, but it seems that I failed, for none of the distinguished speakers who took part in the discussion have discovered this simple tendency in **R.U.R.**

Karel Čapek, "The Meaning of 'R.U.R.'," in The Saturday Review, *London, Vol. 136, No. 3523, July 21, 1923, p. 79.*

How a Play is Produced (1926)

[In the following essay, Čapek engages in a lighthearted discussion of the disparity between the author's conception of a play and its portrayal on stage. Čapek gently mocks the ways in which a work is subjected to the interpretations of the stage manager and actors and is altered to accomodate the limitations of the theatrical company's resources. He also gives a humorous rendition of the roles of various stage personnel connected with the production of a play.]

The producer of a play works on the sound theory that the piece must be given a helping hand, as they say. That means it must be produced quite differently from the way the author has desired it.

'Do you know,' says the author, 'I had imagined a very quiet, naturalistic piece. . . . '

'Oh! That would n't do at all,' replies the producer; 'the play must be given in quite a grotesque manner.'

'Clara is a shy, passive creature,' explains the author further.

'What are you thinking of?' cries the producer, 'Clara is a cruel creature. Look here, on page 37 Danesh says to her, "Do not torment me, Clara!" When he says this line Danesh will writhe on the ground, while Clara will stand by in hysterics. You understand, of course?'

'But that was not my idea at all,' protests the author.

'Why, man, that is just the best scene,' says the producer drily; 'otherwise the second act has no proper curtain. Am I not right?'

'I suppose so,' replies the author dejectedly.

'Good! I knew you'd see my point.'

I will now betray certain deep secrets of the dramatic art. A creative author is one who will not allow himself to be hampered by the theatre, and a creative producer is one who will not allow himself to be hampered by the author. As far as the creative actor is concerned the poor devil has no other choice than that of keeping to the words (in this case the producer gets blamed for bad interpretation) or following the producer's instructions (in which case the bad interpretation is blamed on the actor).

If, by pure chance, no one should stumble in the dialogue on the first night, no badly fixed scenery should suddenly fall down, no reflector should burn itself out, and no other similar misfortune should take place, the producer is then praised in the local press as having 'produced very carefully.' It is pure chance, however, whether any of these things occur.

Of course, before the rehearsals begin, there is the business of casting the play. The author now makes the interesting discovery that this is anything but easy. There are in the play, let us say, three ladies and five gentlemen. For the eight rôles, therefore, the author chooses eight or nine of the best players in the theatre ensemble, and declares that he has written the parts specially for them, and for them alone. So far so good. He now hands his list to the producer, and the matter proceeds, as they say, 'higher up.'

Now, however, the following difficulties ensue:—

1. Miss A. cannot take the principal part because she is just now playing another principal part.

2. Miss B. returns the part the author has chosen for her, protesting in a hurt manner that it is not a suitable part for her.

3. Miss C. cannot be given the part the author has chosen for her, because she had a part last week, and Miss D. must have one now.

4. Mr. E. cannot have the principal part; Mr. F. must have it instead, because the rôle of Hamlet was taken from him, after he had asked for it, and given to Mr. G.

5. On the other hand, Mr. E. might take the fifth part as a substitute, but he is dead certain to return it angrily because the author has not chosen the fourth part for him, which is his own line.

6. Mr. H. must take care of himself because he has a cold owing to a conflict with the producer.

7. Mr. H. cannot play part No. 7 because there is no one else suitable for part No. 5. Although it is not his line, he says he will 'manage it all right.'

8. The eighth part, that of a telegraph messenger boy, will be assigned, by special request, to the player chosen by the author himself.

Thus it comes to pass that the whole affair turns out quite differently from what the inexperienced author imagined. Not only that, but a general bitterness is prevalent among the players, who cannot forgive the author for not having assigned the parts direct to them.

I should like to conduct you through the lives of the players, and reveal to you their pasts, their cares, their sorrows, their sensitiveness, the difficulties of their profession, their superstitions, their loves and hates, their brief joys, which are always being recalled; but I am not writing a novel from life, but only a short guide. I will therefore cease to wander round the dressing-rooms, between scenery, lamps, weapons, and theatrical thrones, and turn my attentions to the mob. They are called supers.

When the author introduces into his play the 'People,' or the 'Workers,' or a 'Mob,' he generally imagines a great mass of individuals, old and young, well-built, broad-shouldered beings with big chests, thick necks, and powerful voices, as the 'People,' the 'Workers,' or a 'Mob' are usually supposed to be. He is visibly disappointed when he sees on the stage instead a small handful of narrow-chested, more or less scrawny fellows, with thin, piping voices, who do not by any manner of means represent the real 'Proletariat' either in weight or substance. As a matter of fact, they are poor students engaged at sixpence a night; and for sixpence one can hardly expect the poor beggars to be strong, broad-shouldered, and sunburned.

True, there are also permanent supers, who move about with a certain arrogance. If the piece is an elaborately mounted play, requiring a very large mob of people, then everyone in the theatre is pressed into service—dressers, sceneshifters, property men, upholsterers, stage managers, electricians, and seamstresses; indeed, it is a wonder that the theatre administration itself does not come on the stage. About fifty people are usually needed. For making a noise one gets paid something extra. The usual murmur of a 'mob' consists of the mysterious word 'rhubarb.'

The stage manager runs to and fro in the wings with the book of words in his hands, pushes the players on the stage at the right moment and through the correct entrance, directs the crowds, produces noises 'off,' and gives the signal for the curtain to rise; further, he rings the bells in all the dressing-rooms, goes along the corridors screaming 'Ready to begin,' plays minor parts, stamps about like a horse when there is one in the play, is on intimate terms with all the actors, and is abused by all and sundry for everything that happens. Just as there are great and lesser producers, so are there great and lesser stage managers.

Certain noises 'off' are produced by various other people: the mechanic unleashes the stage thunder in the stage-machinery loft; the sceneshifter sees to the hail; the rain, bells, sirens, and shots are the business of the property man. But the stage manager imitates the singing of birds, hoots like a motor horn, rattles the crockery, and makes all the remaining necessary noises, except those that are produced by the orchestra.

The curtain man sits in a glass box near the stage. At a sign from the prompter he lowers the curtain. The curtain falls quickly, glides tragically, or descends slowly, according to the way the play ends.

If the theatre is on fire, the curtain man must remain at his post until the iron safety curtain has been let down. He is aware of his heroic duty; his face is the concentrated expression of caution itself, and next to him is a pint of beer. (pp. 419-21)

Karel Čapek, "How a Play is Produced," in The Living Age, *Vol. CCCXXIX, No. 4272, May 22, 1926, pp. 419-21.*

OVERVIEWS AND GENERAL STUDIES

Sam Moskowitz   (essay date 1963)

[*Moskowitz is an American critic, author, educator, and noted authority on science-fiction. He is the author of numerous books on the subject, including* The Immortal Storm: A History of Science Fiction *(1954),* Explorers of the Infinite: Shapers of Science Fiction *(1963), and* Strange Horizons: The Spectrum of Science Fiction *(1976). He has also edited many collections of fantasy stories. In the following excerpt taken from his 1963 work, Moskowitz traces the "brilliant efforts" of Čapek's literary career. He takes particular interest in the development of the robots in* R. U. R. *and their impact on subsequent science-fiction literature.*]

While the passage of the years had given science fiction an unshakable stature as prophecy, and the efforts of Edgar Allan Poe and H. G. Wells had admitted it to the canon of recognized literature, its material had not lent itself readily to theatrical adaptation. Though Mary Shelley's *Frankenstein* enjoyed more than a century of revivals as *Presumption, or the Fate of the Monster,* with script by Richard Brinsley Peake, it scarcely can be treasured as one of the masterpieces of the stage. Nor could the early Tarzan pictures, the several Verne epics, or the Méliès fantasy films be said to have contributed much to dramatic art.

Science fiction as meaningful drama came into its own under the brilliant efforts of Karel Čapek, "father of the Czechoslovakian theater." Together with his brother Josef Čapek, he produced, in the period between World War I and World War II, these science fiction and fantasy plays: *R. U. R., The Insect Story, The Makropoulos Secret, Land of Many Names,* and *Adam the Creator.*

Today there is scarcely a collection of great modern European plays that does not include one of them. Čapek has become the most internationally renowned of all Czech playwrights.

The quality of his plays far exceeds the requirements of dramatic entertainment; the plays distinctly affected the thinking of the western world, and from one of them the word "robot" has entered the language of many nations. Interspersed among his plays were books, three of them science fiction novels which further enhanced his already

glittering reputation and which profoundly changed the direction of science fiction.

Karel Čapek was born January 9, 1890, in Male Svatonvici, northern Bohemia, an area then part of Austria-Hungary. The son of a physician, he found means readily available for his education. He studied at Prague, Paris, and Berlin, finally graduating from the University of Prague in 1917.

Philosophically, he was a disciple of the Americans William James and John Dewey, exponents of pragmatism, which regards "the practical consequences and useful results of ideas as the test of their truthfulness, and which considers truth itself to be a process." Čapek's college thesis was written on the subject of pragmatism.

More immediately, Karel Čapek was influenced by the views of his talented brother Josef, born three years earlier, who was to make a reputation as a playwright, fiction writer, artist, producer, scene designer, and art critic. Their attitudes and outlook were so similar that collaborations were extraordinarily successful.

A series of short stories and sketches, some in collaboration with his brother, created Karel Čapek's first literary reputation. They showed so deft a touch in their handling that he deservedly was termed the Czech Chekov. A collection published in 1916, *Luminous Depths,* is of special importance, for it contains a short story, *L'Éventail,* which utilizes mechanical dolls much in the manner of E. T. A. Hoffmann. An even earlier reference to robots may be found in Čapek's essay, *System,* which appears in in collection, *Krakonos's Garden,* issued in 1918 but actually written between 1908 and 1911. Obviously the idea of the artificially created man intrigued Čapek over a period of years.

In his short stories, Čapek openly acknowledges a debt to Edgar Allan Poe, Oscar Wilde, and Charles Baudelaire. In method he was an experimental modernist, at the forefront of a group of European writers attempting to write what amounted to impressionistic prose. Readers sampling Čapek for the first time are frequently startled by the daring, almost sensational prose. Though his spectacular methods struck a chord of affinity with the youthful generation, it was his subject matter and not his style that brought him fame.

Almost without exception his short stories were off-trail, either in theme or approach. Lovers of the detective story will find his volume *Wayside Crosses,* published in 1917 and later translated as *Money and Other Stories,* to be a bitter but highly original collection of "whodunits" without solutions.

The end of World War I and the creation of the new republic of Czechoslovakia marked the turning point in the career of Karel Čapek. During the war, Karel, with his brother Josef, managed a theater in Vinohrady, in what was later to become Czechoslovakia. With the coming of Czechoslovak independence on October 28, 1918, the National Theater became the cultural center of the new nation and Karel Čapek allied himself with it.

World renown followed unexpectedly and swiftly. The increasing trend toward mechanization, the scientific slaughter of World War I, and the efficient mass-production methods of the United States made a profound impression on Čapek. A modernist in thought and action, he did not feel that the idea of scientific progress in itself was bad. However, he was concerned with the use to which new discoveries were being put and their effects on the lives of people around him.

Čapek conceived the idea of *R. U. R.* "quite suddenly in a motor car when the crowds around him seemed to look like artificial beings," claims Jessie Mothersale, a close friend. The label "robot" for the synthetic men in the play is said to have been suggested to him by his brother Josef and was derived from the Czech word *robititi* or *robata,* meaning "to work" or, in certain connotations, "a worker."

The play *R. U. R.* (Rossum's Universal Robots) opened in Prague, the capital of Czechoslovakia, January 26, 1921, and was a stunning success. Overnight it made Čapek Czechoslovakia's top dramatist, a distinction he was to retain for the remainder of his life. The audacious drama, though even in the narrowest sense bona fide science fiction, still proved magnificently effective theater.

In the near future, on an island whose location is not specified, a formula to produce artificial humans chemically for use as workers and servants has been adapted to mass production, and hundreds of thousands of such creatures are being made and sold annually. These chemical machines are replacing human workers everywhere; the only thing staving off worker revolt is the fact that the lowered cost of labor has dropped prices of the essentials of life to an all-time low. The robots are even increasingly being purchased for armies. The manufacturers justify their position on the grounds that eventually robots will free men from all toil and a utopia will emerge.

Unfortunately, one of the chemists alters the formula and the robots, who have hitherto been without emotions, assume the desires for freedom and domination that previously have been characteristic only of the human race.

The emotionally advanced leaders among the robots organize a revolt of their minions, which now number millions in key positions throughout the world. The rule of man is cast off and the human race is ruthlessly exterminated.

At bay on their little island, the robot manufacturers stave off robot attack, but are betrayed by the misguided Helena Glory, president of the Humanitarian League, who even burns Rossum's original formula for the creation of robots. Since the sexless robots cannot reproduce their kind without it, they might have accepted it in barter for the lives of the remaining human beings.

Remorselessly the robots destroy all but one man, whom they command to rediscover Rossum's formula. They offer him the world if he can help them rediscover the secret of the creation of life. But he is only a builder, not a scientist, and he cannot duplicate the method. Finally, he turns to them in recrimination and asks why they destroyed mankind.

"We had learnt everything and could do everything. It had to be," Radius, leader of the revolt, replies.

"We had to become masters," explains a second robot.

"Slaughter and domination are necessary if you would be human beings. Read history," says Radius.

With almost all hope gone for the continuation of any type of human life, a male and a female robot who apparently have naturally developed sex organs are discovered, and the implication is that they may become the new Adam and Eve of the world.

The fame of *R. U. R.* spread rapidly. It was soon produced in Germany, and Erica Matonek, writing for Britain's *Life and Letters Today,* in 1939 recalled, "that it was a 'smashing success in Germany, too.'" The play opened in London and New York simultaneously, October 9, 1922. The Theatre Guild production at the Garrick Theatre, New York, was the event of the season, and it ran 184 performances. Reviews were enthusiastically provocative:

> It is murderous social satire done in terms of the most hair-raising melodrama. It has as many social implications as the most handy of the Shavian comedies, and it also has so many frank appeals to the human gooseflesh as *The Bat* or any other latter-day thriller. In melodramatic suspense and in its general illusion of impending and immediate doom, this piece from Vienna makes on the alarmed playgoer across the footlights somewhat the same impression as would an infernal machine of which the mechanism had been set and the signal given.—*New York Herald.*

> Bernard Shaw did not write *R. U. R.* but he probably will. Possibly later on we shall have a variation of *R. U. R.* by Mr. Shaw and then what we accepted last night as an exceedingly enjoyable and imaginative fantasy will become a dull diatribe. For *R. U. R.* is Shavian but entertaining. It has force, energy and the sort of "fantasy" that Barrie has striven unsuccessfully to administer in allopathic doses.—*New York American.*

> . . . Like the H. G. Wells of an earlier day, the dramatist frees his imagination and lets it soar away without restraint, and his audience is only too delighted to go along on a trip that exceeds even Jules Verne's wildest dreams. The Guild has put theatregoers in its debt this season. *R. U. R.* is supermelodrama—the melodrama of action plus idea, a combination that is rarely seen on our stage.—*The Evening Sun.*

> There can be no question that in this piece, whether it happens to strike the fancy of the public or not, the Theatre Guild has got something that is worthwhile—but this fantastic composition, even if it is somewhat indebted to the ideas of authors as far apart as Mary Shelley, Hauptmann, and Lord Dunsany, is in form at least a veritable novelty full of brains and purpose.—*The Evening Post.*

Under the critical microscope of the most absolute standards, *R. U. R.* showed some scar tissue holding its components together. Yet time, the supreme judge, finds that, with the possible exceptions of Rostand's *Cyrano de Bergerac* and Molnár's *Liliom,* this is the most frequently anthologized of modern European plays in English translation.

While an acknowledged lightning bolt to world theater, *R. U. R.*'s effect was even greater on the development of science fiction. The theme which had resulted in a few isolated stories of the past about the creation of artificial life, such as Mary Shelley's *Frankenstein* and Ambrose Bierce's *Moxon's Master,* had been given by Čapek such thematic richness that henceforth it would constitute a phase of science fiction exceeded in popularity only by the interplanetary story. Never before, in science fiction, had artificial life been created in wholesale, factory lots. With that as hypothesis, the robot could influence the entire pattern of man's culture and through its numbers create its own culture. The plot potentialities were vast.

If the author wanted to imagine a civilization in which machines gained absolute control, it was now possible; see Miles J. Breuer's novel, *Paradise and Iron,* published in the Summer 1930 *Amazing Stories Quarterly.* On the necessity for built-in safety factors to protect humans from the fate Čapek described, see Isaac Asimov in his book, *I, Robot* (1951). For a metal man with beneficent motives, see the Eando Binder series concerning Adam Link. The possibility of an affectionate relationship between androids (science fiction terminology for humanlike robots as opposed to all-metal ones) was touchingly explored by Lester Del Rey in *Helen O'Loy.* And eventually there came the humorous tale built around robotic machines, notably Lewis Padgett's *Robots Have No Tails,* a swing to the other extreme from that of the Frankenstein-monster concept.

That *R. U. R.* was written in and first electrified audiences of Prague, the home of the Golem, synthetic monster of Hebrew legend, is no coincidence. Not only did Čapek admit to being thoroughly familiar with and influenced by Rabbi Judah Löw's mass of clay cabalistically infused with life, but he had several reminders that may have directly sparked his inspiration.

The Golem was first filmed in Germany by Paul Wegener in 1914, and a second version of the same story, in which Paul Wegener played the monster, appeared in 1920. This later film was widely circulated in Czechoslovakia and 1920 was the year in which Čapek wrote *R. U. R.* (pp. 208-14)

Though Rabbi Löw's Golem is the most famous, it was by no means the first or the last such creature attributed to the children of Israel. The first is credited to Elijah of Chelm, in the middle of the sixteenth century. This golem is reputed to have grown to a monster resembling that created by Frankenstein. Fearing the golem might destroy the earth, Elijah finally managed to extract the *shem* from the forehead of his creation, thereby returning it to dust.

The last golem was said to have been created by David Jaffe, rabbi of Dorhiczyn, Grodno, Russia, about 1800. This golem was manufactured to cut down labor costs. It was intended to replace the gentile who came in to light the ovens of the Jews on the Sabbath. A slight error in instructions resulted in the golem burning the entire town to the ground.

The idea of the golem came to the Jews from general European tradition. In this mass of legends, the Roman poet Virgil took on many of the aspects of a magician, and was said to have described in his writing a statue which moved, spoke, and did his will. There are many other significant points of similarity between this and the golem legends. The statue of Virgil begins an orgy of destruction as a result of an incorrect order by a disciple. This happens in the golem legend from Grodno. The Virgil statue further saves an adulteress in trouble, as does Rabbi Löw's Golem. In this respect it should be noted that golems were sexless, as were Karel Čapek's robots in *R. U. R.*

Attending the opening performance of *R. U. R.* in Prague was Thomas G. Masaryk, founder and first president of Czechoslovakia. He and Čapek became the closest of friends, so close, in fact, that nearly every Friday night was spent by Čapek at Masaryk's palace.

Čapek's success with *R. U. R.* proved no accident. In 1921, in collaboration with his brother Josef, he wrote **The Insect Play,** a fantasy in which he invented a society of insects whose foibles parallel in composite those of humans. Alternatively known as **The Insect Play, The Insects, The Insect Comedy, The Life of the Insect, The World We Live In, And So Ad Infinitum,** and **From Insect Life,** it not only achieved international success, but was hailed by many critics as a better unified piece than *R. U. R.* The critic of the *New York Globe* wrote: "A finer thing than *R. U. R.* Finer in scope, feeling, philosophy. Better than the original production in Prague." (The critic had seen the play abroad.) His feelings were echoed throughout America as the play was taken on a triumphal tour.

The satirical lines of the script are pointed, pungent. Čapek unmercifully flails the shortcomings of humanity; at the same time, the insect characteristics, authentically transferred from J. H. Fabre's *La Vie des insectes* and *Souvenirs entomologiques,* gives the lie to the banality that the animals and insects of the field are more noble or more sensible in their actions than mankind.

Though he gives credit to a theory of Professor Elie Metchnikoff, famous Russian scientist, as the origin of the idea for his next play, **The Makropoulos Secret** (sometimes called **The Makropoulos Affair**), first produced in 1923, actually Čapek has borrowed from the legend of the Wandering Jew. This play did not enjoy the success on the boards of Čapek's previous two efforts, but its effect on the immortality theme in science fiction was at least as emphatic as that of *R. U. R.* on the development of robot stories.

In **The Makropoulos Secret,** a woman is discovered who has lived three hundred years as the result of an elixir perfected by her father. The woman seeks to regain the formula, which is no longer in her hands, so she can renew her life. Others, suspecting the value of the document, vie with her for its possession. Finally, through an appeal for understanding, she convinces her opponents that immortality becomes a frightful vacuum as too much is seen and felt and eventually nothing has value or desirability because there is no end to it. When they give her the formula, she destroys it.

To the well-read individual, even at the time of its appearance *The Makropoulos Secret* might have seemed just another repetition of an old idea. In fact, the charge was brought against Čapek that he had received his inspiration from George Bernard Shaw's *Back to Methuselah* which had appeared several years earlier. Čapek denied ever having read or seen Shaw's play, and pointed out that from what he had heard *Back to Methuselah* regarded the achievement of immortality as a prerequisite of paradise, whereas his play took the opposite view.

In correspondence, he later debated the desirability of longevity with Shaw, finally topping Shaw with: "We still have no experience in this sphere."

While in the early versions of the legend of the Wandering Jew, immortality is a curse which finds its possessor yearning for eternal peace and rest, it is also true that the desire for eternal life is ingrained in humanity. Čapek tries to show that in reproducing its species the human race does have a certain kind of immortality.

Čapek's plot device of the meeting of a lover, grown senile, with the ever-youthful Makropoulos woman, echoes in the achingly beautiful and popular lines of *Mr. Moonlight;* it is sketched poetically in Stanley G. Weinbaum's *Dawn of Flame,* where old Einar totters again into the life of Margaret of Urbs, the immortal woman who loved him in his youth; it appears again in the ironic whim of Naga, heroine of Ross Rocklynne's *The Immortal,* published in *Comet,* March 1941, who commands her lover to go away for "awhile." But how long is "awhile" to an immortal woman?

The same year as *The Makropoulos Secret,* Josef Čapek, without the aid of Karel, produced a science fiction allegory, *Land of Many Names,* which deals with a continent that suddenly rises from the bottom of the sea. This new continent is offered as the land of hope, where each may build anew and achieve his innermost desires.

Nations venture war for its control and possession. Instead of being a land of dreams, the newly risen mass becomes the land of the dead. Finally, when one of the nations has triumphed and while engineers and government officials lay plans for its exploitation, the continent sinks back into the sea.

The moral is obvious: wars are organized by the greedy and selfish and fought by the deluded dreamers who ultimately wake to reality and disillusionment. The play enjoyed only a modest success, possibly because the blank verse which set out to be expressionistic resolved itself into stylized tableau.

The year 1924 was a year of transition for Karel Čapek. He had begun as a lyric poet, made his mark as a short story writer, won international renown as a playwright, and now he would become a novelist. A science fiction idea—the discovery of atomic energy—carried by a daringly experimental narrative technique, combined with his proven artistry at dialogue and characterization, won him success with *Krakatit.*

"And I've discovered atomic explosions," Prokop, the inventor, tells his associate Thomas. In trying to get the secret, Thomas blows himself—and most of the countryside—up, and Prokop loses his memory.

The point Čapek makes is that a discovery that is too big, like atomic energy, can do more harm than good. "It is better to invent something small and useful" is Čapek's credo. Čapek saw clearly, in 1924, the implications of atomic energy and the fact that it was more likely to be used for war than for the betterment of mankind.

He scores the telling point made by L. Frank Baum, author of *The Wizard of Oz,* who, in an earlier book entitled *The Master Key: An Electrical Fairy Tale,* published in 1901, has a demon give to a small boy the power of anti-gravity as well as an offer of force screens, wireless communicators, and life restorers. The demon is the slave of whoever strikes the "master key" of electricity, but is chagrined when, after various misadventures, the boy thrusts his gifts back like an ingrate.

> "Why, oh why did not some intelligent person strike the Master Key!" the Demon moans.
>
> "Accidents are always liable to happen," the boy replies. "By accident the Master Key was struck long before the world of science was ready for it—or for you. Instead of considering it an accident and paying no attention to it you immediately appeared to me—*a mere boy*—and offered your services."

Krakatit was made into a motion picture by Artkino, Czechoslovakia in 1951.

Convinced of the possibility of atomic energy, Karel Čapek wrote a second novel on the theme, *The Absolute at Large,* in 1927. It follows the plot pattern of *R. U. R.* The inventors of the process have set up a company and sell atomic devices to anyone who will pay.

> "The division for atomic motor cars has got the roof on," the company head is informed. "The section for atomic flying-machines will begin work during the week. We are laying the foundations for the atomic locomotive works. One wing of the department for ships' engines is already in operation."
>
> "Wait a minute. You should start calling them atomobiles, atomoters, and atomotives, you know. How is Krolmus getting along with the atomic cannon?"

Atomic energy brings about overproduction and war. The world destroys itself and in the end the secret is lost.

Though clumsily constructed, the fault of many of Čapek's novels, *The Absolute at Large* is written with a light touch and the reader is rewarded with frequent flashes of brilliant wit and shining humanity.

One last time Karel Čapek ventured a fantasy play, again in collaboration with his brother. *Adam the Creator,* which was first produced in 1927, was not a commercial success in the theater. Yet in printed form it possesses undeniable potency, which probably accounts for its frequent appearance in anthologies.

Adam, dissatisfied with the world God has created, wipes the slate clean and begins a new process of creation. However, everything turns out wrong. Some of the outstanding men and women he creates adopt an air of pagan superiority and revile him. Where temples of worship are set up, he finds that he is barred; and commercialism, not piety, seems to be the objective. When, occasionally, humans accept him as their creator, he is reminded that his lack of foresight, not their own actions, is responsible for the plight of the world.

When Adam, in his wrath, threatens to destroy the world with his Cannon of Negation, it is the wretch who personifies the poor and downtrodden who most determinedly acts to prevent him. Finally, Adam realizes that he has botched the matter of creation, and decides the only thing to do is to give the sorry world a chance to work out its problems alone.

To follow was a gracious period during which Karel Čapek traveled and wrote books with such titles as *Letters from Spain, Letters from Holland, Travels in the North;* books on dogs and cats, gardening, fairy tales, newspapers, and the theater. These volumes are filled with a charm, wit, humanity, and sagacity that can only be compared to Mark Twain's.

These were the good years when Čapek was one of the illustrious literary figures of Europe, the epitome of the civilized human being. He had married the beautiful Czech actress Olga Scheinpflugowa, and enjoyed a gracious social life as well.

However, the seeds of his influence were coming to the surface in European literature. As a result of the motion picture produced by her husband, Fritz Lang, for Germany's UFA in 1926, Thea von Harbou's melodramatic but compelling novel, *Metropolis,* became a best-seller across the Continent. A focal figure in the novel was a metal and glass robot, fabricated in the form of a woman, who turns the head of the son of a great industrialist. The basis of the story is enslavement of the workers to the machine by the greedy few.

The all-metal robot appears in the work of American-born author Franz Harper, who made a hit by writing, and having published (1929) in German, his post-Expressionist novel, *Plus and Minus,* later translated into English. The creation of an industry manufacturing homunculi (metal robots) for use as servants and workers serves as the backdrop for a sprightly work of fate and romance.

As the world moved into the thirties, Čapek added two best-sellers about the president of Czechoslovakia to his list: *Masaryk on Thought and Life* and *President Masaryk Tells His Story.*

His trilogy, *Hordubal, Meteor,* and *An Ordinary Life,* won him critical acclaim as a novelist, *Hordubal* generally being regarded as his finest non-fantasy novel. *Meteor* has erroneously been listed as a science fiction novel, but though there is reference to an unspecified chemical discovery and a clairvoyant is a character in the book, it can hardly be considered science fiction.

When it seemed that Čapek's years of writing science fic-

tion were a thing of the past, *War with the Newts,* sometimes called *The Salamander War,* appeared in Czechoslovakia in 1936. This long novel is Čapek's masterpiece of science fiction.

In the sea a strange, nonhuman race called the Newts evolves. The Newts are intelligent creatures, easily taught, with gentle, pliable natures. Gradually, man manages to exploit them for profit, but in the process the Newts learn. The day comes when they revolt and slowly begin to undermine the continents so that they sink into the sea. In the end they have all but destroyed the human race and have set up their own nations and culture.

However, the Newts develop factionalism, warring among themselves, finally exterminating their kind; man comes out of hiding to build anew. There is one puzzling note. The world capitalist tycoon in *War with the Newts,* G. H. Bondy, has the same name as the leading industrialist in *The Absolute at Large.* If the choice was deliberate, it can only mean that Čapek felt that such men were all of the same mold and it was senseless to distinguish them with different names.

Despite his blows against the evils of capitalism, Čapek was anything but a communist. In his book, *On Political Things or Zoon Politics,* published in 1932, Čapek states:

> When all is said, communism is out to rule, not to rescue; its great watchword is power, not help. For it poverty, hunger, unemployment are not an unendurable pain and shame, but a welcome reserve of dark forces, a fermenting heap of fury and loathing.

In addition to his other activities, he worked daily in the editorial offices of a newspaper from 1917 to 1938. To him, a newspaperman, the ominous implications of Adolf Hitler's Germany were frightfully clear. When it became unmistakable that Czechoslovakia's existence was threatened by its warlike neighbor, his friend Eduard Beneš enlisted Čapek's aid.

On June 22, 1938, Karel Čapek addressed the Sudeten Germans over Prague Radio, reasoning for tolerance:

> If we could in one way or another collect all the good that is, after all, in each one of us sinful human creatures, I believe that on it could be built a world that would be surely far kinder than the present one.

Four months later, the robots marched. Goose-stepping, eyes empty of all but hate, they moved on Prague.

As Čapek had predicted, the robots would look like humans.

At the age of forty-eight, on Christmas Day, 1938, Karel Čapek died of pneumonia, his will crushed by the realization "that an alliance of violence and treachery was stronger than truth."

He was spared from knowing that a few years later his brother Josef would be murdered in a Nazi concentration camp. From the earliest years Čapek's work had reflected his fascination with Hebrew thought and legend. In his last hours, he must have realized that his fate and the fate of the Jews were as one. (pp. 216-24)

Sam Moskowitz, "Karel Čapek: The Man Who Invented Robots," in his Explorers of the Infinite: Shapers of Science Fiction, *1963. Reprint by Hyperion Press, Inc., 1974, pp. 208-24.*

R. U. R.

PRODUCTION REVIEWS

Ludwig Lewisohn   (review date 1 November 1922)

[*The world premiere of* R. U. R. *took place on 26 January 1921 at the National Theater in Prague. On 9 October the following year, it made its American debut in a production by the Theater Guild at the Garrick Theater in New York. It was very successful, receiving 184 performances in its initial run. In the following review of the New York staging, Lewisohn expresses some reservations about this work, suggesting that there is a "lack of authentic power in the central idea" of the play which exhibits a "brittleness of argument" and "confusion of the symbolism." Lewisohn regards these shortcomings as* "characteristic of a good deal of minor serious drama of the hour."]

There are two kinds of notions in the world. There is the kind that hits you between the eyes; there is the kind that irradiates the soul. Thus there are two kinds of art. There is the art that dazzles and grows dark; there is the art that shines calmly and forever. It would be a sorry sort of affectation to deny one's natural interest in the merely striking and merely dazzling, especially when it is implicated with powerful forces beyond itself. But it is healthy and necessary to keep the difference in mind. I do not at all blame the Theater Guild for producing **R. U. R.** by the Czechish playwright Karel Capek, especially in view of the quality of the production; I think it well for both the directors of the Guild and for ourselves to remember and, for a space, to realize the precise quality of the drama in question. The central idea has violence rather than creative energy. Punch is not power any more than a pine torch is a star. Punch, indeed, commonly goes with a lack of power. And the lack of authentic power in the central idea of **R. U. R.** is borne out by the execution, which is a strange mixture of wavering brilliance and mere confusion.

What is Capek after? What, in plain language—everything worth saying can be said thus—does he want to tell? Something like this: An industrial civilization with its power concentrated in the persons of the captains of industry and war wants hands not minds, helots not men. It is secure and powerful in the measure in which the pro-

Helena Glory (Kathleen MacDonnell), Harry Domin (Basil Sydney), with the Robot Marius (Myrtland LaVarre) and two Manual Labor Robots. Act I of the 1922 Theatre Guild production of R.U.R.

letariat is degraded, insensitive, supine. That is obviously true and was worked out long ago in a melodramatic but quite telling way by Jack London in one of his not altogether deservedly forgotten books. Now, Capek's argument runs on, if ever this industrial civilization does succeed in reducing the proletariat to the level of mere mechanical helots, then the death of civilization will be upon us. For when these helots revolt they will destroy all things and values that represent the spirit of man. The squint at Russia is obvious; the complete absurdity of the argument equally so. For on the one hand we have the assumption that men can be reduced to the level of mere machines which, in the nature of things, would not revolt at all; on the other hand we are told that these helots will revolt against slavery, oppression, their own soulless estate, which at once reinvests them with all the passions, powers, and thoughts from which the triumphs of civilization—St. Peter's and the Divine Comedy and the Ninth Symphony—draw their origin.

In order to project his argument pictorially and dramatically Capek uses what may be called the Golem-Frankenstein device. Rossum, a great physiological chemist, invents a method of manufacturing man-like creatures who make good workers and soldiers but are without passions or self-originating thoughts. These "robots" are manufactured, bought, and sold as workers and, finally, as cannon-fodder. They soon vastly outnumber mankind whose birth-rate declines to nothing since men cannot compete in cheapness or usefulness with the robots. They revolt—this is the central absurdity—slaughter all men left, but are doomed to extinction in their turn since the secret of their manufacture is lost. This ending, which might be called logical were not the whole thing the reverse, is furthermore stultified by an epilogue in which a male and female robot suddenly become human and enter, a queer Adam and Eve, the dusty paradise left them.

There can be no question but that behind the play, as well as in a hundred details of the execution, a high and powerful passion, a far from ignoble imagination have been at work. *R. U. R.* is no ordinary work, Capek's no ordinary talent or intelligence. I have been at some pains to point out the brittleness of the argument, the confusion of the symbolism, because this brittleness and this confusion are very characteristic of a good deal of the minor serious drama of the hour. These plays come with an intellectual and poetic gesture which, upon analysis, is seen to be merely a gesture. Their turbid symbolism and specious arguments are in danger of making many people undervalue the literature which is humbler and truer, more concrete, and for that very reason more significant, not spectacular but sound.

Whatever the play has of imagination, weirdness, beauty, horror is fully expressed if not indeed heightened by the settings, costumes, acting, directing at the Garrick. As an example of the art of the theater the production is exquisite in skill, sensitiveness, in the unemphatic completeness of its command of all the resources of that art. It deserves the utmost admiration and the closest attention; the play deserves the nine days' wonder of the proverb.

Ludwig Lewisohn, "Helots," in The Nation,

New York, Vol. CXV, No. 2991, November 1, 1922, p. 478.

Kenneth Andrews (review date December 1922)

[*In the following review of the 1922 New York Theater Guild production of* R. U. R., *Andrews finds that the drama "provides a memorable evening" with its "richly sardonic humor." The Theater Guild, however, took the play too seriously, in the critic's judgment, and as a result lost the work's "mood of fantasy."*]

In the Theatre Guild productions of the past one has been conscious of a directing mind extremely sensitive to the mood which the playwright wished to establish. In the case of *Liliom* the delicacy with which the necessary mood was maintained was no doubt responsible for its astonishingly wide popular appeal. The success which *He Who Gets Slapped* achieved was largely due, we think, to the fact that someone had succeeded in imbuing the actors with a sense of the ironical fantasy which was the soul of the play. Everything that happened on the stage, partook of that spirit, and the result was a complete and unified creation which gained its poignancy because its appeal was so clear and definite. The plays themselves were not popular pieces; it was the comprehension of their mood on the part of their producers which made them live. It seems that this quality is lacking in the Guild's production of Karel Capek's *R. U. R.;* and this play, of all the plays they have done, needed it most.

The author takes a perverse and fantastical idea and lets his fancy soar. If some scientist should develop a formula for making human beings by chemical processes, and if all the hard work of the world were turned over to them, he suggests, let's take a night off and try to imagine what would happen. These synthetic beings would be useful to manufacturers, they would eventually be used as the soldiers of the world. They might in the end become so numerous that they would spread over the earth and become more powerful than human beings. Then let us suppose, since we are just supposing, that God should become annoyed at the encroachment on his prerogatives and deprive mankind of the power of reproduction. Suppose then that the "Robots" should form one big union and kill off every human being on earth except one. And suppose—this is something of a stretch—that there is only one copy extant of the priceless formula for making "Robots", and suppose this is destroyed. What would happen then? Indeed it is a theme to fire the imagination, a daring theme for a play, but a splendid one if it is not taken too seriously. The Theatre Guild, astonishingly enough, seemed to take it very seriously, after the first act.

They seemed to lose entirely the mood of fantasy in which the author unquestionably conceived his play, the mood which they themselves established in the beginning. The third act booms as they have staged it. David Wark Griffith could not have improved upon their treatment of the scene where the chief "Robot" stands silhouetted against a fiery sky and sounds his cosmic tocsin. We hope no movie caption writer ever gets a chance at that scene. It is of course possible that the author himself changed his key, and that the play could not have been produced otherwise. One is inclined to that conclusion when he recalls the unwarranted moment of sadism in the epilogue, and the sudden drop to sentimentality at the end. The play provides a memorable evening, there is a richly sardonic humor threaded through it, and there are also keen thrills; but it seems to lack the finished direction which we have come to expect from the Theatre Guild. (pp. 478-80)

Kenneth Andrews, in a review of "R. U. R.," in The Bookman, *New York, Vol. LVI, No. 4, December, 1922, pp. 478-80.*

The Spectator   (review date 5 May 1923)

[R. U. R. *had its London premiere in April 1923. In the following review of the production, the critic offers a mixed evaluation of the play, noting that even though it has "touches of genuine satire," it is nonetheless disappointing. The critic cites numerous faults in the play's construction, with the underdevelopment of the main characters emerging as the most glaring.*]

R. U. R. can hardly be better described than by its own subtitle, "A Fantastic Melodrama." Here and there the fact of its projection into the future, its touches of genuine satire, its digressions into speculation, make one mistake it for a play of ideas. Then it seems disappointing, and we perceive the thin places in plot and characterization. Especially did it seem a "let down" to me, for I have had the pleasure of watching some of the rehearsals of Mr. Karel Capek's other piece, **The Insect Play,** which Mr. Playfair produces at the Regent on May 5th. Here the satire is vivid, and the humour light and delicate. In fine, it is in comparison with **The Insect Play** that we see what is wrong with **R.U.R.,** though it may be that **R.U.R.** will be esteemed the more taking piece. **R.U.R.** has much of the character of an early work. Its whole attitude is tentative and it takes obvious refuge in action and excitement from the difficulties both of sustained characterization and reflection. There is little character drawing in it. All the people are types, somewhat hazily conceived. The exasperating *ingénue,* Helena Glory, is the least successful, and they range up to Dr. Gall (head of the psychological department of Rossum's Universal Robots) and Emma [Nana], Helena Glory's servant, and Jacob Berman, the chief cashier. But really it is a quibble to draw attention to these faults of the play, for once grant that it is to be melodrama, and not a play of ideas, it is extraordinarily good, and holds the spectators from beginning to end. The actual story also is a genuine effort of the imagination.

An old scientist has found out not merely how to produce life, but how to make tissues which can be infused with the life that he has made. He tries to imitate nature and makes an artificial dog. "That took him several years," explains one of the characters, sarcastically, "and resulted in a sort of stunted calf which died in a few days." Then he tried to make a man. But his nephew was a man of very different ideals. He saw that there was money in the idea. He saw that, given a slight twist, the formula would produce not men, but "Robots," living, intelligent, working machines. Young Rossum goes over the human anatomy and

cuts out everything that is "unnecessary." A weaver does not need to play the piano and feel joy or sorrow, or love or hate. Young Rossum, then, produces Robots. The factory is a going concern. Helena Glory comes to the island where the R.U.R. factory is situated on behalf of a sentimental "League of Humanity," who are shocked at the material way in which Robots are looked upon. She sentimentalizes over their hard lot (they are sent back to the stamping mills and ground if they show any signs of inefficiency) and ends by marrying the General Manager, Harry Domain. But Dr. Gall is a scientist and missionary, and carries on the tradition of old Rossum rather than young Rossum. He pushes forward. He endows the Robots with pain, so that they shall not be careless and break their limbs. This is the beginning of the end. Pain proves the beginning of some sort of consciousness. Ten years after the opening scene of the play the Robots are turning upon the men who have made them and conquering the world, for men have ceased to be born, and the Robots now outnumber the human beings by a hundred to one. A thrilling scene ensues in which the humans are besieged by the Robots, and finally overwhelmed, only one man surviving. But the secret of making Robots has been lost through the sentimental action of Helena Glory, who, before the catastrophe, has burned the formula.

Power has made the Robots still more like human beings. They only last twenty years, and their leaders are in agony lest the race of Robots should die out. They are machines and the formula has gone. But the anxiety, in its turn, has had its effect upon them, and the play ends with a young Robot and Robotess going out into the world suffering from new and unaccountable symptoms, such as inability to live without each other, willingness to sacrifice everything for the other's welfare, laughter and a quickened heart-beat. A new Adam and Eve have come back to the world.

An exciting, thrilling play, which everyone will enjoy. But the glamour over, to return to its faults. The part played by old Rossum's formula is ludicrously like that of the "marriage lines" in the old-fashioned Lyceum melodrama. The tragedy is made to turn on their burning by the impulsive sentimental young wife, who has got them out of the strong box where they are kept. Now, Robots are supposed to be turned out by the hundred-thousand. Imagine a play in which the tragedy depends on Mr. Ford losing the formula for his motors! Manufacture in bulk would so patently involve at least some hundred printed copies of the formula that this flaw is worrying, and gives far more sense of unreality than a mere synthetic man. The second drawback is the extremely tiresome character of Helena Glory, played by Miss Frances Carson, whose pretty looks could do no more than make her bearable. The men characters all have a certain touch of imaginative largeness about them. Harry Domain, the manager, wants to make Robots so as to free the human race from the grind of monotonous labour. Dr. Gall is a scientist with enthusiasms. The half-comic cashier is yet a man not without grandeur and a sense of the hugeness of the machine for which he works. But Helena Glory is of the past; she is told nothing about the revolution, and her ten-year anniversary is being celebrated with pearl necklaces, cyclamens and so forth all through the exciting part. Her characteristic speech is, "Oh, Harry, I don't understand!" She would seem out of place in modern London, she is two or three centuries behind the life of the factory between 1950 and 1960. She interrupts the adventure story in the most exasperating way. The adult playgoer will feel almost a schoolboy irritation at the way in which she interferes with our enjoyment of the revolution scene, and in the way in which she is always on the stage. In exasperation we remember that she does not even fulfil the one function of the harem woman; she is childless. All this would be bearable if she were not so constantly in evidence.

Mr. Basil Rathbone looked very handsome as Harry Domain, but acted stiffly. Mr. Brember Wills's acting as Alquist, in the last act was too much reminiscent of his performance in *Heartbreak House*. Mr. Leslie Banks as a Robot, and Miss Beatrix Thomson as a Robotess, were admirable, and the entrance of the Robots at the end was most striking; indeed, I wish we could see more of them— they are really alarming and convincing monsters. I am sorry that Miss Olga Lindo, as Helena II., the Robotess through whom love comes back into the world, should have modelled her costume on the tradition of the opera stage, hair down, backward tilted pose and white nightgown. The result is that to most people she does not look nearly so attractive as Sulla, the unemotional Robotess. (pp. 755-56)

" 'R.U.R.' at St. Martin's," in The Spectator, Vol. 130, No. 4949, May 5, 1923, pp. 755-56.

CRITICAL COMMENTARY

William E. Harkins   (essay date 1962)

[*Harkins is an American critic and educator who has written extensively on Czechoslovakian and Russian literature. In the essay below, he discusses various aspects of* R. U. R., *including its historical and literary contexts, its theme of the dehumanization of humanity, its dramatic structure, and its comic elements.*]

R.U.R., or *Rossum's Universal Robots,* had its première at the National Theater in Prague on January 25, 1921. Within several years, the play was translated and performed in most of the countries of Europe, as well as in the United States and Japan. Čapek's name (in various mispronounced and even misspelled forms) became a household word, along with the term "robot" itself. This word, coined by Josef Čapek [in his story "Opilec"], is derived from the Czech *robota*, "forced labor," "servitude."

The title of the play, *R.U.R.* or *Rossum's Universal Robots,* is the name of a fictitious corporation, and is in English in the original. This would suggest a British or American setting for the play. But the names of the characters are multi-national; here as often later, Čapek tried to create a deliberately international background for his theme. A number of references are made in the play to the commercial interests of Europe, and there is no suggestion that America or Britain alone is guilty of a technological revolution which might submerge the human race.

The idea of a robot, an artificial man, is of course very old. One source is the Jewish legend of the Golem of Prague, which turned against those who misused its sacred power. Mary Shelley's novel *Frankenstein* is another manifest source, closer in that both the robot and Frankenstein's monster are creations not of magic, but of modern technology. Certain details of Old Rossum's experiments, as well as the island setting, may have been suggested by H. G. Wells's novel, *The Island of Dr. Moreau,* in which a scientist operates on animals to make them more nearly resemble men. In Čapek's own work, the robot finds a prototype in the puppets of the early tales.

Nor was Čapek the first to introduce an artificial man on the stage, as is sometimes claimed. Goethe's *Faust,* Part II, is of course no more a play than its Homunculus is really an artificial man. But the mechanical dolls of Delibes' ballet *Coppélia* (1870) and Offenbach's opera *The Tales of Hoffmann* (1881) are earlier examples of stage puppets.

What is new in Čapek's play is the complex meaning of the symbol of the robot, which represents not only the machine and its power to free man from toil but, at the same time, symbolizes man himself, dehumanized by his own technology. From the technical point of view, man is an inefficient instrument, whose emotional and spiritual life only impedes the drive of modern technology. Either he must give way to the machine, or he himself must become a machine. This aspect of the symbol we have already found in the brothers' early story, "The System" (1908). Last, the robot symbolizes man dehumanized by the very freedom from toil which the machine assures him; gone are the struggle of life and the challenge to man's spirit. In *R.U.R.* man loses even his ability to reproduce, the last thing which distinguishes him from the robot. The complexity of the robot symbol must be realized for a proper understanding of Čapek's play. He was too honest a writer to create a superficial melodrama about man-like machines which revolt against man—though this is obviously the aspect of the play which made it so popular.

Another influence on the technological theme of *R.U.R.* was Georg Kaiser's *Gas,* Part I (1918). In both dramas man is seen as an imperfect instrument from the technological point of view: in Kaiser's play the workers become mere expressionistic embodiments of hands or feet, in accordance with the task they must perform at their machines. In *R.U.R.* man's soul is described as standing in the way of mechanical perfection: man plays the violin, goes for walks, and has children—all impediments to his role as an integer in the modern world of industry and commerce. In both plays technology reaches a limit of the irrational which it cannot control: in Kaiser the formula for gas is calculated perfectly, yet the gas explodes; in Čapek, the formula creates mere robots, but in the end robots become men. Man's spirit cannot be regimented, Čapek is saying, even by misapplication of his own reason and science. This theme also reminds us of the brothers' earlier story, "The Luminous Depths."

Both plays end in the apparent victory of technology over spirit: in Kaiser the workers reject the hero's efforts to humanize them; in Čapek, man is destroyed by his own robots. But in both spirit is actually the victor: in *Gas,* the hero has discovered man's true nature—life—and realizes that others, too, will find it; in **R.U.R.,** the robots live and reproduce.

R.U.R. differs strikingly from Kaiser's play, however, in its strong defense of technological utopia—the dream of the factory manager Domin. Kaiser's engineer offers little more to the workers than a picture of a world in which they will have new toys to play with.

Kaiser's play is thoroughly expressionistic in style, while Čapek has blended expressionism with realism. In fact, only the figure of the robot itself (and the final transformation of robots into men) is expressionistic; otherwise Čapek's treatment is conventional and realistic. This mixture of styles was hardly a concession to popular appeal, for it was just the expressionistic symbol of the robot which made the play so popular. What Čapek was seeking, rather, was a humanization of the play, and in this he at least partly succeeded. Today Kaiser's *Gas* seems totally lifeless, while **R.U.R.,** for all its sins against the stage, remains moving and human. Still, in its purity of style, Kaiser's play is surely the more consistent.

R.U.R. opens with a "comedy prologue." Helena Glory, daughter of the president of the firm of Rossum's Universal Robots, comes to visit the island where robots are manufactured. Her ostensible motive is curiosity, but actually she intends to incite the robots to revolt and claim equality with men. All this is quite useless, the directors of the factory assure her, for the robots do only what they are told and have no conception of abstract justice or equality. All the men on the island fall in love with her, and finally she accepts the proposal of Domin, the managing director.

The expository section of the Prologue introduces us to two contrasting aspects of the robot symbol. Their inventor, Old Rossum (the name is derived from Czech *rozum,* "reason") was a rationalist who sought to create life as a proof of the nonexistence of God. He had no interest in the economic exploitation of his discovery. For this type of scientist Čapek always had the warmest praise, though he was fully aware of the limitations of such a point of view. Elsewhere he has described the great scientists of the past as "adventurers and romantics of intellectual discovery," and "Don Quixotes of the nineteenth century." They had the courage of their convictions; their dreams, even their challenges to God, were proud assertions of the human spirit. In his zeal for pure science Old Rossum had striven to create man with everything Nature had given him—even an appendix. It was his nephew, rather, who simplified his discovery, created the robot, and set up manufacture on a mass-production basis.

The "comedy" element of the Prologue arises from Helena's inability to distinguish robots from humans. In one scene she refuses to believe that a robot is not a woman; later she mistakes the directors of the factory for robots, and tries to incite them to revolt. The humor here is not gratuitous; it introduces us directly to the theme of the play. The point is that man is already dehumanized, and so Helena cannot tell the difference. Hence Domin insists that he can afford to wait no more than five minutes for

Helena's reply to his proposal of marriage; he has become a prisoner of his own dream of technological utopia.

The Prologue is set apart from the body of the play because it is comedy, while the play proper is drama. Act I is the kernel of **R.U.R.;** in fact, the dramatic conflict is essentially resolved by its finish, and what follows is largely anticlimax. In this act we learn that robots all over the world have risen against their masters, and that man is doomed. We also learn that man has lost his power to reproduce his kind. Revolted by this news, Helena burns the manuscript of Rossum's formula. But in so doing she destroys herself and those she loves, for the manuscript could have served as the bargaining price for their freedom.

Once we know that man has lost his ability to reproduce, and that the robots have risen against him, the outcome is obvious. Yet Čapek delays the inevitable ending by introducing an electrified barrier which the robots cannot cross until they have taken the factory power plant. This delay is dramatically necessary; otherwise the play would be over by the end of the first act. (Here of course is the reason why Acts II and III seem anticlimactic.) The author needed time to comment on what was happening if the play were to be a drama of ideas, and not a mere melodrama. In the Prologue and Act I the whole burden of argument is against technology. Such an opposition of black and white was foreign to Čapek's purpose. There is no reason to suppose, as some critics have, that he was opposed to human inventiveness as such; in fact, several of his essays welcome new inventions. Moreover, Čapek was a relativist. Domin too has a share of the truth in his dream of a world in which man is freed of toil and his energies are released to pursue the things of the spirit. This dream is depicted in the second act.

Of course, Domin could have described his dream in Act I, and the robots could have launched their attack during Act II. This would have been the more conventional dramatic procedure. But it would have deprived the author of a solemn moment in the symbolic plane of the drama: the awful realization that mankind is passing from the earth.

Čapek later wrote that he conceived **R.U.R.** as a eulogy to man, that he wanted to view human life in retrospect and say, as Hallemeier does in the play, "It was a great thing to be a man." And Čapek adds: "Technology, progress, ideals, faith—all these were rather only illustrations of humanity than the sense of the play."

Of course Čapek exaggerates here; the note of eulogy is not the final one. The end of the play is the miracle of life, the transformation of robots into men. But even if his dramatic means are questionable, Čapek was right to introduce this philosophical note into his play. For the threat to man's existence can be meaningful only if the spectator really grasps that man is about to pass from the earth, if he comprehends what a "great thing" it was "to be a man."

The delay of the electrified screen is also necessary if man is to understand *why* he is doomed to destruction, why the robots have revolted against him. Dr. Gall confesses that he has modified the robots' sensitivity to please Helena. Their coldness had terrified her, and she sought to give them a soul. To gratify her, Gall has increased the "nervous irritability" of the robots. It is this, seemingly, which has produced the revolt. But Gall's hypothesis is far from certain; perhaps it is the fact that there are more robots than people, and the robots are stronger and more intelligent. Perhaps it is because the robots were given arms to fight in national wars. Or perhaps it is because man forgot to create robots with national differences which would turn them against one another. Only at the end of the act do we discover the true cause of the robots' hatred for mankind; they are man's equals, but they work, while man does not.

Both capitalism and communism must share the responsibility for the robot uprising. It is not technology which destroys man, the directors conclude at one point, but greed for profits and the inevitable law of supply and demand. And when Domin reads a manifesto addressed to "robots of the world," he asks who taught them such phrases. Here the robot uprising appears as a symbol of socialist revolution; may not man forfeit even his own humanity to gain a materialist utopia, whether achieved through capitalism or socialism?

The second act culminates in the end of the siege and the massacre of the defenders. The robots kill everyone except the construction engineer, Alquist, who is spared because he still works with his hands.

Act III is also a dramatic anticlimax, but it likewise is necessary for the philosophical point of the play. Alquist is alone, the only human spared by the robots. In despair at man's passing, he tries to discover the secret of manufacturing life. The robot leaders order him to dissect live robots. He attempts this, but his nervous hands cannot hold the scalpel. As he mourns his lack of resoluteness, he observes that his two robot servants, Primus and Helena, have fallen in love. Alquist puts their feeling to the test by suggesting that he intends to dissect one of them. Each begs to be taken in place of the other. Alquist tells them to go and be man and wife to one another. He reads from Genesis how God created man and woman in His own image. "Life will not perish," he concludes.

Ideologically the play thus turns in a circle, denying the very thesis it had asserted for dramatic purposes. This thesis, that modern civilization threatens to destroy man by removing the element of struggle from life, is contradicted: life and love will not perish. This contradiction is no inconsistency, but a deliberate use of a false dramatic resolution followed by the true one. This is why the construction of *R.U.R.*, with its two acts of apparent anticlimax, is so unorthodox.

On June 21, 1923, a public discussion was held in London on the meaning of *R.U.R.* Shaw, Chesterton, and Commander Joseph Kenworthy were among the participants. Shaw made some amusing remarks on the robot element in human nature: man must spend a great part of his life a slave to routine, whether or not it is imposed by modern technology. Better a bit more routine, a bit more "robotry," in order to give man more time for greater spiritu-al independence, Shaw concluded. Chesterton considered the play an eloquent satire on the irresponsibility of modern capitalist civilization. Kenworthy saw in *R.U.R.* a warning against the threat of war and international anarchy. Such interpretations of the play as these last two are popular, and in a sense obvious. Čapek took exception to them, however, and published a rebuttal in *The Saturday Review* [See Author Commentary dated 1923]. (pp. 84-90)

[In his rejoinder] Čapek denies that the play is concerned only with the menace of technology to modern society. The danger, in fact, is civilization itself, which threatens to overwhelm man by its sheer weight and impersonality. Human reason has created civilization, but is manifestly unable to control it.

As Čapek states, the second idea of the play is that of the "comedy of truth," the conflict of pieces of relativist truth, each of them in itself quite valid. There are four such points of view expressed in the play. Domin stands for man as master of the universe (indeed, his name implies this); his is the dream of freedom for man from toil. Opposed to him is Nána, Helena's old nurse, a peasant woman of strict religious persuasion. For her "all inventions are against the Lord God." A more sophisticated variant of her belief is presented by Alquist, the construction engineer. Though he is not certain whether God exists, he recognizes the importance of spirit and moral law, and he prays. He has an almost Tolstoyan faith in work. His profession symbolizes his creativity, which for him is the inner goal of the human need to work. But Alquist forgets that work and creativity are not the same; the drudgery from which Domin seeks to liberate man is not the longing to create.

Alquist's character is developed through an interesting literary reference to Ibsen's *Master Builder*:

> HELENA: What do you do when you feel worried?
>
> ALQUIST: I lay brick. I take off my engineer's coat, and climb up on the scaffolding . . .
>
> HELENA: And don't you feel dizzy on the scaffold?
>
> ALQUIST: No. You don't know how good it feels to hold a brick in your hand, to set it down and knock it into place.

Ibsen's Solness is proud, and feels dizzy because he fears he will fall. Alquist is humble, and climbs the scaffold to do humble work.

Finally, there is Helena's viewpoint. Her name, which is also that of the beautiful robot girl, symbolizes her nature as eternal woman. She acts instinctively, out of feeling, not reason. But she too is doomed, for she does no work, and, though she desires children, she does not have them.

The chief fault in the interplay of these four points of view is that there is no acceptable ideology to counter that of Domin, only the logic of events themselves. Nána's viewpoint, stolidly opposed to all invention as a presumption against God, would return man to an animal existence. Alquist's philosophy of creative work is a personal faith, for not every man is born to create. Helena's intuitive approach to right and wrong has no objective foundation. Though she is in touch with life, she is cut off, paradoxically, from reality, and it is her well-intentioned destruction of the manuscript which brings her own end and the end of those she loves.

The American critic Kenneth Burke has observed [in his *Counter-Statement*] that *R.U.R.* fails primarily because of a lack of eloquence. The intensity of Čapek's ideas is never matched by a corresponding intensity of language. Perhaps Čapek feared to depart too far from everyday speech; here the realistic and expressionistic sides of his play are in conflict. Only the ideas of Domin and Alquist approach eloquence in statement. But Domin's eloquence is sterile, for the logic of events is against him. Alquist's ideas are personal, and stand apart from the drama. Helena, who ought to be the most eloquent person in the play, is the least so. Her speeches have an almost painful banality, while her actions, such as the destruction of the manuscript, appear even more stupid. As one critic has observed [V. Černý, in his *Karel Čapek*], the spectator may conclude from the way the play is constructed that man disappears from the earth because Helena cannot mind her own business.

From the standpoint of realism, there are other faults in the play. It seems impossible that Rossum's manuscript should exist in only one copy. Nor is it likely that Helena should be the only woman on the island, when the men there are well paid. In his need to find a symbol of sterility, Čapek sacrificed probability to the expressionist side of the play. Indeed, may not this picture suggest the existence of psychic conflict within the author himself: an island where six men live with one woman in Platonic love, and where there are no children, only robots? May not the robot symbol have had its origin in a personal fear of sterility?

Čapek was aware of the defects of *R.U.R.,* and liked it least of all his plays. In an interview with Dorothy Thompson [in the *New York Post,* 23 February 1925] he confessed that he was unable to comprehend what people saw in *R.U.R.* But he declined to say what was wrong with it, observing only that the spectator can see for himself. "It is a play that anyone might have written," he added. For years he refused to go to see *R.U.R.,* and gave in only when trapped in a small Czech town by the director of the local theater.

How discerning a prophet was Čapek in *R.U.R.?* If the question touches only man's ability to live with technology and the machine, then his fears were in a sense exaggerated. In spite of the unprecedented rate of technological progress in our times, modern man has demonstrated his ample powers of adaptation. The specter of technological unemployment has largely been dispelled by the discovery that new machines create new responsibilities and new jobs, and by the opening of new areas of employment in personal services. And it can hardly be said that technological "utopia" has decreased the element of toil or conflict in life, as Čapek feared it might; no one is busier than the contemporary American family dwelling in suburbia. If mere survival is easier today than ever before, then the achievement of wealth and prestige costs at least as much in competitive struggle as ever.

But man's ability to adapt does not in itself guarantee his survival. The terrible destructive powers which modern science has created reopen the question and point to the very dilemma of the conflict of motives about which Čapek wrote. Čapek's robots are symbols of modern civilization as a whole. The marvellous instrument of science and technology is only a tool in the grip of uncontrolled forces: the profit motive, supply and demand, competition for markets, the mutual antipathy of nations, the armament race. Modern technology can supply instruments and weapons to serve these forces, but it cannot control them. And it is not only the conflict within man which is at fault, Čapek implies; reason itself errs when it blithely ignores these forces. Reason can forge new weapons of destruction; reason can also fabricate Domin's great dream; reason can create a socialist utopia at the price of dehumanizing man. But reason forgets that it is no absolute, that it is only the servant of the irrational in man, not the master. Reason ought to content itself with a humbler role: to restrain the conflicting forces of civilization, rather than to arm them with new weapons.

The question is of course complicated by the double answer which Čapek gives: man will be destroyed, and he will not be. Today, when the human race still survives, but scarcely knows how long it will go on surviving, it is possible to appreciate the wisdom of this ambiguous answer.

In spite of the faults of *R.U.R.,* it is safe to say that no other play on modern technology has so captured the public's imagination. Perhaps, in view of the great urgency of its theme, it has a just claim to be Čapek's most popular work. (pp. 92-5)

> *William E. Harkins, in his* Karel Čapek, *Columbia University Press, 1962, 193 p.*

James D. Naughton   (essay date 1984)

[*In the following excerpt, Naughton examines the seeming contradiction in* R. U. R. *between its pessimistic vision of the future and its hopeful ending. The critic argues that elements of comedy and lyrical rhetoric as well as a certain vagueness in the plot enable Čapek to end the drama "on what is keenly felt to be a desirable note of optimism."*]

It has been said [by K. Brušák, in the *Penguin Companion to Literature*] of Karel Čapek (1890-1938) that his work 'gives new meaning to the precept of Protagoras, that man is the measure of all things: for he sees how man, noble and wretched, is menaced and mocked in our time.' He wrote of his play *R.U.R.* (1920) that it was concerned 'not with Robots, but with people', declaring, somewhat grandiloquently: 'Imagine yourself standing over the grave of mankind; however jaundiced your view, you would surely realise the divine significance of the extinguished species and say—you too: It was a great thing to be a man.'

Yet the most obvious legacy of the play to the world of man (and the world of science fiction) is the word *Robot* and, to some extent, Čapek's re-created concept of an artificial man, a concept of course with many ancient ramifications including the classical legend of Pygmalion and Galatea and the Jewish Golem. One fairly close ancestor to the Robot is the scientifically-created monster in Mary Shelley's *Frankenstein;* another analogy is to be found in the humanised animals of H. G. Wells's *The Island of Dr. Moreau.* It must be stressed however that Čapek's Robots are quite different from the mechanical devices, automata and Dalek-like monsters for which the term *robot* is now variously applied. Čapek's Robots are biological, not mechanical: they are products of bio-engineering and look just like human beings. At first they are distinguishable on stage only by a certain stiffness of motion and demeanour; later they wear a simple military-style tunic. They are artificial humanoid beings, created by the atheistic inventor, Old Rossum, who wanted to prove that God was unnecessary. His commercially-minded nephew, the real founder of the firm (Rossum's Universal Robots, after which the play is named) simplified his over-complex semi-abortive invention into an efficient, industrially marketable mass-product. Robots are manufactured slave-labour, made in emotionless, sexless, dehumanised, soulless forms suitable for all kinds of industrial, agricultural and domestic labour. They are the ultimate labour-saving device. The word indicates their function. It is derived from the Czech *robota* meaning 'corvée, forced labour, servitude', borrowed also into German as *die Robot,* and related to the Russian *rabota* meaning simply 'work'. Earlier Čapek had apparently considered calling them *Labři*. This term would presumably not have entered the English language, being too close to 'labour' and 'labourer': yet the alternative English term *automaton* is rather too inanimate-sounding to fill the bill. The successful term *Robot* was coined, as Karel Čapek later related, by his brother, sometimes co-author, Josef Čapek. (Incidentally the inventor's name Rossum is similarly based on the Czech word *rozum,* meaning 'reason' given an Anglo-American type spelling appearance suitable for the play's international big-business setting.) The term *Robot* was easily assimilated into the English language as a suitably alien-sounding novelty, a term opaque in derivation, emotionally evocative and specific in its connotations (because of the play). The play, *R.U.R.,* was first produced in London at the St. Martin's Theatre in April 1923 (its professional Czech premiére was on 25th January 1921 at the National Theatre, Prague; its New York Premiére was given by the Theatre Guild on 9th October 1922). The word *Robot,* kept by the translator Paul Selver, and the horror element of the Robot's role in the plot, both seized the public imagination and gave the play its international fame. Today it is only the word *robot* and its semantically shifted and variegated concept that remain familiar to the general public, most of whom have naturally never heard of Karel Čapek.

The plot of *R.U.R.* parallels in several respects that of Čapek's later novel *Válka s mloky* (*War with the Newts,* 1936). Here the newts play the role of the Robots: they build dams, reclaim land, and do all manner of undersea work for man. They are discovered, already existing, not invented, which is one reason why the novel is less futurological in effect; but, like Robots, they bring man to extinction, or to the brink of extinction. In both works the theme of siege and encirclement by alien beings looms large: destruction and encirclement are obsessive themes throughout Čapek's science fiction. In both works, likewise, Čapek portrays the danger that man's inventiveness linked to the materialist economic imperatives presents to his very survival as a species. Yet, of the two, perhaps only the play *R.U.R.* strikes a true futurological note. Both are to be read as dystopian, semi-allegorical fantasies, which display and criticise elements and trends in modern civilisation; but *War with the Newts* comes across as a satirical fantasy-image of the present, rather than a vision set in a future distinctly distanced from the 1930s. *R.U.R.,* can also be seen as a fantasy-image of the present, or a timeless myth. Setting, props and dress need not be (though they may be) overtly futuristic. Apart from the Robots and their manufacture the rest of the technology in the play (guns, transport, etc.) is unblushingly contemporary. This stresses the mythical-allegorical side and rejects the uncompromising (and possibly more glamorous) futuristic approach that another writer might have adopted. However, the more markedly futuristic technological element of the Robots themselves and the historically unrelated setting give a greater sense of temporal distance than we find in *War with the Newts.* Also, unlike *War with the Newts, R.U.R.* seems concerned (in a symbolic, allegorical, non-literal kind of way) with long-distance projection of trends, as well as with satirising, through fantasy, the absurdities and blindness of man's individual and social behaviour.

Disturbing visions of the future, like fantasy images of the present, or visions avoiding any identifiable sense of time, may function as parables, allegories or metamorphoses of the contemporary world, but their specifically future setting and consequent elements of prediction (or quasi-prediction) allow them to function as warnings, as well as critiques. Their prophetic (or quasi-prophetic) qualities enhance their rhetorical exhortative force. Usually, in Western European writing at least (under which heading we include Karel Čapek, since Prague is west of Vienna), the visions of the future are disturbing, seldom uplifting, seldom intended to warm the heart. The Utopias are usually anti-Utopian. Naturally the more optimistic writers— amongst whom Karel Čapek wished to number himself— desire to see their gloomy prognostications avoided. They see their warnings as part of a wider message (not only literary) which may perhaps be heeded. The degree of overt (and covert) optimism or pessimism naturally fluctuates according to various factors including political events of the day, economic and social developments, the author's own experiences, and literary fashions. The relative absence of optimism in *War with the Newts* is clearly attributable to the hardships and absurdities of the Great Depression and the rise of Fascism and Nazism with consequent threats to the independence of Czechoslovakia and the lives of its citizens. All of this left an indelible mark on Karel Čapek's later work, its last pages written under the shadow of Munich. The earlier play, *R.U.R.,* however apocalyptic in tone, and however much partly inspired by the carnage and nationalistic madness of the First World War, exudes in its ending a curiously extraneous, facile optimism. Yet in spite of this, the play can easily be read as if fundamentally pessimistic, simply by finding the optimism hollow and unconvincing. Texts often fail to deliver their intended effect or overt message, and this seems at least partly the case with **R.U.R.** How much the overt, declarative optimism of the final scene is camouflaging a personal *Angst,* linked to a pessimistic analysis of the future human condition, is a question to which we will return briefly at the end of this article. Perhaps it is not merely a biographical question but one relevant to certain features of the text as well.

Before we proceed to analyse **R.U.R.,** as far as possible from the point of view of futurological diagnosis, it should perhaps be noted in passing at least that a number of other works of Čapek contain related futurological elements. However, these works are in the main social satires and fantasies with science fiction elements, some of which have early grasp of the potential of atomic energy. They tend to be set in a fictional present or near-present (with greater or lesser elements of fantasy and unreality) or outside any historical or quasi-historical time-frame. Such works include the novels *Továrna ne Absolutno* (*The Absolute at Large,* 1922) and *Krakatit* (1924, also known in English as *An Atomic Phantasy*), and the play *Bílá nemoc* (*The White Plague,* 1937, translated as *Power and Glory*). Likewise anti-Utopian rather than futurological are the plays *Adam stvořitel* (*Adam the Creator,* 1927, with Josef Čapek), and *Věc Makropulos* (*The Macropulos Secret,* 1925), which deals with the subject of immortality and forms the basis for Janáček's opera of the same name. All these works were published in English versions before the Second World War. Since then Karel Čapek's reputation has faded, to the extent that only the plays **R.U.R.** (1920) and *Ze života hmyzu* (*The Insect Play,* 1921, with Josef Čapek) remain in print in this country today. Both texts printed are adapted stage versions. The following analysis is based on the definitive 1921 Czech text of **R.U.R.,** a shortened and revised version of the original 1920 edition. Attention will be drawn to a number of passages omitted in the English version, translated by Paul Selver and adapted by Sir Nigel Playfair. Some of these markedly affect the tone and symbolic force of the play as a whole.

R.U.R. Rossum's Universal Robots is described beneath its title as a 'collective drama in three acts with a comedy prologue' (in the English version it becomes 'A Play in three acts and an epilogue' and the epilogue is headed as Act IV). The term 'collective' refers to the theme, embracing all mankind; the action on stage is in fact localised, largely semi-domestic and individual in scale: the masses remain firmly offstage. The humour of the comedy prologue is not limited to that part of the play, but spills over into the whole work, or nearly the whole work, a surprisingly large proportion of which is engagingly light-hearted, racy and facetious in tone. This produces a sometimes curious effect when light comedy and satire are blended with quite solemn attempts at lyrical evocations of the nobility of man and the tragedy of his passing. An effect of macabre farce seems to arise from the expression of an apocalyptic warning through whimsically schematic elements of plot and characterisation serving more the purposes of amusement and gentle satire than of engaging our sympathy and self-identification. Čapek's persistent instinct to create verbal and situational fun is aided and

abetted by his enthusiasm for popular 'trashy' fiction—action-packed, full of fantasy, playful, fiction enjoyed as fiction—but the problem in **R.U.R.** is that it is hard to react to the expressionistic lyricism in the text when unable to take the characters or plot seriously, as if real. Moreover, as we shall perhaps demonstrate, the lyrical expressionism is generally insufficiently powerful in its own right: the danger of counter-productive bathos lurks ever-present behind the pathos.

The Prologue is set in the managing director's office at the R.U.R. factory, situated Utopia-style on an isolated island. The managing director Harry Domin (English version: Domain) is dictating letters to his Robot secretary Sulla. (Sulla is only outwardly female: male and female versions of otherwise sexless Robots are only produced for the sake of market demand: e.g. people want female secretaries.) Her sexlessness is emphasised by her inappropriate name: she is paired with another, outwardly male Robot, named Marius, since those who named them imagined that Sulla and Marius were a famous pair of classical lovers.) Helena Glory (ová), young, elegant and naive, daughter of the President of R.U.R., exclusive manufactuers of Robots for the entire world market, arrives on an unannounced visit. She intends to incite the Robots to rebel against their human masters (and creators) and claim equal rights with human beings. (A parallel episode occurs in *War with the Newts.*) But, she is told, her sympathy with the down-trodden is misplaced: the Robots are insensible of justice or equality. They were manufactured without such economically and industrially useless, nay counter-productive, features. Emotions were left out of their make-up: only a sense of pain was found to be of utility. Helena is making the grave though understandable error of treating the Robots like proper human beings, whereas in fact they have no souls; they can contemplate their own destruction with equanimity, and, when they have breakdowns or fits, they can simply be sent (will send themselves) to the pulveriser.

At first Helena has difficulty in distinguishing these Robots from human beings. Later she mistakes for Robots Domin's human colleagues on the island. Her confusion leads us further on towards realising the significance of Čapek's Robots. It becomes clear that the Robots do not only represent the danger of scientific invention, of technology and industry taking over from man, depriving him of his traditional work and responsibilities. They also represent debased, dehumanised man himself, man deprived of essential features (hazily defined, mainly in terms of love and other emotions, creativity, the soul), man treated as a machine, seen as an undifferentiated mass available for exploitation, treated as an object rather than a conscious fellow-being. The concept of Robots maintains a suggestive ambiguity. Robots become multi-faceted symbols of alienation, degradation, 'soullessness', mass uniformity, and technological, industrial, socio-economic, depersonalising threats to individual rights and dignity.

The inventor of the Robots, Old Rossum, had no interest in their economic exploitation; his interest was scientific, philosophic, intellectual. Čapek views him with sympathy, but also with horror at the innocence of science, oblivious of its potential consequences. Domin, in explaining the history of Robot manufacture to Helena, expresses the millenarian view that the Robots will perfect human civilisation. His ideas are distinctly megalomaniac. The introduction of Robots in all branches of work will cause not just mass but total unemployment. Robots will do everything—man will do only what he loves. He will live only to perfect himself. Terrible things will perhaps occur on the way to this paradise on earth, but the ends justify the means—it will all be worth it, for the enslavement of man to man, and of man to matter, will cease. The classless society will have been born, the divisions of labour abolished. Man will be lord of creation, living in the boundless plenty produced for him by the Robots, free to pursue his own desires without encumbrance.

This exposition of ideas is neatly alleviated by the semi-farcical plot. Domin and his five colleagues at once fall in love with Helena, whose name presumably refers to Helen of Troy. There are no other women on the island at the time, though there have been previous female visitors. (Here, as often in the play, the plot is somewhat arbitrary and fanciful, but in the whimsical, almost absurdist atmosphere this seems largely right and proper.) Domin, anticipating and fearing his colleagues' likely designs, and pushed for time (time being money) proposes to Helena after only a few minutes' acquaintance, giving her five minutes to make up her mind once and for all. She is embraced by Domin and assents, and here the Prologue ends.

Act I is set in Helena's boudoir, on the tenth anniversary of her arrival. She is now married to Domin, but childless. The act is built around the dramatic irony of the contrast between the celebration of this anniversary, with gifts from her admirers, and the progressive revelation to the audience (and Helena) that disaster has struck in the world outside. Humans had given up all work and become infertile in the pursuit of pleasure, and because work was no longer necessary. There is an element of mystery or metaphysics here, as well as mere hyperbolic representation of the tendency for affluence to reduce the birth rate. Now the Robots, armed, we learn later, by men first to put down strikes, then to wage wars between nations, have turned, again mysteriously, against their masters. Man seems doomed to immediate as well as long-term extinction. Domin has an emergency plan of escape, to use his warship Ultimus to leave the island, bargaining with the Robots to exchange their lives for the formulae needed to manufacture new generations of Robots, who, as we know, are unable to reproduce themselves in the human manner. This plan is unwittingly foiled by Helena, who (somewhat arbitrarily from the point of view of futurology) burns the only copies of the formulae manuscripts in a bid to prevent further production. She is only partly aware of what has been going on. It is typical of Čapek to make developments in his plot depend on individual acts devoid of a sense of general inevitability (as opposed to some metaphysical or merely authorial hand of fate, operating in this instance through Helena's 'healthy feminine instincts'). However legitimate this may be as an analysis of certain aspects of history—the role played by accident—prophetic effect is certainly diminished by employing such devices which heighten the arbitrary fiction-

ality of the plot (note the artificial dramatic irony of the timing of her action: a typical story-telling device). Act I is permeated lyrically (though not in the English version) by the symbol of the infertile flower Cyclamen Helenae, bred as a gift for Helena (childless, we remember) by the psychologist Dr. Hallemeier (Helman in the English version):

> ALQUIST: . . . . Helena, women will not give birth for men who are unnecessary!
>
> HELENA: Will mankind die out then?
>
> ALQUIST: It will die out. It must die out. It is dropping like a barren flower, and unless—
>
> HELENA: What?
>
> ALQUIST: Nothing. You're right, its fruitless to expect a miracle. The barren flower must perish.
>
> HELENA (*alone*): Oh, barren flower! That's the word! (*Stops beside Hallemeier's flowers.*) Ah, flowers, are some of you barren too? No, no! Why then would you flower?
>
>   . . . . .
>
> HELENA (*beside Hallemeier's flowers*): Gall, are these flowers barren too?
>
> DR. GALL (*inspects them*): Of course, they are infertile flowers. You understand, they are cultured, artificially forced—
>
> HELENA: Poor barren flowers!
>
> DR. GALL: They are magnificent all the same.

The act ends with the arrival of the revolutionary Robots by the first ship to dock for a number of days. It arrives precisely according to the normal timetable of sailings, and this is at first taken as a sign that the rebellion has been quashed. However, the opposite is the case. The punctuality is just what you would expect of the mechanistic Robots. The timetable precision symbolises both comforting regularity and disturbing dehumanised uniformity, as if it is a feature we both need and need to avoid, as human beings:

> DOMIN: Punctuality is a wonderful thing, lads. Nothing fortifies the soul like punctuality. Punctuality means order in the world. (*Raises his glass.*) To punctuality! . . .
>
> HALLEMEIER: When the timetable holds good, human laws hold good, God's laws hold good, the laws of the universe hold good, everything holds good that ought to hold good. The timetable is more than the Gospel, more than Homer, more than the whole of Kant. The timetable is the most perfect effusion of the human spirit.

Act II is again set in Helena's boudoir. Throughout the play there is a curious mixture of drawing-room comedy, blatantly fictional melodrama and horrifying cataclysm,—domesticity and semi-allegorical expressionism. The human beings on the island are now under siege. For a while the Robots are held back behind an electrified fence (rapidly improvised in Heath Robinson style, apparently by connection to the domestic power circuit). When the power station falls to the Robots, the lights go out and they enter the house killing all except one (nearly all off-stage). Only Alquist the Builder is saved, against his will, for, as one of the Robots, Radius, says, 'He is a Robot. He works with his hands like the Robots. He builds houses. He can work.' The symbol of light in this act (and also earlier, through lightbulbs stipulated for the set) is used to express man's essential nature, his creative power, soul, and will to live, his vital spark. A lyrical passage of exchanges between contrasting human voices explores this metaphor and the human connotations of light and fire, casting our minds back across the ages of past human history. This passage is one of the attempts the text makes to attain true pathos and rhetorical power, but it hovers at best on the brink of bathos and counterproductive irony, undermined in addition by the surrounding context. Most of it was cut from the English performing version, presumably because it seemed overdone or incongruous. One might argue that this was the right thing to do, but the omission, along with other similar ones, considerably attenuates the lyrical rhetorical expressionistic atmosphere that the Czech text wishes to create; a certain dimension is lost:

DR. GALL: Do you hear?

DOMIN: Howling. Like the wind.

DR. GALL: Like a distant storm.

FABRY (*lights a bulb on the fireplace*): Shine out, storm candle of mankind! The dynamos are still running, our people are still there—Hold out, men in the power station!

HALLEMEIER: It was a great thing to be a man. It was something immeasurable. A thousand consciousnesses buzz within me like bees in a hive. Millions of souls fly to congregate within me. Friends, it was a great thing.

FABRY: You still shine, ingenious light, still you dazzle, radiant, persistent thought! Knowing science, fine creation of people! Flaming spark of the spirit!

ALQUIST: Eternal lamp of God, fiery wain, holy lamp of faith, pray! Sacrificial altar—

DR. GALL: First fire, branch burning at the cavemouth! Camp bonfire! Watch beacon!

FABRY: You still keep vigil, human star, you glow unflickering, perfect flame, bright inventive spirit. Each of your rays is a great thought—

DOMIN: A torch, which passes from hand to hand, from age to age, eternally onward.

HELENA: The family evening lamp. Children, children, time to sleep.

The bulb goes out.

FABRY: The end.

HALLEMEIER: What's happened?

FABRY: The power station has fallen. Now it's our turn.

Elsewhere the reactions to the siege and feeble defence of

the house are more reminiscent of a schoolboy adventure story. The effect is more comic than awe-inspiring, particularly as the act is punctuated in an absurdist fashion by the commercial manager Busman (English version: Berman) and his obsessive drawing-up of final company balance sheets in the face of the extinction of both himself and the human race. He dies, melodramatically (off-stage), touching the electric fence while endeavouring to trade his life for half a thousand million of useless money. The absurdist hyperbole and lack of an impression of true terror and despair among the besieged (brisk to the last) rob the poetic symbolism of its already flawed emotional force, while at the same time producing a curious amalgam of banality, matter-of-factness, and doom. Man remains hopelessly down-to-earth in the face of extinction and cannot rise to the apocalyptic quality of the occasion. The text's comic, debunking features (compare Hašek's *The Good Soldier Švejk*, so different in other respects) seem in practice to outweigh the desire to move us by man's demise from this earth, to make us say, with Hallemeier: 'It was a great thing to be a man.' The shifts in tone are hard to accommodate, and a persistent sense of dispassionate fictional playfulness is never altogether dispelled.

Act III is set in the factory laboratory on the island, and is the least domestic, least representational. Alquist is alone, the last human being on earth. All searches for others have proved in vain. He has been ordered (as the only creatively thinking being) to re-discover the formulae for making Robots, but he knows it is a hopeless task for which he lacks the requisite knowledge. Absurdly, he is commanded to dissect live Robots, to see if this will reveal the secrets (we feel it unlikely that the Robots would be so stupid). The leading Robot Damon (Domin's double, but Radius in the English version), consents to go on the operating table, without anaesthetic, but when the pacifist Alquist gives up, unable to stomach the deed, even Damon, who had been in charge of the slaughter of humans on the island, declares that he wants to live: it is better to live. Earlier we were told that certain alterations had been made in the manufacture of Robots by Dr. Gall, in order to please Helena by making them more human and appealing (dogs had shunned them too). These alterations have had far-reaching effects—or have they? To be precise, it is pointed out to us by the figures man, Busman, that the numbers of new-style Robots would probably have been too small (a few hundred, according to Dr. Gall) to have much effect. Busman suggests that mere numerical superiority of humans was a more likely cause of the revolt, but this is again unconvincing. We are left in doubt, though obliged in the end to attach some credence to Gall's version. Gall confessed before his death that he had given the new-style Robots emotions, or, as he put it, changed their 'irritability'. Robots rose up against men because of their *hatred* for men, however this may have developed (perhaps metaphysically): they worked, while men did not. Domin declares hatred a quintessential human trait: 'No-one can hate man more than his fellow man! Turn stones into men, and they will stone you to death!' But Robots are also now seen to be capable of *love*. Alquist notices that two have fallen in love with each other, Primus and Robot-Helena (a Helena replica, manufactured by the love-sick Dr. Gall and played by the same actress). The two express their love partly lyrically, partly humorously, and in clichés of popular romance:

> HELENA: Do you hear? The birds are singing. Oh, Primus, I'd like to be a bird!
>
> PRIMUS: Be what?
>
> HELENA: I don't know, Primus. I feel so strange, I don't know what it is: I feel silly, I've lost my head, my body aches, my heart, everything aches—And, oh, I can't tell you what's happened to me! Primus, I think I must die!
>
> PRIMUS: Don't you feel sometimes, tell me, Helena, as if it would be better to die? You know, perhaps we're only sleeping. Yesterday in my sleep I spoke to you again.
>
> HELENA: In your sleep?
>
> PRIMUS: In my sleep. We spoke in a foreign or new language, because I don't remember a word of what we said.
>
> . . . . .
>
> HELENA: (*in front of the mirror*): Me, beautiful? Oh, this simply frrightful hair, if only I had something to put in it! You know, there in the garden I always put some flowers in my hair, but there's no mirror or anyone—

Alquist pretends he wants to dissect one of them: each offers to go in place of the other, and they prove their love in time-honoured fashion, in terms of willingness to sacrifice oneself for the sake of the loved one. Alquist tells them to go and be man and wife, and reads to them from Genesis, telling how God created man and woman in His own image. He brings the play to a close, declaring that 'life will not perish'. This statement is cut in the English stage version, along with much of the life-acclaiming rhetoric of Alquist's final speech, where he declares that 'you, love, will blossom on the rubble and confide the seed of love to the winds'. The text gives no indication as to whether these two Robots have mysteriously acquired or activated the requisite organs of reproduction. Indeed, to provide any such information or explanation would spoil the mystic atmosphere. Strictly speaking, we have only been presented with Alquist's own wishful thinking; yet the declarative effect is not intended to leave us in any doubt on a symbolic, expressionistic level about the desire to end on a note of optimism, affirming the capacity of life to survive the threat of annihilation by the power of love.

Later, in the curiously similar novel, *War with the Newts,* Čapek tackled the problem by leaving the story open. Towards the end the newts, eroding continents for more Lebensraum, approach the last redoubts of humanity, and man's annihilation seems inevitable, according to the logic of the plot. In the final chapter, instead of finishing off the story, Čapek addresses an anti-pessimistic reader and discusses facetiously, almost as a mere gesture, the possibility of an eventual happy ending for mankind, were the newts, say, to turn against one another. (Domin, too, had toyed with the idea of producing nationally antagonistic Robots!) The effect is to leave the situation and the dialogue between pessimism and optimism unresolved, and also to

highlight the fictional nature of the narrative. The doom and gloom in *War with the Newts* is again expressed in terms of comic satire, parody and burlesque, but, one feels, in a more controlled, consistent way. The frequent whimsicality of the narrative serves to avoid the effect of preaching (as in ***R.U.R.***), yet likewise the potential message of warning is muted by the whimsicality of the satire, the fictional playfulness, the lovable cardboard characters one cannot take too seriously.

The characters in ***R.U.R.*** express contrasting ideas and ideals, and indeed consist of little more than bubbling words. Domin (the name refers to *dominus* "master"), represents domination, man as master of the universe; he expresses in part a vaguely Nietzschean will to power, but chiefly a kind of Fabian socialist belief in technical progress emancipating man from enslavement to labour. The somewhat Tolstoyan Alquist, as Čapek called him, a modest version of Ibsen's Solness in the *Master Builder,* believes that 'technical progress demoralises' man by alienating him from work [see Author Commentary]. He is an agnostic, but he prays. He recognises a need for morality and believes in creative work. Busman (= businessman) believes that 'industrialism alone is capable of supplying modern needs'. He is the money-man and represents a financial business attitude to life, an obsession with the power of numbers. Helena is (regrettably, not only from the point of view of the feminist critic) our old friend the intuitive woman, 'instinctively afraid of all this inhuman machinery'. She is seen (somewhat unconvincingly) as representing the positive values and charms of womankind. Her nanny, Nana (not her maid as the English version would have it) represents traditional peasant, Christian values in a primitive, reactionary form: 'all inventions are against the Lord God', she tells Helena. Her position would, taken to a logical conclusion, return man to a primitive state of nature. Lastly, the Robots too have a viewpoint: they see themselves as more intelligent and efficient, and therefore better than man. All of these viewpoints are, as Čapek stated himself, seen as right in their own way: all put forward a certain (partial) truth of their own.

However, Čapek can really only approve of these 'truths' insofar as they are in some way well-intentioned. He had a firm moral sense which made his professed relativism only relatively relativistic. Čapek pleads for tolerance. He dislikes black-and-white judgments, narrow ideologies of the right or left, mass hysteria. He upholds the rights of the individual, and tends to assume that individuals are basically good-natured, all other things being equal. He believes in man's improvability, not perfectibility.

R.U.R. has been seen as conveying a warning that modern civilisation and technology threaten to destroy man, a critique of modern (chiefly *de facto* capitalist) society driven by blind, narrow economic imperatives. The shareholders of ***R.U.R.*** look only to their profits: they care nothing for the ideals of Domin. Čapek's relativism cannot embrace their 'truth', except in the most limited and meaningless of senses. But Čapek is not against science and progress, witness his optimistic ending, however, contrived; not to mention his own statements on the subject elsewhere. He wishes to warn of dangers, not 'throw out the baby with the bathwater'. Equally, he is not a simple denunciator of capitalism and the 'class society', nor is he a Marxist or collectivist. He is horrified by non-individual approaches and doctrines and wishes to see everything as far as possible on a familiar, down-to-earth, individual scale. He suspects intensely the all-embracing abstracts and absolutes of ideologies (a theme of his novel *The Absolute At Large*). Dr. Gall says, speaking partly for Čapek, 'People with ideas should not be given influence in the affairs of this world', (of course, this is to be seen as no more than another partial truth.)

Čapek's vision of the Robots seems, by his own account, to owe much to an acutely personal horror about the unknowability, the insrutability, the facelessness of human beings viewed en masse, from the outside, especially in impersonal modern urban life. He stated that the idea of the Robots had appeared to him during a tramride. One day he had to go to Prague by suburban tram, and it was uncomfortably full. It astonished him how modern conditions had made people disregard ordinary comfort in life. They were packed inside and on the steps of the tramcar not like sheep, but like machines. He began to think about people not as individuals, but as machines, and on the way he searched for an expression which would denote a person capable of working, but not of thinking. The same horror of dehumanising mass-anonymity and its potential for socio-political transformations and human self-destruction is expressed in a letter to his future wife, Olga Scheinpflugová:

> While writing I was struck by a terrible fear, I had wanted somehow to warn against the production of the mass and dehumanised slogans and suddenly I was gripped by the anxiety that it would be like this one day, maybe soon, that I would save nothing by this warning, that just as I the author had led the forces of these dull mechanisms wherever I wanted so one day someone would lead the foolish man of the mass against the world and God. I felt unwell, Olga, and so I looked towards the end almost convulsively for some kind of solution of understanding and love, do you think that one can believe in it, darling?

R.U.R. is a vision of dehumanisation, of men treated like mechanisms and behaving like mechanisms. Man is mocked, victimised and degraded by depersonalised, mechanistic man-made civilisation, his very survival perhaps threatened. Men become Robots; men are destroyed by Robots. If, at the end, the Robots become men, this humanisation is a testament of faith, an expressionist gesture, justified in the logic of the plot only by previous vaguenesses surrounding human infertility and the progress of Robot emotions from nervous 'irritability' towards will, will to live, consciousness and soul. The rhetorical gesture enables the play to end on what is keenly felt to be a desirable note of optimism (witness the letter quoted above), hailing life, created by love, and its power to survive world catastrophe. The final humanisation is denoted by the Robots' acquisition of souls, as Čapek himself wrote, admitting the vagueness involved. 'This (biological) life is only filled when (with the bringing to bear of considerable im-

precision and mysticism) the Robots become *souls.*' However, the subordination of plot-logic to the final apotheosis of the power of life and love undermines the futurological element of prediction, prophecy and warning. The play dissolves into a slightly *kitsch,* vague vitalism. Throughout the play the future setting is fictional, a never-never land, representing in an expressionist, allegorical, metaphorical way, elements of a possible future in which elements of the present are heightened to an extreme: zero birth rate created by affluence, universal automation, total unemployment, mass conformity, mass extermination. (Indeed, most of the common futurological themes seem to be present in some guise or other.) The broad image throughout of man, embattled by the depersonalising, dehumanising trends of his mass civilisation, remains, in spite of everything, perhaps the play's strongest futurological theme. However problematic their dramatic presentation in *R.U.R.,* Karel Čapek's Robotic themes are still alive and troubling, even in this un-1984-like year of 1984. (pp. 72-86)

James D. Naughton, "Futurology and Robots: Karel Čapek's 'R.U.R.'," in Renaissance and Modern Studies, *Vol. 28, 1984, pp. 72-86.*

The triumph of the robots. Act III of the 1922 Theatre Guild production of R.U.R.

AND SO AD INFINITUM

PRODUCTION REVIEWS

Harold Clurman   (review date 21 June 1948)

[*Highly regarded as a director, author, and longtime drama critic (1953-1980) for the* Nation, *Clurman was an important contributor to the development of the modern American theater. In 1931, with Lee Strasberg and Cheryl Crawford, he founded the innovative Group Theatre, which served as an arena for the works of budding playwrights and as an experimental workshop for actors. In addition, he wrote several works on the theater including his acclaimed autobiography* All People Are Famous *(1974). In the following review of a 1948 New York production of* And So Ad Infinitum *(presented under the alternate title* The Insect Comedy), *he judges the play a "pessimistic allegory" in which man "is shown as trivial in his love, paltry in his ambition, predatory and rapacious in his social life." Clurman concedes, however, that the "sting of the play's spleen is sweetened" by its "variety of costume, decor, dance, music and characterization."*]

The reviews I read of *The Insect Comedy,* the final production of the City Center's six-week season of plays, did not seem to me to convey the nature of the event. They expressed disappointment or faint disapproval of the play and respect for the smoothness with which a rather difficult production had been managed after only two weeks of rehearsal. They omitted to note that the first-night audience was unusually enthusiastic. Nor did they stop to consider why.

The Insect Comedy, by the Czech writers Josef and Karel Capek, was first given here in 1922 under the title of *The World We Live In.* It is a pessimistic allegory in which man, presented through a parallel with insect life, is shown as trivial in his love, paltry in his ambition, predatory and rapacious in his social life. The climax of man's struggle is internecine strife, its sum undesired and meaningless death.

Set down this way the play becomes absurd, not because it can be proved false but because it contains the kind of truth that can contribute to nothing except suicide. But *The Insect Comedy* is only partially absurd. There are, it is true, besides moments of sardonic humor, passages in which a kind of Germanic philosophizing is boiled in the heat of that hysteria which prevailed in Central Europe right after the First World War. It represents the combination of despair and fury without any foundation in specific social understanding that inevitably paves the way to another war. The play is nevertheless justified by the fact that it does reflect an atmosphere created by a painfully real historical situation.

The other aspect of the play's significance is that it was written at a time when the Central European theatre was booming with blazing dramatic experiments. It was the time of the theatre theatrical, when plays were scored for the full orchestra of the stage's means: variety of costume, decor, dance, music, characterization. Thus the sting of the play's spleen is sweetened by the glamor of the theatre's magic. The mixture was typical of the twenties, and New York as well as Berlin, Budapest and Prague enjoyed the brew.

Our theatre is now physically impoverished: color and imaginative dimension are relegated either to musical comedy or to essays in Shakespeare. The audiences at the City Center are gratified to see in a straight play something that has a colorful look. It hungers for some of the display and festiveness which our one-set naturalistic drama has all but banished from the theatre. *The Insect Comedy* is a sight for sore eyes.

The audience, in addition, lends a benign intent to the play's rage: it regards it as an anti-war play. I always worry when I see such a play; it is generally followed by a war. But today when anti-war propaganda is almost suspect in many quarters, the good audience at the City Center is to be congratulated on its humane and mildly defiant sentiments.

The production of *The Insect Comedy* is like the reduction of a big score to the range of a harmonica. In this instance, the effect is rather sweet. There is a winning youngness and cordiality about the show.

José Ferrer is amusing when he doesn't act too coquettishly. George Colouris is at his best when he avoids the rhetorical and discloses the sense of pity within the play instead of yielding to the temptations of the playwright's journalistic declamation. The leading butterflies of the first act are played by two very pretty girls: Rita Gam and Phyllis Hill. Annabelle Lyon, as a Female Cricket, strikes a genuine note of chirping poetry. The direction is proficient, but longer pre-rehersal preparation might have led the director to further invention with which to give the production more body. (pp. 28-9)

> *Harold Clurman, "A Dying Sound," in* The New Republic, *Vol. 118, No. 25, June 21, 1948, pp. 28-9.*

John Gassner   (review date July 1948)

[*An American drama critic and theater historian, Gassner was a member of the New York Drama Critics Circle and a professor of playwriting and dramatic literature at Yale University. His commentary reflects his resistance to narrow theoretical frameworks and his emphasis on discovering new and inventive forms of expression within each individual dramatic piece. In the review below, Gassner offers his interpretation of* And So Ad Infinitum (The Insect Comedy), *stressing its pessimism and bleakness, but maintaining that "there is affirmation in negation as intense as this. The world must be loved to be castigated with such passionateness." Gassner concludes that this is "altogether a play . . . that should be toured throughout the nation."*]

Of all the plays produced recently none was more timely or engrossing than *The Insect Comedy* revived by José Ferrer for a brief run at New York's City Center of Drama and Music. The play, it may be recalled, is the work of two notable and noble Czechs, Karel and Josef Capek. After writing his famous fantasy, *R. U. R. (Rossum's Universal Robots)*, in 1921 to protest the soulless regimentation of labor by modern industry, Karel Capek, joined by his sculptor brother Josef, turned a searchlight on all humanity and all nature. *The Insect Comedy,* produced also under the titles, *The World We Live In* and *And so ad infinitum,* was one of several European and American plays during the early 1920's that brought a mature appraisal of the modern world into the theatre.

Employing the device of a Vagrant, who has fled from the horrors of the city—of the human hive—into the forest, only to encounter the horrors of non-human nature, the authors draw a searing parallel between men and insects in terms that Swift would have admired. In fact, it would surprise no one if *Gulliver's Travels* were found to be the direct inspiration of this Slavic *tour de force.* Puzzled by life, harried in spirit, and somewhat inebriated, the tramp sees the eternal round of life in episodes that expose the failure of love, *laissez faire,* collectivist regimentation, imperialism, and life itself. Before him unrolls the panorama of insects behaving like insects, which is frightening enough in itself; and of men behaving like insects, which is an even grimmer nightmare since the human species considers itself superior to the rest of creation by virtue of its capacity for reason and morality. An amoral world of nature is bad enough; an amoral world of man is intolerable. It is possible to forgive the former on the plea that it doesn't know what it is doing and has no standards of right and wrong, but how shall man be forgiven.

The Vagrant watching the procession of life sees the eternal mating under the symbol of butterfly love-making. Disillusionment comes to him as he observes Felix, the butterfly poet, and his female flutterers: "the male pursues the female, the bride allures then slips away, the male follows," until one ardent wooer is snapped up by a bird, whereupon the thoughtless breed returns to its round of folly, Felix spouts more modernistic verse about the "geometry of souls," and the tramp remembers his own insanity.

But no sooner has this fantasy ended than the world grows somber and the butterfly world is supplanted by the obscenely avaricious beetle world, with a male and female beetle pushing their bolus of manure and fondling it as the supreme accomplishment of a lifetime of toil. They have made their "pile," they sniff at it lovingly, they seek ardently for a hole or Fort Knox in which to bury their gold before they go on to make another "pile." The climax comes when another beetle, a marauder, whisks the ball of fertilizer away from them in order to bury it in his own private hole. As played by two members of Mr. Ferrer's cast (Stanley Carlson and the former musical comedy star, Paula Laurence), this scene is a masterpiece of social satire.

It is excelled only by the next episode in which the Ichneumon Fly, brilliantly played by Robert Carroll, exemplifies the predatory instinct in its sentimental parental phase—the Fly captures crickets for his insatiable, precious larvae. His victims, Mr. and Mrs. Cricket, are the little people of the world who seem to have been created only in order

that they may be preyed upon, although the Capek Brothers' pity for them is mingled with the rueful observation that, for all their pathos, the crickets are quite willing to profit by another's misfortune. Mrs. Cricket is snatched by the Ichneumon Fly just as she is gloating over the agonies of the former occupant of her home, another cricket that had been impaled on a thorn. And since the eater is himself eaten in the end, the Ichneumon Fly's pampered larvae make a good dinner for the Parasite who has been biding *his* time while denouncing the Fly as a scoundrel and crying out against the injustice of the world. By the end of the episode the tramp doesn't know where insect ends and man begins, the motives seem the same and the results are the same: "Throughout the Universe feverish jowls are working! Chew, chew, chew! . . . Life is the prey of life."

Wearied of such mandibular individualism, the vagrant observer hopes to find surcease in a well regulated world only to find it too well regulated. A way of life other than "the insect greed of self" is needed, there is great need for being part of a world in which we serve something greater than self. But that which is served turns out to be the juggernaut antheap state that flattens its members into one endless procession of undifferentiated slaves, workers for industry, and soldiers for war. First they fall on the field of speed, then they fall on the field of battle to satisfy the vanity of demagogues and militarists. The inventor ant's head of glass bursts with a new war-machine, and a new war-machine needs a new war. . . . "Nothing serves the State so much as science." The politicians decide that the Red Ants still need a bit of territory "from the birch-tree to the pine-tree, and a road between two blades of grass, the only open road to the South." Up goes the banner of war and 50,000 ants die "to capture twenty paces of latrines." Both Red and Yellow Ants repeat the same barefaced cant and the same slogan of "Women and embryos to be slaughtered." The Yellows win in the end, and their commander is prating about "Justice, our history, our national honor, our commercial interests" when the disgusted Vagrant grinds him to pieces with the heel of his boot.

Throughout the proceedings a Chrysalis has been crying out to be born, unnoticed by rapacious beetles and suicidal ants, and now it is time for it to emerge into the light of life. Perhaps, the Vagrant reflects, the solution will come from life itself (perhaps it is in Shaw's "Life Force," Bergson's *élan vital,* that the disenchanted seeker will find his mystic solace), but he learns only the brevity of life from the moth world into which he is projected. Life emerges from the chrysalis only to droop and drop a moment later, and with this vision death also comes to the Vagrant, who can only cry out "What is this fearful lack of meaning?" Two Snails, very content with the status quo and untouched by the thought of death, watch his death-struggle with indifference, and the response of two human beings, who find his body in the woods, echoes the snails' sense of relief that they are left alive.

So ends this strangely moving, devastatingly satirical drama, born of post-war disillusionment, a play as timely today as it was in 1921 when the world felt the same dismay over a war fought and a peace won only to be lost. It is a great credit to José Ferrer, George Couloris (who plays the tramp), and the large cast. The staging by Ferrer faltered only in the first act and attained imaginative power in the beetle and ant scenes with the aid of excellent lighting by Herbert Brodkin and telling choreography by Hanya Holm. It is altogether a play and production that should be toured throughout the nation, or duplicated, with some improvements wherever possible.

The negativism, the bleakness of a pessimism relieved but in no way altered by the sardonic dung beetle episode and the butterfly antics of the first act, may be shocking. But the world badly needs a shock to rouse it from its schizophrenia. Nor should it be overlooked that there is affirmation in negation as intense as this. The world must be loved to be castigated with such passionateness, and men who cry out against humanity's blunders are themselves representatives of the humanity that transcends the insect world to which we seem so inclined to reduce ourselves. And if the brevity of life cannot be dismissed, it can only spur us on to make the most of it by the exercise of right reason and good will. In the very act of writing a modern *Gulliver's Travels,* founded on J. H. Fabré's *La Vie des Insectes* and *Souvenirs Entomologiques,* the Capek brothers managed to triumph over defeat. They survived to write **The Makropoulos Affair** in 1923, on the dubious desirability of longevity, and **Adam the Creator,** on the theme of rebuilding humanity on its ruins, in 1927. Then in the embattled 1930's, Karel Capek engaged the subject of dictatorship in **The White Scourge** and the problem of averting a second war in **The Mother.** These plays were written in 1937 and 1938, the year of their author's death in his forty-eighth year. If he had survived a little longer, he would probably have died in Hitler's hands as one of Europe's staunchest enemies of Europe's will to death.

The revival of **The Insect Comedy** is, however, an unpleasant reminder that in the theatre, as in the political arena of the atomic age, we are worse off than we were in 1921. The state of our world seems to be unhappily reflected by our dramatists. After 1918, the stage attained an imaginative power that enabled it to engage a war-weary, disenchanted, and confused world. **The Insect Comedy** and **R. U. R.** found such companion pieces as Franz Wefel's vatic *Goat Song,* Ernst Toller's *Masse-Mensch,* Elmer Rice's *The Adding Machine,* O'Neill's *The Hairy Ape,* and O'Casey's *Juno and the Paycock* and *The Plough and the Stars.* Against this galaxy we have virtually nothing to set since Arthur Laurents' *Home of the Brave.* Perhaps we may add the current *Command Decision* and *Mr. Roberts* to make the record seem less meager, but the factual and equivocal nature of the former's indictment of war and the surface showmanship of the latter can hardly be considered substitutes for the plays of the 1920's. The depth and vibrancy of works like **The Insect Comedy,** the expressiveness of theatrical form, the passion of the anguish, and the bite of the protest, seem to have eluded us thus far. Even despair requires a certain straw of optimism to which to cling if it is not to be submerged under the surface, because even despair is purposeful and challenging in creative men. Purpose confounded, confusion compounded, and courage impounded may well be the "obit" written on the flea-bitten soul of an age that betrays its failure in the theatre. (pp. 20-2)

John Gassner, in a review of "The Insect Comedy," in Forum, *Vol. 110, No. 1, July, 1948, pp. 20-2.*

CRITICAL COMMENTARY

William E. Harkins   (essay date 1962)

[*In the excerpt below, Harkins provides a survey of* And So Ad Infinitum (*here called* From the Insect World) *and addresses the question of whether the play is ultimately pessimistic or, as the Čapek brothers have contended, optimistic.*]

In 1920 the Brothers Čapek returned to a collaboration which had been moribund for some eight years, and wrote a comedy revue, **From the Insect World.** The play was published the same year, but received its première at the National Theater only two years later, on March 8, 1922.

The inspiration for the play was suggested in part by a reading of Fabre. The brothers' conception of an insect play satirizing human vices was both original and brilliantly theatrical. True, the fable and beast epos are ancient literary genres, but this form of satire seems to be rarer in the drama. The most specific model for the Čapeks' play is a story by the Russian writer Vsevolod Garšin, "What Never Happened," a philosophical dialogue of the beasts and insects. In the Čapeks' play the figures of the dung beetle, anxiously fondling its ball of manure, and the larva, struggling to be reborn, clearly derive from Garšin's story.

The authors borrowed liberally from the techniques of ballet, revue, film, and pantomime. The play provides ample opportunity for virtuoso acting, speech nuance and movement. The dialogue is colorful, with a rich variety of speech levels.

Though theatrical, the play is essentially undramatic, for the form, a series of scenes taken from the life of different insects, is that of revue and not drama. Moreover, the grotesqueness of the setting, speech, and action might well have turned the play into a spectacle divorced from human life. To unite the individual scenes, the brothers introduced a human character, a tramp, who observes the follies of insect life and comments on them. But this role is more than that of chorus; he is also protagonist, not as *actor,* however, but as *patient.* Only at the end do we discover that the action is about him and has happened to him. He forms a bridge between the audience and the spectacle itself. The tramp—as wanderer—is of course a symbolic figure. As protagonist and chorus together, he is perhaps unique in the modern theater; one must go back to the medieval mystery plays for a parallel. And in fact, the authors were fully conscious of their play's kinship to the mystery and morality dramas.

The tramp is Man. This truth is realized with superlative irony:

> TRAMP: Yes, that's who I am; they know me everywhere.—I am Man, you see. No one calls me anything else. They say, "Man, I'll have you

pinched," "Man, clear up, get it done, bring me that," or "Move along, man!" But I don't take offence because I'm a man. If I were to say, "Man, give me a dime," they'd be insulted. If they don't like it, all right then. I'll think of them as butterflies, or beetles, or ants, whatever they like.

And so we are introduced to the drama of insect life. The first act is laid in the butterfly world. Two fading beauties compete for the attentions of a young poet, who pretends to be a rake, but is at heart inordinately shy. The situation and the cynical wit remind us of *The Garden of Krakonoš* and *The Fateful Game of Love* (indeed, the poet and his beefy rival recall Gilles and Trivalin in the earlier play). Here too there is little more than the deliberate sense of the vanity and monotony of the eternal cycle of falling in and out of love.

In the second act, "The Marauders," we see the virtues and joys of family life as through a concave lens. The reverse image so obtained is that of the insularity of the family, its indifference and cruelty to outsiders, its rapacity and greed in the name of devotion to itself. The first scene is a satire on senseless accumulation of capital:

> *Onto the stage there rolls a great ball of manure, pushed by two beetles.*
>
> MR. BEETLE: Are you sure nothing's happened to it?
>
> MRS. BEETLE: Just suppose! How could it! Ach, what a scare! You're all right, pretty little ball, aren't you? You're our dear little ball!
>
> MR. BEETLE: Haha, our capital! Our dear little dung pile. Our gold! Our all!
>
> MRS. BEETLE: You beautiful dirt, you treasure, you wonderful little ball, you priceless possession!
>
> MR. BEETLE: Our love and our only joy! How we've saved and scraped, the dung we've carried and the stinking scraps we've snatched from our mouths to save up—
>
> MRS. BEETLE: —and ground with our feet and the holes we've dug out, how we've raked it up, before we had it all squeezed together and piled up—
>
> MR. BEETLE: —and rounded out and filled up, our great pretty pearl!
>
> MRS. BEETLE: Our jewel!
>
> MR. BEETLE: Our life!
>
> MRS. BEETLE: Our whole creation!
>
> MR. BEETLE: Just smell it, old woman! The beauty of it! Just weigh it! How much we have!
>
> MRS. BEETLE: The gift of God . . .
>
> MR. BEETLE: I'm crazy with joy. I . . . I . . . I'm crazy with joy. I'm really crazy.
>
> MRS. BEETLE: Why?
>
> MR. BEETLE: With anxiety. Now we have our

> ball! I've looked forward to it so, and now we have it, we must make a new one. The work it'll take!
>
> MRS. BEETLE: Why a new one?
>
> MR. BEETLE: Stupid! So we can have two.
>
> MRS. BEETLE: Ah, two. That's right.
>
> MR. BEETLE: Ha, just think of it: two balls! At least two. Let's say at least three . . .
>
> MRS. BEETLE: Beetle!
>
> MR. BEETLE: What is it?
>
> MRS. BEETLE: I'm afraid. Somebody might steal it from us.
>
> MR. BEETLE: What? Who?
>
> MRS. BEETLE: Our Ball. Our joy. Our all.
>
> MR. BEETLE: Our baaa—ll? For God's sake, don't scare me!
>
> MRS. BEETLE: If . . . if . . . if we can't take it along with us when we're making that other one.

The cuckoo fly and the tramp discuss the responsibilities of family life:

> CUCKOO FLY: Do you have children?
>
> TRAMP: No, I don't think so.
>
> CUCKOO FLY: Ah! Have you seen her?
>
> TRAMP: Who?
>
> CUCKOO FLY: My larva. She's beautiful, isn't she? A clever child. And how she's growing! What an appetite she has, ha ha! Children are a great joy, aren't they?
>
> TRAMP: Everyone says so.
>
> CUCKOO FLY: Isn't it so? At least we fathers know whom we're working for. You have a child, you work hard, you fight! That's life, isn't it? A child wants to grow, it wants to "eaty," to have its goodies, to play, doesn't it? Isn't it so?
>
> TRAMP: A child demands a great deal.
>
> CUCKOO FLY: Would you believe that I bring home two or three crickets a day?
>
> TRAMP: For whom?
>
> CUCKOO FLY: My child. Wonderful, isn't she? And so clever! You think she eats them all up? Not at all, only the tenderest parts, while they're still alive, ha ha! An extraordinary child, don't you think?

The crickets seem an ideal couple; the husband, with his solicitous care for his pregnant wife; the wife with her domesticity and love for curtains. They find an empty house, vacated by another cricket who, impaled on a thorn, is still struggling. But they only congratulate themselves on their luck and snicker at his misfortune. Soon the cuckoo fly strikes them down. Paralyzed, the tramp witnesses this double murder. He is joined by a parasite:

TRAMP: And no one cried out with horror! No one rushed to help them!

PARASITE: Bravo, comrade! Just my opinion.

TRAMP: To perish without any defense!

PARASITE: That's what I say. I've been watching a while, but I wouldn't do that. No, I couldn't do that. Everyone wants to live, doesn't he?

TRAMP: Who are you?

PARASITE: Me? No one special. I'm a poor fellow. An orphan. They call me a parasite.

TRAMP: Can one kill like that?

PARASITE: Just what I say. You think that cuckoo fly needs them? You think he's hungry like me? Go on! He kills to stock up. He's laying in a supply. A scandal, isn't it? Is that justice? Why should he have supplies when someone else goes hungry? Because he has a dagger and I have only my bare hands? Isn't it so?

TRAMP: I'd say so.

PARASITE: That's what I say. There's no equality. For instance, I don't kill anyone. My jaws are too soft. I mean, my conscience is too soft. I don't have the means of suns . . . sunste . . . sustenance. I'm just hungry. Is that right?

TRAMP: One . . . one . . . one shouldn't kill.

PARASITE: My very words, comrade. Or at least you shouldn't accumulate. Eat your fill and that's enough. Accumulation is stealing from those who don't know how to accumulate. Eat your fill and stop! Then there would be enough for all, isn't it so?

TRAMP: I don't know.

PARASITE: That's what I say.

But when the cuckoo fly goes away, the parasite eats up the two crickets and the larva herself in the bargain. Thus both capitalism and communism are rejected.

The tramp reflects that the greed and cruelty of the marauding insects must be due to their anarchist individualism. The authority of the community and state is the answer. The third act takes us to the world of the ants. But here he finds only totalitarian order, the goal of which is greater production for war. Work tempos are increased, though the workers drop from exhaustion in their places. The customary war slogans are paraded, and a pretext is found to wage war on a neighboring hill of yellow ants. But the yellows win, and destroy the whole colony. Contemptuously the tramp crushes them with his foot.

Throughout the second and third acts a chrysalis has been struggling to be born. Solemnly she declares that something new, something transcendant will come into the world with her birth. Now in the epilogue her moment arrives. A chorus of ephemerae dance over the stage, singing the intoxication of life:

We whirl life!
We dance life!

We ourselves are life!
O Life! Life!

Their ecstatic dance endures for a moment, and one by one they sink to the ground, dead. Now the chrysalis opens to bring forth another ephemera, who announces that she brings "a great message" to the world. Before she can pronounce it she too sinks to the earth.

The episode is a parody of the vitalist poetry of the brothers' youth. Life itself is perhaps not the answer either, then, to the tramp's quest, for itself it is meaningless unless man can give it meaning, and it only passes into death.

And now the tramp himself wrestles with death, though he begs pitifully for a respite. Two slugs observe his struggles with interest:

FIRST SLUG: Hey, shlug!

SECOND SLUG: What?

FIRST SLUG: He'sh shtruggling with death.

SECOND SLUG: Let'sh watch, shall we? . . .

TRAMP: You'd choke a man who's down, you coward? Let me go, let me tell—everyone—I want just a little while—Let me—live! Just live! (*Loudly*) No! Go away! I have so many things to say yet! (*Sinks to his knees*) I know—now—how to live. (*Falls on his back*).

FIRST SLUG: Well, he'sh done for.

SECOND SLUG: Mershiful heavensh, what a losh. Woe, woe. Shuch a mishfortune! Why did you deshert ush?

FIRST SLUG: What are you bawling about? It ishn't any of our buishnesh.

SECOND SLUG: But that'sh how you talk when shomeone diesh.

Morning dawns. A woodcutter appears and finds the body of the tramp. A woman comes in, carrying a child for christening.

WOODCUTTER: One is born and one dies.

WOMAN: And always there are people enough.

Thus the epilogue ends on a note of hope: life goes on in spite of death. Yet the phrase, "And always there are people enough" seems a terrible irony in the face of death. For it is man who dies, and only society which goes on. The brothers meant the ending to be optimistic, but it may sound like the final and most cynical note of all. And so the play was taken by reviewers and public all over the world. In answer to their many objectors, the brothers wrote a second ending; the director could decide which to use. In the variant ending the tramp awakes after the departure of the two slugs, to find that he had only dreamt of death. The woodcutter enters, greets him, and asks if he wants work chopping trees. The tramp joyfully accepts.

The choice of endings, therefore, is between life and work. In making such a choice the brothers may seem to have abdicated their responsibility as author, and both these answers to the tramp's question seem irrelevant. The second answer (work) had seemingly been disposed of already in Acts II and III: honest work may be perverted to selfish or self-destructive ends.

As apologists for their play, the brothers wrote a long preface to the second edition:

> During its [the play's] brief existence so many friendly and hostile words have been written, that it is difficult for the authors to add anything to that confusing and many-voiced concert. Their play is "a terrible satire on love, wealth, and war," but also "an ugly, cynical and pessimistic drama, in which there is no truth" (*Christian Science Monitor*), "a play of John the Baptist" (*Freethinker*), and "a cruel, dirty piece of symbolism" (*Sheffield Daily Telegraph*), "an eye-opener for frivolous spectators" and an "image of antediluvian times." "Kill them," one Berlin critic wrote about the authors, while Kerr [the critic of the *Berliner Tageblatt*] enthusiastically greeted the "first pair of brothers," and so on . . .

> Well, to all this the authors have very little to add. They would, however, make one reservation: their comedy may be ugly, but it is not pessimistic. One American critic wrote that the spectator wonders whether he should cut his throat, if the world is as bad as it is depicted in this play. The authors entreat their audiences and readers not to do this, for it was not their intention to cut people's throats. Who the devil compels you to identify yourselves with butterflies or beetles, with crickets or ants or ephemerae? Because these creatures are depicted as loafers and self-seekers, as scoundrels and libertines, militarists and parasites, does it therefore follow that they denote people? Does the demonstration that private, family, or state selfishness is petty, insect-like, brutal and lousy, prove that everything human is lousy? Is there not at least one human being opposed to the insects, the tramp, a creature who sees all, judges and searches for a way? Each spectator or reader may attempt to see himself in the wandering tramp; instead of that—disquieted or scandalized—he has taken it for granted that it is his own image or the image of his society which he sees in these vermin, which in fact do represent—true, with a deliberate bias—certain vices. And just this optical illusion is a testimony that the authors did not write their "ugly and cynical" satire in vain.

> They did not intend to write a drama, but a mystery in a quite antiquated and naive sense. Just as in the medieval mystery play there appeared personifications of Avarice, Egotism, or Virtue, so certain moral concepts are here personified as insects, simply for greater edification. True, Virtue is absent here; if the authors, say, had introduced on their stage a bee as an incarnation of Obedience, or a spider as a personification of Modesty, their piece would no doubt have seemed less pessimistic. If they did not do so, they had their reasons: the mirror which they held up to life was intentionally and tendentiously crooked, and would have distorted the mug

of even the fairest of human Virtues. And lo, their malevolent trick succeeded beyond all expectation, and people without number *recognized* man in that distorted grotesque and realized that there is something ugly, brutal, and worthless even where they were not accustomed to look for it. We did not write about people or about the vermin of the field; we wrote about certain vices. And, God knows, it is not dirty pessimism to find that vice is something wretched and lousy. Of course it is not elevating or original, either, but *that* was really not our end.

> And so those who called the comedy a "worn-out allegory" were right after all. Good heavens, it is terribly worn out, bought, so to speak, from a dealer in second-hand clothing, and then turned once more; but believe us, it is hard to preach morality in a dinner jacket; the morality of dinner jackets would have appeared essentially different from what we wanted to tell people in this play.

In a letter to the editor of the *New York Herald* the brothers added:

> You, the public of our play, you are neither butterflies, beetles, nor ants if you can see the futility of insect life; you yourself are *Tramps;* you are the living, enduring, truth-seeking consciences, just like our own *Tramp.* His life was sad only because he remained in the play alone . . . and this is our pessimistic error, for we too were composing our play in solitude; but if the *Tramp* knew that in other woods—for instance, American woods—other *Tramps* were erring and seeking as he was, he would have bequeathed them his endless quest. For our insect play has another epilogue, printed but as yet not performed on the stage . . . This epilogue in the book edition was written with a deep recollection of your philosopher, William James, whose name is surely a charm against pessimism.

The reader can only agree with the authors that a satire of vice is not pessimistic as such. But this argument hardly disposes of the fundamental problem. The question is not whether vice exists, or even whether virtue and vice may at times actually be opposite faces of the same coin, as the second act suggests. Rather it is how should man live in a world where moral standards are relative? How does one choose when the good of one's family conflicts with the good of society? The tramp finds his answer to this question only when he dies.

Is the failure to give an answer to this question not pessimism? Perhaps there is an escape, after all. Life is not the answer, but the process, the search for an answer. That the question has no ready answer is one of the countless facts of life itself, which man must accept.

Hence the play ends on a note of ambiguity. From here it was possible for Karel Čapek to pursue relativism in one of two directions: as a final answer to all questions, which would ultimately have led him to pessimism; or as a working technique in the search for truth. He himself warned against the first solution when he wrote:

> I do not wish to play with words, but if I have

ever said that all is relative, then something quite unrelativistic has slipped out of me, for that sinful word "all" smells of a buried and concealed absolutism . . . A true, hundred-percent relativism must achieve a finer distinction: almost all is relative.

(pp. 75-83)

William E. Harkins, in his Karel Čapek, *Columbia University Press, 1962, 193 p.*

THE MAKROPOULOS SECRET

PRODUCTION REVIEWS

J. Brooks Atkinson   (review date 22 January 1926)

[*Atkinson was the drama critic for the* New York Times *from 1926 to 1960. Upon his retirement from that post, the Mansfield Theatre in New York was renamed the Brooks Atkinson in honor of his contributions to the theater. His publications include* Skyline Promenades *(1925),* Henry Thoreau: The Cosmic Yankee *(1927), and* East of the Hudson *(1931), as well as many collections of his drama criticism. In the following review of the 1926 New York production of* The Makropoulos Secret *at the Charles Hopkins Theatre, Atkinson asserts that Čapek's use of dramatic irony—in which the audience knows more than the characters on stage—hinders the effectivness of this work. In fact, he claims, the employment of this technical device can "only result in tedium in a philosophical play." Regarding the substance of the play, however, Atkinson states that "abstract though it may be, verbose and argumentative, it holds the interest and appeals to the mind."*]

According to the technical device employed by Karel Capek in *The Makropoulos Secret* put on last evening at the Charles Hopkins Theatre, the characters of the play do not learn what the audience knows until the last scene of the final act. However magic this device may be in certain forms of commonplace drama, it can only result in tedium in a philosophical play written to expound an idea. And the effect in the current comedy is to reduce most of the play to the status of preface, and to confine the most stimulating material to a debating scene, after the climax, where the author expands his thesis completely. Inasmuch as the performance lacks the crispness essential to intellectual drama, *The Makropoulos Secret* does not supply the "lift" we enjoy in the theatre.

As the author of *R. U. R.* and coauthor with his brother of *The World We Live In*, Capek is already well known to American audiences; as the author of prose works in fiction and essay form he is perhaps even more widely known to American readers. Behind the patterns of all his literary works lies a vivid interest in philosophical themes, and not a little humor. No one knows more thoroughly than this Prague theatre manager the fragilities and comic pretenses of human life. Are we proud of our little swarm of civilized

life? Are we vastly superior to the animals? Perhaps we are; but Capek enjoys reminding us that the millennium is not too close at hand. We need not dust off our ascension robes yet.

When his characters in the closing scene of *The Makropoulos Secret* have the elixir of longevity in their hands, the promise—with some risk—of three hundred more years added to their lives, Capek expounds several provocative theses. In the room are an opportunistic lawyer, a radical law clerk, a sweet young girl, an aristocrat and a young man with aristocratic propensities. And more spectacular than any of these moderns—Emilia Marty, the wonder-woman, who was born in Crete in 1587 and still retains her youth and fascination in 1926. Some secret formula has preserved her bodily life all these years, through a long succession of liaisons and worldly entanglements. Only her soul has died; the formula did not provide for spiritual perpetuity. But after she has recounted the disillusioning, inhuman course of her life, its emotional frigidity, none of those eager to live long dares accept the formula. One old roué, already past 70, clutches at it for a moment. But only the fresh young girl has the courage to take the paper and burn it at the candle.

All this quickening of a half-humorous philosophical thesis comes in the aforementioned last scene of the final act. Abstract though it may be, verbose and argumentative, it holds the interest and appeals to the mind. Indeed, in many respects the real qualities of *The Makropoulos Secret* seem barely indicated before the curtain falls; the play that might transport us has only begun. For up to that moment Capek has been content to reveal the enigma of a brilliant opera singer, strangely remote, strangely omniscient, mysterious in every respect, who walks through the hearts of men, cruel and self-contained, cocotte and apparent courtisane. And the contrasts with the mortals who fall transfixed at her feet are merely the obvious ones inherent in that theme.

Capek has a reputation for genial satire. Surely there is irony in this fable; on the stage and in novels we have found it before. But *The Makropoulos Secret* rarely stirs the audience to laughter. Part of the play's impassivity may be laid at the door of a performance that misses the comedies of contrast. Especially in the last act, with a mortal father grieving over the suicide of his son and the capricious singer calmly brushing her hair, the situation should breed a malignant, biting irony. The effect is almost lost in the acting.

As the superhuman Emilia Marty, Miss Menken does not bring to her performance the lustre indicated in the lines. And her acting does not flow with the glamourous verve that might describe this woman in truer proportion. The delivery of the lines, as well as the acting, is broken into particles. Miss Roos as the law clerk's daughter has an appealing sort of beauty. Mr. Vail is pleasing as Bertik. When Mr. Haupt overcomes his tendency to pose he makes an articulate aristocrat, and gives weight generally to the performance. Mr. Mack describes the law clerk, effectively as a soft, rather sentimental old servant. As the truculent attorney Mr. Davenport is satisfactory. But perhaps the most spontaneous performance in the play is the feeble-minded roué by Mr. Williams.

J. Brooks Atkinson, in a review of "The Makropoulos Secret," in The New York Times, *January 22, 1926, p. 12.*

Richard Hayes (review date 27 December 1957)

[*In 1957,* The Makropoulos Secret *was staged by Tyrone Guthrie at the Phoenix Theater in New York. Guthrie was an influential English actor, director, producer, and administrator of London's Old Vic Theatre from 1939 to 1945. He was also one of the founders of the Stratford Festival, Canada and the Guthrie Theatre in Minneapolis. In the following review of this production, Hayes likens the play to nineteenth-century farce: it is, he claims, " 'serious' in its assumptions but intermittently convulsed by wild gleams of the preposterous."*]

Under Mr. Tyrone Guthrie's tutelage, the Phoenix Theatre continues its assumption of the exotic. Neither **The Makropoulos Secret** nor its author, Karel Capek, command quite the animation and fundamental power of Schiller's *Mary Stuart:* the mild audacity of the Czech playwright seems dusty with time, and the dramatic impulse behind **The Makropoulos Secret** could never have been deeply insistent. Yet paradoxes intrude, and one is forced to admit in justice that if the play's intellectual bite is meager, its imaginative force seems nonetheless considerable; if its dramatic vitality is low, it is full still of the interests of theater, and achieves a kind of excellence within self-imposed limits. It gives pleasure, too, as a cultural document, returning us to that fantasy world of *mittel-Europa,* and the spiritual crisis of monocled aristocrats— slimy with class hauteur—and opera singers, legendary images of glamor, exhausted by gusty accesses of passion.

Capek's authority with this stuff of imagination is easy— too easy—and he manipulates it with a gaudy expertise, not too fastidious. Yet his concerns lie obviously elsewhere: ultimately, he employs the motif of bodily longevity as a means to comment on a state of threatened and (he would have it) ideal spirit. It is a usage comparable to Shaw's in *Back to Methuselah,* yet the two plays differ in more than their alien commitments; they share no comparable quality of mind or embodied expressiveness, and one is finally reluctant to admit the claims of **The Makropoulos Secret** as *rigorous* commentary on a philosophic theme. Still, inadequacy need not necessarily exclude worthiness, nor naiveté responsibility, and Capek is in secure possession of these virtues. He makes his plea for unconditioned spirit with eloquent humanism and even a discreet passion; there is, too, an open dignity—a generous response—in his consciousness of the vital possibility of life, and this is a dignity of feeling to which subsequent European dramatists have not often risen.

It is curious to speculate on the attractions such a piece may have had for Mr. Guthrie. **The Makropoulos Secret** permits no scope for his (often rather ghastly) Bright Ideas; it contains no histrionic forces to be deployed, no rhetorical clamors. Indeed, I would suspect Mr. Guthrie

turned to it as an exercise in genre, quite as he sought, in his wholly admirable staging of *The Matchmaker,* to rehabilitate the emptied structure of nineteenth-century farce. **The Makropoulos Secret** is accessible to a similar restatement; it seems the lineal descendant of what one may imagine the theater of Scribe and Sardou to have been like: "serious" in its assumptions, but intermittently convulsed by wild gleams of the preposterous. Mr. Guthrie cannot extinguish these giddy spasms, so he subdues them, guiding the play artfully, in its third act, into a poised climate of emotional eloquence, spiritual authority and melodramatic dash. (He is assisted here by Mr. Norris Houghton's superb last decor, a formal setting of extraordinary aptness and stylistic unity.) Indeed, the success of this production, though not an achievement on any major scale, is yet a thing of distinction, and much to be commended; nor do I imply satiric comment when I suggest that the very absence, from **The Makropoulos Secret,** of anything finely poetic or imaginative, may be an index to Mr. Guthrie's accomplishment with it. (pp. 336-37)

Richard Hayes, "An Exercise in Genre," in The Commonweal, *Vol. LXVII, No. 13, December 27, 1957, pp. 336-37.*

CRITICAL COMMENTARY

William E. Harkins (essay date 1962)

[*Harkins asserts in the following excerpt that although* The Makropoulos Secret *is a "brilliant play," it fails to represent "the tragedy of death" and therefore misses an opportunity to achieve "profound insight into the human situation."*]

In 1922 Čapek published a new play, **The Makropulos Secret.** It had its première at the Prague Municipal Theater on November 21, 1922, under the author's direction. Later it was set as an opera by Leoš Janáček.

The Makropulos Secret is an attack on yet another dream of utopian absolutism: eternal life. The theme is not original, of course. Tithonus, in Greek mythology, received the gift of eternal life at the wish of his spouse Eos, but the goddess forgot to specify that he be given eternal youth as well. The struldbrugs of *Gulliver's Travels* also live eternally, but grow old as quickly as other men. In these tales, as in the legends of the Flying Dutchman and the Wandering Jew, eternal life is only a curse.

Why then did Čapek take up the subject once again? For one thing, the myths dealt with eternal life after youth had been lost; Čapek varies the theme by granting the possibility of eternal youth, at least in appearance. Moreover, the myths were mere fantasies, while Čapek lived at a time when the rapid advance of medical science made a greater span of years entirely possible.

In 1921 Shaw published his "metabiological pentateuch," *Back to Methuselah,* in which he opined that a radically increased life-span would permit man to develop greater intellectual and spiritual maturity. It at first seemed as if Čapek's play were a deliberate rebuttal to Shaw, and, in spite of the author's quite specific statement that he had not read Shaw's play when he wrote **The Makropulos Secret,** critics ever since have regarded his play as an answer to Shaw.

What is likely is that Čapek's play was an answer, not to Shaw, but to H. G. Wells's *Food of the Gods* (1904), in which Wells argues that greater size would benefit man. Čapek, who was influenced very greatly by Wells's science fiction, had almost certainly read *The Food of the Gods.* In **R.U.R.** there is a remark which seems to be a specific counter to Wells's utopian dream. Domin tells Helena that attempts have been made to develop robots larger than men, but that these giants soon fell apart; for some mysterious reason only robots of man's size can survive.

For Čapek titanism is another form of absolutism, and the Wellsian or Shavian superman is a kind of titan. A prolonged life still would not suffice for man to come to absolute truth, but would be sufficiently long for him to become bored with existence. In this Čapek's thought is more modern than either Shaw or Wells; unlike Wells, he is skeptical of dreams nourished by excessive faith in scientific progress. Shavian creative evolution, with its frequent contempt for science, was closer to him, but he could scarcely have agreed with Shaw that conscious will can improve the human race biologically.

In the preface to his play, Čapek writes of its genesis:

> This new comedy began to occupy me some three or four years ago, in other words, before **R.U.R.;** at that time, to be sure, I still conceived of it as a novel. Its subject belongs to a group of themes which I would like to put behind me. One more such task remains if I am to get rid of these old stocks of material [presumably a reference to *Krakatit*, published two years after **The Makropulos Secret**]. The impulse for the play was the theory of Professor Mečnikov, I believe, that old age is autointoxication of the organism.
>
> I mention these two circumstances first, because this winter there appeared a new work by Shaw, *Back to Methuselah,* which so far I know only from a résumé, and which also—on a scale apparently much more grandiose—treats the question of longevity. This coincidence in subject is entirely accidental, and, as it would seem from the résumé, purely superficial, for Bernard Shaw comes to quite opposite conclusions. As far as I may judge, Mr. Shaw sees in the possibility of living for several hundred years the ideal condition of humanity, a kind of future paradise. As the reader will discover, in this book longevity is depicted quite differently, as a condition far from ideal and even quite undesirable. It is difficult to say which view is more correct; on both sides, unfortunately, actual experience is lacking. But perhaps one can at least prophesy that Shaw's thesis will be received as a classical case of optimism, while that of this book will appear to be hopeless pessimism.
>
> No matter, my personal life will obviously be neither happier nor sadder if I am called a pessimist or an optimist. But being a pessimist involves, it would seem, a certain public responsi-

bility, something like a quiet rebuke for bad behavior towards the world and people. Hence I declare publicly that I do not feel guilty in this respect, that I have not committed pessimism, and, if I have, then unconsciously and very unwillingly. In my comedy I intended, on the contrary, to tell people something consoling and optimistic. I do not know if it is optimistic to maintain that to live sixty years is bad, while to live three hundred is good; I only think that to declare that a life of sixty years (on the average) is adequate and good enough is not exactly committing the crime of pessimism. Suppose one says that at some time in the future there will be neither illness nor poverty nor dirty toil—this is certainly optimism. But to say that life today, full of illness, poverty and toil, is not completely bad or cursed, and has something of infinite value, this is—what, actually? Pessimism? I think not. Perhaps there are two kinds of optimism: one which turns away from bad things for something at least a little better, if only dreams. The first looks straight off for paradise; there is no finer direction for the human soul. The second searches here and there for at least some crumbs of relative good; perhaps even this effort is not quite without value. If this is not optimism, then find a better word.

The Makropulos Secret has a complex plot involving an old manuscript and a disputed inheritance. The central character, Emilia Marty, is a mysterious beauty whose detailed knowledge of intimate events of the distant past soon suggests to the spectator that she is older than she looks. In the end her true identity is revealed: she is Elena Makropulos, daughter to the Greek physician of Emperor Rudolph II. Her father discovered a formula for rejuvenation, which he tested on her. The emperor proved too fearful to try it, however, and she alone remained in possession of the secret. She has lived over three hundred years, leading five separate lives under different names, always with the initials E. M. Once she gave the formula to a lover, but now she is aging, and needs desperately to recover it. She admits, however, that eternal life has left her without feeling, only with profound ennui and disgust. She fears death, but in the end comes to the realization that eternal life is a greater terror than death. She offers the formula to whoever will take it. Her visitors cannot agree: one, an aristocrat, insists on reserving it as the privilege of an elite: another, a radical, wants to make it available to all. Finally a young girl, Kristina, acts instinctively by taking the document and burning it in the flame of a candle.

The play is not really an argument against longevity, of course. We can hardly imagine that Čapek would oppose medical science's efforts to prolong human life. Longevity for Čapek is rather a symbol of the absolute. Man's life may be weighed against eternal life:

> EMILIA: Oh, if you only knew how simple life is for you! . . . You are so close to everything! For you everything has meaning. For you everything has some value, because in those few years you have it you will never get enough of it . . . O my God, if I could only . . . once again (*wrings her hands*). Fools, you are so happy. It is sickening how happy you are! And all because of the stu-

pid accident that you are going to die soon! Everything interests you, as if you were monkeys! You believe in everything, you believe in love, in yourself, in virtue, in progress, in humanity, in I don't know what all. You, Max, believe in pleasure; you Kristina, believe in love and fidelity. You believe in strength. You believe in all sorts of nonsense, Vítek. Each one, each one believes in something! You can live, you . . . you madmen!

VITEK (*agitated*): But, excuse me, there really are some kind of . . . higher values . . . ideals . . . duties . . .

EMILIA: There are, but only for you. How can I explain it to you? There may be love, but only in you. As soon as it disappears in you, it does not exist; there is no such thing as love in general . . . anywhere in the universe . . . No man can love three hundred years. Nor hope, nor create, nor even watch three hundred years. He cannot hold out. Everything will disgust him. It will disgust him to be good and to be bad . . . And then you will see that in fact there is nothing. Nothing exists. Neither sin, nor pain, nor earth—nothing. Only that exists which has value. And for you everything has value. O God, I was like you! I was a young girl, I was a lady, I was happy, I—I was a human being!

Emilia's estrangement from life reminds one of that alienation which marks Dostoevski's characters, particularly Svidrigailov [in *Crime and Punishment*] or Stavrogin [in *The Possessed*]. She too has passed beyond good and evil to that point where everything is infinitely boring. But for Dostoevski there are only absolutes: Stavrogin has chosen one logical escape from the dilemma of God as absolute or man as absolute. For Čapek there is no dilemma: man is only relative. Man's "absolutism" is only a discontented yearning for what he cannot have and what would disgust him if he could possess it. Wisdom, then, is to be content with life as it is.

This does not mean, of course, that Čapek is opposed to progress any more than he is opposed to medicine. Progress itself is a part of life as it is, and progress takes place in the world of relative values. It may be asked, however, whether man's incentive to progress might not disappear with loss of faith in absolutes. But this question can hardly be answered: Čapek would argue that, since real knowledge of absolutes is impossible, faith in an absolute can scarcely inspire man to any real progress.

Hence Čapek cannot accept the Shavian ideal of the superman. For him man's present life suffices for him to be human, and that is the most essential thing he can achieve. Man is more noble as man than as a creature on the way to becoming a god. Even a superman would not be wise enough to comprehend the enigma of life, while, as he is, man is sensitive enough to experience the pain and tragedy of existence, as well as its joys.

Čapek described his play as optimistic, but, as with so much of his work, there are two sides to the coin: a deep faith in life and in the "ordinary man," but a despair of real moral progress or essential change. For Čapek,

human progress shares the moral ambivalence of all human action: the same scientific advance which can create new life may in the end destroy us.

Čapek calls his play a comedy; it is not a melodrama, as many critics have considered. Hence it matters little that the audience is aware of Marty's secret long before the personages in the play are initiated. In fact the author's intention seems to be to flatter the spectator by leading him to the solution of the mystery as quickly as possible. Čapek's concern is with character, and Marty is perhaps his most vivid stage figure. A great lady with a contempt for all amenities, beautiful but cold, penetrating but confused, brazen but terrified—her unique personal situation allows Čapek to endow her with a series of paradoxical traits which might seem improbable in any other character. With a great actress in the role, *The Makropulos Secret* is a brilliant play.

In advocating his gospel of relativism, Čapek has overlooked one thing: the tragedy of death. He seeks to persuade us that death is good. But this only can be true as a general law of all humanity; the moment we consider the individual case, we become aware of the profound tragedy of death. Emilia, indeed all the characters of the play fear death, but none of them shows any awareness of its tragic nature. True, such an awareness was opposed to Čapek's real purpose, and would have taken the play outside the realm of comedy. But, by ignoring the tragedy of individual death, Čapek lost an opportunity to achieve a more profound insight into the human situation. Not until (and only in) *An Ordinary Life* did he come to this deeper perception. (pp. 110-15)

William E. Harkins, in his Karel Čapek, *Columbia University Press, 1962, 193 p.*

FURTHER READING

OVERVIEWS AND GENERAL STUDIES

Darlington, W. A. "The Brothers Čapek." In his *Literature in the Theatre and Other Essays,* pp. 137-44. New York: Henry Holt and Company, 1925.

Contends that although Čapek's *R. U. R.* and *And So Ad Infinitum* are "intriguing, arresting, out of the ordinary," neither "represents real progress in the art of writing for the theatre." Darlington insists that both works lack the quality of "knowledge of and love for humanity," which is essential to great drama.

Harkins, William E. "The Real Legacy of Karel Čapek." In *The Czechoslovak Contribution to World Culture,* edited by Miloslav Rechcigl, Jr., pp. 60-7. The Hague: Mouton and Company, 1964.

Survey of Čapek's works, concentrating on "the value of [his] scientific fantasies as art."

———. *Karel Čapek.* New York: Columbia University Press, 1962, 193 p.

In-depth exploration of the life and career of the "father

of Czechoslovakian drama." Harkins provides one of the few book-length English language studies of Čapek's works.

Interview with Karel Čapek. *The Living Age* 319, No. 4142 (24 November 1923): 383-84.
> Brief discussion of *The Makropoulos Secret, The Absolute At Large,* and miscellaneous literary activities.

Manning, Clarence A. "Karel Čapek." *The South Atlantic Quarterly,* XL, No. 3 (July 1941): 236-42.
> Eulogy to Čapek which examines the problems with the author's use of melodrama as the vehicle for expressing his philosophical ideas.

Wellek, René. "Karel Čapek." *The Slavonic Review* 15, No. 43 (July 1936): 191-206.
> Study that divides Čapek's career into three periods and covers all genres in which he wrote. Wellek includes substantial commentary on Čapek's dramatic works.

R. U. R.

Review of *R. U. R. The Literary Digest* LXXV, No. 4 (November 1922): 30-1.
> Account of the reception of the Theater Guild's *R. U. R.,* noting that this "fantastic melodrama" was "presented with astonishing realism" by the company.

Nathan, George Jean. Review of *R.U.R.* In his *The Theatre Book of the Year 1942-1943: A Record and an Interpretation,* pp. 161-62. New York: Alfred A Knopf, 1943.
> Production review that censures the attempts made by some to draw parallels between the events taking place in Europe in 1943 and the action of *R. U. R.* Nathan specifically takes exception to the endeavor to link Nazi soldiers with the robots.

AND SO AD INFINITUM

Beck-Agular, Vera F. de. "Entomological Symbols in the Čapeks and Garcia Lorca." *Literature East and West* 9, No. 2 (June 1965): 96-103.
> Compares *And So Ad Infinitum* with Lorca's *The Spell of the Butterfly* (*El Maleficio de la Mariposa*), noting that both works draw analogies between insects and humans. The critic asserts that through "beetles, snails and but-

terflies, as well as through human spectators," both ask "the eternal questions of life and death."

"An Entomological Morality Play." *Life, Letters, and the Arts* 313 (3 June 1922): 619.
> Finds *And So Ad Infinitum* a "fantastic comedy of an unusual sort."

THE MAKROPOULOS SECRET

Brown, John Mason. Review of *The Makropoulos Secret. Theatre Arts Monthly* 9, No. 5 (May 1925): 348.
> Praises the work as the best-written Čapek play available in English.

Review of *The Makropoulos Secret. The Saturday Review* 11, No. 18 (28 November 1925): 347-48.
> Regards *The Makropoulos Secret* as Čapek's "striking antithesis" to Bernard Shaw's *Back to Methuselah.*

THE MOTHER

Gilder, Rosamond. Review of *The Mother. Theatre Arts Monthly* XXIII, No. 6 (June 1939): 402-03.
> Deems *The Mother* a "dull" work, arguing that "Čapek's mordant wit and his sense of the dramatic foundered in the storm of his passionate rage against a world gone mad."

Review of *The Mother. Life and Letters Today* 24, No. 30 (February 1940): 211-12.
> Claims that the central character in *The Mother* is "a symbol rather than a character" and "not the least interesting as a human being." Although the play is "effective when acted," the critic claims, when read it is "rather a bore."

"*The Mother:* Capek's Fine Work." *The Times Literary Supplement,* No. 1979 (6 January 1940): 8.
> Deems *The Mother* a "strange and moving little play."

Vernon, Grenville. Review of *The Mother. Commonweal* 30, No. 3 (12 May 1939): 76.
> Suggests that *The Mother* is "written with considerable eloquence" and that "there are moments of true poignancy," but notes that "the chief theatrical weakness of the play is the repetition in the conversations with the various ghosts."

Mary Chase

1907-1981

(Full Name: Mary Coyle Chase.)

Chase, an American dramatist and children's story writer, was the author of the 1944-45 Pulitzer prize-winning play *Harvey*. She is most often associated with the vogue of fantasy and escapist drama that developed in the theater in the years surrounding World War II. Like other pieces of the period, such as Joseph O. Kesselring's *Arsenic and Old Lace* (1941) and Noël Coward's *Blithe Spirit* (1941), Chase's phenomenally popular *Harvey* is characterized by exuberance and lighthearted charm. However, despite its whimsical tone, *Harvey* has often been admired for its strong affirmation of the worth of the individual. Chase's other plays, notably *Mrs. McThing* and *Bernardine,* while less enthusiastically received than *Harvey,* are similarly marked by this blending of levity and sensitivity. The success of *Harvey* in its initial run as well as in revival and on film perhaps best testifies to the warm regard audiences hold for Chase and her work and demonstrates the enduring value of her craft.

Born to Irish immigrant parents on 25 February 1907 in Denver, Colorado, Chase was the youngest of Frank and Mary Coyle's four children. The Coyle family cultivated their Irish heritage, especially the rich legacy of folklore from which Chase later drew inspiration for her many plays and children's stories. Young Mary's adventurous spirit and playful personality endeared her to her friends and acquaintances. An exceptionally bright child, Chase achieved academic excellence, graduating from high school at the age of 15. She then attended classes at the University of Denver for two years before transferring to the University of Colorado at Boulder.

Upon her return to Denver, Chase began her career as a journalist with the *Rocky Mountain News.* While at the *News,* she earned a reputation as a dedicated, competitive, and resourceful reporter. She also met and, in 1928, married Robert Chase, a fellow journalist. Described as a fun-loving person, Mary Chase would often play pranks on her co-workers, a penchant that ultimately led to her termination from the *News.* Although the paper eventually offered to reinstate her, she declined, deciding instead to remain at home with her children and to concentrate on writing for the stage.

Her first play, *Me Third,* has a lively plot about a politician who is blackmailed by a former prostitute. Although the comedy was a success in Denver, when producer Brock Pemberton took it to New York under the name of *Now You've Done It,* it had a run of only seven weeks. Undaunted by this experience, Chase continued to write, composing four more plays, none of which played beyond the regional theater. Finally came the inspiration for *Harvey,* and when Pemberton produced the play, Chase had a Broadway hit.

Although *Harvey* provided Chase and her family much-needed income, she experienced great difficulty as she tried to adjust to the sudden wealth and notoriety which accompanied her success. In an interview with Eleanor Harris, she described her experience in these terms: "Any precipitous change is a terrible shock in itself, whether you lose all your money or make a fortune. But nobody seems to realize this. If you lose everything overnight, everyone gives you sympathy. But if you make a great deal of money, no one sympathizes or even seems to understand what a shattering thing has happened to you." This crisis plunged her into a period of depression which lasted for several years. The turning point in her despondency came when she began work on *Mrs. McThing* and *Bernardine,* both of which were staged in 1952. Although the latter work was the last of Chase's plays to succeed on Broadway, she continued to compose pieces for the theater until her final play, *Cocktails with Mimi,* was produced in 1974. In addition to her success as a playwright, Chase earned recognition as a writer of children's stories which are characterized by the same fanciful style that distinguishes her plays.

Throughout the body of Chase's work there is an underlying theme of respect for individuality and human dignity. This is particularly evident in *Harvey,* undoubtedly the dramatist's most widely known piece. Chase has attributed the inspiration for the play's central character to her mother, who once said: "Never make fun of those whom others consider crazy, for they often have a wisdom of their own." Elwood P. Dowd is a gentle tippler whose best friend is Harvey, a six-foot one and one-half inch invisible white rabbit. His sister and niece, greatly embarrassed by his behavior, plan to have Elwood institutionalized. In the end, however, all involved realize that the charming "thirsty soul" Elwood contributes much more to the community than a "perfectly normal human being" because he is charitable and benevolent and highly esteems his fellow man. Broadway audiences were delighted by this droll comedy, and critics, too, were enchanted. Although reviewers pointed out serious flaws in the play's construction, such as unsatisfactory character development and a dragging third act, their notices were almost universally glowing. Lewis Nichols, the *New York Times* reviewer, for example, judged *Harvey* "one of the delights of the season," and the noted critic George Jean Nathan asserted that the play constituted "a delightful theatrical evening." *Harvey* was performed over 1,700 times during its initial engagement, making it one of the longest running plays in Broadway history. In 1947, James Stewart succeeded Frank Fay in the role of Elwood P. Dowd, and in 1950, Stewart was cast for the movie version of *Harvey.* London audiences greeted the production warmly during the 1949-50 season, but British critics were not as enamored of the play as their American counterparts had been. The revivals in New York (1970) and London (1975) both starred Stewart, who had become strongly identified with the part of Elwood.

Shortly after the success of *Harvey,* Chase tried a more serious drama, *The Next Half-Hour.* The play, however, was a dismal failure. Returning to the familiar ground of fantasy, she penned *Mrs. McThing.* In this work, Chase spins the whimsical tale of a wealthy mother and her incorrigible son who learn the value of warm, loving relationships when they lose their riches as a result of an enchantress's spell. Critical reception of *Mrs. McThing* was mixed. For example, while Joseph Wood Krutch claimed it was the "product of an extraordinarily ingenious talent," George Jean Nathan viewed the play as a testament to Chase's inadequacy as a fantasy writer.

Bernardine, inspired by the experiences of Chase's own children, is a coming-of-age account of a group of teenage boys in search of their "dream girl," the mythical Bernardine. Although the work was well-received by the public, the general critical consensus was perhaps best summarized by Brooks Atkinson, who asserted that "the craftsmanship is shaky [but] the material is honest." Thus, the success of *Bernardine* was attributed not to Chase's technical proficiency but to her compassionate portrayal of the struggles of adolescents. In 1957, Twentieth-Century Fox produced *Bernardine* on film.

The eccentric and seemingly capricious qualities which characterize Chase's writing have led some critics to question her capabilities as a craftsman. Yet her mastery of ex-

pressing basic human needs for dignity and respect with both humor and insight has given her plays broad and continuing appeal and has enabled them to thrive before audiences.

(For further information on Chase's life and career, see *Contemporary Authors,* Vols. 77-80, rev. ed., and 105; and *Something about the Author,* Vols. 17 and 29.)

PRINCIPAL WORKS

PLAYS

Me Third   1936 [produced on Broadway as *Now You've Done It,* 1937]
Harvey   1944
Mrs. McThing   1952
Bernardine   1952
Cocktails with Mimi   1974

OTHER MAJOR WORKS

Loretta Mason Potts   (juvenilia)   1958
The Wicked Pigeon Ladies in the Garden   (juvenilia) 1968

OVERVIEWS AND GENERAL STUDIES

W. David Sievers   (essay date 1955)

[*Sievers is the author of* Freud on Broadway *(1955), which examines the influence of psychoanalysis on twentieth-century American theater. In the excerpt below, Sievers surveys Chase's three major plays,* Harvey, Mrs. McThing, *and* Bernardine, *contending that "her style is ingratiating whimsy but beneath it there is the soundly motivated psychology of hallucination."*]

In our predominantly realistic theatre Mary Chase has brought a refreshing sense of fantasy which links her to the earlier American drama of wish-fulfillment—*The Poor Little Rich Girl* [by Eleanor Gates], *The Willow Tree, His Majesty Bunker Bean, Barbara,* and *Lady of the Rose* [by Martin Flavin]. Her style is ingratiating whimsy but beneath it there is the soundly motivated psychology of hallucination.

After an unsuccessful realistic play, ***Now You've Done It*** (1937), Mrs. Chase brought to New York in 1944 the now-immortal ***Harvey,*** in which she explores the inner world of Elwood P. Dowd, a charming bachelor who is to all intents and purposes the most rational person in the play except for his persistent hallucination of a large white pookah rabbit, Harvey. Elwood drinks a good deal, upsets his scatterbrained sister, Veta, and responds to people who anxiously ask if they can do something for him with his disarming, "What did you have in mind?" When Veta attempts to have Elwood committed to a private psychiatric sanitarium, it is she who is committed and forcibly given hydrotherapy. Veta manages to extricate herself and returns comically indignant at the attendant, who she is sure is a white slaver, and the doctor, who asked her a lot of questions, " . . . all about sex-urges—and all that filthy stuff. That place ought to be cleaned up" [Act II, Scene i]. It is not long until the psychiatrist himself is sure that he sees Harvey, for as [Eugene] O'Neill pointed out in *Where The Cross Is Made*, the root of belief is in all of us. By the end of the second act, even the audience is ready to believe that it has seen Harvey cross the stage and open the door of the psychiatrist's office. The doctor himself unburdens to Elwood that he wishes he, too, could escape reality, his private wish being to go to a cool grove outside Akron with a strange young woman who would just stroke his head and say, "Poor thing! Oh, you poor, poor thing" [Act III]. All men apparently need their private Harveys, their ideal creatures to console them and minister to their wants. Few are as frank as Elwood in admitting that need. As Elwood explains to the doctor, "I wrestled with reality for forty years, and I am happy to state that I finally won out over it." When the psychiatrist is about to administer an injection to cure Elwood of Harvey, Veta finally stops him. Neither she nor the audience really wants Elwood any different than he is. If he is happy with Harvey, it is no one else's business; and as the two of them go out together, leaving behind the neurotic, hyper-tense, anxious ones who live in reality, we wonder, as at the end of *Button Button* and *Behold This Dreamer*, just who is crazy?

Mrs. Chase's next play, **The Next Half Hour** (1945), ran only a little longer than its title suggests; utilizing wish-fulfillment again it lacked the happy union of whimsy and humanitarianism that endeared **Harvey**. An Irish woman can foretell the future by listening to the wail of the banshees; she tries to save her eldest son, "a silvercord" boy, from an affair with a married woman and succeeds only in getting her precious younger son shot by the jealous husband. Mrs. Chase went on, however, in her next play, **Mrs. McThing** (1952), to treat the fairy world of witches with somewhat greater success. Here she depicts a never-never-land as it might be imagined in the fantasy of a child, Howay Larue, a poor little rich boy who has all the luxuries except affection, boyhood roughhouse, and companionship. When Howay begins to behave with suspicious perfection, coming in clean and neat, dutifully kissing his mother's guests and refusing candy because it would spoil his dinner, it becomes apparent that a witch, Mrs. McThing, has spirited Howay away and substituted a stick—a child's projection of the impossible ideal mothers would like their children to be. The true Howay turns up at a low dive, the Shantyland Pool Hall, and Mrs. Larue is forced to go there in search of him.

The gang of bad men is also conceived through a child's mind—a mind saturated by comic books and radio programs. The meanest member of the gang goes around looking for an old lady to push under a street car; the cook whimsically refuses to take an order unless he likes the name of the customer; and the boss of the gang is dominated by his old mother who marches in and slaps him for staying out last night. Howay cross-examines his mother to learn if she prefers the stick to him, and decides to stay with the gang. Mrs. Larue becomes a drab scrub woman at the pool hall, while a stick takes her place at home also. The gangsters plot a robbery of the Larue house but are caught by the police, who search them but find no guns, only comic books, Wheatena box tops and bubble gum. Mrs. Larue saves the day by telling the police the boys are her guests, and wins back the good will of the witch by accepting the little girl Howay had wanted to play with. **Mrs. McThing** has amusing moments but is somewhat too heavy a dose of whimsy and witchcraft. If it leaves something to be desired as theatre it is, nonetheless, rewarding in its understanding of the inner logic of the child's world.

With her next play, **Bernardine** (1952), Mrs. Chase steps from the child's world to that of the teen-ager and tries to help the public understand the gang-centered boys, confused, frustrated, sexually eager, who all too often are branded as "juvenile delinquent." They are shown in their native habitat, a back-room of a beer joint, "a world with its own set of rulers, values, dreams, and cockeyed edge to laughter. Here no adult can enter fully—ever." Mrs. Chase captures the strong drive of "belongingness" which motivates boys to seek acceptance by the gang, whose be-bop music, private jargon and talk of sex are rituals of initiation. Mrs. Chase's boys are not vicious, merely keen-minded, imaginative and desperately anxious to express superiority to the adult world in which they are such novices. The leader of the gang, Beau, strives to be blasé, saying of his father, "I barely know the man." Each of the boys has a slogan in terms of a verb—similar to the Stanislavski system of analyzing roles in a play. For one it is "I scheme," for others, "I bull," "I conquer," "I laugh," and for the boy rejected by the gang, "I stink."

The boys also have a creature of wish-fulfillment like Harvey. An objectification of their erotic wants, she is called Bernardine Crudd and is a little older and "beat up looking" but blond, dreamy, and her eyes flash a message. She knows only one word—"yes." The sex-mad member of the gang is Wormy, whose mother is overanxious to be a companion to him. The boys try to get Wormy dates but he is too fast for the girls. He has to be home by ten o'clock, so "Where's the time for technique?" The boys project an ideal world where Bernardine lives, at Sneaky Falls, on the banks of Itching River:

> Up there the mothers have to come to the boys for spending money and permission to leave the house. (Now turns and faces an imaginary mother, placing arms akimbo) So, you say you're going downtown to lunch with women friends and need five bucks? Who are these women? How do I know they're not bums? Go back upstairs. You're not leaving this house and take off that dirty old fox fur.

In search of the mythical Bernardine, Wormy happens upon a stunning blond in a hotel lobby. There is a near-riot in the lobby and they would be arrested but for Beau's glib talking. Wormy ends up in the blond's hotel room, to the envy of the gang. In a hilarious scene, Wormy tries to seduce her but grows frightened when she offers no resistance. The shock of learning that the girl is an old friend of his mother's chills his ardor and he leaves with her gentle reassurance that he will find a nice girl his own age. When he stands up to his mother and announces that he is joining the Navy to escape home, his mother experiences a new emotional awareness, realizing the meaning of their club and their gang outlets. She sees that she had expected and demanded too much of her son:

> Oh, what's the matter with us? Nothing in creation is good enough for you—nothing and no one. We don't want you to live the way we've lived, love the way we've loved, or die the way we'll die. We want the miracle! We want you to walk into the future a brand new way—over a bridge of rainbows.

Wormy finally manages a date with the teen-age girl he admires and the play ends with an epilogue in which the gang leader, now an Air Force flyer, pays tribute to the gang and points out the psychological safety valve which it provided for the boys. It was the gang which understood Wormy better than his own mother and provided him with a steadying force until he could grow to maturity. In *Bernardine,* Mrs. Chase reveals more insight into adolescence than has any other playwright in our theatre today. She dramatizes her insight with the mechanism of projection—the fantasy of imaginary characters and situations that meet the needs of the individual. In spite of its knockabout farce situations, *Bernardine* must not be underestimated as a major contribution to the drama of juvenile psychology. (pp. 356-59)

> *W. David Sievers, "New Freudian Blood," in his* Freud on Broadway: A History of Psychoanalysis and the American Drama, *Hermitage House, 1955, pp. 347-69.*

HARVEY

PRODUCTION REVIEWS

Lewis Nichols   (review date 12 November 1944)

[*In the following review, Nichols finds* Harvey *"one of the delights of the season," concluding that it defies classification.*]

On that somewhat awesome day when the historians get around to poking their grimy fingers into what is the now current theatre they will come on a name which may give them considerable concern. It is Harvey, of course. Historians of the theatre, like historians of everything else, have a meek yearning for tangible facts. Father Day will seem real to them—quite aside from the fact *Life With Father* will be playing the awesome evening in question—and *Strange Interlude* will represent a date, a fact, quite a long fact, as it happens. Harvey is something else again. As they pore over the moldy pages of The Playbill, shared

with their companions, the scholars will be pardoned for muttering to themselves that here was a singular piece of goods. For on Broadway in the autumn of 1944 was an entire play about a rabbit which did not even appear on the cast of characters. Obviously, Harvey will defy classification, although on this sunny side of history the play to which he has given his name does not lack a category. *Harvey* quite simply is one of the delights of the season.

Although it is clear no one could write a comedy about a man and an imaginary rabbit, Mary Chase of Denver has done just that. It is equally obvious that if such a script were arranged no one would produce it. [Producer] Brock Pemberton of Kansas and Times Square has taken the chance and now is reaping the rewards of an affable whirlwind. A few weeks ago it might have been assumed that vaudeville's Frank Fay would prefer lingering death in Shubert Alley to co-starring with a non-existent rabbit six feet one and one half inches tall. Yet Mr. Fay arrives at the Forty-eighth Street Theatre every evening and a couple of afternoons to give amazing performances and bid good-by to vaudeville for years and years. Harvey unquestionably has done things to people, and he will do more as time goes by. Not often does fantasy come so pleasantly to Broadway, and *Harvey* will cheer and move a great many theatregoers before it rings down a final curtain.

Mrs. Chase's play is about a few days in the life of a gentle man named Elwood P. Dowd. Elwood always liked the companionship of the saloons, and one night, while putting a friend in a taxi, he heard a voice calling his name. "I turned and there was this six-foot rabbit learning up against a lamp-post" [Act II, Scene ii]. Elwood was not surprised at either the rabbit or at being correctly addressed for in a small town everyone knows the name of everyone else, but from that time he and Harvey were inseparable companions. The fact that not everyone saw Harvey did not prevent Elwood from introducing him to the neighbors, and after some years of this Elwood's sister thought he should go to a sanitarium, Chumley's Rest. The only trouble was that she, also, saw Harvey occasionally, and so finally did the psychiatrist who set out to examine Elwood. At the end a chance taxidriver casually assures the sister that her brother would be far happier with Harvey than without, so she relents and the family and the rabbit go back home. The precisionists have been bothering their neighbors since the opening to decide whether Elwood is a child of the moon or simply has taken one too many too often. The question remains unimportant; Elwood has Harvey, whatever the cause. And Harvey is quite enough.

Mr. Fay is the perfect player to build Elwood into the charming figure he is. Leisurely and quiet, his voice never rises above a conversational tone, his gestures are calm and reserved. He obviously believes in Harvey and assumes that everyone else will do so. Josephine Hull, who most recently was around town as one of the elderberry wine pourers of [Joseph O. Kesselring's] *Arsenic and Old Lace,* also is excellent as Elwood's sister, who is trying to bring up a marriageable daughter in a household bothered by imaginary rabbits. Mrs. Chase's play is not composed of haphazard gags, but rather offers a warm and gentle humor, which Miss Hull both understands and welcomes. With her wide-eyed, faintly bewildered manner, she can make hilarious such a line as "It's nice to see a room with no one in it but people" [Act III]—Harvey being elsewhere.

Here is the description, as spoken by Elwood, of what he and his friend do to pass the time:

> Harvey and I sit in the bars and we have a drink or two and play the juke box. Soon the faces of the other people turn toward mine and smile. They are saying, "We don't know your name, mister, but you're a lovely fellow." Harvey and I warm ourselves in all those golden moments. We have entered as strangers—soon we have friends. They come over. They sit with us. They drink with us. They talk to us. They tell us about the big, terrible things they have done. The big, wonderful things they will do. Their hopes, their regrets, their loves, their hates. All very large, because nobody ever brings anything small into a bar. Then I introduce them to Harvey and he is bigger and grander than anything they offer me. They get up and leave, but they leave impressed. The same people seldom come back, but that's envy. There's a little bit of envy in the best of us.
>
> [Act II, Scene ii]

Indeed, yes.

Lewis Nichols, "Saga of a Big Rabbit," in The New York Times, *Section 2, November 12, 1944, p. 1.*

Newsweek   (review date 13 November 1944)

[*In the following review,* Harvey *is placed among the few successful Broadway attempts at fantasy. The critic notes that Chase "gives fantasy the lift of subtle humor and charm."*]

Obviously Lewis Carroll took the easy way out when he permitted Alice to see the White Rabbit [in *Alice in Wonderland*]. In Mary Chase's *Harvey,* the new Brock Pemberton comedy about another white rabbit, the animal is not only invisible for all three acts, but, according to Elwood P. Dowd and others who should know, stands exactly 6 feet 1½ inches in his paws. Even if you avoid people and don't drink you're going to hear about Harvey for a long time to come.

Elwood met the rabbit one night after one of his customary sessions in Charlie's place. He was walking home and minding his own business when someone called: "Hello, Elwood." Turning, he saw this abnormally tall rabbit leaning against a lamppost. Elwood wasn't as surprised as you might expect because in a small town everyone knows everyone else's name.

Well, it turned out that the rabbit's name was Harvey. One word led to another, and when Elwood took the rabbit home to live with him, Elwood's sister Veta tried bravely to make the best of it. But then Elwood started introducing Harvey to everyone who came to the house, and somehow the impression got about that Elwood was a little ec-

centric. Veta didn't so much mind Elwood's drinking, but when Harvey seemed likely to ruin the marital chances of her angular daughter, Veta reluctantly decided it was time Uncle Elwood was retired to a nice, homelike sanitarium.

Veta's experience at Chumley's Rest was trying in the extreme, particularly when the fuzzy-brained old lady had to admit that she'd seen Harvey once or twice herself and that he actually was 6 feet 1½. Reasonably enough, a fledgling psychiatrist committed Veta to the institution and sent Elwood off with apologies and a few well-chosen words of commiseration. The final, frenetic chase to get Elwood back where he belongs ended when the famous Dr. Chumley himself had a few quick ones with Harvey at Charlie's place and (no reflection on psychiatrists in general) left the check for the rabbit to pick up.

Every so often Broadway makes a well-intentioned stab at fantasy. The number of successes in any decade can be counted on the fingers of a single, heavy hand. With *Harvey* Miss Chase, a Denver newspaperwoman, gives fantasy the lift of subtle humor and charm. Writing a play about a rabbit is no cinch in the first place; writing a play about a rabbit that is both invisible and somewhat above normal height is a trick that requires more than ordinary skill and understanding. Miss Chase has both. Not that her comedy is perfect, but picking on it is tantamount to quibbling about one of the funniest comedies that has been Broadway's luck in a long time.

However, it's hard to see how she could have reached first fantasy base without the players Pemberton has assembled—notably Josephine Hull and Frank Fay. As sister Veta, Miss Hull, toddling mussed and harried in Harvey's wake and hysterically mistaking white-jacketed psychiatrists for white slavers, is fully as delightful as when she was impersonating the plumper of the two daffy Brewster sisters in [Joseph O. Kesselring's] *Arsenic and Old Lace.* First and last, and for all time, however, *Harvey* is the triumphant pinnacle of Fay's 40-year-old career.

Fay brings to Elwood P. Dowd the superb sense of timing, the droll humor, and ingratiating personality of the only actor who could have made the invisible Harvey and the ineluctable Elwood acceptable to a present-day audience, however literal-minded. If you're the gentle, gregarious sort of person yourself or, alternately, perennially squiffed, Harvey should be looking over your shoulder as you read this. If he isn't, you'd better stand in line outside the 48th Street Theater and hope for the best. (pp. 82-3)

"Harvey the Rabbit," in Newsweek, *Vol. XXIV, No. 20, November 13, 1944, pp. 82-3.*

Kappo Phelan   (review date 17 November 1944)

[*In the excerpt below, Phelan gives a mixed assessment of Chase's* Harvey, *bestowing "a wreath of roses—plus thorns" on both the author and Brock Pemberton, the producer of the Broadway debut. Although he finds the comedy highly amusing, he judges the secondary characters little more than stereotypes and considers it a "serious mistake" to have the rabbit appear to characters off-stage.*]

It is difficult to know whether to lay garlands or a vorpal sword before [producer] Brock Pemberton for having secured the most potentially delicious play of two seasons, [*Harvey*], secured actors capable of a unique performance, and then let the whole thing go through semi-written. I think I will settle for a wreath of roses—plus thorns—to crown his intelligence, since after all, the performance is there and it is unforgettable. But I think Mr. Pemberton and Mary Chase, the author, might have achieved posterity as well as box-office with another careful draft. Harvey is the name of a large busy Rabbit (white), companion to a gentle small-town alcoholic, who lives with his substantial sister and operates from the local bars. His niece, a gangling girl, wishing for some sort of social life, persuades her mother to enlist the help of the nearest psychoanalyst who, with his co-workers, successfully bolloxes everything, only to surrender in the end: the conflict being whether to allow Harvey and his hero to exist as they are; or whether, scientifically, to condemn them to separate realities. It seems important to me as reviewer not to examine too closely the means of the *dénouement;* but as critic, I find myself too truly regretful of the hilarious descent of this human comedy into satire (good), into farce (fair), into confusion (unfair) to be wholly discreet. Where Miss Chase has stumbled, it seems to me, is in allowing the appearance of this extracurricular Rabbit to occur to other movers than the hero, offstage. Not that Harvey must ever be perceptible to the house (the delicate balance here is almost dangerously maintained throughout); but surely we should be present at the Rabbit's conversion of the Doctor in order fully to comprehend the possible parody of the subsequent scenes. This is a serious mistake, I feel, and one complicated by the author's wholesale wandering into exaggeration with her minor characters: a good bit of the motivation of the whole depends upon a sanitorium strong-man impossible of either imagination or fact. This kind of interlocking of farce with fantasy is always wrong, I think. It is a question of suddenly substituting *type* for *character* in order to speed *situation,* and is simply lazy writing. Whole plays can be built in this manner, but the method doesn't ever mix.

But unquestionably no amount of stingy analysis of the play can approximate the production as staged by Antoinette Perry, set by John Root, and principally played by Josephine Hull and Frank Fay. It is, of course, no hyperbole to speak of Miss Hull as the most beloved, round, beaming bundle of vagaries on the street. Here, with her hair *à la* Medusa, another of her sliding satin gowns, still another of her long-stringed handbags, she is adorable, funnier than ever. In the same vein, Frank Fay's portrayal of Elwood P. Dowd, the chosen of Harvey, is a personal triumph. Without once shifting his level affectionate daze, Mr. Fay's gestures, attitudes and quietness are perfect, and he cannot get on or off without prolonged cheers. As the writing of the supplementary characters becomes uncertain, so does the playing suffer, but Jane Van Duser is very good in the part of the Girl, Tom Seidel delivers his neatest job as a young Medic, and exactly as loud and pugnacious as he was planned, Jesse White's Attendant is accurate. An affair which is certain to attract all of the profession as well as the public, my final advice is: when you can get in, go! (pp. 124-25)

Kappo Phelan, "The Stage and Screen," in The Commonweal, *Vol. XLI, No. 5, November 17, 1944, pp. 123-25.*

Joseph Wood Krutch   (review date 18 November 1944)

[*Krutch is widely regarded as one of America's most respected literary and drama critics. Noteworthy among his works are* The American Drama Since 1918 *(1939), which analyzes the most important dramas of the 1920s and 1930s, and* "Modernism" in Modern Drama *(1953), in which he stresses the need for twentieth-century playwrights to infuse their works with traditional humanistic values. A conservative and idealistic thinker, Krutch was a consistent proponent of human dignity and the preeminence of literary art. In the highly favorable review below, Krutch proclaims that Chase's* Harvey *is one of the "miracles which still occasionally occur just when theatergoers have reason to doubt that miracles happen."*]

Even before it opened at the Forty-eighth Street Theater most interested parties already knew that *Harvey* was a play about a man whose best friend is a white rabbit something more than six feet tall. That sounded—and still sounds—like one of those whimsies which delight a few determinedly elfin spirits while generating in most spectators an acute embarrassment, but the fact that *Harvey* has already delighted nearly everyone who has seen it is proof enough that it has unhoped-for qualities. Here is, indeed, one of those miracles which still occasionally occur just when theatergoers have reason to doubt that miracles happen. Here, in other words, is a script so astonishingly fresh in conception and so deft in execution that one is tempted to call it inspired, and here are direction so surefooted and playing so precisely right that one is tempted to call them inspired also. Mary Chase, the author, is—or was—very nearly an unknown. But fortune smiled upon her twice: once when it permitted her to clothe her fantasy in so much unhackneyed wit and humor, so much gaiety and so much tenderness, again when it directed the choice of Frank Fay to impersonate her amiable and touching hero. Not once in a blue moon does it happen that a dramatist realizes his own intention so perfectly, and not once in a moon of even more improbable color does he have also the all but incredible good luck to get for the same play a well-nigh perfect interpretation. Miss Chase, I should guess, is almost scared.

Mr. Fay, as the fortunate friend of the supernatural rabbit, manages somehow to make irresistibly credible the calm happiness, the mellow insanity, and the unshakable amiability of the central character. He is good, one knows, because he is happy but also because his happiness is softened by some memory of a suffering long past, and it is not until near the middle of the play that he clarifies at once both his own character and the theme upon which the whole fantasy is founded by making a quiet remark: "For forty years I struggled with reality; but I am happy to say that I conquered it at last" [Act II, Scene ii]. When that has been said, one realizes that *Harvey* is strong rather than merely whimsical because it is based upon an enduring psychological fact, because there are moments when nearly every man is ready to say with [John] Dryden, "There is a pleasure sure, in being mad, which none but mad men know" [*The Spanish Friar*], or, in our own idiom, "It's great to be crazy."

Let me hasten to add something for the benefit of those few uncompromising souls who will surely rise to protest that traffic with rabbits, real or imaginary, is sheer escapism, and that facing reality is today just what everybody ought to be doing. In the first place, **Harvey** purges the soul. In the second place, it is as much a satire on the realities of the world we have made as it is a defense of those who prefer madness to what, by mere popular vote, has come to be accepted as sanity. Miss Chase, in other words, has given us a sort of Don Quixote in modern dress, and we are about, so I predict, to take him enthusiastically to our bosoms. A man's best friend is not always his dog. Sometimes it is his rabbit. Especially if the rabbit doesn't exist.

Josephine Hull is almost as delightful as Mr. Fay himself in her role of the aunt who talks herself temporarily into the booby hatch while trying to explain why her nephew should be locked up, and the whole play bubbles with sheer—as well as astonishingly unhackneyed—fun. Few surprises on the contemporary stage have ever been more deliriously delightful than that supplied when our hero finally unveils the portrait he has just had painted, and few incidents have been more shrewdly contrived or more quietly meaningful than that of the psychiatrist so overcome by the hypnotic sympathy of the rabbit lover that instead of probing the latter's delusions he goes off into a fantasy of his own involving Akron, Ohio, cool beer, and an unknown siren who will whisper into his ear, "You poor thing, you poor thing." [Act III].

If **Harvey** were less substantial it would probably be unwise to reveal its conclusion, but like all really good plays it loses nothing when we know how it comes out—in this case very satisfactorily indeed. Our hero, because he is too amiable not to try to do whatever will please others, finally consents to the proposal that he be returned to reality by way of the psychiatrist's therapeutic shock treatment. But as the moment approaches, even the members of his family begin to doubt that they would like him any better if he were sane like themselves, and the question is settled finally by the taxi driver who has brought the company to a very efficient sanatorium. This new treatment, so he assures everybody, does really work. In this same cab mad men have driven up and been taken away again with their wits recovered. "He will go into that room for a few minutes. When he comes out he will be a perfectly normal human being—and you know what bastards they are."

> *Joseph Wood Krutch, "Man's Best Friend," in* The Nation, *New York, Vol. 159, No. 21, November 18, 1944, p. 624.*

John Mason Brown   (review date 30 December 1944)

[*Brown, an influential and popular American drama critic during the 1930s, 40s, and 50s, wrote extensively on contemporary British and American theater. He had a thorough knowledge of dramatic history, and his criti-*

From the stage production of Harvey, *starring Frank Fay.*

cism often displays a scholarly erudition in addition to the qualities of popular reviewing. In his review of Harvey, *Mason offers qualified praise of the play, considering it imitative of the works of William Saroyan but conceding that "in wartime, who can complain if oleomargarine is served instead of butter?"*]

There used to be the little man who wasn't there. That was before Mary Chase and Brock Pemberton and Frank Fay had the happy idea of inviting us to read [Charles Jackson's] *The Lost Weekend* in Mr. MacGregor's garden. Now, due to them, lippetty-lippetty (or perhaps more accurately, thumpetty-thumpetty, considering his size) there is the Big Rabbit who isn't there. Or is he?

I raise the question because few characters have been more real of recent seasons than the sizable cottontail who gives **Harvey** its name. He may not actually appear. He is not listed in the cast. His Equity standing may be challengeable. He may be as imaginary as Landor's conversations, and only what a drunk would see who is too pleasant to see pink elephants or snakes. But before the evening is over Harvey does *seem* so real, in a medium where seeming is being, that the soberest drys outfront could swear he existed.

Perhaps the sociologists will someday make much of the fact that, in one of the most terrific of the war years, a novel about a Restoration whore was America's favorite reading, and a comedy about a non-existent rabbit was one of the country's best-loved plays. Perhaps they will even try to establish a connection between the two. If they don't, the psychoanalysts undoubtedly will. In these matters they are apt to be more successful than the historians. Such relationships are not only meat unrationed to the psychoanalysts; but a subject upon which they are glad to mobilize their points.

I mention psychoanalysts because in *Harvey* we are asked to laugh at them as heartily as we do at the imaginary bunny. Of all invitations this is one of the easiest to accept. Its R.S.V.P. is printed in Neon rather than headlines. Because, though they have their place and unquestionably do a needed job well, psychoanalysts, like penguins, pandas, and Joe E. Brown's face, can be just naturally funny. Although they are not nearly as cute as rabbits, they are about as common, have much longer ears, and are not apt to be interested in carrots except when they are raw.

Why are they funny? Not because they don't fill a necessary place, but because they take themselves as seriously as they are taken by the hundred neediest cases among their patients. Why are they funny, when manifestly the mind is worthy of treatment like the body? Because so many of them are anxious to find soot on the cleanest snow. Because emotionally the only infinitives they appear to respect are split. Because the sole twine they tend to recognize is the umbilicus. Because to them everything is apt to be suspect, nothing innocent, all childhood soiled, and adulthood merely the dirty linen of the nursery. Why are they funny? Because so often they seem anxious to make every simple thing complex and to convert every heathy response into an abnormal one.

Let us eavesdrop, for example, on what two Army psychiatrists (which, I admit, is raising the ante) say in all seriousness when, in a recent and in most respects very worthwhile book about the soldier's conversion to civilian life, they try to explain the releases war offers to combatants.

> Battle provides an easy occasion for sundry displacements of hostility and killing in effigy. Hostility, originating in parental or marital conflict, for example, can be shifted on to the enemy and his destruction may symbolize vicarious revenge on wife or parents.

Even *Harvey,* which is very funny, has few laughs to offer which are bigger than that. Certainly the laughs in *Harvey* are franker. Simpler too. Because Miss Chase's is the kind of comedy which is usually described as "unpretentious." This is an adjective meaning only that a pattern which might have been cut in satin has been made up in calico. In this case, however, the calico is more than serviceable.

Harvey has its [William] Saroyan aspects. Its little sermon to the effect that a man nowadays must be either bright or good is advanced in the goofy, giddy, happily cockeyed, and boozy terms upon which Saroyan is generally considered to have taken out a copyright. In the form of its unseen rabbit, too, it makes the same plea for a man's need of his illusions that Mr. Saroyan made with his unseen mice in *The Beautiful People*. But the Saroyan here is cut; diluted for palates not quite ready to take their Saroyan straight.

Once upon a time when he was toying with the idea of being a dramatic critic, Thornton Wilder described a comedy by Philip Barry by saying its lines were of that "bookish sort which people who do not read Charles Lamb imagine to be like him." In the same way *Harvey* is less the real Saroyan than it is vaudeville's idea of him. It lacks his final poignancy, his gift of sudden and deep revelation, and his ultimate magic. But in wartime who can complain if oleomargarine is served instead of butter? In any case, audiences that might be allergic to Saroyan are delighted to accept *Harvey.*

If its individual lines are less uproarious than one might expect and its situations are worked overtime to secure their laughs, it is nonetheless a script that has joy in its heart.

Although one of the season's outstanding successes, and deservedly so, Mr. Pemberton has cast the secondary characters in *Harvey* as if he had been uncertain about the play's run. They seem to have been chosen in much the same way that you choose anything but your best clothes for a walk in the country on a day that may be rainy. They appear to have been selected unconfidently, and act with an expertness more acceptable in a stock company than in a Broadway hit.

But one puts up with them, indeed forgets them, as readily as the wrapping paper on a present is forgotten, because of Josephine Hull's presence in the cast, and because of Mr. Pemberton's inspired choice of Frank Fay as her brother, the dipsomaniac whose best friend is a nonexistent six-foot rabbit.

Miss Hull is one of the country's most lovable and irresistible performers. She may have been Helen Hokinson's model. She could be one of Mrs. Malaprop's [in Richard Brinsley Sheridan's *The Rivals*] lineal descendants. But certainly she must be the comic muse's stand-in at Lane Bryant's. When she waddles into a comedy, she brings not only laughter but surety with her.

As for Mr. Fay, all the skill he possesses as a veteran vaudevillian shines through his performance. Only once does he forget his fellow players and appear to be doing an act by himself at the Palace. This is when he settles down in the second act to ventilate some rather mediocre Saroyan. The rest of the time, however, he plays brilliantly, as an individual and with those near him. His speech is a perfect example of understatement; of points seemingly thrown away, but unfailing in their timing. His voice is used languorously, with a deceptive sense of weariness, almost of resignation and boredom. But its negative tones are among his most positive weapons.

Mr. Fay succeeds in doing wonderful things with his eyes. He uses them sparingly, so that their every measured rotation or sudden brightening is filled with innuendo. Indeed, we not only see Mr. Fay's eyes, but we see what he sees with them.

This is where Harvey, the rabbit, comes thumping in. He becomes for us as genuine a character as he is to Mr. Fay. In no time Mr. Fay establishes his size, indicates his whereabouts, and persuades us that he is truly occupying the vacant chair in which he is supposed to be sitting. Mr. Fay outdoes the usual magician, because the rabbit he produces is pulled out of our hats no less than his. By the evening's end the only way we know that Harvey is not real is because there still remains only one of him. (pp. 10-11)

John Mason Brown, "Out of the Hat," in The Saturday Review of Literature, *Vol. XXVII, No. 53, December 30, 1944, pp. 10-11.*

Rosamond Gilder   (review date January 1945)

[*In the excerpt below, Gilder argues against those attempting to find a profound meaning in* Harvey, *asserting that Chase's play is simply "an evening's pleasant entertainment."*]

If quantity means anything in the theatre, then 1945 should prove auspicious. Broadway has reached the saturation point; every theatre is filled, every box-office running over. The mildest success turns overnight into the maddest triumph. Among those who are foolish enough to care about the quality of the merchandise so lavishly displayed along the Rialto there is less cause for rejoicing. Broadway, suffering from a lack of theatres to house its hits, suffers also paradoxically enough from a singular lack of talents to make those hits important events in the theatre. Yet in spite of a prevalent mediocrity, Broadway has its moments. In the middle of blare and confusion of high pressure production and raucous salesmanship, it can produce as fresh and beguiling a musical as [Rogers and Hammerstein's] *Oklahoma!*, as sensitive and expert a comedy as [John van Druten's] *The Voice of the Turtle* or as humorous and kindly a folk tale as [van Druten's] *I Remember Mama*. It can even be successfully whimsical, as in the creation of Broadway's own peculiar ha'nt, *Harvey.*

For Christmas and New Year's Eve consumption *Harvey* comes first among the mid-season's offerings. Mary Chase dreamed him up, Brock Pemberton escorted him to Broadway, but it is Frank Fay as Elwood P. Dowd in person who evokes his all-but-visible presence on the stage. . . . If you don't see him, lay it to the fact that you are not in the proper holiday mood. Josephine Hull, who plays Elwood's sister, has become so accustomed to having Harvey around the house that she does occasionally see him herself. Of course we must grant that Mrs. Hull is not an entirely trustworthy witness. She has been mixed up for years past in a confusion known as *Arsenic and Old Lace* [by Joseph O. Kesselring]. A lady who poisoned off elderly gentlemen for the kindly purpose of providing them with a decent funeral would have no trouble in discerning a rabbit in someone else's mind's eye. The exact status of Harvey, (who, by the way is a Pooka, which of course explains everything, like the Snark being a Boojum [in Lewis Carroll's *The Hunting of the Snark*]), is left ultimately to the decision of the audience. Mrs. Chase merely presents an episode from the life of that amiable tippler, Elwood Dowd, at a moment when his sister Veta decides that the presence of Harvey is interfering with the matrimonial chances of her daughter Myrtle Mae. Veta's attempts to have Elwood incarcerated in Chumley's Rest form the matter, if any, of an evening's pleasant entertain-

ment. The moral, should anyone misguidedly insist on seeking one, lies in a general plea for kindliness. For Harvey, besides being the tallest of rabbits, is also the best of companions because he is the most understanding, tolerant and wise of creatures.

Mrs. Chase's odd combination of pixy imagination and Broadway hokum derives most of its charm from the performance of Frank Fay who steps from vaudeville to the legitimate stage in a role made for him in an actor's heaven. As Elwood P. Dowd he can make effective use of every asset at his command; his odd personality, dreamy, detached, gently-pathetic, his expert technique trained by years of exercise on the vaudeville stage, his actor qualities of impersonation and projection. None of our comedians, except Victor Moore, can so nicely combine wit and pathos. He is master of understatement; past master of the gentle art of evocation. By a murmured word, a pause, a gesture, a mere glance of the eye, he can convey a fund of meaning—usually, in his vaudeville days, of double meaning. In this play, he can even convey a tall white rabbit. Antoinette Perry has directed *Harvey* skilfully, allowing Mr. Fay latitude for his own individual methods. Since Elwood's absorption in the companionship of Harvey allows Mr. Fay to do most of his acting when technically alone on the stage—Harvey being of course invisible to the audience's duller senses—the one-man quality of his performance is entirely in keeping. He wanders, bemused, through the crude doings of the real world around him, courteous, abstracted, irresponsible, kindly.

Josephine Hull gives him superb support. They are both denizens of the same mad-hatter castle, but whereas you can accept Frank Fay as a dreamer of dreams, a seer of strange sights, Mrs. Hull is superbly concrete. Her rotund figure—which is a delight in itself—her hats, her handbags, the disordered flurry in which she lives are not matters of vision. She arrives at her mad conclusions by the piecemeal practicality of her mind. In each section it makes sense, fitted together it spells confusion thrice confounded. As a middle-aged, middle-western mother, contending with a daft brother, a homely daughter and the staff of a disorganized insane asylum, Mrs. Hull adds another character to her repertory of Hokinson-cum-Bedlam ladies, a list which includes the unforgettable mother in [Moss Hart and George S. Kaufman's] *You Can't Take It With You* and Aunt Abby in *Arsenic and Old Lace*. (pp. 5-6, 9)

Rosamond Gilder, "Holiday Goods: Broadway in Review," in Theatre Arts, *Vol. XXIX, No. 1, January, 1945, pp. 5-16.*

George Jean Nathan   (review date 1945)

[*Nathan has been called the most learned and influential drama critic the United States has yet produced. During the early decades of the twentieth century, he was greatly responsible for shifting the emphasis of the American theater from light entertainment to serious drama and for introducing audiences and producers to the work of Eugene O'Neill, Henrik Ibsen, and Bernard Shaw, among others. Nathan was a contributing editor to H. L. Mencken's magazine the* American Mercury *and coeditor of the* Smart Set. *With Mencken, Nathan belonged to an iconoclastic school of American critics who attacked the vulgarity of accepted ideas and sought to bring a new level of sophistication to American culture, which they found provincial and backward. In the review of* Harvey *below, Nathan observes several weaknesses in the work but nevertheless claims that "Miss Chase's play . . . constitutes a generally delightful theatrical evening."]*

Some thirty-odd years ago H. L. Mencken composed a philosophy to the effect that the Creator had overlooked an idea in not surcharging the atmosphere about us with ethyl alcohol. Had He done so, pondered Mencken, the world would be infinitely happier and more contented than it is or has been; its inhabitants, breathing in the salubrious air, would be constantly maintained in a glowing, expansive, and beneficent state; peace and good will would reign on earth; and heroes would be born, in their own grandiose estimation, by the hour. Much this same philosophy is the core of Miss Chase's play [**Harvey**], which, for all its several lapses, constitutes a generally delightful theatrical evening.

A mixture of fantasy, comedy and farce, that evening concerns a gentleman given to spirituous liquors who, while in a blissful condition, meets up in alcoholic fancy with a rabbit six feet one and one-half inches tall and who enjoys him thereafter as a steady, understanding, and sympathetic companion. So enviable a companion is the rabbit, indeed, that others who have been wont to look askance at the cupful gentleman engage him as well, and find him all that his first discoverer has found him. The latter's family, however, like most unthinking families, presently deem it expedient that their blood-brother rid himself of the beast and to that end have him consigned to a sanitarium. But just as he is about to receive the treatment that will banish the rabbit forevermore they acquire wisdom from a passing taxi driver long versed in the way of humans—the wisdom, to wit, that teetotalers and other such theoretically normal fowl are quarrelsome, grasping, querulous, and miserable—and decide to allow their blood-brother to go on being as kindly, generous, happy, and sans souci as he has been.

As you may gather, what you have here is an extended paraphrase of the familiar skit in the burlesque shows wherein the inebriated low comedian is told that he is sitting opposite a great big beautiful luscious blonde and drinking champagne wine and wherein he thereupon for the next fifteen minutes accepts the delusion as fact and has himself a wonderful time, embroidered with the [Luigi] Pirandello and [John Millington] Synge (*The Well Of The Saints*) theory of the superiority of illusion to reality. In short, what the play dramaturgically is is the character of Joe, the gentle alcoholic out of [William] Saroyan's *The Time Of Your Life,* provided with a rabbit variation of the burlesque blonde. But Miss Chase has added so much of her own and has played over the whole a fantasy at once so paradoxically realistic and basically so in keeping with life that her exhibit, despite an overly long induction and a third act that suffers a bad twelve-minute let-down, amounts in sum to excellent entertainment. Saroyan might on the whole have written a critically much

better play on the theme, one touched with considerably more poetic imagination than Miss Chase's, but, in Saroyan's absence, Miss Chase's will do, and very nicely. What is more, nine people out of every ten (and that includes certain of the professional reviewers) have liked and will like it better than what Saroyan might have made of it. Which is the American theatre's reward, in a manner of speaking, for keeping fancy closer to ground.

Some of Miss Chase's humor is exceptionally fertile. Her account of the barfly's first meeting with Harvey, which is the rabbit's name, after he had solicitously put a brother tosspot to bed is an example. "I saw him leaning against a lamp post when I came out and he called me by name," the lush tells an inquiring psychiatrist. "Didn't you think that rather peculiar?" asks the latter, significantly narrowing his eyes. "No," easily replies Elwood P. Dowd, the lush; "you know how it is in a small town; everybody knows everybody else" [Act II, Scene ii].

Harvey, according to Elwood, has some extraordinary virtues. He can stop clocks and you can go wherever you wish and do anything you please and when you come back you find that not so much as one minute has passed. And he does away with time and space and is better than Einstein, for he does away with time and space—and objections.

In the leading role, Frank Fay, the old vaudeville headliner, is capital. His drunk is not the more usual actor drunk who moves unsteadily about the stage or accompanies his speech with an obbligato of hiccups or engages in any other such ritualistic business, but one in whom a sincere absorption of alcohol has left only a benign fogginess and whose phsyical deportment and locutions are not materially different from those of the average abstemious member of society. Fay underplays as any long experienced lush always underplays, whereas the usual stage lush overplays like an amateur affected by two drinks. And as his sister who, though deeply concerned about him on one occasion also sees Harvey, Josephine Hull is an admirable comic foil.

Mr. Pemberton's physical production, designed by John Root, looks, however, as if it cost all of ten dollars. (pp. 133-35)

George Jean Nathan, "The Year's Productions: 'Harvey'," in his The Theatre Book of the Year, 1944-1945: A Record and and Interpretation, *Alfred A. Knopf, 1945, pp. 133-35.*

Wolcott Gibbs (review date 26 July 1947)

[An American drama critic, editor, journalist, and fiction writer, Gibbs was closely associated with the New Yorker *throughout his career. He was an iconoclastic critic whose ironic reviews pilloried bad plays in general and ineptly sincere portrayals of social problems in particular. Gibbs is widely known for the eloquence of his sardonic appraisals (it has been said that he wrote more brilliantly of bad plays than of good ones) and is considered a master parodist on the order of Max Beerbohm. In the following excerpt, Gibbs contrasts Frank Fay's*

original performance of Elwood P. Dowd in Harvey *with that of James Stewart, who succeeded him in the role, finding that "the rabbit himself seems to take on an entirely new character with a new man playing opposite him."*]

The leading visible character in **Harvey** is a hard problem for an actor, and it is not especially surprising that James Stewart wasn't quite successful with it when he replaced Frank Fay last week. On the surface, Elwood P. Dowd is supposed to be the gentlest of men—a good drunk, chiefly distinguished by his delusion about that enormous rabbit and his nice, boozy affection for all the world. It is an engaging conception, but dangerously close to the kind of whimsey that disfigures so much British humor and even occasionally afflicts practitioners of our own. The ideal performance (Mr. Fay's) produces Elwood as described above, but it also has a hard core of something really ribald, disreputable, and unbalanced underneath. It is all right to love Elwood, but you should also feel that, like almost any drunk, he is watchful, sardonic, and capable of sudden, dark changes. Mr. Fay was able to supply this corrective acidity because, as an old vaudevillian, he is the master of a thousand faintly shady acting tricks that somehow managed to cast some doubt on the perfect sweetness of Elwood's nature, and also because the years have given him a rather rakish and damaged air, which was often strikingly at variance with his tender, lofty lines. Mr. Fay got Elwood's fuzzy benevolence very affectingly, but he made it a good deal funnier by subtly conveying that there was a tough, experienced souse somewhere in the background.

Mr. Stewart, on the other hand, is almost all boyish appeal. He is charming where his predecessor was strange, tentative where he seemed incisive, and simply drunk where he gave a much more difficult effect of total and permanent saturation. His performance, unrelieved by any suggestion that Elwood has his sinister side, has a certain innocent monotony about it, and I have an idea that it subtracts a good deal from the original quality of the play. It is a curious thing, but the rabbit himself seems to take on an entirely new character with a new man playing opposite him. It was easy to think of Mr. Fay's shadowy companion as a rather loud, hard-boiled type, the hero of some pretty rough parties down along the waterfront. Mr. Stewart's is more apt to appear to you huge, soft, and whimsical, right out of [Lewis Carrol's] *Alice in Wonderland.* As a warmup for the projected appearance of Mr. Dowd in the moving pictures, where humor, generally speaking, is also kept rather big and soft, Mr. Stewart's interpretation is probably very sound. On the stage, however, it is a little disappointing, especially when placed in direct comparison with such acting as that displayed by Josephine Hull. There, now, is a great woman. (pp. 40, 42)

> *Wolcott Gibbs, "Old Rip, New Rabbit," in* The New Yorker, *Vol. XXIII, No. 23, July 26, 1947, pp. 40, 42.*

The Times (London)   (review date 6 January 1949)

[*In the following review, the critic compares* Harvey *with*

Noël Coward's Blithe Spirit *(1941) and Joseph O. Kesselring's* Arsenic and Old Lace *(1941), finding that although* Harvey *is enjoyable, it is inferior to the others because it has "no clear comic idea."*]

America, having taught us that murder by ladies wearing old lace and using arsenic may be wildly funny, now invites us to regard dipsomania as a joke; and, to judge from the laughter last night, we shall be willing enough to learn another lesson.

Yet the play, however instructive, is inferior to [Joseph O. Kesselring's] *Arsenic and Old Lace* and to [Noel Coward's] *Blithe Spirit,* other plays in its own kind. It has no clear comic idea. [Charles] Lamb once comforted himself with the reflection that if on his ignominious passage home from a party he thought two and two made five he had done no harm to the eternal verities. They would have the last word on the matter. But the alcoholic's delusion that he is usually accompanied by a white rabbit six feet high is of a nature to threaten the verities, for not only he sees it but his sister supposes that she has seen it on at least one occasion and the rabbit in the end pursues the psychiatrist. The audience itself almost sees Harvey; doors open and close of their own accord as he passes. The roughness of the central idea helps to produce easy laughter; but the mind slowly ceases to be entertained. All is well while the alcoholic reads "Pride and Prejudice" to Harvey and, like the husband in *Blithe Spirit,* appears to be exchanging genial confidences with him over the shoulders of real people, and while we hear that he always pays for the white rabbit's imaginary drinks and buys railway tickets for him when they travel together. But his sister, driven beyond endurance, tries to get him locked up in a home, and in order that the psychiatrists may lock her up instead (an extremely funny scene played deliciously by Miss Athene Seyler) she has to admit having herself seen Harvey. It is from this point that the comic idea begins to lose its clearness of outline, and long before the rather tedious last few scenes the comedy is lamely supporting itself with the crutch of auto-suggestion.

Mr. Sid Field, putting immense restraint on himself, succeeds in giving the alcoholic that sense of simple happiness on which the part depends. When he smiles at Harvey it is with a smile of complete understanding, and Harvey, we do not for a moment doubt, smiles back with equal contentment. It is a good performance given against the grain of temperament. There are occasional flaws: they are caused by the spry, self-confident comedian breaking irrelevantly into the character. Miss Seyler is never out of character. She squeezes all possible fun out of all its phases—that of the perpetually distraught hostess, that of the sister so embarrassed by the need to prove her brother a detainable alcoholic that she is herself detained, or that of the woman whose injured vanity after her release from the padded cell smarts more shrewdly than her shattered dignity. Mr. Ernest Hare and Mr. Jeremy Hawk are amusingly professional as the blundering psychiatrists.

> *A review of "Harvey," in* The Times, *London, January 6, 1949, p. 6.*

J. C. Trewin　(review date 29 January 1949)

[Trewin is a British drama critic, editor, and author whose reviews have appeared in the Observer, *the* Illustrated London News, *the* Sketch, *the* Birmingham Post, *the* Listener *and the* Times Literary Supplement. *In addition, he has written numerous theatrical biographies and dramatic studies, including* The English Theatre *(1948),* Stratford-upon-Avon *(1950),* Mr. Macready: A Nineteenth-Century Tragedian *(1955),* Shakespeare on the English Stage: 1900-1964 *(1964),* Shakespeare's Plays Today *(with Arthur Colby Sprague, 1970), and* Peter Brook: A Biography *(1971). In the excerpt below from a review of the London debut of* Harvey, *Trewin deems Chase's play "some of the strangest moonshine that has glimmered on the stage."]*

I suppose every child now and then has wanted to be invisible, or at least to have the gift of making himself invisible at will. Obviously no device is of more help to a nursery-tale. Once this power is accepted you can whisk people in and out of keyholes and defy every problem of plotting. It is a pleasant confidence-trick, aided usually by the wishful thinking of the reader. On the stage it becomes less easy. Sometimes, when a Puck or Oberon [in Shakespeare's *A Midsummer Night's Dream*] has declared himself invisible, we have wished that this too, too solid flesh would melt. Even so, it is surprising what resolution will do. We can bring ourselves to accept most things. Did not the White Queen [in Lewis Carroll's *Through the Looking Glass*] say that, on occasion, she had believed in as many as six impossible things before breakfast?

Naturally, the cinema or television can manage this better than the theatre. Wells's Invisible Man can have his hour on the screen when he would be impossible on the stage. And yet the stage has now produced a play, in which the title-figure is invisible, that goes as well, I imagine, as it could ever do in the cinema. This is *Harvey,* the fantastic farce at the Prince of Wales. There is no question here of any anxious resolution, of assuming that the portentous fellow at the back of the stage is so much thin air. Harvey is never visible, for though his friend, Elwood P. Dowd, claims to see him constantly, he is no more than a flicker of the imagination. Naughtily, the author has complicated things towards the end of the second act, when she allows doors to open and close, apparently of themselves, as the invisible Harvey makes progress through them. But this is just a whimsical trimming. Harvey, whom we see so clearly in the mind, can exist only in the mind. He is one of the impossible things we are to believe after dinner. He is, indeed, a white rabbit 6 ft. 1½ ins. in height.

We have had curious tanglewood farces from America. But this is, I think, one of the oddest of them all. Mary Chase's principal character is the dipsomaniac, Elwood P. Dowd, who in his town in the Far West is usually to be found down at Charley's Place, forever genial, courteous and sociable, and holding debate with "th' incorporal air." He would deny this: he is, he says, talking to his friend Harvey, and he assumes as a matter of course that everyone can see Harvey as well, one of the most agreeable and well-informed of rabbits. The fellow was leaning against a lamppost on the night Elwood met him first, and Elwood was not at all surprised to be addressed by name: every-

body knows everybody else in these small Western towns. Now here they are, two friends, visible and invisible, almost inseparable companions. We do not see them together at Charley's Place, but we do see Elwood arranging a chair for Harvey, we watch him beckoning and beaming to the empty air, and we see the friends settling down together—one of the friends at least: the other is understood—while Elwood prepares to read aloud the first chapter of *Pride and Prejudice*.

This, undeniably, is some of the strangest moonshine that has glimmered on the stage. The author must have caught her breath when she thought of the idea, and it is a pity that she has not been able to make more of it than a scrambling farce. But the play is quite inoffensive, and Sid Field's performance, one of much charm and control, should endear Elwood Dowd to everyone. He may be remembered when the play itself is just a name in the records.

We have never seen Field before in a "straight" part—that is, always assuming that Elwood can be described as "straight," which is arguable—and he now carries off the business with marked enjoyment. People who dislike the conventional stage drunk scene, with its reeling and writhing and fainting in coils, can go fearlessly to the Prince of Wales. Elwood Dowd remains creamily calm, a kindly bachelor uncle of a man. His eye is a trifle glazed, his walk at once airy and unnaturally precise: that, apart from his acquaintance with Harvey, is all. There is no room, of course, for the artful dodging of Field's Slasher Green, the gibbering of his golfer, the genteel frenzy of his cinema organist: the old Field leaps out only once or twice, like a jack-in-the-box. He is a master of mime, and his admirers will know how much he can put into these eyebrow-jerking, half-smiling, mouth-pursing, silent talks with his devoted and invisible Harvey. Who can wonder that as time passes we, too, catch ourselves "seeing" Harvey and glancing around in guilt? Others in the cast have little to do but dance attendance. Athene Seyler, who could wring farce from the five-times table, charges about delightfully; Ernest Hare booms icily as a psychiatrist in difficulties; and one day we shall hear more of Rosaline Haddon, now with only the dimmest of parts.

No other dramatist of late has tested the problems of invisibility. True, Tinker Bell—played this year by a Miss Jane Wren (promoted from Jenny)—has whisked over the stage of the Scala; and not long ago there was a television revival of [Nöel Coward's] *Blithe Spirit,* with its gay ghost of Elvira, life-and-soul of the realms beyond Styx. But in the West End theatre Harvey—who, I believe, would be called by specialists a "pooka"—holds the stage untroubled.

It was odd that the week that brought *Harvey* should also have produced another fantasy, the Arts Theatre Club revival of Sydney Grundy's *A Pair of Spectacles*. . . .

For the rest, the London stage is deficient in fantasy just now, unless it is the undeclared brand of those farces that pretend with a straight face not to go outside the bounds of the probable and reasonable. Yet, when you examine them, such inventions as, say, *The Happiest Days of Your Life* and *One Wild Oat* are fantastic from beginning to end. Doubtless, the matter-of-fact, no-nonsense playgoer who enjoys them, and who would run miles from fantasy self-confessed, would be horrified to find he had actually been enjoying a complicated game of make-believe. Even so, I think this playgoer will enjoy *Harvey,* for all the dangers of its invisible rabbit. Sid Field has only to lift his finger or crease his face in that sideways smile, and the house—with gratitude—surrenders.

> *J. C. Trewin, "Into Thin Air," in* The Illustrated London News, *Vol. 214, No. 5728, January 29, 1949, p. 152.*

Clive Barnes   (review date 25 February 1970)

[*A British-born American drama and dance critic, Barnes has been called "the first, second and third most powerful critic in New York." He has refrained from wielding his influence, however, and has adopted an informal, conversational writing style in his reviews. Barnes insists that criticism of the arts is a public service; therefore, the function of a reviewer is to advise and inform audiences rather than determine a production's success or failure. As a result, Barnes has also earned the reputation of being "the easiest critic to please." His commentary has appeared regularly in the* New York Times *and the* New York Post. *In the following review, Barnes praises the Broadway revival of* Harvey, *claiming that it "restores . . . a sense of innocence to the American theater."*]

The Phoenix Theater's production of *Harvey,* in a carefully studied re-staging by Stephen Porter, restores James Stewart and a sense of innocence to the American theater. It also gave a certain glamour to the first-night audience, for the ANTA [American National Theater and Academy] Theater last night seemed studded with stars of stage and screen—all of them vintage and some of them of good years.

First for the innocence. It is there right at the beginning, when Miss Chase can open her play with the ringing of a telephone. Any playwright foolhardy enough to do that in these sophisticated times would have half of my critical colleagues deciding the play was already a wrong number and stalking homeward up the aisle.

Imagine a play where not only the unseen, eponymous hero is a white rabbit, 6 feet 2½ inches tall in his paws, but also when the most unseemly word used all evening is seven letters long and could almost—possibly even almost-almost—be used in these seemly pages. Those, gentlemen, were the days. Ah, nostalgia!

Harvey is a darling, cuddly play, meaning nothing but a desire for fantasy in a hard world, no bad thing when *Harvey* was new in 1944. Come to think of it, no bad thing in 1970.

I believe I am right in saying that Mr. Stewart's last stage appearance in our town was also in *Harvey,* when, some quarter of a century ago, he took over as Elwood P. Dowd from the role's originator, Frank Faye. Later, Mr. Stewart played the part in the movie version. Welcome back—even Harvey thanks you.

The charm of Miss Chase's play is not only its sense of fantasy but also in its alert and consistent evocation of the ridiculous. The jokes all flow from Elmer, the most lovable lush ever to lush, who with grave dignity persuades the world that his rabbit is real. Elmer's unfailing faith in Harvey, together with the grave courtesy and unaffected friendliness with which he treats a potentially hostile world, is not only amusing but it also has a beauty to it.

Many actors have played Elmer with love—I personally remember only the great English comedian, the late Sid Field—and you can see why. It is just a great part because it stands for something serious—it stands for all the grown-ups who, like Tinkerbell, want to believe in fairies.

It is difficult to criticize Mr. Stewart's performance—and this is not merely because any adverse comment would presumably have me answering to the Committee on Un-American Activities. The real difficulty is that like many stars of the silver screen returning to the legitimate world, his facial movements are so small that they can easily pass unnoticed. At times you wonder whether he might have dropped off to sleep behind his makeup, but no, that old lovable and familiar growl of voice goes comfortably on.

Mr. Stewart's acting is not so much deadpan as slow-dying-pan, yet as Elmer, his garrulous, gentle, genial presence is a delight. You feel that apart from Harvey himself there is no one that you would rather encounter in your favorite neighborhood bar. However, I did feel—and here Mr. Porter must share responsibility—that the physical impact of the invisible Harvey was never felt. We have now seen Marcel Marceau do miracles in persuading us with mime the reality of an unseen world. If we were looking for a similar miracle from Mr. Stewart and Mr. Porter we would have been disappointed.

Equally as delightful and as charismatic as Mr. Stewart was Helen Hayes. Miss Hayes plays Elmer's sister and wins by a comfortable margin. She epitomizes flustered charm almost as if it were a style of acting—and in her hands, in her face and in her public, it, of course is. She is one of those actors—Laurence Olivier is another, for she keeps the grandest company—where to watch how she is doing something is almost as pleasurable as what she is doing. Her technique is so close to the surface of her acting that it gives it a special blush.

She makes a particularly neat partnership with Mr. Stewart—he ruggedly and rangily immobile and she prancing all around him like a bantam champion looking for a knockout blow. It added to the fun.

Mr. Porter has great style in these revivals, whether they are from the twenties, thirties or forties. He places them in period and yet also makes them live. He knows very well when to let an actor have his head, but also obtains excellent secondary performances. Here, for example, we have most stylish portrayals from Henderson Forsythe as a beleaguered psychiatrist and Peggy Pope as his slightly blowsy wife, and it was a pleasure to note that the authoritative Jesse White as the medical orderly was repeating the role he created in the original production.

At the end there were many, many cheers—most I suppose for Miss Hayes and her new leading man. Yet I hope just a few were for Mary Chase and the restoration of innocence. Mind you, innocence does sometimes pay. Miss Chase was awfully lucky to have won that Pulitzer in the year of *The Glass Menagerie*. Oh well, that's show business.

Clive Barnes, *"Unseen White Rabbit Returns,"* in The New York Times, *February 25, 1970, p. 41.*

Walter Kerr   (review date 1970)

[*Kerr is a Pulitzer Prize-winning American drama critic, essayist, and playwright. Throughout his career, he has written theater reviews for such publications as the* Commonweal, *the* New York Herald Tribune, *and the* New York Times. *In the following review of the 1970 New York revival of* Harvey, *Kerr examines Chase's extraordinary ability to make the invisible six-foot tall rabbit "the production's third fixed star," along with Elwood and his sister Veta.*]

Never mind marijuana. Should Harvey be legalized? In the twenty-eight years since Mary Chase wrote **Harvey** some men have been to the moon, some men have been to psychiatrists, and all men, wherever they've been, have had their knowledge increased, their frontiers expanded, their inhibitions freed. But that rabbit is still around.

It's been good to see him again. And don't think we weren't seeing him. In the delicate, respectful, hilarious, and finally very moving revival of the play at the Anta, it was actually Helen Hayes who saw him first. I know Harvey wasn't supposed to come on until Jimmy Stewart brought him on (it said James Stewart on the program, but the audience was thinking Jimmy and I'm going to leave it at that), gently urging his large white friend through a doorway.

But Miss Hayes happened to appear first, conducting a Wednesday Afternoon Forum in her home (which she described to a newspaper reporter as "festooned with smilax" [Act I, Scene i]), seriously taking thought for a moment to consider whether or not some of her elderly guests might in fact be dead, and hoping against hope that her brother would not arrive with his embarrassing companion until after the neighbors had all gone home.

The thing was, right off, that Miss Hayes was embarrassed not because her brother drank or because he tended to introduce people to his invisible friend. It was the *rabbit* that embarrassed her, his size, his silence, the space he occu-

From the movie Harvey, *starring James Stewart.*

pied, his tenacity, his being or not being there when you didn't know whether he was or not. Harvey rattled this lady because he was real, and that's what Miss Hayes was communicating—fearful eyes darting, fourth and fifth fingers flexing in her outstretched, warding-off hand—all the while she was denying his existence and worrying for her brother's sanity and pretending to all the world that pookas didn't come to parties. Miss Hayes's denial described; her protestations made pictures as incontrovertible as photographs; her alarums had the force of a footman's loudly announcing that Harvey was descending the royal staircase. Miss Hayes brought him to life backwards.

Then, having made the invisible visible simply by looking over her shoulder too often, the actress gave way for a moment and Mr. Stewart took over. For a few minutes now the rabbit was just a bit less real, because he was supposed to be there. Mr. Stewart had to make room for him to waddle past obtrusive chairs (chairs are never that obtrusive, we were being a shade less honest here), he had to urge him to sit, offer him a drink, ask if he was comfortable. Mr. Stewart, shaggier than ever before now that age had tucked in his chins and untidied his hair, was doing all of this very nicely, mind you. But a pooka, it seems, exerts more displacement when he is being doubted than when he is being catered to; looking at him in an empty chair we had to squint harder than when we knew he was waiting just outside the door.

In not too long a time, though—there was a scuffle in a mental home to which Miss Hayes was vainly trying to have Mr. Stewart committed—Harvey, the real Harvey, got lost. He had left his coat and hat behind (the hat made allowance for his alert and rather long ears), but no one knew which local bar he might have wandered off to or why no one could lay eyes on him just now. It was at this point in the play that he joined the cast of characters irrevocably and forever, thick as a church door, heavier than night air, sound as a bell. In everyone's anxiety to find him in order to get rid of him, he became eternally present, the production's third fixed star.

It is necessary to stress the brilliance with which this feat had been accomplished. No one wants to talk about popular comedies, or immensely successful comedies, or comedies so familiar that you feel you could flick them off your overcoat like cigarette ash, as being in any way brilliant. They're just good hack work, aren't they? Lucky strikes, triumphant tricks? ***Harvey,*** my friends, is no trick. As hack work, it wouldn't even be very good: too sloppy in its entrances and exits, too fussed and footloose in its aimless, though inspired, design. What accomplishes ***Harvey*** and Harvey both is not dexterity, not deviousness, not surprise, not chicanery, but—of all things, of all things—simplicity. That is the play's personal, particular genius.

Look. While Harvey was wandering off on his own, Mr. Stewart was being asked (by various doctors, reasonable as cream) to talk about him. Mr. Stewart was happy, in a cooperative and very thoughtful way, to do so. How had he met him? Well, Harvey, late one night, leaning against a lamppost, had called out to him by name. Hadn't this surprised Mr. Stewart? No, not really. You see, he'd lived

a long time in this town, and when you've lived a long time in a town, almost everybody gets to know your name.

Mr. Stewart looked up, having answered the question to his, and I must say to my, satisfaction. I am going to suggest that that is one of the great lines of the American theater and that its greatness stems from its effortlessness, its quiet, its utterly logical escape from the logical. It cannot be faulted, as it could never have been faked. It doesn't depend on a set-up, it's no mere inversion of words. It is an inversion of mind, one man's natural way of thinking about things and accepting them because they fit into his method of grasping reality. There's nothing wrong with it as a means of grasping reality. You just pick the end of a question that strikes you as needing answering, that's all.

The line is perfect and it's not alone. When Mr. Stewart explained that Einstein managed to overcome time and space but that Harvey had managed to overcome time and space and any objections, he (courtesy of Mrs. Chase and her intractably Irish waywardness) had come upon another such. He had also, in those few words, effectively described the way the play works. The play can be as patchy as it likes, it can tread water when it wants, you can raise any objection to it you care to and you can be as right as your wrongheadedness lets you be. Nothing of this will ever matter because Harvey, who just walked through, *has* overcome.

I don't want to go on quoting lines, not even to point out how blissfully superior some of them are. There is, however, one kind of line that acquired a new emphasis in this particular revival and it should be mentioned in order to do full justice to Mr. Stewart. A psychiatrist, probing for a prior association that would explain Mr. Stewart's choice of Harvey as a name for his six-foot crony, asked for the names of his father, his closest childhood playmates, etcetera, etcetera. It turned out—I can feel you're beginning to remember this one—that none of them had been named Harvey. It turned out, in fact, that Mr. Stewart had never known *anyone* named Harvey. "Perhaps," he added reflectively, "that's why I had such hopes for him" [Act II, Scene ii].

I am not going to tell you that this is Mrs. Chase's best or most characteristic line; it is warm and ironically sentimental and just a bit reminiscent, reminiscent of [William] Saroyan perhaps. But as Mr. Stewart read it, and thought it, and began to use it against what was coming, it took on a very special tone. For the actor was himself neither sentimentalizing the role nor the rabbit, he was not being whimsical or nostalgic or wry or, for God's sake, cute.

He was being serious. Almost everything Mr. Stewart did as the evening gathered its wits together for a climax was intensely attentive, listening, relaxed and waiting for the spheres to speak. He meant his engagement with the human race, with the pretty nurse who kissed him without flustering him, with the people who sold him magazine subscriptions on the telephone, with the doctors' wives he hoped to meet at cocktail parties to which he'd never been invited.

He took his own solution, his pal, his pooka, with no grain of salt and no grain of sugar, just with a complete and open earnestness. He had no shield; prove to him that Harvey was hurting someone or something and he would give him up; Harvey wasn't a defense, he was the human imagination honoring itself, enjoying itself, and then surrendering itself when the hard edge of the world so required. In his uncluttered, unidealized, plain ordinary decency, Mr. Stewart made the play's last act astonishingly moving. (Had Frank Fay been funnier? Who can honestly say now? Perhaps. He was nowhere near so touching.)

Being at the Anta became an occasion during the nights of **Harvey,** an odd sort of occasion for what might have been a routine revival of a familiar play, done for a few weeks to kill time by two stars going gray. The audience had come, delight ready in its eyes, not just to see Helen Hayes (you can see Helen Hayes any week of the year, she works all the time) or just to see Jimmy Stewart (stay home and watch television, he's there) but for the most specific purpose of seeing Miss Hayes and Mr. Stewart *together.*

It was a meeting. People came because they thought it was going to be fun to be in on it. They glued those hopeful eyes to each star with each entrance, mouths open in a beginning smile. They didn't overreact or laugh too soon. They waited for the stars to be as good as they should have been. Then, when they were—and that's a kind of miracle, isn't it?—they expanded with joy. They gave the theater their satisfaction. The house filled with assent, with judgment, with a massive gratified relationship. And, because they had come for and were giving such complete concentration to the stars, they could be silently surprised by the play.

Not even the standees left before the last rites, including the curtain call for Harvey, were done. When I got to the parking lot, there was no one ahead of me. (pp. 168-72)

> *Walter Kerr, "Remembrances of Things Past," in his* God on the Gymnasium Floor, *Simon and Schuster, 1971, pp. 161-87.*

Sandy Wilson   (review date June 1975)

[*Wilson is a British drama critic, playwright, and lyricist whose works for stage include* See You Later *(1951),* The Boy Friend *(1953), and* His Monkey Wife *(1971). In the following excerpt, the critic appraises the London revival of* Harvey *as disappointing, maintaining that this play, along with Joseph O. Kesslering's* Arsenic and Old Lace *(1941), is part of a "peculiarly American" genre, "in which the deranged is glorified at the expense of the rational."*]

Curiosity—so my mother used to tell me—killed the cat. A few nights before **Harvey** opened, I saw [Philip Barry's] *The Philadelphia Story,* for about the sixth time, on television, and watched James Stewart give his Oscar-winning performance as Mike Connor, the frustrated novelist sent to cover Katharine Hepburn's high society wedding. A little while before that I had seen him in *That's Entertainment,* singing Cole Porter's *Easy To Love*—not at all badly—to Eleanor Powell. How, I wondered, was Mr Stewart holding up after all these years? Well, my curiosi-

ty didn't kill me, but it gave me—deservedly, I suppose—a pretty awful time.

To begin with, the Prince of Wales must surely be one of the most disagreeable theatres in London, if not the world. To me it resembles a dilapidated Jumbo jet, into which the usherettes wearily cram a new plane-load of passengers—all of whom seem to be heavy smokers—for yet another Delfont package tour. The last time I was on board was for *The Danny La Rue Show,* which struck me, apart from the star and his wardrobe, as a decidedly mingy deal. This trip was much longer and even less exciting, perhaps because I had been on it before, with Sid Field.

As to the play itself, I found myself reflecting on the changing function of alcohol in the American Drama. In the 'thirties it was invariably dealt with humorously: nothing was considered more amusing than to see a star succumbing to endless cocktails. In the film of *The Thin Man,* when William Powell wakes in the middle of the night with a fresh clue to the murderer, Myrna Loy's first reaction is to pour him a hefty scotch from the decanter on the bedside table. In Clare Booth's *The Women* the Countess de Lage, in a state of collapse on hearing of her latest husband's infidelity, demands a gin in her bromo-seltzer, while in *The Philadelphia Story* itself Tracy Lord is wised up through gallons of champagne. Edward Albee changed all that overnight: the drinkers in *Who's Afraid Of Virginia Woolf* sink steadily into the depths of self-hatred and disillusion, and ever since then alcohol has been used in the Theatre to expose the nasty side of human nature. Pity . . . **Harvey,** in which the hero, Elwood Dowd, is so far gone in dipsomania that he not only sees a six-foot white rabbit but has long conversations with it, falls somewhere between the two. It belongs to a period of the American theatre when whimsy was taking over from wit, perhaps as a form of escapism during World War Two, and is of roughly the same genre as *Arsenic And Old Lace* [by Joseph O. Kesslering], . . . in which two dear old ladies are revealed to be homicidal maniacs, to the charmed delight of the audience. This type of parable, in which the deranged is glorified at the expense of the rational, is, I think, peculiarly American, and when Sid Field, the least whimsical of comedians, played in **Harvey,** it was, as I remember, an uneasy combination.

James Stewart, who has portrayed Elwood Dowd on the screen and several times on the stage, is undoubtedly better suited to the role. He was always a touch elfin, but whereas he used to gangle rather charmingly, he now shambles—rather slowly, although his charm inundates the Prince of Wales stage like an avalanche of luke-warm custard. The homely aphorisms of Mary Chase fall like jelly-babies from those india-rubber lips, and every now and then Mr Stewart performs a neat little piece of business—as when Harvey nudges him off his chair and onto the floor—which earns a merited round of applause. But he did make it a long, long evening.

Elwood Dowd's sister, Veta, was played in the previous production by Athene Seyler. Perhaps to accommodate a different class of audience—or, rather, passenger—the Dowd family appears to have dropped a rung or two on the social ladder, and the household is now presided over by Miss Mona Washbourne, in the accents of her native Birmingham, with an occasional short 'a' graciously thrown in by way of acknowledgement that she is appearing in an American play. She and all the other ladies of the cast sport 1960s hemlines, which led me to think that either the play was being presented 'in period'—the wrong period—or that Mr Delfont was using up some of the firm's old wardrobe. Of them all, only Miss Chili Bouchier, as the psychiatrist's wife, managed to project the Thurberesque image of American womanhood which the piece, I think, requires. Her dual obsession with Elwood's predicament and an impending cocktail party was very funny and gave me my only real laughs of the evening. The sets were by Paul Staples and may, for all I know, have belonged to the 1949 version. Their side walls were splayed out at the angle of 160 degrees which the dreadful proportions of the Prince of Wales demands and were as serviceable as the direction of Mr Anthony Quayle (also from the last version) and the lighting of Mr Joe Davis (ditto, I suspect).

The curtain rose at eight o'clock, and it was nearly eleven by the time I staggered out onto the tarmac, leaving the rest of the passengers applauding wildly as Mr Stewart shambled on—rather slowly—for his curtain call.

Sandy Wilson, in a review of "Harvey," in Plays and Players, *Vol. 22, No. 9, June, 1975, p. 26.*

CRITICAL COMMENTARY

Jordan Y. Miller   (essay date 1961)

[*In the excerpt below, Miller delineates the reasons for the success of* Harvey, *arguing that "the signal value comes from the portrayal of Elwood and his friend in a matter-of-fact style."*]

Harvey was one of those sensational New York successes which, by all conventional standards of good theatre, should not have lasted a week. In style it is at once realism and whimsical fantasy; satire alternates with broad, almost slapstick, farce. The play is constructed with a lopsided first act, overweighted with wild improbabilities; afterward, it slows down to an unhurried walk. It has an uninteresting love affair that soon atrophies for lack of nourishment. Though some of the important characters are wonderfully rounded, others enter and exit with little more than sketchy outline of their personalities. The play endures without plot and works a single situation—a question—for its entire length: does or does not a 6-foot-1½-inch white rabbit exist? Fortunately, *Harvey* has something to offer beyond these "violations" of form, and its phenomenal appeal as one of America's longest-running plays can readily be explained.

First of all, the gentle Elwood Dowd and his unseen friend have won sympathetic understanding in nations around the world and in almost every language because of their plea for tolerance of human individuality, however eccentric. There is universal meaning in the play's message about deadening conformity, with its spoof of scientific ef-

fort to eliminate social deviation. The appeal that has carried *Harvey* into every type of civilized community probably remains where it did the first night it opened to a sophisticated New York audience which would be least expected to approve a whimsical fairy tale about talking bunnies. If it is nothing else, *Harvey* is a superb example of modern theatrical escapism.

While it is a play of whimsy, *Harvey* never turns to the unnecessary pursuit of whimsicality for its own sake. Its witty dialogue and its madhouse antics give it a quality best described in words like wacky, cockeyed, or zany, all fittingly descriptive of fine comic escapism. The miracle, so termed by one critic, is in the common sense that comes through it. For all its departure into the delights of pure nonsense, it reveals the fundamental wisdom to be gained from those whose grip on reality is not as deathlike as the rest of us maintain it should be. As Joseph Wood Krutch remarked in his review, *Harvey* makes a good lesson out of the statement "It's great to be crazy" [see review dated 18 November 1944], teaching the lesson in sheer, unhackneyed fun.

The minute the play begins we are in complete sympathy with Elwood. The horrors of a musical afternoon at the Wednesday Forum, full of hypocrisies, fake intellectualism, and childish desires to be properly listed in the society column, are contrasted with Elwood's forthright geniality and innocent sincerity. Everyone can experience a vicarious joy in his intrusion upon the sham of Veta's circle. There are occasions when many of us would be delighted to introduce both our own Harveys and Miss Greenawalt's quart of gin into the midst of these gossiping dowagers. Before we know it, we have accepted Harvey and we are quite willing to sit down with him and listen to Elwood's meticulous reading of Jane Austen.

Mrs. Chase exhibits her finest sense of the comically ludicrous when she gives the confused Veta the duty of explaining Harvey to the young psychiatrist. It is unfortunate that most of the scenes which follow fail to top this wholly preposterous sequence, for it is farce at its very best. By the time Elwood has left the office with his companion and the doctor has discovered the punctured hat, most of the play's highest comic levels have passed. Mrs. Chase has, however, now firmly convinced the most skeptical that Harvey exists. She leaves no doubt at all as Wilson reads the cheerfully mocking greeting in the encyclopedia. By the end of the first act, the audience knows that everybody onstage, except Elwood, is quite, quite mad.

Throughout the rest of the play, Mrs. Chase carries us through a clever satire upon the idea of "normal" life. Elwood remains calmly unperturbed, displays more common sense than all the others, and ends up giving more sound psychiatric advice to the medical profession than it can give to him. The climax occurs in the ingenious twist of forcing the weary doctor, tired of hearing the frustrations of others, to pour out his own dreams of Ohio and idyllic days with lovely maidens to the sympathetic and comprehending Elwood. After all, Elwood has long been able to do what Dr. Chumley dreams of, and he has overcome reality in order to make his own life a thoroughly bearable existence. Chumley, however, is not sure whether to fear or to welcome Harvey, but finally, in desperation, is resolved to capture him by very proper and very underhanded scientific means, even if his method involves the destruction of a happy man. Fortunately, Elwood's loving sister realizes the meaning of his "abnormality" in time to end the threat.

The satire of **Harvey** remains secondary; the signal value comes from the portrayal of Elwood and his friend in a matter-of-fact style that makes the fantasy so enjoyable. After seeing the tryout performances, Mrs. Chase realized that her first strong insistence on using an actor onstage in a monstrous rabbit costume was entirely out of place. There must always be the question of Harvey's existence, regardless of each spectator's private conviction that he is present. The hat, the opening of locked doors, and the accurate predictions of the future of which Elwood is capable are fair proofs,—except that we are never going to admit publicly that Harvey is there. After all, the power of suggestion is strong. Perhaps we are suffering like Dr. Chumley. Or perhaps Dr. Chumley is not suffering anything but only realizing at last that there are facts of life which his training simply cannot tell him. All the professionalism of Dr. Sanderson's attempt to discredit Harvey is lost in Elwood's rational explanations. Harvey cannot be explained away in medical jargon as an alcoholic carryover from delirium tremens. True, Dr. Sanderson's formula can restore Elwood to "normal" living, and Harvey will disappear, but one feels that no scientific process would have exorcised Harvey. Harvey would have departed in disgust, wishing to be no part of the uninteresting but acceptable life of a thoroughly "respectable" person.

As for the "pooka," he is Celtic in origin. Most pookas take the form of horses, but they can be any animal they wish. Normally they are not so congenial as Harvey, and prefer to create disturbances rather than to ingratiate themselves with their human friends. They seldom appear to very many people at once. Some say they cannot be felt to the touch. The nearest equivalent in English lore would be Puck, the mischievous elf who can do good if properly treated, but who prefers to confuse and confound human beings just for the deviltry of it. (pp. 467-69)

> *Jordan Y. Miller, in a review of "Harvey," in his* American Dramatic Literature: Ten Modern Plays in Historical Perspective, *McGraw-Hill Book Company, Inc., 1961, pp. 467-69.*

FURTHER READING

BIOGRAPHICAL INFORMATION ON CHASE

Harris, Eleanor. "Mary Chase: Success Almost Ruined Her." *Cosmopolitan* 136, No. 2 (February 1954): 98-104.
> Relates Chase's struggle to adjust to her sudden fame and new-found wealth after the success of *Harvey*.

Himelstein, Morgan Y. "Mary (Coyle) Chase." In *Contempo-*rary Dramatists, *Second Edition, edited by James Vinson, pp. 145-47. London: St. James Press, 1977.
> Offers a biographical sketch of Chase with an overview of her writing career.

Reef, Wallis M. "She Didn't Write It for Money, She Says." In *More Post Biographies,* edited by John E. Drewry, pp. 50-61. Athens, Ga.: The University of Georgia Press, 1947.
> Profile of Chase containing personal anecdotes told by Reef, Chase's long-time friend and fellow Denver journalist.

"Mary Chase." In *Twentieth Century Authors,* edited by Stanley J. Kunitz, pp. 189-90. New York: The H. W. Wilson Company, 1955.
> Brief overview of Chase's life and career, culminating in the 1944 production of *Harvey* on Broadway.

HARVEY

Atkinson, Brooks. "James Stewart Takes Over in *Harvey.*" *The New York Times* (15 July 1947): 27.
> Compares Frank Fay's and James Stewart's interpretations of the role of Elwood P. Dowd.

Fleming, Peter. Review of *Harvey. The Spectator* 182, No. 6290 (14 January 1949): 45.
> Offers a mixed review of the 1949 London debut of *Harvey*.

Gibbs, Wolcott. "Strange but Wonderful." *The New Yorker* XX, No. 39 (11 November 1944): 40, 42-3.
> Assesses *Harvey* as "touching, eloquent, and lit with fresh surprising humor that has nothing to do with standard comedy formulas."

Lambert, J. W. "Plays in Performance." *Drama,* No. 117 (Summer 1975): 37-55.
> Includes a review of the London revival of *Harvey* that expresses praise for James Stewart's performance as Elwood P. Dowd but censures the rest of the cast. Lambert asserts that although "several of the players have often given excellent performances none of them does so here."

"Harvey." *Life* 17, No. 22 (27 November 1944): 96-8, 101.
> Pictorial review of the Broadway debut of *Harvey*.

"*Harvey* at the Prince of Wales." *New Statesman and Nation* XXXVII, No. 932 (15 January 1949): 55.
> Brief review of *Harvey* in London.

"New Plays in Manhattan." *Time* XLIV, No. 20 (13 November 1944): 60.
> Review of the original Broadway production of *Harvey*, focusing on the actor Frank Fay and his portrayal of Elwood P. Dowd.

"Rabbit with a Mission." *Time* LIII, No. 17 (25 April 1949): 31-2.
> Relates varied responses to the opening of *Harvey* in Vienna, Austria.

"Dearest Rabbit." *Time* 95, No. 10 (9 March 1970): 54.
> Deems the 1970 Broadway revival of *Harvey* "a charmer."

Young, Stark. "New Fanciful Pieces." *The New Republic* 111, No. 21 (20 November 1944): 661.

Describes the original Broadway production of *Harvey* as "happy theatre fun."

OTHER MAJOR WORKS

Atkinson, Brooks. "Authentic Original: *Mrs. McThing* Provides Delightful Fable." *The New York Times* (2 March 1952): II, 1.

Regards Chase's *Mrs. McThing* as a "richer play [than *Harvey*] with a broader point of view, a greater compassion and a more innocent sense of comedy."

——. "Mrs. Chase's New Play: *Bernardine* Is a Portrait of Adolescent Boys." *The New York Times* (9 November 1952): II, 1.

Judges the craftsmanship of *Bernardine* "random" and "floundering" but the material "wonderfully artless and fresh."

Krutch, Joseph Wood. "Drama." *The Nation* 174, No. 11 (15 March 1952): 258-59.

Review of *Mrs. McThing* in which Krutch considers the play "a gimmick" but admits he "enjoyed every minute of it" nonetheless.

Nathan, George Jean. *The Next Half-Hour.* In his *The Theatre Book of the Year: 1945-1946,* pp. 153-55. New York: Alfred A. Knopf, 1946.

Describes Chase's short-running Broadway play *The Next Half-Hour* as "a synthetic and bogus theatrical exhibit."

——. "American Playwrights Old and New." In his *Theatre in the Fifties,* pp. 40-112. New York: Alfred A. Knopf, 1953.

Includes an evaluation of *Mrs. McThing* and *Bernardine* in which Nathan censures Chase's ability as a writer of fantasy.

Review of *Mrs. McThing. Newsweek* XXXIX, No. 9 (3 March 1952): 61.

Compares *Mrs. McThing* with *Harvey,* finding that "if the author had ordered her whimsies with a little lighter touch, she would have had another *Harvey* on hand."

"New Play in Manhattan." *Time* LIX, No. 9 (3 March 1952): 63.

Offers brief mixed review of *Mrs. McThing.*

Alexandre Dumas (*fils*)

1824-1895

Dumas was one of the most popular and prolific French dramatists of the nineteenth century. Born the illegitimate son of the famous novelist Alexandre Dumas (*père*), he secured his own fame in 1852 with the production of *La Dame aux camélias* (*Camille; or, The Fate of a Coquette*), the play for which he is best known today. Based on his novel of the same name, *Camille* is acknowledged by critics as the work that introduced Realism to the modern French stage. Subsequently, in his self-proclaimed role as a social reformer, Dumas used the stage as a tribunal for such contemporary social problems as adultery and divorce. In doing so, he pioneered the development of the modern social drama, and, critics agree, raised the *pièce à thèse,* or thesis play, to an unprecedented level of refinement.

Dumas was raised by his mother, Catherine Labay, until 1831 when the elder Dumas legally recognized his paternity and assumed responsibility for his son's care. After attending a succession of boarding schools, where he was ostracized because of his illegitimacy, Dumas enrolled in the Collège Chaptal, but left without taking a degree. In 1841, he established residence with his father in Paris. He published several volumes of poetry and a picaresque novel entitled *Aventures de quatre femmes et d'un perroquet* in his early years at the Dumas household, where he also adopted his father's extravagant lifestyle and eventually fell into debt. One source of the younger Dumas's insolvency was a two-year liaison with Marie Duplessis, a young Parisian courtesan who died of tuberculosis shortly after Dumas broke off their relationship in 1846. Duplessis's untimely death inspired Dumas to write the novel *La Dame aux camèlias* (*The Lady of the Camellias*); the success of this work, portions of which are based on the Duplessis-Dumas affair, enabled Dumas to repay some of his debts and to provide for the support of his mother. From 1848 to 1852, he produced a spate of novels in an effort to further recover from his financial losses.

Dumas's first and greatest dramatic triumph came in 1852 with the production of his stage adaptation of *Camille* at the Théâtre du Vaudeville. Although censors initially suppressed the play, fearing that audiences would associate Dumas's characters with several of Duplessis's influential admirers, the powerful Duc de Morny intervened on Dumas's behalf, and *Camille* was staged with great success. During the 1850s, Dumas produced several popular dramas including *Le Demi-monde,* a critically acclaimed exploration of the social class existing on the outskirts of respectable Parisian society, and *Le Fils naturel,* a complicated intrigue protesting prejudice against illegitimate children. In 1867, he achieved a popular success with *Les Idées de Madame Aubray* and also began appending detailed explanatory prefaces to his dramatic works. In the 1872 essay *L'Homme-femme: Réponse á M. Henri d'Ideville* (*Man-Woman; or, The Temple, the Hearth, the*

Street), Dumas shocked his compatriots by defending the right of a husband to take the life of an unfaithful and unrepentant spouse. He continued to address controversial social topics in plays and pamphlets during the 1880s, urging specific legal reforms allowing for divorce and woman's suffrage. His popularity as a dramatist, however, began to decline during this later period. He died at Marly-le-Roi in 1895.

Dumas's dramas are typically well-crafted illustrations of his own views on the legal and moral issues of the day. Dumas aspired to invest his dramas with the insight of the sociological novelist Honoré de Balzac and the technical mastery of Augustin Eugène Scribe, inventor of tightly constructed, fast-paced dramas known as "well-made" plays. While Dumas's works are often admired for their brilliant construction, critics note that thematically Dumas appears to have fallen short of his ideal; for, unlike Balzac, he restricted his observations to his own social milieu, earning a reputation as a specialist concerned with the ramifications of illicit love within a small segment of Parisian society. As William Archer has suggested, the playwright approached his subject not as a moralist, but as a sociologist concerned with the behavior of a select

101

class under specific social conditions. Many other critics, however, have focused on Dumas's reforming zeal, characterizing the dramatist as a preacher and his plays as sermons. He is frequently praised in this connection for his masterful and efficient use of moral spokespersons known as *raisonneurs* in such "thesis plays" as *Les Idées de Madame Aubray.* Dumas openly acknowledged the didactic nature of his art, stating, "If I am forbidden to carry on the stage the big questions that interest a living society, I prefer to stop writing."

Two developments in particular are cited as significant factors in the decline of Dumas's popularity: his plays quickly lost their topical appeal among audiences, and his Scribean approach to dramatic construction fell into disrepute among the succeeding generation of dramatists who disdained such theatrical conventions. Émile Zola reflected the prevailing attitude of these writers when he stated that Dumas "never hesitates between reality and a scenic exigency—he wrings the neck of reality." In contrast, British and American commentators initially complained that Dumas was realistic to a fault, especially in his frank treatment of sexual and moral transgressions. Modern critics have tended to acknowledge the limitations of his method and interests while emphasizing his contributions to the development of the modern social drama.

Commentators find that Dumas's best known play, *Camille,* resists comparison with his other works, due to its uncharacteristic sympathy for human frailty and passion. Various critical interpretations have arisen concerning this anomaly, most of which have focused on the Romantic overtones of the courtesan-heroine's redemption through love and suffering. Others, however, have emphasized that the prevailing effect of the drama is to challenge the dominance of Romanticism on the French stage.

Among Dumas's dramas, *Camille* has the additional distinction of continued popular appeal; although consistently described as a work of inferior artistic craftsmanship, its longevity testifies to its status as a story of superior dramatic interest. As Henry James observed, "*Camille* remains in its combination of freshness and form, of the feeling of the spring-time of life and the sense of the conditions of the theatre, a singular, an astonishing production. . . . Some tender young man and some coughing young woman have only to speak the lines to give it a great place among the love-stories of the world."

(For further information on Dumas's life and career, see *Nineteenth-Century Literature Criticism,* vol. 9.)

PRINCIPAL WORKS

PLAYS

La Dame aux camélias 1852
  [*Camille; or, The Fate of a Coquette,* 1853; also published as *The Lady of the Camellias,* 1856]
Diane de Lys 1853

Le Demi-monde 1855
  [*The "Demi-Monde": A Satire on Society,* 1858]
La Question d'argent 1857
  [*The Money-Question* published in the journal *Poet Lore,* 1915]
Le Fils naturel 1858
  [*Le Fils naturel,* 1879]
Un Père prodigue 1859
L'Ami des femmes 1864
Les Idées de Madame Aubray 1867
  [*Les Idées de Madame Aubray,* 1965]
La Princesse Georges 1871
  [*La Princesse Georges,* 1881]
Une Visite de noces 1871
La Femme de Claude 1873
  [*The Wife of Claude,* 1905]
Monsieur Alphonse 1873
  [*Monsieur Alphonse,* 1886]
L'Étrangère 1876
  [*L'Étrangère,* 1881]
La Princesse de Bagdad 1881
  [*The Princess of Bagdad,* 1881]
Denise 1885
  [*Denise,* 1885]
Francillon 1887
  [*Francillon,* 1887]

OTHER MAJOR WORKS

La Dame aux camèlias (novel) 1848
  [*The Camelia-Lady,* 1857; also published as *Camille; or, The Camelia-Lady,* 1860; and *The Lady of the Camellias,* 1902]
Diane de Lys (novel) 1851
L'Affaire Clémenceau: Mémoire de l'accusé (novel) 1866
  [*Wife Murder; or, The Clémenceau Tragedy,* 1866; also published as *The Clemenceau Case,* 1890]
L'Homme-femme: Réponse à M. Henri d'Ideville (essay) 1872
  [*Man-Woman; or, The Temple, The Hearth, the Street,* 1873]
Entr'actes. 3 vols. (essays) 1878-79
La Question du divorce (essay) 1880

AUTHOR COMMENTARY

Preface to *A Prodigal Father* (1868)

[*In the following excerpt from an English translation of his 1868* Préface, Un Père prodigue, *Dumas defines the qualities of the successful playwright and the techniques essential to great drama.*]

To-day, by your leave, we shall discuss technique. We should never fail to attribute to technique the importance due it in dramatic art. Technique is so important that it sometimes happens that technique is mistaken *for* art. Of all the various forms which can be assumed by thought, the drama is that which most nearly approaches the plastic arts; dramatic art cannot be practiced before one knows all the material methods—with this difference, however, that in all the other arts these methods can be learned, but in this, one divines them, or, rather, has them within him.

One may become a painter, a sculptor, even a musician, by study—but not a dramatist. One is a dramatist at the beginning, the way one is dark or light, without wishing it. It is a freak of nature that has so constructed your vision as to enable you to see in a certain way, which is not absolutely the true way, but which for the time being *appears* to be the only way whereby you can make others see what you have seen. The man who is called to write for the stage reveals this very rare faculty at his first attempt, in a farce at school or in a parlor charade. It is the science of optics and perspective which allows him to depict a human being, a character, a passion, an act of the soul, with a single scratch of the pen. The illusion is so complete that it often happens that when the spectator turns reader and wishes to revive for his personal satisfaction the emotion he has experienced together with the crowd, he not only cannot find that emotion in the *written* word and action, but he cannot find the place itself in the play where he experienced it. A word, a look, a gesture, a pause, a purely atmospheric combination of effects had held him spell-bound. That is the genius of technique—if these two words can stand side by side. A play is to other forms of literature what a ceiling fresco is to wall- or easel-paintings. Woe be unto the painter if he forgets that his fresco must be seen from a distance, with the light coming from below!

A man of no value as thinker, moralist, philosopher, writer, may be a first-rate dramatist; that is to say, as manipulator of the purely external actions of human beings; and, on the other hand, in order to be accepted in the theater as thinker, moralist, philosopher, and writer, it is indispensable that he be endowed with the same particular qualities as the man of no value (except as technician). In short, if one would be master in this art he must first be proficient in its technique.

If it be a fact that the natural endowments cannot be given to those who are without them, nothing, on the other hand, is easier than to recognize them in those who do possess them.

The first of these endowments, the most indispensable, the one that dominates and commands, is logic—which includes good sense and clearness. The truth may be absolute or relative, according to the importance of the subject and the *milieu*. But the logic must be implacable from beginning to end; it must never lose sight of this end, while developing the idea and the action. The dramatist must unflaggingly place before the spectator that part of the being or thing for or against which he aims to draw a conclusion. Then comes the science of contrasts; that is to say, the blacks, the shadows, the balancing, the totality of effect, harmony; then conciseness and tempo, which prevent the listener's being distracted or reflecting, or taking a momentary breath, to discuss in his own mind with the author; the knowledge of foreground and background, keep-

ing the figure which ought to stand out in the high-light from falling into the shadow, and those which belong in the middle-distance from assuming a position of too great prominence; and then the mathematical precision, inexorable, fatal, which multiplies scene by scene, event by event, act by act, up to the dénouement, which must be the sum-total, the Q. E. D.; and, lastly, the exact conception of our limitations, which forbid us to make our picture larger than the frame, because the dramatist who has even the most to say must say it all between eight in the evening and midnight, out of which period he must subtract one hour for entr'actes, and repose for the audience.

I have not mentioned imagination, because the theater—besides the author—supplies this in the actors, scenery, and accessories. It puts into flesh and bone, in spoken words, in images, before the spectator, the individuals, places, and things which he would be forced to imagine were he reading a book. Nor have I spoken of invention, because in our profession there is no such thing. We need invent nothing; we have only to observe, remember, feel, coördinate, restore, in a particular form, what every spectator ought to have recalled to him immediately after having felt or seen, without having been conscious of it. As for basis, the real; as for facts, what is possible; as for means, what is ingenious; that is all that can rightfully be asked of us.

Does the art of the drama, which requires a technique all its own, likewise demand a style of its own? Yes. No one is altogether a dramatist unless he has his manner of writing, just as he has his manner of seeing, a manner altogether personal. A play should be written as if it were never intended to be other than read. The production is nothing but a reading by many people who do not care or know how to read. A play succeeds as a result of people's going to the theater; it becomes firmly established as a result of being read. The spectator gives it a certain notoriety, the reader gives it lasting fame. The play that we have no desire to read without having seen, nor to re-read after having seen it, is dead, no matter if it enjoys a run of two thousand nights. Only, it is necessary, if the work is to survive without the aid of the interpreter, that the writer's style be such as to convey to the reader the solidity, proportions, form, and suggestions of tone, which are applauded by the spectator in a theater. The style of the greatest writers can be of no help to the dramatist except as a sort of reference: it can teach him only a few words, and there are even a number of these which he must eschew from his vocabulary, because they lack the relief, strength, character—I had almost said triviality—which are necessary to the end of setting the true human being in action on a false ground. Molière's vocabulary is very limited; he invariably uses the same expressions: he plays the gamut of the whole of the human soul on five octaves and a half.

Written style, that is, thought presented directly to the reader, can be fixed once for all. Whoever writes a story, be it merely a dialogue destined to be read and nothing more, can make use of the form of a master of his own class—Bossuet, Voltaire, Pascal, Jean-Jacques, Sand, Hugo, Lamartine, Renan, Théophile Gautier, Sainte-Beuve, Flaubert, About; and not only will he not be blamed, but rather praised for paying homage to tradition and purism. Perhaps even his original sources will not be perceived, but his influence will be felt; he will be proclaimed a writer, and will actually be one, even if his elegant and pure style fails to contain a single original idea. We see examples of this every day, books in which the style leads one to believe that there is a solid foundation of thought.

There is nothing of the sort in the drama. The moment we imitate the style of one of our masters, we are not hailed as respectful disciples; we are tiresome imitators. What we ought to imitate in those masters is their manner of observing and not of stating. Each of them has his own trademark, which cannot be imitated without our being accused of counterfeiting. Read Corneille, Racine, Molière, Marivaux, Beaumarchais—to speak only of the dead— and notice the difference in their styles. Notice how each one of them has poured his particular essence into the flowing river which is called language! (pp. 383-85)

> *Alexandre Dumas fils, in a preface to "A Prodigal Father," in* European Theories of the Drama, *edited and translated by Barrett H. Clark, revised edition, D. Appleton and Company, 1929, pp. 383-88.*

OVERVIEWS AND GENERAL STUDIES

William Archer (essay date 1896)

[*A Scottish theater critic and playwright, Archer is noted primarily for his English translations of the works of Henrik Ibsen and his efforts to promote the realistic social drama of the 1890s. Archer argued that the drama of his own age was as good or even superior to the work of the ancients and Elizabethans, both of whom he considered overvalued in many respects. In the following excerpt, he offers an unfavorable estimation of the style and content of Dumas's most popular plays, judging them little more than highly-polished "well-made" plays—like those of Augustin Eugène Scribe—overlaid with "social and moral essays."*]

In English-speaking countries, the name of Alexandre Dumas *fils* is more widely known than his works. This fact is entirely to his honour as an artist. It distinguishes him at once from the great majority of his contemporaries and immediate predecessors in the French drama. From the days of Dryden onwards, it has been, and it still is, our habit to adapt French plays instead of translating them; so that, with very few exceptions, the plays which find their way to the English or American stage are those which can be tortured into some sort of distant resemblance to English or American life. Now, the masterpieces of dramatic literature never lend themselves to this Procrustean process. Melodramas, buffooneries, comedies of mechanical intrigue can be forced into the costumes of any country; but plays in which an artist concentrates the essence of character and manners, or a thinker expresses his personal convictions and ideals, are quite intractable to the adapter. Scribe, D'Ennery, and Sardou—the vaudevillistes, the melodramatists, and the practitioners of the clockwork intrigue, warranted to go in any climate—have amused millions of playgoers throughout the Anglo-Saxon world, most of whom have not even heard their names. Dumas, on the other hand, is known by name to all people of culture. They have heard of his ideas, his theses, his paradoxes; they have formed some general conception of his personality; but, if they know his plays, it is either because they have read them or because they have seen them acted in France, or by travelling French companies. Except *La Dame aux Camélias,* which, under the name of *Camille,* has been widely acted in America, none of his plays, so far as I know, has attained any lasting popularity in English dress. Translations of *L'Etrangère* and *La Princesse Georges* have failed utterly. Adaptations of *Le Demi-Monde* and *L'Ami des Femmes,* with all that is really characteristic omitted, have met with a certain success, but only through the personal popularity of Mr. Charles Wyndham. I think I have heard of an adaptation of *Diane de Lys,* but it is certainly long since forgotten. A translation of *Monsieur Alphonse* has shared the same fate. *Denise* has recently been acted, with some acceptance, in the provinces. *La Question d'Argent, Le Fils Naturel, Un Père Prodigue, Les Idées de Madame Aubray, Une Visite de Noces, La Femme de Claude, La Princesse de Bagdad,* and *Francillon* have not, to the best of my belief, been either translated or adapted, at any rate in England.

None the less is Dumas recognised by all students of the drama, whether playwrights or critics, as the master-spirit of the modern French stage. He is not adaptable—thank heaven!—but he is extremely readable. We all know him—all who are in any sense specialists—and some of us greatly delight in him. In brief, he is an influence to be reckoned with, to be accepted or rejected. We hope and believe that we are laying the foundations of an original English drama; but that does not mean that we are to shut ourselves off from the rest of the world, and re-discover all the processes of the art. Rather it behoves us to look carefully around, to study the methods and ideals of foreign masters, and to take example by them—or warning. My present purpose is to inquire in which capacity Dumas can best serve us.

Let me state at once the point towards which my considerations tend. We have something to learn, I think, from Dumas; but we must develop, not imitate, his methods. The drama of the future, not in England alone, must begin where he leaves off, on pain of sinking into puerility and inanition.

First, as to technique. In the preface to *Un Père Prodigue* Dumas gives us his technical confession of faith, concluding that "the dramatist who should know *man* like Balzac and the *theatre* like Scribe, would be the greatest dramatist of all time." To which of these summits of science did Dumas himself most nearly attain? I fear we must answer, to the latter. He knew the theatre very like Scribe—too like Scribe. He is commonly said to have overthrown the supremacy of Scribe, and revolutionised the drama; but, great as was the effect produced by *La Dame aux Camélias,* it is misleading, I think, to call it a revolution. True, the play itself, ran directly enough in the teeth of the Scribe formula. Written, or rather transcribed from the novel, in a few days, without even the guidance of a scenario, it is absolutely simple in its development, and relies for its interest on character and sentiment alone. But Dumas did not consistently follow up this line of advance, which, indeed, he had chosen at haphazard and not on any preconceived theory. He was too truly the son of his father to resist the allurements of ingenuity. In his first mature work, *Le Demi-Monde,* he relapses, to all intents and purposes, not precisely upon the methods of Scribe, but upon those of the plot-school in general. The drama is built on intrigue and counter-intrigue, no less than *Adrienne Lecouvreur* or *Les Pattes de Mouche,* though the artificiality of structure is disguised by the extraordinary latitude of disquisition which Dumas permitted himself. By dint of keen observation and an inexhaustible vivacity of utterance, he persuaded the public to let him add a series of social and moral essays to a story conceived and conducted very much on the ordinary lines. That was the real revolution he effected—he did not shatter the Scribe formula, but expanded it so as to make room for any reasonable quantity of generalisation and theorising. And a reasonable quantity did not suffice him. His theories overflowed into his prefaces, those delightful lay sermons to which the plays will one day, perhaps, be regarded as mere illustrative appendices. Whole pages of these prefaces might quite well be placed in the mouths of the De Jalins, De Ryons, and Thouvenins of the plays, while, on the other hand, whole tirades of the De Jalins and De Ryons might be transferred to the prefaces without leaving any sensible gaps in the dialogue. It was by making room and securing attention for a generalising, not to say sermonising, chorus that Dumas really proved himself an innovator; while of course he chose such themes as provided the chorus with matter for moralisation.

The skeleton of Dumas's plays is so lavishly upholstered with disquisition that it is not always easy to strip off the padding and get at the bare bones of the intrigue. This was once done for me by chance in the case of *Le Demi-Monde.* A play was in rehearsal at the Criterion, known to be an adaptation from the French. A friend who had somehow heard the plot, related it to me, and asked me if I could name the original play. I replied that all this business of compromising letters was common to dozens of plays, but that the conduct of the adventuress-heroine in frankly showing her hand to her antagonist, merely because she happens to have won a single trick, seemed to me of a rare ineptitude. Shortly after, my friend met me again, and said, "I hear the Criterion piece is *Le Demi-Monde.*" I scouted the notion. I had seen the play at the Français three or four times, and read it at least twice; but my memory for plots is not retentive, and this poor, commonplace, and improbable intrigue, stripped of all its trappings, not only did not suggest *Le Demi-Monde,* but seemed to me quite unworthy of Dumas. Yet my friend was right; and in Suzanne's mad frankness to Olivier on the subject of the letters, I now recognise the author's hereditary delight in an instance of preternatural and successful cunning and foresight. Suzanne has laid an elaborate and foolhardy trap for Olivier, into which he has fallen; and the author is so enamoured of her adroitness that he must needs allow her to boast of it, just when she ought to keep her counsel.

The intrigue of *L'Ami des Femmes,* justly reckoned one of Dumas's most characteristic works, is a still more flagrant instance of Scribism. De Ryons is for ever divining great matters from small indications, with the sagacity of a Zadig or a Sherlock Holmes, and making predictions which punctually come true, through the intervention of chances which he did not and could not foresee. Dumas's two avowed romances, or melodramas as some prefer to call them, *L'Etrangère,* and *La Princesse de Bagdad,* are much more simply constructed. In the adroit and highly dramatic awakening of expectancy, the first act of *L'Etrangère* is a masterpiece—as good as (but not better than) the first act of *Lady Windermere's Fan,* and the first act of *The Benefit of the Doubt.* *Francillon* is simply a Palais-Royal vaudeville writ large. It is my favourite among all his works, but it raises no serious technical question. *Le Fils Naturel* is an unblushing fairy-tale. Dumas's most characteristic pieces of construction, to my mind, are *Monsieur Alphonse* and *Denise.* In both, the development of the action from a simple and probable starting-point is incomparably rapid and inevitable. Here he rises far above the Scribe level, and gives proof of personal mastery; but even these plays have no very practical lesson for the English dramatist. The mainspring of their mechanism is one which we, on this side of the Channel, are constitutionally chary of employing—and I am Pharisee enough to think our state the more gracious—I mean deliberate, elaborate, and systematic lying. Nowhere in literature, I am convinced, will you find so many lies to the square inch as in *Monsieur Alphonse.* Everyone concerned, from the god-like Montaiglin to the terrible child, simply wallows in mendacity. Now, we are not all George Washingtons on this side of the Channel; but, whether from hypocrisy or inborn instinct, our gorge rises at such a surfeit of falsehood. It is one of the disabilities of the English playwright, that his characters (his sympathetic ones, at any rate) must not lie with the freedom and facility permitted, and sometimes even enjoined, in France. Hence such an intrigue as that of *Monsieur Alphonse* (and *Denise* is very much in the same case) is to be recommended for avoidance, rather than imitation.

In minor technical points, Dumas is a notoriously bad model. He makes free, and sometimes almost cynical, use of the soliloquy and the aside. For instance, in *Une Visite de Noces,* Lebonnard and De Cygneroi are alone on the stage, Lebonnard suggests that if De Cygneroi goes off with Madame de Morancé, Madame de Cygneroi may take revenge in kind for her husband's unfaithfulness. "She? never!" replies De Cygneroi. "It will never enter her mind. Fortunately, she has her religion; and, besides, women like her never have a lover, my dear fellow. It's women like—," and here Lebonnard positively *interrupts* him with this aside, containing the moral of the play:

> "Admirable! Men think they are jealous of certain women because they are in love with them; and the truth is that they are in love with them because they are jealous of them, which is quite

another matter. Prove to them that they have no reason to be jealous, and they at once perceive that they are not in love."

During the whole aside (six lines in the original text), De Cygneroi stands mute as a fish, and then says "Q'est-ce que tu te racontes-là tout bas?" Can you imagine a more flagrant abuse of this threadbare old convention? Even when they are not asides, but form part of the ordinary dialogue, Dumas's interpolated essays can only be regarded as breaches of strict dramatic form, pardonable in him for the sake of their vivacity, but in nowise to be imitated. As for his style, though delightfully supple in quick exchanges of dialogue, it always tends to become heavily rhetorical, antithetical, and literary, in the bad sense of the word, wherever the length of a tirade allows him to develop his periods and work up dialectical or denunciatory fervour. The other day, I ventured to remonstrate with Mr. Sydney Grundy on the overloaded rhetoric of an otherwise very powerful play, *The Greatest of These—*; but Mr. Grundy's "reasoners" are colloquial in comparison with Dumas's.

Let us turn, now, from form to matter, and try to place Dumas in his relation to the general dramatic movement. Here the first thing to be noted, it seems to me, is that he was not properly a psychologist, but rather a sociologist. M. Bourget, in drawing this obvious distinction, uses a different term, and opposes *moraliste* to *psychologue.* I prefer to say "sociologist," because Dumas was not so much concerned with absolute morality as with conduct under definite social conditions. He was always, from *La Dame aux Camélias* onwards, either combating or reinforcing prejudices. Moreover, he dealt, not really with individuals, but with classes. It is characteristic of the tendency of his mind that he gave a name to two social classes, hitherto innominate, at all events for ears polite: he defined the *demimonde,* and he dissected the genus "Alphonse." Take, for instance, his Suzanne d'Ange in *Le Demi-Monde*—she is not an individual woman, but simply a *demi-mondaine.* Of course she has certain characteristics, but they are only the characteristics demanded by the action. It does not for a moment occur to Olivier de Jalin to take her individual nature into account in considering whether he can suffer a *galant homme* like Raymond de Nanjac to marry her. She is a *pêche à quinze sous,* and that is enough. Again, in *Denise,* though at this later date Dumas was distinctly verging towards a more intimate and penetrating psychology, he posits in his heroine an ideal character with a single flaw in her record, and then he makes André de Bardannes, not a man, but a nobleman—troubled, that is, as to whether his duty to his name and station permits him to overlook the flaw, not at all concerned as to whether he can banish the recollection of it from his own mind, from his own nerves, sufficiently to love her and be happy in her love. That once taken for granted, the world at large is mightily unconcerned about his duty to his ancestors. The problem becomes one of convention, scarcely even of morality, not at all of psychology. Dumas, in short, was always more interested in general rules than in individual cases. He had the lawgiver in his blood. He must have lisped "Thou shalt" and "Thou shalt not" in his cradle; and the "thou" addressed is never an individual, but a member of some determinate social order. And yet, in spite of himself, he establishes his categorical imperatives on the basis of individual character. When he is pleading for leniency, it is a Denise, a Jeannine, a Raymonde that he draws; when he is implacable and rhadamanthine, it is to a Baronne d'Ange, a Femme de Claude, a Duc de Septmonts. Here, again, *La Dame aux Camélias* stands out as an exception. Social policy and the Family are victorious over, and through, the very virtues of poor Marguerite. Perhaps it is the sense of injustice with which her fate afflicts us that has led the censorships of the world, official and otherwise, to denounce the play as immoral. Its residual tendency, so to speak, is humane; and, in questions of sex, "humane" and "immoral" are practically convertible terms.

In one sense, however, the tendency of Dumas's work, as a whole, was really immoral, and should serve as a warning to other would-be moralists. He placed an impassable chasm between the ideal and the actual in conduct. Every play, says Auguste Vitu . . . , should contain *a painting, a judgment, and an ideal.* Now Dumas's pictures were of the life of Paris, or more precisely of a certain sphere of Parisian society, which he represented . . . as fundamentally and almost frenetically polygamous. It was a society, not only based on prostitution, but entirely given over to intrigue and gallantry. And to this picture of unbridled polygamy, Dumas opposed an austerely and rigorously monogamous ideal, which he himself knew and implicitly admitted to be nothing but a pious opinion, far outside the range of practical politics. His magnanimous Gérards, his saintly Claudes, are not the real people of his theatre; they are as fantastic as his father's Monte-Cristo. His Aristide Fressards and his Thouvenins, again, leave us under the impression that virtue and a large family are the concomitants, not to say the rewards, of hopeless provincialism and vulgarity of mind. Dumas himself only pretends to like these personages; he is far from sharing their smug optimism; it is really with his tongue in his cheek that he claims universal validity for their bourgeois ideals. Yet he throws the whole force of his rhetoric into the doctrine that the only alternative to social corruption, decadence, and ruin is a Puritanic monogamy under legal sanctions. Such a message, addressed to the society he depicts in his plays, must have been worse than useless. It must have left people doubtful of the desirability of virtue, and fully persuaded of its impossibility.

And for this sublime morality (exemplified in practice by two engineers, a demigod, and a country notary) he claims the authority, not of science, but of mysticism. True, he talks a good deal about physiology, but his physiology is very much akin to the palmistry and graphology to which he was quite seriously addicted. Regarding Paris—or that Paris within Paris to which his observation was practically confined—as "the crucible in which God makes His experiments," he took his own deductions from these experiments as revelations from on high, and announced them with prophetic unction. His religion was that most convenient of creeds, the theism of the atheist. Quite unconcerned as to the historical or philosophical evidence of religion, he projected his ideal self upon the veil that enshrouds the fountain-head of Causality, and called the simulacrum God. From such a deity, the counterfeit presentment of Dumas's essentially legislative and dogmatic spirit, there naturally proceeded a hard-and-fast system of commandments to be enforced from without upon a society conceived (in its perfect form) as a stationary mechanism. The idea of a morality evolved from within, a taming, and at the same time an enfranchisement, of the individual will, a gradual remodelling of habits of thought and action in ever subtler accordance with the fundamental needs and aspirations of human nature—such an idea was absolutely foreign to Dumas's impatient and imperious intelligence. I sometimes wonder whether the ghost of General Dumas did not "walk" in his grandson oftener than he perhaps suspected. He was apt to regard himself as the heaven-commissioned drill-sergeant of society. But he fortunately inherited from his father the easy-going temper which taught him to laugh and shrug his shoulders when society paid not the slightest attention to his words of command.

Now it is clearly not the drill-sergeant moralist, not the self-consecrated prophet bringing down from—shall we say Montmartre?—a decalogue graven in stone, that is destined to hold the stage of the future, either in England or in Europe. Social distinctions, legal restraints and anomalies, are slowly but surely passing away. It is right and inevitable that the drama should deal with life under its existing forms; but the dramatist who concentrates his study upon castes, classes and institutions, to the neglect of the individual soul, may do effective work in his day, but will scarcely survive it. . . . Thus plays which, like *Le Fils Naturel, Les Idées de Madame Aubray,* and *Denise,* are aimed point-blank at some social institution or prejudice, tend to become obsolete in the direct ratio of their immediate effectiveness. If they have not some more enduring principle of vitality, they will presently be found lying inert, like spent cannon-balls, in the breach they have created. Whatever course civilisation may take—unless, indeed, it relapses into military barbarism—we may confidently foresee a levelling of class inequalities, and a relaxation of those external trammels and tyrannies which supply the social dramatist of to-day with the conflicts he requires. More and more—unless the drama is to become merely historical and fantastic—the playwright of the future will be thrown back on individual psychology. He will find in it an inexhaustible mine of matter, if only he have the skill to manipulate it to dramatic ends. "It is in the soul that things happen," says the old man in Maeterlinck's *Intérieur.* It is in the soul that the great dramas of the world always have happened and always will. "L'art pour l'art," says Dumas, is a formula "absolutely devoid of sense"; and it must be owned that the phrase is rather a discredited one. But if you ask for what other than art's sake *Hamlet, Macbeth,* and *Othello* exist, I am puzzled to inform you. Their direct morality is the veriest commonplace. It needs no Shakespeare to tell us that we ought not to murder our guests, or put instant and implicit faith in the whisperings of reptile malice. Not to enforce such trumpery "theses" were these mighty dramas called into being, but simply to make light in dark places of the human soul. So, too, with *Andromaque* and *Phèdre,* with *Faust* and *Tasso,* with *Hedda Gabler* and *Bygmester Solness:* they are art, if not for art's sake, let us say for light's

sake—for the sake of that light which is indispensable to the growth of a beneficent morality. To this abiding and essential illumination Dumas has not greatly contributed. Here and there, and especially in the single act of *Une Visite de Noces,* he approached the psychological drama. But, as a rule, he worked with a scourge or a battering-ram rather than a torch. (pp. 363-72)

William Archer, "Dumas and the English Drama," in Cosmopolis, *Vol. 1, No. 2, February, 1896, pp. 363-72.*

Hugh Allison Smith   (essay date 1925)

[*In the following excerpt, Smith contends that Dumas's social dramas are superior to his earlier, more popular plays, due to the playwright's later interest in realism and moral issues. This essay was published in a different form as Smith's 1924 Introduction to* La Dame aux camélias.]

More than any other French dramatist of the nineteenth century, Dumas fils was a creator. On most of the roads followed by the French prose drama for the past seventy years he was a pioneer; he even discovered a number of the bypaths into which the theatre has since been occasionally enticed. His restless and independent mind, his self-confidence, and his very lack of background and tradition made him a prolific initiator of new forms, and in most of these his undoubted dramatic gift scored a sensational success. It was inevitable that this originality and this success should impress powerfully his contemporaries and successors. In countries outside of France even, it is surprising how many of his innovations have been followed and exploited during the past fifty years, often without his being given due credit for them, perhaps because so many have been taken second hand, from contemporary French playwrights.

Alexandre Dumas fils was the illegitimate son, recognized and brought up by his father, of Alexandre Dumas, the famous novelist and playwright. He lived his whole life at Paris. While quite young, he began to write novels but soon turned to the stage, and all of his work that has any great importance is dramatic.

The one fact of Dumas's history that is most important in explaining his work was his position in life as an illegitimate child. In his early youth this brought him some painful experiences, and undoubtedly led to a certain bitterness in his attitude toward society, especially when he criticises the conventions and prejudices that bear upon the mother and child in such cases as his own. This experience was also potent in directing his mind to the study of immoral love and its dangers. He has devoted himself to this subject more than any other of the really significant French dramatists.

He was brought up by a good-hearted but prodigal and careless father, in a reckless, dissipated, pleasure-loving group in Parisian society. In due time, something serious in his own character revolted against this life, and he saw all its sins, miseries and falseness. But he is too prone to judge the whole of French society by that one little corner of Paris. In more than one of his plays, he attempts to show that debauchery and libertinism are undermining the morals of all French life, so that, in reading him, at times we almost forget, as he certainly does, that there are honest French people, uncontaminated, and that these make up in France, as elsewhere, the bulk and backbone of the nation.

His lack of a serious education also often betrays him in the discussion of important social problems. However, he was aggressive, determined, capable of great exertion, and gave the most serious and long-continued effort to the writing of his plays. His mind was quick and keen and he was *au courant* of all the questions agitated in his generation. In short, his attitude and mind were largely those of a keen journalist. In addition, he was a man of society, witty, a fine conversationalist, and did not forget that the theatre *must* entertain, whether that be its chief aim or not.

Dumas fils has some of the qualities of his father, particularly a powerful imagination and a love for the unusual. Hence we find him so often choosing subjects that excite or shock, and at times creating characters who are most interesting and striking, but not always true to life, or at least not typical. Nevertheless he had other qualities to offset these. He was, of all that with which he came in contact, a remarkable observer, and he saw more readily a bad motive than a good one. He seems to lack, in most of his plays, the indulgence and charity which have become so prominent in recent writers on social problems. He still believed in individual guilt.

As a rule, the value of Dumas's plays depends much on the balance which he was able to maintain between these qualities just mentioned. Occasionally Dumas the observer is overpowered by his imagination and love for the striking; the elder Dumas gets the upper hand, and we have a play or a character notably false to life.

Finally Dumas's most marked trait is that he does not observe and write *merely* to give us a picture or to amuse us but that he always points the moral. In fact he nearly always chooses his point of view and paints the picture for the sole purpose of teaching the lesson decided upon in advance. In his purpose and mission at least, he is a social reformer, a preacher on the stage, who believes he is called to save man from his many vices. His real interest is in this mission and not simply in literature or in the theatre.

His first play, *La Dame aux Camélias,* finished in 1849 but not played until 1852 on account of difficulties with the censor caused by its realism, was written when he was quite young, in haste, and with no preconceived theories, being in fact adapted from an earlier novel that he had composed following the vein of the Romantic school. In one respect it is an epoch-making play. This life of the courtesan, so often and so falsely portrayed by the Romanticists, is here drawn from personal experience and observation, and presented with a fidelity to actual conditions hitherto unknown on the stage. In spite of its theme and tendency then, this play is the beginning of the modern Realistic drama.

His second significant play, *Le Demi-Monde,* in 1855, is

perhaps his masterpiece and is written with a much firmer dramatic art. Dumas here undertakes the serious study of an important social question, thus inaugurating Social drama, and also, for the first time, takes a conscious stand on the subject of immoral love, a stand which he maintains all his life.

Dumas's *Question d'Argent,* in 1857, cannot be considered among the most important or characteristic of his pieces, but it has a certain interest in evaluating his dramatic work. It is one of the very few plays he wrote not based directly on immoral love; in theme it is more in the usual field of Augier. Dumas is clearly not sufficiently equipped to write a profound study of the money question, but it is interesting to see how skillfully he has popularized his discussion of the problem. In no other play does his witty and clever dialogue show to better advantage. The character of Jean Giraud is also of decided merit and, although imperfectly drawn, proves the capability of Dumas in this feature of drama, a power rarely realized completely owing to his absorption in his themes and plots.

This piece is also one of the best examples to show the dual interest inherent in combining a Balzac study and a Scribe intrigue. Dumas usually succeeds better; here the separation is often clearly marked.

Dumas's third really significant play likewise created a new genre, and the one with which his name is most closely associated, namely the *pièce à thèse,* or Thesis Play. This is *Le Fils Naturel,* in 1858, written to show that the laws and conventions concerning the illegitimate child are harsh and unjust and should be changed.

It is at this time that we find Dumas declaring that the mission of the dramatist is of the highest, that it is even sacred, since it has power over human souls. Undoubtedly this mission assumed by Dumas is sincere and his intentions are commendable. But one may very well question whether the stage, to which people, after all, go primarily for amusement, is a place to propose legislation or to preach the Gospel. Furthermore as we shall see, the Thesis Play and the utilitarian stage, here inaugurated, have been a constant temptation for the theatre to depart from the path of literature, of art, and even of truth into that of propaganda and social reform.

It is impossible to treat adequately in a brief chapter the great variety of Dumas's plays, but the potential significance of certain pieces can perhaps be appreciated by noting their themes and tendencies, since the leads they suggested or opened up have been more fully worked in recent drama.

Un Père Prodigue, in 1859, based on the character of his father, is of no special importance in his work other than to suggest by its title the lack of taste and delicacy of the author, which is evident in a number of his plays and probably in none more strikingly than in the next, *L'Ami des Femmes,* which appeared five years later. But this second play is more remarkable as being one of the pioneer attempts in what might be called formal psychological drama. The psychological study is sufficiently pretentious and, as always with Dumas, very clever, but its serious value may be questioned. The hero, De Ryons, is a sort of psychologic Sherlock Holmes, specializing in running to earth clues in feminine emotions. Dumas's audience did not think this chase led to anything of value, and it might be mentioned that recent audiences have shown the same attitude toward somewhat similar, although abler, studies in some of Curel's plays.

None the less, Dumas returned to the charge with another play of pseudo-scientific import, *L'Etrangère,* in 1876, in which medical science, and particularly physiology, furnishes the chief ammunition. He attempted to give a psychological and physiological explanation for his characters. Perhaps he would have succeeded better—others have done so since—if his characters and his scientific training had both been nearer normal. As it is, the chief interest of the attempt is curiosity in the exhibits of his laboratory *préparateur.* Brieux has entered the same field with his *Damaged Goods* (*Les Avariés*); only with Brieux the gravity of the Doctor and the grewsomeness of his skeleton closet frighten us a little. Here we are at most amused by the medical professor's little wiggling vibrios.

Dumas returns nearer home, and closer to us, in *Les Idées de Mme Aubray,* a sociological study, based on forgiveness and Christian charity. Here Dumas's sympathy for the wronged mother and illegitimate child was so great that he has given the play unusual emotional appeal. His characters doubtless belong in a social Utopia, but they are sincere, on Dumas's part, and touch us by this quality.

In two plays, *Une Visite de Noces* and especially *Monsieur Alphonse,* Dumas has almost, if not quite, anticipated Becque and the later Naturalists, in creating the *Comédie Rosse,* the "tough comedy" that flourished with the Théâtre Libre. The only flaw in his claim to this doubtful honor is that these plays portray a few worthy and sympathetic dramatic figures to offset the contemptible rôles of the leading characters.

A play that deserves special consideration, as an example of the extremes to which his moralistic aim sometimes carried Dumas, is his *Femme de Claude,* in 1873. It is a drama animated by patriotism, and no doubt the dramatist's imagination was abnormally aroused by the recent Franco-Prussian war; its puritanism is as stern as that of John Knox and its symbolism is inspired by the evangelist Saint John. This, however, represents only an occasional aberration of Dumas, and his last two plays, *Denise* and *Francillon,* show a return to his former manner and subjects, without adding anything to them of special value.

Of the several plays, then, in which he turned the drama in new directions, there are doubtless three that stand out for the importance of the forms they created. These are *La Dame aux Camélias, Le Demi-Monde,* and *Le Fils Naturel.* In the first of these, he struck again the realistic note which was to lead the drama back onto the firm ground of observation, after its bewilderment in following the noisy and illusory fanfare of Romanticism; with the second, he opened up the new and vast field of the *comédie de moeurs,* where human nature is studied in connection with, and as affected by, its social environment; and with the third, *Le Fils Naturel,* he created a new model, the *pièce à thèse,* or Thesis Play, with which his name is most

closely associated. The importance of the forms these three pieces inaugurated warrants a more detailed consideration of the plays themselves.

The theme of *La Dame aux Camélias,* which is the poetization or redemption through love of the courtesan, and its effect, which is to magnify largely the importance of love and passion in life, need no comment other than to remind the reader that Dumas took an exactly opposite stand on this question in his later plays. The attitude here is that of the Romantic school, and the genealogy of Marguerite Gautier from Manon Lescaut and Marion Delorme [title characters of works by Abbé Prévost and Victor Hugo, respectively] is obvious. It is easy, then, to explain the origin of the work and its philosophy. What is difficult is to account for the great and enduring success of the play.

In this respect, *La Dame aux Camélias* has always been the despair of the critics. The more they have insisted on finding it weak and unhealthy, false to life, and imperfect in its dramatic construction, the more persistently it has continued to live and to inspire its audiences with its nervous and vibrant vitality.

It is not that the critics are wrong in what they have found to blame in it. It is often puerile. The scenes are sometimes thin and ragged, and certainly some are out of date. The life it portrays is doubtless none too true, and even if it were true is worth little enough; its merit in this respect is its striking external realism. It has no philosophy to speak of, and is so far below Dumas's later standards of dramatic construction that he might very well have written it in a dream.

But with all that, it is, or ought to be, one of the finest object lessons in existence, to the critics as well as to others, to show in what consists one of the greatest dramatic resources. It has the power to reach and move an audience,—and an audience of the most varied sort. In fact, take away the critic's pen and shut him in with the thousand others for an evening, and he also will be moved and grow pale in the scenes between Marguerite and Armand, at the ball after their rupture, and will fight against tears in the final act of Marguerite's death.

Probably Dumas's greatest credit in the history of the French stage is his part in creating a theatre of ideas. Here, however, is a living proof that he, himself, did not need ideas to succeed as a playwright. In fact, this play shows why he did so regularly and so strikingly succeed in spite of his ideas. No dramatist ever preached more to his audiences than Dumas. Usually this would have been fatal and all his logic and all the skill and suspense of the *pièce bien faite* would hardly have saved him. *La Dame aux Camélias* explains how the born dramatist, with his father's instinct for all that holds and moves an audience, was able to carry on his nervous shoulders the triple burden of the moralist, of the preacher, and of the social reformer.

The drama has many weapons with which to win over its hearers, but none is so sure to conquer large numbers as passion. The dramatic thrill that is most general and most frequent is the thrill of deep emotion or feeling. Read the climactic scenes between Armand and Marguerite in the third, the fourth, and the fifth acts of this play as a proof. Admit that these persons are Romanticists or even neurotic sufferers. There are, none the less, situations in life when the emotional soul, be it love, longing, grief, despair, seems to rise to the lips and radiate its power. Dumas has known how to find those occasions and to translate *realistically* this emotion into words and dramatic scenes. It is not easy to find another play which shows more clearly the power of passion and feeling in the drama and demonstrates more conclusively that this quality may cover a multitude of dramatic sins.

Le Demi-Monde is probably Dumas's most important play. With it he inaugurated Social drama, a realistic study of the social problems of his day as he saw them manifested in the society of Paris with which he was acquainted. Moreover, in this play he shows clearly what his own attitude is to be toward the kind of social questions which almost exclusively interested him. He is no longer a follower of the Romanticists. Although obsessed quite as much as they were by the all-absorbing theme of love and passion, his philosophy is exactly the contrary of theirs. Marguerite Gautier, so sympathetically painted in *La Dame aux Camélias,* and known by so many aliases in Romantic literature, has here become Suzanne d'Ange, incapable of real love, heartless, an adventuress endeavoring to break into honorable society. She is judged and condemned by the sternest of moralists. Her attacks on honest society must be thwarted by all means, even, it would seem, by the most dishonorable.

However, *Le Demi-Monde* is not to be praised simply for creating Social drama and for illustrating the philosophy of its author. It has other good qualities and less common ones. Those mentioned above would alone hardly give it the honor, usually accorded, of being Dumas's masterpiece. It is, from the dramatic standpoint, one of his best constructed plays, the one perhaps in which he has put the largest number of his many striking merits as a dramatist and observer, and the fewest of his several faults as a thinker and moralist.

The dramatic technique of Dumas has been described as pouring the contents of Balzac's novels into the mold of Scribe's comedy. Both of these elements have an undeniable merit. With the first Dumas creates a theatre of ideas; or, more exactly, he restores thought to it after it had been emptied by passing through the hands of Scribe. The merit of the well-made play, to a certain extent at least, for the rigid application of its technique may be objected to, is no less certain. Drama is action, and if this is to mean anything and to interest an audience, it must be action with a purpose and goal; it must have a plot.

The chief weakness in Dumas's drama is not in either of these two elements but in the difficulty of combining the two so that the dual purpose may not mar the unity of the play. This fault is sometimes found in his pieces. The moralist occasionally halts the action to preach, or to expound his theories; the showman frequently holds up the performers while he explains the significance of their actions. In *Le Demi-Monde* this dual purpose is rarely, if at all, apparent. The play is most strongly knit. The attempt of Suzanne d'Ange to break into honorable society, her clever-

ness and courage and our more or less natural sympathy for a fight against odds form the plot and hold the interest; and it is this same attempt and its frustration that make the social problem of the play.

It is not the intention to claim that *Le Demi-Monde* is not open to some criticism. It is, but for the most part this criticism is not fundamental. It is true that Olivier de Jalin is the beginning of the long line of reasoners and preachers on the stage. But he is here first of all an actor in the drama, and there is really little to show that he will become unbearable later in the rôle of de Ryons or Rémonin. A worse accusation against Olivier is that the author has been unable to make him as honorable and sympathetic as he intended. Much as we may sympathize with his purpose to save his friend from a heartless and unworthy adventuress, we are unable to approve his methods. Even more, we quite deny his right to throw stones, and when, in the end, his friend calls him *"le plus honnête homme que je connaisse,"* we openly revolt. However, we should not forget that the play is after all primarily about Suzanne d'Ange.

Of all Dumas's plays, probably the one most characteristic of his manner and interests is *Le Fils Naturel.* In the first place, it deals directly with the subject of the illegitimate child, which, because of his own irregular birth, more constantly than any other subject preoccupies him. However, this drama is mainly significant and interesting in the work of Dumas because it represents, as the first and most perfect model of his thesis plays, the final and inevitable phase of Social drama, not only in the hands of Dumas, but in those of nearly every dramatist who has essayed this genre. It is perhaps not sufficiently recognized that the Thesis Play is an almost certain terminus on the road of Social drama, if it be not the precipice over which its authors often fall.

Certainly no one would think of denying the powerful renewal that came in the drama, as well as in the novel, through the study of man affected by his physical and social *milieu*. The analogy, also, with the aims and methods of natural science, by which the drama was considerably influenced, is generally recognized. None the less, it is easily possible to carry this analogy too far and to assume that the scientific spirit and method are equally applicable in literature. This mistake has been made, in theory at least, by the extreme realists, by the Naturalists of the novel, such as Zola, and by some of his counterparts in the drama, such as the extremists of the Théâtre Libre. These theorists overlook the fact—to mention but one difference—that the detached and dispassionate attitude of the scientist, who studies a rock or a plant in his laboratory, is entirely impossible for the dramatist, who studies the human heart; in other words, who confesses his soul and the souls of his hearers before a thousand of his fellow men, and for their delectation. Even could he, by the impossible, attain to this scientific detachment, it is certain that it would be before empty seats. A drama, a study of humanity, must warm by its emotion and its sympathy; the degree of coldness of the audience records its failure or its success.

Social drama, such as Dumas wrote, dealt with the important social problems of his day, with marriage, divorce, immorality, illegitimacy, and in general with many questions that come closest to life. Naturally the dramatist, as well as the audience, had his opinions and convictions on such questions. Under these circumstances, it is too much to expect him to be always judicial, an impartial seeker for the truth. He is making a plea before a jury, and his success is to move them and touch their sympathies. Writing, then, on a social question on which he has strong convictions and prejudices, he is tempted, inevitably, to make a plea, to maintain a thesis. Social drama tends naturally to the Thesis Play.

This inherent situation in Social drama and this inevitable state of mind of the dramatist have created the utilitarian theatre and the propaganda play. Admittedly, no one held such a conception of the mission of the theatre more strongly than Dumas fils, or did more to popularize this view.

"The theatre," he says in the Preface to *Le Fils Naturel,*

> is not the goal; it is only a means to the goal. Moral man has been determined. Social man is yet to be defined. A work that would do for good that which *Tartuffe* has done against evil would be superior to *Tartuffe.*

Let us then, through comedy, through tragedy, through the drama, through burlesque, in whatsoever form suits us best, inaugurate the utilitarian stage, at the risk of hearing rail the apostles of Art for Art's sake, words absolutely devoid of sense. Any literature that does not aim at perfection, moralization, idealism, in short at the useful, is weak and unhealthy, born dead. Pure and simple reproduction of facts and of men is the work of a scribe or a photographer, and I defy anyone to cite a single writer consecrated by time who has not had for purpose the improvement of humanity.

But the rôle of Dumas as a moralist and reformer is too well known to need further comment here. What has not been so clearly recognized, perhaps, is that Social drama tends naturally to become the Thesis Play, and that the Thesis Play is, by definition largely, and by practice certainly, a plea more or less one-sided. However, as one may see with *Le Fils Naturel* as an example, this does not mean that such plays may not be the most moving and effective of dramas.

When *Le Fils Naturel* is looked at critically, we can see that all the virtues and merits have been put on the side of the mother and son, and that all the wrongs and antipathetic qualities are charged to the account of the father and his family. No doubt that is the reason why the play may arouse our sympathy and move us to indignation even, without our feeling in the end entirely satisfied that the last word has been said. Certainly, when we once accept the data of this play, the *donnée,* we find it hard to escape the conclusions of the author. His faultless logic and intense dramatic movement carry us along to the dénouement without a chance, or perhaps even a desire, for escape. It is only if we have the curiosity to return to the point where we were swept into the stream that we become aware how carefully the ways were oiled for our downfall.

It might be expected that the utilitarian stage and the propaganda play, so widely popularized by Dumas, would find a sympathetic reception in America. We are probably inclined, nationally, to the utilitarian in art, as elsewhere, and the success of this form with us is abundantly exemplified in recent years. Every movement, in fact almost every society or organization, be it ever so far removed from literary interests, has had its propaganda play. Whether this gives promise of good drama or not, it is, at least, a striking testimony to our fondness for the dramatic genre, just as it is also evidence of the far-reaching influence of French models.

Dumas was far from being a simple realist. He really escaped from the Romantic fold through being a moralist. But this quality of a moralist, which controls him at all times, may not only carry him into realism, but through and beyond it into the realms of imagination and symbolism. The indignant preacher may dwell on his subject until he becomes the inspired, or perhaps the mad, prophet. Nowhere is this clearer than in tracing the development of Dumas with regard to the one character he has so constantly pictured, the courtesan, from her appearance in his first play to his supreme vision of her in *La Femme de Claude.* Marguerite Gautier was borrowed from Romantic fiction and merely staged realistically by Dumas. Before his next play, the moralist had had time to consider her character seriously and he pictures her in her true light, as Suzanne in *Le Demi-Monde,* cold and self-seeking, although still with the paint and charm of her butterfly stage in Marguerite. In *Un Père Prodigue,* she is Albertine, with the paint rubbed off, not only selfish but mercenary; all pretense of love is dropped. She ruins men with indifference to secure money to maintain her effrontery. In Suzanne and Albertine we have the most realistic conceptions, and perhaps Suzanne is truer to life than Albertine.

In Césarine, the wife of Claude, we find the preacher turned prophet and seeing visions. The courtesan has become a symbol of evil, magnified, a monster of the Apocalypse, threatening destruction to all France. This is not an exaggeration, as will be seen from Dumas's own words in the preface to this play, where he explains his vision of this subject. He looks down at Paris and sees it as "a great melting pot where God makes his experiments."

> I was at this point in my observations, and I was asking myself what would become of us and whether we should not, in the end, be asphyxiated by these poisoners of our atmosphere, when I saw an enormous bubble appear in the cauldron; and there came forth, not simply from the scum and smoke but from the basic matter of the contents, a colossal Beast, which had seven heads and ten horns, and on its horns ten diadems, and on its heads hair of the color of the metal and alcohol which gave it birth. . . .

> At certain moments, this Beast, which I thought to recognize as the one seen by Saint John, gave forth from all her body an intoxicating vapor, through which she appeared radiant as the most beautiful angel of God, and in which came, by thousands, to sport, to tremble with delight, to scream with pain, and finally to evaporate, the

anthropomorphic animalcules whose birth had preceded hers. . . .

This Beast could not be sated. To go faster, she crushed some under her feet, she tore some with her claws, she ground some with her teeth, she stifled some beneath her body. . . .

Now, this Beast was none other than a new incarnation of woman, resolved to revolt in her turn. After thousands of years of slavery and helplessness, in spite of the conventions maintained by the theatre, this victim of man had wished to overcome him, and thinking to break the bonds of her slavery by breaking those of modesty, she had risen up, armed with all her beauty, all her cunning and all her apparent weakness.

This remarkable passage, we must remember, was written by the same hand which drew Marguerite and her companions so realistically that their prototypes were identified by all Paris and the censor refused to pass the play. It was such plays as the one based on this vision and *L'Etrangère* that caused the Naturalists to attack Dumas's realism, and that led Zola to say that Dumas used observation and reality only as a spring-board from which to leap into the realm of theory and imagination. The accusation is not wholly true, for these are not his most characteristic plays, but such flights of theory were always temptations to Dumas.

Dumas himself would have wished to be judged by his moral effect, although it is certain that his influence is primarily dramatic. Some of the tasks he set were: to reconstruct the family code on the basis of justice, equality and love, and to free the woman and child from unfair laws. He attacks the importance of money as vitiating marriage, and all lack of morals that endangers family life. He wishes to reform the prejudices and laws that seem to him unjust, particularly those concerning marriage and divorce, and he uses the stage as a tribune to propose these reforms. In doing this, Dumas often saw only one side of the question, and his attacks are sometimes unjust and his remedies insufficient, but they are always presented with dramatic force, and with a logic that is hard to refute if once we accept the premises.

Dumas's character drawing is subordinate to other interests. In fact, this situation is somewhat inherent in Social drama, although we see in a writer such as his contemporary, Augier, that this subordination is in no way necessary. One character, or rather type, which Dumas has created, is of special interest. This is the reasoner, the moralist of the drama, found in most of Dumas's pieces. It is, of course, Dumas himself, showing his actors and pointing out the lessons of the play. Substantially the entire spiritual life of Dumas can be found in this character.

His women are usually fragile, if not deceitful, and good women are rare in his plays. One might say that he has at least popularized, if he has not created, the modern type of the *femme troublante*. His men are perhaps no better morally than his women, being most frequently egotistic, if not odious. Of course, much of this is inherent in his sub-

jects, which for their presentation most often demand the idle, dissipated or pleasure-loving classes.

Dumas's dramatic art is exceptional, and his plays are among the best constructed of the modern stage. Everything leads straight to the dénouement, which, according to his own words, should be as inevitable as the answer to a mathematical problem. This faultless, and doubtless over-logical construction has been attacked, particularly by the writers of the Théâtre Libre, about 1880-1890, but it is yet to be proved that it is wrong, except in overemphasis.

In judging the final value of Dumas's plays, we must say that they do not present any very complete picture of French life. But what he does give is highly dramatic. His plays are moving—perhaps, also, they irritate and exasperate us with their faultless logic, which does not always satisfy and convince. His greatest contribution is to be found in the works of his contemporaries and successors. If his own work has not always lived, much of it does survive in the writings of others, and it is only after considering some of these, and particularly Augier, that we can fairly pass judgment on the real value and possibilities of this drama of which he was the chief creator.

However, while reserving judgment on many of the possibilities in Dumas's drama, we may draw conclusions at once on some outstanding features. He brought drama back to realities, recaptured it from imagination and impulse, restored it to its traditional French guardian, rationalism, and endowed it with serious thought and purpose.

These are inestimable services which outweigh all his faults, of which some at least are obvious and important. He relied too much on logic and not enough on experience, he turned the drama decisively toward propaganda, and his dramatic success in treating immoral love aided in forming a school where any second-rate author could master the triangle play and find a market for his talents. (pp. 130-50)

> *Hugh Allison Smith, "Dumas Fils and Realistic Social Drama," in his* Main Currents of Modern French Drama, *Henry Holt and Company, 1925, pp. 122-50.*

H. Stanley Schwarz   (essay date 1927)

[*In the following excerpt, Schwarz discusses humor and the use of analogy as important elements in the success of Dumas's plays.*]

"No one has known the theater better than Dumas *fils;* no one has been more thoroughly acquainted with its handling and its manipulation." "No one in our day has been more a master of the theater than Dumas; no one has exercised a more considerable action upon the public." Such are the opinions of Sarcey [in *Quarante ans de théâtre*] and Doumic [in *Essais sur le théâtre contemporain*]. Judgments as unqualified as these certainly justify examination; and it will perhaps prove profitable for us to devote some attention to the main elements of the dramatic technique of Dumas *fils*. Biological dissection, it is true, does not reveal the soul which inhabits the body. A good drama is a work of art; and, in separating it into its elements, we must risk losing for a moment the beauty of the work as a whole. Yet, in order to differentiate the work of Dumas *fils* from that of his fellow dramatists, we must of necessity investigate his methods of workmanship. . . . Many of the elements which constitute the dramatic technique of Dumas *fils* are too subtle to admit of definition and explanation; they are the secret of the dramatist's art. Other features, however, are more tangible, and these we can readily determine. Of them, the most conspicuous are: the *raisonneur*, the interrelation of characters, the "fore-and-aft" arrangement of groups, the "triangle plus," and the *liaison* of scenes. In the present chapter, we shall consider these five elements in the order named, and conclude with a few remarks upon the author's style.

As we survey the entire work of Dumas *fils*, we observe that most of the plays contain a character defined by critics as the *raisonneur* or *porte-parole*. This character develops and elucidates the theories of the author so forcibly as to leave no doubt in the reader's mind concerning the exact thesis which the dramatist is attempting to develop. If some character in the play offers an opinion opposed to the conclusions of Dumas, other characters immediately express contrary opinions, and the *raisonneur* appears who soon solves the difficulty for us and expresses the creed of Dumas on the subject. The *raisonneur* is particularly prominent in the thesis-play; but he is ubiquitous throughout the works of the dramatist. In *Le Demi-Monde,* it is Olivier de Jalin; in *La Question d'argent*, de Cayolle; in *Le Fils naturel,* Aristide Fressard; in *L'Ami des femmes,* de Ryons. One does not have to read far into a play of Dumas *fils* to discover which character is developing the author's ideas; and, in some cases, the author takes it upon himself to indicate in a preface the identity of his spokesman. It is interesting to note that the conception of this character is by no means original with Dumas *fils.* In Molière's *Misanthrope,* he appears in the rôle of Philinte. Petit de Julleville [in his *Histoire de la langue et de la littérature francaise*] indicates that this type was brought back to the French stage with great success by Théodore Barrière in *Les Filles de marbre,* 1853; that the *raisonneurs* are figures of the theater rather than of society; that, in the case of Molière, they represent his characters of lesser stress; and that the dramatist runs the risk of making them mechanical automatons rather than living creatures. This last criticism is unfortunately true of Dumas *fils* in some instances; for the *raisonneur* must at times deliver long monologues in order to do full justice to the ideas emphasized by the dramatist, and thus naturalness is sacrificed. Dumas evidently realized that he was sacrificing dramatic reality to the promulgation of his ideas; for, on one occasion, he attempted to excuse, in the eyes of his audience, two verbose but interesting discourses. In *La Question d'argent,* after a lengthy reply to the ideas of Giraud on nobility and money, de Cayolle terminates his discourse with the following speech which is palpably a dramatic device: "And the proof is that they have listened to me longer than they listened to you, and I have not, like you, a thousand franc note to put into each of my sentences" [I. iv].

Although Dumas *fils* cannot be credited with inventing

the *raisonneur,* he assuredly developed the use of this character to its fullest possibilities. It is, moreover, quite natural that he should have done so; for, with his natural combativeness, his logical mind, and his prodigious energy in argumentation, he had but to convert himself into the character whom he was placing upon the stage. This fact accounts in large measure for the marked similarity that exists between all of the *raisonneurs* of Dumas *fils.* Perhaps the author might have made them distinctive personalities if he had concentrated his attention more upon the emotional side of these men than upon the intellectual side. He had achieved success in differentiating his characters in *La Dame aux camélias,* before social problems obsessed his mind; and, in later plays, those characters which are not vehicles for the development of the author's arguments are the most distinctive of his personages; but even they do not impress us very greatly with their trueness to life. Even in *La Dame aux camélias,* M. Duval lacks the reality which the other participants in the drama possess; and, in subsequent plays, we remember the various *raisonneurs* not as striking individuals but as uniformly patterned orators. It seems that, in the thesis-drama, the *raisonneur* must be, at best, a necessary evil, true to life only when the dramatist can curb his own desire to use the character merely for the promulgation of ideas and endow his spokesman with human qualities other than mere intelligence.

It would be erroneous, however, to assume that the above-mentioned lack of contrast between the *raisonneurs* is characteristic of other personages, either in different plays or in individual dramas. In *La Princesse Georges,* we have Terremonde, who represents passion and who kills, in vivid contrast with Séverine, who represents love and who pardons. In *Le Supplice d'une femme,* the frankness and generosity of Dumont is opposed to the treachery and the ingratitude of Alvarez. So also does the saneness and stability of Dumont gain greater relief when compared with the hot-headedness of Alvarez. In *Les Idées de madame Aubray,* the romantic exuberance of Camille and of Jeannine stands out clearly against the realistic temperament of the older characters in the play. In *La Question d'argent,* a similar contrast is worked out with great skill and delicacy. Here Jean Giraud, practical and unromantic, totally absorbed in figuring out his accounts, is completely oblivious to the romantic scene between René and Mathilde which is taking place in his very presence. In this same play, the truly noble birth of de Cayolle offsets the *parvenu* element in Jean Giraud; and, at the same time, the honesty of de Roncourt counterbalances the unscrupulousness of Jean Giraud. Occasionally the characters in the plays observe these contrasts, as, for instance, Mme Dumont who, in *Le Supplice d'une femme,* remarks upon the difference in character between her husband and Alvarez which we have just indicated. She declares to Alvarez: "Can I help his being just as good as you are cruel, as noble as you are unjust, as devoted as you are ungrateful? Can I help comparing you, the one with the other, can I help repenting and finding him superior in every way to you and particularly to me?" [I. ii].

Not only was Dumas skillful in contrasting one character with another; he also met with success in projecting a character against a background of an entirely different color. In *Les Idées de madame Aubray,* the innocent Lucienne, fifteen years of age, who speaks of *amants* without knowing the true meaning of the term, forms a pretty contrast to the dismal drama which is going on in the house. In *Le Demi-Monde,* the sweet, innocent youth of Marcelle is bright and colorful against the drab and desolate background of the *demi-monde.*

Further instances of contrast abound in the plays of Dumas *fils;* but the examples above are sufficient evidence of how fully the dramatist worked out in his plays the theory of oppositions to which he refers in the preface to *Un Père prodigue* [see Author Commentary]. As most people are aware, a camera is capable of recording two very different reproductions of the same image. If we open wide the diaphragm and give a short exposure, we must expect to obtain a picture in soft tones with a blurred background against which a few salient features stand out in light contrast. If, on the other hand, we diminish the aperture of the diaphragm and give a long exposure, we have as our result a picture in which there is an equal amount of detail in both foreground and background, and we obtain clear, sharply cut, contrasting images. With Dumas, the camera is "stopped down" and the picture which he gives us is one of marked contrasts and of great definition.

Photographic precision, however, does not necessarily produce trueness to life. Dumas, with all of his skill in contrast, rarely produced major characters of real flesh and blood. His talent does not lie in the creation of living characters, but rather in the dramatic interrelation of his personages. His *raisonneurs,* with their verbose tirades, would be laughed off the stage were it not for the fact that the dramatist had already so connected them with other characters as to give promise of a struggle which is, of course, the essence of drama. Thus, in *Le Demi-Monde,* Olivier de Jalin is worked into a dramatic contention of forces with de Nanjac and Suzanne; in *Le Fils naturel,* Aristide Fressard is inseparably linked with Sternay, Clara Vignot, Jacques, and Hermine. Dumas shows unusual ability in his constant association of individuals throughout the action of a play. The characters are manipulated much like the men on a chess-board: each move involves a new situation; and the aggressive dramatist, never permitting any piece of consequence to remain idle, concentrates his forces in a relentless attack which culminates in an inevitable checkmate.

In connection with the interrelation of characters, we notice that Dumas occasionally develops what has been termed the "fore-and-aft" arrangement of personages. In several plays, there is not only a prominent group immediately occupied with a certain problem, but an older group which has finished with it and gives advice, and a younger group which finds itself on the threshold of the problem. This is true particularly of *Le Demi-Monde* and *La Question d'argent,* as the reader will recall to mind. Such an arrangement gives the audience the impression that the problem under discussion is not an exceptional one, of transitory importance, but one which is so fundamental that successive generations find themselves confronted with the same difficulties. It likewise results in greater con-

centration of interest; for the public is eager to observe the reactions of the various groups.

Another point of interest in connection with the arrangement of characters in the plays of Dumas *fils* is . . . [the] "triangle plus." Before the "triangle" play was fully developed, Dumas had already given examples of the triangle with an additional character woven into the main action. Besides the one lover (actual or potential), we have either an additional one, or even several. Thus, in *L'Ami des femmes,* to the triangle of de Ryons, Jane, and de Simerose, there is added de Montègre. In *Francillon,* Lucien and Francine form the two sides of the triangle; but the spectators are not quite sure whether the third side is to be represented by Pinguet or Rosalie Michon. The audience is also interested to ascertain whether three other characters, Stanislas de Grandredon, Jean de Carillac, and Henri de Symeux are to have a part in the formation of the three-sided figure. Other dramatists have given us, shortly after the rise of the curtain, the fully formed, geometrically drawn triangle. Dumas occasionally marks in heavy strokes but two sides of the figure, leaving the third side either in light pencil or else a blank to be filled in later. The very incompleteness of the drawing is suggestive and invites speculation. Will it become necessary later to draw in ink the faintly traced pencil line; shall we have to erase it and substitute another; or will the third line never need tracing, and will the other two sides of the angle, with nothing further to keep them apart, fall together and point in one direction? The possibilities of variety and suspense under this dramatic arrangement of Dumas become limitless.

Having examined the manner in which Dumas interrelates his characters, let us now review for a moment his procedure in gaining dramatic effect by the *liaison* of scenes. (pp. 121-26)

Notice, first of all, that Dumas *fils* does not use the system of balance of [Emile] Augier, but directs his plot logically and unremittingly toward the crisis of events. Professor Hugh A. Smith remarks concerning Dumas:

> His faultless logic and intense dramatic movement carry us along to the dénouement without a chance, or perhaps even a desire, for escape. It is only if we have the curiosity to return to the point where we were swept into the stream that we become aware how carefully the ways were oiled for our downfall [see overview dated 1925].

It is precisely by the dovetailing of scenes that Dumas "oiled the ways for our downfall," or at least kept us from coming to rest.

In any system which depends upon momentum for its force, a pause is fatal. The fall of the curtain at the end of an act marks a breathing spell which the dramatist is compelled to grant his audience. No one was more conscious than Dumas of the danger involved in allowing intermissions to divert the interest of the spectators. He therefore terminated individual acts in a point of high interest. If the reader will turn [to] the first part of *La Princesse Georges* . . . , he will notice that as Séverine, at the end of the first act, pronounces the words: "Oh! je suis une lâche et une malheureuse," Dumas has whetted our interest by the sudden reversal of feeling on the part of the Princess, leaving us eager to learn which emotion is to determine her future actions. Again, at the end of the second act, when Séverine announces to Agénor the fact that his wife has a lover, instead of telling him who the lover is, she replies to his demand for the name of the person: "Cherchez!" Immediately, a host of inquiries arise in our mind. Will Agénor discover that this man is the husband of Séverine? If so, what will be his course of action? Then what will the Prince do? And how will this complicate the situation of Séverine?

Dumas *fils* again displays great talent in sustaining interest by his treatment of the first act of **Les Idées de madame Aubray.** During the act, we have been led to believe that Jeannine is a widow with an only son, Gaston. The little boy, through references to the "Black Prince," has revealed the only name by which we know his father, apparently deceased. Mme Aubray has become acquainted with Jeannine because the latter is earning her living by playing at private concerts. The fact that she, too, is a widow with an only son forms a bond of sympathy between her and Jeannine. But suddenly the act ends with the appearance of Tellier, who has been sitting on the stage holding a newspaper so as to cover his face. When Tellier speaks to Jeannine, little Gaston inquires of his mother who this stranger is. She replies sadly as the curtain descends: "He is the Black Prince, my child." Our interest is immediately awakened. This, then, is the father of the child. But we thought him dead. What reason has Jeannine for concealing the fact? The child must be illegitimate. Then Jeannine is not a widow. This fact may snap asunder the bond between Jeannine and Mme Aubray, who was just about to welcome the visits of Jeannine and create an atmosphere of happiness in her saddened life. Will Mme Aubray discover the deception? If so, what will she do? The entire play will be determined by the answer to these conjectures.

Let us now turn to the end of the third act of this same play. Jeannine has confessed to Mme Aubray that she is unmarried. Mme Aubray has expressed her views on the subject with great frankness and with unusual charity. She sees no reason why Jeannine, repentant, and thoroughly chaste since her first fault, should not marry a young man of good family. She has even told Valmoreau that she knows a young woman, charming in every respect, who has committed a fault, and suggests that she would make a good wife for him. As the act ends, Camille, Mme Aubray's only son, declares his love to Jeannine and cannot understand her refusal to marry him. She tells him to talk the matter over with his mother. Upon his inquiry as to whether she will marry him if he gains the consent of his mother, she replies that she will do whatever Mme Aubray wishes. The act ends:

> CAMILLE, *to Valmoreau:* Ah! my friend, I am eager to see my mother.
>
> VALMOREAU, *to himself:* There is a young man who is going to suffer, but how willing I would be to suffer like that!

Will Mme Aubray have the courage to follow her conviction that a young woman in Jeannine's situation would make an acceptable wife for a young man of good family, when she discovers that it is her own son who wishes to marry Jeannine? If not, will Camille then be doomed to suffering as Valmoreau predicts? Will Valmoreau change his views and he himself marry Jeannine?

Les Danicheff [a work written in collaboration with M. de Corvin and presented under the pseudonym "Pierre Newski"] presents another interesting instance of suspense of interest. The Countess Danicheff, discovering that her son Wladimir loves her serf, Anna Ivanowna, whom she has reared almost as her own daughter, secretly frees both Anna and the coachman Osip and forces them to marry. Wladimir, the reader will remember, is sent to Moscow to spend some months there, the Countess promising that he may marry Anna upon his return if, after seeing many noble-born girls of marriageable age, he still persists in his resolution. The Countess has already determined upon Lydia Walanoff as the bride destined for her son, although gossip has freely used the reputation of Lydia as its target. As the curtain goes down on the second act, Wladimir has discovered the treachery of his mother. He tells Lydia frankly that he will not marry her and upbraids his mother for her ill-doing. He departs in search of Anna, threatening to kill Anna, Osip, and himself. Lydia swears vengeance. The melodramatic touch of this climax is perhaps mitigated by French views on Russian character; but, in spite of its exaggeration, the situation is sufficiently tense to cause the spectator to hope that the *entr'acte* may be of short duration.

In a much better constructed play, **Le Supplice d'une femme** [a work written in collaboration with Émile de Girardin and presented anonymously], another point of high interest is reached. The first act reveals the fact that Mathilde, wife of Dumont, has fallen a victim to the wiles of Alvarez, who has saved Dumont from bankruptcy. A child, Jeanne, has been born, whom Dumont adores in the full confidence that she is his own daughter. Alvarez, dissatisfied with eight years of deceit and lying to Dumont, wishes to end the difficulty by persuading Mathilde to desert Dumont and flee with him to a foreign country. She refuses to forsake her husband even though she still loves Alvarez. The curtain falls as she exclaims: "Oh God! what torture!" Which course will she follow in her dilemma? Which will gain the victory, love or duty?

In the second act Dumont learns the truth. In a pathetic scene, alone with Jeanne who is no longer his daughter, he breaks down and weeps, and the act ends:

> JEANNE, *terror-stricken:* What is the matter? (*She takes her handkerchief and wipes Dumont's eyes.*) You mustn't cry, dear father. Men don't cry. Little girls do that.
>
> DUMONT: You are right. (*He rings.*) Run away and play. (*To the servant.*) Go to M. Alvarez and tell him that I am waiting for him.

Upon this interview, of course, will rest the solution of the play.

An analysis of other plays of Dumas *fils* will reveal many more examples of suspense of dramatic interest. We might mention, in passing, the end of the third act of **La Dame** *aux camélias* where the contents of Marguerite's letter remain undisclosed; the end of the fourth act of *Diane de Lys* where Paul, alone on the stage, utters his challenge to the Count; the end of the prologue of *Le Fils naturel* where Clara discovers that Lucien is about to desert her to marry another woman; the end of the first act of the same play where Jacques departs in search of his father; the end of the third act of *Denise* where Brissot, having learned that Fernand has seduced Denise, demands that he send his mother to ask the hand of Denise for her son. These instances, and many others which we might find, would merely give further evidence of a fact which must be readily apparent to the reader; namely, that Dumas handled suspense of interest at the end of acts with remarkable success. It may be noted also that mastery in this element of dramatic technique aided the dramatist greatly in compelling his audience to listen to the instruction and preaching contained in his thesis-plays.

Not only did Dumas *fils* bridge the gap between acts; he also carefully knit together successive scenes within the acts themselves. *Le Fils naturel* is a striking example of this; but so characteristic is this element of Dumas' method of workmanship that it is conspicuous in any of his better plays. It is possible that, in Dumas' own time, individuals may have left the theater during the course of the performance because they were shocked at his audacity. I doubt that they ever left because they found the play dull. The clever dovetailing of successive scenes, which, in turn, gaining impetus, sweep one along in an irresistible current, must have compelled the attention of the spectators, sometimes even in spite of themselves, for many members of Dumas' audiences were thoroughly hostile to his doctrines.

Now that we have viewed in this chapter the characters and the framework of the plays of Dumas, let us conclude with a brief examination of his style. (pp. 127-31)

Dumas *fils* was quick to perceive the value of the doctrine *castigat ridendo mores,* a maxim which Augier was utilizing, but with genial mildness, at the same time that Dumas was writing his plays. In proportion as Dumas turned from the comedy of manners to the thesis-drama, as he ceased to be a mere observer and became a moralist and a reformer, his wit became more trenchant than that of Augier, and yet equally effective. Wit is ever present in the dramatic works of Dumas *fils* and lends to his last plays the glow of youth which pervades his earliest dramatic efforts. If we were, however, to choose one play in which this element of the dramatist's talent is most evident, our selection would doubtless fall upon his *Ami des femmes.* It is in this work that, in three different statements, de Ryons practically sums up the views of Dumas on the subject of humor which was one of the author's most valuable assets. "Oh, God!" he declares, "how good thou art to have made men so amusing!" [V. vii]. "It is not I who created the world; I take it as it is. But I prefer to laugh at it rather than weep over it" [V. v]. "The humorous along side of the serious, that is life" [V. vii]. It is this last mentioned juxtaposition of the humorous and the serious that Dumas handles with uncommon dexterity. Not only is humor an integral part of our existence, but it constitutes

an actual need; and thus, for the dramatist, "there is no better action than that of causing men, both respectable and otherwise, to laugh and of lifting from their shoulders for the few hours preceding retirement and sleep the burden of existence" [Préface, *Mariage dans un chapeau, Théâtre des 'Autres*].

What are, more definitely, the characteristics of the wit of Dumas *fils?* In the first place, he has a happy facility for coining epigrams and facetious generalities. We append a few of these in order to indicate how prevalent is this type of wit in his plays:

> Men, my dear, are like kites; the more string you give them the tighter you hold them.
> [*Francillon,* I. i]

> One should be married just as one should be vaccinated; it is a preventive.
> [*L'Ami des femmes,* I. v]

> Nothing can waken the wise man from his slumber.
> [*L'Ami des femmes,* I. i]

> One can always live with his wife provided that he has something else to do.
> [*L'Ami des femmes,* I. v]

> The first reason for adoring respectable women is that you should adore them, and the second reason is that you may say anything you wish to them; they blush less readily than the others.
> [*Les Idées de madame Aubray,* I. ii]

> Do you know what pardon is? It is indifference toward that which does not affect you.
> [*Les Idées de madame Aubray,* II. iv]

> BERTHE: There are three of them?
>
> VALENTINE: Including the husband. But a husband is like the *entre-sol* in large mansions; he doesn't count.
> [*La Princesse Georges,* II. ii]

Secondly, Dumas derives humor from a shift from the sublime to the ridiculous, as the following citation will indicate:

> Love is spontaneous. People who believe that it comes on little by little, like gout or baldness, are greatly in error.
> [*Les Idées de madame Aubray,* I. i]

A third, and very effective element of the wit of Dumas *fils* is the clever turn of phrase for which he is justly famous. In *L'Ami des femmes,* de Chantrin is an exemplary young man who gives up smoking because his mother objects to the odor of tobacco. As he is showing some views to Balbine through a stereoscope he says: "Now here we have Castellamare and Sorrento. There is Vesuvius, always smoking." At this point Leverdet remarks: "It couldn't have been brought up by its mother" [II. ii]. Some other instances of this type of witticism are:

> OLIVIER: And how about Maucroix? We have chatted about everything except him.
>
> HIPPOLYTE: That's true, we forgot him. How foolish we are!

OLIVIER: Would you kindly use the singular?

HYPPOLYTE: Of course. How foolish you are.
[*Le Demi-Monde,* I. iii]

LUCIEN: Thank you, gentlemen, perhaps I won't deny that. If it were only the intelligent people in the world who formed public opinion there would be too many fools.

THE MARQUIS (*shrugging his shoulders*): That's true, and there is almost always one more than people believe.
[*Francillon,* II. vii]

BARANTIN: Miss Capulet! Does she descend from the well-beloved Romeo?

VALMOREAU: By the balcony, perhaps.
[*Les Idées de madame Aubray,* I. i]

DE RYONS: And suppose she runs away with a gentleman?

LEVERDET: Oh, the poor gentleman.
[*L'Ami des femmes,* I. v]
(pp. 131-33)

In a word, wit is a most effective element in the plays of Dumas *fils*. He believes it to be one of the most valuable assets of the realistic dramatist. To him, men are amusing and life is characterized by an admixture of the serious and the grotesque. Epigrams, witty contrasts, cleverly turned phrases, all enter into his repertoire. Before we leave this subject, however, let us not fail to observe that Dumas often utilizes wit as a pleasant method of promulgating a serious idea. Those who will take the time to read his thesis-plays will discover that characters in these plays frequently present with a whimsical or humorous touch ideas of very vital import.

The same power of analogy which Dumas utilizes for humorous purposes, he sometimes turns toward more serious ends. Practically every play yields many cases of the evocation of images which greatly accentuate the thought which the author is attempting to emphasize. Take, for example, the following:

MME AUBRAY: First of all, guilty, wicked, and ungrateful people do not really exist; there are only sick people, blind ones, and fools. When we do evil it is not through premeditation, it is through weakness. We believe that the road to the left is more agreeable than the road to the right; and when we are caught in the brambles and in the mire, we call for help. Then it is the duty of the person who is on the safe road to devote his efforts toward saving the other man.
[*Les Idées de madame Aubray,* II. iv]

It is difficult to conceive of a clearer or a more convincing picture of human kindness than the above, a picture which is convincing through the cleverness of the analogy. We have another example of very expressive analogy in *L'Ami des femmes.* De Ryons advises Montègre to leave for China immediately; for, if he does not, de Ryons predicts that before long de Montègre will dishonor the woman he loves. When de Montègre challenges de Ryons to give reasons for this statement the latter replies: "Because you

can't harness a race horse to a plow; because before you have gone the distance of a quarter length of a furrow you will begin to kick against the shafts and will break everything" [III. vi]. In the same play, de Ryons maintains that he has never seen a truly virtuous woman. When Mme Leverdet says: "What! you have never seen a woman who loves her husband, who loves her children, and whose honor is intact?" de Ryons replies: "Yes! but that is not virtue, that is happiness. That is just as if you were to ask me to admire a certain gentleman who has 500,000 francs income and who has never stolen—since he has had them" [I. v]. *L'Ami des femmes* is filled with sparkling images; and it is usually de Ryons who utters them in the course of his conversation. How precisely does he describe de Montègre's voice, "a sonorous and metallic voice, striking off words as a minting-press strikes off coins" [II. i]. What clever comparisons he makes concerning a woman's life: "A well-bred woman does not pass from one passion to another without an interval of time of more or less duration. You never have two successive accidents on the same railroad" [I. v]. "A woman's past is like a coal mine; you must not go into it with a light or there will be an explosion" [II. i].

Lest it seem that we are claiming for the works of Dumas *fils* in general an element of technique that exists in only one or two plays, let us seek other examples in different plays:

FRANCINE: She had spread those diamonds all over her mother who accompanied her and who resembled the constellation of the Great Bear, not only in brilliance but in form.
[*Francillon,* I. iii]

MAXIMILIEN: She is one of those women who spend their lives in lining with a soft padding the ditch into which they intend that their virtue shall fall and who, furious at waiting on the edge for some one to push them in, throw stones at the other women who pass by.
[*Diane de Lys,* II. vi]

PAUL: Am I jealous of the Duke?

DIANE: Did I ever love him?

PAUL: Or of Maximilien? You certainly loved him.

DIANE: As one loves in a convent-school, as every young girl loves, or rather thinks she loves the first man she sees, a love like one's first teeth which have no roots and which come out without any pain.
[*Diane de Lys,* III. viii]

OLIVIER: It is impossible to hold conversation with you; you turn into evil the good that one wishes to do you. At the least word you go off like a cannon, with your reasons like 18-inch cannon balls which break one's arms and legs.
[*Le Demi-Monde,* III. iv]

The best case of analogy in the plays of Dumas *fils* is the oft-cited description of the *demi-monde* by Olivier de Jalin, which is truly a remarkable bit of writing:

Well, some day go into your fruit dealer's, to

Chevet or to Potel, and ask him for his best peaches. He will show you a basket containing magnificent specimens of fruit, each one placed at a little distance from the next piece, separated by leaves so that they may not touch each other or rot each other by contact. Ask him the price and he will answer, "Thirty cents a piece." Look around and you will be sure to see in close proximity to this basket another basket filled with peaches apparently exactly the same as the first ones, but placed closer to one another so that you cannot see all sides of them. The dealer has not shown you this group. If you ask him how much these cost he will answer, "Fifteen cents." Naturally you inquire of him why these peaches, just as beautiful, just as ripe, and just as appetizing as the others, cost less. Then he will pick out one at random, will turn it over, and will show you on its under side a little black spot which will be the reason for the lower price. Well, my dear fellow, you are here in the fifteen cent peach basket. All of the women who surround you have a fault in their past, a spot on their name. They huddle together so that it may be as little in evidence as possible and, with the same origin, the same exterior, and the same prejudices as women of the best society, they find that they no longer belong to that society. They make up what is known as the *demi-monde,* which sails like a floating island in the Parisian ocean and which hails, admits, and accepts all who fall, all who emigrate, all who escape from the mainland, not to mention haphazard wrecks of fortune whose original abode is unknown.

[*Le Demi-Monde,* II. viii]

The brevity of this section is by no means indicative of the extent to which Dumas made use of analogy in his plays. If the reader opens at random any volume of the plays and begins to read at that point, he will not be long in finding instance upon instance of striking analogy. By way of summary, let it suffice to indicate a fact which the reader has already noticed from the perusal of the examples contained in these few preceding pages: we have here a dramatist who, endowed with a tremendous breadth of observation and an unusual keenness of perception, has a peculiar gift for recording in the conversation of his characters the associative images which come so readily to his mind.

We discover, in recapitulating the contents of this chapter, that Dumas' stage-craft is the work of a master hand. He developed to a unique degree the *raisonneur,* even though he made of him a stereotyped character. He displayed unusual skill in the arrangement of his characters, interweaving them ingeniously into the action of the drama. To secure concentration of interest, he arranged a fore-and-aft group of characters, thereby strengthening his main theme. He developed the triangle-play beyond its usual three-sided limitation. He rendered his action dynamic by terminating individual acts with situations of great intensity, thereby bridging the gap caused by intermissions, and also by dovetailing the scenes within the acts so that their strength became cumulative. His style is conspicuous for two elements, wit and analogy; and these features are largely responsible for the brilliance of his dialogue and

for the clarity of what was so dear to his heart, the logical play. (pp. 134-37)

H. Stanley Schwarz, in his Alexandre Dumas, fils: Dramatist, *The New York University Press, 1927, 257 p.*

LA DAME AUX CAMÉLIAS

CRITICAL COMMENTARY

J. Brander Matthews   (essay date 1881)

[*An American critic, playwright, and novelist, Matthews wrote extensively on world drama and served as professor of dramatic literature at Columbia University; he was the first to hold that title at an American university. Matthews was also a founding member and president of the National Institute of Arts and Letters. Because his criticism is deemed both witty and insightful, he has been called "perhaps the last of the gentlemanly school of critics and essayists" in America. In the following excerpt, he suggests that although* Camille *is an unremarkable play in terms of its literary achievement, it is significant for its role in popularizing modern French comedy.*]

Marie Duplessis, the courtesan on whom Dumas based the character Marguerite Gautier in La Dame aux camélias.

With the appearance of M. Alexandre Dumas, *fils,* on the stage, a fresh force came into the French drama. To say this is easy; but to qualify this force adequately and to define its limits is no light task. The two other dramatists, each in his way remarkable, who stand to-day with M. Dumas at the head of French dramatic literature, are comparatively simple problems. In M. Sardou we see the utmost cleverness and technical skill, heightened by a girding wit: he continues the tradition of Scribe, adding all the modern improvements. In M. Augier we behold a high and genuine literary value, a humorous and broad humanity; he inherits by right of primogeniture from Molière, and observes mankind with the large frankness of his master. But M. Dumas continues no tradition; he is that rare thing in literature,—a self-made man. He derives from no one; he expresses himself, and with emphasis; he is a personal force. Not condescending to the ingenious trickery of M. Sardou, and never rising to the lofty liberality of M. Augier, his place in the dramatic hierarchy is not so readily fixed as theirs; his character is not so simple,—in fact, it may fairly be called complex, and even contradictory. Here, for instance, is a bundle of inconsistencies. With a real power of creating character, there is no dramatist who has more often and more boldly brought forward the same faces and figures. While declaring in one volume that he knows no immoral plays, but only ill-made ones, in another volume he asserts that the stage in itself is immoral: setting forth in one piece the right of assassinating the erring wife, he sets forth in the next the duty of forgiving her. In comedies inherently vicious he pauses to preach virtue, but with a bluntness of language at times shocking even to vice. He has written the **Ami des Femmes** and the **Visite de Noces,**—two plays which imply that their author does not suspect what "good taste" means; and yet he has been elected a member of the French Academy, constituted to be a tribunal of taste. The historian of the **Dame aux Camélias** and the discoverer of the **Demi-Monde,**—a word with which he has enriched the vocabulary of the world,— he has stood forward in the name of the Academy to bestow prizes of virtue. The son of a prodigal father always poor, he himself is wealthy and frugal; and finally, brought up in all the looseness of the lightest Parisian society, he has the Bible at his fingers' ends, and quotes the Scripture as freely as an Orthodox New Englander. With such a character and such a career, M. Dumas is one of the most interesting and curiously complex figures of our century.

The literary baggage of M. Dumas is not over bulky. Exclusive of about a dozen juvenile novels of little or no value, it is contained in eleven volumes. The collected edition of his plays, in which each piece was accompanied by a preface in which the author freed his mind, began to appear in 1868; the sixth and, for the present, final volume was issued late in 1879. Under the apt title *Entr'actes* a collection of his miscellaneous essays came out in three volumes in 1878-79. The dramaturgical chapters are of great value, the general literary papers are interesting; and so competent a critic as M. Auguste Laugel has at length, in letters to the *Nation,* praised the political portions. A later novel, the *Affaire Clémenceau,* put forth in 1867, and a discussion of the *Question du Divorce,* published only last winter, complete the list of M. Dumas's acknowledged works. More or less anonymously, he has had a hand in half-a-dozen plays not wholly his own. Chief among these are the **Supplice d'une Femme** of M. de Girardin, and the **Danicheff.** It is as a dramatist only that M. Dumas is now to be considered. (pp. 530-31)

M. Alexandre Dumas, *fils,* was born in Paris in July, 1824, a few days after his father was twenty-one years old, and a few years before his father had begun that career of literary notoriety and inexhaustible production which was to end only with his death. Like his grandfather, he was an illegitimate son,—a fact which seems to have given a congenital bias to his future writings. In one of his many autobiographic fragments, the elder Dumas referred grandiloquently to the birth of his son: "The 29th of July, 1824, while the Duke of Montpensier was coming into the world, there was born to me a Duke of Chartres." M. Dumas himself, in a letter to M. Cuirllier-Fleury, which serves as a preface to the **Femme de Claude,** speaks of the circumstances of his birth with real eloquence. He protests against the law which marked him, an innocent babe, with the stigma of illegitimacy. He says:—

> Happily, my mother was a noble woman, who worked to bring me up,—my father being a petty employé at twelve hundred francs a year; and by a happy chance it turned out that my father was impulsive but good. . . . When, after his first successes as a dramatist, he thought he could count on the future, he formally acknowledged me as his son, and gave me his name. This was much: the law did not compel him; and I was so grateful to him for it that I have borne the name as nobly as I could.

The boy was then put to school under Prosper Goubaux, the author of *Thirty Years of a Gambler's Life.* His schoolfellows bullied him unmercifully because he was a natural son. "My torture, which I have depicted in the *Affaire Clémenceau,* and of which I did [not] speak to my mother so as not to worry her, lasted five or six years." These years of suffering gave him habits of observation and reflection. Removed finally to another school, he regained his strength and his growth. At twenty he was a healthy lad, who, having known misery, was only too eager for pleasure enough to balance the account. His father, making and spending recklessly, was glad to have his son share in his prodigalities; and M. Dumas soon plunged headlong into the vortex of Parisian dissipation. But, to quote again from his letter: "I did not take great delight in these facile pleasures. I observed and studied more than I enjoyed in this turbulent life." Yet he was swept along by the current for several years, writing juvenile novels, more or less imitations of his father's inimitable fictions, gathering a load of debts, and laying up a stock of adventures and experiences for future literary consumption. In all his earlier plays he drew from the living model. The **Dame aux Camélias** and **Diane de Lys,** and even the **Demi-Monde,** were, as he tells us, "the echo, or rather the reaction, of a personal emotion, to which art gave a development and a logical conclusion happily lacking in life." One may perhaps hazard the suggestion that since M. Dumas has exhausted his personal experience, and has to rely altogether on his invention, as in the **Étrangère,** his plays are not nearly so good; whence we may fairly infer that the early adventures of the man were necessary for the full development of the author.

"It was the play of the *Dame aux Camélias,*" he says, "which began to free me from the slavery of debt, and of the society to which I owed both the debt and the success. I promised myself not to fall back either into debt or into this society; and I kept my promise at the risk of being called ungrateful." Written when the author was but little more than twenty-one, the novel of the *Dame aux Camélias* had been published with striking success just before the revolution of 1848. It decked out afresh a figure of which the French seem fonder than any other race. Manon Lescant gave birth to Marion Delorme [title character of works by Abbé Prévost and Victor Hugo, respectively], and Marion Delorme was the mother of the Dame aux Camélias, who in turn can vainly deny her latest offspring, Nana [title character of a work by Émile Zola]. Truly, it is an unsavory brood. The popularity of the novel suggested its dramatization. The elder Dumas thought ill of the project; and it was not until a melodramatist showed the author the *scenario* of a black melodrama, which he had taken from the novel, that—in sheer revolt at such treatment—M. Dumas himself set to work at it. In eight days the play was finished, so the author tells us; and the statement does not seem extravagant. As in the case of the *Supplice d'une Femme,* which he wrote later with extraordinary rapidity, he had his material all under his hand; and the play was not comedy, which calls for slow incubation, but a drama of simple passion, which could be struck off at a white heat. In spite of the speed of its production, the *Dame aux Camélias,* of all plays which any author has made out of his novel, shows least traces of a previous existence.

One would suppose that all the stage-doors in Paris would open wide to receive a dramatization of his successful novel by the son of one of the foremost novelists and dramatists of France; but it was more than three years before the play was tried by the fire of the footlights. Rejected by nearly every theatre in Paris, it was at last accepted at the Vaudeville, only to be vetoed by the censors. Patronized by the Duke of Morny, the government interdict suppressed it until after the *coup d'état* of December, 1851, when the duke himself entered the ministry. He believed in providing sensations for the people of Paris, and if possible in diverting attention from politics to the playhouse. Feb. 2, 1852, the *Dame aux Camélias* appeared at the Vaudeville Theatre, Paris, for the first time on any stage. It was an instant success, holding the stage for a hundred nights or more. It has since been revived in Paris half-a-dozen times, and always with the same success. A mutilated and innocuous alteration of it, prepared by Miss Jean Davenport (afterward the wife of Gen. Lander), was acted by her in America. It was called *Camille, or the Fate of a Coquette,*—a title which shows how the story suffered in the interest of Procrustean morality. Later the piece was taken up by Miss Matilda Heron. An Italian version of the play served Signor Verdi as the book of his *Traviata,*—an opera which the Lord Chamberlain permitted to be performed in London, while prohibiting the acting either of the original French play or of any English alteration of it.

The *Dame aux Camélias* was at once simple, pathetic, and audacious. It emancipated French comedy, and gave it the right of free speech. To judge it fairly, one must consider the comedies which held the French stage before its coming. There were Scribe and his collaborators, with their conventional and machine-made works; and there were Ponsard and M. Augier with their plays, poetic in intent and finely polished, but as yet reflecting nothing vital and actual. The great merit of the *Dame aux Camélias* is that it renewed modern French comedy by pointing out the path back to Nature and the existing conditions of society, and by showing that life should be studied as it was, and not as it had been or as it might be.

There is no need to dwell on the character of the play. As M. Montégut pointed out over twenty years ago in the *Revue des Deux Mondes,* the story of a courtesan's love may be a poetic subject if treated with elevation, or it may be a degrading subject if treated realistically; adding that M. Dumas had chosen a middle course, and that the result was little more than a vulgar melodrama. Before M. Montégut wrote, the subject had been treated poetically in M. Hugo's *Marion Delorme;* since, it has been set forth with unspeakable realism in M. Zola's *Nana.* In M. Dumas' play we avoid the offensiveness of the latter, but we miss wholly the poetry of the former. On one of its revivals, a competent French critic declared that it bore itself, even in its old age, like a masterpiece; and an almost equally competent American critic recorded that he had had a hearty laugh over its "colossal flimsiness." It is, in fact, not to be taken too seriously. It carries one along by the rush of youthful strength; yet one has time to note phrases horribly out of tune, and to detect a sort of sentimentality run mad. In general its morality is cheap, not to say tawdry. In short, the play seems to me youthful,—in the objectionable sense of the word. And I am half inclined to think that the Dame aux Camélias herself is doing exactly what she is best fitted for when she serves as the heroine of an Italian opera. (pp. 531-34)

> *J. Brander Matthews, "M. Alexandre Dumas, Fils," in* The International Review, *Vol. X, June, 1881, pp. 530-49.*

Clayton Hamilton   (essay date 1920)

[*Hamilton was an American playwright and critic. In the following excerpt, he discusses the enduring popularity of* Camille.]

The career of *La Dame aux Camélias* is, in many ways, unique in the annals of the theatre. In the opinion of the best French critics (and the French are very careful in their criticism) this play has never been regarded as a masterpiece, nor was it rated very highly by the author himself; yet, though over sixty years have now elapsed since the date when it was first produced in Paris, *La Dame aux Camélias* is still popular throughout the theatre of the world, and bids fair to be applauded a century from now, when the later and greater plays of the same writer have been relegated to the library.

Alexandre Dumas *fils* was born in 1824; and he was scarcely more than twenty-one when he wrote his first successful novel and called it *The Lady of the Camellias.* The material was drawn directly from his own immediate experience of that "demi-monde" of Paris to which he had been introduced by his prodigal and reckless father. As he said in later years, this youthful narrative was "the echo, or rather, the re-action, of a personal emotion." The book was immature, and sentimental, and immoral; but, in the turbulent days which anteceded the Revolution of 1848, it made a momentous impression on the reading public. The project of dramatization was suggested to the author; and he asked the advice of his famous father, who was perhaps the ablest playwright of the period. The elder Dumas reported to his son, regretfully, that it was impossible to turn the novel into a practicable play; and Alexandre Dumas *père* nearly always had the right idea in regard to questions of success or failure in the theatre.

Nevertheless, the youthful writer decided to waste a week or two in an attempt to dramatize his novel. He retired to the country, and wrote the play in eight successive days. Since the piece is in four acts, it will be noted that he allowed himself precisely two days for the composition of each act. It may be doubted if any other play which has held the stage for more than half a century has ever been written so quickly and so easily; but of course we must remember that the author was already familiar with his plot and with his characters before he sat down to write the dialogue of his play.

Yet, after the play had been completed, there was a doubt for many months that it would ever be produced. Although it had been dramatized from a successful novel, and although it was signed by the son of one of the most famous novelists and dramatists of France, it was rejected by nearly every theatre in Paris. After three years of hopeless wandering, the manuscript was ultimately accepted at the Vaudeville, only to be interdicted by the censorship. After new delays occasioned by political contentions, *La Dame aux Camélias* was finally produced in Paris, at the Vaudeville, on February 2, 1852. The author was, at that time, less than twenty-eight years old. The piece achieved an instantaneous success in France, and has since been added to the repertory of every other nation in the theatre-going world. It may be doubted if any other play composed since the initiation of the modern drama in 1830 has been so continuously popular in every country of the habitable globe.

In the opinion of those disinterested critics whose judgment is not conditioned by the verdict of the boxoffice, *La Dame aux Camélias* has always been regarded as inferior to many of its author's later plays, and especially to his admitted masterpiece, *Le Demi-Monde.* According to the judgment of the present commentor, Alexandre Dumas *fils* wrote, first and last, no less than half a dozen dramas which are more important, from the point of view of art, than this youthful effort that was struck off at white heat. The faults of *La Dame aux Camélias* are many and apparent. The view of life expressed is sentimental, immature, and in the main untrue. The thesis is immoral, because we are asked to sympathize with an erring woman by reason of the unrelated fact that she happens to be afflicted with tuberculosis. In the famous "big scene" between the hero-

ine and the elder Duval, the old man is absolutely right; yet the sympathy of every spectator is immorally seduced against him, as if his justified position were preposterous and cruel. The pattern of the play is faulty, because it rises too quickly to its climax—or turning-point—at the end of the second act, and thereafter leads the public down a descending ladder to a lame and impotent conclusion. In the last act, the coughing heroine—like Charles II—is an unconscionable time a-dying. The writing of the dialogue is artificial and rhetorical. Indeed, this noted play exhibits many, many faults.

Why, then, has it held the stage for more than half a century? And why, if it is not a great drama, does *La Dame aux Camélias* still seem destined to enjoy a long life in the theatre? The obvious answer to this question leads us to explore an interesting by-path in the politics of the theatre. This celebrated piece is continually set before the public because every actress who seeks a reputation for the rendition of emotional rôles desires, at some stage of her career, to play the part of Marguerite Gautier—or, as the heroine is called more commonly in this country, Camille. This part is popular with actresses for the same reason that the part of Hamlet is popular with actors. Both rôles are utterly actor-proof; and anybody who appears in the title-part of either piece is almost certain to record a notable accretion to a growing reputation. No man has ever absolutely failed as Hamlet; and no woman has ever absolutely failed as Camille. On the other hand, an adequate performance of either of these celebrated parts offers a quick and easy means for adding one's name to a long and honorable list, and being ranked by future commentators among a great and famous company of predecessors.

Here, then, we have a drama which is kept alive because of the almost accidental fact that it contains a very easy and exceptionally celebrated part that every ambitious actress wants to play. *La Dame aux Camélias* is brought back to the theatre, decade after decade, not by reason of the permanent importance of the author, but by reason of the recurrent aspirations of an ever-growing group of emotional actresses. (pp. 70-4)

> *Clayton Hamilton, "The Career of 'Camille',"*
> *in his* Seen on the Stage, *Holt, Rinehart &*
> *Winston, 1920, pp. 70-5.*

Stephen S. Stanton   (essay date 1957)

[*In the following excerpt, Stanton compares* Camille *with works by the French dramatist Augustin Eugène Scribe, suggesting that* Camille *possesses the greater emotional appeal.*]

The Broadway critics, reviewing a recent New York production of *La Dame aux Camélias,* or *Camille,* by Dumas *fils,* could only shake their heads over it. "Why *Camille?*" asked Brooks Atkinson of *The New York Times* [19 September 1956]. ". . . it is inconceivable that anyone should have an artistic interest in the old Dumas *fils* rumpus. . . . When [Marguerite] totters and staggers and gasps in the last act one does not suffer as one should." Walter Kerr of the *Herald Tribune* [19 September 1956] finds the play worth knowing historically but no more.

The latter-day consensus is, in fine, that *Camille* is the threadbare romanticism of a bygone day and that any grown-up theatregoer would feel ashamed to be caught tolerating it. Consensus or no, what other dramatist's first play has attained the thousands of performances that *Camille* has been given, and has lasted over a century? Could we name one? A present-day stage historian calls it one of the two most popular plays in America in the nineteenth century [Marvin Felheim, *The Theater of Augustin Daly*], and in the twentieth every year or so still brings forth yet another performance of Dumas' "prodigious moneymaker." Maybe Henry James, who had a pretty discriminating eye for the theatre, knew what he was talking about when he called *Camille* "a singular, an astonishing piece of work" and commented that "the story has never lost its happy juvenility, a charm that nothing can vulgarize" [see Further Reading].

Not that the play is without faults in plenty. Clayton Hamilton rightly pointed them out, and he rightly credited a large share of the play's success to the inveterate ambition of emotional actresses to pass the "test" of *Camille* [see commentary dated 1920]. But the very unanimity of this ambition is no mean tribute to the achievement of a tyro.

On February 2, 1852, at the Théâtre du Vaudeville in Paris, the world greeted the première of Dumas' play with mixed applause and bewilderment. *La Dame aux Camélias* had been adapted in 1849 from his novel of the same name, written two years before when he was only twenty-three. The novel had been smelted out of a personal experience. The play was first produced in sensational circumstances. Both reasons contributed to the tremendous stir that it made. For two and a half years it had been roughly handled by the censors: its frank treatment of a subject previously dealt with only in romantic drama, and thus insulated from real life, seemed immoral. But the Duc de Morny, first minister under Louis Napoleon, foresaw that the play, precisely because it was controversial, would helpfully divert attention from the current political agitations—this on the eve of the *coup d'état* of 1852 that ushered in the Second Empire—and he gave the play his support for production.

The stresses of that original production are, of course, now long forgotten; *Camille* has become merely something to be disparaged as a sentimental by-product of the well-made play. Inasmuch as the French theatre in the first half of the century had been dominated successively by two conflicting genres, the romantic drama and the more logical and satirical *pièce bien faite*, it is natural to see Dumas' first play as falling into the one category or the other. But does it?

Dumas' comment on the speed with which he converted the novel into the play reads: "I have written all my comedies with love and respect for my art, except the first (*La Dame aux Camélias*), which I brought into the world in eight days . . . without quite knowing how—thanks to the daring and luck of youth, impelled by a need for money rather than by divine inspiration" [Foreword to *Théâtre Complet*].

In 1844 Dumas had been captivated by Marie Duplessis, the illustrious fashion-loving courtesan adored by the most distinguished personages of her day. Her love affair with the indigent Dumas lasted until shortly before her death in 1846. The pinch that came of his reckless extravagance drove him in 1847 to the writing of his novel. Partly to ridicule a lurid melodrama concocted from it by a theatre manager, partly to capitalize on the fame that the novel had begun to bring him, he completed the play in the summer of 1849. He wrote at once impetuously and with the resolve to achieve a commercial theatrical success. For the first two acts he drew chiefly on his experience; for the remaining three, which transform and idealize his heroine, he relied on his knowledge of the contemporary stage. Bent on creating a great part for an actress, this frequenter of theatres observed and studied the tragic roles then being performed in Paris.

Rachel, the foremost actress of her time, in one of her rare departures from classical tragedy, was portraying the heroine in *Adrienne Lecouvreur,* the most sensational drama to date of Scribe and Legouvé, which had opened on April 14, 1849. In this play an ill-fated actress, poisoned by her rival for the love of a nobleman, dies in agony on the stage. Rachel amazed Paris with an interpretation so intense, it is recorded, that she frequently wept from exhaustion after performances.

Dumas was unquestionably influenced no little by *Adrienne Lecouvreur,* and the similarity of the two plays is striking. Both present the separation of lovers by a rival. In both first acts one of the lovers meets the future rival. Act II in both contains a scene of local color that halts the main action. In both the jealousy aroused in one of the lovers is assisted by the use of letters. Dumas' peripeteia differs superficially, but in both a separation turns on the withholding of information from one of the lovers. In Act IV each heroine makes a noble sacrifice for her lover. Both heroines faint when insulted or told of their lovers' danger. Each *scène à faire* is engineered by extreme jealousy in one of the lovers, and suspense is broken by a contrived and unexpected diversion. In each play one lover upbraids the other's (or the rival's) duplicity, real or imagined. In each the heroine dies in the last act, and the hero, having learned the truth, arrives just in time to beg forgiveness.

The truth is that both *Camille* and *Adrienne Lecouvreur* illustrate the danger of applying Scribe's methods to tragedy or to serious drama. Character and truthful values are sacrificed, as the list of resemblances shows, to theatrical manipulation. The motivations are the product of coincidence rather than of will. The technique of the well-made play wears best in light or satirical comedy, where an agile, entertaining plot implants the deeper passions or, if they are present, at least does not dissipate them.

Camille, then, has a somewhat ambiguous relation to the well-made play and cannot be said strictly to belong to the genre. It is in some ways better and in others worse constructed than *Adrienne Lecouvreur.* The main action of Dumas' play is simple, direct, and straightforward by comparison with the complex mechanism of Scribe's innumerable contrived entrances and exits, mechanical hide-and-seek claptrap for keeping characters apart, mistaken identifications, and stage business with physical objects. In *Camille* suspense is admirably sustained from the end of Act III almost to the end of Act IV by means of Marguerite's letter to Armand. The kind of theatrical legerdemain that had dominated *The Glass of Water* a decade before has noticeably diminished—a change that is to the credit of a young and inexperienced playwright.

On the other hand, the fourth and fifth acts of *Camille* (*scène à faire* and dénouement) lack the sharp focus and the economy of Scribe. The Scribean obligatory scene always discloses a new and significant truth, up to this moment withheld. Although it is a *coup de théâtre*, it seems indispensable to the action. Some moral weakness is always exposed, though generally not with too solemn an insistence. It is precisely this scene in Scribe's plays that later social dramatists—Ibsen, Shaw, and others—adapted so effectively to their own kinds of ironical revelation. The obligatory scene in *Adrienne Lecouvreur* hinges on the confrontation of women rivals hitherto kept apart and frustrated in their efforts to identify each other. The audience wants the faithful Adrienne to upbraid the calculating and unscrupulous princess for her duplicity, and in this scene Adrienne does explicitly recognize the true character of her rival, setting the record straight as between good and evil. In *Camille* the corresponding scene really adds nothing to the play's effectiveness. It seems contrived, because Armand has already learned the identity of his rival, and we have already had examples of his jealousy, his distrust of Marguerite. Despite her loyalty to Armand, she gets decidedly the worst of it. Since Armand does not learn the truth until after this scene, his contrition in the last act seems over-emphasized and hence sentimentalized. And the obvious interruption two thirds of the way through the fourth act, when dinner is announced, serves merely as a device to relax the mounting tension between Armand and his rival and to bring the lovers together. Again, the death scenes of both *Camille* and *Adrienne Lecouvreur* are too long, the dialogue too rhetorical. Dumas, by weakening his *scène à faire*, deliberately played on the audience's sympathy for Marguerite and at the same time betrayed his determination to contrive, however factitiously, the redemption of the courtesan through love and suffering.

Camille, fuzzy though it may be in structure and content, belongs no more to the romantic world of Victor Hugo's dramas than to the satirical tradition of Scribe. There is a great gulf between Armand Duval's love for Marguerite Gautier and the chivalrous etiquette and daring of the three rival lovers in *Hernani* (1830) or the regenerating devotion of a swashbuckling hero to a courtesan in *Marion Delorme* (1831) and, anyway, both plays are written in a strained and elaborate verse that robs the characters of most of their humanity.

Camille, whatever its shortcomings, has probably exerted a greater leverage on the English and American realistic social drama than any other nineteenth-century French play. The erring woman and her relation to society have held the center of the stage since 1852; and from that year can reasonably be dated the modern comedy of manners. René Doumic, a judicious French critic, was one of the

first to recognize this fact. More recently a biographer of Dumas has described the singular impact of *Camille* on Paris in 1852: "Now came a young man who dared to depict not a courtesan of historical legend, not an adventuress surrounded by a halo of poetic symbolism, but a 'kept woman' of everyday contemporary life, and this author made his subject even more realistic by writing in ordinary prose" [see H. Stanley Schwarz overview in Further Reading].

Eugènie Doche and Charles Fechter, the first artists to play *Camille,* communicated the intended spirit of the play with such subtlety and restraint that Dumas affectionately called them his collaborators. As Marguerite and Armand they commanded from spectators both pity and admiration. Marguerite, as Doche portrayed her in Paris, was "to the last breath, a courtesan," said the great critic Sarcey.

Do American readers know what a courtesan is, or was? The elegant extravagances of European high society have no equivalent in this country. Dumas pointed out in his preface (1867) to the play that in 1830 a Parisian courtesan had been known as a *femme galante*—a fashionable kept woman who had acquired the education and refinement of the wellborn lady. By 1860, however, there had developed the gradations of *femme entretenue, lorette, petite dame, cocotte,* and so on. A good many aristocratic but poor daughters of officers killed in the wars of the Empire had been denied the marriages to which their background, training, and tastes entitled them. However endowed with intelligence, delicacy, and capacity for devotion, they had to exist by amorous liaisons and doubtful enterprises; but many of them had brilliant social gifts and could make their lovers grateful for far more than the pleasures of the voluptuary. For such women Dumas himself coined in 1855 the name that became the title of perhaps his best play, *Le Demi-Monde.*

The realistic acting of Doche and Fechter in *Camille* helped Dumas give greater social meaning to French drama. In 1852 courtesans were not accepted by the middle class, even in France. But at least Marguerite (who is a courtesan, not a *demimondaine*) could be seen as her creator intended her to be. In England and America, however, the true Marguerite was travestied and obscured for years. Matilda Heron, the first famous Camille in the United States, absurdly denatured the part in conformity to squeamish Victorian tastes and in ignorance of Dumas' milieu; she concentrated her interpretation on a harrowing emotional conflict, throwing overboard analysis, suspense, and the comparatively well-ordered plot in order to exaggerate the heroine's high-minded despair and humiliation.

It had been a bold undertaking to show on the stage a courtesan who had been a public celebrity and to make her capable of unselfish love. The author was censured for his idealized version of a free love that made no concession to the world. Having himself been the intemperate lover of a spectacular and wealthy *femme galante,* he now began to take refuge in masochistic apology, in overcompensation for the guilt and insecurity that his recklessness had entailed. In later plays he became more and more the preacher, less and less the man of the theatre. But, though a hint of thesis runs through the play, to the effect that a prostitute cannot be rehabilitated even if she has a regenerating love, Dumas was not yet the moralist of his later *pièces à thèse*. What he did accomplish was to bring the theatre into more direct touch with life and human problems than it had aspired to since before the Romantic Movement. And it was doubtless partly to soften the impact that he resorted to the theatrical machinery of the well-made play, then at the height of its popularity. In the preface to *Camille* he disclaimed the idea of redeeming the courtesan and insisted that Marguerite's love merely illustrated the truism that an act of self-sacrifice can come from an unlikely source.

It is unquestionable that in this first play Dumas wanted to depict the life of the courtesan as it was more than he wanted to reform her. Duval *père,* the voice of respectable morality, who succeeds in separating the lovers, in the last act acknowledges that he was wrong to have done so: yet the play has a sort of implicit corrective undertone that keeps it from being an uncompromising apologia for free love. The courtesan's life is shown to be, after all, trivial and hollow; the men of this milieu are avaricious, irresponsible, and stupid; aside from Marguerite herself, the women are repellent. Several persons in the play frown on this papier-mâché world. The elder Duval is in his way likable and human; and two of the debauchees in the end see the light and marry.

But—the important point in this context—the play achieves a more concentrated dramatic conflict and greater emotional depth than most of the well-made plays of Scribe. The characters have vitality and warmth. We respect Marguerite's frankness, sacrifice, and freedom from hypocrisy. The dialogue is more outspoken and lifelike than the romantics would have ventured to make it. And, as some critics have observed, many faults of construction are atoned for by the emotional power generated through a kind of character altogether new to French drama. (pp. xxv-xxxii)

> *Stephen S. Stanton, in an introduction to* Ca-
> mille and Other Plays, *edited by Stephen S.
> Stanton, Hill and Wang, 1957, pp. vii-xxxix.*

FURTHER READING

AUTHOR COMMENTARY

Dumas, Alexandre. "How to Write a Play." In *Papers on Playmaking,* edited by Brander Matthews, pp. 84-5. New York: Hill and Wang, 1957.

Illuminates the playwright's views on the elements of successful drama.

OVERVIEWS AND GENERAL STUDIES

Arvin, Neil C. "Dumas Fils a Realist?" *The French Review* VI, No. 2 (December 1932): 135-39.

Challenges the commonly accepted interpretation of Dumas as a realist writer.

"Alexandre Dumas." *The Critic* 27, No. 720 (7 December 1895): 379-81.

Appreciation of Dumas's career occasioned by his death.

Fletcher, Jefferson B. "Alexandre Dumas Fils." *The Harvard Monthly* XIII, No. 1 (October 1891): 1-15.

Proposes, regarding Dumas's role as a social commentator, that the dramatist "recognizes that the stage cannot lead us into virtue, but he believes that it can shock us out of vice."

France, Anatole. "M. Alexandre Dumas, Moralist." In his *On Life and Letters,* translated by A. W. Evans, pp. 22-30. London: John Lane, The Bodley Head, 1911.

Discusses Dumas's career as a "spiritual director to the multitude."

James, Henry. "On the Death of Dumas the Younger." *The New Review* 14, No. 82 (March 1896): 288-302.

Assessment of Dumas suggesting that he was "the observer of a special order of things, the moralist of a particular relation as the umpire of a yacht-race is the legislator of a particular sport."

Jerrold, Evelyn. "Alexandre Dumas the Younger." *Temple Bar* 51 (November 1877): 392-408.

Contests Dumas's reputation as a paragon of moral conduct, characterizing the dramatist as "a moral charlatan trading on unclean curiosity, under the cloak of an evangelist."

Lancaster, Charles Maxwell. "Dumas the Younger and French Dramatic Forms Existing in 1850." *Poet Lore* LI, No. 4 (Winter 1945): 345-52.

Highlights Dumas's innovations as a dramatist, praising as realistic his depictions of the social classes.

Nicoll, Allardyce. "From the Medieval to the Materialistic: The Coming of Realism." In his *World Drama: From Aeschylus to Anouilh,* pp. 485-518. New York: Harcourt, Brace and Co., 1950.

Includes a discussion of Dumas's contribution to the development of realism in modern European drama.

Saunders, Edith. *The Prodigal Father: Dumas Père et Fils and "The Lady of the Camellias."* London: Longmans, Green and Co., 1951, 257 p.

Popularized account of the Dumases' lives and careers.

Schwarz, H. Stanley. *Alexandre Dumas, fils, Dramatist.* New York: The New York University Press, 1927, 257 p.

Includes examinations of Dumas's dramaturgy, social beliefs, and debt to the dramatic techniques of Augustin Eugène Scribe and Honoré de Balzac.

Van de Velde, M. S. "Alexandre Dumas Fils and His Plays." *The Fortnightly Review* n.s. 59, No. CCCXLIX (1 January 1896): 94-103.

Acknowledges Dumas's prominence as a dramatist, while finding his career as a moralist partially vitiated by the narrowness of his vision and thematic inconsistencies in his works.

Weinberg, Bernard. "Contemporary Criticism of the Plays of Dumas *fils,* 1852-1869." *Modern Philology* xxxvii, No. 3 (February 1940): 293-308.

> Surveys the reactions of French critics and reviewers to Dumas's plays at the time of their initial performances.

LA DAME AUX CAMÉLIAS

Clark, Roger J. B. Introduction to *La Dame aux camélias,* by Alexandre Dumas *fils,* pp. 7-48. London: Oxford University Press, 1972.

> Discusses the historical background and significance of *La Dame aux camèlias* as well as the moral issues raised therein.

Perkins, Merle L. "Matilda Heron's *Camille.*" *Comparative Literature* VII, No. 4 (Fall 1955): 338-43.

> Compares Dumas's *La Dame aux camélias* with Matilda Heron's popular nineteenth-century English translation of the play.

Charles Fuller

1939-

(Full name: Charles H. Fuller, Jr.)

Fuller, an American playwright, is widely known for his 1982 Pulitzer Prize-winning *A Soldier's Play*. His dramas, which explore racism and discrimination, tackle social concerns while striving to appeal to a wide audience. According to Esther Harriott, Fuller is "almost alone among contemporary American playwrights in focusing attention on social issues."

Born in Philadelphia, Fuller grew up amidst the many foster children taken in by his parents, Charles H. Fuller, Sr. and Lillian Anderson Fuller. He became interested in writing when his father, a printer, let his son proofread works from his press. While at Roman Catholic High School in Philadelphia, Fuller and his friend Larry Neal, who himself became a dramatist and critic, vied to be the first to read every book in the library. But it was at a Yiddish theater that Fuller first became infatuated with drama. "It was fascinating!" he told Jean Ross in an interview in *Contemporary Authors.* "Certainly I attribute my joy in theatre to that first experience—and I didn't understand a word of Yiddish!"

After attending Villanova University from 1956 to 1958, Fuller worked as an Army petroleum laboratory technician in Japan and Korea for four years. He is reticent about this army experience, preferring to reveal his views about military life in his plays. After his return to civilian life, he attended LaSalle College from 1965 to 1968 while continuing to write. Fuller generally accords little attention and praise to these early short stories and plays. Critics agree that he showed promise, however, in *The Village: A Party,* a play in which a community of interracial couples murders its leader, who has fallen in love with a woman of his own race. This, his first professionally produced drama, drew critical attention to Fuller. With *The Brownsville Raid,* however, commentators began to fully recognize his skill as a dramatist.

The Brownsville Raid is based on a 1906 shootup—by unknown assailants—in the town of Brownsville, Texas, that resulted in the dishonorable discharge of 167 soldiers from the all-black 25th Infantry stationed nearby. Fuller's documentary-like recounting of the incident garnered praise for its authenticity, and several critics applauded the play's conclusion, in which the names of the discharged soldiers and their respective fates are read in roll-call fashion. Fuller's *Zooman and the Sign* likewise drew acclaim, and the Off-Broadway production won two Obie Awards. The work recounts a quest for justice after a young black girl accidentally dies at the hands of Zooman, a black teenager. Because the girl's neighbors will not identify the slayer, her family places a sign in their window reading: "The killers of our daughter Jinny are free because our neighbors will not identify them." The production of *Zooman* inspired Gerald Weales to assert that Fuller is "an

obviously talented playwright, ambitious in his attempt to deal with difficult and complex themes." Yet Weales agreed with other critics when he conceded that *Zooman* "never quite succeeds in the ambitious terms in which it is conceived."

With his next production, *A Soldier's Play,* Fuller became only the second black playwright to win the Pulitzer Prize for drama (the first, Charles Gordone, received the honor in 1970). Herman Melville's *Billy Budd* influenced this story of the murder investigation of Technical Sergeant Vernon Waters, a martinet in charge of a unit of black soldiers stationed in Louisiana during World War II. Many critics regard Waters as Fuller's most interesting and complex character to date. A black non-commissioned officer decorated in World War I for his heroism, Waters nevertheless suffers discrimination by his fellow white officers. Yet Waters intentionally echoes Hitler when he suggests that C. J. Memphis, an affable southern black soldier under his command, is a detriment to their race. When C. J. commits suicide, Waters undergoes a transformation, recognizing the futility of his efforts to fully integrate into white society. Several critics observed that the mystery of Waters's murder—discovered to have been perpetrated by one of his black soldiers to avenge C. J.'s suicide—makes audience members examine their own prejudices as they come to conclusions regarding the identity of the murderer. *A Soldier's Play* ran in New York for more than a year, and Fuller received a 1984 Academy Award nomination for his screen adaptation of the play, *A Soldier's Story*.

A Soldier's Play also provoked controversy, however. Amiri Baraka, a dramatist and leading figure in the Black Arts and Theater Movement of the 1960s, accused Fuller of fulfilling the dreams of the white power structure in *A Soldier's Play* and consequently working against his own race. Fuller had long been associated with the Negro Ensemble Company, a rival organization of Baraka's Black Theater Movement. As Harriott wrote: "The [Black Theater] Movement demanded black plays in black theaters in black communities, but Douglas Turner Ward, the actor and director who founded the Negro Ensemble Company in 1967, argued that until the ghettoes were rebuilt, their theaters would be islands." Baraka opposed the Negro Ensemble Company, arguing that it "became a real force in the black community by means of the bourgeoisie's money." He added: "When negro artists say, as did Ward and Fuller recently, that they wanted 'a theatrical rather than a polemical event,' they lie. They have created as political a theater as any in the Black Arts Movement, only it is the politics of our enemies!" Other critics defended the Negro Ensemble Company, however, and praised Fuller for not producing "propaganda" or "agitprop."

Since *A Soldier's Play*, Fuller has opened two seasons for the Negro Ensemble Company with three dramas in an intended five- or six-play series on the black experience during the Civil War and in postbellum America. *Sally* and *Prince*, performed jointly under the title *We*, and *Jonquil* opened successive seasons for the Company. Although these works have received only moderate praise at best, Fuller has continued to portray the plight of blacks in a racially biased society.

(For further information about Fuller's life and career, see *Black Writers; Contemporary Authors*, Vols. 108, 112; *Contemporary Literary Criticism*, Vol. 25; and *Dictionary of Literary Biography*, Vol. 38.)

PRINCIPAL WORKS

PLAYS

The Village: A Party   1968
An Untitled Play   1970
In My Many Names and Days   1972
The Candidate   1974
First Love   1974
In the Deepest Part of Sleep   1974
The Lay Out Letter   1975
The Brownsville Raid   1976
Sparrow in Flight   1978
Zooman and the Sign   1980

A Soldier's Play   1981
*Sally   1989
*Prince   1989
Jonquil   1990

*These works were performed as *We* in 1989.

AUTHOR COMMENTARY

Interview with Charles Fuller   (1982)

[Esther Harriott is the author of the 1988 study American Voices: Five Contemporary Playwrights in Essays and Interviews. *She interviewed a harried Fuller in May 1982, just after he was awarded the Pulitzer Prize for drama. Fuller's responses, delivered with a combination of "amusement, good nature, and fatigue," concerned his works, his thoughts about being a black dramatist, and his current project: the screen adaptation of the prize-winning* A Soldier's Play.]

ESTHER HARRIOTT: *Where do you get the ideas for your plays? History must be one source.*

CHARLES FULLER: Everything I touch, really everything. I can't really point at one thing. I do a lot of reading in history. I read novels. I read all sorts of interesting pieces. For example, right now I'm reading *True Confessions* from 1917 (I think) through 1979, just to see how the magazine has changed, how our tastes have changed.

Do you have certain obligations as a black playwright? Is there pressure put on you to be a spokesman?

No. There never has been any pressure put on me to be a spokesman for anybody. No one has ever come to me and said to me, "Do this. Why don't you consider this or why don't you try looking at this or why aren't you looking at that?" I have been very fortunate in not ever having to deal with that.

So that when you write you're not trying to do anything in your writing other than to write what's inside of you?

I'm trying to capture my experience. I'm translating the kind of contact that I've made with people, most of them black. But how I would write anything that is presumptuous enough to masquerade as being something that speaks for black people is beyond me. I'm just not that sort of person.

What about addressing the audience? I guess that's what my question was getting at. Are you trying to make your audience change in any way?

Oh, of course. There are lots of things that have to change. How people see black people must change. That we are two-dimensional, length-and-width type people that have no depth is simply not true. And I think it's important to display that sense of having more to us than simply the stuff of protest or of being victimized. There's much more to us than that. I'm simply expressing what is real, not what people like to think we are. So far we've been the victims of a compendium of stereotypes about ourselves. The very idea that black people are complex psychological beings is simply not dealt with.

Don't you think that anybody has dealt with that at all? Ralph Ellison, for example?

Yes. But part of the problem with the novel is that it takes a long time to be read by lots of people. The one advantage of working in the theater is that I know I'm going to get an instant response.

On the other hand, if someone writes poetry or fiction, he can count on more people reading him than a playwright can count on people seeing him. And if a play isn't produced, nobody at all is going to know what you've written.

Well, that's never happened. I also don't believe in an age of this great visual explosion that we have, that a whole lot of people take the time to go to a bookstore to find a book. The number of black publications produced every year will certainly attest to that fact. People are not reading a whole lot of black material. But if there's a play that you can come to, sit for two hours, and be moved in some way, and get up and tell your friends, that's a lot easier than spending a week with a book. And then a writer isn't quite sure, after you've read it, what you've got out of it. I'm fairly certain when an audience walks out whether they like or dislike what I've done. I don't want to wait six months, having written for six years.

Do you think, speaking of the visual explosion, that television and movies have hurt the theater?

They might have, but it hasn't been my experience. I think there's a place for all of it. We tend to be very drastic in the way we see things. We say television or the movies are hurting the theater and putting it out of business. The money that the long-running shows have made seems to me to belie the fact that television has cut across a lot of it. Certainly it has taken some money out of the box offices. But there's room enough for everybody.

You sound optimistic. I keep hearing that the theater is in crisis.

Well, that's for people who want to look at the things that used to be. The past is in crisis. The idea that old ways of perceiving the world are still viable in a changed era is in crisis. But that's always been in crisis throughout our history. I was recently reading an article about the theater being in crisis, and ten years before that there was an article about the theater being in crisis. People really don't know what to say about theater, quite frankly. I don't think they've known since Euripides and Sophocles. It's come under fire for ages, constantly under fire.

Then you think it's going to last.

Sure. Crises are things that involve life and death situations. Someone's life is in danger. That's a crisis to me. Anything in the nature of human affairs that can be taken care of tomorrow or in 24 hours or in 48 hours or next month or next year is certainly not in crisis. That's nonsense. If there's a crisis, there was one last year. If there was one last year, then there was one the year before that.

Are you very disciplined?

Yes. When it's time to work, I work. When it's time to do something else, I do that. I never let anything confuse me when I know it's a serious time.

When you're working, do you work all day?

Yes, I work straight through. When I'm not working, I may be doing anything, anywhere. For me, working is really an isolated kind of thing. It's a very steady, long process. Not that it's long in terms of days, but all day every day until the work is finished. It's like the army. When I was in the army, they trained you for six months, but they trained you every day. You got one day off. And you went to school eight hours a day, six days a week. You can't help but learn or get done what it is you set out to do. And that method seems very practical. It works.

But your plays get written fairly quickly, don't they?

Yes. That's why I like them. They don't take long to do.

Have you been drawn to any other forms of writing?

I write short stories and essays.

You mentioned isolation. The collaboration with people in the theater must be pleasant after being isolated at your desk.

It's pleasant for the length of time it takes. It's a kind of closeness that you've got with people for a short period of time. It doesn't mean that you have to do this all year long. I tend to write plays, get them produced, then get out of it for a while. Theater and all the things that attend it are very, very exhausting—the opening, reviews, and all that stuff that goes along with it. So I try to do one a year if I can. And if I can't, I'll do something else. I couldn't do two plays a year. I'd go nuts.

Have you been writing one play a year?

Just about. But I don't think I'll do it next year.

How will you approach your script to make it into a screen play?

What I do is make notes about what I am looking at, and what are some of the things that are going to make sense in terms of this play being translated into pictures. Just pictures, flat, two-dimensional pictures. What do you do to make that happen, as opposed to making it three-dimensional, with depth, and with people moving about, who may trip one night and not trip another? What do you do with something that's always going to be the same every time you look at it?

I read your penciled questions on your script, and one of them that I really liked was "Would I like Davenport?" Do you remember that?

Yes.

Why would you explore his character more for a movie than for a play?

There's more room to do it in. He's the protagonist of the piece. Now when we talk about doing a movie, he's going to be much more real than when we watched him on the stage. And that's the person they're going to put all the money in. And the characters have to be explored more in the film because when their faces are on the screen they're about 40 feet wide and 20 feet high. The concerns that I had with the play are not the concerns that I'll have with the movie. I know the story is going to be the same, but how do you make sure that the people in the seats stay in the seats? That's what I'm basically saying, whatever I'm doing.

You do that very well in the theater. The tension and mood shifts seem to be just right. In movies, though, there's so much less language.

Yes, I know. So, there's that to be considered, too. How do you display this intention without two hundred words, without unnecessary babble, the babble of the theater?

Before you write a play do you write out questions, too?

Yes, generally about the people. Where do they come from? Where were they born? What can I know about them? Is there anything you need to know about them before the play? Is there anything you need to know about them after the play? Those kinds of questions I ask myself all the time. And then I sit in the audience and watch the play take place.

Do you approach it from characters or theme?

I think it's all one and the same. I approach it from the seats, not from on the stage. So I'm guaranteed that what you're watching is what I am watching. And if I like it, I'm praying to God that you do.

I didn't mean that, exactly. I meant, do you create a lot of characters first, and then see what happens? I think Shaw said that he created characters and then let them rip.

No, the characters aren't really separate from the action. I don't see them outside of the story and I don't see the story outside of them. It's all of a piece, a single piece of music. I like to compare this with music.

In what way?

Like, for example, if you go to a concert, you go to hear a piece of music and you don't ask yourself if you want to hear more of that piece of music. You don't say, "My goodness, I wish there was another riff." It begins with an explosion of some sort, and it ends with whatever the musician or composer feels it should end with. For me a play is like that. In *Zooman* [*and the Sign*], for example, I was trying to make a play in which there were no stops. And I wasn't that successful.

What is a play in which there are no stops?

A play with no blackouts, but where time changes take place. Rather than blacking out the lights and shifting from Sergeant Waters back to the barracks. I really wanted to do that in one motion, so that you were part of the past and the present at the same time. You didn't even feel it.

And in that way it's like music?

Yes. In jazz you don't have stops. In the music of the fifties you don't. I come out of the fifties. The music keeps

going, the rhythm section keeps going, the piano keeps playing, the bass player keeps going, and someone stops playing and someone else plays. The actors are like that. They come forward, they play an instrument. Then something else happens. It's like listening to "Round Midnight" with Thelonious Monk, and Miles, and all of them playing at once, to begin the piece. And each one of them settling into their own improvisation until the piece is discovered, until finally you've heard all the music, and it's over. And you go away having felt the entire piece of music. You might remember one solo better than another, but the whole piece of music is what has stirred you. It is the whole piece of music, "Round Midnight," that you care about. And I think plays ought to function in that way. For me they do. If it's not as fluid as I want it to be, then I'm not happy with it. *Zooman* is not as fluid as I want it to be. *A Soldier's Play* comes closer. It's going back and forth in time without any problems with it.

In what way is **Zooman** *not fluid?*

[The character of] Zooman was too isolated out here, and not a part of the whole thing that was going on. Only at the end.

But he always has a connection with Victor.

Yes, there is a visual connection with Victor. And an age connection. But I still felt he was too far away from the family to be effective at the end of the play. What I tried to do this time was to take a character as extreme, as interesting as Zooman and make him integral, connected.

Are there a lot of rewrites?

We didn't rewrite any of it with this play. *Zooman* we rewrote. But with this one, we knew we had something that was exciting when we started. And we went right ahead and did it, you know, with all the gusto we could bring to it. It went so smoothly because the director and I didn't have to deal with all that during rehearsal. The actors were much more confident than they are when you're fooling with the script. And tinkering with it doesn't help the actors that much anyway. They like to get into what they're doing.

I thought that was just part of it, always.

No, that is not always part of it. It doesn't have to be.

Is this something that you discuss with Douglas Turner Ward [artistic director of the Negro Ensemble Company] beforehand?

No, we just normally work things out that way. We tend to agree about the script and where it's going.

You're going to have a lot less of that freedom with the movie, aren't you?

Sure. That doesn't bother me.

It doesn't? Funny that it shouldn't bother you.

Well, lots of things bother me, but these things one can do very little about. The movie is the director's medium. It's foolish for a writer to think that he's going to go to Hollywood and change the way that it has functioned for the last half century.

Writers have been treated very badly in Hollywood.

Yes. I think that you can be treated better. But no one told any writer he can direct a motion picture better than a motion picture director can.

It's just that in the theater the playwright is very important. In the movies you hardly even know who the screenwriter is. In the theater, it's your *play.*

But if you are willing to go into that world and stay there, then you have to suffer those consequences. I have no interest in spending the rest of my life writing movies. Every now and then it might be nice to do that, but going to Hollywood and making a career out of writing movies doesn't interest me at all. I want to write them certainly, but I'm not going to lose any sleep over it. Rest assured. I'm 43 years old, and I know I will never be as good at anything else as I am as a writer. There's not enough time. If I began now, there's not enough time to get as good at being a doctor, for example, as I am as a writer. The older I get the less likely it is that I'm going to have the dexterity necessary to handle an operation. But by reading I can always improve my mind and get better at being a writer. So, I don't concern myself with getting good at being a director or getting good at being this or that. What I'm concerned about is trying to produce the best literary material America has ever seen.

That's pretty ambitious.

Yes, it is. But it's what I'm trying to do. And I think that is an ennobling desire. And I don't think there's anything wrong with it. And I'm not interested in being these other things.

I wonder what will happen to you. You've just won a Pulitzer Prize and sold film rights and are going to Hollywood. The world is running to you, right? I wonder if that could be very seductive and distracting?

Not really. I have a lovely home, two sons that I'm in love with, a wife I love very much, a lifestyle that isn't confusing. It doesn't need all of this. It's nice and very wonderful, but it's not something I'd like to pursue as a life's work. I have more important things to do. I mean, this morning it was so interesting, you know, I was on the Today Show. I thought, "God forbid that my life would depend on having to be on these things every morning." Everyone asks, how can you turn it off? How can you *not?* Remain who you are. After all, it's *that* that I'm concerned about the most, not television, movies. I know that if I write plays there's a reasonable chance that two out of three will get done. That's not a bad average. I won't hassle that. I'm always challenged by the things that I'm doing anyway. So I'm not terribly worried about losing my interest in things.

Did you get discouraged during the period when you didn't think your plays were good?

No. I knew I was doing something different, and that people just didn't like it. It didn't bother me terribly. I was trying to do something enormous. I'm dissatisfied because I wasn't able to do what I set out to do. And it is just discouraging not to make any money. But so what? I keep

wondering sometimes if the myth about American writers is of their own making or the public's.

Which myth?

The myth about being so discouraged and hurt and beaten when your work doesn't succeed. Of course there's pain and problems, but you keep on working. If that stops you, then . . .

Then you're not really a writer?

It's not painful enough to dwell on for any great length of time. I think it's something in the myth we have about writers, that we want them to be more feeling, more compassionate, more everything than we really are. And the truth of the matter is, we simply do something well that very few people can do—put human beings up on the stage. It's a difficult job to do. I don't perceive it as being anything other than that. Suffering is not an unusual human characteristic. You know what I mean? The specialness of writing is simply that not a whole lot of people do it. It's a small category in human affairs. A lot has been written, but not a whole lot of people wrote it. Certainly the things that have been remembered have been written by a very few people.

It sounds as though you constitutionally can't be anything but a writer.

I don't want to be anything but a writer.

I read that you started off wanting to do something in music.

In the fifties we were all caught up in the new wave of jazz—modern jazz, bebop really—Charlie Parker and Dizzy Gillespie. It was something that suggested a most extraordinary future. The music was new, was very exciting. And I wanted to play it. I heard Thelonious Monk one afternoon at my aunt's house and I thought, "My God, where have I been? I haven't heard this before." What he did with the music was so extraordinary. Quite naturally, I wanted to duplicate that. But somewhere along the line, you know, I watched Charlie Parker die of an overdose. It just did not seem like a practical application of one's talents. So many musicians were dying and they suffered so. They had to go through so much about the rights to their music, their jobs. I really didn't want that. And I decided that writing would be a much more realistic endeavor, principally because the foundation of Western civilization was in books. Anything you wanted to know about the proof of Western civilization's power is in the books that Western civilization has written about itself. Such power in words—to be able, with words, to change how people function, how they think. The foundation of our belief in ourselves is the ability to communicate with words and ideas.

Reuben [in **Zooman***] has your faith in language, doesn't he?*

Yes, he understands the value of it. This is what words can do. You can change the whole world, really. If you consider, and I always consider it, and this may be very corny-sounding, but the Declaration of Independence and the Constitution are a group of words that I act on consistently. Once read, you cannot ignore it. Impossible. The words did that.

Whose words do you like? Who are some of the writers you like?

Ellison, Ralph Ellison I like. Albert Murray, a contemporary writer. And classical writers who capture human themes, things that have bothered us for centuries. All the great writers do that. I mean, I can't think of any writer of great worth who hasn't dealt with very fundamental human problems always, always, always. You know the business of nuclear waste materials will go away, but the problem of getting along with one another, the person you love, will never dissipate. There are certain problems that are monumental, because technology has led you that far. The problem of nuclear war is a problem that the people of the fifteenth century didn't have. They still had the problem of dealing with each other. That never disappeared. And when this problem, if we can survive it, disappears, we'll still have the problem of our relationships with one another.

I don't even want to ask this question in view of what you've been saying.

Go ahead and ask it.

Every other black artist I've talked to has been bitter, and it would seem to me that that's unavoidable. But that doesn't seem to be what you're saying.

Well, being bitter would imply that I'm not getting something that I should be getting, or that I feel inadequate somehow. In the reality that I'm faced with there is nothing about me that is not in any way adequate to anything that I have to face. So I'm not afraid of anyone.

I mean a collective bitterness.

About what?

About "the madness of race in America," to use your phrase in **A Soldier's Play.**

Yes, that's part and parcel of the United States. Anyone who wakes up in the morning and doesn't think that racism exists in the United States is crazy. But I don't have time to spend the rest of my life being angry about it. What will serve me, and benefit, certainly, my people more, it seems to me, is actively functioning in a way that everything I do and produce implies that all the nonsense of racism—certainly the stereotyping of racism—is not true. My argument is on the stage. I don't have to be angry. O.K.? I get it all out right up there. There's no reason to carry this down from the stage and into the seats. And it does not mean that I am not enraged at injustice or prejudice or bigotry. It simply means that I cannot be enraged all the time. To spend one's life being angry, and in the process doing nothing to change it, is to me ridiculous. I could be mad all day long, and if I'm not doing a damn thing, what difference does it make?

It could also be very destructive to the art. Not the anger itself, but if it becomes an axe to grind.

I think it can strangle you to death. But I'm certain that every now and then it's important to let people know that things have not been forgotten. Certainly *A Soldier's Play* lets you know that, yes, we lived in a country at one time when the whole army was segregated. But let's not think that oppressing means that the people who are oppressed are not human. O.K.? That is to believe what white people have believed about us. I don't believe that, I'm the human being here. I don't need you to tell me that I'm alive or that I'm human or that I have feelings. But to be angry at the fact that you said that I don't have feelings certainly doesn't mean that I stop feeling, or that I believe you, or care what you say. That's still believing that white people decide for you who you are, or what your impulse is going to be in the future. That's nonsense, and insulting to begin with. I mean, what makes anyone think I cannot do with language all the things they can? And I'm perfectly calm and contented doing it. It's ludicrous.

So many sad, angry people spend so much time arguing this question, and they don't get their work done. They get angry about not being received the way white writers have been received, about not getting the kind of support that white writers have gotten, never understanding that our function in this society has been, since we've been in it, to change how people see things. To go on changing, to go on making America a better place to live in, because the landscape is broad enough for everybody to be on it. If you were to see a black man standing there, you would say, yes, that's the American experience too. That the American experience is not just a white experience. It's black experience and Indian experience, Puerto Rican experience. For anyone to believe that anyone can, by simply telling you that you're no good, make you no good, that's nonsense. My argument is with the people who really believe that only white people have done things that are artistically sensible. That very fact that we create the things that we create simply proves that that's not true. Why should I argue with them all my life? That's nonsense.

It is important that we do things that seem to me to be beneficial to our people, and by doing so, benefit the larger landscape of America. It seems to me that making people more human in their presentation on stage is one way of doing that, rather than making them so two-dimensional that all they do is confront each other in violent terms. That doesn't speak to anything, doesn't move us anywhere. You learn nothing about you, and I learn nothing about me. Finally, I must make it somehow sensible for my sons to live in the twenty-first century. I believe that if I don't do something about that, I've failed. (pp. 112-21)

Charles Fuller and Esther Harriott, in an interview in American Voices: Five Contemporary Playwrights in Essays and Interviews *by Esther Harriott, McFarland & Company, Inc., Publishers, 1988, pp. 112-25.*

A SOLDIER'S PLAY

PRODUCTION REVIEWS

Richard Gilman   (review date 23 January 1982)

[*In the following review, Gilman argues that* A Soldier's Play *is a "flawed but estimable play" that was instrumental in helping the Negro Ensemble Company develop.*]

After fourteen seasons, the Negro Ensemble Company can no longer be regarded as an exotic enterprise on the fringe. The N.E.C. came into being because the established American theater didn't seem to have any place for the black experience. So the group proceeded to carve such a place for itself, with determination if not always a clear notion of what it was doing. It's stance was either aggressive, that of an adversary, or defensive, which meant insular and self-validating; it stumbled, fell, rose and kept going.

Never quite a true ensemble, in that it frequently brings in performers for particular productions, the company has had difficulty creating an identifiable style, a way of doing

things unmistakably its own. If it still has that difficulty, at least its repertory has become much more flexible, so that its socially oriented realism has lost some of the pugnacious, parochial quality that once marred it.

Charles Fuller's *A Soldier's Play,* the opening production of the N.E.C.'s fifteenth season, is exemplary of this change and, as I see it, this growth. A flawed but estimable play, it's about the black experience but is supple enough in its thematic range and social perspectives to treat that experience as part of a complex whole, as part of American reality in its widest sense. To be released from an adversary position may mean a loss of fierceness—it certainly means a reduction in ideological thunder—but it can make for an increase in subtle wisdom and intellectual rigor.

Not that *A Soldier's Play* is a triumph of the dramatic imagination. But it is intelligent and morally various enough to overcome some basic uncertainties and remnants of the N.E.C.'s older confrontational manner, and so commend itself to our attention. Set in a Louisiana army camp in 1944, the play deals with the fatal shooting of a black sergeant (reflecting the times, blacks are called "negroes" or "coloreds"), a martinet who, out of shame

Charles Brown, Peter Friedman, Stephen Zetler, and Cottel Smith in the Negro Ensemble Company production of A Soldier's Play.

at his people's seeming acceptance of their inferior status, is tougher on his own men than are their white officers.

He's far from likable, but when he's killed and the culprits aren't found, the mood turns ugly among the black soldiers. At first, the Klan is suspected, then some white officers, but the brass wants no trouble and the incident is shunted aside. Finally, an investigator is sent from Washington, a black lieutenant with a law degree from Howard University. His relationship with the white captain previously in charge of the case makes up the moral and psychological center of the drama, which on one level proceeds as a moderately absorbing detective story.

The captain, an earnest liberal, is convinced he knows who the killers are but feels his hands are tied, and he grows impatient with the black officer's slow, careful inquiry. The real problem, however, is the dislocation the captain experiences in his abstract good will. "I can't get used to it," he tells the black man, "your uniform, your bars." Still, he comes to accept the investigator, whose mind is much more in tune with reality than his own and who eventually brings the case to a surprising conclusion. Along the way there are some deft perceptions about both political and psychological matters, and a jaunty historical sense: "Look out, Hitler," a soldier says, "the niggers is comin' to get your ass."

The biggest burden the play carries is the direction of Douglas Turner Ward, the N.E.C.'s artistic director, who is also a well-known playwright. Ward manages the many flashbacks, through which the action is propelled, with a heavy hand: lights go up or down with painful slowness, figures from the past *take their places* obediently in the present. There are also some soft spots among the performances and an unpleasant ending, or coda, in which the black officer gratuitously reminds his white colleague of the lessons taught and learned. Yet in its calm concern for prickly truths and its intellectual sobriety, *A Soldier's Play* elicits the audience's approval, if not its boisterous enthusiasm. (pp. 90-1)

Richard Gilman, in a review of "A Soldier's Play," in The Nation, *New York, Vol. 234, No. 3, January 23, 1982, pp. 90-1.*

Leo Sauvage (review date July 1982)

[*Sauvage provides a favorable review of* A Soldier's Play, *noting that "the mystery here ultimately concerns variations in human behavior . . . not methods of crime."*]

Few works this year, on or off Broadway, have been as powerful as Charles Fuller's *A Soldier's Play,* performed by the Negro Ensemble Company, under the direction of Douglas Turner Ward. The show opened November 10, 1981, for a limited run of five weeks, and has been extended ever since. Those who have not yet ventured west of Ninth Avenue on 55th Street to the former church that is the Ensemble's Theater Four are urged to do so.

The scene is the barracks of a black military unit in Fort Neel, Louisiana, in 1944. Without making a speech about it, the author reminds us from the beginning that the Unit-

ed States fought Hitler's Nazis with a racially segregated army. Like many black outfits, this one has some black noncommissioned officers, but all the commanders are white.

All, that is, until something happens in racist Louisiana that has nothing to do with an antiracist World War. A black noncom named Waters (Adolph Caesar) is found dead with two bullets in his body. Concerned about the incident, the top brass at Fort Neel places the investigation in the hands of black Captain Richard Davenport (Charles Brown), who was a lawyer before getting the two bars on his epaulets.

The unit's white commanding officer, Captain Taylor (Peter Friedman), thinks his superiors have made a bad mistake. Taylor is far from the worst racist in the Army, though he does at one point blurt out that "being in charge does not look right on Negroes." In fact, he would like whoever killed Waters to be punished. But because it is generally thought that the crime was committed by the Ku Klux Klan, and there are reasons as well to suspect two white racist officers, Taylor feels a black investigator will never get the cooperation necessary to obtain an indictment, much less a conviction. He tries to convince Davenport to give up the assignment, but Davenport is determined to prove him wrong.

Fuller has said of *A Soldier's Play,* "It may be the first black mystery." He told an interviewer from *Other Stages,* the Off-Broadway counterpart to *Playbill.* "In all my experience, I haven't seen any black writer write a mystery." (Presumably he was thinking only of the stage.) "I wanted to construct a well-made mystery."

And he has, complete with a wholly unexpected solution. True, Captain Davenport's detection is not always fed by satisfyingly hidden, brilliantly uncovered clues. He relies more on guessing than deduction, a shortcoming that, strictly speaking, makes him only third best after Nero Wolfe and Hercule Poirot. The mystery here ultimately concerns variations in human behavior, however, not methods of crime. Interesting people studied in depth offer highly dramatic compensation; we come to know Sergeant Waters, for instance, through what are for once coherent and gracefully introduced flashbacks. Ward's flawless direction, moreover, gives each soldier a specific personality.

Davenport is by far the most delicate role in *A Soldier's Play,* and at first I thought Charles Brown was not right for it. But the uneasiness he conveys on stage soon persuaded me that I was wrong. Brown's difficulties in defending his authority without being smug or arrogant, and in reminding the black enlisted men that they cannot be more familiar with him than with a white captain, accurately mirror the problems a character like Davenport would have had to confront. (p. 21)

Leo Sauvage, "Plays that Got Away," in The New Leader, *Vol. LXV, No. 14, July 12-26, 1982, pp. 21-2.*

Robert Asahina (review date Autumn 1982)

[*In the following review of the N.E.C.'s production of* A Soldier's Play, *Asahina offers a mixed assessment of the drama, stating that "Fuller is to be commended for honestly exposing how racism distorts the soul of not just the oppressor but the victim." He observes, however, several ambiguities in the play's construction that, he claims, lessen its impact.*]

For a change, this year's Pulitzer Prize actually went to the season's most deserving work: Charles Fuller's *A Soldier's Play,* produced by the Negro Ensemble Company and directed by Douglas Turner Ward. But it deserves criticism as well as praise.

Set in 1944, *A Soldier's Play* could also have been written then; it is a straightforward piece of psychological realism that takes the form of a murder mystery. In the first scene, Vernon C. Waters (Adolph Caesar), a Tech/Sergeant in the 221st Chemical Smoke Generating Company, is killed by two unknown assailants. Waters is black, as are the other noncoms and enlisted men at Fort Neal, Louisiana, in the year before the end of World War II. Suspecting that the killers are white and fearing a racial conflict between the soldiers and the residents of the nearby town of Tynan, the white officers restrict their troops to the base and order an investigation.

A black captain, Richard Davenport (Charles Brown), assigned to the military police, arrives at Fort Neal to conduct the inquiry (and to narrate the play, which largely consists of flashbacks). Davenport is reluctantly assisted by a white captain, Charles Taylor (Peter Friedman), a West Pointer who makes known his antagonism by aggressively announcing, "I never saw a Negro until I was twelve or thirteen." Still, it is clear to both of them that the investigation is supposed to fail, since everyone assumes that the murderers are white and will thus be impossible to bring to justice in the South. "Don't take yourself too seriously," Taylor warns Davenport, who sardonically acknowledges that "the matter was given the lowest priority."

Nonetheless, the black captain persists, eventually daring to cast suspicion on two white officers, Lieutenant Byrd (Sam McMurray) and Captain Wilcox (Stephen Zettler). By this time, Taylor has grudgingly come to respect Davenport's efforts; in fact, he is even more eager than his black colleague to bring charges against his fellow whites. But Davenport has begun to believe that the case is more than an incident of racial violence. His questioning of the black soldiers gradually leads him—and us—to the uncomfortable realization that the murder was committed by someone under Waters' command.

As the captain digs deeper, a complex portrait of the dead sergeant emerges from the flashbacks that spring out of the interrogation sessions around which the play is structured. A veteran of World War I, Waters is a career man and a strict disciplinarian who expects his troops to toe the white man's line as squarely as he does. When he busts Corporal James Wilkie (Steven A. Jones) to the rank of private for being drunk on duty, Waters complains, "No wonder they treat us like dogs." His favorite target for abuse is a Southern black, Private C. J. Memphis (David Alan Grier), who represents everything he despises. Pleasant but slow-witted, Memphis is the star of the company baseball team, as well as a mournful blues guitarist and singer. But to Waters, a Northerner, Memphis is nothing but an embarrassing exemplar of a "strong black buck." "Niggers aren't like that today," the sergeant sneers.

Waters is no simple Uncle Tom, however. "This country's at war," he tells his men, "and you niggers are soldiers." To him, they must be more than good soldiers—they must be the best, for their own sake if not the army's. "Most niggers just don't care," he claims. "But not havin's no excuse for not gettin'. We got to challenge the man in *his* arena." In his twisted way, Waters truly believes that the black race can only advance by following his example—by being better than the white man at his own game. "Do you know the damage one ignorant Negro can do?" he asks Memphis. "The black race can't afford you laughin' and clownin'."

Davenport soon learns the lengths to which Waters went to "close our ranks on the chittlins and collard greens style." During the year before his death, the company team had been so successful that a game with the Yankees was in the works if the Fort Neal soldiers were to win their conference title. But the better the troops do on the field, the worse they do on the base. "Every time we beat them at baseball," the soldiers complain about their white opponents, "they get back at us any way they can"—in work details ranging from KP to painting the officers' club. Waters, of course, believes "these men need all the discipline they can get," since he regards their athletic achievements as frivolous, even dangerous, because they reinforce the white man's stereotype of the black.

To his horror, Davenport discovers that Waters found a way of eliminating Memphis while simultaneously sabotaging the team. The sergeant framed the hapless private for a mysterious shooting on the base ("one less fool for the race to be ashamed of"), and when Memphis killed himself in the stockade, the players threw the championship game in protest. But the cost of Waters' demented discipline was a growing desire for vengeance among his troops. As Davenport finally determines, two of them—Private First Class Melvin Peterson (Denzel Washington) and Private Tony Smalls (Brent Jennings)—took matters into their own hands and killed their tormentor. Yet even at the moment of his death, Waters had the last word, or words—the same ones that opened the play. "You got to be like them," he cries in torment. "But the rules are fixed. It doesn't make any difference. They still hate you."

Whatever else can be said about *A Soldier's Play,* Fuller must be credited for creating a truly tragic character for whom those words are an anguished, self-proclaimed epitaph. It is in Waters that the toll of racism is most apparent. To be sure, all the black characters in the drama are representative of different modes of dealing with white oppression: the cautious rationality of Davenport, the self-abasement of Wilkie (brilliantly brought to life by Jones), the unenlightened self-interest of Smalls. Likewise, Memphis embodies the black past, stolid and humble, just as surely as Peterson does the future, or at least one possible future: righteous but also arrogant.

Yet Waters is unique among the men by being both the engineer of his own downfall and the victim of his circumstances; like all genuinely tragic figures, he attains universality because of rather than despite the stubborn reality of his particularity. From the smallest of his affectations—the pompous, gravelly voice, the pipe-smoking, the military carriage, the cultivated disdain for his inferiors—to the enormity of his crimes against his own people in their name, the costs of Waters' unnatural, willful assimilation are painfully apparent. ("Any man don't know where he belongs," says Memphis, "got to be in a lot of pain.") Fuller's resolute writing and Caesar's forceful acting have created a truly unlikeable yet strangely sympathetic character, unpleasant yet unexpectedly revealing of what we fear as the worst accommodationist impulses in ourselves.

Unfortunately, Fuller does not handle the investigation into Waters' violent death as ably as he does the sergeant's tortured life. Somehow the murder mystery comes to dominate the other elements of the play; the larger problems of human behavior in adverse circumstances become secondary to the whodunit questions of motive and opportunity. True, the investigation gives the drama a certain forward momentum, but not enough to disguise the fact that almost everything interesting takes place in the past. The most compelling figure is the victim, whose life is revealed in flashback; the action in the present is, for the most part, structured according to the familiar strategy of revelations leading to further revelations and ultimately to a rather comfortable resolution.

Not too comfortable, mind you; Fuller is to be commended for honestly exposing how racism distorts the soul of not just the oppressor but the victim. For this genuine revelation (as opposed to the convenient revelations that advance the plot) to matter to us, however, it must matter to the character through whose eyes we perceive it. And it is not unreasonable to expect that Davenport's discoveries will change him—somehow. After all, he began his inquiry more or less convinced that the killers were white, and then had to overcome his own prejudices to uncover the truth. He could also see something of himself in Waters. Though younger, the captain must have had to pay the same dues as the sergeant—perhaps even more, to rise to the higher rank.

Yet Davenport maintains an eerie emotional distance throughout (which is underscored by Brown's rather affectless performance; he is so cool that he practically freezes into rigidity). Perhaps Fuller thereby meant to comment on the captain's notion of soldierly conduct, which causes him to be almost color-blind. Indeed, early in the play, Davenport rebuffs Wilkie's presumption of racial familiarity ("You all we got down here," the private claims).

But this sort of irony seems absent elsewhere, particularly from the author's decision to set the play so far in the past. (I do not think the drama required the segregated army, which came to an end after the war; in fact, the play might have been more pointed had it been set after integration.

As for the war itself, it could as easily have been Korea or Vietnam—or no war at all, for all the difference it makes to the action.) Did Fuller believe that the attitudes represented by, say, Memphis and Waters would seem outdated today? That Davenport, too, would seem anachronistic, or even Peterson insufficiently militant? Or did he think (or does he recognize) that setting *A Soldier's Play* in 1944 somehow lets all of us—playwright, cast, audience—off the hook? Or was it that he wanted all concerned to consider the drama as art rather than as "relevant" social comment? It is not that I suspect Fuller's motives—it is just that I don't know what they are. (pp. 439-42)

Robert Asahina, in a review of "A Soldier's Play," in The Hudson Review, *Vol. XXXV, No. 3, Autumn, 1982, pp. 439-42.*

CRITICAL COMMENTARY

Amiri Baraka   (essay date 1983)

[*Baraka is a major figure in the development of contemporary black literature. As a leading dramatist in the Black Arts and Theater Movement of the 1960s, he received world-wide acclaim for his first professional production,* Dutchman *(1964). His subsequent plays have provoked both praise and controversy. In the following essay, he condemns Fuller's "descent into Pulitzerland" with* A Soldier's Play, *a work that Baraka claims caters to the wishes of whites instead of championing blacks.*]

When I saw Charlie Fuller's *Brownsville Raid* in 1976, produced by the Negro Ensemble and directed by Doug Ward, I was generally impressed. Even Ward's acting, which I find rather stylized, was not too much to take that night.

Before that, I had read "Love Song For Seven Little Boys Called Sam" in *Liberator,* Larry Neal and I had even anthologized it in *Black Fire.* The story had a certain poignance that wanted to poke through in the telling of a confrontation between some black youth and white supremacy.

Somehow I always got Charlie Fuller mixed with writer Charlie Russell (maybe because both wrote for the *Liberator* for a minute); at any rate I always try to hook up Fuller to Russell's *Five on the Black Hand Side,* which was a pretty awful movie, an extremely superficial look at the contradictions in the black community, particularly between the "integrationist" sector and the cultural nationalists. What the deep concerns of the majority African American community are—democracy, equality, self-sufficiency—and how different sectors of the black community look at these concerns and why they look at them differently—these would have been what *Five* was about, were it fully drawn. But I could not have written such a play then either. Although Theodore Ward did with his *Big White Fog* almost forty years before. I even had to go back and look through film books to make sure that Fuller did not write *Five.* But, whereas "Love Song" is a sensitive look at the struggle and trauma involved with the desegregation of U.S. society and the African American mind, *Five* simply establishes that its author has not taken enough time to know the black community in any really profound depth.

"Love Song" does deal with the deep feelings of the black community, through the focus of black youth coping with white supremacy, intimidation, and violence, certainly in a more profound and compelling way than does Russell's script. He takes some of the legitimate concerns of the black community and tests them in the context of young black life struggling to develop. This short story was good enough so that when I saw Fuller's *Brownsville Raid* I was prepared for the quality and depth I saw in "Love Song." (If Fuller *had* written *Five on the Black Hand Side* I might have been prepared for what happened after *Brownsville*!)

With *The Brownsville Raid,* it seemed to me that Fuller had grown enormously. Suddenly, I became aware of who he was, of how his mind, articulated through the drama, worked. *Brownsville* was not so slight or so superficial as the other examples of Fuller's work I had seen. It was fully drawn, within the limitations it had set for itself—a courtroom drama with other penetrations. In some ways, *Brownsville* was very much like *A Soldier's Play.* The United States' segregated army was not a metaphor for the U.S.; it was the U.S. black soldiers who, pushed past their limits in remaining "disciplined"—i.e., placid before national oppression—(even unto the murder of their fellow soldiers), rise up to fight against this bloody oppression and are themselves murdered, legally: They are court-martialed and shot for roaring into town in trucks, shooting everything in sight, trying to even the score after some Southern racists have killed one of their number while he was in town on a pass.

The racist process and white supremacy court and government proceedings penetrate to the heart of apartheid America. It shows us America as a courtroom where black people are on trial endlessly with always the same sentence: death by white supremacy! Death comes more swiftly if the victims resist or struggle against it, or demand liberation. Plus, it is always perfectly justifiable and most of the time "legal."

The memory of *Brownsville* stayed with me a long time: I often wished I could see it again. Given this situation, I was completely unprepared for the Negro Ensemble's production of *Zooman and the Sign.* Suddenly here was Charlie Fuller as the voice of the most reactionary sector of the black middle class.

Zooman marked a new low ideologically in black theater. Chas Gordone's abortion *No Place To Be Somebody* could be understood almost as the creation of racists who wished to counter the statements made by the theater of the Black Arts Movement. The awarding of a Pulitzer Prize to Gordone, who is not even a playwright, marking the first time an African American received the award, is pure anti-Black Liberation Movement politics. When Gordone's main character shoots the black gangster figure (Black Power) and then gets into drag announcing he is ecstatic because black militancy has been killed forever, it makes the hair stand up on the back of your neck, but it's obvious

that white supremacy is fighting back. Gordone has never even identified as black, much less become a playwright. Just in terms of the conventions of written drama, *No Place* would get a D in any writing class.

Zooman brought this idea back to me, uglier than ever. Zooman is the black teenage "animal" racists see black youth as. This "animal" epithet is what the sick cops scream as they pump bullets into the back of these kids' heads. It's what the white cops screamed at me as they opened my head with their gun butts and sticks during the 1967 Newark rebellion.

Fuller has his middle-class negroes talk like the most backward negroes on the block. (And I use the term *negro* advisedly.) Because that is what Charlie Fuller seems to want to represent in *Zooman: the Negro Consciousness,* the consciousness of the black people who have been so washed out mentally by white supremacy that they think other blacks are the problem!

Their child has been killed by this black youth, Zooman, but the rest of the community is too frightened to identify him. Fuller's negroes put up a sign accusing the black community of cowardice, in not turning in the youth. The youth comes to take the sign down, and one of Fuller's negroes kills him.

There is no attempt to lay out just what the real causes of black national oppression are, or the ghettos and pathology created by oppression. There are only animals, Zoomen, and they can only be stopped by blacks having the courage to kill them. What about the courage to kill off white supremacy? What about the courage to destroy racism and monopoly capitalism forever? What about even the courage to organize black artists so that they can take an open adversary relationship to this hellish system that has traditionally enslaved and tortured us? No, the only "courage" Fuller speaks of is the "courage" necessary for middle-class negroes to see themselves as a beleaguered elite, beset by a bunch of black animals!

It is no wonder that Chemical Bank immediately put out money to advertise *Zooman,* with huge ads in the *Village Voice, New York Times,* and other newspapers, and initiated a campaign to keep *Zooman* open (to shield it from the problems that most black theater has) so that its "intelligent" message could be spewed out even more broadly.

Zooman not only is backward but, like Gordone's monstrosity, is poorly written as well. Fuller could get maybe a D+ for the writing of *Zooman.* It is awkward and simplistic with old static forms—characters coming to the footlights, etc. Despite its obvious drawbacks, the white supremacists made a great deal of fuss about *Zooman,* all the time allowing as how it could have been better written, etc.

But with *A Soldier's Play,* they scored. It is what such types long for: a play as reactionary as *Zooman* (even more so in the long run) but one well-written, which, as Mao said, makes it even more dangerous since reactionary ideas couched in attractive forms can draw unsuspecting people in.

ASP draws some of its form and thrust from *The Browns-*

ville Raid, but it is ideologically way on the other side. Fuller says he modeled the play, in some ways, on Melville's *Billy Budd.* This idea alone was enough to send negro critic Stanley Crouch into veritable ecstasies. "You know we's into somethin' now, when we can imitate Melville," I can hear him saying.

But the real deadliness of **ASP** is Fuller's point of view. Again, it is the most backward sector of the black middle class, the voice of the negro heard loud and clear.

Adolph Caesar plays a black-hating sergeant who would be at home with a great many negroes, even famous ones, saying, "Stop thinkin' like a nigger," or "You bring us down, boy; we're gonna get rid of you, boy—one less fool for the race to be ashamed of." These comments are said by this sergeant to a young blood from the deep South who represents the oldest, blackest folk ties of the African American. Caesar's character hates this Southern blackness that connects, through slavery, directly back to Africa. When Caesar causes this naive young boy to commit suicide, he is killed. This creates a kind of whodunit mystery aspect to the play and also provides an opening for Fuller's real hero (who he says was modeled on Larry Neal—When? is what I would ask), a black, or is it negro, officer, a captain, who serves as Melville's narrator and at the same time Fuller's prototype of the negro in high places who is qualified to get the job despite the obstruction of white supremacy.

The connection of the black middle class and black bourgeoisie to the black masses is the fact of national oppression. Yes, the qualified negro can be stopped from advancing to his or her proper place, or receiving his or her deserved recognition, by a society based on white supremacy and black national oppression. Caesar's character has been made sick by such obstruction. He, like the negroes in **Zooman,** thinks that the obstruction is other black people, especially Southern black ones who sing the blues. When he is killed, another negro comes on the scene, fundamentally to prove that he is qualified to be an officer in "the man's army."

Of course, the captain is resented and obstructed, even threatened, but in the end he overcomes. He finds the sergeant's murderer, who turns out to be none other than Malcolm X! Not really or literally Malcolm, although the sergeant's killer is the company black militant, a young actor who had played Malcolm X, just weeks before, not so coincidentally, in Laurence Holder's play *When the Chickens Come Home to Roost,* about the conflict between Malcolm X and Elijah Muhammad. Denzel Washington still looked very much like Malcolm—close haircut, glasses, and all.

But what is important, aside from such non-coincidences, is that this black militant, the very opposite of the black-hating sergeant, is given to making militant speeches and condemning the sergeant—although the sergeant takes him out and beats him in a one-on-one combat (you know that all negroes can beat militants). And when the sergeant causes the young boy's suicide, the militant kills the sergeant.

The captain tracks the militant down, condemning him because he lacks compassion for the black-hating sergeant. Fuller says that is our real problem, that the black militants lack compassion for black-hating negroes. Though, interestingly enough, there is no real denouement to the play's ideology. One would expect that there would be the final flaming conflict between Fuller's mouthpiece, the competent, skilled, qualified negro captain, and the militant, in which Fuller would lay out his argument and shoot holes into the concept of black political militance and radicalism. But he does not. There are a few brief remarks, and the militant is led away. No scene of raging ideological confrontation occurs because Fuller hasn't the courage to say, really, anything directly in defense of negro reaction, except what he does say by way of the play's ending.

But then check this as his shattering statement, one he has sneaked away from open ideological confrontation (as even Shakespeare, Dante, or Melville would provide): The negro captain proves his right to be among the white officers by uncovering the militant. Now he belongs. Despite white supremacy, he has proved his mettle, his ultimate worth. He is a soldier, and it is a soldier's play. A soldier "in the man's army"—that's the ultimate aspiration of these reactionary negroes: to be soldiers in the man's army. And their whole lives are nothing but a soldier's play.

The negro captain (Charles Brown, a clumsy quasi-actor) is Fuller and company going off into the sunlight, having proved their right to belong. And let's look at the scorecard: black folk symbol—dead; black folk symbol-hating negro (openly pathological)—dead; black militant—court-martialed, locked up; intelligent, efficient, qualified negro captain—belongs, goes off into the sunlight. Hey, but what about the rest of the troops, the other soldiers, the black masses in the army? Well, they go off to the war, to fight Hitler, to fight against fascism, and they are all killed—to a man, the narrator says! Only I alone lived to tell the tale, said Ishmael (Reed?): the lone surviving negro, who survives because he is an officer in the man's army. All those other non-officer, non-negro blacks perished, fighting white supremacy. Only the negro alone survived to tell the tale and, by the way, win the second Pulitzer Prize any colored playwright ever got!! And Chemical Bank beat the drum louder and longer than ever!! (pp. 51-3)

Amiri Baraka, "The Descent of Charlie Fuller into Pulitzerland and the Need for African-American Institutions," in Black American Literature Forum, *Vol. 17, No. 2, Summer, 1983, pp. 51-4.*

William W. Demastes   (essay date 1987)

[Demastes is the author of the 1988 study Beyond Naturalism: A New Realism in American Theatre. *In the following essay, originally published in* Studies in American Drama, 1945-Present *in 1987, he responds in part to Amiri Baraka's critique of Fuller's career (see commentary dated 1983), asserting that Fuller's strength is his ability to translate "his black experience into an*

idiom that can be more broadly termed an 'American' experience."]

Charles Fuller's recent work as a playwright has marked him as a new voice for an element of American society greatly underrepresented in mainstream theatre today—the black American community. Fuller's talents make him a worthy spokesman, but such a labeling is an uncomfortable one for any artist to bear, given the political implications attached to being a "representative" of such a vastly heterogeneous group. Despite the difficulties, though, Fuller's work has been favorably received by both the general black community and the mainstream theatre world. In fact, Fuller's most noteworthy contribution may be his success at translating his black experience into an idiom that can be more broadly termed an "American" experience.

Throughout his playwriting career, Fuller has been closely connected with the Negro Ensemble Company (NEC), a group that was founded in the late 1960s (first play produced December 1967), because, as critic Richard Gilman puts it, "the established American theater didn't seem to have any place for the black experience." Gilman continues: "So the group proceeded to carve such a place for itself, with determination if not always a clear notion of what it was doing. Its stance was either aggressive, that of an adversary, or defensive, which meant insular and self-validating." Charles Fuller is one of the playwrights responsible for bringing the NEC into mainstream theatre. His ***Soldier's Play*** (1981; Pulitzer Prize, 1982) has capped that struggle to move beyond an adversarial posture and has succeeded at presenting something more than a work that "self-validates" the black perspective. But the result of such a theatre as Fuller and the NEC have created is that there is, as Gilman notes, "a loss of fierceness . . . a reduction in ideological thunder [see review dated 23 January 1982]. It is this lack of thunder that has led one faction of the black community to reject the efforts of the NEC.

Perhaps the most outspoken of that faction is dramatist/activist LeRoi Jones/Amiri Baraka, who, in an essay attacking *A Soldier's Play* in particular, makes the following observation of the NEC in general:

> An oppressed people demand that all their resources be put to the service of liberating them, no matter what these resources are. Certainly art and culture must be seen in such a light. Either we are trying to fashion an art of liberation, whatever its forms, or we are creating an art that helps maintain our chains and slave status (even high, giggling, or in ecstasy). The Negro Ensemble has been, in the main, a skin theater, offering only colored complexion but not sustained thrust in concert with the whole of the BLM [Black Liberation Movement] to liberate ourselves. It has been fundamentally a house slave's theater, eschewing struggle for the same reason that the house niggers did—because they didn't have it so bad [see commentary dated 1983].

Baraka himself approaches the "black condition" advocating one option, "revolutionary violence," as W. D. E. Andrews notes in his study of Baraka's Marxist theatre.

Baraka's is an approach that considers "reformism" or "revisionism" nothing more than "bourgeois double-talk" assisting the white oppressors rather than helping the black oppressed. For Baraka, any approach other than his own is worthy of nothing but contempt, as the above passage clearly illustrates. But upon closer scrutiny, Baraka's theory of art as revolutionary tool has its own limitations. For example, to more clearly draw the line between the perceived antagonists, Baraka's works have relied heavily on "generality and sloganeering," a tactic most noticeable in Baraka's more recent works. And as such, his art becomes didactic and dogmatic, tendencies that Andrews notes damages two of Baraka's more recent dramatic products: "Both *The Motion of History* [1978] and *S-1* [1978] are plays which do not allow the spectator to make his own discoveries or to draw his own conclusions."

Closed to the fuller freedoms that art is capable of utilizing, Baraka has slipped into a realm that may conform to his revolutionary political designs, but one that has also led him to create questionable "art." Fuller's art, on the other hand, is not at all revolutionary in intentions, given Baraka's designs, but neither is it designed to concede the current black condition, as Baraka claims it does. Rather, Fuller's strategy illustrates a subtlety that practitioners such as Baraka either fail to see or fail to acknowledge, a subtlety that, if successful, would bring about its own type of revolution. And it is not a strategy dependent on unsupported generalizations or didacticism. Fuller's dialectic is neither directly confrontational nor in any real sense "agitprop." But though Fuller's works may lack "fierceness" or "thunder," it's a concession that Fuller seems willing to make in order to suggest another approach to the race issue.

The process of change that Fuller advocates begins first with his portrayal of a whole spectrum of character types, revealing subtleties and complexities that black characterization rarely receives, both positive and negative. Such an approach to his characterizations in turn argues that for Fuller the black experience has itself attained a self-assurance and sense of identity that will allow it to be fully included in mainstream American culture without fear of losing itself in the process. Baraka would argue that such a process actually entails losing that black identity, but Fuller's works prove otherwise.

The most noticeable effect of this process is that Fuller helps to break a long tradition of stereotyping blacks—particularly black men—in literature, cinema, drama, and television. Fuller describes the tradition he is challenging as one that portrays blacks as "[i]neffectual types who just can't get themselves together, the kind Hattie McDaniels used to chase out of the kitchen. . . . We speak [in traditional portrayals] one abominable language—hip; we have one interest—women. Our lives have no beginning, no ending. We're highly emotional in terms of reactive violence, and we do not use our minds in any way." Fuller's plays do include such characterizations, but also many others that awaken the audience to a more rounded understanding of blacks as individuals who perhaps have been brought up in different cultural circumstances but who should not be considered some group fundamentally different from others and therefore easily "ghetto-ized."

Fuller's characters, therefore, are no longer racially limited and assume a more "universal" quality. Fuller argues, "I can't see how any growing people would want to be continually portrayed as sweet and innocent," for breaking one stereotype to establish another is not the answer. Stereotypes of any sort isolate people from true understanding, and finally . . . Fuller contends that it is blacks who "have more to lose by staying remote from the White community." Fuller completes the thought: "[Y]ou change or they change or, if nobody changes, somebody loses in this equation, and I'm thinking it's us." Fuller's approach leads to an equation that asks both sides to see and both sides to change. The result is that whites and blacks are shown their common humanity rather than being shown some racial "difference," which is the type of "revolutionary" exacerbation of the factions that Baraka's art must strive for. And it seems Fuller has succeeded. Gilman writes of *A Soldier's Play:* "[I]t's about the black experience but it is supple enough in its thematic range and social perspectives to treat that experience as a part of a complex whole, as part of American reality in its widest sense." Though at one level blacks and whites are seen as two communities, Fuller is striving to illustrate another level where the two communities are, or should be, one.

Fuller's arrival at this conclusion in *A Soldier's Play* is the result of an evolution that can be seen in the thematic progress of his three most successful works, *The Brownsville Raid* (1976), *Zooman and the Sign* (1980), and finally *A Soldier's Play* (1981).

The Brownsville Raid portrays blacks as a minority oppressed by the hatred and misunderstanding of the white majority. Fuller takes an historical event (1906) in which a predominantly white town, Brownsville, Texas, is attacked by a band of unidentified marauders shortly after an all-Negro infantry battalion is bivouacked on its outskirts. The circumstances suggest that the blacks were the marauders. But though the ensuing action, historically and in the play, fails to prove that the blacks were involved in the raid, the black battalion is disbanded in disgrace.

Within this clash of blacks and whites lies a trademark of Fuller's. Amid the public accusations and denials, Fuller has inserted a reasonable cause for private suspicion among the blacks that in their midst may be a guilty party. The richness of ambiguity leaves serious doubt as to who is to blame—retaliating blacks or conspiring whites—and the result in the play is not some reductive "finger pointing" but a more general condemnation of the suspicion itself, the result of mistrust and lack of communication existing between blacks and whites. Interestingly, Baraka applauds the "message" of *The Brownsville Raid,* arguing that "it was the U.S. black soldiers who, pushed past their limits in remaining 'disciplined' . . . rise up to fight against this bloody oppression and are themselves murdered, legally." Baraka, unfortunately, has seen the play without noting the subtleties of doubt and suspicion among the blacks that will more notably mark Fuller's later works. Baraka sees it as merely a play documenting

the injustices blacks have suffered at the hands of the white power structure.

Zooman and the Sign is the play that at least partially clarifies any misinterpretation of Fuller's designs, and understandably Baraka condemns it. The confrontation becomes more focused in *Zooman and the Sign,* virtually eliminating any black-white opposition in favor of studying one half of the problem, namely the struggle within the black community itself. Baraka says of the play, "Suddenly here was Charlie Fuller as the voice of the most reactionary sector of the black middle class." As noted above, however, the action of the play is not a "sudden" shift but a clearer sign of Fuller's designs.

Again an actual event is the germ of the play, a report of a senseless, violent killing of a small black girl by a black hood in the streets of Philadelphia. Frank Rich reports that the play does not illustrate a reactionary black middle-class capitulation to comfort, as Baraka claims, but

> an indictment of black Americans who capitulate to tyrannical punks within their midst. Yet it is much to the playwright's credit that his compassion is not merely reserved for the heroic Reuben Tate [the girl's father]. He also has sympathy for Reuben's frightened friends—and for Zooman, a kid driven into psychosis by the social circumstances of poverty. In **"Zooman and the Sign"** there are no real villains, only victims. Every character is locked in the same cycle of terror, and it's a nightmare only courage can end.

Fuller's play does not argue that since blacks are trapped by white institutions, it is the whites' responsibility to enact change or even that it is the blacks' responsibility to rebel against the system. Rather, it is a treatment of human courage that argues the need to take responsibility for one's life, inasmuch as one can—a message that in fact transcends racial considerations. And Fuller's sensitivity extends to all in this complex situation, victims as well as victimizers. On a more specific level, though, it is a fair but hard and analytic focus on the black community and on the interactions—shortcomings included—of its black residents, and failing to include whites in the action has led to some criticism, Baraka's included.

With *A Soldier's Play,* Fuller strikes the balance that he seems to have been striving for throughout his early works. In very clear terms we see the hatred and prejudices of whites, but more specifically we see the interactions of blacks within that circle. Both halves of the problem are reunited, the result being a study of broad social structures as in *The Brownsville Raid* and a scrutiny of both blacks and whites in a way that included only blacks in *Zooman and the Sign.*

This play has no actual historical source, but Fuller does return to a military setting, for it offers him the opportunity, as he says, to have "men confront men" more honestly, since "[y]ou can't call a man a fool whose principal function is to defend his country." In this camp, set in Louisiana during World War II, an investigation is being conducted into what seems to be a racially motivated murder of a black sergeant. A black investigator, initially convinced of a white conspiracy, eventually discovers the murderer to be a black soldier formerly under the murdered sergeant's charge. In essence the play is a mystery, and designedly so.

A Soldier's Play works to investigate and evaluate racial tensions that have been intensified by the conditions established in the play; for this the mystery form is appropriate. As such, a typical formula would be to look for extreme—and atypical—conditions that would aid in unearthing the mystery: radical blacks confronted by KKK whites, for example. The play, however, challenges the standard, comfortable assumptions that tensions exist only between such radical elements of both races. To overturn such oversimplified assumptions, Fuller works to challenge the cool foundations of reasoned abstraction that lead to these conclusions. The way he challenges these notions is to present standard clues, allow classic and typically stereotypical assumptions to develop—among the investigators—into simple conclusions. Fuller then reveals previously unperceived complexities in the situation, which in turn show how complacent, comfortable solutions/approaches are rooted, finally, in a subtle but pervasive prejudice. The result is that in addition to a murderer's confession and indictment, the process brings out "indictments" of a sort against the entire cast of characters for prejudice and racial/racist behavior.

The modified mystery plot contributes to this unexpected and more encompassing end, but it also has an additional twist. Because audiences are standardly involved in their own process of solving murder-mysteries, if this play succeeds, it will engage the audience, forcing the members to utilize critical instincts—or more accurately, prejudices—which will lead to a complicity similar to that of the onstage investigators. So the play is less concerned with unfolding facts identifying the murderer than it is a work revealing subtle causes of the event under scrutiny that in turn eventually force not only the onstage investigators but also the audience into admitting having taken a superficial approach to the issue, assisted by prejudice and stereotypical assumptions. For Fuller, the play's the thing wherein he will catch the conscience of his audience.

Walter Kerr argues that the play's "particular excitement . . . doesn't really stem from the traditional business of tracking down the identity of the criminal. It comes instead from tracking down the identity of the victim." Fuller focuses on the central character, the murdered Tech/Sergeant Waters, a use of the mystery form that temporarily draws attention away from solving the mystery and toward analyzing a complex and troubling character who is working to improve the image of "his people" but in the end does more to hurt that image.

Waters is a character who has taken upon himself the job of refashioning the black image, assuming a missionary zeal and adopting what he considers a self-justifying posture almost similar to an "amoral" stance of declaring war, where the ends unquestionably justify the means. In World War I, he distinguished himself in actual combat, as did many blacks, but as he says, "[t]he First War, it didn't change much for us," and he feels the time has come for change, though his military background of violent action misdirects him. His intention of bringing about change may be a noble one, but the strategy becomes obsessive to the point of near megalomania. He recounts one event that occurred during the "First War":

> Do you know the damage one ignorant Negro can do? (Remembering) We were in France during the First War. . . . We had won decorations, but the white boys had told all the French gals we had tails. And they found this ignorant colored soldier. Paid him to tie a tail to his ass and parade around naked making monkey sounds. . . . And when we slit his throat, you know that fool asked us what he had done wrong?

This formative incident in Waters's life is followed by others which in turn lead up to Waters's radical act within the play that in turn leads to Waters's murder. That crucial act in the play is Waters's assault on the easygoing C. J., which dramatizes Waters's current as well as former modus operandi.

C. J. is a Southern black, a sort of Billy Budd, by Fuller's account. This innocent "handsome soldier" is a natural athlete (emphasis on natural), the best ball player on the black baseball team, and a simple, unlettered youth who best expresses himself with his guitar, country imagery, and soulful song. His simplicity is the quality that marks him an "ignorant colored soldier" in Waters's eyes.

Waters works to frame the naive and innocent C. J. with an elaborate plot and has him stockaded, thereby singly succeeding in eliminating one more "geech" from the public eye. Waters triumphantly comments:

> I waited a long time for you, boy, but I gotcha! And I try to get rid of you wherever I go. I put two geechies in jail at Fort Campbell, Kentucky—three at Fort Huachuca. Now I got you—one less fool for the race to be ashamed of.

This scheme of purifying his race and the methods used are unethical at best and are especially noted as such when presented with Nazi Germany in the background, complete with the connotations of its own system of purification. But Waters is made to be more complex than this initial response suggests. When discussing his family, for example, we see more precisely the motives behind Waters's actions: to improve the world for future black generations, not necessarily for himself:

> When this war's over [World War II], things are going to change. . . . and I want him [Waters's son] to be ready for it—my daughter, too! I'm sendin' bot' of 'em to some big white college.

So though he appears sinister in executing his plan against C. J., Fuller refuses to offer Waters as a pure source of evil, instead allowing him to be human and even allowing him eventually to express keen remorse upon the ultimate realization of the inhumanity of his plan. Unable to survive walled up in the stockade, C. J. commits suicide, and Waters is driven to drink because he sees the flaws in his "master plan" and realizes he is to blame for this man's death. At first he internalizes the grief, but finally he challenges the source that has so twisted him into his obsession: the white establishment. In a drunken stupor he confronts and attacks two white officers on the night of his murder:

> Followin' behind y'all? Look what it's done to me!—I hate myself. . . . I've killed for you. . . . And nothin' changed! . . . I've tried everything! Everything.

Waters finally realizes his ends in fact have failed to justify the means. He has been misdirected all along. That Waters is murdered/executed in the play is a sort of justice, retribution for all his past crimes, and finally something he himself likely welcomed.

As Kerr says, uncovering the personality of Waters is an intriguing process. Fuller has created a complex "villain" whose rich character can actually trigger a variety of mixed emotions within the audience. This very complexity of character, this creation of an intriguing human being who also happens to be black, greatly contributes to the overall complexity of the issues presented in the play and sheds light on the complexities of trying to "solve" the race problem in general. We accuse and possibly condemn him, only to have to reevaluate at a later time. This mixed reaction occurs throughout the play, onstage as well as offstage, in the audience. And the audience is given its lead by the characters onstage because the structure of the play is such that uncovering the character of Waters occurs throughout the action of the play, through a process of interviewing the various suspects and having their recountings take the form of flashbacks on stage. The audience in turn, engaged in an investigation of its own, responds to the suspects' reactions to Waters as presented on stage.

Within the play, the variety of responses to Waters's character is presented by introducing a variety of characters as suspects, another convenience afforded by selecting the mystery form. Throughout the several interviews, suspicion continually shifts. Any of a variety of suspects could have committed the crime, we realize, and the effect is that uncovering the actual criminal again becomes less important than uncovering the variety of violent responses to Waters's life and what he represents. Presented are white bigots, stereotypically malleable blacks, radically sophisticated blacks, etc. That P. F. C. Peterson, a black, is finally revealed to be the actual culprit is thematically significant, presenting an argument by Fuller that a dangerous "enemy" lies within black ranks rather than without. But it is also a sort of dramatic trick since his guilt is unexpected, which allows for the investigation to continually "misfire" and for the on- and offstage investigators to question the motives for their finally unsupportable conclusions.

A murder of such a nature leads to instant assumptions that it was racially motivated. To a point, it in fact is so motivated, since the death of C. J. was racially motivated and since Waters's murder was the result of C. J.'s death. But that complexity is not at issue in the early investigation, which duly takes the predictable turn of assuming white complicity. The two white officers that Waters confronted on the night of his murder are interrogated, one of whom presents the standard white bigot's view, first insisting that Waters broke with military protocol and then revealing formerly hidden feelings:

> Look—the goddamn Negro was disrespectful! He wouldn't salute! Wouldn't come to attention! And where I come from, colored don't talk the way he spoke to us—not to white people they don't.

But the simple solution of accusing a white is not the actual solution, though it is seriously posed and considered until late in the play, a strategy that succeeds at arousing and keeping alive suspicion that whites are the guilty party. Such serious suspicions stem from prejudiced leanings toward an easy solution, thoughts that Fuller develops in his on-stage investigators and seems to want to allow to develop in the audience, if the tendency exists. Vindicating the whites late in the play gives such presumptions freedom to grow.

The next logical suspect is Private Wilkie, a black man busted to private by Waters from the rank of sergeant, which took him ten years to earn. The revenge motive is there, but Wilkie instead subordinates himself to the will of Waters, a fact not immediately revealed to the audience. This quality leads Waters to take advantage of Wilkie, using him to help frame C. J. That he is such a character, and not some "typically" revenge-ridden emotional stereotype, again provides the opportunity to misinterpret. With Wilkie, too, no simple solution is offered. Wilkie is innocent of murder, though guilty of complicity in framing C. J., guilty of betraying a fellow for his own advancement.

P. F. C. Peterson, the man who finally confesses (along with an accomplice by association, a minor character), places an ironic sense of closure on the mystery. He is strong and opinionated, in many ways the kind of man Waters is trying to make out of all his men. Unlike Waters, though, Peterson maintains his attachment to his black heritage: he's a man from "Hollywood, California—by way of Alabama." But unlike C. J., the suicide from Mississippi, Peterson is a Southerner who has been introduced to a more sophisticated world and has developed the tools to defend himself, to stand up for himself. The confident self-reliance is what Waters admires; the sense of separatism is what Waters wants to beat out of him. The two men's conflicting perspectives on "black destiny" lead first to a fist fight and finally to Peterson murdering Waters for destroying C. J. C. J. represents a kind of innocence that Waters was ashamed of and that Peterson seemed anxious to stand up for and wanted to preserve. The hatred stemming from the confrontation eventually leads to mutual elimination.

To one degree or another, *all* the characters are guilty of racially motivated violence (with the exception of C. J.) an implicit indication that such prejudices are pervasive and not merely restricted to reported acts of violence. Having the least likely suspect turn out to be the actual murderer serves two purposes, as noted above. With Peterson, Fuller makes a statement about the efficacy of a militant stand, a theme he developed in his earlier works. But more significantly, having Peterson be the murderer provides opportunities for misdirected accusations to fly, accusations which are invariably the product of prejudicial conclusions and which condemn the accuser even more than the accused. On stage the accusations come from the two investigators of the murder, men whose efforts to solve the crime force them to come to terms with their own personal prejudices, prejudices that surface because of the work at hand. And if the murder-mystery form succeeds in engaging the audience, the investigators become onstage representatives of their audience equivalents.

To come close to creating audience representatives on stage, Fuller creates two "Everyman" types, characters of equal rank, one white, the other black. The two are the white Captain Taylor and the black chief investigator, Captain Davenport, who is brought in especially to solve the case, and who may have the credentials of an "equal" but who is afforded few of the privileges of his rank, a condition he must continually fight against and which colors his perceptions, almost against his will. Both men's rational attempts to determine the guilty party are constantly clouded by overt prejudices that neutralize their formal efforts to uncover the truth. Taylor considers himself to be a fairly liberal white, concerned about blacks as human beings, though he still considers them his social inferiors, a belief stemming from his "comfortable" upbringing. As a result, his attempts at honesty and sincerity are both comical and revealing: "Forgive me for occasionally staring, Davenport, you're the first colored officer I've ever met." And his observations are stereotypically naive: "Listen, Waters didn't have a fifth grade education—he wasn't a schemer! And colored soldiers aren't devious like that." Blinded by a consequent overzealousness to do right, Taylor falls into a sort of "liberal" trap and overreacts to the facts presented him. In the second interview with the two suspected white officers, he is the one to charge them with murder, proceeding only on an unsound suspicion that the men, obvious bigots, are lying. The charge comes despite Taylor's own earlier insistence that the men had sound alibis: "Consider yourself under arrest, 'gentlemen'! . . . You think I believe that crap—." Davenport, however, at this point releases them.

Though rational during this particular interview, Davenport is not much different from Taylor at other points. For example, feeling like a crusader for his race, Davenport first considers the KKK until common sense evidence eliminates it as a possible force: Waters's insignia would have been stripped from his uniform. Then, even before Taylor does, Davenport attacks the white officers with a conspiracy charge. He blindly argues against fact, claiming that their alibis are "nothing more than officers lying to protect two of their own." When the conspiracy theory extends to having to accuse the camp commander of complicity, Davenport still rages, "They're all lying!" He does eventually settle into looking at the facts, letting the officers go, and finding the actual murderer, almost by accident. Once the crime is solved, he offers a fitting eulogy to those men destroyed by the event and a fitting condemnation to those blinded by color, himself ironically included:

> Two colored soldiers are dead—two on their way to prison. Four less men to fight with—and none of their reasons—nothing anyone 'said' or 'did,' would have been worth a life to men with

larger hearts—men less split by the madness of race in America.

The madness, in fact, has captured all in the play—blacks and whites—and has not just affected the four men directly involved.

But finally what happens onstage, the formal "lesson" Davenport provides, is not nearly as profound as what is hoped to occur in the audience. Fuller turns very specifically to the audience with the final event reported in the play. Davenport reports to the audience that the case itself was subsequently buried and forgotten under more important matters involving the war effort. Also, "[t]hrough a military foul-up," Waters was given a hero's burial, so the affair itself is formally buried. And finally Davenport reports that "the entire outfit—officers [the whites] and enlisted men—was wiped out in the Ruhr Valley during a German advance." Davenport alone is left to tell the tale. It seems that the lessons of the play are to die with the end of the play. None are left to disseminate the lesson unless, of course, the audience itself is to be considered. So, quietly working its way into the audience throughout the course of the production, the play clearly moves into the auditorium at play's end.

The process is ingenious and effective. The murder-mystery plot first forces upon the audience a dramatically leading curiosity to know the victim and to understand the complexities of a conscientious but misguided man in his search for a racial identity. But the stereotypical dramatic expectations (those concerning the murder plot) go further, drawing out hidden prejudices from the investigators onstage and from those "investigators" in the audience as well since they all string together information along a line of individually preconceived notions, which are in turn challenged by the outcome of the event, leaving the various investigators troubled by the various racial prejudices surfaced by the play. And finally the play detaches itself from its stage life and reaches out into the auditorium asking that the audience accept its legacy. Manipulating what may at first have been considered merely a "form of entertainment" is an alarmingly disarming and finally effective technique.

A Soldier's Play deals with a wide variety of "causes" of the race problem, but the "argument" moves to break through prejudices, to shatter barriers, not abstractly but on a personal level. The underlying assumptions are clear. Understanding and psychological change must come on an individual level for any change to be permanent. Group militancy is not the answer. That Waters and Peterson self-destruct clearly argues against either of their brands of militancy and may in fact be read as a subtle comment by Fuller on the inevitable results of the "destiny" that leaders like Baraka are trying to create for blacks. Fuller seems to argue that such visions as Baraka's have their limits and are dreams that are themselves destined to self-destruct.

In *A Soldier's Play,* Fuller has manipulated a theatrical formula to subtly achieve his ends: social awareness not preached but experienced. And with *A Soldier's Play,* Fuller and the Negro Ensemble Company have broken from those former defensive and insular postures to pres-

ent a work that confidently creates not just a black experience, but an "American" experience. (pp. 43-56)

> *William W. Demastes, "Charles Fuller and 'A
> Soldier's Play': Attacking Prejudice, Challeng-
> ing Form," in* Studies in American Drama,
> 1945-Present, *Vol. 2, 1987, pp. 43-56.*

FURTHER READING

OVERVIEWS AND GENERAL STUDIES

Harriott, Esther. "The Quest for Justice." In her *American
Voices: Five Contemporary Playwrights in Essays and Interviews,* pp. 101-11. Jefferson, N.C.: McFarland and Company,
1988.
> Study of *The Brownsville Raid, Zooman and the Sign,*
> and *A Soldier's Play.*

White, Frank, III. "Pushing Beyond the Pulitzer." *Ebony*
XXXVIII, No. 5 (March 1983): 116-18.
> Profile of Fuller's life and career.

A SOLDIER'S PLAY

Demastes, William W. "New Voices Using New Realism:
Fuller, Henley, and Norman." In his *Beyond Naturalism: A
New Realism in American Theatre,* pp. 125-54.
> Explores Fuller's dramatic technique in *A Soldier's Play.*

Hughes, Catharine. "Soldiers at Sea." *America* 147, No. 17
(1 May 1982): 343.
> Laudatory review of *A Soldier's Play.*

Hughes, Linda K. and Faulkner, Howard. "The Role of Detection in *A Soldier's Play.*" *Clues* 7, No. 2 (Fall/Winter
1986): 83-97.
> Examines the mystery in *A Soldier's Play,* determining
> that "the play ultimately asks whether the detective's
> traditional quest for truth is possible when conducted
> amidst a racist society."

Oliver, Edith. "A Sergeant's Death." *The New Yorker* LVII,
No. 42 (7 December 1981): 110, 113-14.
> Praises *A Soldier's Play,* noting that Fuller "moves from
> strength to strength" with each new work.

Weales, Gerald. "American Theater Watch, 1981-1982."
The Georgia Review XXXVI, No. 3 (Fall 1982): 517-26.
> Analyzes Fuller's claim that *A Soldier's Play* parallels
> Herman Melville's *Billy Budd.*

OTHER MAJOR WORKS

Clurman, Harold. Review of *The Brownsville Raid. The Nation* 223, No. 22 (25 December 1976): 701-02.
> Admires *The Brownsville Raid* for its "honestly, inci-
> sively, and often humorously drawn" characters.

Hornby, Richard. "Minority Theatre." *The Hudson Review*
XLII, No. 2 (Summer 1989): 283-89.
> Assessment of *Sally* and *Prince.* Hornby asserts that
> "the ultimate subject" of these pieces "is not history but
> ethics, but they are very good ethical plays indeed."

Oliver, Edith. "A Death in the Streets." *The New Yorker*
LVI, No. 44 (22 December 1980): 55-6.
> Favorable review of the Off-Broadway production of
> *Zooman and the Sign.*

——. "Fuller's Civil War." *The New Yorker* LXIV, No. 47
(9 January 1989): 82.
> Reviews *Sally* and *Prince,* determining, "Although non-
> vintage Fuller, they can be considered the groundwork
> for what lies ahead."

——. "Post-Bellum." *The New Yorker* LXV, No. 50 (29
January 1990): 83.
> Mixed review of *Jonquil,* "a sometimes awkward, some-
> times murky play."

Simon, John. "Maybe in Allentown." *New York* 22, No. 2 (9
January 1989): 56-7.
> Pronounces the production of *Sally* and *Prince* a
> "mighty disappointment."

Nikolai Gogol

1809-1852

(Full name: Nikolai Vasilyevich Gogol-Yanovsky; also transliterated as Nikolay; also Vasilevich, Vasil'yevich, Vasilievich, and Vasilyevitch; also Gogol' and Gógol; also wrote under pseudonyms of V. Alov and Rudy Panko)

A prominent Russian novelist and dramatist, Gogol is considered one of the most innovative and enigmatic writers in Russian literature. He was particularly renowned as an author of multifaceted works that combine elements of realism, romanticism, satire, fantasy, and farce. Reflecting a deep concern with spiritual values and the eccentricities of the author's personality, the complexity of such acknowledged masterpieces as the novel *Dead Souls* (*Mërtvye dushi*) and the short story "Shinel" ("The Overcoat") has inspired a wide range of critical interpretations. Because he often reworked his plays extensively over periods of several years, Gogol wrote relatively few works for the stage; however, he is credited with having displaced the European forms of vaudeville and melodrama prevalent during his era by introducing a uniquely Russian brand of realism to his country's drama. Gogol's most important play, *The Inspector General* (*Révizor*), is broadly regarded as the most enduring and original comedy in the history of Russian theater. Realistic in style, the play was widely perceived at the time of its first production as a politically motivated attack on the corrupt bureaucracy of nineteenth-century Russia; however, the work's ostensibly authentic portrayal of Russian provincial life belies its complexity, which has prompted analysis of the play as a moral or spiritual allegory, a comedy replete with elements of vaudevillian farce, and a commentary on human existence similar in intent to works of the absurdists of the twentieth century.

Gogol was born into a family of Russian landowners who sent him to boarding school as a youth, where he developed an interest in literature and drama. He performed in several amateur productions and hoped, upon graduation, to secure employment as an actor. However, following an unsuccessful audition at the Bolshoi theater in St. Petersburg, Gogol determined instead to become a writer. When he failed to sell his writing, he used his own money to finance the publication of a long epic poem, *Hans Kuechelgärten*. After receiving only negative reviews, Gogol burned all remaining copies of the book and obtained a civil service position in St. Petersburg. His first collection of short stories, *Evenings on a Farm near Dikanki* (*Vechera ná khutore bliz Dikanki*), garnered widespread acclaim and brought Gogol to the attention of both Alexander Pushkin and noted critic Vissarion Belinsky. Gogol found in Pushkin his strongest literary inspiration, and during the highly productive period of their association from 1831 to 1836, he determined to become an author of comedies for the theater.

In the early 1830s, Gogol began writing a play titled *The*

Order of St. Vladimir, Third Class (*Vladimir tret'ei stepeni*), but soon stopped, later commenting that "my pen had touched upon things the censor wouldn't dream of passing. . . . All I can do now is to concoct a subject so innocuous that it couldn't offend even a policeman. Yet what is comedy without truth and fury!" The protagonist of this incomplete work, four scenes of which were worked into final form, is an ambitious government official named Barsukov who aspires to receive a decoration despite the fact that he is an idle braggart and swindler who has recently forged a will. After failing to receive his reward, Barsukov becomes insane and imagines that he has himself become the Order of St. Vladimir, Third Class. Although Gogol abandoned the project, characters in *The Order of St. Vladimir* later served as models for those in his famous short story "Diary of a Madman," and the protagonist bears similarities to the main character of his next work, *The Inspector General*.

According to Gogol, the situation that served as the basis for *The Inspector General* was provided by Alexander Pushkin at his friend's request. In a letter, Gogol wrote: "Do me a favor; send me some subject, comical or not, but an authentically Russian anecdote. My hand is itching to

144

write a comedy. . . . Give me a subject and I'll knock off a comedy in five acts—I promise, funnier than hell." Pushkin replied with a story of mistaken identity that Gogol quickly transformed into the promised comedy. In *The Inspector General,* the prominent figures of a provincial Russian town are alerted that a government inspector will be arriving incognito to assess municipal affairs. An impecunious traveler named Khlestakov, who is mistaken for the expected official, is bribed and fêted, attempts to seduce the mayor's wife and daughter, becomes betrothed to the latter, and departs shortly before the town's residents learn of their mistake and anticipate the arrival of the real government inspector. In this simple plot, constructed within the framework of perverse logic typical of his works, Gogol combined satirical mockery of Russian officialdom with parody of farcical literary conventions and elements of fantasy and satire.

Completed in December 1835, *The Inspector General* was initially denied production by government censors who objected to Gogol's satiric portrayal of bureaucratic corruption. At the behest of the poet Vasily Zhukovsky, however, Tsar Nicholas I read the play and personally overruled the decision. In April 1836 he attended the play's premiere, where he was reported to have laughed heartily and to have remarked, "Everyone has got his due, and I most of all." Although the play proved highly popular in subsequent performances, many audiences reacted with extreme bewilderment and disapproval. Pavel Annenkov noted that at the end of the play, "some people called for the author because they thought he had written a comic masterpiece, others because some of the scenes showed talent, but most because it had made them laugh. The general opinion . . . , however, was that 'this is impossible, this is libel, this is farce'." Subsequent performances caused a sensation in the theater world and prompted heated controversy amongst critics, who were largely divided over the issues of the play's realism and social relevance. While conservative critics denounced *The Inspector General* as a crude, unrealistic farce and a libel against the Russian government, liberal critics praised the play as an artistic rendering of unpleasant social realities. Gogol was deeply offended by both readings; devastated by the indictments of reactionary commentators, he was equally distressed that his defenders viewed the play as either simple farce or a narrow social and political critique. His immediate reaction was to declare the play utterly devoid of social relevance and to feel personally maligned; in a letter to M. S. Shchepkin, he declared: "The reaction to [*The Inspector General*] has been extensive and tumultuous. Everybody is against me. . . . Now I see what it means to be a writer of comedies. The faintest glimmer of truth—and entire classes are up in arms against you."

Gogol modified his position regarding *The Inspector General* several times during his later career. In *Leaving the Theater after the Performance of a New Comedy (Teatral'nyi raz'ezd posle predstavleniia novoi komedii),* a short play estimated to have been written in 1836, several "lovers of art" discuss the artistic approach of a play suspiciously similar to *The Inspector General.* One objects to the drama's lack of plot development, and another, refusing to "affirm or deny the existence of a plot," replies that

"as a rule, people look for a plot centered on private life and prefer not to see the general. Simplemindedly, they have become accustomed to these incessant lovers and their marriages, without which no play can conceivably end. Of course, you have a plot here, but of what sort—something resembling a precise little knot at the corner of a handkerchief. No, comedy should cohere spontaneously, in all its mass, into one great, inconclusive knot." The "Author of the Play," overwhelmed by the diversity of opinion and accusations that all the characters are ignoble, argues that "no one noticed the honorable character who is present in my play. . . . This honorable, noble character is—*laughter.* The kind of laughter that brings out the profundity of its subject, makes vivid what would otherwise go unnoticed, and without whose penetrating power the trivia and emptiness of life would not terrify man so."

In subsequent years, Gogol variously maintained that *The Inspector General* was indeed implicitly critical of social institutions and was therefore a bad play; that the drama was an incisive commentary on social ills and therefore a great work of literature; and that the work was explicitly written as an allegorical representation of humanity's moral condition. The last interpretation is elaborated in *The Dénouement of "The Inspector General" (Razviazka "Révizor"),* a much later play in which two "Men of Society," a "Man of Letters," a "Comic Actor," and a chorus of actors and actresses debate the virtues and problems of *The Inspector General.* The comic actor finally designates the town in which the play is set as "our spiritual city," the real inspector as "our awakening conscience" sent by "command of the Almighty," and the remaining characters as the "passions residing in our souls." However, critics generally agree that *The Inspector General* is free from moral didacticism and dismiss the views expressed in *The Dénouement of "The Inspector General"* as a product of the religious and moral fanaticism of Gogol's later years.

The Inspector General is deeply rooted in theatrical tradition and utilizes such time-honored conventions as mistaken identity, stock characters from eighteenth-century Russian comedy, and elements of slapstick from French vaudeville while adhering closely to the classical unities of time, place, and action. Unencumbered by traditional romantic subplots, the play is often praised for its dramatic structure, in which the action develops frenetically between a startlingly brief exposition and an equally startling denouement. Vladimir Nabokov commented: "The play begins with a blinding flash of lightning and ends in a thunderclap. In fact it is wholly placed in the tense gap between the flash and the crash." The play is also admired for its rich rendering of spoken Russian, in which nuances of speech reflect aspects of character that imply alternate meanings. *The Inspector General* departs from theatrical tradition in its farcical parody of the love intrigue then common to Russian comedy as well as in its rejection of unnatural caricature and the conventional division between virtuous and villainous characters. Gogol's characters are all equally devoid of attractive features, embodying instead such qualities as egocentrism, ignorance, snobbery, and malice. However, they are not generally described as villainous but rather as larger-than-life figures of insignificance and insubstantiality. As Jesse Zeldin asserted, the play "is a remarkable achievement . . . of the portrayal of nothingness, of soullessness. These are all little men who aren't there."

Since Gogol's death, commentary on *The Inspector General* has shifted away from the controversy regarding the play's realism. Although Soviet critics have continued to regard the work as a social document indicting corruption and injustice under tsarist rule, most Western commentators have interpreted the play as an intensely subjective creation. Some scholars, stressing the play's fantastic and grotesque elements and atmosphere of unreality, have examined *The Inspector General* as an absurdist portrayal of human existence in which the meaning of reality remains uncertain. Formalist critics, who consider Gogol the first great Russian prose stylist, approach his play as an exercise in linguistic manipulation. Other commentators, prompted by the drama's religious and spiritual elements, deny that *The Inspector General* conveys any moralistic or political intent and detect diabolic connotations in the character of Khlestakov and biblical parallels throughout the play. Many of these critics have interpreted *The Inspector General* as a parody of judgment day and Khlestakov as either a symbolic false messiah, Antichrist, or the devil himself.

Stung by the criticism of *The Government Inspector*, Gogol moved to Italy in 1836. Except for two brief visits home, he remained abroad for twelve years. Although Gogol's later comedies achieved neither the acclaim nor notoriety of *The Inspector General*, his next play, *The Marriage: An Utterly Incredible Occurrence* (*Zhenit'ba; Sovershenno neveroyatnoye sobitye*), attracted a degree of controversy due to its satirical portrayal of the bureaucratic mercantile class and its coarse, realistic language. Originally written between 1833 and 1835, the play was initially dependent on farcical traditions in the manner of Molière but became increasingly less farcical and more naturalistic following Gogol's extensive revision of the text between 1835 and 1842. Making use of exaggerated characters, the play parodies conventional love stories by focusing on a merchant's daughter who is entertaining suitors at a fair. Mistaken identities, quarrels and reconciliations abound, culminating in the lead suitor's decision to jump out a window and escape the fate of marriage. Critics disagree as to when Gogol actually wrote his final full-length play, *The Gamblers* (*Igroki*). This work contains no female characters and no actual plot, being based on stories of swindles by confidence men and criminals. Although the play has been only rarely performed, *The Gamblers* is generally praised as a nondidactic and authentic depiction of the criminal world. Belinsky considered the play "fully worthy of its author's name," and N. A. Kotlyarevsky commented: "Stories about such stratagems frequently occurred in the literature of Gogol's period. Gogol's merit consisted in that he developed this traditional theme with extraordinary realism and inimitible wit; that he alone succeeded in expressing with equal truth a general tone in several variations; and—most important—that he evaded all didacticism by excluding from the dramatis personae the former hero, the 'victim'!"

Though Gogol's critical appeal waned in his later years, his influence on Russian literature has continued into the twentieth century and is probably best evidenced by the poetry of the Russian Symbolists. Yet many critics maintain that Gogol's blend of realism and satire has proved most influential and remains his greatest achievement. Despite the multiplicity of interpretation, modern critics are nearly unanimous in their praise of *The Inspector General*. The play has remained popular with readers and audiences throughout the world despite its basis in a social milieu that has been largely forgotten. As Henry Ten Eyck Perry concluded, many elements have contributed to the enduring appeal of *The Inspector General*: "Its plot has artistic structure without being rigidly formal. Its texture is a happy combination of individuality and universal truth. Its vitality is extraordinary; its inventiveness never seems to flag; it has the creative quality of life; it lacks only the consistent intellectual meaning which life itself so often seems to lack."

(For further information on Gogol's life and career, see *Nineteenth-Century Literature Criticism*, Vols. 5, 15 and *Short Story Criticism*, Vol. 4.)

PRINCIPAL WORKS

PLAYS

Révizor   1836
  [*The Inspector General*, 1892; also published as *The Government Inspector* in *The Government Inspector and Other Plays*, 1927]
Sochinenya.   2 vols.   (short stories, dramas, and novel) 1842
  [*The Works of Nikolay Gogol*. 6 vols., 1922-1928]
Zhenit'ba; Sovershenno neveroyatnoye sobitye   1842
  [*The Marriage: An Utterly Incredible Occurrence;* published in *The Modern Theatre*, Vol. IV, 1955-1960]
Igroki   1843?
  [*The Gamblers;* published in *The Modern Theatre*, Vol. III, 1955-1960]
Razviazka "Révizor"   1846
  [*The Dénouement of "The Government Inspector"* (partial translation);   published in *The Theater of Nikolay Gogol*, 1980]

OTHER MAJOR WORKS

Hans Kuechelgärten [as V. Alov]   (poetry)   1829
Vechera ná khutore bliz Dikanki [as Rudy Panko]   (short stories)   1831
  [*Evenings in Little Russia*, 1903; also published as *Evenings on a Farm near Dikanka*, 1906]
Arabeski   (essays and short stories)   1835
  [*Arabesques*, 1981]
Mirgorod   (short stories)   1835
  [*Mirgorod*, 1842]
Mërtvye dushi   (novel)   1842

[*Tchitchikoff's Journeys; or, Dead Souls,* 1886; also
   published as *Dead Souls,* 1915]
Vybrannye mesta iz perepiski s druzyami (essays and let-
   ters) 1847
   [*Selected Passages from Correspondence with My
   Friends,* 1969]
Letters of Nikolai Gogol (correspondence) 1967

---

*This publication contains the short play *Teatral'nyi raz'ezd posle
predstavleniia novoi komedii* (Leaving the Theater after the Performance of a New Comedy).*

AUTHOR COMMENTARY

Fragment of a Letter to a Man of Letters   (1836)

[*In the following excerpt from a letter dated 25 May
1836, Gogol expresses his disappointment with the narrow vaudevillian treatment of his characters in the first
stage performance of* The Inspector General *and the
prevailing interpretation of his play as pure farce.*]

The Government Inspector has been performed—and I
have such a troubled and strange feeling. . . . My creation struck me as repellent, bizarre, and not at all mine.
The major role was a failure. . . . Khlestakov . . . turned
into someone from the ranks of those vaudeville rogues,
who have come to us from the theaters of Paris to flit
about our stages. He became the conventional bluffer—an
insipid figure who has appeared in the same guise over the
course of two centuries. Doesn't Khlestakov's part really
speak for itself? Khlestakov doesn't at all bluff; he isn't
a liar by vocation; he forgets he is lying and almost believes what he says. He has become expansive, is in good
spirits, sees that all is going well, people are listening to
him—and as a result his speech becomes more fluent, and
free and easy. He is sincere, completely frank, and in telling lies he shows the stuff he is made of. As a rule our actors are incapable of lying. They imagine that lying is simply chattering away. To lie, one must speak in a tone so
close to the truth, so natural, so naïve as only truth can
be spoken—the comedy of lying consists precisely in this.
I am almost certain that Khlestakov would have fared better had I assigned the part to the most untalented of actors, telling him only that Khlestakov is a sharp fellow,
very *comme il faut,* clever, and perhaps even virtuous, and
that he ought to play him as such. Khlestakov doesn't lie
with calculation or like a theatrical braggart; he lies with
feeling; his eyes convey the pleasure it gives him. It is the
finest and most poetic moment of his life—almost a kind
of inspiration. . . . Of course it is incomparably easier to
caricature elderly officials in their threadbare uniforms
and frayed collars; but to capture those traits that are fairly agreeable and do not markedly differ from what may
be found in conventional society is a task for a powerful
master. Nothing about Khlestakov should be put in sharp
relief. He belongs to a social circle which, apparently, is
in no way distinguishable from those of other young people. At times he even conducts himself properly, speaks

weightily, and only on occasions requiring presence of
mind or character does his somewhat vulgar and paltry
nature reveal itself. The mayor's character is more fixed
and clear. His immutable, hardened exterior designates
him distinctly, and partially attests his character.
Khlestakov's character is extremely fluid, more subtle,
and hence more difficult to grasp. Actually, who is
Khlestakov? A young man, a civil servant, and what we
call an empty fellow, but one who possesses many traits
belonging to people the world does not call empty. . . .
In a word, he should typify many things that are scattered
in various Russian characters, but which have accidentally combined in one, as frequently occurs even in nature.
Everyone, if only for a minute, or even several minutes,
has been or is a Khlestakov, though, of course, he doesn't
care to admit it. . . .

. . . In general the public was satisfied. Half the audience
even received the play sympathetically, while the other
half, as usual, railed against it—for reasons having nothing to do with art. . . .

All in all, it seems to have been the mayor who completely
won over the audience. I was confident of it even
beforehand. . . . I also counted on the servant [Osip], because I had noticed the actor's great attentiveness to the
words and how observant he was. On the other hand, our
friends Bobchinsky and Dobchinsky came off worse than
one might have expected. Although I anticipated it . . . ,
I nevertheless thought their appearance and the situation
in which they find themselves would somehow save them
from caricature. The opposite occurred—namely, caricature. Even before the performance, seeing their costumes,
I gasped. These two chubby little fellows, essentially quite
tidy, their hair decorously sleeked, found themselves in
high, ungainly wigs, disheveled, untidy, rumpled, wearing
enormous elongated dickies. And on the stage they were
so affected that it was simply unbearable. In general, for
most of the play the costumes were very bad and uncon-
scionably caricatured. . . .

One word about the final scene. It did not at all come
across. The curtain fell at a confused moment and the play
seemed unfinished. But I'm not to blame. They didn't
want to listen to me. I'll say it again: the final scene will
not meet with success until they grasp that it is a dumb
scene, that a single frozen group is to be represented, that
the drama has been concluded and replaced by mute mim-
icry, that the curtain must not drop for two to three minutes, and that all this is to be accomplished in the manner
of so-called *tableaux vivants.* But their answer was that
this would restrict the actor; the company would have to
be entrusted to a ballet master; it is even somewhat humiliating for the actor, etc., etc., etc. I caught sight of numerous other *etceteras* on their faces even more vexing than
the verbal ones. Despite all these etceteras, I stand my
ground and say a hundred times: No. It won't restrict the
actor in the slightest, it's not humiliating. . . . Limits do
not stop true talent, just as granite banks do not hold back
a river; on the contrary, when flowing between them, the
waves move more rapidly and with greater fullness. And
in his assigned pose the sensitive actor can express himself
more fully. No one has placed fetters on his countenance;

only the grouping has been arranged. His mien is free to express any emotion. This mute condition holds the possibility of infinite variety. The fright of each of the characters is dissimilar, as are their characters and the degree of their fear and terror, which are a consequence of the magnitude of their individual offenses. The mayor is struck dumb one way, his wife and daughter another. The judge takes fright in his unique way, as do the director of charities, the postmaster, etc., etc. . . . Only the guests may come to a dead stop in an identical manner, but they form the background of a picture which is outlined by one stroke of the brush, and overlaid with a single color. (pp. 178-80)

> *Nikolai Gogol, "Fragment of a Letter to a Man of Letters, Written by the Author Shortly after the First Performance of 'The Government Inspector',"* in The Theater of Nikolay Gogol: Plays and Selected Writings, *edited by Milton Ehre, translated by Milton Ehre and Fruma Gottschalk, The University of Chicago Press, 1980, pp. 178-80.*

The Dénoument of "The Government Inspector" (1846?)

[*The following excerpt is taken from Gogol's short play* The Dénouement of "The Government Inspector," *in which the author attempts to defend himself against widespread criticism by focusing on various characters who share their impressions of* The Government Inspector *as they leave the theater following a performance of the play. In the portion below, a Comic Actor defends the work against accusations of purposelessness by interpreting it not as a realistic portrayal of a typical Russian town but as a depiction of a "spiritual city" intended to "deride whatever dishonors the true beauty of man." Although this piece was not published until after Gogol's death, it is believed to have been written in 1846.*]

FIRST COMIC ACTOR: Very well. . . . Take a close look at the town depicted in the play. Everyone agrees that no such town exists in all of Russia; a town in our country where all the officials are monsters is unheard of. You can always find two or three who are honest, but here—not one. In a word, there is no such town. Do you agree? Now suppose this town is actually our spiritual city and is to be found in each of us? No, let's not look at ourselves through the eyes of a man of the world (after all, it's not he who will pronounce judgment upon us); let us look, as well as we can, with the eyes of Him Who will call all men to account, before Whom the best of us—mark it well— will cast down their eyes in shame. Let us see who will then have enough courage to ask, "Is my face crooked?" Pray we are not alarmed by our own crookedness, just as we felt no fear upon seeing the crookedness of those officials. . . . No, Semyon Semyonych, it's not our beauty that ought to concern us but the fact that our lives, which we are in the habit of regarding as comedies, might very well end in the same sort of tragedy that concluded this comedy. Say what you will, the inspector who awaits us at the portals of the grave is terrible. Can you really be ignorant of this inspector's identity? Why deceive ourselves? He is our awakening conscience, who will force us, once

and for all, to take a long hard look at ourselves. Nothing will remain hidden from this inspector, for he is sent by command of the Almighty. There will be no turning back when his coming is heralded. Suddenly horrors to make a man's hair stand on end will be revealed about and within us. Far better to examine ourselves at the beginning of our lives than at the end. Instead of engaging in idle self-centered chatter and self-congratulation, let us now visit our deformed spiritual city, a city several times worse than any other, where our passions run amuck like hideous officials plundering the treasury of our souls! At the beginning of our lives, let us take an inspector by the hand and examine all that lies within us—a true inspector and not a counterfeit! Not Khlestakov! Khlestakov is a mediocrity; he is the frivolous conscience of the world, venal and deceitful. The passions residing in our souls will buy him off in an instant. Arm in arm with Khlestakov, we will see nothing of our spiritual city. Note how in conversing with him, each official cleverly wriggled out of his difficulties and justified himself. They emerged almost sanctified. Don't you think our every passion, or even a trivial vulgar habit, has more cunning to it than does a swindling official? . . . No, you will not discern anything in yourselves with the superficial conscience of the world: [our passions] will deceive it, and it will deceive them, as Khlestakov duped the officials, and then it will vanish without leaving a trace. You will be in the position of the mayor turned fool, who let his imagination run away with him, began worming his way into a general's rank, announcing he was certain to be top man in the capital, promising positions to others, when he suddenly saw that he had been hoodwinked and played for a fool by a young whippersnapper, a featherbrain bearing no resemblance to the true inspector. No . . . gentlemen, . . . fling aside your worldly conscience. Examine yourselves, not through the eyes of Khlestakov, but those of the true inspector! I vow, our spiritual city is worth the same thought a good ruler gives to his realm. As he banishes corrupt officials from his land sternly and with dignity, let us banish corruption from our souls! There exists a weapon, a scourge, that can drive it out. Laughter, my worthy countrymen! Laughter, which our base passions fear so! Laughter, created so that we might decide whatever dishonors the true beauty of man. Let us restore to laughter its true significance! Let us wrest it from those who have turned it into a frivolous worldly blasphemy that does not distinguish between good and evil! Just as we laughed at the abominations of others, let us laugh at those abominations we uncover in ourselves! Not only this comedy, but everything that ridicules the ignoble and depraved, no matter who the author, must be understood as referring to ourselves, as if written about us personally. . . . Let us not swell with indignation if some infuriated mayor or, more correctly, the devil himself whispers: "What are you laughing at? Laugh at yourselves!" Proudly we shall answer him: "Yes, we are laughing at ourselves, because we sense our noble Russian heritage, because we hear a command from on high to be better than others!" Countrymen! Russian blood flows in my veins, as in yours. Behold: I'm weeping. As a comic actor, I made you laugh earlier, and now I weep. Allow me to think that my calling is as honest as yours, that I serve my country as you do, that

I'm not a light-headed jester created for the amusement of frivolous people, but an honorable functionary of God's great kingdom, and that I awakened laughter in you—not that dissolute laughter stemming from the empty vanity of idle hours by which man mocks man, but laughter born of love for man. Together we shall prove to the world that everything in the Russian land, from small to great, strives to serve Him Whom all things should serve, and that whatever exists in our land is surging upwards (*glancing up*) to the Supreme Eternal Beauty! (pp. 188-90)

> *Nikolai Gogol, in an excerpt in* The Theater of Nikolay Gogol: Plays and Selected Writings, *edited by Milton Ehre, translated by Milton Ehre and Fruma Gottschalk, The University of Chicago Press, 1980, pp. 188-90.*

OVERVIEWS AND GENERAL STUDIES

B. V. Varneke   (essay date 1939)

[*In the following excerpt from his full-length study originally published in Russian in 1939, Varneke presents a biographical and historical overview of Gogol's plays and his experiences as a dramatist. He also assesses Gogol's overall contribution to Russian theater.*]

Even in early childhood Gogol (1809-1852) may have gathered many impressions which contributed to the development of his passion for the theatre: his father Vasily Afanasyevich wrote several comedies in the Ukrainian language—good by the standards of those times—which were staged at the theatres of the neighboring landowners. Two are known: *Dog-Sheep* and *Roman and Paraska,* otherwise called *Simpleton, or Woman's Cunning Outwitted by a Soldier.* The contents of the latter closely remind one of I. P. Kotlyarevsky's famous vaudeville *The Muscovite Enchanter.*

Having matriculated at the Nezhin Lyceum, Gogol had the opportunity of taking part in school performances. Here is what one of his schoolmates tells us about these performances: "We played Fonvizin's comedy, *The Minor,* best of all. I have seen it at Moscow and Petersburg, but I always maintained that no actress played the part of Prostakova as well as the sixteen-year-old Gogol." He also played excellently the part of the nurse Vasilisa in Krylov's comedy *A Lesson to the Daughters.*

This unquestioned dramatic success during his school years was probably one of the principal reasons why later, when he despaired of the possibility of an immediate and brilliant career in Petersburg as a clerk, Gogol remembered the stage, and tried to join the crown company. The attempt was a failure; the administration suggested that he be subjected to an examination, and he was given two excerpts from Khvostov's plays to read. The government official who conducted the examination found that he was reading too naturally, without any expression, and submitted to the director of the theatres a memorandum in

which he asserted Gogol's utter inability to act; he considered it possible to engage his services in the event that the authorities should grant a special favor, "only for parts without speeches."

It seems probable that the sad outcome of the examination was caused merely by the fact that Gogol's natural and unaffected reading had not yet been recognized by the directors of the Petersburg theatre. Not without reason, one of his school friends said: "If he had been accepted for the stage, he would have become a Shchepkin."

Subsequently, Gogol turned to the theatre, no longer as an actor but as a playwright. Ever since 1831 the creation of a comedy had been his cherished and guiding purpose. In his notebooks of that period are outlines of whole plays as well as sketches of individual scenes which he later utilized.

Gogol's dramatic conceptions were closely related to his theoretical views on the theatre, in which he was far ahead of his time. These have considerable interest for us. The lofty social and educational role of the theatre—the theatre as a "school," as a "professorial chair"—was his fundamental postulate.

"The theatre," Gogol maintained, "is in no sense a trifle, and by no means a vain thing, if one considers that a crowd of five or six thousand men at once fill it, and that the people composing this crowd, having nothing in common with one another, may, if broken up into units, suddenly be shaken, may burst into tears, and break into spontaneous laughter. This is a chair from which much good may be imparted to the world." "The theatre is a great school," he reiterated in another passage, "and its significance is momentous; in one breath it preaches a vital and useful lesson to a whole crowd, to thousands of men."

Hence Gogol's profound dissatisfaction with the insignificant and empty repertoire prevailing on the Russian stage, a repertoire which, by promoting "all sorts of ballet leaps, vaudevilles, melodramas, and those tinsel shows that appear magnificent to the eyes but only gratify depravity of taste or corruption of the heart," in no manner helped the theatre fulfill its important mission. "What was being given on the stage?" he asked. "Melodrama and vaudeville, these illegitimate children of the mind of the nineteenth century, complete deviations from nature."

Gogol considered the unnatural and misleading tendencies of the contemporary repertoire as the reason for the lack of outstanding talents in the theatre:

> Complaints about the scarcity of talent among actors are unanimous. But where are talents to develop? On what are they to develop? Do they happen to come across even a single Russian character which they are capable of representing to themselves graphically? Whom do actors impersonate? All kinds of infidels, men who are neither Frenchmen nor Germans, but God knows who—all sorts of giddy persons. It is difficult to describe otherwise the heroes of melodrama, possessing no specific passion whatsoever, and still less a countenance. Is it not strange? Even though we speak about naturalness more

than about anything else, the highest degree of distortion is being thrust under our noses.

In order to restore health to the theatre and to lift it to the level of its lofty aims, Gogol suggested giving it free access to classical drama in lieu of "rotten melodramas" and "ultramodern vaudevilles":

> The stage should benefit by the whole splendor of all the loftiest creations of every age and of every nation. These creations should be given more frequently, as often as possible, and one and the same play should be continually repeated. It is nonsense to say that they have grown too old and that the public has lost taste for them.

Among the great classics whose works should be restored to the contemporary stage Gogol named, in the first instance, Shakespeare, Molière, Schiller, and Beaumarchais. At the same time he most decidedly set as the aim of the Russian theatre the creation of its own original, national repertoire, one that would comprise highly artistic contemporary plays reflecting the life of Russian society and the character of Russian men:

> Russians—this is what we need! Give us our own! What are Frenchmen and all other people beyond the seas to us? Do we lack our own people? Russian characters? Our own characters?— Give us our own!

Gogol extended his insistence on a national tendency in the repertoire beyond drama. Observing the prevalence of foreign influences in opera, he meditated: "What an opera, what music could be composed from our folk tunes!" Thus he was one of the earliest partisans of that school in our music which created the Russian national opera, taking advantage of the wealth of our folk songs which he so pointedly appraised.

The same progressive and fresh character distinguished his ideas on the organization of the theatre, the part of the actor in it, the ensemble, and the technique of the theatre.

Unhesitatingly asserting that the first place in the theatre rightly belongs to the actor-artist, and to him alone, Gogol strongly protested against a situation in which actors, regardless of their talents, found themselves subordinate to aristocratic theatre habitués, such as Kokoshkin, Zagoskin, and Shakhovskoy. During Gogol's time these theatre lovers were headed by Nicholas I himself with his excessive partiality for pseudo-romantic tragedy and vaudeville. The influence of "the august sergeant major" both on the repertoire and on the fate of the actors was boundless. This produced dreadful dramas in the soul of many an actor.

Mercilessly condemning the prevailing lack of coordination, mismanagement, and the thoughtlessness concerning the general plan of the performance, Gogol emphasized the importance of the ensemble in the performance of plays. "There is no effect more crushing," he wrote, "than that produced on man by a perfectly coordinated harmony of all mutually interrelated parts; thus far, however, man has been able to experience such an effect only when listening to a musical orchestra."

From the actor Gogol demanded "truth and naturalness both in speech and in bodily movement," a complete assimilation with the figure "so that the thought and aspirations of the impersonated character be appropriated by the actor himself, and that these stay in his mind during the entire performance of the play."

Acutely aware of all the vices of the contemporary theatre, Gogol even in his earliest plays refused to follow the beaten path, seeking new themes, new images, and novel forms of dramatic expression which would enable him to realize his artistic principles as completely as possible. He wrote to M. P. Pogodin, February 20, 1833:

> I am possessed by the idea of a comedy. While I stayed in Moscow on my journey, and also when I arrived here, it did not leave my mind. However, thus far I have written nothing. Lately, the plot gradually began to take shape; the title *The Order of St. Vladimir, Third Class* is already inscribed in a thick white copybook. And how much bitterness! How much laughter and sting!

This play is said to have been Gogol's first attempt at playwrighting. It was conceived as a bold social satire on bureaucratic customs; the hero was to be the careerist government official Barsukov, seeking by hook or by crook to obtain the decoration of St. Vladimir, third class, and becoming insane because his solicitations come to naught. However, Gogol never carried out this scheme; we have only the several scenes which appeared in print at different times (*The Morning of a Government Official, The Lawsuit, The Cloakroom, Sobachkin*). The principal reason why he did not complete his first comedy was obviously that he realized the impossibility of saving it from censorship. In the same letter to Pogodin he confessed, "I stopped when I noticed that my pen kept knocking against such passages as would never be permitted by the censorship," and added with bitterness: "There remains nothing else for me than to invent a most innocent plot to which even a police precinct officer will take no offense. Yet what is a comedy without truth and indignation!"

Having cut short his work on *The Order of St. Vladimir, Third Class,* Gogol turned to another comedy, with a more "innocent" plot. This was **The Marriage.** On the text—it has five versions—he labored almost nine years (1833-1842). In its original form the comedy was entitled *Bridegrooms.* The action took place in the country, in the landowners' milieu. The fiancée Avdotya Gavrilovna and her fiancés—a retired subaltern officer Yaichnitsa, Zhevakin, and others—were all landowners. Instead of the professional matchmaker Fyokla Panteleimonovna, that wonderful progenitor of Ostrovsky's gallery of matchmakers, there was Marya Savvishna, a lady's companion, who was being sent to a fair for the procurement of bridegrooms. Among the dramatis personae, there was, as yet, no Podkolesin, who subsequently became the central figure in the play.

The theme of the comedy was reminiscent of the Ukrainian novels which Gogol had recently written: *The Sorochinsky Fair, Christmas Eve,* and *Ivan Fyodorovich Shponka and His Auntie.* The whole work bears an obvious farcical stamp in the dramatic situations, in the author's remarks, and in the dialogue.

In the subsequent versions the action of the comedy was transferred to the city. The fiancée was converted into a merchant's daughter, and the fiancés into government officials. The characters of Podkolesin and Kochkarev were emphasized, while the number of vaudeville and farcical episodes steadily decreased. The plot acquired a psychologically justified motivation. The folk quality became more pronounced. One of the most recent research students has made the pointed observation that Gogol's play was converted from a comedy of dramatic situations into a comedy of characters and customs.

In the final variant, which was published in the first collection of Gogol's works (1842), *The Marriage* was a strictly realistic play with a vivid synthetic satirical characterization of the life and the types of the bureaucratic merchant world, in many respects presaging Ostrovsky's portrayals.

The Marriage was first produced on the stage of the Aleksandrinsky Theatre in December, 1842, on I. I. Sosnitsky's benefit night. Notwithstanding the artist's excellent acting, the play was cruelly hissed. Critics who apparently were on the same intellectual level as the audience at that first performance, reproached the author for having written a trivial farce that violated the rules of elegant style and employed coarse words such as "swine" and "scoundrel." Gogol was accused of having presented such government officials as never existed in real life.

Of the fiasco of the play, one of the magazines stated:

> The principal and sole condition of the stage is elegance and decorum. Where this condition is violated, there awakes in the soul of every not altogether perverted man some incomprehensible aesthetic feeling which revolts against this violation and repudiates coarse and filthy nature. Yes, Messrs. Authors, nature and naturalness are requisite to the stage—but in a purified form, in an elegant guise, expressed with delicacy and from a pleasant aspect. However, all of trivial and filthy nature is repugnant. And the public which unanimously hissed down Gogol's play revealed its refinement and its instinct for decency. Honor and praise to it!

The Marriage provided the artists with ample material. In Petersburg, Martynov was particularly fine in the part of Podkolesin, and Guseva in the role of the matchmaker. On Martynov, contemporary critics commented: "The hollow voice in which, with no strain and—it seemed—reluctantly, he speaks, was admirably adapted to the apathetic and indolent figure of Podkolesin." Regarding Guseva we read in one of the reviews:

> Observe how she laughs at Kochkarev when he finds a bridegroom who jumps out of the window. In this somewhat hoarse laughter of the old woman, which blends with the healthy laughter of Kochkarev, there is something original and wicked: you can hear that Kyokla, who has spent a lifetime as a matchmaker, laughs not foolishly or merely in vain, but with a note of anger.

In Moscow the production of *The Marriage* brought no particular laurels to Shchepkin as Kochkarev. According to Belinsky, he revealed in this role "more skill than genuine naturalness." In later days, the part was more effectively taken by Shumsky, whose acting prompted one critic to make the following comments:

> Until now we had seen only M. S. Shchepkin in that role, and we were convinced that it could not be performed better. Everybody was familiar with the type created by this artist. However, having seen Shumsky in the part of Kochkarev, many people have thoroughly revised their opinion: they found that Kochkarev is not an intriguer, not a sly person as he was represented by Shchepkin, but simply a very inconsequential man, an idler, a bustler, a chatterbox, as he was conceived by Shumsky.

Gogol's attempt to write the drama *Alfred,* relating to Anglo-Saxon history, dates from 1835. N. S. Tikhonravov expressed the view that "the idea of writing *Alfred* and the material for the play were suggested to Gogol by his university course on the history of medieval England." This play has survived only in excerpts. N. G. Chernyshevsky's opinion on it is most interesting:

> As far as may be judged by its opening passages, in the drama we should have had something similar to Pushkin's beautiful scenes from the period of Knighthood. In this case simplicity of language and mastery in the unaffected handling of the scenes, ability in portraying characters and the characteristics of the way of life did not fail Gogol. Historical truth is strictly observed.

In a letter to Pushkin on October 7, 1835, Gogol made this request:

> For mercy's sake, give me some funny, or not funny, but genuinely Russian anecdote. Meanwhile my hand shakes with the desire to write a comedy. . . . For mercy's sake, give me a plot: a five-act comedy will be ready in a jiffy, and I swear it will be much funnier than the devil.

It has been suggested that the plot of the brilliant comedy *The Inspector-General*—the zenith of Gogol's playwrighting creative power—was actually based upon an anecdote he had heard from Pushkin. This was to the effect that Pushkin on a journey for the purpose of gathering data on the Pugachyov uprising had been taken by Buturlin, the governor of Nizhny-Novgorod Province, for a government official who had received "a secret commission to collect information concerning irregularities."

It is possible that Pushkin communicated to Gogol the scheme of a play on an analogous theme which he originally meant to write himself, and which was reflected in the following sketch:

> Svinyin (Krispin arrives in NB for the fair) province—he is taken for an ambass(ador). Govern(or) is an honest fool, the govern(or's wife) plays pranks with him. Krisp. proposes to the daughter.

Besides, cases similar to the one depicted in *The Inspector-General* were a frequent occurrence during the Nicholas period, in the atmosphere of utter arbitrariness and irresponsibility of provincial officialdom. Even without Pushkin, Gogol might have known many an episode of this kind.

Molière's remarkable comedies, which Gogol so much admired, were of the greatest importance in the creation of **The Inspector-General.**

The character of Khlestakov closely reminds several critics of Mascarille in *Les Précieuses ridicules:* Molière's hero is as trivial, light-minded, and vainglorious, and he likewise brags about his connections with the *beau monde* and his literary achievements. The scene of the reading of the letter in the last act of **The Inspector-General** is similar to one of the scenes in *The Misanthrope* [Act V, Scene vii]. In the behavior of the officials there is something in common with the comic situations in *Scapin's Deceits.*

In **The Inspector-General** (as well as in other Gogol comedies) we find a kinship not only to Molière, but to the playwrighting technique of the Italian comedy, particularly that of Goldoni; every dramatic situation develops with the participation not of one but of many persons (officials in **The Inspector-General,** fiancés in **The Marriage,** sharpers in **The Gamblers**), and this enables the playwright to paint full character sketches including all the nuances.

It has been long observed that the plot of **The Inspector-General** is similar to that of the comedy of the Ukrainian writer G. F. Kvitka-Osnovyanenko, *The Newcomer from the Capital* or *The Bustle in a County Seat.* This play, written in 1827 but published only in 1840, probably was known to Gogol in manuscript form. His comedy, however, is so superior to its predecessor both from the ideational and from the artistic standpoint that it is impossible to speak of his imitating Kvitka. Kvitka's style fully conforms to the method of comic ridicule which was prevalent in the didactic plays of the eighteenth century. He heaps up a series of droll figures, resorting at every step to exaggeration and caricature; the characters of his comedies are extremely primitive; social satire is lacking. Gogol transferred the handling of the same plot to a new and infinitely higher level; thereby Kvitka's comedy was removed from **The Inspector-General** by nearly the same distance that separates Shakespeare's dramas from Holinshed's chronicles.

The first version of **The Inspector-General** appeared in December, 1835. The comedy subsequently underwent many revisions, which continued until 1842—long after its first production on the stage. The elimination of the vaudeville element; the deepening of the psychological motivations; the emphasized intricacy in characterization; the sharpening of the satirical motif; the marked emphasis on a faster pacing and tension in the development of the action; the adoption of maximum terseness and expressiveness in the text—that was the course Gogol followed

Erast Garin as Khlestakov and Zinadia Raikh as Anna Andreevna in a famous 1926 production of The Inspector General *by Russian director Vsevolod Meyerhold.*

in the improvement and polishing of his comedy. Concerning its theme he wrote to Zhukovsky in 1847: "I made up my mind to put together everything bad I knew, and in one breath to ridicule it all." Such was the origin of *The Inspector-General.*

With enormous power Gogol revealed in *The Inspector-General* the complete abomination and rottenness of the police-bureaucratic regime of the Russia of the period of Nicholas I: the "swine snouts" of the Skvoznik-Dmukhanovskys, the Lyapkin-Tyapkins, and Derzhimordas; the dreadful power of the criminal bureaucratic gang sitting on the people's necks; the unbridled orgy of graft and embezzlement of public funds; the monstrous despotism; the insolent trampling on the most elementary human rights; the coarseness and ignorance. Such was the world that emerged from the pages of Gogol's comedy.

No one prior to Gogol, wrote A. I. Hertzen,

> has given such a complete pathological and anatomical course on the Russian bureaucrat. With laughter on his lips, he pitilessly penetrates to the very depths of the corrupt, wickedly bureaucratic soul: Gogol's comedy *The Inspector-General* . . . is a horrible confession of contemporary Russia, reminding one of the revelations of Katoshikhin in the seventeenth century.

Notwithstanding all its sharpness of delineation and the richness of its colors, and despite its passion for hyperbolism and the grotesque, Gogol's comedy remains one of the greatest examples of realism, mirroring with extraordinary truthfulness social actuality in its most typical manifestations. The satirical genius of Gogol and the mighty synthesizing power of his realistic method are unfolded with particular vividness in his comic characters—the heroes of *The Inspector-General.* Along with the Prostakovs and Skotinins, the Famusovs and Skalozubs, the Town Mayor, Khlestakov, and all the other people in Gogol's comedy—including the sergeants' widow and the police precinct officer Ukhovertov—still retain their significance as artistic symbols with an enormous socio-psychological content. The mere mention of their names evokes in every man a whole complex of ideas and feelings.

As for the skillful development of the comedy intrigue, the symmetry of the dramatic structure, the cohesiveness and rightness of all the constituent parts, *The Inspector-General* has no rivals in all Russian literature. The action in it develops with the naturalness of an organic creation of nature, so that nothing could be either omitted or added without substantial damage to the play.

Equally unsurpassed, from the point of view of artistic power, colorfulness and expressiveness is the language of Gogol's comedy.

Belinsky placed *The Inspector-General,* together with *Dead Souls,* among those "profoundly true creations, by which Gogol so potently contributed to Russia's self-consciousness, enabling her to look at herself as if through a mirror."

It was not easy to obtain permission for the production of *The Inspector-General.* Its appearance on the stage was made possible only by the persistent solicitations of Gogol's influential friends and patrons (Zhukovsky and Vyazemsky). Its first performance in Petersburg, at the Aleksandrinsky Theatre, took place on April 19, 1836. According to P. V. Annenkov, even after the first act

> perplexity was written on all faces: it seemed that no one knew what attitude to take towards the scenes just witnessed. With every new act confusion increased. As if finding relief in the assumption that a mere farce was being given, the majority of the audience—led astray from all theatrical expectations and traditions—embraced this interpretation with unshaken resolve.

It is known that the Minister of Finance, Count Kankrin, remarked after the performance: "What was the use of coming to see this foolish farce?"

Vyazemsky reported:

> The comedy was acknowledged by many people as a liberal manifesto, similar, for instance, to Beaumarchais's *The Barber of Seville,* a political bombshell flung at society under the guise of a comedy. Of course this impression, this prejudice, was apt to divide the public into two contending groups, into two camps. Some people acclaimed the play, were gladdened by it, seeing in it a bold, though veiled, attack upon existing authority. In their opinion, although Gogol had chosen as his battleground a small provincial town, he was in fact aiming higher. Others regarded the comedy as an attempt against the state; they were agitated, frightened, suspecting in the unlucky—or lucky—playwright almost a dangerous rebel.

It was claimed by several eyewitnesses that Nicholas I, who was present at the performance, applauded it and laughed heartily; and he is alleged to have said, when departing from the theatre: "Well, this is quite a play! Everybody got his due—I more than the rest!" The "liberalism" of this comment by the Emperor is nothing more than the hypocrisy and political intrigue habitual in Nicholas.

Gogol himself thus summed up his impressions of the first performance:

> *The Inspector-General* was just performed, and now I am so dazed and perplexed. . . . I knew beforehand how the thing would develop, but with all this, a sad, vexing, and burdensome feeling absorbed me. My own creation appeared to me repulsive and odd, as though it were not mine at all.

Of all the actors only Sosnitsky, in the part of the Town Mayor, satisfied him.

In Moscow the production of the play was fraught with even greater difficulties. To begin with, it was seriously impaired by the fact that Shchepkin, who, in compliance with the author's wishes and quite rightfully, was to have taken charge of it, remained away from it altogether in the end, owing to the stupid interference of the administration. This was apparently the fault of Zagoskin, who at that time was in charge of the Moscow theatres. As a result of the careless staging of the play, only Shchepkin as the Town Mayor, Potanchikov as postmaster, and Orlov as Osip proved satisfactory. All the others were very bad.

The press marked the appearance of **The Inspector-General** by a series of bitterly hostile comments. In *The Reading Library,* which zealously sought to convince the public that the talent of Baron Brambeus far exceeded that of Gogol, it was asserted:

> In **The Inspector-General** there is no picture of Russian society; there are no characters; there is neither intrigue nor denouement; much is unnatural and contrary to truth; while the play *in toto* is nothing but an old anecdote which has been utilized many times in other literatures.

Bulgarin, reiterating all accusations catalogued in *The Library,* added that "everything in the play is implausible"; that "both the officials and the landlords are represented as greatest cheats and fools"; that "coquettes, such as the Town Mayor's daughter and wife, are nowhere to be found"; that "it is incredible that the whole town should be worse than Sodom and Gomorrah"; and that "it is altogether incomprehensible by what miracle this small town, without a single honest soul, can survive on the terrestrial globe." Furthermore, he declared that officials did not at all accept bribes as described in the play, and reproached the author for having used expressions which were not tolerated in good society.

Likewise Polevoy maintained that Gogol's reputation was being inflated without justification. He considered **The Inspector-General** as a mere farce, without discerning in it either drama or purpose, either intrigue or specific characters.

A worthy rebuttal to these accusations was made by Vyazemsky who, in the opening part of his article, placed **The Inspector-General** side by side with *The Minor, The Brigadier, The Slanderer,* and *Woe from Wit.* But Gogol's play was reviewed with particular sympathy in the magazine *Rumor* by an anonymous critic (it is now supposed to have been Belinsky) who wrote:

> Copies of **The Inspector-General,** received at Moscow, have been read through, reread, memorized; they have been converted into proverbs, and out they went far and wide among the people, becoming transformed into epigrams and branding those to whom they were applicable. The names of the dramatis personae in **The Inspector-General,** the very next day, changed into proper names: the Khlestakovs, the Anna Andreyevnas, the Marya Antonovnas, the Town Mayors, the Zemlanikas, the Tyapkin-Lyapkins, arm in arm, started marching along with Famusov, Molchalin, Chatsky, and the Prostakovs. And all this happened overnight, even prior to the performance. Look! They—these ladies and gentlemen—are strolling along the Tverskoy Boulevard, in the Park, throughout the city; and everywhere, everywhere, wheresoever a dozen people are assembled, one among them unfailingly merges from Gogol's comedy. Now why is this so? Who has made this creation come alive? Who has made it so akin to us? Who has corrob-

orated all these nicknames, these phrases, these droll and clumsy expressions? Who? This was accomplished by two great factors: the author's talent and the timeliness of the creation.

The cold public reception of the play at the first performances and the wicked press attacks produced on Gogol's pathologically sensitive soul a most painful impression. This probably explains his departure abroad following the production of **The Inspector-General.** Even though he asserted, "My play disgusts me," still for many years he did not cease pondering over it, revising it, and interpreting its contents to both actors and audiences.

The Inspector-General was followed by **The Departure from the Theatre,** which was so highly regarded by Belinsky; he regarded this polemical play as "a profoundly conceived theory of social comedy"; "a notice of warning to those who would seek properly to perform **The Inspector-General,**" which contained a number of remarkable ideas on the realistic art of acting; and finally **The Dénouement of The Inspector-General.** The latter dates from 1846, that is, from the period when *Selected Portions from the Correspondence with Friends* were written. The pathological crisis in Gogol's ideology which had developed by that time resulted in a most unfortunate interpretation of **The Inspector-General,** suggested in **The Dénouement of The Inspector-General,** an interpretation which assumed a mystical aspect.

In that play the leading comic actor says:

> **The Inspector-General** is our awakened conscience, which will suddenly and spontaneously compel us to look attentively at ourselves. Khlestakov is the giddy-brained fashionable conscience—a venal, deceitful conscience: Khlestakov will be bribed exactly as our own passions dwell in our soul [see Author Commentary dated 1846].

The abrupt change in the attitude of the author towards his play was painfully felt by the same Shchepkin into whose mouth he sought to put this labored and morbid interpretation. The great actor wrote to Gogol:

> In the course of our ten-year friendship, I became so used to the Town Mayor, to Dobchinsky, and Bobchinsky, that it would be a dishonest act to take these and all others away from me. With what are you going to replace them? Leave them alone as they are. I love them. I love them with all their infirmities, as I do all men in general. Do not insinuate to me that they are supposed to be, not bureaucrats, but our passions: no; I do not wish such a transformation; they are genuine persons, live men in whose midst I have grown up and have almost grown old. Do you see what a long-standing acquaintanceship this is! From the world at large you mustered several men to one rallying spot, uniting them in one group; I became closely related to them; and now you try to take them away from me. No; so long as I live, I will not. I will not surrender them to you. After my passing, turn them even into goats, but until that time I will not cede Derzhimorda to you because he, too, is dear to me.

At the first production of *The Inspector-General,* the part of the Town Mayor was performed more successfully than the others, perhaps because in both capital cities it was assigned to artists who were on intimate terms with Gogol, and who for this reason were in a better position to grasp the author's intention. In Petersburg the part was played by I. I. Sosnitsky, and in Moscow by Shchepkin.

We have on record a comparative description of the acting of both artists in that role. The eminent critic D. V. Averkiyev wrote:

> Both artists played with equal excellence, while the difference in their performance was largely due to the difference in the nature of their individual talents. One of them (Shchepkin) was pre-eminently a comic, while the aptitudes of the other (Sosnitsky) came within the compass of the so-called *emploi* of first character parts. With one of the actors the Town Mayor appeared simpler, more cowardly, and wherever there was room for comic rage and anger, for example in the fifth act, Shchepkin performed miracles; in Sosnitsky's impersonation the Town Mayor was more reserved, more shrewd: his very roguery was, one may say, cultivated; it was not, it seemed, a natural appurtenance of the man but reminded one of something acquired through long experience.

Another critic wrote:

> Shchepkin, owing to his southern temperament, his diction, figure, voice and his whole type of talent, based completely on realism, produced a strictly Russian Town Mayor—a carnivorous, cunning blade, and a rascal with the somewhat coarse countenance of a small provincial bureaucrat; one who knows well how to oppress and crush his inferiors, and how to crawl before his superiors. Sosnitsky, brought up on types of the French comedy in adaptations to pseudo-Russian customs of Khmelnitsky, and simply in translations, presented a more common appearance of a shifty and subtle, but cold, swindler with the voice and character of a fox, sweet as honey and bitter as gall.

> Each was excellent in his own way. Of course Shchepkin was more typical; he was, as stated, an ignorant Russian man, ignorant in everything save in the art of outwitting anyone at his discretion. Shchepkin was able to discover one or two almost tragic notes in his role. Thus the words: "Don't ruin me! . . . Wife, children!" were uttered by him with tears in his voice, with a most miserable expression, and with his chin trembling; in fact it seemed that he was about to burst into tears. And for one moment this rogue evoked a feeling of pity. In Sosnitsky the Town Mayor was rather amusing, like that cunning trapped beast which he resembled. Nor were the physical features of the two actors identical; Shchepkin was of small stature, with a broad face; Sosnitsky tall, with elongated features.

After Shchepkin's death, the role of the Town Mayor was given to I. V. Samarin, who was thus faced with a most responsible task—that of appearing before the public which was still under the vivid impression of Shchepkin's brilliant performance. Therefore, strictly adhering to Shchepkin's interpretation of the part, he confined himself to the reproduction of his predecessor's acting in so far, of course, as his physical characteristics permitted. Later, the part of the Town Mayor was played with exceptional brilliance by V. H. Davydov, the successor to Shchepkin's talent, whose traditions he preserved. Prov Sadovsky utterly failed in this part; but, on the other hand, he distinguished himself by the remarkable performance of the role of Osip. In Apollon Grigoryev's words:

> When Osip is on the stage everything lives, but without him it seems empty. One is apt to believe that he continues to live and act behind the stage even when he does not appear before one's eyes. Not even a needle can be stuck under this mask. One feels that it might prick the living body, to such an extent have mask and body grown together. Osip, when he is on the stage, obliterates everything else, even the Town Mayor himself.

Contemporaries have related that Sadovsky in the part of Osip became the character, as it were. By every glance and gesture he inimitably represented Osip's mood; for instance, his resentment against his master in the well known monologue; in brushing back and forth while shining his master's boots and spitting on them in such a manner that all the spectators were fully aware how vexed and irritated he was; his announcement to his master of the Town Mayor's arrival, his joy over the cabbage soup and gruel after a prolonged hunger; and his only too natural urging that the master depart from the town—all these were in truth a triumph of stagecraft. Hence critics were right when they maintained that "in his gestures, sighs, whimperings, and body positions the spectators sensed a whole drama."

The part of Khlestakov was played much less successfully both at the first performance and afterward. Dyur, its first performer on the Petersburg stage, failed to satisfy Gogol because he brought to the role a purely vaudeville interpretation; this was probably due to the rigidity of the theatrical tradition. "The leading role was lost," wrote Gogol, "and this I had expected. Dyur utterly failed to grasp what Khlestakov is. Khlestakov became something in the order of Alnaksarov, similar to a whole range of vaudeville scamps who came to us from the Parisian theatres."

Also, in the course of the subsequent stage history of *The Inspector-General* the actors who played Khlestakov only rarely conveyed correctly Gogol's intentions. In the interpretation of some actors Khlestakov appeared too sedate and too dandyish; in others, too insignificant. According to contemporaries, Samarin was guilty of the former extreme, Maksimov the latter. The role seems to have been best performed by S. V. Shumsky, who acted the scene with the waiter and at dinner particularly effectively. However, he could not at all master excessive bragging, and he had an altogether inappropriate mischievous expression which did not leave him even when he walked restlessly back and forth on the stage, tormented by pangs of acute hunger. But the part of Khlestakov was well performed subsequently by M. P. Sadovsky. Gogol himself realized the great complexity of the role, and wrote to Shchepkin:

> In the whole play the most difficult part is that of Khlestakov. I do not know whether you will succeed in selecting an actor for it. God forbid that it be played in the usual farcical style in which braggarts and theatrical rakes are now impersonated. He is simply stupid: he babbles only because he sees that people are ready to listen to him; he lies because he has lunched heartily and drunk good wine; he is nimble only when he cottons to the ladies. I am very much afraid for this role.

The exact date when Gogol wrote his comedy *The Gamblers* has not been determined. It has been produced on the stage with marked success, though only on rare occasions. Among the performers, critics particularly praised Prov Sadovsky (Zamukhryshkin), Shchepkin (Uteshitelny), Samoilov (Zamukhryshkin), Sosnitsky (Uteshitelny), and Martynov (Ikharev).

N. A. Kotlyarevsky has called *The Gamblers* one of the most perfect dramatic works from the standpoint of technique: "The comedy is not invented but based on stories of actual tricks practiced by different sharpers and crooks." Stories about such stratagems frequently occurred in the literature of Gogol's period. Almost no novel of manners omitted them. Gogol's merit consisted in that he developed this traditional theme with extraordinary realism and inimitable wit: that he alone succeeded in expressing with equal truth a general tone in several variations; and—most important—that he evaded all didacticism by excluding from the dramatis personae the former hero, the "victim"!

Belinsky considered *The Gamblers* to be "fully worthy of its author's name."

A passionate lover of the Ukraine, Gogol one time thought of becoming his father's successor and writing a Ukrainian play. While living abroad, he worked diligently on it, utilizing the historical data which he had gathered earlier, and ordering for study collections of Ukrainian songs. As was his custom, he also took liberal advantage of the counsels given him by his acquaintances. He contemplated writing a play of the Cossack epoch, which, no doubt, would have been a contribution to our drama as valuable as *Taras Bulba* is to another field of poetry. It is to be regretted that nothing came of these labors, and that the preliminary sketches of the play have been burned.

There remains for mention the comedy *The Tutor in a Difficult Position,* translated by Gogol from the Italian. (The original was from the pen of Giordano Giraud.) This play, in which Shchepkin and subsequently V. N. Davydov played with marked success, bears witness to Gogol's interest in the foreign repertoire.

Because he worked on his plays with rare industry, he was unable to produce a large volume of material for the theatre. Neither his sojourn abroad, where it was difficult to keep in contact with the Russian theatre, nor the shockingly unjust attitude of the shortsighted and unimaginative critics, encouraged him to concentrate on the drama.

Nevertheless, in *The Inspector-General* and *The Marriage,* Gogol created the best examples of Russian comedy. These plays introduced realism to the Russian stage. Bringing to a close the entire preceding period of our dramatic development, Gogol became in Russia the progenitor of the realistic theatre, of the theatre of mighty social satire, which in its subsequent phases produced Ostrovsky, Sukhovo-Kobylin, and Chekhov.

"One must ascribe exclusively to Gogol," maintained Chernyshevsky, "the merit of firmly introducing in Russian belles-lettres the satirical, or, to use a more correct term, the critical style."

Gogol also established the same critical tendency in drama, thereby rendering his people an enormous service in their ideological struggle against the sociopolitical regime based upon the autocracy of the Derzhimordas.

Gogol's dramaturgy, replete with profound humanity, genuinely popular and utterly truthful, is also close to us contemporaries of the great socialist epoch—close "through those ideas of Belinsky and Gogol which made these writers dear to Nekrasov, as to every decent man in Russia" (Lenin). (pp. 298-316)

> *B. V. Varneke, "Gogol," in his* History of the Russian Theatre: Seventeenth Through Nineteenth Century, *edited by Belle Martin, translated by Boris Brasol, revised edition, The Macmillan Company, 1951, pp. 298-316.*

THE INSPECTOR GENERAL

CRITICAL COMMENTARY

Janko Lavrin   (essay date 1926)

[*Lavrin is an Austrian-born British essayist, biographer, and critic who is best known for his studies of nineteenth- and twentieth-century Russian literature. These include* An Introduction to the Russian Novel *(1942), in which he combines literary criticism with an exploration into the psychological and philosophical background of a writer. Lavrin is also the author of two critical studies of Gogol:* Gogol *(1926) and* Nikolai Gogol (1809-1852): A Centenary Survey *(1951). In the following excerpt from the former work, he discusses* The Inspector General (Revizor) *as a realistic social satire.*]

[Gogol's *Revizor* is not] a merely exhilarating comedy, but a satire full of gall and hidden indignation. It is saturated with all that "malice, laughter and salt" which he had to suppress when giving up the plan for his *Vladimir.* And as to its technique, it is a work made of one piece. Everything in it is inevitable. Each situation, each figure, is an organic part of the whole. The play abounds in grinning irony and indirect indictments; yet being moral in the best sense as all true art always is, it is not in the least moralizing; there is not a single puppet spluttering out "ideas" and moral recipes. Apart from this, each character speaks a language of his own and, as in *The Marriage,* the comicality of the characters strengthens that of the situations.

Together with Griboyedov's *Gore ot Uma* (The Mischief of being Clever), **The Revizor** belongs to the favourite plays of the Russian stage. And it certainly deserves this honour.

Gogol began to write his **Revizor** in 1834. The play appeared in print in 1836, and its final version was published in 1842. Its motive is almost as old as comedy itself, and Gogol's own variation of a traditional theme was partly suggested to him by Pushkin and partly by other works of a similar kind, Russian and foreign. Kvitka's *Newcomer from the Capital* (1827), for instance, deals (rather clumsily) with almost the same motive; and a thorough scrutiny could discover in Gogol's masterpiece situations reminding us of Molière, or of Corneille's *Menteur.* These resemblances are, of course, casual. But even if they were not so, the main point is not whence an author gets his motives, but whether he can make them his own. In literature one is allowed to steal as much as one can really appropriate; and whenever Gogol takes anything from others he always knows how to make it his own.

The genesis of **The Revizor** is due to an anecdote told by Pushkin of how he himself had been mistaken in Nizhny Novgorod for a high official from Petersburg who had arrived incognito in order to inspect the order of the town. Such a *qui-pro-quo* is in itself only funny. Gogol's imagination, however, transmuted also this incident in such a way as to make it a pretext for showing the whole of Russian life in its most pessimistic aspect—under the mask of fun and laughter. The action of the play takes place in a provincial town whose *gorodnichy* (a kind of town-governor), Anton Antonovitch Dmookhanovsky, is privately informed by a friend that the revizor, or Inspector-General, from Petersburg will visit his town in strict incognito. Thunderstruck by such news, the gorodnichy summons to his house the chief officials of the town, all of whom are prostrate with fear that their transgressions may perhaps be discovered and duly punished. The absurdest and most illogical conjectures are made with regard to the revizor's arrival. The personal situation of each of them looks so serious indeed that they all try to devise various self-protective measures. The gorodnichy initiates even the local postmaster, Ivan Kuzmich, into the whole business:

> Well, I'm no coward, but I *am* just a little uncomfortable. The shopkeepers and townspeople bother me. It seems I am unpopular with them; but the Lord knows, if I've blackmailed anybody I've done it without a trace of ill-feeling. I even think (*buttonholes him and takes him aside*)—I even think there will be some sort of complaint drawn up against me. . . . Why should we have a revizor at all? Look here, Ivan Kuzmich, don't you think you could slightly open every letter which comes in and goes out of your office, and read it (for the public benefit, you know) to see if it contains any kind of information against me or only correspondence? If it is all right, you can seal it up again; or simply deliver the letter opened.

"Oh, I know that game" answers the good-natured postmaster. "Don't teach me *that!* I do it from pure curiosity, not as a precaution. I am death on knowing what's going on in the world. And they're very interesting to read, I can tell you! Now and then you come across a love-letter, with bits of beautiful language, and so edifying. . . . "

But here two worthies, Bobchinsky and Dobchinsky, rush in with rather exciting news. They had seen in the local hotel a young *chinovnik* from Petersburg who was casting very inquisitive looks at everything, even at what people were eating. They found out that the name of the elegant young man was Khlestakov and that he had been staying there for a fortnight under very mysterious circumstances. Who else could he be but the revizor? Both of them are ready to swear he is the revizor himself.

The gorodnichy's panic and confusion increase. On hearing, however, that the dreaded person is still young, he decides to make a professional *tour de force:* to bribe him, and cautiously invite him to be his guest. Trusting in God's mercy, he sets off to the hotel, having first given a few necessary instructions, such as these:

> The police-lieutenant—he is tall, so he's to stand on the bridge—that will give a good effect. Then the old fence near the bootmaker's must be pulled down at once and scattered about, and a post stuck up with a wisp of straw, so as to look like building operations. The more litter there is, the more it will show the Governor's zeal and activity. . . . Good God! though, I forgot that about forty cart-loads of rubbish have been shot behind that fence. What a dirty town this is! No matter where you put a monument, or even a paling, they collect all kinds of rubbish from the devil knows where, and upset it there! . . . And if the newly-come chinovnik asks any of the officials if they are contented, they're to say: 'Perfectly, your Honour,' and if anybody is *not* contented, I'll give him something afterwards to be discontented about . . . (*heaves a sigh*)—ah-h-h! I am a sinner—a terrible sinner! Heaven only grant that I may soon get quit of the matter, and then I'll give such a taper for a thank-offering as has never been given before! I'll levy three *puds* [the equivalent of 108 pounds] of wax from every merchant for it! . . . And if he asks why the hospital chapel has not been built for which the money was voted five years ago, they must mind and say that it began to be built, but was burnt down. Why, I drew up a report about it. But of course some idiot is sure to forget, and let out that the building was never begun. . . . And tell Derzhimorda that he's not to give such free play to his fists; guilty or innocent, he makes them all see stars, in the cause of public order. . . .

The instructions speak for themselves. But while the zealous gorodnichy goes to bribe the imaginary revizor, Khlestakov himself is in terrible straits. To begin with, he is a petty official of the lowest grade, and in addition an irresponsible, naïve charlatan who has lost all his money at cards while on the way to his father's estate. His affairs are so bad, indeed, that he is already refused meals on credit and is even threatened with gaol unless he settles his accounts. Hungry and out of spirits he actually expects to be arrested—he expects this at the very moment when the trembling gorodnichy enters his room. They stare at each other in trepidation.

> GORODNICHY (*plucking up courage a little, and saluting deferentially*): I hope you are well, sir!
>
> KHLESTAKOV (*bows*): My respects to you, sir!
>
> GORODNICHY: Excuse my intruding. . . . It is my duty as chief magistrate of this town, to take all due measures to prevent travellers and persons of rank from suffering any inconvenience.

Khlestakov thinks this is only a polite pretext for arresting him and begins to vent his indignation by accusing the innkeeper who sends him up "beef as hard as a board. And the soup—the devil only knows *what* he'd mixed up with it: I was obliged to pitch it out of the window. He starves me the whole day. . . . And the tea's so peculiar; it smells of fish and nothing else! Why then should I . . . a *fine* idea, indeed!"

The gorodnichy takes Khlestakov's complaint for an accusation of the order in the town and answers in a faltering voice: "I assure you it's not my fault, really. I always get good beef from the market. The Kholmogori drovers bring it, and they are sober and well-principled people. I am sure I don't know where he gets it from. But if anything is wrong . . . allow me to suggest that you come with me and get other quarters."

"No, that I will *not*. I know what 'other quarters' means," shouts Khlestakov, who again interprets the gorodnichy's words in his own way.

> [KHLESTAKOV]: And pray, what right have you—how dare you? . . . Why, I . . . I'm a Government official at Petersburg . . . (*defiantly*). Yes, . . . I . . . I . . . (*aggressively*), that for you and your governorship together! I'll not go with you. I'll go straight to the Minister. (*Bangs his fist on the table*). Who are *you*, pray, who are you?"
>
> GORODNICHY (*starting, and shaking all over*): Have pity on me! Don't ruin me! I have a wife and small children! Don't make me a miserable man! . . . It was only inexperience, I swear, only my inexperience! And insufficient means! Judge for yourself—the salary I get is not enough for tea and sugar. And if I *have* taken any bribes, they were very little ones—something for the table or a coat or two. . . . As for the sergeant's widow, who took to shopkeeping—whom they say I had flogged—it's slander, I swear it's slander. My enemies invented it—they're the kind of people who are ready to murder me in cold blood.

In the end, however, things turn out quite favourably for the gorodnichy, and even more so for Khlestakov, who instead of being arrested is offered money and hospitality. The would-be revizor is solemnly taken to the gorodnichy's house, where he is feasted, admired, idolized. He is led about the town and shown various institutions. All the representatives of the local bureaucracy consider it their duty to introduce themselves to him—one by one, to see whether there will be any orders on his part, to give him bribes, as well as to slander, secretly, of course, their

colleagues and their best friends. Khlestakov, however, is the last man to bother about the real meaning of things and events. He enjoys himself, eats, drinks and boasts. In all this he is full of spontaneity and relish, particularly when he boasts about himself. And he does so with no evil intent, but in the manner of a Russian Tartarin who lies with temperament, even with inspiration because he is the first to believe all he says. His fancies contrive the reality in such a way as to give him at least a moment's illusion of his own importance. Khlestakov is, in short, another Poprischin—Ferdinand VII, without Poprischin's tragedy and madness. He is just an irresponsible braggart with the brains and egotism of a child. Seeing all these provincial worthies staring at him with wondering and open mouths, he simply cannot help displaying before them his own imaginary grandeur. His house is, of course, the first in Petersburg. He gives balls and dinners, the magnificence of which surpasses all description. "On the table, for instance, is a water melon that costs several hundred roubles. The soup comes straight from Paris by steamer in the tureen: there's nothing in the world to be compared with its flavour! I go to a ball every day. We have our whist-clubs there, too: the Foreign Minister, the French Ambassador, the German Ambassador and myself. . . ."

He makes, moreover, love to his host's wife and daughter. To the latter he even becomes engaged. The gorodnichy's excessive fear thus changes into such joy that he almost loses his head. Khlestakov, on the other hand, abandons himself to the course of events without giving a single thought either to their reasons or their possible consequences. The only man who begins to feel somewhat uneasy is his shrewd serf who travels with him. Guessing that the good people must have mistaken his master for somebody else, he urges him to get away as soon as possible. And so, having received considerable "loans" not only from the local chinovniks, but also from the merchants who came to complain of the gorodnichy's misdeeds, Khlestakov makes off—"at a moment's notice, but for a day only"—with his accumulated pleasant memories and money. But before leaving the hospitable town, he posts a letter to a friend of his, with an account of all that has happened to him. Meanwhile, the gorodnichy's triumph over fate and over his "enemies" reaches its zenith. His own daughter betrothed to such a great personage! It is almost past belief, and yet it is true. Swelling with pride and self-importance, he summons the merchants who dared to complain of him. His rage knows no limits. Carried away by moral indignation, he accuses them even of utter lack of gratitude:

> You complained of me? But who was it winked at your jobbery when you built the bridge and charged twenty thousand for less than a hundred roubles' worth of wood? It was I, you goats-beards! Have you forgotten that? If I had rounded on you, I could have sent you to Siberia! What say you to *that*—eh? I have a good mind to . . . but no (*waves his hand condescendingly*). There, may the Lord forgive you! Enough—I bear no malice; only beware and mind your P's and Q's! For I am not giving my daughter to any ordinary gentleman; so see that the wedding presents are . . . you understand? And don't flatter your-

selves you can put me off with your dried fish or
sugar-loaves. . . . There, now, you can go, and
the Lord be with you.

The news of his daughter's engagement rapidly spreads in
the town. All respectable citizens hurry to congratulate
the mighty gorodnichy and his spouse. The gorodnichy's
residence is soon filled with radiant faces, with exclamations of joy, with insinuating compliments. But the mighty
ones feel already so exalted, so high above the level of their
fellow-citizens that they do not consider it necessary even
to hide their disgust with such provincials as their own
friends.

"We intend to live in Petersburg now," says the gorodnichy's wife. "*Here,* there's such an air, I must say . . .
it's really too rustic! . . . I find it excessively
disagreeable . . . my husband, too . . . he will get a general's rank there!"

But soon the postmaster appears. He comes out of breath
and holding a letter in his hand—the very one that
Khlestakov had posted before his departure. The good
man had duly opened it and naturally was puzzled by its
contents.

"Here's an astounding thing happened," he exclaims.
"The chinovnik we took to be the revizor is *not* a revizor."

The news has the effect of a thunderbolt. Yet it is too unexpected to be taken in at once. The stupid postmaster may
be only joking. But here the bearer of the unexpected tid-
ings begins to read the letter, which runs as follows:

> I hasten to let you know, my dear Tryapichkin,
> all about my adventures. On the way an infantry
> captain cleared me out completely, so that the
> innkeeper wanted to send me to gaol; when all
> of a sudden, owing to my Petersburg get-up and
> appearance, the whole town took me for the
> Governor-General. So now I am living at the go-
> rodnichy's. I do just as I please; I flirt madly
> with his wife and daughter, but I can't settle
> which to begin with. Do you remember how
> hard up we were, how we dined at other's folks'
> expense, and how the pastry-cook once pitched
> me out neck and crop, because I had put some
> tarts I had eaten down to the account of the
> King of England? It is quite a different state of
> things now! They all lend me as much money as
> ever I please. They are an awful set of origi-
> nals—you would die of laughing if you saw
> them! You write articles, I know: bring these
> people in. First and foremost, there's the gorod-
> nichy—he's as stupid as a mule. . . .

And so on. Every member of the wonderful company gets
a suitable label taken from the zoological world. While the
letter is being read the scales fall from their eyes; the artificial mist disperses and the barren truth stares them in the
face. The blinded gorodnichy himself is compelled at last
to see it.

"How could I?" he begins to shout as if in a fit of madness.

> There is not such another old blockhead as I am.
> I must be in my dotage, idiot of a mutton-head
> that I am. . . . Thirty years have I been in the
> service; not a tradesman or contractor could

cheat me; rogue after rogue have I overreached,
sharpers and rascals have I hooked, that were
ready to rob the whole universe! Three governors-general I've duped! . . . Pooh! What are
governors-general? (*with a contemptuous wave of
the hand*). They're not worth talking
about. . . . Taking an icicle, a rag, for a man of
rank! And now he is rattling along the road with
his bells and telling the whole world the story!

However, a worse blow follows. While the gorodnichy
curses his own stupidity, a gendarme enters and announces to him in a stern voice:

> The Inspector-General sent by Imperial com-
> mand has arrived and requests your attendance
> at once. He awaits you in the inn.

The whole assembly remains as if petrified. Here the curtain falls.

Such is the skeleton of this comedy, with regard to which
Gogol said later, in his *Author's Confession:*

> I saw that in my former works I laughed for
> nothing, uselessly, without knowing why. If it is
> necessary to laugh, then let us laugh at that
> which really deserves to be laughed at by all. In
> my *Revizor* I decided to gather in one place and
> deride all that is bad in Russia, all the evils
> which are being perpetrated in those places
> where the utmost rectitude is required from
> man.

Corruption, snobbery, stupidity, malice—the whole compendium of vices which could be found in a stagnant provincial existence is focussed in *The Revizor* and whipped
with merciless laughter. Gogol never moralizes nor does
he indulge in direct indictments. He does not even pretend
to swing the whip in his own hands, but makes his characters whip themselves without knowing it, as it were, especially when they talk of their own abuses with a kind of
childlike innocence. He never speaks for the facts, because
he is a great enough artist to understand that facts must
always speak for themselves. He is perhaps at his best
when putting on the mask of an *ingénu* and talking with
a most serious countenance about things which are taken
seriously only by his characters and not by the reader. His
irony consists in his pretending not to see any irony at all,
although indirectly he makes us feel the wide gap between
his own standpoint and that of his characters. The less he
himself emphasizes this gap and pretends to be on the
same level as his characters, the greater the comic-satirical
atmosphere of the play. This atmosphere grows and
grows; but having reached its highest pitch, it suddenly
bursts of itself and dissolves into the sinister last chord,
whose effect is all the stronger because of the previous
comicality. True, Gogol sometimes achieves his effects by
various traditional "tricks"; but in his case they are convincing because he knows how to motivate them psychologically. At the same time, the strictest artistic economy
is preserved throughout, both in the construction and the
details of the play. "In *The Revizor* there are no scenes to
which the word 'better' can be applied, because none of
them is inferior to the rest," wrote Bielinsky; "they are all
excellent; they are the necessary parts forming one artistic
whole, which is rounded up not only by its external form,

but also by its inner contents; and so it is a self-sufficient world of its own."

When this comedy was finished an incredible thing happened: the censor passed it. This miracle was due, however, not to the censors, but to Czar Nicholas I. He read the manuscript of the comedy (brought to him by Zhukovsky) and at once ordered that ***The Revizor*** should be produced on the imperial stage. He himself was present at its first performance (March 19th, 1836), and laughing heartily, remarked: "Everyone has received his due and I most of all."

The play in itself is not a "realistic" copy of Russian provincial life, but an exaggerated picture of all those vices on which Gogol wished to vent his own indignation. It was his conscious craving for a higher form of life that severed him all the more from actual existence. It was his strong but unsatisfied need of reverence coupled with his utter incapacity to revere anything with genuine abandonment and passion that made him all the more aggressive. Hence he indulged at least in his *negative passion*—the passion of indictment, of anger, of laughter through tears. Having collected the necessary objective facts, he modified them according to his own inner need and constructed out of them a picture which he himself took for a mirror of real life. In fact, Gogol had to do so, because this was the only way in which he could attack and refute the reality he loathed. Once more he asserted himself against it— through his art.

The attack made by ***The Revizor*** was strong enough to raise everyone, and most of all, the corrupted officialdom, against Gogol. "The audiences felt the intensity of my anger even while laughing," he said later. But he could have added with equal truth that the production of this play had also been a notable social event: it was the first time that the so-called accusatory literature dared to speak in such terms from the Russian stage. The immediate result of this event was, however, far from being favourable to Gogol. The spectators enjoyed the piece, but they were cross with its author. For everyone saw himself personally insulted. Soon there was raised the hue and cry of the "patriots," who saw in him simply a slanderer of Holy Russia.

"All are against me," wrote Gogol to his Moscow friend, the actor Schepkin, a few days after the first production of the play. "The old and respectable officials are shouting that since I dared to criticize the civil servants in this manner, there is nothing sacred; the police, the merchants, the writers—all are against me."

Soon after this he jotted down his ***Homegoing from the Theatre (Teatralny Razyezd)*** in which he recorded very vividly some impressions of those onlookers who were for or against him. At the same time Gogol made a few interesting remarks of his own, and eventually pointed out that there was at least one honest "character" in his piece—his laughter. He also emphasized the *ethical* significance of laughter.

In spite of all the attacks on Gogol, the piece continued to be played, and the theatre was always crowded. For even those who disliked it could not help enjoying it. But the more they laughed, the more angry they were with the man who was the originator of such double-faced laughter. Things went so far that Gogol soon became tired of the whole affair and decided to go abroad. "A contemporary author who writes comedies and describes manners must be as far from his own country as possible," he wrote to Pogodin before leaving Russia.

> No prophet can earn glory in his own fatherland. I don't mind the fact that all classes of society have risen against me; yet it is somewhat sad and depressing to see my own countrymen, whom I sincerely love, attack me with no justice, to see in what a perverted way they accept and interpret everything.

It was at the beginning of June, 1836, that Gogol left for Western Europe where he stayed until 1848, coming back to Russia only twice during that period. (pp. 137-55)

> *Janko Lavrin, in his* Gogol, *George Routledge & Sons, Ltd., 1926, 263 p.*

Vladimir Nabokov   (essay date 1944)

[*A Russian-born American man of letters, Nabokov was a prolific contributor to many literary fields, producing works in both Russian and English and distinguishing himself particularly as the author of the novels* Lolita *and* Pale Fire. *Nabokov was fascinated with all aspects of creative life, and his works frequently explore the origins of creativity, the relationships of artists to their work, and the nature of invented reality. In the following excerpt from his biographical and critical study* Gogol, *Nabokov discusses the importance of secondary characters and inanimate objects in* The Inspector General *and evaluates the play's artistic merit.*]

1

The history of the production of Gogol's comedy ***The Government Inspector*** on the Russian stage and of the extraordinary stir it created has of course little to do with Gogol, the subject of these notes, but still a few words about those alien matters may be not unnecessary. As it was inevitable that simple minds would see in the play a social satire violently volleyed at the idyllic system of official corruption in Russia, one wonders what hopes the author or anybody else could have had of seeing the play performed. The censors' committee was as blatantly a collection of cringing noodles or pompous asses as all such organizations are, and the mere fact of a writer daring to portray officers of the state otherwise than as abstract figures and symbols of superhuman virtue was a crime that sent shivers down the censors' fat backs. That ***The Government Inspector*** happened to be the greatest play ever written in Russian (and never surpassed since) was naturally a matter infinitely remote from the committee's mind.

But a miracle happened; a kind of miracle singularly in keeping with the physics of Gogol's upside down world. The Supreme Censor, the One above all, Whose God-like level of being was so lofty as to be hardly mentionable by thick human tongues, the radiant, totalitarian Tsar Himself, in a fit of most unexpected glee commanded the play to be passed and staged.

Scene from Vsevolod Meyerhold's 1926 staging of The Inspector General.

It is difficult to conjecture what pleased Nicholas I in *The Government Inspector.* The man who a few years before had red-penciled the manuscript of Pushkin's *Boris Godunov* with inane remarks suggesting the turning of that tragedy into a novel on the lines of Walter Scott, and generally was as immune to authentic literature as all rulers are (not excepting Frederic the Great or Napoleon) can hardly be suspected of having seen anything better in Gogol's play than slapstick entertainment. On the other hand a satirical farce (if we imagine for a moment such a delusion in regard to *The Government Inspector*) seems unlikely to have attracted the Tsar's priggish and humorless mind. Given that the man had brains—at least the brains of a politician—it would rather detract from their quantity to suppose that he so much enjoyed the prospect of having his vassals thoroughly shaken up as to be blind to the dangers of having the man in the street join in the imperial mirth. In fact he is reported to have remarked after the first performance: "Everybody has got his due, I most of all"; and if this report is true (which it probably is not) it would seem that the evolutionary link between criticism of corruption under a certain government and criticism of the government itself must have been apparent to the Tsar's mind. We are left to assume that the permission to have the play staged was due to a sudden whim on the Tsar's part, just as the appearance of such a writer as Gogol was a most unexpected impulse on the part of whatever spirit may be held responsible for the development of

Russian literature in the beginning of the Nineteenth Century. In signing this permission a despotic ruler was, curiously enough, injecting a most dangerous germ into the blood of Russian writers; dangerous to the idea of monarchy, dangerous to official iniquity, and dangerous—which danger is the most important of the three—to the art of literature; for Gogol's play was misinterpreted by the civic-minded as a social protest and engendered in the fifties and sixties a seething mass of literature denouncing corruption and other social defects and an orgy of literary criticism denying the title of writer to anyone who did not devote his novel or short story to the castigation of district police-officers and moujik-thrashing squires. And ten years later the Tsar had completely forgotten the play and had not the vaguest idea who Gogol was and what he had written.

The first performance of *The Government Inspector* was a vile affair in regard to acting and setting, and Gogol was most bitter in his criticism of the abominable wigs and clownish clothes and gross over-acting that the theater inflicted upon his play. This started the tradition of staging *The Government Inspector* as a burlesque; later to this was added a background suggestive of a *comédie de mœurs;* so that the Twentieth Century inherited a strange concoction of extravagant Gogolian speech and dingy matter-of-fact setting—a state of affairs only solved now and then by the personality of some actor of genius. Strange, it was in the years when the written word was dead in Russia, as it has been now for a quarter of a century, that the Russian producer Meyerhold, in spite of all his distortions and additions, offered a stage version of *The Government Inspector* which conveyed something of the real Gogol.

Only once have I seen the play performed in a foreign language (in English) and it is not a memory I care to evoke. As to the translation of the book, there is little to choose between the Seltzer and Constance Garnett versions. Though totally lacking verbal talent, Garnett has made hers with a certain degree of care and it is thus less irritating than some of the monstrous versions of *The Overcoat* and *Dead Souls*. In a way it may be compared to Guizot's tame translation of *Hamlet*. Of course, nothing has remained of Gogol's style. The English is dry and flat, and always unbearably demure. None but an Irishman should ever try tackling Gogol. Here are some typical instances of inadequate translation (and these may be multiplied): Gogol in his remarks about the two squires, Bobchinsky and Dobchinsky, briefly describes them as both having plump little bellies (or, as he says in another place, "they simply must have protruding tummies—pointed little ones like pregnant women have") which conveys the idea of small and otherwise thin and puny men—and this is most essential for producing the correct impression that Dobchinsky and Bobchinsky must convey. But Constance Garnett translates this as "both rather corpulent," murdering Gogol. I sometimes think that these old English "translations" are remarkably similar to the so-called Thousand Pieces Execution which was popular at one time in China. The idea was to cut out from the patient's body one tiny square bit the size of a cough lozenge, say, every five minutes or so until bit by bit (all of them selected with discrimination so as to have the patient live to the nine hundred ninety ninth piece) his whole body was delicately removed.

There are also a number of downright mistakes in that translation such as "clear soup" instead of "oatmeal soup" (which the Charity Commissioner ought to have been giving the sick at the hospital) or—and this is rather funny—a reference to one of the five or six books that the Judge had ever read in his life as "The Book of John the Mason," which sounds like something biblical, when the text really refers to a book of adventures concerning John Mason (or attributed to him), an English diplomatist of the Sixteenth Century and Fellow of All Souls who was employed on the Continent in collecting information for the Tudor sovereigns.

2

The plot of *The Government Inspector* is as unimportant as the plots of all Gogol books. Moreover, in the case of the play, the scheme is the common property of all playwriters: the squeezing of the last drop out of some amusing quid pro quo. It would appear that Pushkin suggested it to Gogol when he told him that while staying at an inn in Nijni-Novgorod he was mistaken for an important official from the capital; but on the other hand, Gogol, with his head stuffed with old plays ever since his days of amateur theatricals at school (old plays translated into indifferent Russian from three or four languages), might have easily

dispensed with Pushkin's prompting. It is strange, the morbid inclination we have to derive satisfaction from the fact (generally false and always irrelevant) that a work of art is traceable to a "true story." Is it because we begin to respect ourselves more when we learn that the writer, just like ourselves, was not clever enough to make up a story himself? Or is something added to the poor strength of our imagination when we know that a tangible fact is at the base of the "fiction" we mysteriously despise? Or taken all in all, have we here that adoration of the truth which makes little children ask the story-teller "Did it really happen?" and prevented old Tolstoy in his hyperethical stage from trespassing upon the rights of the deity and creating, as God creates, perfectly imaginary people? However that may be, some forty years after that first night a certain political émigré was desirous of having Karl Marx (whose *Capital* he was translating in London) know Chernyshevsky, who was a famous radical and conspirator banished to Siberia in the sixties (and one of those critics who vigorously proclaimed the coming of the "Gogolian" era in Russian literature, meaning by this euphemism, which would have horrified Gogol, the duty on the part of novelists to work solely for the improvement of social and political traditions). The political émigré returned secretly to Russia and traveled to the remote Yakoutsk region in the disguise of a Member of the Geographical Society (a nice point, this) in order to kidnap the Siberian prisoner; and his plan was thwarted owing to the fact that more and more people all along his meandering itinerary mistook him for a Government Inspector traveling incognito—exactly as had happened in Gogol's play. This vulgar imitation of artistic fiction on the part of life is somehow more pleasing than the opposite thing.

The epigraph to the play is a Russian proverb which says "Do not chafe at the looking glass if your mug is awry." Gogol, of course, never drew portraits—he used looking glasses and as a writer lived in his own looking glass world. Whether the reader's face was a fright or a beauty did not matter a jot, for not only was the mirror of Gogol's own making and with a special refraction of its own, but also the reader to whom the proverb was addressed belonged to the same Gogolian world of goose-like, pig-like, pie-like, nothing-on-earth-like facial phenomena. Even in his worst writings Gogol was always good at creating his reader, which is the privilege of great writers. Thus we have a circle, a closed family-circle, one might say. It does not open into the world. Treating the play as a social satire (the public view) or as a moral one (Gogol's belated amendment) meant missing the point completely. The characters of *The Government Inspector* whether subject or not to imitation by flesh and blood, were true only in the sense that they were true creatures of Gogol's fancy. Most conscientiously, Russia, that land of eager pupils, started at once living up to these fancies—but that was her business, not Gogol's. In the Russia of Gogol's day bribery flourished as beautifully as it did, and does, anywhere on the Continent—and, on the other hand, there doubtless existed far more disgusting scoundrels in any Russian town of Gogol's time than the good-natured rogues of *The Government Inspector.* I have a lasting grudge against those who like their fiction to be educational or uplifting, or national, or as healthy as maple syrup and olive oil, so that is why I keep harping on this rather futile side of *The Government Inspector* question.

3

The play begins with a blinding flash of lightning and ends in a thunderclap. In fact it is wholly placed in the tense gap between the flash and the crash. There is no so-called "exposition." Thunderbolts do not lose time explaining meteorological conditions. The whole world is one ozone-blue shiver and we are in the middle of it. The only stage tradition of his time that Gogol retained was the soliloquy, but then people do talk to themselves aloud during the nervous hush before a storm while waiting for the bang to come. The characters are nightmare people in one of those dreams when you think you have waked up while all you have done is to enter the most dreadful (most dreadful in its sham reality) region of dreams. Gogol has a peculiar manner of letting "secondary" dream characters pop out at every turn of the play (or novel, or story), to flaunt for a second their life-like existence (as that Colonel P. who passed by in *Shponka's Dream* or many a creature in *Dead Souls*). In *The Government Inspector* this manner is apparent from the start in the weird private letter which the Town-Mayor Skvoznik-Dmukhanovsky reads aloud to his subordinates—School Inspector Khlopov, Judge Lyapkin-Tyapkin (Mr. Slap-Dash), Charity Commissioner Zemlyanika, (Mr. Strawberry—an overripe brown strawberry wounded by the lip of a frog) and so forth. Note the nightmare names so different from, say, the sleek "Hollywood Russian" pseudonyms Vronsky, Oblonsky, Bolkonsky etc. used by Tolstoy. (The names Gogol invents are really nicknames which we surprise in the very act of turning into family names—and a metamorphosis is a thing always exciting to watch.) After reading the important part of the letter referring to the impending arrival of a governmental inspector from Petersburg the Mayor automatically continues to read aloud and his mumbling engenders remarkable secondary beings that struggle to get into the front row.

" . . . my sister Anna Kyrillovna and her husband have come to stay with us; Ivan Kyrillovich [apparently a brother, judging by the patronymic] has grown very fat and keeps playing the violin."

The beauty of the thing is that these secondary characters will not appear on the stage later on. We all know those casual allusions at the beginning of Act I to Aunt So-and-so or to the Stranger met on the train. We all know that the "by the way" which introduces these people really means that the Stranger with the Australian accent or the Uncle with the comical hobby would have never been mentioned if they were not to breeze in a moment later. Indeed the "by the way" is generally a sure indication, the masonic sign of conventional literature, that the person alluded to will turn out to be the main character of the play. We all know that trite trick, that coy spirit haunting first acts in Scribia as well as on Broadway. A famous playwright has said (probably in a testy reply to a bore wishing to know the secrets of the craft) that if in the first act a shot gun hangs on the wall, it must go off in the last act. But Gogol's guns hang in midair and do not go off—in fact

the charm of his allusions is exactly that nothing whatever comes of them.

In giving his instructions to his subordinates in view of preparing and repairing things for the arrival of the Government Inspector, the Mayor refers to the Judge's clerk.

" . . . a knowing fellow, I daresay, but he has such a smell coming from him—as if he had just emerged from a vodka distillery. . . . I meant to mention it to you [to the Judge] long ago but something or other kept putting it out of my head. Remedies may be found if, as he says, it is his natural odor: you might suggest to him a diet of onions or garlic, or something of that kind. In a case like this Christian Ivanovich [the silent District Doctor of German extraction] might help by supplying this or that drug."

To which the Judge retorts:

"No, it is a thing impossible to dislodge: he tells me that his wet nurse dropped him when he was a baby and that there has been a slight smell of vodka hanging about him ever since."

"Well [says the Mayor] I just wanted to draw your attention to it, that is all." And he turns to another official.

We shall never hear about that unfortunate clerk again, but there he is, alive, a whimsical, smelly creature of that "injured" kind over which Gogol smacked his lips.

Other secondary beings have no time to come out in full attire, so impatient are they to jump into the play between two sentences. The Mayor is now drawing the attention of the School Inspector to his assistants:

"One of them, for instance, the one with the fat face . . . can't think of his name . . . well, every time he begins his class, he simply must make a grimace, like this [shows how] and then he starts to massage his chin from under his cravat. Of course if he makes faces only at the boys, it does not much matter—it may be even necessary in his department for all I know of those things; but consider what might happen if he did it in front of a visitor—that would be really dreadful: His Excellency the Government Inspector or anybody else might think it was meant for him. Goodness only knows what consequences that might have."

"What on earth am I to do with him, pray? [replies the School Inspector]. I have spoken to him several times already. Only the other day when our Marshal of Nobility was about to enter the classroom he went into such facial contortions as I have never yet seen. He did not mean anything, bless his kind heart, but *I* got a wigging: suggesting revolutionary ideas to youth, that's what they said."

Immediately afterwards another homunculus appears (rather like the little firm heads of witch doctors bursting out of the body of an African explorer in a famous short story). The Mayor refers to the history teacher:

"He is a scholar, no doubt, and has acquired loads of learning, but there—he lectures with such vehemence that he loses all self-control. I happened to hear him once: so long as he was talking about the Assyrians and the Babylonians it was—well, one could stand it; but when he got to

Alexander the Great, then—no, I simply can't describe his state. Lord, I thought the house was on fire! He dashed out of his desk and banged a chair against the floor with all his might! Alexander the Great was a hero, we all know that, but is this a reason to break chairs? It is wasting Government property."

"Ah yes, he is vehement [admits the School Inspector with a sigh] I have mentioned it to him several times. He answers: whether you like it or not, I can't help forfeiting my own life in the cause of learning."

The Postmaster, to whom the Mayor talks next, asking him to unseal and read the letters that pass through his office (which the good man had been doing for his own pleasure for years), is instrumental in letting out another homunculus.

"It's a great pity [he says to the Mayor] that you don't read those letters yourself: they contain some admirable passages. The other day for instance a lieutenant was writing to a friend and describing a ball he had been to—in a most waggish style. . . . Oh, very, very nice: 'My life, dear friend,' he wrote, 'floats in empyrean bliss: lots of young ladies, band playing, banner galloping . . . '—all of it written with great, great feeling."

Two quarrelsome country squires are mentioned next by the Judge, Cheptovich and Varkhovinsky, neighbors, who have taken proceedings against each other which will probably last all their lives (while the Judge merrily courses hares on the lands of both). Then as Dobchinsky and Bobchinsky make their dramatic appearance with the news that they have discovered the Government Inspector living incognito at the local inn, Gogol parodies his own fantastic meandering way (with gushes of seemingly irrelevant details) of telling a story: all the personal friends of Bobchinsky come bobbing up as the latter launches upon the report of his and Dobchinsky's sensational discovery: "So I ran to see Korobkin [Mr. Box] and not finding Korobkin at home [Jack-in-the-box had left it], I called on Rastakovsky [Mr. Blankety-Blank], and not finding Rastakovsky at home . . . [of all the homunculi only these two will appear as visitors at the end of the last act by special request of the stage management]." At the inn where Bobchinsky and Dobchinsky see the person whom they wrongly suspect to be the Government Inspector they interview the inn-keeper Vlass—and here—among the gasps and splutters of Bobchinsky's feverish speech (trying to tell it all before his double, Dobchinsky, can interrupt him) we obtain this lovely detailed information concerning Vlass (for in Gogol's world the more a person hurries the more he loiters on the way):

" . . . and so Dobchinsky beckoned with his finger and called the inn-keeper—you know, the inn-keeper Vlass—his wife has borne him a child three weeks ago—such a smart little beggar—will keep an inn just like his father does. . . . "

Note how the newborn Anonymous Vlassovich manages to grow up and live a whole life in the space of a second. Bobchinsky's panting speech seems to provoke an intense fermentation in the backstage world where those homunculi breed.

There are some more to come. The room where Khlestakov—the sham Government Inspector—dwells is identified by the fact that some officers who had also chanced to pass through that town some time before had a fight there over cards. One of the Mayor's men, the policeman Prokhorov, is alluded to in the following way.

The Mayor, in blustering haste to the policeman Svistunov: "Where are the others? . . . Dear me, I had ordered Prokhorov to be here, too. Where is Prokhorov?"

The Policeman: "Prokhorov is at the police station, but he cannot be put to any good use."

The Mayor: "How's that?"

The Policeman: "Well, just as I say: he was brought in this morning in a carriage dead drunk. Two buckets of water have been poured over him already, but he has not come round yet."

"But how on earth did you let him get into such a state?" the Mayor asks a moment later, and the Police Officer (incidentally called Oukhovertov—a name which contains the idea of "viciously hitting people on the ear" all in one word) replies: "The Lord knows. There was a brawl in the suburb yesterday—he went there to settle matters and came back drunk."

After this orgy of secondary characters surging at the close of the first act there is a certain respite in the second which introduces Khlestakov. True, a gambling infantry captain, who was great at piling up tricks, appears to the echoes of cheerful card-slapping as Khlestakov recalls the money he lost to him in the town of Pensa; but otherwise the active, ardent Khlestakov theme is too vigorous in this act (with the Mayor visiting him at the inn) to suffer any intruders. They come creeping back in the third act: Zemlyanika's daughter, we learn, wears a blue frock—and so she floats by in between the dialogue, a pink and blue provincial maiden.

When upon his arrival at the Mayor's house Khlestakov, in the most famous scene of the Russian stage, starts showing off for the benefit of the ladies, the secondary characters that come tumbling out of his speech (for at last they had been set rolling by Khlestakov's natural garrulousness and the Mayor's wine) are of another race, so to speak, than those we have already met. They are of a lighter, almost transparent texture in keeping with Khlestakov's own iridescent temperament—phantoms in the guise of civil servants, gleeful imps coming to the assistance of the versatile devil ventriloquizing through Khlestakov. Dobchinsky's children, Vanya, Lisanka, or the inn-keeper's boy existed somewhere or other, but these do not exist at all, as such. The allusions have become delusions. But because of the crescendo of lies on Khlestakov's part the driving force of these metaphysical creatures is more felt in its reaction upon the course of the play than were the idyllic gambols of the little people in the background of Act I.

"Ah, Petersburg!" exclaims Khlestakov. "That is what I call life! Perhaps you think I am just a copying clerk? [which he was]. No, Sir, the head of my section is right chummy with me. Has a way, you know, of slapping me on the shoulder and saying: 'Come and have dinner with me, old chap.' I only look in at the office for a couple of minutes, just to tell them: 'Do this, do that.' And then the copying clerk, old rat, goes with his pen—trrk, trrk, scraping and scribbling away, [in long drawn accents]. It was even suggested that I be made a Collegiate Assessor [again trippingly].—But thought I to myself, what's the use? And there is the office boy [these are bearded men in Russia] running up the stairs after me with a brush—'Allow me, Sir,' he says, 'I'll just give a bit of shining to your shoes.' " Much later we learn that the office "boy's" name was Mikhey, and that he drank like a fish.

Further on, when, according to Khlestakov, soldiers rushed out of the guardhouse as he passed and gave the grand salute: "Their officer whom I knew very well said to me afterwards: 'Well, well, old boy, I am damned if we did not take you for the Commander-in-Chief!' "

When he starts talking of his Bohemian and literary connections, there even appears a goblin impersonating Pushkin: "I hobnob with Pushkin. Many a time have I said to him: 'Well, old Push, how are things going?'—'As usual, my dear fellow,' he says, 'very much as usual.' Quite a character!"

Then other bigwigs come jostling and buzzing and tumbling over each other as Khlestakov rushes on in an ecstasy of invention: Cabinet Ministers, Ambassadors, Counts, Princes, Generals, the Tsar's Advisors, a shadow of the Tsar himself, and "Messengers, messengers, messengers, thirty-five thousand messengers," spermatozoids of the brain—and then suddenly in a drunken hiccup they all fade; but not before a real allusion (at least real in the same sense as the little people of Act I were "real"), the ghost of needy clerk Khlestakov's slatternly cook Mavroosha peeps out for a dreadful instant through a chink of Khlestakov's speech in the midst of all those golden ghosts and dream ambassadors—to help him out of his skimpy overcoat (that "shinel" cloak, to be exact, which later on Gogol was to immortalize as the attribute of a transcendental "chinovnik").

In the next act, when one by one the nervous officials present their respects to Khlestakov, who borrows money from each (they think that they are bribing him) we learn the names of Zemlyanika's children—Nicholas, Ivan, Elizabeth, Mary and Perepetuya: it was probably gentle Perepetuya who wore the pale blue frock. Of Dobchinsky's three children, two have been mentioned already by the Mayor's wife as being her godchildren. They and the eldest boy are uncommonly like the Judge who visits Mrs. Dobchinsky every time her poor little husband is away. The eldest boy was born before Dobchinsky married that wayward lady. Dobchinsky says to Khlestakov: "I make bold to ask your assistance in regard to a most delicate circumstance. . . . My eldest son, Sir, was born before I was married. . . . Oh, it is only a manner of speaking. I engendered him exactly as though in lawful wedlock, and made it perfectly right afterwards by sealing the bonds, Sir, of legitimate matrimony, Sir. Well, now I want him to be, in a manner of speaking, altogether my legitimate son, Sir, and to be called the same as I: Dobchinsky, Sir." (The French "sauf votre respect," though much too long,

would perhaps better render the meaning of the humble little hiss—an abbreviation of "Soodar"—"Sir," which Dobchinsky adds to this or that word at the fall of his sentences.)

"I would not have troubled you," he goes on, "but I feel sorry for him, seeing his many gifts. The little fellow, you see, is something quite special—promises a lot: he can recite verses and such like things by heart, and whenever he happens to come across a penknife he makes a wee little carriage—as clever as a conjuror, Sir."

One more character appears in the background of the act: it is when Khlestakov decides to write about those weird provincial officials to his friend Tryapichkin (Mr. Ragman) who is a sordid little journalist with mercenary and pamphleteering inclinations, a rascal with a knack of making laughing stocks of those he chooses to chastise in his cheap but vicious articles. For one instant he winks and leers over Khlestakov's shoulder. He is the last to appear—no, not quite the last, for the ultimate phantom will be the gigantic shadow of the real Government Inspector.

This secondary world, bursting as it were through the background of the play, is Gogol's true kingdom. It is remarkable that these sisters and husbands and children, eccentric school teachers, vodka-bewitched clerks and policemen, country squires quarreling for fifty years over the position of a fence, romantic officers who cheat at cards, wax sentimental over provincial balls and take a ghost for the Commander-in-Chief, these copying clerks and fantastic messengers—all these creatures whose lively motion constitutes the very material of the play, not only do not interfere with what theatrical managers call "action" but apparently assist the play to be eminently playable.

4

Not only live creatures swarm in that irrational background but numerous objects are made to play a part as important as that of the characters: the hatbox which the Mayor places upon his head instead of his hat when stamping out in official splendor and absent-minded haste to meet a threatening phantom, is a Gogolian symbol of the sham world where hats are heads, hatboxes hats, and braided collars the backbones of men. The hurried note which the Mayor sends from the inn to his wife telling her of the exalted guest whom she must get ready to receive gets mixed up with Khlestakov's hotel bill, owing to the Mayor having used the first scrap of paper that came to hand: "I hasten to tell you, my dearest, that I was in a most sorry plight at first; but thanks to my trusting in the mercy of God 2 salted cucumbers extra and ½ a portion of caviare, 1 rouble 25 kopeks." This confusion is again a piece of sound logic within Gogol's world, where the name of a fish is an outburst of divine music to the ears of gourmets, and cucumbers are metaphysical beings at least as potent as a provincial town mayor's private deity. These cucumbers breed in Khlestakov's eloquent description of his ideal of noble living: "On the table for instance there is a watermelon [which is but a sublimated cucumber]—not an ordinary watermelon but one that costs 700 roubles." The watery soup "with feathers or something floating in it" [instead of golden eyelets of shimmering fat] which Khlestakov has to be content with at the inn is transformed in the speech referring to his life in the capital into a *potage* that comes in a pan "straight from Paris by steamer,"—the smoke of that imaginary steamer being as it were the heavenly exhalation of that imaginary soup. When Khlestakov is being made comfortable in his carriage the Mayor has a blue Persian rug brought from the store room (which is crammed with the compulsory offerings of his bearded subjects—the town merchants); Khlestakov's valet adds to this a padding of hay—and the rug is transformed into a magic carpet on which Khlestakov makes his volatile exit behind stage to the silvery sound of the horse-bells and to the coachman's lyrical admonition to his magical steeds: "Hey you, my winged ones!" ("Hey vy, zalyotnye!" which literally means, "the ones that fly far"): Russian coachmen are apt to invent fond names for their horses—and Gogol, it may be assumed (for the benefit of those who like to know the personal experiences of writers) was to acquire a good deal of viatic lore during the endless peregrinations of his later years; and this gust of poetry, in which Khlestakov—the dreamy infantile swindler—fades out seems to blow open the gates for Gogol's own departure from the Russia he had invented towards distant hazy climes where numberless German watering towns, Italian ruins, Parisian restaurants and Palestine's shrines got mixed up in much the same way as Providence and a couple of cucumbers did in the distracted Mayor's letter.

5

It is amusing to recall that this dream play, this "Government Specter," was treated as a skit on actual conditions in Russia. It is still more amusing to think that Gogol in his first dismal effort to check those dangerous revolutionary allusions to his play pointed out that there was at least one positive character in it: Laughter. The truth is that the play is not a "comedy" at all, just as Shakespeare's dream-plays *Hamlet* or *Lear* cannot be called "tragedies." A bad play is more apt to be good comedy or good tragedy than the incredibly complicated creations of such men as Shakespeare or Gogol. In this sense Molière's stuff (for what it is worth) is "comedy" i.e. something as readily assimilated as a hot dog at a football game, something of one dimension and absolutely devoid of the huge, seething, prodigiously poetic background that makes true drama. And in the same sense O'Neill's *Mourning Becomes Electra* (for what *that* is worth) is, I suppose, a "tragedy."

Gogol's play is poetry in action, and by poetry I mean the mysteries of the irrational as perceived through rational words. True poetry of that kind provokes—not laughter and not tears—but a radiant smile of perfect satisfaction, a purr of beatitude—and a writer may well be proud of himself if he can make his readers, or more exactly some of his readers, smile and purr that way.

Khlestakov's very name is a stroke of genius, for it conveys to the Russian reader an effect of lightness and rashness, a prattling tongue, the swish of a slim walking cane, the slapping sound of playing cards, the braggadocio of a nincompoop and the dashing ways of a lady-killer (minus the capacity for completing this or any other action). He flutters through the play as indifferent to a full compre-

hension of the stir he creates, as he is eager to grab the benefits that luck is offering him. He is a gentle soul, a dreamer in his own way, and a certain sham charm hangs about him, the grace of a petit-maître that affords the ladies a refined pleasure as being in contrast with the boorish ways of the burly town worthies. He is utterly and deliciously vulgar, and the ladies are vulgar, and the worthies are vulgar—in fact the whole play is (somewhat like *Madame Bovary*) composed by blending in a special way different aspects of vulgarity so that the prodigious artistic merit of the final result is due (as with all masterpieces) not to *what* is said but to *how* it is said—to the dazzling combinations of drab parts. As in the scaling of insects the wonderful color effect may be due not to the pigment of the scales but to their position and refractive power, so Gogol's genius deals not in the intrinsic qualities of computable chemical matter (the "real life" of literary critics) but in the mimetic capacities of the physical phenomena produced by almost intangible particles of recreated life. I have employed the term "vulgarity" for lack of a more precise one; so Pushkin in *Eugene Onegin* inserted the English word "vulgar" with apologies for not finding in the Russian language its exact counterpart.

6

The charges directed against **The Government Inspector** by resentful people who saw in it an insidious attack against Russian officialdom had a disastrous effect upon Gogol. It may be said to have been the starting point of the persecution mania that in various forms afflicted him to the very end of his life. The position was rather curious: fame, in its most sensational form, had come to him; the Court was applauding his play with almost vicious glee; the stuffed shirts of high officialdom were losing their stuffing as they moved uneasily in their orchestra seats; disreputable critics were discharging stale venom; such critics whose opinion was worth something were lauding Gogol to the stars for what they thought was a great satire; the popular playwright Kukolnik shrugged his shoulders and said the play was nothing but a silly farce; young people repeated with gusto its best jokes and discovered Khlestakovs and Skvosnik-Dmukhanovskys among their acquaintances. Another man would have reveled in this atmosphere of praise and scandal. Pushkin would have merely shown his gleaming Negro teeth in a good-natured laugh—and turned to the unfinished manuscript of his current masterpiece. Gogol did what he had done after the *Kuechelgarten* fiasco: he fled, or rather slithered, to foreign lands.

He did something else, too. In fact he did the worst thing that a writer could do under the circumstances: he started explaining in print such points of his play as his critics had either missed or directed against him. Gogol, being Gogol and living in a looking-glass world, had a knack of thoroughly planning his works *after* he had written and published them. This system he applied to **The Government Inspector.** He appended a kind of epilogue to it [**The Dénoument of "The Inspector General"**] in which he explained that the real Government Inspector who looms at the end of the last act is the Conscience of Man. And that the other characters are the Passions in our Souls [see Author Commentary dated 1846]. In other words one was supposed to believe that these Passions were symbolized by grotesque and corrupt provincial officials and that the higher Conscience was symbolized by the Government. This explanation has the same depressing effect as his later considerations of related subjects have—unless we can believe that he was pulling his reader's leg—or his own. Viewed as a plain statement we have here the incredible fact of a writer totally misunderstanding and distorting the sense of his own work. He did the same to *Dead Souls*. . . .

He was a strange sick creature—and I am not sure that his explanation of *The Government Inspector* is not the kind of deceit that is practiced by madmen. It is difficult to accept the notion that what distressed him so dreadfully about the reception of his play was his failure to be recognized as a prophet, a teacher, a lover of mankind (giving mankind a warning for its own good). There is not a speck of didacticism in the play and it is inconceivable that the author could be unaware of this; but as I say, he was given to dreaming things into his books long after they had been written. On the other hand the kind of lesson which critics—quite wrongly—discerned in the play was a social and almost revolutionary one which was highly distasteful to Gogol. He may have been apprehensive of the Court suddenly changing its august and fickle mind owing to the too violent praise in radical circles and to the too violent blame in reactionary ones—and thus cutting short the performances and profits (and a future pension maybe). He may have seen his literary career in Russia hampered for years to come by vigilant censors. He may too have been shocked and hurt by the fact that people whom he respected as good Christians (though the "good Christian" theme in its full form was to appear somewhat later) and good officials (which was to become synonymous with the first) were grieved and revolted by what they termed a "coarse and trivial farce." But what seems to have tormented him above all was the knowledge of being talked about by thousands of people and not being able to hear, let alone control, the talk. The buzz that reached him was ominous and monstrous because it was a buzz. The pats he received on his back seemed to him to imply ironic sneers directed at people whom he respected, so that these sneers were also directed at himself. The interest that perfect strangers showed in regard to him seemed alive with dark stratagems and incalculable dangers (beautiful word, stratagem—a treasure in a cave). I shall have occasion to speak in quite a different book of a lunatic who constantly felt that all the parts of the landscape and movements of inanimate objects were a complex code of allusion to his own being, so that the whole universe seemed to him to be conversing about him by means of signs. Something of that sinister and almost cosmic dumbshow can be inferred from the morbid view Gogol took of his sudden celebrity. He fancied a hostile Russia creeping and whispering all around him and trying to destroy him both by blaming and praising his play. In June, 1836, he left for Western Europe.

It is said that on the eve of his departure Pushkin, whom he was never to see again, visited him and spent all night rummaging together with him among his manuscripts and

reading the beginning of *Dead Souls,* a first draft of which had already been made by Gogol about that time. The picture is pleasing—too pleasing perhaps to be true. For some reason or other (possibly from a morbid dislike of any responsibility) Gogol in after years was most anxious to have people believe that all he had written before 1837, that is, before Pushkin's death, had been directly due to the latter's suggestion and influence. As Gogol's art was as far removed from that of Pushkin as could be and as moreover Pushkin had other problems to tackle than guiding the pen of a literary acquaintance, the information so readily supplied by Gogol himself is hardly worth serious consideration. The lone candle lighting up the midnight scene may go out without any qualms on our part. What is far more likely is that Gogol stole abroad without bidding farewell to any of his friends. We know from a letter of his that he did not even say good-bye to Zhukovsky with whom he was on much more intimate terms than with Pushkin. (pp. 35-60)

> *Vladimir Nabokov, in his* Nikolai Gogol, *New Direction Books, 1944, 172 p.*

William Woodin Rowe   (essay date 1976)

[*In the following excerpt, Rowe examines reality and illusion in* The Government Inspector, *typical Gogolian reversals and negations, and associations between the main character Khlestakov and the devil.*]

The Gogolian title of [*The Government Inspector*] is at once both accurate and misleading. Mistaken for the Inspector traveling incognito, a lowly official who has lost all his money is wined, dined, and abundantly bribed by the officials of a small town. Tearing himself away from the mayor's wife and daughter, he rushes off just before the announced arrival of (presumably) the real Inspector.

The mayor opens the play by announcing to the officials of the town: "a Government Inspector is coming to see us." Gogol thus establishes a picture of the Inspector "on his way"—a fitting backdrop for the entire play. The mayor then declares:

> I seemed to foresee it: all night I dreamed of
> these two unusual rats. Really, I've never seen
> the likes of them: black, of an unnatural size;
> They came, sniffed awhile, and went away completely.

Diverted by the dramatic announcement that *one* Inspector is coming, we are apt to miss this preview of Khlestakov and his servant Osip. For they are "two unusual [*neobyknovennye*] rats" indeed, produced by local imagination. As V. G. Belinsky has put it, the mayor's dream releases a series of specters which then comprise the reality of the play. Magnified by the townspeople's fright ("of an unnatural size!"), these unusual rats do come, sniff awhile, and then vanish. This dream is virtually the entire play. Perhaps the most subtle touch of Gogol's trick is the phrase "I seemed to foresee it," which leads us to believe that the prophecy has already been fulfilled (by the mere news that the Inspector is coming). Note also that the mayor announces his prophetic dream as the play opens, to a gathering of all the people it could warn, and none of them ever realizes this.

The mayor goes on to read from a letter he has just received.

> Since I know that you, like everyone else, have a few little sins to hide, because you are an intelligent person and do not wish to lose what is swimming in your hands . . . I advise you to take precautions, because he might arrive at any hour, if only he has not arrived already and is not living somewhere incognito. . . .

Despite this warning, of course, the officials of the town will expend great efforts "to lose what is swimming in their hands" as they desperately force bribes upon Khlestakov. Also ironically, the phrase "he might arrive at any hour" acquires greater and greater accuracy throughout the play. Note also the faintly playful Gogolian negation.

As Scene Two opens, the postmaster arrives and asks if "some sort of official is coming" (again, the Inspector is pictured "on his way"). The postmaster pretends that his sole source of information is Bobchinsky. Later, however, when advised by the mayor to open the mail and read it (as a precautionary measure), the postmaster reveals that he already does this. It is so interesting and "informative," he tells the mayor. "It's such a pity that you don't read the letters. Just recently a lieutenant was writing to his friend and describing a ball most playfully . . ." Act Five, of course, will feature the reading of Khlestakov's outrageously "playful" letter "to his friend," which the mayor "should very much have read" and which contains many "admirable" and "informative" passages. Here, the postmaster even offers to read one letter, which contains, he says, such phrases as "life flows along celestially: many ladies, music plays. . . . " But the mayor has no desire to hear this hidden prophecy, just as he ignored the meaning of his own prophetic dream. Another ironic touch is the mayor's initial reaction to the news that the Inspector is living at the Inn. "It is not he," he fearfully declares.

When we first meet Khlestakov, he is deeply in debt to the Innkeeper, who, Osip reports, has little patience left: "You and your master, says he, are swindlers." Khlestakov then accuses Osip of becoming glad to repeat all this. Thus, Gogol has them both called swindlers in advance and even stresses it. (Similarly, Khlestakov will later repeatedly announce to everyone that he has been mistaken for the Commander in Chief.)

Desperate, Khlestakov assures the Inn servant that he need not worry: "the money will of its own accord. . . . " Later, when the officials thrust bribes upon Khlestakov, even dropping money and pretending it is his, these words prove vividly true. And when Khlestakov starts to pay his bill at the Inn, the mayor tells him: "Now please don't trouble yourself, he'll wait." Khlestakov somehow musters the poise to agree emphatically.

Earlier, when Khlestakov has no idea how to pay his debts, he wishes he had been able to hire a carriage: he could have arrived home in grand style, he declares, even impressing a neighbor's daughter. As the play ends, one can easily project the realization of these idle schemes, for Khlestakov has already rushed off in a carriage laden with loot and a merrily jingling bell. Ironically, the mayor orders that a bell be rung to celebrate his supposed success with Khlestakov.

Addressing his wife in Act Five, the mayor gloats over Khlestakov's proposal to his daughter: "Well, confess honestly: you never even saw it in a dream . . . !" If we recall the mayor's own prophetic dream, his words seem unwittingly ironic indeed. Similarly, the mayor twice emphasizes that he is "not giving" his daughter in marriage to "some kind of simple person." Not only is Khlestakov just such a "simple person"; the daughter is of course "not being given" at all. Again, note the repetition of playful Gogolian negation.

One almost regrets that the marriage fails to take place. Khlestakov's famous pronouncement, "My thoughts have an unusual lightness about them," renders him a perfect match for the mayor's daughter Marya, whose mother tells her: "Some kind of drafty wind is forever playing about in your head." The "love scene" (IV, xiii) between Khlestakov and Marya is thus a meeting of two delightfully empty minds. Their dialogue features amusing Gogolian reversals (of "far" and "near" as he attempts to sit close to her) and "live clothing" (as he wishes to be her "little shawl," to embrace her "lily-white neck").

As we have seen, the mayor's prophetic dream about the antics of two unusual rats tends to slip by unnoticed because only one Government Inspector has been mentioned. But as Erlich suggests, it is possible that the second Inspector is yet another impostor [see Further Reading]. Osip, who seems to have more sense than his master, urges him to depart while there is still time: "or else suddenly some kind of other one will arrive." If this "other one" is indeed an imposter, he himself may be deemed the second "unusual rat" (instead of Osip), and the play, eerily projected, is only half completed at the final curtain. In this respect, *The Government Inspector* may seem to resemble "Shponka and His Aunt," except that here, the projected "second half" seems more a parallel version of the first. Such an interpretation seems quite in keeping with Gogol's constant use of parallelisms. For example, the exclamations that accompany Khlestakov's detection (*Kak revizor?*) parallel the ones when he is exposed (*Kak ne revizor?*); Dobchinsky and Bobchinsky argue to avoid the blame in words that parallel their earlier clamoring for the credit; and when Marya finds Khlestakov on his knees before her mother, she utters exactly the same words (*Akh, kakoj passazh!*) that her mother had, when their roles were reversed.

Perception-expanding reversals in *The Government Inspector* are numerous, even for Gogol. "God himself," the mayor declares at the outset, has arranged it so that "there is no one who does not have some kind of sins behind him." All the patients at the hospital, we learn, "are getting well like flies," a reversal with humorous but disturbing implications. Not only do the "flies" suggest "dying like"; they also suggest unclean, and therefore conducive to dying, hospital conditions. To the judge, who has apparently "reasoned out" some "hair-raising" things about the creation of the world, the mayor declares: "Well, in some cases a lot of mind is worse than none at all."

Reversals are also used in reference to the children of (presumably) the judge and Dobchinsky's wife. While bribing Khlestakov, Dobchinsky makes a request "regarding a certain very delicate circumstance." His eldest son, he explains, was conceived by him before the marriage. But this was done just as "perfectly," he hastens to add, as if the marriage had already taken place. Later, of course, he scrupulously legalized the situation, and now he desires permission to call his "lawful" son "Dobchinsky." The rather dark humor of "perfectly" is thus enhanced by a double reversal: Dobchinsky's "lawful" son, belatedly legalized by marriage, may well be the judge's. The "very delicate circumstance" is therefore doubly indelicate.

The epigraph of *The Government Inspector* is a popular saying, literally: "The mirror should not be blamed if the mug is crooked." The play, wherein the townsfolk blindly force their own image of the Inspector upon Khlestakov, is thus a reversal: The mug (Khlestakov) should not be blamed if the mirror (the imposed image) is crooked. However, both admonitions have this in common: What you see should not be blamed if you expect the wrong thing. Thus, the epigraph is still strangely appropriate. In common usage, moreover, it means: "Don't blame your own faults on others." And this seems good advice for the townspeople, who work so diligently to bestow upon Khlestakov the bribes they presume he seeks.

Just as the epigraph may be deemed reversed, the play itself may be seen as a reversal of Gogol's usual procedure whereby an eerie world gradually invades the "real" one. Here, the patently fantastic world of Khlestakov-as-Inspector is gradually invaded by the grim shadow of the "real" Inspector and by the impending exposé of Khlestakov's obliging masquerade.

In Gogol's later short play, *The Ending of the Government Inspector,* a lachrymose clown boasts a "heart" which offers this "key": *The Government Inspector* is "our spiritual city" [see Author Commentary dated 1846]. Yet as Gippius has put it, we have "grown accustomed to disbelieve Gogol," so characteristic were his "mystifications" [see Further Reading]. In the present writer's view, the only justification for this clown's remarkable interpretation is the notion that art can inspire goodness "negatively." For if a "spiritual" shadow can be discerned in *The Government Inspector,* it seems rather less celestial than demoniac.

As many have observed, the play contains an atmosphere of fright associated with the ominous presence of high officials. And the popular saying applied by Belinsky seems most appropriate: "Fear has large eyes." Inspired by fright, the townspeople create their own "reality." But behind the imagined façade, one can detect a faint background of sinister Gogolian forces.

From the very beginning, the news of the Inspector's visit promotes fear tinged with suspicion. The judge (who humorously misjudges the news as portending war) reacts first: "Yes, the situation is quite . . . unusual, simply unusual. There's some reason for all this." His repetition of

"unusual" (*neobyknovenno*) strangely echoes the mayor's (just recounted) dream of the two "unusual" rats (*neobyknovennye*). Moreover, the word "unusual" (which with Gogol often attends an overlapping of two realities) appears at two other key points in the play. One is Khlestakov's famous pronouncement, discussed above, "My thoughts have an unusual [*neobyknovennaya*] lightness about them." Can this possibly be seen to suggest that his masquerade is somehow supernaturally inspired? In Act Five, just prior to Khlestakov's "unmasking," the judge notes the mayor's "unusual" [*neobyknovennoye*] happiness," which words are repeated by another official.

Is there, then, as the judge suggested earlier, "some reason for all this"? Is there any stronger evidence that Khlestakov's mistaken identity and helpless triumph were encouraged by supernatural forces? Early in the play, the mayor declares that if they fail to impress the Inspector, "the devil knows what may happen." Yet, for Gogol, there are not many such references.

In Act Five, however, there occurs (in Slonimsky's words) "a transition from the comic to the serious." As the fatal climax draws near, mentions of the devil suddenly abound. The mayor's triumphant speeches contain numerous devils (seven in one place alone) and even a witch. When he orders that a bell be rung, for example, he adds "devil take it!," which indirectly associates the devil with a fleeing Khlestakov and his merrily ringing bell. Typically, a merchant explains why he appealed to Khlestakov for help: "The Evil One confused me." The devil then appears in several other speeches, especially often in connection with the mayor's becoming a general, which is of course a doomed plan. There are also two references to people having the faces of pigs, which, if one recalls "The Sorochintsy Fair," may be seen to suggest the devil's presence in this world.

Finally, when the postmaster bursts in with his Gogolian message that "the Inspector is not the Inspector," he claims that "an unnatural force" inspired him to open Khlestakov's letter. It was as if "some demon were whispering, Unseal it, unseal it, unseal it!" And when asked who Khlestakov really is, the postmaster replies: "the devil knows what he is!" After this, the devil is frequently mentioned until the end of the play. The judge exclaims, for example: "The devil knows what it means! If he's only a swindler, that's still good, but perhaps he's still worse." The postmaster even claims that "the devil led" him to give Khlestakov the best troika.

Merezhkovsky aptly adduces several of these allusions as evidence of "a fantastic haze of the devil." He also quotes one of Gogol's letters asserting that the devil was behind the rumors which promoted Khlestakov to Government Inspector.

Is Khlestakov, then, an agent of the devil? If so, he is a playful and unwitting one, to be sure. Nevertheless, all these associations between the devil and Khlestakov tend to render suspect the reasons for his being so forcefully misunderstood. The very creation of his image acquires an eerie tinge. Behind the comic fear which so stimulates local imagination, there seems to be a sinister force, almost completely invisible, at work from the very beginning—a force suggested at first by the characters' strangely intense premonitions; a force sustained when a dream, a letter, an idle plan to escape, and numerous statements become prophetic; and finally, a force suspected by the characters themselves as suggesting the work of the devil. (pp. 135-42)

> *William Woodin Rowe, in his* Through Gogol's Looking Glass: Reverse Vision, False Focus, and Precarious Logic, *New York University Press, 1976, 201 p.*

Milton Ehre   (essay date 1980)

[*In the following excerpt, Ehre analyzes the structure of* The Inspector General *and examines Gogol's use of dramatic technique in order to define the nature of the work's comic effect. To demonstrate Gogol's skillful combination of comedy and apocalyptic terror, Ehre particularly focuses on the play's last act, in which the townspeople dread the imminent arrival of the real inspector general as the coming of a figure of final judgment.*]

Gogol's labored apologias for his great play, written in

Erast Garin as Khlestakov, 1926.

anxious defense against the miscomprehensions of critics, have been largely ignored or ridiculed. In the nineteenth century they were dismissed as the rantings of a religious fanatic; in the twentieth, when our habit is to convert moral judgements into clinical diagnoses, as the symptoms of pathology. The strained style Gogol adopted whenever he felt threatened should not deceive us. He was an acute student of the arts, alert to his own purposes. Any examination of his work must take his views into account.

For Gogol, *The Government Inspector* was a play that should arouse terror as well as laughter. Such is the common thread of his two most important statements about the play, the dramatized essays *Leaving the Theater After a Performance of a New Comedy,* probably written shortly after the historic première of 1836, and the *Dénouement of 'The Government Inspector,'* written a full decade later (1846). He had not intended a balanced "portrait" of contemporary society, he writes in *Leaving the Theater . . . ,* but a heightened image of what he found wrong in Russia: "From all over, from the four corners of Russia, what has been excluded from the truth, moral failings and abuses, have flocked together . . . " in an "ideal" place of assembly so that the audience might experience "an intense, noble disdain for whatever is ignoble." The viewer "shudders in the depths of his being. . . . He must be constantly on guard . . . " lest the objects of his laughter "burst into his soul." These terrifying images should "incessantly haunt the imagination . . . " of the audience.

Though his overwrought rhetoric places him squarely in the Romantic age, Gogol's interpretation of 1836 can still be read in the context of classical theories of comedy, whose purpose was, in a leading Russian classicist's [Sumarakov's] paraphrase of Boileau, "to correct manners through ridicule, / . . . to amuse and serve." The function of comedy is social. It enlightens the public to the ways of the world and acts as a moral prophylactic. Laughter, which Gogol calls "luminous," brings to light the "trivia and emptiness of life," so that these no longer "go unnoticed" but "terrify" us. Fear of ridicule acts as a restraint upon vice. However, the depiction of negative features we find in comedy necessarily implies positive values: an image of a dishonest man potentially conveys an image of an honest man; " . . . deviations from justice and law enable us to perceive clearly the demands of justice, duty, and law." Though laughter has something to do with fear, it is not disturbing—"only what is somber disturbs, and laughter is luminous." Gogol does not explain the paradox whereby comedy can provoke terror and yet not be disturbing—we shall attempt to do so later—but the implication is that it teaches us to fear what should be feared and simultaneously frees us from painful emotions. The final emphasis is on the liberating power of laughter. Proper laughter is "good-natured" and indicates a "magnanimous soul." It frees us from self-righteousness and leads to forgiveness and "reconciliation." The theater creates a community, as "all men come together, like brothers," in a single shared "spirtual motion."

In the 1846 *Dénouement . . .* the emphasis turns from society to the self, from reconciliation and community to preparation for the world's end. Christian allusions had resonated through the metaphors of the 1836 piece; the play is now read as Christian allegory. The earlier "place of assembly," which offered a microcosm of Russian wrongdoing, has become our common "spiritual city." The town's officials are identified with our human passions and "trivial vulgar habits." Khlestakov, the fake government inspector, represents "the frivolous conscience of the world." He blinds us to the identity of the true inspector, who is "our awakening conscience." The religious imagination of the *Dénouement . . .* is, as the title tells us, entirely turned to last things, to death and the grave. Where Gogol saw comedy in *Leaving the Theater . . .* as inhibiting vice and softening self-righteousness, thereby bringing about reconciliation between men here on earth, he now describes an audience that feels "no desire to be reconciled to the characters, but, on the contrary, wishes to repel them unhesitatingly. . . . " Laughter has been transformed from an instrument of community to "a weapon, a scourge" that will drive corruption from our souls and purify us before Last Judgment:

> . . . let us look . . . with the eyes of Him Who will call all men to account, before Whom the best of us—mark it well—will cast down their eyes in shame. . . . Say what you will, the inspector who awaits us at the portals of the grave is terrible. . . . He is our awakening conscience who will force us, once and for all, to take a long hard look at ourselves. Nothing will remain hidden from this inspector, for he is sent by command of the Almighty. There will be no turning back when his coming is heralded. Suddenly horrors to make a man's hair stand on end will be revealed . . . [see Author Commentary dated 1846].

These two readings—the play as social and as apocalyptic satire—anticipate the two tendencies of Gogol criticism: the nineteenth-century (and Soviet) view that locates his art in the actualities of Russian society, and the modernist revision that highlights its demonic aspects (while often ignoring the religious motives, so that Gogol becomes an archetypal "absurdist"). As is often the case in such polemics, the antagonists are responding to different sides of the same object. *The Government Inspector* may be read as social comedy (Gogol's 1836 reading) and as a kind of metaphysical comedy centered on the radical imperfection of human nature (his 1846 revision). It mocks the way of the world but its mockery is part of an effort to obliterate the world as a prelude to final judgement. Nor are the two views mutually exclusive. Apocalyptic terrors result from a sense of social dissolution—even in the *Dénouement . . . ,* where the primary concern is spiritual salvation, Gogol still speaks of "terror at our social chaos." Moreover, his apocalypse is comical, and comedy treats the actualities of human life, which always have a social context. Gogol creates his comic apocalypse by organizing his play so as to reveal the illusory pursuits of his people, the insubstantial character of their society, and the resulting chaos. He brings his world to the brink where final judgment waits. In the following pages we shall examine that organization and, then, the issues posed by a comic apocalypse.

Few who write on *The Government Inspector* fail to point

to the brilliance of the opening two lines: "Gentlemen! I've summoned you here because of some very distressing news. A government inspector is on his way." The obligatory exposition of classical comedy has been compressed into a stunning fifteen words (in Russian). Here is the dramatic situation that governs the entire play, the ineluctable presence that hovers over it from beginning to end. What follows, however, is not an elaboration of that situation, a working out of motive to final resolution as in most drama before Gogol. The situation remains constant for most of the play; the government inspector is a given, an inescapable fact, who elicits, instead of an evolving intrigue, a series of frenzied responses:

> A government inspector?
> An inspector?
>   . . .
> As if we didn't have enough troubles!
> Good God! And with secret instructions!

The work ends on analogous accents of inexorable destiny:

> His Excellency the government inspector has arrived from the capital. In the name of the emperor he demands your immediate presence at the inn.

In Nabokov's felicitous words: "The play begins with a blinding flash of lightning and ends in a thunderclap. In fact it is wholly placed in the tense gap between the flash and the crash" [see commentary dated 1944].

However, it is not only that these lines are dramatically effective, which they are. They also define the structure of the play. The impending arrival of the government inspector is announced in the opening two sentences; he arrives in the final two. These symmetrical pairs, echoing each other in their official bombast and note of irrevocable fact, comprise the only events with the potential to affect the lives of the characters. As a result, the gap between the flash and the crash, which is the duration of the play, acquires a curious status. The life of the play is dislodged from fact, or reality—the true inspector, and shifted to a realm of illusion—the pursuit of a specter: Khlestakov, the unwitting imposter, the False Pretender, a character who, in Gogol's words, is "phantasmagorical."

"Hurry, hurry, for God's sake, hurry" are the last words of Act I, and much of the play is saturated with words of haste, as the townspeople rush headlong to discover the nature of their visitor or cater to his whims.

> MAYOR: Quick, get the police captain. No, wait. [. . .] Tell someone out there to hurry and bring the police captain. [. . .] Go out to the street . . . no, wait! Go get. [. . .] My God! My God! . . . Quick, go to the street; no, wait, first run to my room—do you hear! [. . .] Run, quick; take some men and have each of them grab a . . . Oh hell, the sword's scratched [. . .] Have each of them grab a street—what the!—grab a broom. [. . .] (I, iii-iv.)
>
>   . . .
>
> ANNA: Later? That's a fine piece of news! Later! I don't want your later. Just tell me, what's his rank? Is he a colonel? [. . .]

MARYA: Oh Mama! It doesn't matter. We'll know in a few hours.

ANNA: A few hours! Thank you very much. That's brilliant. Why not a month while you're at it. Avdotya! Avdotya! What have you heard? Has someone arrived? . . . What? They rushed off? You should have run after them. Go now. Hurry! [. . .] Run—ask where they've gone. Find out the details. Who is he, is he handsome? Do you hear [. . .] And come right home. [. . .] Hurry, hurry, for God's sake, hurry! (I, iv.)

The activity on stage rushes along, like Khlestakov's mind, at breakneck speed: policemen and servants rush on stage to receive their orders; Bobchinsky and Dobchinsky tumble on to it with their extraordinary news; the officials slink on to bribe the putative inspector; Khlestakov flits across like a phantom.

But all this rushing is toward an illusion, the false inspector, who in turn won't sit still, whose mind leaps with "extraordinary lightness" from one fabrication to another until he finally flies off in his troika, as if vanishing into thin air. The object of this frenzied bustle is a man without substance, a creature of pure improvisation who can only respond to the signals of the moment, "a nobody and a nothing" in the words of the postmaster (V, viii). Khlestakov's exceptional vacuity has been the subject of much metaphysical and psychological speculation, but it has a dramatic function. Because he lacks character, the townspeople can project their own fears and fantasies upon him. In a sense he is their creation: Khlestakov is "the most empty of men," Gogol wrote, " . . . but the force of general terror has made him into a remarkable comic character." What makes him so comic is the enormous discrepancy between his own inconsequentiality and the importance the terrified town places upon him. Conversely, the frantic rush of the townspeople to placate this illusory phantom deprives their experience of substance. We get the inconsequential in pursuit of the inconsequential; so to speak, nothing heaped upon nothing.

The Gogolian annihilation of experience is particularly thorough-going in the seduction scenes. It has often been said that Gogol's innovation in the tradition of comedy was in eliminating the conventional love story. This is not so. The love story is present, and it is at the center of the play. The action of the "gap" turns around the seeming change in the mayor's fortunes, which is marked by the course of Marya's and Khlestakov's courtship. Before the betrothal the mayor felt himself in danger of destruction; afterwards he is for an instant on top of the world. Instead of dispensing with the conventions of love, Gogol trivializes them so that they become ludicrous. He draws his conventions, not from high comedy, but from popular farce and vaudeville: the ingénue of high comedy is converted into an imbecilic provincial, the paramour into a featherbrained fake, the action into automatized mime. " . . . comedy should cohere spontaneously, . . . " he wrote, and the love scenes are decomposed into a series of hurried accidental gestures, abrupt and unmotivated. Marya wanders aimlessly on to the stage, "going nowhere in particular"; Khlestakov blurts out in his inimitable fashion, "And why, may I ask, weren't you going anywhere in particular?"; he steals a kiss; she is indignant; he falls to his knees to beg forgiveness; Mama bursts in exclaiming, "Oh good heavens"; Khlestakov, not one to be easily put off, again falls to his knees, this time to make a pass at Mama; the daughter walks in with another "Oh good heavens," and so it goes. By reducing action to the quick-paced and bare gestures of farce, Gogol turns his love story into a parody of a love story. The language of love is likewise a parodic *reductio ad absurdum:* "My life hangs by a thread. If you reject my undying love, I no longer deserve to dwell in this vale of tears. My heart ablaze, I ask your hand" (IV, xii-xiv). These inspired words of Khlestakov are addressed not to Marya but to her mother! Such displacements are of course a standard ploy of farce.

If the "love story" goes virtually unnoticed, it is because it was meant to. In *Leaving the Theater . . .* Gogol expressed his disdain for plots that centered on love or "private" life; these were like "a precise little knot at the corner of a handkerchief." Instead he wanted a plot that would tie together all the characters, the whole of society. The "lovers" of *The Government Inspector,* unlike the ingénues and gallants of traditional comedy, offer no alternative image to the comedic world about them. They are as inane as the more conventional comic figures: the gruff and highhanded mayor, his coquettish wife, the bumbling and corrupt officials, all of whom have their prototypes in Russian eighteenth-century comedy. Gogol's great innovation was not to eliminate the love story but to incorporate it into the comic pattern. Instead of two worlds—one fallen; the other of good sense, decorous and decent—he gives us a single universe, tied into "one great knot," all of it ludicrous.

The same integrating power sweeps Khlestakov into the vortex of the play. As classical comedy opposed the comically nonsensical to men and women of good sense, it divided the virtuous and misguided from its authentic villains. *The Government Inspector* is a play without virtuous characters, and it is also a play without villains. Khlestakov comes out of a venerable line of charlatans and imposters, but, as Gogol tirelessly repeated, he is not to be identified with the "braggarts and theatrical rogues" of comedy for the simple reason that he has no idea he's lying. Khlestakov, for Gogol, was a dreamer, a fantasist, for whom imagination and reality have become interwoven into a crazy quilt of illusion. Exposing the ludicrousness of the world about him, he is himself ludicrous. Neither virtuous nor evil, the characters of Gogol's comic works (the melodramas are something else) are merely ridiculous. They reside in a halfway house between redemption and damnation—a comic purgatory.

Besides rushing, the play's other mode is one of performance. Action is speeded up and automatized so that it loses all substance; at the same time, action is transformed into acting, an illusory makebelieve, again lacking in substance. The departure from tradition is once more striking. Where comic masquerades before Gogol divided neatly into deceivers and deceived, confidence men and their gulls, in *The Government Inspector* almost everyone is an impersonator, an actor.

MAYOR: . . . He wants to remain incognito. Fine. We can bluff too, act as if we don't have a hint who he is. (II, viii.)

. . .

ANNA: Osip, dear, I imagine many counts and princes call on your master?

OSIP: *aside.* What do I say? They fed me fine now, and it can only get better. (*Aloud.*) Yes, ma'm, counts and everything. (III, x.)

. . .

KHLESTAKOV: The place is crawling with officials. . . . Seems they've taken me for someone from the ministry. I must have laid it on thick yesterday. (IV, viii.)

Even in those rare moments when Khlestakov is not acting, his every word is taken as performance. The comic routines between him and the mayor are built on this principle: the mayor putting on a show while taking Khlestakov's pedestrian responses for merely another show:

MAYOR: [. . .] Pyotr Ivanovich Dobchinsky and I—Dobchinsky here is one of our local landowners—well, since we were in the neighborhood on official business, we made a point of stopping in to determine whether the guests are being treated properly. Some mayors may not concern themselves with the welfare of others, but I, I . . . insist that a good reception be extended to all persons. Not only because my position demands it, but also out of Christian love for humanity. And now, as if in reward, fortune has afforded me such a pleasant acquaintance.

KHLESTAKOV: I'm also glad. If not for you, I might have been stranded here for ages. I was racking my brains how to pay the bill.

MAYOR: *aside.* Sure, tell it to the birds! Didn't know how he'd pay, did he? (*Aloud.*) May I be so bold as to ask to what parts you are bound?

KHLESTAKOV: Saratov. I'm on my way home.

MAYOR: *aside, an ironic expression on his face.* Saratov, eh? And without a blush! Oh, you've got to be on your toes with him. (*Aloud.*) A most worthy enterprise, sir. (II, viii.)

More frequently the impersonations are duets, as two characters perform ballet-like verbal dances of pretense.

KHLESTAKOV: *bowing.* How delighted I am, madam, to have the pleasure of your acquaintance.

ANNA: It's even more of a pleasure for us to meet you.

KHLESTAKOV: *posturing.* Oh no, madam, not at all. It's far more pleasant for me.

ANNA: How can you say that, sir! You're only trying to flatter us. Please be seated.

KHLESTAKOV: Standing near you, madam, is

joy itself. But if you insist, I'll sit. . . . How delighted I am at last to be sitting beside you.

ANNA: Oh my! I dare not dream your compliments are intended for me. . . . I imagine, after the capital traveling through the provinces must have been quite disagreeable.

KHLESTAKOV: Exceedingly so. Accustomed as I am, *comprenez-vous,* to moving in the best society, and suddenly to find myself on the road—filthy inns, the dark gloom of ignorance . . . I must say, if not for the good fortune . . . (*glancing at* ANNA ANDREEVNA *and posturing*) that has rewarded me for all my trials and tribulations . . .

ANNA: Indeed, how disagreeable it must have been.

KHLESTAKOV: At this moment, madam, everything is most agreeable.

ANNA: You can't mean that, sir! You do me too much honor. I'm not worthy.

KHLESTAKOV: Why aren't you worthy? Madam, you *are* worthy.

ANNA: I live in the country.

KHLESTAKOV: Yes, but the country has its hillocks, its rivulets. (III, vi.)

The characters of the play rush after an illusion—the false inspector—and when they catch up with him, they turn metamorphose into illusory characters, masked selves performing stylized rituals of impersonation.

The ironies of the Discovery and Peripety revolve around metaphors of life as performance. As the town's officials come to the realization that they have foisted an identity upon Khlestakov, that under his mask there is nothing and nobody, the mayor is overcome by the dread that he too may lack substantial identity, that he may be only an actor in a performance.

Oh you thick-nosed idiot! Taking that squirt, that worm, for an important person! . . . He'll turn you into the laughing stock of all Russia. What's more, some cheap hack will stick you into a comedy. That's what hurts. [. . .] And they'll all grin and clap. [. . .] (V, viii.)

Though the play is unremitting in its comic vision, it gives us momentary glimpses of suffering underlying its comedy. Its pathos stems from this sense of loss of selfhood. The townspeople's deepest fears are that they too may be nothings and nobodies:

BOBCHINSKY: [. . .] Your Excellency. I have a very humble request.

KHLESTAKOV: What about?

BOBCHINSKY: I humbly beg you, sir, when you return to the capital, tell all those great gentlemen—the senators and admirals and all the rest—say, "Your Excellency or Your Highness, in such and such a town there lives a man called Pyotr Ivanovich Bobchinsky." Be sure to tell them, "Pyotr Ivanovich Bobchinsky lives there."

KHLESTAKOV: Very well.

BOBCHINSKY: And if you should happen to meet with the tsar, then tell the tsar too, "Your Imperial Majesty, in such and such a town there lives a man called Pyotr Ivanovich Bobchinsky."

KHLESTAKOV: Fine. (IV, vii.)

When performance collapses, when the Discovery unmasks Khlestakov and the townspeople as actors in a comedy of mutual deception, the mode of rush returns. But where the earlier rush was a linear movement toward an end, however illusory, the stage now witnesses a tornado-like whirl of recrimination and abuse. Deprived of an end to action, the townspeople turn upon themselves. As we move from the mayor's expansive rhetorical outburst—the wider end of our tornado's funnel—the language narrows, phrasing becomes terser and hence quicker, compressing finally to one or two-word expletives before Dobchinsky's and Bobchinsky's last effort to get off the hook.

> MAYOR: [. . .] What was there about that birdbrain to make us take him for a government inspector? Nothing! Not that much! (*Shows his little finger.*) And yet everyone was suddenly yapping: "It's the inspector! The inspector!" Who started the rumor? Answer me! Who? [. . .]
>
> JUDGE: You want to know who started it? I'll tell you who—these two geniuses! (*Points at* DOBCHINSKY *and* BOBCHINSKY.)
>
> BOBCHINSKY: Not me, honestly, not me. It never crossed my mind.
>
> DOBCHINSKY: Not me either. I had nothing to do with it.
>
> DIRECTOR OF CHARITIES: Of course it was you!
>
> SUPERINTENDENT OF SCHOOLS: No question about it. They came running from the inn, raving like lunatics. "He's here, he's here, and he won't pay his bill." Some prize you found!
>
> MAYOR: It must have been you! Damned liars, town gossips!
>
> DIRECTOR OF CHARITIES: Go to hell! And take your inspector and your tales along!
>
> MAYOR: Snooping around town, making trouble—that's all you're good for. Windbags, rumor mongers, twittering magpies!
>
> JUDGE: Bunglers!
>
> SUPERINTENDENT OF SCHOOLS: Dunces!
>
> DIRECTOR OF CHARITIES: Potbellied runts! (V, viii.)

The action between the flash and the crash concludes in an image of social dissolution. The society of the play has pursued an illusion, and in the end its fabric is rent. The message of the gendarme, in Gogol's stage directions, "strikes like a thunderbolt." The frenzied whirlwind stops, and all freeze in terror in the dumb scene. The intervention of the central government to set straight a world out of joint provided a standard resolution of comedy before Gogol, but Gogol's inspector is much different from his predecessors. He has no presence in the life of the play. There are no Starodums to speak for him or Pravdins [in Fonvizin's *The Minor*] to act on his behalf. He never appears on stage, and is not even given a name. Though dispatched by the emperor, he is heralded in an (untranslatable) official formula that avoids mention of the word emperor or tsar. More than government or tsar, he represents a generalized and abstract Nemesis finally overtaking a society that has been trivialized into nothingness, its members shown as deceptive masks pursuing illusory goals. It is a society without the cement of affection, kindness, or loyalty. Gogol's apocalypse—his vision of disaster—is not directed toward some external agency. His world is doomed by its own fragmented and insubstantial nature.

"Doom," "apocalypse" are strong words, and we may ask whether comedy can bear their weight. A classic definition of comedy reads as follows: "As for Comedy, it is . . . an imitation of men worse than the average: worse, however, not as regards any and every sort of fault, but only as regards one particular kind, the Ridiculous, which is a species of the Ugly. The Ridiculous may be defined as a mistake or deformity not productive of pain or harm to others" [Aristotle, *Poetics*]. The genius of Aristotle's definition is that it is purely formal: it refrains from prescribing a subject for comedy, so that anything may be comical—hypocrisy, pretension, death, slipping on a banana peel, the apocalypse.

The key phrase is "not productive of pain or harm to others." Comic actions cannot have serious consequences for the observer. The potential for seriousness must be present—the agents make "mistakes" or possess "deformities" of character that may lead to disasters like those of tragedy. We are concerned for their fate, but at some point in the course of the action the grounds of our concern are removed. Pity and terror and other painful emotions are as much part of comedy as of tragedy; in comedy, however, they are provoked only to be shown as baseless. The agent must resemble us in some ways—otherwise he would be monstrous not ridiculous. Nevertheless, his error or deformity is so gross as to make him worse than we are. The pity of tragedy is for undeserved misfortune; its terror, for the fate of one like ourselves. In comedy misfortune is shown as deserved; the terror we feel as unwarranted, even if only in retrospect, because the agent is too unlike ourselves. The pity and terror of tragedy are lived through until they resolve in purgation; pity and terror in comedy, since they are shown to be baseless, resolve in a "relaxation of concern." Unburdened of pity and dread, we laugh. To cite a popular example: Sancho Panza hangs over the edge of a shallow ditch mistaking it for a precipice. In order to laugh we cannot be indifferent to Sancho's fate, for the indifferent do not react in any way. We must have the capacity for a sympathetic apprehension of his terror, and, in addition, the normative knowledge that precipices are indeed dangerous. Perceiving his error, we are released from our anxiety and are free to laugh. The more Sancho writhes in pain, the funnier it gets.

What then is the status of a comic apocalypse? At the end of *The Government Inspector* the world collapses before our eyes and we smile: "What are you laughing at? Laugh at yourselves!" the mayor cries out at us even as everything goes to pieces. The terrors of ultimate disaster remain real for the characters. Their terror is communicated to us, but as the grounds of our concern are removed it dissolves into laughter. The double vision characteristic of comedy comes into play: we witness the heralding of the arrival of the true inspector who, in Gogol's description, is "to destroy them all, obliterate them completely, wipe them from the face of the earth," while we are simultaneously made aware that their catastrophe is as trivial as their lives. What after all has actually happened? A bumbling and foolish mayor has lost his chance to become a bumbling and foolish general; a vain and featherbrained coquette will not realize her ambition to move to the capital; a crowd of corrupt officials may finally receive the punishment they so richly deserve. Both the terror and the laughter are extreme. Like much great comedy *The Government Inspector* veers perilously close to the opposite of comedy, achieving a complexity denied to lesser and more timid talents. It is no great achievement to take us to the edge of the abyss and make us laugh. Gogol's comic genius pushes to a point where comic triviality threatens to shade into a void of meaninglessness, which is a prelude to apocalyptic terror. But his apocalypse also loses substance before the force of his comedy. His characters are ultimately too ridiculous for us to take even their disaster seriously. To borrow Kant's famous formula for explaining laughter [in his *Critique of Judgment*], our terror is "a strained expectation" reduced suddenly to "nothing."

We do not, however, laugh at nothing. "Nothing" and "Nothingness" are valid metaphors for what we experience, but there must be objective facts to compel our reactions. We laugh at something, at distinctively human "mistakes" and "deformities": vanity, arrogance, misplaced ambition, self-serving rationalizations, plain silliness. Comedy is necessarily rooted in the vagaries of actual human life. Without the presence of the recognizably human there would be no concern, and hence no cause for laughter. Remorselessly Gogol has reduced his characters to absurdity, and yet they survive his onslaught to convey a mirror image, however crooked, of the human condition. As such his apocalypse takes on the aspect of an admonition. It was Bergson who pointed out [in his *Creative Evolution*] that the human mind cannot conceive of "Nothing," that it will always see something, even if only a black spot. In moral life "negation aims at someone. . . . It is of a pedagogical and social nature. It sets straight or rather warns. . . ." Thus the "nothings" of *The Government Inspector* are convertible into imperatives of "No" or "Don't." "Don't live like this," the play tells us; say "No" to illusory ambition, false vanity, envy and enmity, or else catastrophe will ensue. Though the 1846 *Dénouement . . .* pointed us to the apocalyptic character of the play, we must conclude that the 1836 *Leaving the Theater . . .* was closer to the mark after all, and comedy is incorrigibly social, "illuminating" the ways of the world, and implying positive values through its negative images. If comedy derives from human error and ugliness, we could never recognize these without a knowledge of the

true and the beautiful. We laugh at what is because we sense what ought to be, and it is of what ought to be that *The Government Inspector,* like all significant comedy, would remind us. The disaster may be final for the characters but it cannot be so for us, for that would be painful, not pleasurable, and laughter is a pleasant thing. Also Gogol tells us that in laughing we reach "reconciliation"—tolerance and forgiveness born of acceptance of our flawed human natures. (pp. 137-49)

> *Milton Ehre, "Laughing Through the Apocalypse: The Comic Structure of Gogol's 'Government Inspector',"* in The Russian Review, *Vol. 39, No. 2, April, 1980, pp. 137-49.*

FURTHER READING

AUTHOR COMMENTARY

Gogol, Nikolay. *The Theater of Nikolay Gogol: Plays and Selected Writings.* Edited by Milton Ehre, translated by Milton Ehre and Fruma Gottschalk. Chicago: University of Chicago Press, 1980, 205 p.

> Consists of translated editions of Gogol's texts *Marriage, The Government Inspector,* and *The Gambler,* as well as an appendix containing numerous personal letters and excerpts from *Leaving the Theater after the Performance of a New Comedy* and *The Dénouement of "The Government Inspector."* This volume also includes an introduction in which the editor discusses Gogol's career as a dramatist and the place of his works in the Russian theater.

OVERVIEWS AND GENERAL STUDIES

Erlich, Victor. *Gogol.* New Haven and London: Yale University Press, 1969, 230 p.

> A valuable general study of Gogol's life and works, designed to provide a complete survey for the English-speaking reader of Gogol.

Gippius, V. V. *Gogol.* Edited and translated by Robert A. Maguire. Ann Arbor: Ardis, 1981, 216 p.

> Regarded as the single most important biographical and critical work on Gogol in any language, this volume contains essays on numerous aspects of Gogol's writing.

Lavrin, Janko. *Nikolai Gogol (1809-1852): A Centenary Survey.* London: Sylvan Press, 1951, 174 p.

> An appreciation of Gogol on the hundredth anniversary of his death.

Magarshack, David. *Gogol: A Life.* London: Faber and Faber, 1957, 329 p.

> Biographical study emphasizing Gogol's artistic development. Magarshack includes lengthy quotations of Gogol and several reminiscences by Gogol's contemporaries.

Peace, Richard. "Theatre." In his *The Enigma of Gogol: An Examination of the Writings of N. V. Gogol and Their Place in the Russian Literary Tradition,* pp. 151-205. Cambridge, Mass.: Harvard University Press, 1981.

> Examines such topics as characters, themes, and comedy in *The Government Inspector* and *Marriage.*

Worral, Nick. *Nikolai Gogol and Ivan Turgenev.* New York: Grove Press, 1982, 207 p.

> An introductory comparison of the dramas of Gogol and Turgenev, with commentary on the plays of both authors and particular emphasis on *The Inspector General.* Worrall includes an extensive critical bibliography.

Zeldin, Jesse. *Nikolai Gogol's Quest for Beauty: An Exploration into His Works.* The Regents Press of Kansas, 1978, 244 p.

> Critical study in which Zeldin argues that "Gogol was primarily interested in the nature of reality, which he identified with beauty."

THE INSPECTOR GENERAL

Cole, Toby, and Chinoy, Helen Krich, eds. "Vsevolod Meyerhold (b. 1873): Rehearsals of *The Inspector-General.*" In *Directing the Play: A Source Book of Stagecraft,* pp. 259-72. Indianapolis: The Bobbs-Merrill Company, Inc., 1953.

> Reprints and combines transcripts of two rehearsals of Meyerhold's production of *The Inspector General* for the purpose of analyzing the director's improvisatory method and changes to Gogol's text. Meyerhold's presentation is often considered one of the most important theatrical productions of the play in the twentieth century.

Coleman, Arthur P. "Humorous Dialogue" and "Humorous Types." In his *Humor in the Russian Comedy from Catherine to Gogol,* pp. 50-8, pp. 59-88. 1925. Reprint. New York: AMS Press, 1966.

> Examines comic dialogue and characters in *The Inspector General,* relating the play to Russian comic traditions.

Fanger, Donald. "Confronting a Public, I." In his *The Creation of Nikolai Gogol,* pp. 125-42. Cambridge, Mass. and London: The Belknap Press of Harvard University Press, 1979.

> Surveys the development of *The Inspector General* and Gogol's reaction to public and critical responses to his play.

Gorelik, Mordecai. "The Tsar Laughed." In *Theatre and Drama in the Making,* Vol. 2, edited by John Gassner and Ralph G. Allen, pp. 743-52. Boston: Houghton-Mifflin Co., 1964.

> An eyewitness account of Vsevolod Meyerhold's production of *The Inspector General.*

Ivanov, Vyacheslav. "Gogol's *Inspector General* and the Comedy of Aristophanes." In *Gogol from the Twentieth Century: Eleven Essays,* edited and translated by Robert A. Maguire, pp. 199-214. Princeton, N.J.: Princeton University Press, 1974.

> Explores the influence of Aristophanes upon Gogol's play.

Kott, Jan. "The Eating of *The Government Inspector,*" translated by Joanna Clark. *Theatre Quarterly* V, No. 17 (1975): 21-9.

> Examines the obsession with food in *The Inspector General* and considers it a prototypical element of "tragic farce," a dramatic genre in which absurdity, reality, comedy, and nightmare are freely intermingled.

Perry, Henry Ten Eyck. "Crosscurrents in Russia: Gogol, Turgenev, and Chekhov." In his *Masters of Dramatic Comedy and Their Social Themes,* pp. 314-58. Cambridge, Mass.: Harvard University Press, 1939.

> General assessment of *The Inspector General,* focusing on characterization and the dramatic function of various figures in the play.

Symons, James M. "Meyerhold's 'Song for Songs.' " In his *Meyerhold's Theatre of the Grotesque: The Post-Revolutionary Productions, 1920-1932,* pp. 149-73. Coral Gables, Fla.: University of Miami Press, 1971.

> Historical overview in which Symons uses Vsevolod Myerhold's production as an example in addressing the problems involved in staging *The Inspector General.*

Worral, Nick. "Meyerhold Directs Gogol's *Government Inspector.*" *Theatre Quarterly* II, No. 7 (July-September 1972): 75-95.

> Attempts to reconstruct from firsthand sources Vsevolod Meyerhold's production of *The Inspector General.*

THE GAMBLERS

Ehre, Milton. "Gogol's *Gamblers:* Idea and Form." *Slavic and East European Journal* 25, No. 1 (Spring 1981): 13-20.

> Analysis of one of Gogol's most critically-neglected plays. According to Ehre, *The Gamblers* "shows Gogol edging toward a new theatrical style, more realistic than his habitual manner."

Lillian Hellman

1905?-1984

(Full name: Lillian Florence Hellman)

One of the most successful and respected American playwrights of the 1930s and 1940s, Hellman is best known as the author of *The Children's Hour* and *The Little Foxes.* She was also a screenwriter, memoirist, short story writer, director, critic, and editor.

Often set in her native South, Hellman's plays explore the human capacity for malice, the allure of power and money, and the conflict between the needs of the individual and the constraints of society. Emerging from the spirit of the consciousness-raising theater projects supported by the government in the 1930s, Hellman earned a reputation as an outspoken writer whose primary concerns were moral and whose works dramatically embody her insight into the socio-economic causes behind the behavior of her characters. Although she has been criticized for melodramatic elements in her plots, she is also favorably compared to Tennessee Williams for her powerful evocation of immorality in the Southern milieu.

Born in New Orleans, Hellman was the only child of a Jewish shoe manufacturer and a Manhattan socialite. She attended New York University and Columbia University, but dropped out after her junior year. Hellman then became a manuscript reader for a publishing house in New York and married publicist and playwright Arthur Kober in 1925. The couple soon moved to Paris where Kober assumed the editorship of the newly founded *Paris Comet,* while Hellman wrote short stories and traveled throughout Europe. Upon their return to the United States in 1929, Hellman accepted a position as a scenario reader in Los Angeles, where she met famed detective novelist Dashiell Hammett. Hammett became Hellman's closest friend and most helpful critic over the next thirty years.

After separating from her husband in 1932, Hellman returned to New York and began writing dramas. Her first attempt, a collaboration with Louis Kronenberger, was never produced. However, her second drama, *The Children's Hour,* was staged in an extremely successful production in 1934, bringing immediate acclaim to the young author. Throughout the next three decades, Hellman continued to write original dramas and screenplays and occasionally adapted the works of others for the stage. In addition to arousing controversy with the explicit social criticism of her work, Hellman was frequently involved in highly controversial political causes. During the 1930s, she raised money for the Spanish loyalists fighting the dictatorship of Generalissimo Francisco Franco. Hellman also visited Russia and other Communist countries and continued to support Soviet premier Joseph Stalin after most American intellectuals and political writers had repudiated his regime.

In 1947, Hellman wrote a scathing editorial published in

the Screen Writers Guild magazine in response to the House Un-American Activities Committee (HUAC) hearings held in Hollywood. Although she was never formally accused of being a Communist, she discovered in 1948 that she had been included on the Committee's blacklist. In 1952, Hellman was served with a subpoena to appear before HUAC and responded with a letter to the Committee indicating that she would testify but would answer only questions relating to her own political activities. Commenting acidly on those former radicals who had chosen to assist the committee's investigations, she stated: "I cannot and will not cut my conscience to fit this year's fashions." During the last twenty years of her life, Hellman devoted her energies to chronicling her political and literary activities in a series of memoirs.

Often considered Hellman's best play, *The Children's Hour* is based on an actual British court case in which two headmistresses of a Scottish girls academy were falsely accused by a student of homosexual activity. Set at a private boarding school, *The Children's Hour* concerns a spoiled and meanspirited girl who seeks retribution for what she feels is unfair treatment by accusing two of her teachers of engaging in a lesbian affair. The girl convinces her grandmother, the school's benefactor, of the existence of this relationship, and the woman in turn influences parents to withdraw their children from the school. Although the charges are eventually proven false, the teachers' lives are ruined by the very suspicion of lesbianism. *The Children's Hour* was a resounding critical and commercial success and was nominated for a Pulitzer Prize. However, several reviewers criticized the second half of the last act as heavy-handed. This scene, in which the grandmother, upon discovering her granddaughter's lie, returns to the school to offer reparation to the teachers just moments after one of them has committed suicide, is one example of Hellman's tendency toward what commentators have labelled melodrama. Nevertheless, many congratulate Hellman's forthright portrayal of intolerance and commend the play as a treatise on mercy and a warning against hasty judgment.

In Hellman's second play, *Days to Come,* she unsuccessfully attempted to incorporate themes regarding the evolving character of labor unions and the conflicts between members of a family. It is generally agreed that the play lacked focus and depth of characterization. *The Little Foxes,* considered one of Hellman's best plays, incorporates these themes more successfully. Ethical business practices and treatment of employees form the subtext in this portrait of the burgeoning industrial South symbolized by the Hubbard family. Set in a small Southern town in 1900, *The Little Foxes* depicts greed and sibling rivalry among members of the affluent Hubbard family who seek to expand their wealth by exploiting the cheap, formerly slave, labor force available in their community. The business venture turns into a catastrophic conflict between Ben Hubbard, his brother Oscar, and their sister Regina, as their quest for power and money results in double-dealings, theft, blackmail, and an act that is tantamount to murder. *The Little Foxes* received widespread acclaim for its strong characterizations, tightly woven plot, and spirited dialogue.

Hellman's next play, *Watch on the Rhine,* for which she won her first New York Drama Critics Circle Award, centers upon a man involved in anti-Nazi activities before the outbreak of World War II. The play asserts the necessity of struggle against both evil and the passivity of bystanders. Similarly, in *The Searching Wind,* Hellman advocates anti-fascist activity in an examination of well-meaning, affluent Americans who fail to use their money and influence to halt the progress of Benito Mussolini and Adolf Hitler. However, many critics contend that this play's multiple scenes and numerous major characters diverted audiences from Hellman's thematic intentions.

In *Another Part of the Forest,* Hellman returns to the Hubbard family twenty years prior to the action of *The Little Foxes* in order to trace the origins of their obsession with money and power. This play centers on the family patriarch, Marcus Hubbard, a self-made man who became rich during the Civil War by charging outrageous sums for necessities. The younger son, Ben, blackmails Marcus into naming him the heir of the family business, when he discovers his father's indirect involvement in the deaths of twenty-seven Confederate soldiers. While not as successful as *The Little Foxes,* Hellman garnered praise for her insights into the sources of human behavior. Particular interest has been shown in the character of Regina, whose purely evil nature is often compared to that of Iago in Shakespeare's *Othello.*

Hellman's last two original dramas, *The Autumn Garden* and *Toys in the Attic,* examine personal relationships. *The Autumn Garden* concerns a group of middle-aged individuals vacationing on the Gulf of Mexico who discover the ramifications of the decisions and compromises they have made. Considered an unusually introspective work in Hellman's canon, this play received positive reviews and drew comparisons to the works of Anton Chekhov for its emphasis on characterization and dialogue. *Toys in the Attic* is a Southern Gothic piece revolving around the obsessive and destructive relationship between spinster sisters and their younger brother, whose sudden wealth and marriage threaten their domination of him. *Toys in the Attic* won the New York Drama Critics Circle Award for best play.

Hellman's dramatic adaptations include *Montserrat,* based on a work by Emmanuel Robles; *The Lark,* based on Jean Anouilh's drama *L'alouette;* and *My Mother, My Father, and Me,* an adaptation of Burt Blechman's novel *How Much?* Hellman also wrote screenplays for the films *Dark Angel,* with Mordaunt Shairp; *Dead End,* adapted from Sidney Kingsley's play of the same title; *The North Star;* and *The Chase.* She adapted several of her own plays for film, including the first cinematic version of *The Children's Hour* (entitled *These Three*), *The Little Foxes,* and *The Searching Wind.* Her three volumes of memoirs, *An Unfinished Woman, Pentimento: A Book of Portraits,* and *Scoundrel Time,* detail her political activities, her renowned relationship with Hammett, her knowledge of several of the most famous writers of her day, and her own career as a dramatist. The praise she originally garnered for these volumes was eventually clouded by the suspicion that Hellman had fictionalized some of the events of her life. Nevertheless, many commend Hellman's memoirs as an illuminating, if somewhat fanciful, account of her carefully reasoned literary and political aims.

(For further information on Hellman's life and works, see *Contemporary Literary Criticism,* Vols. 2, 4, 8, 14, 18, 34, 44, 52; *Contemporary Authors,* Vols. 13-16, rev. ed., Vol. 112 [obituary]; *Dictionary of Literary Biography,* Vol. 7; and *Dictionary of Literary Biography Yearbook: 1984.*)

PRINCIPAL WORKS

PLAYS

The Children's Hour   1934
Days to Come   1936
The Little Foxes   1939
Watch on the Rhine   1941
The Searching Wind   1944

Another Part of the Forest   1946
The Autumn Garden   1951
Toys in the Attic   1960

OTHER MAJOR WORKS

An Unfinished Woman   (memoirs)   1969
Pentimento: A Book of Portraits   (memoirs)   1973
Scoundrel Time   (memoirs)   1976
Maybe   (memoirs)   1980

———————

AUTHOR COMMENTARY

Introduction to *Four Plays*   (1942)

[*In the following essay, Hellman evaluates her early
works upon their publication in the 1942 edition of* Four
Plays.]

Last night I finished reading the proofs of these four plays
[*The Children's Hour, Days to Come, The Little Foxes,*
and *Watch on the Rhine*]. I had never read them before,
nor, beyond the rehearsal period, have I ever seen them
played through. I had, of course, read parts of the plays—
always the parts I liked, and I have seen parts of the plays
once they had opened—always the parts I liked. There is
a blessed door that leads from the orchestra out to the
lobby. With practice you close it without a creak and what
you don't like is behind you. Reading the proofs last night,
carefully, slowly, thinking I was reading for the errors of
the printer, I soon forgot the printer and was reading for
myself.

Long ago I made a rule not to return to finished work:
communion with what was ended seemed to me unhealthy. If you returned too often to what you had already
done, I thought, you would come to like it and yourself
too well, or dislike it and yourself too much. The work of
the years before, or last year, or last month, was as far
away as childhood, and your chance was ahead and not
behind. Stirring the pole of memory in depths long buried,
Henry James said it could be. My extreme dislike of that
pole ended in a kind of pseudo-forgetfulness. I cannot remember: I cannot forget: I have always to be reminded
that I had problems in writing the plays. I have to be told
the first three drafts of *The Children's Hour* had a third
set and three or four more people; *Days to Come* once had
a scene in the town's main street; in *The Little Foxes*
Addie had a daughter and Horace another disease; *Watch
on the Rhine* started out in Ohio. I have always to be told
writing was hard work, and will be again.

Last night, finishing the proofs, I began to examine this
state of forgetfulness with less amusement. There must be
many reasons for it, but one came clear and simple: I have
never before *really* wished to see, to examine, to evaluate
myself. It is true that I, more than many writers, pay polite
lip-service to criticism, to my own and to that of the few
people for whose judgment I would give a penny. I have

thought I was a cold audience for myself only because I
was somewhat less warm than some other writers were
about themselves. But comparative coldness is not necessarily cold at all. Last night, however, I think I saw most
of what was wrong in the plays and—although I do not
like these words, I will not apologize for them—most of
what was right.

I started reading the proofs, as I started writing these
plays, with *The Children's Hour.* It took a year and a half
of stumbling stubbornness to do the play. I remembered,
in the hodge-podge that came back last night, how many
times I tore it up, how many characters I took out and put
back and took out again; how I reached back into my own
childhood and found the day *I* finished *Mlle. de Maupin;*
the day *I* faked a heart attack; the day *I* saw an arm get
twisted. And I thought again of the world of the half-
remembered, the half-observed, the half-understood
which you need so much as you begin to write. It is always
there for you. God help you to use it right. Right? Right
for what? Right to have something to say and to say it
well.

There are, of course, many things wrong with *The Children's Hour.* (Even with my new clarity I have not seen
them all, which is just as well, and better for my health.)
The play probably should have ended with Martha's suicide: the last scene is tense and over-burdened. I knew this
at the time, but I could not help myself. I am a moral writer, often too moral a writer, and I cannot avoid, it seems,
that last summing-up. I think that is only a mistake when
it fails to achieve its purpose, and I would rather make the
attempt, and fail, than fail to make the attempt.

The theme of *The Children's Hour* was good and evil.
The theme of *Days to Come* is good and evil: evil, this time,
in the hands of people who don't understand it. *Days to
Come* was a failure. It got bad reviews in the press, played
six performances, and closed. Reading it now, I have no
apologies for it. I spoiled a good play. I returned to the amateur's mistake: everything you think and feel must be
written *this* time, because you may never have another
chance to write it. I knew a woman like Cora and I hated
her, and *that* hate had to go in the play; I knew a woman
like Julie, I pitied her, and *that* pity had to go in the play;
I had been raised with the Ellicotts of the world, and what
I felt about them had to go in the play, too; I knew Leo
Whalen and I wanted to say how much I respected men
who work for other men. I wanted to say too much. And
I began thinking of new ways to say it. People in life, I told
myself, don't always make the direct answer, or follow the
immediately preceding thought. (That is why, in the play,
people answer, or understand, much later than the question or answer is offered them.) If you had lived in another
place, or been richer or been poorer, or worked harder or
worked less, or read a different book, perhaps you might
have been. . . . And so I gave the leading characters their
counterparts: Leo Whalen is the good Wilkie; Firth the
simple Andrew Rodman; Cora the sick Hannah. I played
this theme all alone: a solitary composer with a not very
interesting quarter note. The subtleties of failures are seldom discovered, and that is just as well.

But with all that is wrong, all the confusion, the jumble,

the attempt to do too much, I stand on the side of *Days to Come.* I am only sorry that the confusion in the script confused the best director in the theatre, who, in turn, managed to confuse one of its most inadequate casts. (There were exceptions, of course.) On the opening night actors moved as figures in the dream of a frightened child. The death-dance of collapse was slow and unreal. It was my fault, I suppose, that it happened. I do not believe actors break plays, or make them, either. And nothing would have affected the play if I had done what the writer must do: kick and fight his way through until the whole is good, and the audience will not stop to worry about the parts. If he cannot do that, he has failed. In that sense, *Days to Come* failed, and only in that sense does its failure matter to me now.

It was with *Days to Come,* or perhaps it was with *The Little Foxes*—this forgetting has its cheery side—that I began to examine the two descriptions that some critics have found so handy for me: the plays are too well-made, the plays are melodramas. By the well-made play, I think is meant the play whose effects are contrived, whose threads are knit tighter than the threads in life and so do not convince.

Obviously, I can have no argument with those whom my plays do not convince. Something does not convince you. Very well, and that is all. But if they convince you, or partly convince you, then the dislike of their being well-made makes little sense. The theatre has limitations: it is a tight, unbending, unfluid, meager form in which to write. And for these reasons, compared to the novel, it is a second-rate form. (I speak of the form, not the content.) Let us admit that. Having admitted it—a step forward, since most of us are anxious to claim the medium by which we earn a living is a fine and fancy thing—we can stop the pretentious lie that the stage is unhampered. What the author has to say is unhampered: his means of saying it are not. He may do without scenery, he may use actors not as people but as animals or clouds, and he still must *pretend* the empty stage is a garden or an arena, and he still must *pretend* that living people are animals. He has three walls of a theatre and he has begun his pretense with the always rather comic notion that the audience is the fourth wall. He must pretend and he must represent. And if there is something vaguely awry, for me, about the pretense of representation—since by the nature of the stage it can never be done away with—it is not that I wish to deny to other writers their variations of the form, but that, for me, the realistic form has interested me most.

Within this form there must be tricks—the theatre is a trick—and they are, I think, only bad when they are used trickily and stop you short. But if they are there, simple, and come to hand, they are justified. In the last act of *Watch on the Rhine,* Kurt Müller is about to leave. He wants to say good-bye to his children who are upstairs. He asks his wife to bring them down. Now it is most probable that in real life a man would go upstairs, find the children in their room, say good-bye there. But it seemed to me, when this problem came up, that kind of un-well-madeness was not worth the candle. It seemed messy to ring in another set, to bring down the curtain, to interfere

with a mood and a temper. The playwright, unlike the novelist, must—and here is where I think the charge of well-madeness should be made—trick up the scene. This is how he has to work. It is too bad, but it is not his fault. If he is good, and drives ahead, it will not matter much. If he is not good, the situation will worry him, and he will begin to pretend it doesn't exist and, by so pretending, fret and lengthen it.

I think the word melodrama, in our time, has come to be used in an almost illiterate manner. By definition it is a violent dramatic piece, with a happy ending. But I think we can add that it uses its violence for no purpose, to point no moral, to say nothing, in say-nothing's worse sense. (This, of course, does not mean, even by inference, that violence plus the *desire* to say something will raise the level of the work. A great many bad writers want to say something: their intention may make them fine men, but it does not make them fine writers. Winning the girl, getting the job, vanquishing the slight foe, are not enough.) But when violence is actually the needed stuff of the work and comes toward a large enough end, it has been and always will be in the good writer's field. George Moore said there was so much in *War and Peace* that Tolstoi must surely have awakened in the night frightened that he had left out a yacht race or a High Mass. There is a needed return to the correct use of the word melodrama. It is only then the critic will be able to find out whether a writer justifies his use of violence, and to scale him against those who have used it.

I do not want to talk here of *Watch on the Rhine.* Only eleven months have gone by since it was finished, and that is not time enough for me to see it clearly. Even now, of course, I know many ideas should have come clearer, many speaches cleaner; many things should have been said with more depth and understanding. I have not wanted to write here any final word on the plays. Some day, perhaps. Some day when I have greater faith that I will be the writer I now, on January 14, 1942, want to be. In any case, while there is much in all the plays that is wrong—and it did not hurt me to see it last night, as it once would have hurt me to half-see it—this much has been right: I tried. I did the best I could do at the time each play was written. Within the limitations of my own mind and nature, my own understanding, my own knowledge, it was the best I could do with what I had. If I did not hope to grow, I would not hope to live. (pp. vii-xii)

Lillian Hellman, in an introduction to her
Four Plays, *Random House, 1942, pp. vii-xiv.*

OVERVIEWS AND GENERAL STUDIES

Barrett H. Clark   (essay date 1944)

[*Clark was a Canadian-born American drama critic who, in his various editorial and advisory capacities, was particularly interested in gaining recognition for the work of young, unknown playwrights and in retrieving forgotten plays from earlier periods, as in his twenty-volume anthology,* America's Lost Plays *(1940-41). In the following excerpt, Clark examines Hellman's first five plays as exemplary works of the moral "propaganda" of the 1930s.*]

The five plays of Lillian Hellman cover exactly one decade in the annals of our contemporary American drama, a period of extraordinary interest and great activity. The first fourteen years of that epoch which opened in the late winter of 1920 with the first full-length drama of Eugene O'Neill saw the establishment of a body of dramatic native work which justified the claim of American critics that the theater had at last come into its own both as an art and as a medium of expression for adult writers. The work of the first decade was less concerned with the intellectual problems of the day than the second, and the playwrights seemed more eager to explore the possibilities of the dramatic medium than to challenge the political status quo. During the early 1930's a number of writers, stimulated to a great extent by the so-called "radical" playwrights of Germany and by a desire to spread the gospel of communism as understood in Soviet Russia, formed groups dedicated to the formula that the drama, whatever else it may be, should, above all, proclaim the brotherhood of man and, by exhibiting the evils of capitalism, hasten the overthrow of our present bourgeois social order. The play of "social significance" was one of the outstanding phenomena of the 1930-40 period. It is not to be wondered at that most of these plays should be mechanical in structure, naïve, and unconvincing, since nearly all of them were inspired rather by their authors' desire to protest against injustice or to plead for some new type of utopia than by an impulse to set forth in terms of beauty or truth some basic concept of human value, without argument and with no concern over its political effect.

To understand one important aspect of the work of Lillian Hellman, it should be pointed out that, while she was never associated with any theater group that discussed, wrote, or produced radical propaganda plays, all but one of her works belong in the camp of the earnest thinkers—the propagandists. To say this without qualification, however, is to miss the point. Though she never wrote a play merely to entertain an audience, to win fame, or to make money, she never wrote a line without trying to say something that would help man to escape or offset the effects of ignorance and wrong thinking. In a word, she is an idealist and a philosopher. But, if that were all, she would hardly be worth talking about: she is also an artist, a playwright whose "message" is invariably, though not always skilfully, integrated into works which hold us by those qualities of truth without which all the good ideas in the mind of man are of no avail.

The first of her plays to be seen in the theater was *The Children's Hour.* Produced and directed by Herman Shumlin (she never had any other producer or director) in November, 1934, this somber drama had a long and successful run. The theme, as the author tells us, is "good and evil." Rather, I believe, evil alone. The evil here, as in the character of Iago, is a kind of unattached and almost meaningless power. It is like a phenomenon of nature, which cannot be eradicated, hardly perhaps even

dealt with. It differs from all the other evils Miss Hellman has so skilfully and meaningfully set forth in her later plays. For instance, in *The Little Foxes* and *Watch on the Rhine,* the forces set in opposition, the good against the evil, are pretty evenly matched, since in each case the evil is shown not only to be rooted in what is understood but to be something about which it is humanly possible to take a definite stand. The child Mary in *The Children's Hour* precipitates a tragedy out of her own malice, yet she is scarcely responsible; she is almost a monster, and, as such, the drama that follows is in a way accidental. True, a part of the responsibility lies with Mrs. Tilford, the child's grandmother, but her responsibility is only indirect and, to that extent, attenuated and weak.

A study in evil, yes, and an amazingly tense and artfully constructed drama, yet weakened because the emotions it precipitates remain partly sterile. What can be done about it all? An almost incredible child invents a tale that the two women who own and operate her school are homosexuals; the story is believed, and the school is put out of business. The child's grandmother accepts the story, and so (evidently) does the fiancé of one of the women. The other then admits that she has always been sexually attracted to her companion, and kills herself. At the very last the grandmother comes to make amends to the woman she has wronged having, in the meantime, learned the whole truth.

Turn now to the revealing Introduction which Miss Hellman wrote in 1942 to the Random House edition of her *Four Plays* [see Author Commentary]. She admits that the play "probably should have ended with Martha's suicide: the last scene is tense and over-burdened." She cannot avoid, she adds, "that last summing up." But if this summing-up had been omitted, most of the irony of the play would have been lost. It might have been better if what is now the summing-up had been made an integral part of the play, but it was not. The author shows simply that there is an irony in things as they happen and *The Children's Hour* is ironic only in the sense that here is evil, and make the best of it. True, she seeks to intensify the human element by causing Karen to say to Mrs. Tilford, "You want to be a 'good' woman again, don't you?"

I believe, though I have no means of knowing, that Miss Hellman's admission about the last scene was perhaps intended to apply not so much to the play under discussion as to all her other plays.

It is a little puzzling that *The Children's Hour,* so effective as pure drama, but so remotely concerned with any issue likely to appeal to anyone so deeply concerned with man and his destiny, should have preceded the other four plays, every one of which is inescapably "moral" in all its implications. Miss Hellman says that she is "a moral writer, often too moral a writer." Which is another way of saying that she writes her plays in order to demonstrate what is wrong with life and how a better way of life may be found and won.

Days To Come, the next of her plays to be produced (1936), was her only failure. It ran for just six performances. "I spoiled a good play," she writes. "I returned to the amateur's mistake: everything you think and feel must be written this time, because you may never have another chance to write it." The whole passage is extremely interesting but too long to quote here. Yet one more sentence must be noted: "I knew a woman like Cora and I hated her, and *that* hate had to go into the play." A reading of all the Hellman plays will show how the author's particularized hatred of this or that individual, this or that fact or idea as exemplified in *The Children's Hour* and *Days To Come,* is in the last three plays, with one or two minor exceptions, attenuated, merged into what closely resembles pity or a remote kind of contempt; "reserved compassion" is perhaps the best phrase. The simple fact of hatred, as it first develops in a writer, may not prevent that writer from seeing his subject whole, but it usually does. Doubtless Miss Hellman learned that to vent her hatred upon anyone or anything tended at the same time to weaken her power to persuade and convince. Notice, for example, how the "villain" Teck, in *Watch on the Rhine,* stands forth a completely rounded characterization, and how Kurt, instead of being opposed by a conventionally wicked man who can be summarily killed and therefore eliminated from the picture, is seen by the audience as pursued by an idea and a philosophy which cannot be so conveniently disposed of.

Days To Come shows a family of more or less well-intentioned Americans confronted by the problem of dealing with organized labor when their employees undertake a strike. Here is no case of labor-baiters versus "good" men—the matter is not so simple. The pattern used is one that the writer was to repeat with variations in each of her next three plays, at least a part of the pattern: on the one hand, a person or a group oppressed by another person or group, the old idea of individualism and the new idea of cooperation for the purpose of achieving justice and human dignity. Now, the playwright, being an observer and a philosopher as well as a special pleader, knows well that in the ranks of each of the opposing forces there are those who are neither villains nor heroes, and she has been at pains to show (particularly among her reactionaries) some man or woman who has been victimized by circumstances, and in some cases a young person not too old to have been corrupted; in a word, someone worth saving, like Alexandra in *The Little Foxes.* What gives *Days To Come* its point is chiefly the character of Julie, a member of the ruling class, who falls in love with Whalen, the labor organizer, the first of the few Hellman "heroes," one of the men who compels her respect, the men "who work for other men." The workers in this play lose the first round in their battle, strikebreakers having been called in; but in "days to come" the story will be different. For Julie it is too late. Her impulse to find a better way of life has been too long delayed. When Whalen tells her that he hates the poor but loves what they could be, Julie answers that she does not hate the poor but that she has no idea what they could be. Nothing can be expected from the man who brought in the strikebreakers, obviously; he is only a stupid, unimaginative, and well-intentioned bungler. As for Cora, she remains a lay figure, the symbol of all that was blind and cruel among the economic royalists who produced her.

I question the artistic validity and effectiveness of the love of Julie for Whalen and of the hesitant confession of the man's attraction toward her. The introduction of a love scene at the climax of the action, no matter what it is intended to do, blurs the outline of the story and obscures the theme. While such things are always happening in life and spoiling the pattern which tidy-minded artists must weave to make themselves articulate, they are too likely to lead us into bypaths, away from the main issue. It was perhaps for this reason and also because of Miss Hellman's desire to find "new ways to say" what she had to say that she felt impelled to pull together the threads of her arguments in the last scene, just as she had done in the earlier play.

There are traces in *Days To Come,* especially in the last act, of the mood that was to sound the note in the entire action of *The Little Foxes.* It is an easy progression into the first act of the latter play, which came to the stage in 1939 and enjoyed a long run. In most respects *The Little Foxes* is the most mature and satisfactory of its author's five plays. Here the artist is nearly always in command of the moralist, or shall we say that the moral backbone of the play is completely fused with the skeleton of the plot. The playwright has, as Henry James phrased it, buried her tools after making good use of them. Details of planting and preparation seem more casual, the direction of the plot is never too obvious, and the dialogue is exactly right. It possesses a rhythmical quality which is never intrusive and a surface realistic quality that makes us forget it is the work of a conscious and determined and scrupulous writer.

Here again, as in *Days To Come* (but note that the action takes place nearly half a century ago), we find a group of old-time royalists, selfish, corrupt, despicable, that join hands with a suave northern capitalist to sell their cotton at an immense profit by exploiting local labor at starvation wages. Oscar Hubbard, his brother Ben and their sister Regina, abetted by the contemptible Leo, Oscar's son, conspire together to put over a deal that will make them all wealthy. They are counting on Regina's husband, Horace, to furnish his share of the capital needed in order that they, the original conspirators, may keep control of the stock. Horace, ill at a distant hospital, is summoned home. He refuses to invest his money, preferring to have no further part in the work of corruption undertaken by his wife and her brothers. But Leo steals negotiable stocks belonging to Horace, and, when the latter learns this, he cleverly devises a plan whereby Regina is given power over the others, or will be given such power after his death. In a most effective scene she allows her husband to die, by refusing him medicine, and immediately demands and gets a lion's share of the stock. Such is the principal plot line. It is the amplifications and undertones, however, that together give the play its "spire of meaning." The "little foxes," the "spoilers of the vines," the corrupt enjoyers of privilege have not seen that "our vines have tender grapes." Regina's seventeen-year-old daughter Alexandra is old enough to understand something of the horror of her situation and young enough, if she escapes in time, to make something of her life. She may perhaps realize what Julie realized too late; and she will almost certainly never become a Cora.

In *The Little Foxes* is the figure of Birdie, who has married into the Hubbard family because of her social standing and her property, and is now a pathetic lost soul—one of the innumerable casualties that strew the path of the spoilers. She, and Horace, and the colored servant Addie, all help Alexandra to break the bonds that hold her, and at the last the child turns to her mother, and tells her she is leaving home. Regina for a moment possibly begins to realize what is happening. But we don't know. Regina asks Alexandra, "Would you like to sleep in my room tonight?" and the latter answers, "Are you afraid, Mama?" At this Regina says nothing, but "moves slowly out of sight," as Addie comes to Alexandra and "presses her arm."

Addie, who in a way speaks for the Negro, is carefully, sparsely, beautifully sketched. How easy it would have been to make her a mouthpiece for the oppressed and thereby have ruined the surface reality of the play and at the same time weakened the plea the dramatist wanted to make! Miss Hellman has learned that in the nice selection of observed phenomena, properly set forth in scenes that are part and parcel of the pattern, she can drive home her argument far more effectively than by stepping outside the framework and mounting the soapbox. Notice how the special pleading for which Addie was introduced is resolved into a simple, almost casual, line of dialogue. When Horace tells her that he is going to leave her something when he dies, Addie answers, *laughing* (that is the stage direction), "Don't you do that, Mr. Horace. A nigger woman in a white man's will! I'd never get it no-how."

Watch on the Rhine, first produced in 1941, was probably even more popular than *The Little Foxes.* It is by all odds the most human of all the Hellman plays, the warmest and in some ways the most understanding. For one thing it has a full-length hero, again a man who "works for other men." He is articulate in a wholly winning manner, and he goes out of his way to stress his unimportance; besides, the enemy is not capitalism, or the privileged members of society, but fascism at its melodramatic worst. Kurt, the little German who gives up his work, his wife and children, and is ready to give up his life in order to crush what threatens all we believe in, could scarcely have been anything but sympathetic.

And again I call attention to the "villain" Teck, the Romanian aristocrat who blackmails his hosts into buying him off when he discovers who Kurt is and what he is trying to do. Teck is no lay figure; he does not even represent fascism: he is no more than a pitiful little rat, himself a victim. But the author wastes no hatred upon him; she even goes out of her way to make him understandable, and she likewise endows him with some remnants of human decency. In a word, she has learned that to symbolize a situation it is not necessary to assume the manner or dramatize the gestures of contempt. The fact speaks for itself when the fact is wholly and understandingly embodied in speech and action.

Certain critics have accused the author of this play and of *The Little Foxes* of being melodramatic. It is true that in both plays there are scenes which, if stripped of their significance, would indeed be pure melodrama. Take the scene in which Kurt kills Teck or, in the earlier play, that in which Regina allows her husband to die while she stands watching him. Pure melodrama, both scenes, in the hands of a writer who conceived them in vacuo, for their own sakes alone; but melodrama is melodramatic not because it is violent or striking but because it uses violence for violence' sake. Miss Hellman seems a little reluctant to use violence as she has consistently done, even apologetic, as though she were saying, "You see what happens in such situations? I didn't invent them; that's what I see." Kurt's words after he strangles Teck reflect, I feel, the playwright's own attitude.

Perhaps, I am not sure, Miss Hellman may have pondered the charge of melodrama when she came to shape the ideas and develop the characters of her latest play, *The Searching Wind.* Here, too, is violence, but a kind of violence only vaguely felt; not a necessary ingredient of that part of her story that was to be told on the stage. Among the elements that go to round out the background are some that we recognize from earlier plays, persons like Moses Taney, the wise old man who closely parallels the deceased but immanent figure of Joshua Farrelly in *Watch on the Rhine;* and Sam, the young generation who speaks for the author as Julie did in *Days To Come,* and the youngsters in *Watch on the Rhine.* The theme in *The Searching Wind* is neither so obvious nor so clearly stated as it was in *Watch on the Rhine,* because by its very nature it is hardly susceptible of perfect definition. When Moses finds himself in the midst of the *fait accompli* of Mussolini's capture of Rome, he says: "I knew most of this years ago. But I should have known before that, and I did. But I didn't know I did. All night long I've been trying to find out when I should have known." There is the heart of the problem Miss Hellman has sought to elucidate, if not to solve. Why have the men of good will and courage and intelligence allowed the destroyers of freedom and the dignity of man to get the upper hand, and how has it come about that little or nothing was attempted besides appeasement? How many of us knew what was happening, and what prevented our killing the evil before it took root and spread? An episodic play of the ordinary kind could do little but remind us of twenty years' newspaper headlines, and an episodic scene would have had to be added to point the moral. So the ever seeking playwright, not content with spinning a little fable and tacking an appendix onto it, conceived a dramatic structure which should combine a personal knot of conflicting wills with a roughly parallel knot showing how a world-wide situation was only an amplified personal drama on a large scale. Cassie, Emily, and Alex, all seeking to understand their relationships one to the other, are in the same sort of dilemma that the world faced twenty years ago and about which the enemies of fascism were unable to do anything effective until a world war resulted.

In order to resolve the personal problem, or rather to merge it into the world problem, the author has faced, and partly solved, technical difficulties far greater than she had ever before tried to handle. It would not do to stress the parallel too strongly, because, after all, the story is told in terms of surface realism, and anything like a *raisonneur* added to the story would destroy the needed illusion. We therefore watch her stalking her prey—her theme—precisely as certain minor characters, like the Negro servant and the French butler, seem to be looking for something they do not themselves understand. The underlying idea is so simple that Miss Hellman approaches it with some hesitancy, and, except for the one passage quoted, she does not return to it directly until the very end of the play. True, Emily is throughout striving to learn how Cassie feels and in what way Cassie's affair with her (Emily's) husband affects all three participants in the situation, and at one point stresses the need for getting things straight, but all she says is: "We've started it; let's finish it.. . . . It's time to find out." But the author, having established on a solid dramatic basis the *personal* drama—a drama in itself complete—resists the temptation to point out that what was wrong with individuals is precisely what is wrong with nations.

When the play is nearly ended, we are in the presence of a situation not unlike those in the concluding scenes of **Days To Come** and **The Little Foxes.** Here Sam, a little like Julie and a little like Alexandra, Sam the young soldier who is heir to the mistakes of his predecessors, cries out upon his parents and grandparents, that is, upon his elders who have caused him to fight in another war and to lose a leg in the process: "I don't want any more of my father's mistakes. . . . I am ashamed of you both, and that's the truth. I don't want to be ashamed that way again. I don't like losing my leg. . . . I'm scared—but everybody's welcome to it as long as it means a little something and helps to bring us out some place."

That **The Searching Wind** is neither so appealing nor so wholly satisfactory as **The Little Foxes** or **Watch on the Rhine,** that its means of achieving revelation are somewhat awkward, and that its implications are not entirely convincing—this is not very important: the play relies to a remarkable extent on the characterization and not on the story, on the dialogue and not on the plot; it needs no violence other than the violence precipitated by the impact of person on person, idea upon idea. Most notable, however, is the author's own attitude toward the problem she wants to set forth. She is no longer the special pleader for this or that type of reform, and she is evidently not ridden by the notion that all you have to do to win the Good Life is to eradicate the evil men and substitute the good. "I love this place," says Sam, and Sam speaks for the author, "and I don't want any more fancy fooling around with it." This place is, of course, our country, or perhaps all those countries in which our way of life is held to be the best.

Lillian Hellman has been writing plays for only a little over a decade; she has pretty well mastered the tools that every dramatist must use in order to gain the attention of the public; she is conscious of the limitations of the drama medium, and she has found out at moments how to make the best of them. She is still unwilling to use her talent except directly in the service of humanity. It is possible, I am convinced, for her to speak just as eloquently on behalf of the oppressed and the blind if she is willing to forget the immediate good to be won by this reform or that and to concentrate on the far more difficult and rewarding task of illuminating the world she knows *as she sees it,* through

the power of her imagination, without insisting too much on guiding and instructing it. It is questionable whether the preacher ever did anything as effectively as the poet. (pp. 127-33)

Barrett H. Clark, "Lillian Hellman," in College English, *Vol. 6, No. 3, December, 1944, pp. 127-33.*

Winifred L. Dusenbury   (essay date 1960)

[*Dusenbury is an American scholar and critic specializing in modern drama. She is the author of* The Theme of Loneliness in Modern American Drama *(1960),* Love as Death in "The Iceman Cometh" *(1967), and* E. G. and E. G. O.: Emma Goldman and "The Iceman Cometh" *(1974). The following excerpt discusses* The Little Foxes *and* Another Part of the Forest *as dramas of the South.*]

Several American dramatists have made valuable contributions to the modern theatre in plays portraying the isolating effects of the particular socioeconomic conditions of the South. Tennessee Williams, frequently an interpreter of the lonely Southern female who lives in romantic dreams of the past but is lost in the modern world, has

Dashiell Hammett and Lillian Hellman.

written two prize-winning plays on the theme: *The Glass Menagerie*, which won the Critics Circle Award for the season 1944-45; and *A Streetcar Named Desire*, which won both the Critics Circle Award and Pulitzer Prize for 1947-48. Although Lillian Hellman's theme in **The Little Foxes** (1939) and **Another Part of the Forest** (1946) is the rapaciousness of a family of rising Southerners, she contrasts them with the ruined aristocracy who now belong nowhere, but who play an important part in the dramas. Paul Green, in a number of plays, notable among which is *The House of Connelly* (1931), has portrayed the loneliness of decay into which the old Southern plantation owners have fallen. All three playwrights emphasize the changing social and economic structure as the basis for a kind of personal near-annihilation of those Southern aristocrats who cannot adapt themselves to changing conditions, and a sense of belonging to those who can.

Although no condemnation of the pre-Civil-War South is explicit in their plays, Williams, Hellman, and Green suggest that the wealthy plantation owners of the South had in them the germs of their own destruction before the Civil War with its aftereffects completed their downfall. Neuroticism or a destructive adherence to dreams and drink is displayed by those characters who do not enter into a healthy relationship with individuals adjusted to present-day society. The playwrights intimate, at least, that the way of life in the South contained elements deleterious to master and slave alike. "Man can adapt himself to slavery, but he reacts to it by lowering his intellectual and moral qualities," as Erich Fromm points out [in his *Man for Himself*]. In a slave-owning society, man treats himself as his own slave, and becomes his own strict taskmaster, so that instead of developing a unified personality at home in the world, he becomes an isolated and haunted character, obsessed by feelings of guilt. Consequently, George Jean Nathan's complaint [in his *Theatre Book of the Year 1948-1949*] that a character like Blanche from *A Streetcar Named Desire* becomes so "psychologically, pathologically, and logically muddled that she gives the effect of three totally different women housed in the same body," may not be justified; for although it is true that Williams attributes the beginning of her downfall to the loss of the family plantation, which loss does not seem to account for all her psychological aberrations, nevertheless, her neuroses may logically be contained in a woman of her social and hereditary background.

The deleterious influence of socioeconomic conditions on Southern characters in American drama, therefore, includes the material loss of the plantations and the depletion of the land, as well as the destruction by the carpetbaggers, after the Civil War itself had wrought much havoc; but it also includes, by inference at least, the moral isolation inherent in the society before its material downfall. In Lillian Hellman's two plays about the Hubbards, they, the up-and-coming money-makers of the South, although filled with physical stamina, suffer as great a moral void as do the real "folks," for inasmuch as they are members of the same social order, they have suffered from its defects. Although the theme of tragic loneliness is carried by Birdie, at the end it is the powerful Regina who pleadingly asks her daughter to sleep with her because of fear

of being alone. In *The Glass Menagerie*, only Tom escapes, and that by running away. In *A Streetcar Named Desire*, Stella adapts herself to a mode of living which might seem unacceptable, but one which removes her from the isolation of Blanche or Laura. In *The House of Connelly*, the remaining members of the family have deteriorated like the plantation. Only young Will is saved by marriage with the daughter of a family of soil-loving tenants. All these plays doubtless portray truthfully the terrifying loneliness of those clinging to a society of the South which has become so debilitated as to be almost nonexistent. (pp. 134-36)

In Lillian Hellman's two plays about the Hubbard family, the emphasis is upon the characters who in a material sense make a success of living, but who are as void of social or moral or spiritual values as a nest of vipers. Contrasted to them, as the DuBois family is to the Kowalskis [in Tennessee Williams's *A Streetcar Named Desire*], are those plantation owners who have been ruined materially by the war and its aftereffects, who are not reprehensible socially or morally, but who have not the stamina to compete in the world around them. Birdie has great similarity to both Laura and Blanche. Mistreated and unloved, she frequently drinks alone in her room as the only compensation for a life of otherwise unbearable isolation. The Hubbards, too, in battling each other for the family wealth, have lost all the affection which the ties of blood should give and the family as a whole is cut off from friendly contacts in the neighborhood.

Lillian Hellman wrote **Another Part of the Forest** in 1946, seven years after **The Little Foxes**, but the later play takes the Hubbard family back to the days of 1880, whereas the play written first begins the family history in 1900. Miss Hellman explains that, although she hated the Hubbards as much as anyone, she became annoyed at the display by the audience of moral superiority to them, and this, she says, "did make me feel that it was worth while to look into their family background and find out what it was that made them the nasty people they were" [in Burns Mantle, *The Best Plays of 1946-1947*]. In her second play she gives great emphasis to the social ostracizing of the Hubbards and their impulse to get ahead financially to compensate for their loneliness. The mother is driven out of her mind by the knowledge of her husband's treachery in aiding Union forces and turns to the Negroes and their church for comfort and understanding. She is loved by them and belongs to them. But the other members of the family compete for the favor of whoever has the upper hand and are mired in their hatred of each other and of the quality folks, who will not speak to them, as well as of the townspeople, who distrust them.

In **The Little Foxes** Regina, at forty, kills her husband and outwits her brothers to become the wealthiest of the Hubbards, but in the end loses the love of her daughter and stands frightened and alone as the final curtain falls. In **Another Part of the Forest**, Regina is portrayed as a girl who has learned at the age of twenty that the way to get along is coquettishly to flatter her father and to play her brothers off against each other. Since she loves John Bagtry, Birdie's cousin, she is anxious to have her father make the Bagtrys a loan to save their plantation, but she is also sincere in wanting to court their favor, for she says,

> I've been kind of lonely here with nobody nice having much to do with us. I'd sort of like to know people of my own age, a girl my own age, I mean— . . .
>
> [Act I]

When he questions her again, she still insists, "I been a little lonesome. No people my age ever coming here—I do think people like that sort of want to forgive you, and be nice to us." As Lillian Hellman probed into Regina's background, she found a lonely girlhood at least partly the cause of her later rapacity. Her lover, who feels he does not belong anywhere except with fighting men, leaves her, explaining her attachment to him with the words, "You're a lonely girl, and I'm the first man you've liked." When Ben contrives to send her lover away, she has nowhere to turn. No wonder the Regina of twenty years later knows only ruthlessness. She has suffered from a feeling of apartness since childhood days and has known nothing to make her appreciate the warmth of human affection.

So hardened has Regina become twenty years later that she says with sincerity of the northern industrialist, Mr. Marshall, "He seems a lonely man. Imagine being lonely with all that money." Lillian Hellman justifiably speaks of the Hubbards as "a nest of particularly vicious diamondback rattlesnakes." A comparison with the work of Franz Kafka, therefore, may be enlightening; for, in *Metamorphosis,* the story of a man's change into an insect, he interprets human psychology in terms of animal symbols. "Kafka's pathos is the pathos of loneliness and exclusion. . . . What it [*Metamorphosis*] represents objectively is the emotion of exclusion from the family and, beyond that, the estrangement of man from his human environment" [Philip Rahv, in the *Kenyon Review* I (1939)]. Although Regina has not the self-recognition of herself that the hero of *Metamorphosis* has, and so does not appear to herself as a despicable insect, it can be questioned whether in a sequel to *The Little Foxes* she might not have some self-revulsion, for there is a challenge in her young daughter's last words to her concerning "people who eat the earth," and certainly by this time she is suffering from a feeling of estrangement from everyone from whom she normally might expect affection.

Some critics have seen in *The Little Foxes* social implications beyond the story of the Hubbards. Richard Watts, Jr., says of the play [in *The Best Plays of 1938-1939*], "Through its thoughtful indignation it becomes a scornful and heartfelt parable of the rise of the industrial South in all its ruthlessness, its savage sense of realism and its fine scorn for the older trappings of Confederate romanticism." Although Lillian Hellman seems more interested in the devastating effects upon the people—both the old families and the wealthy new families—of socioeconomic changes, she does, nevertheless, indicate strongly the nature and importance of these changes. And assuredly she makes them the cause of the isolation of her characters. Miss Hellman's plays have special significance now that a second industrialization of the South seems underway. In "Second Chance for the South" [*Atlantic Monthly*

CXCII (December 1953)], Oscar Handlin points out: "The first New South failed because it could not cope with the problems it inherited from the past." He sees no disadvantage in the use of northern capital except "when it obscures the true interests of the people and perverts public policy on behalf of the outsiders and of their local allies." In the case of the Hubbards' use of outside capital, nobody's interests except their own were served, and the New South that they created ended in deep social inequalities. Miss Hellman's plays are not thesis plays, but the fact that she was interested enough in her characters to study their past and seek out the sociological and moral causes of their rapaciousness proves that she did not consider them mere figures in melodrama. Her further consideration of them also divulged a sense of loneliness, which, while not making them more sympathetic, at least made them better understood.

Marcus Hubbard, when Birdie explains that the people on her plantation are literally starving and that perhaps for a loan the families could be nice friends, replies: "Your mother hasn't bowed to me in the forty years I've lived in this town. Does she wish to be my nice friend now?" Granted that the suspicion about Marcus' war activities was well founded, nevertheless the man had a great love of music and Greek literature and seemingly might have been guided toward higher moral values if he had been helped and not snubbed. Marcus has something to be said for his viewpoint too, in his hot words to John Bagtry, who had been a Confederate soldier.

> Your people deserved to lose their war and their world. It was a backward world, getting in the way of history. Appalling that you still don't realize it.
>
> [Act II]

That the way of the Hubbards—the way of avarice, of robbing and cheating—was worse does not nullify the fact that Hellman and other playwrights suggest the degeneration of the aristocracy of the Old South before socioeconomic conditions brought about its ruin. In one sense Marcus is justified in questioning the tone of moral superiority which the Bagtrys have adopted toward him. He has not lived by the labor of others, nor has he inherited wealth or land. He has stood, in the best American tradition of individualism, on his own two feet.

It is his ruthless march toward wealth that has made him feared by his wife and hated by his children, and when tricked by Ben, "very, very, very—afraid." At one point, Ben appears to have failed and admits,

> I spent twenty years lying and cheating to help make you rich. I was trying to outwait you, Papa, but I guess I couldn't do it.
>
> [Act II]

"Your tricks are getting nasty and they bore me," Marcus tells his oldest child; but in the end, he reaps what he has sown, and becomes Ben's slave. Brooks Atkinson's comment on Tennessee Williams' recent study in hatred among members of a Southern family—*Cat on a Hot Tin Roof*—applies to Lillian Hellman's two plays: "Essentially, each one of them [the family] is living in solitary confinement" [*The New York Times,* 3 April 1955]. In another review Atkinson observes: "There seems to be something in the spiritual climate today that makes loneliness a universal theme. It underlies a good deal of the writing for the stage" [*The New York Times*, 22 May 1955]. The "robber barons," whose rise was made possible during the late nineteenth century by social and economic conditions, apparently taught their sons, as did Marcus Hubbard, that any means to wealth and power was justified; and presumably they were as unloved by their progeny and as isolated finally as he. Ben profits by what he has been taught, however, and even accuses his father of getting soft.

> You were smart in your day and figured out what fools you lived among. But ever since the war you been too busy getting cultured, or getting Southern. A few more years and you'd have been just like the rest of them.
>
> [Act III]

Much has been made of the loneliness of Americans because of the conditons which fostered the competitive spirit and lent an undue prestige to wealth and power. Miss Hellman in her second play illustrates the cause of the rise of the bourgeoisie, for, as D. W. Brogan explains [in *The American Character*], American families from the beginning have risen and fallen according to their ability to compete, and those who made pretensions of surviving on ancient prestige deteriorated.

> The would-be gentry unlearned the idle lessons of gentility or sank into poverty. . . . There was no high plateau of effortless superiority to be attained, by Byrds in Virginia or by Saltonstalls in Massachusetts. A family or an individual had to have what it took to survive—and it took adaptability, toughness, perhaps a not too sensitive moral or social outlook.

The Bagtrys became impoverished and failed, whereas the Hubbards, with a "not too sensitive moral or social outlook," took over.

Miss Hellman's two plays contrast the loneliness of the falling and the rising family, highlighting the two women, Birdie and Regina. At the end of the second play it is hard to say whether Birdie, who must bear the abuse of the Hubbards and lose consciousness in drink, is more isolated than Regina, who, begging her daughter to sleep in the bedroom with her, receives the reply, "Are you afraid, Mama?" Birdie, like Amanda and Blanche in Williams' plays, lives in dreams of the past glory of the plantation, but Regina has no happy memories of the past and her future looks bleak. In warning the young Alexandra, Birdie says,

> In twenty years you'll just be like me. They'll do all the same things to you. In twenty-two years I haven't had a whole day of happiness. . . . And you'll trail after them, just like me, hoping they won't be so mean that day. . . . only you'll be worse off because you haven't got my Mama to remember.
>
> [Act III]

Birdie is so good-hearted that for more than twenty years she has not been able to believe that anyone could be so cruel as the Hubbards, and perhaps hardest of all to bear,

her son has turned out to be like them. She admits ruefully that she likes even her husband better than she does her son. She has been told many times that Oscar married her for the plantation. Ben is frank to say, in front of her, "Lionnet now belongs to *us*. Twenty years ago we took over their land, their cotton, and their daughter." Birdie, living in this nest of rattlesnakes, is tragically lonesome, and has broken under the strain. But Birdie has the love of Alexandra, which Regina has lost so irretrievably that the girl hurls her a parting challenge after announcing that she is leaving her mother forever. Proclaiming that she is not going to stand around while the Hubbards eat the earth, she shouts,

> Tell him [Uncle Ben] for me, Mama, I'm not going to stand around and watch you do it. Tell him I'll be fighting as hard as he'll be fighting some place where people don't just stand around and watch.
>
> [Act III]

In Lillian Hellman's story a humanitarian with the tenderness of Birdie and the forcefulness of Regina arises to sound a new war cry.

To some extent John Bagtry and Ben Hubbard are contrasted as are the women of the two families. John has no place in the post-Civil War South, whereas Ben is in his element. Explaining that business is almost a religion with him, Ben frankly expounds, "A man ain't only in business for what he gets out of it. It's got to give him something here," as he places his hand upon his breast. But to John Bagtry, life on the failing plantation is torture. "I was only good once—in a war," he tells Regina, as he explains he is going to enlist in Brazil. "I want to be with fighting men again. I'm lonely for them." To the Hubbards he seems "A dead man, a foolish man, an empty man from an idiot world. . . . A man in space." Ben claims, "The Southern aristocrat can adapt himself to nothing. Too high-toned to try." John spends as much time as possible with Birdie and her mother because, as he sympathetically explains, "They are lonely," but he cannot feel he belongs to the plantation. John's loneliness is tragic, as is Birdie's; but Lillian Hellman convinces her audiences that there is also tragedy in belonging to nothing but business. The devotion of the Southern gentry to a way of life brings grief, but a deeper loneliness may be in store for those "who eat the earth," than for those who stand around and watch. (pp. 143-49)

Winifred L. Dusenbury, "Socioeconomic Forces," in her The Theme of Loneliness in Modern American Drama, *University of Florida Press, 1960, pp. 113-54.*

Jacob H. Adler   (essay date 1961)

> [*Adler is an American scholar and critic who has written on modern drama, eighteenth-century literature and literary criticism, in addition to being the author of* The Reach of Art: A Study in the Prosody of Pope *(1964), and* Lillian Hellman *(1969). In the following excerpt, Adler examines the portrayals of the South in Hellman's dramas. Furthermore, the critic assesses the playwright's depictions of characters as individual, regional, and uni-*

versal figures and compares her dramatic techniques to those of Tennessee Williams and Anton Chekhov.]

While the modern outburst of Southern writing in fiction, poetry, and criticism has been amply sufficient to be called a golden flood, the flow of Southern drama, though at its best hardly less golden, has been by comparison little more than a trickle. Reasons are not hard to find. Countless novels and short stories may be published almost countlessly; even poetry and criticism have many, though often obscure, outlets. But a play scarcely counts in this country unless it appears on (or "off") Broadway, and the number of plays which Broadway can absorb—and the variety it *will* absorb—are unfortunately limited. A novel lacking popular appeal and selling only a few copies may nevertheless have permanently recognized literary value. The unproduced play, or the play which fails, will all too probably disappear into an oblivion from which it is unlikely to emerge, even in the dramatist's collected works. Such a situation hardly encourages young writers to become playwrights, and playwrights anywhere are almost certain to be fewer than the writers of fiction or poetry.

Serious drama is, moreover, almost inevitably an urban phenomenon—as witness not only New York, but London, Paris, Moscow, ancient Athens. It is probably significant that of the only three prolific dramatists identified with the South, one (Lillian Hellman) grew up in New Orleans and New York; one (Tennessee Williams) was taken from a childhood in Mississippi to an adolescence in St. Louis and early became a cosmopolitan wanderer; and one (Paul Green) is a folk dramatist and college professor who turned rather soon from the writing of plays for New York to the creation of historical pageants designed for non-metropolitan audiences. To be sure, Southern fiction—short and long—has been turned into drama, but so has non-Southern fiction; and plays from the works of Faulkner and Wolfe and Caldwell and Eudora Welty can be matched and overmatched by plays from the works of Henry James, Edith Wharton, Hemingway, Lewis, Marquand, and such lesser lights as William March, Thomas Heggen, Joseph Hayes, and James Michener. Significantly, too, almost the only Southern playwrights to add to the three already named are Faulkner himself (with *Requiem for a Nun*), Carson McCullers, and Truman Capote—all primarily writers in other forms. Very likely the only truly important drama to come from all this prose fiction, or from the producers of both drama and prose fiction, is Marc Connelly's transformation of Roark Bradford's *Ol' Man Adam an' His Chillun* into the tender and beautiful mystery play *The Green Pastures,* which may well be among the few American plays to survive the century. Much more evanescent but still worth mentioning is Carson McCullers' delicate adaptation of her own *Member of the Wedding.* And, in quite a different category, a play of permanent importance for reasons other than its own considerable worth is Du Bose Heyward's *Porgy.*

By almost any standards—literary, dramatic, commercial, or national identification with the South—the first among Southern playwrights is Tennessee Williams. He has had nine productions on—in one case "off"—Broadway, all but one of them, *Camino Real,* about the South: *The Glass Menagerie* (1945), *A Streetcar Named Desire* (Pulitzer

Prize, 1947), *Summer and Smoke* (1948), *The Rose Tattoo* (1950), *Camino Real* (1953), *Cat on a Hot Tin Roof* (Pulitzer Prize, 1954), *Orpheus Descending* (1957), *Garden District* (1958), and *Sweet Bird of Youth* (1959). Almost all have been highly successful with the majority of both critics and the public, though his violence and his addiction to what might be called four-letter actions have brought him detractors. His work has literary as well as commercial-dramatic value, and his reputation—and productions—extend throughout the Western world.

Second-place honors raise a more difficult question. Lillian Hellman's range is greater than Paul Green's, perhaps greater than that of Williams. Her standards of dramaturgy are rigorously high, her commercial success unquestionable. Her identification with the South, though less sure, is built upon four plays dealing directly with Southerners (***The Little Foxes,*** 1939; ***Another Part of the Forest,*** 1946; ***The Autumn Garden,*** 1951; and ***Toys in the Attic,*** 1960) and two more (***Watch on the Rhine,*** 1941; ***The Searching Wind,*** 1944), which, while they breathe the atmosphere of the aristocratic Upper South, have no particular Southern connections. At least one of these five, ***The Little Foxes,*** has considerable power of survival. (Her first play, ***The Children's Hour,*** which also seems likely to outlive its author, was not laid in the South.) On the other hand, while Miss Hellman's plays are almost as fascinating to read as they are to see, they scarcely qualify as literature. In contrast to all this, Paul Green was never more than a mild success in New York; even *In Abraham's Bosom,* which won the Pulitzer Prize—an honor stubbornly withheld from Miss Hellman—had only a brief run on Broadway and achieved a respectable run in downtown New York partly on the basis of the Prize-winning. Green's commercial success and his public identification belong to his popular pageants, like *The Lost Colony* and *Wilderness Road,* which seem of more interest to folklorists, historians, and analysts of culture in the broad sense than to the critic of drama or literature. Yet Green's earlier plays—*In Abraham's Bosom* (1926), *The Field God* (1927), *Roll, Sweet Chariot* (1935)—are the profoundest portrayals of the Southern Negro and poor white that we have in dramatic form; and *The House of Connolly* (1931), his greatest success, perceptively analyzes a decaying upper-class family. Almost all his dramas are in a sense folk dramas—this country's best folk dramas—and this genre depends far less than the usual play upon commercial success for survival.

Still, the feeling persists that all these works are more successful as poetic, powerfully imagined literary "studies" (based firmly on Green's early observations in eastern North Carolina) than as plays. Admittedly deficient in dramaturgy, Green is probably destined to see his plays, like his pageants, survive as precious documents for the cultural historian and the folklorist rather than for the student of drama. This hardly seems the fate reserved for Williams or Miss Hellman, who stand or fall as dramatists. In listing the *dramatists* of the South I am convinced that Miss Hellman deserves second place. (pp. 349-51)

Lillian Hellman's picture of the South resembles Tennessee Williams' in a number of interesting ways; but the story that Dorothy Parker suggested the title of *The Little Foxes* at once illuminates a difference in method. For Miss Hellman's symbolic title, unlike those of Williams, is a comment on the play, not an integral part of it; the same can be said for *Another Part of the Forest.* In these first two of Miss Hellman's plays about the South the method is straightforward realism, to such an extent that even when Miss Hellman wants her characters, the Hubbards, to be representative of something beyond themselves, she does not succeed in making them so. Miss Hellman's plays therefore lack a kind of complexity typical of Williams, and while she too deals with the culture-power dichotomy, she does so in much simpler terms. By and large the cleavage is between aristocrat and Hubbard, with the Negro—much more prominent than in Williams' plays—often admirable and always a victim. Poor whites lie off in the background as further victims, and there are hints of an incipient non-Hubbard middle class; but except for the poor-white Laurette Sincee in *Forest,* there are in the foreground only the three groups: aristocrats, Negroes, Hubbards.

The primary fact is the Hubbards; and perhaps the primary fact about them for present purposes is that, while to any audience they would seem Southern-born, they do not, in their central acquisitive "foxiness," seem typically of the South. (Historically they may be quite representative, but that is not the point; the point is that they do not seem so.) This is rather an odd phenomenon; it becomes especially odd when one compares the Hubbards to similar characters in Faulkner and in Williams. In external phenomena, the Hubbards are thoroughly Southern. They display in wide variety, for example, Southern attitudes toward the Negro—all the way from the guilt feelings which make the demented Lavinia in *Another Part of the Forest* want to devote her entire life to Negroes and even identify herself with them, to the Ku Klux Klanism of her son Oscar in the same play; and, in between, the combination in Ben (in *The Little Foxes*) of loyalty to an old servant—his cook is bad, but he will keep her because she was his mother's—and the grossest economic exploitation of Negroes in the mass; while beyond the Hubbards there is the greater loyalty and sensibility, the *noblesse oblige,* of the old aristocrats, as represented by Birdie and Horace. The Hubbards are rooted historically in the South; much more is made of this than it is regarding anyone, even Blanche, in Williams' plays. They are rooted geographically in the South; they look out onto the North as a different world in which Chicago is to Regina a distant and infinitely desirable Vanity Fair and even Baltimore is remote and incomprehensible. They are Southern in their stubborn family loyalty against the world; they are even Southern in their small habits, so that it seems perfectly natural, neither exaggerated nor ludicrous, to find grits on Regina's breakfast table. Yet Miss Hellman's central purpose, as the title, the historical period, and several key speeches in *The Little Foxes* suggest, was to make them typical of a rising Southern class of exploiting industrialists, and, beyond that, of such a class in America generally. In this, by common critical consent, Miss Hellman fails.

Why does she fail? The usual reason given is that she makes the Hubbards so completely and circumstantially evil, so utterly individual in their depravity, as to make it impossible for them to be typical of anything. But this criticism flounders at the feet of Flem Snopes, as avaricious, hypocritical, calloused, and depraved as any Hubbard, and yet at least as successful as a Southern type as he is as an individual. Furthermore, Faulkner shows Snopes doing just what the Hubbards do—exploiting Negro, poor white, and aristocrat in a rise to power which begins in precisely the same year (1900) as *The Little Foxes.*

The answer, I believe, lies in Miss Hellman's failure to achieve symbolism. (Other dramatic techniques extending beyond realism would serve, but the titles of *Foxes* and *Forest* suggest that symbolism is the one Miss Hellman would use, if any.) This is not the place to determine how Faulkner makes Flem Snopes a symbol or what techniques Faulkner uses to get beyond documentary realism; but Williams too succeeds in making a character like Blanche exist at several levels—as a vividly real and complex individual, as a symbol for the South, and as a symbol for the modern world: precisely what Miss Hellman tries to do with the Hubbards and fails. Archibald MacLeish once contrasted the actual and the real in the drama, feeling that straight "realistic" techniques could achieve only the actual. Thornton Wilder has denied the possibility of achieving the genuinely, permanently true, the essence of reality, through the realistic effects of the picture-frame stage. And even in so naturalistic a play as *Streetcar,* Williams uses the various non-realistic techniques of symbolism, impressionism, and even expressionism. Similarly, even at his more realistic, Ibsen, the more important of Miss Hellman's two dramatic masters (the other is Chekhov), almost always used techniques extending his dramatic picture beyond the actual; and Miss Hellman's inspiration for the character of Regina seems, significantly, to be Hedda Gabler, out of a play which of all Ibsen's major plays seems most actual and least representative. Miss Hellman fails in a way that earlier American dramatic realists failed: it is not that the mother in *The Silver Cord* or the wife in *Craig's Wife* is too individual to be the type she is obviously intended to be; it is that both are too rooted in the actuality of realistic dramatic techniques to escape from it. This is not to deny that Miss Hellman's Hubbards are vivid and fascinating dramatic creations; it is merely to say that they succeed at only one level, as actual individuals, where they were obviously intended to succeed at more than one.

At that one level, there are interesting comparisons and contrasts with Williams. In Williams, the principal symbol of "power" in the culture-power dichotomy is sex. Even in the Big Daddy of *Cat on a Hot Tin Roof,* whose power derives from money and who represents money to almost all who surround him, sexuality is prominent; there is the latent suggestion that without the sexuality the drive which resulted in tremendous aggrandizement could not have existed; and in Brick the achievement of normal sexuality is the *sine qua non* of his inheriting his father's wealth. In Miss Hellman, on the contrary, prominent sexuality almost always attaches to the weak, or if it appears in the relatively strong (as in Horace, and as in David in *Watch on the Rhine*), it is a weaker element in them. Only in Oscar, the weakest of the three Hubbards of the middle generation, is sexuality even active. Of the other two, Ben (like Faulkner's Flem Snopes) has apparently always been sexless, and Regina has become frigid after an unhappy love affair in her youth. Both are thus free to pursue power with a single-mindedness which Oscar lacks. Their father, Marcus, always subordinated love to money, and it is perhaps indicative of his coming fall from power in *Another Part of the Forest* that he has allowed his control to slacken in an incestuous affection for Regina.

The symbol of power, and the principal motivating force, in these two plays—and, to a surprising extent, even in the idealistic *Watch on the Rhine*—is money. And while money is necessary to the preservation of culture (Birdie's family is destroyed through poverty; the wealth in *Watch on the Rhine* represents culture at its best), it can also be destructive of it. Culture, in other words, is neither consistent nor inconsistent with the symbol of power. It resides in the financially successful Horace, who has a broken violin in his safe deposit box, and in the weak Birdie, who treasures a Wagner autograph. It lies in the dominant and wealthy aristocratic matriarch in *Watch on the Rhine,* and in her strong, penniless, idealistic German son-in-law. It is particularly complex in Marcus Hubbard, who learned Greek as a boy doing manual labor, who has a real appreciation for music and literature, who patterned his house after the very Southern culture he despises and has betrayed, who has raised his children in a tyranny bound to make them hate anything he represents, except money; and who has allowed his life to be ruled by money and the power it conveys.

Culture and power are not, then, in necessary opposition. Both are good, though both can exist in the wrong hands, and they are necessarily related only to the extent that money—and culture!—are essential to the preservation of culture. (For indeed culture itself is a sort of power in Miss Hellman; and there is hope that, through Alexandra, it will defeat the power of money in the tribe of Hubbards, and, through Kurt and his kind, the power of fascism in *Watch on the Rhine.*) Between weakness and the wrong kind of strength—the kind conveyed by money alone—lies the well-integrated person who puts culture and money (and sex too) in their proper place: the Farrellys and Kurt in *Watch on the Rhine;* Horace in *The Little Foxes;* no one—not even Birdie, who sells herself for money and clings to a dead past—in *Another Part of the Forest.* Williams too believes that there can be an integration; but sex as the symbol for power is a much more prominent element in the synthesis, and there is probably no example in his plays of the synthesis actually achieved in perfect, self-sustaining balance; such achievement is future or ideal, not actual.

There are many other parallels with Williams. Miss Hellman, for example, gives attention to foreigners in a Southern environment in *Watch on the Rhine* and *The Autumn Garden.* The conflict of cultural ideals and bitter reality has led Lavinia in *Forest,* like Blanche in *Streetcar,* to dementia; and, like Mrs. Winemiller, she has been kept at home, even though the dementia is an embarrassment to her family. Marcus Hubbard and Big Daddy are both poor whites who have gained financial power, and both domi-

nate their families overwhelmingly. Miss Hellman even provides us with insights into typical important Southern phenomena. In the 1880 Oscar we see exactly the process of the Klan's changing from what it was immediately after the war to what it later became; in Ben we see precisely the almost unconscious sanctimoniousness which enables a certain kind of man to get away with exploitation and even theft. In Birdie and her cousin we see distinctly why certain aristocrats declined and disappeared. There are sudden startling realizations, such as the fact that Horace cannot leave the colored Addie money in his will, since in the South of that day she could never collect it. Yet it is curious how little all this has to do with an *interpretation* of the South. These happen to be Southern individuals, and Miss Hellman is clearly interested in interpreting them both as individuals and as Southerners; but the result is no more an interpretation of the South than a play containing Englishmen is necessarily an interpretation of England.

The story ought to be different when one reaches Miss Hellman's next-to-the-last play about the South: *The Autumn Garden.* First, the technique is different. The tightly constructed plots are abandoned. Chekhov takes over as the dominant influence. Money, while still prominent, is no longer such a dominant force and motivation. And this is the first of Miss Hellman's specifically Southern studies which takes place in the present. Moreover, one long suspected advantage over Williams is made finally unmistakable: Miss Hellman is at home in dealing with *genuine* aristocrats, with a genuine upper-class society, which Williams can treat (if at all) only when it has fallen. Indeed, it is hard to believe that any of Williams' fallen aristocrats—Amanda, Blanche, Carol Cutrere in *Orpheus Descending*—were ever *really* upper-class. They lack an essential breeding which, however degraded Miss Hellman's characters become, they never lose. In *The Autumn Garden,* Constance Tuckerman contrasts *breeding* with *gentility,* which she was taught by her mother to believe was its opposite. One cannot help feeling that *gentility* is what Blanche and the others had. Whatever it is, they are self-conscious about it; in Miss Hellman's characters self-consciousness about basic behavior is impossible, since the quality is innate.

But for all this, Miss Hellman's study of a collection of visitors, mostly Southern aristocrats, at a guest home on the Gulf is no more a study of the *South* than are any of her earlier plays. Here are individuals who, unable to take positive action, waste their lives and wither away, and come by various means to a realization of their plight. But their problem is a problem of individual personalities, not specifically Southern at all—a point made clear by the fact that one of the major examples of personality decay is General Griggs, who is not a Southerner. What Miss Hellman is saying is that most of us are like that; and here she does succeed in getting beyond her specific people to a general (though not a special Southern) theme. But, unlike Williams and unlike Faulkner, she still cannot make her themes Southern, though her characters are; hence she cannot show that the truths she sees so clearly are both typical of the South *and* universal. This is especially surprising in *The Autumn Garden,* because Miss Hellman had Chekhov so unmistakably in mind in changing her technique, and because her theme of attrition of the will is so typical of Chekhov; however, Chekhov's characters and problems alike succeed in being as universal as they are unmistakably Russian.

Reminders of Chekhov are everywhere in *The Autumn Garden.* As with Chekhov, the frustration is general, but there are exceptions to it—old Mrs. Ellis and the French-raised Sophie Tuckerman fight the world and win. As with Chekhov, there is compassion—no one is a villain, which is unusual in Miss Hellman's plays. And as with Chekhov, those who give up are sometimes pleasanter, more graceful people than those who never dream of doing so. Also numerous technical similarities are visible: the de-emphasis (but not absence) of plot, the subtle personality clashes, the use of arrivals and departures, as is usual with Miss Hellman, for emotional tension. But the big difference, besides her failure to achieve three levels—individual, regional, universal—is that she continues to stick to straight realism. What Miss Hellman derives from Chekhov is somewhat different from what Williams derives. More genuine than Williams' as aristocrats, Miss Hellman's creations are less genuine as symbols, less profound as human beings, precisely because Williams develops Chekhov's non-realistic techniques (not only the use of symbol but the careful, subtle employment of sound effects and sets for the establishment of mood and personality) and Miss Hellman does not. Miss Hellman's characters are crisp and clear, in *The Autumn Garden* as everywhere. For all their wavering in purpose and lack of self-knowledge they have no blurred edges. They weigh so much, measure so much; the whole is the neat sum of the perceptible parts. This is no mean accomplishment: Miss Hellman is justly praised for her characterization. But at his best Williams is not like this. Blanche is bared to the very soul, yet who is to say that there are not still unplumbed depths, or even unpresented surfaces? A more complex creation than Miss Hellman's characters, Blanche is presented in greater complexity, and our reaction to her is more complex.

The truth is that Miss Hellman employs an old-fashioned technique and succeeds, within her special limits, too well at it. She performs to a "T" the feat she learned from Ibsen—an almost miraculous ability to make characters live and breathe within the confines of a strict plot which ought to, and does not, turn them into puppets. In *Watch on the Rhine* she further succeeds in making her characters and their problems representative; but at the time one might have wondered if this result was not in part fortuitous. This was a war play, and in time of war, large groups of people have attitudes—easily recognizable attitudes—in common. She had not yet succeeded, as Ibsen did, in using the same technique to focus on characters and "problems" of much less obvious general applicability. So Miss Hellman turned to Chekhov's dramatic style—as Shaw tried to in *Heartbreak House*—but the result is still Miss Hellman, just as the result was still Shaw. Her characters function somewhat more complexly than before, but they are still, for all their genuineness, relatively simple and superficial.

Her latest play, *Toys in the Attic,* does represent an advance. She retains what she gained in the functioning of characters in *The Autumn Garden.* Her story is out of Chekhov, bearing various resemblances to the story of *The Three Sisters,* but she has made it her own. (People who see signs in the New Orleans setting and in some of the play's gaudier details that Miss Hellman was capitalizing on Williams apparently forget that Miss Hellman has never hesitated to call a spade by its most accurate name, or to look into any cranny of life which pertains to her dramatic idea.) She does at last prove that *Watch on the Rhine* was not fortuitous: that she can use Ibsen's methods, and strict realism, and money as a dominant motivation and symbol, to present a theme of universal significance and power. But while Miss Hellman's style seems as welcome as a crisp apple after a surfeit of French cookery—and after the later, more decadent Williams—she still fails, and for the reasons given, to equal Williams' earlier performances.

There is a danger, of course, in carrying this view of Miss Hellman's work too far. We believe today that realism has its limitations; it probably does, but there are many different "realisms," and at various times one or another of them has seemed the final answer to the artistic problem. Today we prefer other answers, or at least consider other answers more profound. We believe more in Chekhov's methods than in those of the Ibsen of the middle period, the Ibsen we know best. We prefer the blurred edge to the clearcut outline, the piercing depth to the rounded solidity. We prefer sex to money as the ultimate motivation. So it is really no surprise to find us concluding that Williams is an artist, though not necessarily a skilled craftsman, while Miss Hellman is a tremendously skilled craftsman, though probably not an artist. Like the fox which is her most famous symbol, she traces her quarry with—for our taste—too obvious cleverness and too accomplished skill.

I have myself, of course, written out of these conclusions, even through they must remain faintly suspect because they so thoroughly flatter our own taste. Williams is probably better as a craftsman than we generally believe. In her over-all production, Miss Hellman's scope is much broader, though shallower, than Williams'. Williams tells us far more about the South, though Miss Hellman deals with an aspect of it apparently not available to him. In any case, regionalism is not necessarily a virtue. Yet in the last analysis, what makes the difference, what makes us accept Williams as the profounder of the two, and what makes us almost surely right in doing so, is a wider variety of technique and a far greater ability to make characters function both as characters and as multiple symbols.

At the height of its bloom the rose is—as it should be—in better odor than the fox. (pp. 366-75)

Jacob H. Adler, "The Rose and the Fox: Notes on the Southern Drama," in South: Modern Southern Literature in its Cultural Setting, *edited by Louis D. Rubin, Jr., and Robert D. Jacobs, Doubleday, 1961, pp. 349-75.*

Allan Lewis   (essay date 1965)

[*Lewis is an American scholar specializing in the history of drama. He has published* The Contemporary Theatre *(1962),* American Plays and Playwrights of the Contemporary Theatre *(1965), and* Ionesco *(1973), as well as several plays for stage and screen. The following excerpt explores the influence of the social-propaganda theater of the 1930s on Hellman's major plays.*]

The three most prominent playwrights to come out of the economic depression of the thirties were Lillian Hellman, Clifford Odets, and Irwin Shaw. All were committed writers, deeply concerned with the fight for social justice, and critical of long-held myths that induced complacency in times of success and panic in the face of disaster.

The decade was not a pleasant one. It began with industrial chaos, the collapse of the financial structure, and mass unemployment. It ended with a second world war. A re-examination of the basic structure of the American way of life was in order. The belief that rugged individualism and free enterprise, left unfettered, would result in the greatest good for the greatest number gave way to demands for state planning and government controls. The New Deal instituted Social Security and Federal Works Projects to replace the dole and the breadline. Militant trade unions insisted on a voice in management policies. The issues were critical and the fate of the nation at stake. The theatre became an active participant in the struggle to arouse a disheartened people to renewed conviction. It was sobered, socially conscious, seeking constructive belief to oppose national disintegration. The plays of Hellman, Odets, and Irwin Shaw were a response to a special period of American history.

The advent of another war restored the economy to full production and united a divided nation in the common struggle against totalitarianism. Almost every serious writer was responsible for at least one anti-Hitler play, passionate and partisan—and rarely produced today. The war itself was fought out of a sense of duty, out of a dogged determination to get a job done, rather than from devotion to a crusade. Few war plays of merit resulted. *Mr. Roberts,* the popular comedy by Thomas Heggen and Joshua Logan, deals with the boyish pranks and sexual adventures of sailors caught in the boredom of an isolated supply ship. It has little reference to the cause for which men are fighting. *A Bell for Adano,* the dramatization of the novel, by Paul Osborn and *The Home of the Brave* by Arthur Laurents are accounts of human relations intensified by war. No World War II plays, however, equaled the lusty laughter of *What Price Glory?* by Laurence Stallings and Maxwell Anderson, or the grim plea for peace of Irwin Shaw's *Bury the Dead* or Paul Green's *Johnny Johnson,* all written long before Pearl Harbor.

With the unprecedented prosperity after the second world war, the theatre of social protest fell into disrepute. A public enjoying a booming economy preferred not to be reminded of the terrifying days of the Depression and Hitler's rise to power. The United States in a position of world leadership needed leadership in the arts as well, to rally reluctant and divided allies. Instead, during the days of Senator McCarthy, it fostered the suppression of critical dissent and created a climate hostile to the free expression of the artist. The writer, in particular, fearful of ubiquitous investigating committees, remained silent or was silenced. The theatre concentrated on light comedy, lush musicals, and case studies of psychological frustrations. Advocacy of social issues was suspect. Plays dealing with the results of economic dislocation gave way, in a society of affluence, to dramas of personal dislocation. The future of the nation became less important than the preservation of the self.

The writers of the thirties found it difficult to make the transition. Hellman was the most resilient. She has also been the most active, even though she once said of the theatre,

> It is a tight, unbending, unfluid meager form in which to write, and for these reasons, compared to the novel, it is a second-rate form [see Author Commentary].

After an adult libretto for the musical play *Candide,* she reappeared in 1960 with an original play, *Toys in the Attic,* followed in 1963 by a satirical comedy, *My Mother, My Father, and Me.* (pp. 99-101)

The strength and the weakness of the writers of the thirties derive from the forces that molded them. Critical judgments, as Mr. Dooley said of the Supreme Court, follow the elections. Lillian Hellman, not associated with the Group Theatre or any other collective organization—her plays were produced and often directed by Herman Shumlin, a representative of Broadway's commercial theatre—has best withstood the test of time. In recent years she demonstrated her versatility by writing a delightfully sophisticated and witty book for Leonard Bernstein's musical play *Candide* (1956). Voltaire's theme that "all is for the best in this best of all possible worlds" was rich material for Hellman's acid humor. As a musical play *Candide* is superior to most. . . . The gullible Candide is beset by villainy at every turn, yet keeps on singing his optimistic refrain. He sees evil in the world but refuses to recognize it.

The problem of good and evil is basic to all of Hellman's work, but in her own plays the well-intentioned are destroyed by "the little foxes," who are always around to "eat the earth." The evidence of a satiric touch, so rare in contemporary theatre, was reinforced by her dramatization later of *My Mother, My Father, and Me.* Her adaptation of Emmanuel Robles' *Monsterrat* (1949) and Jean Anouilh's *The Lark* led to the charge that her talent was exhausted and she had been reduced to rewriting the works of others. *Toys in the Attic* (1960) put such fears to rest.

In *The Children's Hour* and *The Little Foxes* the forces of evil are clearly marked. Mary Tilford, the malicious brat, destroys good people in a world where evil is too prone to be accepted. In Regina, all human values have been destroyed by the lust for power and money. Mary confesses, but the harm has already been done. Regina triumphs, and her only defeat is her rejection by her daughter. In *Toys in the Attic,* Cyrus Warkins, the millionaire, is the one consciously malicious character, and he never appears. People who are outwardly good, who presumably sacrifice their lives for others, are now the instruments of human suffering. Misplaced or possessive love can destroy. Julian is beaten up physically and his pride broken through the actions of a spinster sister who secretly prefers to keep him close to her, and by a silly, sex-hungry wife who mistakenly fears Julian will leave her. Both loves are selfish and devastating. The innocent are the tragic victims—Karen and Horace and Anna.

Hellman's dark world of those who triumph through a calculated disregard of moral values is as grim and full of pain as in the most extreme theatre of the absurd. Her dramas differ in that they are portraits of people and not of abstract symbols. Events are causative, and the individual the product of his environment. Her one effort to dramatize immediate social forces resulted in her weakest play, *Days to Come,* an obeisance to the times, in which workers and capitalists line up in opposing ranks.

In her best plays, the cycle of New Orleans family dramas, specific historic events are left in the background, implying the conditions of modern civilization which alter human motives, and the major interest is focused on richly developed, multi-faceted characters involved with forces they dimly understand. Rarely are these protagonists heroic. Kurt in *Watch on the Rhine* is an exception. In the fervent years, his heroism stirred a willing audience. Today he is far too noble to be convincing. His cause is just, but his absolute certainty of righteousness removes him from tragic stature. Regina, her most memorable creation, is a savage, determined woman. Carrie, of *Toys in the Attic,* is quietly obsessive. Julian is a well-intentioned, none too capable young man who finds an easy way to get rich and runs foul of a husband's jealousy and his own wife's innocence. Good characters are more difficult to portray dramatically. Albertine, the wealthy southern aristocrat, and Henry, her Negro consort, are admirable in their philosophic calm and mature understanding, but are nebulous figures.

Lillian Hellman's strength lies in the dramatic power she can extract from the realistic form. *The Little Foxes,* like [Henrik Ibsen's] *Ghosts,* is almost flawless in economy and structure, realization of character, and pertinence of dialogue. Characters generate events and in turn are influenced by them. *Toys in the Attic* has a weak first act with too much preparation for what follows, but its final resolution is explosive. Hellman's mastery of technique has led to the accusation that her plays are too contrived, too adroitly arranged by the author. Such charges are valid, but it is a pleasure to watch the work of a skilled craftsman. All writers rearrange life and impose their own will on the chaos of reality. The test in the realistic theatre is whether the characters appear to be self-propelled, as they do in *The Little Foxes,* a masterpiece of the Ibsen-influenced theatre. *Toys in the Attic* shows bits of the machinery, perhaps because family plays of psychological insight have become too familiar, but is so artfully contrived that it becomes compelling drama. Hellman does not use her skill to exhibit technical prowess, but to expose the extent to which greed and avarice have corrupted the human soul. She strives for a Chekhovian complex of frustrated and unhappy people, but her use of violence and sexuality

brings her closer to Tennessee Williams. At the end of the second act, Anna, the older sister, tells Carrie that her need for Julian is incestuous. Carrie has asked for the truth, which is what she least wants to hear: "When you love, truly love, you take your chances on being hated by speaking out the truth." Anna replies, "All right. I'll take my chance and tell you that you want to sleep with him and always have."

Hellman's bitter complaint is that greed and avarice have eroded love, and that the cause is a social system in which human relations are a product for sale. She is a moralist, and her major weakness, by her own confession, is the obvious addition of the moral, either by an all too obvious explanatory speech or through an arranged resolution that borders on the melodramatic. *The Children's Hour* could have ended with Martha's suicide. The visit of the grandmother, which follows, and the hammering away by Karen that she has come to relieve her conscience are superfluous and aesthetically disturbing. Kurt's final speech in *Watch on the Rhine* about the need to kill if necessary, to destroy Hitlerism, has already been implicitly stated in what went before. *Toys in the Attic* avoids this weakness, and as Julian moans that he "will have to start all over again," we know that he will forever be cared for by his sisters.

Most writers who master the well-made play can ill afford to experiment in other directions. Failure on Broadway is too catastrophic. Odets never varied. Hellman took a chance in *My Mother, My Father, and Me,* and though the piece was not a financial success, it indicated a surprising gift for humor. The play is a travesty of American middle-class life, with abundant laughter, absurd situations, and high comedy, and is expressionist in form. It was probably poorly received because of its failure to concentrate on a few targets, for it lashes out bitterly on all fronts, bordering at times on the petulant and vindictive without reason. Hellman deserted her psychological introspection to concentrate on comic-strip stereotypes in a wild extravaganza of the Jewish family plagued by wealth and removed from dedication to any vital issue. The dominant mother, the complaining and submissive father, the crazy grandmother who is more sane than the rest, the bohemian son, are all here. The scenes shift from the family home to an old folks' asylum, to an Indian reservation to which the young Berney escapes to find American roots. He will spend the rest of his life making silver bracelets and selling blankets to middle-class tourists. He informs the audience that his father

> is back in the shoe business, and seems to be doing all right with what he calls an "Honor" shoe, a shoe to be buried in, a shoe in honor of the dead,

and that his mother was wild when he left and sent him a postcard saying:

> The eye that mocks the father and does not obey the mother, the ravens shall pick it out, and the young eagles shall eat it.

He giggles and adds, "There are plenty of eagles and ravens here, but nothing's happened." "Nothing's happened" distinguishes the comfortable sixties from the Depression era. Most writers of the thirties had something to say, but didn't say it too well. Most writers of today have little to say and say it extremely well.

Hellman's alert sensitivity is able to find varying means to express her major theme. Her problem is her loss of certainty. Her attacks have become negative and as impotent as Rona in *My Mother, My Father, and Me.* When she was stimulated by the social upheaval of the thirties she wrote a powerful drama in human terms, *The Little Foxes,* in which an entire society in decay is revealed. It ranks with Gorky's *Yegor Bulitchev* and Henry Becque's *Les Corbeaux.* (pp. 105-09)

> *Allan Lewis, "The Survivors of the Depression—Hellman, Odets, Shaw," in his* American Plays and Playwrights of the Contemporary Theatre, *Crown Publishers, Inc., 1965, pp. 99-115.*

THE CHILDREN'S HOUR

PRODUCTION REVIEWS

Brooks Atkinson   (review date 21 November 1934)

[*As drama critic for the* New York Times *from 1925 to 1960, Atkinson was one of the most influential reviewers in America. In this review of the opening night of* The Children's Hour, *Atkinson praises the play, its production, and its actors, but faults Hellman for forcing an overly theatrical conclusion.*]

If the author and the producer of *The Children's Hour,* which was acted at Maxine Elliott's last evening, can persuade themselves to ring down the curtain when their play is over, they will deserve the admiration and respect of the theatregoer. For Lillian Hellman has written a venomously tragic play of life in a girls' boarding school—cutting in the sharpness of its dramatic style and in the deadly accuracy of the acting. In the last ten or fifteen minutes of the final act she tries desperately to discover a mettlesome dramatic conclusion; having lured *The Children's Hour* away from the theatre into the sphere of human life, she pushes it back among the Ibsenic dolls and baubles by refusing to stop talking. Please, Miss Hellman, conclude the play before the pistol shot and before the long arm of coincidence starts wabbling in its socket. When two people are defeated by the malignance of an aroused public opinion, leave them the dignity of their hatred and despair.

The point is that Karen Wright and Martha Dobie, headmistresses of a girls' boarding-school, are innocent. After many years of industry they have developed a country school with an enviable reputation. Among their students, however, is Mary Tilford, granddaughter of their chief patroness, and Mary is a diabolical adolescent. Miss Hellman has drawn that evil character with brilliant under-

standing of the vagaries of child nature. Purely as a matter of malicious vanity, Mary spreads the rumor that the headmistresses have an unnatural affection for each other. Horrified and convinced, her grandmother withdraws Mary from the school and warns the parents of other students. The scandal destroys the school and turns the two headmistresses into social exiles. To recover their self-respect, as well as the prestige of the school, they bring a libel action against Mrs. Tilford, but they cannot prove their innocence. That dazed and defeated situation seems to this correspondent to be the logical as well as the most overpowering conclusion to the play.

Having a lamentable respect for the theatre, Miss Hellman then pushes on into suicide and footlights remorse. She gilds the lily until it loses its freshness. For up to that moment *The Children's Hour* is one of the most straightforward, driving dramas of the season, distinguished chiefly for its unflinching characterization of little Mary. She is a vicious maid, but her strength and courage are tremendous. Her capacity for lying, cruelty and sadistic leadership is almost genius. That is the crucial character for two acts of the play. It has not only been ruthlessly drawn in the writing, but it is superlatively well acted by Florence McGee, who forces every drop of poison out of it. She plays it with as much spirit as a wildcat and considerably more craft and intelligence. In fact, you do not know whether to admire Miss McGee for her headlong acting or to fear the tyrannical part she is acting.

Nor is that the only piece of acting to admire in this piercingly directed production. Mr. Shumlin has chosen his actors thoughtfully and directed them with a clear mind. Anne Revere's reticent Martha Dobie and Katherine Emery's broken Karen Wright are portraits of dramatic significance. Robert Keith plays the part of a manly fiancé with splendid decision, and Katherine Emmet plays the sanctimonious patroness with womanly pride and genteel rectitude. As a supercillious and vile-tempered aunt, Alice McDermott gives an excellent performance. All the girls are well acted, especially Barbara Beals's overwrought little Rosalie.

In short, Miss Hellman has written and Mr. Shumlin has produced a pitiless tragedy, and both of them have daubed it with grease-paint in the last quarter of an hour. Fortunately, they can remove that blemish. Instruct the guardian of the curtain to ring down when the two young women are facing a bleak future. That will turn *The Children's Hour* into vivid drama.

> *Brooks Atkinson, in a review of "The Children's Hour," in* The New York Times, *November 21, 1934, p. 23.*

The Literary Digest   (review date 1 December 1934)

[*In the following review, the critic expresses unqualified approval of* The Children's Hour].

Here is a play to wring the heart and fire respect, an adult, steadfast play so conspicuously fine and intelligent that, beside it, much of the theater's present crop becomes shoddy and futile. This is the first play of this erratic sea-

Act II, scene ii of the original production of The Children's Hour: *Robert Keith as Dr. Cardin, Ann Revere as Martha Dobie, Florence McGee as Mary Tilford, Katherine Emery as Karen Wright, and Katherine Emmet as Mrs. Tilford.*

son in which power, intellect, and a glowing sense for theater combine for a terrifying and ennobling experience. The new play is ***The Children's Hour,*** a first play by Miss Lillian Hellman, and overnight, by the force of its own stature, it has become the most important play in New York.

Here is a play that shines with integrity. It is, definitely, the first play of the season in which for two whole, consuming acts the First Audience sat completely silent, held taut by the richness and reality of the tragedy which it describes.

In ***The Children's Hour*** there is conspicuous and magic correlation between the author, the producer, and the cast. It is evident that each contributed a positive majesty of sincerity to it and that all three together determined to make this a play to command the appreciation of its audiences.

Once more Herman Shumlin brings to the theater vivid testimony that he is a man of profound talents, liquid, engrossing talents in which sensitivity and deep understanding are the gifts made eagerly to a play which might easily have withered without them. His thoughtful treatment

and skilled direction, together with Miss Hellman's abiding honesty, construct a production in which the theater, these times, and the audiences may enrich themselves.

By the author's own evaluation, this is the tragedy of considerate age for impetuous youth, youth in which there is headlong disregard for the rights of others. The bleak story is of two finely-reared young women, heads of a private school for girls, whose characters are wrecked and whose enterprise is destroyed by a satanic child, a poisonous young viper whose whole, disordered life is devoted to cruelty, falsehood, and appalling mischief. An orphan, under the guardianship of an indulgent grandmother, she makes the days of her schoolmates hideous with horrible deeds of evil. She traps them in childish thefts and, thereafter, enslaves them through threats of exposure. She takes their money, the pitiful little allowances sent by their parents, and she bullies them when they revolt and refuse further to be hurt by her.

This type of child magnifies all discipline into the shape of injustice. Thus, when punished for a small fraud and threatened with further thwarting of her demoniac acts, she runs away and goes back to her grandmother. This old woman, consummately fond of her troublesome charge, is moved first to send her back to school and discipline. Frightened by this, the little girl invents a monstrous accusation against her teachers. The grandmother first is contemptuous, but the sly, forceful brat becomes so hysterical that the old woman virtually is browbeaten into belief. As a result, she withdraws support from the school and, recklessly, telephones the story to mothers of the other pupils. These, too, are withdrawn and the helpless, despairing young women see their lives grow cold and cruel about them.

The grandmother refuses to listen to explanations; closes her doors to the teachers, envelops her sadistic child with maudlin safety. In all reasonableness, there has not been a more malevolent character in the theater in years than this twelve-year-old marplot. Miss Hellman has poured into the making of the figure a resolute, unswerving honesty. And, in all reasonableness, there have not been in the theater in years any two characters more tragic than the two teachers whose lives are burned down around them by the evil of the wicked child. Ruined by slander, struck helpless by implacable gossip, they seize the only defense at hand—and they lose. They sue for libel and the cowardice of the key-witness completes their ruin.

The Misses Anne Revere and Katherine Emery play these two broken women tautly, humanly, and with an overwhelming sensitivity. Their performances are so absorbing and flawless that audiences sit before them tense, motionless, and silent, forced to complete attentiveness by what they are saying and the way they are saying it.

Scarcely less to be admired for performance, tho the character is unspeakable, is Miss Florence McGee in the rôle of the bullying, lying, venomous brat.

And, strangely, the bleakness and poignancy of the situation increase when, toward the close of the play, one of the teachers discloses that the child had had some measure of justice in her accusations. Here Miss Hellman set herself a difficult problem and solved it magnificently with the help of ten minutes of the most heart-breaking acting to be found in the theater.

This well may be the most important play of the entire season, tho six more months stretch away before the season ends. Certainly, it will be the most controversial. It must earn and merit the unchecked respect of every intelligent theatergoer.

"The Thunderbolt of Broadway," in Literary Digest, *New York, Vol. 118, No. 22, December 1, 1934, p. 20.*

Joseph Wood Krutch   (review date 5 December 1934)

[*Krutch is widely regarded as one of America's most respected literary and drama critics. Noteworthy among his works are* The American Drama since 1918 *(1939), in which he analyzed the most important dramas of the 1920s and 1930s, and* "Modernism" in Modern Drama *(1953), in which he stressed the need for twentieth-century playwrights to infuse their works with traditional humanistic values. A conservative and idealistic*

thinker, he was a consistent proponent of human dignity and the preeminence of literary art. In the following review, Krutch calls the final act of The Children's Hour *"forced, improbable, and monotonous," and offers an explanation of its failure. He contends that Hellman conceived of the play as the story of the two schoolmistresses, but the character Mary Tilford became the central interest as the drama was written. The absence of the "realest and most vivid person in the play" from the last act, Krutch claims, "leaves the audience cheated as well as bored."*]

For two of its three acts **The Children's Hour** (Maxine Elliott Theater) is an unusually well-written play about one of the most vicious and hateful little girls ever known in literature or, I hope, in life. The darling of a doting grandmother, she has a genius far beyond her years for making everyone with whom she comes in contact miserable, and with the disinterested malice of an Iago she cajoles or threatens her way from one despicable triumph to another until she crowns her slighter achievements in the way of making other children wretched by the wreck of four adult lives. What is more, Florence McGee plays the role with such fiendish intensity that the spectator passes rapidly from the state where he is conscious of an overmastering desire personally to administer a beating, to the state where he is firmly convinced that capital punishment for children is an urgent social necessity.

So much for the first two acts, which end on a tense scene where the juvenile villain dramatically extricates herself from cross-questioning in an inquisition which is about to expose her, and once more wins her perverse success. Up to that point the play has not been pleasant but it has been powerful and increasingly gripping. There then follows a third act so strained, so improbable, and so thoroughly boring that the effect is almost completely destroyed, and one is left to wonder that anything so inept was ever allowed to reach production.

The situation is as follows: Mary Tilford, liar, cheat, and tyrant, has progressed in the art of trouble-making to the point where, in feigned innocence and terror, she has suggested a Lesbian relationship between the two proprietors of her school. All the pupils are withdrawn by horrified parents, and the physician fiancé of one of the proprietors undertakes to expose the plotter. He almost succeeds, but the demon, blackmailing a schoolfellow, gets direct though perjured testimony, and ruin falls. Now the whole of the dramatic interest is centered upon the perverse child, and the only real concern of the audience is with her. At this point, however, she completely disappears from the play, and the indescribably tedious last act concerns itself exclusively with the two teachers—one of whom loses her fiancé while the other commits suicide. The wonder is, not merely that this last act seems forced, improbable, and monotonous with a deliberate forcing of the cumulative woe, but that the play could have been rehearsed without someone's becoming aware that the third act was simply not the real conclusion of the play as previously developed. The character unceremoniously dropped is incomparably the realest and most vivid person in the play, as well as dramatically the center of the action. Moreover, all the real tension has developed around her, and the solution of the play lies inevitably in her fate. Emotions might have been released in one way if she had finally been defeated; another effect might have been achieved if she had herself been shown in a final vicious triumph. But the actual last act is merely corollary to the main action and leaves the audience cheated as well as bored.

Only one explanation, I think, is possible. The play must have begun as the story of two girls wrongly accused of Lesbian love. In the writing, what was originally intended as merely a device to precipitate the situation developed into the principal action without the author's becoming fully aware of the fact. Hence this author never noticed that the last act was the last act of the play as originally conceived instead of being, as it should have been, the last act of the play as actually written. Something of the sort happens fairly frequently in the theater, and obvious as the result is, neither author nor director seems always to be aware of it. Nor is that the only reason why the defect is worth pointing out. If the public does not respond to *The Children's Hour* it will be accused of an indifference to truth, power, and intelligence. I suspect, however, that a sound last act would have done wonders for the chances of a play which ought to succeed. (pp. 656-57)

> *Joseph Wood Krutch, "The Heart of a Child,"*
> in The Nation, *New York, Vol. CXXXIV, No. 3622, December 5, 1934, pp. 656-57.*

Euphemia Van Rensselaer Wyatt   (review date January 1935)

[*Wyatt asserts that the inclusion of a "taboo" subject in* The Children's Hour *is justified by the important lesson the play imparts regarding hasty judgments.*]

We admit that [*The Children's Hour*] is a difficult play to review. The most discussed production of the season, it touches upon a subject which we have always felt should be taboo but it tiptoes across unholy ground with such unrelenting loathing of the slime and is so saturated with truth that it seems at times not to be the theater at all, and the question prickles in one's ears—"Have I—may I—by my hasty judgment ever brought—or ever bring—so much suffering to anyone by an unjust word?" That—and not the forbidden implication—is the important content of the tragedy. Two college friends, Karen and Martha, have pinched and saved for years to organize the boarding school for younger girls which, under the patronage of the important Mrs. Tilford, has been successfully opened in a smart suburb of—we should say, Boston. Unhappily Mrs. Tilford's granddaughter is a horrid little girl and in trying to frustrate the kindly discipline of Karen and Martha, Mary's impish malice fastens upon the one weakness of the school; a weakness caused by the generosity of the young head mistresses who have unwisely given shelter to Martha's impossible old Aunt, a third-rate ex-actress.

Eavesdropping at the library door, Mary understands enough of the base insinuations in the vulgar abuse that Aunt Lily hurls at Martha to stimulate her precocious imagination. Extracting a dollar from her room mate by the simple expedient of physical torture, Mary runs away

to her grandmother where she whispers such hideous suggestions in the poor lady's unwilling ear that, losing all sense of fairness or proportion, Mrs. Tilford telephones to all her friends, advising them to remove their children at once from the school. Her sense of responsibility and her shock are so sincere that one can understand her standpoint even when she refuses to listen to the bewildered young teachers who come to their old friend to demand an explanation in a scene of taut agony.

There has been much diversity of opinion about the last act which though lacking the terse intensity of the first two, does convey the devastating consequences when Martha and Karen, disregarding Mrs. Tilford's warning, lose their suit for libel and find themselves not only ruined but outcast. Through it all, Karen's *fiancé* (Mrs. Tilford's nephew) has stood stanchly by the two girls but suddenly Karen realizes that the hideous shadow has also fallen across their relationship and she dismisses him. It is then that Martha shoots herself. She has found some hidden basis of truth in her Aunt's evil insinuations. Perhaps it is here that the curtain should fall, but the author prolongs the suffering until Mrs. Tilford arrives to offer reparation. The child witness, terrorized into perjury by Mary, has confessed her lie. Mrs. Tilford creeps out, a broken woman, where many an unguarded tongue might lead us all.

As far as acting and production are concerned, Miss Katharine Emory as Karen and Miss Emmet as Mrs. Tilford are superb. As Mary, Florence McGee is unique. This child, who seems quite plausible, is an uncanny creation. Her small soul reflects the Renaissance tyrant, crafty, malign and cruel. Louis XI might have had just such juvenile qualities. (pp. 466-67)

> *Euphemia Van Rensselaer Wyatt, in a review of "The Children's Hour," in* The Catholic World, *Vol. CXL, January, 1935, pp. 466-67.*

George Jean Nathan   (review date February 1935)

[*Nathan has been called the most learned and influential drama critic the United States has yet produced. During the early decades of the twentieth century, he was greatly responsible for shifting the emphasis of the American theater from light entertainment to serious drama and for introducing audiences and producers to the work of Eugene O'Neill, Henrik Ibsen, and Bernard Shaw, among others. Nathan was a contributing editor to H. L. Mencken's magazine the* American Mercury *and coeditor of the* Smart Set. *With Mencken, Nathan belonged to an iconoclastic school of American critics who attacked the vulgarity of accepted ideas and sought to bring a new level of sophistication to American culture, which they found provincial and backward. In the following essay, Nathan defends Hellman's often-criticized conclusion of* The Children's Hour.]

Lillian Hellman's *The Children's Hour,* . . . remains still, up to the moment of writing, the one material contribution of the season to American playwriting. It was my pleasure to read it in manuscript, back in early September, at which time I allowed myself to comment upon its considerable virtues in the public prints. The stage production, save in the final passages, is a credit to the text. Those final passages themselves, indeed, may be a discredit to the stage production, for while they may be, as the author convincingly contends, in the key of truth and hard fact, they nevertheless constitute dubious theatre. People, thousands, ten thousands of them, still commit suicide when the grimness of fate staggers them, but the modern drama at its best is a philosopher or a wit or a psychoanalytical professor which credibly argues its own fate-struck children out of doing it. However, the play merits your devoted attention. Its theme you doubtless already know: the ruin and tragedy that befall two young women teachers in a girls' school following a whispered accusation,—on the part of a maleficent little pupil—that they are Lesbians.

In the loud insistence of several of my critical colleagues that the title of the play is unduly misleading and that the play is assuredly not for children, I fear that I cannot entirely concur. It assuredly is for children, as well as for adults, unless it be deemed expedient to bring up American youngsters in the belief that dramatic art is solely either something with Fred Stone and his family in it or something in which the characters are dressed as playing-cards, rabbits and walruses. Children may not like it, true enough, any more than they like castor oil, but it will be equally good for them. Nevertheless, in the pretty general insistence that the last half of the last act is defective, I can—as noted—concur fully, though it seems to me that several of the arguments advanced in company with that insistence are disingenuous. One of these arguments is that, in this latter section of the manuscript, none of the adults involved displays a modicum of common sense. That they do not, as charged, display a modicum of common sense is true, but their failure to display it is certainly logical, and dramatically sound enough. It is seldom the gift of mortals to display acute common sense when emotion overwhelms them, save perhaps in the plays of Bernard Shaw. Common sense is rarely present on such occasions in actual life, and its arbitrary introduction into drama in emotional crises would have wrecked a great many of the finest plays ever written.

This silly longing for common sense in drama is often part and parcel of the passion for the so-called realistic drama, itself so largely fraudulent and bogus. There is a true romance in fuddled feeling, and true drama, and realism and logic have no place and no welcome on that side of the footlights. One too many touches of adult common sense, let such critics reflect, would make *Antony and Cleopatra*, aside from its poetry, dramatically indistinguishable from one of John Drinkwater's masterpieces.

Another contention against the final moments of Miss Hellman's play is the re-introduction of the apologetic grandmother and the explanation of the brat's malfeasance. Here, again, truth and the theatre are critically divorced. What Miss Hellman has written down is essential to the integrity of her theme, even if in stage practise it be discommodious to an audience's patience. Her show may be over and done with before the aforesaid re-introduction and explanation, but her play—that is, her manuscript in all its honesty—is not. What she has written is necessary.

So we come, myself along with the others, once again to the reluctant conclusion and admission that the theatre must woefully often forego fact and truth to make good plays better than they are and to satisfy even the more intelligent audience.

> *George Jean Nathan, in a review of "The Children's Hour," in* Vanity Fair, *Vol. 43, No. 6, February, 1935, p. 37.*

CRITICAL COMMENTARY

Anita Block   (essay date 1939)

[*In the following excerpt, Block asserts that a primary theme in* The Children's Hour *is society's bigoted attitude toward homosexuality.*]

In November, 1934, Lillian Hellman's play bearing the innocuous title of **The Children's Hour** opened in New York. It created immediate and wide discussion which continued during the play's long run of six hundred and ninety-one performances. And, what is most unusual in a world lacking in play-consciousness, where the end of the play *as theatre* almost invariably means the end of interest in it, **The Children's Hour** still lives in the minds of those who saw it. Discussion ranges from doubts as to the fitness of the subject of homosexuality for presentation in the theatre to questions as to the motivation for the behavior of the characters and the logic of the play's denouement. I know that the seeing of **The Children's Hour** was for thousands their first impact with the subject of homosexuality. Breaking through the accumulated darkness with simple, yet illuminating, directness, **The Children's Hour** is a striking example of the vital play, profoundly integrated with its own time. Finally, so far as American audiences are concerned, here is a play that does not deal with an aristocratic Parisian young lady or with a plutocratic London gentleman, but with two ordinary American girls, earning their own living as schoolteachers, exactly like everybody's sisters and cousins and sweethearts, who nevertheless become tragically entangled in a hideous situation. It is to Miss Hellman's credit that she makes the crux of her play not the question of homosexuality itself, but society's savage treatment of the homosexual, arising out of cruelly persisting ignorance. Thus in this play we see again how an individual conflict may serve to focus attention on its crucial social implications.

Karen Wright and Martha Dobie have, through eight years of work and self-sacrifice, established their school for girls near a typical American town. They are progressive college women who thoroughly understand the disturbing behavior of the adolescent girl, and so they have been more than patient with their fourteen-year-old pupil, Mary Tilford. This girl is almost subject enough in herself for a play, although here she is used only as the entirely credible instrument responsible for the drama's catastrophe. Mary is an orphan, spoiled by a grandmother who adores her and whom she dominates. In the world outside, symbolized by the school, which she instinctively senses is hostile to her, she expresses her will to power by trickery and lies so far as her teachers are concerned, and by a sadistic cruelty toward her fellow pupils which makes of them her abject slaves. Last, but not least, her awakening interest in sex takes the form of a prurient pursuit of its abnormal aspects. It is she who secretly circulates a volume of *Mademoiselle de Maupin*. On the fatal day on which the play opens, Mary, in furious resentment at the discipline meted out to her for reprehensible conduct, announces to a few of the pupils that she intends to run away at once to her grandmother. To the astounded question: "What are you going to tell your grandmother?" Mary replied: "Oh, I'll think of something to tell her." And we have little doubt that she will. . . .

At almost the same time Martha, who has, for economic reasons, tolerated, as a teacher in the school, a narrow-minded aunt who is dependent on her and of whose unfitness she is on this disturbed day especially conscious, informs her she must leave; and the aunt, turning on her, blames Martha's action on the fact that "he" is in the house that day. "He" is Dr. Joe Cardin, Karen's fiancé, and the aunt continues:—

> I know what I know. Every time that man comes into the house you have a fit. It seems like you just can't stand the idea of them being together. God knows what you'll do when they get married. You're jealous of him, that's what it is. . . . And it's unnatural, just as unnatural as it can be. . . . You were always like that, even as a child. If you had a little girl friend you always got mad when she liked anybody else. . . .

Startled by a noise at the door, Martha discovers some eavesdropping girls, who promptly report what they have overheard to Mary. And Mary's miserably deformed mind tells her that here she has found her story for her grandmother, her weapon for release from the hated school.

So Mary goes to her grandmother, the respectable Mrs. Tilford, with a whispered tale of horror, detailing the abnormal love-life of the innocent Karen and Martha. And kindly Mrs. Tilford, now hardened by the ignorant repulsion of millions like her, is incapable not only of the shadow of doubt, but also of the shadow of pity. Overcome with disgust, she telephones the shocking news to all the mothers she can reach, so that they may hurry their daughters away from the school. All her previous knowledge of the two admirable young women is at once blotted out by the mention of what to her uninformed mind is unpardonable moral depravity. Incredulous, Karen and Martha appear; and together with the Doctor they insist on questioning Mary. And when Mary's story is finally shaken, she shrieks that it was another girl who "saw them." Whereupon this child, having been previously terrorized by Mary's threats, corroborates her vindictive lies. But Martha and Karen, determined to be cleared publicly, inform Mrs. Tilford that they will sue her for "libel."

When the last act opens, their "libel" suit has been lost and Karen and Martha, hopeless, have hidden themselves away in their empty school. They are publicly branded, and they feel that wherever they may go they will be pariahs. The Doctor, outwardly cheerful, has a plan for their

all going to Vienna, where he studied and can get work; but Karen knows how he longs to stay in his home town with his own practice. And to her bitter grief she knows another thing, too—that in the heart of the man she loves there lurks a doubt, that on his lips there trembles the question she finally compels him to ask. Gently she answers it: "No. Martha and I have never touched each other." But shaken as she is, she feels that he and she can never again believe each other, never again be natural and joyous together. So she sends him away "to think this all over," although she is convinced that their relation is at an end.

It is Martha, however, who is the real victim of the tragedy. Whether she has been shocked by her experiences into a clarifying knowledge of her true nature, or whether she has been so shattered as to believe herself abnormal, Martha now confesses to Karen that she does love her "the way they said" and that she probably always did. And feeling that she has ruined Karen's life and her own, and above all that they can now no longer stay together, Martha steps quietly into the next room and shoots herself.

A few moments later there appears at the school none other than Mrs. Tilford herself. She has come to tell them that, through the other girl, Mary was finally compelled to confess her diabolical lies, and that her grandmother is now here to make amends, including a public apology arranged by the judge who had found them "guilty." But Martha is dead, and to Karen there seems no reason for living. Yet when she sees the remorseful woman, Karen's bitterness falls from her; she understands that Mrs. Tilford, herself a victim of society's ignorance, could not have acted otherwise. Wearily she promises to accept her help, even "perhaps" later to go back to the Doctor. . . . At least we are left with the consolation that Karen will find her way out of this nightmare of medieval torture into a life and love enlarged by new understanding. . . .

This play has broken down, in thousands, their antipathy against its subject and aroused in them the desire for further knowledge. The suicide of Martha, immolated on the altar of cruelty toward the invert, raises the important question of the tragic needlessness of her death and of the right of the homosexual to the fullest personal happiness. *The Children's Hour* is not flawless, but the playwright deals with a subject of grave human import in such a way as to carry the theatre forward and to give it its deepest meaning and significance. (pp. 122-26)

> *Anita Block, "Contemporary Drama: The Individual in Conflict with Changing Sexual Standards," in her* The Changing World in Plays and Theatre, *1939. Reprint by Da Capo Press, 1971, pp. 76-132.*

Eric Bentley   (essay date 1953)

[*Bentley is considered one of the most erudite and innovative critics of the modern theater. He was responsible for introducing Bertolt Brecht, Luigi Pirandello, and other European playwrights to America through his studies, translations, and stage adaptations of their plays. In his critical works, Bentley concentrates on the*

*playwright and the dramatic text, rather than on pro-
duction aspects of the play. Thus in his first important
critical study,* The Playwright as Thinker *(1946), Bentley distinguishes between "art" and "commodity" in the
American theater, basing his definition of commodity on
the premise that most producers are more attentive to
box office receipts than to the artistic quality of a play,
and, as a result, the dramatist is often neglected as a true
artist. Some critics consider this approach an attempt to
compensate for Bentley's unwillingness to accept drama
as a form of popular entertainment. Bentley's finest
work,* The Life of Drama *(1964), is a comprehensive
study of the development of dramatic form, specifically
examining aspects of melodrama, farce, comedy, tragedy, and tragicomedy. Other critical works include anthologies of reviews written during his years as drama
critic (1952-56) for the* New Republic, *and a collection
of his essays on Brecht—*The Brecht Commentaries:
1943-80 *(1981). In the following essay, written on the occasion of a 1953 revival of* The Children's Hour, *Bentley
finds numerous flaws in the drama, charging that Hellman is "less concerned to see life than to manipulate
it."*]

It isn't that one asks her to be Shakespeare. The genre to
which *The Children's Hour* belongs is an honorable, if not
a major, one. Call it the publicist's drama, the drama of
indignation. In such drama we shall not expect to feel the
emotion of characters as strongly as the author's animus.
We shan't ask what such a dramatist has created, we ask
who is the enemy this time, and how clearly the dramatist
has made us see him.

The material from which *A Children's Hour* is made suggests two stories. The first is a story of heterosexual teachers accused of Lesbianism; the enemy is a society which
punishes the innocent. The second is a story of Lesbian
teachers accused of Lesbianism; the enemy is a society
which punishes Lesbians. Now, since either one of these
stories could make an acceptable indignant play, we could
scarcely be surprised if a playwright tried to tell them both
at once. But this is not quite what Miss Hellman does. She
spends the greater part of the evening on the first story.
In fact the indignation she arouses in us has but one
source—our impression that the charge of Lesbianism is
unfounded, an impression reinforced by everyone's holy
horror whenever the subject comes up. Then, in the last
few minutes, we learn that one of the teachers *is* Lesbian.
But it is too late for Miss Hellman to tell Story Two and
spell out its moral. The "guilty" teacher kills herself, and
the curtain comes down. Taking the play as a technical exercise, we could praise this ending as clever, or damn it as
clumsy, but if we are interested in Miss Hellman's indignation, and especially if, during the evening, she has induced
us to share it, we are bound to feel cheated. We are told
that the play has been revived because of the current red
scare. Now suppose it had been about teachers accused of
communism, that for over two acts we had been asked to
boil with indignation at the wrongness of the accusation,
only to find, towards the close of act three, that one of the
pair *did* harbor communist sympathies? Of course, a play
can favor communism; a non-communist play can favor
the toleration of communists; but these very different

plays cannot be squeezed into the last ten minutes of a play
protesting at the incrimination of non-communists.

Or can they? The political analogy suggests not only the
logical weakness of Miss Hellman's position but also the
historical and psychological path along which she reached
it. Is it not in politics, rather than the theatre, that we have
witnessed this drama before? Mr. A would say it was infantile to accuse Mr. B of communism—"after all you're
accused of communism nowadays if your hair is red"—
and yet, later, when Mr. B did come out with communist
views, Mr. A was neither displeased nor surprised. In the
thirties, Mr. A would have said that of course an Alger
Hiss was not a spy and then, if the espionage had been
proved, he would have said, well, the Soviet Union is a
special case . . . *The Children's Hour* has nothing directly
to do with communism, but it was written in the thirties,
and is the product of the dubious idealism of that time.
Commenting on the play, Miss Hellman wrote: "I am a
moral writer, often too moral a writer" [see Author Com-
mentary]. As a man's feeling of being moral increases, his
awareness of moral issues declines. The "too moral" writer takes everything for granted.

For example, her antagonists. In *The Children's Hour*
there are three: cowardice (Mrs. Mortar), credulity (Mrs.
Tilford), and sheer evil (Mary). In each case, Miss Hellman counts on our having our response ready. Our hatred
of cowardice is to put the flesh and blood on the skeleton
from Broadway farce which is all the author provides. Our
understanding of credulity is relied on to make plausible
an old lady's believing the villian's unplausible accusations: no character is created of whom we must say, "*she*
of course would have believed." Finally, our being against
sin is supposed to assure our hatred of a villain's unex-
plained villainy. I for one would not insist on a psychological explanation of evil (though such an explanation would
be in place in drama of this sort) but if you don't explain
it psychologically, you must either explain it some other
way, or *create* it, as the Elizabethans did. Miss Hellman's
villain is a *diabolus ex machina* not simply lowered onstage at the end but smuggled in at the outset.

This villain is a child. Instead of the sweet little chee-ild
done to death by the tyrannical teacher we have the sweet
little teacher done to death by the tyrannical child—an inversion of orthodox melodrama which would be all very
well if the values of melodrama, as well as the roles, were
inverted. But Miss Hellman is a melodramatist, first, in
seeing life as a melodrama insofar as she sees it at all and,
second, in being less concerned to see life than to manipulate it. Admittedly, the audience at the Coronet is not concerned with the moral ambiguities I find inherent in the
play. As far as I could observe, they are busy being delightedly shocked at two phenomena: Lesbianism and
wickedness in a child. (pp. 30-1)

Eric Bentley, "Hellman's Indignation," in
The New Republic, *Vol. 128, No. 1, January
5, 1953, pp. 30-1.*

Philip M. Armato   (essay date 1973)

[In the following essay, Armato discusses the concept of mercy as the central message of The Children's Hour.*]*

Critics have often called *The Children's Hour* a melodrama. Those who have done so, see Karen Wright and Martha Dobie as "good" characters who are victimized by "evil" Mary Tilford. To Barrett H. Clark [see overview dated 1944] and Brooks Atkinson [in the *New York Times,* 19 December 1952], Mary Tilford is a "monster." Even Hellman's most perceptive critic [Jacob H. Adler, in his *Lillian Hellman*] calls her "the embodiment of pure evil." If *The Children's Hour* is the story of a "sweet little teacher done to death by . . . [a] tyrannical child" [Eric Bentley; see commentary dated 1953], then we must concur with Barrett Clark's reading of the play's ultimate meaning: " . . . here is evil . . . make the best of it."

With great patience, Lillian Hellman has defended her play against the attacks of those who have labelled it a melodrama. In a 1965 interview [in the *Paris Review* 9], for example, she said that it is wrong to view her characters as being entirely good or evil: "You [the author] have no right to see your characters as good or bad. Such words have nothing to do with people you write about. Other people see them that way." The interviewer reminded Hellman that in the preface to the 1942 edition of her plays she had said that *The Children's Hour* was about goodness and badness. To this she replied, "Goodness and badness is different from good and bad people isn't it?" Her assertions suggest that Hellman did not intend to portray a melodramatic conflict between two "good" teachers and an "evil" child when she wrote her play. To clarify the play's substance, we should ask what, within the world of the play, is good and what evil.

Playwrights seldom underestimate the dramatic value of the visual-aural impact at curtain rise. The opening of *The Children's Hour,* in a study-room of the Wright-Dobie school, seems undramatic. Mrs. Lily Mortar, Martha Dobie's aunt, is sleeping, the students are sewing. The action which would catch the eyes of the audience is that of Evelyn Munn, "using her scissors to trim the hair of Rosalie, who sits, nervously, in front of her. She has Rosalie's head bent back at an awkward angle and is enjoying herself." However, the audience sees this stark visual image of the infantile pleasure of exercising cruelty while hearing about mercy, for the first words are those of a student reciting Portia's famous speech in *The Merchant of Venice.* Portia's plea for mercy should make an exceedingly strong impression on the audience, for portions of it are interpolated six times between the dialogue of Mrs. Mortar and her pupils. The visual image of cruelty is juxtaposed with the words "pity" and "mercy," which are repeated seven times during the opening moments of the play.

In *The Children's Hour* Hellman posits mercy as an ultimate good and merciless cruelty as an ultimate evil. But to understand the merciless world of Lancet and its cruelty, one must move beyond the notion that Mary Tilford is the embodiment of it.

The rancorous structure of interpersonal relationships in *The Children's Hour* is patterned after the structure of human association in the Venice of Shakespeare's *Merchant.* This can best be described as a victim-victimizer syndrome, the most concrete representation of which is the relationship between Antonio and Shylock. Antonio is convinced that his harsh treatment of Shylock is "just," because the Jew's interest rates are harsh. As victim, Shylock suffers from spiritual agony, feelings of persecution, and desires revenge. If he is able to consummate his wish, Shylock will become the victimizer of the man who originally victimized him. That the victim-victimizer syndrome is finally self-destructive is seen in the courtroom scene, when each victimizer in turn is reduced to the position of victim. Shylock's demand for Antonio's life is turned against him when Portia reminds the court that an alien Jew must suffer the death penalty if he plots against the life of a Venetian citizen. The Duke and Antonio destroy the vicious circle by showing mercy to Shylock.

In the first two acts of her play, Hellman develops three relationships which are characterized by the circular form and destructive content of the victim-victimizer syndrome; these pairs are: Karen Wright—Mary Tilford, Martha Dobie—Lily Mortar, and Amelia Tilford—Wright/Dobie. In *The Merchant,* a Jew who is socially inferior to a Christian is mistreated by the Christian and attempts to use the Duke—the land's highest authority—as a vehicle for his revenge. In *The Children's Hour,* an adolescent pupil who is socially inferior to an adult teacher is mistreated by the teacher and proceeds to use Lancet's most influential citizen—the powerful matron Amelia Tilford—as a vehicle for her revenge. Finally, in the much criticized third act, Hellman, like Shakespeare, posits mercy as the only solution to the moral dilemma which is created when we deal justly with each other.

Karen Wright's treatment of Mary Tilford has never been sensitively evaluated. No one has noticed that immediately preceding their initial confrontation, Hellman suggests that Karen is perhaps not as compassionate as a teacher of young children should be. For when Mrs. Mortar complains that one of her students does not "appreciate" Portia's plea for mercy, Karen replies: "Well I didn't either. I don't think I do yet." The harshness of her discipline will demonstrate the truth—on a far more literal level than she suspects—of her remark.

Mary Tilford's offense is a minor one. She attempts to excuse her tardiness by saying that she was picking flowers for Mrs. Mortar. The flowers, Karen knows, were "picked" from the top of a garbage can, and Mary's stubborn refusal to admit the truth convinces Karen that she must be punished. First, Mary is told to take her recreation periods alone for two weeks; then, that her friend Evelyn will no longer be her roommate, and that she must now live with her enemy Rosalie. Mary is also ordered not to leave the grounds for any reason. Hellman emphasizes Karen's harshness by adding details—Mary is specifically forbidden participation in hockey and horse-back riding—and by one further prohibition. Mary hopes that Karen's rules apply only to weekdays; if so, she may still be able to attend an event she has been looking forward to, the boat-races on Saturday. Unfortunately, she is told that she cannot attend them. While these restrictions might not be extreme deprivation for an adult, they are so for a child.

Mary feels—and rightly—that she is being persecuted. From wanting to tell her grandmother "how everybody treats me here and the way I get punished for every little thing I do," she moves to a sense of her inner agony, objectified in her hysterical "heart problems," and finally to a rebellious attitude: "They can't get away with treating me like this, and they don't have to think they can." She sets out to take her revenge, as is the victim's wont. She accuses Karen and Martha of lesbianism, and persists in her lie. Her behavior is ugly, but has been provoked by Karen's earlier ugliness: she seeks an eye for an eye, a tooth for a tooth.

Karen's inability to deal compassionately with Mary Tilford is paralleled in Act I by Martha Dobie's attitude toward her aunt Lily. Karen and Martha decide that she must be relieved of her teaching duties, and literally thrown out of school. Their decision is just, for Mortar is a nuisance and an incompetent, yet they do not consider for a moment the effect such a dismissal may have on an old woman whose life has been the school. Again, justice is untempered by mercy, and again Hellman emphasizes the rigidity of the decision's administration. Martha not only tells Lily that she must leave, but makes fun of her— "We don't want you around when we dig up the buried treasure"—and threatens that "You ought to be glad I don't do worse." Mortar pathetically attempts to save face: "I absolutely refuse to be shipped off three thousand miles away. I'm not going to England. I shall go back to the stage. I'll write my agents tomorrow, and as soon as they have something good for me—." This is essentially a plea for mercy cast in a manner that will allow her to retain some semblance of dignity. The old crone is finished on the stage, her "agents" are imaginary, and if she does not leave until they find her a part, she will never leave at all, which is her wish. Her suggestion is brusquely rejected. As Karen isolates Mary, Martha exiles Mortar. Lily's reaction is the same as Mary's: "You always take your spite out on me." As she exits, she casts toward Martha a "malicious half-smile" and the malice of revenge is realized when she refuses to testify on Martha's behalf at the libel trial.

In Act II, Karen and Martha suffer an ironic reversal of fortune; the victimizers become victims themselves. Amelia Tilford, an influential figure in the community of Lancet, misuses her authority over Karen and Martha just as surely as they had taken advantage of the weaker positions of Mary and Lily. When Mary tells Amelia that her two teachers are lesbian, the dowager immediately phones the parents of the children who are enrolled at Wright-Dobie and repeats the charges, thus destroying the school. When Karen and Martha come for an explanation, Amelia makes it clear that she does not want these two lepers in her house: "I don't think you should have come here. . . . I shall not call you names, and I will not allow you to call me names. It comes to this: I can't trust myself to talk about it with you now or ever." Her condescension and her revulsion in the face of her visitors' suspected abnormality pervades the scene: "This—this thing is your own.

Go away with it. I don't understand it and I don't want any part of it." Ironically, Karen and Martha now suffer from the same humiliation and ostracism that they so rigorously inflicted on others.

To make the ironic parallel—and thus the lesson—even more explicit, Hellman shows Karen and Martha reacting just as Lily and Mary had. Both think that they are being unjustly persecuted: "What is she [Amelia] trying to do to us? What is everyone doing to us?" Both feel spiritual agony: "You're not playing with paper dolls. We're human beings, see? It's our lives you're fooling with. *Our* lives." Finally, they feel the need for revenge: "What can we do to you [Amelia]? There must be something— something that makes you feel the way we do tonight. You don't want any part of this, you said. But you'll get a part. More than you bargained for."

In Act II, then, Hellman presents a change in relationships, but not a change in the structure of relationships. The rancorous victim-victimizer syndrome is as pervasive in this act as it was in the previous one, the difference being that relationships have now come full circle; those who mistreated others are now mistreated themselves. Clearly, Hellman implies that when one mistreats another, he plants the seeds of his own destruction. This insight is made even more explicit in the third act.

Martha admits to herself that she has always been physically attracted to Karen. Her attitude toward herself is just as harsh as it had been towards others—or as Amelia Tilford's attitude had been towards lesbianism. Indeed, Martha's rancorous attitude toward the imperfections of others is but a reflection of her own self-condemnation. Hellman is making the same crucial point that Sartre makes in *Dirty Hands,* when he has Hoederer say to Hugo, "You, I know you now, you are a destroyer. You detest man because you detest yourself."

As in the other two acts, there is a parallel action, but this time it is the difference that is instructive, not the similarity. Martha's self-condemnation is matched by a new-found self-disgust in Amelia Tilford. She discovers that Mary has lied about her two teachers, and realizes that her hasty phone calls have destroyed two people who are innocent of the charges. Her discovery propels her into the same kind of guilt and self-laceration that we have just seen driving Martha to suicide. Amelia begs Karen to allow her to "do something" for her so that she can in part expiate her sin. Karen extends mercy.

Hellman counterpoints Karen's new-found benevolence with the by now familiar infantile hostility of Lily Mortar, who protests against Amelia Tilford even setting foot in the school: "With Martha lying there? How can you be so feelingless? . . . I won't stay and see it. I won't have anything to do with it. I'll never let that woman—." Martha's suicide, however, has for Karen been both harrowing and educative. Because of it she is, she tells Amelia, "Not [young] any more." The brief statement implies that she feels sadness at the loss of her own innocence, but also suggests that Martha's death has introduced her to a new maturity. Her horror at the guilt that caused Martha's suicide leads her to sympathize with the plight of "guilt-ridden"

Amelia. In the last moments of the play, she accepts Amelia's atonement and thereby extends compassion—the ultimate good in the world of the play.

> MRS. TILFORD: You'll be all right?
>
> KAREN: I'll be all right, I suppose. Goodbye, now. (*They both rise.* MRS. TILFORD *speaks, pleadingly.*)
>
> MRS. TILFORD: You'll let me help you? You'll let me try?
>
> KAREN: Yes, if it will make you feel better.
>
> MRS. TILFORD: (*With great feeling.*) Oh, yes, oh, yes, Karen. (*Unconsciously* KAREN *begins to walk towards the window.*)
>
> KAREN: (*Suddenly.*) Is it nice out?
>
> MRS. TILFORD: It's been cold. (KAREN *opens the window slightly, sits on the ledge.* MRS TILFORD *with surprise.*) It seems a little warmer now.
>
> KAREN: It feels very good. (*They smile at each other.*)

Karen has destroyed the vicious circle that has characterized human relations; her compassion is the ultimate good in the world of the play.

The two traditional criticisms of *The Children's Hour*'s last act are that Mary Tilford is the central interest of the play and so should not be missing at its conclusion; and that the final "summing up" (Hellman's words) is tedious. However, Mary Tilford is not the central interest of the play; a certain perverse structure of human relationships is. Moreover, if critics paid more attention to what Hellman is "summing up," they would find that the conclusion of the play is a structurally necessary resolution, not a tedious reiteration of previous materials. Jacob H. Adler has noted that *The Children's Hour*, like *The Wild Duck*, "ends not with . . . [a] suicide but with a brief discussion pinning down the issues as a result of the suicide."

Works as diverse as Aeschylus' *Oresteia*, Shakespeare's *Measure for Measure*, and Melville's *Billy Budd* have dealt with the dichotomy between primitive justice and mercy. Although *The Children's Hour* is certainly a less monumental work of art than any of these, it is within its limits a wholly successful moral play. Hellman suggests that adults are too often "children." While infantile revenge is matter of course in men's dealings with each other, Hellman shows a last-act discovery—Karen Wright's discovery of a more mature concept of compassion. (pp. 443-47)

> *Philip M. Armato, " 'Good and Evil' in Lillian Hellman's 'The Children's Hour',"* in Educational Theatre Journal, *Vol. 25, No. 4, December, 1973, pp. 443-47.*

THE LITTLE FOXES

PRODUCTION REVIEWS

Brooks Atkinson   (review date 16 February 1939)

[*While praising* The Little Foxes *in the production review below, Atkinson ranks it below* The Children's Hour, *due to its melodramatic rather than tragic execution.*]

As a theatrical story-teller Lillian Hellman is biting and expert. In *The Little Foxes,* which was acted at the National last evening, she thrusts a bitter story straight to the bottom of a bitter play. As compared with *The Children's Hour,* which was her first notable play, *The Little Foxes* will have to take second rank. For it is a deliberate exercise in malice—melodramatic rather than tragic, none too fastidious in its manipulation of the stage and presided over by a Pinero frown of fustian morality. But out of greed in a malignant Southern family of 1900 she has put together a vibrant play that works and that bestows viable parts on all the members of the cast. None of the new plays in which Tallulah Bankhead has acted here has given her such sturdy support and such inflammable material. Under Herman Shumlin's taut direction Miss Bankhead plays with great directness and force, and Patricia Collinge also distinguishes herself with a remarkable performance. *The Little Foxes* can act and is acted.

It would be difficult to find a more malignant gang of petty robber barons than Miss Hellman's chief characters. Two brothers and a sister in a small Southern town are consumed with a passion to exploit the earth. Forming a partnership with a Chicago capitalist, they propose to build a cotton factory in the South, where costs are cheap and profits high. The Chicago end of the deal is sound. But Miss Hellman is telling a sordid story of how the brothers and the sister destroy each other with their avarice and cold hatred. They crush the opposition set up by a brother-in-law of higher principles; they rob him and hasten his death. But they also outwit each other in sharp dealing and they bargain their mean souls away.

It is an inhuman tale. Miss Hellman takes a dextrous playwright's advantage of the abominations it contains. Her first act is a masterpiece of skillful exposition. Under the gentility of a social occasion she suggests with admirable reticence the evil of her conspirators. When she lets loose in the other two acts she writes with melodramatic abandon, plotting torture, death and thievery like the author of an old-time thriller. She has made her drama air-tight; it is a knowing job of construction, deliberate and self-contained. In the end she tosses in a speech of social significance, which is no doubt sincere. But *The Little Foxes* is so cleverly contrived that it lacks spontaneity. It is easier to accept as an adroitly designed theatre piece than as a document in the study of humanity.

One practical advantage of a theatre piece is the opportunities it supplies to the actors. In a perfectly cast performance, none of them fumbles his part. Sometimes our Tallulah walks buoyantly through a part without much feeling for the whole design. But as the malevolent lady of *The Little Foxes* she plays with superb command of the entire character—sparing of the showy side, constantly aware of the poisonous spirit within. As a neurotic victim of circumstances, Miss Collinge also drags the whole truth out of a character, and acts it with extraordinary lightness and grace. Frank Conroy plays the part of a tired man of the house with patient strength of character. Florence Williams is singularly touching in the part of a bewildered, apprehensive daughter of the family. There are also vivid characterizations in the other parts by Charles Dingie, Abbie Mitchell, Carl Benton Reid, Dan Duryea, Lee Baker and John Marriott.

Howard Bay has provided a setting that conveys the dark stealthiness of the story, and Aline Bernstein has designed suitable costumes for a period narrative. As for the title, it comes from the Bible: "Take us the foxes, the little foxes, that spoil the vines; for our vines have tender grapes." Out of rapacity, Miss Hellman has made an adult horror-play. Her little foxes are wolves that eat their own kind.

Brooks Atkinson, in a review of, "The Little Foxes," in The New York Times, *February 16, 1939, p. 16.*

George Jean Nathan   **(review date 27 February 1939)**

[*In the following review, Nathan asserts that* The Little Foxes *assures Hellman's place as the most skillful female playwright of her time.*]

Lillian Hellman's new play, **The Little Foxes,** provides fresh evidence of its author's high position among American women writers for the stage. Both in **The Children's Hour** and in this exhibit—even, indeed, in certain phases of her defective **Days to Come**—she indicates a dramatic mind, an eye to character, a fundamental strength, and a complete and unremitting integrity that are rare among her native playwriting sex. Her dramaturgic equipment is infinitely superior to Susan Glaspell's; her surgery of and grip on character are infinitely superior to Lula Vollmer's; and compared with her Rachel Crothers is merely a shrewd damsel in a box-office dispensing prettily water-colored parlor tracts. Some of her other sisters enjoy pleasant little talents but there is none in the whole kit and caboodle whose work shows so courageous and unflinching an adherence to the higher and better standards of drama. Once she has succeeded in mastering her present weaknesses—a periodic confusion of melodramatic bitterness with suggestive tragedy, intensified and unrelieved acerbity with mounting drama, and a skeletonization of episode

Act II of the 1939 production of The Little Foxes: *Regina (Tallulah Bankhead), her husband Horace Giddens (Frank Conroy), nephew Leo Hubbard (Dan Duryea), and brothers Ben Hubbard (Charles Dingle) and Oscar Hubbard (Carl Benton Reid).*

with dramatic economy—she will find herself occupying a really distinguished critical place in our theater.

Her latest play, admirably staged by Herman Shumlin and given the best performance of her career by Tallulah Bankhead, to say nothing of being further assisted on its course by a supporting company with hardly a flaw in it, is a scrutiny of social and economic changes in the South at the turn of the present century. Related in terms of a middle-class family of rapacious and conniving knaves bent upon out-doing not only one another but upon sacrificing all that is proud and fine in the tradition of the old southland to the new economic slavery and the new capitalistic greed, it may flippantly be described as a Dodie Smith nightmare. It may also be less flippantly described as the very best illustration of the difference between the current cheap and squashy family drama calculatedly manufactured by English female pastry cooks and the fond intention, at least, of American women like this Hellman to bring to the stage that inner inviolable dramatic vitality and thematic meat which London critics on brief excursions to these shores so offendedly and patriotically minimize and derogate. From first to last, *The Little Foxes* betrays not an inch of compromise, not a sliver of a sop to the comfortable acquiescence of Broadway or Piccadilly, not the slightest token that its author has had anything in her purpose but writing the truest and most honest play on her theme that it was possible for her to write.

The central characters are a woman and her two brothers who individually and apart brook no interference with their selfish determinations to get for themselves what they want out of family, community, finance, and worldly position. The woman is hard, disillusioned, and merciless to the point of contributing to the death of her invalid husband in order to perch herself on top of the heap. The brothers descend to perjury, theft, and even to veiled threat of murder accusation to dislodge her from it. In the handling of character, the ghost of Strindberg here and there peers over Miss Hellman's shoulder as in the treatment of theme the ghost of Ibsen—momentarily and paradoxically, too, the ghost of the Pinero of *The Thunderbolt*—here and there edges the spook of Strindberg to one side. The conclusion resolves itself into a temporary triumph for the wily, slate-hearted female but with the evil of the money-hungry brothers' machinations a cloud darkening her future. And out of the parable of boiling acid there emerges the disgust and defiance of a new, young generation that throws into the face of mankind the challenge of human decency, fairness, equity, and honor.

Where the play partly defeats its potential, proper, and full effect is in the grinding monotony of its emotional drive, in its periodic over-elaborate melodramatic countenance, and in its failure to invest its explosion with that complete sense of tragic purge which is the mark and nobility of the drama of Melpomene. It strikes the note of bitterness so steadily and loudly that, when the moment for purging exaltation comes, the psychic and emotional ear is too deadened to hear it even were it there. But just the same it is a play 'way above the general and, though it must by its very nature prove anathema to popular audiences, a credit to its author and to American dramatic writing.

George Jean Nathan, "Dour Octopus," in Newsweek, *Vol. XIII, No. 9, February 27, 1939, p. 26.*

John Mason Brown   (review date 11 March 1939)

[*Brown, an influential and popular American drama critic during the 1930s, 40s, and 50s, wrote extensively on contemporary British and American theater. He had a thorough knowledge of dramatic history, and his criticism often displays a scholarly erudition in addition to the qualities of popular reviewing. In the following review, which was first published in the 11 March 1939 issue of the* New York Post, *Brown suggests that the actors' fine performances in* The Little Foxes, *especially Tallulah Bankhead's as Regina, distract the audience from flaws in Hellman's play.*]

If *The Little Foxes* gave us no other cause for gratitude, the mere fact that it at last provides Tallulah Bankhead with a part in this country which reveals her full splendors as an actress would be enough to put us all in Miss Hellman's debt. Miss Bankhead is a player who has abundantly deserved her present good fortune. The faults of her Cleopatra have long since slipped into ancient history and been forgotten. Even at their worst they had nothing to do with Miss Bankhead's extraordinary powers as a realist.

For some years, in such insufficient scripts as *Dark Victory, Forsaking All Others, Something Gay,* and *Reflected Glory,* she has been giving tantalizing glimpses of these powers. All of us have admired her sullen beauty, and applauded the versatility she has shown in realism as she has turned emotional cartwheels from tragedy to comedy and back again.

As we have listened to her husky laugh, or heard her release her throbbing voice, we have sensed the vibrancy which is hers. We have noted the restless energy which has granted uncommon strength in her playing. We have observed her grace and responded to the explosive force of her personality. We may have regretted the lack of discipline which has marred some of her effects. Always, however, we have realized, as we have watched her pacing through unfortunate plays like a caged pantheress, that before us was an actress so gorgeously endowed that it would be one of the true theatrical misfortunes of our time were she to be unable to find a script permitting her to do justice to herself.

Fortunately for all of us, *The Little Foxes* brings Miss Bankhead her long-awaited opportunity. As the despicable Southern wife who is the central figure of Miss Hellman's drama, she gives the performance we have been waiting impatiently for her to give. She creates the kind of villainess even the Grand Guignol has never matched. Her technical resourcefulness is put to superb use. Her smoldering strength galvanizes the attention. Her quality of immediate ignition, of incessant combustibility enslaves the interest. In her torrid presence one understands why it is that theatres have to have asbestos curtains. One watches her fascinated, as if confronted by a cobra. To see her is to see Sargent's Madame X come to life, possessed of a clammy heart into which flows the black blood of Clytemnestra, Medusa, Lady Macbeth, and Mrs. Danvers.

If one has the time, even while sitting breathlessly before **The Little Foxes,** to keep on thinking of how magnificent a Hedda Gabler Miss Bankhead would make, the fault is not Miss Bankhead's. Hers is a brilliant performance throughout. It is Miss Hellman who by her very overcompetence forces the mind to wander.

It is Miss Hellman because, engrossing as is her play, it suffers from being far too well contrived for its own enduring health. Much of its writing is too expert in the worst manner of Ibsen, which is only another way of saying in the best manner of Pinero. It is not only a play that is wellmade (as if that in itself were not something to date it); it is a play that is too-well-made. This in no way detracts from its fascination in production. But as a drama which pretends to sociological significance and abiding literary importance, it does put **The Little Foxes** in precisely the same category in the the the theatre which *Rebecca* occupies on the list of best-sellers in fiction.

Just as *Rebecca* forces you to feel as if you were about to shake hands with the Brontës on any page, so **The Little Foxes** seduces you into believing that at almost any minute all of Ibsen's and Strindberg's most unattractive heroes and heroines, having crossed the Atlantic without suffering a sea change, will suddenly bob up on the stage as Sons and Daughters of the Confederacy, in convention met near Atlanta. Do not misunderstand me. The literary skill of both Miss Du Maurier's novel and Miss Hellman's melodrama is such that, while their spell is upon you, you are willing to believe you are getting literature, although in both cases your better judgment insists upon informing you at every turn that all you are receiving is super-Crime Club stuff.

As a *fleurs du mal* dramatization of the profit motive below the Mason-Dixon line, I do not for a moment doubt that, if it were badly acted, Miss Hellman's absorbingly unpleasant guignol would evoke snickers because of the very boldness with which she has dipped her pen in sulphur. Miss Hellman has a genius for plotting. Such closeknit plotting as she is adept at is more than slightly oldfashioned in the theatre; it is a lost art.

One grows suspicious of it, even as one tires of the way in which Miss Hellman unrolls a red carpet before every scene in her play, hell-bent upon turning each one of them into what, in the language of "Sardoodledom," used to be called a "big scene." Her costumes of the turn of the century help her in protecting the excesses of her storytelling. So does the commendable validity of much of her observation and the way in which she *seems* to look into the hearts of evil characters and goad these people into action.

Most of all, it is Miss Hellman's actors who endow her play with its final effectiveness. It is Charles Dingle as a sinister brother. It is Carl Benton Reid as a loathsome husband. It is Patricia Collinge who gives one of the season's most poignant performances as a silly Southern wife driven by despair into becoming a secret drinker. Above all, it is Tallulah Bankhead. These players are all of them so expert that, even while they keep Miss Hellman's play the

superlatively "good theatre" it is, they are able for the most part, with her Machiavellian aid, to make it seem much more than that. The result is an evening of extraordinary interest and almost anguishing tension. (pp. 116-20)

> *John Mason Brown, "The Only Honest Hypocrites," in his* Broadway in Review, *W. W. Norton & Company, Inc., 1940, pp. 105-131.*

Euphemia Van Rensselaer Wyatt   (review date April 1939)

[*In the following excerpt, Wyatt considers* The Little Foxes *a parable directed at those who stand by and watch others destroy the earth.*]

> Catch us the little foxes that destroy the vines;
> for our vineyard hath flourished.
>   [Canticle of Canticles, ii. 15]

Gone with the wind may be the ugly era of reconstruction and the Northern carpetbaggers but the exploitation of the South is not ended for, as Miss Hellman shows in her latest play [**The Little Foxes**], the South can now exploit itself. It is not written, however, for any particular locality, but as a general exposure of those foxes who run amuck through our social order careless of the vines they may destroy to reach the grapes of their desire. The parable is directed towards those who watch the little foxes at their work but who build no fences and set traps too late to ensnare them.

We are not told how long ago Horace Giddens had recognized the vixen in his wife, the ambitious Regina, but he did know the foxiness of the Hubbard family and his two brothers-in-law and apparently the acquaintance had something to do with the heart attacks and his visit to the Johns Hopkins Hospital where he is a patient when the play opens. The Hubbards, a product of the new South, have become the leading capitalists of a small Southern town by the shrewd advantage they have taken of their neighbors. To dispose more profitably of their raw cotton, they point out to a Western banker the low wage scale that could be maintained in a local factory by playing off the darkies against the white crackers. The deal is concluded except for the capital that Horace may contribute. Regina already sees herself in Chicago society and undertakes to pledge herself for Horace. Their sixteen-year-old daughter is dispatched to Baltimore to fetch him home where he arrives in Act II, feeble in body but very firm in spirit and determined to enter into no deal with the Hubbards. The situation grows more tense as Regina, thwarted, openly proclaims her contempt and hatred for her husband and decides that no price is too dear to pay for her ambition and proves it. But how heavy the price we will not say as that would spoil the story. Horace has let the little foxes gnaw at the roots of his own well-being and has seen them destroy the vineyard of his sister-in-law and of his neighbors but he is determined to save his daughter. He does not count on the vindictive power of Regina.

The old South is represented by the pathetic Birdie who married Oscar Hubbard. Birdie thought that Oscar was a handsome young man although he had no ancestral portraits like the ones on her plantation. Later she discovered that it was only the plantation that he wanted. Except for Horace, she is ignored by the entire family. Birdie clings to her niece for her only happiness but although we are given hope that the young girl may escape, there is none held out for Birdie. The gentle old South that has no weapons for defense is ended.

Tallulah Bankhead has created in Regina, a heroine with whom Ibsen had bowing acquaintance in Hedda and Rebecca. Regina, however, is vixen, not feline. She does not bother to play with her victims. Only at the end does she show a touch of compassion towards her daughter. She is not a very complicated character but she has a forceful sense of direction that elicits admiration even from her brothers when she conquers. Her terms are cash and no compromise. But it is partly her beauty that has ruined her husband. On all of this Miss Bankhead has set her seal. The play is hers except for Frank Conroy as Horace and for Miss Patricia Collinge, whose Birdie is a delicate and matchless study. Birdie's unpleasantly retrograde son is also a masterpiece. The others are adequate. Technically this is a better play than Miss Hellman's *Children's Hour.* It offers keen interest but not much pleasure. (pp. 87-8)

> *Euphemia Van Rensselaer Wyatt, in a review*
> *of "The Little Foxes," in* The Catholic World,
> *Vol. CXLIX, April, 1939, pp. 87-8.*

CRITICAL COMMENTARY

Elizabeth Hardwick (essay date 1967)

[*Hardwick is an American novelist and critic. In the following essay, occasioned by the 1967 revival of* The Little Foxes, *she attacks the popular notion that Hellman's plays are technically well-wrought.*]

Among the contented subscribers at the Lincoln Center revival of Lillian Hellman's *The Little Foxes,* I felt the same unease and restlessness that often afflict me at the performances of the APA. Affirmation, enjoyed by that which passes beyond the claim of mere entertainment, will inevitably be a statement of principle, a rebuttal to counter-claims. The *de luxe* conventional gives the greatest possible pleasure to the public and the critics—you can almost reach out and touch the joy our people feel when these two things, in any aspect of our national life, come together. All we ask is to be left alone, with a certain amount of style.

And yet how wearying is the air in which *The Little Foxes* drifts, the sky rich with stars, the earth voluptuous with stuffs, the setting heavy and dark, pampered like some plum-plushy whorehouse in which the girls are no longer young but ripe and experienced in giving customer-satisfaction. It was too much from the beginning. What was being produced? Well, a successful production was being produced, a sort of Lincoln or Cadillac.

What is the play about? I don't think it would have occurred to us to ask that in 1939 when it was first presented.

The answer was clear. *The Little Foxes* was about Tallulah Bankhead—a greedy bitch who, along with her coarse brothers, Ben and Oscar Hubbard, was the very spirit of ruthless Capitalism and ravening Big Business. This family preyed upon some pleasantly pastoral persons, who chattered aimlessly, drank too much, and were innocently, graciously impractical. The extremity of the pastoral weakness is embodied in the condition of Horace Giddens, Regina's husband, who is dying of heart disease. The play was a melodrama, mechanically put together, but redeemed as a composition by the energy of Regina and the brutal yet enjoyable piracy of the brothers, Ben and Oscar.

But what odd things time has done to the text—or to us. It appears to me now—perhaps because of a world around us begging for "development"—that the play is about a besieged Agrarianism, a lost Southern agricultural life, in which virtue and sweetness had a place, and, more strikingly, where social responsibility and justice could, on a personal level at least, be practiced. It is curious what a catalogue of sentiment about the Old South the play turns out to be. I do not know whether this represents the author's conviction, conscious or unconscious, or whether it is the by-product of the plot. First of all the play is divided into Good Characters and Bad Characters. The Good and the Bad cling together in tribal clusters, never tempted to cross the boundaries or to intermingle. Bad are Regina, Oscar and Ben, and Oscar's son, Leo; Good are Oscar's wife, Birdie, Horace Giddens, and Alexandra (Regina's daughter), and the Negroes.

The Hubbards represent the beginning, in 1900, of the industrialization of the South. Birdie and Horace represent "good families" in decline, the planters, ruined by the Civil War. It is hard to think of Regina and her brothers as Southern. They differ from Faulkner's Snopes family in that there is little of the rural in their nature or in their cunning. In *Another Part of the Forest,* written later but concerning itself with an earlier period in the Hubbard family, with the previous generation coming to an end ten years before, we learn that the Hubbard father had been scorned by his neighbors for the money he made during the Civil War, money made by selling salt to a desperate people at a huge profit. True, all the Hubbards have what amounts to an inherited craving for money, but they crave even more the pleasure of the pursuit. In the earlier play, Ben Hubbard manages to outwit his own father by getting the "goods" on him, finding the proof of his dishonesty. This advances Ben's fortunes, but also gives him a sort of aesthetic delight. "Yet I glory more in the cunning purchase of my wealth, than in the glad possession . . . " Volpone says. The Hubbard brothers and sisters have no illusions about the outside world and yet they treat each other as rival firms.

In *The Little Foxes,* the plot has to do with the Hubbard family's desire to invest in a mill that will "bring the machine to the cotton, and not the cotton to the machine." That this was a sound business idea—and the "wave of history"—I gather from W. J. Cash's *The Mind of the South,* in which he writes, "The total number of bankruptcies among the early cotton mills in the South can literally be reckoned on the fingers of one hand." True, the conditions in the mills were dreadful and in them the terrible division between the poor mill-hand whites and the rural Negroes began to harden. Yet as threatening to provincial manners as the mills were, it is hard to be confident about setting above them a decaying agricultural life. (John Crowe Ransom, who had been an Agrarian, got the point when the world greeted as immoral Morgenthau's plan of sending the defeated Germans back to the land.) The spring of the action in **The Little Foxes** is Regina's determination to have a share in the new industrial prosperity by getting her dying husband, Horace, to release his money for the cotton mill. This is an idea of great interest, and in Lillian Hellman's failure to do justice to its complications so much about our theater and our left-wing popular writers of the Thirties is revealed.

To return, for a moment, to the picture of the South in **The Little Foxes**. It is what you might expect and what many serious historians believe to be a legend, not to say a cliché. Culture and fineness of feeling, indifference to mere money—these are the claims of the plantation tradition. At the very opening of the play, we find Birdie representing Culture. She is looking for her album, in which there is a photograph of Mama and Papa meeting of all people, Richard Wagner, indeed Mr. and Mrs. Wagner. (The mind refuses to imagine the hash that singular culture-hero would have made of Mama and Papa.) Other more profound virtues accompany the love of music. Birdie blurts out pitifully, "We were good to our people!" "Our people!" were their slaves, the Negroes, and later their servants. This could perfectly well have been true. Lionnet, the plantation Birdie's family lost to the Hubbard family, was good land with feckless management, a combination that can sometimes be agreeable to the helpless. Nostalgia in unlucky women is common, and while Birdie is not truly interesting we would not say that she is a serious defect in the play.

What *is* serious is the lack of tragic conflict or intellectual complication in Regina's husband, Horace Giddens. Horace was of "good family" again, but he had started as a clerk and worked into being a bank owner. He is dying and leaving an adored daughter. He refuses to give Regina the money to invest in the mill. His reasons are unbelievably idealistic and startling in a man of his time and experience. Stubbornness and hatred of the Hubbards no doubt play some part, but to these Horace adds a straining nobility, an indifference to mere advantage that make him appear to be simply a puppet in the service of an idea. We are told that in his safety deposit box Horace has his 88,000 dollars and an old cameo, his daughter's baby shoe, and a piece of an old violin. This iconography is as pure a distillation of the sentimental Old South as one could find. But the truth was, to quote Cash once more, "Hundreds of planters poured into the rising towns to take advantage, in their own persons, of the promised opportunities of industrialism and commerce; and the sons of the planters came in even greater numbers." It turns out that Horace is against cheaper wages in the South, against exploiting Negroes, against "ruining" the town by industrialization. But we have no reason to associate him with all these fine, advanced ideas. It is as if Madame Ranevsky in *The Cherry Orchard* had been a militant conservationist!

Horace's failure to feel, even for a moment, the seductive power of the investment in the mill robs the play of all genuine seriousness. Imagine what Ibsen could have done with a man who had the experience of a banker and yet who had genuine hatred for his wife's greedy desire to make money on a sound and sensible business investment. But Horace rises like an empty balloon of didactic goodness above all the possibilities of his situation. He is, we see, just one of The Good, and nothing will be asked of him.

The Negroes are another deviation, from probability and observation. In **Toys in the Attic,** Irene Worth comes wandering into the New Orleans sunlight on the arm of her Negro chauffeur and lover, not risking her life, and his, as we would think, but simply in their supreme casualness making a point. The servants in **The Little Foxes** are frequently ready with moral comment peculiarly sententious and convenient. Addie sums up for us, "Yeah, they got mighty well off cheating niggers. Well, there are people who eat the earth and eat all the people on it like in the Bible with the locusts. Then there are people who stand around and watch them eat it. . . . Sometimes I think it ain't right to stand and watch them do it." (Addie is talking to Birdie and Horace, not to her preacher.)

It seems to me that these lectures, in Lillian Hellman's plays and in others of this tradition, are addressed as much to the authors' conscience as to that of the audience. This was also true of some of the popular movies of the period, written by Leftists. In the midst of an effort to fashion an acceptable, successful work, the author's political beliefs cry out for some part of the stage. It is necessary for the writers to prove something to themselves. The strike leader, the Negro servant, the old Jew will carry the message back to the author that he is really a good man. This problem becomes especially necessary, I think, in Lillian Hellman's plays because they are an unusual mixture of the conventions of fashionable, light, drawing room comedy and quite another convention of realism and protest. In most of her plays there are servants, attractive people, money, expensive settings, agreeable surroundings and situations for stars. It is typical of her practice that when she writes in **Watch on the Rhine** of a German refugee coming to America in 1940, he goes not to the Bronx or Queens or even to Fort Washington Avenue, but to a charming country house near Washington. "Large French doors leading to an elevated open terrace." The play opens with a French housekeeper and a Negro butler.

It is nearly always said that Lillian Hellman's plays are triumphs of craftsmanship. Actually the question of motivation, the construction of a plot, are quite awkwardly managed in most of them. In **Autumn Garden** the plot finally turns on a disgrace supposedly brought about by a drunken man's falling asleep on a sofa and thereby compromising the honor of a priggish girl. The plays are full of thefts and letters discovered. The basic plot device is so often unfortunate that the efforts to work it out, skillful enough in a technical sense, become more and more visible and disturbing. This craftsmanship of climaxes and curtain lines and discoveries is a sort of know-how, useful enough in the commercial theater, but paralyzing to the natural development of characters in action. We are too often asked more on behalf of the plot than we can sensibly give assent to.

Behind Lillian Hellman's plays there is a torn spirit: the bright stuffs of expensive productions and the hair-shirt of didacticism. Between these two, her genuine talent for characterization is diminished. Regina and the brothers go too far. (Why the absurd idea of the marriage between Leo and Alexandra should be added to all the other treacheries one can't decide.) But they are alive and interesting. The little prostitute in **Another Part of the Forest** is a striking vignette. That these characters and others should be squeezed to death by the iron of an American version of Socialist Realism and the gold of a reigning commercialism is a problem of cultural history. (pp. 4-5)

Elizabeth Hardwick, "The Little Foxes Revived," in The New York Review of Books, *Vol. IX, No. 11, December 21, 1967, pp. 4-5.*

Lillian Hellman later in life.

FURTHER READING

AUTHOR COMMENTARY

Bryer, Jackson R. *Conversations with Lillian Hellman.* Jackson: University Press of Mississippi, 1986, 298 p.
    Collects interviews from Hellman's entire career. Includes an index and chronology of Hellman's life and career.

Hellman, Lillian. "Theatre." In her *Pentimento: A Book of Portraits,* pp. 149-209. Boston: Little, Brown and Company, 1973.
    Hellman recounts her memories of the productions of her plays, including the influence of Dashiell Hammett.

Phillips, John and Anne Hollander. "Lillian Hellman: An Interview." *The Paris Review* 9, No. 33 (Winter-Spring 1965): 65-95.
    Hellman discusses her relationship with Dashiell Hammett and the state of the arts.

OVERVIEWS AND GENERAL STUDIES

Adler, Jacob H. *Lillian Hellman.* Austin, Texas: Steck-Vaughn Co., 1969, 44 p.
    Brief overview of Hellman's life and writings.

Estrin, Mark W. *Lillian Hellman: Plays, Films, Memoirs.* Boston: G. K. Hall, 1980, 378 p.
    Exhaustive annotated bibliography of primary sources. Indexed.

Falk, Doris V. *Lillian Hellman.* New York: Frederick Ungar Publishing Co., 1978, 180 p.
    Sets Hellman's plays and memoirs in their biographical and historical contexts.

Friedman, Sharon. "Feminism as Theme in Twentieth-Century American Women's Drama." *American Studies* XXV, No. 1 (Spring 1984): 69-89.
    Includes a discussion of the character of Regina from *The Little Foxes* and *Another Part of the Forest* as a feminist creation whose quest for power highlights her exclusion due to her gender.

Gassner, John. "Lillian Hellman: The Autumn Garden." In his *Theatre at the Crossroads: Plays and Playwrights of the Mid-Century American Stage,* pp. 132-39. New York: Holt, Rinehart and Winston, 1960.
    Reevaluates Hellman's works on the basis of the stylistic and technical innovations evidenced in *The Autumn Garden.*

Holditch, W. Kenneth. "Another Part of the Country: Lillian Hellman as Southern Playwright." *The Southern Quarterly* XXV, No. 3 (Spring 1987): 11-35.
    Finds traces of Southern culture throughout Hellman's works.

Lederer, Katherine. *Lillian Hellman.* Boston: Twayne Publishers, 1979, 159 p.
    Critical assessment of Hellman's plays and nonfiction works. Includes a brief chronology and biography of the author.

Moody, Richard. *Lillian Hellman: Playwright.* New York: Pegasus, 1972, 372 p.

    Highly detailed, well-respected biography.

Riordan, Mary Marguerite. *Lillian Hellman: A Bibliography 1926-1978.* Metuchen, N. J.: The Scarecrow Press, 1980, 210 p.

    Annotated list of works by and about Hellman. Includes an index and extensive chronology of Hellman's life and career.

Wright, William. *Lillian Hellman: The Image, The Woman.* New York: Simon and Schuster, 1986, 480 p.

    Attempts to reconcile the evidence presented by the public record and Hellman's associates with the Hellman's autobiographical writings.

WATCH ON THE RHINE

Patraka, Vivian M. "Lillian Hellman's *Watch on the Rhine:* Realism, Gender, and Historical Crisis." *Modern Drama* XXXII, No. 1 (March 1989): 128-45.

    An interpretation that attempts to place *Watch on the Rhine* in its historical context, with particular attention paid to gender as theme.

THE AUTUMN GARDEN

Brown, John Mason. "A New Miss Hellman." *Saturday Review of Literature* XXXIV, No. 13 (31 March 1951): 27-9.

    Discusses the differences between *The Autumn Garden* and Hellman's previous plays.

Clurman, Harold. Review of *The Autumn Garden,* by Lillian Hellman. *New Republic* 124, No. 13 (26 March 1951): 21-2.

    Attempts to elucidate Hellman's "subtle" intentions in this play.

————. "Miss Hellman's New Play: No Message, But a Meaning." *New York Herald Tribune* (4 March 1951): 1-2.

    Clurman enumerates the plot strands of *The Autumn Garden.*

Felheim, Marvin. "*The Autumn Garden:* Mechanics and Dialectics." *Modern Drama* 3, No. 2 (September 1960): 191-95.

    Explores the nature of Hellman's stylistic and technical innovations in *The Autumn Garden.*

TOYS IN THE ATTIC

Adler, Jacob H. "Miss Hellman's Two Sisters." *Educational Theatre Journal* XV, No. 2 (May 1963): 112-17.

    Compares *Toys in the Attic* to Chekhov's *The Three Sisters.*

Driver, Tom F. Review of *Toys in the Attic,* by Lillian Hellman. *The Christian Century* LXXVII, No. 17 (27 April 1960): 511-12.

    Asserts that this play is melodrama that fails as propaganda.

Kerr, Walter. "Miss Hellman." In his *The Theater in Spite of Itself,* pp. 235-38. New York: Simon and Schuster, 1963.

    Praises Hellman's facility with language in *Toys in the Attic.*

Christopher Marlowe

1564-1593

(Also Kit; also Marlow, Marlo, Merling, Merlin, Marlin, Marley, and Morley)

Marlowe, an English dramatist and poet, is the author of such renowned plays as *Doctor Faustus; Tamburlaine, Parts I* and *II; The Jew of Malta;* and *Edward II.* Scholars recognize him as the first English dramatist to reveal the full potential of blank verse poetry, and as one who made significant advances in the genre of English tragedy through keen examinations of Renaissance morality. Although his achievements have been generally overshadowed by his exact contemporary William Shakespeare, many critics contend that had he not died young, Marlowe's reputation would certainly have rivaled that of the more famous playwright.

Marlowe was born in February 1564, the son of a prosperous shoemaker in Canterbury. He received his early education at the King's School in Canterbury and at the age of seventeen was awarded a scholarship to study for the ministry at Cambridge. He obtained his Bachelor of Arts degree in 1584, but controversy surrounded his attempt to graduate with a Master of Arts degree three years later. Scholars have learned that Cambridge officials attempted to withhold Marlowe's degree based on reports that he had visited a Catholic seminary at Rheims, France, and that he was planning to be ordained a Catholic priest upon graduation. Queen Elizabeth's Privy Council intervened, however, and declared that Marlowe had in fact been sent to Rheims on matters related to national security. Some modern critics interpret this remarkable occurrence as evidence that Marlowe served as a spy for the government on this occasion and perhaps others as well. Ultimately, the Cambridge officials relented and awarded Marlowe his degree, but controversy continued to follow him, this time to London, where he took up residence after graduation. Contemporary accounts indicate that he adopted a bohemian lifestyle and continually abused social norms with boorish and repugnant behavior. During this time Marlowe was implicated in a murder and spent two weeks in jail until he was acquitted as having acted in self-defense. In other clashes with the law, he was accused of atheism and blasphemy and was awaiting a trial verdict on such charges when he was killed in 1593. The circumstances surrounding his death puzzled scholars for centuries until records discovered in the early twentieth century revealed that Marlowe died of a stab wound to his forehead received during a brawl with a dinner companion with whom he had been arguing about the tavern bill. A critical dispute remains, however, over the question of whether Marlowe's death was really inadvertent or if he was assassinated by his companions.

Marlowe wrote during the Elizabethan period, an unsettled age of remarkable change, and one in which the spirit

Portrait of a young man, possibly Christopher Marlowe. No authenticated portrait of the playwright exists.

of both the Renaissance and the Protestant Reformation predominated. Society had begun to liberate itself from restrictive medieval institutions and to celebrate the ascendancy of the individual. These revolutionary advances inspired an intellectual and artistic awakening that had not been seen since the Classical Age. Marlowe was a man very much of his time. He witnessed these developments first-hand and, though deeply affected by them, began to explore the potential consequences of this newfound freedom. In his dramas, Marlowe often created distinctively Renaissance characters, providing them with such attributes as great strength, wealth, or knowledge. These virtues initially appear to give them unlimited potential, but as events unfold they are inevitably consumed by pride and ultimately corrupted. The dangers of excessive ambition and the apparent compulsion to strive for more than one already has forms a major theme in Marlowe's plays. The philosophy of Machiavellianism constitutes another important—and related—theme for Marlowe, for his characters commonly strive to achieve their ambitions with the single-minded, ruthless, and amoral cunning described by Niccolo Machiavelli in his controversial political manifesto *The Prince* (1512-13).

Scholars speculate that Marlowe wrote his first play in 1586, just seven years before his death. In this brief period, he composed *The Tragedy of Dido Queen of Carthage; Tamburlaine the Great: Divided into two Tragicall Discourses; The Famous Tragedy of the Rich Jew of Malta; The Massacre at Paris: with the Death of the Duke of Guise; The Troublesome Raigne and Lamentable Death of Edward the Second, King of England;* and *The Tragicall History of the Life and Death of Doctor Faustus.* In addition, he began the narrative poem *Hero and Leander,* a project that he had not completed at the time of his death. Because Marlowe's literary career was so brief yet prolific, scholars have found that the accurate dating of many of his works is extremely difficult.

While a critical consensus on the dating of Marlowe's works is lacking, some scholars maintain that *Dido Queen of Carthage* is his first play. Although *Dido* was not published until 1594, these critics assert that it was composed perhaps as early as 1586, when Marlowe was still a student at Cambridge. The title page of the first edition states that the play had already been performed by the company of boy actors known as the "Children of Her Majesties Chappell." The first of Marlowe's plays to appear on the London stage was most likely Part I of *Tamburlaine,* which was probably presented around 1587. It was a great success among Elizabethan theater goers and in fact was so popular that Marlowe produced a sequel no more than a year later. As the Prologue to Part II states, "The generall welcomes *Tamburlain* receiv'd, / When arrived last upon our stage, / Hath made our Poet pen his second part."

Marlowe wrote *Tamburlaine* as a direct challenge to his audience to rise above the "jigging veins of riming mother wits / And such conceits as clownage keeps in pay" (Prologue, Part I) often found in early Elizabethan drama. Marlowe thus introduces the Scythian shepherd Tamburlaine, a figure of heroic dimensions who epitomizes "Renaissance man" and who single-handedly orchestrates the forging of an empire. According to Gāmini Salgādo, *Tamburlaine* represents "the saga of the self-made man, triumphing through no advantages of birth or inheritance, but entirely through qualities of character." As such, the play reflects transitions in Marlowe's society, in which the dependence of personal advancement upon matters of birthright was gradually giving way to advancement earned through individual achievement. Tamburlaine accomplishes an unbroken series of military and political triumphs by sheer strength—not just physical power as demonstrated by his military prowess, but also by his forceful and eloquent rhetoric. These traits combined with a ruthless will to dominate identify him as a consummate Machiavellian, one who is able to assume and sustain leadership by force of personality. In Part I, Marlowe defies theater goers' expectations, for Tamburlaine pays no tragic retribution for his overweening pride. The dramatist follows a more classical approach in Part II, however, which is pervaded by a theme of death and decay. With the defeat of all human opposition and his massive consolidation of power, Tamburlaine gradually succumbs to megalomania

and attempts to defy Death, his last and most significant adversary. Death slowly erodes Tamburlaine's resolve, first by taking his beloved wife, Zenocrate, and finally by afflicting Tamburlaine himself. Marlowe thus demonstrates that for all the hero's striving and accomplishment, he is nevertheless human; ultimately he must face death, the final limiter of human aspiration.

As already noted, the two parts of *Tamburlaine* were first staged around 1587-88. Their first publication was in a 1590 edition containing both parts, here called "two Tragicall Discourses." Interestingly, although this edition represents the only known printing of any of Marlowe's plays in his lifetime, his name is nowhere given. His next play may have been *The Jew of Malta,* perhaps performed around 1590, though not published until 1633, long after the dramatist's death. The title page of the first edition of *The Jew of Malta* designates the play a tragedy, but critics have often described it as a black comedy or, in the words of T. S. Eliot, a "savage farce."

As he does in *Tamburlaine,* Marlowe explores the implications of Machiavellianism in *The Jew of Malta;* but while Barabas, the central figure of the latter drama, shares Tamburlaine's ruthlessness, he manifests none of the earlier character's heroic grandeur. Indeed, nearly all the characters in this bitterly ironic piece are remarkable for their meanness. In *The Jew of Malta,* according to Eric Rothstein, Marlowe creates a world where "all values are inverted by a central diabolism in grotesque form, expressing itself through materialism . . . and a Machiavellian ethic." The inversion of values and the "diabolism" of the play are evident in the confrontation between the wealthy Jew Barabas and his antagonists, the Roman Catholic rulers of Malta. (Significantly, both groups, Jews and Catholics, were objects of fear and distrust to Elizabethan England.) The Governor of Malta, Ferneze, in financial straits, hypocritically denounces Barabas and confiscates his wealth, depriving him not only of his money but also of the love and mercy which Christianity supposedly represents. Barabas seeks revenge with unnerving viciousness, and a profusion of brutal murders ensues until Barabas, caught in one of his own traps, dies cursing. Critics maintain that although there is tragedy inherent in Barabas's fall, his overreaching himself in his quest for revenge, the viciousness of his ignoble motives, and his cruel conduct preclude sympathy for him and therefore deprive him of tragic definition.

The Massacre at Paris exhibits similarities of tone and style to *The Jew of Malta* and was perhaps written around the same time. Although it is known to have been performed in 1593, it could not have been composed until after 1589, since it depicts the death of Henry III of France, who died in August of that year. This play survives only in an undated octavo edition that provides what critics commonly regard as a corrupt and unreliable text.

Many scholars consider *Edward II*—probably written during the winter of 1592-93, but not published until 1594—the first great English history play, and possibly Marlowe's most accomplished drama in any genre. George L. Geckle maintains that of Marlowe's major plays, "*Edward II* stands out as the most coherent in terms of structure and as the most complex in terms of the interrelationship between theme and character." Although *Edward II* is not one of Marlowe's best-known plays, critics have identified numerous factors contributing to what they regard as its remarkable literary success. Marlowe's sensitive construction of the relationships between this play's chief characters marks a significant advance from his earlier work, in which a play's most important motifs are typically centered around one dominant figure. Marlowe's merging of such elements as the selfish, hedonistic relationship between Edward and Gaveston, with its subtle suggestion of homosexuality, and Mortimer's Machiavellian ambition, commentators agree, give *Edward II* unprecedented dimension. Marlowe's eloquent dramatic verse, variously lyrical, comedic, and tragic, additionally draws the play's many elements into a cohesive whole. Commentators have also praised Marlowe's masterful compression of twenty-three years of history into a five-act dramatic structure. It is commonly held that Shakespeare himself was aware of the exceptional literary achievement of *Edward II,* for his *Richard II* (1595) displays marked similarities to Marlowe's drama.

Although it is apparent that *Doctor Faustus* was not widely popular with Elizabethan audiences, today it is generally considered Marlowe's greatest drama. Written in the tradition of medieval morality plays, *Doctor Faustus* explores the implications of one man's pact to sell his soul to the devil for twenty-four years of power and knowledge. Salgādo observes that "built into the very bones of the story is the element of the cautionary tale, with Faustus as the horrible example of what happens when creatures rebel against their lot and aspire to the condition of their Creator." Critics agree that Faustus represents a Renaissance man whose intellectual ambitions cause him to overstep his human bounds. Marlowe masterfully illustrates how Faustus, although he aspires to divinity, is gradually debased throughout the play by the devil Mephistophilis. Succumbing to pride, avarice, and physical gratification, Faustus never realizes he has been duped into trading his soul for a life of triviality, and he refuses to avail himself of numerous chances to repent. The explicitly religious theme of *Doctor Faustus* continues to perplex critics, for many consider it uncharacteristic of Marlowe to treat theological issues in his works. Whether or not *Doctor Faustus* is meant to convey a particular religious message, it nevertheless presents a penetrating philosophical analysis of the consequences of human aspiration.

The dating of *Doctor Faustus* is especially difficult, as two conflicting texts are extant. The earliest recorded performance was in 1594, but it is known that the theatrical manager Philip Henslowe hired two writers to revise the play for this production. Scholars speculate that an edition of 1616 represents *Doctor Faustus* in this form. However, a differing, shorter, version was printed some years earlier, in 1604. This text, researchers postulate, may be the play before it was revised, and may reflect its unfinished state at the time of the dramatist's death.

Marlowe's dramatic works are suffused with the spirit of the Elizabethan age, clearly reflecting the intellectual enlightenment of the Renaissance as well as exhibiting the

profound political impact of Machiavellianism. In play after play, Marlowe examines various aspects of these revolutionary changes in an effort to better understand their influence on the human condition. In addition, Marlowe's verse greatly improves upon the crude style of his predecessors and vastly expands the scope and power of dramatic representation. Michael Drayton, the eminent English man of letters, paid tribute to his contemporary's literary genius in the poem entitled "Of Poets and Poesie." He wrote, "Neat *Marlow* bathed in the *Thespian* springs / Had in him those brave translunary things, / That the first Poets had, his raptures were, / All ayre, and fire, which made his verses cleere, / For that fine madnes still did he retaine, / Which rightly should possesse a Poets braine." Similarly, no less a judge than Ben Jonson hailed the force and beauty of "Marlowe's mighty line." Beyond question, Marlowe, in his brief but brilliant career, helped guide English drama to an unprecedented level of artistic maturity.

(For further information on Marlowe's life and career, see also *Dictionary of Literary Biography,* Vol. 62.)

PRINCIPAL WORKS

PLAYS

The Tragedy of Dido Queen of Carthage 1586? [published 1594]
Tamburlaine the Great: Divided into two Tragicall Discourses 1587, 1588 [published 1590]
The Famous Tragedy of the Rich Jew of Malta 1590? [published 1633]
The Massacre at Paris: with the Death of the Duke of Guise 1590? [published 1594?]
The Troublesome Raigne and Lamentable Death of Edward the Second, King of England 1592-1593 [published 1594]
The Tragicall History of the Life and Death of Doctor Faustus 1593? [published 1604, 1616]

OTHER MAJOR WORKS

Hero and Leander (poetry) 1593? [incomplete; published 1598]

OVERVIEWS AND GENERAL STUDIES

Harry Levin (essay date 1964)

[*Levin is an American educator and critic whose works reveal his wide range of interests and expertise, from Renaissance culture to the contemporary novel. He has long been an influential advocate of comparative litera-*

ture studies, and he has written seminal works on the literature of several nations, including The Power of Blackness: Hawthorne, Poe, Melville *(1958) and* The Gates of Horn: A Study of Five French Realists *(1962). In the following essay, written on the occasion of the 400th anniversary of the playwright's birth, Levin addresses major themes in Marlowe's dramatic works. He also examines Marlowe's influence on other literary figures—most notably Shakespeare and the Romantic writers—and assesses his reputation among modern audiences. This essay was later reprinted in Levin's* Shakespeare and the Revolution of the Times *(1976).]*

On his four-hundredth anniversary, as at all other moments of critical judgment, it is Marlowe's peculiar destiny to be reconsidered in a Shakespearean context. His strongest claim is bound to be the fact that he did so much more than anyone else to bring that context into existence. This was the high point of A. C. Swinburne's eulogy in the *Encyclopaedia Britannica:* "He is the greatest discoverer, the most daring and inspired pioneer, in all our poetic literature." Yet even Swinburne qualified his superlatives: "The place and the value of Christopher Marlowe as a leader among English poets it would be almost impossible for historical criticism to over-estimate." The implicit qualification is underlined by our realization that the Victorian poet was far from being a historical critic. Marlowe must abide the question of history, which Shakespeare has all but outflown. Yes, he is for all time, we must agree with Ben Jonson. And Marlowe then, was he primarily for his age? Certainly he caught its intensities, placed its rhythms, and dramatized its dilemmas as no Elizabethan writer had previously done, and as all would be doing thereafter to some extent. Shakespeare, two months younger, could have emerged only by way of Marlovian discipleship. Had he likewise died at twenty-nine, he would have left us no more than Marlowe's seven plays. Most of Shakespeare's comparable sheaf of erotic poems seem likely to have been composed shortly afterward. In 1593 the Shakespearean corpus probably comprised three or four of the cruder histories and two or three of the lighter comedies, plus *Titus Andronicus.*

Neither of these matchless contemporaries, at twenty-nine, was a schoolboy; and it would be presumptuous for us to set them in retroactive competition, awarding Marlowe a special palm for higher achievement to date. Yet it is reciprocally poignant that Shakespeare, who retired early and was not destined to live beyond middle age, had at least twenty years left in which to compose about thirty more plays and thereby to round out the full assertion of his uniqueness. One is almost tempted, on sentimental grounds, by Calvin Hoffman's silly theory [in *The Man Who Was Shakespeare*] that Marlowe was not really killed in a tavern brawl, but was whisked away to a secret retreat wherefrom he proceeded to turn out Shakespeare's plays. As against the other anti-Stratfordian theories [which propose that someone other than the man from Stratford composed the plays of "Shakespeare"], this one has the merit of naming the single alternate who had actually demonstrated a dramaturgic flair. However, such temptations are easily brushed aside, not merely by the documents attesting Marlowe's death and Shakespeare's life, but by the contrasting patterns of their respective careers.

Marlowe's was meteoric in its development, and in its expression as well. In that sense his end was not untimely, and it is futile to sentimentalize now over his fragments and unwritten masterworks. Shakespeare needed maturity to express ripeness, although he could never have matured without assuming first the youthful stance that Marlowe has made permanently his own. Insofar as he must seem forever young, we are inclined to feel old as we belatedly reread him. Michael Drayton set the angle for all backward glances at Marlowe, when he described him as having primordial qualities: "those brave translunary things / That the first poets had."

Drayton went on to amplify this description with a famous chemical formula, which implies again as much as it states: "His raptures were / All air and fire . . ." Significantly enough, they are not said to have been compounded of earth or water, which are after all the elements of flesh and blood, and hence are major components for literature. Shakespeare seems to have marked the passing of Marlowe through his own *Richard III,* where he proved himself to be past master of the Marlovian attitudes and tonalities, even while he was ranging on toward richer complexities and subtler nuances of human relationship. To be sure, *Richard II* would be unthinkable without the example of **Edward II,** or *The Merchant of Venice* without **The Jew of Malta.** Speaking more broadly, *Hamlet* owes a certain amount to the precedent of **Doctor Faustus,** and *Coriolanus* to **Tamburlaine.** Yet, in each of these instances, Shakespeare moves on a wholly different plane—and appeals to a wholly different mode—of experience. *Titus Andronicus* itself, perhaps his most derivative work and surely his least effective, already shows a few of his humanely original touches. The ear that has been attuned to Marlowe, of course will catch reverberations throughout the whole repertory. Incongruously Barabas, under a balcony, prepares the ground for Romeo's advances:

> But stay! What star shines yonder in the east?
> The lodestar of my life, if Abigail.
>
> [*J of M,* II.i]

Ophelia's madness would have been less plaintive, had she not been preceded by Zabina:

> Let the soldiers be buried. Hell! Death! Tamburlaine! Hell!
> Make ready my coach, my chair, my jewels! I come, I come, I come.
>
> [*1T,* V.ii]

And Hamlet might not have contemplated the other world so intensively, if it had not been for Mortimer,

> That scorns the world, and, as a traveller
> Goes to discover countries yet unknown.
>
> [*E2,* V.vi]

Nor would Milton's Satan have spanned quite so wide an arc, if Mephistophilis had not declared:

> Hell hath no limits, nor is circumscrib'd
> In one self place, but where we are is hell.
>
> [*F,* II.i]

But the very echo sounded increasingly hollow as the theatre gained in depth, and as the histrionic manner of Marlowe's [Edward] Alleyn gave way to the modulated acting of Shakespeare's [Richard] Burbage. Within a decade after the prologue to *Tamburlaine* had so proudly vaunted its forthcoming innovations, they were looked upon as old-fashioned fustian, mouthed by such seedy playgoers as Ancient Pistol [in *2 Henry IV*], and burlesqued by many lesser playwrights. Shakespeare and others paid incidental tribute to the Dead Shepherd; gossip about Kit's wild escapades and shocking opinions continued to spread; and the final stab carried with it an obvious moral to be heavily labored. As for the plays themselves, except for the debasement of *Doctor Faustus* into a puppet show, they went unperformed through the latter seventeenth and eighteenth centuries. They were passionately rediscovered by the Romantics, who saw in Marlowe himself a fellow Romantic, and read him for such purple passages as Charles Lamb extracted in his *Specimens of the English Dramatic Poets.* Signs of growing appreciation included Edmund Kean's revival of *The Jew of Malta,* as well as Alexander Dyce's scholarly edition of the collected works. During the later years of the nineteenth century, Marlowe came into his own—and possibly into something more. His "Best Plays," edited by Havelock Ellis with a general introduction by J. A. Symonds, inaugurated the popular Mermaid Series in 1887. Their artistic novelty, their sensual coloring, their intellectual boldness, along with their underlying legend of genius misunderstood, held an especially powerful appeal for the *fin de siècle* and for the first generation of the twentieth century.

Marlowe was hailed, in Swinburne's panegyric, as "Soul nearest ours of all, that wert most far." We might wonder whether he stands any nearer to, or farther away from, ourselves at his quadricentennial; and we may well ask ourselves what characteristics found so strong an affinity in his admirers of two or three generations ago. The image of the Superman was then in the air, we recall, and it must have seemed more glamorous than it has subsequently become. Symonds and Ellis both talked about *L'amour de l'impossible* as if it embodied an imminent possibility. Ellis was a professional nonconformist, dedicated to sexual reform, French Naturalism, and the iconoclastic side of many other controversial issues of the day. Symonds was the principal English interpreter of the Renaissance, and his interpretations stressed those tendencies which meant most to the advanced thinkers among his contemporaries: neo-pagan aestheticism, hedonistic individualism, secularistic liberalism, naturalistic skepticism. Further reinterpretation, influenced in its turn by some disillusionment over such tendencies, has more recently veered toward the other extreme, stressing the heritage of the Middle Ages and the continuity of its orthodox traditions. Consequently the question, "How modern was Marlowe?" entails the counter-question, "How modern are we?" If we entertain the more conservative view of his period, we can no longer view him as its characteristic spokesman. Douglas Bush would treat him, with some cogency, as a highly idiosyncratic figure. This should not lessen the interest we take in him as a writer, and it should increase his importance as a historic voice, whose dissents from orthodoxy were pioneering affirmations of modernism.

Such may be the most satisfactory placement that we can

make for Marlowe's position today, but the anti-modernists would press the argument further. Not content with turning back the clock on the Renaissance itself, they would reinterpret Marlowe's outlook in conformity with the canons of traditional belief. Unlike Rimbaud's apologists, they can tell no tale of deathbed conversion to invest the poet with an aura of posthumous respectability. Marlowe's heresies, for better or worse, are matters of legal record. We may not altogether trust his accusers; and we must distinguish their hostile testimony from the considered purport of Marlowe's writing; yet the cloud of suspicion surrounding the man lends credence to the more radical impression of his work. Paul H. Kocher has traced his thought through his dramaturgy on the justifiable assumption that he was a subjective dramatist. This is something of a contradiction in terms, since we ordinarily assume that the drama is—or should be—an objective medium. But objectivity, in the presentation of ideas, emotions, and characters, is at best an approximation. Shakespeare seems most unique in his "Negative Capability," his capacity for effacing his own personality behind his varied and vivid *dramatis personae.* Marlowe's more insistent and limited gift might be characterized, by inevitable comparison, as positive capability. Where Shakespeare is everybody, Marlowe is always himself. The critical method suggested by David Masson, the detection of "fervors" and "recurrences," proves elusive and hazardous for Shakespeare. But for Marlowe it works, because he keeps obsessively returning to certain themes, rising to particular occasions, and modifying his material in distinctly personal ways.

Consider what Mario Praz has called the Ganymede complex. Whether or not Marlowe was a homosexual can be no concern of ours; it is somewhat more relevant that his conversations, as reported by Thomas Kyd and Richard Baines, consistently exhibit a preoccupation with homosexuality; and it is of real significance, in the history of western literature, that few writers have so candidly dwelt on that theme, between the ancients and the epoch of Proust and Gide and Jean Genet. Both in *Dido, Queen of Carthage,* and in *Hero and Leander,* the conventionally heterosexual plot is augmented by the interpolation of a homosexually motivated episode. It has not passed without remark that Marlowe's one sustained treatment of amorous passion appears in the love of Edward II for Gaveston—a relation adumbrated in Henry II and his minions. One of the ironies of Marlowe's fate, under the circumstances, has been his repute among casual readers as a sort of laureate for young lovers. This may be due in part to his premature demise and to the discredited rumors involving a lovers' duel, but it has mainly resulted from that small handful of quotations from him which have circulated very widely: his much anthologized lyric, "The Passionate Shepherd to his Love"; the rapturous invocation of Doctor Faustus to Helen of Troy, detached from its austere context; and, above all, the quasi-proverbial line about love at first sight that Shakespeare echoed in *As You Like It.* More in the distinctive Marlovian vein is the cynical twist of Barabas' response to the charge of fornication, which T. S. Eliot culled for an epigraph, and which has since provided a title for Ernest Hemingway and latterly James Baldwin:

> . . . But that
> Was in another country; and besides
> The wench is dead.
>
> [*J of M,* IV.i]

Lamb could not, and would not, have gone into concrete details; yet he pointed in the prevailing direction, when he spoke of Marlowe's disposition "to dally with interdicted subjects." His contemporary reputation for "daring God out of Heaven," in Robert Greene's phrase, clearly echoed fervent lines and mirrored recurrent scenes. We need not forget that those heretical speeches and blasphemous gestures were put into the mouths of protagonists on whose heads they brought down the most exemplary damnations. But if Marlowe is not—what Ellis claimed—his own hero, then his typical heroes tend to be committed heretics, as well as self-made moderns; and *Doctor Faustus,* with a black magic still potent in the curses and conjurations of *Moby Dick* or *Ulysses,* comes perilously close to prefiguring Marlowe's own tragedy: the cut branch, the burnt laurel. The playwright not only takes part in the scholar's blasphemy, but also seems to enjoy his anathema. True, the pagan vision of Helen dissolves before the Gothic grotesquery of the hell-mouth. But it is the perpetual curiosity, rather than the terminal agony, that survives in our minds as the peculiarly Faustian posture. Similarly, we go on thinking of Don Juan as an unrepentant libertine, rather than as a sinner burning in hell. Since the interdiction is duly scheduled to win out over the dalliance, *Doctor Faustus* would have the stark outline of a morality play, if an outline were all that we looked for in it. Neoorthodox moralists would indeed reduce the mighty *Tamburlaine* to the abject level of a cautionary fable, as Roy W. Battenhouse has attempted to do, by emphasizing the dogmatic background at the expense of the dramatic foreground, though the latter expressly flouts the former.

Since every drama is perforce dialectical, there is much that has to be said on both sides; and where opinion was strictly regulated, it would be the right thinkers who had to say the last word; yet though they reaffirm the appropriate taboo, it has been challenged in the process by more fascinating spokesmen. These unbelievers maintain a tense atmosphere of moral ambiguity, made explicit by the theatrical caricature of Machiavelli. The Latin warrant that brings about Edward's murder would make a suggestive paradigm for the reading of Marlowe as a whole. It could convey an innocuous piety: "Kill not the king, 'tis good to fear the worst" [*E2,* V.iv]. Or, as repunctuated and retranslated by Mortimer, it could have a subversive and sinister meaning: "Fear not to kill the king, 'tis good he die" (V.iv). So it sounds with Marlowe's ambiguous situations. There is not impiety, from a Christian standpoint, when Tamburlaine burns the Koran; his ensuing death, in any case, might well be regarded as Mohammed's revenge. When the Christian armies break their oath, the Mohammedan leader calls upon Christ, who avenges their just cause against his own adherents. It is in this connection that the infidel Orcanes makes the most elevated of Marlowe's religious pronouncements, affirming the existence of a transcendent God who—like the hell that accompanies Mephistophilis—is not "circumscriptible." This is as far from Marlowe's alleged atheism as it is from any theo-

logical dogma; and it does not exclude a thoroughgoing anticlericalism, or a skeptical feeling that few religionists live up to the creeds they profess. As a study in comparative ethics, *The Jew of Malta* is more anti-Christian than anti-Semitic. Here again it is the Christians who do the oath-breaking, and their Governor outdoes the Jew in Machiavellian blackmail and double-dealing.

The gods themselves are pantheistically pluralized by Marlowe, with room among them for both Christ and Mohammed under the ultimate deity of Jove. That classical ruler, who coalesces at times with the Old Testament visage of Jehovah, is likewise seen as the Olympian revolutionary who overthrew the Titans; Tamburlaine cites him as an illustrious forerunner in an eternal conflict; and it is revealing to compare this triumphal account of a perpetually dynamic cosmos, where nature teaches men to have aspiring minds, with the hierarchical conception of order and degree that Ulysses elucidates in *Troilus and Cressida.* The individual movement is upward, with Marlowe; the total framework is more balanced, with Shakespeare. Tamburlaine's be-all and end-all, "The sweet fruition of an earthly crown," becomes, for the Lancastrian kings, the mere beginning of responsibility: "O polish'd perturbation, golden care!" [*2 Henry IV*]. Marlowe's later heroes, though they are no less monomaniacal or megalomaniacal, have more sublimated ambitions—capital, sorcery—than the kingship, which Edward so pathetically loses. Yet even Tamburlaine, in the midst of his amoral drive to power, can pause to speculate on "What is beauty?" Though he remains untouched by his cruel slaughter of the Damascene virgins, he is finally moved by Zenocrate's tears for her father, and he expends the utmost Marlovian eloquence in expressing the problem of poetic inexpressibility. More pointedly, when Faustus apostrophizes Helen, his aesthetic rapture is framed by the ethical situation. And the delights of music and poetry are frankly envisioned as snares to be manipulated by Gaveston, whose introductory monologue concludes by describing an ominous masque, wherein Actaeon will be stricken down for having observed the naked goddess.

Marlowe's chastened and penitential mood, so ambivalently interwoven with his exaltations and exuberances, might be summed up in this distich from a posthumous poem by e. e. cummings:

> where climbing was and bright
> is darkness and to fall.

These are not the inert and untragic falls of medieval tragedy; for the overriding emphasis is upon the intellectual pride, the extreme *hubris,* the dazzling brightness that went before them and virtually made the price worth paying. Nonetheless it is acknowledged and paid, and herein lies the sharp difference between Marlowe and the Romantics. His psychic pattern is not Titanic, like theirs, but Icarian, since it encompasses both the limitless aspiration and the limiting consequence: both infinitude and fragmentation. His Faust is much less close to Goethe's hero, who gets out of his diabolic bargain with such Romantic casuistry, than to the guilt-ridden genius of Thomas Mann's *Doktor Faustus.* We cannot read Marlowe as naïvely today as our predecessors could in the nineteenth century; and he might make us happier if we could stick to his bright surfaces; but his stature as a tragic playwright is enhanced by the darker and deeper meanings we may now be finding in his tragedies. The note of triumph that runs through them, Renaissance triumph uncontrolled, rings false already in *Edward II* and takes on an ironic reverberation for us. Among their spectacular properties, which symbolize aspects of the human predicament, Tamburlaine's chariot fascinates us less than Bajazet's cage. Standing—as we do—somewhat closer to Kafka than to Nietzsche, alas, we comprehend the reaching of limits as well as the testing of potentialities. Capitalism seethes in the self-prepared caldron of Barabas. Science itself is tormented by the flames that Faustus has conjured up.

Thus Marlowe still has resonance, albeit in an unexpectedly minor key, for a time which terms itself the Age of Anxiety; and it might not be unduly hopeful to look for a restaging of his drama in the light of what we sometimes term the Theatre of the Absurd. Its anti-heroic characters have more in common with the exceptional Edward, standing beardless and bemused in his puddle, than with the more flamboyantly Marlovian figures. It may indeed be no accident that Bertolt Brecht, in his earliest playwriting days, collaborated on a German adaptation of *Edward II*. Marlowe seems to have naturally obtained that effect for which Brecht has been so consciously striving: alienation rather than identification, estrangement and not endearment—and this must be our last and clinching distinction between Marlowe's art and Shakespeare's. Yet we live in a world, and in a universe, where a sense of strangeness may be more pertinent than the illusion of being at home. Every day remote and obscure nations clamor to be heard, vaunts of ever more menacing weapons are thunderously exchanged, while intrepid voyagers are being launched on interplanetary flights. Marlowe, with his insatiable urge to prove cosmography, to confute the geographers, and to transform history into modernity, might have gained more pleasure from such spectacles than many of us may do. To reread him now is to be reminded of the exotic breeds and barbaric hordes that migrate across the poems of St. John Perse, or of those half-forgotten civilizations whose emergences and declines have been so categorically passed in review by Arnold Toynbee. Marlowe is forever the lone explorer. (pp. 22-31)

> *Harry Levin, "Marlowe Today," in* The Tulane Drama Review, *Vol. 8, No. 4, Summer, 1964, pp. 22-31.*

Gāmini Salgādo   (essay date 1971)

[*A Ceylonese-born British educator, scholar, and editor, Salgādo has written works on D. H. Lawrence and the modern English novel, as well as several books on Shakespeare and Elizabethan drama. His publications include* A Study of Sons and Lovers *(1965),* Eyewitnesses to Shakespeare *(1975),* The Elizabethan Underworld *(1977), and* A New Introduction to English Drama *(1980). He is also the editor of* Three Jacobean Comedies *(1965),* Three Restoration Comedies *(1968), and* Othello *(1975). In the excerpt below, Salgādo presents a biographical and critical survey of Marlowe, re-*

constructing the playwright's historical background and providing commentary on the sources and themes of each of his plays. For his quotations, Salgādo employs slightly modernized versions of the original editions of Marlowe's works.]

Merling, Merlin, Marlin, Marley, Morley, Marlowe—the man who died by a stab wound from his own hand in a tavern brawl at Deptford Green on the night of 30 May 1593 was known during his lifetime by all these names. In his one surviving signature he signs himself 'Marley'. His name first appears as 'Christopher, the sonne of John Marlow' in the baptismal register of St George's Church, Canterbury on 26 February 1564—two months to the day before the baptism at Stratford-upon-Avon of William Shakespeare. In the records of Corpus Christi College, Cambridge, where he was a student for six years, he is listed as 'Merling'; and the Middlesex jury which held the inquest on his death identifies him as 'Christopher Morley'.

The John Marlow who was Christopher's father was a prosperous shoemaker from a family whose connections with Canterbury go back at least one hundred and fifty years before the dramatist was born. John married Catherine Arthur, possibly the daughter of a Canterbury vicar. The year Christopher was born his father became a freeman of the city, having served less than the usual period of apprenticeship. Christopher was one of nine children, two of whom died in infancy—a circumstance which was by no means unusual at the time.

Sixteenth-century Canterbury had changed little from the medieval Cathedral town of Chaucer's day, though the Reformation had put an end to the practice of making pilgrimage to the shrine of St Thomas à Becket. The town was on the main Dover—London road and offered a convenient resting place for travellers to the capital and the port, as well as for soldiers to and from the European wars. Like many large towns, its activities included bull-baiting and public executions—by 1576 there were three gibbets in the town, and men were also hanged from the city walls. City records show that during the reign of Henry VIII religious and political rebels in Canterbury were tortured by being boiled. Thus the atmosphere of cruelty, intrigue and violent death which is an immediately striking aspect of Marlowe's plays needs no special explanation in terms of the dramatist's personality—it was part of the air he breathed as a child.

But only part of it. Coming as he did from a comfortable 'middle class' background, Marlowe's early life was inevitably cushioned against many of the dangers and hardships of Elizabethan life. As a freeman of the city, his father could not be tried by any but a Canterbury jury, or imprisoned anywhere but in Canterbury. In his mother's will, the bequests include gold and silver rings, silver spoons and christening linen as well as sums of money.

In January 1579, Christopher Marlowe entered the King's School, Canterbury. He was within a few weeks of his fifteenth birthday, which was fortunate, as the School Statutes barred any boy over fifteen from admission. As a King's scholar he received an allowance of £1 each quarter from the funds of the Cathedral, in whose account book he appears as 'Christopher Marley'. Though it was laid down that the pupils of the school were to be confined to 'fifty poor boys, both destitute of the help of friends, and endowed with minds apt for learning, who shall be sustained out of the funds of the Church', this was a statute more breached than observed. Marlowe was typical of the majority of the school's pupils in being the son of a prosperous citizen.

Like most Tudor educational institutions, the King's School laid greatest emphasis on the teaching of Latin. The object was to impart a reasonable knowledge of Latin grammar and proficiency in speaking and writing the language. Among the methods used to achieve this end was the acting of plays in Latin. These school plays form part of the earliest secular drama in England.

The school day was, by modern standards, long and arduous. Lessons began and ended with psalms and ran from six in the morning till five in the afternoon. Marlowe stayed at the school till the Michaelmas term of 1580 when, at the age of sixteen, he went up to Corpus Christi College, Cambridge.

Marlowe's education at Cambridge was paid for by one of the scholarships endowed by Archbishop Parker of Canterbury, who was also Master of Corpus Christi, one of the oldest of the Cambridge Colleges. In the main, the Parker scholarships were granted on the understanding that holders should eventually take holy orders. Marlowe (or 'Merling') first appears on the college books, however, not as a student of theology but of dialectics.

He remained at Cambridge for six years, though his attendance during this period was erratic. His reading at the University brought him into contact not only with the Latin classics, but also with contemporary Italian and French literature and, even more importantly, with the writings of the sixteenth-century Florentine diplomat and political philosopher, Nicolo Machiavelli. Only a year before Marlowe went up to Corpus Christi, the Cambridge scholar Gabriel Harvey had written to the poet Edmund Spenser about his Cambridge contemporaries:

> And I warrant you some good fellows amongst us begin now to be pretty well acquainted with a certain parlous book called, as I remember me, Il Principe di Nicolo Machiavelli, and I can peradventure name you an odd crew or two that are as cunning in his Discorsi, in his Historia Fiorentina, and in his Dialogues della Arte della Guerra too . . .
>
> [*The Works of Gabriel Harvey,*
> ed. A. B. Grosart].

Machiavelli introduced a new realism into European political thinking, being a keen analyst of the actualities of statecraft and the real, as opposed to the professed motives that guided those who sought or retained political power. When, in his play *The Jew of Malta,* Marlowe has the Prologue spoken by Machiavelli in person, he not only puts into his mouth nearly all the commonplaces associated with Machiavelli in the popular mind, but creates a character, the intriguer whose whole existence is based on never revealing his real character or motives to anyone but the audience, whose descendants are legion in the drama of the next few decades, and who include Shakespeare's

Richard III, Edmund [in *King Lear*] and Iago [in *Othello*]. The Machiavellian world of double dealing and realpolitik also provides the characters and atmosphere of Marlowe's *The Massacre at Paris.*

But Marlowe's acquaintance with the world of political intrigue was by no means merely academic and theoretical. During at least three of his six years at Cambridge he was absent from the University for several weeks at a time, and it seems reasonably certain that at least some of these absences were on secret state business—in other words, as a member of the vast anti-Catholic espionage system operated by Mr Secretary Walsingham. One of the places most closely watched was the English Catholic seminary at Rheims where missionary priests were given a training which often involved subversive religious and political activity in England. (The distinction between these two spheres, never very clear until modern times, was virtually obliterated, as far as English Catholics were concerned, by Pope Pius V's excommunication of Queen Elizabeth in 1570.) Among those who spied for Walsingham at the Rheims seminary were the dramatist and pamphleteer Anthony Munday and Richard Baines, possibly the same man who informed against Marlowe in 1593. A few months before he was due to receive his M.A. degree the rumour spread that Marlowe himself had decided to join the Catholic seminary at Rheims as a novice-priest. The university authorities took this and other rumours about Marlowe seriously enough to refuse him permission to take his degree, but were evidently uninformed about the real nature and scope of Marlowe's activities. At any rate a Privy Council resolution dated 29 June 1587 fairly brusquely directed that the degree be granted, while at the same time giving some indication of Marlowe's true profession:

> Whereas it was reported that Christopher Morley was determined to have gone beyond the seas to Rheims and there to remain their Lordships thought good to certify that he had no such intent, but that in all his actions he had behaved himself orderly and discreetly whereby he had done Her Majesty good service, and deserved to be rewarded for his faithful dealing. Their Lordships request that the rumour thereof should be allayed by all possible means, and that he should be furthered in the degree he was to take this next commencement: Because it was not Her Majesty's pleasure that anyone employed as he had been in matters touching the benefit of his country should be defamed by those that are ignorant of the affairs he went about.

'The affairs he went about' and the people with whom he went about them (such as Robert Poley, one of the men with him in the last few hours of his life), were the counterparts in real life of the characters and action Marlowe portrayed in *The Jew of Malta* and *The Massacre at Paris.* (Richard Baines had even made the suggestion that the entire Jesuit seminary at Rheims could be eliminated by poisoning the well, which is Barabas's bright idea in *The Jew of Malta.*) The University authorities naturally did as they were told and Marlowe took his M.A. in July 1587. But his dramatic career had already begun. *Tamburlaine the Great,* his first play, had been staged in London and had been so overwhelmingly successful that it had been speedily followed by a sequel.

The exact nature of Marlowe's espionage activities will, in the nature of the case, probably remain obscure. They certainly involved him closely in the state affairs of France, Spain and probably the Low Countries. These were the feverish years before the Great Armada and Elizabeth's Government was more than usually interested in the activities abroad of English Catholics, one of whose main centres was the seminary at Rheims. It is difficult to imagine that Marlowe's work for Walsingham did not bring him into contact with the Catholics abroad, at Rheims and elsewhere. (*The Massacre at Paris* contains an explicit reference to 'a sort of English priests' who 'hatch forth treason 'gainst their natural Queen'.) And if he did have such contact, the hazy knowledge of it in the outside world would be quite sufficient to give rise to the rumour that he himself was a Catholic, or on the point of becoming one. We have Baines' word for it that Marlowe said 'That if there be any God or good religion, then it is in the papists, because the service of God is performed with more ceremonies, as elevation of the Mass, organs, singing men, shaven crowns etc'. But in its context this passage seems to indicate only the dramatist's regard for ritual and pageantry rather than any real religious sympathy for Catholicism.

Marlowe's career as a spy accounts, in part, for his comparatively small literary output (he wrote seven plays, an unfinished narrative poem, some translations and a handful of lyrics). At the same time it provides the dark and violent world of plays such as the *Jew of Malta* and more specifically the detailed knowledge of recent French political history revealed in *The Massacre at Paris.* It seems that the roots of Marlowe's attachment to the life of a secret service agent were social and economic as well as temperamental. The hostility towards Catholic Spain and the consequent suspicion of English Catholics and their activities abroad has already been mentioned as a feature of the social climate. This attitude must be seen against the background, not of England as a first class world power, which she was not to be until the beginning of the eighteenth century, but as a small island nervously aware of the hostility of an immensely rich Catholic superstate just across the ocean. Next we have to remember that the professional dramatist (and indeed, the professional secular writer) was only just beginning to emerge in Marlowe's day. The old secure system of literary patronage was breaking down and the impersonal relations between writer and public which we take for granted today were a long way in the future. Despite the fact that the first London theatre had been established a full decade before Marlowe began to write for the stage, and was quickly followed by several others, the economic position of the young men who came down from the universities and began to write plays was by no means secure. This can be clearly seen when we consider that most of them had to turn out plays at a rate which would be regarded today as consistent only with hackwork, but also from the fact that many of them had to resort to other activities than playwriting to earn a living—Robert Greene to 'coney catching' (confidence tricks), Thomas Nashe to pamphleteering and so on. Finally we have a certain amount of evidence which suggests that Marlowe was by nature drawn to a life of intrigue and violence. The dramatist Thomas Kyd, with whom Marlowe shared a room for some time, spoke of his 'rashness in attempting sudden privy injuries to men,' while Marlowe's continued association with such sinister figures as Robert Poley is also significant. In this part of his life Marlowe is nothing if not typical of his time and place.

Marlowe's spying activities must have taken him through much of northern and western Europe, though it is impossible to be certain just where and when. In October 1587, a letter to Lord Burghley written from Utrecht refers to a certain 'Morley' as a messenger though this may have been the musician Thomas Morley who was in the Low Countries at this time. In 1592 one 'Marlin' figures as a courier between the Government and the British Ambassador in Paris, Sir Henry Unton. But the next time we come across Christopher Marlowe unmistakably is in September 1589 when he was arrested, during a sword fight within the City precincts, together with Thomas Watson who today survives only in anthologies, but was the most celebrated Latin poet of his day and ranked by his contemporaries as the equal of Philip Sidney and Edmund Spenser. Marlowe was remanded (along with Watson) in Newgate prison and the prison register accords him the rank of 'yeoman' living in the prosperous suburban district of Newton Folgate. The grim conditions of Newgate prison have been vividly recorded in a contemporary pamphlet, *The Black Dog of Newgate* by Luke Hutton. They may be guessed at from the fact that more prisoners died of gaol fever than were executed. Marlowe, who was discharged with an admonition to keep the peace in December 1589, undoubtedly recalled his own experiences when he came to write the brief but unforgettable prison scenes in *Edward II.*

In addition to his familiarity with intrigue abroad and violence at home, Marlowe appears also to have been connected with a group of radical thinking young men of his day who gathered round the enigmatic figure of Sir Walter Ralegh. This group sometimes called The School of Night, which included Ralegh's half-brother Carew, the astronomer John Dee, the mathematician Thomas Harriot and several others, was associated in the popular imagination with atheism, necromancy and other sinister goings on. When Ralegh lost the Queen's favour in 1592 by marrying one of her Maids of Honour, he retired from the court to Sherborne Abbey in Dorset (a gift from the Queen in happier days) and the house soon acquired a reputation as a centre of freethought, blasphemy and worse. Marlowe's direct connection with Ralegh cannot be established with certainty, though the latter did write a reply to Marlowe's 'Passionate Shepherd' and according to an informer's report, Marlowe's friend Richard Chomley said that 'Marlowe told him that he had read the atheist lecture to Sir Walter Ralegh and others'. What is probable is that Marlowe's fascination with the movement of the planets and heavenly light and infernal darkness derives in some part from the activities and interests of men like Harriot, while John Dee's contemporary reputation seems to have been one of the sources of inspiration for the figure of Doctor Faustus.

Marlowe's fascination (if such it was) with Ralegh hardly needs any special explanation, for Ralegh fascinated most of his contemporaries. Courtier, poet, patron, explorer, polemicist, historian—Ralegh not only embodied the many-sidedness of his age, but in his failure to achieve real fulfilment in any of his activities and interests was typical of the 'aspiring mind' of his generation. In comprehensiveness of imagination and scepticism of intellect, as well as in the manner of his death Ralegh resembled not only the heroes of Marlovian drama but their creator.

It is probable that at Ralegh's London house in the Strand, where he played host to such men as the Italian humanist Giordano Bruno and John Florio, the translator of Montaigne, Marlowe came into personal contact with members of 'The School of Night'. He was certainly associated in the public mind with this group and one of its members, the poet and dramatist George Chapman, wrote a continuation of *Hero and Leander,* a narrative poem which Marlowe left unfinished at his death.

What with his mysterious dealings with suspected traitors abroad and his open association with known unbelievers at home, it was not at all surprising that within a few years Marlowe had acquired a reputation as an intriguer, a blasphemer and a libertine. Everything we know or can infer about his personality suggests that it was not a reputation which he took the least trouble to live down; indeed, it is likely that he gloried in it, though this was a dangerous thing to do, as subsequent events proved.

In 1593, five years after the defeat of The Great Armada, fears of a Catholic invasion (possibly based on the Isle of Man) were still prevalent and Elizabeth's Government very sensitive to the slightest suspicion of a Catholic plot against the Queen. Feeling against foreigners was very strong within the city and the tension was hardly lessened by a violent outbreak of plague which spread across London.

In May the dramatist Thomas Kyd was arrested, apparently on suspicion of having had a hand in the vituperative libels against foreigners which, appearing on city walls, were a principal cause of unrest among London apprentices and others. Though nothing was found to connect Kyd with these activities, the authorities did find papers which they described as 'vile and heretical conceits denying the deity of Jesus Christ'. Kyd was interrogated and his examination included the customary torture, under which he declared that the papers in question had belonged to Marlowe and dated from a time some two years earlier when they had shared a room; many people, he added, would swear that Marlowe was an atheist. In letters written later, Kyd went into some detail about his fellow-dramatist's blasphemous and heretical opinions.

Kyd's evidence led to a warrant being issued against Marlowe, which the latter duly answered. He was ordered to attend on the Privy Council. He seems to have been treated by the Council much better than Kyd (as a University graduate Marlowe was entitled to the rank of gentleman). The Council now instructed Marlowe to be available while they made further inquiries as to his activities and opinions. The principal upshot of these inquiries was a report

by the informer Richard Baines, headed *A Note containing the opinion of one Christopher Marly concerning his damnable judgment of religion and scorn of God's Word.* This 'note' (which, together with Kyd's letters referred to above and some references in Greene's *Groatsworth of Wit* forms the chief source for our knowledge of Marlowe's religious views) is undated. But by the time the Queen received her copy of it Marlowe had already been dead two days.

Thanks to Mr Leslie Hotson's discovery, some forty years ago, of the proceedings of the inquest on Marlowe's death, it is now possible to reconstruct almost hour by hour the events which took place at the widow Eleanor Bull's tavern in Deptford Green on 30 May 1593. (This has not however prevented Mr Calvin Hoffman from claiming, in his book *The Man Who Was Shakespeare,* that Marlowe did not die that evening at all, but escaped and lived on to write plays under the pseudonym of—guess who?)

Besides Marlowe himself, there were three other people who met on the morning of 30 May at Mistress Bull's house. All four men were associates of Thomas Walsingham, and three of them were secret service agents. There was the sinister Robert Poley already mentioned, and Nicholas Skeres, who had worked with Poley before. The fourth man was Ingram Frizer who earlier that year had been Skere's partner in defrauding a young gentleman to the benefit, among others, of Thomas Walsingham whose business agent Frizer then was. A contemporary account tells us that it was Frizer who invited Marlowe to Deptford.

After an early dinner the four men walked about in the garden and went in for supper at about six in the evening. The meal over, Marlowe rested on a bed while the others sat playing backgammon. A dispute then arose about the bill and Marlowe suddenly sprang up, drew Frizer's dagger from his belt and began beating him on the head with it. Frizer struggled to retrieve his weapon and drove the point of the dagger into Marlowe's skull just over the right eye. Death was apparently instantaneous.

Nearly 300 years after his death, a memorial was erected at Canterbury though even then it was felt that there should not be one in Westminster Abbey on account of 'his acknowledged life and expressions'. At St Nicholas' Church, Deptford, a brass plate put up in 1919 refers 'To the Immortal Memory of Christopher Marlowe, M.A., The Founder of Grandiloquent Blank Verse'.

Christopher Marlowe died before he was thirty. His writing career lasted just over five years. During that time, in addition to producing an outstanding, though uncompleted, narrative poem and a vigorous translation of Lucan's *Pharsalia* (and a less satisfactory version of Ovid's *Amores*), Marlowe virtually single-handedly changed the nature and scope of the English drama. Of his contemporaries, only Shakespeare clearly surpasses him in achievement. And as an influence, it could be claimed that he is more important than Shakespeare, not least for his influence on Shakespeare himself. (pp. 103-11)

. . . . .

The world of classical legend was one to which writers of the Renaissance returned time and again, and Marlowe's attachment to it is shown once more in **Dido, Queen of Carthage,** possibly his earliest play, though he may have revised it at a later date before production. When Shakespeare's Hamlet discusses contemporary plays with the First Player, Marlowe's **Dido** seems to be in his mind, for though not popular ('caviare to the general') he says it was 'an excellent play, well digested in the scenes, set down with as much modesty as cunning'.

Marlowe found the simple plot in Virgil's *Aeneid* and Ovid's *Metamorphoses.* Aeneas, escaping from the sack of Troy, is wrecked on the Libyan coast where Dido, the Carthaginian queen falls in love with him, although she is already pledged to Iarbas, one of her noblemen. In a vision Mercury tells Aeneas that his destiny is to found Rome and he must therefore leave Dido. After one unsuccessful attempt he does this, whereupon Dido kills herself for sorrow, followed by her sister Anna and Iarbas.

Parts of the play are almost word-for-word renderings of passages from the first, second and fourth books of Virgil's epic but elsewhere Marlowe adapts his source material with the greatest freedom, which is one of the reasons for thinking that the play as we have it is the work of different periods of Marlowe's career. The title page of the only extant early edition (1594) tells us that **Dido** was acted by the Children of the Chapel and names Thomas Nashe as co-author of the play. It is very difficult indeed to see what part, if any, Nashe had in the composition of **Dido.** It bears no resemblance to the only dramatic work definitely known to be by Nashe, *Summer's Last Will and Testament.* Though collaboration between playwrights was very much the rule in Marlowe's day, Marlowe himself seems to have been an exception in this respect. Perhaps the partnership in this case dated from Marlowe's Cambridge days, when Nashe was his contemporary.

What is indisputable is that **Dido, Queen of Carthage** bears the unmistakable signature of Marlowe both in its language and its stage technique. Though unique among Marlowe's plays in being the only one with a central love interest, it has many links with the other plays and shows in cruder form the restlessness of spirit, the exuberance of imagination and that capacity to evoke horror by pushing the grotesque almost, but not quite, to the point of caricature, which T. S. Eliot singled out as Marlowe's peculiar strength:

> Then from the navell to the throat at once,
> He ript old Priam: at whose latter gaspe
> Joves marble statue gan to bend the brow,
> As lothing Pirrhus for this wicked act:
> Yet he undaunted tooke his fathers flagge,
> And dipt it in the old Kings chill cold bloud,
> And then in triumph ran into the streetes,
> Through which he could not passe for slaugh-
> tred men: . . .
>
> [lines 550-57]

Single lines break loose from their context and haunt the memory—

> We saw Cassandra sprauling in the streetes
>
> [line 569]

> At last the souldiers puld her by the heeles,
> And swong her howling in the emptie ayre
>
> [lines 542-43]
>
> . . . heele make me immortall with a kisse.
>
> [line 1329]

(A line that found its definitive and unforgettable context when Marlowe adapted it for Faustus' words to the phantom Helen of Troy.) Occasionally, there is an odd anticipation of Shakespeare, as in:

> See what strange artes necessitie findes out.

Dido is too static and too predictable in its development to be a successful drama, but occasionally we hear in it the voice of a great dramatist, confident in his capacity.

Marlowe wrote four great tragedies: **The Massacre at Paris** is not one of them. As it stands it is undoubtedly his worst play. The text, as given in the only (undated) early edition that survives, is so short and often so garbled that it is almost certainly based on an actor's memory or a theatrical abridgement. But it is not difficult to account for the contemporary popularity of the play (the great Elizabethan actor Edward Alleyn had one of his outstanding successes in the principal role of the Guise in it) for its rabid and unvarying anti-Catholicism was a faithful reflection of popular sentiment at the time.

The play, sometimes called *The Guise,* covers a period of some seventeen years, from the notorious massacre of the Huguenots on St Bartholomew's Eve 1572, to the death of Henri III in 1589, probably just a year or two before Marlowe wrote the play. The action opens with the murder of Admiral Coligny in his bed which is a prelude to the massacre of the Protestants, which in turn is followed by a series of individual killings culminating in the death of the Guise followed by that of the new king. The only variations from the unending sequence of stabbings, stranglings and poisonings are a grotesque scene where a cutpurse has his ears chopped off for trying to steal gold buttons from a wedding guest, and a hackneyed and irrelevant sub-plot dealing with the adultery of the Guise's wife.

The anti-Catholic bias of **The Massacre of Paris** seems to have been strong enough to overcome the customary ban on the presentation of political and religious topics on the Elizabethan stage. But for all the bitter strife between Protestants and Catholics which forms the staple of his play, Marlowe appears to be singularly uninterested in the rights and wrongs of the religious debate. The Huguenots (twice referred to as Puritans) are portrayed as pathetic victims without much courage or dignity, and the dying king's concluding injunction to the English agent to

> Salute the Queene of England in my name,
> And tell her Henry dyes her faithfull freend.
>
> [lines 1256-57]

sounds more like an obligatory flourish than a deeply felt patriotic utterance. The only real interest in the play lies in the character of the Guise, who is presented as a thoroughgoing Machiavellian, using religion, kinship, personal loyalty and anything else that comes to hand in the service of a relentless and single-minded self-seeking. In his great opening soliloquy (the longest in any of Marlowe's plays) we recognize the authentic accent of the Marlovian would-be superman:

> Oft have I leveld, and at last have learnd,
> That perill is the cheefest way to happines,
> And resolution honors fairest aime.
> What glory is there in a common good,
> That hanges for every peasant to atchive?
> That like I best that flyes beyond my reach.
> Set me to scale the high Peramides,
> And thereon set the Diadem of Fraunce,
> Ile either rend it with my nayles to naught,
> Or mount the top with my aspiring winges,
> Although my downfall be the deepest hell.
>
> [lines 94-104]

'That like I best that flyes beyond my reach'—it could be the motto of Tamburlaine, the first Marlovian hero, who took the stage by storm and became a theatrical legend even within the brief span of his creator's lifetime. There is an appropriate irony in the fact that the two parts of **Tamburlaine the Great,** stamped as they are in every line with Marlowe's characteristic genius, are the only works by Marlowe for which documentary evidence of his authorship is lacking. No author's name appears on the title page of any of the three early editions.

From the very first lines of the Prologue it is clear that the young dramatist knows exactly what he wants to do:

> From jygging vaines of riming mother wits,
> And such conceits as clownage keepes in pay,
> Weele lead you to the stately tent of War,
> Where you shall heare the Scythian Tamburlaine
> Threatening the world with high astounding te-arms
> And scourging kingdoms with his conquering sword.

The first two lines glance disparagingly at the buffoonery and the jogtrot verse typical of the early years of Elizabethan drama. But taken together these opening lines serve to define the action of Marlowe's own play: it is precisely a progress from the 'jigging veins' of the ineffectual Mycetes to the stately verse of Tamburlaine's utterance. In finding a new kind of hero Marlowe also finds the speech that gives him life; or rather, he discovers the character through the language.

Marlowe had five principal sources for his play. These were George Whetstone's *The English Mirror* (1586); a life of Tamburlaine published in Florence in 1553; Lonicerus's *History of the Turks;* the famous atlas by Abraham Ortelius (*Theatrum Orbis Terrarum*); and Paul Ive's *Practice of Fortification,* from which Marlowe took most of the details of military strategy. The real life original of his hero was Timur the Lame who ruled in Samarcand in the late fourteenth century, and whose vast empire was looked on with awe and admiration by the monarchs of Europe.

But the historical figure was little more than a point of departure for the dramatist's soaring imagination. Marlowe saw in Tamburlaine the very image of Renaissance man, entranced by the variety of the world he lived in and boundlessly confident in his ability to bend it to his will. It is no accident that the hero begins life as a humble shep-herd. Drama (other than comedy) had hitherto dealt with the exploits of kings and nobles: here we have the saga of the self-made man, triumphing through no advantages of birth or inheritance, but entirely through qualities of character. (We meet a similar figure in Doctor Faustus.) Tamburlaine's attitude and career are a continuous challenge to the traditional scheme of things, where a man's life was determined by the station to which he was born, and the cardinal virtue, in religion as in politics, was humble obedience. The 'world' which Tamburlaine threatens with 'high astounding terms' is nothing less than the socioreligious order which was the medieval heritage of the Elizabethan age:

> I am a Lord, for so my deeds shall proove,
> And yet a shepheard by my Parentage: . . .
>
> [lines 230-31]

At every point Tamburlaine challenges the ethic of 'the fall of princes' as expounded in such popular treatises as *The Mirror for Magistrates* (a new edition of which appeared in 1587, the year **Tamburlaine** was first performed). Marlowe is simply not interested in enforcing the old moral that pride goeth before a fall; this is especially true if we remember that the two parts of the play were not conceived together; and that the first part concluded not with Tamburlaine punished for his pride but rather when he 'takes truce with all the world' at the height of his triumph.

Tamburlaine's physical conquests are of course an emblem of the spiritual discoveries, the 'thirst for the infinite' of Renaissance man. The language in which Tamburlaine speaks of himself leaves us in no doubt that his territorial expansion is not merely the result of squalid political ambition:

> For Fates and Oracles [of] heaven have sworne,
> To roialise the deedes of Tamburlaine:
> And make them blest that share in his attemptes.
> And doubt you not, but if you favour me,
> And let my Fortunes and my valour sway
> To some direction in your martiall deeds,
> The world will strive with hostes of men at armes
> To swarm unto the Ensigne I support.
> The host of Xerxes, which by fame is said
> To drinke the mightie Parthian Araris,
> Was but a handful to that we will have.
> Our quivering Lances shaking in the aire,
> And bullets like Joves dreadful Thunderbolts,
> Enrolde in flames and fiery smoldering mistes,
> Shall threat the Gods more than Cyclopian war-res,
> And with our Sun-bright armour as we march,
> Weel chase the Stars from heaven, and dim their eies
> That stand and muse at our admyred armes.
>
> [lines 605-22]

Throughout the play Tamburlaine is identified with the sun and likens himself repeatedly to the gods. But his blasphemy goes unpunished and he climbs from victory to victory, while his enemies are shown to be pathetic, self-divided weaklings. The deeply traditional image of the wheel of Fortune with whose fickle movement men rise and fall is given a new ironic twist by Tamburlaine:

I hold the Fates bound fast in yron chaines,
And with my hand turne Fortunes wheel
        about. . . .

                                    [lines 369-70]

He is Fortune, controlling his own destiny and those of others; and insofar as the play shows every character's fate dependent on Tamburlaine's will or whim while he himself is not subject to control, it confirms Tamburlaine's view of himself.

Marlowe is clearly fascinated by the energy, the resolve and the visionary imagination of his hero. Tamburlaine's capacity to give utterance to his ambition becomes, in the words of the play, the guarantee that the ambition is achieved. To put it in another way, Tamburlaine's eloquence is the dramatic equivalent of his military prowess; the 'high astounding terms' and the 'conquering sword' are exactly interchangeable. It is significant that the weakling Mycetes, at the very beginning of the play, finds himself 'insufficient to express' his feelings about his country because 'it requires a great and thundering speech'—the speech, in other words, of a Tamburlaine. The Marlovian hero is distinguished by his eloquence, or magniloquence, as we might expect in a theatre where the spoken word was the most powerful resource of stagecraft; the weaklings are always at a loss for words.

No doubt Marlowe's original audience, as soon as they heard Tamburlaine's arrogant utterances and saw his acts of cruelty (such as the sack of Damascus and the slaughter of the virgins), would have sat back in their seats and waited for a proper retribution to overtake him for his *hubris* in rejecting his appointed place in society and setting himself up as a rival to the gods. An audience accustomed to moralizing tracts of the *Mirror for Magistrates* variety could hardly be expected to react otherwise. But the great dramatist, though he may take his audience's stock responses into account, does not necessarily satisfy them. (Shakespeare, in his History plays, shows his awareness of the idea of the Great Chain of Being, but he is not shackled by it.) One of the reasons for the immense popularity of *Tamburlaine the Great* may well have been precisely the fact that it did *not* satisfy the audience's expectations; instead, it deflected them in a new and surprising direction. But to put it this way is also slightly misleading. For the Elizabethan age was, more than most, an age of transition. Counterpoised in the Elizabethan mind with the medieval sanctions against 'over-reaching' was the Renaissance admiration for the 'aspiring mind'. And it is in the tension between these two that *Tamburlaine the Great* lives, moves and has its being.

If the first part of *Tamburlaine the Great* is a celebration of Renaissance individualism, the second is something like a lament for its limitations. Since he had already exhausted most of his source material in Part I, Marlowe was compelled to elaborate on Tamburlaine's further conquests in the sequel. But Part II is not simply the massacre as before. There is a dramatic development, as we see the hero becomes more and more drunk with power, seeing himself now not merely as 'the scourge of God' but as the rival and even the superior of the gods. Tamburlaine's growing madness, the death of his beloved wife Zenocrate

and finally his own death are the shadows cast by the bright sun of Tamburlaine's imperial conquest. It is not weakness of character nor any twist of Fate that brings about Tamburlaine's downfall, if such it is. It is the very nature of man, and of human existence. Tamburlaine is a finite creature with a longing for infinity. The frustration of his *ultimate* aspiration—divinity—is implicit in the aspiration itself. It has been well said by M. M. Mahood [in *Poetry and Humanism*] that *Tamburlaine* is the only drama in which the death of the hero constitutes the tragedy. And the hero himself expresses this in his final piercing moment of tragic awareness:

        For Tamburlaine, the Scourge of God must die.

Like Tamburlaine, Marlowe's next hero Doctor Faustus is a man of humble birth who, when the Chorus first introduces him to us at the beginning of the play, has already established himself in the world of learning through his native abilities. This opening chorus is a cunningly contrived piece of stagecraft for it not only gives us, in a nutshell, 'the form of Faustus' fortunes good or bad' (with a brief backward glance at *Tamburlaine*) but, with that freedom of movement through space and time which was second nature to the Elizabethan dramatist, concludes by zooming down on Faustus, at this moment, with the fateful choice still before him—'And this the man who in his study sits'. This shuffling together of past, present and future gives some sense of the inevitability of Faustus' progress to damnation while preserving inviolate the hero's capacity to choose.

In some ways *The Tragicall History of The Life and Death of Doctor Faustus* is a more deeply traditional play than *Tamburlaine.* Marlowe's immediate source was probably an English translation of the contemporary German *Faustbuch,* but the story itself was part of European mythology. It tells how Faustus, thirsting for supreme power, sold his soul to the devil in exchange for twenty-four years of absolute dominion on earth. Built into the very bones of the story is the element of the cautionary tale, with Faustus as the horrible example of what happens when creatures rebel against their lot and aspire to the condition of the Creator. The Chorus stresses this aspect of the fable, and behind the immediate allusion to Icarus looms the distant shadow of the first rebel, Satan himself:

        Till swolne with cunning, of a selfe conceit,
        His waxen wings did mount above his reach,
        And melting heavens conspirde his overthrow.
                                    [lines 20-2]

The Good and Evil Angels who embody the struggle with Faustus' soul come straight out of medieval Morality drama and the concluding warning of the Chorus, after Faustus has met his awesome fate, is undeviatingly orthodox:

        Faustus is gone, regard his hellish fall,
        Whose fiendful fortune may exhort the wise,
        Onely to wonder at unlawful things,
        Whose deepenesse doth intise such forward wits,
        To practice more than heavenly power permits.
                                    [lines 1481-85]

But, as with *Tamburlaine,* the play invites us to regard its hero from more than one point of view. The Chorus was for Marlowe a convenient means for directing the audience's interests, but it no more represents the total tragic experience of *Doctor Faustus* than, say, Edgar's tidy moralizings represent the final judgement of *King Lear*. It is not irrelevant to remember that Marlowe himself was probably the friend of men such as John Dee, whose life's aim was 'to practise more than heavenly power permits' (at least insofar as heavenly power was incarnated in the ecclesiastical authorities), but we do not need to go outside the world of the play to be powerfully aware of the dramatist's imaginative sympathy with his protagonist. In *Tamburlaine* the hero's territorial conquests are a metaphor for the scope of his imagination, and his military and political ascendancy the outward sign of his soaring spirit. With *Doctor Faustus* we are dealing with the thing itself. The story deals directly with Faustus' spiritual ambition and its consequences. In his very first speech he surveys and rejects contemptuously the whole body of traditional learning—logic, medicine, law, theology. The Biblical reference 'The reward of sin is death' underlines the nature of the offence Faustus is about to commit, but it is difficult not to hear in his subsequent lines something more than the dramatist's creative sympathy for any of his characters:

> O what a world of profit and delight,
> Of power, of honor, of omnipotence
> Is promised to the studious Artizan?
> All things that move betweene the quiet poles
> Shal be at my commaund . . .
>
> [lines 81-5]

When Faustus, in this opening speech, rejects theology he takes the first fateful step towards damnation, but it is in no spirit of vindictive moralizing that Marlowe follows his hero's descent into hell. Though the outcome is certain, the tension is maintained by a series of choices throughout the action by means of which Faustus confirms himself in sin and finally puts himself beyond the reach of divine mercy. After his first rejection of God's teaching, there is his refusal to heed the Good Angel, the signing of the blood bond with Lucifer, his refusal, (or inability, perhaps, at this stage) to follow the Old Man's exhortation to repent, and his effort to forget his desperate spiritual predicament in the gratification of physical desire. Though the fable deals with aspiration and damnation at the literal level, the dramatist still has to find adequate embodiment of this conflict in word and gesture. Marlowe's verse rises magnificently to every dramatic occasion, from the opening self-assurance of Faustus rejecting all human learning, through the desolate eloquence of Mephistophilis—

> Why this is hel, nor am I out of it:
> Thinkst thou that I who saw the face of God,
> And tasted the eternal joyes of heaven,
> Am not tormented with ten thousand hels,
> In being depriv'd of everlasting blisse?
>
> [lines 312-16]

—to the final desperate writhings of Faustus' tormented soul:

> The starres moove stil, time runs, the clocke will strike,
> The divel wil come, and Faustus must be damnd.

O Ile leape up to my God: who pulles me downe?
See see where Christs blood streames in the firmament.
One drop would save my soule, halfe a drop, ah my Christ.
Yet wil I call on him: oh spare me Lucifer!

[lines 1429-35]

The imagery is resonant with memories of all the great rebels of myth and religion, the Titans, Phaeton, Icarus, up to Lucifer himself, so that the hero's progress becomes in some sense the progress of the European consciousness. And though Marlowe's language carries the greatest charge of meaning and implication, the action and spectacle have retained undiminished their capacity to hold an audience enthralled. Already in *Tamburlaine* Marlowe had shown his ability to make telling use of the theatre's non-verbal resources. Tamburlaine's triumphal entry in a chariot drawn by four deposed Asian kings and the scene where the captured monarch Bajazeth is brought on in a cage against whose bars he dashes out his brains were two of the most famous 'set-pieces' in Elizabethan drama. Perhaps for us today their bravura tends to spill over into comedy. But the same cannot be said of the great moments of *Doctor Faustus*—Faustus holding his hand over a flame because the blood in which he has to sign the bond has congealed, the pageant of the Seven Deadly Sins (no less effective for being profoundly traditional), above all, the great scene where Faustus confronts his paramour, the incarnation for all Europe of a world ill lost, Helen of Troy, and utters the most poignantly ironic line in all Elizabethan drama:

'Sweet Helen, make me immortal with a kiss'

—in scenes such as this the visual presentation matches superbly the incandescent blank verse which is Marlowe's legacy to the English stage.

Though not as popular as *Tamburlaine* in Marlowe's own day, *Doctor Faustus* is the play by which its author is best known today, and it has a strong claim to be considered his best in spite of a comic sub-plot which is not completely woven into the main action. The text has come down to us in two quite different forms, the earlier, and probably more authentic of which, is found in the Quarto editions from 1604 to 1611. The Quartos from 1616 to 1631 print a version which is half as large again (though some of the original matter has been omitted or recast), but it is generally believed that most of the new material is not in fact by Marlowe at all. For the most part, it consists of crude incidents taken from the Faustbook and is probably the work of a well-known Elizabethan hack called Samuel Rowley. There is also a Quarto of 1633, containing many comic scenes adopted from Marlowe's next play *The Jew of Malta*, but this has no textual authority whatever.

To pass from *Tamburlaine* and *Doctor Faustus* to *The Jew of Malta* is like leaving the open air or a spacious palace to enter a prison cell. For this setting Marlowe abandons the freedom of Renaissance Europe and the wide plains of Asia for a tight little island in a land-locked sea. And for his hero, instead of a warrior who sweeps all before him in his triumphal progress, or a thinker whose dreams are boundless, he chooses a devious and calculating Jew, a friendless outsider in a hostile community.

Nor is this restriction of scope limited to character and setting. In both the earlier tragedies the actions and utterances of the hero evoke a world of absolute values, even if only to reject it. When Tamburlaine boasts:

> I hold the Fates bound fast in yron chaines,
> And with my hand turne Fortunes wheel
>   about, . . .
>
>   [lines 369-70]

he recalls, however scornfully, the forces in human life which set a limit to human aspiration and achievement, forces later to be embodied in the death of Zenocrate. In the same way Faustus' words—

> Thinkst thou that Faustus is so fond, to imagine,
> That after this life there is any paine?
> Tush, these are trifles and meere olde wives tales.
>
>   [lines 565-67]

gain their dramatic force from the incompleteness of Faustus' commitment to them. But the mean and narrow world of *The Jew of Malta* is the only reality with which the play deals directly or by implication. It is a world whose manifesto is spoken by Machiavelli appearing as Prologue:

> And let them know that I am Machevill,
> And weigh not men, and therefore not mens
>   words:
> Admir'd I am of those that hate me most.
> . . . .
> I count Religion but a childish Toy,
> And hold there is no sinne but Ignorance.
> . . . .
> Might first made Kings, and Lawes were then
>   most sure
> When like the Dracos they were writ in blood.
>
>   [lines 7-21]

There is a world of difference between Faustus' professed disbelief in an afterlife and Machiavelli's cynical definition of religion. For all his defiance, the former teeters between faith and doubt and the play in some sense proves his words wrong. The action and motivation of *The Jew of Malta* on the other hand confirm at every point that we are in a society where force and fraud are the ruling principles and lip-service to religion a handy instrument of policy.

Barabas the Jew is undoubtedly the villain of the piece, but, while Marlowe amply satisfied the audience's desire to see the Jew as scapegoat, the entire play turns on the fact that Jew, Christian and Turk without exception act in the same ruthlessly egotistic way in their pursuit of wealth and power, whatever their pious avowals. On the evidence of the play Barabas has the 'right' on his side when he declares:

> Thus loving neither, will I live with both,
> Making a profit of my policie;
> And he from whom my most advantage comes,
> Shall be my friend.
> This is the life we Jewes are us'd to lead;
> And reason too, for Christians doe the like.
>
>   [lines 2213-18]

It is impossible not to feel the savage irony which, unknown to the speaker, comes through the words of the Christian Governor as he piously admonishes the Jew, having just confiscated all his possessions—

> Excesse of wealth is cause of covetousnesse:
> And covetousnesse, o 'tis a monstrous sinne.
>
>   [lines 356-57]

There is something deeper than the desire to pander to the popular taste for anti-clerical satire in the scene where the two friars, fooled by Barabas's protestations that he wishes to turn Christian, try to get their hands on his fortune. In the end Barabas is left, literally, to stew in his own juice, but only because he is not Machiavellian enough: he makes the fatal error of trusting a Christian.

The Jew of Malta cannot be called a tragedy in any but the crudest sense, the sense in which we may call any play a tragedy in which the chief character dies. Barabas dies, but utterly without tragic illumination, and nowhere else does the play offer even the faintest glimmer of such illumination. The staple of its plot is the sheerest melodrama—poisoned porridge, poisoned flowers, stranglings, boilings in oil and the like follow one another in bloodthirsty succession. There is an undeniable comic relish in the way Marlowe depicts this world, a relish which black comedy and sick jokes may make more accessible to the modern audience:

> As for my self, I walke abroad a nights
> And kill sicke people groaning under walls:
> Sometimes I goe about and poyson wells;
> And now and then, to cherish Christian theeves,
> I am content to lose some of my Crownes;
> That I may, walking in my Gallery,
> See 'em goe pinion'd along by my doore.
>
>   [lines 939-45]

Barabas never attains the near-tragic stature of Shylock any more than the play itself ever emerges from its worm's eye view of human motivation. With neither tragic insight nor comic liberation, the laughter it provokes is thoughtful and disturbing and its peculiar quality is aptly summarized in T. S. Eliot's phrase 'savage farce'.

In spite of its title, Marlowe's *Edward II* is not a 'history play', certainly not in the sense in which the phrase is applied to Shakespeare's plays dealing with kings of England. Like Shakespeare, Marlowe found his raw material in Holinshed's *Chronicles* and the *Annals* of John Stow, but there is little similarity in the use which the two dramatists made of their sources. Marlowe has little of the concern for the suffering land which runs through Shakespearean history plays, and nothing at all of the Shakespearean sense of historical change. He covers a period of over twenty years (1307-30) but we have little sense of what happens to England during this time. The dramatist's centre of interest is the relationship between the weak and frivolous Edward and his favourite, Gaveston. It has been suggested that in the figure of Gaveston Marlowe came closest to drawing a self-portrait, and certainly the dramatic character has the personal charm, the panache and the touch of cruelty which we tend to think of as the leading traits of his character, in addition to being a partner in a homosexual relationship. (According to Baines,

Marlowe held that 'all they that love not tobacco and boys were fools'.) Unfortunately for the unity of the play, Gaveston disappears from it about halfway through, put to death by the nobles whom he has offended. Though Edward immediately takes new favourites, these have neither the attractiveness nor the force of personality of Gaveston, and the dramatic impact of the Gaveston—Edward relationship is gone. The lack is partly compensated for by the emergence of Mortimer as a fully fledged Machiavellian (though Marlowe has to do a certain amount of violence to his earlier portrayal of Mortimer to achieve this). The latter part of the play is largely taken up by the combined efforts of Mortimer and Queen Isabella to oust Edward from power, efforts which eventually succeed in forcing the king to abdicate in favour of his son. Mortimer tries various means of getting rid of the king and when everything else fails hires Lightborn, a specialist in ingenious means of murder. Lightborn is discovered and Mortimer put to death by the young king who also sends his mother to the tower.

Though it bears all the marks of Marlowe's impatient genius, *Edward II* is in some ways his most ambitious play. To begin with, he shows a certain amount of skill in choosing and ordering character and events from the fairly substantial material provided by his sources. Sometimes the very swiftness of the 'cutting' carries its own penalty, as for instance when we suddenly hear, towards the end of the play, of '*old* Edward', when we still think of him (as the play has made us do) as a pleasure-loving young man. But most of the time the plot, in spite of being 'broken backed' after Gaveston's exit, moves rapidly enough.

Then again, the dialogue of the play spans the entire Marlovian range, from the youthful lyricism of *Dido* (here finely tuned to the immediate dramatic occasion, as in Gaveston's account of the diversions he has planned for the king, lines 50-71) through the horror-comedy of *The Jew of Malta* to the austere splendour of *Doctor Faustus,* as in Mortimer's last words, with their anticipation of *Hamlet:*

> Farewell faire Queene, weepe not for Mortimer,
> That scornes the world, and as a traveller,
> Goes to discover countries yet unknowne.
>
> [lines 2632-34]

There is even, for Marlowe, a new kind of dialogue, a dialogue that gets its power not from splendidly extravagant statement but rather from a bare and chilling matter-of-factness applied to a grim situation (see for instance, the exchange between Lightborn, Matrevis and Gurney, lines 2476-85).

But the most distinctive thing about *Edward II* is that it is not a 'one character' play, as *Tamburlaine, Doctor Faustus* and *The Jew of Malta* tend to be. Apart from the king himself we have Gaveston and Mortimer as characters in their own right. And among the minor figures, Lightborn, the professional killer, has a deadly and totally convincing dramatic presence. (He is not found in Marlowe's sources; it is not fanciful to assume that the dramatist modelled him on some real-life acquaintance encountered in the course of his secret service activities.)

Edward II attempts, within the limits imposed by its historical sources, to discover the alternatives in human action to the self-seeking hedonism of a Gaveston and the Machiavellian cynicism of a Mortimer. The world-ranging conquests of a Tamburlaine have shrunk here to the pathetic dimensions of an imprisoned king standing in the filth of sewers in a dungeon below the earth. The play has little to offer in positive terms, other than the Stoic defiance of death expressed in the last words of Mortimer. This attempt to invest the acceptance of death with an autonomous significance, as a reaction against the emptiness of a life drained of value, is one that will be made repeatedly in drama in the two or three decades following Marlowe's death. We see it, for instance, in the two great tragedies of John Webster, *The White Devil* and *The Duchess of Malfi,* and in the plays of John Ford. In this, as in so much else, Marlowe first sounded the note that was to be taken up by later dramatists. But Marlowe's claim to greatness does not rest merely on his influence on others, nor on his own brilliant promise, but on a solid and varied achievement to which a fellow poet, Michael Drayton, paid a splendid tribute in his poem 'To Henry Reynolds, Of Poets and Poesy':

> . . . Marlowe, bathed in the Thespian springs,
> Had in him those brave translunary things
> That your first poets had; his raptures were
> All fire and air, which made his verses clear,
> For that fine madness still he did retain
> Which rightly should possess a poet's brain.
>
> (pp. 115-30)

Gāmini Salgādo, "Christopher Marlowe," in English Drama to 1710, *edited by Christopher Ricks, 1971. Reprint by Peter Bedrick Books, 1987, pp. 103-30.*

TAMBURLAINE, PARTS I AND *II*

CRITICAL COMMENTARY

G. I. Duthie (essay date 1948)

[*In the excerpt below, Duthie disagrees with U. M. Ellis-Fermor's statement in her book* Christopher Marlowe *(1927) that* Tamburlaine *offers "no progress, crisis, or solution" (see Further Reading). Duthie asserts, however, that despite the fact that* Tamburlaine *seems to depict the hero's uninterrupted—and therefore undramatic—rise to power, Marlowe creates in each of the two parts a "single coherent dramatic structure" that generates suspense and interest. In Part I, Duthie claims, the playwright opposes Zenocrate's plea for mercy to Tamburlaine's ruthless concept of honor, and in Part II, he focuses on the hero's confrontation with death. Act, scene, and line references are taken from Ellis-Fermor's edition of* 1 *and* 2 Tamburlaine *(1930).*]

According to the Prologue to Part II of *Tamburlaine,* Marlowe wrote Part II as a result of the popularity of Part

Tamburlaine

the Great.

Who, from a Scythian Shephearde,

by his rare and woonderfull Conquests,

became a most puissant and migh-
tye Monarque.

And (for his tyranny, and terrour in
Warre) was tearmed,

The Scourge of God.

Deuided into two Tragicall Dif-

courses, as they were sundrie times
shewed vpon Stages in the Citie
of London.

By the right honorable the Lord

Admyrall, his seruantes.

Now first, and newlie published.

LONDON.

Printed by Richard Ihones: at the signe
of the Rose and Crowne neere Hol-
borne Bridge. 1590.

Title page from the 1590 edition of Tamburlaine, *Part I.*

I. Part I is, then, a complete play in itself, and in the following study I propose in the first place to speak of Part
I *per se.*

I

What are the essentials of the plot-material out of which
I Tamburlaine is made? The following answer might perhaps be given. A Scythian shepherd, endowed with a mind
of astonishing power and with a uniquely compelling personality, and inspired by a soaring ambition, embarks on
a career of ruthless conquest with the aim of becoming a
pre-eminent ruler. He achieves success after success, and,
to round off the play, finally "takes truce with all the
world" and marries the lady whom he loves: he had taken
her prisoner at the beginning of his career, and, some time
after her capture, she had come to love him. The main
content of the play, according to this view, consists of the
amazing series of triumphs which Tamburlaine enjoys,
these being presented as a result, on the one hand, of the
operation of Fate, and, on the other, of the tremendous
strength of Tamburlaine's ambition, his overwhelming
confidence in his own destiny (which he communicates to
others too), and the extraordinary energy and mental vitality which he brings to his warmaking.

If this is a fair summary of the essential stuff of *I Tamburlaine,* it must, I think, be granted that Marlowe has set
himself to make a play out of dramatically unpromising
material. Unchecked development along a straight, even
although upward-slanting, line can hardly be called truly
dramatic development. The aspiring mind hardly furnishes promising psychological material for drama if there is
no conflict in that mind, no interplay of opposing motives.
And it has been claimed that the content of *I Tamburlaine*
is in fact undramatic. In her very interesting book on Marlowe [see Further Reading], Professor U. M. Ellis-Fermor
writes as follows:

> *Tamburlaine,* so far from interpreting life by in-
> dicating its form, appears as formless and inco-
> herent as life itself. The first part, in this, errs less
> than the second, but even the first has no prog-
> ress, crisis or solution. The final triumph and
> marriage of Tamburlaine is perhaps a climax,
> but it is too long deferred to have a direct con-
> nection with the original impulse, and the idea
> has been anticipated and handled so often that
> it has lost its freshness. Tamburlaine's rise to
> power cannot fill five acts of a play without com-
> plications, and a complication would be a denial
> of the very nature of Tamburlaine's genius,
> which triumphs, not after a struggle, but with-
> out it. Thus, before his play was begun, Marlowe
> had committed himself to a theme that was in
> its essence undramatic. It is a foregone conclu-
> sion, then, that there will be no dramatic
> form. . . . It is obvious that, of all the emotions
> that may be roused in an audience by the action
> of a play, almost the only one possible to the plot
> of *Tamburlaine* is surprise, an emotion that can
> only be evoked to a limited degree. The audience
> is in a state of suspense during the earliest acts
> of the double play, and suspense gives way to
> amazement as triumph follows triumph. As
> soon as the point is reached at which there is no
> longer any uncertainty in the mind of the audi-
> ence—that is, as soon as repetition of the tri-
> umph has made the situation familiar and
> caused it to be expected, there is no more sus-
> pense. There are, in point of fact, about two
> more acts, but they have to be helped out with
> Bajazeth and the Virgins of Damascus—
> episodes which are irrelevant to the too simple
> original theme.

For myself, I cannot help disagreeing with this estimate
of *I Tamburlaine.* I cannot agree that the play has "no
progress, crisis or solution", nor that the final triumph and
marriage of Tamburlaine has no "direct connection with
the original impulse", nor that "a complication would be
a denial of the very nature of Tamburlaine's genius, which
triumphs, not after a struggle, but without it", nor that the
episodes of Bajazeth and the Virgins of Damascus are "irrelevant to the too simple original theme", nor that the
play has "no dramatic form".

It is clear that at one crucial point there is a very real conflict in the hero's mind. This is at V.ii.72-127, a soliloquy
by Tamburlaine in which we find him caught between two
possible courses of action. Is he to continue in his former
ways as a ruthless conqueror? He would like to. But he
cannot help being affected by Zenocrate's grief for her

country and her father. Is he to allow this to deflect him
from his habitual inexorability? The struggle in his mind
is severe: in her tear-filled eyes

> Angels in their christal armours fight
> A doubtfull battell with my tempted thoughtes,
> For Egypts freedom and the Souldans life:
> His life that so consumes Zenocrate.
>
> [V.ii.88-91]

The words "tempted" and "doubtfull" are significant—
we have mental conflict in the hero and we have genuine
dramatic suspense. Zenocrate's anxiety for her father is a
most powerful inducement to Tamburlaine to change his
ways. The irresistible conqueror has never stood in such
danger of defeat as he now stands—Zenocrate's sorrow is
more likely to turn him from his ruthless course than any
enemy he has previously encountered: her sorrows, he
says,

> lay more siege vnto my soule,
> Than all my Army to Damascus walles.
> And neither Perseans Soueraign, nor the Turk
> Troubled my sences with conceit of foile,
> So much by much, as dooth Zenocrate.
>
> [V.ii.92-6]

Is he going to allow her to deflect him, or is he going to
resist her?

This conflict in Tamburlaine's mind is resolved, and its
resolution conditions the nature of the conclusion of the
play. Tamburlaine not only spares the Soldan's life but
also declares to him that he will

> render all into your hands.
> And ad more strength to your dominions
> Then euer yet confirm'd th' Egyptian Crown.
>
> [V.ii.385-87]

His own words make it clear that the course he is taking
is the result of Zenocrate's influence—

> Come happy Father of Zenocrate,
> A title higher than thy Souldans name:
> Though my right hand haue thus enthralled thee
> Thy princely daughter here shall set thee free.
> She that hath calmde the furie of my sword.
> Which had ere this bin bathde in streames of
>   blood,
> As vast and deep as Euphrates or Nile.
>
> [V.ii.371-77]

Had it not been for the influence of Zenocrate, Tamburlaine would have behaved otherwise towards the conquered Soldan. But what Marlowe presents us with is not
a simple matter of Tamburlaine abrogating his old principles and substituting new ones for them. Having declared
that he is going to "render all" into the Soldan's hands,
he goes on—

> The God of war resignes his roume to me,
> Meaning to make me Generall of the world,
> Ioue viewing me in armes, lookes pale and wan,
> Fearing my power should pull him from his
>   throne.
> Where ere I come the fatall sisters sweat,
> And griesly death by running to and fro,
> To doo their ceaslies homag to my sword
>
> [V.ii.388-94]

He still claims that his "honor" consists

> in sheading blood,
> When men presume to manage armes with him.
>
> [V.ii.415-16]

This is the sort of thing that he has been saying from the
beginning of the play. The resolution of the mental struggle of V.ii.72ff. consists of a determination by Tamburlaine
not to give up his old principles, but to maintain them
though allowing them to be modified to some extent by the
influence of Zenocrate.

Zenocrate signifies Beauty. Beauty sits in her face
[V.ii.80-1]. Now in the crucial soliloquy at V.ii.72ff. Tamburlaine declares that a warrior must admit Beauty as an
influence upon him—

> And euery warriour that is rapt with loue,
> Of fame, of valour, and of victory
> Must needs haue beauty beat on his conceites.
>
> [V.ii.117-19]

But the influence of Beauty must not be excessive—

> But how vnseemly is it for my Sex
> My discipline of armes and Chiualrie,
> My nature and the terrour of my name.
> To harbour thoughts effeminate and faint?
> Saue onely that in Beauties just applause,
> With whose instinct the soule of man is toucht.
> And euery warriour etc.
>
> [V.ii.111-17]

And he declares that he, Tamburlaine, will both "conceiue" and "subdue" Beauty [V.ii.120]—he will both admit
and resist its influence. Beauty can influence a warrior in
two directions. First, it can encourage him in his warlike
career. Zenocrate has encouraged Tamburlaine unhesitatingly up to the point where Damascus is besieged and the
Soldan is threatened, and at the end Tamburlaine can still
think of her as "adding more courage to [his] conquering
mind" [V.ii.453]. But secondly, Beauty can also urge a
warrior towards clemency: it can try to arouse compassion
in him, to exert a softening influence upon him. And Tamburlaine believes that it is possible to give way too much
to this softening influence, so that one is degraded from
the status of great warrior. That, he insists, he himself
must avoid.

On the face of it, the upshot of this soliloquy is that Tamburlaine determines to allow Beauty to affect him as far
as its encouraging influence goes, but that he determines
to resist its softening influence. On the face of it, that is
what he means when he says that he will both "conceiue"
and "subdue" Beauty. If that is the entire result of the soliloquy, however, we must surely be prepared at the end
to find him refusing to be lenient to the Soldan. But that
is just what we do not find. We find him sparing the Soldan
and declaring that it is Zenocrate who has calmed the fury
of his sword. Moreover it is very shortly after the soliloquy
that he first avows his intention to spare the Soldan, and
in making this avowal he indicates that the decision has
been made for the sake of Zenocrate:

THER.: We know the victorie is ours my Lord,

But let vs saue the reuerend Souldans life,
For faire Zenocrate, that so laments his state.
TAMB.: That will we chiefly see vnto, Therida-
mas.
For sweet Zenocrate, whose worthinesse
Deserues a conquest ouer euery hart.
[V.ii.140-5]

The word "conquest" here points back to "battell" in
V.ii.89. Now I do not think it could be seriously suggested
that in the soliloquy Tamburlaine resolves to resist the influence of Zenocrate's grief, and then, almost immediately, decides briskly, after Theridamas's short plea on her
behalf, to give in after all. I believe that by the end of the
soliloquy he has decided to be merciful to the Soldan.
When he declares that he will both "conceiue" and "subdue" Beauty, I believe that by "conceiuing" it he means
more than admitting its influence as an encouragement in
his martial exploits. He means that, doubtless: but I think
he also means that he will admit its moderating influence
as far as the sparing of the Soldan is concerned. He will
admit its moderating influence—but not beyond the point
where that ceases to be consistent with his honour as a
warrior. Should Beauty ever tempt him to be weak, spine-
less, effeminate, he would refuse to give in to it: but he may
spare the Soldan without pusillanimity. I believe that this
solution of his problem is implied in the soliloquy itself:
it is at any rate certainly the solution at which he has arrived by the end of the play when, at V.ii.371, he enters
leading the captive Soldan.

The modifying effect of Beauty on Tamburlaine in the end
is to create in him a disposition to show pity in a greater
degree than he has been willing to do before. We may say
that what is opposed to Beauty during the conflict in his
mind is Honour as he has up to now conceived it—that
is, a conception of Honour which excludes Pity after a certain point. Before the psychological crisis it has been his
custom on the first day of an engagement to pitch white
tents in his camp, indicating to his enemies that if they surrender now all their lives will be spared. It is not until the
third day, when his tents are black, that his wrath demands the blood of all "without respect of Sex, degree or
age" [IV.i.63]. Under certain circumstances, then, he is already prepared to be merciful. But it seems clear that what
is required of him at the critical moment in V.ii is that he
shall be merciful beyond the limits to which he has previously been willing to go. When he announces that he is
going to spare the Soldan he says, as we have seen, that
had not Zenocrate calmed the fury of his sword it

had ere this bin bathde in streames of blood,
As vast and deep as Euphrates or Nile.
[V.ii.376-77]

Tamburlaine modifies his old ideal of Honour. But he does
not jettison it. The old ideal had been imperfect: it had not
allowed sufficient scope to Pity. Now, revised, adjusted, it
can still stand. And, inasmuch as Beauty has not only a
softening but also an encouraging influence on a warrior,
Zenocrate remains an inspiration which adds more courage to Tamburlaine's conquering mind [V.ii.453].

It is to be noticed that after the soliloquy Tamburlaine immediately asks "Hath Baiazeth bene fed to day?"

[V.ii.129]. And when, shortly afterwards, he asserts that
Zenocrate "deserues a conquest ouer euery hart", he goes
on immediately to speak insultingly to Bajazeth [V.ii.146].
There is not much evidence here of any change in Tamburlaine in the direction of lenity! But we must remember
that though he has accepted the idea of the moderating effect of Beauty he has also insisted that it shall not be allowed to derogate from his honour as a warrior, and we
may suggest that in making him persist in his former attitude to Bajazeth Marlowe is simply emphasizing the fact
that Tamburlaine is not giving up his role of conqueror—
he is not by any means altogether revoking his former values. In the same way, we may be somewhat disconcerted
to find at the end of the play that no sooner has Tamburlaine shown his leniency to the Soldan in deference to
Zenocrate than he goes on to rant about the god of war
resigning his room to him—his old bombast rings out
again unaltered. But what the audience or reader has to
do here [V.ii.371-416] is, I think, to imagine a combination
of the two attitudes which are indicated side by side—the
willingness of the hero to be merciful beyond his former
wont, and his insistence on the fact that he will not allow
himself to be reduced to anything less than a great warrior. I believe that at the end we are meant to see a Tamburlaine who is ready to admit in due proportion the moderating and encouraging influences of Beauty—a Tamburlaine animated by a single new ideal consisting of a modification of his original conception of Honour. But apparently all that Marlowe can do to convey this is to make him
speak now in terms indicating a resolve to be merciful and
generous as not before, and now in terms exactly like those
he was in the habit of using before.

At V.ii.72ff., then, we have a psychological crisis in the
hero, and its resolution conditions the nature of the conclusion of the play. Now the direct preparation for this crisis begins at the end of IV.ii, where Zenocrate first begs
Tamburlaine to be merciful to Damascus—

Yet would you haue some pitie for my sake,
Because it is my countries, and my Fathers.

But Tamburlaine's reply is uncompromising—

Not for the world Zenocrate, if I haue sworn.

He will not be merciful contrary to his oath—his honour
demands that he shall keep his oath. The oath consists of
the declaration that if the city is surrendered while Tamburlaine's tents are white all inside will be spared—if it is
surrendered while the tents are red those inside who are
armed will be slain—and if it holds out until the tents are
black not one of the inhabitants shall escape. Tamburlaine
will not, even for Zenocrate's sake, be compassionate beyond the bounds of his established practice—and it is clear
that that is what she is asking him to be, for her "Yet
would you haue some pitie" comes immediately after his
threats as to what will happen "when they see me march
in black aray".

Then in IV.iv. Zenocrate appears sad. Tamburlaine asks
her why, and she replies—

My lord, to see my fathers towne besieg'd,
The countrie wasted where my selfe was borne,
How can it but afflict my verie soule?

If any loue remaine in you my Lord,
Or if my loue vnto your maiesty
May merit fauour at your highnesse handes,
Then raise your siege from faire Damascus wal-
les,
And with my father take a frindly truce.
[IV.iv.67-74]

But again Tamburlaine is firm—

Zenocrate, were Egypt Ioues owne land,
Yet would I with my sword make Ioue to stoope.
[IV.iv.75-6]

He will not give up the aim and the methods that have brought him to the point where he now is. He will not buy Zenocrate's father's love with the sacrifice of his ambition. Zenocrate is submissive, and yet at the same time she pleads again, this time for her father himself—

Honor still waight on happy Tamburlaine:
Yet giue me leaue to plead for him my Lord.
[IV.iv.87-8]

And now Tamburlaine makes a concession to her—

Content thy selfe, his person shall be safe.
And all the friendes of faire Zenocrate,
If with their liues they will be pleasde to yeeld,
Or may be forc'd to make me Emperour.
For Egypt and Arabia must be [m]ine.
[IV.iv.89-93]

But it is a grudging concession—witness that "If " and the ring of the last line.

Then in V.i and ii we have the episode of the Virgins of Damascus. Here we see the idea of genuine pity arising in Tamburlaine's mind for the first time: but it arises only to be rejected, unhesitatingly if regretfully. He is sincerely sorry for the Virgins—

What, are the Turtles fraide out of their neastes?
Alas poore fooles, must you be first shal feele
The sworne destruction of Damascus.
They know my custome: could they not as well
Haue sent ye out, when first my milkwhite flags
Through which sweet mercie threw her gentle
beams
Reflexing them on your disdainfull eies:
And now when furie and incensed hate
Flings slaughtering terrour from my coleblack
tents.
And tels for trueth, submissions comes too late.
[V.ii.1-10]

There is real compassion here. But he cannot and will not break his oath: he must give full scope to his idea of Honour—

Virgins, in vaine ye labour to preuent
That which mine honor sweares shal be per-
form'd:
Behold my sword, . . .
[V.ii.43-5]

And after he has ordered their deaths he reiterates his old principle emphatically—

I will not spare these proud Egyptians.
Nor change my Martiall obseruations,

For all the wealth of Gehons golden waues.
Or for the loue of Venus, would she leaue
The angrie God of Armes, and lie with me.
They haue refusde the offer of their liues,
And know my customes are as peremptory
As wrathfull Planets, death, or destinie.
[V.ii.58-65]

He has felt pity. (And we may ask ourselves whether the idea of pity would have occurred to him had it not been for Zenocrate's previous pleading.) He has felt pity: but he is still unprepared to allow himself to be merciful beyond the bounds laid down in his former practice. We see his old imperfect conception of Honour being assailed by the idea of Pity, but it is still not seriously threatened by that idea, and it stands firm. Then comes the soliloquy at V.ii.72ff., showing that now there is a conflict in Tamburlaine's mind. This conflict is led up to from the end of IV.ii, from which point onwards the principal interest is, in my opinion, the clash between the idea of Pity, suggested by Zenocrate, and Tamburlaine's old idea of Honour according to which pity cannot be exercised contrary to the warrior's previous oath. Tamburlaine has no difficulty in resisting the idea of Pity up to the soliloquy: but in connection with the Virgins of Damascus he for the first time feels a certain inclination towards Pity. Thus the episode of the Virgins of Damascus is definitely relevant to the dramatic development. So also is the episode of Bajazeth, who is Tamburlaine's last and most conspicuous victim before the question of Honour versus Pity arises.

I am claiming that Acts IV and V are thoroughly dramatic. There is a working up to a psychological crisis—the crisis involves suspension—there is a solution of the crisis—and so the play comes to a dramatically satisfying conclusion. But it may be suggested that the play *as a whole* does not have satisfactory dramatic shape. It may be suggested that Marlowe set out to produce a play from material essentially undramatic (simply the successive victories of a conqueror endowed with an aspiring mind), that by the end of Act III he found that he had done all that could be done with that material, and that in Acts IV and V he proceeded to a new theme which he could and did treat in truly dramatic fashion. This is essentially the view taken by Miss Leslie Spence [in *Publications of the Modern Language Association of America* XLII (1927)].

"As early as the end of Act II," she says, "the audience is convinced that no one can defeat him,

Whose smiling stars give him assured hope
Of martial triumph ere he meet his foes
[III.iii.42-3]

His early insistence on the invincibility of Tamburlaine left Marlowe under the dramatic necessity of furnishing for the remaining three fifths of his drama elements of conflict other than military struggle, even though military success was the only ambition of the historic conqueror. Act III, in which Marlowe tried to subordinate concern for the outcome of the battle to humorous debate and farcical treatment, lacked intensity and was dramatically unsuccessful. It was clear that the dramatist must create another interest. Searching the universe for something which had a chance of conquering his invincible, heaven-guarded hero, Marlowe seems to have made the choice determined on by Seneca's desperate Juno, when she sought to overcome Hercules, whom nothing on sea, on earth, or under the earth could conquer:

> sed vicit omnes, quaeris Alcidae parem?
> nemo est nisi ipse. bella iam secum gerat
> (*Hercules Furens,* 84-5.)

The dramatist decided that only Tamburlaine could conquer Tamburlaine. From the elements of character furnished by history—military invincibility, ambition, and wrath—no momentous inner struggle could be evolved. Accordingly, Marlowe added love and some pity to oppose the fiercer propensities of the great Scythian. Against a background of military rigor, which the display of ensigns, the torture of Bajazeth, the slaying of the maidens, and the destruction of Damascus all accentuate, the emotions of Tamburlaine fight, till, in the conflict of his passions, he admits the sorrows of Zenocrate

> lay more siege unto my soul,
> Than all my army to Damascus' walls.
> [V.ii.92-3]

Shall he adhere to his military rules in dealing with Zenocrate's father? Not until the very end of the play is this question settled. On the struggle of Tamburlaine with himself was built the dramatic conflict of the last two acts. . . . By the end of Act II Marlowe had made Tamburlaine so gloriously invincible that the centre of interest could no longer be physical strife. Hence the inner struggle and the love story.

In my opinion Miss Spence does excellently to point out how Marlowe endows Tamburlaine with emotional complexity. But I am not happy about the suggestion that Marlowe found himself at the end of Act II in an apparent impasse, that he tried in Act III to get out of it by one way and failed, and that he tried in Acts IV and V to get out of it by another way and this time succeeded. I believe that the entire play was conceived from the start as a single coherent dramatic structure.

I am sure that when Marlowe composed the soliloquy at V.ii.72ff. he himself had the beginning of the play in mind. The soliloquy ends as follows:

> I thus conceiuing and subduing both:
> That which hath stopt the tempest of the Gods,
> Euen from the fiery spangled vaile of heauen,
> To feele the louely warmth of shepheards flames.
> And martch in cottages of strowed weeds,
> Shal giue the world to note for all my byrth,
> That Vertue solely is the sum of glorie,
> And fashions men with true nobility.
> [V.ii.120-27]

Now there appears to be some textual corruption here. It does not make very good sense to say that something has "stopt the tempest of the Gods to feele the louely warmth of shepheards flames". Various emendations have been proposed, and the best thing to do in my opinion is to emend "stopt" to "stoopt" (Dyce) and "tempest" to "top-

most" (Deighton). Both of these emendations postulate scribal or compositorial errors of a likely enough kind. "Stopt" may be a case of the accidental omission of a single letter: "tempest" may show a double misreading of a manuscript "o" as "e" (quite likely in Elizabethan script) and also a metathesis—a scribe or compositor, thinking that his copy read "tepmest", might very well emend to "tempest". It seems to me that these two emendations are suggested by the passage as it stands. It may be that the line "And martch in cottages of strowed weeds" also requires emendation: but it does make sense—in the note in her edition Miss Ellis-Fermor suggests the interpretation "and move in spheres no higher than weed-strown cottages".

Now the second to the fifth lines of this passage, with the two emendations we have accepted, at once remind us of a passage near the beginning of the play in which Tamburlaine says

> Ioue sometime masked in a Shepheards weed,
> And by those steps that he hath scal'd the heauens,
> May we become immortall like the Gods.
> [I.ii.198-200.]

The reference is probably to Jove's love for Mnemosyne: in Ovid's *Metamorphoses,* vi.114, we are told that Jove tricked Mnemosyne in the guise of a shepherd. At I.ii.198-200 Tamburlaine is still at the beginning of his career: it is only a short while since he has taken off his shepherd's clothing: and he is determined to raise himself from the humble position to which he was born. At I.ii.198-200 he declares that he may ultimately become godlike, for, after all, Jove himself at one time appeared outwardly as a shepherd. Tamburlaine has appeared outwardly as a shepherd—has actually been a shepherd—and he may end up as an immortal like Jove. Always conscious of his humble birth, Tamburlaine takes comfort from the principle that, in the career of a conquering warrior (i.e. as regards Honour), what counts is not birth but a man's qualities—his manliness, bravery, energy, strength, his abilities: in a word, "virtue". To his chief supporters he says at IV.iv.128-32:

> Deserue these tytles I endow you with.
> By value and by magnanimity.
> Your byrthes shall be no blemish to your fame.
> For vertue is the fount whence honor springs.
> And they are worthy she inuesteth kings.

This idea inspires him from the start. At I.ii.198-200 he takes comfort from the fact that Jove "sometime masked in a Shepheards weed". But by V.ii.72ff. he has risen to a position of eminence and he is now afraid that he may lose it and fall back into the humble position he was born to. And in this soliloquy he again refers to Jove's disguising himself as a shepherd. But this time he does not take comfort from that, but a warning. What induced Jove to disguise himself as a shepherd was his love for Mnemosyne—his love of her beauty. Jove was influenced by Beauty to degrade himself. Tamburlaine must not let that happen to him. And so he must (on the one hand) "subdue" Beauty. Beauty sits in Zenocrate's tearful face—Beauty, "mother to the Muses" (V.ii.81): and in Greek mythology the mother of the Muses was Mnemosyne. Beauty "stoopt the topmost of the Gods . . . to feele the louely warmth of shepheards flames". That must not happen to Tamburlaine. And so, while he has by V.ii.120 already resolved that he will admit the softening influence of Beauty as far as the sparing of the Soldan is concerned, he finishes the soliloquy with a passage which clearly indicates that he will not allow that influence to prevail to the extent of destroying his "virtue"—he will not allow it to degrade him from the status of great warrior to the humble status from which he started out. He declares that in spite of his lowly birth he will by his deeds show the world that "Vertue solely is the sum of glorie". He will still allow his own "virtue" scope.

There can be no doubt, I think, that when he wrote V.ii.72ff. Marlowe had I.ii.198-200 in his mind. And I think that the spectator or reader is meant to recall that earlier passage. But furthermore, if we consider that when in I. ii he wrote the line "Ioue sometime masked in a Shepheards weed" Marlowe was thinking of Jove's love for Mnemosyne and of how it caused Jove to humble himself, and if we consider that already before that he has shown us that Tamburlaine has fallen in love with Zenocrate, can we not say that as early as I. ii Marlowe has at any rate at the back of his mind the situation that will arise in Acts IV and V?

It seems to me significant that in I.ii, the first scene in which Tamburlaine appears, we see him in the company of Zenocrate. In his speech at I.ii.34ff. he indicates his military ambitions—to conquer Asia, to be a terror to the world, to rise far above his humble origin: and it is, I think, significant that he does this in a speech in which he avows his intention of marrying Zenocrate and sharing with her the exalted position at which he is aiming. He had obviously conceived his military aspirations before he captured her; but, by showing him at his first appearance declaring his love for her and his intention of making her his consort when he shall have risen to eminence, Marlowe contrives to give the audience the impression that she is from the start a source of inspiration to him in his pursuit of military glory. He takes off his shepherd's clothing and puts on complete armour as befits a man with his ambition: and I think that Marlowe knew what he was doing when he placed the passage in which Tamburlaine does this in between two passages in which he declares his determination to wed Zenocrate:

> I am a Lord, for so my deeds shall prooue,
> And yet a shepheard by my Parentage:
> But Lady, this faire face and heauenly hew,
> Must grace his bed that conquers Asia:
> And meanes to be a terrour to the world,
> Measuring the limits of his Emperie
> By East and west, as Phaebus doth his course:
> Lie here ye weedes that I disdaine to weare,
> This compleat armor, and this curtle-axe
> Are adiuncts more beseeming Tamburlaine.
> And Maddam, whatsoeuer you esteeme
> Of this successe, and losse vnvallued,
> Both may inuest you Empresse of the East:
> And these that seeme but silly country Swaines,
> May haue the leading of so great an host,

> As with their waight shall make the mountains quake.
> Euen as when windy exhalations,
> Fighting for passage, tilt within the earth.
> [I.ii.34-51.]

We are here given the impression that Beauty encourages Tamburlaine to raise himself. At the crisis in V.ii the question arises whether it will cause him to lower himself again. Here in I.ii the inspiration of Zenocrate is suggested in connection with Tamburlaine's doffing of his shepherd's weeds: and this points forward to V.ii.120-27.

At the outset, then, our attention is directed to the relationship of Tamburlaine and Zenocrate. At the end of IV.ii Marlowe begins to prepare for the crisis in V.ii which also, of course, has to do with their relationship. What happens between I.ii and IV.ii? We see Tamburlaine's succession of triumphs, presented as the work partly of Fate and partly of his own "virtue". It cannot, of course, be denied that Marlowe is intensely interested in the aspiring mind whose ambitions are directed to "the sweet fruition of an earthly crowne"—that he is intensely interested in that in itself. It would be remarkable if Zenocrate did not drop into the background to some extent during the hero's rise to power. But the audience is, I think, meant to recall her significance from I.ii; and in any case she does step into the foreground from time to time between I.ii and IV.ii. In III.ii she avows her love for Tamburlaine. And after this she approves of his military ambitions and of his methods of warfare. When he is about to fight against Bajazeth she hopes for victory for him—

> And may my Loue, the king of Persea
> Returne with victorie, and free from wound.
> [III.iii.132-33]

She speaks scornfully to Zabina, as Tamburlaine would have her do. She prays that he may be strengthened against Bajazeth—

> And let his foes like flockes of fearfull Roes,
> Pursude by hunters, flie his angrie lookes,
> That I may see him issue Conquerour.
> [III.iii.192-94]

She has the same sort of blind confidence in his success as he himself has—

> If Mahomet should come from heauen and sweare,
> My royall Lord is slaine or conquered.
> Yet should he not perswade me otherwise.
> But that he liues and will be Conquerour.
> [III.iii.208-11]

One part of the influence of Beauty upon a warrior is to encourage him in his warlike exploits, and Zenocrate does this up to the point where her own country and her own father are affected. It is only after Tamburlaine has laid siege to Damascus that she seeks to have him modify his ideals, and even as she does so she shows by her words that she does not want him to give them up—

> Honor still waight on happy Tamburlaine:
> Yet giue me leaue to plead for him my Lord.
> [IV.iv.87-8]

The second aspect of the influence of Beauty has begun to emerge. After the fall of Damascus Zenocrate's own feelings of pity rise to a climax at V.ii.257ff., and she repents of Tamburlaine's and her own treatment of Bajazeth and Zabina—

> Ah myghty Ioue and holy Mahomet,
> Pardon my Loue, oh pardon his contempt,
> Of earthly fortune, and respect of pitie, . . .
> And pardon me that was not moou'd with ruthe,
> To see them liue so long in misery.
>   [V.ii.301-03, 307-08]

Even here she has no thought of swerving from her loyalty to Tamburlaine: in this speech [V.ii.285-309] she is very much concerned for his welfare. But she has undergone a change of heart: and shortly afterwards we find her speaking compassionately to the dying Arabia [V.ii.350-54]. She has undergone a change of heart: she has come to realize that a conqueror should be merciful. In the earlier portion of the play, in his presentation of Zenocrate, Marlowe emphasizes exclusively the power and desire of Beauty to encourage the warrior. Then in the later portion of the play, where we have this change of heart in Zenocrate, Marlowe conveys the idea that Beauty is essentially compassionate, and emphasizes its desire to induce clemency in the warrior—though at the same time it also remains an encouraging influence. The change of heart in Zenocrate ultimately results in a change in Tamburlaine; and their marriage symbolizes the establishment of the ideal relationship between Beauty and the warrior.

At the end we have a Tamburlaine changed by the influence of Zenocrate who has herself changed. The play is throughout concerned with the relationship between these two characters. I think it is true to say that we are never intended to forget Zenocrate during Tamburlaine's rise to power. In the note on III.ii.9-10 in her edition Miss Ellis-Fermor comments: "The figure of Zenocrate is substantially an addition of Marlowe's and the story of her relations with Tamburlaine is skilfully interwoven with that of his rising career, serving both to indicate the passage of time and to give variety." But it does much more than that. I agree as to the skilful interweaving; but that is part of the very theme of the play. Again, in her book on Marlowe [*Christopher Marlowe*] Miss Ellis-Fermor says that "as far as Zenocrate is anything at all she is a virtuous, god-fearing Elizabethan matron": but she is much more than that—she is Beauty incarnate. Miss Ellis-Fermor states [in her edition of *Tamburlaine*] that in Part I Zenocrate "only speaks effectively once . . . when, in the absence of Tamburlaine, she chants the moving lament over the Turkish monarchs and the prayer against Tamburlaine's worship of the glory of the world". It must be agreed that she becomes a much more living character after the conflict of loyalties, to Tamburlaine on the one hand and to Damascus and the Soldan on the other, has arisen in her mind: she becomes psychologically much more interesting then. This is only to be expected. Before conflict arises in Tamburlaine's mind he is made interesting by virtue of his aspiring mind and his astonishing series of victories: there is no way of making Zenocrate interesting to anything like the same extent in the first half of the play. But that does not alter the fact that all through

she is of fundamental importance as regards the main theme.

If we took the Prologue as indicating the theme of *I Tamburlaine* we should have to say that the theme was simply the successive conquests of its hero:

> From jygging vaines of riming mother wits,
> And such conceits as clownage keepes in pay,
> Weele lead you to the stately tent of War.
> Where you shall heare the Scythian Tamburlaine:
> Threatning the world with high astounding tearms
> And scourging kingdoms with his conquering sword.
> View but his picture in this tragicke glasse,
> And then applaud his fortunes as you please.

But I believe that in this Prologue Marlowe refers to only a portion of the plot-material. He refers to that portion which would doubtless be the most popular. I suggest that the complete plot-design he conceived from the outset was, briefly, as follows. Tamburlaine, a Scythian shepherd, endowed with an aspiring mind, determines to become a world potentate by military conquest; at the beginning of his career he comes under the spell of Zenocrate, whose beauty inspires him further in his original ambition; he proceeds to raise himself by triumph after triumph; meanwhile Zenocrate falls in love with him, they become betrothed, and she supports him in his aspirations and approves of his methods; but then these aspirations and methods threaten her own country and kindred, and, without being disloyal to Tamburlaine, she tries to persuade him to be merciful; she regrets his and her own previous want of pity; at first Tamburlaine resists her pleas; but then a conflict arises in his mind; he resolves it in a way of which she can approve; and the play concludes with their marriage. On the symbolic level the theme of the play is the nature of the influence that Beauty should have on the conception of Honour held by a man whose aspiration is directed towards the achievement of empire by conquest. It is, of course, an essential part of a drama embodying the above plot-design that the successive victories of the hero should be actually shown. It may be that there is a danger right from the start that this will overshadow the rest in its appeal to the audience's imagination. If it actually does, then Marlowe has failed. I can only say that in my opinion it does not. The play seems to me to be from beginning to end a coherent dramatic structure.

II

We may say that at the crisis of *I Tamburalaine* Marlowe shows us the hero assailed by Beauty and the outcome is that the hero suffers a defeat at its hands and at the same time wins a victory over it. (We are entitled to use this metaphor because Tamburlaine speaks in military terms at V.ii.88-96.) He suffers a defeat inasmuch as he allows the influence of Beauty to persuade him to change his ways. But he wins a victory inasmuch as he is still prepared to "subdue" Beauty whenever that shall appear to him to be necessary. Of course, as we have seen, Zenocrate has had no desire to persuade him to *abandon* his ideal of Honour: but if she should ever do so he would firmly withstand her, and he has won a victory inasmuch as he has come to this decision.

What now about the plot-material of *2 Tamburlaine*? The popularity of Part I induced Marlowe to write Part II. But what a task he set himself when he embarked on this sequel! How was he to treat Tamburlaine dramatically this time? Does he in fact do so? I think he does. And it is by imitating to some extent the design of Part I. In Part I the most dangerous foe that Tamburlaine had to face was Zenocrate (see V.ii.88-96). In Part II Marlowe confronts him with an even more dangerous foe—Death himself.

The description of the dramatic culmination given in the Prologue to Part II is misleading. We are there told that in this Part

> death cuts off the progress of his pomp.
> And murdrous Fates throwes al his triumphs
> down.

This implies that the play is to have a "falls of princes" theme—that Tamburlaine's death is to be a defeat and nothing else. But that is not the impression we are left with at the end of the play.

The first occurrence of his distemper is at V.i.217. From this point on we are concerned with Tamburlaine's attitude to his inexorably approaching death. His attitude to Death changes between the onset of his sickness and his death itself. He feels himself distempered at V.i.217. His first reaction is "Sickness or death can neuer conquer me" [V.i.221]. When next we see him (in V.iii) he is determined to resist Death—to oppose him by force and win this fight as he has before won so many:

> What daring God torments my body thus,
> And seeks to conquer mighty Tamburlaine,
> Shall sicknesse prooue me now to be a man,
> That haue bene tearm'd the terrour of the
>   world?
> Techelles and the rest, come take your swords,
> And threaten him whose hand afflicts my soul,
> Come let vs march against the powers of heauen,
> And set blacke streamers in the firmament,
> To signifie the slaughter of the Gods.
>   [V.iii.42-50]

We have had Tamburlaine threatening the gods before; but now there is a pathetic twist to it:

> Ah friends, what shal I doe I cannot stand,
> Come carie me to war against the Gods,
> That thus inuie the health of Tamburlaine.
>   [V.iii.51-3]

Tamburlaine goes on speaking of his intention to combat Death, though in the midst of it he seems to be convinced that Death will win after all. Techelles says that Tamburlaine's "griefe" cannot last, it is so violent; and with grim humour Tamburlaine replies

> Not last Techelles, no, for I shall die.
>   [V.iii.66]

But shortly after this his physician gives him some hope and he is momentarily comforted: he will

> liue in spight of death aboue a day.
>   [V.iii.101]

Up to this point we might well suppose that Marlowe was preparing us to regard Tamburlaine's death as a total defeat. Tamburlaine seems so to regard it as it approaches; and we remember the words of the Prologue.

But now Tamburlaine's attitude to death changes. He accepts the fact that it is inevitable, but now he regards it as a translation to higher spheres:

> But I perceiue my martial strength is spent,
> In vaine I striue and raile against those powers,
> That meane t'inuest me in a higher throane,
> As much too high for this disdainfull earth.
>   [V.iii.119-22]

And he speaks of his spirit as being too fiery for his body to contain [V.iii.168-70]. He now regards death as a gateway to a higher life. But what of his plans for earthly conquest? There are parts of the world which he has still not conquered:

> And shall I die, and this vnconquered?
>   [V.iii.150, 158]

Allowing that for him death is not a defeat inasmuch as it is an entrance to a nobler life, is it not still the case that it is a defeat inasmuch as he has not yet fulfilled all his earthly ambitions? Not altogether: for he is convinced that, though he himself is to die, his spirit will live on in the world in the breasts of his two surviving sons:

> But sons, this subject not of force enough,
> To hold the fiery spirit it containes,
> Must part, imparting his impressions,
> By equall portions into both your breasts:
> My flesh deuided in your precious shapes,
> Shal still retaine my spirit, though I die,
> And liue in all your seedes immortally.
>   [V.iii.168-74]

In his belief it is not even true to say that his flesh is about to perish, for his sons are his flesh. His spirit will survive on earth in his flesh—his sons will continue his career of conquest—and he himself will pass to a higher existence. Thus, essentially, Death has not defeated him: he has defeated death: he has shown that he is immortal on earth.

Tamburlaine triumphs in death. But at the same time it is, of course, true that Death *has* won a victory of a sort. For Tamburlaine did not will his own death: it was forced upon him: he was in this respect passive, a victim. And, having proclaimed his own triumph, Tamburlaine admits that nothing can prevent his actual departure: his last words emphasize the defeat aspect—

> For Tamburlaine, the Scourge of God must die.
>   [V.iii.248]

In Part I he was assailed by Beauty and the result was that he partially submitted to and partially triumphed over it. In Part II he is assailed by Death and the result is similar—he is in one sense defeated by it and in another sense triumphs over it. In the act of giving in to it he proclaims his immunity to it: in the act of proclaiming his immunity to it he has to submit to it.

But what of Part II as a whole? From the point where

Tamburlaine first feels distempered it has a coherent dramatic shape. Does the play as a whole have a coherent dramatic shape?

In dealing with Part I we saw that the conclusion concerns Tamburlaine's attitude to Zenocrate and that at his first appearance in the play he enters along with her. In a similar way in Part II Marlowe at the outset prepares us for the main theme. In Part II we first encounter Tamburlaine in I.iv. In his very first speech he refers to his and Zenocrate's sons and their hoped-for future—they "shall be Emperours" [I.iv.7]. In his next speech he expresses his love for them [lines 18-19] but fears that their looks are not "martiall as the sons of Tamburlaine" [line 22]. Zenocrate declares that "when they list, [they have] their conquering fathers hart" [line 36]. Tamburlaine goes on to speak of his youngest son's future, and at lines 59-60 he says

> When I am old and cannot mannage armes,
> Be thou the scourge and terrour of the world.

Already in the first scene the attention of the audience is drawn to the idea of Tamburlaine's sons as his successors, continuing after him to pursue his aims by his methods—Calyphas will not have a foot of land from his father unless he bears a "mind corragious and inuincible" [line 73]; and he that would place himself in Tamburlaine's chair must "armed wade vp to the chin in blood" [line 84]. All this is in I.iv. Tamburlaine's illness first attacks him at the end of V.i. And in between Marlowe gives much attention to Tamburlaine's sons, their education in his methods of waging war, his concern to imbue them with his own ambitions in their role of successors to him. Zenocrate dies in II.iv. Almost her last words are to her sons—a plea to them to resemble in their lives their father's excellence [line 76]. Then in III.ii Tamburlaine lectures his sons on the technique of waging war [lines 53ff.]. His ambition is to make them soldiers

> And worthy sonnes of Tamburlain the great.
>   [line 92]

He wants to teach them not only the art of war but also

> to beare couragious minds,
> Fit for the followers of great Tamburlaine.
>   [lines 143-44]

("Followers" presumably means "successors".) Then in IV.i, to the defeated Turkish kings, he says

> See now ye slaues, my children stoops your pride
> And leads your glories sheep-like to the sword.

And he continues—

> Bring them my boyes, and tel me if the warres
> Be not a life that may illustrate Gods,
> And tickle not your Spirits with desire
> Stil to be train'd in armes and chiualry?
>   [lines 76-81]

When Tamburlaine is riding in his chariot drawn by the captive kings, his son Amyras wants to be similarly drawn [IV.iii.27-8]. And a little later Tamburlaine speaks of his son Celebinus to the captive King of Jerusalem—

> I Turke, I tel thee, this same Boy is he,

> That must (aduaunst in higher pompe than this)
> Rifle the kingdomes I shall leaue vnsackt.
> If Ioue esteeming me too good for earth,
> Raise me to match the faire Aldeboran,
> Aboue the threefold Astracisme of heauen,
> Before I conquere all the triple world.
>   [IV.iii.57-63]

The idea of Tamburlaine's sons as his successors, imbued with the same spirit as he is, pursuing, after him, the same aims by the same methods, runs right through the play, and cannot anywhere be very far from the audience's mind as it watches Tamburlaine's own further career of conquest as unfolded in this second drama. The material concerning Calyphas is, of course, extremely relevant to this theme and is not introduced simply to give variety. Calyphas refuses to be another Tamburlaine, and rejects his father's values. I do not think that Marlowe can be said to be altogether unsympathetic to Calyphas: he sees that there are different possible points of view: but, as regards his dramatic design as a whole, he intends his audience to accept Tamburlaine's point of view and not that of Calyphas. As far as the total plan of the play is concerned it is Tamburlaine's and not Calyphas's values which emerge triumphant. Calyphas is the unworthy son: unfit to succeed his father, he is killed ignominiously.

Before we can state in full the dramatic design of Part II we must say something about the Tamburlaine-Zenocrate relationship, which forms part of it.

The Zenocrate of Part II is essentially the same character as the Zenocrate of Part I. She at the same time commends Tamburlaine's values and seeks to mitigate extravagance and immoderation in him. Considering the nature of the conclusion of Part I we might perhaps have expected that in Part II there would be no contrariety of attitude whatever between Tamburlaine and Zenocrate, no pull at all between them in opposite directions. But this is not so. The nature of the conclusion of Part I made it possible for Marlowe in Part II to show the two characters again in partial opposition and partial agreement. Tamburlaine had decided both to "conceiue" and to "subdue" Beauty. At the end of Part I he succeeded in balancing the conceiving and subduing of it. But he is resolved that in the future he must be careful not to "conceiue" it too much. He must always be on guard in case he (still the aspiring conqueror) should ever be influenced by Zenocrate to go too far in the direction of gentleness. And so, while still admitting her double influence, he is always prepared to resist its moderating element if necessary. As for her: we may imagine her deciding that she must still keep urging Tamburlaine to moderation, there being always a danger that he may return to courses of utter ruthlessness. And so, while still supporting him in his role as conqueror, she must always be prepared to restrain him if necessary. These are in fact the attitudes we find in them in Part II. In Part II Zenocrate's first speech [I.iv.9-11] is an implied plea to Tamburlaine to give up his war-making because of the perils involved—

> Sweet Tamburlain, when wilt thou leaue these
>   armes
> And saue thy sacred person free from scathe:
> And dangerous chances of the wrathfull war.

And Tamburlaine in circumlocutory fashion declares that he never will. Shortly afterwards, Tamburlaine having delivered a bloodthirsty speech, Zenocrate protests—

> My Lord, such speeches to our princely sonnes,
> Dismaies their mindes before they come to
>   prooue
> The wounding troubles angry war affoords.
>
> [I.iv.85-7]

She still wants to restrain him. But at the same time she still admires and encourages him as a conqueror. On her deathbed she speaks her hopes that he will continue to live in his resplendent glory—

> Liue still my Lord, O let my soueraigne liue,
> And sooner let the fiery Element
> Dissolue, and make your kingdome in the Sky,
> Than this base earth should shroud your majes-
>   ty.
>
> [II.iv.57-60]

And she bids her sons in their lives resemble their father's "excellency" [II.iv.76]. In Part II she still exerts herself when necessary to restrain immoderation in Tamburlaine, but she still encourages him in his martial career.

When she dies, Tamburlaine feels lost. He needs her: he is not self-sufficient. In Part I he had declared at the end that she added "more courage to [his] conquering mind" [V.ii.453]. As a conqueror he needed the help of her encouragement (cf. Part I, V.ii.117-19). Now that she has been removed by Death he has been deprived of an essential part of his inspiration as a warrior. He tries to keep this inspiration alive by carrying her body with him as he proceeds further in his conquests; and, apostrophizing her picture, he says

> At euery towne and castle I besiege,
> Thou shalt be set vpon my royall tent.
> And when I meet an armie in the field,
> Whose looks will shed such influence in my
>   campe,
> As if Bellona, Goddesse of the war
> Threw naked swords and sulphur bals of fire,
> Upon the heads of all our enemies.
>
> [III.ii.36-42]

But this attempt to defeat Death (for that is what it is) fails miserably: what happens is that Tamburlaine becomes filled with a fury greater than any he has shown heretofore. The moderating influence of Zenocrate is removed. And though Tamburlaine wants her encouraging influence to persist, and tries to make it persist, it does not—he now shows not courage so much as blind rage. Zenocrate is dead: both elements of her influence are gone: Death has attacked Tamburlaine in the first instance through Zenocrate, and Death has won the day. Death will attack him a second time later on, and its second victory will be counterbalanced by a triumph on the part of Tamburlaine.

The Tamburlaine of Part II is certainly a less impressive figure than the Tamburlaine of Part I. Miss Ellis-Fermor rightly speaks of the Tamburlaine of Part II as "marked by a savageness, an ever-increasing extravagance, a lack at once of inspiration and of balance". "The freakish, unrestrained moods of these later scenes," she says, "have lit-

tle or nothing to do with the glittering figure of the earlier part. . . ." Her view is that in Part II Marlowe had embarked on an undertaking which by its very nature entailed a debasing of the character of Tamburlaine even against the playwright's will. His savagery and frenzy, she says, "are the logical outcome of the situation that Marlowe created when he set out to write a 'second part' to the study of a character who can, by the very nature of his being, only have a first part. For Tamburlaine lives in the future and the essence of his spirit is the forward reach and the aspiration which must continue 'still climbing' if they are to live, and fail, even as Marlowe's interpretation failed, when they reach 'the ripest fruit of all'." But I think that Marlowe knew what he was doing, and that Tamburlaine's later frenzy, related to his loss of Zenocrate, is relevant to the dramatic design of Part II. It is part of Death's initial victory in a drama the main theme of which is Tamburlaine versus Death.

The figure of Zenocrate, then, is relevant to the dramatic design of Part II because she is the first object of Death's attack on Tamburlaine. She is also relevant to it because his sons are her sons too. As she dies she urges them to resemble their father's excellence. We may be sure that she would not have approved of Calyphas's conduct after her death. At I.iv.65-6 Calyphas says

> But while my brothers follow armes my lord
> Let me accompany my gratious mother.

This suggests that his mother represents complete opposition to the following of arms; but, as we have seen, she does not. Calyphas is presented not only as an unworthy son of Tamburlaine but also as an unworthy son of Zenocrate. The other two sons, Tamburlaine's successors, do try to resemble their father, and do thus try to obey their mother's final request.

Miss Ellis-Fermor, holding that Part I has "no progress, crisis or solution", believes that Part II is to an even greater extent lacking in dramatic structure. "In the second part of the play," she says, "where the original impulse is gone, the difficulty of giving any appearance of structural unity increases enormously". "Marlowe's error", she maintains, "is really a very simple mathematical one; the rise of Tamburlaine's career throughout the second part could be practically formulated as an arithmetical progression, whereas that of the first part has the more rapid rise of a geometrical progression, and it is this last formula alone which can be relied upon to outrun the anticipations of an audience and create surprise and interest." This would be a perfectly sound condemnation of Part II if the theme were simply the continued military triumphs of a world conqueror. But I believe that this is only a portion of the theme and that Part II, like Part I, has a coherent dramatic pattern.

I should summarize the essentials of the plot of Part II as follows. Tamburlaine continues his career of conquest, still loving and inspired by Zenocrate, but still resolved to resist any attempt by her to influence him excessively, as he sees it, in the direction of gentleness. Early in the play he shows that he is conscious that he will grow old and that he will die: and so he concerns himself to prepare his sons to be worthy successors to him (i.e. he prepares to win a victory over Death). He encourages and trains them. One is unworthy (both as a son of Tamburlaine and as a son of Zenocrate): the other two he finds satisfactory. Meanwhile Death attacks Tamburlaine in the first instance through Zenocrate, and she dies. Her restraining influence is now removed. Tamburlaine tries to keep her encouraging influence alive by carrying her body and her picture with him on his martial journeys; but it is gone too, and Tamburlaine becomes, instead of a type of inspired courage and mental fire, a type of fury and savage rage. Death has won this initial bout. Then Death attacks Tamburlaine directly. At first Tamburlaine attempts resistance (foolishly, of course), but then he acquiesces, and his death, a defeat in one sense, is a triumph in another, since his two surviving sons, his own flesh containing his own spirit, will continue his work on earth while he himself steps on to a higher plane of being. All this is surely a well-conceived dramatic design.

In so far as Death is a more terrible adversary than Zenocrate (or Beauty) was, the conclusion of Part II cannot be said to leave us with an impression of bathos. Nevertheless it is certainly true that Marlowe's imagination is much more powerfully at work in Part I than in Part II. Part II is a much inferior play to Part I. I have in this essay been concerned with one point only. There is much more which I believe should be said about these plays. But I have been concerned only to argue that both have coherent dramatic structure. However much they may offend us by their rant and bombast and by their bloodthirstiness and violence, they are at any rate dramas in the true sense of that word.

(pp. 101-26)

> *G. I. Duthie, "The Dramatic Structure of Marlowe's 'Tamburlaine the Great', Parts I and II," in* English Studies, *London, n.s. Vol. 1, 1948, pp. 101-26.*

Eugene M. Waith   (essay date 1962)

[*Waith is an American scholar and editor specializing in English drama of the Elizabethan and Restoration periods. His publications include* The Pattern of Tragicomedy in Beaumont and Fletcher *(1952),* The Herculean Hero *(1962), and* French and English Drama of the Seventeenth Century *(with Judd D. Hubert; 1972). He has also produced editions of Shakespeare's* Macbeth *(1954) and Ben Jonson's* Bartholomew Fair *(1963). In the essay below, Waith extensively examines the character of Tamburlaine, particularly as he relates to the classical tradition surrounding the Hercules legend. The critic demonstrates that Tamburlaine is Marlowe's contribution to the long history of stage representations of the popular Greek demigod. "Hercules, as he appears in Sophocles, Euripides, and above all Seneca," Waith asserts, "is revitalized in Tamburlaine." All act, scene, and line references are taken from U. M. Ellis-Fermor's 1951 revised edition of* Tamburlaine.]

> His looks do menace heaven and dare the gods,
> His fiery eyes are fixed upon the earth,
> As if he now devis'd some stratagem,
> Or meant to pierce Avernas' darksome vaults
> To pull the triple headed dog from hell.

The brilliance of the heroic image Marlowe created in *Tamburlaine* has proved to be both attractive and blinding. The glittering verse, the sound of trumpets, the movement of armies across the stage, seem to have concealed more than they have revealed of one essential part of the play's meaning, the author's attitude towards his hero. The question of whether this extravagantly unconventional protagonist is presented with approval or disapproval has received answers so various and contradictory that a reader of the criticism might easily conclude that the play contains no sure indications of attitude—that Tamburlaine is whatever his audience makes of him. However, one point on which all critics agree is that Marlowe had a well-defined attitude towards his hero. It is worth seeking again even at the cost of another reconsideration of a play which has been much discussed.

The spectacular circumstances of Marlowe's life have figured in the interpretation of his plays from his own times down to ours, for if he was an atheist, a homosexual, a spy, a scoffer and a quarreller, it seems more than a coincidence that he chose for principal characters an atheistical warrior, a scholar who sold his soul to the devil, a homosexual king, a Machiavellian schemer. An older group of critics emphasized what might be called the brighter side of Marlowe's unconventionality by interpreting Tamburlaine's boundless ambition as a joyous assertion of Marlowe's Renaissance paganism—a celebration of human worth in general and of his own aspirations in particular. To more recent critics this sort of interpretation has seemed to rest upon a romanticized view of the Renaissance. Hence a somewhat grimmer picture has been drawn of a Tamburlaine who is the mirror image of a resolute defier of convention, remarkably "advanced" in his freedom of thought, but pathologically attracted by cruelty, and characterized, as one critic has put it, by "abnormal nervous energy" and "uncoordinated personality factors" [T. M. Pearce in his "Christopher Marlowe, Figure of the Renaissance," *University of New Mexico Bulletin, English Language and Literature Series* I, No. 1 (1934)].

The difficulties which attend upon such identifications of Marlowe and Tamburlaine may be illustrated from the most impressive of these studies, Paul H. Kocher's *Christopher Marlowe.* Looking at the play for the light it may throw on the mind and character of Marlowe, Kocher finds that Part I is dominated by two religious conceptions: one, that the law of nature commands Tamburlaine and others to seek regal power; the other, that in his conquest Tamburlaine is acting as the scourge of God. Though the first conception is thoroughly anti-Christian, the second is, of course, perfectly compatible with Christianity, so that Kocher is faced with a conflict in Marlowe's thought as he understands it. He asks whether these ideas may not be harmonized "by simply amputating the Christian appendages" but concludes that even then some inconsistency remains. In considering the character of Calyphas, Tamburlaine's cowardly son in Part II, Kocher finds that in certain scenes the boy is made ridiculous but that in the first scene of Act IV his mockery of the warrior code of conduct is "a personal outburst by the dramatist". Kocher speculates that Marlowe was "thoroughly satiated and weary with excess" by this time but that Calyphas' mockery "cannot have been any part of Marlowe's plan for the drama". The dangers of this method of interpretation are obvious. Although it would be naive to expect perfect consistency of an Elizabethan play, it is an act of critical desperation to discount or "amputate" whatever does not fit with a predetermined picture of Marlowe's opinions, or to explain all discordant elements as lapses and unpremeditated changes in the artist's plans. Such an interpretation takes the opinions of Marlowe as reported by his contemporaries, Thomas Kyd, Richard Baines, and others, as fixed points of reference and, rather than explain any contradictory ideas which appear in the play, explains them away. Whether or not Marlowe held the opinions ascribed to him (a matter which has never been established beyond doubt), the attitudes expressed in **Tamburlaine** should be determined by a careful weighing of all the evidence given in the play. The knowledge of Marlowe's reputation hinders almost as much as it helps such a process.

Unfortunately, the refusal to identify Marlowe with his hero by no means solves the problem of interpretation. The crucial problem remains: is Tamburlaine presented with approval or disapproval? As J. C. Maxwell says [in his "Plays of Christopher Marlowe," in *The Age of Shakespeare,* ed. Boris Ford], "No one can ever have doubted that Marlowe displays in a high degree the imaginative sympathy with his hero which is required for successful dramatic presentation," but sympathy does not mean approval, and even the critics who agree on Marlowe's objectivity in creating Tamburlaine differ as to the attitude the play presents. It has been said that Marlowe makes his hero both physically and morally more admirable than he appears in the sources, but it has also been suggested that Part II, where the sources provide much less of the action, shows a progressive disenchantment with the hero. The two parts of the play together have been read as a chronicle of the Renaissance discovery that human nature cut off from its divine source is not emancipated but impoverished, or even as an indictment of Tamburlaine from a conservative Renaissance point of view, and hence "one of the most grandly moral spectacles in the whole realm of English drama." Roy Battenhouse, from whose study these last words are quoted, sees Tamburlaine's death as the divine punishment such as a "scourge of God" was inevitably given, once his mission had been accomplished [see second Further Reading entry for Battenhouse].

There could scarcely be greater diversity of opinion, yet through it all runs a discernible pattern. The critics who believe that Marlowe approves of Tamburlaine either try to show that he passes over his hero's disagreeable qualities to emphasize others (such as the aspiration for knowledge and beauty) or believe that Marlowe, as a rebel against the morality of his time, approves of Tamburlaine's cruelty, pride, atheism and ruthless exercise of power. Those who believe that Marlowe disapproves of Tamburlaine assume that such behaviour must be recognized as bad, and that Marlowe's frank portrayal of it indicates his moral condemnation. Neither group of critics suggests the possibility that Tamburlaine's faults might be an integral part of a kind of heroic nature familiar to Marlowe and his audience and unlikely to offend anyone but "precise" churchmen or the poet's enemies. It is possible,

of course, that Marlowe's attitude toward his hero shifts from scene to scene, or from Part I to Part II, but it seems to me more likely that his concept of heroic character is sufficiently complex to include what appear to be contradictory elements and that his attitude, going beyond simple approval or disapproval, remains constant.

Hercules, as he appears in Sophocles, Euripides, and above all Seneca, is revitalized in Tamburlaine. No one of the older plays was used as a model, but Hercules was often in Marlowe's mind as he wrote. Several allusions in the play make this fact indisputable, and, as Mario Praz pointed out many years ago [in his "Machiavelli and the Elizabethans," *Proceedings of the British Academy* XIV (1928)], there are striking resemblances between Tamburlaine and Hercules Oetaeus. However, it is finally less important to decide whether Marlowe was deliberately fashioning a Herculean hero than to remember that the traditional depictions of Hercules, especially those from Rome and Renaissance Italy, were thoroughly familiar to him. It is not surprising that Tamburlaine, who had already been used by Louis Le Roy and others as a symbol of the physical and intellectual vigour of the Renaissance, should suggest the Greek hero to him. I believe that his attitude towards Tamburlaine, as expressed in the play, is very similar to the attitudes found in some of the portrayals of Hercules [by Marlowe's predecessors]. The images created by Seneca and Pollaiuolo can be of great assistance to the spectator of the twentieth century, partially cut off from the traditions in which Marlowe wrote; for they prepare the eye to discern the outlines of Marlowe's heroic figure.

The figure is vast. The very structure of the play conveys this impression, for the succession of scenes—some of them might almost be called tableaux—stretching over great expanses of time and space, presents the man in terms of the places he makes his and the time which at the last he fails to conquer. It is no accident that we always remember the effect of Marlowe's resounding geography, for earthly kingdoms are the emblems of Tamburlaine's aspirations. At the end of his life he calls for a map, on which he traces with infinite nostalgia his entire career and points to all the remaining riches which death will keep him from:

> And shall I die, and this unconquered?
> [Part II, V.iii.150]

To be a world-conqueror in the various senses which the play gives to the term is the essence of Tamburlaine's character. That this insight is conveyed in part by the sprawling structure of the play is an important advantage to weigh against some of the obvious disadvantages of such a structure in the theatre. Although complication and even conflict in its fullest sense are almost missing, each successive episode contributes something to the dominant idea—the definition of a hero. There is a forward movement of the play in unfolding not only the narrative but the full picture of the hero. When the play is well acted and directed, it has ample theatrical life, no matter how much the form is indebted to epic.

The first view we have of Tamburlaine is a kind of transformation scene. It is preceded by the brief, and basically snobbish descriptions given at the court of Mycetes, the ludicrously incompetent king of Persia, to whom Tamburlaine is a marauding fox, a "sturdy Scythian thief", and the leader of a "Tartarian rout" [I.i.31, 36, 71]. The Tamburlaine who walks on the stage dressed as a shepherd and leading Zenocrate captive has some of the outward appearance suggested by these descriptions, and the earlier impression of social inferiority is conveyed in the words of Zenocrate, who at first takes him for the shepherd he seems to be [I.ii.8]. However, his words and actions reveal a strikingly different man: he boasts like a genuine hero if not a gentleman, and exchanges his shepherd's weeds for complete armour and curtle-axe. Before our eyes he assumes the outward appearance which matches his warrior's spirit.

Tamburlaine is a proud and noble king at heart, yet his Scythian-shepherd origins give a clue to the absolute difference between him and the world's other kings. His is the intrinsic kingliness of the hero, associated with the ideal of freedom, whereas other kings are presented as oppressors, the products of a corrupt system. The garb of the Scythian shepherd, even though he discards it, relates Tamburlaine to the simpler world of an earlier, mythical time. The king he becomes carries with him into a decadent world something of this primitive simplicity. Like his successors, Chapman's Bussy and Dryden's Almanzor, he is an early edition of the "noble savage".

Thus far Tamburlaine appears as a hero in the classic

A 1584 depiction of Tamburlaine by André Thevet.

mode, but when he tells Zenocrate that her person "is more worth to Tamburlaine / Than the possession of the Persian crown" [ll.90-1], the influence of the romance tradition is apparent. In fact, for the moment it seems that the "concupiscible power" of his soul dominates the "irascible power", though the subsequent action shows that this is not true. Tamburlaine's love, expressed in the poetry of the famous speech beginning "Disdains Zenocrate to live with me?" [ll.82-105], further distinguishes him from his rival warriors. Their pride and their ambition are not accompanied by the imagination which informs his promises to Zenocrate:

> With milk-white harts upon an ivory sled
> Thou shalt be drawn amidst the frozen pools,
> And scale the icy mountains' lofty tops,
> Which with thy beauty will be soon resolv'd.
>   [ll.98-101]

The cold fire of this speech is the first testimony of Tamburlaine's imaginative scope and of the paradoxes of his nature; the icy mountain tops are the first memorable image of his aspiration.

The arrival of Theridamas with the Persian forces provides for another surprising revelation of the hero. We have just seen him in the guise of a lover; we now see him as an orator, overcoming Theridamas with words. Marlowe insists on the unexpectedness of these aspects of the hero. "What now? in love?" says Techelles [l.106], and, when Tamburlaine asks whether he should "play the orator", replies disdainfully that "cowards and faint-hearted runaways / Look for orations" [ll.130-31]. In defiance of this advice, Tamburlaine delivers his brilliantly successful oration, winning from Theridamas the tribute that even Hermes could not use "persuasions more pathetical" [l.210]. Yet, surprising as this eloquence is to Tamburlaine's followers, it is not alien to the Renaissance concept of the Herculean hero. [Vincenzo] Cartari [in his 1556 work *Imagini de i Dei degli Antichi*] specifically reminds his readers that Hercules, like Mercury, whom he has just discussed, has been called a patron of eloquence. It is, so to speak, perfectly proper to present a Herculean hero as orator.

Tamburlaine begins his oration with a complimentary picture of Theridamas, but soon turns to himself with the famous boast, "I hold the Fates bound fast in iron chains", and the comparisons of himself to Jove. The effect of the speech is double, for though it displays the hero as orator, it also presents, by means of eloquence, his self-portrait as conqueror of the world and even as demigod. Such self-praise might be taken as Marlowe's way of portraying a man who will say anything to get ahead or of pointing to the ironical contrast between a man's pride and his accomplishment, but one of the puzzling features of *Tamburlaine* is that the hero's actions also show him in the guise of a demigod, and only his death proves that he does not control the fates. Even death is not presented unequivocally as defeat. Tamburlaine's extravagant boasts, like those of Hercules, are largely made good, so that he and his followers become the amazement of the world. In Usumcasane's words, "These are the men that all the world admires."

Before Tamburlaine unleashes his persuasive forces Theridamas comments on his appearance in words which emphasize the importance of visual impressions in this play:

> Tamburlaine! A Scythian shepherd so embellished
> With nature's pride and richest furniture!
> His looks do menace heaven and dare the gods,
> His fiery eyes are fixed upon the earth,
> As if he now devis'd some stratagem,
> Or meant to pierce Avernas' darksome vaults
> To pull the triple headed dog from hell.
> [I.ii.154-60]

Again we have the transformation of the Scythian shepherd into a noble warrior, but here even the armour appears as part of nature's endowment of the hero. The eyes fixed on the earth are the symbolic equivalent of one of Tamburlaine's best-known speeches, in which he makes an earthly crown the ultimate felicity, but this fixation on the earth is accompanied by looks which menace heaven and also suggest a Herculean conquest of hell. The description is perfect, though to use it when the character described stands before the audience is to risk a ludicrous incongruity. Marlowe depends on unhesitating acceptance of the verbal picture.

Marlowe's heavy dependence on description is again illustrated in the next scene, when Menaphon gives Cosroe an even fuller account of Tamburlaine's looks than we have had from Theridamas. In this speech the hero's body is made symbolic of his character. He is tall like his desire; his shoulders might bear up the sky like Atlas; his complexion reveals his thirst for sovereignty; he has curls like Achilles; and his arms and hands betoken "valour and excess of strength" [II.i.7-30].

One of Tamburlaine's most important traits, his infinite aspiration, receives its first major treatment in a much discussed speech in the second act about the "thirst of reign and sweetness of a crown" [II.vii.12-29]. Menaphon's encomium of Tamburlaine's physical beauty provides a clue to the understanding of this passage. Just as his body seems beautiful not simply in itself but in that it expresses his character, so Tamburlaine extols the "sweet fruition of an earthly crown" not because anything the earth has to offer has final value for him, but because domination of the earth represents the fulfilment of his mission—the fulfilment of himself. The speech is about the infinite aspiration taught us by nature and the never-ending activity to which the soul goads us. "The sweet fruition of an earthly crown" is indeed bathos, as it has often been called, unless the earthly crown means something rather special in this play.

There is a good deal of evidence that it does. In an earlier scene Usumcasane says, "To be a king, is half to be a god", and Theridamas replies, "A god is not so glorious as a king" [II.v.56-7]. Tamburlaine never puts it quite thus, for it is clear that like Hercules he already considers himself partly divine, yet kingship is obviously glorious to him. The "course of crowns" which he and his followers eat in Act IV, Scene iv, is the visual equivalent of the constant references to sovereignty. The earth itself is despicable—inert—the negation of heroic energy, as appears in the speech of Theridamas immediately following the lines about the earthly crown:

> For he is gross and like the massy earth
> That moves not upwards, nor by princely deeds
> Doth mean to soar above the highest sort.
> [II.vii.31-3]

but ruling the earth is not an end in itself. It is a manifestation of the will to "soar above the highest sort". When Tamburlaine seizes his first crown, the crown of Persia, he makes the act symbolic of his will:

> Though Mars himself, the angry god of arms,
> And all the earthly potentates conspire
> To dispossess me of this diadem,
> Yet will I wear it in despite of them . . .
> [II.vii.58-61]

His contempt for earthly potentates and the assertion of his will combine in his conception of himself as the scourge of God, a conception which he shares with Hercules [III.iii.41-54]. He is the avenger, nemesis to the mighty of the world, contemptuous demonstrator of the absurdity of their claims, liberator of captives. He is not so much the instrument as the embodiment of a divine purpose. His serene confidence that his will is seconded by destiny gives him the magnificence of the hero who transcends the merely human. The activities of such a hero are always confined to the earth, though always pointing, in some sense, to a goal beyond. Thus Seneca's Hercules Oetaeus, while rejoicing in his earthly deeds, never forgets that he is destined to become a star. Toward the end of Part II Tamburlaine begins to speak of an otherworldly goal, but even before this time the thrones and crowns of the world stand for something which though *in* the earth is yet not *of* it. Their importance to Tamburlaine lies in taking them away from tyrants like Bajazeth, for whom they have intrinsic value. Tamburlaine's last instructions to his son are to sway the throne in such a way as to curb the haughty spirits of the captive kings [Part II, V.iii.234-41]. An earthly crown represents the sweet fruition of his purpose in being.

Tamburlaine's moving description of the aspiration for sovereignty has the utmost value in the play in presenting his double attitude towards the earth. And as he both seeks and despises earthly glory, he both claims and defies the power of the gods. "Jove himself" will protect him [I.ii.179]; not even Mars will force him to give up the crown of Persia [II.vii.58-61]. He does not belong entirely to either earth or heaven. Though he has distinctly human characteristics, both good and bad, he has something of the magnificence and the incomprehensibility of a deity.

Tamburlaine speaks of Mars as "the angry god of war", and the words might serve as self-description, for when he is angry the awe that his looks inspire is almost that of a mortal for a god. Agydas, when Tamburlaine has passed, "looking wrathfully" at him, expresses a typical reaction:

> Betrayed by fortune and suspicious love,
> Threatened with frowning wrath and jealousy,
> Surpris'd with fear of hideous revenge,
> I stand aghast; but most astonied
> To see his choler shut in secret thoughts,
> And wrapt in silence of his angry soul.

Upon his brows was pourtrayed ugly death,
And in his eyes the fury of his heart,
That shine as comets, menacing revenge,
And casts a pale complexion on his cheeks.
[III.ii.66-75]

Later a messenger speaks of "The frowning looks of fiery Tamburlaine, / That with his terror and imperious eyes / Commands the hearts of his associates" [IV.i.13-15], and the Governor of Damascus calls him "this man, or rather god of war" [V.i.1]. Anger is the passion most frequently displayed in his looks, his words, and the red or black colours of his tents.

Not only is he a man of wrath, as the Herculean hero characteristically is; he is also fiercely cruel. This trait of character receives a continually increasing emphasis; it is strikingly demonstrated in Tamburlaine's treatment of Bajazeth. In Scene ii of Act IV the defeated emperor is brought on in his cage, from which he is removed to serve as Tamburlaine's footstool. But Scene iv is even more spectacular. Tamburlaine, dressed in scarlet to signify his wrath towards the besieged city of Damascus, banquets with his followers while the starving Bajazeth in his cage is insulted and given scraps of food on the point of his conqueror's sword. In the midst of these proceedings Tamburlaine refuses Zenocrate's plea that he raise the siege and make a truce with her father, the Soldan of Egypt. In the last act of Part I we see Tamburlaine order the death of the virgins of Damascus, who have been sent to beg for mercy after the black colours have already indicated Tamburlaine's decision to destroy the obstinate city. With inhuman logic he points out that it is now too late and that they "know my customs are as peremptory / As wrathful planets, death, or destiny" [V.ii.64-5]. At the end he says that his honour—that personal honour which is the basis of the hero's *areté* [ideal of nobility]—"consists in shedding blood / When men presume to manage arms with him" [V.ii.415-16]. Tamburlaine's is a cosmic extension of the cruelty Achilles shows to Hector or Hercules to the innocent Lichas. Though it is a repellent trait, it is entirely consistent with the rest of the character. Instead of passing over it, Marlowe insists on it. One need not assume, however, that Marlowe himself loved cruelty nor, on the other hand, that he is depicting here a tragic flaw. It is an important part of the picture, a manifestation of Tamburlaine's "ireful Virtue", to use [Torquato] Tasso's phrase [in his *Allegory of Jerusalem Delivered*], and one of the chief occasions for wonder. One may disapprove and yet, in that special sense, admire.

Marlowe's method of constructing his dramatic portrait is essentially dialectical. Not only is love balanced against hate, cruelty against honour, but these and other traits are constantly brought out against a background of parallels or contrasts. Tamburlaine is contrasted with other monarchs and with Zenocrate. In the last act an entire city is his antagonist. Throughout the play his followers are like variations on the Tamburlaine theme, imitating his ferocity and zest for conquest, but incapable of his grandeur. The first three monarchs with whom the hero is contrasted are the foolish Mycetes, his brother, Cosroe, and the emperor Bajazeth. Mycetes is a grossly comic foil in his inability to act or speak well, to control others or himself.

In the opening speech of the play he deplores his own insufficiency to express his rage, "For it requires a great and thundering speech" [I.i.1-3], a thing Tamburlaine can always provide.

In a low-comedy scene in the first act, he comes alone on to the battlefield, the picture of cowardice, looking for a place to hide his crown. This action in itself takes on great significance when we come, three scenes later, to Tamburlaine's praise of crowns. Mycetes curses the inventor of war and congratulates himself on the wisdom that permits him to escape its ill effects by hiding the crown which makes him a target. To put the censure of war and the praise of scheming wisdom in the mouth of such a character inclines the audience to see virtue in the hero's pursuit of war and in a kind of wisdom more closely allied to action.

The contrast with Cosroe is another matter. Patently superior to his brother Mycetes, Cosroe appears to be an ordinarily competent warrior and ruler. In fact, his one crippling deficiency is his inability to recognize the extraordinary when he sees it in the person of Tamburlaine. His attempt to pat Tamburlaine on the head, and reward him for a job well done by giving him an important post in the kingdom, as any normal king might do, is as inept, given the nature of Tamburlaine, as the feckless gesturing of Mycetes. Cosroe is perfectly familiar with the rules of the game as it is generally played in the world, where the betrayal of a Mycetes is venial and competence has at least its modest reward. His cry of pain when Tamburlaine turns against him, "Barbarous and bloody Tamburlaine" [II.vii.1], expresses the outrage of one who finds that the rules he has learned do not apply. Tamburlaine's strategy is so much more daring and his treachery so much more preposterous that they are beyond the imagination of Cosroe.

Bajazeth, Tamburlaine's third antagonist, is no mere moderately successful king. A proud and cruel tyrant, he rejoices in the sway of a vast empire. With his first words a new perspective opens up: "Great kings of Barbary, and my portly bassoes" [III.i.1]. Here is a ruler served by kings. "We hear the Tartars and the eastern thieves, / Under the conduct of one Tamburlaine, / Presume a bickering with your emperor." The tone is superb. One notes the condescension of "one Tamburlaine" and the hauteur of "presume a bickering". He is assured ("You know our army is invincible"); he is used to command ("Hie thee, my basso . . . Tell him thy lord . . . Wills and commands, for say not I entreat"); and he is obeyed by thousands ("As many circumcised Turks we have, / And Warlike bands of Christians renied, / As hath the ocean or the Terrene sea / Small drops of water").

If Cosroe is a little more like Tamburlaine than is his foolish brother, Bajazeth is decidedly more so. He speaks of "the fury of my wrath" [III.i.30], and shows his cruelty by threatening to castrate Tamburlaine and confine him to the seraglio while his captains are made to draw the chariot of the empress. The famous (and to a modern reader ludicrous) exchange of insults between Zabina and Zenocrate reinforces the parallel. Yet Marlowe emphasizes the ease with which this mighty potentate is toppled from his throne. The stage directions tell the story: "BAJA-ZETH *flies and he pursues him. The battle short and they enter.* BAJAZETH *is overcome*" [III.iii.211 ff.]. This contrast brings out what was suggested by the contrast with Cosroe, the truly extraordinary nature of Tamburlaine. For Bajazeth is what Mycetes would like to be but cannot be for lack of natural aptitude. He is what Cosroe might become in time with a little luck. As a sort of final term in a mathematical progression, he presents the ultimate in monarchs, and in himself sums up the others. That even he should fall so easily defines the limitations of the species and sets Tamburlaine in a world apart. He is not merely more angry, more cruel, more proud, more powerful. Though sharing certain characteristics with his victims, he embodies a force of a different order.

Zenocrate, by representing a scale of values far removed from those of the warrior or the monarch, provides further insights into Tamburlaine's character. Something has already been said of his courtship of her in the first act, when, to the surprise of Techelles, he shows that he is moved by love. The inclusion in his nature of the capacity to love is a characteristic Renaissance addition to the classical model of the Herculean hero. One recalls that Tasso's Rinaldo [in the *Allegory*], though chiefly representing the "ireful virtue", is susceptible to the charms of Armida. Yet Zenocrate is not an enchantress like Armida nor is Tamburlaine's love for her presented as a weakness. Love, as opposed to pure concupiscence, is a more important part of Tamburlaine than of Rinaldo. As G. I. Duthie has pointed out [see commentary dated 1948], it modifies considerably his warrior ideal, leading him to spare the life of the Soldan and "take truce with all the world" [V.ii.467].

Marlowe leaves no doubt that the commitment to Zenocrate is basic and lasting, but it is not allowed to dominate. Tamburlaine refuses Zenocrate's plea for Damascus, and when he also refuses the Virgins of Damascus he says:

> I will not spare these proud Egyptians,
> Nor change my martial observations
> For all the wealth of Gihon's golden waves,
> Or for the love of Venus, would she leave
> The angry god of arms and lie with me.
>
> [V.ii.58-62]

This clear evaluation of the claims of Venus as opposed to those of Mars precedes by only a few lines the long soliloquy in which he extols the beauty of Zenocrate. Here he admits that he is tempted to give in to Zenocrate, who has more power to move him than any of his enemies. By implication it is clear that this power is due to her beauty, which is so great that if the greatest poets attempted to capture it,

> Yet should there hover in their restless heads
> One thought, one grace, one wonder, at the least,
> Which into words no virtue can digest.
>
> [V.ii.108-10]

But on the verge, as it might seem, of capitulating to this softer side of his nature, he first reproves himself for these "thoughts effeminate and faint", and then presents beauty as the handmaid of valour. This passage is a textual crux, and its syntax is so treacherous that a close analysis of the meaning is nearly impossible, but I think it is fair to say

that Tamburlaine's convictions about the role of beauty are given in the lines:

> And every warrior that is rapt with love
> Of fame, of valour, and of victory,
> Must needs have beauty beat on his conceits . . .
>
> [V.ii.117-19]

The conclusion of the speech looks forward to what beauty may inspire Tamburlaine to do, and it is as important a part of his mission as the scourging of tyrants. This is to show the world "for all my birth, / That virtue solely is the sum of glory, / And fashions men with true nobility" [V.ii.125-27]; that is, that the hero's goal is to be attained by an innate power which has nothing to do with the accidents of birth. To Theridamas, Techelles and Usumcasane he has said much the same thing, assuring them that they deserve their titles

> By valour and by magnanimity.
> Your births shall be no blemish to your fame;
> For virtue is the fount whence honour springs.
>
> [IV.iv.129-31]

In several ways the power of love and beauty is subordinated to Tamburlaine's primary concerns. The encomium of Zenocrate leads to the statement of beauty's function in the warrior's life and then to Tamburlaine's intention of demonstrating true nobility. Furthermore the entire soliloquy is carefully framed. Before it begins, Tamburlaine orders a slaughter, and after his lines about true nobility he calls in a servant to ask whether Bajazeth has been fed. Tamburlaine's love for Zenocrate, extravagant as it is, is part of a rather delicately adjusted balance of forces.

Zenocrate is a pale character beside the best heroines of Shakespeare and Webster, but her attitude towards Tamburlaine is an important part of the meaning of the play. After her initial mistake—not wholly a mistake—of thinking he is just the Scythian shepherd he seems to be, her feelings towards him change rapidly. When she next appears she defends him to her companion, Agydas, who still sees Tamburlaine as a rough soldier. He asks:

> How can you fancy one that looks so fierce,
> Only disposed to martial stratagems?
>
> [III.ii.40-1]

Zenocrate replies by comparing his looks to the sun and his conversation to the Muses' song. When Tamburlaine enters he rewards each of them with behaviour suited to their conception of him: *"Tamburlaine goes to her, and takes her away lovingly by the hand, looking wrathfully on Agydas, and says nothing"* [III.ii.65 ff.].

Zenocrate enters enthusiastically into the exchange of insults with Bajazeth and Zabina, but it is her speeches after the sack of Damascus and the suicides of Bajazeth and Zabina which truly reveal her attitude towards Tamburlaine. Sorrowing for the cruel deaths of the Virgins of Damascus, she asks:

> Ah, Tamburlaine, wert thou the cause of this,
> That term'st Zenocrate thy dearest love?
> Whose lives were dearer to Zenocrate
> Then her own life, or aught save thine own love.
>
> [V.ii.273-76]

His cruelty is recognized for what it is without its impairing her love. Similarly, when she laments over the bodies of the emperor and empress, she acknowledges Tamburlaine's pride, but prays Jove and Mahomet to pardon him. This lament is a highly effective set-piece, whose formality gives it a special emphasis. Its theme, the vanity of earthly power, is resoundingly stated in the refrain, "Behold the Turk and his great emperess!" which occurs four times, varied the last time to "In this great Turk and hapless emperess!" [V.ii.292, 295, 300, 306]. But within the statement of theme there is a movement of thought as Zenocrate turns from the most general aspect of the fall of the mighty to what concerns her more nearly, its bearing on Tamburlaine. The orthodoxy of the moral she draws from this spectacle of death is conspicuous, and nowhere more so than in the central section:

> Ah, Tamburlaine, my love, sweet Tamburlaine,
> That fightst for sceptres and for slippery crowns,
> Behold the Turk and his great emperess!
> Thou that, in conduct of thy happy stars,
> Sleep'st every night with conquest on thy brows,
> And yet wouldst shun the wavering turns of war,
> In fear and feeling of the like distress,
> Behold the Turk and his great emperess!

The culmination of the speech is its prayer that Tamburlaine may be spared the consequences of "his contempt / Of earthly fortune and respect of pity" [V.ii.302-03].

When Tamburlaine's enemies inveigh against his pride and presumption, their protests have a hollow ring, and Marlowe may seem to be laughing at the point of view they express. He is certainly not doing so when he puts criticism of the same faults in the mouth of Zenocrate. Through her an awareness of the standard judgment of Tamburlaine's "overreaching" is made without irony and made forcefully. Through her it is also made clear that such an awareness may be included in an unwavering devotion, just as Deianira's devotion can digest even the grave personal slight she suffers from Hercules. Zenocrate both presents the conventional view of hubris more convincingly than any other character, and shows the inadequacy of this view in judging Tamburlaine.

A contrast on a larger scale forms the final episode of Part I: Tamburlaine is pitted against the great city of Damascus. Since Zenocrate pleads for the city, this is an extension of the contrast between the hero and heroine. Since the city is ruled by Tamburlaine's enemies, it is the climax in the series of contrasts between him and the representatives of corrupt worldly power. His first three enemies are individuals of increasing stature, but the Governor of Damascus and his allies, the Soldan and Arabia, are none of them imposing figures. Instead, the city of Damascus becomes the collective antagonist, to which Tamburlaine opposes his personal will. Much more than the individual monarchs of the first acts, the city seems to represent the point of view of society, which Zenocrate also adopts when she becomes the spokesman for conventional morality. When the delegation of virgins asks the conqueror for mercy, the appeal is in the name of the whole community:

> Pity our plights! O, pity poor Damascus!
> Pity old age . . .

> Pity the marriage bed . . .
> O, then, for these and such as we ourselves,
> For us, for infants, and for all our bloods,
> That never nourished thought against thy rule,
> Pity, O pity, sacred emperor,
> The prostrate service of this wretched town . . .
>   [V.ii.17-37]

Tamburlaine's refusal is based on the absolute primacy of his will—of the execution of whatever he has vowed. He is as self-absorbed as Hercules, whose devotion to his areté obliterates any consideration for Deianira or Hyllus, in *The Women of Trachis.* Homer portrays the hero's uncompromising adherence to his own standard of conduct in the refusal of Achilles to fight. In Book IX of the *Iliad,* when he is waited on by the delegation of warriors, including his old tutor, Phoenix, heroic integrity directly opposes obligation to others—to friends and allies in war. The "conflict between personal integrity and social obligation" was inherent in the story of the Wrath of Achilles, according to Cedric Whitman [in his *Homer and the Heroic Tradition*], but Homer gave it special importance, seeing it "as an insolubly tragic situation, the tragic situation *par excellence*". In the Renaissance it is not surprising to find "social obligation" represented by the city, but in this case it is an enemy city. Instead of being urged to fight for friends Tamburlaine is urged to spare citizens whose only fault is the acceptance of the rule of their foolish, and finally weak, Governor. Hence the social obligation denied by Tamburlaine is not that of supporting his friends' cause but of conforming to an ideal of behaviour which places mercy above justice. The code of Tamburlaine is a more primitive affair. His word once given is as inflexible as destiny, and the imposition of his will upon Damascus is also the carrying out of a cosmic plan. To the demands of a segment of society he opposes a larger obligation to free the world from tyrants. Marlowe's setting him against Damascus reaffirms both his colossal individuality and his god-like superiority. The siege of this city is used to present the core of the problem of *virtus heroica.*

Marlowe puts far less emphasis upon the benefactions of his hero's career than was put upon the benefactions of Hercules; the punishment of the wicked is what Tamburlaine himself constantly reiterates. Nevertheless, the punishment of Damascus is balanced by the hero's generosity in sparing the Soldan. This is not a matter of just deserts. It is Tamburlaine's god-like caprice to spare Zenocrate's father. Because he does so the end of Part I suggests a positive achievement. Zenocrate's greeting of her "conquering love" is a mixture of wonder and gratitude, and even the vanquished Soldan joins in the general thanksgiving.

Whether Part II was planned from the first, as some have thought, or written in response to the "general welcomes Tamburlaine receiv'd", as the Prologue says, its general conception is strikingly similar to that of Part I. Its structure is again episodic, though the episodes are somewhat more tightly knit. The pattern is again a series of encounters between Tamburlaine and his enemies, leading at last to the one unsuccessful encounter—with death. To Mycetes, Cosroe and Bajazeth correspond the vaster alliance of Bajazeth's son Callapine and his allies. To the conflict between the factions in Persia corresponds the fight between Orcanes and Sigismund after a truce has been concluded. Here again, but even more circumstantially, we have the jealous struggles, the hypocrisies and the betrayals of conventional kings. Sigismund is a despicable figure, Orcanes a rather sympathetic one—even more so than his structural counterpart, Cosroe. He is portrayed as a religious man, is given some fine lines on the deity, ". . . he that sits on high and never sleeps, / Nor in one place is circumscriptible" [II.ii.49-50], and, though born a pagan, acknowledges the power of Christ. That religion spares him none of the humiliations accorded to the enemies of Tamburlaine suggests that his religion, like his statecraft, is conventional. He is far from being the worst of men or the worst of rulers, yet, like the kings in Part I, he is given to boasting of his power and position and making snobbish remarks about Tamburlaine's lowly origin. It may be significant that he offers his partial allegiance to Christ as a means of obtaining the victory over Sigismund, who is a perjured Christian. This bargaining religion is the foil to Tamburlaine's impious self-confidence.

Other elements of the pattern of Part I are also imitated here. The siege of Damascus is matched by the siege of Babylon; Bajazeth in his cage is matched by the conquered kings in harness, to whom Tamburlaine shouts the famous "Holla, ye pampered jades of Asia!" [IV.iii.1], so often parodied. Tamburlaine in his chariot, actually whipping the half-naked kings who draw him, is a powerful theatrical image. Preposterous as the scene may be, it is satisfyingly right as a visual symbol of one of the principal themes of the play. Part II develops the theme more fully than Part I, giving it a prominent place in the dying hero's instructions to his eldest son:

> So reign, my son; scourge and control these
>   slaves,
> Guiding thy chariot with thy father's hand.
>   .   .   .   .   .
> For, if thy body thrive not full of thoughts
> As pure and fiery as Phyteus' beams,
> The nature of these proud rebelling jades
> Will take occasion by the slenderest hair,
> And draw thee piecemeal, like Hippolytus . . .
>   [V.iii.228-29, 236-40]

Another theme developed in Part II is the cruelty of Tamburlaine. It is so prominent here that it may seem to mark a loss of sympathy for the hero. Certainly the brutality to the conquered kings and to the Governor of Babylon, and above all Tamburlaine's murder of his son, constitute more vivid and more shocking examples than even the treatment of Bajazeth. Yet one need not conclude that Marlowe has changed his mind about his hero. All of these scenes may be understood as part of a rhetorical amplification of a theme which is, after all, unmistakable in Part I. Furthermore these scenes serve to emphasize other aspects of Tamburlaine's character indicated in Part I. The portrait is not changed: its lines are more deeply incised.

The scenes presenting Calyphas, the cowardly son, are perhaps the most shocking of all, and may be used as examples of the amplified theme of cruelty in Part II. In the first of them [I.iv] Celebinus and Amyras, the two brave sons, win paternal approval by vying with each other in promises to scourge the world, while Calyphas is furiously

rebuked for asking permission to stay with his mother while the rest are out conquering. As in all the scenes with the three sons, the patterning is obvious to the point of being crude, and the humour in the depiction of the girlish little boy not much to our taste. Nevertheless, the scene does more than show how hard-hearted Tamburlaine can be. For members of the audience who have not seen Part I it presents Tamburlaine's relationship to Zenocrate, and for the rest it restates that relationship in different terms. The scene opens with a loving speech to Zenocrate, who replies by asking Tamburlaine when he will give up war and live safe. It is this question which the scene answers by asserting the primacy of the irascible powers in Tamburlaine's nature. In spite of his love he identifies himself with "wrathful war", and as he looks at her, surrounded by their sons, suddenly thinks that his boys appear more "amorous" than "martial", and hence unworthy of him. Zenocrate defends them as having "their mother's looks" but "their conquering father's heart" [I.iv.35-6], and it is then that they proclaim their intentions. Tamburlaine's rebuke to Calyphas is a statement of his creed, glorifying the "mind courageous and invincible" [I.iv.73], and drawing a portrait of himself comparable to several in Part I:

> For he shall wear the crown of Persia
> Whose head hath deepest scars, whose breast
>   most wounds,
> Which, being wroth, sends lightning from his
>   eyes,
> And in the furrows of his frowning brows
> Harbours revenge, war, death and cruelty . . .
>   [I.iv.74-8]

The furrowed brows belong to the angry demigod of Part I, and if the picture is somewhat grimmer, it is partly because of the hint that the demigod must suffer in the accomplishment of his mission.

The next scene with Calyphas [III.ii.] takes place after the death of Zenocrate, and like the former one, makes its contribution to the development of Tamburlaine's character. As the earlier scene began with the praise of Zenocrate, so this one begins with her funeral against the background of a conflagration betokening Tamburlaine's wrath. Again Calyphas is responsible for an unexpected note of levity when he makes an inane comment on the dangerousness of war just after his father has concluded stern instructions to his sons how to be "soldiers / And worthy sons of Tamburlaine the Great" [III.ii.91-2]. The consequence is not only a rebuke but a demonstration. Never having been wounded in all his wars, Tamburlaine cuts his own arm to show his sons how "to bear courageous minds" [III.ii.143]. Here his cruelty and anger are turned against himself, as perhaps they always are in some sense in the scenes with Calyphas.

The last of these scenes [IV.i] is the most terrible and by far the most important, for Calyphas here prompts Tamburlaine to reveal himself more completely than ever before. In the first part of the scene the boy has played cards with an attendant while his brothers fought with their father to overcome the Turkish kings. He has scoffed at honour and, like Mycetes, praised the wisdom which keeps him safe [IV.i.49-50]. When the victors return, Tamburlaine drags Calyphas out of the tent and, ignoring the pleas of his followers and of Amyras, stabs him to death. It is almost a ritual killing—the extirpation of an unworthy part of himself, as the accompanying speech makes clear:

> Here, Jove, receive his fainting soul again;
> A form not meet to give that subject essence
> Whose matter is the flesh of Tamburlaine,
> Wherein an incorporeal spirit moves,
> Made of the mould whereof thyself consists,
> Which makes me valiant, proud, ambitious,
> Ready to levy power against thy throne,
> That I might move the turning spheres of heaven;
> For earth and all this airy region
> Cannot contain the state of Tamburlaine.
> [IV.i.111-20]

To interpret this murder as merely one further example of barbarous cruelty is to accept the judgment of Tamburlaine's enemies. The cruelty is balanced against one of the most powerful statements of the spirituality of Tamburlaine. It is the "incorporeal spirit" which makes him what he is, a hero akin to the gods, and which, because it cannot bear to be other than itself, pushes him to the execution of his cowardly son. As the great aspiring speech of Part I obliges us to see an earthly crown as the goal to which Tamburlaine's nature forces him, so this speech and its accompanying action oblige us to accept cruelty along with valour, pride and ambition as part of the spirit which makes this man great. The soul of Calyphas, by contrast, is associated with the "massy dregs of earth" [IV.i.123], lacking both courage and wit, just as Theridamas described the unaspiring mind as "gross and like the massy earth" (Part I, II.vii.31).

So far does Tamburlaine go in asserting his affinity to heaven and contempt for earth, that for the first time he hints that sovereignty of the earth may not be enough for him. It is an idea which has an increasing appeal for him in the remainder of the play. He makes another extreme statement in this scene when his enemies protest the barbarity of his deed. "These terrors and these tyrannies," he says, are part of his divine mission,

> Nor am I made arch-monarch of the world,
> Crown'd and invested by the hand of Jove,
> For deeds of bounty or nobility . . .
> [IV.i.150-52]

To be the terror of the world is his exclusive concern.

The emphasis on terror is consistent with the entire depiction of his character. The denial of nobility is not. It is an extreme statement which the emotions of the moment and dialectical necessity push him to. Allowing for an element of exaggeration in this speech, however, the scene as a whole, like the other scenes with Calyphas, presents a Tamburlaine essentially like the Tamburlaine of Part I, and not seen from any very different point of view. As he grows older, as he encounters a little more resistance, his character sets a little more firmly in its mould. It remains what it has always been.

The death of Zenocrate is, as every critic has recognized, the first real setback to Tamburlaine. In view of her association with the city in Part I it is appropriate that Tamburlaine makes a city suffer for her death by setting fire to it.

His devotion to her and to the beauty she represents appears in the speech he makes at her deathbed [II.iv.1-37], in his raging at her death, in the placing of her picture on his tent to inspire valour [III.ii.36-42], and in his dying address to her coffin [V.iii.224-27]. As G. I. Duthie says, death is the great enemy in Part II, and his conquest of Zenocrate is in effect his first victory over Tamburlaine. As he had to make some concessions to Zenocrate in Part I, so in Part II he has to come to terms with the necessity of death. The process begins with the death of Zenocrate, to which his first reaction is the desire for revenge. Not only does he burn the town where she died; he also orders Techelles to draw his sword and wound the earth [II.iv.97]. This prepares us somewhat for his later order, when death has laid siege to him, to "set black streamers in the firmament, / To signify the slaughter of the gods" [V.iii.49-50]. By keeping always with him the hearse containing her dead body he refuses wholly to accept her death as he now defies his own.

Only in the last scene of Act V does cosmic defiance give way to acceptance, and when this happens, Tamburlaine's defeat by death is partially transformed into a desired fulfilment. I have already mentioned his hint that the earth cannot contain him. It is followed by a suggestion that Jove, esteeming him "too good for earth" [IV.iii.60], might make a star of him. Now he says:

> In vain I strive and rail against those powers
> That mean t'invest me in a higher throne,
> As much too high for this disdainful earth.
> [V.iii.120-22]

and finally:

> But sons, this subject, not of force enough
> To hold the fiery spirit it contains,
> Must part . . .
> [V.iii.168-70]

Like Hercules Oetaeus, he feels that his immortal part, that "incorporeal spirit" of which he spoke earlier, is now going to a realm more worthy of him, though imparting something of its power to the spirits of his two remaining sons, in whom he will continue to live. In these final moments we have what may be hinted at earlier in his self-wounding—a collaboration with death and fate in the destruction of his physical being. For the psychologist the drive towards self-destruction is latent in all heroic risks; it is the other side of the coin of self-assertion. Though Marlowe could never have put it this way, his insight may be essentially similar.

From the quotations already given it will be apparent that Tamburlaine's attitude toward the gods changes continually. He boasts of their favour or defies them to take away his conquests; likens himself to them, executes their will, waits for them to receive him into their domain, or threatens to conquer it. Tamburlaine's religious pronouncements, especially his blasphemies, have attracted a great deal of critical comment from his day to ours. Since Marlowe himself was accused of atheism, the key question has been whether or not Tamburlaine is a mouthpiece for his author. Some critics emphasize Tamburlaine's defiance of Mahomet and the burning of the Koran, but these episodes are surely no more significant than his "wounding" of the earth. As [Paul H.] Kocher has pointed out [in his *Christopher Marlowe*], his line, "The God that sits in heaven, if any god" [V.i.200] contains in its parenthetical comment more blasphemy for a Christian than does the whole incident of the Koran. Yet even this questioning of God's existence is only one of the changes of attitude just cited. To try to deduce Marlowe's religious position from these speeches is a hopeless undertaking, and to try to decide on the basis of the biographical evidence which of them Marlowe might endorse is risky and finally inconclusive. Somehow the relationship of these opinions to the rest of the play must be worked out. Either their inconsistency is due to carelessness (in this case carelessness of heroic proportions) or it has some bearing on the heroic character. Seneca's Hercules displays a similar variety of attitudes. In the earlier play [*Hercules Furens*] he thanks the gods for their aid in his victory over the tyrant, Lycus, and offers to kill any further tyrants or monsters the earth may bring forth. Moments later, as his madness comes upon him, he says:

> To the lofty regions of the universe on high let me make my way, let me seek the skies; the stars are my father's promise. And what if he should not keep his word? Earth has not room for Hercules, and at length restores him unto heaven. See, the whole company of the gods of their own will summons me, and opens wide the door of heaven, with one alone forbidding. And wilt thou unbar the sky and take me in? Or shall I carry off the doors of stubborn heaven? Dost even doubt my power?
>
> (*Hercules Furens*, ll.958-65)

In the first lines of *Hercules Oetaeus* he again boasts of his activities as a scourge of tyrants and complains that Jove still denies him access to the heavens, hinting that the god may be afraid of him. Later [ll.1302-03] he almost condescends to Jove, remarking that he might have stormed the heavens, but refrained because Jove, after all, was his father. Greene could quite properly have inveighed against "daring God out of heaven with that atheist Hercules". At the end of *Hercules Oetaeus* the hero accepts his fate with calm fortitude and even helps to destroy himself amidst the flames. These changes in attitude are perhaps more easy to understand in Hercules, since his relationship to the gods was in effect a family affair. Tamburlaine is not the son of a god, but his facile references to the gods, sometimes friendly, sometimes hostile, may be interpreted as part of the heroic character of which Hercules is the prototype. He has the assurance of a demigod rather than the piety of a good man.

Such assurance, rather than repentance, breathes in the lines in which Tamburlaine advises his son Amyras:

> Let not thy love exceed thine honour, son,
> Nor bar thy mind that magnanimity
> That nobly must admit necessity.
> Sit up, my boy, and with those silken reins
> Bridle the steeled stomachs of those jades.
> [V.iii.199-203]

The advice to admit necessity may reflect Tamburlaine's own acceptance of his death, but in context it refers primarily to the necessity for Amyras to take over Tamburlaine's throne. The whole speech shows Tamburlaine's conviction of the rightness of what he has done. The place of love is again made subordinate to honour, the hero's chief concern. Magnanimity is stressed as it is in Tamburlaine's advice to his followers to deserve their crowns "by valour and magnanimity" [Part I, IV.iv.129]. Even the bowing to fate is to be done nobly, as Tamburlaine himself is now doing. Finally, the heroic enterprise of controlling tyrants is to be continued. There is no retraction here, no change in the basic character. He has come to terms with death, but this is more a recovery than a reversal. He has spoken earlier in the play of his old age and death, but, very humanly, has rebelled when death struck at Zenocrate and then at himself. Now he has regained calm with self-mastery.

Though the suffering of Tamburlaine is so prominent from the death of Zenocrate to the end, retribution is not what is stressed. The last scene of the play presents a glorification of the hero approaching apotheosis. It opens with a formally patterned lament, spoken by Theridamas, Techelles and Usumcasane, the last section of which expresses the theme of the scene, Tamburlaine as benefactor:

> Blush, heaven, to lose the honour of thy name,
> To see thy footstool set upon thy head;
> And let no baseness in thy haughty breast
> Sustain a shame of such inexcellence,
> To see the devils mount in angels' thrones,
> And angels dive into the pools of hell.
> And, though they think their painful date is out,
> And that their power is puissant as Jove's,
> Which makes them manage arms against thy
>   state,
> Yet make them feel the strength of Tamburlaine,
> Thy instrument and note of majesty,
> Is greater far than they can thus subdue;
> For if he die, thy glory is disgrac'd,
> Earth droops, and says that hell in heaven is
>   plac'd.
> [V.iii.28-41]

His sons live only in his life, and it is with the greatest reluctance that Amyras mounts the throne at Tamburlaine's command. When he speaks in doing so of his father's "anguish and his burning agony" [V.iii.209], he seems to imply that Tamburlaine's sufferings are the inevitable concomitants of his greatness and his service to humanity. It is he who pronounces the final words:

> Meet heaven and earth, and here let all things
>   end,
> For earth hath spent the pride of all her fruit,
> And heaven consum'd his choicest living fire!
> Let earth and heaven his timeless death deplore,
> For both their worths will equal him no more.
> [V.iii.249-53]

Full of Herculean echoes, the lines form a perfect epitaph for the hero, the product of earth and heaven.

Three times in this scene Tamburlaine adjures his son to control the captive kings and thus maintain order. He compares the task with Phaëton's:

> So reign, my son; scourge and control those
>   slaves,

Guiding thy chariot with thy father's hand.
As precious is the charge thou undertak'st
As that which Clymene's brain-sick son did
    guide
When wandering Phoebe's ivory cheeks were
    scorched,
And all the earth, like Aetna, breathing fire.
Be warned by him, then; learn with awful eye
To sway a throne as dangerous as his;
                                                [V.iii.228-35]

Despite his ambition and pride, Tamburlaine is no Macbeth to seek power "though the treasure / Of nature's germens tumble all together, / Even till destruction sicken . . . " [*Macbeth,* IV. i. 58-60]. Rather, he identifies himself with universal order, as does Seneca's Hercules. The very chariot which is a symbol of his cruel scourging is also the symbol of control and hence of order. Compared to the chariot of the sun, it is also the bringer of light.

In the depiction of the Herculean hero there is no relaxation of the tensions between his egotism and altruism, his cruelties and benefactions, his human limitations and his divine potentialities. Marlowe never lets his audience forget these antitheses. In the first scene of Act V this great benefactor orders the Governor of Babylon to be hung in chains on the wall of the town. He rises from his deathbed to go out and conquer one more army. It is Marlowe's triumph that, after revealing with such clarity his hero's pride and cruelty, he can give infinite pathos to the line, "For Tamburlaine, the scourge of God, must die" [V.iii.248].

In obtaining a favourable reception for his hero among the more thoughtful members of his audience Marlowe could no doubt count on not only some familiarity with the heroic tradition in which he was working, but also on the often-voiced regard for the active life. Gabriel Harvey, it will be recalled, asks who would not rather be one of the nine worthies than one of the seven wise masters. He also expresses another attitude on which Marlowe could count, the Stoic regard for integrity—truth to oneself. Harvey prefers Caesar to Pompey because Pompey deserts himself, while Caesar remains true to himself. He notes that it was Aretine's glory to be himself [*Gabriel Harvey's Marginalia,* ed. G. C. Moore Smith].

The last moments of the play appeal to the spectator's pity by insisting on the tragic limitation of Tamburlaine as a human being. "For Tamburlaine, the scourge of God, must die" is comparable to Achilles' lines: "For not even the strength of Herakles fled away from destruction, / although he was dearest of all to lord Zeus . . . " But the play's dominant appeal is to the wonder aroused by vast heroic potential. The very paradoxes of Tamburlaine's nature excite wonder, and this was supposed in Marlowe's time to be the effect of paradox. Puttenham, in his familiar *Arte of English Poesie,* calls paradox "the wondrer". Tamburlaine's "high astounding terms", for which the Prologue prepares us, clearly aim at the same effect. Many years later, Sir William Alexander, the author of several Senecan tragedies, wrote [in *Anacrisis*] that the three stylistic devices which pleased him most were: "A grave sentence, by which the Judgment may be bettered; a witty

Conceit, which doth harmoniously delight the Spirits; and a generous Rapture expressing Magnanimity, whereby the Mind may be inflamed for great Things." The last of these three he found in Lucan, in whose "Heroical Conceptions" he saw an "innate Generosity"; he remarked the power of "the unmatchable Height of his Ravishing Conceits to provoke Magnanimity". Marlowe was undoubtedly influenced by the style of the *Pharsalia,* the first book of which he had translated, and in any case Alexander's words might justly be applied to *Tamburlaine.* The epic grandeur of the style, with its resounding catalogues of exotic names, its hyperboles, and its heroic boasts and tirades, "expresses magnanimity", that largeness of spirit so consistently ascribed to the great hero. Alexander testifies that such a style may inflame the mind "for great things", and general as this description is, it serves well for the feeling aroused by the play. Another name for it was admiration. (pp. 60-87)

> *Eugene M. Waith, "Marlowe," in his* The Herculean Hero in Marlowe, Chapman, Shakespeare and Dryden, *Chatto & Windus, 1962, pp. 60-87.*

Mark Thornton Burnett (essay date 1987)

[*Burnett examines the theme of honor in* Tamburlaine, *claiming that various characters hold conflicting interpretations of the concept. The clash in the play between these opposing definitions, he maintains, reflects the evolving conception of honor in Renaissance society at large. The quotations and line references are taken from* Tamburlaine the Great, *edited by J. S. Cunningham (1981).*]

Honour was widely discussed in the sixteenth and seventeenth centuries in England, in drama, pamphlets, conduct books and popular literature. Esteem accorded to one of high rank, an exalted position or a reward for services to the state—these, and other meanings, were part of the traditional definition of honour. Virtue, a closely associated concept, could refer to moral worth or excellence, physical strength, valour or power. Critics have recognized that honour is a major thematic concern in Shakespeare, but have failed to notice that it is as important an issue in Marlowe's plays. In *Tamburlaine the Great* (1587-88), individual codes of honour determine the lives of all the characters. The conflict that arises when these codes come together accounts, in part, for our difficulty in directly engaging with the play and for the contradictory critical responses that it has provoked. *Tamburlaine* can be seen as an exploration or anatomization of honour at a time when the concept, affected by the processes of social, economic and political change, was undergoing a transformation, loosing old meanings and acquiring new associations and importance.

Honour is constantly alluded to in the speeches and protestations of Tamburlaine's enemies. On being crowned by Ortygius and Ceneus, Cosroe vows:

And Jove may never let me longer live
Than I may seek to gratify your love
And cause the soldiers that thus honour me

To triumph over many provinces . . .
                          [I:I.i.170-73]

Cosroe's invoking of divine authority is specious and hypocritical. He is ostensibly honoured by his soldiers when
they offer him the Persian crown, but we are not allowed
to forget that the gift is the result of his plot to usurp his
brother, Mycetes. The scheming that has gone before undermines Cosroe's expressions of love and fellowship. As
the play reveals, Jove does not permit him to live, and his
promise to "triumph over many provinces" remains un-
fulfilled.

Marlowe further discredits the claims of Tamburlaine's
foes to honour when Meander proposes his plan for defeating the Scythian's invading army. Gold will be strewed
about the battlefield, and then the Persian soldiers

             fighting more for honour than for gold,
         Shall massacre those greedy-minded slaves.
                          [I:II.ii.66-7]

The implication is that Tamburlaine's followers, seeing
war as no more than a means to pillage and acquire booty,
will be easily led astray and corrupted. Motivated by
higher principles, the Persian army will win the day. This,
however, is another idle speculation; Meander defects to
Cosroe's side, and Tamburlaine shows his magnificent disdain for material possessions when, shortly afterwards, he
hands back the Persian crown to Mycetes with a lordly audacity.

Honour, then, at least as far as Tamburlaine's enemies are
concerned, is a means to justify rebellion and the pursuit
of power. Their individualistic interpretation is set against
Tamburlaine's view: when he makes his first appearance
the more conventional aspects of honour are stressed. He
speaks of the "friends that help to wean my state"
[I:I.ii.29], and creates fellowship by his persuasive rhetoric
rather than political conspiracy. Theridamas, entranced
by his words, promises "To do you honour and security"
[I:I.ii.250]. The honour with which Tamburlaine is graced
commands the greater respect and admiration. And contrary to Meander's accusations, Tamburlaine is liberal, almost dismissive, in his attitude towards wealth. "Not all
the gold in India's wealthy arms / Shall buy the meanest
soldier in my train" [I:I.ii.85-6], he maintains, and flatters
Zenocrate by saying she is of "more worth" [I:I.ii.90] than
the Persian crown. Contemporary conduct book writers
thought it essential for the honourable man to be liberal
and magnanimous. James Cleland advised in 1607 [in *The
institution of a young noble man*]: "To giue is the most
honourable & proper vse of your goods, you can[n]ot im-
ploy the[m] better." "Generositie doth lead vs to honour",
added Thomas Gainsford in 1616 [in *The rich cabinet furnished with varietie of excellent descriptions, exquisite
characters*]. Tamburlaine seems to conceive of himself at
the start of the play in terms of the behaviour the ideal
gentleman was urged to cultivate.

Sixteenth- and seventeenth-century writers took a dim
view of the upstart who imitated the conduct of his social
superiors. There was some disagreement, but most authorities held that an individual below the rank of "esquire"
was unfit to entertain a desire for honour. "Gentrie . . .

may be accounted the lowest Shrube or vnder Branch of
Honor", wrote Francis Markham in 1625 [in *The booke
of honour*]. Virtue and high birth were regarded as the
most important attributes. A profound contradiction becomes increasingly apparent for Cosroe and Meander, of
royal and noble descent, abuse honour even while they
profess to uphold it. It is Tamburlaine, the *arriviste,* who
appears to embody what honour demands. But clearly a
"base born" shepherd cannot argue that his origins support his claim to honour, and Tamburlaine must employ
other means if he is to be accounted honourable in the eyes
of society.

Tamburlaine prides himself on his "love of arms"
[I:II.i.20] and on the glory that accompanies his military
conquests. He fights for the "honour of . . . wondrous victories" [II:IV.ii.206] and, pointing to the bodies of Bajazeth, Zabina and the King of Arabia, exclaims:

         And such are objects fit for Tamburlaine,
         Wherein as in a mirror may be seen
         His honour, that consists in shedding blood
         When men presume to manage arms with him.
                          [I:V.i.476-79]

The stage tableau dramatically realizes the ruthless and
inflexible code of honour to which Tamburlaine sub-
scribes. He seems here, however, also to be drawing on the
ideal of the honourable soldier described by several contemporary writers. An anonymous tract of 1579 [*Cyuile
and vncyuile life*] argued that "honour is . . . our want or
desire to excel . . . in . . . Armes", and Gervase Markham, using a typically Marlovian image, said of the soldier
in 1624 [in *Honour in his perfection*]: "it is his Actions
which must make vp the myrror wherein true *Honour* is
to be seene." Through military success Tamburlaine hopes
to win the honours which, due to his birth, he is denied.

Tamburlaine seems ultimately to be motivated by the insatiable desire for sovereignty and dominion. Crowns and
thrones, the symbols of power, are the objects he seeks.
The height of his ambition is, as Menaphon states, "the
throne / Where honour sits invested royally" [I:II.ii.17-
18]. In these lofty aspirations, Tamburlaine can be likened
to the honourable man in that he argues his triumphs have
been preordained [II:IV.i.150-56]. As John Norden said
in 1597 [in *The mirror of honour*]: "*no man can be honorable without diuine inspiration . . .* " But for Tamburlaine, being perceived as honourable also implies the acceptance of his controversial identity. Critics have drawn
attention to the importance of names and naming in the
play, but the social implications of the theme have not
been fully explored. Tamburlaine freely appropriates the
"names and titles" [I:IV.ii.79] of those he conquers, and
anticipates seeing his "name and honour . . . spread / As
far as Boreas claps his brazen wings" [I:I.i.204-05]. Acquiring honour will enable Tamburlaine firmly to establish
himself in a society founded on rigid rank distinctions and
lineage.

The immortality for which Tamburlaine longs is also associated with the winning of honour. He is, in his own
words, a "warrior . . . rapt with love / Of fame"
[I:V.i.180-81], and strives to be "immortal like the gods"
[I:I.ii.200]. Geoffrey Fenton wrote in 1582 [in *Golden epis-

tles], "honour and good renoune . . . after our death . . . lift vs to immortalitie", and Robert Ashley in 1596-1603 [in *Of honour*] thought it honourable to "haue the glorie of" one's "name commended to eternitie." If he can secure honour, Tamburlaine will be able to enjoy a god-like omnipotence and overcome his human limitations and mortality.

The play repeatedly, however, exposes Tamburlaine's boasts as hollow and illusory. Honour motivates other characters apart from the central protagonist, and the cumulative effect is to undermine and damage his exhilarating claims. Agydas, fearing death at Tamburlaine's hands, decides he will be accorded "More honour and less pain" [I:III.ii.97] if he accepts Techelles' Mephistophelian offer of the dagger and commits suicide. Usumcasane, impressed by his "manly" [I:III.ii.109] behaviour, will "honour" [I:III.ii.113] Agydas by giving him a noble burial. Bajazeth, too, kills himself, as he can no longer endure to see "my crown, my honour, and my name / Thrust under yoke and thraldom of a thief" [I:V.i.260-61]. When Olympia, afraid that Theridamas will "dishonor" [II:IV.ii.7] her, fails in her suicide attempt, she tricks her lover into killing her; she, like Agydas, will be interred with the "pomp" [II:IV.ii.97], ceremony and honour that befits her death. In certain circumstances during this period, suicide was seen as honourable. Although Agydas' death reflects favourably on Tamburlaine's ability to terrify his opponents, even when he chooses not to speak, the later scenes in which an individual takes his or her own life have a more disturbing effect. Olympia's demise, for instance, points to Theridamas' failure with words and, by extension, to Tamburlaine's growing cruelty and waning power and authority.

The fates of these characters, and the suffering they experience, prompt us to resist identifying too closely with Tamburlaine's self-consuming project. Tamburlaine's drive to be regarded as honourable is undermined by the violent indignities and dishonour he inflicts upon his enemies. It is an "honour" [I:IV.ii.21], he claims, that Bajazeth should be forced to serve as his footstool, but his grand sentiments are contradicted by the scene of physical humiliation. Tamburlaine states that his officers deserve the titles he bestows upon them

> By valour and by magnanimity:
> Your births shall be no blemish to your fame
> For virtue is the fount whence honour springs,
> And they are worthy she investeth kings.
> [I:IV.iv.129-32]

The ideas expressed in the speech are conventional. Sir John Ferne observed in 1586 [in *The blazon*]: "a true nobilitye, hath no other fountaine, from whence to fetch her source, then onley vertue." From "a lively fountaine floweth everie vertuous and praise-woorthie action, practised by a prudent man", added Pierre de La Primaudaye in the same year [in *The French academie*]. Tamburlaine acts as the dispenser of honour, rewarding his followers with the trappings of power. But the speech is also unsettling and uncomfortably reminds us of the results of Tamburlaine's attempts to achieve his ends. The victims of his ambition are all too apparent on the stage—Bajazeth and Zabina,

caged and starving. Tamburlaine sees virtue in terms of *virtù* or prowess, glorifying but brutal and unaccommodating. Marlowe encourages an enthusiastic response to Tamburlaine and at the same time makes us aware of his destructive potential.

Those obstructing Tamburlaine's path to power are cruelly slaughtered as his concept of honour, his conviction of his own ability, demands that he conquer and rule. The "honours" of the Virgins of Damascus "rely" [I:V.i.19] on Tamburlaine, and their "love of honour" [I:V.i.35] determines that they will plead for their town to be spared. Tamburlaine, however, unable to brook opposition to that "which my honour swears shall be performed" [I:V.i.101], refuses to listen to their request. The Virgins go to their deaths, symbolically raped on soldiers' spears, their honour lost, innocent victims of Tamburlaine's will to triumph over the world. Calyphas, Celebinus says, "dost dishonour manhood and thy house" [II:IV.i.32]. In his pleasure-loving and unmanly behaviour he fails to measure up to Tamburlaine's rigorous standards. He puts to shame his father's "name and majesty" [II:IV.i.90] and the honour for which he has striven. The cowardly son is consequently savagely executed.

But at the end of both parts of the play Tamburlaine's excesses are left to one side, the positive aspects of honour are affirmed and social norms, temporarily abandoned, are reinstated. In the final scene of Part One, the Soldan is delighted that Tamburlaine "hast with honour used Zenocrate" [I:V.i.485]. The respect that Tamburlaine has shown for Zenocrate's virginity is an important element in his acceptance into the establishment. The hero's generosity re-emerges in his promise, "with honour", to "entomb" Bajazeth and Zabina, "this great Turk and his fair emperess" [I:V.i.532-33]. In death, Tamburlaine gives Amyras some parting words of counsel:

> Let not thy love exceed thine honour, son,
> Nor bar thy mind that magnanimity
> That nobly must admit necessity . . .
> [II:V.iii.199-201]

Tamburlaine's recognition of "necessity", of the fact that he must die, ennobles him; like Agydas, Bajazeth and Olympia, he displays calm, resolve and fortitude in the face of death. The gift of an empire to his son is a superb gesture of liberality. He becomes "an honour to the heavens" [II:V.iii.12] which are everlasting, and will live on in the "seeds" of his sons, "immortally" [II:V.iii.174]. Immortality, the highest honour of all, seems to have been achieved at last.

The play does not, however, simply progress towards reinforcing a more conventional reading of honour, and this does not answer to its total effect. Honour in ***Tamburlaine*** is in a constant state of flux. Tamburlaine, handicapped by the problem of his low birth, practises, in many respects, a false claim to honour. The mark of an honourable soldier, at least according to Thomas Gainsford in 1616, was a quality of compassion and forgiveness; he should spare those taken prisoner in battle. But Tamburlaine cares little for such principles, and destroys with no compunction those who stand in his way. Moreover, he is liberal with wealth that is not his own, and towards the end develops traits of covetousness (in robbing the Governor of Damascus of his gold and afterwards ordering his execution). Tamburlaine's code of honour is repeatedly challenged by and comes into conflict with that of the other characters; it is, for example, set against the feminine perspective of Olympia (and to a lesser extent, of Zenocrate). Like Shakespeare in *Henry IV, Part I* (c 1597) and *Troilus and Cressida* (c. 1602), Marlowe may well be showing up the emptiness of honour, presenting the figure of Machiavellian tyrant who, to legitimize his actions, draws on aristocratic paradigms and modes of conduct.

To explain the prominence of honour in Marlowe's play, however, we need to turn to considerations that are more complicated and difficult to interpret. Marlowe is not only concerned with highlighting the hero's "honourable" opportunism. Tamburlaine does not force Zenocrate to yield him her chastity. Furthermore, in their unscrupulousness and fickleness, many of his enemies cannot be said to be morally superior, and fully deserve their fates and our contempt. We might find that studies of primitive cultures assist us in determining the place of honour in *Tamburlaine.* The conferring of honour is the community's sign of recognizing an individual's superiority. Honour is the "essential prerequisite of prestige", and reflects the proper "status relationships between individuals or groups". The correct behaviour of the family of the honourable man increases his standing and influence [J. K. Campbell, *Honour, Family and Patronage*]. Honour, in short, is the "value of a person . . . in the eyes of his society" [Julian Pitt-Rivers, "Honour and Social Status," in *Honour and Shame: The Values of a Mediterranean Society,* ed. J. G. Peristiany]. Theories such as these have a direct bearing on Tamburlaine's relationship with the other characters, on his aspirations and on his quest for power.

Historical factors are also important. It has been argued [by Mervyn James, in *English Politics and the Concept of Honour 1485-1642*] that less emphasis during this period was placed on traditional concepts of honour (fidelity, rank and blood), and more on the adhesion to a specific style of behaviour. A movement from "communal sentiment" to a "focus on the individual" was taking place [Martin Dodsworth, *Hamlet Closely Observed*]. The "rise of the gentry" and of the new, professional classes into a hereditary governing élite undermined the reliance on a hierarchical view of society. As a recent article points out, in the sixteenth and seventeenth centuries in England, the language used to describe the social order was changing—the vocabulary of "estates" and "orders" was giving way to that of class. It was difficult to establish hard and fast criteria of status, no clear consensus of opinion existed as to what characterized a gentleman and to define honour presented a problem that seemed intractable and irresolvable. *Tamburlaine* engages with this linguistic shift, and can be regarded as a play in which concepts of honour are still in a process of transition. Traditional interpretations are at odds with speeches in which honour is referred to divorced from its usual meanings and associations. Contemporary writers, like Marlowe, seemed unable to decide if Tamburlaine's glorious career should ultimately be seen as honourable. In 1586 Sir John Ferne praised Tamburlaine for "his vertues", and for rising from a "Hogheard"

to be "King of Scythians." George Gifford, possibly recollecting Marlowe's play, wrote in a confused state in 1594 [in *A treatise of true fortitude*]: Tamburlaine is portrayed as a "valiant and expert souldiour" but also a "cruell . . . Tyrant . . . " John Norden expressed his criticism more strongly in 1597, saying that Tamburlaine's "vices" had sealed his "eternal ignominie" rather than gaining him "honor." Marlowe shares the uncertainty of these authors. For in *Tamburlaine,* no single view of honour is eventually granted approval or condemnation. Typically, Marlowe poses many questions but provides few answers. (pp. 201-05)

Mark Thornton Burnett, " 'Tamburlaine' and the Renaissance Concept of Honour," in Studia Neophilologica, *Vol. LIX, 1987, pp. 201-06.*

THE JEW OF MALTA

CRITICAL COMMENTARY

Harry Levin (essay date 1952)

[*In the following essay, Levin analyzes* The Jew of Malta *in relation to the historical and literary traditions concerning the depiction of Jews, quests for revenge, and Machiavellianism; and he examines the unusual mixture of these elements with comedy in Marlowe's play. The critic describes the drama as "a tragedy of humours" in which Barabas is "a scoundrel who is too clever for his own good, the cheater cheated, wily beguiled." Furthermore, Levin observes, "In getting out of hand, [Barabas's] counterplots exceed the proportions of tragedy, and his discomfiture is more like the happy endings of melodrama."*]

What next? That has always been the crucial question for the creative mind. How can it continue to surprise the audience captured by its early boldness? The Renaissance could offer more in the way of unrealized potentialities, could open wider and smoother channels to innovation, than the age of Joyce, Picasso, and Stravinsky. But Marlowe, like the most original artists of our century, strives to surpass himself with every effort. After his triumphant arrival with *Tamburlaine,* all his viceroys—Peele, Lodge, Greene, and the rest—duly gained their contributory crowns. But Marlowe's own hyperbolic impetus had carried him as far as he could possibly go on the naïvely imperialistic plane. The next step he took, in whatever direction, would involve some kind of strategic retreat *pour mieux sauter.* Because his works were produced within so brief a span, we are not quite certain which of them came next. Each of them, however, introduces novelties of conception and execution which range them in a fairly logical order, proceeding from simplicity toward complexity and coinciding with the chronological sequence, as nearly as it can be inferred from the external evidence. *Tamburlaine,* the simplest, laid down the outline of a new dramat-

The Famous
TRAGEDY
OF
THE RICH IEVV
OF *MALTA.*

AS IT WAS PLAYD
BEFORE THE KING AND
QVEENE, IN HIS MAJESTIES
Theatre at *White-Hall,* by her Majesties
Servants at the *Cock-pit.*

Written by CHRISTOPHER MARLO,

LONDON;
Printed by *I. B.* for *Nicholas Vavasour,* and are to be sold
at his Shop in the Inner-Temple, neere the
Church, 1633.

Title page of the 1633 edition of The Jew of Malta.

ic genre, the tragedy of ambition—an ascending line propelled by the momentum of a single character, whose human relationships are incidental to his ulterior goal, and whose conflicts are literal, overt, and invariably successful. If Tamburlaine had been more evenly matched against other characters, if his victims had been presented more sympathetically, if his path had been crossed by more effectual foes, if Callapine rather than heaven had avenged the death of Bajazeth, *Tamburlaine* would have fitted into a more elaborate and conventional genre, the tragedy of revenge.

That form arrived, not long after *Tamburlaine,* with Marlowe's gloomy colleague, Thomas Kyd, and his *Spanish Tragedy.* It gave to the enlarging repertory a role of comparable stature and much greater emotional range; for, while Tamburlaine threatened and acted, it remained for Hieronimo to lament and suffer, to "shew a passion" [III.xiia.145]. While Tamburlaine was a superhuman antagonist, driven by some sort of inner urge, Hieronimo is more of a human protagonist, responding to the outer situation; but since he is rather the challenged than the challenger, it is the situation that predominates—the vendetta thrust upon him when his son is murdered while seeking to avenge a previous murder. While Marlowe had been

concerned with the individual who is a law unto himself, Kyd's concern was with the more general laws of God and man. *Tamburlaine* is an esthetic spectacle, framed by an equivocal morality, which is flouted more emphatically than it is asserted. *The Spanish Tragedy,* though it is intermittently heroic, is consistently ethical; in subordinating love and war to revenge, it measures private motives against public sanctions. To take the law into one's own hands may be "a kinde of Wilde Iustice," as Bacon defined it; but it implies an ethos, however primitive, which the hero imposes on others instead of rejecting. It was ambition that animated character, on the vast scale of Elizabethan drama; but it is revenge that motivates plot; and plot is the main thing, for technicians like Aristotle. For the Elizabethans, a plot was originally a piece of ground or the design of a house; and Shakespeare is fully conscious of the metaphor, when his plotters conspire in the second part of *Henry IV* [I.iii.42]. Thence the term was used more abstractly for any scheme, especially for a conspiracy against the established order, as when "the plot is laide" in *The Massacre at Paris* [l.165]. By a later extension, after many such intrigues had been hatched upon the stage, it was neutrally applied to the plan of a literary work.

Thus plot is a moral as well as a technical concept, which presupposes some responsible agent. As George Meredith, in *Modern Love,* discerned:

In tragic life, God wot,
No villain need be! Passions spin the plot:
We are betray'd by what is false within.

But when the heroine of *The Spanish Tragedy* cries out, "We are betraide" [II.iv.50], the hero is eminently justified in suspecting malice aforethought. So is Navarre, when the same cry goes up in *The Massacre at Paris* [l.202]. In short, we are in the presence of the villain—that ingenious theatrical figure who, by pulling the wires of the story, determines the structure of the play. Properly, his name has a low origin in the feudal term *villein,* a peasant or base fellow, which was easily transferred from a social to a moral context, and thence to the theater. The role that it stigmatizes is closely related to that of the Vice, the mischievous tempter in the moralities, or to the clever slaves and parasites who manipulated Roman comedy. Where Tamburlaine enacted the *Alazon* or proud man, your villain must enact the *Eiron* or sly man. The irony lies in the difference between his conduct upstage and his machinations behind the scenes, as it were. But what he conceals from the other characters must be revealed directly to the audience, and this convention tends to be less and less convincing. Thus Richard III, the Shakespearean heir of Marlovian invention, soliloquizes at his first appearance:

I am determined to proue a Villaine.

[I.i.30]

Life would be considerably less tragic, God wot, if villainy announced itself in such resounding tones. The villains of actuality are readier to invest themselves, like Tamburlaine, with the sense of a lofty mission. Few, if any, of them are cold-blooded hypocrites; what is false in our world is largely perpetrated by men who sincerely believe that it is true, and launch indignant countercharges at all who doubt the nobility of their intentions. The problem of evil would be no problem at all, if good and bad were clearly labeled in black and white. The difficulties of choice are the source of tragedy. "In the twilight," Jean-Paul Sartre has reminded us, "it takes sharp eyesight to distinguish God from the Devil." To Macbeth, confounding the colors of good and evil, fair seems foul and foul seems fair. When Othello puts his trust in honest Iago, it is the blackamoor who is truly noble, the white man who is blackhearted. Yet when Shakespeare attempted his first tragedy, *Titus Andronicus,* he explicitly painted his Moorish villain as black as the traditional devil. By the time he came to *Julius Cæsar,* he had acquired his comprehensive awareness of the endless jar between right and wrong. A contemporary witness, John Weever, tells us:

> The many-headed multitude were drawne
> By *Brutus* speach, that *Cæsar* was ambitious,
> When eloquent *Mark Antonie* had showne
> His vertues, who but *Brutus* then was vicious?

Antony's vices would be shown up by Octavius, with the next revolution of Fortune's wheel; and Brutus, retrospectively, could claim to have been revenging Pompey's death. The question of war guilt can be pushed back indefinitely, and the blood feud is handed on from one generation to another. So it goes, with ambition and revenge acting as stimulus and reacting as response. The rising and falling lines are crisscrossed and paralleled in a symmetrical pattern of motivation. Sympathies shift when the erstwhile villain is hailed as a fallen hero, or when the revenger turns out to be a villain. With the give-and-take of injuries, gore is bound to flow in ever-increasing amounts. The ethic of revenge is the *lex talionis,* the Mosaic code of an eye for any eye, a thumb for a thumb. On the grim but equable assumption that "blood asketh blood," *Gorboduc* sacrifices a life for a life, a Ferrex for a Porrex (IV, Chorus, 17). But to right a grievous wrong by retaliating is to provoke the loss of further lives. Furthermore, revengers usually try to better the instruction, as Shylock would, if not for the intervention of a more merciful kind of justice.

> Thou never dost enough revenge the wronge,
> Exept thou passe,

says Atreus in Jasper Heywood's translation of Seneca's *Thyestes;* and his cruelty to his brother's children is so surpassing that it brings down a curse upon the heads of his own. Warmed over by Shakespeare, it provides the cannibalistic catastrophe for *Titus Andronicus.* Though Kyd's Hieronimo is more punctilious, he cannot rest until he is "reuenged thorowly" [IV.iv.172]. And Kyd's Soliman, at a similar consummation, rejoices in having revenged a friend's death "with many deaths" [V.iv.148]—a total of thirteen in the play, *Soliman and Perseda,* as compared with eleven in *The Spanish Tragedy.* The fact that nine of the dramatis personæ do not survive the last act of *Hamlet* evinces Shakespeare's relative moderation. There are sixteen corpses in the two parts of *Tamburlaine,* not counting the casualty lists from the battlefields. Apart from the off-stage carnage in *The Massacre at Paris,* such as the hundred Huguenots drowned in the Seine, twenty characters

are killed *coram populo* during an unusually abbreviated play—an average of one killing for every sixty-three lines.

Numbers, at that rate, mean all too little; it is taken for granted that an Elizabethan tragedy will terminate in many deaths; there is more significance in the manner of them. Here the fine Italian hand of Machiavellianism is discernible; and *The Jew of Malta* is notable, not for its twelve fatalities—exclusive of the poisoned convent and the exploded monastery—but for the perverse ingenuity with which they are conceived and executed. Marlowe might well be expected to outdo Kyd's theatricalism, to sharpen the formula for the tragedy of revenge, to discipline its wallowing emotions by his ruthless intellectuality. But, in the process, he seems to have learned a good deal from *The Spanish Tragedy:* from its complicated plotting, its interplay of motive, and above all its moralistic tone. He was still too much of an intellectualist to let himself be constricted by this framework, and too much of a hero-worshiper to let his hero suffer very acutely. Barabas the Jew is a man with a grievance, but his retaliation outruns the provocation. His revenges, augmented by his ambitions, are so thoroughgoing that the revenger becomes a villain. He is not merely less sinned against than sinning; he is the very incarnation of sin, the scapegoat sent out into the wilderness burdened with all the sins that flesh inherits. *Tamburlaine* dealt with the world and the flesh, but not with the devil; that was to be the sphere of *Doctor Faustus.* Somewhere between the microcosm of *Doctor Faustus* and the macrocosm of *Tamburlaine* stands *The Jew of Malta.* Contrasted with the amoral Tamburlaine, Barabas is an immoralist, who acknowledges values by overturning them. Contrasted with the devil-worshiping Faustus, he is more consistently and more superficially diabolical. His is a test case for the worldly logic, if not for the spiritual consequences, of the Satanic decision: "Evil be thou my Good" (*Paradise Lost,* IV, 110).

In Shakespeare, as critics have noted, it is the villains who expound free will and take a skeptical view of planetary influences. In Marlowe the villains are heroes, by virtue—or perhaps we should say *virtù*—of their unwillingness to accept misfortune. As soon as he is left "to sinke or swim" [l.503], Barabas defies his "lucklesse Starres" [l.495]. Like Tamburlaine and the rest, he considers himself to be "fram'd of finer mold then common men" [l. 453]. His attitude toward others is that of Lorenzo, the villain of *The Spanish Tragedy:*

> Ile trust my selfe, my selfe shall be my freend.
> [III.ii.118]

This fundamental premise of egoism is stated even more incisively by Richard III:

> *Richard* loues *Richard,* that is, I am I.
> [V.iii.184]

Barabas makes the same affirmation, somewhat more deviously, by misquoting slightly from the *Andria* of Terence:

> *Ego mihimet sum semper proximus.*
> [l.228]

The articles of his credo have been more bluntly set forth

in the prologue, where Machiavel makes a personal appearance to bespeak the favor of the spectators for his protégé. It was a bold stroke, which undoubtedly thrilled them, with a different thrill from the one they felt at beholding Marlowe's resurrection of Helen of Troy. Marlowe based his speech on a Latin monologue by Gabriel Harvey, and both scholar-poets were in a position to know how grossly they distorted Machiavelli's doctrine and personality. Yet, in misrepresenting him, they voiced a state of mind which he anticipated and which Nietzsche would personify: the impatience with words and ideas, the special fascination with brutal facts, that marks the disaffected intellectual. Might could be right, snarls Machiavel, and fortification more important than learning. Marlowe must also have enjoyed the occasion for shocking the middle class, which wanted improving precepts from the drama. Instead, with Cæsarian flourishes and Draconian precedents, he propounds a series of maxims which Blake might have included in his "Proverbs of Hell." These reflect the English suspicions of popery and of other Italianate observances, recently intensified by the persecution of the French Protestants and by the indictment that Gentillet had itemized in his *Anti-Machiavel.*

> I count Religion but a childish Toy,
> And hold there is no sinne but Ignorance.
>
> [ll.14-15]

This last is a Machiavellian corollary to the Socratic equation of knowledge and virtue. As for religion, it is dismissed by Atheism with a peculiarly Marlovian monosyllable. Just as polysyllables are a means of aggrandizement, "toy"—which in Marlowe's day meant trifle or frivolity—is the ultimate in belittlement.

The Jew of Malta, continuing Marlowe's studies in *libido dominandi,* emphasizes conspiracy rather than conquest—or, in the terms laid down by *Tamburlaine,* policy rather than prowess. From the roaring of the lion we turn to the wiles of the fox. "Policy," the shibboleth of political realism, is mentioned thirteen times, and serves to associate Barabas with Machiavelli. Barabas is well qualified to speak for himself, speaking more lines than any of Marlowe's other characters, indeed, about half of the play. Whereas Machiavel has his "climing followers," they have theirs, from Tamburlaine's viceroys to Edward's favorites; and even Barabas, in his egoistic isolation, takes up with an alter ego. The knight of Lope de Vega has his *gracioso;* the rogue of the picaresque novel commonly squires a fellow-traveler; and Barabas the Jew finds a roguish accomplice in Ithamore, the Turkish slave. They are well aware, from their first encounter, of what they have in common: "we are villaines both . . . we hate Christians both" [ll.979-80]. Barabas announces another key-word when he asks Ithamore's profession, and the answer is "what you please" [l.931]. For "profession," like "vocation" or "calling," signified a way of life in a double sense: religious conviction and practical employment. The ambiguity is the key to much controversy, which dwelt with particular bitterness on what was known as "the profession of usury." Barabas confides to Ithamore what professions he has practiced, starting in Italy as a Machiavellian doctor who poisoned his patients, carrying on the self-appointed task of destruction as a military engineer in the wars of the Em-

pire, and reaching the climax of this protean and predatory career as "an Usurer." After mastering all the shady tricks of all the dubious trades, his culminating crime has been the taking of interest. Later we learn the percentage: "A hundred for a hundred" [l.1563].

The paradox of his notorious harangue is that it so crudely expresses a vaunted subtlety:

> As for my selfe, I walke abroad a nights
> And kill sicke people groaning under walls.
>
> [ll.939-40]

And, in the same vein of horrific gusto, further revelations are divulged. Reality is so callowly assailed that the modern reader thinks of the so-called comic books. These, we think, are the nightmares of spoiled children rather than the misdeeds of wicked men. Yet we know how audiences were impressed, and that Marlowe again was paid the compliment of imitation by Shakespeare. The parallel monologue of Aaron the Moor in *Titus Andronicus* throws light back upon *The Jew of Malta,* since it is wholly preoccupied with pointless mischief:

> Tut, I haue done a thousand dreadfull things
> As willingly, as one would kill a Fly.
>
> [V.i.141-42]

If this conveys any point, it is an echo from an earlier scene, where Titus objects to the killing of a fly. Though the cross-reference seems to bring out the worst in both Shakespeare and Marlowe, it manages to be characteristic of both. The real basis of distinction is that, while Aaron is merely gloating over his macabre practical jokes—including one which has been borrowed from an episode in *The Jew of Malta*—Barabas is trenchantly satirizing the professions and institutions of his day. In sketching such a violent self-portrait, he belatedly lives up to the introduction of his Florentine patron and departs from the tragic dignity that he has maintained throughout the opening scenes. There we hear the note of lamentation that we heard in the threnodies of *Tamburlaine;* but it has been transposed to the minor harmonics of the Old Testament, notably the Book of Job. When the three Jews fail to comfort Barabas, he invidiously compares himself with Job, who, after all, lost a less considerable fortune; and Marlowe even diminishes Job's five hundred yoke of oxen to two hundred.

> For onely I haue toyl'd to inherit here
> The months of vanity and losse of time,
> And painefull nights haue bin appointed me.
>
> [ll.429-31]

By catching the lilt—and, in this case, the very language—of the Bible, Marlowe has modulated and deepened his style. Barabas is lighted with scriptural grandeur at the beginning of the second act. There he is still in part what Edmund Kean was apparently able to make him: a sympathetic figure, the injured party about to seek redress, no Atheist but an anti-Christian praying to the wrathful deity of his tribe, a prophet imprecating the avenging Jehovah. The darkness of the night is accentuated by the flicker of his candle, and the heavy images are sustained by the tolling rhythms:

> Thus like the sad presaging Rauen that tolls

The sicke mans passeport in her hollow beake,
And in the shadow of the silent night
Doth shake contagion from her sable wings;
Vex'd and tormented runnes poore *Barabas*
With fatall curses towards these Christians.
The incertaine pleasures of swift-footed time
Haue tane their flight, and left me in despaire.

[ll.640-47]

This is an extraordinary departure from the swiftness and brightness of Tamburlaine's forensics. It has more in common with the speeches of Dr. Faustus—and with the lamenting Kyd, the infernal Seneca, the nocturnal *Macbeth*. Shakespeare's puzzling reference to "the School of Night" in *Love's Labour's Lost* [IV.iii.225] may indeed be a side glance at such rhetorical tendencies. But Marlowe looks upward, with the imprecations of Barabas:

Oh thou that with a fiery piller led'st
The sonnes of *Israel* through the dismall shades,
Light *Abrahams* off-spring.

[ll.651-53]

Marlowe was never more the devil's advocate than when he chose a wandering Jew for his hero. His working model was less a human being than a bugbear of folklore, inasmuch as the Jews were officially banished from England between the reign of Edward I and the protectorate of Oliver Cromwell. In certain regions of the Mediterranean, Jewish financiers and politicians had risen to power in the sixteenth century; and Marlowe, whose play has no literary source, must have come across anecdotes about them. In his selection of a name there is a deeper significance, for Barabbas was the criminal whom the Jews preferred to Jesus, when Pilate offered to release a prisoner. One of the witnesses against Marlowe's Atheism, Richard Baines, quotes his assertion: "That Crist deserved better to dy then Barrabas and that the Jewes made a good Choise, though Barrabas were both a thief and a murtherer." It could also be said that, if Christ died for all men, he died most immediately for Barabbas; and that Barabbas was the man whose mundane existence profited most immediately from Christ's sacrifice. From the perspective of historical criticism, Barabbas actually seems to have been an insurrectionist. Marlowe, in instinctively taking his side, identifies his Jew with the Antichrist. Hence the crude cartoon becomes an apocalyptic monstrosity, whose temporal kingdom is the earth itself. It is no idle jest when Ithamore remarks of Barabas: "The Hat he weares, *Iudas* left vnder the Elder when he hang'd himselfe" [ll.1988]. When Alleyn wore it with the accustomed gabardine, the red beard, and the hyperbolic nose, he must have seemed the exemplification of guile, acquisitiveness, and treachery.

Nature seemed to be imitating art when, a year after Marlowe's death, the Jewish physician, Roderigo Lopez, was executed for plotting against the Queen. This had some bearing on the success of the play; and, what is more, the play may have had some bearing on the outcome of the trial—where doubtful evidence was strengthened by prejudice. The animus that flared up on such occasions was kindled by the twofold circumstance that many Jews, forbidden to hold property, lived by trading in money; and that the profession of usury stood condemned by the orthodox tenets of Christianity. The gradual adaptation of Christian tenets to the rise of modern capitalism, through the diverging creeds of the Protestant Reformation, has been much scrutinized and debated by social historians. There seems to be little doubt that Jewish moneylenders, whose international connections enabled them to organize some of the earliest stock exchanges, performed an indispensable function in the developing European economy. The myth of the elders of Zion, controlling Europe from their treasuries, finds some degree of confirmation in Barabas.

Thus trowles our fortune in by land and Sea,

[l.141]

he exults, cognizant that this blessing of Abraham entails the curse of anti-Semitism.

Or who is honour'd now but for his wealth?

[l.151]

he retorts, to the assumption that there have been other standards. Yet, as a self-made merchant prince, he speaks not so much for his race as for his epoch—an epoch when consumption was more conspicuous than it had ever been before. This timeliness keeps him from being quite alien in mercantile England. Though Malta was not to be a British colony for more than two centuries, it occupied a strategic position on the old trade routes and in the new struggle for markets. The polyglot Maltese, descended from the Phoenicians, mixed in their Levantine melting pot with Italians and Spaniards, were mainly Semitic in blood and Latin in culture. On their island, if anywhere, East met West. The Knights Hospitallers of Saint John—formerly of Jerusalem—had settled at Malta when Rhodes fell to the Turks in 1522, and successfully held out when besieged in 1565, presumably the period of the drama. Their baroque capital, with its bastioned port, was both an outpost of Christendom and a citadel against Islam; but the spirit of the crusaders who founded it had yielded to the emergent interests of the merchant adventurers.

The starting point of the play is the exit of Machiavel, who pulls back the arras that curtains the inner stage and thereby discovers Barabas in his counting-house. We are not asked to believe that this shallow recess is anything more than concretely strikes the eye. This is a back-room, not the façade of a palace. True, the stage direction indicates heaps of coins; but we are less impressed by them than by Barabas' gesture of dismissal.

Fye; what a trouble tis to count this trash.

[l.42]

We are dazzled, not because riches are dangled before us, but because they are tossed aside; because precious stones are handled "like pibble-stones" [l.58]. Not that Barabas is indifferent to them; soon enough he makes it evident that gold is to him what the crown is to Tamburlaine, "felicity" [l.689]; and he completes that blasphemy by marking his buried treasure with the sign of the cross. But it vastly increases the scale of his affluence to reckon it up so dryly and casually. Barabas out-Herods Tamburlaine by making hyperboles sound like understatements; he values the least of his jewels at a king's ransom. His will to power is gratified less by possession than by control. In this he does not resemble the conqueror so much as he adumbrates the capitalist; and Marlowe has grasped what is truly imaginative, what in his time was almost heroic, about business enterprise. To audit bills of lading for Indian argosies, to project empires by double-entry bookkeeping, to enthrone and dethrone royalties by loans—that is indeed "a kingly kinde of trade" [l.2330]. In the succinct formulation of Barabas,

> Infinite riches in a little roome,
>
> [l.72]

Marlowe sublimates his expansive ideal from the plane of economics to that of esthetics. The line itself is perfect in its symmetry; each half begins with the syllable "in" and proceeds through antithetical adjectives to alliterative nouns; six of the ten vowels are short *i*'s; and nothing could be more Marlovian than the underlying notion of containing the uncontainable. It is hard to imagine how a larger amount of implication could be more compactly ordered within a single pentameter. Ruskin once categorically declared that a miser could not sing about his gold; James Russell Lowell, on the contrary, has described this line as "the very poetry of avarice"; and if that be a contradiction in terms, it matches the contradictions of Marlowe's theme.

To pursue this theme, *libido dominandi,* we now take the fox's path through the realms of high finance. Barabas warns us that it is more complex, if less spectacular, than the lion's path across the battlefield:

> Giue vs a peacefull rule, make Christians Kings,
> That thirst so much for Principality.
>
> [ll.172-73]

His policy spins a plot for **The Jew of Malta** which can be pursued on three interconnecting levels. The conventions of English drama prescribed an underplot, which is ordinarily a burlesque of the main plot; clowns are cast as servants and play the zany to their respective masters; and the stolen sheep is a symbolic counterpart of the infant Jesus in the *Second Shepherds' Play* of Wakefield. With the full development of tragedy, there is a similar ramification upwards, which might conveniently be called the overplot. That is the stuff of history as it impinges upon the more personal concerns of the characters; thus the events of *The Spanish Tragedy* are precipitated by wars between Spain and Portugal. Thus, with *Hamlet,* the overplot is conditioned by the dynastic relations of Denmark with Norway and Poland; while the main plot concentrates upon Hamlet's revenge against Claudius; and the underplot—which, in this instance, is more romantic than comic—has to do with the household of Polonius, and most particularly with Ophelia. **The Jew of Malta** is similarly constructed, and probably helped to fix this triple method of construction. The overplot, framed by the siege, is the interrelationship between the Christians and Jews, the Spaniards and Turks. It is connected with the main plot through the peculations of Barabas, who is caught up in the underplot through his misplaced confidence in Ithamore. The bonds of self-interest connect the central intrigue, which involves usury, with power politics upon the upper level and with blackmail upon the lower. Blackmail is the tax that Barabas pays on his ill-gotten hoards; but his rear-guard ac-

tions against the blackmailers are more successful than his efforts to beat the politicians at their own game.

Morally, all of them operate on the same level, and that is precisely what Marlowe is pointing out. In order to sell a cargo of Turkish slaves, the Spanish Vice-Admiral talks the Governor into breaking the treaty between Malta and the Turks. It is not merely in the slave market, but in the counting-house and the senate chamber, that men are bought and sold. As for the traffic in women, Ithamore becomes ensnared in it; soon after Barabas buys him, he falls into the hands of the courtesan Bellamira and her bullying companion, Pilia-Borza—whose name, meaning "pick-purse," denotes the least sinister of his activities. The confidence game that this nefarious couple practices on Barabas, through their hold over Ithamore, was known in the Elizabethan underworld as "crossbiting." By whatever name it goes, it reduces eroticism to chicanery; it debases Marlowe's *libido sentiendi* to its most ignoble manifestation. Ithamore addresses Bellamira as if she were Zenocrate or Helen of Troy, instead of a woman whose professional habit is to do the persuading on her own behalf. The invitation to love, as he extends it, is sweetened for vulgar tastes; the classical meadows of Epicureanism now "beare Sugar Canes"; and rhetorical enticements sink into bathos with a couplet which burlesques "The Passionate Shepherd":

> Thou in those Groues, by *Dis* aboue,
> Shalt liue with me and be my loue.
>
> [ll.1815-16]

The subversion of values is finally enunciated in **Tamburlaine** when, with the chorus of lesser Kings, "hell in heauen is plac'd" [l.4408]. Here the confusion that exalts to the skies the god of Hades, and of riches likewise, is a final commentary upon an ethos turned upside down. When everything is ticketed with its price—an eye, a thumb, man's honor, woman's chastity—values turn inevitably into prices. The beauty of Helen herself is devalued, a decade after Marlowe's apostrophe, with the epic degradation of *Troilus and Cressida:*

> Why she is a Pearle,
> Whose price hath launch'd aboue a thousand
>   Ships,
> And turn'd Crown'd Kings to Merchants.
>
> [II.ii.81-3]

The principle of double-dealing, which prevails on all sides in Malta, is established in the scene where the Governor summons the Jews to raise funds for the Turkish tribute. Distinguishing somewhat pharisaically between his profession and theirs, he offers the alternative of conversion, which none of them accepts. When he mulcts them of half their estates, the other Jews comply at once; and since Barabas refuses, his wealth is entirely confiscated. To him, therefore, his co-religionists are Job's comforters; yet, from the outset, his devotion has centered less on his race than on his selfish interests. He finds a justification in observing that Christians preach religion and practice opportunism.

> What? bring you Scripture to confirm your
>   wrongs?
> Preach me not out of my possessions.
>
> [ll.343-44]

From one of the Knights, he picks up the catchword that seems to explain the disparity between what they profess and what they really do:

> I, policie? that's their profession.
>
> [l.393]

In endeavoring to recover his lost fortune, he resolves to "make barre of no policie" [l.508]. He justifies his next stratagem on the grounds that "a counterfet profession" [l.531], his daughter's pretended conversion, is better than "vnseene hypocrisie," than the unexposed perfidies of professed believers. He admonishes his daughter that religion

> Hides many mischiefes from suspition.
>
> [l.520]

His cynicism seems altogether justified when the Knights break a double faith, refusing to pay the Turks the money they have seized for that purpose from Barabas. Their argument, the one that the Christians used in *Tamburlaine* when they violated their oath to their Mohammedan allies, proves a useful rationalization for Barabas:

> It's no sinne to deceiue a Christian;
> For they themselues hold it a principle,
> Faith is not to be held with Heretickes;
> But all are Hereticks that are not Iewes.
>
> [ll.1074-77]

Ithamore, going over to the other side, can quote this dangerous scripture against his master:

> To vndoe a Iew is a charity, and not sinne.
>
> [l.2001]

After the Christians have broken their league with the Turks, Barabas leagues with the Turks against the Knights. His fatal mistake is to betray his new allies to his old enemies, the Christians, by whom he thereupon is promptly betrayed. He is repaid in kind; but his Turkish victims have been comparatively honorable; and he ends as an inadvertent defender of Christendom. Meanwhile, by craftily pitting infidels against believers, one belief against another, fanaticism against Atheism, Marlowe has dramatized the dialectics of comparative religion.

Is there, then, no such thing as sincere devotion? Perhaps some unfortunate person, Barabas is willing to allow,

> Happily some haplesse man hath conscience.
>
> [l.157]

If so, he does not appear on the Maltese horizon. But by chance, by that ironic destiny which Thomas Hardy calls "hap," there is one woman,

> one sole Daughter, whom I hold as deare
> As *Agamemnon* did his *Iphigen*.
>
> [ll.175-76]

Though Agamemnon is less relevant than Jephtha might have been, the simile is an omen for Abigall, the single disinterested character in the play, who is characterized by the first four words she speaks: "Not for my selfe . . . " [l.462]. Her father lovingly repeats her name as David repeated the name of Absalom. His policy dictates her profession, when in filial duty she reënters his former house, which has been converted into a nunnery. When she rec-

ognizes that she has been the unwitting instrument of his revenge, "experience, purchased with griefe," opens her eyes to "the difference of things" [l.1285]. She now experiences a genuine vocation, perceiving that

> there is no loue on earth,
> Pitty in Iewes, nor piety in Turkes.
>
> [ll.1270-71]

By taking the veil, she extinguishes the latent spark of tenderness in Barabas, who retaliates by poisoning all the nuns. Stricken, she has the moral satisfaction of confessing that she dies a Christian. But the pathos of these last words is undercut by the cynical dictum of her confessor:

> I, and a Virgin too, that grieues me most.
>
> [l.1497]

Abigall's honesty, in the Elizabethan sense of chastity as well as sincerity, is confirmed by her death; but she finds no sanctuary among the religious. Her innocent lover, Don Mathias, has been slain while slaying the Governor's son, Don Lodowick, in a duel contrived by the vengeful Barabas. This contrivance gives a Marlovian twist to one of the strangest obsessions of the European consciousness, the legend of the Jew's daughter, who serves as a decoy in luring a Christian youth to his doom by her father's knife in their dark habitation: The story is deeply rooted in those accusations of ritual murder, which seem to result from misunderstandings of the Jewish Passover rite, and have left a trail of bloodier revenges—across whole countries and over many centuries—than could ever be comprehended within the theatrical medium. Created out of hatred to warrant pogroms, thousands of lurid effigies swing behind Barabas; and Abigall's sacrifice is one of millions, which have not yet atoned for the Crucifixion. In medieval versions the martyrdom commonly flowers into a miracle, as in the ballad of Hugh of Lincoln or the tale of Chaucer's Prioress [in *The Canterbury Tales*]. The latter points an old moral, "Mordre wol out," which is expressly rejected by Marlowe's Machiavel:

> Birds of the Aire will tell of murders past;
> I am asham'd to heare such fooleries.
>
> [ll.16-17]

But Barabas invokes the birds of the air, the raven before and the lark after Abigall has aided him to regain his moneybags. The night scene, in its imagery and staging, curiously foreshadows the balcony scene in *Romeo and Juliet*. When Abigall—who, like Juliet, is "scarce 14 yeares of age" [l.621]—appears on the upper stage, Barabas exclaims:

> But stay, what starre shines yonder in the *East*?
> The Loadstarre of my life, if *Abigall*.
>
> [ll.680-81]

When Shakespeare copies this picture, he brightens it, in accordance with the more youthful and ardent mood of Romeo:

> But soft, what light through yonder window
>   breaks?
> It is the East, and *Iuliet* is the Sunne.

[II.ii.2-3]

There is another moment which looks ahead to Shakespeare's romantic tragedy; and that comes after the duel, when the Governor eulogizes the rival lovers and promises to bury them in the same monument. If this midpoint had been the ending, the drama might have retained its equilibrium; there would have been enough grievances and sufferings on both sides. With the disappearance of the fragile heroine and of the lyrical touches that cluster about her, tragedy is overshadowed by revenge. But we might have realized, when Abigall introduced herself to the Abbess as

> The hopelesse daughter of a haplesse Iew,
>
> [1.557]

that Marlowe was shaping his play by the sterner conventions of *The Spanish Tragedy* and Kyd's Hieronimo,

> The hopeles father of a hapless Sonne.
>
> [IV.iv.84]

Between revenge and romance, between tragedy and comedy, *The Merchant of Venice* provides a Shakespearean compromise. It gives the benediction of a happy ending to the legend of the Jew's daughter; and it allows the Jewish protagonist, for better or for worse, his day in court. Legalism both narrows and humanizes Shylock, in contradistinction to Barabas, who for the most part lives outside the law and does not clamor for it until it has overtaken him. In rounding off the angles and mitigating the harshness of Marlowe's caricature, Shakespeare loses something of its intensity. The mixed emotions of Shylock, wailing, "O my ducats, O my daughter" [II.viii.15], are muted by being reported at second hand. We see and hear, we recall and recoil from the unholy joy of Barabas:

> Oh girle, oh gold, oh beauty, oh my blisse!
>
> [1.695]

If the comparison is not with Shakespeare but with Marlowe's earlier writing, *The Jew of Malta* registers enormous gains in flexibility. Except when Barabas mutters to himself in a *lingua franca* of Spanish and Italian, the diction is plainer and much saltier. The average length of an individual speech is no more than 2.8 lines, as differentiated from the second part of *Tamburlaine,* where it runs to 6.3. This implies, theatrically speaking, more than twice as many cues in the later play, with a consequent thickening of the dialogue and a general quickening of the action. It follows that there are fewer monologues, although Barabas delivers a number of them—in that Biblical vein which transforms the basic modes of Tamburlaine's rhetoric, the threat and the plea, into the curse, the jeremiad, the prophecy. The Prophets had spoken English blank verse in Greene and Lodge's *Looking-Glass for London,* as had the Psalmist in Peele's *David and Bethsabe.* But *The Jew of Malta* requires some means of private comment, as well as public speech, to express the cross-purposes between policy and profession, deeds and words. It leans much more upon the soliloquy, which the extroverted Tamburlaine hardly needed, and its characteristic mode is the aside. Marlowe did not invent this simplistic device; actors had voiced their thoughts to audiences before they had exchanged them with each other; and characterization of the

villain was, for obvious reasons, peculiarly dependent upon that convention. It could not be disregarded by a playwright who had to guide introverted characters through the Machiavellian province of false declarations and unvoiced intentions. *"I must dissemble,"* says Barabas [1.1556], and the italics alert the reader to what the spectator feels when the spoken words are aimed at him in a stage whisper. The actor is professionally a dissembler, etymologically a hypocrite. The histrionics of Barabas are not confined to his role in the disguise of a French musician. Except for his unwarranted confidences to his daughter and to his slave, he is always acting, always disguised. We, who overhear his asides and soliloquies, are his only trustworthy confidants. We are therefore in collusion with Barabas. We revel in his malice, we share his guilt. We are the "worldlings" to whom he addresses himself [1.2332].

This understanding is the framework of Marlowe's irony. When Barabas is first interrogated by the Knights, his replies are deliberately naïve; we know that he knows what they want from him; but he dissembles his shrewdness, plays the *Eiron,* and fences with the Governor. Often he utters no more than a line at a time, and engages in stichomythy—in capping line for line—with his interlocutors. Repartee is facilitated by Marlowe's increasing willingness to break off a speech and start upon another at the cæsura, without interrupting the rhythm of the blank verse. Speeches of less than a line are still rather tentative, and prose is a more favorable climate than verse for the cultivation of pithy dialogue. Possibly the most striking advance beyond *Tamburlaine* is the transition from a voluble to a laconic style, from Ciceronian periods to Senecan aphorisms. Effects depend, not upon saying everything, but upon keeping certain things unsaid. The climax of ironic dissimulation comes with the scene where the two Friars "exclaime against" Barabas [1.1502]. In their association with the nuns, Marlowe has lost no opportunity for anticlerical innuendo; now the "two religious Caterpillers" hold the upper hand over Barabas, since they have learned of his crimes from the dying Abigall; but since they are bound by the seal of confession, they cannot lodge a downright accusation. He has both these considerations in mind, as do we, when he parries their hesitating denunciations.

> Thou art a—,
>
> [1.1539]

says one Friar; and Barabas admits what is common knowledge, that he is a Jew and a usurer.

> Thou hast committed—,
>
> [1.1549]

says the other, and again the admission is an evasion:

> Fornication? but that was in another Country:
> And besides, the Wench is dead.
>
> [ll.1550-51]

For anyone else there might be, for others there have been, romance and even tragedy in the reminiscence. For Barabas it is simply an alibi, a statute of limitations. He is content to remind the Friars, with a legalistic shrug, that the Seventh Commandment is not to be taken as seriously as the Sixth. Deploring his callousness, we are tempted to admire his cheerful candor, and are almost touched by the emotional poverty of his life.

At this impasse he takes the initiative, with the dissembling announcement that he stands ready to be converted. His renunciation is actually a temptation, to which the Friars easily succumb, enticed by his Marlovian catalogue of the worldly goods he professes to renounce.

> Ware-houses stuft with spices and with drugs,
> Whole Chests of Gold, in *Bulloine,* and in
> Coyne . . .
> All this I'le giue to some religious house.
>
> [ll.1573-84]

Pretending to be persuaded, it is he who persuades and they who do the courting. Their courtship is the most grotesque of Marlowe's variations on the tune of "Come live with me and be my love." The vistas of opulence that Barabas has just exhibited contrast with the cheerless asceticism of their monkish vows. While Barabas ironically aspires toward grace, they fall into the trap of worldliness that he has so lavishly baited for them.

> You shall conuert me, you shall haue all my
> wealth,
>
> [l.1590]

he tells one. Whereupon the other tells him,

> Oh *Barabas,* their Lawes are strict . . .
> They weare no shirts, and they goe bare-foot too,
> [ll.1591-93]

and is told in turn,

> You shall confesse me, and haue all my goods.
> [l.1595]

By playing off one monastic order against the other, he divides and conquers. He murders one Friar and pins the blame on the other, with a threadbare trick which Marlowe may have encountered in a jestbook. The fact that the same trick occurs in a play of Thomas Heywood's, *The Captives,* plus the fact that Heywood sponsored the publication of **The Jew of Malta,** have led some commentators to infer that he may have added these scenes to Marlowe's play. It would seem more probable that **The Jew of Malta** influenced *The Captives.* Clearly it influenced *Titus Andronicus,* where the jest of a leaning corpse is mentioned by Aaron in his imitative monologue. Since we owe the text of **The Jew of Malta** to Heywood's quarto of 1633, published more than forty years after the drama was written, it may well have been retouched here and there. But the Friars are integral to Marlowe's design; Abigall's death would go unrevenged without them, and Machiavel's contempt for the clergy would go undemonstrated. Furthermore, in the canon of Heywood's extant works, there is no passage which is comparably sharp in tone or audacious in matter. Closer affinities might be sought in the sardonic tragicomedy of Marston or in the baroque tragedy of Webster.

It seems wiser—and is certainly more rewarding—to accept **The Jew of Malta** as an artistic whole, noting its incongruities and tensions, than to take the easy course of ruling them out as interpolations by a later hand. Criticism is warranted in stressing the disproportion between the two halves of the play; but the very essence of Marlowe's art, to sum it up with a Baconian phrase, is "strangenesse in the proportions." The "extreme reuenge" [l.1265] of Barabas runs away with the play, egregiously transcending the norms of vindictiveness; but it is the nature of the Marlovian protagonist to press whatever he undertakes to its uttermost extreme. As Barabas progresses, the Old Testament recedes into the background, and the foreground is dominated by *The Prince.* Effortlessly, his losses of the first act are made good by the second; and the third repays, with compound interest, his grudge against the Governor. Here, with the disaffection of Abigall, he abandons any claim upon our sympathy and vies with his new accomplice, Ithamore, in the *quid pro quo* of sheer malignity. In the fourth act he is blackmailed, not only by Bellamira and her bravo, but by the pair of Friars. His countermeasures lead him, in the fifth act, upward and onward into the realms of the higher blackmail, where Turks demand tribute from Christians and Christians from Jews.

> Why, was there euer seene such villany.
> So neatly plotted, and so well perform'd?
> [ll.1220-21]

Ithamore asks the audience. Yet who should know, better than he, that the performance of each plot somehow leaves a loose end? Murder is not postponed from act to act, as it is in the bungling *Arden of Feversham;* rather, as in a well-conducted detective story, every crime is its own potential nemesis. Barabas does not count on Abigall's love for Mathias when he calculates the killing of Lodowick. He does away with her and her sister religionists without expecting the Friars to inherit his guilty secret. When he silences them, he comes to grips with the complicity of Ithamore and with the extortions of Pilia-Borza. In settling their business, he incriminates himself; and, though he survives to betray the entire island, his next and final treason is self-betrayal.

To show the betrayer betrayed, the engineer hoist in his petard, the "reaching thought" [l.455] of Barabas overreached, is the irony of ironies. Marlowe's stage management moves toward a *coup de théâtre,* a machine which is worthy of all the machination that has gone before. Barabas can kill with a poisoned nosegay, can simulate death with "Poppy and cold mandrake juyce" [l.2083], and—thrown to the vultures from the walls of the town—can let the enemy in through the underground vaults, the subterranean corridors of intrigue. His hellish broth for the nuns is brewed from the recipes of the Borgias, seasoned with "all the poysons of the Stygian poole" [l.1405], and stirred with imprecations from the classics. "Was euer pot of Rice porredge so sauc't?" comments Ithamore [l.1409]. The sauce of the jest is that poetic justice takes, for Barabas, the shape of a boiling pot. He is shown *"aboue"*—from which coign of vantage he likes to look down on the havoc he engineers—*"very busie"* in his "dainty Gallery" [l.2316], explaining his cable and trapdoor to the Governor. When the signal is given, and the monastery blown up with the Turks inside, it is Barabas who falls through the trap. The curtain below is flung open, *"A Caldron discouered,"* and in it Barabas fuming and hissing his last. He implores the Christians to help him, but they are "pittilesse" [l.2354]. Once he merely professed "a burning zeale" [l.850], but now he feels "the extremity of heat" [l.2371]. He dies cursing. The steaming caldron in which he expires, like the "hell-mouth" of ***Doctor Faustus,*** was a property in the lists of Alleyn's company. But, like the human pie in *Titus Andronicus,* today it excites more ridicule than terror. In the age of *Macbeth,* however, a caldron was no mere object of domestic utility. It was the standard punishment for the poisoner. It had betokened a city of abomination in the flaming vision of Ezekiel. And in the *Emblems* of Geoffrey Whitney, printed in 1586, it illustrates the humbling of aspiration and amplifies the gospel of Luke (xviii, 14), *Qui se exaltat, humiliabitur:*

> The boyling brothe, aboue the brinke doth swell,
>   And comes to naughte, with falling in the fire:
> So reaching heads that thinke them neuer well,
> Doe headlong fall, for pride hathe ofte that hire:
>   And where before their frendes they did dispise,
> Nowe beinge falne, none helpe them for to rise.

Barabas stews in the juice of his tragic pride, foiled and foiled again, like the melodramatic villain he has become. Malta is preserved; murder will out; crime does not pay; the reward of sin is death; vengeance belongs to the Lord. This is exemplary but commonplace doctrine, and we have clambered through a labyrinth to reach it. Can Machiavel's introductory proverbs of hell be conclusively refuted by such copybook didacticism? Barabas is a consistent Machiavellian when, at the very pinnacle of his career, he soliloquizes on Turks and Christians:

> Thus louing neither, will I liue with both,
> Making a profit of my policie.
>   [ll.2213-14]

The words "live" and "love" jingle strangely amid this concentration of cold antipathy. Yet they are in character—or rather, Barabas steps out of it at the crisis, when he willfully departs from the teaching of his master. Machiavelli, in his chapter on cruelty and pity, had counseled: "Both dowbtlesse are necessarie, but seinge it is harde to make them drawe both in one yoake, I thinke it more safetie (seinge one must needes be wantinge) to be feared then loved, for this maybe boldlie sayde of men, that they are vngratefull, inconstante, discemblers, fearefull of dayngers, covetous of gayne." This may unquestionably be said of Barabas, and he is all too painfully conscious of it; he is conscious of being hated, and wants to be loved. To be loved—yes, that desire is his secret shame, the tragic weakness of a character whose wickedness is otherwise unflawed. His hatred is the bravado of the outsider whom nobody loves, and his revenges are compensatory efforts to supply people with good reasons for hating him. Poor Barabas, poor old rich man! That he should end by trusting anybody, least of all the one man who wronged him in the beginning! He has authority now, but Malta hates him. Instead of playing upon the fear of the islanders, he proposes to earn their gratitude by ridding them of the Turks. As Governor, he is anxious to make his peace with the former Governor, to whom he says: "Liue with me" [l.2192]. It is worse than a crime, as Talleyrand would say; it is a blunder.

The original miscalculation of Barabas was his failure to reckon with love. Then Abigall, sincerely professing the vows she had taken before out of policy, declared that she had found no love on earth. Having lost her, holding himself apart from the "multitude" of Jews, Barabas must be his own sole friend: "I'le looke vnto my selfe" [l.212]. Yet he would like to win friends; he needs a confidant; and for a while he views Ithamore, much too trustingly, as his "second self" [l.1317]. It is the dilemma of *unus contra mundum,* of the egoist who cannot live with others or without them. Since he conspires against them, they are right to combine against him; but their combinations frequently break down, for each of them is equally self-centered.

> For so I liue, perish may all the world.
>   [l.2292]

When every man looks out for himself alone and looks with suspicion on every other man, the ego is isolated within a vicious circle of mutual distrust. The moral of the drama could be the motto of Melville's *Confidence-Man,* "No Trust." Without trust, sanctions are only invoked to be violated; men live together, not in a commonwealth, but in an acquisitive society, where they behave like wolves to their fellow men. Barabas, who is fond of comparing himself to various beasts of prey, announces in his most typical aside:

> Now will I shew my selfe to haue more of the Serpent
> Then the Doue; that is, more knaue than foole.
>   [ll.797-98]

This is taking in vain the injunction of Jesus, when he sent forth the Apostles "as sheepe in the middest of wolues" (Matthew, x, 16). They were enjoined to remain as innocent as doves, but also to become as wise as serpents, so that they might distinguish between vice and virtue. Bacon amplified this precept in his *Meditationes Sacræ,* but in his career he did not exemplify it very happily. The innocence of the dove can scarcely preserve itself unless it is armed with the wisdom of the serpent; but it is difficult to acquire such worldly wisdom without being somewhat corrupted in the process. *Columbinus serpens: serpentina columba,* by whichever name Gabriel Harvey designates that hybrid creature, it is engendered in the humanist's mind by the crossbreeding of innocence and experience. Experience, as the dovelike Abigall discovers, is purchased with grief. The serpentine Barabas, too, comes to grief; and the difference between his caldron and Tamburlaine's chariot, between feeling pain and inflicting it, may well betoken Marlowe's advancing experience in the ways of the world. He is awakening to a vision of evil, though he innocently beholds it from the outside. The devil obligingly identifies himself by wearing horns and a tail.

But the devil is no diabolist; he sees through himself; he knows that men have invented him to relieve themselves of responsibility for those woes of the world which the Governor attributes to "inherent sinne" [l.342]. The devil's disciple, Machiavel, holds that there is no sin but ignorance; and Machiavel's disciple, Barabas, prefers the role of the knave to that of the fool. Thus, in letting other knaves get the better of him, he commits the only sin in his calendar, the humanistic peccadillo of folly. He acts out the Erasmian object lesson of a scoundrel who is too clever for his own good, the cheater cheated, wily beguiled. In getting out of hand, his counterplots exceeded the proportions of tragedy, and his discomfiture is more like the happy endings of melodrama. T. S. Eliot endows the play with a kind of retrospective unity by interpreting it as a comedy, a "farce of the old English humour." Though the interpretation is unhistorical, it has the merit of placing **The Jew of Malta** beside the grotesquerie of Dickens and Hogarth and—most pertinently—Ben Jonson's *Volpone, or the Fox.* Jonson's comedy of humours begins where Marlowe's tragedy of humours leaves off; Volpone and Mosca continue the misadventures of Barabas and Ithamore; and the Fox of Venice has learned not a few of his tricks from the Jew of Malta. The atmosphere of both plays is conveyed, and both playwrights are linked together, by a couplet upon an earlier comic dramatist which Jonson revised from Marlowe's translation of Ovid:

> Whil'st Slaues be false, Fathers hard, & Bauds
> be whorish,
> Whilst Harlots flatter, shall *Menander* flourish.
> [I.xv.17-18]

The hard-bitten types of New Comedy are perennially recognizable: miser, impostor, parasite, prostitute. Whether in Malta or Venice, Athens or London, their outlook is always a street and never a landscape. Social intercourse is, for them, a commercial transaction; self-interest is the universal motive; everything, every man's honesty and every woman's, has its price; all try to sell themselves as dearly, and to buy others as cheaply, as possible. The moral issue is the simple choice between folly and knavery—in Elizabethan terms, the innocence of the gull and the wisdom of the coney-catcher. The distance between these extremes, as **The Jew of Malta** demonstrates, can be precariously narrow. Barabas, for all his monstrous activism, inhabits a small and static world. Though Marlowe would not be Marlowe without a cosmic prospect, he seems to be moving centripetally through a descending gyre toward a core of self-imposed limitation. But, even as potentialities seem to be closing in, actualities are opening up. The room is little, the riches are infinite. (pp. 56-80)

> *Harry Levin, in his* The Overreacher: A Study of Christopher Marlowe, *Cambridge, Mass.: Harvard University Press, 1952, 204 p.*

EDWARD II

CRITICAL COMMENTARY

Robert Fricker   (essay date 1953)

[*A Swiss scholar and educator, Fricker has written a number of books on English drama, covering the period from Elizabethan to modern times. In the following*

The troublesome
raigne and lamentable death of
Edward *the second, King of*
England: with the tragicall
fall of proud Mortimer:

As it was sundrie times publiquely acted
in the honourable citie of London, by the
right honourable the Earle of Pembrooke his seruants.

Written by Chri. Marlow *Gent.*

Imprinted at London for *William Iones*
dwelling neere Holbourne conduit, at the
signe of the Gunne. 1694.

Title page from an early edition of Edward the Second.

essay, Fricker offers a scene-by-scene analysis of Edward II, *claiming that this work represents a significant advance in Marlowe's dramatic method. Unlike the earlier plays, which link together various episodes around a dominant central figure,* Edward II, *the critic argues, features a cohesive plot structure involving several characters engaged in a unified action. Fricker uses act, scene, and line references from the H. B. Charlton and R. D. Waller edition of* Edward II *(1933).*]

It has been generally recognised that the structure of Marlowe's chronicle play [**Edward II**] differs from that of his other dramas in many respects, but the question in what exactly this difference consists, has not been thoroughly examined so far. [Paul H.] Kocher, in his valuable biographical interpretation of Marlowe's work [*Christopher Marlowe, a Study of his Thought, Learning, and Character*], sees it in, and explains it by, the growing interest of the poet in the human world outside his ego which led him to abandon the one-man structure of **Tamburlaine** and, first, to take into consideration the ethical code and the religious opinions of this world and, secondly, to extend his sympathy to a number of other dramatis personae. In its ultimate result this opinion coincides with the one offered by Charlton and Waller in the introduction to their edition of *Edward II,* but they explain the change of Marlowe's technique not by a corresponding development of his character but by the example set by his contemporary and disciple Shakespeare in *2* and *3 Henry VI,* which made him rely less on 'transport and rhetoric' than on 'the interplay of human character'.

Both explanations of the same phenomenon may be right, and each ultimately rests on a hypothesis, the hypothesis namely that Marlowe—like a romantic poet and unlike what seems to have been the attitude of the Elizabethan playwrights—expressed himself through his work so that his plays may be regarded as the mirror of his thought, and on the hypothesis that Shakespeare wrote his chronicle plays before Marlowe created his *Edward II.* The aim of this paper is not to discuss the question whether the change of dramatic technique in *Edward II* was the result either of the development of Marlowe's character or of the influence of Shakespeare, but to investigate some aspects of the dramatic method which he used in this play. I shall be less concerned with Marlowe's verse and his character-drawing than with the structure of the play, though in a highly organic work of art like *Edward II,* the three aspects are inextricably mixed and cannot be completely isolated from one another. The study of the verse and the characters should therefore yield results similar to those obtained by the study of the structure of the play.

The dramatic method which Marlowe used in his other plays may be roughly summed up in the following way: he juxtaposed a number of episodes which form the body of the drama, and linked them together by the figure of the hero, which he represented by means of either a lyrical portrait as in *Tamburlaine* or, as in *Doctor Faustus,* a spiritual conflict which is clearly separated from the rest of the play. The different episodes are further connected by their causal relationship as in *The Jew,* where Barabas revenges himself on the Governor through the death of the latter's son and then tries to rid himself of those who know about the part he played in the duel between Lodowick and Matthias; or by a common religious and political interest as in *The Massacre,* where the play deals with the struggle between the Catholics and the Huguenots.

Thus the principle of the construction of these plays is rather juxtaposition than subordination to a central idea or motif, although the will to create a whole can be felt even in *Tamburlaine.* But, in his earlier dramas, Marlowe never achieved the impression of unity by the handling of the plot; he rather achieved it by the dominant position he gave to the hero. The impression is left that character and plot exist side by side and do not completely explain each other. Nowhere is the character fused into the action of the play and revealed by the action alone. There still remains a part of his portrait which is not, and cannot be, expressed by the plot and therefore exists for its own sake.

This is no longer the case, however, in *The Massacre,* where the Guise's aspirations are purely political and are completely absorbed by the drama. [Frederick S.] Boas was the first to insist on the importance of this play because it represents in many respects a precedent to *Edward II* [see Further Reading]. He limits his observations, however, to parallels between characters and to verbal echoes,

whereas the relationship includes the structure of the plays: *The Massacre* shows the same merging of the character into the plot, the violent clash between the hero (Guise) and at least one antagonist (Henry III) which leads to the death of both, and the high speed of the action. But this play—leaving aside the question of the artistic level—still falls into two episodes, the massacre and the struggle between the Guise and Henry III, and the only links between them—the figure of the hero and the politico-religious nature of the conflict—are not strong enough to make it an organic whole. *Edward II* possesses the dramatic qualities of the earlier play without sharing its weaknesses, and it has the further advantage that it is preserved in a good text.

Most readers will find it difficult to get a clear idea of the plot of the other plays, whereas it is comparatively easy to sum up the action of *Edward II* it is the struggle between a king and his peers about a minion, which leads to the latter's death and is followed, first, by the king's revenge and, secondly, by the struggle for power carried on by his antagonist which ends with the death of both the hero and his adversary. This clear outline of the plot is the result of the envisagement and subsequent handling of the material not as a series of episodes but as a whole. Marlowe did not merely condense the material which he found in Holinshed and other chroniclers with a view to reducing the events of 23 years to the 'two hours traffic of the stage', but he selected only those episodes which fitted into the pattern of the play as he conceived it, bound them together and gave prominence to certain minor characters, while he rejected other events which would have made excellent theatre. He eliminated all that would have spoilt his design, namely the prolonged conflict lifting up now the king and now the barons, while it inevitably draws to its tragical conclusion.

This pattern differs widely from that of the other plays where the hero, as in *Tamburlaine* and *The Jew,* inflicts a series of defeats on those who successively oppose him, and finally is either 'hoist with his own petar' or meets with his accidental or tragical fate. In *The Massacre* alone the Guise is defeated by a human antagonist; his death is not, however, the result of the development of a uniform action, but is dealt out to him by a man who rises to eminence only in the second half of the play and only at the end identifies himself with the religious and political forces against which the Guise has spent his fury. Nor is Henry of Navarre his antagonist in the proper sense of the word; although he represents the party hostile to him, he is not the direct cause of his overthrow and his character is too dimly conceived for this part. In *Edward II* the man and the cause are identical from the beginning, and for the first time in Marlowe's plays the hero is confronted with an enemy of equal stature, namely Mortimer, who, as will be shown by the analysis, fully deserves this title.

The play opens, not with a clamorous state scene or the aftermath of a pitched battle as in *2* and *3 Henry VI,* but with Gaveston's soliloquy, which is skilfully broken in the middle by a dramatic passage. This quiet and strictly personal opening is significant in that it prepares the way for a play which is not concerned with political issues and warlike events alone, but with private and intimate relations as well that will lead to actions in the heroic sphere. At the same time this opening focuses our interest on the man who is the object of strife and the cause of the hero's tragical overthrow. With the exception of this scenic section Gaveston remains in the background of the play; his is a passive part and his activity is limited to being banished, recalled and hunted to death, and to cynical sallies of his Gascon wit. Marlowe reveals his character only so far as it concerns the King, to whom he is devoted, though his devotion is not free from egoistical motives. His treatment of the three Poor Men shows that he does not care for the people, whom he considers only so far as they serve his selfish interests. His thoughts are centred in the King

> . . . upon whose bosom let me die,
> And with the world be still at enmity.
> [I.i.14-5]

In order to remain in his lord's favour he will gladly risk the hatred of all other men, and he will separate the King from them by his love. In the second part of his soliloquy he gives free rein to the sensuous imagination with which he will satisfy Edward's craving for 'music and poetry'. It is just the kind of entertainment he describes here that fascinates the King, and it is important that we should recognise the dramatic function of this soliloquy because it silences the possible objection that nowhere in the play does Marlowe give any reason for the infatuation of the King. The principle of economy which Marlowe observes strictly in this drama, is responsible for the fact that this is the only place where he introduces any motive. The comparative amplitude of the passage—one of the very few descriptions in *Edward II*—is fully justified by its dramatic function.

On this quiet introductory section of the first scene which, translated into musical terms, might be called sostenuto, follows the violent clash between the king and his rebellious peers which, for all its conciseness, recalls the numerous scenes of this kind in the first chronicle plays of Shakespeare. Here Edward shows his headstrong character and professes his determination to have his will and Gaveston. Among his opponents the interest at once concentrates on the young Mortimer who, by his impetuous temperament and craving for immediate action, resembles Richard, the later Duke of Gloucester, in *3 Henry VI*.

This rapid and stormy section of I, i is followed by the meeting of the two friends. The king has his wish and feels he has reached the height of bliss. Transported as they are they take to swift action and mishandle the Bishop of Coventry who was the main cause of Gaveston's banishment. By ill-treating the spiritual peer they add fuel to the fury of the nobles whose cause slowly gathers impetus in I, ii. The speed of the counteraction, however, is checked by the short intervention of the Queen who, siding with her husband, acts as a clog and, at the same time, prepares us for the part she is to play later on.

The controlled movement of this scene is interrupted by the ironic thumbnail sketches of the nobles which Gaveston gives in I, iii. After this brief suspense, and rendered more effective by it, I, iv begins at top speed: the peers hurriedly put their signatures to the order banishing the favourite. The counteraction thus reaches a first culminating point, and by its concentrated power and momentum the two friends are separated, the King being forced to sign the order. Edward who had his will in the first scene now has to bow to the barons; but he is not prepared to brook the insult and it is he who keeps the action going through the Queen. He threatens not to acknowledge her as his wife if she does not succeed in making the peers recall Gaveston. So she sets about accomplishing this difficult task. It is the young Mortimer whom she selects among the nobles to plead for her cause and through him she effects the recall of the King's minion. Thus this scene witnesses, in its first half, the triumph of the antagonists and, in the second half, the swift rise of the hero to a state of generosity and glad expectancy. At the end of act I the dramatic struggle seems to be decided in his favour.

The dialogue of the two Mortimers which ends the scene, and II, i where Baldock and Spencer make up their minds to offer their services to Gaveston, and the King's niece expects the return of her betrothed, mark the time which elapses between his sailing to Ireland and his return. It is a period of political inactivity—although Mortimer Senior departs for the Scottish wars—and a lull in the movement of the drama, the interest being shifted to the private sphere of life. A minimum of tension is preserved, however, by the aristocratic pride of the young Mortimer, who emphasizes his determination not to 'yield to any such upstart' and 'dapper Jack so brisk' as Gaveston. Rebellion is still smouldering.

The tension becomes more acute in II, ii where Edward impatiently expects his minion, while the nobles vent their hatred of Gaveston. The latent conflict at once explodes into open hostility after the King has saluted his friend. It is the lords who take the initiative and Mortimer who, first, wounds Gaveston and then forces his way into the King's presence to denounce his disastrous foreign policy. Thus, from a complete lull, the counter-action breaks out in its most violent form. Compared to the similar situation in I, iv the development of the play is marked by the change from threats and more or less peaceful means to immediate action and war. The section of this scene which is devoted to the open conflict is again followed by one of comparative quiet: after the indignant Kent has left his brother, Baldock and Spencer are accepted into Edward's service, and the King thinks not of war but of the marriage of Gaveston to his niece. The interest once more shifts to the private sphere of life and the tempo slackens.

Action is resumed with increasing speed in the following scenes (II, iii—III, i): they sketch the renewed and successful attempt of the barons to separate the King from his minion—this time not by written order but by an act of force. The assault on Tynmouth Castle and the succeeding separation of Edward and Gaveston is represented against the background of Isabella's feelings: the infatuated King neglects her entirely and it is she who directs the peers in their pursuit of the favourite. Her two short soliloquies interrupt the speed of the action and create a fine rubato movement. The private and the political elements are skilfully combined and the first serves as a lyrical or emotional foil to the latter. At the same time the Queen's affection is shown to shift definitely towards Mortimer, although Marlowe has taken care not to hurry this process, as is witnessed by her resolution in the second soliloquy once more to attempt to gain Edward's favour.

It is characteristic of the technique used in this play that the author has prepared this development from the moment when the Queen first appears on the stage in I, iv. Here she is immediately addressed by Mortimer and it is to him that she speaks last. The accusations of Edward and Gaveston concerning her intimacy with the young lord—which have no foundation in the play so far—and her choosing Mortimer as a means to change the minds of the peers, are the stages which lead up to the open declaration of love in this scene. From now on she ceases to clog the activity of the lords and becomes, next to Mortimer, the main antagonist of the King and a decisive factor in his overthrow.

Marlowe has skilfully regulated the movement of Gaveston's downfall in II, v and vi where, immediately after his capture, Arundel asks the barons for a last interview of the King with their prisoner. The author thus brings about, on the one hand, a conflict among the nobles similar to that in I, iv, where the Queen entreats them to recall Gaveston, on the other hand a slight delay of the counter-action and a corresponding upward movement of the cause of Edward and his friend. The lull at the end of II, v where Pembroke and Arundel, in whose custody the prisoner has been left, decide to visit the former's wife, is immediately followed by the vigorous movement of III, i: Warwick forces Pembroke's servants to yield Gaveston up to him and has him hurriedly put to death. The considerable space Marlowe has allowed for this episode is fully justified when we consider its rhythmical function in the pattern of the play. It can be understood as an experiment in the regulation of dramatic speed which is repeated—on a larger scale—in the series of scenes representing the hero's fall from power.

III, ii develops with increasing speed. Edward is uncertain about Gaveston's fate and apprehends the worst. The two Spencers are trying, not without success, to rouse him from his dejection. The Queen takes leave to go to France and thus introduces at an early date the territory which is to serve as a jumping-board for the final onset of the counter-action. When Arundel announces the death of Gaveston, the King temporarily relapses into his humour:

> O shall I speak, or shall I sigh and die!
> [III.ii.122]

It is again young Spencer who urges him to resist so that Edward vows a terrible vengeance for the death of his friend. When therefore the rebels' herald asks him to deliver up his new minion, he sends the messenger back, promising to follow 'with sword and fire at (his) heels'. He is now the revenger of Gaveston and bent on swift and ruthless action.

The next scene opens with a breathing pause during the battle of Boroughbridge. It shows Edward ready to 'pour vengeance with (his) sword On those proud rebels', fretting to get back into action. The defiant speeches of the leaders of the two hosts which follow lead the conflict at

once to its intellectual pitch. The King will sacrifice everything, even his country, to revenge; he is firmness itself and resolved 'rather to Make England's civil towns huge heaps of stones' than to give in. This 'desperate and unnatural resolution', as Warwick calls it, leads to immediate victory and in the following section of the scene Edward is shown as the implacable judge of his adversaries.

It is again Mortimer on whom Marlowe focuses the interest by placing his speech last when the barons are led to their respective dooms:

> What, Mortimer! can ragged stony walls
> Immure thy virtue that aspires to heaven?
> No, Edward, England's scourge, it may not be;
> Mortimer's hope surmounts his fortune far.
> [III.iii.71-4]

The cause of his rebellion has been removed by Gaveston's death, but imprisonment becomes a new cause for further resistance—if we are allowed to speak of a cause, for he rather follows an irrational yearning which revolts against the prison-bars and will not be satisfied until he has annihilated the tyrant. His aristocratic pride which made him hate the upstart Gaveston, transforms itself into the deadly hatred of the soaring intellect against its oppressor.

To make Edward's victory more complete Spencer, in the last section of III, iii, frustrates the efforts of the Queen to win the French King for her cause. The counter-action thus is at a standstill at the beginning of act IV, the heart of the resistance lying 'immured' in the Tower. Then it gathers force slowly.

Marlowe begins the new act with two scenes which are marked by their parallel structure—an andante followed by an allegro—and by a significant increase of size and implication. Kent, in a soliloquy which is set in a fine lyrical frame—'Fair blows the wind for France: blow, gentle gale'—is waiting for Mortimer to escape from the Tower. When he arrives they set sail for France. Here the Queen is shown in a state of dejection after the French King's refusal of her demand for help. As soon as Mortimer joins her and Hainault, the action takes a directed course and gains speed.

In IV, iii the King revels in his victory and he makes up his mind at once when he hears of the activity of his enemies in France. Like his antagonist Mortimer he thirsts for immediate action and expresses his impatience in the time-devouring verses:

> Gallop apace, bright Phoebus, through the sky,
> And dusky night, in rusty iron car,
> Between you both shorten the time, I pray,
> That I may see that most desired day,
> When we may meet these traitors in the field.
> [IV.iii.45-9]

The onward urge of these words is at once bridled by the speeches of the Queen and Mortimer who, in the following scene, land in England. It is significant that the latter no longer primarily thinks in terms of action but of policy. His verse has lost the youthful ring of the earlier scenes and it is strange to hear him gently rebuke the Queen:

> if you be a warrior
> You must not grow so passionate in speeches.
>
> [IV.iv.15-16]

And then follows his own speech on the legality of their enterprise which, by its formal coldness, rings false and shows the Machiavellian man of power hiding behind the mask of the loyal subject. As long as the King was governed by his minions, the sympathy of the audience was rather drawn towards his antagonist. Now Mortimer is shown as a usurper and therefore appears in a less favourable light. The development of his character should, no doubt, be understood primarily as a necessity to which the dramatist had to submit in order to have his play performed on the public stage; it is less motivated by the lapse of time because Marlowe, at least up to this moment, does not create the impression that a period of many years is covered by the play. The perfunctory delineation of Mortimer's development causes a flaw in his dramatic portrait which shows that the author was not interested in this aspect but rather hurriedly proceeded to what was of more concern to him: Mortimer's Machiavellian rule and the tragedy of the hero.

Thus he does not dwell on Edward's attempt to oppose his enemies but represents, in the rapid opening of IV, v, his reluctant flight to Ireland. Then, after the quiet movement of Kent's soliloquy, who is shown to waver in his allegiance and thereby prepares us, in time, for his part in act V, we see the victorious antagonist having the old Spencer put to death and giving order, in spite of the compassion of Kent, the Queen, and the Prince for the fugitive King, to trace him to his hiding place. It is again Mortimer who represents the driving force of the counter-action which, in the course of this scene, gradually gathers speed.

IV, vi opens quietly with the King seeking 'this life contemplative' in the Welsh Abbey of Neath. That the lull in the action is going to be of short duration only and the calm introduces the tempest, is shown by Edward's haunting suspicion and the uneasy remark of Spencer about 'a gloomy fellow in a mead below' who 'gave a long look after (them)'. When the hero's spirits have drooped lowest and he puts his head 'laden with mickle care' in the abbot's lap, wishing he may 'never again lift up this drooping head', the emissaries of Mortimer, led by the very mower who had watched the fugitives, intrude into this pseudo-idyll which, by its unique mixture of quiet and unrest, of fearful apprehension and an intense craving for security, belongs to the finest rubato scenes of the play. Edward is separated from his friends and forced back into the political strife. This time he stands alone.

Act V witnesses the continuation, on the one hand, of the slow but steady decline of the hero and, on the other, the gradual rise to supreme power of the antagonists. In the abdication scene we still hear the Edward who could scarcely await Mortimer's coming to England in order to crush him. He compares himself to the 'imperial lion' who

> Highly scorning that the lowly earth
> Should drink his blood, mounts up into the air.
>
> [V.i.13-14]

He feels 'pent and mew'd in a prison' while his wings carry him 'soaring up to heaven'. Thus he strongly resembles his antagonist when put in prison himself in III, iii. At the same time, however, his weaker self is ready to submit to the pressure of the situation and to deliver the crown to the emissaries of his enemy. We have been prepared for this struggle between his nobler and weaker selves already in I, iv where, in a manner as showy as here, he oscillated between furious protest against, and submission to, the exigencies of the hour. But the object or alter ego for which he struggles is no longer his friend whom he stands in danger to lose, but his crown. Like Faustus he clings to something which does not belong to him any more and, like the magician, he asks the 'watches of the elements' to stand still. 'All times and seasons, rest you at a stay' [V.i.67], he cries, but time, for Edward as for Faustus, moves on relentlessly and cannot be stopped. Here it is not marked by the striking of a clock but by the short and pressing remarks of Mortimer's emissaries which interrupt the monologue. Having changed his mind six times, the King hands over the crown and expects death as a welcome deliverer.

The steady decline of the hero's fortunes is further interrupted—or lengthened—by the futile effort of Kent to rescue him, for which we have been prepared by his change of sympathy in IV, v and by the mention made of his attempt in V, ii. A last delay in the movement towards the catastrophe occurs in the murder scene where Edward, harping upon his suffering and trying to bribe Lightborne, strives to escape the clutches of the murderer who is feigning compassion and tears until, throwing off his human mask, he suddenly reveals his murderous intention to his victim and executes it with all speed—an action which is all the more effective because of the delay.

It has been generally recognised that Edward's end is hardly heroic: it is actually as unheroic and pitiful as that of Faustus and reveals, when held against his valorous behaviour in the struggle with Mortimer, the full extent of his bipolar character which mirrors the two-fold vision of man in Renaissance philosophy. Both heroes give a truer, more comprehensive and, at the same time, more objective and dramatic picture of the Renaissance man than Tamburlaine, who illustrates only the optimistic and modern alternative.

In the meantime (V, ii), Mortimer has further strengthened his position, first by taking the young Prince from the protection of his uncle Kent, secondly by giving Lightborne the ambiguous order to kill the imprisoned King, and thirdly by having Prince Edward crowned. He expects to rule through the puppet king and he proves his superiority by sentencing Kent against the will of his sovereign. The latter's resistance, however, when compared to the feeble attempt of the Prince in V, ii to stay under his uncle's protection, shows that the forces antagonistic to Mortimer's rule are increasing and concentrating upon the young King. Marlowe has prepared us for his part by introducing him early into the action (III, ii) and stressing certain features in his character: thus in IV, ii it is he who speaks affectionately of his father while the Queen and Mortimer are taking the first steps towards his ruin.

In the final scene of the play, which follows hard upon the

hero's death, Mortimer feels he has reached the goal of his aspiration:

> As for myself, I stand as Jove's huge tree,
> And others are but shrubs compar'd to me.
> All tremble at my name, and I fear none.
> [V.vi.11-13]

From this zenith of his power he is pushed down by the young King who, supported by the nobles, confronts him and the Queen with a determination which is not to be shaken, though it is distinguished by its humanity.

Thus the play ends with the rapid rise to triumph of the forces which represent poetic justice. Looked at from a distance, *Edward II* shows—in the first two acts or, more exactly, until III, ii—the struggle for Gaveston with the culminating points for the hero in I, i and at the end of I, iv, and the lowest points in the middle of scenes I, iv and III, ii. In the latter scene the struggle for Gaveston is ended and immediately followed by Edward's revenge which is achieved at the end of act III where, as in a classical tragedy, the hero seems to have secured the victory over his antagonists. The play about Gaveston now changes into the struggle for power which is caused, directly, by this very vengeance (itself rooted in Edward's love of Gaveston) and indirectly by the change of Mortimer's character. During act IV the counter-action gathers force and approaches its climax at the beginning of the last scene of the play where Mortimer exults in his absolute power. This gradual rise is accompanied by the slow decline of the hero's fortunes which, after many oscillations, reach their lowest point in the death scene. Then we witness the swift rise to power of the hero's son which is accompanied, again in a contrasted sense, by the sudden fall of the antagonists.

In spite of a certain weakness of the link between the two movements of the action, the play forms an organic whole. Its structure is characterized by what may be called dramatic rhythm. It would be easy to represent this movement, which I have tried to express in the terms of the drama and—tentatively—of music, graphically by lines tracing, by their varying inclination, the speed with which the actions led by the hero and his antagonist proceed. The result would be, roughly speaking, the rapid fall and rise of the hero's line in the first act, the much slower decline in act II which ends in III, ii and is followed by a vigorous rise in the second half of this act. The last two acts show the undulating falling line of the hero's fate, to which is attached, in the last scene, a steep rise. The line thus described would be accompanied, but in a contrasted sense, by that of the antagonist. The play conceived in this manner would consist of three successive waves and counter-waves which differ from one another only by their growing size. Translating the dramatic structure into terms of music, we may say that the first act gives the tragic theme, which is followed by two variations in each of which the theme is brought nearer to its tragic conclusion.

Thus *Edward II* forms a strongly and closely knit whole from which no part, however loosely joined to the body of the play it may seem, can be separated without either changing the rhythm of the action or weakening its logical structure. It is true that Marlowe might have used a differ-

ent technique altogether to obtain this result, and given it more outward unity by using, for instance, the messenger's report of classical drama. But the effect would have been entirely different and *Edward II* would not have been acted on the Elizabethan stage for which it was written. Marlowe knew what was expected of him and represented all the episodes of the play on the stage, i.e. he adopted the *ab ovo* technique of the popular drama. Although he selected from the vast body of material offered to him by the sources only those incidents which had a direct bearing on the gradual unfolding of Edward's tragedy, the amount he used is nevertheless enormous when we consider the length of the play. He conquered the difficulties by speed and concentration.

The structural unit of *Edward II* is neither the act nor the scene, but what may be called the scenic section, and in this respect Marlowe was not an innovator but could follow the example set by Kyd in *The Spanish Tragedy*. Yet even from this point of view the difference between the two plays is far greater than their similarity. *The Spanish Tragedy* is a very slow drama in which the action is carried forward simultaneously on three different levels: on the political, where it seems to develop slowly towards a happy ending, namely the marriage of Bel-Imperia and Balthasar: on the private, where Hieronymo gradually changes from a passive into an active hero; and on a level where the fate of Lorenzo's servants is shown. Action and counter-action only meet at the end of the play in the catastrophe. In *Edward II* the private and the political spheres of the action are not separated but mingle from beginning to end, and we witness a rapid series of clashes between the hero and his antagonist. The structure of the two plays is entirely different: the scenic units in *The Spanish Tragedy* help to erect a stately and three-dimensional building, whereas in *Edward II* they form a rapid succession which creates the impression not of space but of time.

The main functions of the scenic units in *Edward II* are the regulation of the rhythm of the action and the reception of a vast material. The action passes swiftly from one unit to the next, and often the impression of speed is heightened by the abrupt opening of scenes which suggests that the action represented has been going on for some time before. The beginning of the play shows Gaveston reading the King's letter. He limits himself to picking out the two most significant lines and proceeds straight to the heart of the matter. Without turning back to what has passed he looks ahead to what is to come. The next section presents the king in the full course of a hot dispute with the barons.

K. EDW.:	Lancaster!
LAN.:	My lord?
GAV.:	That Earl of Lancaster do I abhor. (*Aside.*)
K. EDW.:	Will you not grant me this? In spite of them I'll have my will; and these two Mortimers, That cross me thus, shall know I am displeas'd. (*Aside.*) [I.i.74-9]

The essence of the dispute which has taken place before

they enter, is contained in these few lines which introduce the hero. We do not not know what his will is—but that is of secondary importance: he is crossed in his will by Lancaster and the Mortimers, and Gaveston by his asides shows that he hates them. It is his will the king will have, and it is one of the men he names that will block it. The dramatic conflict is foreshadowed in this breathless passage, the beginning of the drama properly speaking.

It has been noticed that Marlowe, true to his classical training and contrary to the stage customs of his time, does not represent the traffic of the battles on the stage. Thus, of the battle of Boroughbridge he only gives a breathing-space filled in with the defiant speeches of the leaders, and the result: the condemnation of the rebels. The second armed conflict between the King and Mortimer he omits completely and proceeds straight to the moment when Edward and his favourites 'shape [their] course to Ireland'. What he gains by this technique is again speed and concentration: the attention of the audience is not diverted by noisy 'alarums and excursions' but remains fixed on the intellectual conflict.

Marlowe's grip on the attention of the audience is further tightened by the reduction to a minimum of the elements creating relief from the forward urge of the action. He gives us neither comic scenes nor descriptions but concise soliloquies which contain a lyrical element, and short scenic sections which do not allow for a lengthy breathing-space. The dynamic force of the play is intensified by the almost complete lack of retrospective passages and descriptions. Rarely do the characters look back on their past experience: their attention—and with it that of the audience—is bent on the immediate future, and when they remember the past it is only in short snatches like Edward's

> Tell Isabel, the queen, I look'd not thus,
> When for her sake I ran at tilt in France,
> And there unhors'd the Duke of Cleremont.
>
> [V.v.67-9]

Here, of course, the reminiscence has a dramatic function: by its associations with glorious deeds of chivalry it creates a sharp contrast to the miserable situation in which the King now lives who is timorously facing his murderer.

It is the powerful rhythm of the action which captures the mind of the modern reader perhaps more than the rational exposition of causes and motives. The sacrifice of the earlier heroes' aspiring minds and of the poetry depending on it is compensated for by this dramatic element, and what the characters lack in that respect they gain in outline and impetuosity. The cosmic element gives way to the dynamic; lyrical poetry is transformed into the dramatic poetry of action.

Once we have realised the dynamic quality of this play, the relationship to Shakespeare's first chronicle plays becomes clearer. In both we witness the repeated and violent clash of opposed characters, and the development of Richard, the later Duke of Gloucester, resembles that of Mortimer. The general structure of *3 Henry VI* shows the rise and fall of the conflicting parties in much the same way as that of *Edward II.* But the bareness and onward sweep of the lat-

ter play contrast strongly with the breadth of the former, the concise directness of the verse which Marlowe uses here with the exuberant imagery and rhetoric of the early Shakespeare. It is probable that Shakespeare wrote—or rather revised—his plays first, but when he sat down to work he had the clash of defiant speeches and the rhetoric of *Tamburlaine* before him and the aspiring mind, not of the cosmic poet *Tamburlaine,* but of the man who is fascinated by the glittering crown much in the same way as his own Duchess of Gloucester, Jack Cade, the old Duke of York and his two sons. Marlowe, in *Edward II,* seems to have been influenced by the dramatic structure of *2* and *3 Henry VI*—whoever was responsible for that—but it was Shakespeare's turn to fall under the spell of *Edward II* when he wrote *Richard II,* although the total result was something entirely different. Perhaps he got nearest to the dramatic method of *Edward II* in *Romeo and Juliet, Othello, Macbeth,* and *Antony and Cleopatra*: here we find the dynamic quality of Marlowe's play, and many things besides which we do not get in *Edward II.* (pp. 204-17)

> *Robert Fricker, "The Dramatic Structure of 'Edward II',"* in English Studies, *London, Vol. 34, 1953, pp. 204-17.*

DOCTOR FAUSTUS

CRITICAL COMMENTARY

W. W. Greg   (essay date 1946)

[*An English literary scholar and librarian, Greg was a pioneer in establishing modern bibliographical scholarship. Combining bibliographical and critical methods, he developed an approach to editing Shakespeare and other Elizabethan dramatists. Greg closely examined the physical evidence of external documents, such as records of the English court and private journals, and analyzed the mechanical errors in the printing of early editions in an effort to recapture the original form of a dramatist's text. In the following essay, Greg examines several aspects of the hero's downfall in* Doctor Faustus, *particularly how Faustus's pact with Mephistophilis leads not to a rise in grandeur and power, but to mere worldly gratification. Ultimately, the critic claims, Faustus "commits the sin of demonality, that is, bodily intercourse with demons." The quotations are taken from Greg's own collation of the 1604 and 1616 quarto editions of* Doctor Faustus.]

When working lately on the text of *Doctor Faustus,* I was struck by certain aspects of the story as told in Marlowe's play that I do not remember to have seen discussed in the editions with which I am familiar. I do not pretend to have read more than a little of what has been written about Marlowe as a dramatist, and it may be that there is nothing new in what I have to say; but it seemed worth while to draw attention to a few points in the picture of the hero's downfall, on the chance that they might have es-

Title page of the 1628 edition of Doctor Faustus.

caped the attention of others, as they had hitherto escaped my own.

As soon as Faustus has decided that necromancy is the only study that can give his ambition scope, he seeks the aid of his friends Valdes and Cornelius, who already are proficients in the art—

> Their conference will be a greater help to me
> Than all my labours, plod I ne'er so fast.

Who they are we have no notion: they do not appear in the source on which Marlowe drew—'The historie of the damnable life, and deserued death of Doctor John Faustus . . . according to the true Copie printed at Franckfort, and translated into English by P. F. Gent.'— and Cornelius is certainly not the famous Cornelius Agrippa, who is mentioned in their conversation. But they must have been familiar figures at Wittenberg, since on learning that Faustus is at dinner with them, his students at once conclude that he is 'fallen into that damned art for which they two are infamous through the world'. The pair are ready enough to obey Faustus' invitation, for they have long sought to lead him into forbidden ways. 'Know', says Faustus—

> Know that your words have won me at the last
> To practise magic and concealed arts.

At the same time, though they are his 'dearest friends', he is anxious not to appear too pliant, adding, a little clumsily (if the 1604 text is to be trusted)

> Yet not your words only, but mine own fantasy,

and he makes it plain that he is no humble seeker after instruction, but one whose personal fame and honour are to be their main concern—

> Then, gentle friends, aid me in this attempt,
> And I, that have with concise syllogisms
> Gravelled the pastors of the German church,
> And made the flowering pride of Wittenberg
> Swarm to my problems, as the infernal spirits
> On sweet Musaeus when he came to hell,
> Will be as cunning as Agrippa was,
> Whose shadows made all Europe honour him.

His friends are content enough to accept him on these terms. Valdes, while hinting that common contributions deserve common rewards—

> Faustus, these books, thy wit, and our experi-
> ence
> Shall make all nations to canonize us—

paints a glowing picture of the possibilities before them, adding however—in view of what follows a little ominously—

> If learned Faustus will be resolute.

Reassured on this score, Cornelius is ready to allow Faustus pride of place—

> Then doubt not, Faustus, but to be renowmed,
> And more frequented for this mystery
> Than heretofore the Delphian oracle—

but only on condition that the profits of the enterprise are shared—

> Then tell me, Faustus, What shall we three
> want?

However, it soon appears that for all their sinister reputation the two are but dabblers in witchcraft. They have, indeed, called spirits from the deep, and they have come—

> The spirits tell me they can dry the sea
> And fetch the treasure of all foreign wracks,
> Yea, all the wealth that our forefathers hid
> Within the massy entrails of the earth—

but they have made no use of this knowledge, they have never become the masters—or the slaves—of the spirits. Even to raise them they must, of course, have run a mortal risk—

> Nor will we come unless he use such means
> Wherby he is in danger to be damned—

but they have been careful not to forfeit their salvation for supernatural gifts; they have never succumbed to the temptation of the spirits or made proof of their boasted powers. Nor do they mean to put their own art to the ultimate test. When Faustus eagerly demands,

> Come, show me some demonstrations magical,

Valdes proves himself a ready teacher—

Then haste thee to some solitary grove,
And bear wise Bacon's and Albanus' works,
The Hebrew Psalter, and New Testament;
And whatsoever else is requisite
We will inform thee ere our conference cease—

and guarantees to make him proficient in the art—

First I'll instruct thee in the rudiments,
And then wilt thou be perfecter than I.

Knowing the depth of Faustus' learning, and satisfied of his courage and resolution, they are anxious to form a partnership with one whose potentialities as an adept so far exceed their own. But Cornelius leaves us in no doubt of their intention to use Faustus as a cat's-paw rather than run into danger themselves—

Valdes, first let him know the words of art,
And then, all other ceremonies learned,
Faustus may try his cunning by himself.

The precious pair are no deeply versed magicians welcoming a promising beginner, but merely the devil's decoys luring Faustus along the road to destruction. They serve their purpose in giving a dramatic turn to the scene of his temptation, and except for a passing mention by the students, we hear no more of them.

Faustus goes to conjure alone, and alone he concludes his pact with the devil. What use will he make of his hazardously won powers? His dreams, if self-centred, are in the heroic vein:

Oh, what a world of profit and delight,
Of power, of honour, and omnipotence,
Is promised to the studious artizan!
All things that move between the quiet poles
Shall be at my command; emperors and kings
Are but obeyed in their several provinces,
But his dominion that exceeds in this
Stretcheth as far as doth the mind of man:
A sound magician is a demi-god!

More than mortal power and knowledge shall be his, to use in the service of his country:

Shall I make spirits fetch me what I please?
Resolve me of all ambiguities?
Perform what desperate enterprise I will? . . .
I'll have them read me strange philosophy
And tell the secrets of all foreign kings;
I'll have them wall all Germany with brass, . . .
And chase the Prince of Parma from our
  land . . .

Whatever baser elements there may be in his ambition, we should, by all human standards, expect the fearless seeker after knowledge and truth, the scholar weary of the futilities of orthodox learning, to make at least no ignoble use of the power suddenly placed at his command.

Critics have complained that instead of pursuing ends worthy of his professed ideals, Faustus, once power is his, abandons these without a qualm, and shows himself content to amuse the Emperor with conjuring tricks and play childish pranks on the Pope; and they have blamed this either on a collaborator, or on the fact of Marlowe's work having been later overlaid and debased by another hand.

The charge, in its crudest form, involves some disregard of the 1616 version, which is not quite as fatuous as its predecessor, but in broad outline there is no denying its justice. As to responsibility: it is of course obvious that not all the play as we have it is Marlowe's. For my own part, however, I do not believe that as originally written it differed to any material extent from what we are able to reconstruct from a comparison of the two versions in which it has come down to us. And while it is true that the middle portion, to which objection is mostly taken, shows little trace of Marlowe's hand, I see no reason to doubt that it was he who planned the whole, or that his collaborator or collaborators, whoever he or they may have been, carried out his plan substantially according to instructions. If that is so, for any fundamental fault in the design Marlowe must be held responsible.

The critics' disappointment is quite natural. Although it is difficult to see how any dramatist could have presented in language and dramatic form the revelation of a knowledge beyond the reach of human wisdom, there is no question that much more might have been done to show the wonder and uphold the dignity of the quest, and so satisfy the natural expectation of the audience. Marlowe did not do it; he deliberately turned from the attempt. Instead he showed us the betrayal of ideals, the lapse into luxury and buffoonery.

And what, in the devil's name, would the critics have? I say 'in the devil's name', because all that happens to Faustus once the pact is signed is the devil's work: 'human standards' are no longer relevant. Who but a fool, such a clever fool as Faustus, would dream that any power but evil could be won by a bargain with evil, or that truth could be wrung from the father of lies? 'All power tends to corrupt, and absolute power corrupts absolutely,' is indeed an aphorism to which few Elizabethans would have subscribed; but Marlowe knew the nature of the power he put into the hands of his hero and the inevitable curse it carried with it.

Of course, Faustus' corruption is not a mechanical outcome of his pact with evil. In spite of his earnest desire to know truth, and half-hidden in the Marlowan glamour cast about him, the seeds of decay are in his character from the first—how else should he come to make his fatal bargain? Beside his passion for knowledge is a lust for riches and pleasure and power. If less single-minded, he shares Barabbas' thirst for wealth—

I'll have them fly to India for gold,
Ransack the ocean for orient pearl,
And search all corners of the new-found world
For pleasant fruits and princely delicates . . .

Patriotism is a veil for ambition: he will

chase the Prince of Parma from our land
And reign sole king of all our provinces . . .

I'll join the hills that bind the Afric shore
And make that country continent to Spain,
And both contributary to my crown:
The Emperor shall not live but by my leave,
Nor any potentate in Germany.

His aspiration to be 'great emperor of the world' recalls Tamburlain's vulgar desire for

> The sweet fruition of an earthly crown.

But Faustus' ambition is not thus limited; the promptings of his soul reveal themselves in the words of the Bad Angel:

> Be thou on earth, as Jove is in the sky,
> Lord and commander of these elements.

If there is a sensual vein in him, it is hardly seen at this stage; still his demand to 'live in all voluptuousness' anticipates later desires—

> Whilst I am here on earth let me be cloyed
> With all things that delight the heart of man;
> My four and twenty years of liberty
> I'll spend in pleasure and in dalliance—

and it may be with shrewd insight that Valdes promises 'serviceable' spirits,

> Sometimes like women or unwedded maids
> Shadowing more beauty in their airy brows
> Than in the white breasts of the Queen of Love.

But when all is said, this means no more than that Faustus is a man dazzled by the unlimited possibilities of magic, and alive enough to his own weakness to exclaim:

> The god thou serv'st is thine own appetite . . .

After Faustus has signed the bond with his blood, we can trace the stages of a gradual deterioration. His previous interview with Mephostophilis struck the note of earnest if slightly sceptical inquiry with which he entered on his quest:

> This word Damnation terrifies not me,
> For I confound hell in Elizium:
> My ghost be with the old philosophers!

He questions eagerly about hell, and the spirit replies:

> Why, this is hell, nor am I out of it:
> Think'st thou that I who saw the face of God
> And tasted the eternal joys of heaven,
> Am not tormented with ten thousand hells
> In being deprived of everlasting bliss? . . .
> FAU.: What, is great Mephostophilis so passion-
>   ate
> For being deprived of the joys of heaven?
> Learn thou of Faustus manly fortitude,
> And scorn those joys thou never shalt possess.

After the bond is signed the discussion is renewed, but while the devil loses nothing in dignity of serious discourse, we can already detect a change in Faustus; his sceptical levity takes on a more truculent and jeering tone. Asked 'Where is the place that men call hell?' Mephostophilis replies:

> Within the bowels of these elements,
> Where we are tortured and remain for ever.
> Hell hath no limits, nor is circumscribed
> In one self place, but where we are is hell,
> And where hell is, there must we ever be:
> And to conclude, when all the world dissolves
> And every creature shall be purified,

> All places shall be hell that is not heaven.
> FAU.: Come, I think hell's a fable.
> MEPH.: Ay, think so still, till experience change
>   thy mind. . . .
> FAU.: . . . Think'st thou that Faustus is so fond
>   to imagine
> That after this life there is any pain?
> Tush! these are trifles and mere old wives' tales.
> MEPH.: But I am an instance to prove the con-
>   trary;
> For I tell thee I am damned and now in hell.
> FAU.: Nay, and this be hell, I'll willingly be
>   damned:
> What? sleeping, eating, walking, and disputing!

In the next scene there follows the curiously barren discussion on astronomy. It has probably been interpolated and is not altogether easy to follow, but the infernal exposition of the movements of the spheres calls forth an impatient,

> These slender questions Wagner can decide

and at the end Mephostophilis' sententions

> Per inaequalem motum respectu totius

and Faustus' half-satisfied

> Well, I am answered!

leave in the mouth the taste of dead-sea fruit. The quarrel that follows on the spirit's refusal to say who made the world leads to the intervention of Lucifer and the 'pastime' of the Seven Deadly Sins. There seems to me more savour in this than has sometimes been allowed; still it is a much shrunken Faustus who exclaims:

> Oh, this feeds my soul!

He had been no less delighted with the dance of the devils that offered him crowns and rich apparel on his signing the bond: we do not know its nature, but from his exclamation,

> Then there's enough for a thousand souls!

when told that he may conjure up such spirits at will, we may perhaps conclude that it involved a direct appeal to the senses. That would, at least, accord with his mood soon afterwards; for while it would be rash to lay much stress on his demanding 'the fairest maid in Germany, for I am wanton and lascivious' (this being perhaps an interpolation) we should allow due weight to Mephostophilis' promise:

> I'll cull thee out the fairest courtesans
> And bring them every morning to thy bed;
> She whom thine eye shall like, thy heart shall
>   have,
> Were she as chaste as was Penelope,
> As wise as Saba, or as beautiful
> As was bright Lucifer before his fall.

So far Faustus has not left Wittenberg, and emphasis has been rather on the hollowness of his bargain in respect of any intellectual enlightenment than on the actual degradation of his character. As yet only his childish pleasure in the devil-dance and the pageant of the Sins hints at the depth of vulgar triviality into which he is doomed to descend. In company with Mephostophilis he now launches forth into the world; but his dragon-flights

> To find the secrets of astronomy
> Graven in the book of Jove's high firmament,

and

> to prove cosmography,
> That measures coasts and kingdoms of the earth,

only land him at last in the Pope's privy-chamber to

> take some part of holy Peter's feast,

and live with dalliance in

> the view
> Of rarest things and royal courts of kings . . .

It is true that in the fuller text of 1616 the rescue of 'holy Bruno', imperial candidate for the papal throne, lends a more serious touch to the sheer horse-play of the Roman scenes in the 1604 version, and even the 'horning' episode at the Emperor's court is at least developed into some dramatic coherence; but this only brings out more pointedly the progressive fatuity of Faustus' career, which in the clownage and conjuring tricks at Anhalt sinks to the depth of buffoonery.

If, as may be argued, the gradual deterioration of Faustus' character and the prostitution of his powers stand out less clearly than they should, this may be ascribed partly to Marlowe's negligent handling of a theme that failed to kindle his wayward inspiration, and partly to the ineptitude of his collaborator. But the logical outline is there, and I must differ from Marlowe's critics, and believe that when he sketched that outline Marlowe knew what he was about.

Another point to be borne in mind is that there is something strange and peculiar, not only in Faustus' situation, but in his nature. Once he has signed the bond, he is in the position of having of his own free will renounced salvation. So much is obvious. Less obvious is the inner change he has brought upon himself. Critics have strangely neglected the first article of the infernal compact: 'that Faustus may be a spirit in form and substance'. Presumably they have taken it to mean merely that he should be free of the bonds of flesh, so that he may be invisible at will, invulnerable, and able to change his shape, ride on dragons, and so forth. But in this play 'spirit' is used in a special sense. There is, of course, nothing very significant in the fact that, when the 'devils' dance before him, Faustus asks:

> But may I raise such spirits when I please?

that he promises to

> make my spirits pull His churches down

and bids Mephostophilis

> Ay, go, accursed spirit to ugly hell!

or that the latter speaks of the devils as

> Unhappy spirits that fell with Lucifer—

though it is noticeable how persistently devils are called

spirits in the play, and it is worth recalling that in the *Damnable Life* Mephostophilis is regularly 'the Spirit'. What is significant is that when Faustus asks 'What is that Lucifer, thy lord?' Mephostophilis replies:

> Arch-regent and commander of all spirits

which Faustus at once interprets as 'prince of devils'; and that the Bad Angel, in reply to Faustus' cry of repentance, asserts:

> Thou art a spirit; God cannot pity thee

—a remark to which I shall return. And if there could be any doubt of the meaning of these expressions, we have the explicit statement in the *Damnable Life* that Faustus' 'request was none other than to become a devil'. Faustus then, through his bargain with hell, has himself taken on the infernal nature, although it is made clear throughout that he still retains his human soul.

This throws a new light upon the question, debated throughout the play, whether Faustus can be saved by repentance. Faustus, of course, is for ever repenting—and recanting through fear of bodily torture and death—and the Good and Bad Angels, who personate the two sides of his human nature, for are ever disputing the point:

> FAU.: Contrition, prayer, repentance: what of these?
> GOOD A.: Oh, they are means to bring thee vnto heaven.
> BAD A.: Rather illusions, fruits of lunacy

and again:

> GOOD A. Never too late, if Faustus will repent.
> BAD A. If thou repent, devils will tear thee in pieces.
> GOOD A. Repent, and they shall never raze thy skin.

There are two passages that are particularly significant in this respect: and we must remember, as I have said, the double question at issue—Faustus' nature, and whether repentance can cancel a bargain. First then, the passage from which I have already quoted:

> GOOD A.: Faustus, repent; yet God will pity thee.
> BAD A.: Thou art a spirit; God cannot pity thee.
> FAU.: Who buzzeth in mine ears, I am a spirit?
>   Be I a devil, yet God may pity me;
>   Yes, God will pity me if I repent.
> BAD A.: Ay, but Faustus never shall repent.

The Bad Angel evades the issue, which is left undecided. Later in the same scene, when Faustus calls on Christ to save his soul, Lucifer replies with admirable logic:

> Christ cannot save thy soul, for he is just:
> There's none but I have interest in the same.

Thus the possibility of Faustus' salvation is left nicely poised in doubt—like that of the archdeacon of scholastic speculation.

It is only when, back among his students at Wittenberg, he faces the final reckoning that Faustus regains some measure of heroic dignity. Marlowe again takes charge.

But even so the years have wrought a change. His faithful Wagner is puzzled:

> I wonder what he means; if death were nigh,
> He would not banquet and carouse and swill
> Among the students, as even now he doth . . .

This is a very different Faustus from the fearless teacher his students used to know, whose least absence from the class-room caused concern—

> I wonder what's become of Faustus, that was
> wont to make our schools ring with *sic probo*.

One good, or at least amiable, quality—apart from a genuine tenderness towards his students—we may be tempted to claim for him throughout: a love of beauty in nature and in art:

> Have not I made blind Homer sing to me
> Of Alexander's love and Oenon's death?
> And hath not he that built the walls of Thebes
> With ravishing sound of his melodious harp
> Made music—?

and the climax of his career is his union with the immortal beauty of Helen, to measures admittedly the most lovely that flowed from Marlowe's lyre. Is this sensitive appreciation something that has survived uncorrupted from his days of innocence? I can find no hint of it in the austere student of the early scenes. Is it then some strange flowering of moral decay? It would seem so. What, after all, is that 'ravishing sound' but the symphony of hell?—

> Made music—with my Mephostophilis!

And Helen, what of her?

Here we come, if I mistake not, to the central theme of the damnation of Faustus. The lines in which he addresses Helen are some of the most famous in the language:

> Was this the face that launched a thousand ships
> And burnt the topless towers of Ilium?
> Sweet Helen, make me immortal with a
>   kiss! . . .
> Here will I dwell, for heaven is in these lips,
> And all is dross that is not Helena
> I will be Paris, and for love of thee
> Instead of Troy shall Wittenberg be smoked;
> And I will combat with weak Menelaus,
> And wear thy colours on my plumed crest:
> Yes, I will wound Achilles in the heel,
> And then return to Helen for a kiss.
> Oh, thou art fairer than the evening's air
> Clad in the beauty of a thousand stars,
> Brighter art thou than flaming Jupiter
> When he appeared to hapless Semele,
> More lovely than the monarch of the sky
> In wanton Arethusa's azured arms;
> And none but thou shalt be my paramour!

In these lines Marlowe's uncertain genius soared to its height, but their splendour has obscured, and was perhaps meant discreetly to veil, the real nature of the situation. 'Her lips suck forth my soul', says Faustus in lines that I omitted from his speech above. What is Helen? We are not told in so many words, but the answer is there, if we choose to look for it. When the Emperor asks him to present Alexander and his paramour before the court, Faustus

(in the 1604 version) laboriously explains the nature of the figures that are to appear:

> My gracious lord, I am ready to accomplish your request so far forth as by art and power of my spirit I am able to perform. . . . But, if it like your grace, it is not in my ability to present before your eyes the true substantial bodies of those two deceased princes, which long since are consumed to dust. . . . But such spirits as can lively resemble Alexander and his paramour shall appear before your grace in that manner that they best lived in, in their most flourishing estate . . .

He adds (according to the 1616 version):

> My lord, I must forewarn your majesty
> That, when my spirits present the royal shapes
> Of Alexander and his paramour,
> Your grace demand no questions of the king,
> But in dumb silence let them come and go.

This is explicit enough; and as a reminder that the same holds for Helen, Faustus repeats the caution when he presents her to his students:

> Be silent then, for danger is in words.

Consider, too, a point critics seem to have overlooked, the circumstances in which Helen is introduced the second time. Urged by the Old Man, Faustus has attempted a last revolt; as usual he has been cowed into submission, and has renewed the blood-bond. He has sunk so low as to beg revenge upon his would-be saviour—

> Torment, sweet friend, that base and aged man,
> That durst dissuade me from thy Lucifer,
> With greatest torments that our hell affords.

And it is in the first place as a safeguard against relapse that he seeks possession of Helen—

> One thing, good servant, let me crave of thee
> To glut the longing of my heart's desire;
> That I may have unto my paramour
> That heavenly Helen which I saw of late,
> Whose sweet embraces may extinguish clear
> Those thoughts that may dissuade me from my
>   vow,
> And keep mine oath I made to Lucifer.

Love and revenge are alike insurances against salvation. 'Helen' then is a 'spirit', and in this play a spirit means a devil. In making her his paramour Faustus commits the sin of demoniality, that is, bodily intercourse with demons.

The implication of Faustus' action is made plain in the comments of the Old Man and the Angels. Immediately before the Helen episode the Old Man was still calling on Faustus to repent—

> Ah, Doctor Faustus, that I might prevail
> To guide thy steps into the way of life!

(So 1604: 1616 proceeds:)

> Though thou hast now offended like a man,
> Do not persever in it like a devil:
> Yet, yet, thou hast an amiable soul,

If sin by custom grow not into nature . . .

But with Faustus' union with Helen the nice balance between possible salvation and imminent damnation is upset. The Old Man, who has witnessed the meeting (according to the 1604 version), recognizes the inevitable:

> Accursed Faustus, miserable man,
> That from thy soul exclud'st the grace of heaven
> And fliest the throne of his tribunal seat!

The Good Angel does no less:

> O Faustus, if thou hadst given ear to me
> Innumerable joys had followed thee . . .
> Oh, thou hast lost celestial happiness . . .

And Faustus himself, still haunted in his final agony by the idea of a salvation beyond his reach—

> See, see, where Christ's blood streams in the firmament!
> One drop would save my soul—

shows, in talk with his students, a terrible clarity of vision:

> A surfeit of deadly sin, that hath damned both body and soul. . . . Faustus' offence can ne'er be pardoned: the Serpent that tempted Eve may be saved, but not Faustus.

and Mephostophilis echoes him:

> Ay, Faustus, now hast thou no hope of heaven!

It would be idle to speculate how far the 'atheist' Marlowe, whom gossip accused of what we call 'unnatural' vice, may have dwelt in imagination on the direst sin of which human flesh is capable. But in presenting the fall and slow moral disintegration of an ardent if erring spirit, he did not shrink from depicting, beside Faustus' spiritual sin of bartering his soul to the powers of evil, what is in effect its physical complement and counterpart, however he may have disguised it in immortal verse. (pp. 97-107)

> *W. W. Greg, "The Damnation of Faustus," in* The Modern Language Review, *Vol. XLI, No. 2, April, 1946, pp. 97-107.*

C. L. Barber   (essay date 1964)

[An American linguist, scholar, and educator, Barber was one of the most important modern critics of Shakespearean comedy. His Shakespeare's Festive Comedy *(1959) was a highly influential comparison of Elizabethan holiday celebrations and Shakespearean comedy. He also produced editions of several works by the Elizabethan playwright Thomas Middleton and numerous teaching guides to Shakespearean drama. His later works include* Poetry in English *(1983), and* The Theme of Honour's Tongue *(1985). Here, Barber claims that* Doctor Faustus *is an expression of the Protestant Reformation, "profoundly shaped by sixteenth-century religious thought and ritual." However, Marlowe's hero perverts religious ceremony in the play and "makes blasphemy a Promethean enterprise, heroic and tragic, and expression of the Renaissance." The line references are taken from C. F. Tucker Brooke's* The

Works of Christopher Marlowe, *first published in 1910.]*

Doctor Faustus tends to come apart in paraphrase. It can be turned into a fable about a Modern Man who seeks to break out of Medieval limitations. On the other hand, when one retells the story in religious terms, it tends to come out as though it were Marlowe's source, *The History of the Damnable Life and Deserved Death of Doctor John Faustus.* The truth is that the play is irreducibly dramatic. Marlowe dramatizes blasphemy, but not with the single perspective of a religious point of view: he dramatizes blasphemy as heroic endeavor. The play is an expression of the Reformation; it is profoundly shaped by sixteenth-century religious thought and ritual. But in presenting a search for magical dominion, Marlowe makes blasphemy a Promethean enterprise, heroic and tragic, an expression of the Renaissance.

The emergence of a new art form puts man in a new relation to his experience. Marlowe could present blasphemy as heroic endeavor, and the tragic ironies of such endeavor, because he had the new poetic drama, which put poetry in dynamic relation to action—indeed he himself had been the most important single pioneer in creating this form, in *Tamburlaine.* This creation, in turn, depended on the new professional repertory theatre to which, when he came down from Cambridge in 1587, he brought his talents, and his need to project possibilities of human omnipotence. The London theatre was a "place apart" of a new kind, where drama was not presented as part of a seasonal or other social occasion but in its own right. Its stage gave a special vantage on experience:

> Only this (Gentlemen) we must perform
> The form of Faustus' fortunes good or bad.
> To patient judgements we appeal our plaud . . .
> [ll.7-9]

Marlowe, with characteristic modernity, calls his play just what we call it—a form. He has an audience which includes gentlemen, to whose patient judgments he appeals. In this new situation, blasphemy can be "good or bad."

Professor Lily B. Campbell [in her "*Dr. Faustus*: A Case for Conscience," *PMLA* LXVII, No. 2 (March 1952)] has related *Doctor Faustus* to fundamental tensions in Reformation religious experience in an essay which considers Marlowe's hero, against the background of Protestant casuistry, as "a case of Conscience." She focuses on Faustus' sin of despair, his inability to believe in his own salvation, a sin to which Protestants, and particularly Calvinistic Protestants, were especially subject. They had to cope with the immense distance of Calvin's God from the worshipper, and with God's terrifying, inclusive justice, just alike to the predestined elect and the predestined reprobate. And they had to do without much of the intercession provided by the Roman church, its Holy Mother, its Saints, its Masses and other works of salvation. Faustus' entrance into magic is grounded in despair. He quotes crucial texts, regularly heard as part of the Anglican service:

> Jerome's Bible, Faustus, view it well.
> *Stipendium peccati mors est:* ha, *Stipendium peccati mors est.*
> The reward of sin is death: that's hard.

Si peccasse negamus, fallimur, et nulla est in nobis veritas.
If we say that we have no sin,
We deceive ourselves, and there's no truth in us.
Why then belike
We must sin, and so consequently die.
Ay, we must die an everlasting death:
What doctrine call you this, *che sera, sera,*
What will be, shall be? Divinity, adieu,
These metaphysics of magicians
And necromantic books are heavenly: . . .
                                                                [ll.65-78]

Faustus leaves out the promises of divine grace which in the service go with "the reward of sin is death"; here, as always, he is unable to believe in God's love for him. But he does believe, throughout, in God's justice.

Miss Campbell observes that it was peculiarly the God-fearing man who was vulnerable to despair, dragged down, like Spenser's Red Cross Knight in the Cave of Despair, by a sense of his sins [in *The Faerie Queene*]. What Despair in his cave makes Spenser's knight forget, by insisting on his sinfulness, is God's love; as Una tells him in snatching away the dagger: "Where Justice grows, there grows eke greater Grace." Faustus forgets this too: vivid as is his sense of the lost joys of heaven, he never once expresses any sense that God could love him in spite of his sins. ". . . Faustus will turn to God again. / To God? he loves thee not" [ll.440-41]. Lucifer himself points to divine justice: "Christ cannot save thy soul, for he is just" [l.697].

Miss Campbell parallels Faustus as Marlowe presents him with the experience of Francis Spira, a historical case of conscience which became an exemplar of despair for Protestants. This Italian lawyer, who in 1548 died of no outward cause, surrounded by counseling Catholic doctors but miserably certain of his own damnation, had recanted Protestant views under Catholic pressure. Earlier he had been enthusiastic in his conviction of the truth of justification by faith. In his last weeks, Spira was tormented by a burning physical sensation of thirst which no drink could assuage.

Spira, dying in terror, could no longer believe in the efficacy of the Roman rites. Faustus embraces magical rituals; they are something he can *do*. It can help in understanding his turning to magic—and, indirectly, Marlowe's turning to poetic drama—if we consider the tensions which were involved, for the Elizabethan church, in the use and understanding of Holy Communion. Faustus near the end expresses his longing for communion in imagery which reflects these tensions:

O I'll leap up to my God: who pulls me down?
See, see, where Christ's blood streams in the firmament.
One drop would save my soul, half a drop, ah, my Christ.
Ah, rend not my heart for naming of my Christ,
Yet will I call on him: O, spare me, Lucifer!
Where is it now? 'tis gone: and see, where God
Stretcheth out his arm, and bends his ireful brows.

                                                                [ll.1431-38]

The immense distance away that the blood is, streaming in the sky like the Milky Way, embodies the helplessness of the Protestant who lacks faith in his own salvation. Calvin taught that communion could come by the lifting up of the soul to heaven, that it was not necessary that the essence of the flesh descend from heaven. But Faustus must try to leap up by himself, without the aid of Grace. His focus on the one drop, half a drop, that he feels would save his soul, expresses the Reformation's tendency to isolate the individual in his act of communion, and to conceive of it, as Dom Gregory Dix underscores in his great history, *The Shape of the Liturgy,* "as something passive, as a reception." At the same time, the cosmological immensity of the imagery embodies Marlowe's characteristic sense of the vastness of the universe and, here, of the tremendousness of the God who rules it and yet concerns himself with every life, stretching out his arm and bending his ireful brows.

The piety of the late Middle Ages had dwelt on miracles where a host dripped actual blood, and had depicted scenes where blood streamed down directly from Christ's wounds into the chalice on the altar. The Counter-Reformation, in its own way, pursued such physical imagery and literal conceptions, which remained viable for the Roman Catholic world as embodiments of Grace. A hunger for this kind of physical resource appears in the way that Faustus envisages Christ's blood, visibly streaming, in drops to be drunk. But for the Elizabethan church, such thinking about Communion was "but to dream of a gross carnal feeding," in the words of the homily "Of the worthy taking of the Sacraments." We have good reason to think that Marlowe had encountered Catholic ceremony during his absences from Cambridge, when the reasonable assumption is that he was working at intervals as a secret agent among Catholic English exiles and students on the Continent. The letter from the Privy Council which secured him his degree is best explained on that hypothesis, since it denies a rumor that he is "determined to have gone beyond the seas to Reims and there to remain" (as secret Catholics were doing after graduation) and speaks of his having been employed "in matters touching the benefit of his country." To have acted the part of a possible student convert would have involved understanding the Catholic point of view. And we have Marlowe the Scorner's talk, filtered through Baines, "That if there be any god or any good religion, then it is in the Papists' because the service of god is performed with more ceremonies, as elevation of the mass, organs, singing men, shaven crowns, etc. . . . That all protestants are hypocritical asses. . . . "

What concerns us here is the way *Doctor Faustus* reflects the tension involved in the Protestant world's denying itself miracle in a central area of experience. Things that had seemed supernatural events and were still felt as such in Reims, were superstition or magic from the standpoint of the new Protestant focus on individual experience. Thus the abusive Bishop Bale calls the Roman priests' consecration of the elements "such a charm of enchantment as may not be done but by an oiled officer of the pope's generation." Yet the Anglican church kept the basic physical gestures of the Mass, with a service and words of administration which leave open the question of how Christ's body and blood are consumed. And Anglican divines, while occasionally going all the way to the Zwinglian view of the service as simply a memorial, characteristically maintained a real presence, insisting, in Bishop Jewell's words, that "We feed not the people of God with bare signs and figures." Semantic tensions were involved in this position; the whole great controversy centered on fundamental issues about the nature of signs and acts, through which the age pursued its new sense of reality.

In the church of the Elizabethan settlement, there was still, along with the Reformation's insistence that "Christ's Gospel is not a ceremonial law . . . but it is a religion to serve God, not in bondage to the figure and shadow," an ingrained assumption that the crucial physical acts of worship had, or should have, independent meaning. This was supported by the doctrine of a real though not physical presence of Christ. But for many worshippers the physical elements themselves tended to keep a sacred or taboo quality in line with the old need for physical embodiment. We can, I think, connect the restriction of the impulse for physical embodiment in the new Protestant worship with a compensatory fascination in the drama with magical possibilities and the incarnation of meaning in physical gesture and ceremony: the drama carries on, for the most part in secular terms, the preoccupation with a kind of realization of meaning which had been curtailed but not eliminated in religion. In secular life, the cult of royalty, as for example Elizabeth's magical virginity, carried it on also—bulking of course far larger than the drama for the age itself if not for posterity.

In *Doctor Faustus* we have the special case where religious ritual, and blasphemous substitutes for ritual, are central in a drama. The Prayer Book's admonition about the abuse of Holy Communion strikingly illuminates Marlowe's dramatization of blasphemy:

> Dearly beloved in the Lord: ye that mind to come to the holy Communion of the body and blood of our Saviour Christ, must consider what S. Paul writeth to the Corinthians, how he exhorteth all persons diligently to try and examine themselves, before they presume to eat of that bread, and drink of that cup: for as the benefit is great, if with a truly penitent heart and lively faith we receive that holy sacrament (for then we spiritually eat the flesh of Christ, and drink his blood, then we dwell in Christ and Christ in us, we be one with Christ, and Christ with us:) so is the danger great, if we receive the same unworthily. For then we be guilty of the body and blood of Christ our Saviour. We eat and drink our own damnation, not considering the Lord's body.

To eat and drink damnation describes not only Faustus' attitude but the physical embodiment of it, as we shall see in considering the ramifications of gluttony in the play.

Blasphemy implies belief of some sort, as T. S. Eliot observed in pointing, in his seminal 1918 essay, to blasphemy as crucial in Marlowe's work; blasphemy involves also, consciously or unconsciously, the magical assumption that signs can be identified with what they signify. Ministers were warned by several rubrics in the Tudor Prayer Books against allowing parishioners to convey the bread

of the sacrament secretly away, lest they "abuse it to superstition and wickedness." Such abuse depends on believing, or feeling, that, regardless of its context, the bread is God, so that by appropriating it one can magically take advantage of God. Spelled out in this way, the magical thinking which identifies sign and significance seems so implausible as to be trivial. But for the sort of experience expressed in *Doctor Faustus,* the identifications and displacements that matter take place at the levels where everyone is ignorant, the regions where desire seeks blindly to discover or recover its objects. Faustus repeatedly moves through a circular pattern, from thinking of the joys of heaven, through despairing of ever possessing them, to embracing magical dominion as a blasphemous substitute. The blasphemous pleasures lead back, by an involuntary logic, to a renewed sense of the lost heavenly joys for which blasphemy comes to seem a hollow substitute—like a stolen Host found to be only bread after all. And so the unsatisfied need starts his Ixion's wheel on another cycle.

The irony which attends Faustus' use of religious language to describe magic enforces an awareness of this circular dramatic movement. "Divinity, adieu! / These . . . necromantic books are heavenly" [l.76-7]. What seems to be a departure is betrayed by "heavenly" to be also an effort to return. "Come," Faustus says to Valdes and Cornelius, "make me blest by your sage conference" [ll.126-27]. And Valdes answers that their combined skill in magic will "make all nations to canonize us" [l.149]. In repeatedly using such expressions, which often "come naturally" in the colloquial language of a Christian society, the rebels seem to stumble uncannily upon words which condemn them by the logic of a situation larger than they are. So Mephistophilis, when he wants to praise the beauty of the courtesans whom he can give to Faustus, falls into saying:

> As wise as Saba, or as beautiful
> As was bright Lucifer before his fall.
>
> [ll.589-90]

The auditor experiences a qualm of awe in recognizing how Mephistophilis has undercut himself by this allusion to Lucifer when he was still the star of the morning, bright with an altitude and innocence now lost.

The last and largest of these revolutions is the one that begins with showing Helen to the students, moves through the Old Man's effort to guide Faustus' steps "unto the way of life," [l.1274] and ends with Helen. In urging the reality of Grace, the Old Man performs the role of Spenser's Una in the Cave of Despair, but Faustus can only think "Hell calls for right" [l.1287]. Mephistophilis, like Spenser's Despair, is ready with a dagger for suicide; Marlowe at this point is almost dramatizing Spenser. Faustus asks for "heavenly Helen," "To glut the longing of my heart's desire" and "extinguish clean / Those thoughts that do dissuade me from my vow" [ll.1320-24]. The speech to Helen is a wonderful poetic fusion of many elements, combining chivalric worship of a mistress with humanist intoxication over the project of recovering antiquity. In characteristic Renaissance fashion, Faustus proposes to relive classical myth in a Medieval way: "I will be Paris . . . wear thy colors" [ll.1335, 1338]. But these secular elements do not account for the peculiar power of the speech; the full awe and beauty of it depend on hoping to find the holy in the profane. the prose source can provide a useful contrast here; Helen is described there so as to emphasize a forthright sexual appeal:

> her hair hanged down as fair as the beaten gold, and of such length that it reached down to her hams, with amorous coal-black eyes, a sweet and pleasant face, her lips red as a cherry, her cheeks of rose all colour, her mouth small, her neck white as the swan, tall and slender of personage . . . she looked round about her with a rolling hawk's eye, a smiling and wanton countenance . . .

On the stage, of course, a full description was not necessary; but Marlowe in any case was after a different kind of meaning. He gives us nothing of the sort of enjoyment that the Faust book describes in saying that Helen was "so beautiful and delightful a piece" that Faustus "made her his common concubine and bedfellow" and "could not be one hour from her . . . and to his seeming, in time she was with child." There is nothing sublime about this account, but it has its own kind of strength—an easy, open-eyed relishing which implies that sensual fulfillment is possible and satisfying in its place within a larger whole. The writer of the Faust book looked at Helen with his own eyes and his own assumption that the profane and the holy are separate. But for Marlowe—it was his great, transforming contribution to the Faust myth—the magical dominion and pleasures of Dr. Faustus ambiguously mingle the divine and the human, giving to the temporal world a wonder and excitement which is appropriated, daringly and precariously, from the supernatural.

The famous lines are so familiar, out of context, as an apotheosis of love, that one needs to blink to see them as they fit into the play's motion, with the play's ironies. (Eartha Kitt, telling *Life* magazine about playing Helen opposite Orson Welles, ignored all irony, saying simply "I made him immortal with a kiss.") By contrast with the Helen of the source, who has legs, Marlowe's Helen is described only in terms of her face and lips; and her beauty is *power*:

> Was this the face that launch'd a thousand ships,
> And burnt the topless towers of Ilium?
> [ll. 1328-29]

The kiss which follows is a way of reaching this source of power; it goes with a prayer, "Make me immortal with a kiss," and the action is like taking communion, promising, like communion, a way to immortality. It leads immediately to an ecstacy in which the soul seems to leave the body: "Her lips suck forth my soul: see where it flies!" The speech ends with a series of worshipping gestures expressing wonder, awe, and a yearning towards encountering a fatal power. It is striking that Helen comes to be compared to Jupiter, god of power, rather than to a goddess:

> O thou art fairer than the evening air
> Clad in the beauty of a thousand stars;
> Brighter art thou than flaming Jupiter
> When he appeared to hapless Semele;
> More lovely than the monarch of the sky
> In wanton Arethusa's azured arms;

> And none but thou shall be my paramour.
> [ll.1341-48]

Upward gestures are suggested by "the evening air" and "the monarch of the sky"; Faustus' attitude towards Helen is linked to that of hapless Semele when Jupiter descended as a flame, and to that of the fountain nymph Arethusa when she embraced Jupiter in her spraylike, watery, and sky-reflecting arms. Consummation with the power first described in Helen's face is envisaged as dissolution in fire or water.

I can imagine a common-sense objection at this point to the effect that after all Faustus' encounter with Helen is a sexual rhapsody, and that all this talk about it does not alter the fact, since after all a kiss is a kiss. Mistresses, it could be added, are constantly compared to heaven and to gods, and lovers often feel, without being blasphemers, that a kiss makes mortality cease to matter. But it is just here that, at the risk of laboring the obvious, I want to insist that Marlowe's art gives the encounter meaning both as a particular kind of sexual experience *and* as blasphemy.

The stage directions of the 1604 text bring the Old Man back just at the moment when Faustus in so many words is making Helen into heaven:

> Here will I dwell, for heaven be in these lips
> And all is dross that is not Helena:
> > *Enter old*
> > *man.*
> > [ll.1333-34]

This figure of piety is a presence during the rest of the speech; his perspective is summarized after its close: "Accursed Faustus, miserable man, / That from thy soul exclud'st the grace of Heaven."

Another perspective comes from the earlier scenes in the play where the nature of heaven and the relation to it of man and devil is established in conversations between Mephistophilis and Faustus. For example, the large and final line in the later scene, "And all is dross that is not Helena," has almost exactly the same movement as an earlier line of Mephistophilis' which ends in "heaven."

> And, to be short, when all the world dissolves,
> And every creature shall be purified,
> All place shall be hell that is not heaven.
> [ll.556-59]

One does not need to assume a conscious recognition by the audience of this parallel, wonderfully ironic as it is when we come to hear it as an echo. What matters is the recurrence of similar gestures in language about heaven and its substitutes, so that a meaning of heaven, and postures towards it, are established.

The most striking element in this poetic complex is a series of passages involving a face:

> Why, this is hell, nor am I out of it:
> Think'st thou that I, that saw the face of God,
> And tasted the eternal joys of heaven,
> Am not tormented with ten thousand hells,
> In being depriv'd of everlasting bliss?
> [ll.312-16]

Just as Faustus' rapt look at Helen's face is followed by his kiss, so in the lines of Mephistophilis, "saw the face of God" is followed by "tasted the eternal joys of heaven."

Both face and taste are of course traditional religious imagery, as is motion upward and downward. Marlowe's shaping power composes traditional elements into a single complex gesture and imaginative situation which appears repeatedly. The face is always high, something above to look up to, reach or leap up to, or to be thrown down from:

> FAUSTUS: Was not that Lucifer an angel once?
>
> MEPHISTOPHILIS: Yes, Faustus, and most dearly lov'd of God.
>
> FAUSTUS: How comes it then that he is prince of devils?
>
> MEPHISTOPHILIS: Oh, by aspiring pride and insolence;
> For which God threw him from the face of heaven.
>
> [ll.300-04]

A leaping-up complementary to this throwing-down, with a related sense of guilt, is expressed in Faustus' lines as he enters at midnight, about to conjure and eagerly hoping to have "these joys in full possession":

> Now that the gloomy shadow of the night,
> Longing to view Orion's drizzling look,
> Leaps from th' antarctic world unto the sky,
> And dims the welkin with her pitchy breath,
> Faustus, begin thine incantations . . .
>
> [ll.235-39]

Here the reaching upward in *leaps* is dramatized by the word's position as a heavy stress at the opening of the line. There is a guilty suggestion in *gloomy*—both discontented and dark—linked with *longing to view.* An open-mouthed panting is suggested by *pitchy breath,* again with dark associations of guilt which carry through to Faustus' own breath as he says his *incantations* (itself an open-throated word). The whole passage has a grotesque, contorted quality appropriate to the expression of an almost unutterable desire, at the same time that it magnificently affirms this desire by throwing its shadow up across the heavens.

A more benign vision appears in the preceding scene, where the magician Valdes promises Faustus that "serviceable spirits" will attend:

> Sometimes like women, or unwedded maids,
> Shadowing more beauty in their airy brows
> Than has the white breasts of the queen of love.
>
> [ll.156-58]

Here we get an association of the breast with the face corresponding to the linkage elsewhere of tasting power and joy with seeing a face. The lines suggest by "airy brows" that the faces are high (as well as that the women are unsubstantial spirits).

The complex we have been following gets its fullest and most intense expression in a passage of Faustus' final speech, where the imagery of communion with which we began is one element. To present it in this fuller context, I quote again:

> The stars move still, time runs, the clock will strike,
> The devil will come, and Faustus must be damn'd.
> O I'll leap up to my God: who pulls me down?
> See, see, where Christ's blood streams in the firmament.
> One drop would save my soul, half a drop, ah, my Christ.
> Ah, rend not my heart for naming of my Christ,
> Yet will I call on him: O, spare me, Lucifer!
> Where is it now? 'tis gone: and see, where God Stretcheth out his arm, and bends his ireful brows:
>
> [ll.1429-37]

Here the leap is discovered to be unrealizable. Faustus' blasphemous vision of his own soul with Helen—"See, where it flies"—is matched now by "See, see, where Christ's blood streams." It is "in the firmament," as was Orion's drizzling look. A paroxysm of choking tension at once overtakes Faustus when he actually envisages drinking Christ's blood. And yet—"one drop would save my soul." Such communion is denied by the companion vision of the face, now dreadful, "ireful brows" instead of "airy brows," above and bending down in overwhelming anger.

When we turn to consider the presentation of the underside of Faustus' motive, complementary to his exalted longings, the Prayer Book, again, can help us understand Marlowe. The Seventeenth of the Thirty-Nine Articles contains a warning remarkably applicable to Faustus:

> As the godly consideration of Predestination, and our election in Christ, is full of sweet, pleasant, and unspeakable comfort to godly persons. . . . So, for curious and carnal persons, lacking the spirit of Christ, to have continually before their eyes the sentence of God's Predestination, is a most dangerous downfall, whereby the Devil doth thrust them either into desperation, or into wretchlessness of most unclean living, no less perilous than desperation.

Faustus is certainly a "curious and carnal person," and he has "the sentence of God's Predestination" continually before his eyes, without "the spirit of Christ." The Article relates this characteristically Calvinist predicament to the effort to use the body to escape despair: "wretchlessness" (for which the New English Dictionary cites only this instance) seems to combine wretchedness and recklessness. The phrase "most unclean living" suggests that the appetites become both inordinate and perverse.

The psychoanalytic understanding of the genesis of perversions can help us to understand how, as the Article says, such unclean living is spiritually motivated—like blasphemy, with which it is closely associated. We have noticed how blasphemy involves a magical identification of action with meaning, of sign with significance. A similar identification appears in perversion as Freud has described it. Freud sees in perversions a continuation of the secondary sexual satisfactions dominant in childhood. The pervert, in this view, is attempting, by repeating a way of using the body in relation to a certain limited sexual object, to recover or continue in adult life the meaning of a relationship fixed on this action and object in childhood.

So, for example, the sucking perversions may seek to establish a relationship of dependence by eating someone more powerful. Faustus lives for twenty-four years "in all voluptuousness," in "wretchlessness of most unclean living": it is the meanings that he seeks in sensation that make his pleasures unclean, violations of taboo. We have seen how what he seeks from Orion or from Helen is an equivalent for Christ's blood, how the voluptuousness which is born of his despair is an effort to find in carnal satisfactions an incarnation. Perversion can thus be equivalent to a striving for a blasphemous communion. In the same period that T. S. Eliot wrote the essay in which he pointed to the importance of Marlowe's blasphemy, his poem *Gerontion* expressed a vision of people in the modern world reduced to seeking spiritual experience in perverse sensuality and aestheticism:

> In the juvescence of the year
> Came Christ the tiger
>
> In depraved May, dogwood and chestnut, flow-
>   ering judas,
> To be eaten, to be divided, to be drunk
> Among whispers; by Mr. Silvero,
> With caressing hands, at Limoges
> Who walked all night in the next room;
> By Hakagawa, bowing among the Titians;
> Madame de Tornquist, in the dark room,
> Shifting the candles; Fräulein von Kulpe,
> Who turned in the hall, one hand on the door.

As I read the elusive chronology of Eliot's poem, Marlowe would have envisaged Helen in the luxuriance of a "depraved May" associated with the Renaissance, from which we come down, through a characteristically telescoped syntax, to the meaner modern versions of a black mass. What immediately concerns us here is the seeking of incarnation in carnal and aesthetic satisfactions. The perverse has an element of worship in it.

When we consider the imagery in **Doctor Faustus** in psychoanalytic terms, an oral emphasis is very marked, both in the expression of longings that reach towards the sublime and in the gluttony which pervades the play and tends towards the comic, the grotesque, and the terrible. It is perhaps not fanciful to link the recurrent need to leap up which we have seen with an infant's reaching upward to mother or breast, as this becomes fused in later life with desire for women as sources of intoxicating strength: the face as a source of power, to be obliviously kissed, "airy brows" linked to "the white breasts of the queen of love." The two parents seem to be confused or identified so that the need appears in fantasies of somehow eating the father, panting for Orion's drizzling look. This imagery neighbors directly religious images, Christ's streaming blood, the taste of heavenly joys.

It is because Faustus has the same fundamentally acquisitive attitude towards both secular and religious objects that the religious joys are unreachable. The ground of the attitude that sustenance must be gained by special knowledge or an illicit bargain with an ultimately hostile power is the deep conviction that sustenance will not be given freely, that life and power must come from a being who condemns and rejects Faustus. We can see his blasphe-

mous need, in psychoanalytic terms, as fixation or regression to infantile objects and attitudes, verging towards perverse developments of the infantile pursued and avoided in obscure images of sexual degradation. But to keep the experience in the perspective with which Marlowe's culture saw it, we must recognize that Faustus' despair and obsessive hunger go with his inability to take part in Holy Communion. In Holy Communion, he would, in the words of the Prayer Book, "spiritually eat the flesh of Christ, and drink his blood . . . dwell in Christ . . . be one with Christ." In the Lord's Supper the very actions towards which the infantile, potentially disruptive motive tends are transformed, for the successful communicant, into a way of reconciliation with society and the ultimate source and sanction of society. But communion can only be reached by "a truly contrite heart" which recognizes human finitude, and with "a lively faith" in the possibility of God's love. Psychoanalytic interpretation can easily lead to the misconception that when we encounter infantile or potentially perverse imagery in a traditional culture it indicates, *a priori*, neurosis or degradation. Frequently, on the contrary, such imagery is enacted in ritual and used in art as a way of controlling what is potentially disruptive. We are led by these considerations to difficult issues about the status and limits of psychoanalytic interpretation beyond the scope of this essay, and to ultimate issues about whether worship is necessary which each of us must settle as we can.

But for our purposes here, the necessary point is the perspective which the possibility of Holy Communion gives within Marlowe's play. Tragedy involves a social perspective on individual experience; frequently this perspective is expressed by reference to ritual or ceremonial acts, acts whose social and moral meaning is felt immediately and spontaneously. The hero one way or another abuses the ritual because he is swept away by the currents of deep aberrant motives associated with it, motives which it ordinarily serves to control. In **Doctor Faustus** this public, social ritual is Holy Communion. How deeply it is built into sensibility appears, for example, when Faustus stabs his arm:

> My blood congeals, and I can write no more.
> . . . .
> *Faustus gives thee his soul.* Ah, there it stayed.
> Why shouldst thou not? Is not thy soul thy own?
>   [ll.494, 499-500]

This is the crucial moment of the black mass, for Faustus is imitating Christ in sacrificing himself—but to Satan instead of to God. A moment later he will repeat Christ's last words, "Consummatus est." His flesh cringes to close the self-inflicted wound, so deeply is its meaning understood by his body.

The deep assumption that all strength must come from consuming another accounts not only for the desperate need to leap up again to the source of life, but also for the moments of reckless elation in fantasy. Faustus uses the word "fantasy" in exactly its modern psychological sense:

> . . . your words have won me at the last,
> To practice magic and concealed arts:
> Yet not your words only, but mine own fantasy,

Which will receive no object, for my head
But ruminates on necromantic skill.

[ll.129-33]

Here "ruminates" carries on the imagery of gluttony. Moving restlessly round the circle of his desires, Faustus wants more from nature than nature can give, and gluttony is the form his "unclean living" characteristically takes. The verb "glut" recurs: "How am I glutted with conceit of this!" "That heavenly Helen . . . to glut the longing. . . . " The Prologue summarizes his career in the same terms, introducing like an overture the theme of rising up by linking gluttony with a flight of Icarus:

Till swoll'n with cunning, of a self conceit,
His waxen wings did mount above his reach,
And melting heavens conspir'd his overthrow.
For falling to a devilish exercise,
And glutted now with learnings golden gifts,
He surfeits upon cursed Negromancy.

[ll.20-5]

On the final night, when his fellow scholars try to cheer Faustus, one of them says, " 'Tis but a surfeit, never fear, man." He answers, "A surfeit of deadly sin, that hath damn'd both body and soul" [ll.1364-67]. How accurately this exchange defines the spiritual, blasphemous motivation of his hunger!

Grotesque and perverse versions of hunger appear in the comedy. Like much of Shakespeare's low comedy, the best clowning in **Doctor Faustus** spells out literally what is metaphorical in the poetry. No doubt some of the prose comedy, even in the 1604 Quarto, is not by Marlowe; but when the comic action is a burlesque that uses imaginative associations present in the poetry, its authenticity is hard to doubt. Commentators are often very patronizing about the scene with the Pope, for example; but it carries out the motive of gluttony in a delightful and appropriate way by presenting a Pope "whose *summum bonum* is in belly cheer" [l.855], and by having Faustus snatch his meat and wine away and render his exorcism ludicrous, baffling magic with magic. Later Wagner tells of Faustus himself carousing and swilling amongst the students with "such belly-cheer / As Wagner in his life ne're saw the like" [ll.1343-44]. The presentation of the Seven Deadly Sins, though of course traditional, comes back to hunger again and again, in gross and obscene forms; after the show is over, Faustus exclaims "O, this feeds my soul!" One could go on and on.

Complementary to the active imagery of eating is imagery of being devoured. Such imagery was of course traditional, as for example in cathedral carvings of the Last Judgment and in the Hell's mouth of the stage. With being devoured goes the idea of giving blood, also traditional but handled, like all the imagery, in a way to bring together deep implications. To give blood is for Faustus a propitiatory substitute for being devoured or torn in pieces. The relation is made explicit when, near the end, Mephistophilis threatens that if he repents, "I'll in piece-meal tear thy flesh." Faustus collapses at once into propitiation, signalled poignantly by the epithet "sweet" which is always on his hungry lips:

Sweet Mephistophilis, intreat thy Lord

To pardon my unjust presumption,
And with my blood again I will confirm
My former vow I made to Lucifer.

[ll.1307-10]

By his pact Faustus agrees to be devoured later provided that he can do the devouring in the meantime. Before the signing, he speaks of paying by using other people's blood:

The god thou servest is thine own appetite,
Wherein is fix'd the love of Belsabub.
To him I'll build an altar and a church,
And offer luke warm blood of new born babes.

[ll.443-46]

But it has to be his own blood. The identification of his blood with his soul (a very common traditional idea) is underscored by the fact that his blood congeals just as he writes "gives thee his soul," and by Mephistophilis' vampire-like exclamation, as the blood clears again under the influence of his ominous fire: "O what will I not do to obtain his soul."

Faustus' relation to the Devil here is expressed in a way that was characteristic of witchcraft—or perhaps one should say, of the fantasies of witchhunters about witchcraft. Witch lore often embodies the assumption that power can be conveyed by giving and taking the contents of the body, with which the soul is identified, especially the blood. To give blood to the devil—and to various animal familiars—was the ritual expression of submission, for which in return one got special powers. Witches could be detected by the "devil's mark" from which the blood was drawn. In stabbing his arm, Faustus is making a "devil's mark" or "witch's mark" on himself.

The clown contributes to this theme in his role as a commonsense prose foil to the heroic, poetic action of the protagonist. Between the scene where Faustus proposes a pact to buy Mephistophilis' service and the scene of the signing, Wagner buys a ragged but shrewd old "clown" into his service. He counts on hunger:

. . . the villain is bare, and out of service, and
so hungry that I know he would give his soul to
the Devil for a shoulder of mutton, though it
were blood raw.

[ll.358-61]

We have just heard Faustus exclaim:

Had I as many souls as there be stars,
I'd give them all for Mephistophilis.

[ll.338-39]

But the clown is not so gullibly willing to pay all:

How, my soul to the Devil for a shoulder of mutton, though 'twere blood raw? Not so, good friend, by 'rlady I had need to have it well roasted, and good sauce to it, if I pay so dear.

[ll.362-65]

After making game of the sturdy old beggar's ignorance of Latin tags, Wagner assumes the role of the all-powerful magician:

Bind yourself presently unto me for seven years,
or I'll turn all the lice about thee into familiars,
and they shall tear thee in pieces.

[ll.377-80]

But again the clown's feet are on the ground:

> Do you hear sir? you may save that labour, they
> are too familiar with me already. Swounds, they
> are as bold with my flesh, as if they paid for me
> meat and drink.

This scene has been referred to as irrelevant padding put in by other hands to please the groundlings! Clearly the clown's independence, and the *detente* of his common man's wit which brings things down to the physical, is designed to set off the folly of Faustus' elation in his bargain. Mephistophilis, who is to become the hero's "familiar spirit" (as the Emperor calls him later at line 1011), "pays for" his meat and drink, and in due course will "make bold" with his flesh. The old fellow understands such consequences, after his fashion, as the high-flown hero does not.

One final, extraordinarily complex image of surfeit appears in the last soliloquy, when Faustus, frantic to escape from his own greedy identity, conceives of his whole body being swallowed up by a cloud and then vomited away:

> Then will I headlong run into the earth:
> Earth gape. O no, it will not harbour me:
> You stars that reign'd at my nativity,
> Whose influence hath allotted death and hell,
> Now draw up Faustus like a foggy mist
> Into the entrails of yon labouring cloud,
> That when you vomit forth into the air,
> My limbs may issue from your smoky mouths,
> So that my soul may but ascend to heaven:
> [ll.1441-49]

Taken by themselves, these lines might seem to present a very far-fetched imagery. In relation to the imaginative design we have been tracing they express self-disgust in terms exactly appropriate to Faustus' earlier efforts at self-aggrandizement. The hero asks to be swallowed and disgorged, anticipating the fate his sin expects and attempting to elude damnation by separating body and soul. Yet the dreadful fact is that these lines envisage death in a way which makes it a consummation of desires expressed earlier. Thus in calling up to the "stars which reigned at my nativity," Faustus is still adopting a posture of helpless entreaty towards powers above. He assumes their influence to be hostile but nevertheless inescapable; he is still unable to believe in love. And he asks to be "drawn up," "like a foggy mist," as earlier the "gloomy shadow," with its "pitchy breath," sought to leap up. The whole plea is couched as an eat-or-be-eaten bargain: you may eat my body if you will save my soul.

In the second half of the soliloquy Faustus keeps returning to this effort to distinguish body and soul. As the clock finally strikes, he asks for escape in physical dissolution:

> Now, body, turn to air,
> Or Lucifer will bear thee quick to hell:
>   *Thunder and lightning.*
> Oh soul, be chang'd into little water-drops,
> And fall into the ocean, ne'er be found:
> [ll.1470-73]

It is striking that death here is envisaged in a way closely similar to the visions of sexual consummation in the Helen speech. The "body, turn to air," with the thunder and lightning, can be related to the consummation of hapless Semele with flaming Jupiter; the soul becoming little water-drops recalls the showery consummation of Arethusa. Of course the auditor need not notice these relations, which in part spring naturally from a pervasive human tendency to equate sexual release with death. The auditor does feel, however, in these sublime and terrible entreaties, that Faustus is still Faustus. Analysis brings out what we all feel—that Faustus cannot repent. Despite the fact that his attitude towards his motive has changed from exaltation to horror, he is still dominated by the same motive—body and soul are one, as he himself said in the previous scene: "hath damned both body and soul." The final pleas themselves confirm his despair, shaped as they are by the body's desires and the assumptions those desires carry.

I said at the outset that because Marlowe dramatizes blasphemy as heroic endeavor, his play is irreducibly dramatic. But in the analytical process of following out the themes of blasphemy and gluttony, I have been largely ignoring the heroic side of the protagonist, the "Renaissance" side of the play. It is high time to emphasize that Marlowe was able to present blasphemy as he did, and gluttony as he did, only because he was able to envisage them as something more or something else: "his dominion that exceeds in this / Stretcheth as far as doth the mind of man." We have been considering how the play presents a shape of longing and fear which might have lost itself in the fulfillment of the Lord's Supper or become obscene and hateful in the perversions of a witches' sabbath. But in fact Faustus is neither a saint nor a witch—he is Faustus, a particular man whose particular fortunes are defined not by ritual but by drama.

When the Good Angel tells Faustus to "lay that damned book aside . . . that is blasphemy," the Evil Angel can answer in terms that are not moral but heroic:

> Go forward, Faustus, in that famous art
> Wherein all nature's treasury is contain'd:
> Be thou on earth as Jove is in the sky,
> Lord and commander of these elements.
> [ll.102-05]

It is because the alternatives are not simply good or evil that Marlowe has not written a morality play but a tragedy: there is the further, heroic alternative. In dealing with the blasphemy, I have emphasized how the vision of magic joys invests earthly things with divine attributes; but the heroic quality of the magic depends on fusing these divine suggestions with tangible values and resources of the secular world.

This ennobling fusion depends, of course, on the poetry, which brings into play an extraordinary range of contemporary life:

> From Venice shall they drag huge argosies
> And from America the golden fleece
> That yearly stuffs old Philip's treasury.
> [ll.159-61]

Here three lines draw in sixteenth-century classical

studies, exploration and commercial adventure, national rivalries, and the stimulating disruptive influence of the new supply of gold bullion. Marlowe's poetry is sublime because it extends desire so as to envisage as objects of passion the larger life of society and nature: "Was this the face that . . . "—that did what? " . . . launched a thousand ships." "Clad in the beauty of . . . "—of what? " . . . a thousand stars." ***Doctor Faustus*** is a sublime play because Marlowe was able to occupy so much actual thought and life by following the form of Faustus' desire. At the same time, it is a remorselessly objective, ironic play, because it dramatizes the ground of the desire which needs to ransack the world for objects; and so it expresses the precariousness of the whole enterprise along with its magnificence.

Thus Faustus' gluttonous preoccupation with satisfactions of the mouth and throat is also a delight in the power and beauty of language: "I see there's virtue in my heavenly words." Physical hunger is also hunger for knowledge; his need to depend on others, and to show power by compelling others to depend on him, is also a passion for learning and teaching. Academic vices and weaknesses shadow luminous academic virtues: there is a fine, lonely, generous mastery about Faustus when he is with his colleagues and the students; and Mephistophilis too has a moving dignity in expounding unflinchingly the dreadful logic of damnation to Faustus as to a disciple. The inordinate fascination with secrets, with what cannot be named, as Mephistophilis cannot name God, includes the exploring, inquiring attitude of "Tell me, are there many heavens above the moon?" The need to leap up becomes such aspirations as the plan to "make a bridge through the moving air / To pass the ocean with a band of men." Here we have in germ that sense of man's destiny as a vector moving through open space which Spengler described as the Faustian soul form. Faustus' alienation, which we have discussed chiefly as it produces a need for blasphemy, also motivates the rejection of limitations, the readiness to alter and appropriate the created universe—make the moon drop or ocean rise—appropriating them for *man* instead of for the greater glory of God, because the heavens are "the book of Jove's high firmament," and one can hope for nothing from Jove. Perhaps most fundamental of all is the assumption that power is something outside oneself, something one does not become (as a child becomes a man); something beyond and stronger than oneself (as God remains stronger than man); *and yet* something one can capture and ride—by manipulating symbols.

Marlowe of course does not anticipate the kind of manipulation of symbols which actually has, in natural science, produced this sort of power; Mephistophilis answers Faustus with Ptolemy, not Copernicus—let alone the calculus. But Marlowe was able to exemplify the creative function of controlling symbols by the way the form of poetic drama which he developed uses poetry. He made poetic speech an integral part of drama by exhibiting it as a mode of action: Faustus can assert about himself, "This word damnation terrifies not him, / For he confounds hell in Elysium." The extraordinary pun in "confounds hell in Elysium" suggests that Faustus is able to change the world by the way he names it, to *destroy* or *baffle* hell by *equating* or *mixing* it with Elysium.

Professor Scott Buchanan, in his discussion of tragedy in *Poetry and Mathematics*, suggested that we can see tragedy as an experiment where the protagonist tests reality by trying to live a hypothesis. Elizabethan tragedy, seen in this way, can be set beside the tentatively emerging science of the period. The ritualistic assumptions of alchemy were beginning to be replaced by ideas of observation; a clearcut conception of the experimental testing of hypothesis had not developed, but Bacon was soon to speak of putting nature on the rack to make her yield up her secrets. Marlowe knew Thomas Harriot: Baines reports his saying "That Moses was but a juggler, and that one Heriots being Sir W. Raleigh's man can do more than he." Faustus' scientific questions and Mephistophilis' answers are disappointing; but the hero's whole enterprise is an experiment, or "experience" as the Elizabethans would have termed it. We watch as the author puts him on the rack.

> FAUSTUS: Come, I think hell's a fable.
>
> MEPHISTOPHILIS: Ay, think so still, 'till experience change thy mind.
>
> [ll.559-60]

In ***Tamburlaine,*** Marlowe had invented a hero who creates himself out of nothing by naming himself a demigod. By contrast with the universe assumed in a play like *Everyman,* where everything has its right name, ***Tamburlaine*** assumes an open situation where new right names are created by the hero's combination of powers: he conceives a God-like identity for himself, persuades others to accept his name by the "strong enchantments" of an Orphic speech, and imposes his name on stubborn enemies by the physical action of "his conquering sword." This self-creating process is dramatized by tensions between what is expressed in words and what is conveyed by physical action on the stage: the hero declares what is to happen, and we watch to see whether words will become deeds—whether, in the case of Tamburlaine, man will become demigod.

The high poetry, the bombast, of Marlowe and kindred Elizabethans is not shaped to express what is, whether a passion or a fact, but to make something happen or become—it is incantation, a willful, self-made sort of liturgy. The verbs are typically future and imperative, not present indicative. And the hero constantly talks about himself as though from the outside, using his own name so as to develop a self-consciousness which aggrandizes his identity, or cherishes it, or grieves for it: "Settle thy studies, Faustus, and begin . . . " [l.29]; "What shall become of Faustus, being in hell forever?" [ll.1382-83]. In the opening speech, Faustus uses his own name seven times in trying on the selves provided by the various arts. In each unit of the speech, the words are in tension with physical gestures. As Faustus "levels at the end of every art," he reaches for successive volumes; he is looking in books for a miracle. But the tension breaks as he puts each book aside because "Yet art thou still but Faustus and a man." When finally he takes up the necromantic works, there is a temporary consummation, a present-indicative simultaneity of words and gestures: "Ay, these are those that

Faustus most desires." At this point, the actor can use gesture to express the new being which has been seized, standing up and spreading his arms as he speaks the tremendous future-tense affirmation: "All things that move between the quiet poles. / Shall be at my command. . . . " At the very end of the play Faustus' language is still demanding miracles, while the *absence* of corroborating physical actions makes clear that the universe cannot be equated with his self: "Stand still, you ever-moving spheres of heaven. . . . " King Lear in the storm, at the summit of Elizabethan tragedy, is similarly trying (and failing) to realize a magical omnipotence of mind: ". . . all-shaking thunder, / Smite flat the thick rotundity of the world. . . . "

The double medium of poetic drama was peculiarly effective to express this sort of struggle for omnipotence and transcendent incarnation along with its tragic and comic failure. The dramatist of genius can do two things at once: Marlowe can "vaunt his heavenly verse," animating the reach of Faustus' motive—and putting into his hero much that, on the evidence of his other plays and of his life (beyond our scope here), was in himself. At the same time he is judge and executioner, bringing his hero remorselessly to his terrible conclusion. At the end of the text of *Doctor Faustus,* Marlowe wrote "*Terminat hora diem, Terminat Author opus.*" As my friend Professor John Moore has remarked, it is as though he finished the play at midnight! The final hour ends Faustus' day; but Marlowe is still alive. As the author, he has been in control: *he* has terminated the work and its hero. This is another kind of power from that of magical dominion, a power that depends on the resources of art, realized in alliance with the "patient judgements" in an audience. It has not been a drumhead trial and execution, moreover, based on arbitrary, public-safety law. Though the final Chorus pulls back, in relief, to such a position, we have seen in detail, notably in the final soliloquy, how the fate of the hero is integral with his motive. In *Tamburlaine,* it was the hero who said "I thus conceiving and subduing both. . . . Shall give the world to note for all my birth, / That Vertue solely is the sum of glorie." Fundamental artistic limitations resulted from the identification of Marlowe with his protagonist in that play. But now, at the end of *Doctor Faustus,* Marlowe has earned an identity apart from his hero's—he is the author. He has done so by at once conceiving and subduing the protagonist.

The analogy between tragedy and a scapegoat ritual is very clear here: Faustus the hero has carried off into death the evil of the motive he embodied, freeing from its sin, for the moment, the author-executioner and the participating audience. The crop of stories which grew up about one devil too many, a real one, among the actors shows how popular tendencies to project evil in demons were put to work (and controlled, so far as "patient judgements" were concerned) by Marlowe. Popular experience of public executions provided, as Mr. John Holloway has recently pointed out [in his *The Story of the Night*] (and Wyndham Lewis before him [in his *The Lion and the Fox*]), another paradigm for tragedy. We can add that, in Marlowe's case at least, some of the taboo quality which tends to stick to an executioner attached to the tragedian, a

sense of his contamination by the sin of the victim. He proudly claims, in classical terms, the prerogative of the author who terminates the work, has done with it. But in his own life what was working in the work caught up with him by the summons to appear before the Privy Council, and the subsequent death at Deptford—whether it was a consequence of his own tendency to give way to "sudden cruelty," or a successfully camouflaged murder to get rid of a scandalous client of Thomas Walsingham. Art, even such austere art as *Doctor Faustus,* did not save the man in the author. But the author did save, within the limits of art, and with art's permanence, much that was in the man, to become part of the evolving culture in which his own place was so precarious. (pp. 92-119)

C. L. Barber, "The Form of Faustus' Fortunes Good or Bad," in The Tulane Drama Review, *Vol. 8, No. 4, Summer, 1964, pp. 92-119.*

A. Bartlett Giamatti   (essay date 1972)

[*Giamatti was an American educator and author whose special areas of study were the medieval and Renaissance periods in England and Italy. He was also the president of Yale University and, from 1988 until his death a year later, he served as the commissioner of baseball. In the following essay, Giamatti postulates that* Doctor Faustus *examines the repercussions of Renaissance man's conviction that he could "remake or change or transform himself." The critic maintains that this play addresses the problem: "Given man's basic urge and potential for transformation, would man re-form himself in a good sense and be one of the blest, or would he de-form himself and become a monster?"*]

George Sabellicus was pleased to call himself, a contemporary tells us in 1507, "the younger Faust, the chief of necromancers, astrologer, the second magus, palmist, diviner with water and fire, second in the art of divination by water." But even this billing did not smooth the way, for Dr. Faust, as Sabellicus came to be called, was constantly forced to move on. City after city, nervously or defiantly, expelled him. It had always been so for the man called to the arts of illusion.

From antiquity through the seventeenth century, if no farther, the mummer, the mime, the juggler, the actor, the mountebank, the magician, even the scientist as astrologer or alchemist—all were suspect for their solitary or their irregular lives. But even more, they were profoundly distrusted for their varying and various capacities for irreverence. By irreverence, I mean not only their blasphemous conditions and conversation; I mean essentially their abilities to imitate and to transform, their gifts for changing shape and surpassing limits in ways which seemed to threaten Divine plan or Divinity itself. The historical Faust played to all these fears. By the time he disappears as an actual figure, around 1540, even his name has changed from George to Johann Faust—a harmless image within the historical records of his alleged sinister powers to manipulate appearances.

The Faust story is a product of the Protestant Reformation when, in Germany, men saw clearly the price of sin, the power of evil, and above all the limits of man. It was a time when the religious impulse, always ambiguous and now obsessed with purity and reform, precipitated out and identified its own darker side, the urge to magic and deformation. The Faust story is a Reformation story because it implies deformation as the result of any human impulse beyond or outside the strictly interpreted norm.

The Faust story sees both reformation and deformation as springing from the same source: the impulse to be at one with God—the difference being that the former results from submission to God, the latter from trying, like Faust, to assume Godhead. But the Faust story has even deeper roots than the Reformation. It draws its radical potency from that great Renaissance (and hence modern) myth which says that spiritual reformation and deformation derive from man's innate power of formation, the capacity of the self to shape the self. The Faust story is firmly rooted in Renaissance man's profound conviction that he is a Proteus, that he can remake or change or transform himself.

The problem in this attitude, a problem crystallized by the Faust story, is this: Given man's basic urge and potential for transformation, would man re-form himself in a good sense and be one of the blest, or would he de-form himself and become a monster? What shape would he fashion for himself? Would he be Hyperion, or a satyr? Both were in him. Finally, once he unleashed the process of transformation, could he stop it? This was the most haunting question of all, and is the issue in *Doctor Faustus.*

> we must now perform
> The form of Faustus' fortunes, good or bad.

So the chorus to Marlowe's play. And here Renaissance art offers itself as one solution to the massive ambiguities of Renaissance life. Performing is one way of forming, for the theatre can safely release the human desire for new shapes. It provides an arena for limitless aspiration and multiple shapes while containing this impulse within the physical limits of the theatre and the arbitrary structure of art. This is no final answer, because now the theatre becomes simply a public image, a public language, for man's private agonies. "The great Globe" is a theatrical place and an individual's head, and both are reservoirs in their way for the energy to change and to remake human form. Both are dangerous places. The final solution is to purify the mind and the place; it is to have another Reformation, a Puritan Revolution, and close down the theatres. You return to radical principles, write a poem justifying the ways of God to man, and go back to calling Faustus Satan or Eve. But that was all ahead. In the early 1590's, the theatre was still being fashioned as the medium for manageable metamorphosis. And Marlowe takes a giant step when he transforms the material from the English translation (1592) of the German *Faustbuch* (1587) into a play about how the splendid urge to aspire to new form can deform past salvation if the shape you want is that of God Himself.

Renaissance man felt he had the power to transform himself because he had the power of language. Words were units of energy. Through words man could assume forms and aspire to shapes and states otherwise beyond his reach. Words had this immense potency, this virtue, because they were derived from and were images of the Word, the Word of God which made us and which was God. Used properly, words could shape us in His image, and lead us to salvation. Through praise, in its largest sense, our words approach their source in the Word and, therefore, we approach Him.

Because words, like men, were fallen, however, they contained, as we do, shapes of evil within them. Fallen words, like men, are unstable elements; thus they are, as we are, such dangers to us. As we must always check that impulse to deformation in ourselves, so we must constantly be aware of the beast in language—Spenser calls it the Blatant Beast, whose rabid bite is vicious slander—and we must know that when we unleash a word and let it soar, we run the risk of loosing an evil force as well, one that we cannot control. We, as men using words, must stay within our limits, or what we master may master and misshape us.

This is simply to say that the power of words and the power in words reflect our fallen state—above the beasts, below the angels, and capable of assuming either form. As a power, language is neither good nor bad. It all depends upon how we convert this energy, upon how we transform this power, in the mind with the mind. We are what we are depending upon how we shape ourselves with words; depending on whether we use words as God intended us to use them, or we use words to set ourselves up in His place and assume His knowledge and power.

Because all men are users of the magic power, language, because all men are performers with words and transformers through words, the Renaissance could figure all men under the single image of the *magus,* the magician. And as there were two ways of using language to project new shapes, a good and a bad, the Renaissance distinguished two kinds of *magus.* One is the "goetic" or black magician. This is Faustus, or Spenser's Archimago, or—in his own fashion—Iago, who imposes a nightmare on the island of Love, Cyprus, and who transforms the shape of Desdemona in the head of Othello. The other kind of *magus* and magic is represented by the "natural" or white magician. In harmless form, this is Puck, who can take whatever shape he wants—"Sometime a horse I'll be, sometime a hound, / a hog, a headless bear, sometime a fire" [Shakespeare's *Midsummer Night's Dream*]—but whose power to transform finally will amend and harmonize all the divisions of love and the law. In Spenser's *Faerie Queene,* opposed to Archimago, there is Merlin in Book III who can project in his magic glass the true shape of love in Britomart's Artegall. Finally, there is the great white magician of Elizabethan literature, Prospero [in Shakespeare's *Tempest*], who controls not only form and substance in Ariel and Caliban, and fashions justice and love, but who also can recognize the limits of his art and drown his book. This knowledge of white Prospero—where his knowledge stops—is acquired by black Faustus much too late.

In the black-and white magicians, the Renaissance poets and thinkers saw concentrated the black dangers and the white glories of that single power, language, and that single urge, self-transformation. In the *magus,* they saw man;

through the One, they perceived the Many. Therefore Renaissance Faustus differs from all those other magicians who stand behind him in grand and receding array, Roger Bacon and Piero d'Albano (***Doctor Faustus*** I.i.155), the medieval Virgil (III.i.13), the sinister sorcerer Simon Magus, who offered to buy the power of the Holy Ghost (Acts viii:9-24; the apocryphal Acts of Peter), for Faustus is not simply doing tricks or trying to buy magic power. Faustus is any of us, any man using (and misusing) power in the quest for all knowledge and total control. Faustus is no trickster; he is modern man who would play the role of God.

In our play, the warring impulses for good and evil in the mind of everyman are visualized by the Good and Bad angels which hover around Faustus. Again, the single human head is the source for the double drive. And when we first meet those angels, the first words of the Good angel are:

> O, Faustus, lay that damnèd book aside,
> And gaze not on it. . . .
> Read, read the Scriptures. That is blasphemy.
> > [I.i.71-4]

Here, at the outset, is an indication of the way the play is a battle of books. We see how the deepest issue in the play is words, the language of black magic versus the language of Scripture. We see how the power of words to shape for good or ill, and how that power is used and how that power can use you, is the pivot on which the play turns. We see how, at bottom, the problem of language remains.

Throughout his career, as he struggled to shape a new idiom for the nascent English stage, Marlowe wrestled with the multiform angel (or demon) of language. He made his problem as a playwright the subject of his plays. He expanded the limits of the stage by writing of the human mind in its battle to surpass human limitation. He used soaring words as symbols of man's aspiring mind. And he used the lurking dangers in words to image the terrors of aspiring too far.

Only ***Doctor Faustus*** fully exploits the glories and terrors in language to illuminate the full ambiguity of the human condition, though even as early as *Hero and Leander* one can hear Marlowe exploring through words the terrain of human potential, its mountain peaks and dark ravines:

> And fruitful wits that in aspiring are,
> Shall discontent, run into regions farre.
> > [I.477-78]

In the earlier plays, however, the emphasis is heavily on man's mind as it soars beyond human limits—the dangers are not at issue yet—and thus the emphasis is on what language can do and not yet on what it can do to you. So we hear of the "aspiring mind" of Tamburlaine, and of his "conquering mind," whose foil is Bajazeth's "conquered head." Marlowe's great heroes all live in the present participle and the future tense. So in *Edward II* we hear of Mortimer's "virtue that aspires to heaven," but because we hear of it as he goes to prison, the ambiguities begin to emerge. And the ambiguities of the human condition are fully clear when we hear the Duke of Guise, whose

"aspiring thoughts aim at the crown" (***The Massacre at Paris,*** xix.24):

> That I like best that flies beyond my reach.
> Set me to scale the highest pyramidès
> And thereon set the diadem of France;
> I'll either rend it with my nails to naught
> Or mount the top with my aspiring wings,
> Although my downfall be the deepest hell.
> > [ii.42-7]

There is what the Marlovian hero always knows: that his superb urge to transcend may also damn him deep.

Even more interesting is the image of Icarus submerged in the metaphor of flight in the last two lines. This myth fascinated Marlowe all his life, for like winged words themselves, it was another way of imaging the glories and terrors of transcendence. We first meet Icarus in Marlowe's earliest play, ***Dido Queen of Carthage,*** when Dido passionately laments Aeneas' parting:

> I'll frame me wings of wax like Icarus,
> And o'er his ships will soar unto the sun,
> That they may melt and I fall in his arms.
> > [V.i.243-45]

Dido will be Icarus so that she may fall, but later in the words of the Duke of Guise Marlowe exploits the myth as an image of the act of reaching per se and he comes back to Icarus one last time—if ***Doctor Faustus*** is his last play—in the chorus' description of Faustus, who excelled in theological disputes:

> Till swoll'n with cunning of a self-conceit,
> His waxen wings did mount above his reach,
> And melting, heavens conspired his overthrow.
> > [Prol.20-2]

To say the Icarus myth has informed the substance of Marlowe's plays all along is a way of suggesting that Faustus, under various guises, has been all Marlowe's study. I am not implying Marlowe knew about Faust before he wrote of Faustus, though he may have, nor that Marlowe writes the same play over and over, for in crucial ways they are different. What I am suggesting is that in ***Doctor Faustus*** Marlowe's life-long obsessions with the language of aspiration found their perfect vehicle. However, there is another sense in which ***Doctor Faustus*** reveals Marlowe's life-long absorption in problems of language, and that emerges throughout the plays not in a Faust-like figure, but in a Faust pattern.

By Faust pattern, I mean that the crucial act in the Faust story is the consummation of a pact which promises a soul for twenty-four years of omnipotence. And in all the plays a pact or pledge has a critical role by representing that limit which the hero either rejects or overreaches. In ***Dido,*** it is the marriage pledge (Marlowe makes much of what his Virgilian source says is only a figment of Dido's imagination), which Aeneas superhumanly ignores to Dido's despair; in ***I Tamburlaine,*** there are Zenocrates' letters of safe conduct from the Great Cham himself which Tamburlaine, as his first act before us, countermands to prove himself "a greater man"; in ***The Jew of Malta,*** there are two pacts: the decrees Barabas refuses to sign which then deprive him of his goods (and goad him on) and the pledge between him and the Governor to betray the Turk, which both plan to break. In *Edward II,* the King is forced to sign a document banishing Gaveston, and in *The Massacre at Paris,* various pacts in the form of letters propel the Duke of Guise to his excesses, but none so much as the pledge of marriage—the "union and religious league"— between the King of Navarre and Margaret.

It would serve no purpose to push this pattern, if pattern it is, too hard. Still it is striking that in each play the hero defines himself and his role (or roles), his form and his performance, in terms of what for a better term we can call a verbal institution—some pact or pledge, letter, contract, or decree, whose validity as binding the hero at some point denies and which he tries to overcome. In all the plays, words supply a limit which the heroes' language attempts to supersede, an image of the mind trying to surpass our human limitations.

In *Doctor Faustus,* the verbal institution Faustus wants to overcome is language itself, language as it codifies, regulates, controls. And simply with his words, he can do this. He can send his words past the limits of other men's knowledge and control. But while his words are soaring, what about his deeds? What about the issue, the shapes, created by those flying words? If language is the power to form new realities, what are they? At the beginning of his career, with *Tamburlaine,* Marlowe saw no problem. "Go stout Theridamas; thy words are swords," says Mycetes. We change words to swords by prefixing an *s,* and for Tamburlaine things were almost that easy. He needed only to say he was a King to be one. In *Tamburlaine,* there is no gap between word and deed, no tragic lag between what you want and what you can have. But Tamburlaine is a figure of romance, the shepherd who becomes a knight and gets the girl. By the end of his career Marlowe had thought hard on our fallen state, and language; and tragedy, not romance, is the result.

In *Doctor Faustus,* the gap between word and deed widens and widens until it yawns like the mouth of Hell. As Faustus' language soars higher, the products of language— events, shapes, actions—become lower and lower, in the sense of trivial, in the sense of approaching Hell. What his words express and what they effect could not be more tragically separated. As we witness the widening gap between the mental spectacle the words conjure and the theatrical spectacle actually unfolding, between the way one thing is said and a very different effect is communicated or results, we see how Marlowe dramatizes the terrible ambiguities in the power of self-transformation through the magic of words.

First, the difference between what Faustus' words say and what his words actually do. In I.i we find Faustus alone in his study, about to "settle" his studies. He then speaks for some sixty-five lines. Now, according to his own words, he is a most learned man and very deep thinker; but according to what we see as a result of his words, Faustus has very patchy learning and a superficial mind. For while his words tell us he has soared above all organized human knowledge, they actually show us deep ignorance, particularly in the simple and central matters of the soul.

For instance, when Faustus dismisses Philosophy at line 10—he has attained its end; when he considers Medicine, finds it wanting, and dismisses it at line 27; when he says Law is all "paltry legacies," "external trash," and waves it away at line 36; and when he regards Theology and then, in the first of many unintentionally sinister puns (and there resides the issue of the play) bids it "adieu" at line 49—when he is saying all this, what do we actually see? When he says Philosophy is limited, we see a man who confounds Aristotle and Peter Ramus, a man who treats the deep questions of being and not being and the technique of disputing well as if they were the same. When he says Medicine is limited, we see a man who confuses gold and health, alchemy and physic, and who finds medicine wanting because it is not miracle, a lack he will remedy by turning to magic, miracle's parody. The soaring language does not offer us an ennobling spectacle; rather, the opposite.

When Faustus dismisses Law, something more sinister commences. To prove Law is really only legalism, Faustus quotes Justinian twice in Latin. In the first citation, Faustus misquotes Justinian. But if the ironic spectacle of misquoting what you claim is far beneath you were not enough, further ironies attend the second citation, which is: "The father cannot disinherit the son except . . ." (line 31). Faustus leaves the citation unfinished, but the rest of the play completes it. God the Father cannot disinherit man His son except when man chooses to will his soul to Satan. What Faustus considers legalistic trash far beneath his soaring mind is in reality an abiding principle which eludes his grasp.

Nowhere does Marlowe's technique of having Faustus dismiss a body of knowledge by a partial quotation have more devastating effect than in Faustus' denial of Theology. Faustus says Theology only teaches that we must sin and die, thus *che serà, serà,* and he wants no part of a doctrine whose lesson is that necessity hangs over us. Nowhere do we see his limitations through his statements of mastery more clearly than here and in his citations from Scripture. He cites, in Latin, Romans vi:23, "The wages of sin is death," but as with Justinian's words he fails to finish the line: "But the gift of God is eternal life through Jesus Christ our Lord." He cites the first Epistle of John, "If we say we have no sin, we deceive ourselves, and there is no truth within us," but he fails to finish the passage, "If we confess our sins he is faithful and just to forgive us our sins, and to cleanse us from all unrighteousness." It is certainly to convert, and abuse, the power of the Word through one's own words when the Bible is misshaped to justify turning to "heavenly" "necromantic books." The play's techniques and issues are concentrated in this first speech and projected into the rest of the drama. The more Faustus transforms himself into a god through language, looking down on all human experience and knowledge, the more we see his very words transform him into something foolish, ignorant, superficial; the more Faustus tells of total mastery, the more we see a process of enslavement. Finally, we begin to understand how Marlowe's irony operates through the techniques of partial citation; for when Faustus only partially quotes Justinian or the Bible, language releases a meaning which Faustus does not pursue but which throughout the action of the play pursues Faustus. That is the problem with language, and is the issue Marlowe probes.

Faustus has dismissed Philosophy, Medicine, Law, and Theology. He has embraced the "metaphysics of magicians." Then he exclaims:

> A sound magician is a demi-god.
> Here try thy brains to get a deity!
> Wagner—

Here are those crucial lines where Faustus says in effect that through magic he will assume powers only God has. Immense and potent lines. Then, "Wagner"—and Wagner, his servant and disciple, enters. The joke is verbally juxtaposing "deity" and "Wagner"; the joke is visually juxtaposing mighty Faustus and foolish Wagner, calling upon godhead and getting a goon. The terrifying implications of this process (and scene) develop in Act II.ii, when Faustus cries out to Christ, and Lucifer springs up. But that is tragedy, and later. This is still funny—challenging Heaven and getting Wagner—and here, in I.i, we really initiate the subplot.

The function of a subplot is to burlesque the concerns of a main plot by mirroring those concerns in lower form; not simply to reduce mighty concerns to absurdity but also to show us that no man's mighty self is immune to human fallibility, to foolishness, to flaw. The subplot is the great equalizer, savagely reducing or gently jesting the main concerns as the dramatist sees fit. The subplot's ironic spectacle and perspective make it a crucial element in **Doctor Faustus,** and in Act I, Marlowe introduces us to its uses. In Scene ii, Wagner and the two scholars, but mostly Wagner, burlesque Faustus and his two accomplices in magic in Scene i; in Scene iv, the actions of Wagner and Robin, the clown, provide farcical, shrewd commentary on Faustus and Mephistophilis in Scene iii. In Act II, the subplot begins to provide more than burlesque.

Scenes i and ii of Act II show us Faustus assuming the awesome powers of the devil, and at the end of Scene ii Lucifer gives Faustus a gift: "peruse this book and view it thoroughly, and thou shalt turn thyself into what shape thou wilt." But we really only understand the implications of this Satanic gift of words which shape when immediately in the following scene, Robin and Dick enter with one of Faustus' conjuring books. They mumble and jumble, parodying what has just preceded, and then make for a tavern where we meet them again three scenes later at Act III.iii. There, the Vintner searches them for a stolen cup. Robin decides to conjure. And Mephistophilis appears. This is suddenly no joke. As Mephistophilis is the first to say:

> To purge this rashness of this cursèd deed,
> First be thou turnèd to this ugly shape,
> For apish deeds transformèd to an ape. . . .
> Be thou transformed to a dog, and carry him
>   upon thy back.
>
>   [III.iii.40-2, 45]

The two clowns go off chattering and baying: in the devil's word, and by his word, transformed.

Here in the midst of farce, something serious has happened. The subplot's burlesque of the main plot's mighty concerns has been gradually acquainting us, in visual terms, with the way foolish shapes are latent in Faustus' aspiring words. But with the appearance of Mephistophilis at Robin's conjuring, this larger issue is clarified. We suddenly see clearly the way language releases meaning the user—here the clown—cannot control, and the way this meaning—here Mephistophilis—shapes or transforms the user. We see the transformer transformed, precisely what was suggested on the basis of Faustus' opening speech would happen to Faustus by the end. The seemingly simple contrast of subplot and main plot leads back to the central problem of the play: how the power to shape—language—can also misshape. And we have been led to this because the clown, transformed, is only a version of what Faustus, mighty magician, will become.

Or, indeed, what Faustus is rapidly becoming before our eyes. For there is that ever-growing split between Faustus' mighty words and his trivial deeds, between the shapes his language envisions and the shapes it actually creates. This larger movement, like the subplot which it parallels and meets in Act IV, begins in Faustus' second long speech in Act I.i, just after Wagner has appeared.

Beginning at line 79, we see the way Faustus' words fly up while their effects remain below. Faustus says he will create spirit servants. They will fly to India—for gold; ransack oceans—for pearls; search the corners of the earth—for fruits and delicacies. His servants will read him strange philosophies—and tell him royal secrets; they will dress schoolboys in silk, and invent new war machines. Here indeed is the language of aspiration—and the spectacle of naked appetite. Superb words—which show a taste for jewels, food, gossip, fashion, grim destruction. While we hear the flying words, we also see a man changing himself, through those words, from a magician to a dabbler in luxury to a general agent of death.

And when, over the course of the play, we see what Faustus does with those splendid powers; when we see how Faustus only uses them to vex the Pope and his retinue (III.i-ii), produce a dumbshow and put horns on a courtier (IV.ii), fool a fop with a false head (IV.iii) and a horse-courser with a false horse and leg (IV.v), and gather grapes for a pregnant Duchess (IV.vii)—then we see that what Faustus does with his power totally undercuts what we heard Faustus claim for his power. But not only does the power to be a god make trivia; much worse, that very power makes Faustus trivial. Over the play, the magician metamorphoses himself to a court jester, a fool. The process dramatized in the language of Act I.i is dramatized in the spectacle of the whole play.

The overall effect of this process is to trivialize everything, finally to trivialize main plot to the level of subplot. We see this happening when the characters of the subplot begin to enter the main plot—Wagner entering after Faustus gulls the horse-courser; Robin and Dick talking to the horse-courser and carter about Faustus' mighty deeds, like turning horses to hay. This merging of the two levels of life is completed in IV.vii when, after Faustus brings off his last piece of tremendous trivia—grapes for the Duchess—Robin, Dick, and Company burst in and one by one

Faustus charms them dumb. Now subplot is main plot; there is no difference. With his power to gain a deity, Faustus has reduced the world to its lowest level. Instead of learning the secrets of the universe, he has turned reality to farce. Finally, even the power of language, the power of transformation, is itself dramatically trivialized before our eyes when, without a word, Faustus denies the gulls the power of speech. That mighty power of language is so abused it no longer even communicates on a simple level; it only produces silence in the mouths of fools.

When we ponder the spectacle of the last scene, V.ii, in comparison with the statement of I.i, we notice that we see at the end precisely what we heard at the beginning. In both scenes, a universe, an unlimited existence, is unfolded. But, of course, similarities only underscore differences, and here the difference between the scenes is all the world. Where at the outset Faustus was a creator, at the end he is a creature; where before he dreamed of unlimited power and glory, now he is assured of limitless torment.

The words by which he reshaped himself into a demi-god at the beginning have now exploded into horror all about him. What we see on stage are the contents of his head—the Hell he will possess forever, the Heaven he will shortly lose. He brought it on himself, this deformed world, when he converted, when he turned to magic from God, when he turned the power of words from God's praise to his own. It does him no good to shriek "I'll burn my books" at the very end. The power in his books has swallowed him, and he is now himself only a misshapen symbol, another occult sign, in Satan's ledger.

More than any other play, Marlowe's **Doctor Faustus** celebrates that God-like power of language, and shows us how words can soar, and tempts us to dizzying heights within our heads. But all the time, Marlowe is in control. He knows too much about the shaping power of words to be a Faustus. Marlowe is a *magus* too, all poets are, but one who tells us in this play to use that awesome power of words to fashion ourselves in God's image. Else, like his hero, we will be deformed by the servant we abuse. (pp. 530-43)

> *A. Bartlett Giamatti, "Marlowe: The Arts of Illusion," in* The Yale Review, *Vol. LXI, No. 4, Summer, 1972, pp. 530-43.*

FURTHER READING

OVERVIEWS AND GENERAL STUDIES

Boas, Frederick S. *Christopher Marlowe: A Biographical and Critical Study.* Oxford: Oxford University Press, 1940, 336 p.
 Seminal analysis of Marlowe's life and literary career.

Bradbrook, M. C. "Christopher Marlowe." In her *Themes and Conventions of Elizabethan Tragedy,* pp. 137-64. Cambridge: Cambridge University Press, 1935.
 Describes how the dramatic conventions Marlowe used

in his major works are reflective of the Elizabethan period.

Brooke, Nicholas. "Marlowe the Dramatist." In *Elizabethan Theatre,* edited by John Russell Brown and Bernard Harris, pp. 87-105. London: Edward Arnold (Publishers) Ltd., 1966.
 Explores Marlowe's use of poetry for dramatic effect and examines the structures of his major plays.

Brooke, Tucker. "Marlowe's Versification and Style." *Studies in Philology* XIX, No. 2 (April 1922): 186-205.
 Textual analysis of Marlowe's innovations of blank verse in his major dramas.

Brown, John Russell. "Marlowe and the Actors." *Tulane Drama Review* 8, No. 4 (Summer 1964): 155-73.
 Discusses various technical approaches to producing and acting Marlowe's plays, citing some of the most famous performances in the Marlovian stage history.

Courtney, W. L. "Christopher Marlowe: I and II." *The Fortnightly Review* n.s. LXXVIII, Nos. CCCCLXV and CCCCLXVI (September and October 1905): 467-84, 678-91.
 Extensive critical analysis of Marlowe's life and literary career.

Danson, Lawrence. "Christopher Marlowe: The Questioner." *English Literary Renaissance* 12, No. 1 (Winter 1982): 3-29.
 Examines the use of various kinds of questioning as a dramatic technique in Marlowe's plays.

Dowden, Edward. "Christopher Marlowe." In *Modern English Essays,* Vol. 1, edited by Ernest Rhys, pp. 216-40. London: J. M. Dent & Sons, 1922.
 Compares Marlowe's dramatic style to those of Shakespeare and other Elizabethan playwrights and surveys major themes in his plays.

Eliot, T. S. "Notes on the Blank Verse of Christopher Marlowe." In his *The Sacred Wood: Essays on Poetry and Criticism,* pp. 86-94. 1920. Reprint. London: Metheun & Co., 1960.
 Assessment of the blank verse composition in Marlowe's major dramas.

Ellis-Fermor, U. M. *Christopher Marlowe.* 1927. Reprint. Hamden, Conn.: Archon Books, 1967, 172 p.
 Critical analysis of Marlowe's works by a noted scholar. G. I. Duthie objects to Ellis-Fermor's interpretation of *I* and *II Tamburlaine* as having "no progress, crisis, or solution" (see *Tamburlaine* commentary dated 1948).

Friedenreich, Kenneth; Gill, Roma; and Kuriyama, Constance B., eds. *"A Poet and a filthy Play-maker": New Essays on Christopher Marlowe.* New York: AMS Press, Inc., 1988, 376 p.
 Anthology of critical essays on Marlowe's works and literary career by prominent Elizabethan scholars.

Geckle, George L. *Tamburlaine and Edward II: Text and Performance.* London: Macmillan Education, Ltd, 1988, 107 p.
 Provides commentary on both the texts and significant performances of *Tamburlaine, Parts I* and *II* and *Edward II.*

Knights, L. C. "The Strange Case of Christopher Marlowe." In his *Further Explorations,* pp. 75-98. Stanford, Calif.: Stanford University Press, 1965.

Comprehensive overview of Marlowe's life and major plays in relation to the political and religious conventions of the Elizabethan period.

Leech, Clifford. "Marlowe's Humor." In *Essays on Shakespearean and Elizabethan Drama in Honor of Hardin Craig*, edited by Richard Hosley, pp. 69-81. Columbia, Mo.: University of Missouri Press, 1962.

Discusses the comedic aspects of Marlowe's plays.

Lowell, James Russell. "Marlowe." *Harper's New Monthly Magazine* LXXXV, No. DVI (July 1892): 194-203.

Critical overview of Marlowe's literary works.

Ribner, Irving. "Marlowe and the Critics." *Tulane Drama Review* 8, No. 4 (Summer 1964): 211-24.

Traces scholarly reaction to Marlowe's works from 1774 to 1962.

Stroup, Thomas B. "Ritual in Marlowe's Plays." *Drama in the Renaissance: Comparative and Critical Essays*, edited by Clifford Davidson, C. J. Gianakaris, and John H. Stroupe, pp. 21-44. New York: AMS Press, 1986.

Examines Marlowe's use of formal and ceremonial processions in his plays, analyzing the effect they have on the dramatic action.

Swinburne, Algernon Charles. "Christopher Marlowe and Some Minor Contemporaries." *North American Review* CCIII, No. 726 (May 1916): 742-48.

Offers a laudatory appraisal of Marlowe's contribution to English literature, deeming him "the father of English tragedy and the creator of English blank verse."

TAMBURLAINE, I AND II

Battenhouse, Roy W. "Tamburlaine, The 'Scourge of God.' " *PMLA* LVI, No. 2 (June 1941): 337-48.

Explores the origin of the concept "scourge of God" and how Marlowe used this tradition to portray Tamburlaine as a Renaissance hero.

————. *Marlowe's Tamburlaine: A Study in Renaissance Moral Philosophy.* Nashville, Tenn.: Vanderbilt University Press, 1941, 266 p.

Influential analysis of Marlowe's play, focusing on its intellectual background, Elizabethan literary context, and dramatic structure.

Brooks, Charles. "*Tamburlaine* and Attitudes toward Women." *ELH: A Journal of English Literary History* 24, No. 1 (March 1957): 1-11.

Maintains that in keeping with the Renaissance concept that identifies women with "prizes that must be seized" by a "triumphant hero," the women in *Tamburlaine* embody the men's aspirations.

Leech, Clifford. "The Structure of *Tamburlaine*." *Tulane Drama Review* 8, No. 4 (Summer 1964): 32-46.

Close examination of the dramatic structure of *Tamburlaine*.

Levin, Richard. "The Contemporary Perception of Marlowe's *Tamburlaine*." In *Medieval & Renaissance Drama in England: An Annual Gathering of Research, Criticism, and Reviews*, edited by J. Leeds Barroll, III, pp. 51-70. New York: AMS Press, 1984.

Argues that, contrary to prevailing critical opinion,

Marlowe's *Tamburlaine* is an artistic failure because it inadequately conveyed its major themes to its contemporary audiences.

Richards, Susan. "Marlowe's *Tamburlaine II*: A Drama of Death." *Modern Language Quarterly* XXVI, No. 3 (September 1965): 375-87.

Surveys the effects of Tamburlaine's "death-dealing power" and the results of his own confrontation with death.

THE JEW OF MALTA

Friedenreich, Kenneth. "*The Jew of Malta* and the Critics: A Paradigm for Marlowe Studies." *Papers on Language and Literature* 13, No. 3 (Summer 1977): 318-35.

Records various critical interpretations of *The Jew of Malta* by prominent Elizabethan scholars.

Rothstein, Eric. "Structure as Meaning in *The Jew of Malta*." *JEGP: Journal of English and Germanic Philology* LXV (1966): 260-73.

Analyzes Marlowe's parodic technique throughout the dramatic structure of *The Jew of Malta*. The critic asserts that the dramatist has created a grotesque setting in the play where all values are "inverted by a central diabolism."

EDWARD II

Voss, James. "*Edward II*: Marlowe's Historical Tragedy." *English Studies* 63, No. 6 (December 1982): 517-30.

Demonstrates how intensely personal and emotional desires precipitate key political crises, which in turn lead to Edward's downfall. This dramatic structure forms a unique literary genre which the critic deems "historical tragedy."

DOCTOR FAUSTUS

Empson, William. *Faustus and the Censor: The English Faust-book and Marlowe's* Doctor Faustus. London: Basil Blackwell, Ltd, 1987, 226 p.

Unorthodox interpretation of *Doctor Faustus* that regards the play not as a tragedy, but as a subversive burlesque of the social and religious issues of Marlowe's England.

Heilman, Robert B. "The Tragedy of Knowledge: Marlowe's Treatment of Faustus." *Quarterly Review of Literature* II, No. 4 (1945): 316-32.

Examines the ramifications of Faustus's quest for knowledge, concluding that the tragedy of knowledge is that it leads to "pride" and "wilfulness," which cause "blindness to the nature and destiny of man."

Hunter, G. K. "Five-Act Structure in *Doctor Faustus*." *Tulane Drama Review* 8, No. 4 (Summer 1964): 77-91.

Argues that *Doctor Faustus* possesses a five-act structure, despite the absence of any such divisions in its early editions and the general critical reluctance to apply this framework to the drama.

Kocher, Paul H. "The Witchcraft Basis in Marlowe's *Faus-*

tus." *Modern Philology* XXXVIII, No. 1 (August 1940): 9-36.

> Demonstrates that in addition to using the *English Faust-book* as a source for *Doctor Faustus,* Marlowe also drew heavily upon the European witch tradition.

McAlindon, T. "Classical Mythology and Christian Tradition in Marlowe's *Doctor Faustus.*" *PMLA* LXXXI, No. 3 (June 1966): 214-23.

> Describes how in *Doctor Faustus* classical mythology plays more than the merely aesthetic role it assumes in Marlowe's other plays. Here, the critic maintains, mythology acts as an agent for Faustus's demise in that it represents the evil alternative to Christianity.

———. "The Ironic Vision: Diction and Theme in Marlowe's *Doctor Faustus.*" *The Review of English Studies* n.s. XXXII, No. 126 (May 1981): 129-41.

> Focuses on the ways in which Marlowe's use of diction contributes to an overall ironic theme in *Doctor Faustus.*

Morgan, Gerald. "Harlequin Faustus: Marlowe's Comedy of Hell." *The Humanities Association Bulletin* XVIII, No. 1 (Spring 1967): 22-34.

> Views *Doctor Faustus* as a comic satire on Classical and Medieval myths and traditions surrounding the concept of Hell.

Ornstein, Robert. "The Comic Synthesis in *Doctor Faustus.*" *ELH: A Journal of English Literary History* 22, No. 3 (September 1955): 165-72.

> Contends that the scenes with coarse humor in *Doctor Faustus* "unite with the seemingly fragmented main action to form a subtly ironic tragic design."

Ricks, Christopher. "*Doctor Faustus* and Hell on Earth." *Essays in Criticism* XXXV, No. 2 (April 1985): 101-20.

> Analyzes the effect that living in a plague-ridden society may have had on Marlowe's composition of *Doctor Faustus.*

Arthur Miller

1915-

The author of *Death of a Salesman, The Crucible,* and numerous other dramatic works, Miller is ranked among the most important and influential American playwrights since World War II. He is also known as an essayist, scriptwriter, short story writer, nonfiction writer, and novelist.

Miller was born and raised in New York City, the son of a prosperous businessman who lost his wealth during the Great Depression. A mediocre high school student with little interest in academic pursuits, Miller was rejected upon his initial application to the University of Michigan. He then spent several years at various manual labor jobs, during which time he developed an interest in literature, almost by accident. Miller was deeply impressed by Fedor Dostoevski's classic novel *The Brothers Karamazov,* a work he had mistakenly thought was a detective story. He later reapplied to the University of Michigan and was this time accepted as a journalism student. It was at Michigan that Miller first began writing for the stage, showing distinct promise as a dramatist and winning several student awards. For a short time after college, he was employed writing scripts for radio plays. While he found the demands of broadcast writing restrictive and confining, this period, together with his college years, served as a valuable apprenticeship for Miller. His first Broadway play, *The Man Who Had All the Luck* was produced in 1944. Although it lasted only four performances, it nevertheless won a Theater Guild award and established Miller as an important young playwright.

Throughout his career, Miller has continually addressed several distinct but related issues in both his dramatic and expository writings. In his early plays and in a series of essays published in the 1940s and 50s, Miller first outlined a form of tragedy applicable to modern times and contemporary characters, challenging traditional definitions that hold that only kings, queens, princes, and other members of the nobility can be suitable subjects for tragedy. In "Tragedy and the Common Man," Miller asserts that the "underlying struggle" of all such dramas "is that of the individual attempting to gain his 'rightful' position in society." Consequently, "the tragic feeling is evoked in us when we are in the presence of a character who is ready to lay down his life, if need be, to secure one thing—his sense of personal dignity" within a society that inhibits such endeavors. According to this view, even ordinary people—like Willy Loman, the protagonist of *Death of a Salesman*—can achieve truly tragic stature. It is this issue of the individual's relationship to society, and its representation on stage, that forms the second of Miller's abiding concerns. Throughout his work, Miller has sought to fuse the moral and political messages of "social" plays with the realism and intensity of psychological dramas that focus on the individual. In work after work, from *All My Sons* and *The Crucible* to *Incident at Vichy,* Miller has pres-

ented dilemmas in which a character's sense of personal integrity or self-interest conflicts with his or her responsibility to society or its representatives. Finally, Miller has repeatedly returned to the theme of family relations, particularly interactions between fathers and sons. The families depicted in Miller's plays often serve as vehicles for the author's analyses of the broader relations between individuals and society.

These issues are discernable in *All My Sons* and clearly evident in *Death of a Salesman,* widely considered Miller's masterpiece and recognized as a classic of contemporary American theater. In *All My Sons,* set during World War II, the truth about Joe Keller's past is gradually revealed. Keller has sold defective parts to the United States Air Force, resulting in the death of several American pilots. When his sons learn of this, one, a pilot himself, commits suicide by crashing his plane; the other demands that Keller take responsibility for his actions. As the play closes, Keller accepts his obligation to society, recognizing that all the lost pilots were, in effect, his "sons." He then takes his own life to atone for his crime. *All My Sons* was considerably more successful than *The Man Who Had All the Luck,* enjoying a long run and winning the New York

Drama Critics Circle Award in 1947. With the production of *Death of a Salesman* in 1949, Miller firmly established his reputation as a profound writer of American dramas. This play, which represents his most powerful dramatization of the clash between the individual and materialistic American society, chronicles the downfall of Willy Loman, a salesman whose misguided notions of success result in disillusionment and, ultimately, his death. Throughout his life, Willy has not only blindly pursued society's version of success, he has based his own identity and self-worth on social acceptance—on how "well-liked" he is. At the drama's end, he commits suicide, convinced that the settlement on his life insurance policy will provide his son Biff the wealth that had eluded Willy himself; however, Biff's ideals have already been tarnished by the same forces that destroyed his father.

Critics have generally agreed that *Death of a Salesman* is an important dramatic work. Upon its debut in New York, Brooks Atkinson hailed it as a "rare event in the theatre," and Harold Clurman similarly claimed that *Death of a Salesman* "marks a high point of significant expression in the American theatre." Some commentators, however, took issue with Miller's insistence that *Death of a Salesman* is a modern tragedy and that Willy is a tragic hero. The noted dramatic critic Eric Bentley argued that the elements of social drama in *Salesman* keep "the 'tragedy' from having genuinely tragic stature." Describing Willy as a "little man," Bentley insisted that such a person is "too little and too passive to play the tragic hero." Bentley and others charged that, according to Miller's own definition, Willy's death is merely "pathetic" rather than tragic. Other critics argued that, to the contrary, the salesman does attain tragic dimensions by virtue of what Miller terms the tragic hero's "total compulsion" to preserve his humanity and dignity. John Mason Brown characterized *Death of a Salesman* as "a tragedy modern and personal, not classic and heroic." Willy Loman is, he observed, "a little man sentenced to discover his smallness rather than a big man undone by his greatness."

Whether or not *Salesman* can be classified as a true tragedy, it has been generally praised for its innovative structure, which merges elements of both realism and expressionism. Reviewers admired the drama's interweaving of the "past" with the "present" and of events inside Willy's mind with those outside. While not "realistic," this technique nevertheless produces a penetrating psychological examination characteristic of dramatic realism. It is appropriate, several critics noted, that Miller's working title for the play was *Inside of His Head*. *Death of a Salesman* earned Miller a Pulitzer Prize as well as his second New York Drama Critics Circle Award.

Miller followed *Salesman* with an adaptation of Henrik Ibsen's *An Enemy of the People* and, in 1953, *The Crucible*. Although the latter work won the 1953 Tony Award for best play, it received generally lukewarm responses from critics, and the piece had a run that, while respectable, was only one-third the length of *Salesman*'s premier production. Perhaps Miller's most controversial drama, this work is based upon the witch trials held in 1692 in Salem, Massachusetts. Featuring historical characters drawn

from this period, *The Crucible* addresses the complex moral dilemmas of John Proctor, a man wrongly accused of practicing witchcraft. Through his depiction of the mass frenzy of the witch hunt, Miller examines the social and psychological aspects of group pressure and its effect on individual ethics, dignity, and beliefs.

When *The Crucible* was first staged, a number of critics maintained that Miller failed in his characteristic attempt to merge the personal and the social. Many of the figures in the play are poorly developed and merely serve as mouthpieces for Miller's social commentary, they claimed. The play was commonly interpreted as a thinly disguised critique of Joseph McCarthy's Senate investigations of communism in the United States, and it was judged preachy and overly political. Walter Kerr, the *New York Times* critic, considered *The Crucible* a "mechanical parable . . . the sort of play which lives not in the warmth of humbly observed human souls but in the ideological heat of polemic." Similarly, Eric Bentley regarded it as a "story not quite told, a drama not realized." Furthermore, Bentley questioned the validity of the parallels Miller established between the Salem trials and the congressional investigations. The relationship between the historical events depicted in the play and the events of the 1950s has continued to be the subject of much debate among subsequent critics of *The Crucible*.

Miller was himself called to testify before the House Committee on Un-American Activities in 1957. Although he admitted that he had attended a meeting of communist writers, he refused to identify anyone he had met there and denied ever having been a member of the Communist Party. As a result, he was found guilty of contempt of Congress, a conviction that was later overturned. A year later, after much of the furor over communist activity in the United States had died down, *The Crucible* was revived off-Broadway. This time, freed from much of its association with "current events," the play was warmly received by critics and enjoyed a run of over six hundred performances. It was now seen to have a more lasting and universal significance than had earlier been apparent. As Robert Martin later maintained, *The Crucible* "has endured beyond the immediate events of its own time. If it was originally seen as a political allegory, it is presently seen by contemporary audiences almost entirely as a distinguished American play by an equally distinguished American playwright."

Miller's next offering, produced in 1955, consisted of two one-act plays: *A Memory of Two Mondays*—a semi-autobiographical piece reflecting Miller's own experiences as a young man working in an auto parts warehouse—and *A View from the Bridge*, for which the playwright won his third New York Drama Critics Circle Award. He later expanded this play to two acts. Given Miller's attempts to establish a new, modern form of tragedy, *A View from the Bridge* is significant in that it exhibits many similarities to classical Greek tragedy. Eddie Carbone, the play's central character, unconsciously harbors an incestuous love for his niece, Catherine. Jealous of her attraction to an illegal alien the Carbones are hiding, Eddie exposes the man to immigration authorities and becomes involved in a fatal confrontation with the man's brother. Critics have often noted that, like such Greek dramatic heroes as Oedipus, Eddie brings about his own downfall through his ignorance and inability to see the consequences of his actions.

A nine year break from playwriting followed, during which period Miller embarked on his highly publicized marriage to, and subsequent divorce from, Marilyn Monroe. Before they separated, however, Miller adapted one of his short stories into the screenplay *The Misfits* as a vehicle for his wife. He returned to the theater in 1964 with two works, *After the Fall* and, near the end of the year, *Incident at Vichy. After the Fall* is considered Miller's most experimental and, perhaps, most pessimistic piece. This play takes place, as Miller has stated, "in the mind, thought, and memory of Quentin," a guilt-ridden man who tries to come to terms with his past through conversations with an imaginary listener. In the course of Quentin's examination of the ruins of two failed marriages, the individual, the family, and society are all subjected to harsh criticism. Nearly every character in the play betrays love for the sake of his or her own survival. Reviewers were sharply divided over *After the Fall.* While some considered its structure a brilliant experiment in stagecraft, others faulted Miller for pretentious theorizing and artificial characterizations. In addition, the drama was commonly considered autobiographical, and audiences and critics were often occupied in trying to identify in it people and events from the playwright's own life. In *Incident at Vichy,* Miller continued his exploration of the conflicts between individual and societal responsibility. Set in occupied France during World War II, this play features seven men who, awaiting interrogation by their Nazi captors, discuss their fate and the importance of social commitment to maintaining group freedom. The drama suggests that those who fail to resist oppression are as guilty as the Nazis of crimes against humanity.

In 1968, Miller returned to realistic family drama with *The Price.* In this work two brothers, Victor and Walter Frank, are brought together after many years by the death of their father. Like the characters in *All My Sons* and *Death of a Salesman,* these two men recall the past, trying to come to an understanding of their lives and the choices they have made. *The Price* represents Miller's last major Broadway success. His next work, *The Creation of the World and other Business,* a series of comic sketches based on the Biblical Book of Genesis, met with severe critical disapproval when it was first produced on Broadway in 1972, and it closed after only twenty performances. All of Miller's subsequent works premiered outside of New York. Miller staged the musical *Up from Paradise,* an adaptation of *Creation of the World,* at his alma mater, the University of Michigan. *The Archbishop's Ceiling,* presented in 1977 at the Kennedy Center in Washington, D.C., is a work more typical of the playwright. Set in a communist European country, the drama concerns Sigmund, an outspoken dissident novelist who openly condemns the actions of his government. Forced to choose either exile or a trial for treason, Sigmund must consider the effect of his decision not only on his own life, but on the lives of those around him. His decision to remain and fight oppression has led critics to consider *The Archbishop's*

Ceiling a celebration of the power of the human will and perhaps Miller's most optimistic work.

In the 1980s, Miller produced a number of short pieces. *The American Clock* is based on Studs Terkel's oral history of the Great Depression, *Hard Times,* and is structured as a series of vignettes that chronicle the hardship and suffering that occurred during that period. *Elegy for a Lady* and *Some Kind of Love Story* are two one-act plays that were staged together in 1982. Similarly, 1986's *Danger, Memory!* is comprised of the short pieces *I Can't Remember Anything* and *Clara.* Reviewers have generally regarded these later plays as minor works, inferior to Miller's early masterpieces.

Despite the absence of any notable theatrical success since the mid-1960s, Arthur Miller remains an important voice in contemporary American drama. Such early works as *Death of a Salesman* and *The Crucible* are still frequently performed, thereby reaching succeeding generations of playgoers. And though less compelling, his later works have continued to probe and explore the nature of the individual, not in isolation, but as an innately social, interactive creature. Much of Miller's work displays his deep and abiding concern with conscience and morality, with one's dual—and often conflicting—responsibilities to oneself and to one's fellow human beings. It is only through relationships with others, Miller's plays suggest, that our humanity truly emerges.

(For further information on Miller's life and career, see *Contemporary Literary Criticism,* Vols. 1, 2, 6, 10, 15, 26, 47; *Contemporary Authors,* Vols. 1-4, rev. ed.; *Contemporary Authors New Revision Series,* Vol. 2; *Dictionary of Literary Biography,* Vol. 7; and *Concise Dictionary of American Literary Biography, 1941-1968.*)

PRINCIPAL WORKS

PLAYS

The Man Who Had All the Luck   1944
All My Sons   1947
Death of a Salesman: Certain Private Conversations in Two Acts and a Requiem   1949
An Enemy of the People   [adaptation of Henrik Ibsen's play]   1950
The Crucible   1953
A View from the Bridge   [one-act version]   1955
A Memory of Two Mondays   1955
A View from the Bridge   [two-act version]   1956
After the Fall   1964
Incident at Vichy   1964
The Price   1968
The Creation of the World and Other Business   1972
Up from Paradise   [musical adaptation of *Creation of the World*]   1974
The Archbishop's Ceiling   1977

The American Clock   [adaptation of Studs Terkel's *Hard
    Times*]   1980
†*Elegy for a Lady*   1982
†*Some Kind of Love Story*   1982
Danger, Memory!   [two one-act plays, *I Can't Remember
    Anything* and *Clara*]   1986

OTHER MAJOR WORKS

Situation Normal   (nonfiction)   1944
Focus   (novel)   1945
The Misfits   (screenplay)   1961
I Don't Need You Any More   (stories)   1967
The Theater Essays of Arthur Miller   (essays)   1978
Timebends: A Life   (autobiography)   1987

*These two works were first performed together in a single produc-
tion.

†These two works were first performed together in a single production. *Elegy for a Lady* was published in the United States in 1982;
Some Kind of Love Story was issued the following year. They were
published together in Great Britain as *Two-Way Mirror* in 1984.

AUTHOR COMMENTARY

Tragedy and the Common Man   (1949)

[*Miller published the following essay shortly after the
premiere of* Death of a Salesman. *He here disputes traditional definitions of tragedy, in which only individuals
of noble rank are considered suitable subjects for such
dramas, and he attempts to formulate a theory in which
ordinary people—like Willy Loman—can qualify as
tragic heroes. Critics have regarded this essay as a significant attempt to establish modern standards for tragedy
and have often judged Miller's own works, including*
Salesman, *by its precepts.*]

In this age few tragedies are written. It has often been held
that the lack is due to a paucity of heroes among us, or else
that modern man has had the blood drawn out of his organs of belief by the skepticism of science, and the heroic
attack on life cannot feed on an attitude of reserve and cir-
cumspection. For one reason or another, we are often held
to be below tragedy—or tragedy above us. The inevitable
conclusion is, of course, that the tragic mode is archaic,
fit only for the very highly placed, the kings or the kingly,
and where this admission is not made in so many words
it is most often implied.

I believe that the common man is as apt a subject for tragedy in its highest sense as kings were. On the face of it this
ought to be obvious in the light of modern psychiatry,
which bases its analysis upon classic formulations, such as
the Oedipus and Orestes complexes, for instances, which
were enacted by royal beings, but which apply to everyone
in similar emotional situations.

More simply, when the question of tragedy in art is not

at issue, we never hesitate to attribute to the well-placed
and the exalted the very same mental processes as the
lowly. And finally, if the exaltation of tragic action were
truly a property of the high-bred character alone, it is inconceivable that the mass of mankind should cherish tragedy above all other forms, let alone be capable of understanding it.

As a general rule, to which there may be exceptions unknown to me, I think the tragic feeling is evoked in us
when we are in the presence of a character who is ready
to lay down his life, if need be, to secure one thing—his
sense of personal dignity. From Orestes to Hamlet, Medea
to Macbeth, the underlying struggle is that of the individual attempting to gain his "rightful" position in his society.

Sometimes he is one who has been displaced from it, sometimes one who seeks to attain it for the first time, but the
fateful wound from which the inevitable events spiral is
the wound of indignity, and its dominant force is indignation. Tragedy, then, is the consequence of a man's total
compulsion to evaluate himself justly.

In the sense of having been initiated by the hero himself,
the tale always reveals what has been called his "tragic
flaw," a failing that is not peculiar to grand or elevated
characters. Nor is it necessarily a weakness. The flaw, or
crack in the character, is really nothing—and need be
nothing—but his inherent unwillingness to remain passive
in the face of what he conceives to be a challenge to his
dignity, his image of his rightful status. Only the passive,
only those who accept their lot without active retaliation,
are "flawless." Most of us are in that category.

But there are among us today, as there always have been,
those who act against the scheme of things that degrades
them, and in the process of action everything we have accepted out of fear or insensitivity or ignorance is shaken
before us and examined, and from this total onslaught by
an individual against the seemingly stable cosmos surrounding us—from this total examination of the "un-
changeable" environment—comes the terror and the fear
that is classically associated with tragedy.

More important, from this total questioning of what has
previously been unquestioned, we learn. And such a process is not beyond the common man. In revolutions
around the world, these past thirty years, he has demonstrated again and again this inner dynamic of all tragedy.

Insistence upon the rank of the tragic hero, or the so-
called nobility of his character, is really but a clinging to
the outward forms of tragedy. If rank or nobility of character was indispensable, then it would follow that the
problems of those with rank were the particular problems
of tragedy. But surely the right of one monarch to capture
the domain from another no longer raises our passions,
nor are our concepts of justice what they were to the mind
of an Elizabethan king.

The quality in such plays that does shake us, however, derives from the underlying fear of being displaced, the disaster inherent in being torn away from our chosen image
of what and who we are in this world. Among us today
this fear is as strong, and perhaps stronger, than it ever

was. In fact, it is the common man who knows this fear best.

Now, if it is true that tragedy is the consequence of a man's total compulsion to evaluate himself justly, his destruction in the attempt posits a wrong or an evil in his environment. And this is precisely the morality of tragedy and its lesson. The discovery of the moral law, which is what the enlightenment of tragedy consists of, is not the discovery of some abstract or metaphysical quantity.

The tragic right is a condition of life, a condition in which the human personality is able to flower and realize itself. The wrong is the condition which suppresses man, perverts the flowing out of his love and creative instinct. Tragedy enlightens—and it must, in that it points the heroic finger at the enemy of man's freedom. The thrust for freedom is the quality in tragedy which exalts. The revolutionary questioning of the stable environment is what terrifies. In no way is the common man debarred from such thoughts or such actions.

Seen in this light, our lack of tragedy may be partially accounted for by the turn which modern literature has taken toward the purely psychiatric view of life, or the purely sociological. If all our miseries, our indignities, are born and bred within our minds, then all action, let alone the heroic action, is obviously impossible.

And if society alone is responsible for the cramping of our lives, then the protagonist must needs be so pure and faultless as to force us to deny his validity as a character. From neither of these views can tragedy derive, simply because neither represents a balanced concept of life. Above all else, tragedy requires the finest appreciation by the writer of cause and effect.

No tragedy can therefore come about when its author fears to question absolutely everything, when he regards any institution, habit or custom as being either everlasting, immutable or inevitable. In the tragic view the need of man to wholly realize himself is the only fixed star, and whatever it is that hedges his nature and lowers it is ripe for attack and examination. Which is not to say that tragedy must preach revolution.

The Greeks could probe the very heavenly origin of their ways and return to confirm the rightness of laws. And Job could face God in anger, demanding his right and end in submission. But for a moment everything is in suspension, nothing is accepted, and in this stretching and tearing apart of the cosmos, in the very action of so doing, the character gains "size," the tragic stature which is spuriously attached to the royal or the highborn in our minds. The commonest of men may take on that stature to the extent of his willingness to throw all he has into the contest, the battle to secure his rightful place in his world.

There is a misconception of tragedy with which I have been struck in review after review, and in many conversations with writers and readers alike. It is the idea that tragedy is of necessity allied to pessimism. Even the dictionary says nothing more about the word than that it means a story with a sad or unhappy ending. This impression is so firmly fixed that I almost hesitate to claim that in truth

tragedy implies more optimism in its author than does comedy, and that its final result ought to be the reinforcement of the onlooker's brightest opinions of the human animal.

For, if it is true to say that in essence the tragic hero is intent upon claiming his whole due as a personality, and if this struggle must be total and without reservation, then it automatically demonstrates the indestructible will of man to achieve his humanity.

The possibility of victory must be there in tragedy. Where pathos rules, where pathos is finally derived, a character has fought a battle he could not possibly have won. The pathetic is achieved when the protagonist is, by virtue of his witlessness, his insensitivity or the very air he gives off, incapable of grappling with a much superior force.

Pathos truly is the mode for the pessimist. But tragedy requires a nicer balance between what is possible and what is impossible. And it is curious, although edifying, that the plays we revere, century after century, are the tragedies. In them, and in them alone, lies the belief—optimistic, if you will, in the perfectibility of man.

It is time, I think, that we who are without kings, took up this bright thread of our history and followed it to the only place it can possibly lead in our time—the heart and spirit of the average man. (pp. 1, 3)

> *Arthur Miller, "Tragedy and the Common Man," in* The New York Times, *February 27, 1949, pp. 1, 3.*

OVERVIEWS AND GENERAL STUDIES

M. W. Steinberg   (essay date 1960)

[*Steinberg is a Canadian scholar, critic, and editor. Included among the numerous publications he has edited is* Aspects of Modern Drama *(1960). In the essay below, he assesses Miller's major plays,* All My Sons, Death of a Salesman, The Crucible, *and* A View from the Bridge, *in light of the playwright's own definition of tragedy as a conflict between an individual and the dehumanizing forces of society. Although the critic observes a consistent focus on this opposition throughout Miller's work, he also discerns a progressively greater "emphasis on character, . . . making the protagonist a worthier opposite to the forces he struggles against."*]

"Anyone who dares to discuss the making of tragedy," cautions Maxwell Anderson, "lays himself open to critical assault and general barrage"—a warning that has not deterred modern scholars, if we are to judge by the many books and articles on the subject. On reading the critical literature on tragedy, one is impressed by the number of widely differing definitions. One finds the assertion, for example, put forward by Joseph Wood Krutch and others, that virtually no modern play is tragic because the protagonist is not of exalted rank. At the other extreme, we find more tolerant critics who are willing to accept as tragedies almost any serious play that must perforce involve conflict and suffering. F. L. Lucas, in his book *Tragedy,* says that if we attempted to remould the Aristotelian definition in the light of the history of tragedy, we would get something like this tautology: "Serious drama is a serious representation by speech and action of some phase of human life." And he adds, "If there is an unhappy ending, we may call it tragedy; but if the play is a serious attempt to represent life, it makes no great difference whether or not good fortune intervenes in the last scene." In many articles during the past ten or eleven years Arthur Miller has attempted to formulate an acceptable modern definition, and an examination of his plays and his essays on tragedy will not only reveal the terms of his definition, but may also indicate something of the relation between modern tragedy and that of earlier periods.

As the twentieth century approached, various forces were making for realism in drama with its emphasis on people and situations drawn from ordinary life. In part this interest reflected the growth of democracy and the extension of education to the masses which introduced the era of the common man. Perhaps an even more important aspect of the new drama was the post-Darwinian emphasis on environment as a shaping force in life. Man was seen as the product, and from one point of view the victim, of his surroundings. Increasingly, writers became preoccupied with social institutions, political and economic issues, and these they presented as best they could objectively, or "scientifically." The primary concern was with the external factors that operated on the protagonist, rather than with the inner crisis experienced by him when challenged by his conditions. In [Henrik] Ibsen's *A Doll House,* for example, the central concern is with the social forces that unfortunately made women dependent and limited. We are not invited to witness and vicariously participate in a personal tragedy with universal application, but rather we are directly involved and made aware of our guilt, our responsibility for the social milieu that makes for tragedy. A blow is aimed at us; the dramatist uses his characters to compel us to consider a social problem. [Bernard] Shaw, following in this pattern, makes his purpose clear in his Preface to *Plays Unpleasant.* He writes,

> I must, however, warn my readers that my attacks are directed against themselves, not against my stage figures. They cannot too thoroughly understand that the guilt of defective social organization does not lie alone on the people who actually work the commercial makeshifts which the defects make inevitable, and who often, like Sartorius and Mrs. Warren, display valuable executive capacities and even high moral virtues in their administration, but with the whole body of citizens whose public opinion, public action, and public contribution as ratepayers, alone can replace Sartorius's slums with decent dwellings, Charteris's intrigues with reasonable marriage contracts, and Mrs. Warren's profession with honorable industries guarded by a humane industrial code and a 'moral minimum' wage.

This concern with the social problem, the social injustice

and its effect on the lives of the characters, is found in Miller's plays too. The economic basis of social mischief is as obvious in **All My Sons** as in Shaw's *Widowers' Houses* or Ibsen's *An Enemy of the People;* in **Death of a Salesman** the common man is crushed by forces outside himself and by illusions, false ideals, spawned by those forces; and in **The Crucible** the political motif is clear. Miller refused to regard this emphasis as in any way negating the high seriousness of his plays or diminishing their tragic quality.

On the other hand, it is sometimes charged that such plays are not really tragic because they rub our noses in the social mire and depress rather than exalt; because they end with a stated or implied call to action rather than with a feeling of catharsis, a sense of "all passion spent"; or because they conclude with a note of question rather than with a sense of our being reconciled to life. According to such a view, the tragic hero through his struggle and the recognition of his own shortcoming reveals man's essential or potential nobility, and we are ennobled, uplifted by the spectacle. While this view undoubtedly holds true for some of the finest tragedies ever written, we may not only doubt its comprehensiveness but even question its application to plays that are unquestionably accepted by these same critics as tragedies. Are we, for example, reconciled to the death of Othello or uplifted by it? Here is a good man whose goodness has been imposed upon. Though he recognizes his error, there is no evidence of amendment or opportunity for it. He has already killed Desdemona, so any effective amendment in that direction is obviously impossible. His suicide indicates that he accepts his guilt, but certainly the compounding of corpses cannot reconcile us to the tragic situation. While it is true that the action brings out a flaw in Othello's character, it is not of such a nature that it merits his death: the punishment does not fit the crime or, rather, weakness. Our sense of justice is shocked—or ought to be; we are morally offended at the disparity between what we consider just and what "fate" metes out. Furthermore, even if we accept Othello's death as just, what about the death of Desdemona, the innocent? What about the death of Cordelia [in *King Lear*], of Duncan [in *Macbeth*], of Lady Macduff and her children [*Macbeth*]? The superb poetry at the end of *Hamlet* and *Lear,* which diverts us and cushions the shock of the horrors revealed, does not really change the fact that this is a world in which Hamlet is treacherously poisoned and Cordelia is found hanging. On what basis can we be reconciled to such a scheme of things? Within the terms of our earthly existence, only by confirmed pessimism, bitter or passive stoicism, and a kind of grim satisfaction—or a sense of exaltation if we are romantics—at our capacity for struggle and endurance. But even where such a sense of exaltation or reconciliation existed in the traditional tragedy, it could be achieved only by focussing on the hero and ignoring the world in which he moved, for in that world there is injustice and unmerited suffering—unless one postulated a God or gods whose ways, though incomprehensible to us morally, were accepted as just. This kind of reconciliation the modern dramatist, with the exception perhaps of T. S. Eliot, is unwilling to accept. But, at the same time, he is not willing to accept the initial situation, that of man in a sorry world, as fixed and final. He makes no clear distinction between the order of things and man in the order.

For him there is a continuing inter-relationship, a possibility of development. The dramatist, as Arthur Miller insists, must not conceive of man as a private entity and his social relations as something thrown at him, but rather he must come to see that "society is inside of man and man is inside society, and you cannot even create a truthfully drawn psychological entity on the stage until you understand his social relations and their power to make him what he is and to prevent him from being what he is not" ["The Shadow of the Gods," included in *The Theater Essays of Arthur Miller;* see Further Reading]. Man is seen as constantly in the process of becoming, shaped and not merely stimulated by his environment, his fate. But there is nothing fixed about his fate—it too is subject to change; it has no eternal metaphysical basis. Tragedy, says Miller, must question everything; from the total questioning we learn. Hence the onslaught on social conditions in post-Ibsen drama and the optimistic premise underlying the tragedy: earth and high heaven do not ail from the prime foundation, and the troubles that beset us are not visited on us from on high by mysterious or vengeful deities. Implied is the social reformer's call to take up arms against our troubles, and his confidence that we can by opposing end them. The possibility of a way to the better, however, does not alter the fact that the full look at the worst, at the moment, reveals tragedy.

In one of his earliest essays on drama, "Tragedy and the Common Man" [see Author Commentary], Arthur Miller formulated his position on the nature and function of tragedy. The tragic feeling, he writes, is evoked in us when we are in the presence of a character who is ready to lay down his life, if need be, to secure one thing—his sense of personal dignity. From Orestes to Hamlet the underlying struggle is that of the individual attempting to gain his rightful place in his society. Sometimes he is displaced, sometimes he seeks to attain it for the first time, but the fateful wound from which all events spiral is the wound of indignity. Man's failure to achieve or to maintain this needed sense of personal dignity is, according to Miller, the fault of society. He cautions us not to exclude the personal factor, for the hero must not be flawless, nor ought we to exclude social factors and seek the source of misery solely in our minds. His emphasis, however, is undoubtedly on the social forces, not on the hero's inner weakness. Tragedy need not preach revolution, but since its theme is man's need to wholly realize himself, whatever confines man and stunts his growth is "ripe for attack and examination." Man's destruction in his effort to evaluate himself and to be evaluated justly, says Miller, "posits a wrong or an evil in his environment." This truth, he adds, is the morality of a tragedy and its lesson, and the enlightenment of a tragedy consists in this discovery of the moral law, not the discovery of some abstract or metaphysical quality. This emphasis on social forces is seen also in Miller's brief but revealing comment on the nature of the tragic flaw. Since the tragic action stems from the questioning of the stable and stifling environment, the importance of the personal flaw is diminished. Indeed, for Miller, this factor in the hero's composition is not necessarily a weakness. It is, he says, man's inherent unwillingness to remain passive in the face of what he conceives to be a challenge to his dignity, his image of his rightful status. Only the passive or submissive are flawless. Thus the accepted notion of the tragic flaw as a shortcoming in the hero's character which precipitates the catastrophic action and which, theoretically at least, makes morally tolerable his defeat, is transformed by Miller into what would seem to be a condition of the hero's greatness.

Thus, for the most part in this essay, Miller sees the human situation as the product of forces outside the individual person and the tragedy inherent in the situation as a consequence of the individual's total onslaught against an order that degrades. The function of tragedy is to reveal the truth concerning our society, which frustrates and denies man his right to personal dignity; and the enlightenment of tragedy is the discovery of the moral law that supports this right. Basically the aesthetic position formulated in "Tragedy and the Common Man" is influenced, perhaps even determined, by Miller the social critic, and while the terms of this definition of tragedy are acceptable, they are also limited.

Miller's first play, **All My Sons,** reveals this concern with social issues. It is most clearly and simply in the tradition of the social problem plays of Ibsen, Shaw, and [John] Galsworthy. An aspect of the tragedy arises out of the character of the son, Chris Keller, out of an inner conflict between the affection and loyalty he had for his father and his concept of justice and universal brotherhood which the father offended. The persons in the play, however, exist mainly to illustrate the unhappy consequences of a disaster generated by a selfish, materialistic society which respects economic success as it flaunts underlying moral law. At the climax of the play, Joe Keller comes to realize that all the young soldiers killed or endangered by his selfish action are his sons as much as are his own two boys for whom he was building up his business. And in reply to the mother's cry at the end of the play, "What more can we be?", Chris, the remaining son, says, "You can be better! Once, for all, you can know there's a universe of people outside and you're responsible to it, and unless you know that, you threw away your son because that's why he died" [Act III]. The play advances clearly to this punch-line.

In **Death of a Salesman** we find the same emphasis on social forces as the source of tragedy, though the issue here is somewhat confused by Miller's attempt to make of Willy Loman a tragic hero. The essay "Tragedy and the Common Man", published in 1949, the same year that **Death of a Salesman** appeared, has obvious application to the play. Miller in general terms defends the use of the common man as a fit subject for tragedy in the highest sense, as rank is not a measure of human greatness. Insistence upon rank, he says, is but a clinging to outward forms of tragedy. In the conflict the hero gains "size", that tragic stature that is spuriously attached to the high born in our minds. The commonest of men may take on that stature to the extent of his willingness to throw all he has into the contest—the battle to secure his rightful place in his world. The idea that a tragedy can be based on the lives of ordinary folk is not new in the modern period. Ibsen's drama and [John Millington] Synge's *Riders to the Sea* are obvious examples. What is interesting here is that Miller in the essay makes a case for the common man protagonist, the low man, as tragic hero. He is a man who struggles against "a seemingly stable cosmos" to secure what he conceives his rights, to preserve his dignity. This is closer to the traditional view of tragedy, with its focus on the individual. But, while we may be prepared to accept the argument that a common man, that is, one without rank, may achieve heroic stature, the tragic nature of *Death of a Salesman* does not stem from this possibility. Willy Loman does not gain "size" from the situation. He is seen primarily as the victim of his society; his warped values, the illusions concerning the self he projects, reflect those of his society. His moments of clear self-knowledge are few, and even fewer are the moments when he asserts with strength and dignity his worthwhileness—that of the common man—as he does when he angrily rejects Biff's estimate of himself and his father ("Pop, I'm a dime a dozen and so are you") with his cry "I am not a dime a dozen! I am Willy Loman and you are Biff Loman!" [Act II]. Though there are occasions, too, when Willy emerges from the fog of self-deception and illusion, when he sees himself clearly—and at the end he does realize that Biff loves him for himself alone—he goes to his death clinging to his illusions. He is a pathetic figure, yet Miller in his essay written at this time says that there is no place for pathos in real tragedy. Pathos, he remarks, is the mode for the pessimist, suitable for the kind of struggle where man is obviously doomed from the outset. And earlier in the essay Miller postulated that tragedy must be inherently optimistic. In Miller's view of the nature of tragedy and his expression of it in his plays, there seems to be some confusion that needs to be examined.

In *All My Sons* we have a tragedy in the manner of the modern problem play. After this Miller seemed to be moving towards a greater emphasis on character. In "Tragedy and the Common Man" not only does he say that the common man may have heroic stature, but he implies that in tragedy he must have it, and that the tragic effect stems from the hero's struggle against the conventions, persons, and institutions ranged against him. But Miller's concern is still largely with those forces which he wished to condemn and with establishing the underlying moral law or a principle that could serve as an alternative to the prevailing social condition which shapes, or rather maims us. This is made clear in a passage in the Introduction to his *Collected Plays* [included in *Theater Essays*], where Miller says that the tragedy in *Death of a Salesman* grows out of the fact that

> Willy Loman has broken a law without whose protection life is insupportable if not incomprehensible to him and to many others; it is a law which says that a failure in society and in business has no right to live. Unlike the law against incest, the law of success is not administered by statute or church, but it is very nearly as powerful in its grip upon men. The confusion increases because, while it is a law, it is by no means a wholly agreeable one even as it is slavishly obeyed, for to fail is no longer to belong to society, in his estimate. Therefore, the path is open for those who wish to call Willy merely a foolish

man even as they themselves are living in obedience to the same law that killed him.

And so in *Death of a Salesman,* though Willy is as prominent as a tragic hero in the action, he never achieves heroic stature because of Miller's too strong concern with criticism of his society. The social problem play that would express this criticism leads him to present Willy as a nearly always deluded victim rather than as a sufficiently clear-sighted heroic challenger.

The same dichotomy persists in *The Crucible* between the concept of tragedy evidenced in the problem play, with the focus of interest on social conditions that are expressed through characters and their interactions, and the pre-modern, or what has been called the Christian tragedy, in which the focus of attention is on the tragic hero and the social context is given what significance it has through its bearing on him. Though *The Crucible* is a very powerful drama, structurally it suffers from Miller's failure to resolve this confusion. The introduction which outlines the social context, the opening scene, and large sections of the play later provide more than a background before which the protagonist acts. They have a significance greater than necessary for the playing out of the tragedy of John Proctor. The diffusion of the tragic force that results from the dramatist presenting the evil in society crushing Giles Corey, Rebecca Nurse, and others, as well as John Proctor, supports this view. Miller is clearly interested in showing the larger social effects of the particular blight that concerns him here. Even though we can agree with him that *The Crucible* is not merely a response to McCarthyism, or an attempt to cure witch-hunting, any more than the intention of *Death of a Salesman* is to improve conditions for travellers, nevertheless the concern with the political problem was obvious when the play appeared in 1953. Indeed Miller, in an article on *The Crucible,* reiterates his earlier statement that the dramatist cannot consider man apart from his social context and the problems that his environment presents. "I believe," he writes, "that it is no longer possible to contain the truth of the human situation so totally within a single man's guts as the bulk of our plays presuppose" ["Brewed in *The Crucible,*" included in *Theater Essays*]. It is not merely that man and the environment interact, but that they are part of each other—"The fish is in the water and the water is in the fish." We in the twentieth century, Miller adds, are more aware than any preceding generation "of the larger units that help make us and destroy us. . . . The vast majority of us know now—not merely as knowledge but as feeling, feeling capable of expression in art—that we are being formed, that our alternatives in life are not absolutely our own, as the romantic play inevitably must presuppose." Then, with specific reference to *The Crucible,* he says further, "The form, the shape, the meaning of *The Crucible* were all compounded out of the faith of those who were hanged. They were asked to be lonely and they refused. . . . It was not good to cast this play, to form it so that the psyche of the hero should emerge so 'commonly' as to wipe out of mind the process itself, the spectacle of that faith. . . ."

And yet the play, after the opening scene, becomes increasingly concerned with the role of one man, John Proc-

ompted by out-
sults from this
ual, the tragic
vhole tragic sit-
the play com-
y not always),
Miller's theme,
etween a man's
the question of
t of the human
over not mere-
to one's friend
t *The Crucible*
ciousness than
onsciousness is
he hero, makes
iore significant
issue and sees
a clear expres-
ill is conscious
ie more than a
esist degrading
nce of them—
mited vision.

ompted in part
hich the Salem
though Miller
oblem play, he
seems to have become increasingly concerned with and
even carried away by the tragedy in individual human
terms. Indeed in the Introduction to his *Collected Plays*
Miller tells us that it was an individual's crisis, not a social
issue, that precipitated the play:

> I doubt that I should ever have tempted agony
> by actually writing a play on the subject (the
> Salem witch-hunt) had I not come upon a single
> fact. It was that Abigail Williams, the prime
> mover of the Salem hysteria, so far as the hyster-
> ical children were concerned, had a short time
> earlier been the house servant of the Proctors
> and now was crying out Elizabeth Proctor as a
> witch; but more—it was clear from the record
> that with entirely uncharacteristic fastidiousness
> she was refusing to include John Proctor, Eliza-
> beth's husband, in her accusations despite the
> urgings of the prosecutors.

Miller's increasing concern with the individual rather
than with the social issue, or rather his attempt to express
the issue primarily through a clearly and intensely conceived character with heroic qualities, while evident in
The Crucible, is carried even further in *A View from the
Bridge.* Here too fate is seen to some extent as external to
man, a condition of environment. But here it is expressed
largely through individual persons rather than conventions and institutions, through a coming together of persons whose presence takes on dramatic significance only
in relation to the protagonist. And Miller has no easy explanation for the fateful interplay. In an article which appeared in the *New York Times* (September 25, 1955), he
wrote:

> There was such an iron-bound purity in the au-

tonomic egocentricity of the aims of each of the
persons involved that the weaving together of
their lives seemed almost the work of a fate. I
have tried to press as far as my reason can go toward defining the objective and subjective elements that made that fate, but I must confess
that in the end a mystery remains for me.

The illegal immigrants, the two women in the play—
Eddie's wife and his niece—important as they are to the
plot, even the moral law by which Eddie lives and of which
he runs afoul, all take their importance from the way in
which they precipitate Eddie's passion and are the agency
of his destruction. Eddie's attractiveness or unattractive-
ness, his rightness or his essential wrongness become relatively unimportant. What counts is that here is a man
who, as Miller says, "possesses or exemplifies the wondrous or humane fact that he too can be driven to what
in the last analysis is a sacrifice of himself for his conception, however misguided, of right, dignity, and justice."
Unlike the ending of *All My Sons* with its moral tag that
we are all one family and that a selfishness which is prepared to destroy others leads to self-destruction, and unlike the ending of *Death of a Salesman* with Charley's concluding remarks blaming society ("Nobody dast blame
this man. A salesman is got to dream, boy" [Requiem]),
the conclusion of *A View From the Bridge,* spoken by Alfieri, who serves as a Chorus in the play, emphasizes the
tragedy potential in man himself:

> Most of the time now we settle for half and I like
> it better. But the truth is holy, and even as I
> know how wrong he was, and his death useless,
> I tremble, for I confess that something perverse-
> ly pure calls to me from his memory—not purely
> good, but himself purely, for he allowed himself
> to be wholly known and for that I think I will
> love him more than all my sensible clients. And
> yet, it is better to settle for half, it must be! And
> so I mourn him—I admit it—with a certain
> alarm.
>
> [Act II]

It is interesting to note that in his early essay, "Tragedy
and the Common Man", in which Miller stresses the external factors as the source of tragedy, he mentions only
the emotion of terror as provoked by the spectacle of the
"total onslaught by an individual against a seemingly stable cosmos." He makes no mention of pity. Here, however, in the last play, where his emphasis has shifted and
tragedy is seen not as in the problem play as a product of
a social condition that can be altered by resolute action but
rather as a condition of a great man's nature, the feeling
of pity is powerful.

In an essay that appeared in 1945, W. H. Auden remarked
that at the end of a Greek play we say "What a pity it had
to be this way", while at the end of a Christian tragedy we
say "What a pity it had to be this way when it might have
been otherwise." In this pithy but somewhat oversimplified generalization Auden points to a significant distinction between the tragedies of the two cultures. In Greek
drama the sense of fate, residing for the most part in forces
outside of man, is overwhelming. The destiny of the hero
is foretold by oracles, or, as we are often reminded, made
the consequence of actions by the gods—of their quarrels

and judgments. Their action, moreover, is prompted often by events for which the hero is not responsible. In Christian tragedy there is a sense of greater personal freedom implied—man is free, according to a basic assumption commonly accepted, to act morally. The battleground, in the main, is in the hero's soul. In Greek drama the situation is given, fixed, and the dramatist concentrates on the way in which his characters respond to the grip events have on them. In Christian tragedy the situation is not given, or its givenness is irrelevant; the situation is created and destiny is not known beforehand. But there is a fixed system of moral imperatives resting on divine authority, there is an established order, and the tragedy works itself out largely in terms of the hero's conscious or accidental violation of that order. Arthur Miller in his plays combines elements of both. As in Christian drama the situation is not given; but as in Greek drama, the forces making for tragedy are often outside the protagonist—he is caught in circumstances not of his own making. But unlike Greek drama, these forces that determine or are the fate of the protagonist are not beyond his reach. Hence the possibility of decisive action is held out, and the will of the hero is called into play. Furthermore, Miller becomes decreasingly concerned with external factors until in *A View from the Bridge* the focus of attention is almost entirely on the central character, Eddie Carbone, and the way in which he confronts his situation. Yet in other respects *A View from the Bridge* is the most classical of Miller's tragedies. The use of the engaged narrator, or Chorus, to underline the generalized significance of the play and the depiction of the hero as a man almost possessed, driven beyond the ultimate bound of caution to destruction by an overwhelming force, strongly reminds us of Greek tragedy. But we do not feel that he is destined to defeat. As in Christian drama, we feel that the possibility for self-mastery is there—that is, it might have been otherwise.

Miller's tragedies then tend to fluctuate, often uneasily, between Greek drama with its emphasis on external causes (though Miller tries to avoid its fatalism) and Christian drama, which involves freedom and responsibility and which seeks the source of tragedy in the individual. His drama is unlike both in that for the most part it rejects a religious framework. Miller, like most modern tragedians, has been seeking a new explanation of the human situation with its tragic aspects. He seeks it in naturalistic and humanistic terms, not transcendental ones. Our ignorance, our lack of consciousness, is remediable. Our man-made ethical system, though incomplete and faulty, can be improved. Our environment, which restricts and defeats us, which prevents us from realizing ourselves (a failure which to Miller is the heart of the tragic experience) can be changed—if we will. The modern dramatists have to postulate a free will in what appears as an otherwise mechanistic world. This is one of the dilemmas faced by the writers of problem plays. Insofar as they regard external factors as the source of tragedy and regard man as largely the product and victim of his environment, they would seem to negate the idea of an effective free will. But this they are disinclined to do. For the most part the determinism that is implied in the naturalist view of man is ignored, and instead the view is presented that man is not merely a part of nature, but apart from it; that he is not

simply subject to its laws and forces, but can and should resist his environment or fate and seek to change it. The underlying position is optimistic: that man, an object of nature, is more than nature; that Willy Loman, for example, can somehow be more than the force that made him. The dilemma, which is clearly seen in *Death of a Salesman,* was recognized by Arthur Miller in the concluding paragraphs of his recent and fullest statement, the Introduction to his *Collected Plays:*

> A drama worthy of its time must first, knowingly or by instinctive means, recognize its major and most valuable traditions and where it has departed from them. Determinism, whether it is based on the iron necessities of economics or on psychoanalytic theory seen as a closed circle, is a contradiction of the idea of drama itself as drama has come down to us in its fullest developments. The idea of the hero, let alone the mere protagonist, is incompatible with a drama whose bounds are set in advance by the concept of an unbreakable trap. Nor is it merely that one wants arbitrarily to find a hero and a victory. The history of man is a ceaseless process of overthrowing one determinism to make way for another more faithful to life's changing relationships. And it is a process inconceivable without the existence of the will of man. His will is as much a fact as his defeat. . . .

> The idea of realism has become wedded to the idea that man is at best the sum of forces working upon him and of given psychological forces within him. Yet an innate value, an innate will, does in fact posit itself as real not alone because it is devoutly to be wished, but because, however closely he is measured and systematically accounted for, he is more than the sum of his stimuli and is unpredictable beyond a certain point. A drama, like a history, which stops at this point, the point of conditioning, is not reflecting reality. What is wanted, therefore, is not a poetry of escape from process and determinism, like that mood play which stops where feeling ends or that inverted romanticism which would mirror all the world in the sado-masochistic relationship. Nor will the heightening of the intensity of language alone yield the prize. A new poem will appear because a new balance has been struck which embraces both determinism and the paradox of will. If there is one unseen goal toward which every play in this book strives, it is that very discovery and its proof—that we are made and yet more than what made us.

On this note of faith, which well reflects the direction in which Arthur Miller has been moving, it might be well to end. In most respects Miller's position now is what it was ten years ago. He has been consistent in rejecting an exclusive preoccupation with the individual in terms of his neuroses or other purely private concerns, or with an exclusive preoccupation with social forces. He was always conscious not merely of their interplay, but of their fusion. But there has been an appreciable alteration in his angle of vision that has resulted in a sharper focussing on the individual and the subordination of the social issue to the inner crisis. As he moves towards greater emphasis on character, Miller has been making the protagonist a worthier opposite to the forces he struggles against. He has been giving his common man tragic stature, and the result has been a strengthening and an intensifying of the tragic quality in his plays. (pp. 329-40)

M. W. Steinberg, "Arthur Miller and the Idea of Modern Tragedy," in The Dalhousie Review, *Vol. 40, No. 3, Fall, 1960, pp. 329-40.*

Orm Överland   (essay date 1975)

[*Överland is a Norwegian scholar, critic, and editor specializing in American literature. He has edited the journal* American Studies in Scandinavia *and has written* The Making of an American Classic: James Fenimore Cooper's "The Prairie," *and* America Perceived: A View from Abroad in the Twentieth Century. *In the following essay, Överland detects two oppositions in Miller's plays. The first is the gap between what the writer wishes to express and the responses of audiences and reviewers. This has led, the critic maintains, to Miller's "radical distrust" of the theater as a means of communication. The second opposition is that between the elements, present in many of Miller's works and discussed in his theoretical writings, of both social drama and psychological drama of the individual. In this analysis, Överland focuses particularly on* All My Sons, Death of a Salesman, The Crucible, A View from the Bridge, After the Fall, *and* The Creation of the World and Other Business.]

"There are two questions I ask myself over and over when I'm working," Arthur Miller has remarked [in *Arthur Miller: Portrait of a Playwright*, by Benjamin Nelson]. "What do I mean? What am I trying to say?" The questions do not cease when a play is completed but continue to trouble him. In the "Introduction" to his *Collected Plays* [included in *The Theater Essays of Arthur Miller;* see Further Reading] Miller is constantly asking of each play: "What did I mean? What was I trying to say?" These questions and the playwright's attempts to answer them are directly related to his account of how he planned and wrote his next play.

The process of playwriting is given a peculiar wavelike rhythm in Miller's own story of his efforts to realize his intentions from one play to the other. Troughs of dejection on being exposed to unexpected critical and audience responses to a newly completed play are followed by swells of creativity informed by the dramatist's determination to make himself more clearly understood in the next one. This wavelike rhythm of challenge and response is the underlying structural principle of Miller's "Introduction" to his *Collected Plays*. Behind it one may suspect the workings of a radical distrust of his chosen medium. The present essay will consider some of the effects both of this distrust of the theater as a means of communication and of Miller's theories of dramatic form on his career as a dramatist.

Arthur Miller is not alone in asking what he is trying to say in his plays, nor in being concerned that they may evoke other responses than those the playwright thought he had aimed at. From the early reviews of *Death of a*

Salesman critics have observed that a central problem in the evaluation of Miller's work is a conflict of themes, real or apparent, within each play.

The case for the prosecution has been well put by Eric Bentley [see Further Reading]:

Mr. Miller says he is attempting a synthesis of the social and the psychological, and, though one may not see any synthesis, one certainly sees the thesis and the antithesis. In fact, one never knows what a Miller play is about: politics or sex. If *Death of a Salesman* is political, the key scene is the one with the tape recorder; if it's sexual, the key scene is the one in the Boston hotel. You may say of *The Crucible* that it isn't about McCarthy, it's about love in the seventeenth century. And you may say of *A View from the Bridge* that it isn't about informing, it's about incest and homosexuality.

John Mander points to the same conflict in his analysis of *Death of a Salesman* in his *The Writer and Commitment:*

If we take the "psychological" motivation as primary, the "social" documentation seems gratuitous, if we take the "social" documentation as primary, the "psychological" motivation seems gratuitous. And we have, I am convinced, to choose which kind of motivation must have the priority; we cannot have both at once.

Mr. Mander's own image of this conflict of themes within Arthur Miller's play is the house divided and its two incompatible masters are Freud and Marx.

More sympathetic critics find that the plays successfully embody the author's intentions of dramatizing a synthesis of the two kinds of motivation. Edward Murray, for instance, has made the same observation as have Bentley and Mander, but in his view the difficulty of branding Miller either a "social" or a "psychological" dramatist points to a strength rather than to a flaw in his work: "At his best, Miller has avoided the extremes of clinical psychiatric case studies on the one hand and mere sociological reports on the other. . . . he has indicated . . . how the dramatist might maintain in delicate balance both personal and social motivation" [see Further Reading].

Miller himself has often spoken of modern drama in general and his own in particular in terms of a split between the private and the social. In the 1956 essay, "The Family in Modern Drama" [included in *Theater Essays*], he claims that the various forms of modern drama "express human relationships of a particular kind, each of them suited to express either a primarily familial relation at one extreme, or a primarily social relation at the other." At times he has pointed to his own affinity with one or the other of these two extreme points of view on human relationships, as when he talks of the forties and fifties as "an era of gauze," for which he finds Tennessee Williams mainly responsible: "One of my own feet stands in this stream. It is a cruel, romantic neuroticism, a translation of current life into the war within the self. The personal has triumphed. All conflict tends to be transformed into sexual conflict" [conversation with Miller, in Henry Brandon's *As We Are*]. More often, as in "The Shadow of the

Gods" [included in *Theater Essays*], Miller has seen himself primarily in the social tradition of the Thirties. It is in this essay that Miller makes one of his most explicit statements on the need for a synthesis of the two approaches:

> Society is inside of man and man is inside society, and you cannot even create a truthfully drawn psychological entity on the stage until you understand his social relations and their power to make him what he is and to prevent him from being what he is not. The fish is in the water and the water is in the fish.

Such synthesis, however, is fraught with problems which are closely connected with Miller's medium, the theater.

Indeed, for Miller synthesis has largely been a question of dramatic form, and the problem for the playwright has been to create a viable form that could bridge "the deep split between the private life of man and his social life." In addition to his frustration with audience responses and his desire to make himself more clearly understood, part of the momentum behind Miller's search for new and more satisfactory modes of expression after the realistic *All My Sons* has been the conviction that the realistic mode in drama was an expression of "the family relationship within the play" while "the social relationship within the play" evoked the un-realistic modes ["The Family in Modern Drama," included in *Theater Essays*].

In retrospect Miller found that the theme of *All My Sons* (1947) "is the question of actions and consequences," and the play dramatizes this theme in the story of Joe Keller, for whom there was nothing bigger than the family, and his son Chris, for whom "one new thing was made" out of the destruction of the war: "A kind of—responsibility. Man for man." When Miller is slightly dissatisfied with his first successful play, it is because he believes that he had allowed the impact of what he calls one kind of "morality" to "obscure" the other kind "in which the play is primarily interested." These two kinds of "morality" are closely related to the two kinds of "motivation"—psychological and social—that John Mander and other critics have pointed to. The problem may be seen more clearly by observing that the play has two centers of interest. The one, in which Miller claims "the play is primarily interested," is intellectual, the other emotional. The former is mainly expressed through the play's dialogue, the latter is more deeply embedded in the action itself.

Joe Keller gradually emerges as a criminal. He has sold defective cylinder heads to the air force during the war and was thus directly responsible for the deaths of twenty-one pilots. The horror of this deed is further brought home to the audience by the discovery that Keller's elder son was a pilot lost in action. This is what we may call the emotional center of interest, and most of the plot is concerned with this past crime and its consequences for Keller and his family. But it is this emotional center that for Miller obscures the real meaning of the play.

Miller wanted his play to be about "unrelatedness":

> Joe Keller's trouble, in a word, is not that he cannot tell right from wrong but that his cast of mind cannot admit that he, personally, has any viable connection with his world, his universe, or his society. . . . In this sense Joe Keller is a threat to society and in this sense the play is a social play. Its "socialness" does not reside in its having dealt with the crime of selling defective materials to a nation at war—the same crime could easily be the basis of a thriller which would have no place in social dramaturgy. It is that the crime is seen as having roots in a certain relationship of the individual to society, and to a certain indoctrination he embodies, which, if dominant, can mean a jungle existence for all of us no matter how high our buildings soar.

This, then, is the intellectual center of the play. Any good drama needs to engage the intellect as well as the emotions of its audience. Miller's problem is that these two spheres in *All My Sons* are not concentric. When a play has two centers of interest at odds with each other, the emotional one will often, as here, have a more immediate impact on the audience because it is more intimately related to the action of the play. Invariably action takes precedence over the sophistication of dialogue or symbols.

Death of a Salesman (1949) may serve as further illustration of the point made about the two centers of interest in *All My Sons.* Bentley wrote that the key scene of the play could be the one in Howard Wagner's office or the one in the hotel room depending on whether the play was "political" or "sexual." There is no doubt, however, as to which scene has the greater impact in the theater. The hotel room scene is carefully prepared for. The constant references to stockings and the growing tension around the repeated queries about what had happened to Biff after he had gone to ask his father's advice in Boston are some of the factors that serve to high-light this scene. A more immediate impression is made on the audience by the mysterious laughter and the glimpse of a strange woman quite early in the first act. The point is, however, that it is primarily on the stage that this scene makes such an overwhelming impact that it tends to overshadow the other scenes that together make up the total image of Willy's plight. If the play is read, if one treats it as one would a novel, balance is restored and a good case may be made for a successful synthesis of "psychological" and "social" motivation as argued, for instance, by Edward Murray.

Miller seems to have become increasingly aware of the difficulty of making a harmonious whole of his vehicle and his theme. His story would have sexual infidelity (consider for instance the prominence this factor must have in any brief retelling of the plot of *Death of a Salesman* or *The Crucible*) or another personal moral failure at its center, while the significance the story held for the author had to do with man's relationship to society, to the outside world. The one kind of "morality" continues to obscure the other. When starting out to write *A View from the Bridge* (1955), Miller had almost despaired of making himself understood in the theater: no "reviews, favorable or not," had mentioned what he had considered the main theme of *The Crucible* (1953). Since he, apparently, could not successfully merge his plots and his intended themes, he arrived at a scheme that on the face of it seems preposterous: he would "separate, openly and without concealment, the action of the next play, *A View from the Bridge,* from its generalized significance."

With such an attitude to the relationship between story and theme or "action" and "significance" there is little wonder that Miller was prone to writing plays where critics felt there was a conflict of themes. For while Miller's imagination generates plots along psychoanalytic lines, his intellect leans towards socio-economic explanations.

The story was, according to his own account, his starting point for *A View from the Bridge:*

> I had heard its story years before, quite as it appears in the play, and quite as complete. . . . It was written experimentally not only as a form, but as an exercise in interpretation. I found in myself a passionate detachment toward its story as one does toward a spectacle in which one is not engaged but which holds a fascination deriving from its monolithic perfection. If this had happened, and if I could not forget it after so many years, *there must be some meaning in it for me, and I could write what had happened, why it had happened, and to one side, as it were, express as much as I knew of my sense of its meaning for me. Yet I wished to leave the action intact so that the onlooker could seize the right to interpret it entirely for himself and to accept or reject my reading of its significance.* (my italics)

This decision, Miller explains, led to the creation of "the engaged narrator," the role played by Alfieri in *A View from the Bridge.*

The narrator is hardly an innovation in the history of dramatic literature, especially when seen in relation to the chorus in Greek drama. In our own time widely different playwrights like Thornton Wilder (*Our Town*) and Bertolt Brecht (*The Caucasian Chalk Circle*) have made successful use of the narrator. Such historical antecedents and the widespread use of narrators in modern drama should not be lost sight of when considering this aspect of Arthur Miller's plays. Miller's narrators, however, are closely connected with his reluctance to let his plays speak for themselves. They are born from his long and troubled struggle with dramatic form.

Arthur Miller had tried his hand at fiction as well as drama before he achieved success on Broadway with *All My Sons* in 1947. When he thought of his next play, his aim was to achieve "the density of the novel form in its interchange of viewpoints." Again and again he comments on *Death of a Salesman* in terms of a prose narrative, as when he contrasts its sense of time with that of *All My Sons* : "This time, if I could, I would have *told the whole story* and set forth all the characters in one unbroken speech or even one sentence or a single flash of light. As I look at the play now its form seems the form of a confession, for that is *how it is told*. . . . " Although this may merely be a manner of speaking, as suggested by his own critique of the movie version where "drama becomes narrative," it does point to an attitude that in certain respects runs counter to drama: the story as something to be *told* as opposed to something to be *shown* or dramatised.

In fact, however, *Death of a Salesman* succeeds precisely

because Willy's story is shown on the stage, not told. The possible uncertainty as to motivation does not detract from the intense and unified impact of the drama in the theater. The characters reveal themselves through action and dialogue supported by what Miller has called the play's "structural images." All the more striking then, the need Miller evidently felt to have the characters stand forth and give their various interpretations of Willy's life after the drama proper has closed with Willy's death. The chorus-like effect of the "Requiem" is obviously related to Miller's conscious effort to write a tragedy of "the common man," a drama which places man in his full social context, which in his essay "On Social Plays" [included in *Theater Essays*] is so clearly associated in Miller's mind with Greek drama. From another point of view the "Requiem" may also be seen as the embryo of the narrator figure who becomes so conspicuous in *A View from the Bridge* and *After the Fall* : after the play is over the characters stand forth and tell the audience what the play is about.

Miller's reluctance to let a play speak for itself became even more evident in his two attempts to add extra material to the original text of *The Crucible* after its first production in 1953. The first of these additions, a second scene in Act Two, helps to explain Abigail's behavior in Act Three, but, as Laurence Olivier told the playwright, it is not necessary. Although Abigail's psychotic character is brought out entirely in action and dialogue, in an encounter with John Proctor on the eve of the trial, and there is no suggestion of extra-dramatic exposition, the added scene is nevertheless evidence of Miller's sense of not having succeeded in making himself understood in the original version of the play.

More striking is the evidence provided by the series of non-dramatic interpolated passages in the first act, where the playwright takes on the roles of historian, novelist and literary critic, often all at once, speaking himself *ex cathedra* rather than through his characters *ex scena*. There is an obvious difference in intent as well as effect in writing an introductory essay to one's play and writing a series of comments that are incorporated in the text itself. The material used need not be different. For example, some of the comments on Danforth in the "Introduction" to the *Collected Plays* are quite similar to those on Parris or Hale incorporated in the play. In the one instance, however, he is looking at his play from the outside, as one of its many critics, in the other he has added new material to the play and has thus changed the text.

In effect the play has a narrator, not realized as a character but present as a voice commenting on the characters and the action and making clear some of the moral implications for the reader/audience. The director of the 1958 Off Broadway revival of *The Crucible* drew the consequences of the revised text and introduced "a narrator, called The Reader, to set the scenes and give the historical background of the play." Besides his function as one of the minor characters, this is what Alfieri does in *A View from the Bridge.* The introduction of a "narrator" element in *The Crucible* is closely related to Miller's attempts to have a separate voice present the author's view of the "generalized significance" of the "action" in the later play.

The interpolated expository passages of *The Crucible* serve two different purposes. Frequently the comments on a character merely repeat points made in that part of the drama which may be acted on the stage. Indeed, the opening words of the following paragraph on John Proctor are suggestive of the Victorian novelist guiding his readers through his story, making sure that no point, however obvious, may be missed:

> But as we shall see, the steady manner he displays does not spring from an untroubled soul. He is a sinner, a sinner not only against the moral fashion of the time, but against his own vision of decent conduct. These people had no ritual for the washing away of sins. It is another trait we inherited from them, and it has helped to discipline us as well as to breed hypocrisy among us. Proctor, respected and even feared in Salem, has come to regard himself as a kind of fraud. But no hint of this has yet appeared on the surface, and as he enters from the crowded parlor below it is a man in his prime we see, with a quiet confidence and an unexpressed, hidden force. Mary Warren, his servant, can barely speak for embarrassment and fear.

Proctor's sense of guilt is central to any understanding of him as a dramatic character, but certainly this is made sufficiently clear by, for instance, the several explicit remarks made by Elizabeth as well as by his behavior on the stage.

While such passages are further instances of Miller's apparent distrust of his medium as a means of communication, other passages speak of an impatience with the limitations of the dramatic form. Miller had researched this play thoroughly, and it is as if on second thought he has regretted that he had not been able to bring as much of his research and his historical insights into the play as he would have liked. But when he in the interpolated passages takes on the roles of historian and biographer he tends to confuse the sharp line that must be drawn between the characters in a play called *The Crucible* and a group of late seventeenth century individuals bearing the same names as these characters. Thus, in the first of the two paragraphs that serve to introduce Proctor as he enters on the stage, Miller tells us:

> Proctor was a farmer in his middle thirties. He need not have been a partisan of any faction in the town, but there is evidence to suggest that he had a sharp and biting way with hypocrites. He was the kind of man—powerful of body, even-tempered, and not easily led—who cannot refuse support to partisans without drawing their deepest resentment. In Proctor's presence a fool felt his foolishness instantly—and a Proctor is always marked for calumny therefore.

The change in tense in the paragraph that follows (quoted above) suggests that Miller had a different Proctor in mind in each paragraph: the historical Proctor and the character in the play. This confusion runs through the various character sketches or brief essays on for instance Parris, Putnam and Rebecca and Francis Nurse. It should further

be noted that these interpolated expository passages are often concerned with motivation, and that both psychological, religious and socio-economic explanations of the trials are given. While the information is interesting in itself and throws light on the Salem trials, it cannot add to our understanding of the drama as acted on the stage. Whatever needs to be known about these characters and their motives by the audience must be expressed in action and dialogue. That is, if we do not accept the dichotomy of "action" and "significance," with the latter element presented by a representative of the author, a "Reader" or a narrator.

The assumption of such a dichotomy, according to Miller, lies at the heart of the structure of his next play, *A View from the Bridge.* Here, and in *A Memory of Two Mondays,* the one-act play originally presented on the same play bill, Miller thinks of himself as having followed "the impulse to present rather than to represent an interpretation of reality. Incident and character are set forth with the barest naïveté, and action is stopped abruptly while commentary takes its place." On the face of it, however, it is difficult to see why such commentary should be found necessary, unless the playwright had given up trying to make himself understood through "action" alone or, rather, to let his "action" carry the full weight of the "significance" he saw in it.

In his "Introduction" Miller claims at the outset that his "approach to playwriting and the drama itself is organic," and he insists that "the play must be dramatic rather than narrative in concept and execution." When towards the end of the "Introduction" he explains that "the organic impulse behind" his early plays was "split apart" in *A View from the Bridge,* it is as if he admits the failure of this approach. The organic structure of the early *All My Sons,* however, has already been questioned by Miller in his critique of its two centers of interest. As in this earlier play, the emotional center of *A View from the Bridge* is embedded in the action. But in the latter play Miller explains that he deliberately tried not to have the dialogue of the characters involved in the action carry any burden that goes beyond this action. The aspect of the play that dialogue attempted to express in *All My Sons* is now delegated to the narrator. The more explicit splitting apart of "the organic impulse" has been observed in *Death of a Salesman* with its concluding "Requiem." Moreover, Miller has also been seen to depart from the second of his two basic principles of playwriting in introducing narrative and expository passages into *The Crucible*. With *A View from the Bridge* he wrote a play that approaches illustrated narrative.

Alfieri, the lawyer-narrator, opens the play by telling a little about himself and his neighborhood and suggesting some of the themes of the play to follow. When Eddie appears on the stage, the verbal tense Alfieri makes use of is striking in its implications: "This one's name *was* Eddie Carbone" (my italics). Later in the play Alfieri consistently refers to Eddie in the past tense. The story is obviously Alfieri's story. What we see on the stage is Alfieri's memory of Eddie as he ponders on its significance: "This is the end of the story. Good night," he concludes the original one act version of the play. The past tense is the mode of narrative; drama is enacted in the present.

The title *A Memory of Two Mondays* is in itself interesting in this connection as it suggests an implied narrator, someone whose memory is projected on the stage as is Alfieri's. This technique is developed to its furthest extreme in *After the Fall,* where *"the action takes place in the mind, thought, and memory of Quentin."* The play has become illustrated narrative, and is essentially a two act monologue which the narrator and main character Quentin, directs at the audience. Significantly, since the flow of narration is essential to the play and the many dramatizations of situations in the narrative are incidental, Quentin's audience is in Miller's stage directions defined as a *"Listener, who, if he could be seen, would be sitting just beyond the edge of the stage itself."*

The images presented on the stage are illustrations of Quentin's consciously controlled discourse or of the working of his sub-consciousness as he struggles for self-understanding and self-acceptance. In either case, the device of giving characters within *"the mind, thought, and memory of Quentin"* a semi-independent status on the stage and allowing them to speak for themselves, makes possible an objective view of the self-image projected by Quentin in his discourse. Essentially, however, Miller has placed a character on the stage and given him the opportunity of examining his life and motives and explaining himself to a Listener through a monologue that lasts the whole length of a two act play. From point of view of genre the result is a cross between expressionist drama, stream of consciousness novel and dramatic monologue. The result, however, is good theater: it works on the stage. The critical attacks on *After the Fall* have mainly been concerned with Miller's subject matter and theme, not his experiment with dramatic form.

Rather than add a clarifying "Requiem," as he did with *Death of a Salesman;* rather than interpolate expository passages in the published play to make himself more readily understood, as he did in *The Crucible;* and rather than introduce a narrator, somewhat to the side of the central plot, who could explain the author's "reading of its significance," Miller in *After the Fall* made the narrator's attempt to arrive at the significance of his own life and explain himself directly to the audience the center of the play. Ironically, Miller may never have felt himself so misunderstood by audiences and critics alike as after the first production of *After the Fall* in 1964, the play that may be seen as the culmination of a series of efforts to develop a form that would allow him to present his intentions unmistakably and clearly to his public.

Some years earlier, in his "Introduction" to the *Collected Plays,* Miller had observed that "the intention behind a work of art and its effects upon the public are not always the same." His answers to the question of how to avoid this communication gap could not, finally, have struck him as successful in practice. In his next play, at least, *Incident at Vichy,* written immediately after the critical disaster of *After the Fall,* he returned to the form of the straightforward, realistic play. By concentrating on one of the two poorly integrated themes of *After the Fall,* that

represented by the concentration camp tower, the later play, moreover, avoids the conflict between two different kinds of "morality" or "motivation" many critics have found in his plays up to and including *After the Fall. Incident at Vichy* may be too much the drama of ideas (and not very new or original ones at that) to be successful in the theater, and Von Berg's development may not be quite convincing on the stage; but at least there is no need for any "Requiem," explanatory footnotes or narrator to express the play's dominantly public theme.

Four years later Miller returned to the material of *All My Sons, Death of a Salesman* and *After the Fall* in another family drama, *The Price.* The play is also a return to the realistic style and retrospective technique of *All My Sons.* But of course Miller had traveled a long distance since 1947. There is a greater economy of characters and incidents, a more subtle and dramatically integrated use of symbols, no more need for manipulative, mechanistic devices like surprise arrivals or unsuspected letters. Two hours in an attic with old furniture and four people—and the experience in the theater is of something organic, something that comes alive and evolves before us on the stage. The playwright appears relaxed, confident that the "action" expresses its "generalized significance": the characters speak for themselves and the play speaks for Arthur Miller.

The critics who found, I think rightly so, a confusion of private-psychological and public-political themes in Miller's plays were addressing themselves to the very Problem Miller has repeatedly pointed to as the central one for the dramatist in our day: how to create a form that can bridge "the deep split between the private life of man and his social life." Miller's belief, expressed in several essays in the mid-fifties, that it is the unrealistic modes of drama that are capable of expressing man's social relationships, as opposed to the realistic drama which is best suited to present the private life, is seen most clearly at work in *A View from the Bridge* from 1955. The "bridge," however, is rather crudely built: to the side of the realistic action stands the narrator, who in the first version of the play spoke in verse—poetry, according to Miller, being the style most closely related to public themes. In the light of such theories the author's misfired intentions with *After the Fall,* his most "unrealistic" play, may be more easily understood; and the irony of its reception as his most embarrassingly private play more readily appreciated. There is further irony in the successful synthesis of the public and the private spheres in *The Price.* For according to Miller's theory, the realism of this or any other play "could not, with ease and beauty, bridge the widening gap between the private life and the social life." But in his essay on "The Family in Modern Drama," Miller had also wondered: "Why does Realism always seem to be drawing us all back to its arms? We have not yet created in this country a succinct form to take its place." This was written at a time when Miller was trying to break away from realism. This movement, however, had its temporary conclusion in *After the Fall,* the play that more than any other must have led Miller to despair of communicating his intentions to his audience.

The ironies of Arthur Miller's career as a dramatist were further compounded with the production of *The Creation of the World and Other Business* in 1973. In spite of the success, with audiences as well as with critics, of *The Price,* following the disastrous reception of his experiments in *After the Fall,* Miller seems unable to rest comfortably in the strong and protective arms of Realism. His latest play is his first attempt to express himself through comedy and pure fantasy, and in this his most radical departure from realism his earlier concern with the problems of integrating man's private and social life has given way to teleological speculation. Behind the fanciful cosmological draperies, however, one may discover the playwright's old story of the two sons and familial conflict. Indeed, the new play serves as a reminder that the Cain and Abel story is an archetypal pattern in *All My Sons, Death of a Salesman, After the Fall* and *The Price.*

In a different guise the old question of the two centers of interest is also raised by Miller's attempt at comedy. While God and Lucifer incessantly come together on the stage to discuss the Creator's design, Miller's alleged theme, the audience, who cannot but grow restless after two acts with God, his Angels and a boring couple named Adam and Eve, are finally given the two sons, the responsible and respected Cain and the irresponsible and loved Abel. The rather simplistic psychological presentation of the conflict between them is the kind of dramatic material Miller has successfully handled before, and both because it is welcome relief from the overall tediousness of the rest of the play and because it has dramatic potential, it will easily lay claim to the attention and the interest of the audience at the expense of the play's concern with the human dilemma. Miller's latest Broadway venture thus is not only thematically related to his first one but shows that the playwright has still not been able to solve the problem of dramatic form he then felt had served to obscure his main theme.

The story of Arthur Miller's struggle with dramatic form had its beginning in his realization of the two centers of interest in *All My Sons.* His subsequent theories of social drama and its relationship to the realistic and unrealistic modes of drama should be regarded primarily as rationalizations of his own attempts to express himself clearly, to bridge the gap not so much between the social and the private as between his conscious intentions and the audience and critical responses. This was fully demonstrated in his attempts deliberately to separate the action of a play from its significance. His distrust of the realistic drama as a usable medium was thus properly a distrust of the theater itself as a medium, as evidenced in his use of intermediary commentary and narrators and in his tendency towards illustrated narrative. Realism nevertheless has proved to have a strong hold on Miller, and it is the mode with which, the evidence of his plays suggests, he is most at home. *The Creation of the World and Other Business* marks a break with the tone and style of all his previous plays, but it is impossible at this point to guess whether it will turn out to be a new departure in his career or a dead end. Although Miller, like the devil in [Henrik] Ibsen's *Peer Gynt,* has not always been able to reckon with his audience, he has demonstrated that he has been ex-

tremely sensitive to their responses. He may therefore accept the common verdict of critics and audiences and return to the kind of work that has placed him in the front rank of contemporary dramatists. (pp. 1-12)

Orm Överland, "The Action and Its Significance: Arthur Miller's Struggle with Dramatic Form," in Modern Drama, *Vol. XVIII, No. 1, March, 1975, pp. 1-14.*

DEATH OF A SALESMAN

PRODUCTION REVIEWS

Brooks Atkinson   (review date 11 February 1949)

[*Atkinson was the drama critic for the* New York Times *from 1926 to 1960. Upon his retirement from that post, the Mansfield Theatre in New York was renamed the Brooks Atkinson in honor of his contributions to theater. His publications include* Skyline Promenades *(1925),* Henry Thoreau: The Cosmic Yankee *(1927), and* East of the Hudson *(1931), as well as many collections of his drama criticism. In the following review, Atkinson hails the premier of* Death of a Salesman *as a "rare event in the theatre," claiming that "Mr. Miller's elegy in a Brooklyn sidestreet is superb."*]

Lee J. Cobb and Mildred Dunnock as Willy and Linda Loman.

Arthur Miller has written a superb drama. From every point of view *Death of a Salesman,* which was acted at the Morosco last evening, is rich and memorable drama. It is so simple in style and so inevitable in theme that it scarcely seems like a thing that has been written and acted. For Mr. Miller has looked with compassion into the hearts of some ordinary Americans and quietly transferred their hope and anguish to the theatre. Under Elia Kazan's masterly direction, Lee J. Cobb gives a heroic performance, and every member of the cast plays like a person inspired. . . .

Two seasons ago Mr. Miller's *All My Sons* looked like the work of an honest and able playwright. In comparison with the new drama, that seems like a contrived play now. For *Death of a Salesman* has the flow and spontaneity of a suburban epic that may not be intended as poetry but becomes poetry in spite of itself because Mr. Miller has drawn it out of so many intangible sources.

It is the story of an aging salesman who has reached the end of his usefulness on the road. There has always been something unsubstantial about his work. But suddenly the unsubstantial aspects of it overwhelm him completely. When he was young, he looked dashing; he enjoyed the comradeship of other people—the humor, the kidding, the business.

In his early sixties he knows his business as well as he ever did. But the unsubstantial things have become decisive; the spring has gone from his step, the smile from his face and the heartiness from his personality. He is through. The phantom of his life has caught up with him. As literally as Mr. Miller can say it, dust returns to dust. Suddenly there is nothing.

This is only a little of what Mr. Miller is saying. For he conveys this elusive tragedy in terms of simple things—the loyalty and understanding of his wife, the careless selfishness of his two sons, the sympathetic devotion of a neighbor, the coldness of his former boss' son—the bills, the car, the tinkering around the house. And most of all: the illusions by which he has lived—opportunities missed, wrong formulas for success, fatal misconceptions about his place in the scheme of things.

Writing like a man who understands people, Mr. Miller has no moral precepts to offer and no solutions of the salesman's problems. He is full of pity, but he brings no piety to it. Chronicler of one frowsy corner of the American scene, he evokes a wraithlike tragedy out of it that spins through the many scenes of his play and gradually envelops the audience.

As theatre *Death of a Salesman* is no less original than it is as literature. Jo Mielziner, always equal to an occasion, has designed a skeletonized set that captures the mood of the play and serves the actors brilliantly. Although Mr. Miller's text may be diffuse in form, Mr. Kazan has pulled it together into a deeply moving performance.

Mr. Cobb's tragic portrait of the defeated salesman is acting of the first rank. Although it is familiar and folksy in the details it has something of the grand manner in the big size and the deep tone. Mildred Dunnock gives the performance of her career as the wife and mother—plain of speech but indomitable in spirit. The parts of the thoughtless sons are extremely well played by Arthur Kennedy and Cameron Mitchell, who are all youth, brag and bewilderment.

Other parts are well played by Howard Smith, Thomas Chalmers, Don Keefer, Alan Hewitt and Tom Pedi. If there were time, this report would gratefully include all the actors and fabricators of illusion. For they all realize that for once in their lives they are participating in a rare event in the theatre. Mr. Miller's elegy in a Brooklyn sidestreet is superb.

> *Brooks Atkinson, in a review of "Death of a Salesman," in* The New York Times, *February 11, 1949, p. 27.*

John Mason Brown   (review date 26 February 1949)

[*Brown, an influential and popular American drama critic during the 1930s, 40s, and 50s, wrote extensively on contemporary British and American theater. He had a thorough knowledge of dramatic history, and his criticism often displays a scholarly erudition in addition to the qualities of popular reviewing. In the following assessment, Brown lauds* Death of a Salesman *as "the most poignant statement of man as he must face himself to have come out of our theatre."*]

George Jean Nathan once described a certain actress's Camille as being the first Camille he had ever seen who had died of catarrh. This reduction in scale of a major disease to an unpleasant annoyance is symptomatic of more than the acting practice of the contemporary stage. Even our dramatists, at least most of them, tend in their writing, so to speak, to turn t.b. into a sniffle. They seem ashamed of the big things; embarrassed by the raw emotions; afraid of the naked passions; and unaware of life's brutalities and tolls.

Of understatement they make a fetish. They have all the reticences and timidities of the over-civilized and undemonstrative. They pride themselves upon writing around a scene rather than from or to it; upon what they hold back instead of upon what they release. They paint with pastels, not oils, and dodge the primary anguishes as they would the primary colors.

Their characters belong to an anemic brood. Lacking blood, they lack not only violence but humanity. They are the puppets of contrivance, not the victims of circumstance or themselves. They are apt to be shadows without substance, surfaces without depths. They can be found in the *dramatis personae* but not in the telephone book. If they have hearts, their murmurings are seldom audible. They neither hear nor allow us to hear those inner whisperings of hope, fear, despair, or joy, which are the true accompaniment to spoken words. Life may hurt them, but they do not suffer from the wounds it gives them so that we, watching them, are wounded ourselves and suffer with them.

This willingness, this ability to strike unflinchingly upon the anvil of human sorrow is one of the reasons for [Eugene] O'Neill's pre-eminence and for the respect in which we hold the best work of Clifford Odets and Tennessee Williams. It is also the source of Arthur Miller's unique strength and explains why his fine new play, *Death of a Salesman,* is an experience at once pulverizing and welcome.

Mr. Miller is, of course, remembered as the author of *Focus,* a vigorous and terrifying novel about anti-Semitism, and best known for *All My Sons,* which won the New York Critics Award two seasons back. Although that earlier play lacked the simplicity, hence the muscularity, of Mr. Miller's novel, it was notable for its force. Over-elaborate as it may have been, it introduced a new and unmistakable talent. If as a young man's script it took advantage of its right to betray influences, these at least were of the best. They were [Henrik] Ibsen and [Anton] Chekhov. The doctor who wandered in from next door might have been extradited from *The Three Sisters.* The symbolical use to which the apple tree was put was pure Ibsen. So, too, was the manner in which the action was maneuvered from the present back into the past in order to rush forward. Even so, Mr. Miller's own voice could be heard in *All My Sons,* rising strong and clear above those other voices. It was a voice that deserved the attention and admiration it won. It was not afraid of being raised. It spoke with heat, fervor, and compassion. Moreover, it had something to say.

In *Death of a Salesman* this same voice can be heard again. It has deepened in tone, developed wonderfully in modulation, and gained in carrying power. Its authority has become full-grown. Relying on no borrowed accents, it now speaks in terms of complete accomplishment rather than exciting promise. Indeed, it is released in a drama which is not only by all odds the best play to have been written by an American this season, but a play which provides one of the modern theatre's most overpowering evenings.

How good the writing of this or that of Mr. Miller's individual scenes may be, I do not know. Nor do I really care. When hit in the face, you do not bother to count the knuckles which strike you. All that matters, all you remember, is the staggering impact of the blow. Mr. Miller's is a terrific wallop, as furious in its onslaught on the heart as on the head. His play is the most poignant statement of man as he must face himself to have come out of our theatre. It finds the stuffs of life so mixed with the stuffs of the stage that they become one and indivisible.

If the proper study of mankind is man, man's inescapable problem is himself—what he would like to be, what he is, what he is not, and yet what he must live and die with. These are the moving, everyday, all-inclusive subjects with which Mr. Miller deals in *Death of a Salesman.* He handles them unflinchingly, with enormous sympathy, with genuine imagination, and in a mood which neither the prose of his dialogue nor the reality of his probing can rob of its poetry. Moreover, he has the wisdom and the insight not to blame the "system," in Mr. Odets's fashion, for what are the inner frailties and shortcomings of the individual. His rightful concern is with the dilemmas which are timeless in the drama because they are timeless in life.

Mr Miller's play is a tragedy modern and personal, not classic and heroic. Its central figure is a little man sentenced to discover his smallness rather than a big man undone by his greatness. Although he happens to be a salesman tested and found wanting by his own very special crises, all of us sitting out front are bound to be shaken, long before the evening is over, by finding something of ourselves in him.

Mr. Miller's Willy Loman is a family man, father of two sons. He is sixty-three and has grubbed hard all his life. He has never possessed either the daring or the gold-winning luck of his prospector brother, who wanders through the play as a somewhat shadowy symbol of success but a necessary contrast. Stupid, limited, and confused as Willy Loman may have been, however, no one could have questioned his industry or his loyalty to his family and his firm. He has loved his sons and, when they were growing up, been rewarded by the warmth of their returned love. He loves his wife, too, and has been unfaithful to her only because of his acute, aching loneliness when on the road.

He has lived on his smile and on his hopes; survived from sale to sale; been sustained by the illusion that he has countless friends in his territory, that everything will be all right, that he is a success, and that his boys will be successes also. His misfortune is that he has gone through his life as an eternal adolescent, as someone who has not dared to take stock, as someone who never knew who he was. His personality has been his profession; his energy, his protection. His major ambition has been not only to be liked, but well liked. His ideal for himself and for his sons has stopped with an easy, back-slapping, sports-loving, locker-room popularity. More than ruining his sons so that one has become a woman chaser and the other a thief; his standards have turned both boys against their father.

When Mr. Miller's play begins, Willy Loman has reached the ebbtide years. He is too old and worn out to continue traveling. His back aches when he stoops to lift the heavy sample cases that were once his pride. His tired, wandering mind makes it unsafe for him to drive the car which has carried him from one town and sale to the next. His sons see through him and despise him. His wife sees through him and defends him, knowing him to be better than most and, at any rate, well-intentioned. What is far worse, when he is fired from his job he begins to see through himself. He realizes he is, and has been, a failure. Hence his deliberate smash-up in his car, in order to bring in some money for his family and make the final payment on his home when there is almost no one left who wants to live in it.

Although *Death of a Salesman* is set in the present, it also finds time and space to include the past. It plays the agonies of the moment of collapse against the pleasures and sorrows of recollected episodes. Mr. Miller is interested in more than the life and fate of his central character. His scene seems to be Willy Loman's mind and heart no less than his home. What we see might just as well be what Willy Loman thinks, feels, fears, or remembers, as what we see him doing. This gives the play a double and successful exposure in time. It makes possible the constant fusion of what has been and what is. It also enables it to achieve a greater reality by having been freed from the fetters of realism.

Once again Mr. Miller shows how fearless and perceptive an emotionalist he is. He writes boldly and brilliantly about the way in which we disappoint those we love by having disappointed ourselves. He knows the torment of family tensions, the compensations of friendship, and the heartbreak that goes with broken pride and lost confidence. He is aware of the loyalties, not blind but open-eyed, which are needed to support mortals in their loneliness. The anatomy of failure, the pathos of age, and the tragedy of those years when a life begins to slip down the hill it has labored to climb are subjects at which he excels.

The quality and intensity of his writing can perhaps best be suggested by letting Mr. Miller speak for himself, or rather by allowing his characters to speak for him, in a single scene; in fact, in the concluding one. It is then that Willy's wife, his two sons, and his old friend move away from Jo Mielziner's brilliantly simple and imaginative multiple setting, and advance to the footlights. It is then that Mr. Miller's words supply a scenery of their own. Willy Loman, the failure and suicide, has supposedly just been buried, and all of us are at his grave, including his wife who wants to cry but cannot and who keeps thinking that it is just as if he were off on another trip.

"You don't understand," says Willy's friend, defending Willy from one of his sons. "Willy was a salesman; and for a salesman, there is no rock bottom to the life. He don't put a bolt to a nut, he don't tell you the law, or give you medicine. He's a man way out there in the blue, ridin' on a smile and a shoeshine; and when they start not smilin' back—boys, that's an earthquake. And then you get yourself a couple a spots on your hat, and you're finished. Nobody dast blame this man. A salesman is got to dream, boys; it comes with the territory" [Requiem].

The production of **Death of a Salesman** is as sensitive, human, and powerful as the writing. Elia Kazan has solved, and solved superbly, what must have been a difficult and challenging problem. He captures to the full the mood and heartbreak of the script. He does this without ever surrendering to sentimentality. He manages to mingle the present and the past, the moment and the memory, so that their intertwining raises no questions and causes no confusions. His direction, so glorious in its vigor, is no less considerate of those small details which can be both mountainous and momentous in daily living.

It would be hard to name a play more fortunate in its casting than **Death of a Salesman.** All of its actors—especially Arthur Kennedy and Cameron Mitchell as the two sons, and Howard Smith as the friend—act with such skill and conviction that the line of demarcation between being and pretending seems abolished. The script's humanity has taken possession of their playing and is an integral part of their performances.

Special mention must be made of Lee J. Cobb and Mildred Dunnock as the salesman, Willy Loman, and his wife, Linda. Miss Dunnock is all heart, devotion, simplicity.

She is unfooled but unfailing. She is the smiling, mothering, hardworked, good wife, the victim of her husband's budget. She is the nourisher of his dreams, even when she knows they are only dreams; the feeder of his self-esteem. If she is beyond whining or nagging, she is above self-pity. She is the marriage vow—"for better for worse, for richer for poorer, in sickness and in health"—made flesh; slight of body but strong of faith.

Mr. Cobb's Willy Loman is irresistibly touching and wonderfully unsparing. He is a great shaggy bison of a man seen at that moment of defeat when he is deserted by the herd and can no longer run with it. Mr. Cobb makes clear the pathetic extent to which the herd has been Willy's life. He also communicates the fatigue of Willy's mind and body and that boyish hope and buoyancy which his heart still retains. Age, however, is his enemy. He is condemned by it. He can no more escape from it than he can from himself. The confusions, the weakness, the goodness, the stupidity, and the self-sustaining illusions which are Willy—all of these are established by Mr. Cobb. Seldom has an average man at the moment of his breaking been characterized with such exceptional skill.

Did Willy Loman, so happy with a batch of cement, when puttering around the house, or when acquaintances on the road smiled back at him, fail to find out who he was? Did this man, who worked so hard and meant so well, dream the wrong dream? At least he was willing to die by that dream, even when it had collapsed for him. He was a breadwinner almost to the end, and a breadwinner even in his death. Did the world walk out on him, and his sons see through him? At any rate he could boast one friend who believed in him and thought his had been a good dream, "the only dream you can have." Who knows? Who can say? One thing is certain. No one could have raised the question more movingly or compassionately than Arthur Miller. (pp. 30-2)

John Mason Brown, "Even as You and I," in
The Saturday Review of Literature, *Vol.
XXXII, No. 9, February 26, 1949, pp. 30-2.*

Harold Clurman   (review date 28 February 1949)

[*A celebrated director and theater critic, Clurman founded, in association with Lee Strasberg and Cheryl Crawford, the Group Theatre in 1931. For the next ten years, as its managing director, he helped create many notable productions, particularly of American plays. Clurman directed the premiere of Miller's* Incident at Vichy *in 1964. In addition, he served the* Nation, *the* New Republic, *and the* Observer *as drama critic from 1949 to 1963. His publications include* The Fervent Years: The Story of the Group Theatre *(1945),* Lies Like Truth: Theatre Essays and Reviews *(1958),* On Directing *(1973), and* The Divine Pastime: Theatre Essays *(1974). In the review below, Clurman echoes the general critical consensus that* Death of a Salesman *"marks a high point of significant expression in the American theatre of our time."*]

"Attention must be paid to such a man. Attention!" [Requiem] The man his wife refers to is Willy Loman, the central figure of Arthur Miller's *Death of a Salesman.* Perhaps the chief virtue of the play is the attention that Miller makes us pay to the man and his problem, for the man represents the lower middle class, the $50-a-week-plus-commission citizen, whose dream is to live to a ripe old age doing a great volume of business over the telephone. It was not unusual to hear of this person in the thirties, but in the theatre of the forties he has once more become the forgotten man.

The play has tremendous impact because it makes its audience recognize itself. Willy Loman is everybody's father, brother, uncle or friend, his family are our cousins; *Death of a Salesman* is a documented history of our lives. It is not a realistic portrait, it is a demonstration both of the facts and of their import. "We had the wrong dream," says Biff, Willy Loman's son, and what Miller is saying in terms few can miss is that this wrong dream is one the greater part of America still cherishes.

"The only thing you got in this world is what you can sell," the prosperous man next door tells Willy [Act II]. This is the harsh fact, but Willy, the poor dear fellow, is not satisfied with it. He wants to be *well-liked*. It is natural and healthy to harbor this desire, but the philosophy of Willy's economic situation denatures this desire to the hope of being well-liked or "known" as a way to security, success, salvation. To be a "personality" is to cultivate those traits which make one sufficiently "well-liked" to do a greater volume of business so that one may achieve a brighter place in the sun.

The competition Willy encounters is too tough for his modest talents; the path he has chosen denies his true being at every step. He idolizes the dream beyond the truth of himself, and he thus becomes a "romantic," shadowy nonentity, a liar, a creature whose only happiness lies in looking forward to miracles, since reality mocks his pretensions. His real ability for manual work seems trivial and mean to him. "Even your grandfather was more than a carpenter," he tells Biff [Act I]. From this perpetual self-denial he loses the sense of his own thought; he is a stranger to his own soul; he no longer knows what he thinks either of his sons or his automobile (he boosts and denounces them both in almost the same breath); he cannot tell who are his true friends; he is forever in a state of enthusiastic or depressed bewilderment. "That man never knew who he was" [Requiem], Biff says of him. He never owns anything outright till his death by suicide (committed to give Biff a foundation of $20,000); he has never been free.

His sons suffer the guilt of the father: Biff, the older, with increasing consciousness; Hap, the younger, stupidly. Hap seeks satisfaction as a coarse ladies' man. Biff cannot find any satisfaction because, being more trusting and sensitive than his brother, he tries to live according to his father's dream with which he has nothing in common—the boy yearns to live on the land. Only toward the end does Biff discover the spiritual hoax of his father's life, the corruption of heart and mind to which his father's "ideals" are leading him. With his father's death, Biff has possibly achieved sufficient self-awareness to change his course; Hap—like most of us—persists in following the way of his

father. He will go on striving "to come out No. 1 man." . . . The point of all this is not that our economic system does not work, but that its ideology distorts man's true nature. Willy's well-adjusted neighbor "never took an interest in anything" [Act II] and has no aspiration beyond the immediately practicable.

Arthur Miller is a moralist. His talent is for a kind of humanistic jurisprudence: he sticks to the facts of the case. For this reason his play is clearer than those of other American playwrights with similar insight whose lyric gifts tend to reflect the more elusive and imponderable aspects of the same situation. There is poetry in *Death of a Salesman*—not the poetry of the senses or of the soul, but of ethical conscience. It might have been graven on stone—like tablets of law. *Death of a Salesman* stirs us by its truth, the ineluctability of its evidence and judgment which permits no soft evasion. Though the play's environment is one we associate with a grubby realism, its style is like a clean accounting on the books of an understanding but severe sage. We cry before it like children being chastised by an occasionally humorous, not unkindly but unswervingly just father. *Death of a Salesman* is rational, dignified and profoundly upright.

Elia Kazan's production conveys these qualities with a swift and masterful thrust—like a perfect blow. He has cast the play admirably, and the entire occasion might be cited as an example of real theatre: meaning and means unified by fine purpose. Lee J. Cobb, who plays Willy Loman, is surely one of the most powerful and juicy actors on our stage today. He displays a tendency in this part to sacrifice characterization to a certain grandiosity. Willy Loman's wife speaks of his exhaustion, and Willy himself refers to his having grown fat and foolish-looking. None of these textual indications is taken into sufficient account, and what is gained in general impressiveness is lost in a want of genuine pathos.

Indeed the tone of histrionic bravura tends to make the others in the cast—for instance, Arthur Kennedy, the beautifully sensitive actor who plays Biff—push a little too hard. The production therefore pays for its virtues by a lack of intimacy, which is the dimension needed to make the event complete. Mildred Dunnock, in her simplicity and delicacy of feeling, is like the symbolic beacon of everything sound in the production. Tom Pedi, as a waiter, is as real and tasty as a garlic salad; Hope Cameron, in the smallest role in the play, suggests a remarkably touching naïveté. Both have a specific reality that I should have liked to see carried through all the longer parts. But virtually everyone in *Death of a Salesman* is better than good; and the whole marks a high point of significant expression in the American theatre of our time. (pp. 26-8)

> *Harold Clurman, in a review of "Death of a Salesman," in* The New Republic, *Vol. 120, No. 9, February 28, 1949, pp. 26-8.*

Joseph Wood Krutch   (review date 5 March 1949)

[*Krutch is widely regarded as one of America's most respected literary and dramatic critics. Noteworthy among his works are* The American Drama since 1918 *(1939), which analyzes the most important plays of the 1920s and 30s, and "Modernism" in* Modern Drama *(1953), in which he stresses the need for twentieth-century playwrights to infuse their works with traditional humanistic values. A conservative and idealistic thinker, Krutch was a consistent proponent of human dignity and the preeminence of literary art. In the following review, he offers a negative opinion of* Death of a Salesman. *The play is "prosy and pedestrian," he contends, and lacks "new insight, fresh imagination, or individual sensibility."*]

It has been a good many years since any serious play has provoked enthusiasm as unqualified and as nearly universal as that which greeted Arthur Miller's **Death of a Salesman** (Morosco Theater). That it is powerful, veracious, and theatrically effective can hardly be denied; but perhaps a reviewer who has the privilege of making a delayed report may be forgiven if he undertakes to suggest that, like every work of art, it is good only in its own particular way and that there are virtues which it does not exhibit.

The action recounts the last few days in the life of a traveling salesman who has outlived his usefulness and is discharged by the firm for which he has worked all his life. Behind him lie the memories of a drab and unsuccessful existence which was sustained by a shabby illusion of his own importance and by a belief in what I suppose it would now be fashionable to call his "myth"—that is to say, in a philosophy of life which assumes that "self-confidence" and "influence" are the instruments and "being well liked" the outward sign of success. His wife is exhausted by years of attempting to meet instalment payments, and his two sons, whom he has encouraged to believe that importance on the high-school football team will open all doors, are flashy fakers. Now that he can no longer believe that he has "influence" or that he is "well liked," nothing lies before him except confession of failure. He chooses therefore to commit suicide in order that the wife may at least have his insurance money to live on.

This being 1949, one naturally assumes that such a story is most likely to be told in order to expose the evils of our social system. No doubt in some very general way **The Death of a Salesman** may be taken to do just that. But I was unable to perceive anything in the slightest degree doctrinaire, and at least as much stress seems to be laid on the intellectual and moral weakness of the central character as upon any outward necessity determining his fate. The moral can be taken to be merely "Know Thyself," since the only positive suggestion seems to be that the hero would have been a good deal better off if he had realized that what he calls "success" is not for such as he and that he could have been humbly happy cultivating the soil or working with a carpenter's tools—two things he actually enjoys doing. Like the central character in [Eugene O'Neill's] *The Ice Man Cometh* Mr. Miller's salesman dies when he loses his illusions, but **Death of a Salesman** is without the mystical suggestions of O'Neill's play and is actually in theme and effect a good deal closer to Elmer Rice's *The Adding Machine*, which, indeed, it seems to me to resemble more closely than has so far been recognized.

Like *The Adding Machine* it has as hero a Mr. Zero, and it employs nonrepresentational techniques. Thus the ad-

mirable set designed by Jo Mielziner is multiple like the same designer's set for [Tennessee Williams's] *Summer and Smoke*, and the action involves many flash-backs presented as recalled in the memory of the principal personage. But—still more consistently than in *The Adding Machine*—the material is strictly naturalistic, and it is this fact which limits its effect upon this one spectator at least. All the action and all the characterizations are recognizably true to life, but almost every feature of either is both familiar and without other than literal meaning. To me there is about the whole something prosy and pedestrian; a notable absence of new insight, fresh imagination, or individual sensibility. The dialogue serves its purpose as well as the dialogue of a [Theodore] Dreiser novel, but it is also almost as undistinguished, as unpoetic, as unmemorable, and as unquotable. Among the performances that of Mildred Dunnock seems to me the best, while that of Lee Cobb, though hailed with unbounded enthusiasm by the audience, struck me as being—necessarily perhaps—as convincing but also as heavy-footed as the dialogue itself.

Since Tennessee Williams is the only other recently emerged playwright who has awakened even remotely similar enthusiasm, certain comparisons will inevitably be made between them. Against Williams it will be said that he is eccentric and neurotic and that he has so far dealt exclusively with abnormal people, whereas **Death of a Salesman** involves characters and situations true to life as everyone has observed it and presented with an objectivity which everyone can recognize. But to me it seems equally evident that in Mr. Williams's work there are unique qualities which are absent from Mr. Miller's earlier **All My Sons** and from his present play, both of which, by the way, turn so closely around a father-son relationship as to permit almost as strongly as in the case of the Williams plays the objection that the author is obsessed with one theme. Almost hysterical though [Williams's] *A Streetcar Named Desire* may sometimes seem, it offers moments of new insight, and it reveals, as **Death of a Salesman** does not, a unique sensibility as well as a gift for language, sometimes misused and precious, but increasingly effective as it is increasingly purified. That Mr. Miller's new play is extremely good in its own way I have already said, and that it will appeal to an even larger audience than was attracted to either *A Streetcar* or *Summer and Smoke* seems probable. But to me at least it seems, nevertheless, relatively old-fashioned. (pp. 283-84)

Joseph Wood Krutch, in a review of "Death of a Salesman," in The Nation, *New York, Vol. 168, No. 10, March 5, 1949, pp. 283-84.*

Eric Bentley   (review date November 1949)

[*Bentley is considered one of the most erudite and innovative critics of the modern theater. He was responsible for introducing Bertolt Brecht, Luigi Pirandello, and other European playwrights to America through his studies, translations, and stage adaptations of their plays. Bentley's critical works concentrate on the playwright and the dramatic text, rather than on the production aspects of the play. In his first important critical study,* The Playwright as Thinker *(1946), he charges that most producers are more attentive to box office receipts than to the artistic quality of a play and, as a result, the dramatist is often neglected as a true artist. Bentley's most important work,* The Life of Drama *(1964), is a comprehensive study of the development of dramatic form, specifically examining aspects of melodrama, farce, comedy, tragedy, and tragicomedy. His recent works include anthologies of reviews written during his years as drama critic (1952-56) for the* New Republic, *and a collection of his essays on Brecht:* The Brecht Commentaries: 1943-80 *(1981). In the following assessment, Bentley judges* Death of a Salesman *muddled and self-contradictory, divided between the dual concerns of a the tragedy of a "little man" and a critique of American life. "The 'tragedy'," he insists, "destroys the social drama; the social drama keeps the 'tragedy' from having a genuinely tragic stature."]*

News of **Death of a Salesman** reached me in Germany some months ago. Arthur Miller, I was told, had heretofore been kept off the boards in the western zones and played only in the Russian zone—as anti-American propaganda. Now he had been greeted in New York as the important American playwright. **Death of a Salesman** was the first play I went to see on coming ashore. It was an exciting evening. In the auditorium there was an infectious feeling, unusual in the theatre, that the occasion was an important one. On the stage, apparently, was a pretty savage attack upon what in Germany is being held up as an idyllic "American way of life." The New York audience seemed impressed, even if I didn't see "strong men weeping" as I had been told I would.

To my mind, **Salesman** is first and foremost an occasion, a signal event in New York theatrical life. In the second place, it is one man's performance, a rock of a performance, strong enough to hold up any play. I mean Lee Cobb's rendering—unless creation is a better word—of Willy Loman.

If American actors give very poor renditions of Frenchmen and Englishmen, they often give a marvelously nuanced account of their own countrymen; and none more brilliantly, with more body and bounce, than those who worked with [Harold] Clurman and [Clifford] Odets in the Group Theatre. Lee Cobb's work in this play is a most triumphant vindication of the Group's method. He brings to the drama a knowledge of the salesman's character (as expressed in his limbs, the hunch of his shoulders, in vocal intonation, in facial expression) which is not provided in the script. What an idiom represents in language, Mr. Cobb can manifest in stance or vocal color. Each small movement seems to come welling up from the weary, wounded soul. According to plan, Mr. Cobb strongly identifies himself with the role; and the audience identifies itself with Mr. Cobb. Thus an attempt is made at what Mr. Miller himself has called the tragedy of the common man. We all find that we are Willy and Willy is us; we live and die together; but when Willy falls never to rise again, we go home feeling purged of (or by) pity and terror.

Meanwhile what has become of the attack on "the American way"? Has it been successfully subsumed under the larger heading "the human way"? This is what Mr. Miller's admirers tell us. The impression I had was not of the

small purpose being included within the large, but of the two blurring each other. The "tragedy" destroys the social drama; the social drama keeps the "tragedy" from having a genuinely tragic stature. By this last remark I mean that the theme of this social drama, as of most others, is *the little man as victim*. The theme arouses pity but no terror. Man is here too little and too passive to play the tragic hero.

More important even than this, the tragedy and the social drama actually conflict. The tragic catharsis reconciles us to, or persuades us to disregard, precisely those material conditions which the social drama calls our attention to. Political antagonists of Mr. Miller have suggested that he is a Marxist who, consciously or unconsciously, lacks the courage of his convictions—or is it that "Stalinism" today welcomes a sentimental haze? Certainly, had **Salesman** been written a dozen years earlier, it would have ended with a call to revolt and would thus have had more coherence than the play Mr. Miller has written. Or is Mr. Miller a "tragic" artist who without knowing it has been confused by Marxism? Whatever the truth, there is no need to turn any criticism of the play into special accusation against its author, since its confusions are those of a whole class, a whole generation.

It is interesting that critics who have never shown any love for poetry praise **Salesman** as a great poetic drama. The poetry they like is bad poetry, the kind that sounds big and sad and soul-searing when heard for the first time and spoken very quickly within a situation that has already generated a good deal of emotion. I think it was Paul Muni who made the classic comment that in this play you can't tell where the prose leaves off and the poetry begins. You can tell, though, that the prose is relatively satisfactory, the poetry ham; mere rhetorical phrasing, as witness any of the longer speeches. Indeed, this kind of poetry contributes very liberally to that blurring of lines which enables Mr. Miller to write a social drama and a tragedy at the same time and thus please all.

Absolutely everything in the production, as a matter of fact, contributes to the same end. The great vice of Mr. Miller's style is a false rhetorical mode of speech heard only on Broadway and in films, radio and political speeches. There is an equivalent of this rhetoric in Mr. Kazan's directing and Mr. Mielziner's designing and lighting. Things move fast in a Kazan show. So fast you can't see them. If anything is wrong you don't notice. If a false note is struck its sound is at once covered by others. One has no time to think. "Drama isn't 'time to think'," the director seems to be saying, "it's action that sweeps you off your feet!" The Mielziner staging reinforces the effect. It is above all murky. It reveals, or hints at, a half-world of shadows and missing walls and little spotlights that dimly illuminate the corridors of time. As to this last point, Mielziner is of course staying close to the form of the play Mr. Miller gave him, a play in which the chief formal device is the flashback. There is no reason why time in a play shouldn't go back instead of forward. The thing is that the device of going-back has always, up to the present, been used to create one sort of emotional state: a mood of nostalgia, mystery, phantasmagoria. (I have in mind examples as different as *Double Indemnity* and *Red Gloves*.) In fact the flashback has become primarily a way of rendering these moods, and there is usually something portentous and false about it. We never know where we are. "Light," the designer seems to be saying, "makes of the stage a magic carpet, carrying us wherever we wish." But *where* do we wish? Mr. Mielziner helps Mr. Miller to be vague.

If it is too much to ask that Mr. Miller know which of two feasible plays he wanted to write, one can ask that he clear aside rhetorical and directorial bric-a-brac and look more closely at his people. Has he given us a suitable language for his tarts, in the whoring sequence? Are the sons of Willy *seen* with the eye or just constructed from the *idea* that the present generation is "lost"? Is Uncle Charlie of Alaska more than a sentimental motif? Is Willy's marriage *there* for us to inspect and understand down to its depths? It would be unfair to push these questions to include Willy himself, for he could not be a satisfactory character while the central contradiction of the play stands unresolved. Is his littleness the product of the capitalist system? Or is it Human Nature? What attitude are we to have to it? Pity? Anger? Or just a lovely mish-mash?

Mr. Miller seems to be a serious writer. He is therefore, among playwrights, a man in a thousand. He knows what the other playwrights know: how to shape up a story for actors. But he wants to write truthfully. He knows that there is more drama in the actual facts than in the facts as modified by threadbare rhetoric and directorial legerdemain. If he can in future act more resolutely on this knowledge, **Death of a Salesman** will *not* be the great American drama of the mid-century. (pp. 12-14)

> *Eric Bentley, "Back to Broadway," in* Theatre Arts, *Vol. XXXIII, No. 10, November, 1949, pp. 12-14.*

CRITICAL COMMENTARY

Arthur Miller and Others   (symposium date 1958)

[*The following discussion of* Death of a Salesman *is a transcript of a radio broadcast originally produced by the scholar and educator Philip Gelb, who served as moderator. The participants in this symposium included Miller himself; Richard Watts, the drama critic for the* New York Post; *John Beaufort, reviewer for the* Christian Science Monitor; *the* Progressive *magazine critic Martin Dworkin; scholar David W. Thompson; and noted writer and commentator Gore Vidal.*]

GELB: This series is concerned with "Ideas and the Theatre," and we feel Arthur Miller is qualified both as a thinker and as a dramatist. Actually, I think he also qualifies as a kind of prophet. He is a prophet in the sense that he warns us of the possible bitter harvest that may be reaped from our present limited ways; he calls attention to the moral and ethical decisions that must be made; and he dramatizes the problem and the need for individuality and will. These may well prove to be the ultimate meanings of hope. But why hope? **Death of a Salesman** is gener-

ally thought to be Mr. Miller's most important play; is it an affirming one? Let's refresh our memories.

WATTS: The title, **Death of a Salesman,** has the virtues not only of being striking and provocative, but also of telling forthrightly what the drama is about. Mr. Miller is describing the last days of a man who is forced to face the terrible fact that he is a failure; that his vague ideal of success has crumbled; that his sons, on whose respect and success he has counted, have only contempt for him. With the utter collapse of Willy Loman's world, there is nothing for him to do but die. The story is as simple as that, and there is such truth in it that it is hard to see how any sensitive playgoer can fail to find something of himself in the mirror that it holds up to life. Only the most fatuous observer could think of **Death of a Salesman** as a propaganda play, and yet it manages to go so deeply into contemporary values that it becomes a valid and frightening social criticism. Mr. Miller looks upon the salesman ideal of success with an angry but discerning eye, and he sees its hollowness and treachery. Poor Willy Loman, who thought that for a successful salesman popularity and good fellowship were all and tried to teach his sons what he believed was his wisdom, is a completely credible victim of a prevailing code as the encroachment of old age destroys its shabby plausibility. Set down with frank emotions (this) play is, I suspect, something to make strong men weep and think.

GELB: Mr. Watts, that was an excerpt from your review of the play when it first opened in 1949; do you think the play still stands up?

WATTS: Oh yes, I think so. The curious thing about this play is that it really was a tragedy for extroverts. The more extroverted people were that went to it, the more they seemed to be moved by it. Usually with a tragedy here, the wives drag their protesting husbands along and the husbands have an awful time and the wives cry. But I saw again and again that it would be the husband who would be moved by **Death of a Salesman.** He would see something of himself in it. He would get far more out of it usually than his wife did.

GELB: If **Death of a Salesman** is so starkly pessimistic, what is so special about it?

DWORKIN: The play is special and Miller's most meaningful work, because he really hit something deep in America when he made that play. The great American idea of the salesman goes back to the old Yankee trader of the Sam Slick type and exists today in the modern huckster who doesn't carry a suitcase or a sample-kit but sells, and in selling he has to take a part of what is human and make it marketable and put a price on it. I consider this Miller's greatest play because his own great skill, his dramatic sense, his artistry, gets beyond his argument so successfully. He has some severe criticisms to make of our society, and yet **Death of a Salesman** criticizes without being propaganda because the characters are so real. The play is an illustration of that paradoxical problem, that so often emerges when discussing works of art, in which the more valid the particularity gets, the more universal it is an exemplification. Willy Loman comes to represent a certain danger, a certain menace, a certain integral nature in salesmanship in general, because he is so much a particular Willy Loman and not simply a slogan out of the 1930's. He represents a condition where a man necessarily has to go out into space with nothing but a smile and a shoe shine and that packet of samples he is selling and get that order! This strange man, out in space, completely divorced from the fundamental productive processes which manufacture the merchandise that he is selling, not quite the friend and not quite the enemy and not quite the instrument of the people to whom he is selling, somehow, this strange intermediary must sell himself in order to sell things.

VIDAL: I disagree! I don't think the play is about salesmanship and money. Rather I think it is more concerned with a human being who tries to live by a certain set of standards to which he cannot measure up and what happens to him as he fails. I think money is a part of it, but it is much more simply keeping up with the Joneses, and bit by bit failing, and what happens. And Mr. Miller is quite beautifully saying that attention must be paid to this sort of failure in our society. I think Miller in a sense sentimentalizes it because I don't think the problem is all that great. I think people adjust to failure quite beautifully, since that is the lot of nearly all of us. It is not as tragic as that, even in this society at the level of a salesman on the Boston route. But except for a certain sentimentality in the handling of it, I think it showed a situation which nobody else had showed on the stage.

BEAUFORT: I am not sure I agree here. I do not believe Willy Loman is a tragic character. I think that he is a sad character. I think he is a vicious character. The trouble with Willy Loman, as a figure in dramatic tragedy, is that he never starts with any ideals to begin with. He is a man who, from the very beginning of the play, says it is a question of whether you're liked or whether you're well-liked. He encourages his sons to steal and cheat. He has no moral values at all.

GELB: But what if one asks, isn't this Americana? Isn't this the common man?

BEAUFORT: It's one phase of Americana; but if Willy Loman truly represented the whole mass of American civilization of today, I think that the country would be in a terrible state. I just can't accept Willy Loman as the average American citizen. I can accept him as a specimen of a certain aspect of society. We all know that people like Willy Loman exist, and Miller has every right to write about him. I'm perfectly willing to accept him as a dramatic character on the stage; but I will not for a minute accept Willy Loman as the American "Everyman." I think that is nonsense.

GELB: What reasons are there for people doing things in our mid-twentieth century other than to be liked or well-liked or to realize more material benefits? I suppose what I'm asking is how much of an influence, if any, do you think the moral and spiritual factors are in our time?

BEAUFORT: I think they're still very substantially influential. I'm not a social historian; I'm not a sociologist. All I'm willing to say is that I believe that for the most part the people in the United States are motivated by many

such things or other and many finer things than Willy Loman was motivated by: love of country, religious principles, and ethical values. . . . I mean you only have to consider in any situation the response of the American people to a disaster and the need for help to see that we are not an indifferent people. We are a concerned people. Oh, I don't mean to say that we never manifest indifference, we do; but all I'm trying to say is that you couldn't, at least I couldn't, accept Willy Loman as the reflection of the mean of American society in terms of the individual citizen. It just wouldn't be possible.

GELB: Arthur Miller, how valid and pertinent are Mr. Beaufort's observations?

MILLER: The trouble with Willy Loman is that he has tremendously powerful ideals. We're not accustomed to speaking of ideals in his terms; but, if Willy Loman, for instance, had not had a very profound sense that his life as lived had left him hollow, he would have died contentedly polishing his car on some Sunday afternoon at a ripe old age. The fact is he has values. The fact that they cannot be realized is what is driving him mad—just as, unfortunately, it's driving a lot of other people mad. The truly valueless man, a man without ideals, is always perfectly at home anywhere . . . because there cannot be a conflict between nothing and something. Whatever negative qualities there are in the society or in the environment don't bother him, because they are not in conflict with what positive sense one may have. I think Willy Loman, on the other hand, is seeking for a kind of ecstasy in life, which the machine-civilization deprives people of. He's looking for his selfhood, for his immortal soul, so to speak. People who don't know the intensity of that quest, possibly, think he's odd. Now an extraordinarily large number of salesmen particularly, who are in a line of work where a large measure of ingenuity and individualism are required, have a very intimate understanding of this problem. More so, I think, than literary critics who probably need [to] strive less after a certain point. A salesman is a kind of creative person (it's possibly idiotic to say so on a literary program, but they are), they have to get up in the morning and conceive a plan of attack and use all kinds of ingenuity all day long, just the way a writer does.

GELB: What about this, Mr. Miller? John Beaufort made the statement that if Willy Loman represented the whole mass of American civilization today, the country would be in a terrible state. He would not for a moment accept Willy Loman as an average American man.

MILLER: Well, it's obvious that Willy Loman can't be an average American man, at least from one point of view; he kills himself. That's a rare thing in society, although it's more common than one could wish. But this "being average" is beside the point. As a matter of fact, the standard of averageness is hardly valid. It tells neither whether a character is a truthful character, as a character, nor a valid one. It's ridiculous. Hamlet isn't a typical Elizabethan either. Horatio probably is. What's the difference? It has no point unless we are not talking about literature but about patriotism. I did not write *Death of a Salesman* to announce a new American man, or an old American man. Willy Loman is, I think, a person who embodies in him some of the most terrible conflicts running through the streets of America today. A Gallup poll might not indicate that they are the majority conflicts; I think they are; but then what is the difference?

GELB: Earlier, Martin Dworkin said that he feels the play makes a statement about the average American man because Willy Loman is such a particular Willy Loman. Do you feel that the best way to present a universal is in terms of a really specific story?

MILLER: It is the best way! It is the hardest way, too! The ability to create the universal from the particular is not given to many authors, nor to any single author many times. You have to know the particular in your bones to do this. But it is the best way. As the few plays that are repeatedly done over generations and centuries show, they are generally, in our Western Culture anyway, those plays which are full of the most particular information about the people.

GELB: What about this question of hope and hopelessness? I mean, is there a chance to make the positive value in drama dramatic? Or is drama, by its very nature, only an attack upon things?

MILLER: Not only drama, but literature in general—and this goes back a long, long distance in history—posits the idea of value, of right and wrong, of good and bad, high and low, not so much by setting forth, but by showing so to speak, the wages of sin. In other words, when, for instance in *Death of a Salesman,* we are shown a man who dies for the want of some positive, viable human value, the play implies—and it could not have been written without the author's consciousness that the audience did believe something different. In other words, by showing what happens where there are no values, I at least, assume that the audience will be compelled and propelled toward a more intense quest for the values that are missing. I am assuming always that we have a kind of civilized sharing of what we would like to see occur within us and within the world. I think that the drama, at least mine, is not so much an attack but an exposition of "the want." This kind of drama can be done only if the audience itself is constantly trying to supply what is missing.

GELB: Although critic John Beaufort and playwright Arthur Miller seem to be in some disagreement over the character of Willy Loman, I think it is even more significant to note that Mr. Beaufort, in his earlier comments, came up with the very conclusion that Mr. Miller wanted from his play—the conclusion that there is a better way than Willy's way, that we can act on more meaningful values. In other words, John Beaufort supplies some of what Arthur Miller seems to be suggesting as the missing moral links between the *Death of a Salesman* and the Life of a Man. The day I first interviewed Arthur Miller was shortly after the Russians had launched the first satellite. This led me to ask Mr. Miller as to whether or not the various sciences, from nuclear physics to psychology, hadn't made the contemporary artist's job too difficult by giving him too many facts and views to consider. Under this deluge of knowledge, weren't apathy, anxiety and cynicism the natural results? Could any creative writer take even most

of the available information and insights into consideration and still write creatively?

MILLER: Well, whether it can be done remains for me or somebody else to prove. But let me put it this way: we're living, or I'm living anyway, with a great consciousness of the incredible force of objective thought. As we speak, there is an object flying around in the sky passing over this point every, I think it's one hundred and some minutes, which was put up there by thinking men who willed it to go up there. The implications of this are as enormous as any statement by or on the part of Zeus, or Moses, or Shakespeare, or any feeling man. Now, it may be a great bite to take, but I think the only thing worth doing (whether one can do it or not is an entirely different story, but aims are important) today in the theatre, from my point-of-view, is to synthesize the subjective drives of the human being with what is now demonstrably the case. Namely, that by acts of will he can and has changed the world. It is said that nothing is new under the sun. This is! It's right under the sun, and it's new! But it's only one of many things that are new. I've seen communities transformed by the act of a committee. I've seen the interior lives of people transformed by the decision of a company, or of a man, or of a school. In other words, it is old fashioned to simply go on asserting the helplessness of the individual.

GELB: You're not in the large "artistic" camp then of those who write of, by, and for despair.

MILLER: Well, for myself I can't write anything if I'm sufficiently unhappy. A lot of writers write best when they're most miserable. I suppose my sense of form comes from a positive need to organize life and not from a desire to demonstrate the inevitability of defeat and death.

GELB: Do you think this becomes a kind of final analysis of many issues in life—social, political, economic, psychological? You made a statement putting you on the side of life against death. Aren't many "final answers" dependent upon whether this is or is not a basic commitment?

MILLER: It is a commitment on my part. I don't see the point in proving again that we must be defeated. I didn't intend that in *Salesman.* I was trying in *Salesman,* in this respect, to set forth what happens when a man does not have a grip on the forces of life and has no sense of values which will lead him to that kind of a grip; but the implication of it was that there must be such a grasp of those forces—or else we're doomed. I was not, in other words, Willy Loman. I was the writer, and Willy Loman is there because I could see beyond him.

THOMPSON: In summary then, "The curious thing" about Arthur Miller's *The Death of a Salesman* is, as Mr. Watts said, that it really is "a tragedy for extroverts." In older drama, for example in Moliere, a bumbling, simpleminded hustler is always a figure of fun. He is the object of satiric criticism. Mr. Miller does criticize his salesman but earnestly, without a trace of the older comic view. And what is really curious is that the play, besides criticizing Willy Loman's dishonesty and vulgarity, asks that a great deal of sympathy and attention be paid to the failure himself. Willy is shown to be wrong in every respect of human decency but is still expected to be a great tragic figure. This asking for more sympathy than the facts seem to deserve is what gives, as Mr. Vidal said, "a certain sentimentality" to the play. As Mr. Beaufort put it, "I think that Willy Loman is not a tragic character. I think that he is a sad character. I think he is a vicious character. The trouble with Willy Loman, as a figure in dramatic tragedy, is that he never starts with any ideals to begin with. . . He has no moral values at all."

This word "values" set off the big controversy in today's program. In his reply to Mr. Beaufort's charge, Mr. Miller at first insisted that Willy Loman "has tremendously powerful ideals. . . The fact is that he has values . . . (he) is seeking for a kind of ecstasy in life." (One might note here in passing that the universal, primitive egotism of a child always leads to a generalized "seeking for a kind of ecstasy in life"—its worth depends entirely upon what specific values and forms mark that search, especially in adult life). Later, Mr. Miller seemed to contradict himself by saying that his play shows "what happens where there are no values," and that Willy Loman has "no sense of values" which will lead him to "a grip on the forces of life." This contradiction, of course, proves very little, except perhaps that Mr. Miller, fortunately for us, is a playwright and not a dramatic theorist.

There was, after all, general agreement among the participants as to Mr. Miller's important, even leading, position as a contemporary American dramatist. There was no denying that his ***Death of a Salesman*** is a powerful play giving a true-to-life portrayal of a certain type of American, who, as Mr. Dworkin said, is as old as the Sam Slick Yankee trader and as current as the modern huckster. If some of us, like Mr. Vidal, and Mr. Beaufort, feel the play is marred by a certain sentimentality in its demanding so much sympathy for Willy, this may only mean that we are neither salesmen or extroverts.

Perhaps in older, tougher days the subject of a foolish, childish salesman, plus Mr. Miller's keen sense of realistic detail, would have produced a biting social satire. Today, however, it is certainly not Mr. Miller's fault that his audience, composed mainly of hucksters, will accept criticism only in a sympathetic "tragedy for extroverts." (pp. 63-9)

> *Arthur Miller and others, " 'Death of a Salesman': A Symposium," in* The Tulane Drama Review, *Vol. 2, No. 3, May, 1958, pp. 63-9.*

Winifred L. Dusenbury   (essay date 1960)

[*Dusenbury is an American scholar and critic, specializing in modern drama. She is the author of* The Theme of Loneliness in Modern American Drama *(1960),* Love as Death in "The Iceman Cometh" *(1967), and* E. G. and E. G. O.: Emma Goldman and "The Iceman Cometh" *(1974). In the following excerpt from the first-named work, Dusenbury analyzes Willy Loman's isolation, loneliness, and limited awareness. It is his lack of insight into himself and the world around him, the critic maintains, that accounts for his failure: "Although Willy might be representative of many, it is nonetheless his own failure—not that of America—which brings his*

downfall. If many are in the same dilemma, the place to look for a solution is not in society, but in themselves," she insists.]

In [one] of the most popular American dramas of recent years, ***Death of a Salesman,*** is to be found exemplification of what David Riesman [in *The Lonely Crowd*] calls the other-directed individual, who, living in hope of the approval of his peers, is seldom free of a diffuse anxiety lest this approval be withheld. [Willy Loman, whose aim in life is to be not just "liked," but "well liked," is too pitifully wrong to be tragic, perhaps, but he represents a failure typical of the times.] As Riesman points out, the economy of the country, especially in the past few decades, has given particular emphasis to consuming, for production is able to take care of itself. But to increase consumption, more and better salesmen are needed. In Willy Loman, boxed in his Brooklyn house by towering apartment buildings, trying in vain to grow a few seeds in the darkness of the shadows, is portrayed the lonely traveling salesman, who is not successful because he holds that to be "well liked" is the *aim* of living rather than the *result* of unselfish thoughtfulness of others.

"I was lonely, I was terribly lonely" [Act II], Willy says to Biff in explaining the woman "buyer" in his hotel room. Wonderingly, on the verge of tears, Willy says to his old neighbor, "Charley, you're the only friend I got. Isn't that a remarkable thing?" [Act II]. To Linda, he says, "On the road—on the road I want to grab you sometimes and just kiss the life outa you. 'Cause I get so lonely—. . . " [Act I]. No doubt Willy as a salesman is susceptible to a kind of loneliness which to men in other work might not be so keen, for he is "a man way out there in the blue, riding on a smile and a shoeshine" [Requiem]. But Willy's isolation and failure come about because, as Biff perceptively says after his death, "He had the wrong dreams. All, all wrong" [Requiem]. To see the surface of life was his undoing. Perceiving that the men who made good were well liked (for their money if nothing else) he assumed that to be well liked was to make good and that making good was the end of all living.

On the last day of his life he still did not see beyond that. He recognized his failure in himself and in his sons, but even at the end of his life he had no vision of the truth. His final words to the rich brother he imagines stands before him—"Ben! Ben, where do I . . .? Ben, how do I . . . ?" [Act II]—indicate that he had no insight of where he had gone wrong. Willy's lonesomeness is of his own making but it is of his times as well, for a century ago there was a chance to own a sunny lot large enough to raise a garden, and a man was likely to be in creatively productive work. The play's popularity is testimony to the effectiveness of its characterizations and its dramaturgy, but most of all perhaps to its dramatization of the plight of many Americans today.

Willy, at one point, in explaining that he did not know his father and that he would like advice from his older brother, says to himself, "I still feel—kind of temporary about myself " [Act I]. This is Willy's way of expressing his loneliness. As Erich Kahler, in his book explaining the trans-

Mildred Dunnock, Lee J. Cobb, Arthur Kennedy, and Cameron Mitchell in the original production of Death of a Salesman.

formation of the individual in the present age [*The Tower and the Abyss*], points out:

> The estrangement between human beings in daily life, the lack of immediacy in human contacts and the resulting loneliness we frequently witness today, have their roots in man's alienation from his own personal human center. Since his "commodity" or functional self has taken on such importance, his individually human self is left to wane. The perfectly legitimate question, "who are you?" . . . is usually answered with a description of one's work; while a feeling of emptiness and falsehood, a feeling that one has not at all given an answer to the question usually remains.

So Willy, feeling his lack of success as a "functional self" in the economic world, cannot answer the question of who he is and consequently has only a sense of temporariness about himself. How to attain the "individually human self" which would give Willy a feeling of identity and permanency he does not know.

The play, which might be called "Failure of an American" as well as **Death of a Salesman,** conveys the idea that, although Willy might be representative of many, it is nonetheless his own failure—not that of America—which brings his downfall. If many are in the same dilemma, the place to look for a solution is not in society, but in them-

selves. Willy's affair with a woman on his selling trips is excusable, at the worst a sordid reminder of the flesh in mankind. Not so, his encouraging Biff to steal the football; not so, his boasting of the expensive lumber his boys have taken from a nearby lot; not so, his flouting the integrity of the school in proclaiming that the principal would not dare flunk an athlete like Biff; not so, his thanking "Almighty God" that his sons are built like Adonises because they will therefore be well liked.

No wonder Willy feels "kind of temporary" about himself. His sense of honesty is badly distorted, and his recognition of the values of integrity, truth, and responsibility is very slight. His loneliness results partly from his inability to understand the moral principles, which to a man like his neighbor, Charley, are innate. It is certain, too, that he exaggerates the extent of the hard work which he has devoted to the New England territory. Personality, in his thinking, has always been more important than work. Like Willy, the successful American from the time of the pioneers has had grandiose visions of success, but unlike Willy he has labored to bring them to reality.

The pitiful thing about Willy is his belief that, more than for wealth or fame, he longs for friendship. All his dreams are of friendship and comradeship, and his thoughts of the past include the happy relationship between himself and his boys. His memories of the 84-year-old salesman, who was so successful that he called his buyers to come to his hotel room, revolve not upon the money he made, but upon the friends he had.

> 'Cause what could be more satisfying than to be
> able to go, at the age of eighty-four, into twenty
> or thirty different cities, and pick up a phone,
> and be remembered and loved and helped by so
> many different people?
>
> [Act II]

In those days, recalls Willy, there was comradeship in selling. The actual fact of his not being able to make a living at the end of his life did not hurt Willy half so much as the fact that nobody knew him. His final sacrifice was made so that Linda might have the insurance money, but also in hopes that hundreds of imagined friends would come to his funeral from "Maine, Massachusetts, Vermont and New Hampshire" [Act II].

Throughout his life Willy had compensated for his failure by dreams of personal popularity, the success of his sons, and recognition by his company. Finally forced to acknowledge that reality has clashed irrevocably with his dreams, Willy at the end makes a fruitless but valiant effort to save himself by feverishly planting carrot, beet, and lettuce seeds in his dark back yard. Even in his distraught state he recognizes that if he can make a little plant grow, he may be saved. With suicide strongly in his mind, getting close to the dirt may make him want to live. If seeds will grow, he still can grow. Although he has sometimes had idealistic dreams of natural scenes of beautiful growing trees and grass in the New England countryside, and of lilac and wisteria and peonies around his own house, he now turns to the soil, not sentimentally, but with a terrible hunger for reality. Imagination has failed him, but in the earth there is still hope—not dreams, but food. It is too late, however. Willy senses that his company does not know him; his buyers do not know him; his sons do not know him; a heartbreaking loneliness tells him it is time to die.

An analysis of the play from the point of view of the function of the theme of loneliness which runs through it must be made with Arthur Miller's statement [in *The Burns Mantle Best Plays of 1948-1949,* edited by John Chapman] about the play in mind: "the remembered thing about *Salesman* is really the basic situation in which these people find themselves." The situation is of importance in itself, not as a background for the growth of character or for dramatic action. The situation in which a father is separated from his sons, and a mother from both sons and father in trying to mediate between them, is basic to the play. How the family became separated is the story of the play. Told in flashbacks as they come to Willy's mind, the incidents reveal the deleterious effect upon the family relationship of the false ideals which Willy holds and instills in his sons. As the play is constructed, Willy has reached a state of isolation in the first scene, which results in his suicide in the last. In between, the explanation for his plight is revealed in remembered incidents. The situation itself is not dramatic, but the revelation of the causes for it is very dramatic.

Many of these revelatory incidents are plays in miniature with a rising action and climax of their own. For example,

the series of incidents which lead up to the climactic scene in which Biff finds his father with a cheap woman in his hotel room are all dramatic. In the opening scene Willy becomes irate when Linda mentions that Biff is finding himself. "Not finding yourself at the age of thirty-four is a disgrace," he shouts. With illogical contradiction in his reasoning with regard to Biff, he continues, "The trouble is he's lazy, goddammit!" and a few speeches later he surprisingly adds, "And such a hard worker. There's one thing about Biff—he's not lazy." Willy's irritation toward Biff for his antagonism carries over into the conversation with Linda in a series of contradictions: "Why do you get American when I like Swiss? . . . Why am I always being contradicted?" Later he says, "Why don't you open a window in here, for God's sake?" She replies, "They're all open, dear." Complaining about the stifling neighborhood in which they live, he says, "there's more people now." To Linda's gentle reply, "I don't think there's more people," he yells, "There's more people! That what's ruining this country." This first scene, in which it is made obvious that an intense feeling has split father and son, lays the groundwork for the following ones concerning Biff and Willy.

The next scene in this series takes place between the mother and sons, who have been wakened by Willy's muttering and have come downstairs to talk to their mother. She berates Biff for his lack of consideration for his father. Biff replies: "He threw me out of the house, remember that." Linda asks, "Why did he do that? I never knew why." Biff's explanation indicates the bitterness of his feeling toward his father. "Because I know he's a fake and he doesn't like anybody around who knows! . . . Just don't lay it all at my feet. It's between me and him. . . . " It is an unusual situation in which a mother does not know why a father has thrown out their son. The question raised is still unsettled as the scene rises to a pitch through a happy interlude of planning for the future, which is abruptly ended as Willy berates Linda for interrupting him in his violent enthusiasm for the boys' plans. Biff rises to his mother's defense: "Don't yell at her, Pop, will ya?" Willy, angered, replies, "What're you, takin' over this house?" Biff is furious. "Stop yelling at her." Willy leaves "beaten down, guilt ridden." The cause of the hatred between them is still unrevealed, but the fact of its existence is made unmistakably evident.

The separation of father and son is revealed in a later scene involving a character outside the family, Bernard, Biff's friend, who has become a nationally known lawyer. Questioning Willy as to why seventeen-year-old Biff seemed to quit trying to be anything after visiting his father in Boston, Bernard explains:

> When he came back—I'll never forget this, . . .
> it always mystifies me. Because I'd thought so
> well of Biff, . . . I knew he'd given up his life.
> What happened in Boston, Willy?
>
> [Act II]

Willy furiously replies, "Nothing. What do you mean, . . . What's that got to do with anything?" The feeling aroused in Willy by Bernard's mention of the Boston visit is as intense as that he shows in the scenes with Linda and with his sons. It is apparent that the rift between Biff and Willy is recognized outside the family as well as within, but that its cause is not known either within or without by others than the two involved.

The climactic scene of the series, the scene that reveals the cause of the separation of Biff and Willy, comes unexpectedly in a restaurant washroom, where Willy relives the Boston hotel scene in which Biff finds him with a woman to whom he gives silk stockings. Biff in bitter tears exclaims, "You—you gave her Mama's stockings! . . . You fake! You phony little fake!" and runs out [Act II]. Willy is kneeling on the washroom floor, pounding with his fists and yelling to Biff to come back, when a waiter enters and Willy realizes where he is. The remembered scene is hardly more sordid than the present one, for Willy's two sons have gone off with two common women, and left the sick man alone in the washroom with no thought for his welfare. Willy's lonesomeness has reached its peak. With dramatic acumen Arthur Miller has imposed the remembered scene, in which father and son are split apart, upon the action of the play, so that one incident reinforces the other, and Willy, although Biff has left with an appeal to Happy to save his father, is deserted by his son in this scene, as in the first.

This melodramatic scene is not the last between Biff and Willy. The reasons for the situation in which the characters find themselves at the beginning are still to be revealed. The series of incidents has reiterated the situation. From various viewpoints it has been made clear that there is an unbridgeable gulf between Willy and his son. Suspense has been created by the obvious emotion of the characters concerning the situation, and by their uncertainty of its cause. "Spite" is the key word of the final scene, which may be called anticlimactic in a dramatic sense but which is absolutely essential to the meaning of the play, for in it comes Willy's explanation for Biff's failure and Biff's countercharge to Willy. Not the affair of the woman, but the basic controversy of their lives is exposed. "You ruined your life to spite me," is the basis of Willy's argument. "You blew me so full of hot air and false ideals of honesty that I'm a nobody," responds Biff. Willy truly believes his own reiterated charge that Biff ruined his life to get revenge, and in a sense Willy is right—but it is not revenge on Willy for having a woman in his hotel room but revenge for the falsity of the ideals which Willy has espoused throughout his life. Willy shouts,

> Spite, spite, is the word of your undoing! And when you're down and out, remember what did it. When you're rotting somewhere beside the railroad tracks, remember, and don't dare blame it on me!
>
> [Act II]

Biff answers,

> I stole myself out of every good job since high school! . . . And I never got anywhere because you blew me so full of hot air I could never stand taking orders from anybody! That's whose fault it is!
>
> [Act II]

Feeling still, however, that his dream of the West, of a ranch, of the open air represents happiness, Biff continues,

"All I want is out there, waiting for me the minute I say I know who I am! Why can't I say that, Willy?" Thornton Wilder [in "The American Loneliness," *The Atlantic Monthly,* August 1952] claims that the American cannot say who he is except in terms of his accomplishments. Indeed, how can Biff then say who he is? How can Willy tell him who he is, since Willy cannot tell who he, the father, really is.

Separating Willy and Biff is an irreparable loneliness, which is made all the more poignant by a momentary revelation of the love which could have been between them. Crying in his father's arms at the sordid failure of his life, Biff moves Willy to wonder and amazement that his son loves him; but Biff has already gone upstairs with the words, "I'll go in the morning," before Willy makes his discovery, "That boy—that boy is going to be magnificent!" Willy is immediately dreaming of Biff's success as a high school football star—"There's all kinds of important people in the stands,"—just before he drives off to kill himself.

In experiencing a "suffering self-recognition of separateness," Willy exemplifies the individual whose only aim is that kind of success which will gain him social approbation. The playwright, while highlighting the separation of Willy and Biff through a series of emotionally charged incidents, has packed the play with supporting scenes which, in other ways and through other characters, reflect and reiterate the lonesomeness of a character with Willy's lack of understanding. He could have been a good craftsman; he could have belonged by seeing around him his own creations. He could build a porch; he could plaster a ceiling; but a misguided idea of success led him to salesmanship with the mistaken thought that there was "comradeship" in it. Instead there was in it for Willy only biting lonesomeness.

The other characters, through whom the theme is emphasized, appear and disappear as Willy's mind switches back and forth from present to past. The play opens and closes with the music of the flute, thin and poignant, representing the unknown musical father, for whose guidance Willy longs, and whose presence he cannot remember. Uncle Ben, the epitome of false standards of conduct, appears momentarily several times to misguide Willy and to isolate him further from the ideals to which he might have belonged. Charley and Bernard are a contrasting father and son to Willy and Biff. Through ideals of honesty and progress through hard work, Bernard attains the standing of a highly respected lawyer, to whom Charley points with modest pride, and at whom Willy can only shake his head and marvel. The contrast between Bernard and Biff is devastating even to Willy's dream of his son's success. The young boss, Howard, who fires Willy, completes Willy's separation from his work, and isolates him economically, as the others have psychologically. Howard's role is really only the technical fulfillment of the deterioration of Willy as a salesman, and is actually of minor importance.

Happy and Linda, the most important characters next to Willy and Biff, are unattached like them at the beginning and at the end, but in the flashbacks they appear as part of the unified family, reveling in the prospects of future attainments of the hero-sons. It is said of Linda in the stage directions that behind Willy's violence and his need for her she has always sensed in him

> a hovering presence which for thirty-five years
> she has never been able to predict or understand
> and which she has come to fear with a fear so
> deep that a moment ago, in the depths of her
> sleep, . . . she knew this presence had returned.
>
> [Act I]

And in the end, in spite of the relief which it might seem she would feel after living so long "from day to day," she is really desolated by his death. Although her ideals were always higher than Willy's—for example, she detested the action of Uncle Ben in tripping up Biff—she never wished to impose them upon her husband. She followed where he led, even encouraging his dreams of success, although she recognized what Willy did not—that the facts did not support the dream. "She had developed an iron mastery of her objections to her husband," according to the playwright, and her encouragement of his idea of himself as an important salesman led only to an essential separation between them. Her reiteration, "Willy, darling, you're the handsomest man in the world" [Act I], only brings to his mind a woman in a hotel room, as does her mending her stocking recall his gift of stockings to the woman. There is no companionable discussion between them, but only a boosting of Willy's ego by his wife who fears him, yet longs to please him.

Happy, likewise, adds emphasis to the theme of the loneliness of Willy, for Happy is a rubber stamp of Willy. He has not, like Biff, "ruined his life for spite," but he lives in the dream of being a much more important man than he is. Without aim in life or high standards of conduct, he lives on the pleasures of women and drink, and at Willy's funeral his philosophy is still

> He [Willy] had a good dream. It's the only
> dream you can have—to come out number-one
> man. He fought it out here, and this is where I'm
> gonna win it for him.
>
> [Requiem]

Misguided, lonesome—"My own apartment, a car, and plenty of women. And still, goddammit, I'm lonely" [Act I]—Happy will never be different from his father. In him are seen the results of Willy's teaching personified in a second Willy. Whereas Biff in a sense revolted against his father's materialism, and deliberately became a failure, Happy is not even aware of the faults of his father's ideas and lives by them himself.

Thus Biff is alienated from Happy, who still lives in a dream of the future, and the two boys are alienated from Linda, who berates them for their lack of respect for Willy.

> . . . there's no leeway any more. Either he's
> your father and you pay him that respect, or else
> you're not to come here.
>
> [Act I]

And Linda is alienated from Willy because she knows no way to get along except to give in to him. When Bernard warns that if Biff doesn't buckle down, the football hero

will flunk math, Linda says, "He's right, Willy, you've gotta—" whereupon Willy explodes in anger at her, "You want him to be a worm like Bernard? He's got spirit, personality . . . " and Linda, almost in tears, leaves the room [Act I]. And, of course, the alienation of Willy and Biff plays the central part in the plot. The relationship of Willy and Happy, while not so clearly defined, obviously indicates a lack of friendship, for Willy feels he cannot turn to Happy for help when he loses his job, and says to Charley, who gives him money, "You're the only friend I got" [Act II].

Thus each member of the family feels an isolation from the others, and thus the play is logically constructed so that the memories which appear upon the stage are those which come to Willy's mind as a result of the impact of his unhappiness. The lonesomeness of the hero is emphasized by this technique, for to him alone come the thoughts which are dramatized in incidents explaining the situation in which he finds himself. All the other characters of the play take part as he wills. The action, however, follows no casual plan in its forward movement. The careful design of the play is illustrated, for one example, by the build-up of suspense in the Willy-Biff series; but the theme of loneliness is emphasized by the fact that in essence the scenes are played by Willy alone with his dreams.

Arthur Miller has skillfully created a drama in which the action and form and purpose all cooperate to the same end. Measured by Francis Fergusson's statement [in *The Idea of Theater*] that "in any given tragedy (if it is good) action, form and purpose are one," **Death of a Salesman** qualifies; for the action, which is made up of the incidents, is appropriate to the form, which reveals the mind of the central character, and both serve the purpose of illustrating the situation (and its causes) in which Willy and many of his fellow Americans find themselves. Study of the meaning of the term "action" as used by critics has led Fergusson to conclude that it can be defined and understood only with reference to a particular play and that, making use of plotting, characterization, and speech, the action points to the object which the dramatist is trying to show. As the action of [Sophocles's] *Oedipus* might be indicated by the phrase "to find the culprit," so the action of **Death of a Salesman** might be described as an attempt "to discover how to be well liked." The skill of Arthur Miller lies in the fact that he has taken this idea—a concept which is in itself not dramatic, not full of possible plot situations—and composed a drama in which that idea is made the main purpose of the action by the exemplification in plot, character, and speech of the situation of the misguided American salesman.

With artistry the playwright has created a coherence between the action and the form. Disavowing that he makes use of flashbacks, Miller says

> It is simply that the past keeps flowing into the
> present, bringing its scenes and its characters
> with it—and sometimes we shall see both past
> and present simultaneously.
>
> [Act I]

The action of the play itself consumes hardly more time than would be allowed by the neoclassicist [who would insist that the time represented in a play not exceed one day], but the range covers many years as the scenes recalled in Willy's mind emerge. Many times, as, for example, when Linda's laughter merges with that of the woman in the hotel room, we see past and present simultaneously. By perhaps no other technique could we be made so aware of the reason for Willy's failure "to be well liked" as by the flow of scenes from past to present, whereby we view Willy's mistakes in the light of the present and whereby we are made aware of the lack of moral stamina in his character through the years, which has resulted in his present irrational behavior. The stream-of-consciousness form of the play is the proper medium for the action. Form and action cohere to express the playwright's desired purpose.

Arthur Miller has made doubly sure that his purpose will not be lost by concluding the play with a requiem—a mass for the repose of a soul—in which the theme of the play is reiterated as various characters express their opinions of Willy. "He had the wrong dreams," says Biff. "There's more of him in that front stoop than in all the sales he ever made." Willy could have "belonged" by reveling in the creations of his own hands. He couldn't belong by aspiring to be well liked and chesting his way across New England. According to Charlie, he couldn't help himself, "A salesman is got to dream. . . ." America needs salesmen, and they've got to ride on "a smile and a shoeshine." Nobody can blame Willy, for there is no "rock bottom" to a salesman's life. Willy had nothing solid under his feet, and no inner strength sustained him. His failure represents, says Arthur Miller, "a situation which I have seen repeated throughout my life," and its application becomes broader for Americans as the number of salesmen increase in this land of a consumer society. (pp. 16-26)

> *Winifred L. Dusenbury, "Personal Failure,"*
> *in her* The Theme of Loneliness in Modern
> American Drama, *University of Florida Press,*
> *1960, pp. 8-37.*

Barry Edward Gross   (essay date 1965)

[*Gross closely examines the "motifs of peddler and pioneer" in* Death of a Salesman. *Willy Loman strives to imitate both his father and the traditional American ideal of the Yankee peddler by uniting the spirit of the frontiersman with that of the salesman, the critic argues. Ironically, Gross observes, he succeeds only with his death: he is then both the "peddler, selling his life for a profit" and the "pioneer, penetrating unknown and dangerous territory."*]

Although much has been written about **Death of a Salesman,** the use to which Arthur Miller has put the American frontier tradition—especially the motifs of peddler and pioneer—has not been sufficiently discussed.

First of all, Willy Loman thinks of himself as, in his own right, a pioneer:

> WILLY: When I went north the first time, the Wagner Company didn't know where New England was.
> [Act I]

This characterization of Willy as pioneer is not sarcastic or ironic. It is consistent with the small scale of Willy's life that his frontier is not, say, the Northwest Territory but—quite literally, in the salesman's jargon—the New England Territory. However, such a frontier is not enough for Willy. He must try to create a literal one:

> WILLY: It's Brooklyn, I know, but we hunt too.
>
> BEN: Really, now.
>
> WILLY: Oh sure, there's snakes and rabbits and—that's why I moved out here. Why, Biff can fell any one of these trees in no time!
> [Act I]

But why should it be necessary for Willy Loman, an easterner, in the nineteen-forties, to create a frontier in the backyards of Brooklyn? Why should he feel the need to be a pioneer? If the answer were only that Willy is an American and that the frontier is a significant force in the American consciousness, then the play would not be nearly so effective and Willy would not be nearly so moving. True, Willy Loman *is* a contemporary Everyman—or, at least, Everyamerican—but he must also be, at the same time, a particular human being, if **Death of a Salesman** is to be anything more than a dissection of a national disease. No, Willy Loman must need a frontier for particular, as well as universal, reasons.

The father-son relationship is one of the major motifs in **Death of a Salesman.** In addition to the most important relationship between Willy and his sons, there is neighbor Charley and his son Bernard, and Willy's dead boss Wagner and his son Howard. But it is too frequently forgotten that Willy, too, has a father. And it is his father, the exemplar of the Yankee peddler, who helps to explain, in large part, Willy's need for a frontier and to suggest some of the reasons for Willy's failure:

> BEN: Father was a very great and wild-hearted man. We would start in Boston, and he'd toss the whole family into the wagon, and then he'd drive the team right across the country; through Ohio, and Indiana, Michigan, Illinois, and all the Western states. And we'd stop in the towns and sell the flutes that he'd made on the way. Great inventor, Father. With one gadget he made more in a week than a man like you could make in a lifetime.
> [Act I]

And it is certainly true that some of this spirit survives in Willy. He, too, wanders a territory peddling wares. But they are not his own wares made with his own hands. Nor can he choose his own territory: Willy has started and ended in Boston. The fault is not Willy's: given the tradition in which he was raised, Willy Loman is simply in the wrong place at the wrong time. A man can no longer wander the country selling what he makes with his own hands. If a man is to be peddler, he cannot, as his father was, be pioneer as well.

Willy can boast of his heritage and his pioneer tradition—

> WILLY: My father lived many years in Alaska. He was an adventurous man. We've got quite a

little streak of self-reliance in our family.

[Act II]

—but the self-reliance of the Yankee peddler is useless to the modern peddler. Willy's world places value on getting along with others, not on getting along on one's own. One source of Willy's failure is his inability to apply the values of his father's world to his own, the impossibility of being both peddler and pioneer, and of realizing the eternal creativity that "pioneer" suggests to Willy.

Willy might have been different if his father's values had not been passed down to him so indirectly. It is quite easy for Ben to simply walk off into the wilderness in search of his father. Ben, a teenager at the time of his father's desertion, knew his father well. He was tutored in the frontier tradition, and he had a living example to follow. But Willy was not yet four when Ben walked "away down some open road" to find his father in Alaska [Act I]. It is impossible to speculate on what sort of influence Willy's mother had on him, but it is safe to say that Willy was deprived of the masculine influence which allowed Ben to so blithely head for Alaska and wind up in Africa. Furthermore, imagine Willy just wandering off, leaving Linda alone with Happy and Biff, as his father had left his mother alone with two sons. It is unthinkable in modern society. Willy accepts his father's and Ben's desertion as the mark of a man, but his sons, brought up in a different tradition, would not have so honored him had he followed his father's lead.

That the feminine influence continues to be dominant in Willy's life is made clear when Linda discourages him from accepting the one opportunity which would allow him to fulfill his pioneer yearnings. Linda, who is usually thought of as passive, quite actively frustrates the pioneer in Willy because she fears it. She represents the values of modern society, not the values Willy would be able to apply in Alaska:

> BEN: Now, look here, William. I've bought timberland in Alaska and I need a man to look after things for me.

> WILLY: God, timberland! Me and my boys in those grand outdoors.

[Act II]

Ben needs a *man,* and this is, at heart, all that Willy has dreamed of being. Both Biff and Happy are wrong at the end of the play when the former says that Willy dreamed of being "number-one man" and the latter that Willy's dreams were all wrong [Requiem]. All Willy has ever wanted is to be a *man,* in the sense that he understands that word, a man as his father was; Ben offers him the opportunity to be that man. Willy also conceives of the frontier as purely a man's world; in his initial excitement, he gives no thought to Linda but thinks only of "me and my boys."

> BEN: You've got a new continent at your doorstep, William. Get out of these cities, they're full of talk and time payments and courts of law. Screw on your fists and you can fight for a fortune out there.

> WILLY: Yes, yes! Linda, Linda!

LINDA: Oh, you're back?

BEN: I haven't much time.

WILLY: No, wait! Linda, he's got a proposition for me in Alaska.

LINDA: But you've got—*To Ben:* He's got a beautiful job here.

WILLY: But in Alaska, kid, I could—

LINDA: You're doing well enough, Willy.

BEN, *to Linda:* Enough for what, my dear?

LINDA, *frightened of Ben and angry at him:* Don't say those things to him! Enough to be happy right here, right now. *To Willy while Ben laughs:* Why must everybody conquer the world? You're well liked, and the boys love you, and someday—*to Ben*—why, old man Wagner told him just the other day that if he keeps it up he'll be a member of the firm, didn't he, Willy?

[Act II]

What Linda does not understand is that Willy was brought up in a tradition in which one had worlds to conquer and that the attempt to conquer them was the mark of a man. Hers is the voice that Ben refers to, the voice representative of the time payments which punctuate the play and become the dominant symbol of modern society. Even at Willy's death, Linda does not understand how little and yet, in this society, how much Willy really wanted. Charley, who throughout the play seems so insensitive to Willy's problems, understands, but Linda cannot:

> LINDA: I can't understand it. At this time especially. First time in thirty-five years we were just about free and clear. He only needed a little salary. He was even finished with the dentist.

> CHARLEY: No man only needs a little salary.

> LINDA: I can't understand it.

[Requiem]

Indeed, in Linda's farewell to Willy, the time payment becomes an epitaph. Linda's parting words are doubly ironical if one thinks of Willy as frustrated pioneer—in modern society, the last payment on the house always comes too late, and a man, while he lives, is never free. One is obliged, at this point, to compare Willy with his father, whose house was a wagon on wheels which he owned utterly, and whose freedom was such that he could abandon this symbol of mobility and independence in search of an even greater freedom:

> LINDA: Forgive me, dear. I can't cry. I don't know what it is, but I can't cry. I don't understand it. Why did you ever do that? Help me, Willy, I can't cry. It seems to me that you're just on another trip. I keep expecting you. Willy, dear, I can't cry. Why did you do it? I search and search and I search, and I can't understand it, Willy. I made the last payment on the house today. Today, dear. And there'll be nobody home. . . . We're free and clear. . . . We're free. . . . We're free. . . . We're free. . . .

[Requiem]

Willy has succeeded in passing on his inherited values to his sons, but they are of as little value to Happy and Biff as they are to Willy. Indeed, their failures can be understood in terms of the same conflict between peddler and pioneer that ruins Willy. Quite simply, there is a good deal of the peddler in Happy, but there is also some of the pioneer in him, too, and the pioneer frustrates the peddler in him:

> HAPPY: Sometimes I want to just rip my clothes off in the middle of the store and outbox that goddam merchandise manager. I mean I can outbox, outrun, and outlift anybody in that store, and I have to take orders from those common, petty sons-of-bitches till I can't stand it any more.
>
> [Act I]

The reverse is true of Biff: he is predominantly pioneer but there is enough peddler in him to frustrate the pioneer:

> BIFF: Hap, I've had twenty or thirty different kinds of jobs since I left home before the war, and it always turns out the same. I just realized it lately. In Nebraska when I herded cattle, and the Dakotas, and Arizona, and now in Texas. It's why I came home now, I guess, because I realized it. This farm I work on, it's spring there now, see? And they've got about fifteen new colts. There's nothing more inspiring or beautiful than the sight of a mare and a new colt. And it's cool there now, see? Texas is cool now, and it's spring. And whenever spring comes to where I am, I suddenly get the feeling, my God, I'm not getting anywhere! What the hell am I doing, playing around with horses, twenty-eight dollars a week! I'm thirty-four years old, I oughta be makin' my future. That's when I come running home. And now, I get here, and I don't know what to do with myself.
>
> [Act I]

That the attempt to wed the peddler and pioneer is fatal is dramatized by Willy's suicide, for only in death can they be successfully combined. In committing suicide, Willy is still the peddler, selling his life for a profit, bartering his existence for a legacy for Biff; but he is also a pioneer, penetrating unknown and dangerous territory. Ben tells him, "It's dark there, but full of diamonds" [Act II]—Africa-black, Alaska-white, one suspects.

In some way, Willy's death liberates both Biff and Happy in that it kills that frustrating element in each of them. Willy's death kills the pioneer in Happy, in whom the peddler has always dominated, forever:

> HAPPY: I'm staying right here in this city, and I'm gonna beat this racket! . . . I'm gonna show you and everybody else that Willy Loman did not die in vain. He had a good dream. It's the only dream you can have—to come out number-one man. He fought it out here, and this is where I'm gonna win it for him.
>
> [Requiem]

And it kills the peddler in Biff: at the end of the play, Biff goes West, presumably for good. Biff's liberation is more positive because, by embracing the pioneer, he embraces that part of Willy he has always loved:

> BIFF: There were a lot of nice days. When he'd come home from a trip; or on Sundays, making the stoop; finishing the cellar; putting on the new porch; when he built the extra bathroom; and put up the garage.
>
> [Requiem]

One immediately recalls Biff's statement in Act I, ". . . we don't belong in this nut-house of a city! We should be mixing cement on some open plain. . . . " However much the pioneer in Willy is stifled, it is the little expression he does give it—making repairs on the house—that guarantees him a small modicum of immortality:

> BIFF: You know something, Charley, there's more of him in that front stoop than in all the sales he ever made.
>
> [Requiem]

Death of a Salesman, then, is, from one viewpoint, a search for identity, one man's attempt to be a man according to the frontier tradition in which he was raised, and a failure to achieve that identity because in this time and in this place that identity cannot be achieved. That is what Biff means when he says, "He never knew who he was" [Requiem]. But it is also, in the end, a search for identity that succeeds, for Willy in death, but for Biff in life. And that is what Biff means when he says, "I know who I am, kid" [Requiem]. (pp. 405-10)

> *Barry Edward Gross, "Peddler and Pioneer in 'Death of a Salesman',"* in Modern Drama, *Vol. VII, No. 4, February, 1965, pp. 405-10.*

Guerin Bliquez   (essay date 1968)

[*Bliquez analyzes the character of Linda Loman in* Death of a Salesman. *Her adulation of her husband, the critic contends, leads her to support his unrealistic dreams and minimize his faults and thus, ironically, contribute to his downfall.*]

Mrs. Willy Loman has a more forceful role in ***Death of a Salesman*** than most commentators have thus far noted. To overlook the part she plays in her husband's pathetic downfall is to miss one of the most profound levels in Arthur Miller's subtle structuring of his tragedy. Linda's facility for prodding Willy to his doom is what gives the play its direction and its impetus.

Death of a Salesman is more than the story of one man's failure. Its theme includes the disintegration of a family in a particular social world, brought about by self-blindness and a refusal to know or to acknowledge others. It demonstrates how a fear of the responsibilities of knowledge can lead only to ruin. Miller's ironic rendering of Linda as the bulwark deserves closer examination.

The Lomans have been married almost thirty-five years. They have reared two sons. Although during most of that time Willy was on the road for as much as five days every week, his absences cannot provide sufficient reason for the terrible mutual ignorance that he and Linda share. This couple is not alienated, in the usual sense of that term. They never fight or disagree. All outward appearances demonstrate an intimate relationship and a secure marriage. Even their sons are unable to see that a great part of Linda's married life has been devoted to the task of helping Willy shirk the responsibilities of the kind of knowledge needed to hold himself and his family together.

Willy is a dreamer. What joys he has are always projections into a friendly heaven that is ignorant of a hostile earth. This salesman never learns to know his territory, his ideals of the workaday world notwithstanding. His labors are heroic, almost, and always aimed at financial-social success. But faithful Linda helps to insure only their marginal return.

Objectively Linda is the proof of her husband's ability as provider and subjectively the negation of it. She is his security symbol. Centered as she is in the house and garden, she is in a way identical with these as the empirical fact of Willy's success as a breadwinner. But subjectively, Linda makes demands. Thematically, she is the source of the cash-payment fixation. Like the house and garden, she must be constantly secured, maintained, planted, and cultivated. She is the goal of the salesman's futile activity as a man, a goal that can never be achieved.

Willy of course is unaware of this. He thinks his sons are the principal reason for his drive. But all he can give them is his platitudes and a punching bag. He has no real time for them; he is still trying to woo their mother.

In his stage directions Miller explains that "Linda . . . has developed an iron repression to Willy's behavior—she more than loves him, she admires him" [Act I]. These two characteristics—repression and love—transcending admiration—are the forces by which Willy is seriously undermined at home.

To appreciate Linda's repression demands an understanding of the difference between acceptance and acquiescence. Significantly, it is a difference in degrees of knowledge. Acceptance of reality is an active state of cognition. Acquiescence is passive. Understanding plays no part. A wife cannot acquiesce morally to a husband's serious faults. If Linda accepts Willy for what he is shown to be, she accepts a liar, a cheat, and a pompous fraud. Such attributes cannot be explained away, as Linda tries to do, by her husband's exhaustion. Add the note of potential suicide, which Linda is "ashamed" to expose because it would be an "insult," and we are all the more suspicious of her real conception of Willy. To acquiesce in all of Willy's weaknesses is to be a failure as a wife and mother, and to share in the responsibility of her husband's fall.

The second characteristic of Linda's relationship to her husband is even more destructive. How is it possible in marriage for admiration to reach a point of "more than" love? If all admiration is grounded in love—if not love of a particular person, at least love of the values exemplified—how can admiration be transcendent? But if in this marriage admiration does transcend love, then it follows that for Linda the superiority of her husband is more important than any marital equality. This is hero projection on her part. It is to insure this superiority that Linda does not support her husband where he is weak. To do this would confirm her status as an equal partner with her own specific role and would provide a dialectical "other" that

would synthesize Willy as a complete man. Instead, Linda "has developed an iron repression" that constantly belittles Willy's weaknesses, thereby encouraging them. Linda does more than acquiesce in her husband's faults; she encourages him to dream.

So Willy does not dream alone. He is the victim of Linda's ambition as well as his own. Just as Willy unconsciously projects Biff against reality as a living vindication of himself as man and father, so Linda projects Willy as her own ideal of all that a man should be, an ideal she must foster, protect, and defend if she is to be secure and, perhaps, tolerate the husband she has married. Contrary to the rules for good business, Willy is pulling more than his own weight.

Ben is Willy's hero, his ideal of economic and personal success. When he points to Alaska, Linda dissuades Willy from going. Willy needs a Ben figure; but if he has him, he does not need a Linda. So she sees to it that Willy repeatedly turns back to her as his "foundation and support."

Linda is a strong support, therefore, not for Willy but for his dream; a support that Willy is all too prone to accept. She may be right in her judgment that Willy can never be a Ben, a splendid opportunist in dark jungles; but she will never admit that her "more than" love for her husband cannot sustain him either. So by making himself radically dependent on his wife, while at the same time being unfaithful to her, Willy hopes to establish himself as independent in society. But betrayal exposes the basic dishonesty of the entire marriage relationship; it shows Willy to be even less a man. His marriage is not a fulfillment, it is an emasculation. Willy in effect has been stripped of his true self. With such a loss there is more meaning than he knows in his lame excuse to Biff in the hotel room in Boston: "I was lonely; I was terribly lonely" [Act II].

Some of the scenes on which this analysis of Linda is based are recollections from the past, a past that is portrayed as Willy's alone. But these memories are not invalid because they are only Willy's. While he is often self-inspired to prophesy the future, Willy is wholly incapable of modifying the past. It is apparent especially toward the end of the play that Willy can see better when he remembers than he can in his present consciousness. These recollections are ironically out of the control of Willy's dream. The past becomes the only reality for Willy, the only part of his world that we can trust.

Finally, Willy does not vindicate his suicide by an appeal to Biff's welfare alone. A constantly recurring epigram proclaims, "Because the woman has suffered." This is the only confession Willy makes which can imply a personal fault rather than an unlucky inability to find "the secret." Exactly what Linda has suffered is a failure, and the failure is Willy himself. He knows this instinctively and it only heightens his anxiety and his helplessness. When Biff in the final scene suggests that Willy come inside to Linda, he recoils and, "with guilt in his voice," says, "No, I don't want to see her" [Act II]. There is no consolation left in this marriage because there is no dream left, except Willy's dream of total escape. Reality has come home not just for

Willy but for Linda too. At the grave she cannot cry because she cannot understand. She never has understood.

Is Linda a conscious instrument of Willy's undoing? Is she a plotter or a schemer? No. Like her husband, she is merely weak; she shares his fear of truth. They are both guilty of self-blindness and the refusal to know and accept each other.

Like all domestic tragedy, **Death of a Salesman** has far-reaching social implication. Its portrayal of ignorance of personal values is the picture of a muddled and perverted social world of values, caused by the refusal of its citizens to assert their own individuality. In such a world particular involvement is basically unhealthy. In such a world disillusioned men like Willy Loman, abetted by such wives as Linda, are always afraid to "take that phony dream and burn it before something happens" [Act II]. (pp. 383-86)

> Guerin Bliquez, "Linda's Role in 'Death of a Salesman'," in Modern Drama, Vol. 10, No. 4, February, 1968, pp. 383-86.

B. S. Field, Jr. (essay date 1972)

[*In the following essay, Field investigates Willy Loman's "sin" or "crime" that justifies his tragic downfall. The crime, Field maintains, is that Willy has molded Happy and Biff "in his own image"; he has raised sons who, like himself, are "morally and socially castrated."*]

I

One of the things one looks for in any play, be it comedy, tragedy, or garrago, is the propriety of the catastrophe. How does the final disaster, the embarrassment or the agony of the protagonist, which it is the play's business to recount, stand as an appropriate consequence to the protagonist's sin, his fault, his *hamartia*? A critic's struggle to "explain" a play is often in large measure simply the attempt to verbalize that relationship, to describe the poetic justice of the plays, the propriety of matching that *hamartia* with those consequences.

In Arthur Miller's **Death of a Salesman,** how does Willy's catastrophe stand as a poetically just consequence of his *hamartia*? Many answers to that question have been suggested, and many of them help in some measure to describe why the play succeeds. My thesis is modest enough. It is offered not in any attempt to displace other explanations, but as an addition to the multiple cause-effect relationships in that modern drama: Willy committed a crime for which he is justly punished.

II

The criticism of **Death of a Salesman** falls into two schools, that which feels it necessary to explain why the play fails, and that which feels it necessary to explain why the play succeeds. Since it seems to me that the play succeeds, and since it seems fruitless to attempt to argue people into liking something that they do not like, let what follows be addressed exclusively to those who agree that the play succeeds.

For it does succeed. In the court that has final provenance in such a case, the stage, the verdict is that **Death of a Salesman** is a success. Most of the adverse criticism of this play, and there is a lot of it, tries to argue that because the play is not unified and coherent in the way a classical tragedy is coherent, it is a failure, not only as a tragedy, but as a work of art of any kind. Alfred Schwarz [in an essay in *Modern Drama* IX, 1966] has pointed out while reviewing the discussions of this issue by Hebbel, Büchner, Luckács, and by Miller himself, that there is not even a theoretical necessity for a modern tragedy to be unified and coherent in the same ways we have learned to expect in a classic tragedy. A modern realistic tragedy, even in theory, is a multiple device. Such tragedy is anchored not in eternal conditions, as man's relation to fate, but in the immediate and ever shifting conditions of men's relations with each other and with their institutions. Thus a modern play, to be successful, even to be effective tragedy, needs not even theoretically to be singular. On the contrary, according to the poetic that Schwarz describes, a modern drama will present manifold causes of a manifold catastrophe illustrating a manifold theme.

It is clear enough from all the criticism that **Death of a Salesman** has a theme that is open to various interpretations. One large group insists that it is, or ought to be, about Willy's isolation from nature. Others point out that Willy suffers from a lack of love, a loss of identity, a worship of the False God of Personality. The causes of Willy's disaster are presented with equal variety: he is defeated by society; he is too weak and immoral for any social conditions; he once made a wrong choice of careers; he married a woman who tried to stifle his sense of adventure; or simply that he got too old. And the condition that constitutes Willy's catastrophe is also variously described: he suffered a miserable and pointless death; he suffered the agony of seeing that he had worthless sons; he suffered the agony of the whole twenty-four hours of insane self-torture which takes up the supposed "real" time of the play's performance; or simply that he had a miserable funeral.

It is pointless to argue that because one of these can be a correct analysis, the others must be wrong, even though in Miller's play, in the "Requiem" which closes it, Charley, Biff, Happy, and perhaps Linda, too, argue as if their explanations of Willy's catastrophe were mutually exclusive. They may all be right, even Linda, who says, "I don't understand," that is, that it is inexplicable.

III

Elements of the play that have not received the attention from critics that they deserve are those scenes which display Willy training his sons. [Barclay W.] Bates suggests that one of the roles in which Willy tries to function is that of the "dutiful patriarchal male intent upon transmitting complex legacies from his forebears to his progeny" [see Further Reading]. The episodes which support that generalization, however, do not indicate that Willy has any clear ideas what legacy he has received from his forebears. He speaks vaguely of his father who was "better than a carpenter," who made flutes, and in the scenes with Ben he pleads with his brother to tell him something that he can transmit.

Please tell about Dad. I want my boys to hear.
I want them to know the kind of stock they
spring from. All I remember is a man with a big
beard, and I was in Mamma's lap, sitting around
a fire. . . .

[Act I]

Later he complains to Ben of his fears, that "sometimes
I'm afraid that I'm not teaching them the right kind of—
Ben, what should I teach them?"

Part of this tragedy is that what he has taught them does
not look to him like what he wanted them to have learned.
Miller drops suggestions into the first part of the play that
while Biff is a charismatic young man, he has also the
makings of an amoral punk. In the bedroom with Happy
near the beginning of the play, Biff speaks of going to see
Bill Oliver.

BIFF: I wonder if Oliver still thinks I stole that
carton of basketballs.

HAPPY: Oh, he probably forgot about that long
ago. It's almost ten years. You're too sensitive.
Anyway, he didn't really fire you.

BIFF: Well, he was going to. I think that's why
I quit. I was never sure whether he knew or not.

[Act I]

Biff's first speech suggests that he feels aggrieved at being
suspected; his second speech suggests that Oliver was right
to suspect him. Moments later in the script Willy brings
home a new punching bag. Then Biff shows off the new
football that he has "borrowed" from the locker room.
Willy, laughing, tells him that he has to return it.

HAPPY: I told you he wouldn't like it!

BILL: (Angrily) Well, I'm bringing it back!

WILLY: (Stopping the incipient argument, to
HAPPY) Sure, he's gotta practice with a regulation ball, doesn't he?" (To BIFF) Coach'll probably congratulate you on your initiative.

[Act I]

The boys are not mean boys. Indeed, they are cheerful and
eager. They carry Willy's bags in from the car. They help
Linda carry up the wash. But they steal things, they cheat.
Bernard complains that Biff doesn't study.

WILLY: Where is he? I'll whip him, I'll whip
him!

LINDA: And he'd better give back that football,
Willy, it's not nice.

WILLY: Biff! Where is he? Why is he taking everything?

[Act I]

Moments later in the script, Willy complains again:

Loaded with it. Loaded! What is he stealing?
He's giving it back, isn't he? Why is he stealing?
What did I tell him? I never in my life told him
anything but decent things.

[Act I]

Miller underscores these same issues again later on in the
same act when Charley suggests that it is a poor idea to

steal building materials, and, of course, again in the second half of the play when Biff walks out of Bill Oliver's
office with Oliver's pen and then cannot go back and face
the man.

BILL: I took those balls years ago, now I walk
in with his fountain pen? That clinches it, don't
you see? I can't face him like that!

[Act II]

Among the more famous analyses of *Death of a Salesman*
is the one published by a psychiatrist while the original
production was still on the Broadway stage. Daniel E.
Schneider saw the play as an expression of Willy's aggression against his older brother Ben, as Happy's aggressions
against Biff. Schneider speaks of the meeting of the father
and his sons in the bar as a "totem feast," the whole play
as "an irrational Oedipal bloodbath," of Willy's sudden
need to go to the bathroom in that barroom sequence as
"castration panic," and points out the possible sexual significance of that stolen pen, those stolen basketballs and
footballs [see Further Reading]. Most commentators on
Death of a Salesman seem to have found Schneider's analysis of the play of little use. At any rate, few of them mentioned him. And indeed Schneider's attempt to point out
a pattern seems perhaps a bit forced, that is, a bit psychoanalytic. But he makes some telling points.

There is a pattern, one I think, that has not been pointed
out before. It is worth remembering how often, in scenes
involving Willy's training of his sons, that balls, footballs,
basketballs, punching bags, appear. If Schneider's suggestion is valid that these balls are images of a concern with
castration, the implication follows that Willy is guilty of
a crime that can serve as the *hamartia* for which his catastrophe is poetically just.

Willy's crime is that he has tried to mould his sons in his
own image, that he has turned them into wind-bags and
cry-babies. They are not sexually impotent, no more than
Willy is, but they are impotant in a larger sense. Happy
complains of the meaninglessness of his life.

Sometimes I sit in my apartment—all alone.
And I think of the rent I'm paying. And it's
crazy. But then, it's what I always wanted. My
own apartment, a car, and plenty of women.
And still, goddammit, I'm lonely.

[Act I]

The boys are not impotent sexually, but morally and socially. Willy himself has no basis for making moral
choices. It is not so much that he chooses or has chosen
evil, but that he has no idea how to choose at all. Everyone, himself included, is constantly contradicting him. He
lives in a morally incoherent universe, an incoherence that
is the most striking element of the play which describes his
torments. And because he is morally incapacitated, he is
socially incapacitated. Everything is against him. The city
is killing him. The competition is killing him. He cannot
get along with the son he loves most. The very seeds he
plants no longer grow. Nothing he does has any consequences. He simply cannot make anything happen.

One may, in describing a person like Willy who has no
"character," in the vulgate employed in Miller's dialogue,

say of Willy that "he's got no balls." And neither have his sons. Willy's efforts to mould these boys in his own image have not been a failure but a success. They are just like him. They offer two aspects of the same personality, Happy taking more after his mother, perhaps, but both sharing the same defect with their father. They cannot make anything happen. They are morally and socially castrated.

To the other causes of Willy's catastrophe, then, to Willy's weakness, his incompetence to deal with a society too cruel to pay him the attention that he cannot wrest from it with his own strength, to his isolation from nature, to his incapacity to explain his own situation to himself, to his feelings of a loss of identity, of spiritual dryness, of lack of love, to his erroneous worship at the altar of personality, I suggest we may add to all these his crime: he has made moral eunuchs of his own sons. His is a criminality, a *hamartia,* for which the punishment, that miserable life, that miserable death, and that miserable funeral too, are appropriate and decorous consequences. (pp. 19-24)

> *B. S. Field, Jr., in a review of "Death of a Salesman," in* Twentieth Century Literature, *Vol. 18, No. 1, January, 1972, pp. 19-24.*

THE CRUCIBLE

PRODUCTION REVIEWS

Brooks Atkinson   (review date 23 January 1953)

[*In his review of the premier of* The Crucible, *Atkinson maintains that, although "powerful," this work is inferior to* Death of a Salesman. *Compared to the earlier play, the critic insists, "there is too much excitement and not enough emotion in* The Crucible.*"*]

Arthur Miller has written another powerful play. *The Crucible,* it is called, and it opened at the Martin Beck last evening in an equally powerful performance. Riffling back the pages of American history, he has written the drama of the witch trials and hangings in Salem in 1692. Neither Mr. Miller nor his audiences are unaware of certain similarities between the perversions of justice then and today.

But Mr. Miller is not pleading a cause in dramatic form. For *The Crucible,* despite its current implications, is a self-contained play about a terrible period in American history. Silly accusations of witchcraft by some mischievous girls in Puritan dress gradually take possession of Salem. Before the play is over good people of pious nature and responsible temper are condeming other good people to the gallows.

Having a sure instinct for dramatic form, Mr. Miller goes bluntly to essential situations. John Proctor and his wife, farm people, are the central characters of the play. At first the idea that Goodie Proctor is a witch is only an absurd rumor. But *The Crucible* carries the Proctors through the

whole ordeal—first vague suspicion, then the arrest, the implacable, highly wrought trial in the church vestry, the final opportunity for John Proctor to save his neck by confessing to something he knows is a lie, and finally the baleful roll of the drums at the foot of the gallows.

Although *The Crucible* is a powerful drama, it stands second to *Death of a Salesman* as a work of art. Mr. Miller has had more trouble with this one, perhaps because he is too conscious of its implications. The literary style is cruder. The early motivation is muffled in the uproar of the opening scene, and the theme does not develop with the simple eloquence of *Death of a Salesman.*

It may be that Mr. Miller has tried to pack too much inside his drama, and that he has permitted himself to be concerned more with the technique of the witch hunt than with its humanity. For all its power generated on the surface, *The Crucible* is most moving in the simple, quiet scenes between John Proctor and his wife. By the standards of *Death of a Salesman,* there is too much excitement and not enough emotion in *The Crucible.*

As the director, Jed Harris has given it a driving performance in which the clashes are fierce and clamorous. Inside Boris Aronson's gaunt, pitiless sets of rude buildings, the acting is at a high pitch of bitterness, anger and fear. As the patriarchal deputy Governor, Walter Hampden gives one of his most vivid performances in which righteousness and ferocity are unctuously mated. Fred Stewart as a vindictive parson, E. G. Marshall as a parson who finally rebels at the indiscriminate ruthlessness of the trial, Jean Adair as an aging woman of God, Madeleine Sherwood as a malicious town hussy, Joseph Sweeney as an old man who has the courage to fight the court, Philip Coolidge as a sanctimonious judge—all give able performances.

As John Proctor and his wife, Arthur Kennedy and Beatrice Straight have the most attractive roles in the drama and two or three opportunities to act them together in moments of tranquillity. They are superb—Mr. Kennedy clear and resolute, full of fire, searching his own mind; Miss Straight, reserved, detached, above and beyond the contention. Like all the members of the cast, they are dressed in the chaste and lovely costumes Edith Lutyens has designed from old prints of early Massachusetts.

After the experience of *Death of a Salesman* we probably expect Mr. Miller to write a masterpiece every time. *The Crucible* is not of that stature and it lacks that universality. On a lower level of dramatic history with considerable pertinence for today, it is a powerful play and a genuine contribution to the season.

> *Brooks Atkinson, in a review of "The Crucible," in* The New York Times, *January 23, 1953, p. 15.*

Walter F. Kerr   (review date 23 January 1953)

[*Kerr is a Pulitzer Prize-winning American dramatic critic, essayist, and playwright. Throughout his career, he has written theater reviews for such publications as the* Commonweal, *the* New York Herald Tribune, *and*

Jenny Egan as Mary Warren accusing Arthur Kennedy as John Proctor in Act III of the 1953 production of The Crucible.

the New York Times. *In his assessment of the opening night performance of* The Crucible, *Kerr focuses on the drama's social and political content, judging it a "mechanical parable . . . the sort of play which lives not in the warmth of humbly observed human souls but in the ideological heat of polemic."*]

Arthur Miller is a problem playwright, in both senses of the word. As a man of independent thought, he is profoundly, angrily concerned with the immediate issues of our society—with the irresponsible pressures which are being brought to bear on free men, with the self-seeking which blinds whole segments of our civilization to justice, with the evasions and dishonesties into which cowardly men are daily slipping. And to his fiery editorializing he brings shrewd theatrical gifts: he knows how to make a point plain, how to give it bite in the illustration, how to make its caustic and cauterizing language ring out on the stage.

He is also an artist groping toward something more poetic than simple, savage journalism. He has not only the professional crusader's zeal for humanity, but the imaginative writer's feeling for it—how it really behaves, how it moves about a room, how it looks in its foolish as well as in its noble attitudes—and in his best play, **Death of a Sales-**

man, he was able to rise above the sermon and touch the spirit of some simple people.

In **The Crucible,** which opened at the Martin Beck last night, he seems to me to be taking a step backward into mechanical parable, into the sort of play which lives not in the warmth of humbly observed human souls but in the ideological heat of polemic.

Make no mistake about it: there is fire in what Mr. Miller has to say, and there is a good bit of sting in his manner of saying it. He has, for convenience's sake, set his troubling narrative in the Salem of 1692. For reasons of their own, a quartet of exhibitionistic young women are hurling accusations of witchcraft at eminently respectable members of a well-meaning, but not entirely clear-headed, society.

On the basis of hearsay—"guilt by association with the devil" might be the phrase for it—a whole community of innocents are brought to trial and condemned to be hanged. As Mr. Miller pursues his very clear contemporary parallel, there are all sorts of relevant thrusts: the folk who do the final damage are not the lunatic fringe but the gullible pillars of society; the courts bog down into travesty in order to comply with the popular mood; slander becomes the weapon of opportunists ("Is the accuser always holy now?" [Act II]); freedom is possible at the price of naming one's associates in crime; even the upright man is eventually tormented into going along with the mob to secure his own way of life, his own family.

Much of this—not all—is an accurate reading of our own turbulent age, and there are many times at the Martin Beck when one's intellectual sympathies go out to Mr. Miller and to his apt symbols anguishing on the stage. But it is the intellect which goes out, not the heart.

For Salem, and the people who live, love, fear and die in it, are really only conveniences to Mr. Miller, props to his thesis. He does not make them interesting in and for themselves, and you wind up analyzing them, checking their dilemmas against the latest headlines, rather than losing yourself in any rounded, deeply rewarding personalities. You stand back and think; you don't really share very much.

Under Jed Harris' firm and driving hand, a large and meticulously cast company performs expertly. Arthur Kennedy brings integrity and candor to a role that is not really not much more than a banner for Mr. Miller's thought. But when he is shaking his head over the greediness of a minister and muttering "It hurt my prayer it hurt my prayer" [Act II], or when he is laboriously naming the Ten Commandments and forgetting the one he has most recently broken, he invests a two-dimensional figure with great perception.

Beatrice Straight is a fine complement to him as the wife who has centered too much of her life on her husband's single infidelity, and Walter Hampden gives a beautifully varied, fiercely powerful performance as a wily judge who is jealous of his authority and bent on turning an official investigation to his own preconceived ends.

In lesser roles, Jean Adair is especially striking as an old woman of unquenchable honor, E. G. Marshall supplies a needed subtlety in the role of a man of God who must begin to doubt his own devils, Joseph Sweeney is rousing as a crusty villager with genuine common sense and Madeleine Sherwood finds a believable intensity for her venomous trouble maker.

Boris Aronson has designed four spare, clean settings which succeed in evoking that Salem which Mr. Miller has not been patient enough to create.

> *Walter F. Kerr, in a review of "The Crucible,"*
> *in* New York Herald Tribune, *January 23,*
> *1953, p. 12.*

Eric Bentley   (review date 16 February 1953)

[*Bentley questions the validity of parallels, evident in* The Crucible, *between the Salem trials and congressional investigations into communist activities. Moreover, he finds this work a rather lifeless "story not quite told, a drama not realized" as a result of its overt political content.*]

The first thing to say about Arthur Miller's **The Crucible** is that it is worth discussing, a fact that sets it off from all other English and American plays of the season. I found the occasion a moving one. To begin with, it is moving to see so many good American actors, or perhaps what I mean is that it's moving to see them permitted to act. Above all, at a moment when we are all being "investigated" or about to be "investigated," it is moving to see images of "investigation" before the footlights. It seems to me that there ought to be dozens of plays giving a critical account of the state of the nation, yet the fact of one such play, by an author who is neither an infant, a fool, or a swindler, is enough to bring tears to the eyes.

"Great stones they lay upon his chest until he plead aye or nay. They say he gives them but two words. 'More weight,' he says, and died" [Act IV]. Miller's material is magnificent for narrative, poetry, drama, meaning. The fact that we sense its magnificence suggests that either he or his actors have in part realized it, yet our moments of emotion only make us the more aware of half-hours of indifference or dissatisfaction. This is a story not quite told, a drama not realized. Pygmalion has labored hard at his statue but it has not come to life. There is a terrible inertness about this play. The individual characters, like the individual lines, lack all fluidity and therefore all grace. There is an O'Neill-like striving after a poetry and an eloquence which the author cannot achieve. "From Aeschylus to Arthur Miller," say the textbooks. The world has made this author important before he has made himself great; the reversal of the natural order of things weighs heavily upon him. It would be all too easy, script in hand, to point to weak spots. The inadequacy of particular lines and characters, is of less interest, however, than the mentality from which they come. It is the mentality of the unreconstructed liberal.

There has been some debate as to whether this story of 17th century Salem "really" refers to our current "witch hunt" but since no one is interested in anything *but* this reference, I pass on to the real point at issue, which is: the validity of the parallel. It is true in that people today are being persecuted on quite chimerical grounds. It is untrue in that communism is not, to put it mildly, merely a chimera. The word communism is used to cover, first, the politics of Marx, second, the politics of Stalin, and, third, all the activities of liberals as they seem to illiberal illiterates. Since Miller's argument bears only on the third use of the word, its scope is limited. Indeed, the analogy between "red-baiting" and witch hunting can seem complete only to communists, for only to them is the menace of communism as fictitious as the menace of witches. The non-communist will look for certain reservations and provisos. In **The Crucible,** there are none.

To accuse Mr. Miller of communism would of course be to fall into the trap of over-simplification which he himself has set. For all I know he may hate Stalin with all the ardor of Eisenhower. What I am maintaining is that his view of life is dictated by assumptions which liberals have to unlearn and which many liberals have rather publicly unlearned. Chief among these assumptions is that of general innocence. In Hebrew mythology, innocence was lost at the very beginning of things; in liberal, especially American liberal, folklore, it has not been lost yet; Arthur Miller is the playwright of American liberalism. It is as if the merely negative, and legal, definition of innocence were extended to the rest of life: you are innocent until proved guilty, you are innocent if you "didn't do it." Writers have a sort of double innocence: not only can they create innocent characters, they can also write from the viewpoint of innocence—we can speak today not only of the "omniscient" author but of the "guiltless" one.

Such indeed is the viewpoint of the dramatist of indignation, like Miss [Lillian] Hellman or Mr. Miller. And it follows that their plays are melodrama—a conflict between the wholly guilty and the wholly innocent. For a long time liberals were afraid to criticise the mentality behind this melodrama because they feared association with the guilty ("harboring reactionary sympathies"). But, though a more enlightened view would enjoin association with the guilty in the admission of a common humanity, it does not ask us to underestimate the guilt or to refuse to see "who done it." The guilty men are as black with guilt as Mr. Miller says—what we must ask is whether the innocent are as innocent. The drama of indignation is melodramatic not so much because it paints its villains too black as because it paints its heroes too white. *Othello* is not a melodrama, because, though its villain is jet black, its hero's white radiance is not unstained. **The Crucible** is a melodrama because, though the hero has weaknesses, he has no faults. His innocence is unreal because it is total. His author has equipped him with what we might call Superinnocence, for the crime he is accused of not only hasn't been committed by him, it isn't even a possibility: it is the fiction of traffic with the devil. It goes without saying that the hero has all the minor accoutrements of innocence too: he belongs to the right social class (yeoman farmer), does the right kind of work (manual), and, somewhat contrary to historical possibilities, has the right philosophy (a distinct leaning towards sceptical empiricism). . . .

The awkwardness I find in Mr. Miller's script is duplicated in Mr. Harris's directing. [He has not] . . . taken this script up like clay and re-molded it. He [has not] . . . struck fire from the individual actor . . . [nor] brought one actor into the liveliest relationship with another. Arthur Kennedy is not used up to half his full strength in this production; E. G. Marshall and Walter Hampden give fine performances but each in his own way, Hampden's way being a little too English, genteel, and 19th century; the most successful performance, perhaps, is that of Beatrice Straight because here a certain rigidity belongs to the character and is in any case checked by the performer's fine sensibility. (pp. 22-3)

Eric Bentley, "Miller's Innocence," in The New Republic, *Vol. 128, No. 7, February 16, 1953, pp. 22-3.*

Richard Hayes (review date 20 February 1953)

[*Hayes offers guarded praise of* The Crucible, *considering it "a drama of arresting polemic distinction" which states its political theme with "admirable concision and force." As a whole, however,* The Crucible *is a work of lesser "tragic force" than* Death of a Salesman *in Hayes's opinion.*]

It is altogether possible that Mr. Arthur Miller was prompted to the composition of his latest play by the malign politico-cultural pressures of our society, but whatever the impulse, it has issued in a drama of arresting polemic distinction.

The Crucible does not, I confess, seem to me a work of such potential tragic force as the playwright's earlier *Death of a Salesman;* it is the product of theatrical dexterity and a young man's moral passion, rather than of a fruitful and reverberating imagination. But it has, in a theatre of the small success and the tidy achievement, power, the passionate line—an urgent boldness which does not shrink from the implications of a large and formidable design.

With the Salem witchcraft trials of 1692 as a moral frame and point of departure, Mr. Miller has gone on to examine the permanent conditions of the climate of hysteria. The New England tragedy was for him, dramatically, a fortuitous choice because it is accessible to us imaginatively; as one of the few severely irrational eruptions American society has witnessed, it retains still its primitive power to compel the attention. And it exhibits, moreover, the several features of the classically hysterical situation: the strange moral alchemy by which the accuser becomes inviolable; the disrepute which overtakes the testimony of simple intelligence; the insistence on public penance; the willingness to absolve if guilt is confessed.

It is *imaginative* terror Mr. Miller is here invoking: not the solid gallows and the rope appall him, but the closed and suffocating world of the fanatic, against which the intellect and will are powerless.

It is a critical commonplace that the commitments of Mr. Miller's plays are ideological rather than personal—that he does not create a world so much in its simple humanity, or its perceptible reality, as in its intellectual alarms and excursions. *The Crucible* reinforces this tradition.

Despite the fact that he is often at his best in the "realist" vein, Mr. Miller, like any good heir of the thirties, is preoccupied with ideology. He has a richer personal sense of it than comparable writers, but the impulse remains unaltered. His characteristic theme is integrity, and its obverse, compromise. In earlier plays, Miller frequently brought to this subject a distressing note of stridency; one often felt that, really, the battle had long since been won, and that this continued obsession with it was an indication not of seriousness, but perhaps of some arrested moral development.

In *The Crucible,* however, he has stated his theme again with a wholly admirable concision and force. His central figure is John Proctor, another spokesman for rational feeling and the disinterested intelligence. Proctor is so patently the enemy of hysteria that his very existence is a challenge to the fanatic temperament, and he is consumed by its malice. What gives the situation a fresh vitality is Miller's really painful grasp of its ambiguities: the dilemma of a man, fallible, subject to pride, but forced to choose between the "negative good" of truth and morality, and the "positive good" of human life under any dispensation. Around this crisis of conscience, Mr. Miller has written an exhaustive, exacerbated scene—one of his most truly distinguished, and one which most hopefully displays the expanding delicacy of his moral imagination.

It is difficult, however, to feel that the political complexities inherent in *The Crucible* have been approached by Mr. Miller with any comparable sensitivity. He has, admittedly, disclaimed intent of contemporary reference in the play, choosing to see in it only the tragedy of another society. But it would be fatuous of Mr. Miller to pretend that our present cultural climate had not always a place in the foreground of his mind. Surely then, he can see that the Salem witch-hunts and our own virulent varieties are parallel only in their effects, not in their causes.

Dramatically, *The Crucible* maintains always that provocative interest and distinction one has come to associate with the work of this playwright. Mr. Miller has, on the whole, handled the Puritan idiom discreetly, despite the somewhat "official" taint of the weak prologue, and several unfortunate lapses into the contemporary. Mr. Miller *will* have his poetry, though; in *Death of a Salesman* he often resorted to a kind of bastard [Walt] Whitman rhetoric, while *The Crucible,* especially in its hysterical imagery, owes an inordinate debt to the King James Bible. But language is handled here generally with considerable skill and sensibility.

Of the production at the Martin Beck, one can have very little criticism. Arthur Kennedy plays Proctor with all his assured style and intense virility, while Walter Hampden, Beatrice Straight and E. G. Marshall lend a grave and sober excellence to other figures in this Salem landscape. Mr. Jed Harris has directed boldly, with no shyness of scenes and curtains operatic in their intensity (and what a splendid opera might be made out of the Salem trials, incidentally). What *The Crucible* enriches and again asserts is the range, the variety and continuing interest of the American polemic tradition.

> *Richard Hayes, in a review of "The Crucible,"*
> *in* The Commonweal, *Vol. LVII, No. 20, Feb-*
> *ruary 20, 1953, p. 498.*

CRITICAL COMMENTARY

George Jean Nathan   (essay date 1953)

[*Nathan has been called the most learned and influential drama critic the United States has yet produced. During the early decades of the twentieth century, he was greatly responsible for shifting the emphasis of the American theater from light entertainment to serious drama and for introducing audiences and producers to the work of Eugene O'Neill, Henrik Ibsen, and Bernard Shaw, among others. Nathan was a contributing editor to H. L. Mencken's magazine the* American Mercury *and coeditor of the* Smart Set. *With Mencken, Nathan belonged to an iconoclastic school of American critics who attacked the vulgarity of accepted ideas and sought to bring a new level of sophistication to American culture, which they found provincial and backward. In his discussion of* The Crucible, *Nathan observes several shortcomings in the play. Firstly, it fails to adequately communicate its powerful theme to the audience. Secondly, the critic charges, the drama suffers from poor character development and an "air of propaganda." Lastly, the work is, in Nathan's judgment, badly constructed: when "the call is for emotional excitement and explosion," he asserts, the play becomes "fizzed out and flat." For a refutation of Nathan's views, see Philip G. Hill's commentary dated 1967.*]

Though I am scarcely known as a congenital optimist, since in my old definition any such sugarteat is the kind of person who believes a housefly is looking for a way to get out, I can not entirely disbelieve that patience sometimes has its reward, even in the theatre. And so it has presently come about that, just as we all were more or less convinced that our American playwrights in the aggregate and with small exception had eyes only for the box-office, a man of some rather higher pride and ambition has made a reappearance on the cheapjack scene. His name, Arthur Miller, and his play, **The Crucible.** It was not, true, altogether a surprise, since though a pair of his earlier efforts, excursions into [Henrik] Ibsen, were critically questionable, even they indicated his independent resolve, and since his excellent **Death of a Salesman,** that happily turned out to be box-office in spite of itself, indicated it even more. So it is that, while his newest play is very far beneath the merit of the last named and is in fact an out of hand dramatic performance, it provides us with the encouragement in respect to our theatre that we badly stand in need of. It may go down under critical gunnery, but its author's flag keeps flying, brightly.

Dealing with the historical Salem witch-hunts and witch-craft trials in the late years of the seventeenth century and wringing from them a lashing philippic against superstition and ignorance and the bigotry that is their offspring, the play's chief fault is that its fire remains within it and does not communicate itself to its auditors. It has a powerful theme and its general direction by Jed Harris and some of its acting have an internal power as well but little energy comes out of it, as in the case of a powerhouse operating at full blast in a preliminary test and as yet with no outside connection. At one point in its second act when the group of girls in the grip of hysteria shriek a repetition of their witchcraft imaginings and overcome one of their hesitant number a touch of real drama quivers across the footlights. But the rest fore and aft, while dynamic in intention, boils only within itself and gives off little external steam.

The reasons are several. Miller has been remiss in developing character of any close approximation to recognizable warm humanity and has thus denied his audience any of the necessary sympathetic contact with his two central figures, the husband and wife victims of the witch-hunt. What he has contrived are simply a pair of spokesmen who serve as sounding-boards for his theme, which is volleyed against them and returned much like a damp tennis ball. They, and in particular the persecuted husband, do their full duty by the written speeches but the effect is of two obedient actors in passionate recitation rather than of two human characters that better playwriting might have made them. One listens to them with some interest but without that measure of conviction which would result were they less tape recordings and more flesh and blood. As they stand, they give the impression of figures out of mechanical old melodrama coldly intellectualized.

A second flaw in the writing, no less than in the direction by the otherwise qualified Jed Harris, is a too great intensity in the early stages of the play which reduces the tension that should properly come later. The prologue, indeed, is so overwrought and conducted at so high a pitch that what follows, when the call is for emotional excitement and explosion, becomes fizzed out and flat, save alone for the one episode noted. The performances, in short, are previously so excessive that, even were the play more shrewdly composed, it would take phenomenal acting, accompanied by a spectacular chariot race, dramatically to top them. And thirdly there is the matter of contemporary parallels. Though Miller has been studiously careful not to finger-point and emphasize them and is to be critically endorsed in this respect, one nonetheless gets the feeling they are his primary concern and that the concern has here and there colored his treatment of his theme not to its advantage. There is consequently an underlying air of propaganda in the play that stubbornly permeates it for all the author's wish that it should not and, as with propaganda drama in the aggregate, the result is discommodious.

It is discommodious because what are unquestionably designed as parallels are not always rational parallels. It may be wholly true that what are currently referred to as political witch-hunts now and then proceed from mass hysteria and are grounded in fear, and also that they are sometimes cruel, irresponsible and deplorable. But the author's hoped for parallel between the Salem of 1692 and conditions today bogs down when the consideration extends to religious superstition and ecclesiasticism. This may be drawing the line pretty fine, since there are other points well taken, but there is a considerable difference between persecution based on ignorant superstition and prosecution, however extremely and at times eccentrically conducted, in time of national peril. The general dramatic idea may be valid but particularized analysis devitalizes it.

The realest figure in the play is that created by Walter Hampden as the deputy-governor who presides at the protagonist's trial. With his thorough grounding in the old-time school of acting, he brings to the role precisely those qualities that, while they would seem ham in a play laid in modern times, are perfectly suited to one like this laid in a long past era. Fred Stewart is also acceptable as the pivotal church bigot, and two or three others, among them the young Jenny Egan when you can make out what she is talking about in her hysterical scenes, are commendable. But both Arthur Kennedy and Beatrice Straight, who have the roles of the hounded married couple, present all the attributes of marionettes save only the energizing wires, though the impression may conceivably be the fault of the direction.

As [August] Strindberg was the most positive influence on [Eugene] O'Neill so Ibsen is the most positive on Miller. O'Neill as a consequence was primarily interested in analyzing the grinding effect of those emotions of man and woman that lie below the calmer surface emotions; Miller as a consequence is primarily interested in man's sociological aspects. Above all, O'Neill as a dramatist was concerned with character, whereas Miller seems in large part to be concerned with theme and with character only incidentally. Though in his worthy **Death of a Salesman** he achieved character, it still and nevertheless occasionally had the effect of being inserted into his theme rather than emerging naturally and easily out of it; and in this latest play we find all theme and no character. His people are ventriloquial spokesmen for him, not for themselves. They possess humanity, when they possess it at all, only in the distant sense that a phonograph recording of it does. They speak and act at an obvious turning of his crank. And the result is a play impressive as a lecture may be impressive but for the major part equally remote from the listener's heart and feeling. It may be, of course, that he thought he had worked out his thesis in terms of character and so would insinuate it into an audience's emotions. That I can not tell. But, if he did, he has failed. And if, on the other hand, he believed that the sheer vitality of his theme would satisfactorily infiltrate itself in his audience independent of any recognizable and pulsing character to assist it, he has not yet sufficiently educated himself in dramatic eccentricity.

The Crucible, in sum, is an honorable sermon on a vital subject that misses because the sting implicit in it has been disinfected with an editorial tincture, because it does not succeed in ridding itself of dialectic chill and in resolving itself, for all its fury, into even the mild fever of affecting drama, and because, though it contains the potential deep

vibrations of life, it reduces them to mere superficial tremors. (pp. 105-09)

George Jean Nathan, "American Playwrights, Old and New," in his The Theatre in the Fifties, *Alfred A. Knopf, 1953, pp. 40-112.*

Henry Popkin   (essay date 1964)

[*Popkin examines the issue of tragic guilt and responsibility as it relates to* The Crucible. *In classical tragedy, the hero must have committed an act which deserves punishment. In the Salem witch trials, Popkin notes, the victims were innocent; they had committed no such act. Thus, he argues, Miller must "invent" for John Proctor "a new sort of guilt"—adultery—so that he may fulfill the role of tragic hero in* The Crucible.]

Although **The Crucible** is set in seventeenth-century America, Arthur Miller intended it as a comment on American life of his own time. For several years before the play opened in 1953, public investigations had been examining and interrogating radicals, former radicals, and possible former radicals, requiring witnesses to tell about others and not only about themselves. The House Committee to Investigate Un-American Activities evolved a memorable and much-quoted sentence: "Are you now, or have you ever been a member of the Communist Party?" Borrowing a phrase from a popular radio program, its interrogators called it "the $64 question."

Senator Joseph McCarthy built his international fame on his presumed knowledge of subversion in government and added a new word to our vocabulary—"McCarthyism," meaning ruinous accusation without any basis in evidence. A few months before **The Crucible** reached Broadway, McCarthy had helped to elect a President of the United States, and, two days before the premiere, that President was inaugurated. The elections had made McCarthy chairman of an important congressional subcommittee; his power was greater than ever. The film and television industries gave every sign of being terrified by McCarthyism—but by the atmosphere that McCarthy created, more than by his own subcommittee. Show business found itself of more interest to the House Committee to Investigate Un-American Activities than to Senator McCarthy's subcommittee. Blacklists barred certain actors and writers from working in the popular media. Actors who refused to give testimony disappeared both from the large film screen and the small television screen, but "friendly witnesses" continued to work. On the other hand, the New York stage, since it was and still is a relatively chaotic enterprise, was comparatively unmanaged and untouched. Nevertheless, **The Crucible** was a bold as well as a timely play, written at a time when the congressional investigators had the power to do considerable damage. Senator McCarthy's personal authority wilted in the following year, but Miller was a somewhat unfriendly witness before a congressional committee in 1956. He described his own flirtation with Communism but refused to give the names of Communists he had known. He was ultimately absolved of the charge of contempt of the committee.

The Crucible dramatized the phrase that was popularly

being used to describe the congressional hearings—"witch hunts." In the Salem witch trials, Miller chose an unmistakable parallel to current events. He has never permitted any doubt that the parallel was deliberate. In his Introduction to his *Collected Plays* [included in *The Theater Essays of Arthur Miller;* see Further Reading] and in his interpretative remarks scattered through the text, he calls attention to the play's contemporary reference and invites comparisons between the two widely separated hearings.

The Salem witch trials are, equally, a historical event. In 1692, in Salem, Massachusetts, twenty people were found guilty of witchcraft and hanged; others who had been accused saved themselves by confessing to witchcraft and accusing others. As in the unhappy occurrences of the 1950's, naming others was taken to be a guarantee of sincerity and of a laudable desire to tell all. Also, the witchcraft scare was violent, alarming, and brief, like an epidemic and, again, like the Communist scare of the 1950's. It will be easy enough to discover and to expound still other parallels as we examine the play, but one preliminary difficulty needs to be stated: the parallel fails at one important point. There is such a thing as Communism; there is no such thing as witchcraft. This distinction indicates that the psychological state of the victims of the Salem trials is somewhat different from that of the victims of the investigations of the 1950's. Of course, people suffered equally in both centuries, and, while it may seem callous to weigh one anguish against another and to say that one man's suffering means more than another's, it is necessary to observe that the situation of our own time is more complex and therefore potentially more useful to the artist.

The distinction I am making is the same one that Aristotle made in our first treatise on literature, the *Poetics.* Aristotle writes that we are appalled by the suffering of the entirely blameless; such suffering, says Aristotle, is too disturbing to be a suitable subject for tragedy. Instead, we expect our tragic characters to exhibit some weakness, some sort of flaw. Scholars have disagreed for centuries as to the kind of flaw that Aristotle meant, but it is safe to say that the tragic hero is somehow imperfect and that his imperfection has some connection with his tragic catastrophe.

The unfortunate condemned innocents of Salem did nothing to bring on their ruin, nothing, at least, that had anything to do with the charge against them. Let me qualify that statement: it is conceivable that one aged eccentric or another actually thought she was in communication with the devil. That delusion is too special—not to say too lunatic—to be a very likely, interesting, or useful state of mind for a serious character. Miller seems to be of this opinion, since the only person in *The Crucible* who believes herself to be a witch is Tituba, who is not fully developed as a character and remains a minor figure. Furthermore, she confesses and is not executed; she need not suffer any pangs of conscience over her presumed witchcraft. If she thinks she has been a witch, she must also think she has atoned by confessing. The others, the true martyrs of Salem, had the consolation of knowing that they were innocent. Certainly, they were heroic in maintaining their innocence at a time when false confession was likely to save their lives. But to be heroic is not necessarily to be the complex, dramatic character who gives life to drama.

The events of the 1950's provided a more logical connection between character and fate. The American Communist Party existed, and, for a long time, its legality was unquestioned. It was perfectly possible and legal to join it— for any of a variety of reasons, both good and bad—for idealistic reasons, out of a desire for power, out of an instinctive interest in conspiracy, out of a general dissatisfaction with society, or even, as many later said, in order to offer effective opposition to Fascism. It was possible for many, like Miller himself, to have some association with Communism and Communists without joining the party. Great numbers of those accused in the 1950's came from the ranks of these party members and their non-member "fellow traveller" associates. Still others among the accused had no connection with the Communist Party; for the purposes of our comparison, they are exactly like the innocent victims of the Salem trials.

I have set up these elementary categories in order to demonstrate that the actor or director who was blacklisted and so lost his job in the 1950's was likely to have made some commitment in the 1930's that affected his subsequent fate. This was not necessarily so, but it was likely. He had not made a commitment to Satan, and few will now say that such a man deserved to be banished from his profession because of his past or present politics, but, in his case, we can say that character and fate roughly, very roughly, fit together, that there is a meaningful connection between what the man did and what later happened to him. Life is not always so logical, as the Salem trials tell us. The witchcraft trials in Salem were wild, unreasonable offenses against justice; they present intrinsic difficulties for any dramatist who wants to make an orderly drama out of them. Art tends to be neater and, superficially, more logical than the history of Salem. In contrast, the corresponding events of the 1950's have a cruel and inaccurate logic; their injustice is, in a sense, logical, even though the logic is reprehensible.

If we were not able to point out that the historical parallel in *The Crucible* is imperfect, we might still justifiably object that the impact of a sudden and undeserved punishment upon entirely innocent people is a difficult subject for drama. Aristotle's criticism of the entirely blameless hero continues to be valid. In apparent recognition of this principle, Miller has constructed a new sort of guilt for his hero, John Proctor. In the play, Proctor has been unfaithful to his wife, and Miller goes out of his way to assure us directly that his infidelity violates his personal code of behavior. The girl whom he loved, jealous and resentful of being rejected, accuses Proctor's wife of witchcraft, and so Proctor, who has, in this peculiar fashion, caused his wife to be accused, has a special obligation to save her. In trying to save her, he is himself charged with witchcraft. So, he does suffer for his guilt—but for a different guilt, for adultery, not for witchcraft.

But it must be remembered that a play is not merely an exercise in ideas or even in characterization. It is a creation that moves forward in time, catching interest and creating suspense. While the historical context is useful to any preliminary understanding of a play, any full understanding and any proper evaluation must follow a close look at its plot. The plot presents to us an ebb and flow of argument and incident, an alternation of crises, turning, in *The Crucible,* about the issue of witchcraft.

The Crucible begins with a crisis, a moment of excitement that shows the false witnesses in full cry—one child on stage and another of whom we are told, both of them displaying the different but equally convincing symptoms of demonic possession. We note a number of fatuous adult responses to the children's behavior, and then the adults conveniently leave the stage to the children, who effectively clear up any mysteries by frankly discussing their deceitful actions. They incidentally, and very usefully, provide us with Abigail's special motive, her jealous hatred of Elizabeth Proctor. Directly upon this cue, John Proctor enters, and, perhaps a bit improbably revealing too many intimate secrets in the presence of a child feigning possession, he and Abigail tell us most of what we need to know about their love affair and its present consequences. In quick succession, then, we have seen the central disorder of the play, demonic possession, and the explanation for it; in the children's malice, we have also noted a particular form of malice that is to breed results to come—Abigail's jealousy. The main exposition has been effected, and the main lines of action are ready.

At once the skeptic, Proctor, clashes with Parris, the believer in witchcraft. The argument between the skeptical and the credulous, and the ensuing effort to convince the community dominate all of the play. Like other works by Miller, *The Crucible* has something of the quality of a trial, of a court case, even before the formal hearings begin. Throughout, the exponents of both views are arguing their cases, making their points, and, inadvertently, revealing their real motives. Proctor and Parris now engage in just such a dispute, showing us their own personal hostility and helpfully bringing in some additional exposition concerning the land war, the rivalry over ministerial appointments, and the issue of Parris's salary. These are the real, underlying issues that motivate the men of Salem.

Once the local prejudices have been established, we have reached the appropriate moment for the arrival of the guileless outsider, the idealistic seeker of witches, John Hale. In theory, Hale is perfectly equipped to combat witchcraft, and he even enters carrying visible evidence of his qualifications, the heavy books that have enlightened him. In practice, he is as helpless as a child, much more helpless than the children of the play. He is totally unequipped, precisely because he is an outsider with a load of irrelevant academic knowledge, precisely because he has missed the informative conversations that just precede his entrance. He has pursued the wrong study; instead of demonology, he should have applied himself to economics, the psychopathology of children, and eavesdropping. Hale is the simple, eager man of good will, the human *tabula rasa* upon whom the experience of the play will write. His simplicity makes him the ideal audience for the wholesale charges of witchcraft that begin to be made as the curtain falls upon the first act. As we should expect, these

charges proceed inevitably from the circumstances that the previous action has painstakingly interpreted.

After some preliminary exposition of the cool relationship between John Proctor and his wife, the second act provides, in order, Elizabeth Proctor's interrogation of her husband, the Proctors' joint interrogation of Mary Warren, and, finally, the real goal of the scene—Hale's examination of the Proctors. One incidental effect of this repeated use of courtroom technique is to show us that Elizabeth Proctor's justice to her husband is as lacking in mercy and understanding as the public justice of Salem. The crime of adultery that Elizabeth continues to probe and to worry over has already been adequately punished and repented for, but Elizabeth will never permit herself to forget it.

Following the troubled exchange between the Proctors comes the only courtroom procedure that brings out the truth, the Proctors' joint examination of Mary Warren. A suitable rigor on the part of the questioners and the threat of a whipping bring the whole truth out of her fast enough. Then Hale takes the initiative, less successfully. He is a sufficiently experienced investigator to hunt out a crime, but, without knowing it, he has found the wrong crime— adultery, not witchcraft. He causes Proctor to miss the seventh commandment and evidently takes that failure as a sign of the man's general impiety when it is really a sort of Freudian slip, an unwilling confession of his infidelity. In addition, Hale rightly sniffs out the general atmosphere of guilt and notes "some secret blasphemy that stinks to Heaven." He is responding to the chilly atmosphere that Elizabeth Proctor maintains and to the shame that it produces in John Proctor. His suspicion has an ironically appropriate result: it is Elizabeth herself who is the victim of her own heavy insistence on the reality of guilt. In a sense, Hale is right to arrest her. She is guilty of pharisaism, which is a more serious charge than witchcraft or adultery, and Miller gives the unmistakable impression that he considers pharisaism a very serious offense indeed. (Pharisaism appears again and is again made to seem obnoxious in a later play of Miller's, *After the Fall,* where it is once more the trait of a wife whose husband has been unfaithful.)

The third act revolves about John Proctor's effort to save his wife; when the accusation is at last directed against him, the principal forward action of the play has come to an end. The charges of witchcraft have begun by hitting out blindly in all directions, but then, in accordance with the painstaking preparations that informed us of Abigail's jealousy of Elizabeth, the accusations fix upon Elizabeth. Proctor tries to reverse them by charging Abigail with adultery, but, in consequence, he is himself accused of witchcraft. Up to this time, slander has been spreading in all directions, attaching itself at random to one innocent victim after another, but now it finds its true and proper target. The real, the ultimate victim in this play is John Proctor, the one independent man, the one skeptic who sees through the witchcraft "craze" from the first. As if instinctively, in self-defense, the witchcraft epidemic has attacked its principal enemy. This is a climactic moment, a turning point in the play. New witches may continue to be named, but *The Crucible* now narrows its focus to John

Proctor, caught in the trap, destroyed by his effort to save his wife, threatened by the irrationality that only he has comprehended.

The third act has an incidental function; it is climactic for Hale as well as for Proctor. Hale first appears as a zealous specialist; in the second act, he is shown going industriously about his work; in the third act, shaken by the obvious injustice of what he has brought to pass, he denounces the hearings. That is the crucial step for him, and, from that moment, his personal drama does not take any new direction, just as the general development of the play takes no distinctive new steps following these turning points for Proctor and Hale.

In addition, the third act is a carefully organized unit of argument and counter-argument. Concerned to protect their authority, the judges promise a long period of safety for Elizabeth Proctor, and, when this stratagem fails, they start bullying the turncoat Mary Warren. Proctor counterattacks with the same low tactics that his enemies use—charging Abigail, the primary accuser, with the crimes that do her reputation the most damage; they are specifically anti-Puritan crimes, laughing during prayer and dancing. These are curious accusations from a skeptic, but he is learning, too late, to play his enemies' game. Abigail responds by attributing witchcraft to Mary Warren. This give-and-take continues when Proctor calls out "Whore! Whore!" After three acts of fencing, the real truth is out; the burden of establishing it rests with the one person whose truthfulness can be fully guaranteed—Elizabeth Proctor. All attention goes to her as she is asked the critical question. And, for once, in a moment of high excitement and suspense, this model of truthfulness lies because she values something more than the truth—her husband's good name.

The value Salem attributes to a good name has been indicated previously in the play; it becomes critically important in the last act. From the beginning, Salem has been presented as a community in which mutual evaluation is a generally popular activity. Prying, slander, and recrimination are unpleasant but persuasive testimonials to the value that attaches to a good name. Living in this environment and sharing its values, Elizabeth Proctor must value reputation even more than truth. This decision has disastrous results, for Mary Warren, facing serious punishment as a turncoat and possible witch, must defend herself by making a new charge—against the man who got her into this sorry mess, John Proctor. The path of the accusations has been circuitous, but Proctor is, in effect, being punished for his hostility to Salem's obsession with sin—in particular, his wife's obsession with adultery and the community's obsession with witchcraft. We may suspect a tacit hint that the two fixations are closely linked.

In the last act, public opinion has shifted: Andover is in revolt, even Parris is shaken, and more pressure is being applied to obtain confessions. Proctor can be saved only by a dishonest confession to witchcraft. Life is sufficiently dear for him to make the confession, but he will not let it become a public document. The issue is, once again, his good name. Previously preferred over truth, his good name is now preferred to life itself. This issue seems now

to dominate the play, but, as we have observed, it has been prominent throughout, for accusations of witchcraft are harmful to the reputation as well as to the individual life. The citizens of Salem have been concerned with scoring points against one another, with establishing their own superior virtue and the depraved character of their enemies. To use the word "depraved" is to remind ourselves that this state of affairs is well suited to the Puritan theology, which held that divine election was the one balm for innate human depravity. Reputation served as an indispensable guide to the state of grace, for it was an outward sign of election. As a result, Proctor is not only expressing a characteristically modern concern for his good name, a concern equally important to the twentieth-century protagonist of Miller's next full-length play, *A View from the Bridge;* he is exhibiting a typically Puritan state of mind.

Proctor dies, then, for his good name; but to return to the troubling issue, his good name was not, in the most serious sense, threatened by the charges brought against him. His good name was, in fact, being threatened by his fear of death and by his knowledge of his own adultery, but it was shaken only in the most superficial way by the charge of witchcraft. Proctor is not merely innocent; he is *an* innocent, and his guilt as an adulterer is irrelevant, except insofar as it supplies Abigail with her motive for slandering his wife. We can see why Proctor's adultery had to be invented; surely it came into existence because Miller found himself compelled to acknowledge the Aristotelian idea that the blameless, unspotted hero is an inadequate protagonist for a serious play.

This problem may be further illuminated by reference to some of Miller's other works. In his first two Broadway successes, a relatively unsullied hero (played in each case by an actor named Arthur Kennedy) is present, but he does not have the leading role. The chief character in each of these plays, *All My Sons* and *Death of a Salesman,* is a guilty older man, who has lived by the wrong values. In this last respect at least, he resembles Hale of *The Crucible,* but he is more complex and more serious. Now, however, in *The Crucible,* the younger, unsullied hero (again played in the original production by Arthur Kennedy) moves into the foreground. Of course, Proctor is deeply conscious of his infidelity to his wife, but this fact does not affect his fundamental freedom from guilt; in a sense, he is unsullied, significantly less guilty than the sinful older men of the earlier plays. We are obviously expected to apply a modern "psychological" judgment to him and say that he was driven to adultery by a cold wife and by the irresistible attraction of the conscienceless girl who seduced him. Abigail is not made "a strikingly beautiful girl" (in the stage directions [Act I]) for nothing. We must exonerate Proctor, just as we are required to exonerate a similar character in a later play by Miller, another man who stands between a cold, complaining wife and an irresistible child-woman—Quentin in *After the Fall.* (Eddie Carbone in *A View from the Bridge* is another married man fascinated by a child-woman, but he is exonerated in another way: he is "sick.")

Miller expresses regret, in the Introduction to his *Collected Plays* [included in *Theater Essays*], that he failed to make his villains sufficiently wicked; he thinks now that he should have represented them as being dedicated to evil for its own sake. I suspect that most students of *The Crucible* will feel that he has made them quite wicked enough. For one thing, he has established their depravity by inserting a number of clear references to the investigators and blacklisters of his own time. He has made Proctor ask, significantly: "Is the accuser always holy now?" [Act III]. To the automatic trustworthiness of accusers he has added the advantage of confession (always efficacious for former Communists), the necessity of naming the names of fellow-conspirators, the accusation of "an invisible crime" (witchcraft—or a crime of thought), the dangers threatening anyone who dares to defend the accused, the prejudice of the investigators, the absence of adequate legal defense for the accused, and the threat that those who protest will be charged with contempt of court. Most of these elements constitute what might be called a political case against the accusers and especially against the magistrates, Danforth and Hawthorne. Miller builds an economic case as well, suggesting that the original adult instigators of the witchcraft trials were moved by greed, particularly by a desire for the victims' lands. The whole case is stated only in Miller's accompanying notes, but much of it is given dramatic form.

The viciousness of the children, except for Abigail, is less abundantly explained. We are evidently to assume that when they make their false charges they are breaking out of the restrictive forms of proper, pious, Puritan behavior to demand the attention that every child requires. The same rebelliousness has led them to dance in the moonlight and to join in Tituba's incantations. The discovery of these harmless occupations has led then to their more destructive activity. Curiously, Miller chooses not to show us any good children—a category to which the Proctors' offspring surely belong. We hear of "Jonathan's trap" for rabbits, but these children are as absolutely banished from the stage as the protagonists' children in [Bernard] Shaw's *Candida*. Most modern dramatists are less self-conscious about presenting children than Shaw was, but Miller makes a similar omission in *After the Fall*. At a climactic moment, Quentin is confronted with his written statement that the only person in the world whom he has ever loved is his daughter, and yet this child is never seen in the play.

Over against the bad individual, the vengeful adults, and the lying children, Miller sets the basically sound community, in which the saintly Rebecca Nurse's benefactions are known even to the stranger Hale. At best, Salem is a bad, quarrelsome place; the good community is more warmly depicted in Miller's earlier plays, but even in Salem it exists, and it furnishes twenty honest souls who will not confess to witchcraft, even to save their lives. The underlying presence of the good community, however misruled it may be, reminds us that Miller, even in face of his own evidence, professes to believe in the basic strength and justice of the social organism, in the possibility of good neighbors. If he criticizes society, he does so from within, as a participant and a believer in it.

The deliberately antique language surely reflects Miller's self-consciousness regarding his emphatically heroic hero and the extreme situation in which he finds himself. Issues are never made so clear, so black and white in any of Miller's other plays. And so, naturally, the statement of these issues must be colored, must be, to use Bertolt Brecht's term, "alienated" by quaint, unfamiliar ways of speech. Certainly, the peculiar speech of *The Crucible* is not a necessity, even in a play set in the seventeenth century. (Christopher Fry's fifteenth-century Englishmen in *The Lady's Not for Burning* speak a language closer to our own.) The purpose of the quirkish English of *The Crucible* is not only to give the impression of an antique time, although that is part of it; the purpose is to alienate us, to make us unfamiliar in this setting, to permit distance to lend its enchantment to this bare, simplistic confrontation of good and evil, and also to keep us from making too immediate, too naive an indentification between these events and the parallel happenings of our own time. The issues are too simple, much more simple than the modern parallels. Language imposes a necessary complexity from without.

Any final comment must dwell upon *The Crucible* as a play of action and suspense. It falls short as a play of ideas, which is what it was originally intended to be. It falls short because the parallels do not fit and because Miller has had to adulterate—the pun is intentional—Proctor's all too obvious innocence to create a specious kind of guilt for him; he is easily exonerated of both crimes, the real one and the unreal one, so easily that no ideas issue from the crucible of this human destiny. And yet, *The Crucible* keeps our attention by furnishing exciting crises, each one proceeding logically from its predecessor, in the lives of people in whom we have been made to take an interest. That is a worthy intention, if it is a modest one, and it is suitably fulfilled. (pp. 139-46)

> Henry Popkin, "Arthur Miller's 'The Crucible'," in College English, *Vol. 26, No. 2, November, 1964, pp. 139-46.*

Philip G. Hill   (essay date 1967)

[*An American theater scholar, educator, and critic, Hill has written numerous essays on drama and published* The Living Art *in 1971. In the following essay, Hill refutes point by point George Jean Nathan's charges that* The Crucible *fails to communicate its theme to audiences, that its characters are poorly developed, that it is propagandistic, and that it is badly constructed (see commentary dated 1953). Contrary to Nathan's view, Hill finds* The Crucible "*a thoroughly successful, provocative, and stimulating theater piece.*"]

The Crucible is too often spoken of as one of Arthur Miller's less successful plays. Its relative merits as compared with *Death of a Salesman* need not be argued here, but unquestionably the calumny that has been heaped upon it by well-meaning critics is little deserved—the play, however short it may fall of being *the* great American drama, is nevertheless a thoroughly successful, provocative, and stimulating theater piece. When competently performed, it can provide a deeply moving experience for the theatergoer.

The criticism of George Jean Nathan is perhaps typical [see commentary dated 1953]. Nathan levels four principal charges at the play, charges that in one form or another have been brought against it again and again by other critics. Nathan at least speaks from the advantageous position of having seen the play performed in New York, but too often it appears that wild charges are being flung at the play by critics who have never seen it staged—who have tried, perhaps inexpertly, to capture its full effectiveness from the printed page. This is a hazardous procedure at best, and in the case of *The Crucible* it has led to some gross distortions of what the play says and what it does. Let us examine each of Nathans' four charges and attempt to measure the validity of each.

In the first place, Nathan maintains that the power of the play is all "internal," that it is not communicated to an audience. If we take this criticism to imply that the action occurs within the mind and soul of the protagonist, then of course the statement that the play's power is internal is accurate, but that this in any sense damns the play is belied by the large number of plays throughout dramatic literature that have their action so centered and that are regarded as masterpieces. Most of the plays of Racine can be cited at once in support of this contention, together with selected plays of Euripides, Shakespeare, and Goethe, to name but a few. That *The Crucible* does not communicate this power to an audience is an allegation regarding which empirical evidence is lacking, but the long lines at the box offices of most theaters that have produced it since it "failed" on Broadway constitute, at least in part, a refutation of the charge. At one recent production of which the writer has first-hand knowledge, all previous attendance records were broken, and experienced theatergoers among the audience testified that they had enjoyed one of the rare and memorable theatrical experiences of their lives. This hardly describes a play that fails to communicate its power to the audience, whatever the quality of the production may have been.

The second charge brought by Nathan against *The Crucible,* and one that is almost universally pressed by those who are dissatisfied with the play, is that it suffers from poor character development. To this charge even the most vehement of its supporters must, in all justice, admit some truth. Elizabeth Proctor is a Puritan housewife, an honest woman, and a bit straight-laced; beyond this we know little of her. John Proctor is an upright and honest farmer confronted by a challenge to his honesty; more can and will be said of the struggles within his soul, but the fact remains that the multifaceted fascination of a Hamlet, an Oedipus, or even of a Willy Loman is indeed lacking. Danforth, on the other hand, is an all-too-recognizable human being: not at all the embodiment of all that is evil, but a conflicting mass of selfish motives and well-intentioned desires to maintain the status quo; not the devil incarnate, but a man convinced that a "good" end (maintaining the theocracy in colonial Massachusetts) can justify the most dubious means—in this case, the suborning of witnesses, the twisting of evidence, and the prostitution of justice. Reverend Hale, too, is a well developed and many-faceted character, a man who arrives upon the scene confident of his power to exorcise the Devil in whatever form he may

appear, and who by the end of the play can challenge every value for which a hero ever died: "Life is God's most precious gift; no principle, however glorious, may justify the taking of it" [Act IV].

Still, it must be admitted that the principal power of *The Crucible* does not lie in its character development. The characters are entirely adequate for the purposes for which Miller designed them, and no immutable law requires that every play depend upon characterization for its success, but certainly there is some justice in suggesting that *The Crucible* exhibits only a moderate degree of character development.

Nathan's next point of criticism is one that was heard from many of the New York critics at the time of the play's original production, but that has ceased to have much potency since the McCarthy era has passed into history. It was loudly proclaimed in 1953 that *The Crucible* was essentially propagandistic, that it struck too hard at an isolated phenomenon, and that thus it was at best a play of the immediate times and not for all time. The thirteen years that have passed since this charge was leveled, and the continued success of the play both in this country and abroad in the interim, drain from the assertion all of the efficacy that it may once have appeared to have. From the short view inescapably adopted by critics themselves caught up in the hysteria of McCarthyism, the play may well have seemed to push too hard the obvious parallels between witch-hunting in the Salem of 1692 and "witch-hunting" in the Washington and New York of 1952. If so, then we have simply one more reason to be grateful for the passing of this era, for unquestionably the play no longer depends upon such parallels. A whole generation of theater-goers has grown up in these intervening years to whom the name McCarthy is one vaguely remembered from newspaper accounts of the last decade, and who nevertheless find in *The Crucible* a powerful indictment of bigotry, narrow-mindedness, hypocrisy, and violation of due process of law, from whatever source these evils may spring. Unquestionably, if the play were tied inextricably to its alleged connection with a political phenomenon now buried (a connection that Miller denied all along), it would even today not have a very meaningful effect upon its audiences. And yet it does.

The fourth charge against the play, and the one brought by the more serious and insightful of the critics dealing with *The Crucible,* is at the same time the most challenging of the four. For Nathan, together with a host of other critics, attacks the basic structure of the play itself, claiming that it "draws up its big guns" too early in the play, and that by the end of the courtroom scene there is nowhere to go but down. This charge, indeed, gets at the very heart of the matter, and if it can be sustained it largely negates further argument regarding any relative merits that the play might exhibit. I submit, however, that the charge cannot be sustained—that, indeed, the critics adopting such an approach reveal a faulty knowledge of the play's structure and an inaccurate reading of its meaning. Indeed, Miller appears to me to have done a masterful job of sustaining a central action that by its very nature is "internal" and thus not conducive to easy dramatic development, and of sustaining this central action straight through to its logical conclusion at the end of the play.

The term "central action" is being used here in what I take to be its Aristotelian sense: one central objective that provides the play's plot structure with a beginning, a middle, and an end; when the objective is attained, the play is over. This central action may be described in the case of *The Crucible* as "to find John Proctor's soul," where the term "soul" is understood to mean Proctor's integrity, his sense of self-respect, what he himself variously calls his "honesty" and (finally) his "name." Proctor lost his soul, in this sense of the term, when he committed the crime of lechery with Abigail, and thus as the play opens there is wanted only a significant triggering incident to start Proctor actively on the search that will lead ultimately to his death. That this search for Proctor's soul will lead through the vagaries of a witch-hunt, a travesty of justice, and a clear choice between death and life without honor is simply the given circumstance of the play—no more germane to defining its central action than is the fact that Oedipus' search for the killer of Laius will lead through horror and incest to self-immolation. Thinking in these terms, then, it is possible to trace the development of this central action in a straight-forward and rather elementary manner.

The structure of the play can conveniently be analyzed in terms of the familiar elements of the well-made play. The initial scenes involving Parris, Abigail, the Putnams, and the other girls serve quite satisfactorily the demands of simple exposition, and pave the way smoothly for the entrance of John Proctor. We learn quickly and yet naturally that a group of girls under Abby's leadership have conjured the Devil and that now at least two of them have experienced hysterical reactions that are being widely interpreted in terms of witchcraft. We also learn, upon Proctor's entrance, of the sexual attraction that still exists between him and Abby, and of the consummation of this attraction that has left John feeling that he has lost his soul. The inciting incident then occurs when Abby assures John that the girls' hysteria has "naught to do with witchcraft," a bit of knowledge that is very shortly to try John's honesty and lead him inevitably to his death.

The rising action of the play continues, then, through the arrival of Hale, Abby's denunciation of certain of the Puritan women (taking her cue from Tituba's success) in order to remove any taint of guilt from herself, and eventually, in the next scene, to the accusation of witchcraft being directed at Elizabeth Proctor. The significant point here, however, is that the rising action continues through the bulk of the courtroom scene, as horror piles upon horror, accusation upon accusation, and complication upon complication, until the action reaches not a climax but a *turning point* when Elizabeth, who purportedly cannot tell a lie, does lie in a misguided attempt to save her husband. This act on her part constitutes a turning point because, from that moment on, Proctor's doom is sealed; no device short of a totally unsatisfactory *deus ex machina* can save him from his inevitable fate. The *central action* of the play is not yet completed however; Proctor has not yet found his soul, and even moderately skillful playing of the play's final scene can demonstrate quite clearly that this struggle

goes on right up to the moment at which Proctor rips up his confession and chooses death rather than dishonor. Thus, this prison scene does not, as some critics have charged, constitute some sort of extended denouement that cannot possibly live up in intensity to the excitement of the courtroom scene, but rather the scene is, in technical terms, the *falling action* of the play, moving inevitably from the turning point to the climax.

This structural significance of the prison scene may be observed in a careful reading of the play, but it is more readily apparent in a competent production. Thus, it is the business of the actor playing Proctor to convey to the audience the fact that signing the confession and then refusing to hand it over to Danforth is not, as has so often been charged, a delaying action and an anti-climactic complication on Miller's part, but rather a continuing and agonizing search on Proctor's part for his honesty—for the course of action that will be truest to his own honor and will recover for him his lost soul. In a dilemma for which there is no simple solution, Proctor first sees the efficacy of Hale's argument, that once life is gone there is no further or higher meaning. Feeling that his honesty has long since been compromised anyway, Proctor seriously feels a greater sense of dishonor is appearing to "go like a saint," as Rebecca and the others do, than in frankly facing up to his own dishonesty and saving his life. On the strength of this argument, he signs the confession. Yet, as Proctor stands there looking at his name on the paper (and here the way in which the actor works with this property becomes all-important), we have a visual, tangible stage metaphor for the struggle that is going on within him. Proctor, unable fully to express the significance of his own plight, cries out:

> Because it is my name! Because I cannot have another in my life! Because I lie and sign myself to lies! Because I am not worth the dust on the feet of them that hang! How may I live without my name? I have given you my soul; leave me my name!
>
> [Act IV]

The audience must see that this cry for his "name" is still the same search that has been at the heart of the entire play, and that here it has reached not some kind of anti-climax, but rather *the* climactic moment of the play.

But in stating outright that his confession is a lie (and this is the first moment at which he says so in so many words), Proctor triggers in Danforth the one reaction that seals his own doom. For Danforth, however narrow-minded and bigoted he may be, does indeed believe in the fundamental fact of witchcraft, and he cannot allow a confession that is frankly and openly a lie:

> Is that document a lie? If it is a lie I will not accept it! What say you? I will not deal in lies, Mister! . . . You will give me your honest confession in my hand, or I cannot keep you from the rope. . . . What way do you go, Mister?
>
> [Act IV]

Thus stretched to the utmost on the rack of his dilemma, Proctor makes the decision that costs him his life but restores to him his soul: he tears up the confession. The denouement following this climactic moment consumes not a whole scene as has frequently been charged, but a mere twelve lines. Proctor is led out to die, and Elizabeth speaks the epitaph that once again, finally, sums up the central action and significance of the play: "He have his goodness now. God forbid I take it from him!"

Thus, a close structural view of *The Crucible* reveals that this fourth charge against it is also an unfair and inaccurate one. The play, however it may appear in the reading, does not, in performance, rise to a climax in the courtroom scene that cannot be equalled. Certainly the tension of the courtroom scene is great; certainly the prison scene, if poorly performed, could be a letdown. But in a competent performance the inevitable movement from the turning point toward a climax, technically called the "falling action" but certainly involving no falling interest or intensity, continues through the prison scene to that moment at which Proctor rips up his confession, after which a quick denouement brings us to a satisfactory, and at the same time stunning, conclusion.

The play is certainly not one of the great plays of all time. Still, it has been maligned unduly by a series of critics who apparently were either too close to their critical trees to see the theatrical forest or were relying on an inadequate understanding of the play's structure. That this structure is not immediately apparent to the reader, but rather must be brought out in performance, may suggest some degree of weakness in Miller's dramaturgy, but is certainly not a damning weakness in itself. Plays are, after all, written to be performed on a stage, and the ultimate test of their success is their effectiveness under production conditions. *The Crucible* stands up very well to this test. (pp. 312-317)

> *Philip G. Hill, "The Crucible: A Structural View," in* Modern Drama, *Vol. X, No. 3, December, 1967, pp. 312-17.*

Robert A. Martin   (essay date 1977)

[*Martin is an American critic, educator, playwright, and noted Miller scholar. He has edited several works on theater, including* The Theater Essays of Arthur Miller *(1978),* Arthur Miller: New Perspectives *(1981), and* The Writer's Craft *(1982). In the following essay, Martin compares Miller's depiction of the witchcraft trials in* The Crucible *to seventeenth-century records and documents relating to the actual events. He defends Miller's revisions of the historical record in the play and contends that* The Crucible *"stands virtually alone as a dramatically coherent rendition of one of the most terrifying chapters in American history."*]

When *The Crucible* opened on January 22, 1953, the term "witchhunt" was nearly synonymous in the public mind with the Congressional investigations then being conducted into allegedly subversive activities. Arthur Miller's plays have always been closely identified with contemporary issues, and to many observers the parallel between the witchcraft trials at Salem, Massachusetts in 1692 and the current Congressional hearings was the central issue of the play.

Miller has said that he could not have written *The Cruci-*

ble at any other time, a statement which reflects both his reaction to the McCarthy era and the creative process by which he finds his way to the thematic center of a play. If it is true, however, that a play cannot be successful in its own time unless it speaks to its own time, it is also true that a play cannot endure unless it speaks to new audiences in new times. The latter truism may apply particularly to *The Crucible,* which is presently being approached more and more frequently as a cultural and historical study rather than as a political allegory.

Although *The Crucible* was written in response to its own time, popular interest in the Salem witchcraft trials had actually begun to surface long before the emergence of McCarthyism. There were at least two other plays based on the witchcraft trials that were produced shortly before *The Crucible* opened: *Child's Play* by Florence Stevenson was produced in November, 1952 at the Oklahoma Civic Playhouse; and *The Witchfinders* by Louis O. Coxe appeared at about the same time in a studio production at the University of Minnesota. Among numerous other works dealing with Salem witchcraft, a novel, *Peace, My Daughter* by Shirley Barker, had appeared as recently as 1949, and in the same year Marion L. Starkey had combined an interest in history and psychology to produce *The Devil in Massachusetts,* which was based on her extensive research of the original documents and records. Starkey's announced purpose was "to review the records in the light of the findings of modern psychology," and to supplement the work of earlier investigators by calling attention to "a number of vital primary sources of which they seem to have been ignorant."

The events that eventually found their way into *The Crucible* are largely contained in the massive two volume record of the trials located in the Essex County Archives at Salem, Massachusetts, where Miller went to do his research. Although he has been careful to point out in a prefatory note that *The Crucible* is not history in the academic sense, a study of the play and its sources indicates that Miller did his research carefully and well. He found in the records of the trials at Salem that between June 10 and September 22, 1692, nineteen men and women and two dogs were hanged for witchcraft, and one man was pressed to death for standing mute. Before the affair ended, fifty-five people had confessed to being witches, and another hundred and fifty were in jail awaiting trial.

Focusing primarily upon the story of John Proctor, one of the nineteen who were hanged, Miller almost literally retells the story of a panic-stricken society that held a doctrinal belief in the existence of the Devil and the reality of witchcraft. The people of Salem did not, of course, invent a belief in witchcraft; they were, however, the inheritors of a witchcraft tradition that had a long and bloody history in their native England and throughout most of Europe. To the Puritans of Massachusetts, witchcraft was as real a manifestation of the Devil's efforts to overthrow "God's kingdom" as the periodic raids of his Indian disciples against the frontier settlements.

There were, surprisingly, few executions for witchcraft in Massachusetts before 1692. According to George Lyman Kittredge in his *Witchcraft in Old and New England,* "not more than half-a-dozen executions can be shown to have occurred." But the people of Salem village in 1692 had recent and—to them—reliable evidence that the Devil was at work in the Massachusetts Bay Colony. In 1688 in Boston, four children of John Goodwin had been seriously afflicted by a "witch" named Glover, who was also an Irish washwoman. In spite of her hasty execution and the prayers of four of the most devout Boston ministers, the Goodwin children were possessed by spirits of the "invisible world" for some months afterward. One of the leading Puritan ministers of the time was Cotton Mather, who in 1689 published his observations on the incident in "Memorable Providences, Relating to Witchcrafts and Possession." Although the work was intended to warn against witchcraft, Mather's account can also be read as a handbook of instructions for feigning possession by demonic spirits. Among numerous other manifestations and torments, Mather reported that the Goodwin children were most often afflicted by "fits":

> Sometimes they would be Deaf, sometimes Dumb, and sometimes Blind, and often, all this at once. One while their Tongues would be drawn down their Throats; another-while they would be pull'd out upon their Chins, to a prodigious length. They would have their Mouths opened unto such a Wideness, that their Jaws went out of joint; and anon they would clap together again with a Force like that of a strong Spring Lock.

Four years later, in February, 1692, the daughter and niece of the Reverend Samuel Parris of Salem village began to have "fits" very similar to those experienced by the Goodwin children as reported and described by Mather. According to Marion Starkey, Parris had a copy of Mather's book, and, in addition, "the Parrises had probably had first-hand experience of the case, since they appear to have been living in Boston at the time. The little girls might even have been taken to see the hanging."

In spite of an apparent abundance of historical material, the play did not become dramatically conceivable for Miller until he came upon "a single fact" concerning Abigail Williams, the niece of Reverend Parris:

> It was that Abigail Williams, the prime mover of the Salem hysteria, so far as the hysterical children were concerned, had a short time earlier been the house servant of the Proctors and now was crying out Elizabeth Proctor as a witch; but more—it was clear from the record that with entirely uncharacteristic fastidiousness she was refusing to include John Proctor, Elizabeth's husband, in her accusations despite the urgings of the prosecutors. Why? I searched the records of the trials in the courthouse at Salem but in no other instance could I find such a careful avoidance of the implicating stutter, the murderous, ambivalent answer to the sharp questions of the prosecutors. Only here, in Proctor's case, was there so clear an attempt to differentiate between a wife's culpability and a husband's [Introduction to the *Collected Plays,* included in *The Theater Essays of Arthur Miller;* see Further Reading].

As in history, the play begins when the Reverend Samuel Parris begins to suspect that his daughter Betty has become ill because she and his niece Abigail Williams have "trafficked with spirits in the forest" [Act I]. The real danger Parris fears, however, is less from diabolical spirits than from the ruin that may fall upon him when his enemies learn that his daughter is suffering from the effects of witchcraft:

> PARRIS: There is a faction that is sworn to drive me from my pulpit. Do you understand that?
>
> ABIGAIL: I think so, sir.
>
> PARRIS: Now then, in the midst of such disruption, my own household is discovered to be the very center of some obscene practice. Abominations are done in the forest—
>
> ABIGAIL: It were sport, uncle!

As Miller relates at a later point in the play, Parris was a petty man who was historically in a state of continual bickering with his congregation over such matters as his salary, housing, and firewood. The irony of the above conversation in the play, however, is that while Parris is attempting to discover the "truth" to prevent it from damaging his already precarious reputation as Salem's minister, Abigail actually is telling him the historical truth when she says "it were sport." Whatever perverse motives may have subsequently prompted the adult citizens of Salem to cry "witch" upon their neighbors, the initiators of the Salem misfortune were young girls like Abigail Williams who began playing with spirits simply for the "sport" of it, as a release from an emotionally oppressive society. A portion of the actual trial testimony given in favor of Elizabeth Proctor (John Proctor's wife) by one Daniel Elliott suggests that initially, at least, not everyone accepted the girls' spectral visions without question:

> the testimony of Daniel Elliott, aged 27 years or thereabouts, who testifieth and saith that I being at the house of lieutenant Ingersoll on the 28 of March, in the year 1692, there being present one of the afflicted persons which cried out and said, there's Goody Proctor. William Raiment being there present, told the girl he believed she lied, for he saw nothing; then Goody Ingersoll told the girl she told a lie, for there was nothing; then the girl said that she did it for sport, they must have some sport.

Miller's addition in *The Crucible* of an adulterous relationship between Abigail Williams and Proctor serves primarily as a dramatically imperative motive for Abigail's later charges of witchcraft against Elizabeth Proctor. Although it might appear that Miller is rewriting history for his own dramatic purposes by introducing a sexual relationship between Abigail and Proctor, his invention of the affair is psychologically and historically appropriate. As he makes clear in the prefatory note preceding the play, "dramatic purposes have sometimes required many characters to be fused into one; the number of girls . . . has been reduced; Abigail's age has been raised; . . . " Although Miller found that Abigail's refusal to testify against Proctor was the single historical and dramatic "fact" he was looking for, there are two additional considerations that make adultery and Abigail's altered age plausible within the historical context of the events.

The first is that Mary Warren, in the play and in history, was simultaneously an accuser in court and a servant in Proctor's household. If an adulterous affair was probable, it would more likely have occurred between Mary Warren and Proctor than between Abigail Williams and Proctor; but it could easily have occurred. At the time, Mary Warren was a fairly mature young woman who would have had the features Miller has represented in Abigail: every emotional and sexual impulse, as well as the opportunity to be involved with Proctor. Historically, it was Mary Warren who attempted to stop the proceedings as early as April 19 by stating during her examination in court that the afflicted girls "did but dissemble": "Afterwards she started up, and said I will speak and cried out, Oh! I am sorry for it, I am sorry for it, and wringed her hands, and fell a little while into a fit again and then came to speak, but immediately her teeth were set, and then she fell into a violent fit and cried out, oh Lord help me! Oh Good Lord save me!" As in the play, the rest of the girls prevailed by immediately falling into fits and spontaneously accusing her of witchcraft. As her testimony of April 21 and later indicates, however, she soon returned to the side of her fellow accusers. On June 30, she testified:

> The deposition of Mary Warren aged 20 years here testifieth. I have seen the apparition of John Proctor senior among the witches and he hath often tortured me by pinching me and biting me and choking me, and pressing me on my Stomach till the blood came out of my mouth and also I saw him torture Mis Pope and Mercy Lewis and John Indian upon the day of his examination and he hath also tempted me to write in his book, and to eat bread which he brought to me, which I refusing to do, Jno Proctor did most grievously torture me with a variety of tortures, almost Ready to kill me.

Miller has reduced Mary Warren's lengthy and ambiguous trial testimony to four pages in the play by focusing on her difficulty in attempting to tell the truth after the proceedings were under way. The truth that Mary has to tell—"It were only sport in the beginning, sir"—is the same that Abigail tried to tell Parris earlier; but the telling has become compounded by the courtroom presence of Proctor, Parris, Hathorne and Danforth (two of the judges), the rest of the afflicted girls, and the spectators. In a scene taken directly from the trial records, Mary confesses that she and the other girls have been only pretending and that they have deceived the court. She has never seen the spirits or apparitions of the witches:

> HAWTHORNE: How could you think you saw them unless you saw them?
>
> MARY WARREN: I—I cannot tell how, but I did. I—I heard the other girls screaming, and you, Your Honor, you seemed to believe them, and I—It were only sport in the beginning, sir, but then the whole world cried spirits, spirits, and I—I promise you, Mr. Danforth, I only thought I saw them but I did not.
>
> [Act III]

The second, additional consideration is that although Miller has raised Abigail's age from her actual eleven to seventeen, and has reduced the number of girls in the play to five only, such alterations for purposes of dramatic motivation and compression do not significantly affect the psychological or historical validity of the play. As the trial records clearly establish, individual and family hostilities played a large role in much of the damaging testimony given against those accused of witchcraft. Of the ten girls who were most directly involved in crying out against the witches, only three—Betty Parris (nine years old), Abigail Williams (eleven years), and Ann Putnam (twelve years)—were below the age of sexual maturity. The rest were considerably older: Mary Walcott and Elizabeth Booth were both sixteen; Elizabeth Hubbard was seventeen; Susanna Sheldon was eighteen; Mercy Lewis was nineteen; Sarah Churchill and Mary Warren (Proctor's servant) were twenty. In a time when marriage and motherhood were not uncommon at the age of fourteen, the hypothesis of repressed sexuality emerging disguised into the emotionally charged atmosphere of witchcraft and Calvinism does not seem unlikely; it seems, on the contrary, an inevitable supposition. And it may be worth pointing out in this context that Abigail Williams was not the only one of the girls who refused to include John Proctor in her accusations against his wife, Elizabeth. In her examination of April 21, Mary Warren testified that her mistress was a witch and that "her master had told her that he had been about sometimes to make away with himself because of his wife's quarreling with him, . . ." A few lines later the entry reads: "but she would not own that she knew her master to be a witch or wizzard."

With the exception of Abigail and Proctor's adultery, the events and characters of *The Crucible* are not so much "invented" data in a fictional sense as highly compressed representations of the underlying forces of hatred, hysteria, and fear that paralyzed Salem during the spring and summer of 1692. And even in this context Abigail Williams's characterization in the play may be more restrained in the light of the records than Miller's dramatization suggests. For example, one of the major witnesses against John Proctor was twelve year old Ann Putnam, who testified on June 30 that "on the day of his examination I saw the apparition of Jno: Proctor senior go and afflict and most grievously torture the bodies of Mistress Pope, Mary Walcott, Mercy Lewis, Abigail Williams. . . ." In projecting several of the girls into Abigail, Miller has used the surface of the trial records to suggest that her hatred for Proctor's wife is a dramatic equivalent for the much wider spread hatred and tension that existed within the Salem community. Abigail, although morally corrupt, ironically insists upon her "good" name, and reveals at an early point in the play that she hates Elizabeth Proctor for ruining her reputation:

> PARRIS: [*to the point*] Abigail, is there any other cause than you have told me, for your being discharged from Goody Proctor's service? I have heard it said, and I tell you as I heard it, that she comes so rarely to the church this year for she will not sit so close to something soiled. What signified that remark?

ABIGAIL: She hates me uncle, she must, for I would not be her slave. It's a bitter woman, a lying, cold, sniveling woman, and I will not work for such a woman!

[Act I]

On a larger scale, Miller brings together the forces of personal and social malfunction through the arrival of the Reverend John Hale, who appears, appropriately, in the midst of a bitter quarrel among Proctor, Parris, and Thomas Putnam over deeds and land boundaries. Hale, in life as in the play, had encountered witchcraft previously and was called to Salem to determine if the Devil was in fact responsible for the illness of the afflicted children. In the play, he conceives of himself, Miller says, "much as a young doctor on his first call":

[*He appears loaded down with half a dozen heavy books.*]

HALE: Pray you, someone take these!

PARRIS: [*delighted*] Mr. Hale! Oh! it's good to see you again! [*Taking some books*] My, they're heavy!

HALE: [*setting down his books*] They must be; they are weighted with authority.

[Act I]

Hale's entrance at this particular point in the play is significant in that he interrupts an argument based on private and secular interests to bring "authority" to the question of witchcraft. His confidence in himself and his subsequent examination of the girls and Tituba (Parris's slave who inadvertently started the entire affair) represent and foreshadow the arrival of outside religious authority in the community. As an outsider who has come to weigh the evidence, Hale also helps to elevate the issue from a local to a regional level, and from an unofficial to an official theological inquiry. His heavy books of authority also symbolically anticipate the heavy authority of the judges who, as he will realize too late, are as susceptible to misinterpreting testimony based on spectral evidence as he is:

HALE: [*with a tasty love of intellectual pursuit*] Here is all the invisible world, caught, defined, and calculated. In these books the Devil stands stripped of all his brute disguises. Here are all your familiar spirits—your incubi and succubi; your witches that go by land, by air, and by sea; your wizards of the night and of the day. Have no fear now—we shall find him out if he has come among us, and I mean to crush him utterly if he has shown his face!

[Act I]

The Reverend Hale is an extremely interesting figure historically, and following the trials he set down an account of his repentance entitled "A Modest Inquiry into the Nature of Witchcraft" (Boston, 1702). Although he was at first as overly zealous in his pursuit of witches as everyone else, very much as Miller has portrayed him in *The Crucible,* Hale began to be tormented by doubts early in the proceedings. His uncertainty concerning the reliability of the witnesses and their testimony was considerably heightened when his own wife was also accused of being a witch. Hale appears to have been as tortured spiritually and as

dedicated to the "middle way" in his later life as Miller has portrayed him in *The Crucible.* Five years after Salem, he wrote in his "Inquiry":

The middle way is commonly the way of truth. And if any can shew me a better middle way than I have here laid down, I shall be ready to embrace it: But the conviction must not be by vinegar or drollery, but by strength of argument. . . . I have had a deep sence of the sad consequence of mistakes in matters Capital; and their impossibility of recovering when compleated. And what grief of heart it brings to a tender conscience, to have been unwittingly encouraging of the Sufferings of the innocent.

Hale further commented that although he presently believed the executions to be the unfortunate result of human error, the integrity of the court officials was unquestionable: "I observed in the prosecution of these affairs, that there was in the Justices, Judges and others concerned, a conscientious endeavour to do the thing that was right. And to that end they consulted the Presidents [Precedents] of former times and precepts laid down by Learned Writers about Witchcraft."

In *The Crucible,* Hale's examination of Tituba is very nearly an edited transcription of her testimony at the trial of Sarah Good, who is the first person Abigail accuses of consorting with the Devil. At the time of the trials, Sarah Good had long been an outcast member of the Salem community, "unpopular because of her slothfulness, her sullen temper, and her poverty; she had recently taken to begging, an occupation the Puritans detested." When she was about to be hanged, her minister, the Reverend Nicholas Noyes, made a last appeal to her for a confession and said he knew she was a witch. Her prophetic reply was probably seen later as proof of her guilt when she said to Noyes: "you are a lyer; I am no more a Witch than you are a Wizard, and if you take away my Life, God will give you Blood to drink." A few years after she was hanged, Reverend Noyes died as a result of a sudden and severe hemorrhage.

Largely through the Reverend Hale, Miller reflects the change that took place in Salem from an initial belief in the justice of the court to a suspicion that testimony based on spectral evidence was insufficient for execution. This transformation begins to reveal itself in Act Two, as Hale tells Francis Nurse that the court will clear his wife of the charges against her: "Believe me, Mr. Nurse, if Rebecca Nurse be tainted, then nothing's left to stop the whole green world from burning. Let you rest upon the justice of the court; the court will send her home, I know it." By Act Three however, Hale's confidence in the justice of the court has been badly shaken by the arrest and conviction of people like Rebecca Nurse who were highly respected members of the church and community. Hale, like his historical model, has discovered that "the whole green world" is burning indeed, and fears that he has helped to set the fire.

Partially as a result of Hale's preliminary investigation into the reality of Salem witchcraft, the Court of Oyer and Terminer was appointed to hear testimony and conduct the examinations. The members of the court immediately encountered a serious obstacle: namely, that although the Bible does not define witchcraft, it states unequivocally that "Thou shalt not suffer a witch to live" (Exodus 22:18). As Proctor attempts to save his wife from hanging, Hale attempts to save his conscience by demanding visible proof of the guilt of those who have been convicted on the basis of spectral testimony:

> HALE: Excellency, I have signed seventy-two death warrants; I am a minister of the Lord, and I dare not take a life without there be a proof so immaculate no slightest qualm of conscience may doubt it.
>
> DANFORTH: Mr. Hale, you surely do not doubt my justice.
>
> HALE: I have this morning signed away the soul of Rebecca Nurse, Your Honor. I'll not conceal it, my hand shakes yet as with a wound!
>   [Act III]

At first, the witches who were brought to trial and convicted were generally old and eccentric women like Sarah Good who were of questionable character long before the trials began. But people like Rebecca Nurse and John Proctor were not. As Miller has Parris say to Judge Hathorne in Act Four: "it were another sort that hanged till now. Rebecca Nurse is no Bridget that lived three year with Bishop before she married him. John Proctor is not Isaac Ward that drank his family to ruin." In late June, Rebecca Nurse was found guilty and sentenced to hang after an earlier verdict of "not guilty" was curiously reversed. Her minister, the Reverend Nicholas Noyes again, decided along with his congregation that she should be excommunicated for the good of the church. Miller seems to have been especially moved by her character and her almost unbelievable trial and conviction, as he indicates by his comments in the "Introduction" and his interpolated remarks in Act One. On Tuesday, July 19, 1692, she was hanged on Gallows Hill along with four others, all women. She was seventy-one years old. After the hanging, according to Starkey:

> The bodies of the witches were thrust into a shallow grave in a crevice of Gallows Hill's outcropping of felsite. But the body of Rebecca did not remain there. Her children bided their time . . . and at night when the crowds and the executioners had gone home again, they gathered up the body of their mother and took it home. Just where they laid it none can know, for this was a secret thing and not even Parris, whose parsonage was not a quarter of a mile up the road past the grove where the Nurses buried their dead, must see that a new grave had been opened and prayers said. This was the hour and the power of darkness when a son could not say where he had buried his mother.

Historically, Proctor was even more of a victim of the laws of his time than Miller details in *The Crucible.* Although the real John Proctor fought against his arrest and conviction as fervently as anyone could under the circumstances, he, like Miller's Proctor, was adamant in his refusal to confess to witchcraft because he did not believe it existed.

And although fifty-two of his friends and neighbors risked their own safety to sign a petition in his behalf, nothing was done to re-examine the evidence against him. Ironically, Proctor's wife—in whose interest he had originally become involved in the affair—had become pregnant and, although sentenced, would never hang. She was eventually released after enduring her husband's public execution, the birth of her child in prison, and the seizure and loss of all her possessions.

Under the law, the goods and property of witches could be confiscated after their trial and conviction. In Proctor's case, however, the sheriff did not wait for the trial or the conviction. A contemporary account of the seizure indicates that neither Proctor nor his wife were ever expected to return from prison:

> John Proctor and his Wife being in Prison, the Sheriff came to his House and seized all the Goods, Provisions, and Cattle that he could come at, and sold some of the Cattle at half price, and killed others, and put them up for the West-Indies; threw out the Beer out of a Barrel, and carried away the Barrel; emptied a Pot of Broath, and took away the Pot, and left nothing in the House for the support of the Children: No part of the said Goods are known to be returned.

(The Proctors had five children, the youngest of whom were three and seven.) Along with three other men and one woman, John Proctor was hanged on August 19. On September 22, seven more witches and one wizard were hanged, and then the executions suddenly ended.

Miller has symbolized all the judges of the witchcraft trials in the figures of Danforth and Hathorne (Nathaniel Hawthorne's ancestor), and presented them as being more "official" in a legal sense than their historical models actually were. None of the judges in the trials had any legal training, and, apparently, neither had anyone else who was administering the law in the Massachusetts Bay Colony. According to Starkey, the curious nature of the trials was in part due to the Puritans' limited understanding of the law, their contempt for lawyers, and their nearly total reliance on the Bible as a guide for all matters of legal and moral authority:

> The Puritans had a low opinion of lawyers and did not permit the professional practice of law in the colony. In effect the administration of the law was in the hands of laymen, most of them second-generation colonists who had an incomplete grasp of current principles of English jurisdiction. For that matter, this chosen people, this community which submitted itself to the direct rule of God, looked less to England for its precepts than to God's ancient and holy word. So far as was practicable the Puritans were living by a legal system that antedated the Magna Carta by at least two millennia, the Decalogue and the tribal laws codified in the Pentateuch.

As historians occasionally have pointed out, the executions did not stop because the people in Massachusetts suddenly ceased to believe in either the Devil or witchcraft; they stopped, simply and ironically, because of a legal question. There never was any doubt for most people living in New England in 1692 whether or not witchcraft was real or whether witches should be executed; the question centered around the reliability of spectral evidence coming from the testimony of the afflicted. It was largely through the determinations of Increase Mather and fourteen other Boston ministers that such testimony was declared to be insufficient for conviction and therefore became inadmissable as evidence. It was better, they concluded, to allow ten witches to escape than to hang one innocent person. In late October, Governor Phips officially dismissed the Court of Oyer and Terminer, and—although the trials continued through the following April—in May, 1693 he issued a proclamation discharging all the remaining "witches" and pardoning those who had fled the colony rather than face arrest, trial, and certain conviction.

Miller has said that if he were to rewrite *The Crucible,* he would make an open thematic issue of the evil he now believes to be represented by the Salem judges. His altered viewpoint toward the play may be accounted for partially as a reconsideration of his intensive examination of the trial records which, he has said, do not "reveal any mitigation of the unrelieved, straightforward, and absolute dedication to evil displayed by the judges of these trials and the prosecutors. After days of study it became quite incredible how perfect they were in this respect."

Miller's subsequent view of evil, however, did not come entirely from his study of the trial records. Between writing *The Crucible* in 1952 and producing the "Introduction" to the *Collected Plays* in 1957, he underwent a personal crucible when he appeared before the House Un-American Activities Committee in 1956. Although the experience was understandably not without its effect on his later attitude toward Congressional "witchhunters," it should, nevertheless, be considered in relation to his comments on the judges and evil quoted above. A more accurate reflection of Miller's attitude while writing *The Crucible* appears perhaps most clearly in the account published in February, 1953 of his thoughts while standing on the rock at Gallows Hill:

> Here hung Rebecca, John Proctor, George Jacobs—people more real to me than the living can ever be. The sense of a terrible marvel again; that people could have such a belief in themselves and in the rightness of their consciences as to give their lives rather than say what they thought was false. Or, perhaps, they only feared Hell so much? Yet, Rebecca said, and it is written in the record, "I cannot belie myself." And she knew it would kill her. . . . The rock stands forever in Salem. They knew who they were. Nineteen ["Journey to *The Crucible,*" included in *Theater Essays*].

Like the rock at Salem, *The Crucible* has endured beyond the immediate events of its own time. If it was originally seen as a political allegory, it is presently seen by contemporary audiences almost entirely as a distinguished American play by an equally distinguished American playwright. As one of the most frequently produced plays in the American theater, *The Crucible* has attained a life of its own; one that both interprets and defines the cultural

and historical background of American society. Given the general lack of plays in the American theater that have seriously undertaken to explore the meaning and significance of the American past in relation to the present, *The Crucible* stands virtually alone as a dramatically coherent rendition of one of the most terrifying chapters in American history. (pp. 279-90)

> *Robert A. Martin, "Arthur Miller's 'The Crucible': Background Sources," in* Modern Drama, *Vol. XX, No. 3, September, 1977, pp. 279-92.*

Jean-Marie Bonnet   (essay date 1982)

[*In the following essay, Bonnet demonstrates how in* The Crucible *Miller bridges the gap between social drama and drama of the individual. In this work, the critic argues, "Proctor's own problem is inseparable from that of the community: his own personal dilemma is transformed into a social crisis."*]

The Crucible presents us with the picture of a small village falling prey to a collective fear that witchcraft is about, lurking in some of its citizens. A specialist in demonology, the revered Hale, is summoned to seek out the devil and a court of justice is set up to root out the evil by hanging witches. The play constantly shifts between two related poles: the individuals must be purged separately so that the community as a whole may be preserved. We then may wonder whether the play is about an individual's discovery of his true self or about a whole community getting out of hand. As Northrop Frye has pointed out [in *Fables of Identity: Studies in Poetic Mythology*], *The Crucible* has the 'content' of 'social hysteria' but the 'form' of a 'purgatorial or triumphant tragedy'. Arthur Miller himself is of no help for the critic in this matter since he has made two entirely contradictory statements on the subject. In the preface to his *Collected Plays* [included in *The Theater Essays of Arthur Miller;* see Further Reading], he wrote: 'The central impulse for writing at all was not the social but the interior psychological question of the guilt residing in Salem', and, a few years later, in his interview with Richard I. Evans [in Evans's *Psychology and Arthur Miller*] he said that ' . . . the predominant emphasis in writing the play was on the conflict between people rather than the conflict within somebody'.

As Miller's statements clearly show, it is quite difficult to situate the play in a fixed traditional pattern: is it tragic drama involving a hero confronting more than human forces, or drama involving a whole group of people? Miller's play seems in fact to straddle both types and it would be hard to draw a clear line between the two. I shall endeavour here to analyze this fundamental duality in *The Crucible,* and show that the play is highly successful though not easily classified within the traditional categories of drama.

That *The Crucible* is a play about the individual and society is obvious if only by the wide scope of characters presented to the audience: they range from farmers and maids to ministers and court-officials. There are twenty-one characters in all, not to mention the people referred to in the course of the play. A whole town is involved, not simply one family whose drama might be representative of the plight of the community.

The twofold nature of the drama is stressed right from the beginning by Miller himself in his authorial statements accompanying the first act. In a fairly long disquisition sketching out the main features of Salem, Mass., in 1692, Miller is very careful to give his reader a few necessary facts concerning the life of the community. (Miller's statements are available to the reader of the play only; nothing is mentioned of the background when the play is performed on stage). His comments are not those of the 'objective' historian, however, for they serve to prepare the readers for the crisis to come. Miller's commentary is a selection of facts chosen primarily for their significance at the time of the crisis, not for their intrinsic importance. Miller first lays stress on the importance of the sense of 'community'. The action takes place in 1692 at a time when people were living in a very closely knit society, based on Puritan principles, and, consequently, prone to a certain amount of intolerance towards any form of opposition or dissent. Discipline and obedience were the primary rules, for society was based on an implicit motto saying that ' . . . in unity lay the best promise of safety' [Act I]. Such an adamantly rigid society of course implies that any form of individuality will be considered subversive and dangerous. Thus, paradoxically, such a society is likely to generate suspicion among its members, to develop, as Miller points out, ' . . . a predilection for minding other people's business' [Act I]. We have therefore an essentially explosive situation where unity at once ensures and endangers the individual's safety. It is precisely the potentially explosive situation which triggers off the whole drama in *The Crucible,* where the general tragedy can be seen as a magnification of petty, selfish quarrels occasioned because the individual's desires are curbed by the authoritative state. Those squabbles gradually develop into a wider, extensive quarrel that soon gets out of hand both for the individuals and for the society, and becomes impossible to control—the result being, of course, an intensification of the already exaggerated authority. In other words, the play seems to portray some sort of malignant process in which essentially personal grievances are inflated to socially important hatreds.

The main cause of this gangrenous process is a mixture of individual and social forces. It first appears to be Abigail, a girl who has an 'endless capacity for dissembling' [Act I], out of lust for John and out of jealousy for Elizabeth Proctor. Then, this malignancy gradually feeds on the grievances of all the other inhabitants of the community and becomes a social phenomenon: thus we have the Putnams' greed for land, the thirst for revenge aimed at Martha Corey because of a sick pig, the boundary disputes between the Putnams and the Nurses, the argument over lumber between the Proctors, the Coreys and the Putnams, and Mrs. Putnam's cantankerous bitterness at having been able to keep only one of her numerous children alive. All these squabbles seem to be occasions seized upon by individuals in order to assert their rights in a basically oppressive society. A constant lust for power and a pervasive acquisitiveness compensate for their low station. For the women, such as Abigail, witchcraft may be a way of asserting their will and their power in a system centered on and dominated by men.

Thus we see how a society, because of its tight unity, may be subject to ruin as soon as a breach occurs in its defences. This kind of extreme order generates its own undermining germs: the slightest gap in the bulwark is an outlet for all individual and hitherto pent-up passions. Thus jealousy or envy can be seen to fragment friendship and mutual respect, the true cement of unity. Such a rigid state is open to all forms of betrayals and accusations. Every single person can avail himself of the opportunity to wreak his own personal vengeance on his neighbour. At the same time that fallen state of things becomes a social matter, in which even justice is infected by the same process and becomes twisted, warped in its turn.

If one leaves out the first act, which serves as an overture, the three remaining acts all take place—literally or symbolically—in court. At the Proctors', the scene of Act Two, the house is soon equated to a court: in Proctor's own words, it is ' . . . as though he comes into a court when [he comes] into his house'. The same idea is carried on a few moments later in his reiterated 'I confessed, I confessed', which prefigures the future confessions to be exacted from all the victims. The equation with the court is pushed even further when Miller makes Elizabeth describe her husband as having to appear before the tribunal of his own conscience: 'The magistrate sits in your heart that judges you', she tells him; and there we touch the core of the drama, Proctor's case being both an entirely personal drama as well as a social one. This arraignment of Proctor in his own house and in his own conscience helps to convey how closely privates lives are linked with society. Proctor's own problem is inseparable from that of the community: his own personal dilemma transformed into a social crisis, is thereby intensified to a dramatic pitch.

This heightening is clearly demonstrated by situating the fourth act in a prison cell, for it enhances the symmetry of the picture. The fourth act is a pendant to the second act, in that it reverts intensively to Proctor's case. There is a narrowing focus, after the third act, which is placed in an official court with the community at large attending and which culminates in hysteria at the close. The fourth act is not only a static pendant to the second act, but the outcome of what was latent in it, that is, an individual's hesitations between preserving his own integrity at the expense of his life or abandoning it to save his life. It illustrates how conscience, which is the essential being of any man, is manipulated by society. And ending the play in a prison cell is the fitting symbolical way of showing it: for a cell is a limited space and therefore retains some sort of privacy coordinate with matters of private importance; but, at the same time, it is also an official place that can be invaded by the official authorities. Conscience, then, is 'no longer a private matter but one of state administration'. If the play ends with the personal victory of an individual, it also stresses the victory of social authorities over him. Thus the end is double-edged and the two aspects cannot be separated without running the risk of splitting the play in half, forcing a needless dichotomy.

The role of each individual in the development of the hysterical crisis 'walking' Salem can be pointed out by studying Miller's way of depicting his townspeople. As Edward Murray has suggested, most of them appear as static individuals, whereas Proctor and to a lesser extent Elizabeth, are well-rounded characters undergoing a process of evolution [see Further Reading]. All characters, except Proctor, are presented either as anonymous victims, as people whose pleading for honesty must appear as totally inadequate before a warped court, or as people with rigid unbending attitudes, whether for honest (Rebecca Nurse) or dishonest (Danforth, Abigail) reasons. The static character of individuals is most clearly observed through a study of the language of the play. The whole drama, we could say, is set off, conducted and concluded by the mere force of language.

Language can first be seen as the mainspring of the action. For, the witch hunt does not get its initial impulse from fact; it is based merely on a report: 'the rumour of witchcraft is all about', as Abigail has it [Act I]. A whole community is thus endangered by hearsay which develops into hysteria. Even Danforth perceives it although he fails to rightly understand this basic truth:

> . . . witchcraft is ipso facto, on its face and by its nature, an invisible crime, is it not? Therefore who may possibly be witness to it? The witch and the victim.
>
> [Act III]

There is never any palpable evidence of anything throughout the play, and each individual is required to tell a lie if he wants to save his life. In that sense, language is the demonic force of the play; everything rests on it, and this is true for all characters, on whichever side they stand. Thus Abigail's power over the girls and also over Danforth and the whole community ('Let *you* beware, Mr. Danforth' [Act III]) is essentially verbal. Everyone knows how mobs can easily be mesmerized by the mere power of words, by oratorical gifts which devilishly seduce rational minds. This is precisely the way she acts: at the end of Act One, her hysterical (or rather mock-hysterical) incantatory repetitions of the single phrase 'I saw [so and so] with the Devil', simply degenerate into a cascade of accusations. It is through her perverted use of language that she kindles the fire of hysteria and retains power over the party of deluded girls. She also makes use of language as a way of ensuring her own safety. By pretending she is offended by Danforth's suspicion ('Why this—this—is a base question, sir' [Act III]), she averts his questions and shamefacedly secures her purpose and her life.

Her attitude contrasts with that of Proctor, who is too honest to be artful and delude the judges. Proctor's speech, like those of many other of the accused (like Rebecca's, for instance), is too frank and honest and is no match for the corrupted language of justice. In the court-scenes, language has reached a point when it is of no help to anyone; all means of communication (and understanding) between the individual and society through this medium are blocked. The authorities suggest the answers, or distort and discard all evidence by the mere reply: 'This is contempt of the court.' They thereby cut all answers short, do not allow the accused to express their opinion fully, or lead them into mazes of syllogisms: as Proctor sees it clearly, it is a dead end, 'the accuser is always holy' [Act II].

Hence the necessity of confessing and the misunderstanding over the idea of 'name' between Proctor and the Judges. The word 'name' means at once something entirely personal, but also something social, for it has a value in so far as it distinguishes each individual in society. Besides, it also implies fame, reputation, and, for Proctor, self-integrity. It is in the conjunction of all these aspects that there is a discrepancy between Proctor's view and that of the judges. In other words, when the authorities exact confessions, their preoccupation is with the actual 'saying' of it, even if this means lying on the part of the individual confessing. Confessing a lie is the new institutionalized type of social adjustment as well as a safeguard for life. Those opposing it are inevitably endangering their lives, and Proctor's courage lies precisely in his rejection of a society which institutionalizes falsehood. For him his 'name' does not only mean reputation, but truth to oneself and others. When he refuses to give away other people's names it is because he 'likes not to spoil their names' [Act IV]; and when he refuses to 'sign his name', it is to save his own integrity before God and himself.

This linguistic misunderstanding sums up the conflict between both parties; it is highly ironical since Elizabeth's one lie is tragically believed by the court and, for once, taken as truth.

The play is thus bi-focal, and continually shifting its view from the personal to the public; individuals trying to assert their individuality are strangled by the web of social constraints. The structure seems to point to the personal victory of one character, who has come to a heightened self-awareness and prefers to preserve his own dignity rather than live in a society where falsehood has achieved the status of an institution. We may wonder, however, if this sacrifice will prove beneficial to the community as Hale's doubting words tend to suggest: 'What profit him to bleed. Shall the dust praise him? Shall the worms declare his truth?' [Act IV].

Indeed nobody, even Proctor, is allowed to come out whole at the end of the play, and the 'crucible' seems to be that of society, as well as that of its individuals. (pp. 32-6)

> *Jean-Marie Bonnet, "Society vs. The Individual in Arthur Miller's 'The Crucible'," in* English Studies, *Netherlands, Vol. 63, No. 1, February, 1982, pp. 32-6.*

FURTHER READING

AUTHOR COMMENTARY

Carlisle, Olga and Rose Styron. "Arthur Miller." In *Writers at Work: The "Paris Review" Interviews,* Third Series, edited by Alfred Kazin, pp. 197-230. New York: The Viking Press, 1967.

> Reprint of a wide-ranging 1966 interview, covering such topics as Miller's own plays and theories of drama, the works of other writers, and the relationship of politics to art.

Martin, Robert A. "Arthur Miller and the Meaning of Tragedy." *Modern Drama* XIII, No. 1 (May 1970): 34-9.

> Interview with Miller in which the playwright discusses the relation of his dramas to his own theories of tragedy.

———— and Richard D. Meyer. "Arthur Miller on Plays and Playwriting." *Modern Drama* XIX, No. 4 (December 1976): 375-84.

> Conversation held in 1974 between Miller and students and faculty of the University of Michigan.

Miller, Arthur. *The Theater Essays of Arthur Miller,* edited by Robert A. Martin. New York: The Viking Press, 1978, 401 p.

> Essential collection of Miller's theoretical writings, including "Tragedy and the Common Man," "On Social Plays," "The Family in Modern Drama," "Introduction to the *Collected Plays,*" and other pieces. This volume includes newly written introductions by Miller and the editor as well as a bibliography of Miller's works and cast lists for the original productions of his plays.

Roudané, Matthew C. "An Interview with Arthur Miller." *Michigan Quarterly Review* XXIV, No. 3 (Summer 1985): 373-89.

> Interview conducted in 1983 in which the author discusses his works from 1947's *All My Sons* to 1982's *Elegy for a Lady* and *Some Kind of Love Story.*

OVERVIEWS AND GENERAL STUDIES

Bentley, Eric. *What is Theatre? Incorporating the Dramatic Event.* New York: Limelight Editions, 1984, 491 p.

> Influential study by the noted critic that features discussions of several of Miller's works, including *Salesman, Crucible, A View from the Bridge,* and *After the Fall.*

Corrigan, Robert W., ed. *Arthur Miller: A Collection of Critical Essays.* Englewood Cliffs, N.J.: Prentice-Hall, 1969, 176 p.

> Significant collection of essays about Miller and his works written by a variety of critics up to the mid-1960s.

Hogan, Robert. *Arthur Miller.* University of Minnesota Pamphlets on American Writers, No. 40. Minneapolis: University of Minnesota Press, 1964, 48 p.

> Concise overview of Miller's life and works.

Martin, Robert A., ed. *Arthur Miller: New Perspectives.* Englewood Cliffs, N.J.: Prentice-Hall, 1982, 223 p.

> Updates Corrigan's collection (see entry above), featuring more recent analyses.

Martine, James J. *Critical Essays on Arthur Miller.* Boston: G. K. Hall & Co., 1979, 217 p.

> Worthwhile anthology that includes reviews of Miller's plays in performance as well critical studies.

Moss, Leonard. *Arthur Miller.* New York: Twayne Publishers, 1967, 160 p.

> Valuable work that includes both biographical and critical material as well as a selected bibliography.

Murray, Edward. *Arthur Miller, Dramatist.* New York: Frederick Ungar Publishing Co., 1967, 186 p.

> Important study featuring individual chapters on seven of Miller's works, including *All My Sons, Salesman, Crucible, A Memory of Two Mondays, A View From the Bridge, After the Fall,* and *Incident at Vichy.*

Sievers, W. David. "Tennessee Williams and Arthur Miller." In his *Freud on Broadway: A History of Psychoanalysis and the American Drama,* pp. 370-99. New York: Hermitage House, 1955.

> Contains psychological analyses of the father-son relationships in *All My Sons* and *Death of a Salesman,* and of the social hysteria in *The Crucible.*

DEATH OF A SALESMAN

Bates, Barclay W. "The Lost Past in *Death of a Salesman.*" *Modern Drama* XI, No. 2 (September 1968): 164-72.

> Claims that Willy Loman is "anachronistic," a character who cherishes out-of-date values. The salesman, Bates maintains, "was born as the American frontier era drew to a close. Growing up in a transitional period, he found no suitable identity" and thus has become an outcast in his own time.

Eisinger, Chester E. "Focus on Arthur Miller's *Death of a Salesman:* The Wrong Dreams." In *American Dreams, American Nightmares,* edited by David Madden, pp. 370-99. Carbondale: Southern Illinois University Press, 1970.

> Examines the theme of dream versus reality in *Salesman,* paying particular attention to the competition between the "urban dream of business success" and the "rural-agrarian dream of open space, a right relation to nature."

Jacobson, Irving. "Family Dreams in *Death of a Salesman.*" *American Literature* XLVII, No. 2 (May 1975): 247-58.

> Investigates the Lomans' hopes and aspirations relating to family and home. Jacobson demonstrates Willy's failure to "transform a relatively impersonal social world into a home that offered familial warmth."

Koon, Helene Wickham, ed. *Twentieth-Century Interpretations of "Death of a Salesman."* Englewood Cliffs, N.J.: Prentice-Hall, 1983, 115 p.

> Anthology of ten essays providing a variety of critical approaches to *Salesman.*

Lawrence, Stephen A. "The Right Dream in Miller's *Death of a Salesman.*" *College English* 25, No. 7 (April 1964): 547-49.

> Argues that Willy does indeed have the "right dream"; however, his problem is that "he is human enough to think that the same things that matter in the family—especially his love for his son—matter everywhere, including the world of social success."

Miller, Arthur. *Death of a Salesman: Text and Criticism,* edited by Gerald Weales. New York: The Viking Press, 1967, 426 p.

> Contains, in addition to the text of the play, critical commentary, reviews of productions, and a selection of other literary portraits of salesmen.

Schneider, Daniel E. "Play of Dreams." *Theatre Arts* XXXIII, No. 9 (October 1949): 18-21.

> Psychoanalytic interpretation of *Salesman* that regards the action as an Oedipal struggle for dominance between Willy and his sons.

THE CRUCIBLE

Calarco, N. Joseph. "Production as Criticism: Miller's *The Crucible.*" *Educational Theatre Journal* 29, No. 3 (October 1977): 354-61

> Offers "an interpretation of *The Crucible* achieved through the complete production—from the initial study of the script through performance with an audience," by a director who staged the play in repertory for two seasons.

Miller, Arthur. *The Crucible: Text and Criticism,* edited by Gerald Weales. New York: The Viking Press, 1971, 484 p.

> Contains, in addition to the text of the play, critical commentary, reviews of productions, documents relating to both the Salem trials and the congressional hearings, and other materials.

Morgan, Edmund S. "Arthur Miller's *The Crucible* and the Salem Witch Trials: A Historian's View." In *The Golden and the Brazen World: Papers in Literature and History 1650-1800,* edited by John M. Wallace, pp. 171-86. Berkeley: University of California Press, 1985.

> Judges Miller's depiction of Puritanism as the "antagonist" in *The Crucible* an unfair distortion of both the religion and the issue of oppression. According to Morgan, Miller allows audiences to think that "John Proctor asserted the dignity of man against a benighted and outworn creed. Proctor did nothing of the kind. Proctor asserted the dignity of man against man. Man is the antagonist against which human dignity must always be defended; not against Puritanism" or any other set of beliefs.

Warshow, Robert. "The Liberal Conscience in *The Crucible:* Arthur Miller and His Audience." *Commentary* 15, No. 3 (March 1953): 265-71.

> Charges that *The Crucible* over-simplifies the issues at stake in the original witch trials and that Miller "reveals at every turn his almost contemptuous lack of interest in the particularities—which is to say, the reality—of the Salem trials."

Yukio Mishima

1925-1970

(Pseudonym of Kimitake Hiraoka)

The provocative and colorful Mishima is commonly considered one of the most important modern Japanese writers. Both prolific and versatile, Mishima composed over forty dramas, including *Five Modern Nō Plays* (*Kindai nōgakushū*) and *Madame de Sade* (*Sado kōshaku fujin*), as well as novels, short stories, essays, and screenplays. Although the works best known in the West are his novels, he achieved great critical success in all genres and was as highly esteemed in Japan for his plays as for his fiction. Mishima received many literary awards in his country and was nominated for the Nobel Prize in 1965.

Mishima's works often reflect his dedication to the traditional values of imperialist Japan and are further characterized by a preoccupation with aggression and eroticism. Scholars have thus found it unsurprising that he was drawn to the formal, stylized violence of the traditional dramatic forms of Kabuki and Nō (also rendered in English as No or Noh). Mishima's pieces in these genres are, however, also esteemed for their updating of traditional works while preserving the spirit of the originals. Commentators also agree that Mishima's *shingeki* or "new theater" plays successfully combine the finest aspects of Eastern and Western dramatic traditions with the author's own distinctive voice to create some of Japan's most highly acclaimed modern theater pieces. In addition to many Nō, Kabuki and *shingeki* plays, Mishima also composed other performance works, including a *Bunraku* (puppet theater) piece and a ballet. From 1953 to 1970 he composed one full length play per year while continuing to produce his novels, magazine serials, and short stories. "Plays awaken a different part of my desire," Mishima once said; "that part which is unsatisfied by writing novels. Now, when I write a novel, I want to write a play next. Plays occupy one of the two magnetic poles of my work."

Mishima was born Kimitake Hiraoka in 1925 in Tokyo, where his father was a senior government official. Kimitake was the eldest of his parents' three children. His paternal grandmother Natsu was obsessively protective of the young Kimitake and would not allow him to live with the rest of the family on the upper level of their home; instead, she kept him with her in her darkened sickroom until he reached the age of twelve. Perhaps because of this extreme isolation, Mishima had difficulty forming social relationships as a youth, and many biographers and critics have attributed the source of his homoerotic and nihilistic tendencies to these formative early years. Before she died in 1939, Natsu introduced Kimitake to the Kabuki theater, taking him to one play a month—an activity he continued the rest of his life.

A gifted student, Kimitake immersed himself in Japanese and Western classical literature, as well as the works of such European authors as Jean Racine and William Butler

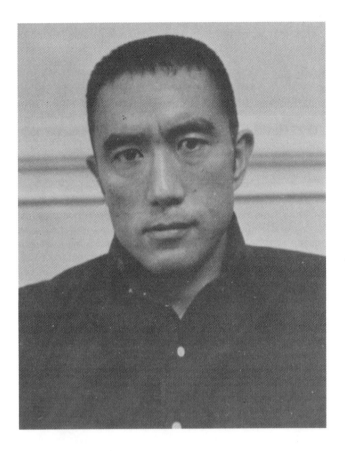

Yeats. He began writing stories in middle school and had his first work published while he was still a high school student. It was upon this occasion in 1941 that Kimitake was given the pen name Yukio Mishima. He later studied law at Tokyo University and subsequently accepted employment in the government's Finance Ministry. Within a year, however, he resigned in order to write full-time. With the great success of his first novel *Confessions of a Mask* (*Kamen no kokuhaku*) in 1949, he firmly established himself as an important voice in Japanese literature.

Throughout his adult life, Mishima was disturbed by what he felt was Japan's moral vacuum and "effeminate" image as "a nation of flower arrangers." He became increasingly consumed by a desire to revive "the way of the warrior" (*bushidō*), the traditional values and morals of the samurai, and he vehemently opposed the Westernization of his country. A supporter of *Literary Culture* (*Bungei Bunka*), the small nationalist magazine that had printed his early short fiction, introduced Mishima to the *Nihon Roman-ha,* a prominent group of Japanese Romanticist intellectuals who stressed the "value of destruction" and called for the preservation of Japanese cultural traditions. The *Nihon Roman-ha* had a profound effect on Mishima, who found reinforcement of his personal ideals in the group's emphasis on death and violence. Thus, Mishima's later works reflect his growing conservative political orientation and his philosophy of "active nihilism," which regards self-sacrifice as essential to achieving spiritual fulfillment.

In 1967, Mishima formed the Shield Society, or *Tate no kai*, a private army dedicated to restoring the prestige of the nation and reestablishing its old imperial glory. The Shield Society consisted of one hundred university students pledged to defend the Emperor—traditionally, the source of all Japanese culture—with their lives. The organization was ridiculed or ignored by the press, and Mishima was accused by some of fascism and cultural elitism. On 25 November 1970, Mishima submitted to his publisher the last installment of *The Decay of the Angel* (*Tennin gosui*), the final section of his novel tetralogy *The Sea of Fertility* (*Hōjō no umi*). He and his followers then attacked the commander of the Japanese Self-Defense Forces (*Jietai*). They held him hostage, barricading themselves in his office and demanding that Mishima be allowed to address an assembly of defense personnel. After repelling a rescue attempt by *Jietai* officers, Mishima gave a speech exhorting a return to imperial ideals. He advocated overthrowing the American-imposed constitution and restoring the Emperor to his former position of preeminence. Receiving only laughter and jeers in response, Mishima returned to the commander's office humiliated. Aware that his values were not shared by the majority of his countrymen and having failed to incite a coup, Mishima, in affirmation of his personal convictions, committed *seppuku*, a uniquely Japanese form of ritual suicide that involves disembowelment and beheading. *Seppuku* in the samurai ethos served as a respected form of protest or as a way of preserving personal honor in an otherwise dishonorable situation.

The passion and violence that characterized Mishima's personal life is conveyed throughout his writing. Indeed, critics often interpret Mishima's writings from a biographical perspective and routinely detect apparent contradictions between and within the man and his literature. An ardent supporter of distinctively Japanese values, he was also steeped in Western aesthetic traditions and lived in a Western-style house. A master of traditional dramatic forms, he yet created some of his country's most notable modern theatrical pieces. A tireless writer, bodybuilder, and swordsman, who possessed a vibrant and charismatic personality, Mishima nevertheless in his works displayed a markedly erotic fascination with death. Married and the father of two children, he created some of the most vivid and realistic depictions of homosexuality in literature. *Confessions of a Mask*, an uninhibited account of the protagonist's struggle to come to terms with his homoerotic and aggressive feelings, contains a passage critics believe unifies many of these oppositions in a single literary aesthetic: since childhood, he recalls, the "heart's yearning was for Death and Night and Blood." This statement thus points to Mishima's tendency to regard violence and death as sources of passion.

In 1953, Mishima became affiliated with the prominent

Bungakuza theater group. This association continued for ten years until the group stopped production of one of Mishima's plays because of its political content. Outraged, Mishima published a scathing open letter of resignation, calling the group members hypocrites. He soon joined the New Literature Theater but left in 1969 to form the Romance Theater (*Roman Gekijo*), where his final dramatic pieces were performed. Most of Mishima's plays for these companies were written in the *shingeki* or modern style. *Shingeki* is the Japanese dramatic form most accessible to Western audiences, featuring fully developed psychological characterization and realistic settings. While the form is frequently considered immature by Western standards, Mishima did not conceive of his *shingeki* dramas as "naturalistic" in the Western sense. He clearly distinguished drama from the more realistic genre of the novel, in which "strong emotion bears down upon the details and marches forward, treading the details underfoot." Conversely, "the modern play," he stated, "is far, far removed from the chaotic world of the novel, as I see it. It must look like a paper cathedral floating in the sky." Mishima is often judged the finest *shingeki* dramatist since World War II and is possibly the most widely translated, although only a few are available in English. These include *Tropical Tree* (*Nettaiju*), *Madame de Sade* (*Sado kōshaku fujin*), and *My Friend Hitler* (*Waga tomo Hittorā*).

Tropical Tree is a story of incest and murder, in which a mother who dominates her son, both sexually and psychologically, attempts to incite him to murder his father for his money. The daughter, who similarly controls him, urges him to kill their mother. In this work, Mishima welds elements of Greek tragedy and Aristotelian unities of time, place, and action with the traditional Japanese "double suicide" play to create what he termed an expressionistic "Japanese Electra." *Madame de Sade* addresses the question of why the Marquise de Sade—wife of the notorious figure whose beliefs gave rise to the term "sadism"—remained absolutely faithful to her husband while he was imprisoned during the French Revolution, but left him the moment he was freed. The play is, Mishima said, "Sade seen through women's eyes," and all six characters are female: the Marquis himself is never seen. The women variously symbolize wifely devotion, society, religion, carnal desires, guilelessness, and the common people. This work is typical of the *shingeki* style, which rejects the theatricality of traditional Japanese dramatic forms. Marguerite Yourcenar judged it a "tour de force," and it was extremely successful in Tokyo. However, it never gained the status Mishima had hoped for it in the United States. *My Friend Hitler* concerns the supposed friendship of Hitler and Ernst Roehm, a close associate of the German leader and a co-founder of the Nazi party who was purged in 1934. The play warns that, at its inception, totalitarianism often hides behind the façade of mainstream liberalism. *My Friend Hitler* is often interpreted as Mishima's mocking of left-leaning Japanese intellectuals and critics.

Many of Mishima's significant *shingeki* works have never been translated into English, including the 1955 drama *Shiro ari no su*, which won the Kishida Drama Prize. Although Mishima published his first "modern" play, *Kataku*, in 1948, it wasn't until he composed *Shiro ari no su* that he firmly established himself as an important *shingeki* dramatist. This piece takes place on a post-World War II Brazilian coffee plantation. It depicts the involvement of an aristocratic Japanese émigré couple and their two servants in a web of adultery and attempted suicide. Although *Rokomeikan,* Mishima's next work, has been dismissed by Henry Scott-Stokes as "not an interesting play," it is one of the dramatist's most popular. *Tōka no kiku* which won the Yomiuri Prize in 1962, evokes the theme of betrayed loyalty and has been read as an attack upon sentimental conservatism. Mishima's increasing political awareness manifests itself in *Yorokōbi no koto,* the work that created the playwright's rift with the *Bungakuza.* The play concerns the Matsukawa Incident—a 1949 train derailment by never-identified saboteurs—and contains politically charged rhetoric that the *Bungakuza* found objectionable. *Raiō no Terrasu* is among the last plays Mishima wrote. Based on a Khmer legend of King Jayavarman III, a leper who built the temple of Bayon at Angkor Wat in Cambodia, the play has been seen as "a metaphor for the life of an artist who transfuses a work of art with his entire existence and then perishes."

Mishima also composed many Nō pieces, including the works that were later translated as *Five Modern Nō Plays: Kantan, The Damask Drum (Aya no tsuzumi), Sotoba Komachi, The Lady Aoi (Aoi no ue),* and *Hanjo.* Nō is a performance art that developed out of traditional dance forms and integrates music, dance, and speech to evoke a general mood rather than a specific response in spectators. Reflective of Buddhist thought, it is subtle and oblique in both its text and presentation. According to generations of Japanese critics, Nō should suggest a realm of truth that is indefinable yet perceptible. Nō actors are masked, as in classical Greek drama, and they strike symbolic poses to communicate. Typically, a well-known story or situation is presented indirectly, using allusions to past events. A ghost figure is commonly featured looking back on his or her life. Historically, Nō theater was patronized by the Shogun Ashikaga Yoshimitsu (1358-1408) and subsequent rulers and thus acquired aristocratic associations.

"For me," Mishima wrote, "the Nō theatre is a temple of beauty, the place above all wherein is realized the supreme union of religious solemnity and sensuous beauty." In his own Nō works, Mishima updates time-honored pieces by combining the linguistic grace and the mood of classical Nō with modern situations and character complexity to create, in the opinion of many critics, the most successful contemporary Nō plays. His use of traditional material varies from piece to piece. In some, he freely adapts the customary theme to a modern setting, while in others he closely follows the details of the older work. Mishima's *Damask Drum* revises a piece about an older lower class man who falls in love with a young girl of a higher class. In both versions the man is told that he will win her love if he succeeds in beating a drum loudly enough for her to hear. However, the drum's head is made of damask instead of skin and thus makes no sound. Brought to despair, the man commits suicide. The play's second half shows his return as a ghost to haunt the young woman. In the traditional work, the ghost torments the woman with the incessant beating of his drum, but in Mishima's

version, the woman is undisturbed. She is equally insensible to love and the spectral beating of the drum. As a result, the ghost is driven again to despair. *Kantan*—unlike *The Damask Drum,* in which the playwright handles his source freely—follows the Nō original closely. In both stories, a young man napping on a magic pillow dreams of a glorious life. Traditionally, the young man envisions himself the Emperor of China; Mishima's selfish youth dreams of riches and power as a financial tycoon and dictator. In *Sotoba Komachi,* however, Mishima again inverts the ending of his source. This work tells the story of a poet who encounters an old woman who was once the renowned beauty Komachi. As a young woman, Komachi refused to yield to her lover until he visited her on one hundred consecutive nights. The poet and Komachi reenact this scene, but whereas at the end of the older work it leads to the possibility of reconciliation and revival, in Mishima's play Komachi remains the same—cold, haughty, and alone. In *The Lady Aoi* Mishima substitutes Freudian psychology for the demonic possession suggested by the traditional work: the central figure now suffers from sexual repression rather than possession by the spirit of her former rival. *Hanjo* retains only the theme of the original while revising the ending. In the Nō model, the mad girl Hanako is restored to sanity by the appearance of the lover who had once abandoned her. Mishima's young woman, however, does not recognize him and turns him away. She remains insane, and the play ends on a bleak note.

A form of popular entertainment that developed in the seventeenth and eighteenth centuries, Kabuki appropriates elements of Nō, *Bunraku,* and folk dance to create a highly ornate and colorful theatrical form. The action occurs on a large, plain stage, and all the roles are filled by men. Mishima wrote eight Kabuki plays in the traditional style, and, according to John Nathan, actors agree that he was "the only contemporary playwright capable of handling 'grand Kabuki' conventions and language authentically." Mishima's last theatrical work was the Kabuki play *Chinsetsu yumiharizuki* (the title means "The Moon Like a Drawn Bow"). It is an adaptation of a nineteenth-century novel by Bakin Takizawa and is possibly the best-known of Mishima's Kabuki works. He manages the romance's complex plot by reducing it to the scenes that excited him, including a bloody battle in the snow and the climactic *seppuku* of the protagonist. Mishima himself produced and directed a spectacularly gory staging of this play, which was, in the words of one critic, "a failure, but an impressive one."

Among Mishima's fiction, the novels *The Temple of the Golden Pavilion (Kinkakuji)* and *The Sailor Who Fell from Grace with the Sea (Gogo no eikō)* are perhaps the most famous, along with the works in his *Sea of Tranquility* tetralogy: *Spring Snow (Haru no yuki), Runaway Horses (Homba), The Temple of Dawn (Akatsuki no tera),* and *The Decay of the Angel (Tennin gossui).* The only collection of his short stories available in English is *Death in Midsummer and Other Stories (Manatsu no shi).* It contains his best-known, and ultimately prophetic, story "Patriotism" ("Yukoku"). In this piece, a young military officer and his wife commit *seppuku* because he feels disgraced by his comrades. The suicide is described in extraordinary, almost sensuous detail. Mishima characterized "Patriotism" as "neither a comedy nor a tragedy, but a tale of bliss." Many critics have found that this story further exemplifies Mishima's tendency to blend death and eroticism.

Although the circumstances surrounding his own spectacular suicide and his reputation as a novelist have often overshadowed his work as a playwright, Mishima consistently maintained that drama occupied an important place in his creative life. "Novels are like my literary wife," he once said, "but plays are like mistresses. I've got to do at least one a year." Mishima's drama also represents a significant contribution to Japanese literature. Translations of his plays have helped introduce the traditional forms of Nō and Kabuki to the world and have provided evidence of the thriving state of the *shingeki* theater in Japan. Even more importantly, Mishima's successful melding of Oriental and Occidental, modern and traditional aesthetics has resulted in a series of timeless dramas that transcend cultural boundaries.

(For further information on Mishima's life and career, see *Contemporary Authors,* Vols. 97-100 and Vols. 29-32, rev. ed.; *Contemporary Literary Criticism,* Vols. 2, 4, 6, 9, and 27; and *Short Story Criticism,* Vol. 4.)

PRINCIPAL WORKS

PLAYS

Kataku   1948
*Kantan   1950
*Aya no tsuzumi   1951
  [*The Damask Drum,* 1957]
*Sotoba Komachi   1952
  [translated 1957]
Muromachi hangonkō   1953
Yoru no himawari   1953
  [*Twilight Sunflower,* 1958]
*Aoi no ue   1954
  [*The Lady Aoi,* 1957]
Wakaudo yo, yomigaere!   1954
*Hanjo   1955
  [translated 1957]
Shiro ari no su   1955
Yuya   1955
Kindai nōgakushū   1956
  [*Five Modern Nō Plays,* 1957]
Rokumeikan   1956
Dōjōji   1957
  [translated in *Death in Midsummer and Other Stories* 1966]
Bara to kaizoki   1958
Nettaiju   1959
  [*Tropical Tree;* published in *Japan Quarterly,* 1964]
Tōka no kiku   1961
Yorokobi no koto   1963
Sado kōshaku fujin   1965

  [*Madame de Sade*   1967]
Yoroboshi   1965
  [*Yoroboshi: The Blind Young Man;* published in *Modern Japanese Drama: An Anthology,* 1979]
Suzaku-ke no metsubō   1967
Waga tomo Hittorā   1968
  [*My Friend Hitler;* published in *St. Andrews Review,* 1977]
Raiō no Terrasu   1969
Chinsetsu yumiharizuki   1969

OTHER MAJOR WORKS

Kamen no kokuhaku   (novel)   1949
  [*Confessions of a Mask,* 1958]
Manatsu no shi   (short fiction)   1953
  [*Death in Midsummer and Other Stories,* 1966]
Kinkakuji   (novel)   1956
  [*The Temple of the Golden Pavilion,* 1959]
Gogo no eikō   (novel)   1963
  [*The Sailor Who Fell from Grace with the Sea,* 1965]
Taiyo to tetsu   (essay)   1968
  [*Sun and Steel,* 1970]
Hōjō no umi   (novel tetralogy)   1969-1971
  [*The Sea of Fertility: A Cycle of Four Novels,* 1972-1974]
  Haru no yuki   1969
    [*Spring Snow,* 1972]
  Homba   1969
    [*Runaway Horses,* 1973]
  Akatsuki no tera   1970
    [*The Temple of Dawn,* 1973]
  Tennin gosui   1971
    [*The Decay of the Angel,* 1974]

*These works are included in *Kindai nōgakushū* and are translated in *Five Modern Nō Plays.*

AUTHOR COMMENTARY

"The Japan Within"   (1970?)

[*In the following posthumously published essay, Mishima explores his attraction to Nō, declaring that the drama serves as a refuge from the "frantically paced" modern industrialized Japan and provides a focus for what he terms the "quietism of the soul." The year of Mishima's death has been used to date this piece.*]

Once every month without fail, I go to a *noh* theatre to see the *noh* drama. There, one may see in its original form a classical stage art that dates from the fifteenth century, an art that, complete and perfect in itself, admits of no meddling by contemporary man. There, actors and chorus, in a masked drama similar in many respects to the Greek, display a technical accomplishment that is the distillation of a training and an experience that command unquestioning confidence. For me, the *noh* theatre is a temple of beauty, the place above all wherein is realized the supreme union of religious solemnity and sensuous beauty. In no other stage art has such an exquisite refinement been achieved.

Let me recall one experience at a *noh* theatre. The main offering that day, a play called *Kayoi Komachi,* is based on an ancient legend that tells how Fukakusa-no-Shōshō, a young man of noble birth, conceives a passion for Komachi, a noblewoman celebrated for her beauty. The proud Komachi demands that he come to her house for 100 nights in succession; on the 100th night, and not before, she will accept his advances. For 99 nights, he continues his unrewarded pilgrimage, only to expire, clinging to her carriage, on the 100th night when the goal is all but within reach. In the *noh* play, the ghosts of the two lovers appear to an itinerant monk in a dream and re-enact for him the pitiful tale of their earthly love.

The play begins, and soon the sound of the flute summons onto the stage a beautiful woman who carries a basket of nuts that she has been gathering. Questioned by the monk, she identifies herself as a countrywoman living in the neighbourhood; but, in fact, she is the ghost of Komachi.

The actor playing Komachi wore the mask known as *ko-omote,* representing a beautiful young woman, and a rich robe with patterns of butterflies and cherry blossoms woven on a bright red ground. His white socks and the flame-red of the costume reflected in the highly polished cryptomeria boards of the stage. As the actor appeared, the chorus began to chant: "What are these nuts you are gathering . . . ?"

All the while Komachi was on the stage, my eyes remained riveted on her form, following every delicate movement as it emerged from the background of music—the remote, mysterious music of the *noh.* Softly moving, the beautiful apparition began softly to sing; and my mind fell under the spell of Komachi. Prisoner of her fascination, it yielded up its all to her.

And it was not only my mind of which I was so willingly robbed. For did she not rob me, also, of the time that I usually consider my own? That hour that elapsed between the start of *Kayoi Komachi* and its end was an hour of my life I would never know again; in surrendering it so utterly to Komachi, I had savoured an experience very similar to that of the ill-fated Fukakusa-no-Shōshō.

In thus wiping out a certain period of time with the intensity of her beauty, Komachi was an embodiment of the eternal aspect of time; but more than that, she also, for me, obliterated the whole world beneath a single, consistent beauty. Thanks to her, a space of time, for me irreplaceable, had become the monopoly of beauty. And yet, why should beauty have such a right? By what right did beauty rob me and my life so irrevocably?

I do not, fortunately, have the *bourgeois* habit of passively enjoying beauty as a kind of nourishment for the mind. The *bourgeois* likes to follow a typically mammalian procedure in everything: ingestion, mastication, digestion, elimination. It is the same whether he is tackling Shakespeare, Cezanne, or *noh:* it is this that is known as "culture" in *bourgeois* society.

True beauty is something that attacks, overpowers, robs, and finally destroys. It was because he knew this violent quality of beauty that Thomas Mann wrote *Death in Venice.* Culture is no more than a kind of life insurance taken out against the dangerous blandishments of beauty.

The long line of dramatists and actors beginning with the fifteenth-century *noh* dramatist Zeami was, I suspect, thoroughly familiar with this terrifying quality inherent in beauty. That, indeed, is why they took care to seek beauty only in the ruined, shutting up beauty within the confines of dreams, of reminiscence, and of death. It was their rule that even the most perilously seductive beauty should be nothing but an apparition from the dead, that it should be already over, with no power to threaten us in actuality and no existence in reality outside the bones lying in the grave.

Nowhere else in the world can there be such a strange dramatic form as this "dream" type of *noh.* Usually, this form calls for a monk to appear and fall into a doze at some spot associated with some tale of old. In his dreams, he encounters a beautiful ghost—still fettered by the chains of illusion forged by her earthly love—talks with her, and finally, by his prayers, helps the ghost to attain enlightenment and thus escape into nirvana at last.

Superficially, the point of such plays would seem to lie in Buddhist proselytizing, but what interests the audience in practice is the beauty of the spirits in distress that they show. Even so, since these are tales told by ghosts, their plots do not, as in most dramas, form a present progressive but depend on the evocation of the past, so that by the time a *noh* play begins, the drama is already over. *Noh* cannot begin until after the drama is ended and beauty lies in ruins.

One might even liken this (to use a rather outrageous metaphor) "necrophilous" *noh* aesthetic to that of works by Edgar Allan Poe, such as *Ligeia* or *Berenice.*

Whatever its precise aesthetic nature, however, the fact remains that the beauty of *Kayoi Komachi* did not merely captivate my mind, by summoning up the dead with overwhelming sorrow, but, with its moment-to-moment evocation of beauty, took possession of my time as well.

Later, I could not refrain from attempting to analyze the ingredients of this aesthetic experience.

Since I am a Japanese, familiar with the Japanese tongue since infancy and familiar too, since boyhood, with the classical literature, I am unquestionably captivated by the elegant linguistic beauty of *noh,* by the dignified, remote beauty of its style and by the overlapping images created by its frequent use of "pivot words."

I am equally attracted by the unique technique of chanting used by the principal actor in *noh,* by the voice that, coming from within a mask, sounds so profoundly mysterious, the voice that is indisputably that of a man yet, far from destroying the illusion of a beautiful young woman, actually succeeds in portraying feminine emotions more objectively than would a real woman's voice. And I am moved, beyond doubt, by the beauty of the masks, the magnificence of the costumes, the ineffable mystery of the flute and drum, the voices of the chorus, soughing like a night-breeze in autumn. . . .

A still more important element, however, is the way in which each movement of the beautiful young woman Komachi and every word that she utters has been completely fixed, stylistically polished to utter perfection, since ancient times. Whichever actor of a particular school performs a particular role, he is not permitted to deviate from tradition either in movement or in emotional expression. The performer's scope for freedom is restricted to the utmost degree—though the emotional overtones of a performance vary greatly, of course, according to his command of technique. An actor's skill lies in the degree to which he brings out these subtler nuances of the piece.

The essence of beauty, I suspect, lies in this use of prescribed form. *Komachi* is a piece of fluid sculpture; its form in each successive moment is totally unrelated to the visually displeasing looseness of form of the human being. Every moment is part of a continuous succession of moments, each of which presents a perfect image of beauty. In ballet, the dancer has time to rest and respond to applause. In *noh,* no such thing is permitted. So long as the actor playing Komachi is on the stage, he is an incarnation of beauty and emotion in its purest form; when he is still, he is absolutely still; when he moves, there is no movement other than that necessary for shifting from perfect form to perfect form.

Only by being stolen thus from us by beauty can the slipshod time that makes up our daily lives be endowed with perfect order. It goes without saying that such a fragile, easily disrupted order could never survive for weeks, or even days. Yet it is only when we find forcibly imposed on us an order never to be found in our daily lives that our fear resolves into intoxication, and the perilous fascination of beauty can resolve itself into a quiet elegy based on reminiscence of the distant dead.

Generally speaking, I set little store by the kind of "Japanese culture" promoted by the Foreign Ministry and the Education Ministry. When they sent *noh* to London, they chopped down to half an hour a piece that should take an hour and a half on the theory that foreigners would be too bored to sit through the whole thing. The actors found themselves rushing about the stage at an unseemly pace, deprived of the intense slowness that is one of *noh*'s quintessential elements.

In an age such as the present, slowness in itself comes to constitute a major element of beauty. The slower the "Japan" within me becomes, in relation to the unnatural speed of the Japan outside, the more beautiful I find it. If this frantically paced industrialization, modernization, and urbanization—the half-crazed rush of daily life in the cities—is indeed the "Japan outside," then I feel a compulsion to restore the balance by guarding ever more jealously the leisurely pace of my "Japan within." *Noh* is the ideal focus for this quietism of the soul. In it lies the only type of beauty that has the power to wrest "my" time away from the "exterior" Japan of today—that outside world that, given its own way, would fragmentize it so thoroughly—and to impose on it another, different regime. And be-

neath its mask that beauty must conceal death, for some day, just as surely, it will finally lead me away to destruction and to silence. (pp. 54-55)

> *Yukio Mishima, "The Japan Within," in* This
> is Japan, *Vol. 18, 1971, pp. 54-5.*

OVERVIEWS AND GENERAL STUDIES

Henry Scott-Stokes   (essay date 1974)

[*As a Tokyo-based journalist, Scott-Stokes became a friend of Mishima in 1968. In the excerpt below from his full-length biography of the writer, he provides a survey of Mishima's career as a dramatist.*]

> Once the theater was like a jolly party I enjoyed attending after a hard day's work. There I could find another world—a world of glittering lights and colors, where the characters of my own creation, clad in alluring costumes, stood in front of a handsome set, laughed, screamed, wept, and danced. And to think that I, as a playwright, governed and manipulated all these theatrical worlds from behind the scenes!
>
> Yet such delights gradually turned bitter. The magic of the theater—to give people the illusion of life's noblest moments and the apparition of beauty on earth—began to corrupt my heart. Or was it that I grudged being an alienated playwright? Theater, where a false blood runs in the floodlights, can perhaps move and enrich people with much more forceful and profound experiences than anything in real life. As in music and architecture, I find the beauty of the theater in its abstract and theoretical structure, and this particular beauty never ceases to be the very image of what I have always held in the depth of my heart as Ideal in Art.
>
>   Yukio Mishima, Catalogue to the Tobu
>   Exhibition

The modern theater had a slow start in Japan. Whereas Japanese writers were attracted to the Western novel in the decades that followed the Meiji Restoration of 1868, and the first "modern" novels were written in Japan in the late nineteenth century, Western-style theater did not become established until after the Pacific War. Valiant attempts were made by small groups of actors and actresses to create a modern theater long before the war; the beginning of Shingeki is customarily traced to 1906, when a society for the promotion of the arts, the Bungei Kyokai, which specialized in drama, was founded. But the theater suffered cruelly from official censorship and, after a brief flowering in the 1920's, succumbed to government control. There were always small, politically radical groups ready to brave the authorities' disapproval—but scarcely any permanent achievements were made before the onset of the Pacific War. (An exception is the establishment of the Bungakuza—Literary Theater—in 1938. It survived the war, taking as its slogan "Art for art's sake.") In addi-

Mishima with the Kabuki actor Utaemon in 1958.

tion to all this, modern theater had strong competition from both the traditional Japanese theater, the Kabuki, a form established in the seventeenth and eighteenth centuries, and the successful lowbrow theater known as Shinpa, which had none of the intellectual appeal of Shingeki and drew large audiences, catering to a popular taste for Western-style, sentimental drama.

After the war, Shingeki benefited from a relaxation of censorship. The radical character of modern theater in Japan was apparent in the choice of plays made by the leading theatrical groups: works by Ibsen, Gogol, Tolstoy, Chekhov, and a number of Japanese writers who drew on the Russian tradition. The prestige of Western writers was great. Among the most popular Shingeki productions in the 1950's were Tennessee Williams's *A Streetcar Named Desire* and John Osborne's *Look Back in Anger*. The Western classical repertoire was also drawn upon; in 1955 the Bungakuza played *Hamlet* with great success. For the first time, good translations of the plays of Shakespeare were available and Shakespeare was for a time the height of fashion; veteran Kabuki actors vied for the honor of playing Hamlet. Few Japanese writers of the older generation rose to the challenge of the Shingeki in the late 1940's. It was left to the young men—among them Yukio Mishima

and Kobo Abé—to respond. Abé did so in a manner consonant with the tradition of Shingeki, in which radical, proletarian protest had played so large a part before the war. In one of his early plays, *Dorei Gari* ("Slave Hunt," 1952), he satirized the business world in Japan—describing a particularly bizarre form of postwar commerce (a trade in the remains of the war dead). Mishima, by contrast, showed no taste for ideology; his forte was style. These two young playwrights, the most successful newcomers to Shingeki after the war, were far apart in politics, which was equally apparent in their novels and in the translations of their works (Abé was taken up by the Soviet literary world; Mishima was translated exclusively in the West). Mishima showed a taste for the Western classical tradition—he was to write plays modeled on works by Racine and Euripides; Abé had a taste for Brecht.

Mishima's first work for the Shingeki was the one-act play **Kataku** ("Fire House," 1949). This was performed by the Haiyuza, one of the two leading Shingeki groups, and he was gratified to hear well-known actors and actresses speaking his lines. His first major success came the following year, in a genre which he made his own, the modern No play. Since its establishment in the fifteenth century as the theatrical form of the feudal aristocracy and the Imperial Court, No has attracted many writers, even in modern times. According to Keene's preface to **Five Modern Nō Plays,** published by Alfred A. Knopf: "Some have fashioned pastiches on the traditional themes, others have tried to fit modern conceptions into the old forms. The hysteria of wartime propaganda even led to the composition of a *Nō* play about life on a submarine. Some modern works have enjoyed temporary popularity, but they were essentially curiosities, having neither the beauty of language and mood of the old plays, nor the complexity of character delineation we expect of a modern work. The first genuinely successful modern *Nō* plays have been those by Yukio Mishima." As an example of Mishima's success, Keene takes **Kantan,** the first of his modern No plays, written in 1950; he compares the classical original with Mishima's work. In the classical No,

> a traveler naps on a magic pillow, and during the brief time that it takes his hostess at the inn to cook a bowl of gruel, he dreams of a glorious life as Emperor of China. He awakens to the realization that life is but a dream. In Mishima's play, instead of a traveler, we have a spoiled young man of today who sleeps on the magic pillow while his old nurse prepares the breakfast. His dreams are not of ancient China but of riches and power as a financial tycoon and a dictator [see commentary dated 1957].

Mishima wrote many modern No plays. The second book of his to be translated was a collection of these plays, which had a great success overseas. They were performed in many European countries and in Australia and Mexico as well as in North America, eventually being staged Off-Broadway late in 1960; that production ran for two months and had good notices. It was partly through these short plays—all are one-act dramas—that Mishima first acquired a measure of fame in the West; the dialogue is taut and the playwright retains sufficient of the ghostly quality of the classical No to give his works a unique character. Their appeal was considerable in Japan itself. The plays were produced by Shingeki companies and also appeared on the classical No stage. One play, **The Lady Aoi,** was sung as a Western-style opera. Translations of the classical No plays were long ago done by Arthur Waley, but they can scarcely be performed without the settings of the genuine No—the uniquely shaped stage, the gorgeous costumes and masks, and the musicians and chorus—often compared to classical Greek drama. Mishima's modern No plays gave the West a taste for No some time before it was possible for No companies to travel to foreign cities to perform the superb repertoire of the classical Japanese theater.

Some insight into Mishima's character is afforded by his attitude toward the classical No. While he was in Tokyo he would go "once a month without fail" to see a No play. But his attitude toward the No was peculiar; I do not believe that he really enjoyed No performances—during which he often fell asleep. A month before his suicide, he sent me a copy of an article on the No published in *This Is Japan* for 1971 [see Author Commentary]:

> There [at the No] one may see in its original form a classical stage art that dates back to the

fifteenth century, an art that, complete and perfect in itself, admits of no meddling by contemporary man . . . The No theater is a temple of beauty, the place above all wherein is realized the supreme union of religious solemnity and sensuous beauty. In no other theatrical tradition has such an exquisite refinement been achieved . . . True beauty is something that attacks, overpowers, robs, and finally destroys. It was because he knew this violent quality of beauty that Thomas Mann wrote *Death in Venice* . . . The No cannot begin until after the drama is ended and beauty lies in ruins. One might liken this . . . 'necrophilous' aesthetic of the No to that of works by Edgar Allan Poe, such as *Ligeia* or *Berenice* . . . In No lies the only type of beauty that has the power to wrest 'my' time away from the 'exterior' Japan of today . . . and to impose on it another regime . . . And beneath its mask that beauty must conceal death, for some day, just as surely, it will finally lead me away to destruction and to silence.

Mishima also wrote plays for the Kabuki theater in the early 1950's—before he had established himself as a Shingeki playwright. He had a unique advantage over his contemporaries: he alone had mastered classical Japanese and knew sufficient of the difficult language used in Kabuki to write plays in this genre. A photograph taken in 1953 shows him seated with Mantaro Kubota, a grand old man of the Japanese theater with a special affection for Kabuki. Mishima is going over a draft of a play, perspicaciously racing through the script. Kubota looks over one shoulder with a perplexed expression of admiration on his face, while an acolyte of the old man regards the youthful prodigy between them from the other side. Mishima loved the Kabuki; the baroque bloodletting and fierce swordplay appealed to his instincts. So, too, did the theme of many a Kabuki play—that true love may end in a shinju, or double suicide. His attitude toward the No was reverent and a little constricted, even ridiculous; his admiration for Kabuki was unrestrained. Many of the great actors of the day were his friends and he spent long hours backstage conversing with them. . . . Mishima's Kabuki plays are of no great importance; during his life, however, they attracted much attention. In some ways the most successful was his last work for the theater, **Chinsetsu Yumiharizuki** (whose title is untranslatable). He wrote it in 1969 and himself produced it at the National Theater. Mishima was a good mimic and an able Kabuki actor. After this production, he made a record of the play in which he took all forty parts.

Mishima defined his approach to Shingeki, for which he wrote most of his forty plays, in his essay "The Play and I" (1951):

> The modern play is far, far removed from the chaotic world of the novel, as I see it. It must look like a paper cathedral floating in the sky. No matter how naturalistic a play may be, the theme which makes for dramatic tension is such that it never suits the novel form. Strong emotion bears down upon the details and marches forward, treading the details underfoot.

His first successful long play was *Shiro Ari no Su* ("The Nest of the White Ant," 1955), set on a Brazilian coffee plantation where an aristocratic Japanese couple have taken refuge with two servants—a chauffeur and his wife—after the war. The structure of the play, a tale of adultery and suicide attempts, is excellent, and *Shiro Ari no Su*—the hollow nest of a white-ant colony is the symbol of the empty lives of the Japanese émigrés—established Mishima's reputation as a Shingeki dramatist. Not long after completing this work, for which he won a dramatic award, Mishima declared: "My ideal life would be to write one long novel a year and no short stories at all. Or, if I have to, then nothing longer than twenty pages. Otherwise, I would devote my time to plays." And on the relationship between his novels and his plays he commented: "Plays awaken a different part of my desire, that part which is unsatisfied by writing novels. Now, when I write a novel, I want to write a play next. Plays occupy one of the two magnetic poles of my work."

Mishima never achieved his ideal. He continued to write two or three novels a year, and some of his most striking works—for example, "Patriotism," the tale of hara-kiri—were to be longish short stories. For the remainder of his life, however, with the exception of the last year, he alternated continually between writing plays and novels. In 1956, for instance, he wrote *The Temple of the Golden Pavilion* in the early part of the year and followed it with a play, which he completed in time for the autumn season—*Rokumeikan*. This drama, the most frequently performed of Mishima's plays, is not an interesting play, in my opinion.

Toka no Kiku ("Tenth-Day Chrysanthemums," 1961) was the great triumph of Mishima's career as a dramatist. September 9 is a day of festival in Japan, on which exhibitions of chrysanthemums are staged. Tenth-day flowers would be too late for the show—they would be wasted. The chrysanthemum is a symbol of loyalty in Japan (the Imperial crest is composed of a thirty-two-petaled chrysanthemum). Thus, Mishima's play has as its theme wasted loyalty.

The principal character is a politician, a former Finance Minister named Mori, who had once, before the war, in the 1930's, been the target of an assassination attempt by rightwing terrorists. Mori's attitude toward the incident is brought out during a visit paid him by Kiku, the faithful maidservant who saved his life sixteen years before, who has not seen him since the assassination attempt (described in the play as if it were a minor detail in one of the numerous unsuccessful coups d'état of the 1930's). The old man states that the most honorable day of his life—which he prizes more highly than the day on which he was appointed Finance Minister, his highest office—was the day on which patriotic youths tried to kill him. The most fortunate accident that can befall a statesman, Mori implies, is to be struck down by the hand of an assassin. Death in the service of the nation and the Emperor is to be preferred to life, if that life has no meaning. Mori spends his days pursuing a lonely hobby, the growing of cacti; his activities as a cactus fancier are much dwelt upon in Mishima's play. The old man is depicted as one who,

like the cactus, has no blood; his existence is without meaning. The political background to the play is the murderous struggle which took place in the 1930's between those whose prime objective was order—politicians, men of business, and civil servants—and those who put a premium on honor. Mori has belatedly realized that he belongs, at heart, to the latter camp. In Mishima's play, Kiku gives Mori short shrift at their meeting. *Toka no Kiku* may be read as an assault upon sentimental conservatism; the dramatic action favors such an interpretation. The playwright himself, however, had a streak of sympathy for Mori's attitudes; the play was based on the Ni Ni Roku Incident of February 26, 1936, carried out by rebel army officers with whom Mishima later claimed he had much in common.

Not that *Toka no Kiku* is a political play. The dramatic interest lies in the relationship between Kiku and her former master and employer, Mori. The part of Kiku was taken by Haruko Sugimura in the production given by the Bungakuza in November 1961, on the occasion of the twenty-fifth anniversary of the foundation of the theatrical group, and this was one of the most distinguished performances by an actress generally regarded as the finest of Shingeki players. How far the Bungakuza, whose dominant personality was Miss Sugimura, was from regarding *Toka no Kiku* as an ideological drama was made apparent two years later when the group rejected a fairly mild play of Mishima's on ideological grounds, precipitating a furious quarrel between the Bungakuza and Mishima that ended in his resignation from the group with which he had worked, almost exclusively, for nearly a decade. Had *Toka no Kiku* been sympathetic to the right in the eyes of the Bungakuza, it would scarcely have been selected by them for performance at an anniversary.

The play which caused a rupture between Mishima and the Bungakuza was *Yorokobi no Koto* ("The Harp of Joy," 1963), and it is not one of Mishima's important works. It is set in postwar Japan and is based on the Matsukawa Incident—the derailment of a train in 1949 by saboteurs whose identity was never established, although the authorities believed for a time that they were from the left. The principal character is a senior police officer, Matsumura, a veteran who is popular with his subordinates, one of whom, Katagiri, he instructs to investigate the derailment of a train (the Matsukawa Incident is not identified as such in the play). The zealous Katagiri arrests several men and is astonished by their immediate release, when it has been ascertained that they are rightists. There are frequent left-wing demonstrations in the streets, the object of which is to show popular discontent with a government which is trying to pin the blame for the train derailment on the left, without any proof. A strange incident then occurs at the police station where Katagiri and his men work. A young policeman says he has heard the sound of a koto (a classical musical instrument) while on duty. The others laugh at him—how, in the midst of noisy demonstrations, could he have heard such a thing? Shortly afterward the investigation of the sabotage takes a totally unexpected turn. Matsumura, the man who is carrying out the police inquiry, is himself accused of having organized the sabotage; the police chief is said to have been an undercover Communist agent. The faithful Katagiri is shattered by this. Later the charges against Matsumura are shown to have been fabricated by the right; nonetheless, the younger man loses his faith in his superior. One day, when Katagiri is on duty in the streets, with demonstrators surging about him, he hears the beautiful sound of a koto. A man who had placed his faith in absolute authority, in the immutable system of the law, seeks refuge in fantasy after the collapse of his belief in order.

The turning point in the play comes when Katagiri realizes that Matsumura, his revered leader, has exploited him for his own ends—though these are not political. The Bungakuza, after starting rehearsals of *Yorokobi no Koto* in mid-November 1963, and following the return of Haruko Sugimura from travels in China, suddenly suspended rehearsal and informed Mishima that the production was off. Some of the actors, it was explained to Mishima by a succession of delegations which visited him at his home to give reasons for the suspension of rehearsals, objected to the right-wing lines spoken by the policemen in the play. Mishima was incensed. His angry rebuttal of the Bungakuza was printed as an open letter to the group; it appeared in the *Asahi Shimbun* a few days later, following his resignation from the Bungakuza. It read in part:

> Certainly *Yorokobi no Koto* is quite different from my other works and includes an element of danger. But what have you been thinking about me all this while that you should be astonished by a work such as this? Have you been making a fool of me, saying that Mishima is a playwright . . . who writes harmless dramas which gather large audiences? You set up such safe criteria as 'Art' and conceal within yourselves a vague political inclination [to the left], dropping the phrase 'art for art's sake' from time to time . . . Isn't this just hypocrisy and commercialism? I would like you to understand this: there is always a needle in art; there is also poison; you can't suck honey without the poison too.

The break was complete. Shortly afterward, Mishima joined another theatrical group, the NLT (New Literature Theater). It was a sad moment. Mishima never again found a group as effective to work with as the Bungakuza and the Bungakuza lost their best playwright.

The quarrel is a puzzling one. Within three years Mishima was to profess political beliefs which would have fully justified the Bungakuza in breaking with him. He was to assert that *Toka no Kiku* was in fact a play about the Ni Ni Roku Incident. He was also to state that he shared the patriotic attitude of the fanatically imperialist young officers who staged the Ni Ni Roku Incident. But his imperialism did not surface clearly in his writing until the summer of 1966, when he wrote *Eirei no Koe* ("The Voices of the Heroic Dead"). Nevertheless, there was a surprising violence to the quarrel. Mishima had very few squabbles with people or with organizations during his life. There were disagreements, but Mishima avoided public hostility on almost all occasions. Like many Japanese—and however un-Japanese he may have been in many respects—he abhorred public fracas.

Madame de Sade, the next play, again showed Mishima to be far more interested in problems of structure than in political matters. He wrote it after becoming intrigued with the problem of why the Marquise de Sade, who was absolutely faithful to her husband during his many years in prison, left him the moment he was free. The play was an attempt to provide a solution to the problem; it was "Sade seen through women's eyes." All six characters are women and the action is controlled exclusively through dialogue. Mishima intended that visual appeal would be provided by the rococo costumes of the women; the five characters must form a precise, mathematical system around Madame de Sade. Keene has described the debt owed by Mishima to Racine: "Mishima's classicism . . . is given its most extreme expression in the play *Madame de Sade* . . . Here he adopted most of the conventions of the Racinian stage—a single setting, a reliance on the *tirade* for the relation of events and emotions, a limited number of characters each of whom represents a specific kind of woman, and an absence of overt action on the stage."

Madame de Sade was a considerable success in Tokyo, although the subject matter was a little too recherché. After its translation into English, Mishima hoped that it would be produced on Broadway and pressed his agent in New York, Audrey Wood, to find a theater for it. *Madame de Sade,* however, proved to have no appeal to American actresses; the absence of overt action on the stage was the major problem. Quite possibly, none of Mishima's long plays will ever be performed on the Western stage. Certainly, it is unlikely that Mishima's subsequent major plays, *Suzaku Ke no Metsubo* ("The Fall of the House of Suzaku," 1967)—a play based on Euripides—and *Wagatomo Hitler* [1969, *My Friend Hitler,* 1977], would have great appeal to Western audiences. The latter is set in Germany in 1934; in it Mishima describes the events before and after the Night of the Long Knives. It makes the point that Hitler steered a "neutral" course between the Brownshirts and the conservative forces—the regular army and big business—on that occasion. Mishima neither praises nor criticizes Hitler; nor does he develop the character of the dictator in the play. Mishima treats the Night of the Long Knives as an incident in a struggle for power, a technical operation. The title of the play refers to Roehm, the head of the Brownshirts, one of Hitler's victims on the Night. In the play Roehm believes the Führer is "my friend"—until it is too late. At the première, held in Tokyo on January 19, 1969, Mishima distributed a note to the audience: "The dangerous ideologue, Mishima, dedicates an evil ode to the dangerous hero, Hitler." His intention was to mock the critics and the vaguely leftist neutralism of Japanese intellectuals. Neutralism, the play said, can lead any where.

Mishima's last play for the modern theater was *Raio no Terrasu* ("The Terrace of the Leper King," 1969). He invited me to the première and I remember how he looked that evening—he was wearing all-white evening attire and was accompanied by [his wife] Yoko. Tennessee Williams was supposed to put in an appearance and there was an empty seat next to Mishima where he should have been. The performance itself went well enough. *Raio no Terrasu* is an untranslated play about the Khmer king Jayavarman III, the builder of the temple of Bayon at Angkor Wat. The monarch suffered from leprosy; Bayon is his monument. Mishima used the tale to make the point that the material triumphs over the immaterial, the Body over the Spirit—Bayon alone remains. He was especially proud of the last scene, an exchange on the steps of the newly constructed Bayon between the Body—the youthful image of the king—and the Spirit, represented by the voice of the dying, leprous king (a sepulchral, tape-recorded voice in the Teigeki production we saw).

> BODY: King, dying king. Can you see me?
>
> SPIRIT: Who is calling me? I remember the voice. That brilliant voice.
>
> B: It's me. Do you see?
>
> S: No. Of course not. I'm blind.
>
> B: Why should the Spirit need eyes? It has been your source of pride that you see things without using your eyes!
>
> S: Such harsh words. Who are you?
>
> B: I'm the king.
>
> S: Absurd! That's me.
>
> B: We share the same name. King, I am your Body.
>
> S: Who am I then?
>
> B: You are my Spirit. The Spirit that resolved to build this Bayon. What is dying is not the Body of the king.
>
> S: My Body was rotten and has vanished. You cannot be my Body, speaking so proudly and boldly.

The actor who played the part of the Body was heavily suntanned and wore a short tunic with straps across his bare chest. As he spoke his lines, he strode about the terrace of the temple, flourishing his arms. Behind him was a giant face made of foot-high blocks of stone, one of many such faces at the temple of Bayon. The actor, Kinya Kiyaoji, was slightly overweight; his voice boomed out cheerfully, while the groaning Spirit endeavored to reply:

> B: It's not true. Your Body was never rotten. Your Body is here, shining with youth, full of vigor, like an immortal golden statue. The cursed illness is an illusion of the Spirit. How could such a triumphant king as I be affected by illness?
>
> S: But what could the Body achieve? What imperishable things can he construct? It is not stones that planned and constructed this imperishable Bayon. Stones are nothing but materials. It's the Spirit that made this.
>
> B (*laughing aloud with pride*): The Spirit cannot see Bayon any more, because even the Spirit depended on the Body.
>
> S: No. I don't need to see it. The finished Bayon shines in my spirit.

> B: Shining? It's only a small streak of light, which is about to be put out. Think, if it is enough to be shining in the Spirit, why was it necessary to construct Bayon with such an enormous quantity of stones?
>
> S: The Spirit always longs for a shape.
>
> B: That's because you are shapeless. Shape always takes its model from a beautiful body like me. Did you use as a model of this temple the rotten body of a leper?
>
> S: Rubbish! The body of a leper is nothing.
>
> B: Nothing? You suffered for so long.
>
> S: No, nothing. The Spirit is everything.
>
> B: What are they, the rotten, the shapeless, and the blind? They are the shape the Spirit takes. It's not you that suffered from leprosy. Your very existence is leprous. You are a born leper.
>
> S: Sharpness, clarity, and the power to see through to the bottom of this world constructed Bayon. The Body cannot have such power. You are only a slave captured by the Body.
>
> B: You say that you are more free than me? Are you? More free because you cannot run, cannot jump, sing, laugh, or fight?
>
> S: I run through one hundred years. You run only in space.
>
> B: There is light in space. Flowers bloom, bees hum. A beautiful summer afternoon stretches ahead. But what you call time is a damp and dark underground tunnel.
>
> S: Oh, Bayon, my love.
>
> B: Why do you leave it here? Bayon is the present. The forever-shining present. Love? Were you ever so beautiful as to be loved?
>
> S: I'm dying. Each breath is agony. Oh, my Bayon.
>
> B: Die! Perish! . . . You planned and constructed. That was your illness. My breast, like a bow, shines in the sun. Water flows, sparkles, and is still. You didn't follow me. That was your illness.
>
> S: My Bayon . . .
>
> B: The Spirit perishes, as a kingdom perishes.
>
> S: It's the Body that perishes. The Spirit is imperishable.
>
> B: You are dying . . .
>
> S: Bayon . . .
>
> B: You're dying.
>
> S: . . .
>
> B: What has happened?
>
> S: . . .
>
> B: No answer. Are you dead?

S: . . .

B: You are dead.

(*The sound of bird song*)

Look. The Spirit has died. A bright blue sky!
Beautiful birds, trees, and Bayon protected by
all these! I will reign over this country again.
Youth is immortal. The Body is imperishable. I
won. It is I that am Bayon.

Early in 1970, Mishima surprised his friends by announcing that he would write no more plays. The drama had been such an important part of his life for so many years that his decision was incomprehensible: some put it down as a foible; others believed that he was tired by his struggle with *The Sea of Fertility* and had decided to concentrate all his strength on that single novel.

Not long before he killed himself, Mishima arranged a shelf of objects in his upstairs sitting room at home in Magome. These were a Greek vase, a small bronze nude of himself, a collection of translations of his books, and a stage model for the last scene of *Raio no Terrasu.* One evening he showed this display to some friends. "How do you like it?" he asked them in an ironic tone. "This really sums up my life, don't you think?" And he burst into laughter. (pp. 201-16)

> *Henry Scott-Stokes, in his* The Life and Death of Yukio Mishima, *Farrar, Straus and Giroux, 1974, 344 p.*

Marguerite Yourcenar (essay date 1980)

[*Yourcenar is the author of* Mishima: A Vision of the Void, *a highly-acclaimed discussion of the biographical aspects of Mishima's writing. It was first published in French in 1980. In the following excerpt from that work, the critic briefly assesses* Five Modern Nō Plays *and* Madame de Sade. *The latter drama, she declares, is "a tour de force."*]

Most of Mishima's plays, as successful in Japan as were his novels, and sometimes even more so, have not been translated; we can refer, therefore, only to his *Five Modern Nō Plays,* from the fifties, and to *Madame de Sade,* written toward the end of his life. To give a modern equivalent of the Nō play presents more or less the same dangers and attractions as transposing a Greek tragedy from the ancient to the modern world: the attraction of a theme already worked out, known to everyone, a theme which has moved generations of poetry lovers, and whose form has been, so to speak, polished over the centuries; it carries the danger of falling into flat pastiche or exasperating paradox. Cocteau, Giraudoux, Anouilh, and D'Annunzio before them, as well as a few others in our time, conducted this experiment, with varying success. The difficulty with Nō plays is the greater in that they are works steeped in the sacred, an element which in Greek drama is hardly felt by us, since it belongs to a religion which the spectator believes dead. Nō, on the contrary, mingling Shinto mythology and Buddhist legend, is the product of two religions which are still alive, even if their influence today seems to be waning. Its beauty comes, in part, from its combining

before our eyes living creatures and ghosts, who are practically the same thing in a world where impermanence is the rule, but who rarely seem convincing in our modern mental setting. In most cases, Mishima succeeds. In *The Lady Aoi,* it is difficult to remain unmoved when Prince Genji (who here has become a rich and important businessman), standing in the room of a clinic where his wife, Aoi, is dying from a severe shock, sees a ghostly yacht glide through one door and exit through another. Bewitched, almost against his will, he climbs aboard it with a mistress from the past, Rokujō, the very same "living phantasm" who slowly submits the unfortunate Aoi to torture and death. Even more extraordinary, if possible, is the setting of *The Damask Drum:* a blue empty space, a chasm of sky seen between the top floors of two buildings. The one on the left is a fashion designer's salon, patronized by a cold and frivolous woman customer; that on the right is a law office where an old love-sick employee sits at the window, watching. As in the original Nō, the "damask drum," which is sent to the old man as a joke, emits, as one might guess, no sound—a symbol of the beautiful woman's indifference when faced with the innocent old lover, who exhausts himself in vain, beating harder and harder on the drum, like a wild heart about to burst.

Madame de Sade is a tour de force. Composed, like Racine's plays, only of dialogue, with no action except offstage or as reported by the characters, the play is built entirely on a counterpoint of female voices: the loving wife; the conventional mother-in-law upset by the excesses of her daughter's husband; the sister who has become the mistress of the guilty and persecuted man; a discreet maid; a pious woman, friend of the family; and, less agreeable to listen to than the other women, a female Sade, a follower of the Marquis, a sort of more violent Madame de Merteuil reeling out cynical monologues written, it would seem, to impress the spectator. The play has the strange fascination of any novel or drama centered on a character who does not appear. Sade is invisible to the very end, as is the Percival worshipped and loved by all the other characters in Virginia Woolf's *The Waves.* The faithful wife who, for love (or for some other, darker reason?), ends by taking part in a cruel and degrading orgy moves us, even though we grow uncomfortable listening to her glorify Sade as a kind of hypostasis of Evil destined to create new values, as a grandiose and maligned rebel, somewhat like Satan in the eyes of Baudelaire and Bakunin. This almost Manichaean opposition of Good and Evil, alien to Far Eastern thought, has, for the modern Western reader, been entirely exhausted in this form: we have seen the real powers of darkness at too close range to be still excited by a romantic evil. The Europeanized Mishima, playing his theatrical trumps, seems thereby to fall into easy rhetoric. But the scene that follows is a great moment of theater: the wife, who has not failed to visit the prisoner behind bars in the darkness of his cell, who has read *Justine* with passion, and who has just delivered to us an ardent encomium to its author, is interrupted by the arrival of the maid, announcing to the ladies that Monsieur le Marquis de Sade, freed by the revolutionaries (we are in 1790), is at the door. "I hardly recognized him. He is wearing a black woolen coat with patched elbows and a shirt with a collar so dirty—excuse me for saying so—I took him at first for an old beggar. And he's become so stout! His face is puffy and looks deathly pale, and his body's grown so fat that his clothes are too small for him . . . You can see when he mumbles that he's only got a few yellowish teeth left in his mouth. But when he gave his name, it was with dignity. He said . . . 'I am Donatien-Alphonse-François, Marquis de Sade.' " Madame de Sade's reply is that the Marquis should be refused entry and told she will never see him again in her life. On this verdict, the curtain falls.

What has happened? Does Madame de Sade, who has loved in him the ideal of Evil Incarnate, dimly glimpsed in the darkness of a cell, not want anything more to do with this fat and flabby man? Does she believe it is wiser— as she stated a few moments earlier—to retire to a convent and pray at a distance, not for the soul of her husband, as a pious friend suggests, but for him to continue the career of cursed demiurge which God has chosen for him? Or is she simply afraid, now that prison bars no longer separate them? The mystery, deeper than before, closes on Madame de Sade. (pp. 42-7)

> *Marguerite Yourcenar, in her* Mishima: A Vision of the Void, *translated by Alberto Manguel and Marguerite Yourcenar, Farrar, Straus and Giroux, 1986, 151 p.*

FIVE MODERN NŌ PLAYS

CRITICAL COMMENTARY

Donald Keene   (essay date 1957)

[*Keene is one of the foremost American translators and critics of Japanese literature. Mishima's friend for almost twenty years, he has translated numerous of the author's works, including* Five Modern Nō Plays *(1957),* After the Banquet *(1963), and three pieces in* Death in Midsummer and Other Stories *(1966). In the introduction to his translation of the Nō plays, Keene gives a brief history of the dramatic form and discusses Mishima's works, calling them "the first genuinely successful modern Nō plays."*]

One of the first non-Japanese ever to see a Nō play was Ulysses S. Grant. In 1879 he stopped in Tokyo on a goodwill journey around the world, and his hosts, rather at a loss what to offer in the way of entertainment to the rare visitor from abroad, asked the great Nō actor Hōshō Kurō to perform. It would not have been altogether surprising if the grizzled old ex-soldier had fallen asleep as he watched the solemn, hieratic movements of this subtle and symbolic art. It is recorded instead that after the performance he turned to his hosts in admiration and declared: "You must preserve this."

Grant probably did not know that it was a real question at the time whether or not the Nō would survive. It had been associated intimately since its creation in the four-

teenth century with the Shogunate government, which was finally overthrown in 1868, and for that reason if no other it had fallen into marked disfavor with the victorious enemies of the old regime. This was, moreover, an age when Western things were frantically being imported and adapted into Japanese life. It appeared inevitable that a dramatic art which in 1879 was distinctly an archaic survival should have been one of the first victims of modernization. The fashionable people of the day, far from patronizing the Nō, flocked at night to the celebrated Rokumei Hall to dance to the strains of the waltz or to display their mastery over the mysteries of the knife and the fork. It seemed indeed that the future of the art was in peril. But Grant urged that it be preserved, and the recommendations of so distinguished a visitor were not lightly to be dismissed in those days of uncritical respect for all things foreign. Other support came from Japanese who, when traveling abroad, had witnessed performances of opera, and had concluded that since Nō rather resembled the opera it might be worth saving. The few Nō actors who had persevered in their art during the years of neglect gradually began to win audiences again, and gifts from the court and the nobility ensured that this unique dramatic form would continue.

Nō was preserved, but it was not free from the danger of turning into a kind of museum exhibit, to be accorded, like the operas of Monteverdi, pious and infrequent revivals. Certainly there was no great popular appeal in the Nō. It had been supported largely by the court of the Shogun, the military ruler of Japan, and it had steadily grown farther and farther away from the ordinary public. With the rise in the sixteenth century of the puppet theater and the Kabuki, dramatic forms with a braoder appeal, Nō had become almost exclusively a court entertainment. Only infrequently were benefit performances open to the public. The court spectators were connoisseurs able to detect the slightest variation—good or bad—from the usual stage movements or sounds. The traditions were so strong that Nō tended to become almost a ritual, and so well versed in the texts were the audiences that it was unnecessary and even undesirable to make the plays dramatically convincing. The dialogue was pronounced in a deliberately muffled manner, and the gestures became completely stylized. A hand slowly lifted to the face denoted weeping, the stamp of a foot might mean a ghost had disappeared. That Grant should have been impressed by this remote and difficult art is little short of astonishing.

Nō originally was much simpler. It stemmed from various playlets performed at temples and shrines as part of harvest and other celebrations, or whenever the people of a village happened to congregate. In the fourteenth century this rustic entertainment was developed by the genius of two men, a father and son, into one of the world's great dramatic forms. These men were Kan'ami Kiyotsugu (1333-84) and Zeami Motokiyo (1363-1443). As established by them, only four or five actors normally appear in a Nō play: the principal speaker-dancer, a personage (often a priest) who does not dance, and various accompanying figures. The climax of each play is an extended dance which occurs near the end, and toward which the text from the outset has pointed. The plays themselves are

The Poet and Komachi in Sotoba Komachi.

seldom as long as a single act of a Western work, but a Nō drama requires about an hour to perform because of the final dance and the deliberate manner of recitation. There is a chorus and a musical accompaniment consisting of a flute and several kinds of drums, which serve to heighten moments of intensity.

In some respects Nō suggests ancient Greek drama: there are few characters; there is a chorus, dances, and masks (worn by the principal dancer in many cases), and an abundant use of traditional or legendary themes. However, unlike Greek drama, which became increasingly realistic, Nō developed into an essentially symbolic theater, where both the texts of the plays and the gestures of the actors were intended to suggest unspoken, indefinable realities. Some of the surviving works by Kan'ami indicate that in his day Nō was closer to European drama in that it was representational, but Zeami and his successors wrote plays in which the relation of the expressed part to the whole is like that of the visible surface to the entire iceberg. Zeami himself wrote a good deal on symbolism in the Nō. He believed that Nō should attempt through beautiful movements and words to point at an indefinable and limitless world beyond them. The nature of this world would depend both on the capacities of the actor to suggest and of the audience to comprehend.

Nō plays are usually divided into two sections. Often in the first part a character appears as an old woman, a fisherman, a reaper, or some other humble person, but in the second part the same character returns in his true appearance as a great warrior or a beautiful woman. Frequently we have to do with a ghost, a tormented spirit who asks to be prayed for, or one whose dreadful wrath must be exorcised. The world of the dead was perhaps uniquely suited to the peculiarly remote, symbolic nature of Nō, and the separation between life and death, the dead and the living, has never been more touchingly depicted than in Nō.

Once the form had been evolved and brought to its highest perfection by Zeami, Nō underwent few important changes. A seventeenth-century Nō play, in much the same way as one written in the fourteenth century, was likely to begin with a priest on a journey to some holy spot. There he meets a person of the vicinity whose strangely poetic words belie his humble appearance. The priest questions the unknown reaper or fishergirl, who gradually reveals the story of his former glory, and leads us to understand that some unsatisfied attachment to the world has kept his spirit behind. At the end of the play a hope of salvation, of deliverance from the attachment, is offered, and the ghost fades away. This was a typical form, and it enabled a playwright to give in a very abbreviated compass a poetic and complicated story. The reluctance of Japanese dramatists to abandon it is understandable. Nō plays continued to be written, but all the good ones of the sixteenth century and afterward when put together would not bulk as large as the work of Zeami alone. In the seventeenth century the puppet theater became the outlet for the dramatic genius of the country. It is not to be wondered at that Nō was forsaken by later dramatists: European composers did not go on writing madrigals when once the golden age had passed, and only seldom today does a composer choose to write for the harpsichord in preference to the potentially more expressive piano.

Yet Nō has continued from time to time to attract leading Japanese writers. Some have fashioned pastiches on the traditional themes, others have tried to fit modern conceptions into the old forms. The hysteria of wartime propaganda even led to the composition of a Nō play about life on a submarine. Some modern works have enjoyed temporary popularity, but they were essentially curiosities, having neither the beauty of language and mood of the old plays, nor the complexity of character delineation we expect of a modern work.

The first genuinely successful modern Nō plays have been those by Yukio Mishima. Indeed, we may say that if the medium is given a new lease of life it will be because of Mishima and his work. Despite his youth—he was born in 1925—Mishima is a man of exceptional breadth of knowledge, and he has drawn freely on both Japanese and Western sources in writing his novels and plays. His brilliantly successful novel *The Sound of Waves,* for example, had its genesis in the ancient Greek romance *Daphnis and Chloe,* and another novel concludes with a scene obviously suggested by Maupassant's *La Maison Tellier.* Some of Mishima's plays are on entirely modern themes, others in the style and language of the seventeenth-century Kabuki, and there is even a puppet play in the traditional idiom which is based on Racine's *Phèdre.*

Mishima seems to have been attracted both by the structure and the subject matter of the Nō plays. His adaptations have, of course, been free, for it has been his intent that these plays be wholly intelligible and completely contemporary. He has in fact suggested that if these modern Nō plays are performed in the United States, the adaptation should be carried one step farther. For example, the park where we first see Komachi gathering cigarette butts should be Central Park in New York, and for the Rokumei Hall, Delmonico's or some other famous spot should be substituted. There is no reason why so violent an adaptation cannot be made with complete success, and there is no question but that these plays have in their own right an immediate and powerful appeal even to people who are normally indifferent to Japanese drama.

The five plays of the collection were written between 1950 and 1955. They have been presented as modern plays on the Tokyo stage. *The Damask Drum* was performed in 1955 in traditional Nō style. *The Lady Aoi* was sung in 1956 as a Western-style opera.

Mishima's use of the original Nō dramas varies from play to play. Sometimes he has chosen only the general themes, at other times he has followed even the details of the originals. For example, the old man of the original *Damask Drum* who sweeps the garden of a palace becomes in the modern version a janitor who sweeps a law office in downtown Tokyo. The latter falls in love not with a princess but with the client of a fashionable couturière in the building across the way. In both versions the old man is told that he will win the favor of his beloved if he succeeds in beating a drum loud enough for her to hear it; in both cases the covering of the drum is damask instead of skin, and the drum makes no sound. The janitor, like the gardener, commits suicide. The Nō ghost returns to torment the cruel princess with the ceaseless beating of the drum, but in the modern play the lady's inability to love makes her deaf to the beating of the drum, and the janitor's ghost is driven a second time to despair.

Kantan follows the same story as the Nō progenitor. A traveler naps on a magic pillow, and during the brief time that it takes his hostess at the inn to cook a bowl of gruel, he dreams out a glorious life as Emperor of China. He awakens to the realization that life is but a dream. In Mishima's play, instead of a traveler, we have a spoiled young man of today who sleeps on the magic pillow while his old nurse prepares breakfast. His dreams are naturally not of ancient China but of riches and power as a financial tycoon and a dictator.

In *Sotoba Komachi,* Mishima has replaced the priests who dispute with Komachi by a poet. The priests are angry to discover Komachi sitting on a stupa (a *sotoba*), "the holy image of the Buddha's incarnation." The poet in Mishima's play berates Komachi for sitting on a park bench at night, when lovers want to be left alone. The main theme of the play, the story of the heartless beauty, Komachi, who refuses to yield to a lover unless he comes to visit her a hundred nights, is followed in Mishima's version. Here the poet asks the old hag about her life eighty years before, and gradually he finds himself re-enacting the part of her old lover on the hundredth night. The original Komachi was offered at the end of the play a promise of salvation, but the modern Komachi is at the end as she was at the beginning, a miserable old woman counting her nightly haul of cigarette butts.

In *The Lady Aoi,* a nurse in a modern hospital who talks not of demons but of sexual repressions is the counterpart of the priest who exorcises the living phantasm of Rokujō. Prince Genji, the husband of Aoi, who does not figure in the Nō play, appears in Mishima's as Hikaru: Hikaru, "The Shining One," had been an epithet of the dazzling Genji. The carriage in which Rokujō and Aoi contested the place of preference at the Kamo Festival becomes here a sailboat on which Rokujō and Hikaru recall the memory of their first meetings.

Hanjo is the farthest removed from the original play, which is almost the only Nō drama that has a happy ending. Hanako, the mad girl, is restored to sanity by the appearance of the man who had once abandoned her. In the modern play Hanako does not recognize her lover when he finally comes, and she turns him away.

The world of the psychiatric hospital, of the law office, and of the public park certainly seems a far cry from the dreamlike realms of the Nō, but however free Mishima's use of the original material, the dramatic situations remain identical. What Mishima has done principally is to add a modern understanding to the situations and to explore possibilities only vaguely adumbrated in the fifteenth-century texts. In *The Damask Drum,* again, the trick of asking the old man to beat a soundless drum is the invention of a spiteful dancing-teacher. The others who abet him in the cruel joke are a self-important diplomat, a foolish young man, and the worldly proprietress of a dressmaking establishment, all of whom are given sharply defined personalities. In the original the act was little more than the whim of a moment.

Mishima's use of the dramatic themes of the past may be likened to similar practices of European and American dramatists, such as Cocteau's treatment of the Œdipus story in his *Infernal Machine,* or O'Neill's adaptation of the Oresteia for his *Mourning Becomes Electra,* or even Brecht's *Threepenny Opera,* a modern version of Gay's *Beggar's Opera.* In none of these instances is it necessary to be acquainted with the original play in order to appreciate the new one. Each stands on its own merit, but at the same time a knowledge of the earlier work adds a dimension and permits us to measure the workings of a modern intelligence against a familiar background. Sophocles would have been startled to discover that in Cocteau's play the Sphinx is in love with Œdipus and herself yields the answer to her riddle; this unexpected turn not only attracts us but assuages our modern curiosity. (Why else should Œdipus have been the first to supply the answer to the riddle?) Similarly, the original Nō play offers no explanation as to why the princess should have caused the old man to beat a damask drum. Inevitably we feel that the story makes better sense as told by Mishima, whose use of the old story is at once respectful and courageous.

Again, the conclusion to Zeami's *Hanjo* shows the exchange of the fans by which the separated lovers pledge to marry. This is much too abrupt for us today. We have not even been prepared for Hanako's regaining her sanity, and the whole change is effected in a single line though, to be sure, the dance which accompanies it helps to clarify the situation. In Mishima's play even the exchange of fans cannot shake Hanako out of the madness into which she has been plunged by Yoshio's desertion. We can imagine her continuing to go every day to the railway station to wait for a lover she has in fact rejected.

The nature of our response to these modernized Nō plays is bound to differ from our response to a performance of the traditional ones. We are, for one thing, far more intellectually absorbed. The plays have the wit and invention we expect from an extraordinarily gifted writer. Oddly enough, Mishima manages somehow to suggest much of the uncanny symbolic quality of the originals, even in the tawdry modern surroundings of a public park or a downtown office. The five plays all have powerful overtones which even the uninitiated can feel. Hanako and Jitsuko looking into a future of waiting and non-waiting; the sinister tinkle of the telephone by Aoi's sickbed; the kaleidoscopic visions of Jirō as he sleeps on the magic pillow; the tortured ghost who cannot make his beloved hear the drum even when it actually sounds; the old woman left in grim loneliness: all these evoke much the same sensations as the ancient plays and suggest why Mishima should have turned to them and their particular themes after having written numerous entirely new works.

The Japanese may well congratulate themselves on having been able to preserve the Nō through the period of greatest danger to it, when Western things seemed on the point of overwhelming all the native traditions. There are today larger audiences than ever for Nō plays, and new theaters are being built in Tokyo, Kyoto, and other cities. Most encouraging of all, perhaps, is the fact that an outstanding young writer has devoted himself to this traditional dramatic art, and in so doing has created works of unusual and haunting beauty. (pp. vii-xvii)

> *Donald Keene, in an introduction to* Five Modern Nō Plays *by Yukio Mishima, translated by Donald Keene, Alfred A. Knopf, 1957, pp. vii-xvii.*

Anthony Thwaite   (essay date 1958)

[*The following essay is Thwaite's review of Donald Keene's translation of* Five Modern Nō Plays. *The critic expresses several reservations about Mishima's treatment of the traditional Nō material but admits that the writer has "managed to inject some fresh and youthful blood into one of the oldest and most austere of dramatic forms."*]

In many ways, the *No* seems to be treated in Japan today as a pseudo-art, like flower arrangement and the tea ceremony: its purposeful remoteness, fossilisation, exclusiveness, obscurity and irrelevance put it in that class, despite its far greater literary and historical importance, which is basic. My students at Tokyo University found it boring, scorned it, and in general were very ignorant about it; they preferred Shakespeare, by whom they were genuinely excited, and Eliot, on whose *Murder in the Cathedral* more university theses have been written in Japan than in England.

Their rejection of *No* is, of course, no good reason for us to reject it too; and one cannot pretend, either that the traditional *No* is dying, for as Donald Keene says in his introduction to Mishima's plays, 'There are today larger audiences than ever, and new theatres are being built in Tokyo, Kyoto and other cities.' But these audiences are not made up of young people, and the force behind the building of theatres is often official—Japanese governments are very conscious of a duty to preserve the native artistic past.

The fact that Mishima, a man in his early thirties, has attempted to revive the *No* in a modern form is therefore interesting in itself, and is the more interesting because he is an extremely successful and sophisticated writer of novels, short stories and film scripts; the golden boy of contemporary Japanese literature, with a reputation something like that of Somerset Maugham, Dylan Thomas and Scott Fitzgerald combined, if such a hybrid can be imagined. Unfortunately, the only complete work of his which has previously been seen in England is *The Sound of Waves,* a trivial idyll which no Japanese I ever met took seriously. These five plays are obviously an attempt at something much bigger. That on the whole they fail, in English and in print, is only what one would expect; the language, the background, the assumptions—these account for some of the trouble. On the other hand, to say that 'the construction isn't good' (and such a criticism leaps up at once) would be like criticising a Japanese room for not having chairs: the Japanese write plays and they sit down, just like us, but the context is different. And the one play I have seen acted of these five, **Hanjo,** presented in Dr. Keene's translation, performed by amateurs and produced by Mishima himself, came across astonishingly well. On the page, I still find it, as I did before the performance, rather empty and even pretentious; but it has a strange, inactive poetry of its own, which lies, perhaps, in the gestures and silences the words assume rather than in the words themselves, and which therefore must be stag^d before it can be seen.

Two of the plays make a less qualified impression simply at a reading: **The Damask Drum** and **Kantan.** Here, the modern situations are defined with greater precision, the characterisation is clearer (particularly in **The Damask Drum,** with the firmly differentiated old caretaker, dance-teacher, *couturier,* Foreign Office type and callow postwar youth), and the typical *No* juxtaposition of bleak tragedy and witty comedy (which in the traditional *No* is split into separate but consecutively performed plays—the *No* play proper followed by the *kyogen*) is given more emphasis. These plays retain few of the qualities that Yeats saw in *No,* and those English readers whose knowledge of *No* is based on *At the Hawk's Well* and the Waley translations may feel them to be a different genre. But Mishima has, however remotely and with whatever overall impression of failure, managed to inject some fresh and youthful blood into one of the oldest and most austere of dramatic forms.

> *Anthony Thwaite, "Golden Boy," in* The Spectator, *Vol. 200, No. 6758, January 3, 1958, p. 24.*

Bettina L. Knapp   (essay date 1980)

[*Knapp is the author of numerous books on French drama, including* Jean Cocteau: A Critical Study *(1970), and* French Theatre 1918-1939 *(1985). In the following essay, she traces the philosophical traditions of Zen Buddhism, Shintoism, and Taoism as they intertwine within* The Damask Drum. *Furthermore, she praises the "intensity of sustained emotion" that this work provides.*]

Yukio Mishima (1925-70), novelist, poet, dramatist, film director, and head of a personal army numbering approximately 100 men, was also the author of successful Noh plays. Rooted in Japanese philosophy, history and culture, characteristics of this form of theatre, Mishima's Noh dramas expanded their focus: they were transposed into modern terms, thereby answering contemporary spiritual needs. Past and present are blended into one symbolic dramatic ritual in **The Damask Drum** (1955): image, line, color and tonality lure and allure the viewer into a complex of mysterious elements.

The product of samurai upbringing, Mishima was educated according to the tenets of his class: the code of strength was uppermost. Courage, will and loyalty to the Emperor had been impressed upon him since his earliest days. Spartan in his ways, honorable in his acts, humble in his attitudes, Mishima was also a specialist in the martial arts of *kendo* (dueling with bamboo staves) and karate. There

was, however, another side to this man of iron: that of the poet. Endowed with extraordinary sensitivity, Mishima understood and reacted to the exquisitely delicate aspects of Japanese art. He felt the *livingness* of the Oriental's nuanced universe and entered into complicity with nature in its most elemental ramifications. Mishima set down his thoughts and feelings when a student at Tokyo Imperial University (1944) in a collection of short stories. Kawabata, the future Nobel Prize winner who became Mishima's mentor, encouraged him to pursue a literary course. His advice was accepted by the acolyte. The author of 257 books (fifteen novels, some of which have been translated into English), Mishima emphasized Japan's rich heritage and the poignancy of the confrontation which his culture had to undergo in modern times. At the age of forty-five, Mishima committed *seppuku* (ritual suicide), thus effecting in the real world what had been imagistically and symbolically portrayed in his premonitory work *Runaway Horses.*

The Damask Drum introduces audiences to two different acting areas on stage: the third floors of two office buildings in downtown Tokyo. A law office is visible on one side of the acting area; on the opposite is a couturière's establishment. A street below separates the two: it is marked with the hustle and bustle, neon lights and other brash elements of contemporary life. An old janitor, Iwakichi, is sweeping out the law office. A pretty young clerk, Kayoko, is talking to him. She complains about the difficulties involved in earning a living. During the course of the conversation we learn that Iwakichi has fallen in love with one of the clients of the fashionable dressmaker on the other side of the street whom he had observed only through the window. Kayoko derides the old man for his passion. Suddenly the lights switch off in the law office, only to be turned on in the dressmaking establishment. We now listen to the conversations of a heartless dance master, an unfeeling young man, an arrogant member of the Ministry of Foreign Affairs and the self-satisfied owner of the dressmaking establishment. Irony and satire mark their discourse. We are informed about Iwakichi's love letters, which Kayoko has been delivering daily to the dressmaker's establishment. They mock him, and the dance master creates a plan. He will use one of his props, a drum, to which he will attach a note informing Iwakichi that if he beats the drum his lady-love will hear the sound and be forever his. They throw the drum through the window. Iwakichi receives it, reads the note and is thrilled at the prospect. What he does not know is that the drum is not made of skin but of damask. No matter how hard he pounds, no sound is emitted. His despair drives him to suicide; and unseen by the audience, he jumps out of the window.

Like many Noh plays, **The Damask Drum** is constructed in two parts, the second of which features Iwakichi's return as a ghost. His ladylove, now present, is no longer the pure idealized image he had believed her to be, but a "whore." Unrequited in her love experiences, she longs for Iwakichi's "real" love as he does for hers. He beats the drum once again, fervently and passionately. Owing to the woman's heartlessness throughout life, however, she is unable to hear the sound. Iwakichi's ghost dies of despair.

In accordance with traditional Noh theatre, *The Damask Drum* is a combination of dance, song and poetic recitation. Although it brings to the stage specific situations and individual beings, an ambiguous condition is experienced. The characters are archetypal in nature; they bathe in a mythical world beyond the space/time continuum. Like weightless entities, they articulate their tensions, and pain grips them in spasmodic sequences. *The Damask Drum* is a play in which the unexpressed is more important than the revealed, silence more predominant than the articulated word, the void prevails over the filled and the amorphous is preferred to the formed.

As traditional Noh drama is religiously oriented, so *The Damask Drum* is imbued with the three most important Japanese philosophical traditions: Taoism, Shintoism and Zen Buddhism. According to the tenets of these sects, the transcendental rather than the individual sphere is experienced—the eternal and not the mortal, the life force (cosmic energy or breath) and not the concrete deity. Noh plays therefore do not bathe in linear time but in cyclical schemes. Although *The Damask Drum* takes place in April, it could be the spring season of any year in any place in the world—that period when the aridity of winter burgeons into hope. Decors are likewise vague; always symbolic, they reflect a mood, a vision, an idealized love, as in *The Damask Drum:* the awakening of powerful emotions which lead directly into pain, controlled yet burning inwardly, altering in accordance with the cosmic life force, so important to the Oriental metaphysician and poet. The visible element on stage reflects not the exterior world, but an inner spiritual and emotional climate. Because of the profoundly spiritual focus, viewers apprehend Noh drama in general and *The Damask Drum* in particular; they penetrate its world intuitively. During the course of its stage life, insights are released, enlightenment is experienced, the mystery of matter becomes discernible—not perhaps in the phenomenological world, but in the deeply spiritual universe of the Japanese soul.

The Damask Drum has maintained the formulae of Noh theatre in its spiritual outlook, its themes, characters, relationship to nature and use of symbol. Like Zen Buddhism and Taoism, *The Damask Drum* is meditative, introspective, slow-paced, subtle and suggestive. The depth and meaning of Iwakichi's love may be apprehended in sudden flashes of illumination; it is not brash or aggressive, but turned inward, felt, sensed. Like conventional Noh drama, *The Damask Drum* has no real plot, and therefore it may take an infinite amount of patience for a Westerner to understand the series of complex images which make up its song-and-dance sequences, tonalities and the inflections included in its choral and orchestral accompaniments. Of import are Iwakichi's sensations; the feelings evoked during the course of the performance; the tensions aroused by the images implicit in his discourse, his gestures and pace (the timing, for example, between the sweeping sequences and the apostrophe to the potted laurel tree in the office which he personifies and cares for with love and affection). All aspects of Iwakichi's stage life, as well as that of the other protagonists, are stylized and predetermined: spatial patterns woven about the stage, poses, interpretations—all add to the fascination of the theatrical experience.

Important in *The Damask Drum,* as it had been in ancient Noh theatre, is the relationship between the stage proceedings and nature. Although the play takes place in two office buildings, there is a symbolic correlation between Iwakichi's feelings and attitudes and nature in general: a correspondence between the cosmic domain and its interaction with regard to the individual in the phenomenological world. These two realms inspire resonance and infinite patterns and distillations of sensations and moods.

The notion of timelessness and eternal becoming implicit in traditional Noh drama is clearly discernible in *The Damask Drum.* Iwakichi lives in a three-dimensional as well as in a four-dimensional sphere. He experiences these worlds interchangeably. In the phenomenological domain, matter and spirit only seem to operate antithetically; in reality, they are manifestations of the Taoist's yin/yang principles, a single universal cosmic force. Since matter and spirit are one in the atemporal sphere, death and life coincide, as do image and reality, fiction and fact. Duality and multiplicity exist only in the existential domain, in Iwakichi's world. The conflicts which arise are stressed by Mishima throughout *The Damask Drum* not only for dramatic purposes, but also for metaphysical reasons: age as opposed to youth, inanimate and animate objects, life and death, outer and inner domains, solitude and society, business and poetry. These divergent ways are forever intruding one upon the other. "They've switched off the light," Iwakichi says. "Every day at the same time. . . . When this room dies that one comes to life again. And in the morning when this room returns to life, that one dies." The continuity of this duality expresses the eternal play of conflicting forces which must be endured in life.

Iwakichi's "feeling" world stands for ancient ways, spiritual climes as opposed to the harshness of a burgeoning industrial society which is determined to destroy tradition. As the member of the Ministry of Foreign Affairs says when talking about Iwakichi and the world he represents: "It is essential to make him realize that where he lives is a little room nobody will enter." Iwakichi's world is closed, gone, dead to the agents of contemporary culture. Yet the two domains are linked, connected in the form of the clerk Kayoko, who, although a product of twentieth-century ways, still understands traditional views, the nuanced sensitivity of a bygone world. It is she who delivers Iwakichi's love letters to the woman across the way. It is she who can feel the pain involved when one has outlived an age, an approach to life, a society. Two forces which make up the universe according to Taoist doctrine are part of the cosmic flow: it is Kayoko who becomes the catalyst, forcing fusion or dissolution.

That Mishima has situated his drama on the third floor of two office buildings is not surprising. Verticality was always an important factor in Noh drama. The height of the office building corresponds to the mountains which figure so prominently in early Noh theatre. Motionless, still, mountains represent ethereal spheres: heaven, spirit, light circulating about the universe. So the office building in *The Damask Drum* reveals Iwakichi's vision: his love which is too absolute; his desire, overly encompassing; his idealization. The dichotomy between the purity of this image—that is, his ladylove (height)—and the earthiness of the woman of reality (ground) is too great to take on existence in the phenomenological sphere. It can only come to life in the imagination. Iwakichi's earthly fall in suicide at the conclusion of the first part of *The Damask Drum* compels him to take stock of the polarities between fantasy and reality and to rework his vision. Only in death does divergency vanish and oneness prevail.

In the collective and cosmic world of Noh theatre, nature is neither crushed nor violated, nor is it used exclusively for man's benefit, as is so frequently the case in the Western world. In *The Damask Drum* nature is experienced as part of a whole. It is loved and appreciated spiritually, esthetically and physically. When, for example, Iwakichi looks at the potted laurel tree in the office, he cares for it, loves it, personifies it, apostrophizes it. He grasps its spirit, its superworldly aspects; understands its beauty, its mobile attitudes and pulsations.

In accordance with the close correspondence between man and nature characteristic of Noh drama, Mishima's use of natural forces is implicit in his work. Wind, for example, to which Iwakichi alludes when he opens the window, is alive; it enters into the stage ritual as a turbulent force, a catalyst. Iwakichi describes his feelings in terms of the wind, thus emphasizing their transpersonal nature: "I can't stand that dusty wind that blows at the beginning of spring." He longs for "the calm of the evening." Spring, although specific, takes on universality because of the successive seasons implied, the death/rebirth cycle of which it is a part. It reflects the rhythms of life; the lives of the societies and civilizations to which the protagonist belongs. Spring is the symbol of eternal renewal. It mirrors the notion of perpetual becoming: of love forever burgeoning and vanishing.

Iwakichi fears inner chaos, and the wind is an outer manifestation of this state: a world with which he cannot cope: "the dusty wind" which forces up the dross and earthiness of life as well as its spiritual counterpart. He rejects the frightening and sinister character of a wind which alters nature's seeming stability and longs for the stillness of the clouds which endow the world with serenity. As the wind dies down, images of softness and tenderness appear in Iwakichi's mind's eye, immersing him in the tranquil climate of his own being: "The wind's died down since evening."

Inasmuch as Noh theatre is archetypal and bathes in the collective domain, specifics such as characters and sets are to be considered symbolically. Characters in traditional Noh theatre are fixed for the most part. Iwakichi, the Old Man, corresponds to the *shite,* the main actor. Although he does not wear a mask (nor does he under certain circumstances in ancient Noh plays), his face itself remains expressionless: it virtually becomes a mask. Because of its immobility it stands out in sharp contrast to his bodily movements, vocal tones and complex of sculptured spatial forms which he weaves about the stage as he sweeps the room, tends to the laurel tree and writes his letters. Iwakichi's expressionless face severs him from the outside world. He must therefore look inward. In so doing, he injects his part with "emotional coloring" by means of a va-

riety of poses of the head and neck and by downward or upward glances and intricate gestures. The ensemble of accessories used by Iwakichi, such as his broom, the laurel plant to which he talks, the letter-writing ceremony and his nuanced vocal emissions, are integrated into a new unity, thus making for a total effect. The individual character takes part in a cosmic drama.

Iwakichi in many respects is reminiscent of a Zen Buddhist priest who is detached from the material world, which he considers meaningless. He has swept it all away, symbolically speaking, and has rid himself of the dross, the material encumbrances which tie him to life. His inner riches—his fantasy world, his dream—the realm of the absolute, are of higher value to him. Only in the spiritual sphere does he feel the pulsations, the breath and cosmic rhythms of the universe about him; only in this domain does he experience the dynamism of life and feelings of belonging. The opposite world is expressed in the dressmaking establishment across the way: artifice, materialism, arrogance and cruelty—all forces with which Iwakichi must contend.

Kayoko, the young letter-carrying clerk, may be considered a kind of contemporary *waki,* a wanderer throughout the temporal and atemporal realm. She sets up the dialogue or chemical interchange between the two views of life. Although specific, the repetition of her activity takes on cyclical import: that of a perpetual death/birth ritual. Hope is injected into Iwakichi's life when she delivers the letters, and despair when no answer is forthcoming. Not only does Kayoko act as a link between Iwakichi's world and society at large, but she herself also straddles two civilizations: past and present. Beset by economic difficulties, she too is a victim of spiritual crisis: that of the individual who has not yet discovered her groundbed.

The dancing master, the young man, the government official and the owner of the dressmaking establishment are ironic, satiric and humorous in a rather grotesque manner. They are modern counterparts of the *kyogen,* those ancient clowns who kept audiences amused by their farces and laughable ways. Anonymous beings who emerge from nowhere and vanish into darkness, they serve to heighten tension, to explain the stage happenings in less than poetic language. They infuse comedy as well as cruelty into Iwakichi's poignant love situation by relating vignettes and revealing unusual incidents associated with letters delivered by Kayoko.

Although only a stage prop, the damask drum, as a symbol, is steeped in tradition. It is representational and yet remains functionless. Comparable to the *koan,* a device used by Zen Buddhists to banish rational and syllogistic reasoning (techniques so dear to Western mentality), it serves as a basis for experience. It allows Iwakichi to become exposed to the mysteries of existence, to intuit undreamed-of truths, to transcend individual understanding. The drum leads to Iwakichi's sudden awakening to the realization of his situation and its impossibility—hence his suicide. When he first takes hold of the drum after it has been tossed out of the office window into his own, he thinks he can win his beloved by pounding on it. He has not yet been initiated into the atemporal sphere of the *koan* and so is incapable of entering into that dimension which would allow him to understand the "foolishness" of his passion.

When Iwakichi strikes the drum—attempting to use it for his own purposes in the existential sphere—he is doomed to failure. As a *koan,* it bathes in its own logic; it participates in cosmic consciousness, which is incompatible with that of worldly spheres. Had Iwakichi been trained by a Zen master, his comprehension of the meaning and focus of this object would have been deeper. As stage property, the drum belongs to the logical and rationally oriented universe, the intellectual sphere and not the archetypal realm. In that it was sent to Iwakichi by those living in the temporal world, the drum represents formalism, convention, geometrical and causal reality. The dimensionless universe sought by Iwakichi and implicit in Zen Buddhism and Taoism implies a world *in potentia*—the notion of perpetual becoming.

The drum which Iwakichi beats, but which remains soundless because of its material, is as alive in his mind as is the potted laurel tree. In keeping with Shinto belief, everything in nature, whether animate or inanimate, is alive. Shinto deities (*kami*), in the form of spirits of trees, mountains, flowers, ancestors, heroes, the sun or the moon, breathe, act and react in the existential sphere. Man approaches the *kami* without fear and in friendship. A force or *kami* therefore inhabits both the essence of the drum and the laurel tree. Although the drum did not respond to Iwakichi's pleadings, the laurel tree does. It has been transformed in his fantasy world into a princess that takes on life in a garden inhabited by the moon: "She's the princess of the laurel, the tree that grows in the garden of the moon." All the poetry, sensitivity and creative impact of his feelings emerge in this one symbol. Its beauty and gentleness become consoling forces for Iwakichi, who feels his loneliness with such desperation.

The laurel and the moon are recurrent images in Iwakichi's world: they usher in a mood of melancholy. The moon, symbol of transformation, represents biological rhythms and cyclical states. Frequently evoked by Japanese poets, the moon is associated with indirect rather than direct experience and knowledge: passivity, receptivity, and the dream. As it makes its way in the night world of Iwakichi's unconscious, this celestial force conjures up a domain inhabited by spirits, ghosts and images which would allow him to embrace his beloved.

The Japanese have always been "Moon lovers." Iwakichi is no exception. The eerie and mysterious light which emanates from this force suggests a dim, insinuating, shaded domain. It is never brilliant nor filled with glaring lights; rather it is remote, distant, already lived. Objects illuminated by moonlight are not individualized but blend into the environment—hazy, essentially obscure, hiding through the branches of the laurel, stirring the feelings of the onlooker. Its soft light falls lovingly on the complex designs and forms inhabiting the stage. A shadowy world emerges, paving the way for the ghostly encounter in the second part of *The Damask Drum.*

The moon and the laurel are one for Iwakichi. Each injects a sense of belonging or *participation mystique* into the proceedings; each endows the events with painful feeling tones, underscoring the bleakness of Iwakichi's temporal existence and the beauty of his idealization. Yet when Iwakichi's spirit returns, his beloved is no longer that pure being he had created in his mind's eye, but rather a "whore" who longs for the purity of an unborn—unmanifested—love. As he beats the drum once again, hoping this time to breach the gap—to link dichotomies between the invisible and visible spheres—the cold rays of an unfeeling moon envelop the atmosphere, divesting the world of all its warmth and, in so doing, leading to another painful demise.

In contrast to Western theatre, where characters attempt to mark their roles with individuality, the Noh actor focuses his efforts on the creation of emotion—love, anger, revenge, hate—in order to go beyond the individual personality. The facts of the situation to be enacted are stated at the outset of the drama; the atmosphere, mood and poetry conveyed by the role rather than the being itself must be portrayed during the course of the spectacle. For the Westerner, *The Damask Drum* may lack action and conflict. For the Oriental, tension is concentrated and distilled in the images, poetry, gesture and plastic forms which move about the stage. The spatial compositions create the mood, develop and pursue the single emotion which is the sine qua non of Noh theatre.

Just as the Zen painter uses the fewest possible brushstrokes to express the world of multiplicity, so Zen poetry is also known for its sparseness. Mishima maintains this tradition. A word in *The Damask Drum* stands alone, bare, solitary, divested of adjectives and adverbs, and becomes an entity unto itself. As in Bashō's haiku poems, the image delineated becomes "the agent" of cosmic force, bringing illumination to the phenomenological world, making a more profound reality known.

The Damask Drum reflects the Taoist's and the Zen Buddhist's calmness of mind and oneness with nature. It is a manifestation of the Shintoist's animistic beliefs which endow inanimate objects with a *livingness,* thereby enlarging the scope and depth of the dramatic spectacle. Noh theatre, whether ancient or as recreated by Mishima, is unique. It varies from all other forms of performing arts such as song, mime, dance, verse and drama; yet it includes them all. It is the intensity of sustained emotion in *The Damask Drum* which moves audiences and not the realistic portrayals, the sublimated passion with its exquisitely nuanced poetry and its cosmic purpose and design which forces its impress upon the viewer. (pp. 383-87)

        Bettina L. Knapp, "Mishima's Cosmic Noh Drama: 'The Damask Drum'," in World Literature Today, *Vol. 54, No. 3, Summer, 1980, pp. 383-87.*

John K. Gillespie   (essay date 1982)

[*In the essay below, Gillespie explores Mishima's "aesthetic pessimism" as seen in* Hanjo, The Damask Drum, *and* Sotoba Komachi. *These works, the critic argues, demonstrate Mishima's rejection of the modernist*

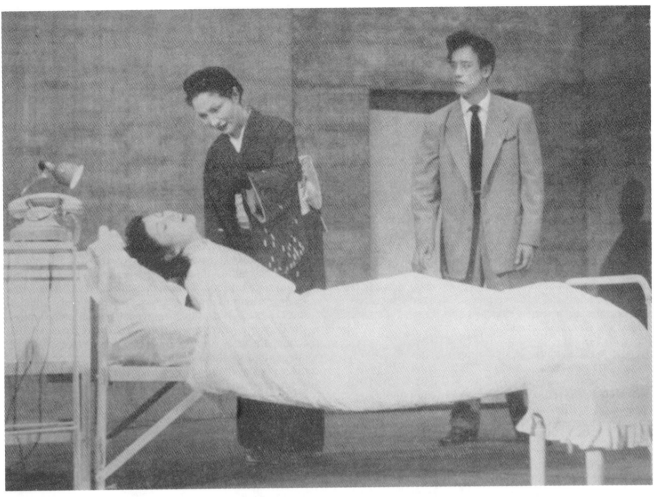

Aoi, Mrs. Rokujo, and Hikaru in The Lady Aoi.

view—particularly as expressed in William Butler Yeats's "Sailing to Byzantium"—that art is eternal and thus provides a refuge or sanctuary from mundane life. Although "Mishima denies the very sufficiency of art to fulfill life's needs," Gillespie adds, "ironically, he achieves his end with stunning artistry" in these three pieces. Japanese characters given by the critic in names and titles have been silently deleted.]

In 'Sailing to Byzantium', William Butler Yeats articulates an important mood in modern artistic endeavors. The unageing Byzantine monuments provided, for him, an alluring harbor, a compelling raison d'être. Yeats perceived the monuments of Byzantium, indeed, the very aesthetic atmosphere of the city, as sufficient unto themselves: art preserves for eternity and itself becomes eternal. Such a mood characterizes the work of a number of modern writers such as Oscar Wilde and Walter Pater in Britain, Stefan George and Gottfried Benn in Germany, Stéphane Mallarmé and Paul Verlaine in France. So enamored was Gustave Flaubert of this aesthetic *Weltanschauung* that he wrote what amounts to a pithy manifesto: 'Life is so horrible that one can only bear it by avoiding it. And that can be done by living in the world of Art.' Irving Howe [in *The Idea of the Modern in Literature and the*

Arts] affirms this view as peculiarly modern: 'The idea of art as a sanctuary from the emptying-out of life is intrinsic to modernism. . . .'

Nor were Japanese writers immune to the delights of Byzantium. At certain periods in their lives, Takayama Chogyū, Tanizaki Jun'ichirō, Nagai Kafū, Miki Rofū, Yokomitsu Riichi, Nishiwaki Jun'zaburō, and Yoshioka Minoru, among others, were all mesmerized by what Yeats calls 'the artifice of eternity'. Nishiwaki typifies this aesthetic mood when he writes in *Shi to Shiron*: 'The beauty I seek allows us to forget everything. . . . We are to think of nothing, but just to be receptive of that very abstract sense which comes purely from the sense of sight. Meanwhile, we should not feel any "meaning" in life. . . . We should simply live in a world of color, a world of form, a world of light and darkness.'

But Mishima Yukio shatters the mood of Byzantium. He rails against 'the artifice of eternity', crying out with an anguished voice that art alone cannot provide a safe haven. Listen to him in *Kinkakuji*: 'The eternality of beauty surely obstructs our lives and poisons existence.' And 'beauty, beautiful things are now, for me, deadly enemies.' Although at one time he might have savored the delights of

Byzantium, Mishima makes it clear that his journey cannot end there; he must sail beyond.

Mishima makes this journey in his so-called modern noh plays, which are certainly more modern than noh. Although he adopts the titles and basic dramatic situations of the older plays, his versions have far more in common with, say, the theatre of the absurd. For he adheres to few of the conventions of the traditional noh theatre, utilizing instead contemporary speech, naturalistic gestures, stage settings, and make-up. While Zeami [an early Muromachi period noh actor, playwright, and critic (c. 1364–c. 1443)] evokes passionate feeling, Mishima elicits intellectual response. While noh nurtures in the spectator a spiritual reassurance with overtones of life, Mishima's modern noh often gives rise to vague anxieties with overtones of death; while Zeami's flower must bloom, Mishima's already is dead and withered. Ultimately, Mishima denies the very sufficiency of art to fulfill life's needs, although, ironically, he achieves his end with stunning artistry. The purpose of this article is to examine Mishima's pessimistic view of art in the three of his modern noh plays which are structured by this notion: *Aya no Tsuzumi* [*The Damask Drum*], *Hanjo,* and *Sotoba Komachi.*

In [*Aya no Tsuzumi*], Mishima reveals his essentially modern artistic preoccupation as he undertakes to penetrate the nature and function of the aesthetic spirit. This he achieves by crystallizing onstage the attempts at human expression of the unfortunate old janitor Iwakichi. Iwakichi's dilemma is his uncontrollable passion for Hanako, a paragon of beauty, whom he frequently observes making purchases at the dress shop across the street. He writes love letters to her, but they are suppressed by Madame, the shop owner, fearing the loss of a good customer. Three friends of Madame finally reveal to Hanako the contents of the thirtieth letter, which ends in a plea for a single kiss. One of the friends devises a plan to deal with Iwakichi: they will toss a damask drum to the old janitor urging him to strike it, and, if the sound is heard across the street, Hanako will grant his wish. Alas, the damask drum emits no sound; in despair, Iwakichi jumps to his death. In the second part of the play, he returns in proper noh form as a ghost and confronts Hanako directly. But his despair is rekindled for she still does not hear the beat of the damask drum. The play ends on this non-note.

How does such action probe the nature and function of the aesthetic spirit? Mishima effects this by placing the aesthetic spirit on the vehicle of the old janitor's fanciful, poetic love. Early in the play, for example, Iwakichi muses on Hanako as he composes his thirtieth letter: 'You are the laurel in the midst of the moon.' But the futility of his efforts is immediately evident when we witness Iwakichi's relationship with the potted laurel tree to which he compares Hanako. Affectionately watering the plant, he caresses its leaves, murmuring, 'A little bit more and your leaves will soon have a lustrous gloss. Poets used to speak of black hair lustrous as leaves. . . . ' Clearly indicated in Iwakichi's tender relationship with this potted plant is his pitiable inability to communicate with other human beings.

Mishima juxtaposes Iwakichi's lyrical reverie with the prosaic dialogue in the dress shop (on the other side of the stage). This division serves to clarify Iwakichi's dilemma, for the conversation of the bourgeois clones in the dress shop is at every point inimical to Iwakichi and what he represents. For example, the bureaucrat Kaneko establishes his essential superficiality by pontificating of Iwakichi that 'weirdos who believe in real feelings' are not to be tolerated. For, he says, 'love begins from the tongue.' To this, Madame interjects, 'My, how erotic!' Such insensitive, anti-aesthetic banter provides sharp counterpoint to the genuine, if simple, emotion of Iwakichi. He wants to communicate with Hanako, but how is he to combat such overwhelming forces?

We arrive at the crux of the problem in an ironic statement by Fujima, who, as a dance instructor, is a bourgeois artist figure: ' . . . I have learnt that the only condition for dance is that there be uninhibited freedom for the movements of the hands. That old man is really trying hard to head up his own school [he moves his hands as if dancing about] . . . he thus is neglectful of the free and uninhibited ecstasy of love.' With this, Fujima completely undermines aesthetic indulgence, making of art a merely mechanical reaction, the only stipulation for which is that there be room enough to move about. The irony is that he and his confreres are so hemmed in by bourgeois convention that any unprescribed movement is for them impossible. In fact, they let their own 'freedom' infringe upon Iwakichi's, who is trying to free his love from the bonds that fetter it. The foul trick which they perpetrate on him is a matter of course for them; we have come to expect such behavior on their part. And so they toss him the damask drum.

Excited about this turn of events, Iwakichi drapes the drum—itself an exquisite art object worthy of Byzantium's unageing monuments—about his laurel tree and begins to beat it. After a time, however, hearing no sound at all, he loses hope and leaps to his death. In this way, Mishima symbolically illustrates the hapless plight of the aesthetic spirit in the modern world. But this does not yet spell irrevocable death for the aesthetic spirit; Iwakichi reappears as a ghost and confronts Hanako. This ghost scene is shrewdly conceived, for when Iwakichi re-enters this life as a supernatural being still in possession of the aesthetic spirit, still yearning to communicate his love, that spirit is rendered for a brief moment as a phenomenon embodying a power greater than that of merely human life.

At this point, Mishima's play gains depth by the obvious parallel to Zeami's. In that play, Iwakichi's prototype, an old gardener, finds that his desire to express love for the princess merely by casting his eyes upon her (an action that would make him her equal) is rewarded by the damask-drum treatment. He too dies of despair but returns as the ghost of a demon, complaining, 'My heart is spent . . . consumed in glimpsing moon rays thinly slanting through the trees.' Similarly, even the rejuvenated expressions of love for Hanako by Iwakichi as ghost slip away unanswered, spent, as though he too were attempting to seize elusive moon rays. But Mishima counterpoints sharply his conclusion with Zeami's; while Zeami's princess ultimately repents of the evil inflicted on the old gardener, Hanako and Iwakichi have a different experience:

> HANAKO: I've come at your behest. But you still don't know me. You don't know how I was able to come here.
>
> IWAKICHI: Because I drew you.
>
> HANAKO: No. Without human strength, doors . . . don't open.
>
> IWAKICHI: Would you deceive even a ghost?

Hanako remains impervious to Iwakichi's plight. She fails to perceive his ghostly presence as proof of his more-than-human passion, as a manifestation of the power of the aesthetic spirit. There is no genuine communication between them. The modern age, Mishima appears to say, is no longer capable of genuine communication, no longer capable of apprehending the aesthetic spirit.

This truth is even more apparent in the ensuing dialogue when Hanako claims that Iwakichi's love has been insufficient and for that reason no sound came from the drum. Desperately, the ghost pounds the drum: 'My love will make the damask drum sound! [The drum sounds clearly.] It sounded! It sounded! Didn't you hear it?' But Hanako, 'smiling slyly', says, 'I can't hear anything.' Although the drum is now sounding clearly, Iwakichi's love is crushed under Hanako's negative reaction. Doubting his own ears, he intones the death knell of the aesthetic spirit: 'It's no good, useless. Won't this drum make any sound at all? Even when I pound it, the damask drum is silent, useless.' What is the use of the aesthetic spirit? How is it relevant to life? Only negative answers are possible when the beating stops after the hundredth stroke and Iwakichi's ghost disappears. Hanako's final words have a hollow ring: 'I could have heard if only he had beat it one more time.' Surely, this utterance marks the futility of human endeavor and the sterility of the aesthetic spirit as represented in the play as a whole. Moreover, it is made by Hanako, whose very name is clearly a play on Zeami's notion of the flower; whereas for Zeami this term signified supreme aesthetic achievement, for Mishima it has anti-aesthetic import. For Hanako is hardly receptive of the aesthetic spirit. Another drumbeat, we can be certain, would have changed nothing. In this way, Mishima thrusts the aesthetic spirit, overlaying Iwakichi's passion, into the realm of real-life human expression and finds it wanting.

The problem of **Hanjo** is perhaps suggested by the manner in which old Iwakichi had fallen in love. For, as with Zeami's gardener, it is by a mere glimpse, and it is in this single, initial moment that his love is unconscious of external, destructive forces, untarnished by anxiety and despair. Iwakichi says,

> . . . then I saw her for the first time. If I were to tell you about the beauty of her face, well, it was like the moon. Right around it everything was shining brilliantly. She said something and then she smiled. My whole body was shaking. She smiled! I stood staring at her from behind this window. . . . That's the moment it began.

Kanze Hideo, comparing Zeami and Mishima [in "Noh Business," *Concerned Theatre in Japan* 1 (Winter-Spring 1970-1971)], explains Mishima's interest in such a momentary event: 'Zeami talked about a "flower of youth", which he regarded as something extremely beautiful yet fleeting. Zeami tried to think of something eternal in contrast to this passing beauty. Mishima, however, remained interested only in the flower of youth, only in momentary beauty.'

In *Hanjo,* Mishima creates such a moment. There are three characters: Hanako, a mad woman; Honda Jitsuko, an artist; and Yoshio, erstwhile lover of Hanako. Yoshio has had a brief affair with Hanako several years ago and has exchanged fans with her as promise of his return. He fails to return and Hanako, while continuing to await him, gradually loses her sanity. Jitsuko, enraptured with Hanako's beauty, keeps her in Tokyo, fearing Yoshio might actually return and take Hanako away from her. But when Yoshio suddenly appears on the scene, the distraught Hanako does not recognize him. Yoshio departs and Hanako continues to hope for the return of her lover.

Mishima creates his 'momentary beauty' through the character of Hanako. Shortly before Yoshio arrives, Hanako lyrically reveals her inner thoughts to Jitsuko:

> HANAKO: Then I'll surely look like a little island. I'll look like a little island lost in sleep . . . waiting and wondering with each passing day whether a boat, its sails transparent against the deep red horizon of the setting sun, won't head this way. On that island, even by day the moon comes out, even by night the sun shines, and clocks are useless. I'm getting rid of mine, as of today.
>
> JITSUKO: [dolefully] Why?
>
> HANAKO: Because then the train will never leave.

In this way, Hanako attempts to revert permanently to the moment of bliss when her lover was by her side. Aesthetically imagining herself as 'a little island', she isolates herself from the possibility of grievous experience; abandoning her clock, she halts the flow of time that would sap the vitality of her one, fleeting moment of happiness. Clearly, we must count her among the 'lords and ladies of Byzantium'.

At this point, Yoshio appears in the doorway, thus shaking the foundation of Hanako's attempt to arrest time; his appearance verifies that the train on which he took his leave from her indeed departed. Yet, steeped as she is in her obsession for the preservation of a single, past moment in time, Hanako fails to recognize Yoshio when he finally returns. For she has kept him fettered in that instant of time. How, then, could he be anywhere else? After a strained attempt to make her recognize him, Yoshio leaves. It is as if he had never come. Hanako says to Jitsuko: 'In the evening the morning sun shines and the cocks crow, don't they? On an island you don't need a clock or anything, do you?' Thus, Hanako remains within her isolated moment, determined, as Yeats says, 'to sing . . . of what is past, or passing, or to come.'

Again, Mishima adds depth by the Zeamian reference

points. Principally, there is the matter of the *hana* of Hanako. If Zeami's *hana* involved the creation of something eternal by which to contrast the fleetingly beautiful 'flower of youth', Mishima's flower involves the human futility of the effort to eternalize. For Hanako's attempt to halt time is surely bleak; Yoshio in fact returns, thus assuring us of Hanako's ultimate failure. Moreover, Hanako's effort to arrest time is artfully conceived; she is for Mishima an artist figure. And her effort, although bleak, is so successful that the reality of Yoshio, the object of her artistry who continues unarrested in time's advance, becomes lost to her forever. Sealing Hanako's dilemma is the fact that as she haplessly waits within her isolated moment, she grows older; she therefore loses her flower of youth, a principal ingredient in that moment. Finally, Jitsuko, a professional artist, yields Hanako nothing but her empty obsession for Hanako's beauty; she does nothing to mitigate Hanako's deepening madness and endless waiting for the cherished Yoshio.

Certainly, then, Mishima places himself at odds with the Zeamian aesthetic. He perceives no virtue in the ill-starred attempt to arrest time for some vague, eternal experience. Rather, he envisions only an ephemeral flower of youth, a momentary experience, uncontrasted by anything eternal. In the last analysis, this is the kind of moment Hanako experiences—a moment seizable but, having passed, irretrievable.

In [*Sotoba Komachi*], we are invited again to witness the modern impasse in human communication, the plight of the aesthetic spirit, and the modern obsession for the intensity of experience contained within a single moment. Here again Mishima makes pronouncement on the relationship between art and life.

The main characters are an old woman, who calls herself Komachi, and a poet. The old woman sits on a park bench counting cigarette butts. The poet approaches and the old woman tells of her youth when she was an acclaimed beauty and had a lover whose desire she promised to fulfill on the hundredth night of their courtship. The poet is taken by this and suggests that he pretend to be her lover on the hundredth night. They partially re-enact that fateful experience, but afterward the poet continues to behold the ugly old Komachi as beautiful, just as if the pretense had not ended. He yearns for that wonderful, fleeting moment when Komachi will finally grant him the desire of his heart. Komachi warns against the futility and even danger of his obsession. But for the poet it is a moment of such beauty that he claims he would gladly die for it. And so he does, although with a sudden loss of enthusiasm for death. Meanwhile, Komachi returns to her original task, counting cigarette butts.

A salient aspect of this play is the accuracy of Komachi's observations. When the poet first approaches, she recognizes him immediately as a poet. A few lines later she perceives the mark of death on his face. She complements this observation by asserting that all who have called her beautiful in the past have died; therefore, the poet should beware lest he meet the same fate. Such accuracy casts in a curious mold her other observations, as well as Mishima's own aims which are couched in those observations. Her

negative view of life is thus analogous to Mishima's skeptical view of the aesthetic spirit as providing sanctuary for human life. Komachi recalls her past:

> . . . when I was young, unless I felt myself spinning about, I never felt I was really alive. I sensed I was really alive only when I forgot myself. Since then I've become aware of my mistake. When every last girl's face looks like that of an empress, when you feel as if roses bloom on dead rose trees . . . idiotic things like that happened when I was young. But when I think about such times now, I know I was really dying. The worse the liquor, the quicker you get drunk. In the midst of my drunkenness, in the midst of my mushy feelings and maudlin tears, I was dying. Since then, I've been determined not to drink. This is the secret of my long life.

By this remarkable statement, Komachi repudiates the aesthetic spirit, the very value of inspiration, of art and its passion. Although in Byzantium Yeats would subsume himself aesthetically as 'a perne in a gyre', Komachi considers those moments when she felt herself 'spinning about' to be essentially useless. Thus, for Komachi, the wine of aesthetic inspiration yields not life but death. She prefers not the giddy heights of artistic creation but the predictable boredom of her daily existence: 'I know the face of a person come back to life. . . . It's a face of horrible boredom. And that very face, that's the one I like.' All this is the secret of her long life; even if she does not proclaim her happiness, she is nevertheless content to exist in an uneventful life completely purged of the aesthetic spirit.

Although the pretense of their reenactment is for Komachi merely a game, it becomes for the poet a tangible artistic achievement in which the flow of time is arrested. This artistry yields for the poet a single moment in which he valiantly expects a paroxysm of aesthetic ecstasy:

> . . . within a few minutes, a moment not possible in this world will come. When it does, the sun will shine in the dead of night. A big ship will sail into the middle of the courtyard. The trees will roar like the sea. In dreams like this, I feel I'm so happy my heart will stop beating.

The poet would sail to Byzantium, but the old woman senses the madness of his journey, terming him 'drunk', which, of course, aesthetically he is. She attempts in vain to steer him free of his dangerous obsession. The moment falls upon the poet, he calls Komachi 'the most beautiful woman in the world', and he dies.

What does Mishima accomplish by this? The similarity to *Hanjo* and Hanako's obsession with a clockless island is quickly apparent. The futility of Hanako, therefore, may well be the futility of the poet. More poignant, however, is the fact that this poet is merely a mediocre poet, if not a downright bad one. He is moved by such events in the play as the activities of the miserable lovers on a park bench. Komachi, of course, whose observations throughout the play are unerringly accurate, sees through the poet's imperceptive, mushy romanticizing. 'Utter foolishness,' she says. 'Why do you respect such things?' We thus are clearly invited by Mishima to judge as 'utter foolishness' the poet's sacred moment, his attempt at meaningful aesthetic expression. If the poet is a failure in one aesthetic area, he can hardly be expected suddenly to become a master in another. And so he pitifully constructs a vague moment in which he calls the obviously ugly Komachi beautiful. Moreover, he dies immediately, unable to probe the inner recesses of his created moment.

In his *Guide to Aesthetics,* Benedetto Croce casts in bold relief the particular dilemma of the poet in this play: 'Our thought is historical thought about an historical world, process of development about a development; and no sooner has the attribute of a reality been articulated than the attribute no longer holds because it has itself produced a new reality which awaits a new attribute.' Croce perceives that once a creator moves outside an aesthetic moment, thereby becoming conscious of its implication, the moment crumbles and loses its vitality, its inner necessity, and a new one must be created either to take its place or to sustain an analogous experience. Mishima's poet indeed creates an aesthetic moment and of such importance that he vows to remain within the moment by his willingness to die for it. Surely, he is convinced, death at the height of such aesthetic ecstasy would prolong the moment for eternity. But, alas, mediocre poet that he is, he fails in his artistic design by jumping outside his moment just prior to his death. Even before realizing the ineffable rapture of his moment, he suddenly divulges a 'disheartening feeling', which is his lurking fear of death. 'I don't want to die . . . ,' he says. As we sense his anxious tone of voice, we see him no longer at one with his moment; as he becomes conscious of his moment's implication, it crumbles before him. The attribute of his aesthetic reality, having been articulated, cries out for the new attribute of the consequent new reality. All too conscious now of himself and the implication of his endeavor, the poet is unable to comply.

Croce further rails against the ugliness born of extra-aesthetic concerns in a work of art, asserting that such ugliness 'rebels against the pure passion of art' and serves only to introduce 'dissonances and discords'. Thus, Mishima's poet further contributes to the crumbling of his moment by including Komachi in it. For she is the paragon of ugliness, of extra-aesthetic concerns, who condemns the poet's meager attempt at subsuming himself aesthetically and who seems most preoccupied with the mundane business of gathering and counting cigarette butts. Moreover, her attitude toward life is one of thorough-going pessimism—witness, in this respect, her reason for continuing in her wretched existence: 'Existing as I am, isn't that reason enough to keep on living?' In view of all this, the poet's failure is hardly surprising. Mishima indicates that the poet's aesthetic failure is also his human failure since the result of his aesthetic endeavor yields nothing more than an unwanted, unhappy death.

A brief look at the original noh play, by Kan'ami [Nambokuchō era actor and author (1333-84) and father of Zeami], serves to emphasize Mishima's point. Early in the play, the Shingon priests intone the line: 'Our lives we pass as in a fleeting dream-lull.' The aesthetic implication is that art itself is in a definite sense a non-material sur-

passing of reality, occurring in a dream-lull. The artist is the one who defines the dream-lull. Komachi, lamenting the loss of her beauty and her cruelty to her lover, seeks to make just such a definition: 'Although I am a lowly shard of driftwood, there are yet flowers at my heart. . . .' The phrase 'flowers at my heart' (*kokoro no hana*), synonymous in Japanese for 'poetry', reveals Komachi as receptive of the poetic spirit which propagates insight within her: 'In a fleeting instant, one thought can yield Buddhahood in the heart' (*ichinen hokki bodaishin*). We discern from this the prototypical attitude of Mishima's poet who feels that his one moment can deliver him from imperfection. Kan'ami's lofty perspicacity is evident here in that just as a flower grows from a sown seed, so Buddhahood, or salvation, flowers from a sown thought; hence, 'flowers at my heart' sow 'salvation in the heart'; in other words, the poetic or aesthetic spirit leads to human fulfillment.

Here once again the notion of the flower appears. Mishima's Komachi observes of the park-bench lovers:

> Don't they look like dead bodies? They're actually dying as they make out. [She sniffs the air]. . . . At night the flowers in the park smell nice. Exactly like those in a coffin. Those lovers are perfectly dead, buried in the smell of flowers. The only ones alive here are you and me.

The contrast with Kan'ami is sharp. The modern Komachi's denunciation of the lovers is made the more effective in her relegating the classical Komachi's life-yielding flower to the death-aura of a coffin. Mishima thereby expresses the folly of hoping that 'flowers at the heart' will yield 'salvation in the heart'; rather, he understands with his Komachi that such flowers sow, as in the poet, unhappiness and death.

In these three plays, Mishima sees the aesthetic spirit as an insufficient haven for human repose, as unequal to the task of coping with the rigors of real life. At least two corollaries emerge from his view. First, isolating oneself within the dream-like realm of art can lead to loss of rational contact with real life and a consequent growth of anxiety, unhappiness, obsession, madness, and even death. Second, the once-exalted position of the artist in society must now be considered as one enfeebled position among many. What, for example, do Iwakichi's attempts at aesthetic self-expression profit him? Very little, save despair, death, and further despair as a ghost after death. By her aesthetic efforts in *Hanjo,* Hanako gains the loss of the lover whom she so patiently, and unavailingly, will continue to await. The poet suffers an unwanted death.

Mishima's pessimistic view of these aesthetic endeavors is overwhelming. Indeed, in a manner similar to some observers in the modern West, he perceives the sterility of the modern artist. Rainer Maria Rilke's analogous insight, for example, can bring Mishima's perception into sharper focus. In his novel *Die Aufzeichnungen des Malte Laurids Brigge,* Rilke chronicles the musings of a certain Malte, a modern man of decidedly aesthetic bent. At one point, Malte inadvertently enters a theatre in which the stage is set for the impending performance. He has a vision of time ineluctably marching toward death, and he feels a strong need to take his proper place upon the stage. But, alas, he finds himself, as he puts it, 'completely unprepared'. He is unprepared to play his role, to fulfill his capacity as an artist within the artistic setting of the theatre, unprepared to delve into the poetics of the imagination. Suddenly, struck by the immensity of this dilemma, Malte admits: 'I yielded to a violent shock of pleasure.' This is surely the pleasure that Malte takes in avoiding the spiritual discomfort of resolving the conflict of the stage, in soothing the itch of his own human, finite weakness; it is the pleasure of abandoning the agonizing incoherence of poetic imagination for the sweet clarity of prosaic thought. Thus, for Rilke, as for Mishima, the real-life dilemma posed by the tension between the fleeting and the eternal is ultimately unresolved through the aesthetic spirit.

This kind of perception is boldly evident in **Aya no Tsuzumi** where Mishima has pared the odyssey of the aesthetic spirit down to its barest essentials by placing it on the almost laughable love of the old janitor Iwakichi. Such a technique makes Iwakichi's abandonment of his love-aesthetic efforts by suicide more penetrating; returning in ghostly form, Iwakichi bespeaks Mishima's view that the modern artist in his mere humanity is somehow shorn of that high artistic capacity once possessed in former times. Malte's musings also illuminate Mishima's insight in **Hanjo** where Hanako, too, is so obviously 'completely unprepared' that she cannot have what she yearns for even when the very real Yoshio appears before her. Moreover, Hanako, like Malte, also yields to 'a violent shock of pleasure' as she eagerly succumbs to the sweet temptation of her isolated, clockless island, thereby avoiding the painful conflicts of life itself as symbolized by Yoshio. Hers is the brittle balance struck by Malte.

Finally, in **Sotoba Komachi** the poet closely resembles Rilke's anti-hero Malte. Like Malte upon entering the theatre, he is indulgent of his aesthetic inclination as he stands on Komachi's bench, a kind of stage, and calls it a 'ladder reaching to the heavens' and 'a lofty lookout.' But, like Malte, who is unprepared to perform, the poet's artistry from his celestial stage is far less than lofty. His aesthetic vision allows but a paltry view: 'Lots of benches over there. Some ragpickers by a fire. A car full of flowers. Coming from . . . a funeral. [He climbs down from the bench and sits.] That's it, that's everything I can see.' Moreover, upon the approach of his magic moment, the poet also yields to 'a violent shock of pleasure'. And, just as Malte's pleasure is transient as he goes sadly away—'What should I do there? Today our plays fall in fragments . . . collect in heaps and are swept away. . . . '—so the poet's joy is also brief, for he, too, relinquishes his moment, ultimately avoiding the demands of art which he earlier accepted, and sadly faces death. And Komachi, after the poet's death, calmly pursues her business, relinquishing all claims to the aesthetic spirit, and, if not precisely caught within a 'shock of pleasure', is at least content to count out the moments of her life in so many stamped-out cigarette butts. Ours being the 'ambition of a sardine', as another Mishima character comments in this play, perhaps our chief reason for living is, as Komachi tersely states: 'Existing as I am, isn't that reason enough to keep on living?'

Thus, Mishima concludes that art is not enough for the happy confrontation with and pursuit of real life. He is not mesmerized by 'the artifice of eternity'. He rejects Yeats's aesthetic vision that 'once out of nature I shall never take / My bodily form from any natural thing'; he finds 'the holy city of Byzantium' sterile, unresponsive to deep human needs. But this conclusion is steeped in irony and perhaps subject to question. For Mishima renders his view through a startling aesthetic brilliance. Even Zeami—and Yeats—would applaud Mishima's consummate skill as he lures us, lulls us, by appropriating aspects of traditional noh, then sharply shocks us by transforming these into a modern setting. Yet Mishima appears to have lived his life in accordance with the salient perception of these plays: art was inadequate to sustain him. (pp. 29-39)

> *John K. Gillespie, "Beyond Byzantium: Aesthetic Pessimism in Mishima's Modern Noh Plays," in* Monumenta Nipponica, *Vol. XXXVII, No. 1, Spring, 1982, pp. 29-39.*

FURTHER READING

Calta, Louis. "Theatre: Two Noh Plays by Mishima." *The New York Times* (16 November 1960): 51.

>   Favorable review of a production of *Hanjo* and *The Lady Aoi* (here called *The Lady Akane*). Calta calls Mishima a "versatile, subtle and effective author" and praises his literary style.

Keene, Donald. "Mishima." *The New York Times Book Review* (3 January 1971): 4, 24-5.

>   Memorial tribute to Mishima in which Keene reflects on their friendship and comments on the artist's suicide.

———. "Mishima and the Modern Scene." *The Times Literary Supplement* (20 August 1971): 989-90.

>   Discusses Mishima's personal philosophy, reputation, and suicide. Keene notes contradictions between Mishima's lifestyle and his professed ideals.

Mishima, Yukio. *Tropical Tree. Japan Quarterly* 11, No. 2 (April-June 1964): 174-210.

>   English translation of *Nettaiju* by Kenneth Strong. Mishima also provides a "Note by the Author" in which he discusses his conception of the play.

Nathan, John. *Mishima: A Biography.* Boston: Little, Brown and Company, 1974, 300 p.

>   Portrait by a translator and one-time friend of Mishima. Nathan had the cooperation of Mishima's family, and much of the description of the artist's early life is based on a biographical reading of *Confessions of a Mask.*

Petersen, Gwen Boardman. "Mishima Yukio." In her *The Moon in the Water: Understanding Tanizaki, Kawabata, and Mishima,* pp. 201-336. Honolulu: University Press of Hawaii, 1979.

>   Introduces the major themes in Mishima's works and comments on the stylistic elements of his fiction within the context of Japanese literature.

Pronko, Leonard C. Introduction to his *Guide to Japanese*

Drama, second edition, pp. 1-21. Boston: G. K. Hall & Co., 1984.

 Concise history of traditional Japanese theatrical forms.

Scott-Stokes, Henry. *The Life and Death of Yukio Mishima.* New York: Farrar, Straus and Giraux, 1974, 344 p.

 Account by a friend that attempts to explain Mishima's suicide in terms of the complex contradictions present in his life and evidenced in his works.

Takaya, Ted T. Introduction to *Modern Japanese Drama: An Anthology,* edited and translated by Ted T. Takaya, pp. xv-xxxvii. New York: Columbia University Press, 1979.

 Gives a history of modern Japanese theater and places Mishima within its context.

Wolfe, Peter. *Yukio Mishima.* New York: Continuum, 1989, 200 p.

 Biocritical study that exposes the unresolved conflicts of the writer's life and works. Wolfe concentrates on Mishima's novels but also considers the dramatic works, which, he observes, encompass some of the author's more controversial ideas.

Richard Brinsley Sheridan

1751-1816

(Born: Thomas Brinsley Sheridan)

During his brief career as a dramatist, the Irish-born Sheridan rose to remarkable prominence in the English theater. His brilliant wit and stagecraft were enormously popular with contemporary audiences, and some critics have considered him the most significant British playwright in the period from Shakespeare's death until Bernard Shaw's debut. By the age of twenty-eight, when he embarked on a career in politics, Sheridan had completed all his major works for the stage, including *The Rivals* and *The School for Scandal*. In these and other plays, Sheridan was strongly influenced by the English Restoration comedy of manners, which depicts the amorous affairs of wealthy society. Commentators agree that Sheridan was a gifted theatrical craftsman who utilized yet transcended the conventions of Restoration comedy and thus was able to create supremely entertaining pieces of enduring appeal. As Rose Snider observed, Sheridan captured the spirit of his predecessors William Congreve and William Wycherley in his presentation of "heartless women, scheming men, and, in general, a cold and worldly-wise society." He differed from them, however, in balancing these harsh representations with a "genuine warmth of tone," which was lacking in the works of the earlier writers.

Sheridan was born in Dublin to Thomas Sheridan, a prominent actor, and his wife Frances, a noted author. When the younger Sheridan was eight, the family moved to Paris, but he himself was sent to boarding school in London. Although failing to distinguish himself academically, he displayed a talent for literature when he began writing poetry at an early age. He continued to show promise in the dramatic sketches and verse he composed with friends. During his adolescence, Sheridan made known his desire to become a playwright. Thomas Sheridan, however, had different plans and arranged for his son to study law. Richard submitted to his father's wishes, but, shortly after his marriage to the renowned singer Elizabeth Linley, he abandoned his legal studies to devote himself to writing.

Sheridan's work was enthusiastically greeted by the audiences of his time. Many echoed the sentiment expressed by Lord Byron, a younger contemporary of the playwright: "Whatever Sheridan has chosen to do it has been *par excellence*, always the *best* of its kind. He has written the *best* comedy, (*School for Scandal*,) the *best* opera, (*The Duenna*,) [and] the *best* farce (*The Critic*,) . . . ever conceived or heard in this country." Subsequent generations of theatergoers have continually praised Sheridan's works for their sparkling dialogue and clever construction. As Robert Hogan asserted, Sheridan's comedies have become "a perennial source of linguistic delight."

Although *The Rivals* and *The School for Scandal* have remained popular successes, some critics have offered sharp-

ly negative appraisals of their literary merit. Marvin Mudrick, for example, judged Sheridan's comedies mere "miscellanies of stagey, actable situations incorporating sentimental and stock-comic types." He further charged that Sheridan was neither responsible for a revival of English comedy nor particularly innovative. Such critics claim that the "staginess" of Sheridan's works detracts from their artistic value. Countering these arguments, scholars such as John Loftis have contended that Sheridan's deliberate aim was to exaggerate and burlesque these stock figures. This technique, they claim, not only heightens the theatricality of the plays, but also satirizes the artificiality of Restoration stage conventions.

Sheridan's rise to theatrical prominence was swift, despite a shaky beginning. In 1775, his first year of writing for the stage, he produced three highly acclaimed works: *The Rivals, The Duenna; or, The Double Elopement,* and *St. Patrick's Day; or, The Scheming Lieutenant.* The success of these pieces quickly established him as a prominent dramatist. *The Rivals,* Sheridan's first play, premiered at Covent Garden Theatre. The initial performance was a dismal failure due to miscasting and excessive length. Undaunted by the poor reception, Sheridan recast several roles, abbreviated sections of the play, and reopened it ten days later to a nearly unanimous positive response. According to Mark Auburn, the success of *The Rivals* derives from Sheridan's effective manipulation of familiar dramatic techniques, including "complex, fast moving, amiably comic plots peopled by probable yet theatrical characters." Jack Durant adds that the "distinction Sheridan boasts is not that he managed these techniques first but that he managed them better than anyone else did." Perhaps the most memorable character in *The Rivals* is Mrs. Malaprop, whose hilariously inappropriate word usages have continually delighted audiences and resulted in the entrance of the word "malapropism" into the English language.

Sheridan's next work was *The Duenna,* an opera for which his father-in-law, Thomas Linley, composed the music. The initial run of this piece lasted an impressive seventy-five performances. It was followed by *St. Patrick's Day,* a work that was highly praised in its time but is now judged a minor effort. Later in 1775, when David Garrick retired as owner and manager of the Drury Lane Theatre, Sheridan formed a partnership to purchase the playhouse and became its manager. During the next two years, he revived a number of Restoration comedies and wrote and staged his most successful work, *The School for Scandal.*

This play is both Sheridan's most popular and the most strongly reminiscent of the Restoration period. As a burlesque of a gossip-loving society, the comedy provides the dramatist's most brilliant display of wit, though its strong reproof of scandal differs sharply from the gentle tone of *The Rivals. The School for Scandal* is also noted for its double plot lines, as well as for its superb command of language and its technical refinement. The continued revival of the play throughout the world attests to its reputation as one of England's best-loved and most enduring comedies.

In 1779, Sheridan produced *The Critic; or, A Tragedy Rehearsed.* Strongly influenced by the Duke of Buckingham's *The Rehearsal* (1671), the play provides a satirical look at the world of the theater and parodies the vanity of artists and critics. Though *The Critic* never achieved the popularity of *The Rivals* or *The School for Scandal,* many commentators consider it Sheridan's most intellectual work. The dramatist later stated that he had hoped to sum up in this piece all that previous comic poets had achieved in the satirizing of tragedy. Sheridan's last play was *Pizarro,* an adaptation of August von Kotzebue's *Die Spanier in Peru oder Rollas Tod* (1796). A historical drama, *Pizarro* met with popular acclaim but this recognition was short-lived, and the play is routinely dismissed by critics, who consider it an anticlimactic conclusion to Sheridan's theatrical career.

Sheridan was elected in 1780 to the House of Commons, where he excelled as an orator. His speeches are considered brilliant; in particular, the four-hour oration denouncing his fellow statesman Warren Hastings is regarded as a masterpiece of persuasion and verbal command. However, Sheridan's interest in politics kept him from his theatrical endeavors and his management of Drury Lane became haphazard. In an attempt to beautify the aging

theater, he rebuilt the interior, but it burned down shortly thereafter, leaving Sheridan penniless. Not only was the loss of the playhouse disastrous, but the devastation of his resources made funding another Parliamentary campaign impossible. This compounded Sheridan's financial woes by eliminating his only remaining source of income. His last years were spent in poverty and disgrace. However, shortly before his death in 1816, his reputation as a distinguished statesman and dramatist was restored and he was buried with honor in the Poet's Corner of Westminster Abbey.

(For further information on Sheridan's life and career, see *Nineteenth-Century Literature Criticism,* Vol. 5)

PRINCIPAL WORKS

PLAYS

The Rivals   1775
The Duenna; or, The Double Elopement   1775
St. Patrick's Day; or, The Scheming Lieutenant   1775
The School for Scandal   1777
The Critic; or, A Tragedy Rehearsed   1779
Pizarro [adaptor; from the drama *Die Spanier in Peru oder Rollas Tod* by August von Kotzebue]   1799

OVERVIEWS AND GENERAL STUDIES

Cecil Ferard Armstrong   (essay date 1913)

[*In the following excerpt, Armstrong surveys Sheridan's life and career as a playwright, tracing in particular the development of Sheridan's stagecraft from its beginning in* The Rivals *to its culmination in* The School for Scandal.]

Richard Brinsley Sheridan was born in Dublin in 1751. His father, Thomas Sheridan, was famous as an actor, a manager, a lexicographer, and the biographer of [Jonathan] Swift. As an actor, though never in quite the first flight, he was considered very good indeed. As a manager in Dublin, he was a reformer and improved the conditions behind the scenes in the theatre very considerably during his eight years of management. Moreover he was famous for having brought the great little David Garrick to his senses, and to terms, in something less than five minutes. As a lexicographer he wrote a pronouncing dictionary which was for a very long time regarded almost as a standard work. As a pedagogue, he had ambitions to found a school of oratory, and delivered lectures on elocution in London and at Oxford. His wife, the mother of Richard Brinsley, achieved some fame as a novelist and dramatist. In the latter capacity she wrote three plays, *The Discovery,* which was produced at Drury Lane under the management of David Garrick, who played in it himself, playing the part of a tiresome prig and bore in a manner that certainly did not bore his audience. Coleman the Younger said that "he made those eyes which nature had stuck like twin stars in his head look like two coddled gooseberries". Mrs. Sheridan's husband also appeared in the play. Her other plays were *The Dupe* and *The Trip to Bath,* which has been thought by some to have afterwards suggested **The Rivals** to her son. Her plays are, on the whole, very poor, and their existence would have been forgotten long ago, but for her son's better ones.

Sheridan was the third child, and second son of this talented couple. When he was three years old his father and mother were practically driven out of Dublin and their theatre by an infuriated mob, who considered, as Irish audiences sometimes do to this day, that the politics were more important than the play, and wished certain lines in Miller's version of Voltaire's *Mahomet* encored, because they soothed their tender national spirit. Sheridan, who was a genuine artist, absolutely refused, and the mob tore up his benches, invaded his stage, and did deeds of incredible bravery and ferocity amongst his scenery, with their swords. Two years later Thomas Sheridan returned to Dublin and entered management again, but was this time ousted by the success of his rivals, Barry and Woodward. Then he took to lecturing on elocution and worked hard at his pet project, the foundation of an Academy of Oratory. In this he had the cordial support of the Lord Lieutenant, Lord Chesterfield. Some such academy was afterwards founded, but Sheridan was given no hand in it, and it is not surprising that, disgusted with his treatment at the hands of his countrymen, he shook the dust of Dublin from his feet and betook himself to London. Up till this time his two sons had been to a day school in Dublin. Now it was decided to send Richard to Harrow whilst Charles, the elder, remained at home, to be the object of his parents' experiments in upbringing and education. And so Richard began life with all the advantages of a younger son! However, he did not do much with them at first. At Harrow he was popular with masters and boys alike on account of his sunny and lively disposition, but left behind him no particular reputation for intelligence. When fifteen years old he lost his mother, who died at Blois, whither she and her husband had fled from creditors. The father returned to London, and at the age of eighteen Richard Brinsley left Harrow and joined his brother to be "finished" by his father. The finishing process consisted of lessons in fencing and riding, oratory and English grammar, taught them by their father, and Latin and mathematics, taught them by an old Irish tutor.

Sheridan had made friends at Harrow with a boy named Halhed. They had formed a literary partnership which was not dissolved when their ways diverged, for though Halhed went to Oxford, Sheridan and he collaborated upon a three-act farce, with the significant and sonorous title of *Jupiter.* They reckoned to get this produced by Foote and to clear a sum of at least £200 by it, but neither eventuality occurred! They then produced and published a little book containing an English verse adaptation of the prose works of a little-known Greek author called Aristænetus. The Sheridan-Halhed version caused his work to be known no better, and gave no one any desire for a further acquaintance with him.

The Sheridans were now living at Bath, whither the father had moved in 1770, his circumstances made a little more easy by a pension of £200 a year, obtained for him by Lord Bute. He also earned a little by paying another visit to Dublin and teaching certain members of the Irish Parliament elocution, a task which must have been about as difficult as teaching ducks to swim.

In Bath lived one Thomas Linley, an English musician of no mean order. His daughter Elizabeth was the greatest of all the great beauties of Bath. And she seems to have been as good as she was beautiful. But she was a professional singer, and her public position caused her to be much pestered by undesirable and desirable lovers. Amongst the desirables were both the Sheridans, Charles and Richard, and Richard's friend Halhed. Amongst the undesirables was an elderly gentleman to whom Eliza, as she was called, was engaged at the age of sixteen, but she broke off the engagement, and her father tactfully arranged matters so that the old gentleman settled £3000 upon her as a compensation for breach of promise! Another undesirable was one Captain Matthews, a wealthy Welsh landowner, whose intentions seem to have been neither honourable nor remote. To escape them and also those of many others, whose names were legion, Miss Linley, acting under the advice of Richard Brinsley, decided to flee to France and there take refuge in a convent. Richard Brinsley chivalrously offered to escort her. This he did, and to complete the picture of ancient chivalry, claimed the rescued damsel as his reward, and got her. They were married first and afterwards Miss Linley, or Mrs. Sheridan, took refuge in a convent at Lisle, and Sheridan returned to Bath and faced the music of Linley père's wrath which was not so sweet as his other music. Not only did the irate parent sternly refuse to recognize the match, but Bath was in a ferment, and Captain Matthews challenged Sheridan to a duel. The first duel was fought in Hyde Park and seems to have been an absurd fiasco. They found it so difficult to escape observation that they finally adjourned to a coffee-house, where Sheridan seems to have disregarded all the rules of duelling and to have rushed in under his opponent's guard almost before the seconds had given the word, smashed his sword and then demanded an apology at the point of his own. This led to a second duel which was fought at Bath, which seems to have developed into a sort of rough and tumble, both combatants rolling upon the ground and pummelling each other. Sheridan seems to have had his share of wounds, but whether they were caused by his own or his opponent's blade, hilt or fists; or whether the blood that freely flowed was the genuine article, or merely some claret which Sheridan had been drinking to excess previous to the duel, will never be known. Various versions, each entirely different from the others, were published by various persons who had been present on both occasions, and if anyone is sufficiently interested in the ridiculous and unimportant event to try and get at the true facts of it, they have plenty of work before them. The final result was that apologies were tendered and honour somewhat easily satisfied. Sheridan was also satisfied, for Mr. Linley now consented to the match. Miss

Linley had returned from France and had been singing in public and having clandestine meetings in private with Sheridan, who is said sometimes to have disguised himself as her coachman and driven her to the opera. The two were re-married, with the parental blessing, on 13 April, 1773, and retired to love and live in a cottage at East Burnham, on the interest of £3000, paid to Miss Linley as compensation for her first escape from matrimony! This marriage, which reads like a romance, or rather a comedy by Sheridan, which indeed it was, culminated in a really happy, though all too short married life.

The young couple lived barely a year at East Burnham, and then moved to a house in Orchard Street, Portman Square, and here Sheridan wrote **The Rivals.** It was written for Covent Garden where it was produced for the first time on 17 January, 1775. The story of its first night failure is a familiar piece of theatrical history, and the actor Lee, to whose ill success in the part of Sir Lucius O'Trigger the failure was mainly due, has achieved immortality on that account! The fact that the failure of one part, and that by no means the most important one, wrought so much mischief, says a very great deal for the artistic value of the play as a whole. Especially at the present time when the reverse sometimes happens and the too striking performance of one part has sometimes been known to upset the equilibrium of a whole play. But in Sheridan's plays, at any rate, the part never equals or exceeds the whole! As a comedy, **The Rivals** has plenty of faults. It is, I think, too long and too loquacious, and there are too many subsidiary interests, and the main intrigue is, in itself, really almost too slight to carry a five-act comedy. In any other hands but those of a genius such a mistake was bound to spell disaster. It is the kind of play, more or less, that is fashionable at the present day, 1913, depending more for success upon style, humour, characterization than upon actual drama, as drama is generally understood. And the style, atmosphere, humour and characterization of **The Rivals** are perfect. Although producing an effect of spontaneity, as all works of genius do, a close examination reveals the presence of immense care and pains in the working out of the play. Nothing is omitted, nothing is left to chance, and, as was the custom of those days, little is left to the imagination. The notion that **The Rivals** is a happy-go-lucky farce, seems to me entirely misleading. Like its great successor, **The School for Scandal,** it is practically a play of one situation, and of that situation Sheridan never once loses sight. Everything plays up to the absurd duel scene, a scene which was probably suggested to him by his own ridiculous adventures in that direction.

All the characters, grave, gay, and ridiculous, converge to this great scene, and a careful study of the dialogue and events of the preceding acts, shows how Sheridan kept it before him constantly. At the same time he knows his road so well that having no fear of losing it, or wandering off down by-ways and lanes, he can stop to pick the flowers by the way, and regale us with chit-chat and familiar studies of tales of men and things, like a Canterbury Pilgrim. An artist who knows the road is a delightful companion. This singleness of purpose has another admirable effect in that it keeps the author's sense of proportion just, and the wood is not obscured by the trees, the characters

and incidents all fall naturally into their right places and the result is a design, a complete work of art. This result is certainly achieved in **The Rivals,** and, in my opinion, is the chief glory of the play. The characterization and humour are both, I think, a little obvious, if not strained. Bob Acres and Mrs. Malaprop, delightful though they both are, seem yet to bear traces of the prentice hand, as indeed does the play as a whole in spite of its success as a work of art. One may be an artist before one can draw, but till one can draw and gain a free hand one can never give others the full benefit of one's art. Sir Anthony Absolute and Sir Lucius O'Trigger are both types which seem to have been fairly common in plays and novels of the period, and in Bath. But Sheridan has immortalized them. But Falkland and Julia are the characters that really give one pause. Here, surely, Sheridan touched a really live wire. Falkland's doubts and fears and moroseness are very annoying, and one wonders why Julia has not sent him to the right about long ago. But deep down in her heart she loves him, and that love probably tells her that his doubts are not altogether unworthy, or unreasonable, that he is desperately anxious to have nothing but the genuine article and that the fact of her being under an obligation to him is the thorn in his side. After all he is only anxious to assure himself that he is loved for himself alone, or perhaps it would be better to say in spite of himself. And that is what we all want, and what Julia, with her large forgiving, maternal heart, gives him. I think that in these two characters Sheridan gives a hint of some of the deep things latent within him, and shows us what he might have been had he never deserted the stage for the platform.

I have said that in some of the humour and characterization there are marks of the prentice hand. And so there are in the play as a whole, just as there are in Shakespeare's *Richard III*, but it is the prentice hand of a genius. In **The Rivals** it seems to me to take the usual form of great anxiety to tell the audience everything, of fear that they will miss something important.

This ultra-anxiety is a characteristic of the young, untried author, and it is refreshing to see a great man sharing it. Like Lady Teazle's consciousness of her own innocence, Sheridan's consciousness of his own inexperience made him guilty of a thousand little explanations, justifications, hints and amplifications that are quite unnecessary and had quite disappeared by the time he came to write **The School for Scandal.** Intuition and genius may tell one many things, but experience tells one more. And Sheridan was quick to profit by it. The next play that he wrote was a farce entitled **St. Patrick's Day or the Scheming Lieutenant.** It was written entirely for Clinch, the actor who had saved the situation and the play of **The Rivals** by his performance of Sir Lucius O'Trigger. Otherwise there is nothing remarkable about the play, which would have been dead and buried long ago, but for its author.

His next serious effort was **The Duenna,** an operatic play, nowadays it would be a musical comedy, written for Covent Garden, and the music composed by Thomas Linley, Sheridan's father-in-law. Sheridan's own father had quarrelled with him about something, or more probably nothing, and hence did not assist in any way at the rehearsals, many of which took place at Sheridan's home in Orchard Street.

And what rehearsals those must have been, brightened with his own wit, and sweetened with his wife's voice and exquisite beauty. The play was first produced on 21 November, 1775, and was an instantaneous and, for those days, lasting success, being performed seventy-five times during that season.

It is a charming comedy, interspersed with beautiful little lyrics, duets and quartettes. The music is said to have been exquisitely lovely, and I believe that if the play were well produced and mounted to-day, with the right atmosphere of Old Spain, it would command a very large measure of success and interest.

The story is simple in the extreme and easily told. Don Jerome has a daughter. They always do in Spain! That daughter has a lover. They always do in Spain! But the lover is disapproved of by her father. They always are in Spain! And his father has his own idea for his daughter's marriage. They always have in Spain. This idea is wealthy. It always is in Spain. It is also unattractive! The daughter has a Duenna, as daughters do in Spain. And the Duenna has her eye upon Mendoza's money-chest. Fortunately for the play and those concerned, there is a custom in Spain of wearing a mantilla or veil, and concealed under these the Duenna and the daughter are enabled to exchange identities. For the Duenna wants to marry the Jew for his money-bags, as much as the daughter wants the hero for his heart.

There is a secondary hero and a secondary heroine, a convent and some rascally priests. Thus we have all the material for a charming comedy of intrigue and romance, whose end is foretold from the beginning. Things fall out as we hope they will fall out, and then fall in as we hope they will fall in. As I have already said, here is a charming comic opera ready to hand for anyone who is on the lookout for such a thing. It would not be an expensive production of its kind. The cast is a small one, the mounting would gain nothing by lavishness, but everything by taste. The present generation has not, unless I am very much mistaken, had the opportunity to see and hear this charming opera. I am sure they would not be in a hurry to miss it.

The success of **The Duenna** raised Sheridan to the pinnacle of fame, and made him, not yet twenty-four, the fashionable dramatist of the hour. With a keen eye to business, David Garrick produced *The Discovery,* Sheridan's mother's play, at Drury Lane, but the reflected glory was not sufficient to turn it into a success. It was almost the great little actor's last speculation, for he was now sixty years old and had practically made up his mind to retire. Sheridan, riding upon the crest of the wave, saw what he thought was his opportunity, seized it and, as things turned out, was eventually swamped by it. He determined to step into Garrick's shoes as part manager of Drury Lane, and in June, 1776, had found, heaven, or hell, only knows how, £10,000 to pay for two-fourteenths of Garrick's holding. His father-in-law Linley became responsible for a like number of shares, and other members of the

public were found willing and even eager to invest their money in a venture with the witty and brilliant Mr. Sheridan at the head.

The world went very well for Sheridan then. At home his wife had presented him with a beautiful boy, Tom, upon whom the father doted and dilated. The relations between the two afterwards became very much like those between Sheridan and his own father. Young Tom was a thorough chip of the old block, and the encounters between him and his father were delicious. Young Tom once complained that he had no money, whereupon his father suggested that he should try the King's highway! To this young Tom retorted that he had done so, but had had no luck, as he had stopped a company of Drury Lane players, who had no money, not yet having been paid their salaries. Another version of the story has it that young Tom said that he had tried the highway, but had had no luck, having stopped Peake, Sheridan's treasurer at the theatre, who was, of course, quite empty-handed, Sheridan having been to the till before him! But the son did not always have things his own way. Speaking of party humbugs, young Tom remarked that if he went into the House he should join no party, but write upon his forehead the words "To be let". "And under that," said his father, "unfurnished."

The next production from Sheridan's pen was a play called **A Trip to Scarborough,** which was a version of Vanbrugh's play, *The Relapse,* and it proved one, but Sheridan quickly made amends, for about three months later, on the 8th of May, 1777, was produced his greatest play, **The School for Scandal.** It was an immediate and unqualified success, and has remained so ever since. Sheridan had been working very hard and carefully upon it for a long time, as his manuscripts showed. It was originally two separate plays, which he had boiled down into one and then strained very carefully through the sieve of his experience. It is interesting to compare the original drafts with the play as completed, and to notice the improvements. Sir Peter Teazle was originally a widower, and plain Mr. Solomon Teazle, whose first marriage had been a disastrous failure, lasting, fortunately for him, barely two years. He came on and told the audience this in a soliloquy at the very opening of the play, thus losing their sympathy and robbing the main situation of half its charm and interest. So Solomon was turned into Peter and Peter was knighted, or baroneted whichever it was, and the little country miss became Lady Teazle; the situation gained in contrast and distinction, and the audience have the additional and pleasurable sensation of watching an old bachelor losing his crust.

Moreover, Sheridan had learnt that it is not wise to divulge the main situation too early in the proceedings. There are artistic reasons for this, as well as the purely practical one that at the opening of a play there is probably still a good deal of movement going on among the audience. And it is a serious mistake to spring the main situation upon an audience, before they have had the time or opportunity to appreciate it at its full value.

The fact that Lady Teazle has been transplanted from the country to new surroundings is more impressive when we know what these new surroundings are like. So Sheridan first of all shows us the company she has come into, before Sir Peter comes on and describes to us that which she came out of. The position of his soliloquy is altered very much for the better in the new version, would that it had been altered still further and been entirely done away with! The quarrel that follows brings the important facts out quite as clearly and much more piquantly. Sir Peter's soliloquy, in accordance with an old stage custom, now mercifully exploded, only prepares us for what is coming, waters the glass before we get the grog. The element of surprise was entirely lacking in the old drama, but surely it is one of the most important elements, and the unexpected or unrealized is essential to live drama. I know that, as a matter of fact, in old Greek tragedy and in Shakespeare, the audience are practically never surprised. They are merely lookers-on, contemplators of the drama. Nowadays they expect to share in it to some extent, and if the object of a play is to create an illusion, surely that is as it should be. In any case it must enlarge their sympathies, and appreciation, and interest.

The family name of the Surfaces had been at different stages of the manuscript Plausible, Pliable, and Pliant. Excellent names, all of them, but not so good as Surface. They are too obvious. Surface seems to express the characters of both, for both are distinctly superficial. That is to say, that the characters they present to the world are not at all their real ones. Each is striving to be popular and effective. Joseph believes in sentiment and morals, Charles in sentimentalism and immorals. Joseph is sleek and Charles is slack. Joseph parades the popular virtues, Charles the popular vices, and they are easier to live up to. It would be difficult to say which brother did the more mischief or caused the more suffering.

I find it easier to believe in the insincerity of Joseph than the sincerity of Charles. Charles had a fine eye for effect. His refusal to sell his uncle's portrait seems rather plausible. His uncle, if he had any character at all, would probably have liked him all the better if he had been knocked down with the rest. Joseph is far more consistent in his villainy, but perhaps such consistency is hardly a virtue! I cannot help thinking that Charles, with his habits and his keen eye for dramatic and telling effect, must have been an unconscious portrait of Sheridan himself, and Joseph Surface a portrait of his "familiar". Charles Surface what he succeeded in being, Joseph Surface what he succeeded in avoiding. When all is thought, said and done, there is not really very much to be said for these two beauties, or very much difference between them, except that they are both masterpieces of characterization. And so is Lady Teazle. She is as true as the two brothers are false. Sir Peter has obviously been a self-centred, self-indulgent old bachelor, or he would never have been taken in by her print dress, modest mien and demurity, prettiness and simplicity. It may be unchivalrous to say so, but I simply do not believe that these things exist in young ladies, old ladies, or ladies of any age, time, or place. Girls never have been and never will be kittens. The so-called homely virtues of submission and docility never did and never will exist in any girl's heart, though they may be donned with her gowns. The demure, downcast eye, behind the poke-bonnet of the early Victorian era as often as not hid very

quick intelligence or silent suffering. Like many an old, and young self-satisfied silly fool before and since his day, Sir Peter thought he had got what he wanted and found he had got what he *needed;* something that would shake him out of himself and give him no rest until he was thoroughly cured.

Lady Teazle is a splendid warm-hearted creature who never humbugs herself and would have been torn into a thousand pieces ere she yielded to Joseph's insinuations. She plays with fire, it is true, but it is because of her upbringing, not her inclinations. Folk who have been brought up in an ice-house may be forgiven for going too near the flame at first.

Sir Peter Teazle has no character at all to speak of at the opening of the play. He is a crusty old bachelor, but he will have plenty of character, and very nice character, by the end of the chapter.

The other characters in the play are all types. Maria is the best of them, morally I mean. She sticks to her chosen hero in the face of much opposition and some facts.

The construction of the play is, according to the canons then in vogue, perfect. It is obviously worked out with immense care, and, as in *The Rivals,* Sheridan never loses sight of his main situation. Everything is subordinated to it, leads to it, depends upon it and falls away from it at the end.

The plays open, in Shakespearean style, with the entrance of the villains and hatching of the plot. Joseph Surface comes in behind his screen, and Sheridan then and there begins to knock it down and goes on doing so metaphorically, until Charles Surface does so actually. And the pious screen of learning and sentiment that hides Joseph is not the only screen that is knocked down, but the scandalous one that conceals the real Lady Teazle from her friends, and that of his own making, which hides her from her husband, also falls. In fact the whole play is a knocking down of screens.

From the villains we come by natural steps to the victims, but not before we have a little hint through Rowley of the eventual victors. In the short second act this is carried still further, and the God in the Car comes on the scenes in the person of Sir Oliver, acquaints himself fully with the situation, and expresses his opinion thereon. In the third act he is satisfied that his opinion is the right one (the God in the Car generally is), and in the fourth act everybody else is. People and things come out in their real colours.

The fifth act shows us that this has had the desired and expected effect, and there is a general tying up all round. The end is conventional, it is, in a sense, a conventional comedy, and bears no sign of raggedness, although it was written under great pressure. *"Finished at last. Thank God!"* wrote Sheridan at the foot of the manuscript. *"Amen!"* wrote the prompter, W. Hopkins; small blame to him!

The fact that Joseph Surface never reforms is refreshing, and mitigates the accusation of artificiality which has, not altogether unjustly, been levelled against the play. But it is a comedy of manners. An artificial comedy of artificial times. The situations, telling and effective though they are, are not very real. But many telling situations happened in those days, and happen now, which are not real. Sheridan was always contriving them. He contrived one when he escorted the beautiful and talented Miss Linley to a conventual retreat in France, far removed from the world, the flesh, and the devil. But it was not real, or else he would have left her there! The situations of *The School for Scandal* were quite a possibility, if they did not actually happen, in Sheridan's day. And belike the quaint, stilted, periodical manner of talking was real. The dialogue of *The School for Scandal* is light, witty, and airy, but it is also literary, and few characters open their mouths without giving expression to a carefully rounded or phrased sentence or period.

In the same way Shakespearean characters talk blank verse, and yet they talk very naturally, because the thoughts they utter are natural. And so it seems to me with Sheridan, and that *The School for Scandal* is an extraordinarily true, faithful, and plausible picture of the times. It is, in every sense of the word, a real comedy and work of art, depending upon something more than mere journalism, although journalism should, and must, play a very important part in every play; but *The School for Scandal* is more than that, or it would have died a natural death years ago. It is immortal with the immortality of Art.

Two years after its production Sheridan produced his last original play, *The Critic; or a Tragedy Rehearsed.* In the meantime Garrick had died, and Sheridan had followed him to the grave as chief mourner, written a monody to his memory, and practically acquired the whole of his share in Drury Lane Theatre. Although, in a sense, topical and typical of its time, *The Critic* has maintained its popularity up to the present day, though of quite recent years it has only been spasmodically produced and still more spasmodically played at special performances. But in Charles Mathews's day it was popular and one of his favourite drawing cards.

Some of the point of *The Critic* has, of course, been lost by the disappearance from the scenes of the originals of some of the characters. Sir Fretful Plagiary thinly veiled the petty personality of Cumberland, the dramatist. Dangle is supposed to have been one Vaughan, one of those busy-bodies who professed to be behind all the scenes. Puff gave rise to much discussion at the time, and by some is thought to have found his prototype in Woodfall, the publisher, but this is so manifestly unjust to that high-minded and high-principled person, that it is quite impossible to think of Sheridan as being guilty of such an inartistic mistake. The probability is that Puff did not stand for a person at all, but for a profession. There are very many Puffs today. They are officially known as Press Agents. But Sir Fretful Plagiary's peculiarities are not so much professional as personal. Like W. S. Gilbert's *Patience,* however, the extreme popularity of *The Critic* depended upon more permanent grounds than mere personalities. Its wit and humour and admirable parody of Shakespeare are mingled with not a little common sense and sound advice to dramatic authors. If some of them would study carefully

the dialogue between Sir Walter Raleigh and Sir Christopher Hatton at the opening of *The Spanish Armada,* there would be an immediate improvement in the methods they employ to give information to their audience. Moreover, Sheridan has something to say anent the little way that some authors have of ignoring the human element and practical considerations, and also has a dig at the actors who arrange among themselves how, why, and where the play shall be "cut".

In short, as a study of "how not to do it," *The Critic* or rather *The Spanish Armada* forms a splendid object-lesson. It might be maintained that *The School for Scandal* is an equally good model of how to do it. But that is not at all the case. Fashions in plays change, and the device that deceives to-day is seen through to-morrow. I have read a modern play carefully written, constructed and studied upon the lines of Sheridan, and the effect was ludicrous.

There is very little variation in our mistakes, but infinite variety in our achievements.

I once heard a would-be dramatist remark that there was only one vice, but uncountable virtues, a remark that was worth all the plays she had ever written up to date, and probably ever will write.

After *The Critic* Sheridan laid down his pen, and excepting for a translation of Kotzebue's bombastic and idiotic play *Pizarro,* wrote no more for the theatre. He took the opportunity of a dissolution of Parliament to contest and win the constituency of Stafford. The brilliant playwright now became a brilliant politician. That is to say, as an orator. As a minister, he began well, but ended disastrously, being altogether too casual, indolent, and happy-go-lucky for the drudgery and responsibility of office. His career as a politician is only interesting to us as it throws light upon his dramatic and artistic ability. And it throws considerable light upon them. His speeches and their dramatic effect were as carefully studied as were his plays. His wonderful speech at the impeachment of Warren Hastings was the greatest thing he had done since *The School for Scandal,* and the conclusion of it, when he sank fainting into the arms of Burke, was most effective. But his career as a statesman does not leave an impression of deep sincerity. He was a witty as well as a brilliant orator, but many of his best "impromptus" and repartees seem carefully to have been led up to and engineered beforehand. In short, he was a born dramatist, and it is a thousand pities he did not content himself with remaining one. Even management was a mistaken step, and he who could not do his share properly in the management of a theatre was scarcely likely to do it in that of a kingdom! But had he confined himself to writing plays, one wonders where an author who had begun with *The Rivals* and *The School for Scandal* would have ended. He was a "morning glory" if ever there was one. He started life in a halo of romance, prosperity and promise, and ended it in debt, squalor and disgrace. His first wife, the beautiful Miss Linley, predeceased him in 1792, his second, Miss Esther Ogle, the daughter of the Dean of Winchester, survived him.

His character could never keep pace with his talents. He

died on 7 July, 1816, and was buried, with great pomp, beside David Garrick in Westminster Abbey. A grave in that hallowed spot needs no epitaph, but they might have carved upon the tomb of Sheridan—

> Here lies one of life's greatest successes, and greatest failures!

As a dramatist his fame seems to depend almost as much upon what he might have done as upon what he did. His finished works, incomparable though they are, are only forerunners. They bear traces of infinite individuality. One feels that the mine from which they were drawn was inexhaustible. In spite of the immense care with which they were obviously written, there is yet all the ease and facility of a great genius. It has been said that Sheridan owed much to the dramatists who preceded him, especially those of the Restoration period. But a comparison with the best of them, Congreve, is immensely in Sheridan's favour. Congreve . . . was a most careful workman, a man who bound himself strictly with the conventions of his trade, who had imagination, wit and liveliness, but no heart. He represented a heartless period. Sheridan came at a time when the human heart was beginning to be recognized as essential to the human art, if art was to live, and his plays have got that touch of sympathy, and a hankering after better things, which makes them live. Lady Teazle, Julia, Falkland, Maria and Sir Peter, are live characters which are seldom if ever found in the drawing-rooms, gardens, or bed-chambers of Congreve, Wycherley or Vanbrugh.

Sheridan certainly owes something to the Restoration dramatists, but they owe more to him. Their nomenclature, their methods, and their style he has, to a certain extent, adopted and copied, but he has improved upon it, he has toned down their extravagances, curtailed their fopperies, fripperies and indecencies, and refined their spurious and base metal into gold and silver that is pure enough and has enough of the genuine ring to pass currency for ever. (pp. 147-67)

> *Cecil Ferard Armstrong, "Richard Brinsley Sheridan," in his* Shakespeare to Shaw: Studies in the Life's Work of Six Dramatists of the English Stage, *1913. Reprint by Books for Libraries Press, 1968, pp. 147-67.*

Aubrey de Sélincourt   (essay date 1960)

[*In the following excerpt, de Sélincourt surveys Sheridan's dramatic career, paying special attention to the playwright's method of composition. Although he considers the stories that Sheridan's plays were "tossed off with the utmost casualness and ease," more myth than fact, he nevertheless detects some signs that these works were hastily constructed.*]

Other people's financial affairs are always, I find, a little mysterious, and Sheridan was certainly no exception. His wife, when she married him, had . . . a small fortune of £3,000. He himself had nothing, and the first thing he did was to forbid Elizabeth to continue her career as a singer. No doubt Elizabeth's father helped to set them up in London; but there was no money coming in, and the house in

Engraving of Sheridan by R. Hicks, based on a portrait by Sir Joshua Reynolds.

Orchard Street is said to have been fitted up regardless of expense. A life of lavish entertaining immediately began. There is a story that a friend of Sheridan's remonstrated with him on his extravagance, urging that his means were totally inadequate to such a life of fashionable display. 'My dear friend,' Sheridan replied, 'it *is* my means.'

Fortunately, however, a seed had been lying for a year or two past in Sheridan's mind, and it now suddenly germinated. This seems a fairer way of putting the matter than Sheridan's own, who always liked to pretend that his productions were tossed off with the utmost casualness and ease, hardly interrupting his life of fashionable indolence and pleasure. 'There will be a comedy of mine', he wrote to Linley, 'in rehearsal at Covent Garden within a few days . . . I had not written a line of it two months ago, except a scene or two which I believe you have seen in an odd act of a little farce.' The comedy was *The Rivals*, and it was performed at Covent Garden in the January of 1775. On the first night the piece failed; but the manager of the theatre had confidence in its qualities, and after very considerable and judicious cutting, and the substitution of a different actor from the one who had played the part of Sir Lucius, it was brought back upon the stage, and succeeded. A month later it was produced in Bath where it was received enthusiastically. Since then its popularity has never declined.

The Rivals was a return to the old Comedy of Manners, modified by a certain concession to the changed taste of the time for the 'sentimental'. Happily the sentiment— introduced mainly through the character of Faulkland—is handled with sufficient lightness and gaiety not to spoil the whole. But any formal criticism of the play seems pedantical, and beside the point. The thing is a bubble—a nothing; yet it has its place in the dramatic literature of the world. Without roots in reality, it lives, and will continue to live; of irrepressible gaiety, it is made of laughter which is wholly devoid of irony and leaves no sting. One is the better for such laughter.

The plot is ingenious enough. The two rivals (as most of my readers will know) are but one man, Captain Absolute pretending to be the penniless ensign Beverley in order to win the affection of the romantic Lydia, who cannot endure the prospect of a safe and conventional love affair, while his rich father, Sir Anthony, wishes to marry him to her in his own, and unacceptable, person. But who cares about the plot? The delightfulness of the play is wholly in the dialogue, with its unfailing effervescence, its featherlight touch and heady sparkle like the bubbles in wine. 'Yes, Jack' (says Sir Anthony to his son), 'the independence I was talking of is by a marriage—the fortune is saddled with a wife—but I suppose that makes no difference.

> JACK: Sir! Sir! You amaze me!
>
> SIR ANTH.: Why, what the devil's the matter with the fool? Just now you were all gratitude and duty.
>
> JACK: I was, Sir—you talked to me of independence and a fortune, but not a word of a wife.
>
> SIR ANTH.: Why—what difference does that make? Odds life, Sir, if you have the estate, you must take it with the live stock on it, as it stands.
>
> JACK: If my happiness is to be the price, I must beg leave to decline the purchase. Pray, Sir, who is the lady?
>
> SIR ANTH.: What's that to you, Sir? Come, give me your promise to love, and to marry her directly.
>
> JACK: Sure, Sir, this is not very reasonable, to summon my affections for a lady I know nothing of.
>
> SIR ANTH.: I am sure, Sir, 'tis more unreasonable in you to *object* to a lady you know nothing of. . . .'

[Act II, Scene i]

Sir Anthony, despite such bursts of unanswerable, Alice-in-Wonderland logic, is, one must admit, a stage father of very familiar pattern, as is Captain Jack Absolute, his son. Indeed, all the characters of the play are conventional characters; but they have passed through the crucible of Sheridan's wit, and come out new. Even Mrs. Malaprop (whose name has given a new word to our language) had her fore-runners—yet she stands unchallenged in her kind through the sheer fertility of Sheridan's delighted invention. He cannot let her alone; he plays with her like a child with a toy, tosses her up and catches her, twists her about and tries again—hit or miss, but nearly always hit—to our unflagging entertainment: whether she assures Sir Lucius

that her love shall never be miscellaneous and that female punctuation forbids her to say more, exclaims that the Captain is the very pineapple of politeness, reprehends the use of her oracular tongue and a nice derangement of epitaphs, sighs that Lydia is as headstrong as an allegory on the banks of the Nile, or shudders, when the duel is in prospect, at the thought of the fine suicide, paracide and salivation going on in the fields. Moreover, by a delicate touch of dramatic art, dear Mrs. Malaprop is allowed in the end to show herself to be by no means wholly a fool.

Yet, in all this nonsense, there is a picture of a society, now for ever gone. I said the play has no roots in reality: neither has it; but a better image might be to call it cut flowers— for a brief moment as bright as when they grew. The thing has style: it is as *civilized* as Molière, though without a trace of Molière's wisdom or knowledge of the human heart.

In the same year Sheridan produced two other plays— both now forgotten: the farce **St. Patrick's Day** and the light opera, **The Duenna.** Personally, I cannot quite forget **St. Patrick's Day,** if only for Mrs. Bridget's reason for deprecating soldier husbands: 'O barbarous! to want a husband that may wed you today, and be sent the Lord knows where before night; then in a twelve-month perhaps to have him come *like a Colossus,* with one leg at New York and the other at Chelsea Hospital . . . No, give me a husband that knows where his limbs are, though he wants the use of them.' **The Duenna,** strangely enough, was immensely successful, and considered superior to [John Gay's] *The Beggar's Opera* which had first appeared nearly fifty years before, and which Byron in his letters refers to as 'that St. Giles' lampoon.' The music (of which I know nothing) for **The Duenna** was written by Sheridan's father-in-law, Linley. Perhaps it was that which made it popular, for the lyrics are nothing much. Public taste has surely been right in preserving *The Beggar's Opera* for posterity.

It was at this time, the end of the year 1775, that Garrick announced his intention of selling his share in the patent of Drury Lane Theatre. Sheridan, now twenty-four years old, had made money by his successes and seemed to have a brilliant future before him, so with characteristic rashness he determined to acquire a controlling interest in the theatre himself. He managed in some unspecified way to raise £10,000—what he had earned by his plays, though considerable, could hardly have paid for more than his current expenses—and with the assistance of Linley and of a certain Dr. Ford, who each put up a similar sum, he bought Garrick out and took upon himself, with the consent of his partners, full responsibility for the control of the great enterprise. Garrick had made a fortune out of Drury Lane, and as Covent Garden was the only other licensed theatre in London at that time, any other competent person ought to have been able to do the same. Sheridan, however, lacked all the qualities of a man of business; brilliant, sanguine and feckless, the best talker in London and the gayest companion, a man of genius able to work only when some unpredictable spark set his mind on fire, he was incapable of the drudgery and close attention to detail which a business enterprise requires. Garrick wanted

Sheridan to succeed him; but Garrick did not know his man. Sheridan's control of the great theatre consisted for the most part in doing nothing whatever and hoping for the best.

Nevertheless, before serious decay set in, there was to be one triumph, and that a great one. In the early summer of 1777, rather more than a year after Sheridan had assumed control, *The School for Scandal* was produced.

The actual writing of *The School for Scandal* was even more hurried than that of *The Rivals,* the last act being put into the hands of the players only five days before the opening night. But in another sense the play had been the work of years. Sheridan had pecked at it, and brooded over it, ever since he first discovered his talent for comedy; he had written scenes, and sketches for scenes, some of which were retained, others discarded. Two separate plots seem to have been running concurrently in his head, one in which the scandalmongers controlled the action and another concerning an old man and his young wife and two brothers, one virtuous, the other a hypocrite, who entangle themselves in her destiny. Had all been well at Drury Lane, nobody knows how much longer Sheridan would have played with his ideas; but all was not well: actors and the other shareholders alike were impatient for something which would steal the glory of *The Rivals* from Covent Garden and restore the already diminished lustre of Drury Lane. Sheridan knew that the effort must be made, and, in characteristic fashion, made it. The two plots were amalgamated, and the work which had occupied his thoughts for so long was rapidly completed. The play, which is Sheridan's masterpiece, was received with acclamation.

The greatest comedies of the world are based upon a perception of the real anomalies of human character. Alceste, for instance, in Molière's *Misanthrope,* is a good man: how is it, then, that he can also be absurd? Falstaff [in Shakespeare's *1* and *2 Henry IV*] is a rogue and a libertine, soaked in sack; yet we laugh ourselves into loving him. One cannot, it seems, judge a man by an arithmetical assessment of his virtues and vices: the sum, for some delightful reason, always comes out wrong. Of this quality of perception there is in *The School for Scandal* not a trace, any more than there is in its predecessor, *The Rivals.* The chief characters are all stock characters of comedy—the elderly husband, the giddy young wife, the spendthrift young man with a heart of gold; but though the play does not illuminate the heart, as the greatest comedies do, with laughter, it does present a picture of a certain aspect of society with unsurpassed brilliance and precision. The world it presents is, of course, the world of idle fashion—like that of [William] Congreve; but whereas Congreve painted society as if it were a thing-in-itself, self-sufficient, and with no threads, visible or invisible, to connect it with another life beyond, Sheridan, catching the altered tone of his day, stands a little apart from his creation, casts upon it an eye of half-whimsical criticism, and allows us to believe, even while the play is playing, and we are enjoying the polished wit of the scandalous tongues, that fashionable society, with its inevitable boredoms and frivolities, is, however gay and brilliant the picture it presents, both

corrupt and corrupting. Sheridan himself might well have denied this: but it is true—it was the debt which he had perforce to pay to the Sentimental Comedy which had held the stage for so long.

The School for Scandal makes one laugh less than *The Rivals*—and less, perhaps, than certain pieces of inspired nonsense which occur in Sheridan's minor plays, like for instance poor Dr. Rosy's lament, in *St. Patrick's Day,* over his wife who was carried off by an inhuman dropsy: 'gone never to return, and left no pledge of our loves behind—no little babe to hang like a label round papa's neck'; but the *inward* laughter is subtler and more all-pervading, and for plot and stage-effect it is greatly superior. Sheridan had the true playwright's eye for a situation, and in the whole range of comedy there are few better contrived or more amusing scenes than the 'screen' scene of this play, in which all the chief characters are brought together at the crisis of their fortunes, and the knots are untied. But, when all is said, it is the unfailing point, wit and polish of the dialogue which make *The School for Scandal* a classic of the English stage; the talk is as bright as a button and as sharp as a rapier; it keeps the audience on edge with expectation, which it continually satisfies. 'What makes you impatient of Sir Peter's temper,' says Joseph to Lady Teazle, 'and outrageous at his suspicions'? Why, the very consciousness of your innocence.'

> LADY T.: 'Tis very true.
>
> JOSEPH: Now, my dear Lady Teazle, if you would but once make a trifling *faux pas,* you can't conceive how cautious you would grow, and how ready to humour and agree with your husband.
>
> LADY T.: Do you think so?
>
> JOSEPH: Oh I am sure on 't; and then you would find all scandal would cease at once; for, in short, your character at present is like a person in a plethora, absolutely dying from too much health.
>
> LADY T.: So, so; then I perceive your prescription is, that I must sin in my own defence, and part with my virtue to preserve my reputation?
>
> JOSEPH: Exactly so, upon my credit, ma'am.'
> [Act IV, Scene ii]

Taste changes, the forms of society—and hence the themes upon which comedy is built—shift and dislimn like the architecture of clouds, but this play keeps its point and freshness. The infallible preservative is style.

The success of *The School for Scandal* put Drury Lane temporarily on its feet again. Sheridan, who had sunk all he possessed and all he could borrow in the venture, now looked forward to a golden future. He lived the life of a wealthy man, and entertained an increasing number of friends and acquaintances on a more and more lavish scale, visiting, in his turn, the houses of the great, where his talk and his charm always found him a welcome. His ambition grew. A successful playwright, or man of letters of any other kind, enjoyed less consideration from society in the eighteenth century than perhaps he does today, and

Sheridan was determined, if he could, to win fame and fortune and position in a wider field. His thoughts accordingly began to turn towards politics. But meanwhile his brief but brilliant literary career was to have one more triumph, though a minor one. In the same year as *The School for Scandal* Sheridan's last play of any importance, *The Critic,* was produced.

It may well be that the stories, which all Sheridan's biographers tell, of the haphazard manner in which his plays were flung together at the last minute were encouraged by Sheridan himself, who liked to adopt the pose of 'writing like a gentleman', much as Byron liked his friends to believe that he composed his *Giaour* and *Lara,* and so on, while he was shaving in the morning after a night of revelry at some ball or rout. There is in most of us a touch of snobbery which finds a certain seductiveness in the idea of such dandified brilliance. Sheridan had no desire to appear as the professional man of letters; much more to his taste was the reputation of a society wit whose by-work chanced to be the best comedy of his century. Nor was the pose, if pose it was, without foundation in reality, and it helps to account both for virtues and for the limitations of his work. The method of composition of *The Critic* seems by all accounts to have been 'gentlemanly' to excess: three days before the play was due to appear, the last scene was still unwritten. Sheridan's co-proprietors, Linley and Ford, were on tenterhooks with anxiety; the actors were in despair. For weeks past King, who was stage-manager and was to play Puff, had been pestering the reluctant author to do his duty, but in vain. 'At last,' we are told, 'Mr. Linley hit upon a strategem. A night rehearsal was ordered, and Sheridan having dined with Linley was prevailed upon to go. When they were on the stage, King whispered to Sheridan that he had something to communicate, and begged that he would step into the second greenroom. Accordingly Sheridan went, and found there a table with pens, ink and paper, a good fire, an armchair at the table and two bottles of claret, with a dish of anchovy sandwiches. The moment he got into the room, King stepped out and locked the door, immediately after which Linley and Ford came up and told the author that until he had written the scene he would be kept where he was. Sheridan took this decided measure in good part; he ate the anchovies, finished the claret, wrote the scene, and laughed heartily at the ingenuity of the contrivance.'

The Critic or A Tragedy Rehearsed is a skit on the most abject aspect of the contemporary theatre. For us, some of its point is inevitably blunted, as our own theatre, even when it is abject, is abject in a different way. We no longer write tragedies in mock-Elizabethan fustian. Nevertheless Sheridan cannot fail to be entertaining. The skit is as high-spirited as *The Rivals,* and reads like a glorified charade. The first act, with the admirably devised portrait of Sir Fretful Plagiary and the explications of Mr. Puff of the fine art of puffing a forthcoming play, is as sparkling and as tart in flavour as anything Sheridan wrote, and the second act, in which Mr. Puff's new tragedy is rehearsed, with a running commentary from the author himself and two unsympathetic critics, is a splendid joke.

PUFF: Now enter Tilburina!

SNEER: Egad, the business comes in quick here.

PUFF: Yes, Sir—now she comes in stark mad in white satin.

SNEER: Why in white satin?

PUFF: O Lord, Sir, when a heroine goes mad, she always goes into white satin—don't she, Dangle?

DANGLE: Always—its a rule . . .

(*Enter* Tilburina and Confidant, *mad, according to custom*)

SNEER: But what the deuce—is the confidant to be mad too?

PUFF: To be sure she is—the confidant is always to do whatever her mistress does . . .

TILBURINA: . . . Is this a grasshopper? Ah, no, it is my Whiskerandos—you shall not keep him—An oyster may be crossed in love—who say's
> A whale's a bird? Ha! did you call, my love?
> He's here! He's there! He's everywhere!
> Ah me! He's nowhere!
(*Exit* Tilburina)

I think one is aware, reading that passage, of the anchovy sandwiches and the two bottles of claret.

Apart from the plays I have mentioned, Sheridan, before he wrote *The School for Scandal,* had adapted a comedy of Vanburgh's, which he called *A Trip to Scarborough,* and he produced, after *The Critic,* a dreary bread-and-butter tragedy called *Pizarro,* which is deservedly forgotten, being much the kind of stuff which was so effectively burlesqued in *The Critic. The Critic* was his last farewell to the stage which for a few short years he had so brilliantly adorned. He still had thirty-seven years to live, but to literature he contributed nothing more. (pp. 116-27)

> *Aubrey de Sélincourt, "Sheridan," in his* Six Great Playwrights: Sophocles, Shakespeare, Molière, Sheridan, Ibsen, Shaw, *Hamish Hamilton, 1960, pp. 105-31.*

Robert Hogan   (essay date 1986)

[*In the essay below, Hogan examines the plot, characterization and comic language in Sheridan's* The Rivals, The School for Scandal, *and* The Critic. *He concludes that, despite the "academically slovenly" nature of the plotting and the lack of "original elements" in the characterization and comic writing of these plays, Sheridan's manipulation of the familiar material make them fresh and "a perennial source of linguistic delight."*]

Oliver Goldsmith and Richard Brinsley Sheridan—these two Irishmen are inevitably considered the preeminent comic talents of the English-speaking theater in the eighteenth century. Indeed, many literary historians have said that from the retirement of Congreve and the death of Farquhar early in the eighteenth century, until the appearance of Oscar Wilde, Bernard Shaw, and W. B. Yeats late in the nineteenth century, there were no dramatists who even approached the quality of Goldsmith and Sheridan.

Like all generalizations, this one is a bit too general. This long period hardly saw the profusion of masterpieces that appeared during the reign of Elizabeth I or of Charles II, and an overwhelming number of the plays produced between 1700 and 1890 now strike us as too full of high fustian and low theatrics, and too evocative of easy tears and brainless belly laughs. Still, John Gay's *The Beggar's Opera* has outlasted Sheridan's **The Duenna,** and Henry Fielding's *Tom Thumb* stands up nicely to Sheridan's **The Critic,** while some of the straight comic work of Macklin, Murphy, Garrick, Colman the Elder, and Sheridan's own mother Frances did not in the eighteenth century fall that far short of the best of Goldsmith and Sheridan themselves. And even from the more arid nineteenth century, Dion Boucicault's *Old Heads and Young Hearts* and T. W. Robertson's *Caste* might be revived with pleasure, while the airy operettas of Gilbert and Sullivan have never been out of favor.

Still, when all of the qualifications have been made, Goldsmith and Sheridan remain unlikely to be challenged in their historical preeminence, just as their best works remain unlikely to lose their popularity on the stage.

When Sheridan's first play, **The Rivals,** was initially produced at Covent Garden in 1775, it failed. It was too long, insufficiently rehearsed, and in one instance badly cast. Sheridan quickly cut the play and replaced the offending actor with a better, and in less than two weeks, **The Rivals** had become a solid success. The play has never lost its popularity. It is one of those plays that takes a perverse genius to do badly. It is almost actor-proof and director-proof, and mediocre or even distinctly bad productions can still arouse delight. It has, nonetheless, been generally considered a lesser work than **The School for Scandal.** Yet, if there is to be any revision in the critical opinion about Sheridan, it can only be in the upgrading of **The Rivals,** and a convincing case can be made that **The Rivals** in many ways equals and in some surpasses the worth of **The School for Scandal.**

Neither play is what one would call well made, and, indeed, construction was never Sheridan's strong point. However, a tidy plot construction is probably an overrated quality in comedy, and even in tragedy the English-speaking theater has preferred Elizabethan sprawl to neoclassical trimness. Sheridan's faults in plotting **The Rivals** have been no better isolated than by the perceptive Tom Moore, who noted that

> For our insight into [the] characters, we are indebted rather to their confessions than their actions. Lydia Languish, in proclaiming the extravagance of her own romantic notions, prepares us for events much more ludicrous and eccentric, than those in which the plot allows her to be concerned; and the young lady herself is scarcely more disappointed than we are, at the tameness with which her amour concludes . . . and the wayward, captious jealousy of Faulkland, though so highly coloured in his own representation of it, is productive of no incident answerable to such an announcement [see Further Reading].

This point can be applied to the relations of other charac-

ters in the play. Bob Acres and Lydia are never brought together for a confrontation; little is made of the "love affair" of Mrs. Malaprop and Sir Lucius. Despite his usefulness to the "real" plot, Acres might just as well be cut out of the play. It would have been dramaturgically tidier for the Jack-Lydia-Mrs. Malaprop-Sir Lucius imbroglio if Jack confronted Sir Lucius without the distraction of Acres. Acres's cowardice is, however, so delicious that one would no more sacrifice it than one would the windmill episode in *Don Quixote.* Such academic strictures are sometimes just theatrically beside the point. Despite, then, the omission of several "obligatory scenes," an audience does not miss or even note what Sheridan might or should have done, because what he has done is totally absorbing and increasingly delightful: he has written a series of irresistible scenes, based either on ludicrous situations or characterizations. As each droll scene is succeeded by another of equal or greater interest, the audience remains so caught by the pleasure of the moment that the static or erratic quality of the plot is simply not noticed. Nevertheless, the plot must at least seem to move, and in **The Rivals** Sheridan's plot does lurch on toward the aborted duel. A difficulty of **The School for Scandal** is that for the first two acts the plot *seems* static.

Tom Moore sets up a persuasive but wrong-headed comparison between the language and characterization of the two plays:

> With much less wit, it [**The Rivals**] exhibits perhaps more humour than **The School for Scandal,** and the dialogue, though by no means so pointed or sparkling, is, in this respect more natural, as coming nearer the current coin of ordinary conversation; whereas, the circulating medium of **The School for Scandal** is diamonds. The characters of **The Rivals,** on the contrary, are *not* such as occur very commonly in the world; and, instead of producing striking effects with natural and obvious materials, which is the great art and difficulty of a painter of human life, he has here overcharged most of his persons with whims and absurdities.

This view—that the dialogue is natural but the characters are exaggerated—strikes me as only half true. Sheridan was dealing with "humours," types, exaggerations, but the characters were not extravagant exaggerations, and so, for instance, the stage-Irishness of Sir Lucius was played down when Sheridan revised the play. The excellence of Sheridan's comic characterizations is that his types are handled with such a verve, freshness, and panache that they reinvigorate their stockness. Sir Anthony is basically the tyrannical father; Mrs. Malaprop, the superannuated dame; Sir Lucius, the Stage Irishman; and Bob Acres is a combination of rustic booby, false beau, and braggart soldier. Among the comic characters (as opposed to the straight characters of Jack and Julia), Lydia and Faulkland are the most touched with originality. Both possess the dull youth and handsomeness of innumerable young heroes and ingenues, but in Sheridan's treatment they become comic rather than straight characters because their admirable qualities are exaggerated until they become faults. In Lydia, romance becomes exaggerated to absurdity; in Faulkland, love becomes exaggerated to neurosis.

Even the stock servant—a figure that has a centuries-old provenance and is little different in Wodehouse, Wilde, Vanbrugh, Machiavelli, or Terence—is made original in Sheridan. What he adds to the character of the pert servant is a charming falsity of language that the audience finds both refreshing and novel, and this addition revivifies most of Sheridan's otherwise stock characterization.

The individuality of Lydia, Faulkland, and all the less original characters, then, is established largely by their language. Rather than the natural dialogue that Tom Moore saw, the play contains a dazzling degree of unnatural and absurd dialogue. Sheridan took great pains with the writing of *The Rivals,* and it has throughout a graceful fluency that gives the impression of naturalness. It is, however, the unimportant parts of the play that are the most easy, natural, and realistic. The strongest parts, with the biggest laughs, are those in which a character uses language in a finely foolish fashion.

To take the most obvious example: the great comic lines of Mrs. Malaprop spring from an inspired misuse of words that is far too outlandish to be thought realistic or natural. Set in a surrounding dialogue of fluent naturalness, her marvelous mistakes of diction appear in bold relief. Mrs. Malaprop is funny because she is doubly pretentious: she is an aging woman who regards herself as still young and beautiful enough to be the object of a romantic love affair, and she is a stupid and vain woman who regards herself as a bluestocking. Her first pretension is deflated by the plot and by how the other characters regard her; her second pretension is deflated by her own language and by how the audience regards it. A character using the wrong word has long been a source of theatrical and fictional comedy. The laughter has traditionally come from the character using a wrong word that sounds like the right one. Mrs. Malaprop's best mistakes improve on this device, for the word that she chooses not only sounds like the word she meant, but it also contains a meaning that either reduces her thought to inspired nonsense or makes her say the opposite of what she intended. In her great speech about the education of young women [Act I, Scene ii], she desires Lydia to know "something of the contagious countries," and her choice of "contagious" for "contiguous" contains a brilliant bit of nonsense that, of course, indicates her own ignorance and delights the audience.

If Mrs. Malaprop's language deflates her claims to learning, Sir Anthony's deflates his own false reasoning. In his attempts to persuade Jack to be married, Sir Anthony is thwarted, and, instead of becoming more cogent and reasonable, he becomes more incoherent and emotional. So far Sheridan follows tradition: a stock father who would be the repository of wisdom, reason, and tolerance is shown to be dense, irrational, and splenetic. Sheridan again goes beyond tradition, however, for Sir Anthony's language does not merely become incoherent with anger; at its climactic and funniest it actually becomes a parody of reasoning. His brilliant exit speech of act 2, scene 1, uses the trappings of reason but winds up in the depths of infantilism.

The success of these scenes requires two characters: the faulty speaker and the clear-eyed critic. The critic is a straight character who helps the audience see what is wrong with the comic character's language and, therefore, with his character. Thus, after Sir Anthony's great outburst, Jack acts the role of critic with his ironic remark:

> Mild, gentle, considerate father—I kiss your hands—What a tender method of giving his opinion in these matters Sir Anthony has!
> [Act II, Scene i]

Or, in Mrs. Malaprop's great scene in act 1, it is Sir Anthony, elsewhere himself a faulty speaker, who acts the role of critic and says:

> I must confess, that you are a truly moderate and politic arguer, for almost every third word you say is on my side of the question.
> [Act I, Scene ii]

In the Faulkland-Julia scenes, Julia acts as the critic, and so her language needs to contrast sharply with Faulkland's. In contrast to his circuitous, emotional floridness, she must be direct, simple, and reasonable. To emphasize what is wrong with his language and character, her language and character must set the rhetorical and the moral norm. Early in their first meeting [Act III, Scene ii], Sheridan controls her language well, and she makes direct and terse remarks: "I had not hoped to see you again so soon," for example, or, "Nay then, I see you have taken something ill. You must not conceal from me what it is." Such sentences contrast effectively with Faulkland's purple effusions:

> For such is my temper, Julia, that I should regard every mirthful moment in your absence as a treason to constancy:—The mutual tear that steals down the cheek of parting lovers. . . .

Although the young Sheridan was already a master of comic language and here effectively mocks the language of sentiment, he was far from a master of serious language used to convey emotional intensity. Consequently, Julia's later, more intense speeches become as stiff, florid, and false as Faulkland's, and we find her saying in act 5, scene 1:

> Then on the bosom of your wedded Julia, you may lull your keen regret to slumbering; while virtuous love, with a Cherub's hand, shall smooth the brow of upbraiding thought and pluck the thorn from compunction.

Aside from the failure of serious language, the play is the performance of a virtuoso of dialogue fit to be ranked with Wilde and Shaw. The play may have a rather untidy plot, but the plot does provide a multitude of effective comic situations. The play may use stock types, but it also works original variations on these types. Finally, the play does provide a variety of false language hardly seen in English drama since the comedies of Congreve and Ben Jonson. The language of *The Rivals* has secured the play its high position in the English theater. It is a language that civilizes by involving its audience. It is a language that makes its audience become active critics of false language and, therefore, of false behavior.

* * *

The two main kinds of comic language are the language of humor and the language of wit. The language of humor predominates in *The Rivals,* and the language of wit in *The School for Scandal.* The language of humor misuses grammar and sentence structure and rhetorical devices to produce speech that amusingly and ignorantly diverges from a norm of commonly accepted good speech and writing. The language of wit uses grammar and sentence structure and rhetorical devices with such uncommon fluency that its speech diverges from a norm of good speech and writing by its more considerable excellence. In other words, the language of humor is purposely bad writing, and the nature of its badness is a symptom of what is wrong with the speaker. The language of wit, on the other hand, is purposely superb writing, and the nature of its excellence is a symptom of what is right with the speaker. Using the language of humor, the speaker may fail to attain a civilized norm by innate stupidity such as Dogberry's [in Shakespeare's *Much Ado about Nothing*], or by lack of education such as Sam Weller's [in Charles Dickens's *Pickwick Papers*], or by provincial ignorance such as the quaint dialect flaws of the stage Irishman and Scotsman or Frenchman. Using the language of wit, as Shakespeare's Benedick and Beatrice do poorly [in *Much Ado*], or as Congreve's Millamant and Mirabell [in *The Way of the World*] do well, or as Shaw's Don Juan and Devil [in *Don Juan in Hell*] do consummately, the speaker exceeds the civilized norm and makes us admire his urbanity, insight, and wisdom. In the language of humor, the audience perceives a misuse of words that stems from a character fault, and the resultant laughter is critical. In the language of wit, the audience perceives a consummate use of words that stems from excellences of character, and the resultant laughter is admiring. More simply, the language of humor occasions critical laughter at stupidity, and the language of wit occasions admiring smiles at brilliance.

As the appreciation of wit is of higher worth than the perception of stupidity, so the language of wit is thought of greater worth than the language of humor. Thus a play like *The School for Scandal* is more highly regarded than a play like *The Rivals.* Yet this attitude may be suspect, for both comic languages actively engage the judgment of their auditors, and both comic languages use quite complex techniques. If there is an innate difference of value between the two comic languages, it must lie in the content. The language of wit has occasionally been used, notably in some plays by Shaw, to discuss more complex themes than the drama usually handles.

The School for Scandal, largely because of its witty language, has been Sheridan's most admired play. The play was first produced at Drury Lane on 8 May 1777 and has held the boards ever since. The scandal scenes in particular have been considered a triumph of witty language, and they will only work, indeed, because they are witty. The danger of these scenes, particularly in a poor production, is that they are static. Nothing happens in them. The plot does not advance, and one of the viewers at the play's brilliant premiere was even heard to grumble that he wondered when the author was going to get on with the story.

But, of course, the stories themselves are not well structured. To take only one example, the heroine, Maria, has quite a small part. She is off the stage through most of the crucial acts and, amazingly, is not even confronted with the hero until the very denouement in act 5. As with *The Rivals,* one could pile up a dozen instances of what Sheridan had to do with his plot and did not do. But, also as with *The Rivals,* one must admit that what he did do instead is so delightful and absorbing that his audience is thoroughly satisfied.

Sheridan makes some use of more individualized characterization in this play. There are well-defined stock types such as Mrs. Candour and Sir Benjamin Backbite, but Sir Peter and Lady Teazle are rather fuller than types, and in Charles and particularly in Joseph, Sheridan cuts beneath the surface and finds contradictions and something approaching complexity. Joseph, the apparently good but actually hypocritical brother, was regarded by Sheridan's sisters as a sketch of their own older brother, Charles. In any event, Joseph is a meaty acting role, even if not quite a fully fleshed-out one. He is, however, closer to reality than the great comic monsters of a Volpone [title character of a play by Ben Jonson] or a Tartuffe [title character of a play by Molière]. In Charles, it may not be stretching a point to see some of Richard Sheridan's own carelessness and casual mismanagement. But, like everyone, Sheridan had a good deal of tolerance for his own foibles, and so does his audience have a good deal of tolerance for the erring but basically good-hearted Charles. From this crucial attitude, much of the sunniness of the play can be traced.

The rhetorical showpieces of the play are the great scandal-mongering scenes of acts 1 and 2, in which the chorus of gossips, with bubbling spirits and brilliant technique, rends and shreds reputations. It is curious that the strength of these scenes arises from exquisitely phrased malice. Lady Sneerwell says in explanation that "there's no possibility of being witty without a little ill nature: the malice of a good thing is the barb that makes it stick" [Act I, Scene i].

Certainly it is true that Maria and Sir Peter, the unmalicious characters in the scandal scenes, are able to counter the witty malice with no more than direct statement, which is ineffective, and with honest dignity, which appears stuffy. Yet, while neither Maria nor Sir Peter is a match for witty malice, that does not mean that a match could not be found. A well-equipped Shavian wit, such as Sidney Trefusis or Don Juan, could have more than upheld the side of sense and worth with equal rhetorical cleverness and by substituting gaiety for malice.

It seems generally taken for granted that Sheridan's scandalmongers are deplorable, but it has not been much noticed that their critiques are correct. An audience would not laugh at their jokes unless their victims deserved laughter. Mrs. Evergreen, discussed in act 2, is mutton trying to pass as lamb; Miss Simper and Miss Prim are foolishly vain; Mrs. Pursy, although too fat, attempts to appear slim; Lady Stucco, although too old, attempts to appear beautiful. All of these victims deserve the lash of satire, and the audience laughs at popular pretensions deservedly deflated. The scandalmongers, then, are joke makers and, like all joke makers, are necessarily moralists. Why, then, are they themselves funny?

The reason, of course, is that they live in glass houses. The delight they take in other people's failings is wedded to their perfect ignorance of their own. Once again Sheridan worked a new twist upon old material and conveyed his truths by the vehicles of folly.

In the language of humor, which Sheridan basically used in *The Rivals,* the audience laughs at language faultily used and so becomes, en masse, a literary critic. In the language of wit, which Sheridan frequently used in *The School for Scandal,* the audience laughs at language cleverly used and becomes a literary appreciator. The point might be proved by taking any of *The School for Scandal*'s well-turned jokes and rephrasing them. Almost invariably the rephrasing lessens—if not, indeed, destroys—the strength of the joke. For instance, in act 1, the poetaster Sir Benjamin Backbite unknowingly makes a joke against his own vapid verses when he describes the appearance of his forthcoming slim volume: "a beautiful quarto page, where a neat rivulet of text shall meander through a meadow of margin" [Act I, Scene i]. The delight of the joke comes from two sources, one obvious and one rather subliminal. The obvious point is the originality of the metaphor; the subtler point is the reinforcement of sound, first in the *t's* of "neat Rivulet of text," and next in the *m's* of "meander through a meadow of margin." To rephrase the remark in unmetaphorical and unalliterative statement is to arrive at something like: "a beautiful quarto page, where a few lines are set off by a wide margin."

We catch Sheridan's neatly conceived and deftly turned statement on the wing, and our appreciative laughter is instantaneous. It is, therefore, unnecessary as well as uncivilized to spend more space in reducing clearly successful jokes to baldly tedious statements. However, it might be noted that Sheridan pushes his audience to appreciate wit in another way, and he does so by smoothly inserting some literary criteria. Several times he actually ensures that his audience will laugh by telling them what and even how to appreciate.

For instance, in the play's opening dialogue, Snake and Lady Sneerwell almost immediately launch into a rhetorical consideration of Lady Clackitt's gossip:

> LADY SNEERWELL: She certainly has Talents, but her manner is gross.
>
> SNAKE: 'Tis very true—she generally designs well—has a free tongue and a bold invention—but her colouring is too dark and her outline often extravagant. She wants that delicacy of Hint—and mellowness of sneer which distinguish your ladyship's Scandal.
>
> [Act I, Scene i]

In a similar manner, Sheridan sets up the rhetorical techniques of Crabtree and Mrs. Candour.

But perhaps to say more about the high quality and the manifold techniques of Sheridan's comic language would be tedious. A good joke does not need to be explained. It startlingly explodes into perfect and unexpected obviousness, and our instantaneous laughter results from our per-

fect but unexpected perception. Let it merely be asserted, then, that Sheridan's command of the widest variety of rhetorical techniques is consummate. When one thinks of the flabby badinage that passes for wit between Shakespeare's Beatrice and Benedick, one can only turn with relief and delight to a Congreve, a Wilde, a Shaw—or a Sheridan.

But perhaps the greatest quality of Sheridan's comic writing is one that he shares with Goldsmith—a sunny good nature deriving from a benevolent tolerance. Neither Sheridan nor Goldsmith says much in his plays, but in their one shared, pervasive quality they imply an attitude that imparts to their work something often lacking in the work of even their greatest colleagues. That attitude is charm. Charm is usually an underrated quality, assigned to minor writers such as Charles Lamb or Kenneth Grahame. Perhaps it is easier to allow them a trivial excellence than to analyze their excellence seriously. But is charm so trivial? In Sheridan, are we not charmed because we are reminded of the vital fact that it is awfully nice to be alive? This humanity, as Virginia Woolf noted [in her *Books and Portraits*], "was part of his charm" and "still warms his writing."

* * *

It is too arbitrary to limit comic language to two kinds only, the language of humor and the language of wit. There is at least one other, albeit minor, kind. What of the language of imitation, the language of parody that satirizes presumptive excellence by exaggerating its faults? This is a rarer use of comic language, limited mainly to the criticism of literary forms, but it certainly does appear in plays.

The three great examples of parody or burlesque in English drama are Buckingham's *The Rehearsal* (1671), Fielding's *Tom Thumb* (1731), and Sheridan's *The Critic* (1779). *The Critic* pushed *The Rehearsal* off the stage, and Fielding's delightful play presents such problems of staging that it has always been more popular in the study than on the boards. Only *The Critic* is still occasionally performed today, even though the stage style it lampooned is two centuries out of date.

Sheridan's second and third acts in *The Critic* have some brilliantly bad writing, although not nearly the profusion found in Fielding. Sheridan compensates, however, by satirizing the complete theatrical experience. Thus, he has many more visual and aural gags than does Fielding. Indeed, if we are to consider the play solely as literature, it tails off disappointingly because Sheridan does not rely on words at the conclusion but, rather, on a parody of excessive stage spectacle. In the original staging at Drury Lane, the spectacular visual conclusion satisfyingly topped everything that had gone before. On paper, little of this effect can be apparent: on the modern stage, all of this effect can be a problem.

The purely literary content, however, is so fine that the play has always been admired as the third of Sheridan's masterpieces. Indeed, he himself regarded the first act as the most finished piece of dramatic writing he had done. The act is a brilliant piece of work, and a chief excellence is that it gets its laughs while actually establishing the rules for laughing. Some of the generalizations established in act 1 are also aids for judging the ineptitudes of the play-within-the-play of acts 2 and 3.

Act 1 falls into three major scenes: the dialogue between Mr. Dangle and Sneer, the baiting of Sir Fretful Plagiary, and the rhetorical exhibition of Mr. Puff. In the Dangle-Sneer dialogue, some criticisms are made about the incompatibility of comedy and overt moralizing, which had been joined in popular sentimental comedies of Richard Steele and others. There is briefly even some criticism of the bad writing of sentimental comedy. It has too much nicety: "No double entendre, no smart innuendo admitted; even Vanburgh [*sic*] and Congreve obliged to undergo a bungling reformation!" [Act I, Scene i]. The Sir Fretful scene is a humorous criticism of a poor but egotistical playwright, *à la* Buckingham's Bayes, and the character is something of a cartoon of Richard Cumberland. But even in this scene a number of axioms about false and inflated language are insinuated. For example:

> In your more serious efforts . . . your bombast would be less intolerable, if the thoughts were ever suited to the expression; but the homeliness of the sentiment stares thro' the fantastic encumbrance of its fine language, like a clown in one of the new uniforms!
>
> [Act I, Scene ii]

Later, in the play-within-the-play, this fault is illustrated abundantly and with delightful inanity. Then, after the broad interlude of non-English and broken English in the little scene of the Italian singers and the French interpreter, comes the great scene in which Mr. Puff analyzes the varieties of false language that composed contemporary advertising. The passage is too long to quote in full, but in it Sheridan bombards his audience with false fluency and, in effect, forces each member to see that it is false and to become a literary critic. For instance, part of Mr. Puff's illustration of the Puff Direct reads:

> Characters strongly drawn—highly coloured—hand of a master—fund of genuine humour—mine of invention—neat dialogue—attic salt! Then for the performance—Mr. DODD was astonishingly great in the character of SIR HARRY! That universal and judicious actor Mr. PALMER, perhaps never appeared to more advantage than in the COLONEL;—but it is not in the power of language to do justice to Mr. KING!—Indeed he more than merited those repeated bursts of applause which he drew from a most brilliant and judicious audience! As to the scenery—The miraculous power of Mr. DE LOUTHERBOURG'S pencil are universally acknowledged!—In short, we are at a loss which to admire most,—the unrivalled genius of the author, the great attention and liberality of the managers—the wonderful abilities of the painter, or the incredible exertions of all the performers!
>
> [Act I, Scene ii]

Sheridan has set up Mr. Puff's lecture on Puffing so that the audience is primed to look closely at language that Puff asserts will be effective and seem sincere in any instance. Hence, all of the descriptive phrases and all of the admiring epithets stand out in bold relief as indications of insincerity and gush. This is a considerable achievement and a healthy one.

To test Sheridan's feat, I took down from my shelves the first four volumes of contemporary dramatic criticism I put my hands on; books by Kenneth Tynan, Robert Brustein, Stanley Kauffman, and Martin Gottfried. Still seeing with a Brinsleyan clarity, I opened each volume at random and was astonished to see that certain phrases now leapt off the page. From Mr. Tynan: "admirable, transfigured, one of the noblest performances I have ever seen, marvelously characterized, I shall never forget the skill with which . . . " [*Curtains*]. From Mr. Brustein: "a spirited performance, the season's triumph, and a triumph for the American theatre. Though superlatives have a habit of sticking in my throat, I must not temporize here: this was the finest production of a Shakespeare comedy I have ever seen" [*Seasons of Discontent*]. From Mr. Kauffmann: "production is outstandingly happy, setting is almost miraculous, vitality of the born actor and the fine control of the skillful one, we will be allowed to watch an extraordinary career develop" [*Persons of Drama*]. From Mr. Gottfried: "wonderfully fluid use of stage possibilities, genuinely poetic, apt and funny, hilarious, brilliant. He is part of our theater's great tomorrow" [*Opening Nights*].

We have seemingly wandered far afield here, but the difference between the muddy fustian of the critics and the piercing clarity of the dramatist may indicate not only how pertinent Sheridan's strictures still are but also how valid his excellence still is. It may also suggest that the clearest, shortest way to truth is not through criticism but through the work of art itself.

The language of the remaining two acts of ***The Critic*** illustrates, by broad parody, various kinds of bad dramatic writing. Particularly droll is the flat and intentional inadequacy of the blank verse in the "butler-maid" scene of exposition between Raleigh and Hatton. Here, of course, Sneer's axiom about homely sentiment and fine language is illustrated. Such a prosaic lameness of thought couched in words of pseudo-Shakespearian grandeur is not far-fetched. Many worthless tragedies with scarcely less awful language have succeeded for the moment on the stage: see much, if not quite all, of the work of Sheridan's young kinsman, James Sheridan Knowles.

An equally fine parody is Tilburnia's lyric purple passage that begins with the superbly stale

> Now has the whispering breath of gentle morn,
> Bad Nature's voice, and Nature's beauty rise;
> While orient Phoebus, with unborrow'd hues,
> Cloaths the wak'd loveliness which all night slept
> In heav'nly drapery! Darkness is fled.
>
> [Act II, Scene ii]

The speech ends with a lengthy catalogue of birds and flowers. Ophelia has a lot to answer for.

A chief symptom of Sheridan's parodic success is that quoting it is so irresistible. Here, then, is one final, fine, brief parody, this time of the language of rant and fustian:

WHISKERANDOS: Thou liest—base Beefeater!
BEEFEATER: Ha! Hell! the lie!
  By heav'n thou'st rous'd the lion in my heart!
  Off, yeoman's habit!—base disguise!—off!
  off!

                        [Act III, Scene i]

By precept and example, Sheridan has established what bad theatrical language is. One does not need to be a scholar to appreciate his fun, but he has joked and punned so well that he has momentarily created an audience of laughing pundits. *The Critic* is not about life or human nature. It is about good and bad literary form; it is about taste. That fact must make it a work of lesser import than *The Rivals* or *The School for Scandal,* but it is not a work of lesser pleasure.

* * *

Three conclusions and a concluding generalization sum up Sheridan's accomplishments in his three great plays.

The plotting, although academically slovenly, is so continuously absorbing in its successive incidents that it is theatrically irresistible.

The characterization contains no original elements and scarcely ever diverges from the stereotypes worked over by Congreve, Molière, Shakespeare and Jonson, Goldoni and Plautus; upon these stock figures, however, Sheridan has mixed such new combinations and insinuated such fresh fancies of detail that they have not lost the illusion of bloom for the last two hundred years.

The comic writing, similarly, contains no original elements; and indeed, I suspect that no writer in the last two thousand years—with the dubious exception of Beckett—has discovered a new way of making a joke. What Sheridan's comic writing does is to utilize each of the comic modes—humor, wit, and parody—and to invest these traditional manners with such fresh inventiveness of detail as to make the three great plays a perennial source of linguistic delight and even of civilized apprehension.

Sheridan wrote in one of the most constricting, simplistic, and naive forms of art, the drama. Unlike Ibsen or Strindberg or Chekhov or Granville-Barker, he did not attempt to expand the form either in technique or in content. He was a traditionalist, albeit a consummate one. A greater comic artist who did attempt to expand the form but who also thoroughly understood its traditionalism, was Bernard Shaw who remarked—not with entire truth—that dramaturgically he himself merely appropriated the characterization of Dickens and the plotting of Molière. But what Shaw further said of himself [in his *Sixteen Self Sketches*] is an appropriate final generalization about Brinsley Sheridan: "He touches nothing that he does not dust and polish and put back in its place much more carefully than the last man who handled it." (pp. 274-84)

> *Robert Hogan, "Plot, Character, and Comic Language in Sheridan," in* Comedy from Shakespeare to Sheridan: Change and Continuity in the English and European Dramatic Tradition, *edited by A. R. Braunmuller and J. C. Bulman, Associated University Presses, 1986, pp. 274-85.*

THE RIVALS

PRODUCTION REVIEWS

The Town and Country Magazine   (review date January 1775)

[*On 17 January 1775,* The Rivals *was presented on stage at Covent Garden Theatre for the first time. The play received scathing reviews which prompted Sheridan to withdraw the work for significant revisions. The debut of the second version took place on 28 January. The reworked comedy was nearly universally admired. In the following review of the first performance of* The Rivals, *the play is judged to be "long, in many parts uninteresting, and of course tedious." The critic particularly condemns the work's "many low quibbles and barbarous puns that disgrace the very name of comedy" but concedes that* The Rivals *might be salvageable if it is "properly pruned."*]

If we examine this comedy [*The Rivals*] by the rules of criticism, many objections may be made to it. Few of the

Sheridan the political orator, 1788.

characters are new, and scarce any well supported: those of Falkland and Miss Melville are the most *outré* sentimental ones that ever appeared upon the stage: the acts are long, in many parts uninteresting, and of course tedious. But the most reprehensible part is in the many low quibbles and barbarous puns that disgrace the very name of comedy. Nevertheless, there are some scenes lively, spirited, and entertaining; and if it were properly pruned by a competent judge of what is called the *Jeu de théatre,* it might probably go down with less opposition.

It was believed by the friends of the author that it would meet with opposition from a certain quarter, as it was thought by many to have a close connexion with a certain affair at Bath, in which the celebrated Miss Linley (now Mrs. Sheridan) was the subject of rivalship; but in this respect they seem to have been mistaken, as no comedy that we recollect has met with fairer play. After a pretty warm contest towards the end of the last act, it was suffered to be given out for the ensuing night. (p. 43)

> *A review of "The Rivals," in* The Town and Country Magazine, *Vol. VII, January, 1775, pp. 41-3.*

The Public Ledger   (review date 18 January 1775)

[*In the review below of the first performance of* The Rivals, *the critic censures the work, judging the dialogue "defective to an extreme," the plot bizarre, and the character of Lucis O'Trigger "an absolute exotic in the wilds of nature."*]

The Rivals, as a Comedy, requires much castigation, and the pruning hand of judgment, before it can ever pass on the Town as even a tolerable Piece. In language it is defective to an extreme, in Plot outré and one of the *Characters* is an absolute exotic in the wilds of nature. The author seems to have considered puns, witticisms, similes and metaphors, as admirable substitutes for polished diction; hence they abound in every sentence; and hence it is that instead of the *'Metmorphosis'* of Ovid, one of the characters is made to talk of Ovid's 'Meat-for-Hopes,' a Lady is called the 'Pine Apple of beauty,' the Gentleman in return 'an Orange of perfection.' A Lover describes the sudden change of disposition in his Mistress by saying, that 'she flies off in a tangent born down by the current of disdain'; and a second Tony Lumkin, to describe how fast he rode, compares himself to a 'Comet with a tail of dust at his heels.'

These are shameful absurdities in language, which can suit no character, how widely soever it may depart from common life and common manners.

Whilst thus censure is freely passed, not to say that there are various sentiments in the Piece which demonstrate the Author's no stranger to the finer feelings, would be shameful partiality. . . .

Many of the parts were improperly cast. Mr. Lee [Sir Lucius O'Trigger] is a most execrable Irishman. Miss Barsanti [Lydia Languish] is calculated only for a mimic; she has the archness of look and manner, that shrug of the shoulders, which must for ever unqualify her for genteel

Comedy; and when she is represented as a girl of thirty thousand pounds fortune, we curse the blind Goddess for bestowing her favours so absurdly; then she has the agreeable lisp of Thomas Hull, and cannot be expected to articulate her words so as to be understood, unless her tongue first undergoes a cutting. (pp. 313-14)

> *A review of "The Rivals," in* The Major Dramas of Richard Brinsley Sheridan, *edited by George Henry Nettleton, Ginn & Company, 1906, pp. 313-14.*

The Morning Chronicle   (review date 30 January 1775)

[*The following review of the second version of* The Rivals *lauds Sheridan's alterations and affirms the play's ability to "stand its own ground."*]

We heartily wish it was a general custom for authors to withdraw their pieces after a first performance, in order to remove the objectionable passages, heighten the favourite characters, and generally amend the play. The author of **The Rivals** has made good use of his time; his comedy is altered much for the better since it was first acted. The cast of it is improved, and all the performers are now perfect, and better acquainted with their several parts. It comes within a reasonable compass as to the time taken up in the representation, and the sentiments thrown into the mouth of Sir Lucius O'Trigger produce a good effect, at the same time that they take away every possible idea of the character's being designed as an insult on our neighbours on the other side of St. George's Channel. In the room of the objectionable and heavy scenes which are cut out, two new ones of a very different turn are introduced, and we remarked more than one judicious alteration in the Prologue.—**The Rivals** will now stand its ground; and although we cannot pronounce it, with all its amendments, a comic chef-d'ouvre it certainly encourages us to hope for a very capital play from the same writer at a future season; he therefore, from motives of candour and encouragement, is entitled to the patronage and favour of a generous public.

> *A review of "The Rivals," in* The Major Dramas of Richard Brinsley Sheridan, *edited by George Henry Nettleton, Ginn & Company, 1906, p. 317.*

The Monthly Review   (review date February 1775)

[*In the review of the revised version of* The Rivals *below, the critic praises Sheridan and anticipates "much future entertainment from the rays of genius that shine through particular passages of his Comedy."*]

The Author of this Comedy [**The Rivals**] speaks so modestly of his performance, presumes so little on supposed abilities, and so candidly acknowledges his youth and inexperience, that even remorseless critics are inclined rather to promise themselves much future entertainment from the rays of genius that shine through particular passages of his Comedy, than to censure with acrimony its irregularities and defects. The fable indeed is neither new nor probable, nor the characters original or well sustained; but there are many just observations on human life and manners, many beauties of sentiment, and much excellent dialogue.

> *A review of "The Rivals," in* The Major Dramas of Richard Brinsley Sheridan, *edited by George Henry Nettleton, Ginn & Company, 1906, p. 318.*

CRITICAL COMMENTARY

Mrs. Oliphant   (essay date 1883)

[*Margaret Oliphant was a prolific Victorian novelist and critic. In her biographical and critical study of Sheridan, from which the following excerpt is drawn, she admires the writer's stagecraft in* The Rivals, *finding the play to be a "brilliant dramatic sketch." She particularly praises the character Mrs. Malaprop, whose "delightful absurdities," she claims, "have never been surpassed."*]

The Rivals—to the ordinary spectator who, looking on with uncritical pleasure at the progress of that episode of mimic life, in which everybody's remarks are full of such a quintessence of wit as only a very few remarkable persons are able to emulate in actual existence, accepts the piece for the sake of these and other qualities—is so little like a transcript from any actual conditions of humanity that to consider it as studied from the life would be absurd, and we receive these creations of fancy as belonging to a world entirely apart from the real. But the reader who has accompanied Sheridan through the previous chapter of his history will be inclined, on the contrary, to feel that the young dramatist has but selected a few incidents from the still more curious comedy of life in which he himself had so recently been one of the actors, and in which elopements, duels, secret correspondences, and all the rest of the simple-artificial round, were the order of the day. Whether he drew his characters from the life it is needless to inquire, or if there was an actual prototype for Mrs. Malaprop. Nothing, however, in imagination is so highly fantastical as reality; and it is very likely that some two or three ladies of much pretension and gentility flourished upon the parade and frequented the Pump-room, from whose conversation her immortal parts of speech were appropriated; but this is of very little importance in comparison with the delightful success of the result. *The Rivals* is no such picture of life in Bath as that which, half a century later, in altered times, which yet were full of humours of their own, Miss Austen [in her novel *Northanger Abbey*] made for us in all the modest flutter of youthful life and hopes. Sheridan's brilliant dramatic sketch is slight in comparison, though far more instantly effective, and with a concentration in its sharp effects which the stage requires. But yet, no doubt, in the bustle and hurry of the successive arrivals, in the eager brushing up of the countryman new-launched on such a scene, and the aspect of the idle yet bustling society, all agog for excitement and pleasure, the brisk little holiday city was delightfully recognisable in the eyes of those to whom "the Bath" represented all those vacation rambles and excursions over the world which amuse our leisure now. Scarcely ever was play so full of liveliness and interest constructed upon a slighter machinery. The Rivals of the title, by means of the most simple yet amusing of mystifications, are one person. The gallant young lover, who is little more than the conventional type of that well-worn character, but a manly and lively one, has introduced himself to the romantic heroine in the character of Ensign Beverley, a poor young subaltern, instead of his own much more eligible personality as the heir of Sir Anthony Absolute, a baronet with four thousand a year, and has gained the heart of the sentimental Lydia, who prefers love in a cottage to the finest settlements, and looks forward to an elopement and the loss of a great part of her fortune with delight: when his plans are suddenly confounded by the arrival of his father on the scene, bent on marrying him forthwith in his own character to the same lady. Thus he is at the same time the romantic and adored Beverley and the detested Captain Absolute in her eyes; and how to reconcile her to marrying peaceably and with the approval of all her belongings, instead of clandestinely and with all the *éclat* of a secret running away, is the problem. This, however, is solved precipitately by the expedient of a duel with the third rival, Bob Acres, which shows the fair Lydia that the safety of her Beverley, even if accompanied by the congratulations of friends and a humdrum marriage, is the one thing to be desired. Thus the whole action of the piece turns upon a mystification, which affords some delightfully comic scenes, but few of those occasions of suspense and uncertainty which give interest to the drama. This we find in the brisk and delightful movement of the piece, in the broad but most amusing sketches of character, and the unfailing wit and sparkle of the dialogue. In fact, we believe that many an audience has enjoyed the play, and, what is more wonderful, many a reader laughed over it in private, without any clear realisation of the story at all, so completely do Sir Anthony's fits of temper, and Mrs. Malaprop's fine language and stately presence, and the swagger of Bob Acres, occupy and amuse us. Even Faulkland, the jealous and doubting, who invents a new misery for himself at every word, and finds an occasion for wretchedness even in the smiles of his mistress, which are always either too cold or too warm for him, is so laughable in his starts aside at every new suggestion of jealous fancy, that we forgive him not only a great deal of fine language, but the still greater drawback of having nothing to do with the action of the piece at all.

Mrs. Malaprop's ingenious "derangement of epitaphs" [Act III, Scene iii] is her chief distinction to the popular critic; and even though such a great competitor as Dogberry [in Shakespeare's *Much Ado about Nothing*] has occupied the ground before her, those delightful absurdities have never been surpassed. But justice has hardly been done to the individual character of this admirable if broad sketch of a personage quite familiar in such scenes as that which Bath presented a century ago, the plausible, well-bred woman, with a great deal of vanity, and no small share of good-nature, whose inversion of phrases is quite representative of the blurred realisation she has of surrounding circumstances, and who is quite sincerely puzzled by the discovery that she is not so well qualified to enact the character of Delia as her niece would be. Mrs. Malaprop has none of the harshness of Mrs. Hardcastle, in [Oliver Goldsmith's] *She Stoops to Conquer,* and we take it unkind of Captain Absolute to call her "a weather-beaten she-dragon" [Act III, Scene iii]. The complacent nod of her head, the smirk on her face, her delightful self-satisfaction and confidence in her "parts of speech," have nothing repulsive in them. No doubt she imposed upon Bob Acres; and could Catherine Morland [in *Northanger Abbey*] and Mrs. Allen have seen her face and heard her talk, these ladies would, we feel sure, have been awed by her presence. And she is not unkind to Lydia, though the minx deserves it, and has no desire to appropriate her fortune. She smiles upon us still in many a watering-place—large, gracious, proud of her conversational powers, always a delightful figure to meet with, and filling the shop—keeping ladies with admiration. Sir Anthony, though so amusing on stage, is more conventional, since we know he must get angry presently whenever we meet him, although his coming round again is equally certain; but Mrs. Malaprop is never quite to be calculated upon, and is always capable of a new simile as captivating as that of the immortal "allegory on the banks of the Nile" [Act III, Scene iii].

The other characters, though full of brilliant talk, cleverness, and folly, have less originality. The country hobble-dehoy, matured into a dandy and braggart by his entrance into the intoxicating excitement of Bath society, is comical in the highest degree; but he is not characteristically human. While Mrs. Malaprop can hold her ground with Dogberry, Bob Acres is not fit to be mentioned in the same breath with the "exquisite reasons" of that delightful knight, Sir Andrew Aguecheek [in Shakespeare's *Twelfth Night*]. And thus it becomes at once apparent that Sheridan's eye for a situation, and the details that make up a striking combination on the stage, was far more remarkable than his insight into human motives and action. There is no scene on the stage which retains its power of amusing an ordinary audience more brilliantly than that of the proposed duel, where the wittiest of boobies confesses to feeling his valour ooze out at his finger-ends, and the fire-eating Sir Lucius promises, to console him, that he shall be pickled and sent home to rest with his fathers, if not content with the snug lying in the abbey. The two men are little more than symbols of the slightest description, but their dialogue is instinct with wit, and that fun, the most English of qualities, which does not reach the height of humour, yet overwhelms even gravity itself with a laughter in which there is no sting or bitterness. Molière sometimes attains this effect, but rarely, having too much meaning in him; but with Shakspeare it is frequent amongst higher things. And in Sheridan this gift of innocent ridicule and quick embodiment of the ludicrous without malice or *arrière-pensée* reaches to such heights of excellence as have given his nonsense a sort of immortality.

It is, however, difficult to go far in discussion or analysis of a literary production which attempts no deeper investigation into human nature than this. Sheridan's art, from its very beginning, was theatrical, if we may use the word, rather than dramatic. It aimed at strong situations and highly effective scenes rather than at a finely constructed story, or the working out of either plot or passion. There is nothing to be discovered in it by the student, as in those loftier dramas which deal with the higher qualities and developments of the human spirit. It is possible to excite a very warm controversy in almost any company of ordinarily educated people at any moment upon the character of Hamlet. And criticism will always find another word to say even upon the less profound but delightful mysteries of such a poetical creation as Rosalind [in Shakespeare's *As You Like It*], all glowing with ever varied life and love and fancy. But the lighter drama with which we have now to deal hides no depths under its brilliant surface. The pretty, fantastical Lydia, with her romances, her impatience of ordinary life, her hot little spark of temper, was new to the stage, and when she finds a fitting representative can be made delightful upon it; but there is nothing further to find out about her. The art is charming, the figures full of vivacity, the touch that sets them before us exquisite: except, indeed, in the Faulkland scenes, probably intended as a foil for the brilliancy of the others, in which Julia's magnificent phrases are too much for us, and make us deeply grateful to Sheridan for the discrimination which kept him—save in one appalling instance—from the serious drama. But there are no depths to be sounded, and no suggestions to be carried out. While, however, its merits as literature are thus lessened, its attractions as a play are increased. There never was a comedy more dear to actors, as there never was one more popular on the stage. The even balance of its characters, the equality of the parts, scarcely one of them being quite insignificant, and each affording scope enough for a good player to show what is in him, must make it always popular in the profession. It is, from the same reason, the delight of amateurs. (pp. 49-55)

Mrs. Oliphant, in her Sheridan, *Harper & Brothers Publishers, 1883, 199 p.*

Joseph Quincy Adams   (essay date 1910)

[*Adams was an American scholar and editor, specializing in the works of Shakespeare. He produced a number of works on the dramatist and served as the director of the Folger Shakespeare Library from 1931 to 1946. In the following excerpt, Adams offers an overview of* The Rivals, *including a discussion of the play's use of "sentimentality" in the Julia-Faulkland subplot.*]

The Rivals is "a comedy of intrigue" in which the action turns upon humorous deception. The audience is let into the secret at the outset, and thus allowed to enjoy the pleasure of witnessing those not in the secret make themselves ridiculous; of anticipating the surprise of the ultimate discovery; of relishing the innumerable *double-entendres;* and of sympathizing with the hero when he is treading, so to speak, on thin ice. There is a continual bustle of action, mixed with surprises, and an ever-complicating plot. In many respects the play is strikingly like the comedies of Terence and Plautus, in which the young hero and heroine, by a series of ingenious devices, outwit their parents or guardians; and the similarity is heightened by the presence of clever servants.

Secondly, *The Rivals* is "a comedy of humours," a type developed by Ben Jonson and frequently employed throughout the seventeenth and eighteenth centuries. The term "humour" was applied to some habitual oddity of character or of manner which rendered a person more or less absurd. In *The Rivals* most of the *dramatis personæ* exhibit for our amusement clearly marked "humours": Acres in his foppishness and his "referential oaths"; Mrs. Malaprop, in her misuse of big words, and her refrain "don't become a young woman"; Sir Anthony Absolute in his irascibility—his "absolutism"; Lydia Languish in her ultra-romantic temperament; Sir Lucius O'Trigger, in his self-assurance and his love of quarrels; and Faulkland, in his absurd jealousy and alternating moods. These "humours" are well sustained throughout the play.

Thirdly, *The Rivals* is "a comedy of wit." Interest, it is true, is maintained in the plot; but the life of the play is in the dialogue. We delight primarily in the volleys of wit, in the keen but good-natured satire, and in the all-pervading spirit of fun. Many of the epigrammatic sayings of the characters have passed into our ordinary speech, and others, we find, linger pleasantly in our memory.

Finally, *The Rivals* is "a comedy of society"; that is, the mirror is held up to the fashionable world in its distinctively social functions. Perhaps *The School for Scandal* is an even better example of this type of comedy. The two plays together, it may be said, reflect the contemporary fashionable life of the two great capitals of English society,—Bath, with its free and easy cosmopolitanism, and London, with its brilliant drawing room artificiality.

"The scope and immediate object of a play," says Sheridan in his Preface, "is to please a mixed assembly in Representation." Judged by this standard, *The Rivals* has thoroughly succeeded. For nearly a century and a half it has kept its place in our theatrical repertory, always effective when adequately presented. Its sudden surprises, clever groupings of persons, strong contrasts of character, keen thrusts of satire, and rapid fireworks of wit make it in action a grand *tour de force* that is well-nigh irresistible.

But the play must be submitted also, as Sheridan grants, to "the cooler tribunal of the Study." Here it does not fare quite so well, for the reader who judges the play as literature finds along with its excellent qualities certain grave faults. These faults are due primarily, it would seem, to the inexperience of the author. Indeed, from a young man of twenty-three, unfamiliar with the theatre, and composing his first play, we could not expect the finish of a master. The remarkable thing is that the play is so excellent.

To inexperience, surely, is due the first fault that we observe: the machinery of the play is too evident. We realize too often that the characters are talking not to each other, but at the audience; we see constantly the dramatist striving through asides and monologues to convey to us certain necessary information; and we feel throughout the general movement of the plot the presence of some one behind the scenes. In short, the young playwright had not yet acquired "the art that conceals art."

A second fault, obvious on reading the play, is the artificiality of the language. The servants, for example, are far too keen at repartee, and their wit is of a nature quite impossible in country menials. This in some measure may be ex-

cused, perhaps, on the plea that the whole play moves on a level of wit much higher than in actual life, and that in the midst of the general display of cleverness even the servants may indulge in epigram and repartee. The explanation, however, does not fully excuse. Again, in quite a different way, Faulkland and Julia are artificial. They speak in stilted rhetoric and elaborate figures. Take, for example, Julia's closing speech:—

> Then let us study to preserve it so: and while Hope pictures to us a flattering scene of future Bliss, let us deny its pencil those colours which are too bright to be lasting.—When Hearts deserving Happiness would unite their fortune, Virtue would crown them with an unfading garland of modest, hurtless flowers; but ill-judging Passion will force the gaudier Rose into the wreath, whose thorn offends them, when its Leaves are dropt!
>
> [Act V, Scene iii].

Certainly no young lady ever spoke in this fashion, and even the fact that Faulkland and Julia represent the sentimental muse does not condone such artificiality. The other characters, also, are apt now and then to speak rhetorically.

Again, the humor of the play is often exaggerated to the point of improbability, or sheer impossibility. For example, Mrs. Malaprop's misuse of words is at times overdone:

> I laid my positive *conjunction* on her, never to think on the fellow again;—I have since laid Sir Anthony's *preposition* before her;—but, I'm sorry to say, she seems resolved to decline every *particle* that I enjoin her.
>
> [Act III, Scene iii]
> Well, Sir Anthony, since *you* desire it, we will not anticipate the past;—so mind, young people—our retrospection will now be all to the future.
>
> [Act IV, Scene ii]

Surely there is too much method in this "derangement of epitaphs." Moreover, Bob Acres's "referential oaths," though invariably humorous, leave an impression that they are "above the speaker's capacity."

> DAVID: But put the case that he kills me!—by the Mass! I go to the worms, and my honour whips over to my enemy!
>
> ACRES: No, David—in that case!—Odds crowns and laurels! your honour follows you to the grave.
>
> [Act IV, Scene i]
>
> SIR LUCIUS: Would you chuse to be pickled and sent home?—or would it be the same to you to lie here in the Abbey? I'm told there is very snug lying in the Abbey.
>
> ACRES: Pickled!—Snug lying in the Abbey!— Odds tremors! Sir Lucius, don't talk so!
>
> [Act V, Scene iii]

We smile at these ingenious oaths, yet at the same time are quite aware of their improbability.

The English stage in the latter half of the eighteenth century was overrun with the so-called Sentimental Comedy—the French *comédie larmoyante*. It presented to the audience impossible characters, speaking in an artificial, "genteel" language, and moving in an atmosphere surcharged with virtue. Apparently its main purposes were to teach morality, and to make the spectators "weep a flood." Against this prevailing sentimental comedy a warfare had been waged for some years. Goldsmith, in *The Good Natur'd Man* (1768) and *She Stoops to Conquer* (1773), had struck the hardest blows. But others, also, had joined in the battle; notably Samuel Foote, who had produced at the Haymarket Theatre in 1773 an amusing burlesque of the sentimental in his farce *The Handsome Housemaid; or Piety in Pattens,* in which "a maiden of low degree, by the mere effects of morality and virtue, raised herself to riches and honours." *The Rivals* carried on the work of Goldsmith and Foote, and helped to give the finishing blows to the prevailing moral-lachrymose comedy. This fact Sheridan clearly acknowledges in his second prologue, in which he makes fun of

> The goddess of the woful countenance—
> The sentimental Muse.

Yet, as a concession, it would seem, to those who demanded sentimentality, Sheridan introduced in the characters of Julia and Faulkland a sentimental sub-plot. The actor Bernard, who witnessed the first performance of *The Rivals,* wrote some years later:

> It must be remembered that this was the English 'age of sentiment,' and Kelly and Cumberland had flooded the stage with moral poems under the title of comedies, which took their views of life from the drawing-room exclusively, and coloured their characters with a nauseous French affectation. *The Rivals* was an attempt to overthrow this taste, and to follow up the blow which Goldsmith had given in *She Stoops to Conquer.* My recollection of the manner in which the former [*The Rivals*] was received, bears me out in the supposition. The audience on this occasion were composed of two parties—those who supported the prevailing taste, and those who were indifferent to it and liked nature. The consequence was that Faulkland and Julia (which Sheridan had obviously introduced to conciliate the sentimentalists) were the characters which were the most favourably received.

It must not be overlooked, however, that Faulkland and Julia serve also as foils to Captain Absolute and Lydia, and as such have full dramatic justification. The romantic courtship of the one pair of lovers stands out vividly and humorously against the sentimental courtship of the other pair. Each gains much from the contrast. Furthermore, the sub-plot may be regarded as comic. It approaches, indeed, very near to a satire on the sentimental, a fact recognized by the critic of *The Morning Chronicle* (January 18, 1775), when he wrote: "The characters of Faulkland and Julia are even beyond the pitch of *sentimental* comedy." In modern productions of the play this sub-plot is commonly reduced to a minimum: yet there is no reason why the present-day reader should not enjoy the parts of

Faulkland and Julia, both as a foil to Absolute and Lydia, and as a comic satire on the sentimental.

In the preface to *The Rivals* Sheridan says: "Many other errors there were, which might in part have arisen from my being by no means conversant with plays in general, either in reading or at the theatre. Yet I own that in one respect I did not regret my ignorance: for as my first wish in attempting a Play was to avoid every appearance of plagiary, I thought I should stand a better chance of effecting this from being in a walk which I had not frequented, and where consequently the progress of invention was less likely to be interrupted by starts of recollection." From this we might infer that a discussion of the sources of *The Rivals* would be superfluous. Such, however, is not the case, for though Sheridan did not borrow much from outside sources, he did utilize material from within the family.

Part of the play, we know, came from an earlier attempt. On November 17, 1774, he wrote to his father-in-law, Mr. Linley: "I had not written a line of it two months ago, except a scene or two, which, I believe, you have seen in an odd act of a little farce." Of this "little farce" we know absolutely nothing. Apparently it was an early attempt at a play, resembling *The Rivals* in some of its scenes.

Again, part of the play came from his mother's unfinished and unpublished comedy, *A Journey to Bath*. Here, in the character of Mrs. Tryfort, "the fondest of hard words, which without *mis*calling, she always takes care to misapply," he found Mrs. Malaprop, with "her select words so ingeniously *misapplied,* without being *mispronounced.*" He has Mrs. Malaprop repeat in *The Rivals* eight of the word blunders made by Mrs. Tryfort. Moreover, he got from Mrs. Tryfort Mrs. Malaprop's character-tag, "don't become a young woman." It is more than possible, too, that he found in Ned Bull, of Bull Hall, the suggestion of Bob Acres, of Clod Hall; compare, for example, *The Rivals,* ii, 1 and iii, 4, with *A Journey to Bath,* iii, 1 and iii, 11. Actual verbal borrowings are obvious in at least two places:

> "If I had Blunderbus Hall here, I could show you a range of ancestry."
> —*The Rivals* [Act III, Scene iv]

> "If I had your ladyship at Bull-hall, I could show you a line of ancestry."
> —*A Journey to Bath*

> "Though the mansion-house and dirty acres have slipped through my fingers, I thank heaven our honor and the family-pictures are as fresh as ever."
> —*The Rivals* [Act III, Scene iv]

> "Why the land and the Mansion house has slipped thro' our fingers, boy: but thank heaven the family pictures are still extant."
> —*A Journey to Bath*

To a much less extent Sheridan was indebted to his mother's novel, *The Memoirs of Miss Sidney Bidulph.* The name Faulkland undoubtedly came from this source, with possibly some suggestion of his character. The Faulkland of the novel is thus described: "His ideas of love, honour, generosity, and gratitude, are so refined, that no hero in romance ever went beyond him." From the novel also, perhaps, came a few "starts of recollection" that embodied themselves in the play. Thus, in *Sidney Bidulph* Faulkland, after having killed a man, rushes before the woman he loves and dramatically exclaims: "You see a man whose life is forfeited to the law." In *The Rivals* Faulkland appears before Julia under the pretense of having killed a man, and declares: "You see before you a wretch, whose life is forfeited." The situations are quite similar. Again, in the novel, Faulkland, the second, is represented as jealous of his beloved Cecilia's being "the life of the whole family" and exhibiting a "constant flow of spirits." This occurs also in *The Rivals,* [Act II, Scene i]. In general, however, the indebtedness of the play to the novel is slight.

Attempts have been made to prove that Sheridan was indebted to numerous other sources. It may be true that he had read, or seen on the stage, a number of plays, and that "faded ideas" from these plays "floated" in his memory "like half-forgotten dreams." But that he was guilty of any close borrowing seems altogether doubtful. (pp. xv-xxii)

> *Joseph Quincy Adams, in an introduction to* The Rivals: A Comedy *by Richard Brinsley Sheridan, Houghton Mifflin Company, 1910, pp. iv-xxvi.*

Marvin Mudrick   (essay date 1955)

[*In the essay below, Mudrick castigates Sheridan's works as merely "miscellanies of stagey, actable situations incorporating sentimental and stock-comic types." He particularly attacks* The Rivals *for its contrived "stage tricks" and wooden characterizations and concludes that Sheridan is "a second-rate and second-hand playwright."*]

It is by now safe to assert that Sheridan . . . had a passive audience and no cult of manners; that this audience, bottle-fed on sermons and sentimental comedy, refused to recognize entire continents of vitality; that sex was inadmissible and irony incomprehensible; that good nature—which tended to be defined, dramatically, as an incapacity for thought—had replaced good manners; that Sheridan, the presumptive inheritor of the tradition of [William] Congreve, found his inheritance dissipated before he could lay his hands on it, and was in fact writing, not comedies of manners, but—patched out with hasty reconstructions of Jonsonian and Restoration types—good-natured sentimental dramas of comic intrigue and situation, which [Henry] Fielding had acclimated to fiction, in the guise of anti-sentimentalism, a generation before.

It may be that *The School for Scandal* is a better play than *The Rivals;* but both are miscellanies of stagey, actable situations incorporating sentimental and stock-comic types, and the former is, characteristically, indifferent enough toward motive and design to leave the scandalmongers of the title without function or effect in the play. *The Rivals,* in any case, is not much worse; and it is a more candid and melancholy epitaph on the comedy of manners, indeed on the English comic drama.

The most obvious quality of *The Rivals* is its literariness:

its remoteness from live situations seen and live conversations recorded; its dependence on formula, contrivance, tips to the audience, plot summaries, scene-shifting and stage-business, playable circumstances and playable characters at the expense of consistency and subtlety, the comfortable simplifying echo of dead authors' perceptions—all the paraphernalia of the well-made popular play of any age.

Sheridan falls back on formula even while he affects to attack it. The sitting duck of the play is the Julia-Faulkland relationship; but its embarrassing woodenness will exceed the expectations of the most ill-disposed critic. Faulkland is ostensibly a satire on the sentimental hero of the novels Lydia borrows from the lending libraries—all nerves, doubt, sophistry, and remorse. Unluckily, however, he is presented at such length and with such abundant self-justification that Sheridan seems to be soliciting sympathy, or at least fatiguing our attention, on behalf of as windy a bore as any sentimental novel offers. And Julia, whom Sheridan exerts himself to contrast approvingly with her lover, is as smug and dreary a copybook of eighteenth-century posies as might be culled from the collected works of Charlotte Lennox:

> My heart has long known no other guardian—I now entrust my person to your honour—we will fly together. When safe from pursuit, my father's will may be fulfilled—and I receive a legal claim to be the partner of your sorrows and tenderest comforter. Then on the bosom of your wedded Julia, you may lull your keen regret to slumbering, while virtuous love, with a cherub's hand, shall smooth the brow of upbraiding thought, and pluck the thorn from compunction.
> [Act V, Scene i]

To return from this preening flaccidity to any remark, however casual, by any of the women in [William Congreve's] *The Way of the World* is to measure interplanetary distances. Nor is Sheridan more successful when he attempts to manufacture—as a foil to Julia, that sober and responsible heroine—an up-to-date Millamant, her head turned by the reading of novels. The affectation of Congreve's Millamant has a purpose and is subordinated to her wit; the best Sheridan can do by way of expressing Lydia's affectation is to preface her otherwise characterless remarks with a "Heigh-ho!" and to feed the audience on curiously mixed, interminable catalogues of lending-library fiction, in which [Tobias] Smollett is equated with [Laurence] Sterne and both with the true-romance writers of the time—as if Sheridan, acquiescing in the eighteenth-century snobbery toward the novel, is himself incapable of making the distinctions. (One is reduced to looking for signs of the *author's* personality when he gives us no impression of personality, motive, or value in his characters.)

Even Sheridan's theatrical machinery makes alarming noises. In the opening scene two servants labor, during an implausibly crammed and hearty chat, to identify in detail all the characters and relationships of the play. The audience, as it doubtless deserves, is occasionally treated like an idiot with an ear trumpet: "Ye powers of impudence, befriend me!" [Act IV, Scene ii] says Absolute in an aside, preparing to be impudent, or, preparing to act repentant,

"Now for a penitential face" [Act III, Scene i]; and, fearful that we may not deduce the magnitude of Lydia's silliness from the incompetence of its presentation, he nudges us with bogus good humor—"Ha! ha! ha! one would think now that I might throw off all disguise at once, and seize my prize with security; but such is Lydia's caprice, that to undeceive were probably to lose her" [Act III, Scene iii].

Conventions are not to be trusted, either. Setting up his recognition scene, in which Lydia looks forward to the prompt exposure of a deception that has in fact been practised only on her, Sheridan has Lydia turn her face from the door and keep it turned away through half the scene, while she wonders why "I han't heard my aunt exclaim yet! . . . perhaps their regimentals are alike, and she is something blind" [Act IV, Scene ii], and later, "How strangely blind my aunt must be!" The suspense is not in the dramatic use of a frankly theatrical device—to throw light, for example, on the cumulative extravagance of self-deception—but simply in waiting for Lydia, whose turning away has made the scene possible if not credible, to turn round and see what is there. Sheridan is working, here as elsewhere, not with live conventions but with stage tricks only.

The only figures Sheridan enjoys are his bullies and blusterers: Sir Anthony, the comic-tyrannical father; Acres, the good-natured, swearing country squire with an aversion to dying; Sir Lucius, the obsessed and doctrinaire duelist—"Pray, sir, be easy; the quarrel is a very pretty quarrel as it stands; we should only spoil it by trying to explain it" [Act IV, Scene iii]. They are the only characters who speak with an approximation of personality, and they do their amusing vaudeville stunts with a verve that recalls to us, by unhappy contrast, the nullities in the leading rôles.

If Mrs. Malaprop is less consistently amusing (and she does have one Miltonic simile: "as headstrong as an allegory on the banks of Nile" [Act III, Scene iii]), it is because her "nice derangement of epitaphs" is an unfunctional, isolated humor, usually a rambling collection of improbable errors interrupted by plain sense whenever Sheridan is anxious to advance the plot and not at all a determined flood of self-revelation as with her great predecessor, [Henry] Fielding's Mrs. Slipslop [in *Joseph Andrews*]. Again, though, the shattering comparison is with Congreve, with the impressionable virago of an aunt that Sheridan found in *The Way of the World*: Lady Wishfort and her fishwife eloquence as, for example, when she casts off her scheming maid:

> Away! out! out! Go set up for yourself again! Do, drive a trade, do, with your three-pennyworth of small ware flaunting upon a packthread, under a brandy-seller's bulk, or against a dead wall by a ballad-monger! Go, hang out an old frisoneer-gorget, with a yard of yellow colberteen again. Do; an old gnawed mask, two rows of pins, and a child's fiddle; a glass necklace with the beads broken, and a quilted nightcap with one ear. Go, go, drive a trade! These were your commodities, you treacherous trull! . . .

It is not merely that Lady Wishfort is here speaking with a freedom rather indecorous for Sheridan's stage, but that she speaks always as a character involved in the action, and with an energy and particularity of vision beyond Sheridan's powers entirely.

We must pay our respects, eventually, to talent, for literary history cannot quite conjure it away. There is little enough talent in any age: the run of Restoration comic dramatists, working unimpeded before the same audience and in the same tradition as [William] Wycherley, produced libraries of triviality, dullness, and smut. On the other hand, less satisfactory traditions—the [William] Wordsworthian ruminative blank verse of the nineteenth century, for example—if they inhibit, do not necessarily prevent the operation of talent. Sheridan—after one has deplored his audience and the sentimental tradition it venerates and imposes—remains a second-rate and second-hand playwright: that there is no great playwright in his time may be the fault of the time, but Sheridan himself will have to bear some of the responsibility for being no better than he is. (pp.115-20)

> *Marvin Mudrick, "Restoration Comedy and Later," in* English Stage Comedy, *edited by W. K. Wimsatt, Jr., Columbia University Press, 1955, pp. 98-125.*

THE SCHOOL FOR SCANDAL

PRODUCTION REVIEWS

The London Magazine (review date May 1777)

[The School for Scandal *had its debut on 9 May 1777 at the Drury Lane Theatre, of which Sheridan was part-owner and manager. In the following review of that performance, the critic finds the comedy "one of the keenest and best pointed satires in the English language," even though it suffers from a plot that is "infinitely too complex and overcharged."*]

Last night a phenomenon in the theatrical world made its first appearance at this House [Drury Lane Theatre]: that is, a modern comedy, unaided by the deceptions of scenery, or the absurdities of sing-song and pantomime, received by "a brilliant and crouded audience," with the most universal and continued marks of applause. Before we proceed to give our opinions of its merits and demerits, it will be necessary to lay a short sketch of the piece, and a detail of the characters before our readers.

The characters of ***The School for Scandal*** are as follows, and were thus personated.

Sir Oliver Surface, Mr. *Yates*. Mr. Surface, Mr. *Palmer*. Charles Surface, Mr. *Smith*. Sir Benjamin Backbite, Mr. *Dodd*. Rowley, Mr. *Aickin*. Moses, Mr. *Baddeley*. Snake, Mr. *Packer*. Careless, Mr. *Farren*. Sir Peter Teazle, Mr.

King. Lady Teazle, Mrs. *Abington.* Lady Sneerwell, Miss *Sherry.* Mrs. Scandal, Miss *Pope.* Maria, Miss *P. Hopkins.*

The piece is an assemblage of wit, sentiment, pointed observation, and improbabilities, unconnected by any grand principle of action. To give an account of a plot, where there is none, would be still a more difficult task than to write a good comedy; we shall however, as far as in our power, collect such parts of the piece as bear any relation to each other, together, and serve them up in the way of a plot, story or history, instead of a better. . . . [The critic here gives a detailed summary of the Sir Peter-Lady Teazle plot and the Charles and Joseph Surface "under plot."] (p. 228)

Besides the plot, and under plots, there is a groupe of figures worked into the body of the piece, which form a kind of club, whose sole delight is in propagating scandal, when they have materials; and when they have none, inventing, adding, and misrepresenting everything they hear, or their rage, folly, malice, or prolific brains, can suggest. Lady Sneerwell, Mrs. Scandal, Sir Benjamin Backbite, and Crabtree, constitute this valuable society. Joseph and Lady Teazle, though now and then otherwise engaged, appear to be at least honorary members. It is a pity, that the standing members of the club were not more directly engaged in the business of the piece; but in spite of this objection we do not recollect to have ever heard or read a more just or pointed satire; nor a dialogue fuller of wit than the conversation held up by this very respectable brotherhood and sisterhood of modern mohawks. Besides the general satire, which will hold good as long as the English language is read or understood, the particular application of it to a certain modern daily publication is logically true throughout, and ought to crimson with blushes every cheek which has encouraged such a butchery of male and female reputation.

Snake's character, though not so well known, is a character, we fear, but too frequent in this great town, and his fears lest he should lose it by telling truth, at the conclusion, is happily hit off.

The last scene of the scandal club, in which the various reports relative to Sir Peter and Lady Teazle, is admirably wrought, finely conceived, and drawn by a masterly hand, while it exposes the general rage of scandal, it shews how matters are always exaggerated. The concealment behind the screen is turned into something worse than a bare concealment; the eclaircissement into a duel. The duel at first is a duel with swords. Pistols are introduced as an improvement, till at length Sir Peter Teazle, who is consigned to the dust, as having received a mortal wound in the Thorax, makes his appearance, and gives the lie to every syllable advanced by this seminary of combers and dressers.

Few who are capable of judging of this piece will speak the truth. The friends of the author, and other cotemporary playwrights, have their prejudices. We labouring under none of these impediments of partiality, rivalship, private pique, or an overflow of wit, we flatter ourselves that we are tolerably enabled to pronounce with critical truth on the merits and demerits of *The School for Scandal.* The

great objects of the satire are detraction and hypocrisy, which, according to character and situation, the author has very artfully blended, sometimes in the same person, and sometimes distinct. The person given to detraction is not always an hypocrite, though he often, nay generally, is one; when it is unaccompanied by hypocrisy it is certainly less noxious; the effects are seldom attended to, and seldomer felt in their consequences; whereas the malignant hypocrite scarcely ever deals in scandal, but to effect some sinister or dark purpose. Scandal is made to answer another very natural and obvious end between the extremes of slander aforethought, and the mere rage for tale-bearing, that of reducing every one to the level of the slanderer. This we repeat, as directed to the great end proposed by the author, is one of the keenest and best pointed satires in the English language.

The scene in Joseph's library, the *embarras* upon *embarras,* on the successive intrusion of Sir Peter Teazle and Charles, and the discovery of Lady Teazle behind the sentimental Joseph's screen, is a piece of as fine stage effect as can possibly be conceived.

The auction scene is happily imagined, and is rich in sentiment and nature.

The last scene of the scandalous club, as was before observed, has few equals in the whole circle of the English drama.

The mischief arising from usurious contracts, Moses's instructions to Sir Oliver, in the assumed character of Mr. Premium, and the mode of conducting money negotiations are strongly and faithfully delineated.

The dialogue abounds in wit throughout; the piece produces new and interesting situations in every scene; sentiments the most natural and elevated arise from those situations. Virtue and principle, operating on conduct, is strongly recommended. Vice is described in its most hideous garb; and yet neither one nor the other are effected in a disgusting sermonic stile. Virtue is judiciously blended with its failings and foibles, and even vice is only rendered hateful on account of its effects on society, and its contradiction to the first uncontaminated principles of our nature. These are a few out of innumerable beauties of a less striking nature, that are thickly strewed in every scene almost, in *The School for Scandal.* Let us now perform a very disagreeable part of our duty, that of pointing out some of its leading defects in which it is almost equally fruitful.

The School for Scandal is totally deficient in plot, and of the underplots or incidents, which all ultimately conduce to the *denouement,* and are meant to constitute one complete action, we are still of opinion, that taking the whole business as referable to the end, the plot is still infinitely too complex and overcharged. There is no leading figure on the canvas, no great point seemingly in view. The figures all occupy equal spaces, the incidents equal attention, and the very marriage between the hero and heroine happens as it were by chance. Maria, till almost the very last scene, might be married to the witty Sir Benjamin Backbite, or any one else, as well as to Charles, and Charles to a nabob's daughter, whom he never saw before, as well as to Maria.

The means devised by Rowley and Sir Oliver, are too much dwelt and built on; a great part of that business might be well retrenched, which would have a double good effect; that of shortening the piece, and of melting, softening, and qualifying, the means made use of to depretiate Joseph, and raise Charles, in the esteem of his uncle.

To heap coals on poor Joseph's head, for seducing Lady Teazle, is in our opinion very unfair. If there was any seduction at either side, it seemed to arise on that of the lady. She was not won by his casuistical doctrines, but by something else. She controverted their truth, and the deductions drawn by him from them in his own favour. She was no convert at the time. Her conversion must have arisen previous to Joseph's sentimental sermon, from some more prevailing argument; but she is not the first lady, who made the first advances, and afterwards brought a charge of seduction against the party seduced.—On the whole, there is something very improbable in this love affair, nor can we at all reconcile Lady Teazle's going to see Joseph's library, to any thing which passed before or after.

Sir Peter Teazle's interview and consultation with Joseph, lies liable to the same objection; partly on his consulting a young man on so nice and delicate an affair; but more so, in his strange resolution, of settling an ample separate maintenance, and the reversion of his whole fortune on a woman, who had done every thing in her power to render herself disagreeable to him, and his life miserable and unhappy.

Charles's assisting to push Stanley out of Joseph's chamber, by no means accords with the idea held out of his generous and grateful nature, when in the very instant of this outrage he recognizes him, by the name of little Premium, who had acted so very generously in the purchase of the pictures.

Joseph and Charles, in point of character, are the principal figures in the groupe. Joseph, full of morality and sentiment, is always preaching up virtue and feeling; but is at bottom mean, mercenary, malignant, artful, and designing. Charles, on the other hand, is lively, giddy, profligate, and extravagant. His follies and vices are however qualified with openness and generosity; with an unstrung purse; a heart susceptible for others woes: he sympathizes with the unfortunate and miserable. He does not often confine himself to ineffective lamentation; he augments his own distresses to alleviate those of others. These two are indeed the great characteristic features of human nature, in the early stages of life. Every man under thirty is, in some measure, a Joseph or a Charles. He either acts up to some rules of prudential conduct, arising from native disposition, or dictated by art; or he gives way to his passions, and throwing off all restraint, stands confessed, the gay generous libertine, or the mere profligate sensualist. The characters afford no novelty, though they are newly dressed; and we are ready to allow, on the whole, well dressed. But we should have hardly troubled our readers with observations which are on a level with the meanest capacity, were it not to introduce others, of much more importance. What is

the tendency of this piece? The author's friends will say; to promote active virtue; to disseminate true sentiment, and distinguish it from counterfeit; to detect hypocrisy; and to encourage and deter by punishments and rewards. This may have been his intention, but we will appeal to common sense, to experience, and to a tolerable acquaintance with human nature, whether its incitements to a perseverance in vicious idle habits, and consequential injuries, are not much stronger than to the practice of virtues which cannot be models of imitation to him who does not recognize at least their seeds in his own breast. How will such a model probably operate on the real Charles's of the day? Ruminating in his own mind, says the spendthrift, 'I am extravagant; I have dissipated my patrimony, disposed of my younger brothers and sisters fortunes, because they loved and confided in me. I have ruined the too credulous tradesman. I have rendered myself despicable in the eyes of every sober intelligent man; but then, cannot I trace Charles Surface in every single circumstance almost in my conduct? When my father died, did not I spontaneously add to the provision made for younger children? Have I not exerted my interest as a member of parliament, to serve the deserving and distressed? Has not my pocket been always open to the applications of the miserable? In fine, though ruined and undone myself, and having ruined and undone others, am not I Charles Surface?' Those observations might be multiplied beyond number, and extended to every stage, from seduction to total ruin; to prove that Charles Surface is rather a dangerous character to be held out to the youth of the present age. It reveals a villain, clothed with the outside trappings of morality and sentiment, a compound of hypocrisy and art; no uncommon sight in this designing tricking age; and it conveys pointed instructions to those who are apt to mistake appearances for realities. Granted, it does all this; and delivers its instructions, clothed in the current modes and fashionable language of the day. Joseph's manners delineate the hypocrite more strongly at this time of day, than the affected prowess of Nol Bluff, the dexterity of Count Basset, or the latitudinary, deistical, pretended principles of Tinsel: it is the dramatic Ephemeris for 1777. So far the character has its use; but when all the pretensions of sentiment, as connected with a rule of moral conduct; when every species of morality, arising from incident and situation; when mere animal instinct is preferred to the guidance of reason; when reflexion, comparison, and decision, the leading distinctions between the rational and brute creation, are laughed out of doors, and branded under the general opprobrium of hypocrisy: we rather wish, if it may be presumed that the stage operates on the morals of the people, that the character of Joseph Surface had never been written, at least represented. As on one hand, the fools and rascals may find, without having a genuine spark of Charles's virtue in their frame, a great deal to countenance their follies and vices, in his character, as drawn by the poet; so the brutes in human form, the wolves in sheeps cloathing, by way of keeping clear of the imputation of hypocrisy, sooner than be likened to Joseph Surface, will, in many instances, commence savages in manners, and ruffians in respect of civil society. We shall make no apology to the public, or the author, for saying thus much on the subject. To the first, we can say, it was intended as an act of duty: to the author no apology is necessary; because we think our engagements to the public, so far as we are bound or connected with it, paramount to all other. Secondly, because we are conscious that the singular opinion of an individual will never affect the author in either his profits or his fame, as a first rate dramatic writer.

We cannot dismiss this very important article, without taking some notice of the performers, and the manner of getting up the piece, to borrow a technical expression.

The parts were most judiciously cast, and of course contributed greatly to the uncommon success of the piece. If the company would have admitted it, Maria and Joseph ought have been stronger played. Let us descend to particulars.

Mr. Smith's Charles was one of the most genuine, easy, natural, and elegant played characters we have seen in a new comedy for some years. He keeps fashionable company, it is said, and he has most certainly profited by it. The innocent, good humoured benevolent countenance of such a young man as Charles is represented to be, was well expressed, and left no wish ungratified, but that the fire of youth had not deserted it. It was indeed a fine piece of playing.

Mrs. Abington's Lady Teazle was admirable throughout almost; except, that she exhibited more of the town, than country coquette. She laboured under the same native impediment, we have pointed out in Charles; she wanted that glow of health and youth, which some people would be apt to expect from the lively and amorous Lady Teazle. We would advise this inimitable actress, unless fashion renders it indispensably necessary, at whose shrine all the inferior properties of life should we allow be sacrificed, that she will be more sparing in point of exhibition, and that she will learn to conceal in part, what our grandmothers, out of mistaken, foolish prudery, were wont totally to hide.

Mr. King played the part of Sir Peter with his usual excellence. It is rather a difficult part, and presents a great latitude to the person who fills it. We would advise this gentleman to avoid all those made looks, and unusual exertions of countenance, which neither heighten the performance, nor add to the merit of the performer.

Mr. Yates filled the character of Sir Oliver, most chastely. He was always above par, and in some places, inimitable.

Joseph Surface was tolerably personated by Mr. Palmer; but there is a certain inanity of countenance and manner, and such a want of the *vis comica,* in this gentleman that we would recommend to him, to relinquish the parts that do not fit easily on him; or endeavour by the dint of industry, to substitute art, when nature denies her assistance. This hint is far from being meant as a general censure; as he has great merit in several characters, particularly in tragedy.

Mr. Parson's Crabtree was a horrid piece of playing; happily the author gave him little to do. This favourite of the town should not abuse its indulgence; nor caricature every thing, because some of his real caricatures have succeeded. We will venture to say that such hideous contorsions of

countenance, such horrid looks, upon so slight a provocation, were never exhibited at the Drury, since it was built. He seemed to have copied his attitudes from the Almeary and St. Giles, and his expressions of countenance from the *dramatis personae* in the dance of furies in the Christmas Tale.

Miss Pope was very well in Mrs. Scandal, Mr. Dodd tolerable in Benjamin Backbite, Miss Sherry so so in Lady Sneerwell, and Baddeley great indeed in Moses.

Miss P. Hopkins's Maria was far from being striking. Neither her stile of playing, dress, or person, seemed fully to convey the portrait the author intended to lay before the public. In short, when Maria, Lady Sneerwell, Mrs. Scandal, and Sir Benjamin Backbite were on stage together, it presented something resembling the inside of a Dutch dancing school, where tow daughters, and a maiden aunt of a fat burgomaster were practising, under the instruction of a French dancing master. (pp. 230-32)

A review of "The School for Scandal," in The London Magazine; or, Gentleman's Monthly Intelligencer, *Vol. 46, May, 1777, pp. 228-32.*

CRITICAL COMMENTARY

J. Brander Matthews   (essay date 1877)

[*An American scholar, educator, and novelist, Matthews began his literary career by lecturing, contributing extensively to various periodicals, and writing plays. In 1900 he was appointed professor of dramatic literature at Columbia University, becoming the first person to hold such a title at any American university. His published works, including* The Development of the Drama *(1903),* Molière *(1910), and* The Principles of Playmaking *(1919), reflect his interest in the practical as opposed to the theoretical aspects of drama. In the following excerpt, Matthews suggests that the comic characterizations in* The School for Scandal *are second only to those of "world-wide and all-embracing geniuses" such as Shakespeare.*]

In *The School for Scandal* the construction, the ordering of the scenes, the development of the elaborate plot, is much better than in the comedies of any of Sheridan's contemporaries. A play in those days need not reveal a complete and self-contained plot. Great laxity of episode was not only permitted, but almost praised; and that Sheridan, with a subject which lent itself so readily to digression, should have limited himself as he did, shows his exact appreciation of the source of dramatic effect. But it must be confessed that the construction of *The School for Scandal,* when measured by our modern standards, seems a little loose—a little diffuse, perhaps. It shows the welding of the two distinct plots. There can hardly be seen in it the ruling of a dominant idea, subordinating all the parts to the effect of the whole. But, although the two original motives have been united mechanically, although they have not flowed and fused together in the hot spurt of homogeneous inspiration, the joining has been so carefully concealed, and the whole structure has been overlaid with so much wit, that

Contemporary depiction of the Screen Scene (Act V, scene iii) of The School for Scandal.

few people after seeing the play would care to complain. The wit is ceaseless; and wit like Sheridan's would cover sins of construction far greater than those of *The School for Scandal.* It is "steeped in the very brine of conceit, and sparkles like salt in the fire."

In his conception of character Sheridan is a wit rather than a humorist. He creates character by a distinctly intellectual process; he does not bring it forth out of the depths, as it were, of his own being. His humor—fine and dry as it is—is the humor of the wit. He has little or none of the rich and juicy, nay, almost oily humor of Falstaff, for instance. His wit is the wit of common-sense, like Jerrold's or Sydney Smith's; it is not wit informed with imagination, like Shakespeare's wit. But this is only to say again that Sheridan is not one of the few world-wide and all-embracing geniuses. He is one of those almost equally few who in their own line, limited though it may be, are unsurpassed. It has been said that poets—among whom dramatists are entitled to stand—may be divided into three classes: those who can say one thing in one way—these are the great majority; those who can say one thing in many ways—even these are far fewer than they would be generally reckoned; and those who can say many things in many ways—these are the chosen few, the scant half-dozen who

hold the highest peak of Parnassus. In the front rank of the second class stands Sheridan. The thing he has to say is wit—and of this in all its forms he is master. His wit in general has a metallic smartness and a crystalline coldness; it rarely lifts us from the real to the ideal; and yet the whole comedy is in one sense, at least, idealized; it bears, in fact, the resemblance to real life that a well-cut diamond has to a drop of water.

Yet, the play is not wholly cold. Sheridan's wit could be genial as well as icy—of which there could be no better proof than the success with which he has enlisted our sympathies for the characters of his comedy. *Sir Peter Teazle* is an old fool, who has married a young wife; but we are all glad when we see a prospect of his future happiness. *Lady Teazle* is flighty and foolish; and yet we cannot help but like her. *Charles* we all wish well; and as for *Joseph,* we feel from the first so sure of his ultimate discomfiture, that we are ready to let him off with the light punishment of exposure. There are, it is true, here and there blemishes to be detected on the general surface, an occasional hardness of feeling, an apparent lack, at times, of taste and delicacy—for instance, the bloodthirsty way in which the scandal-mongers pounce upon their prey, the almost brutal expression by *Lady Teazle* of her willingness to be a widow, the ironical speech of *Charles* after the fall of the screen; but these are perhaps more the fault of the age than of the author. That Sheridan's wit ran away here with him is greatly to be regretted. That in the course of his constant polishing of the play he should not have seen these blots, is only another instance of the blindness with which an author is at times afflicted when he has dwelt long on one work.

The great defect of *The School for Scandal*—the one thing which shows the difference between a comic writer of the type of Sheridan and a great dramatist like Shakespeare—is the unvarying wit of the characters. And not only are the characters all witty, but they all talk alike. Their wit is Sheridan's wit, which is very good wit indeed; but it is Sheridan's own, and not *Sir Peter Teazle's,* or *Backbite's,* or *Careless's,* or *Lady Sneerwell's.* It is one man in his time playing many parts. It is the one voice always: though the hands be the hands of Esau, the voice is the voice of Jacob. And this quick wit and ready repartee is not confined to the ladies and gentlemen; the master is no better off than the man, and *Careless* airs the same wit as *Charles.* As Sheridan said in *The Critic,* he was "not for making slavish distinctions in a free country, and giving all the fine language to the upper sort of people." Now, no doubt the characters do all talk too well; the comedy would be far less entertaining if they did not. The stage is not life, and it is not meant to be; it has certain conventions on the acceptance of which hangs its existence; a mere transcript of ordinary talk would be insufferable. We meet bores enough in the world—let the theatre, at least, be free from them; and, therefore, condensation is necessary, and selection and a heightening and brightening of talk. No doubt Sheridan pushed this license to its utmost limit—at times even beyond it—but in consequence his comedy, if a little less artistic in the reading, is far more lively in the acting. It has been said that in Shakespeare we find not the language we would use in the situations, but the language we should wish to use—that we should talk so if we could. We cannot all of us be as witty as the characters of *The School for Scandal,* but who of us would not if he could?

Wit of this kind is not to be had without labor. Because Sheridan sometimes borrowed, it does not follow that he was incapable of originating; or, because he always prepared when possible, that he was incapable of impromptu. But he believed in doing his best on all occasions. If caught unawares, his natural wit was ready; if, however, he had time for preparation, he spared no pains. He grudged no labor. He was willing to heat and hammer again and again—to file, and polish, and adjust, and oil, until the delicate machinery ran smoothly, and to the satisfaction even of his fastidious eye. As he himself said in two lines of *Clio's Protest,* published in 1771—a couplet often credited to Rogers—

> "You write with ease, to show your breeding,
> But easy writing's curst hard reading."

The School for Scandal was not easy writing then, and it is not hard reading now. Not content with a wealth of wit alone—for he did hold with the old maxim which says that jests, like salt, should be used sparingly; he salted with a lavish hand, and his plays have perhaps been preserved to

us by this Attic salt—he sought the utmost refinement of language. An accomplished speaker himself, he smoothed every sentence till it ran trippingly on the tongue. His dialogue is easy to speak as his songs are easy to sing. To add in any way to the lustre and brilliance of the slightest sentence of *The School for Scandal,* to burnish a bit of dialogue, or brighten a soliloquy, could never cost Sheridan, lazy though he was, too much labor. "This kind of writing," as M. Taine says, "artificial and condensed as the satires of La Bruyère, is like a cut vial, into which the author has distilled, without reservation, all his reflections, his reading, his understanding." That this is true of Sheridan is obvious. In *The School for Scandal* he has done the best he could; he put into it all he had in him; it is the complete expression of his genius; beyond it he could not go.

Michael Kelly, hearing that Sheridan had told the queen he had a new comedy in preparation, said to him, "You will never write again. You are afraid to write." "I am afraid?" asked Sheridan; "and of whom?" And Kelly retorted quickly, "You are afraid of the author of *The School for Scandal.*" (pp. 561-62)

J. Brander Matthews, "The School for Scandal," in Appleton's Journal, *Vol. XI, June, 1877, pp. 556-62.*

Louis Kronenberger   (essay date 1952)

[*In the following excerpt, Kronenberger examines the theme of scandal in* The School for Scandal, *observing that, on many levels, the play is concerned with the perception of sin where none actually exists. Significantly, Kronenberger charges Sheridan himself with a type of scandalmongering. In the critic's opinion, the dramatist creates the illusion that immoral acts are occuring between the characters in* The School for Scandal, *but fails to demonstrate any such transgressions on stage.*]

Sheridan was a born satirist and student of manners: he had a sharp eye, especially for detail; a skeptical mind, and a witty tongue. He, like [William] Congreve before him, was a thorough worldling, the difference being that Congreve was an incorruptible one, whose worldliness nothing outward could shake, whose attitude nothing *else* could discolor. Congreve must always, in a sense, portray and never participate. He shows us the way of the world with no more illusion than anger. He quite lacks idealism; he does not fight—he does not even protest—for virtue's sake, but he does have a sort of hard integrity; he does recognize the obligation to tell the truth. Thus though in his worldling's way he scarcely so much as lays a finger on vice, he gives fraud a merciless thrashing.

Sheridan is the successor, the inheritor of Congreve, but he fails to achieve the same success. The reason is not one of talent only, is rather perhaps one of temperament and of the different ages into which the two men were born. There was something more romantic and quixotic about Sheridan, and something more ambitious. Sheridan has quite as much the sense of society, quite as many of a worldling's tastes, as Congreve, but he had much less of a worldling's mind. Sheridan made a romantic elopement. Congreve never married at all. Sheridan, while still young, abandoned the theater for politics; Congreve, while still young went frostily into retirement. Sheridan made what was considered the most brilliant parliamentary speech of England's most brilliant age of oratory; it is difficult to imagine Congreve making any public speech at all.

But the seventy-five years that separate the two men in time possibly create a wider gulf than the qualities that divide them in temperament. Where Congreve's chief concern was to attack appearances, Sheridan had himself some to keep up. Sheridan writes for a considerably more genteel age, and accepts a more genteel tradition. There are some things one can no longer talk about at all; there are many that one cannot talk about with the old frankness and freedom. Immorality may not go unpunished, and indecency must go veiled. The difference between the two ages is most clearly discerned by comparing Vanbrugh's *The Relapse* with Sheridan's cleaned-up version of it, *A Trip to Scarborough.* Not all the disadvantages are on Sheridan's side; his world is often tidier than Congreve's or Vanbrugh's. But it is in every way tamer, at least where truth or revelation is concerned; for sheer superficial glitter it has almost never been equaled.

The glitter hardly flashes out upon us at the start: no one would be likely to use the word to describe **The Rivals.** It would be rather difficult, indeed, to find any one word to describe it: though it satirizes a number of types, the prevailing tone is not really satirical; nor is it quite farcical; nor is it exactly romantic. Nor, though it tells us something about life at Bath in the 1770's, and of fashions and foibles among people generally, is it a comedy of manners. Actually it is a hodgepodge, a pastiche; or we may simply term it a stage piece. To be sure, Sheridan sets out to make fun of sentimental comedy in the person of Lydia Languish, a romantical young lady who sighs for everything out-of-the-ordinary. She would rather elope than be married at church. Captain Absolute in his own person would be too prosaic a choice, but Captain Absolute posing as Ensign Beverley, and conducting a secret and unlicensed courtship, is ideal. There is still some fun in Lydia Languish, but it would be absurd to call such broad spoofing by the name of satire. Bob Acres, again, belongs to so long a line of boastful cowards as to have become, long before Sheridan's day, a mere stage type; Sir Lucius O'Trigger and Sir Anthony Absolute are the merest stage types, too; while Mrs. Malaprop, though no stage type when she first appeared—though no prototype, either: we need only think of Dogberry [in Shakespeare's *Much Ado about Nothing*]—is simply a made-to-order character part. Indeed, **The Rivals** is a perfect paradise of character parts, and as such, has about it much more of the comedy of humors than of manners, and all the paraphernalia—practical joking, mistaken identity, huffing and bluffing—of stock farce.

Amusing though parts of it are, **The Rivals** is on the whole not only a relative failure, but a relative bore. There is too much of everything and everybody, and much too much that is tame and even ladylike. It seems to me completely Victorian, and its great reputation has been made by the Victorian-minded, by people who are as easily amused as they are shocked, and who much prefer the whimsical to

the truly witty. But if the whole thing, for a grown-up taste, is all too vanilla-flavored, *The Rivals,* for a first play, is undeniably talented. The writing may verge on the cute, but one at once gets the sense of a writer, the feel of a playwright. Lydia languishes with a certain verbal adroitness:

> I had projected one of the most sentimental elopements—so becoming a disguise!—so amiable a ladder of ropes—conscious moon—four horses—Scotch parson—with such surprise to Mrs. Malaprop—and such paragraphs in the newspapers.

Sir Lucius, warning Bob Acres that the duel may be the death of him, speculates with a certain verbal adroitness:

> Would you choose to be pickled and sent home?—or would it be the same to you to lie here in the Abbey?—I am told there is very snug lying in the Abbey.

As for Mrs. Malaprop, all her good things long ago passed into the language, and it is hard to have an unhackneyed sense of them: still, there remains something to savor in things like "the very pineapple of politeness" or "a nice derangement of epithets" nor has all the point vanished from "Tis safest in matrimony to begin with a little aversion."

The greatest bore in **The Rivals** is the romance between Falkland and Julia, which is often cited as sounding a note of straight sentimental comedy in a play that sought generally to discountenance it. But Sheridan, I feel sure, knew perfectly well how milksoppish Falkland was, and how excessive and humorless were the pleas and denials on both sides. The truth, I suspect, is that Sheridan was having his joke and concealing it too—making sly fun of Falkland for those who would relish the slyness and giving other people the fodder they liked. But Falkland, whether or not he is made fun of, is yet no fun. Sheridan failed here through playing safe; the whole play, in fact, suffers from playing safe. The targets are of a kind no one could object to, the jokes of a kind no one would blush at; the plot is confected of the most familiar ingredients, and the play no part of Sheridan's true claims to celebrity and brilliance.

They lie pre-eminently, of course, in *The School for Scandal,* which remains the most famous comedy of manners in the language. As a work for the theater, in which plot, characterization, social background, and a kind of characterizing theme are mingled and blended, it can hardly be held unworthy of its fame. As a work, moreover, that constantly flashes with witty thought and polished diction, that has a true drawing-room air and eighteenth-century London lustre, it deserves its fame no less.

The play's characterizing theme is set forth in its title: we are allowed to watch, as it were, the preparation and distribution of scandal all the way from manufacturer to consumer. We are shown scandalmongers who make great oaks from exceedingly little acorns, who make scandal from what they hear, from what they overhear, from what they hear wrong. We are offered scandal for scandal's sake—where the motive is artistic and virtually disinterested; we are shown it equally for the scandalmonger's sake, where the object is to draw suspicion to the wrong person. And such scandalmongers as Lady Sneerwell and Mr. Snake are, we must allow, true artists in their line. It is part of the fun that when they and Mrs. Candour get together, they indulge in the same sort of shop talk and trade secrets that so many booksellers or pastrycooks might go in for. The tone is set right at the start, and scenes like the opening one recur all through the play. They constitute its thematic whalebone; equally they are an illustration of manners and a commentary on society. They give the play spice; they also give it glitter. And it is worth noting that the scandalmongers are Sheridan's only way of providing the play with that sense of naughtiness which is the very atmosphere of Restoration comedy. The play is concerned with the *imputation* of sinning; of sin itself there is absolutely nothing. The famous screen scene is one of circumstantial evidence only, not at all of guilt. Not only is Joseph Surface a villain without being demonstrably a rake, but Sir Peter Teazle is an aging knight without being a cuckold. Even Charles Surface, though the most imprudent of spendthrifts is nowhere shown to be even the mildest of libertines.

There is perhaps good reason why, whenever we find much sin or much scandal, we should find little of the other. In communities that are habitually sinful, there cannot be anything very newsworthy about sin; moreover, in a community of glass houses every one thinks twice about throwing stones. Scandal is a kind of amusement tax that virtue exacts of indecorum. For it really to thrive, there must, in other words, be people who behave no less than people who misbehave. Gossip has a certain fellow-feeling about it, an equalitarian basis of talking about others but realizing that one is also talked about oneself. But scandal constitutes a sort of revenue in self-esteem: scandal concerns people who are not just (like oneself) humanly fallible, but who are socially culpable as well. And scandal, I think, is always predicated of people who have a certain amount of relative position, who are the equals or the superiors of those whom the scandal delights. When a society woman's housemaid gets herself into trouble, it may seem to her employer an outrage or a misfortune or both, but it is not a scandal. I mention all this, not from wishing to elevate scandal to the level of philosophy or impose upon it the rules and laws of science, but because it *is,* on the other hand, a permanent and important social phenomenon that, like snobbery, is often slurred over as not worth serious thought. But it *is* worth serious thought, certainly in any study of the comedy of manners; and here, as the very theme of the most famous social comedy in the English language it is worth a good deal of serious thought, the more so as, in English comedy, a devout interest in scandal has by Sheridan's time superseded the old Restoration absorption in sin.

Sheridan is writing for a straiter-laced, a more squeamishly refined audience than [George] Etherege or Congreve did; he is writing in an age when "taste" is not a matter of how you deal with things, but of what things you may deal with. In *The School for Scandal,* quite as in *The Rivals,* no one sexually sins. But as a result, sin now seems far more wicked and important than it used to. Restoration comedy is an almost tedious succession of ladies and gentlemen thrust behind screens, pushed into closets, hid-den under beds, flung down back stairways; nothing, after a while, could seem more routine. And now here we have Lady Teazle hiding behind a screen—in what is certainly the most famous scene in all English social comedy, just as the moment when that screen is knocked over represents the most climactic moment in all English social comedy. Some of this is doubtless due to Sheridan's great gifts as a playwright, to his building up the scene to get the utmost from it. But some of it is surely due to its being, as similar scenes a century earlier never were, so zestfully scandalous. We are back in an age when sex has become glamorous through being illicit.

Scandal also, at least superficially, harmonizes with the study of manners: for it is not only something that people talk about in drawing-rooms, it is something that taxes all their ability to be clever and insinuating in talk. Scandal is, indeed, most an art in that it seeks to suggest far more than it actually can say. And scandal concocted by artists for the enjoyment of audiences, scandal that not only causes loss of reputation but is leveled at people who have reputation to lose, is one of the worldliest of recreations. Though nothing improper happens in the whole course of **The School for Scandal,** impropriety is yet the very essence of what goes on.

All this bright scurrility and malice is the framework for a story that of itself is almost obstreperously fictional and by no means at the highest level of comedy. It is a good story, to the extent that we regard it as nothing more than one, and it is worked out by somebody who has clearly mastered his medium. The key point about Sheridan—or at least Sheridan's great success—is not his comic but his dramatic sense, the way he can give, even to his scandalmongers, not just the sheen of wit, but the deviousness of spiders; the way he can raise a colloquy into a scene; the general way that he can plot; the specific way that he can unravel or expose. **The School for Scandal** tells, just so, of a well-knit *group:* of Sir Peter and Lady Teazle, and Joseph, Charles, and Sir Oliver Surface; while even Lady Sneerwell and Mr. Snake have their places in the plot, and perhaps only Maria takes less of the limelight than we should expect. The whole thing has the conciseness of good artificial comedy: Maria is Sir Peter's ward; Sir Peter and Sir Oliver are old friends; Maria wants Charles for a husband; Lady Sneerwell wants Charles for a lover; Joseph wants Maria for a wife; Joseph wants Lady Teazle for a mistress. Thus the story is both concentrated and complicated. The plot thickens, as a good plot should. The hero's future darkens, as a proper hero's must. With but two acts to go, Sheridan leaves himself an enormous lot to work out and clear up.

Sheridan solved everything in the fourth act—including the perennial success of the play. And he solved it not just with the ingenuity of some one with a knack for plot, but with the visual magic of some one who has a sense of the footlights. First, Charles Surface's fortune is made in the picture scene, when he refuses to put his uncle's portrait up for auction. Then Joseph's goose is cooked in the screen scene, when Lady Teazle exposes and denounces him. One such scene immediately following and, as it were, capping the other, the two constitute between them a triumph of stagecraft. They also provide an exhilarating contrast, one scene showing how essentially good is the bad boy, the other, how essentially bad is the good one.

They are not quite the same *kind* of scene, however. The screen scene, descending straightforwardly from the Restoration, belongs wholly to the comedy of manners. In altogether classic style, it involves the husband, imperils the heroine, and unmasks the villain; in equally classic style, it maintains the tone of artificial comedy. The picture scene—at least on Sheridan's terms—would be very unusual, would be hardly possible, in Restoration comedy. Its appeal, to the audience quite as much as to Charles's uncle, is unabashedly sentimental; and though audiences in Sheridan's age and forever since have found the appeal irresistible, one may doubt whether audiences would have done so in the age of Charles II. The theme of the good and bad brother is literally the oldest in the world, for it turns up first—and perhaps most forcefully—with Cain and Abel. But the Restoration, which much modified conventional ideas of virtue and vice, rather transformed good and bad brother into better and worse one, and preferred to contrast the two, less in terms of good and bad than of naïveté and sophistication, of gaucherie and grace. Perhaps what I am now going to say argues a Restoration cynicism on my part; but I suspect that had any Restoration playwright thought up the picture scene, *his* Charles would have refused to part with the portrait through being shrewd rather than warmhearted. The effect would have been the same on the story, but not on the audience, who instead of dabbing at their eyes would have knowingly nodded their heads, and—it may be—would less have condemned Charles for his wiliness than Uncle Oliver for his vanity. But more to the point, any young man who would have behaved in an Etherege comedy as Charles Surface does in Sheridan's, would have seemed a very singular fellow. A hundred years later—as well as two hundred years later—and he is simply a conventional hero. In other words, it is the Restoration, not Sheridan, that is anomalous; the Restoration, not Sheridan, that runs counter to popular taste and "normal" sentiment. And though the Restoration stage is as extreme in offering such scanty virtue and decency, as other ages are suspect for offering such an abundance, it is just because the Restoration provides such an offset that we feel a certain gratitude toward it. Lack of feeling is at least superior to fraudulent feeling.

Charles and Joseph Surface are not, indeed, really in descent from characters like [Thomas] Shadwell's Belfond senior and junior; they descend much more plainly and immediately from Tom and Blifil in *Tom Jones.* [Henry] Fielding, a really humane and not really a sentimental man, with his deep hate of hypocrisy and warm sympathy for heedless youth, felt a strong compulsion to contrast a Tom with a Blifil, to insist that goodness was a thing of the heart, that decorum was not virtue, nor animality vice. But for all that, his contrast is too pat, and his dénouement a little too pleasant. Yet though Fielding may be voted over-generous, he was not, like Sheridan, too genteel. Tom's heart might be made of gold, but his will power was made of tinfoil and his moral scruples were scarcely sawdust. For almost two centuries, and in certain quarters perhaps even now, the character and the book alike were

attacked because Tom allowed himself to be kept by Lady Bellaston. Charles Surface, so far as we know, isn't even the lover of any fine lady. There is only enough wrong with him to make him endearing. He drinks—but presumably like a gentleman. He is careless of money and always in debt—but as much from being goodhearted as extravagant. Although he needs money, he won't sell his uncle's picture; though he needs money, he gives much of what he obtains to a struggling kinsman.

One tends to make fun of Charles not because he is particularly implausible, but because he is so exceedingly calculated—and for the light he throws on Sheridan, who begot him, and on the theater, that boasts of him. The theater *may* boast, but art, in the finest sense, must blush. And blush the more for having also something to be proud of. The neatness of the plotting in *The School for Scandal,* the vividness of the scene-writing, the brightness of the dialogue, the brilliance of the scandalmongers, above all the perfect understanding of the tone of artificial comedy—all this is admirable. Call it adroit and scintillating theater, and—with due allowance for the ravages of time—it would be hard to find anything better on the English stage. But that is the most that you *can* call it: it offers neither a genuine point of view, as does all the best Restoration comedy, nor a serious criticism of life, as does all important literature. The trouble is not that it is artificial, but that it is superficial, and not, again, that it snaps its fingers at realistic truth, but that it clicks its heels before conventional morality. A man who acquiesces in the common morality of his age may just escape with his life—by rejecting the usual trickery of his profession. He may escape rather better if, while using the tricks of technique, he preserves his independence of mind. But a man who succumbs to both temptations, who gives in to stage effect and audience effect alike, cannot get off scotfree. What Sheridan wrote here was, I think, the most brilliant box-office comedy in the English language.

His sense of the theater wins out, in the end, over his knowledge of the world. *The School for Scandal* has more motion than Restoration comedy, which is to the good, but it posits more characters whose fortunes are at stake and fewer who express a point of view; it offers more situations that interest us for their story value than that interest us in themselves. And Sheridan, far more than the Restoration playwrights, deals at the end in outright rewards and punishments. And all this is to be sharp and emphatic in the way the theater loves to be and life does not; which, because it harmonizes with the genius of the theater, isn't necessarily a fault. What *does* seem a fault is to combine such sharp and emphatic dramaturgy with such mild and sanctified subject-matter; to indulge only in what is generally acceptable, to inveigh only against what is demonstrably safe. Sheridan satirizes scarcely anything that the world does not condemn; nowhere does he challenge fashionable opinion or shock fashionable complacence. Wycherley may not have shocked his own generation, but he still shocks us. Shaw may not shock us, but he did shock his own generation. So effervescent a writer as Etherege at least touches on much that is true and even tragic about human nature; so ambiguous a dramatist as Oscar Wilde will time and again, if only in an epigram, explode against his trashy plots social criticism that is challenging and even subversive. But Sheridan, though sometimes delightfully impudent, is *never* challenging or subversive. His scandalmongers are a kind of Greek chorus in a play that Sheridan never got round to writing. Their air of iniquity is a false-front for the play's intrinsic innocence. The most brilliant thing about it, perhaps—in terms of Sheridan's mastery of his trade—is not the actual brilliance of its dialogue, but the seeming wickedness of its plot. (pp. 192-202)

> Louis Kronenberger, "Sheridan: 'The Rivals', 'The School for Scandal'," in his The Thread of Laughter: Chapters on English Stage Comedy from Jonson to Maugham, *Alfred A. Knopf, 1952, pp. 191-202.*

Leonard J. Leff   (essay date 1970)

[*In the essay below, Leff explores the disguise motif in* The School for Scandal *and demonstrates how the play is "solidly unified by its pervasiveness."*]

Knowing the value of a good facade, the old widow Ochre paints her face; however, "when she has finished, she joins it so badly to her neck that she looks like a mended statue in which the connoisseur may see at once that the head's modern though the trunk's antique." Several critics feel that such a careless and awkward piece of joining also describes the lack of unity in the play from which the passage is taken, Sheridan's *The School for Scandal* [Act II, Scene ii].

The story of Sheridan's combination of two plays (the Teazle plot and the Slanderers plot) into one is well known. Although the two plots join and climax in the screen scene, most critics feel that the unity is at best superficial. Yet there is unity in *The School for Scandal,* a unity which is to be found not in atmosphere, dialogue, rhythm, or a vital principal situation, but in the use of a fully developed disguise motif. Concerned with gossip—which is malicious talebearing masquerading as truth—*The School for Scandal* is unified through Sheridan's use of a series of disguise images beginning in Act I with Lady Sneerwell's veiled love of Charles Surface and concluding with Snake's plea in Act V that his one good deed remain hidden. It will be the purpose of this article to explore examples of this motif and to show how the play is solidly unified by its pervasiveness.

In the comedy there are two groups of characters: those who mask themselves and those who do not. The first group is divided into those who mask with malevolent intent (Snake, Lady Sneerwell and the scandalmongers, and Joseph) and those who mask without malevolence though not always with noble intent (Lady Teazle, Sir Peter Teazle, and Sir Oliver Surface). The second group consists of Rowley, Maria, and Charles Surface. Though all the characters who wear masks are eventually unmasked, the reader suspects that Joseph, the scandalmongers and Lady Sneerwell, and Snake will once again disguise themselves, and that Sir Oliver and the Teazles will avoid disguise. It is by examining the the language and actions of the two

sets of masqueraders that one can begin to understand how Sheridan unifies his play.

The opening scene of *The School for Scandal* has been attacked for its awkwardness and slowness. "A long scene of clumsy exposition," Schiller calls it [see Further Reading]. Armstrong concedes its failings [in his *Shakespeare to Shaw: Studies in the Life's Work of Six Dramatists of the English Stage*], terming the lack of movement a necessity since during the enactment people were probably coming into the theatre. In their notes to the play [in *Plays of the Restoration and Eighteenth Century*], Dougald MacMillan and Howard Mumford Jones remark on the weighty speeches of Snake and Mrs. Sneerwell, calling the exposition "one of the ill-concealed joints between the two plots of the comedy."

Yet the four critics fail to note the significance of the language that these first two characters are using, language heavily loaded with images of disguise. Snake, the lackey of Mrs. Sneerwell, has been spreading gossip and in his first speech he dutifully reports to the president of the college of scandal that all paragraphs were copied in "a feigned hand." Thus, he and Lady Sneerwell conspire to circulate false reports under an assumed (disguised) name.

As the conversation continues, Snake questions his latest assignment involving Sir Peter and his former guardians. Having assessed the traits of Joseph and Charles, Snake is puzzled by Lady Sneerwell's not linking her fate with that of Joseph, a "most amiable character . . . universally well spoken of." Yet even in his bewilderment, Snake is fully aware of the distinctions between appearance and reality; thus, he tempers his confusion with the expression "now, on the face of these circumstances." Like characters in the play, "circumstances" have a "face," one which may be real or unreal as the situation warrants.

Lady Sneerwell then explains Joseph's attachment to Maria's fortune and reports his need "to mask his pretensions." When Snake is still puzzled, Lady Sneerwell confesses to the shame that she has "concealed" even from her lieutenant: she loves Charles. Seeing her affection for Charles unmasked, Snake concludes that her "conduct appears consistent." Such language—even before the entrance of Joseph, a major character—must be regarded as certainly relevant if not fundamental to an understanding of the disguise motif of the play. To feign, to conceal, to appear are simply to disguise, and the opening scene prepares the audience not only for the development of Snake's and Lady Sneerwell's characters but those of the scandalmongers as well.

The scandalmongers' skill at disguising truth is readily apparent. Though the gossipers claim to be reporters only of what they have heard, theirs is a poorly disguised rationalization to assuage their complicity in masking truth. Indeed, they revel in the faulty, egregious masks of others, for example Miss Vermillion's:

> MRS. CANDOUR: She has a charming, fresh color.
>
> LADY TEAZLE: Yes, when it is fresh put on.

MRS. CANDOUR: Oh, fie! I'll swear her color is natural. I have seen it come and go.

LADY TEAZLE: I dare swear you have, ma'am; it goes off at night and comes again in the morning.

[Act II, Scene ii]

When the conversation turns to the teeth of Mrs. Prim, Lady Teazle adds remarks about the pains she takes "to conceal her losses in front." As dear friends are unmasked, so relatives must certainly be. Mrs. Candour reveals the disguise of her in-law, Miss Sallow: "Let me tell you, a woman labors under many disadvantages who tries to pass for a girl of six-and-thirty." Glibly, the scandalmongers proceed to unmask her, Mrs. Evergreen, Miss Simper, and Lady Stucco.

Among these thieves, there is apparently no honor. Unwisely, Lady Sneerwell showed her "weakness" to Snake and "real view" to Joseph; her reward in Act V, Scene iii, is unmasking by both. Opening the door behind which Lady Sneerwell has been hiding, Joseph announces: "Lady Sneerwell's injuries can no longer be concealed." The one remaining person capable of keeping her somewhat ruffled disguise in place is her other confidant, Snake, who further strips her: "You paid me extremely liberally for the lie in question, but I unfortunately have been offered double to speak the truth." Though undone, she is certainly too clever not to perform cosmetic surgery on her maimed reputation as well as her shattered mask.

Snake—whose movements "should not go unobserved" [according to MacMillan and Jones]—is more devious than Lady Sneerwell. As an inserter of paragraphs, he is perhaps a "new journalist," similar to writers for *The Town and Country Magazine* (founded 1769) or *The Morning Post* (1772). Like them, he is only disguised as a journalist, for his paragraphs contain not facts but gossip and slander; indeed, the *Post* filled every issue with "libellous paragraphs" [as noted by R. Crompton Rhodes in *Plays and Poems of Richard Brinsley Sheridan*]. As a tool for Lady Sneerwell, Snake is essential, for he forges and plants in strategic places letters about Lady Teazle and Charles. He is so valuable to her that she is blinded from seeing his disguise. It is in fact Joseph who warns her against him: "Take my word for 't, Lady Sneerwell, that fellow hasn't virtue enough to be faithful even to his own villainy" [Act I, Scene i]. His mask is constant, while the face behind it is sold to the highest bidder, ultimately Sir Oliver.

Just as it is implicit that Lady Sneerwell will continue to veil her wickedness by inventing stories which make her the injured rather than the injurer, so it is explicit that Snake will continue to design and deceive. Indeed, for his words of truth in Charles's behalf, Snake asks only that he remain anonymous. "I live by the badness of my character. I have nothing but my infamy to depend on" [Act V, Scene iii]. Thus, when the play is over, the scandalmongers, Lady Sneerwell, and Snake leave the distinct impression that their art of disguise has been impaired little if at all.

Joseph is perhaps the best masked character in the play.

The elder brother Surface, he is a master of deceit, and it is no surprise that when he occasionally lapses into metaphor, the figure of speech should sound the note of disguise. After peremptorily dismissing Sir Oliver—disguised as Stanley—Joseph remarks: "The silver ore of pure charity is an expensive article in the catalogue of a man's good qualities, whereas the sentimental French plate I used instead of it, makes just as good a show and pays no tax" [Act V, Scene i]. The image of plate masquerading as silver is an appropriate one to associate with the ostensibly untarnished yet highly superficial character of Joseph.

Unlike his brother Charles, Joseph consciously masks his real character from the world. In earlier drafts of the play, the brothers' surnames were variously Plausible, Pliable, and Pliant, but Sheridan's final choice—Surface—readily suggests the predominant motif in the play. Interestingly, John Palmer, who created the role, was himself but a loosely disguised Joseph Surface. He was a man of superiority as well as a hypocrite. "Very attractive to women, idle, and unscrupulous, he made frequent use of his charming plausible manner to attain his own ends." If as Christian Deelman suggests [in *Review of English Studies*, n.s. XIII, 1962] the characters were inspired by popular eighteenth-century actors, Sheridan chose a fine model from which to draw his hypocritical Joseph.

From beginning to end, Joseph employs disguise. His first words in Lady Sneerwell's house are compliments on Snake, a man of "sensibility and discernment"; yet as soon as Snake exits, Joseph unmasks, mournfully regretting the amount of confidence that Lady Sneerwell has misplaced in Snake. In his own apartment, one sees furnishings which reflect the mask he wears. Not only does the study contain a screen (first used to insure privacy threatened by a neighboring "maiden lady") but it also is furnished with recently acquired books. "Books," Joseph tells Sir Peter, "are the only things I am a coxcomb in" [Act IV, Scene iii]. The extent of Joseph's scholarship is unknown; but since he previously disposed of a "most valuable" library that had belonged to his father, it appears that the coxcomb's principal interest in books is as an aid in creating a false impression. It is indeed easier to visualize Joseph as seasoned hypocrite than Sunday antiquarian.

The same study which allows Sir Peter to interpret Joseph as a man "ever improving himself " becomes an ascetic's retreat as Joseph prepares himself for Stanley's visit. After the screen scene, Joseph's facade is rather battle scarred, and he has hardly time or inclination to mend it: "To suppose that I should now be in a temper to receive visits from poor relations!" Yet he must put a mask in place: "I must try to recover myself and put a little charity into my face, however." And so he disguises himself as the nephew wronged by an otherwise worthy uncle. Unfortunately, it is to Stanley's ears that Joseph complains: "I will tell you, my good sir, in confidence what he has done for me has been a mere nothing, though people I know have thought otherwise" [Act V, Scene i].

Outside his library, Joseph shows further ability to put on a quick face. When the scandalmongers leave him and Maria alone, he renews his quest for her. She turns away from him frowning, so he kneels to commmplete his protestations; then Lady Teazle enters. Joseph quickly masks his intentions by concocting a story about Maria's threats to report to Sir Peter her suspicions about Joseph and Lady Teazle. But Lady Teazle pierces his disguise, and Joseph is unmasked for the first time. Departing, she calls him "an insinuating wretch." Joseph ends the scene in despair of being masked, and in fear of being unmasked: "Sincerely I begin to wish I had never made such a point of gaining so very good a character, for it has led me into so many cursed rogueries that I doubt I shall be exposed at last" [Act II, Scene ii].

After being exposed in Act V, Joseph hides his complicit guilt and trails after Lady Sneerwell to check "her revengeful spirit." Sir Oliver performs the benediction proclaiming the couple "oil and vinegar." Indeed, Joseph is too much the thoroughgoing hypocrite, Lady Sneerwell too much the breaker of reputations (especially after being wounded once more), and Snake too much the mercenary not to continue their masquerading. But another set of characters, who occasionally employ disguise, abandon it once its purpose is complete. They are Lady Teazle, Sir Peter, and Sir Oliver.

Lady Teazle is a descendant of Millamant (Congreve's *The Way of the World*) and Harriet (Etherege's *The Man of Mode*); like them she dislikes the country. Yet in her naive regard for the ways of townlife, she is also very much like Margery Pinchwife (Wycherley's *The Country Wife*). Flirting with Joseph, she confesses: "I have so many of my country prejudices left that, though Sir Peter's ill humor may vex me ever so, it shall never provoke me to—." And Joseph completes the statement: "The only revenge in your power. Well, I applaud your moderation" [Act II, Scene ii].

Encounters with Joseph and the other scandalmongers confused Lady Teazle; thus by the time the play began she had enrolled in, attended, and ultimately graduated "licentiate" from Lady Sneerwell's school. Her proficiency alarms Sir Peter and when he censures her for post-baccalaureate participation in seminars of scandal, she protests that he would "restrain the freedom of speech"—that is, slander in the guise of free speech.

Lady Teazle's pivotal scene is in neither Lady Sneerwell's school nor her own home but in Joseph's apartment. By Act IV, Scene iii, she has experience enough to suspect that Joseph's mask hides his lack of genuine affection for her, a fore-shadowing of her ability to see that Sir Peter's crusty, unaffectionate facade hides an abundance of real love for her. When she enters, she hears the final words of a self-pitying soliloquy in which Joseph contemplates an end to juggling Maria and Lady Teazle. Her interruption and opening remarks cause him to put on a mask of impatience, one which his visitor immediately pierces: "O lud! don't pretend to look grave. I vow I couldn't come before." Rakishly, Joseph initiates an apparently logical plan whereby Lady Teazle will surrender her virtue in order to preserve a reputation previously tarnished by scandal. As Joseph approaches the conclusion of his cock-eyed syllogism, a servant enters to warn the couple of Sir Peter's presence.

Lady Teazle immediately hides herself behind a screen, and overhears her husband tell Joseph of the generous financial settlement he has made upon her. Only the former of Sir Peter's two sides—"tetchiness and ultimate amiability" [Arthur C. Sprague; see Further Reading]—has been previously unmasked before Lady Teazle. Genuinely moved, she repays Sir Peter for his unmasking by doing some unmasking of her own. Once she recovers from the shock of being exposed from behind the screen, she delightedly unmasks Joseph with a single exclamation. Of his lengthy explanation of her presence she remarks: "There is not one syllable of truth in what that gentleman has told you" [Act IV, Scene iii].

In addition to exposing Joseph, she reforms. By the final scene of the play, she has made her peace with Sir Peter; pledging good faith, she forsakes scandal—the central disguise motif in the play. Lady Sneerwell is given back Lady Teazle's diploma "as she leaves off practice and kills characters no longer" [Act V, Scene iii].

Lady Teazle's abandoning disguise means that Sir Peter may do likewise. After all, he has assumed a mask in Lady Teazle's presence only to protect his own feelings. In public, he is open. Mrs. Candour is ostensibly delighted by his arrival at Lady Sneerwell's, for the guests have gotten out of hand with their slander, especially Lady Teazle. But Sir Peter refuses to mask the truth. His asides ("A character dead at every word, I suppose") become more and more audible until he finally infuriates Mrs. Candour and his hostess by saying: "No person should be permitted to kill characters and run down reputations but qualified old maids and disappointed widows" [Act I, Scene ii]. His feelings are in no way disguised, and when he exits, he leaves his true character behind him.

Unlike Pinchwife, Sir Peter is a sympathetic character. Hardly a rake or a cuckolder, "he is the very model of husbandly forbearance, neither living down a lurid past nor contemplating vengeful peccadilloes for the future" [Schiller]. Yet he remains disguised from Lady Teazle. In his first soliloquy he catalogues the faults of his wife; country-bred and city-taught, she has indulged herself beyond luxury, participated in fopperies, and been the cause of his being paragraphed in the newspapers. Despite it all, he loves her. "However, I'll never be weak enough to own it" [Act I, Scene ii].

In Act II, Scene i, Sir Peter and his wife argue a multitude of topics: authority in the household, spending practices, country and city amusements, and of course the "utterers of forged tales, coiners of scandal, and clippers of reputation." Lady Teazle takes delight in the "daily jangle"; she enjoys seeing her husband so disgruntled. But his irritability is only a mask; when she leaves, Sir Peter admits to enjoying the argument: "Yet with what a charming air she contradicts everything I say, and how pleasantly she shows her contempt for my authority! Well, though I can't make her love me, there is great satisfaction in quarreling with her."

Once the screen falls in Act IV, so does Lady Teazle's disguise. By Act V, she has begged Rowley to intercede for her with Sir Peter. At first Sir Peter is unmoved, thinking of the doubled mortification of seeing the newspapers report his reconciliation after all that happened. But he is eventually resolved and vows to live without sentiment, without hypocrisy, without disguise: "I have had enough of them to serve me the rest of my life" [Act V, Scene ii].

Of course, Lady Teazle has not been the only source of embarrassment to Sir Peter. In Act IV, for example, he holds up Joseph as a model for Charles: "He is a man of sentiment. Well, there is nothing in the world so noble as a man of sentiment" [Act IV, Scene iii]. In the important opening scene, however, the audience has learned that hypocrisy is disguised by a mask of sentiment. In Snake's and Lady Sneerwell's presence Joseph sympathizes with the fate of his brother and recognizes the necessity of supporting him despite his misconduct. Lady Sneerwell quickly reproaches him: "O lud! you are going to be moral and forget that you are among friends." And Joseph replies: "Egad, that's true! I'll keep that sentiment till I see Sir Peter." Throughout the play "sentiment" is a euphemism for treachery and hypocrisy. Thus, Sir Peter's words play the fool with him when Rowley and Sir Oliver tease him about being gulled by Joseph's disguise. In the penultimate scene of the play, laughed at by his peers, Sir Peter spits out his mistake: "Yes, yes, his sentiments! Ha! ha! ha! Hypocritical villain!"

From the beginning of the play, Sir Oliver has known more than his old friend wished. Attempting to mask the unhappiness of his marriage from Sir Oliver, Sir Peter begs Rowley not to disclose that he and Lady Teazle are ever in disagreement, for he is afraid of the ridicule he will be subjected to. But when in Act II, Scene iii, Sir Oliver first appears, he is already laughing at his friend who has been seven months on "the stool of repentance!" Thus, he is not only a master of mask but of unmasking as well. When on their first meeting he threatens Sir Peter's tender disguise by raising the topic of his marriage, the former bachelor postpones the discussion. Sir Oliver concedes: "True, true, Sir Peter. Old friends should not begin on grievances at first meeting. No, no, no."

Certain critics have regarded Sir Oliver—whose bluntly stated purpose is "to expose hypocrisy"—as an unfortunate necessity or *deus ex machina*. Rodway calls his test of the brothers' hearts "a piece of structural sentimentality" ["Goldsmith and Sheridan: Satirists of Sentiment," in *Renaissance and Modern Essays*]. Earlier audiences did not need a character of moral judgment to decide the fate of the two brothers, the late eighteenth-century audience did. "Sir Oliver, a-t-on dit, est introduit simplement pour servir de *deus ex machina*. La remarque n'est pas fausse. Mais ce *deus ex machina* n'en est pas moins un personnage fort vraisemblable" [Jean Dulck, *Les Comédies de R. B. Sheridan*].

Upon Dulck's defense of Sir Oliver can be built a discussion of him as an integral part of the disguise motif. Indeed, it is he alone who assumes nominal disguises, first as Premium, then as Stanley. Being successfully masked, he knows that disguise is effective; thus he is not to be fooled by masks in his test of the nephews. He knows Charles to be the subject of gossip, "but I am not to be prejudiced against my nephew by such . . . if Charles has done nothing false or mean, I shall compound for his extravagance." And he knows Joseph to be extremely well spoken of: "I am sorry to hear it; he has too good a character to be an honest fellow" [Act II, Scene iii]. None of his intelligence reports, the audience learns, will mask the truth from him.

Sir Oliver is quite successful. He learns that Charles is much as he appears to be and Joseph quite the opposite. The value of such unmasking is obvious. For himself, he learns the goodness of one nephew and the treachery of another. For Sir Peter, he reveals in Charles a good heart, well-suited for his ward, Maria. For the audience, he provides much of the laughter, especially in his dealings with such minor yet well-drawn characters as Moses and Trip.

With Lady Sneerwell, Snake, Joseph, Sir Oliver Surface, and the Teazles, one completes discussion of the major disguised figures and concentrates on those who avoid masks or unmask others: Rowley, Maria, and of course Charles.

Rowley is the former servant of the brothers' deceased father. Like another "servant" in the play—Snake—he is in many ways superior to his masters. In a play in which most characters find gossip the way of the world and disguise the only method of navigation, he stands out as a man with intuitive powers, a man whose eyes readily penetrate masks. When Sir Peter complains of being ward to a woman who refuses the worthy brother and yearns for the profligate, Rowley takes Charles's side. Sir Peter knows Joseph's mask, but Rowley knows the face behind it and wants to prevent Sir Peter's being fooled by the disguise: "I only wish you [Sir Peter] may not be deceived in your opinion of the elder" [Act I, Scene ii].

The primary reason for Sir Peter's suspicion of Charles is the gossip about him. Rowley tells Sir Oliver: "His [Sir Peter's] prejudice against him is astonishing, and I am sure greatly increased by a jealousy of him with Lady Teazle, which he has industriously been led into by a scandalous society in the neighborhood who have contributed not a little to Charles's ill name. Whereas the truth is, I believe, if the lady is partial to either of them, his brother is the favorite" [Act II, Scene iii]. Yet Sir Peter continues to suspect Charles, and Sir Oliver completes plans for a test of hearts: neither man accepts the advice of Rowley. Such behavior serves to polarize two groups of characters. Sir Oliver and Sir Peter, avoiding Rowley's advice, must mask themselves to unmask others. Charles, having Rowley's devoted support and intuitive sense, remains unmasked yet still unmasks others. Rowley is thus more than a servant. He is a touchstone, an admirable character who fights deceit not with deceit but with intelligence and intuition. Such qualities seem also to belong to the other two characters in his group, Maria and Charles.

Maria, a prim, rather stiffly conceived young woman, is a foil to the gossip-mongers. She is disarmingly candid, thoroughly unhypocritical. Although her behavior should make her a sympathetic, perhaps appealing character, she is neither. Pursued by Joseph, resented by Lady Teazle, admired by Sir Oliver, she avoids a mask; but unlike Rowley and Charles, she suggests stuffiness.

Her dislikes place her outside the circle of scandal. "I take very little pleasure in cards" [Act II, Scene ii], she tells Lady Sneerwell who has asked her to play piquet with Joseph. She takes less pleasure in being followed by the foppish Sir Benjamin Backbite. Entering Lady Sneerwell's, she says: "Oh! there's that disagreeable lover of mine, Sir Benjamin Backbite, has just called at my guardian's with his odious uncle, Crabtree; so I slipped out and ran hither to avoid them" [Act I, Scene i]. Such frankness indicates that she disguises nothing: "How is it possible I should? If to raise malicious smiles at the infirmities or misfortunes of those who have never injured us be the province of wit or humor, Heaven grant me a double portion of dulness!" [Act II, Scene ii].

"Blessée dans sa sensibilité, [elle] nous paraît bien faible" [Dulck]. "Seems" is an important word, for though she appears to be unable to act on her designs in a relationship with Charles, her intractability with Sir Peter is what keeps her free up to Act V. Her lack of disguise, her candor, have insured that when Charles's true worth is realized, she will be available as an appropriate mate for him. And Charles, who has filled "a dozen bumpers" to toast "a dozen beauties," has also remained true to Maria, refusing to blacken her surname by introducing it at the drinking table of his roguish companions. Two plain dealers will eventually marry.

"Plain dealing in business I always think best" [Act III, Scene iii], Charles tells Sir Oliver disguised as Premium. Ironically, he receives dishonest responses from his two hearers (Sir Oliver and Moses). Sir Oliver says he likes him the better for it and Moses vows he scorns to tell lies; both men lie and both are disguised. Thus, Charles's virtue in cataloguing his extravagance and failure is rewarded with craft, deceit, and disguise. Yet he is not a gullible man. Had he known the identity of Premium, he would not have played Sir Oliver's game. He is a great unmasker.

Just as Joseph knows his true worth and hides it, Charles recognizes his and flaunts it. For this reason, he is occasionally surprised by objects and people whose true meaning is masked. After he has concluded the auction of the paintings and Sir Oliver (still disguised as Premium) and Careless the auctioneer have left, Charles shows his bewilderment at the price the paintings have brought: " 'Fore heaven, I find one's ancestors are more valuable relations than I took them for!" [Act IV, Scene i]. In the screen scene [Act IV, Scene iii], he no sooner hears that Sir Peter is hidden in the room than he exposes him. Opening the closet, he says: "I'll have him out. Sir Peter, come forth!" Just as he is later surprised to find that Sir Oliver has disguised himself to test him, he is astonished to discover Sir Peter "turn inquisitor and take evidence *incog.*"

Charles's unmasking the presence of Sir Peter foreshadows the unmasking of Joseph's hypocrisy. When Sir Peter and Charles are left alone, Sir Peter cannot resist telling of Joseph's French milliner standing behind the screen. Charles is disbelieving and immediately wants to expose her also: " 'Slife let's unveil her!" As the screen goes down, Joseph reenters and the trio stands unmasked: Joseph of his sentiment, Sir Peter of his crotchetiness, Lady Teazle of her honor. Using language which touches on the dis-

guise motif, Charles remarks: "Egad, you seem all to have been diverting yourselves here at hide and seek" [Act IV, Scene iii]. On that note, Charles leaves the trio to quickly find some masks to cover its infrequently exposed proper faces. In both pivotal scenes—auction and screen scenes—Charles's amazement implicitly reflects the theme of the drama: appearances are deceiving.

For the première at Drury Lane, Charles was enacted by William Smith, a fancier of hunting and racing. A gentleman who was dismissed from Cambridge for firing an unloaded handgun at a proctor, Smith was somewhat indistinguishable from his character, but Charles's reformation through love perhaps separated actor and role. Although Charles pledges his love to Maria, regarding his reformation he makes no official promises. But as Schiller points out, throughout the play Charles's aim has been marriage not seduction. As a couple Maria and Charles give the lie to the incompatibility of the affectionate and the sensual; together they constitute a victory over scandal and over disguise.

But their proposed marriage also constitutes a victory over the critics who find little unity in the play. Throughout *The School for Scandal* Maria has been passive regarding the unmasking of deceit and pretense. Rather than face Sir Benjamin, she flees to Lady Sneerwell's; still discontented, she feigns illness because she is incapable of staying to expose hypocrisy. Charles, however, is aggressive. Whenever he sees disguise, he acts. His life, as Armstrong says, is "a knocking down of screens." Thus the marriage of the two is more than the transparent unifying device it appears to be. Sir Oliver wishes that their love "never know abatement"; psychologically speaking, it should not for they are an exemplary match. An aggressive, assertive husband is well suited to a passive, unassuming wife; not a match of appearances, it is a marriage founded on unmasked realities. The vital signs are indeed good when the relationship is measured in terms of the disguise motif.

The School for Scandal is thus a well-unified play, one which establishes an attitude toward scandal, manifests it through a series of elaborate disguise motifs, and eventually condemns and dismisses masquerade by presenting the unification of two characters who stand for a world without masks. (pp. 350-60)

> *Leonard J. Leff, "The Disguise Motif in Sheridan's 'The School for Scandal'," in* Educational Theatre Journal, *Vol. XXII, No. 4, December, 1970, pp. 350-60.*

FURTHER READING

OVERVIEWS AND GENERAL STUDIES

Auburn, Mark S. *Sheridan's Comedies: Their Contexts and Achievements.* Lincoln: University of Nebraska, 1977, 221 p.
  Study of Sheridan's works that attempts to "draw to-

gether all the information of source studies, biography, bibliography, literary historical criticism, and theatrical history to provide the context within which to assess Sheridan's achievement as a comic dramatist."

Beers, Henry A. "Sheridan." In his *The Connecticut Wits and Other Essays,* pp. 159-78. New Haven: Yale University Press, 1920.

Attributes Sheridan's continued popularity to the fact that his "cleverness and artistic cunning are such that they keep their freshness."

Byron, George Gordon, Lord. Journal entry for 17-18 December 1813. In *Byron: Selections from Poetry Letters & Journals,* edited by Peter Quennell, pp. 652-53. London: The Nonesuch Press, 1949.

Contains Lord Byron's brief but often-quoted comments, in which he declares: "Whatever Sheridan has done or chosen to do has been, *par excellence,* always the *best* of its kind."

Durant, Jack D. "The Sheridanesque: Sheridan and the Laughing Tradition." *Southern Humanities Review* XVI, No. 4 (Fall 1982): 287-301.

Argues that the longevity of Sheridan's popularity is due not only to his skilled stagecraft but also to his understanding of human nature. Durant deems the dramatist an "earnest moralist" who provokes us to "laugh at . . . melancholy truths about ourselves."

Hazlitt, William. "On the Comic Writers of the Last Century." In his *Lectures on the English Comic Writers with Miscellaneous Essays,* pp. 149-68. London: J. M. Dent & Sons, Ltd., 1819.

Lauds Sheridan's skill as a playwright and comedic writer, finding his works "faultless."

Loftis, John. *Sheridan and the Drama of Georgian England.* Cambridge, Mass.: Harvard University Press, 1977, 174 p.

Maintains that while Sheridan was strongly influenced by his Restoration predecessors, he surpassed them by virtue of his "sensitivity to the rhythms of prose dialogue and . . . his capacity to give familiar dramatic situations intensified force by his mastery of the techniques of burlesque."

Macey, Samuel L. "Sheridan: The Last of the Great Theatrical Satirists." *Restoration and Eighteenth-Century Theatre Research* IX, No. 2 (November 1970): 35-45.

Presents Sheridan as the last in a line of satirical writers who "stood aghast at the upsurge of middle-class manners and taste" for sentimentality.

Moore, Thomas. *Memoirs of the Life of the Right Honorable Richard Brinsley Sheridan,* 2 vols. New York: Excelsior Catholic Publishing House, 1882, 307 p., 335 p.

Considered one of the most reliable biographical accounts of Sheridan. Moore includes commentary on the playwright's works as well as reflections on his life by such prominent associates as Lord Byron and the Prince of Wales.

Nettleton, George Henry. "Richard Brinsley Sheridan." In his *English Drama of the Restoration and Eighteenth-Century (1642-1780),* pp. 291-313. New York: The Macmillan Company, 1932.

Biographical and critical overview of Sheridan's literary career. Nettleton discusses Sheridan's "reaction against sentimental drama" as it is specifically manifested in *The Rivals* and *The School for Scandal.*

———. "Sheridan's Introduction to the American Stage." *Publications of the Modern Language Association of America* LXV, No. 2 (March 1950): 163-82.

Overview of the stage history of Sheridan's works, from their introduction to the New World in 1779 through 1789. By the latter date, Nettleton observes, Sheridan had established "his comprehensive conquest of the American theatre."

Snider, Rose. "Richard B. Sheridan." In her *Satire in the Comedies of Congreve, Sheridan, Wilde, and Coward,* pp. 41-73. New York: Phaeton Press, 1972.

Studies Sheridan's satirical treatment of hypocrisy, sentimentality, and the conventions of genteel comedy. Snider also contrasts Sheridan's portrayal of female characters in his plays with the treatment of women in the works of William Congreve.

THE RIVALS

Auburn, Mark S. "The Pleasures of Sheridan's *The Rivals:* A Critical Study in the Light of Stage History." *Modern Philology* 72, No. 3 (February 1975): 256-71.

Analyzes the text and production history of *The Rivals* to account for the continued success of this "most durable of English stage comedies."

THE SCHOOL FOR SCANDAL

Jordan, Thomas H. *The Theatrical Craftsmanship of Richard Brinsley Sheridan's* The School for Scandal. New York: Revisionist Press, 1974, 193 p.

In-depth study of *The School for Scandal,* focusing on linguistic and dramatic elements of the play. Jordan also examines the cast and audience of the comedy's initial production.

Schiller, Andrew. "*The School for Scandal:* The Restoration Unrestored." *Publications of the Modern Language Association of America* LXXI, No. 4 (September 1956): 694-704.

Examines *The School for Scandal* as an attempt to revive the "comedy of manners," concluding that the play is a "triumphant" fusion of "the wit, bustle and brilliance" of Restoration comedy and "the moral as well as esthetic sensibilities" of Sheridan's own age.

Sprague, Arthur C. "In Defence of a Masterpiece: *The School for Scandal* Re-examined." In *English Studies Today,* Third Series, edited by G. I. Duthie, pp. 125-35. Edinburgh: Edinburgh University Press, 1964.

Examination by a noted theater historian of the dialogue, plot and characters in *The School for Scandal.* Sprague asserts that the play is a "masterpiece" and "a drama of extraordinary theatrical skill."

Sophocles

c. 496 B.C.-c. 406 B.C.

Sophocles is considered one of the greatest dramatists in Western literature. His surviving tragedies attest to his consummate craftsmanship in plot construction, characterization, and versification. The stage conventions that he—along with Aeschylus and Euripides—initiated have become central to dramatic art; in fact, critics acknowledge him as one of the shapers of the genre. From the earliest evaluations of his work, commentators have been especially fascinated with Sophocles' use of irony in his masterpiece *Oedipous Tyrannos* (*Oedipus Rex*), and have followed Aristotle in identifying it as the epitome of effective dramatic technique and characterization. For all these reasons, as critic J. W. Mackail asserted, Sophocles "is the single poet who embodies centrally and completely the spirit of Athens."

As a poet and a public figure, Sophocles truly was representative of "the spirit of Athens." His birth and death dates correspond almost exactly to the beginning and end of the Golden Age of Athens (480 B.C.-404 B.C.), a period when the city enjoyed unprecedented cultural and political supremacy in the Greek world. Born into a wealthy and respected family, Sophocles was renowned for his amiability and gentlemanly behavior. As a member of the Athenian elite, he held important political positions; in addition, he showed his devotion to traditional religion by serving as a priest of the healing deity Amynos.

Sophocles' victories at the Great Dionysia in Athens marked the beginning of his long career as an acclaimed dramatist. Held every spring, the Dionysia, records of which date back to the sixth century B.C., were festivals in honor of the god Dionysus. The high point of these festivals, which included entertainment provided by groups of traveling players, was the renowned tragic competition: the judging of four performed plays (three tragedies and a comic satyr play) by rival dramatists. At the festival of 468 B.C., Sophocles defeated Aeschylus, winning first prize with *Triptolemos*, one of the many lost plays. According to biographical sources, he went on to win first prize more than twenty times, never receiving anything below second prize, a unique feat among Greek dramatists.

Sophocles is believed to have written one hundred and twenty-three tragedies; titles and fragments of ninety exist, but only seven tragedies survive in their entirety. The earliest of these, *Aias* (*Ajax*), dated c. 450 B.C., follows the sufferings of its title hero from his public humiliation by the Greek commanders Agamemnon and Menelaus to his suicide. *Antigonē* (*Antigone*), composed c. 442 B.C., concerns the conflict between the heroine and her uncle, King Creon, stemming from his refusal to allow the burial of Antigone's brother Polyneices, condemned as a traitor to his city. Together with *Oedipous Tyrannos* and *Oedipous epi Kolōnōi* (*Oedipus at Colonus*), *Antigone*

forms the Theban trilogy—plays based on the ancient story of King Oedipus. *Ichneutai* (*The Trackers*), written c. 440 B.C., is a brief comic fragment dealing with the theft of Apollo's cattle by Hermes. Dating from around 440-30 B.C., *Trakhiniai* (*The Trachiniae*) recounts the story of Deianeira, who learns of her husband's infidelity and, hoping to remedy the situation with a magic robe, unknowingly kills her husband and later takes her own life. Next in the chronology of surviving works comes *Oedipous Tyrannos*, written c. 425 B.C. Perhaps the most famous play ever written, it describes the tragic events that lead Oedipus to murder his father and marry his mother, unaware of their true identities. *Ēlektra* (*Electra*), which Sophocles wrote between 425 and 410 B.C., also focuses on an extreme example of family misfortune. Electra convinces her brother Orestes to avenge their father's murder by killing their mother Clytemnestra. *Philoktētēs* (*Philoctetes*) is the only one of Sophocles' plays whose date of performance is certain, for it was awarded first prize at the Great Dionysia of 409 B.C. Afflicted by a horrible wound which refuses to heal, Philoctetes lives in exile on the island of Lemnos. He is sought by Odysseus and Neoptolemus because a prophecy has foretold that Troy cannot be captured without the aid of Philoctetes' bow and arrows.

Sophocles' last play *Oedipus at Colonus* was posthumously produced by his grandson Sophocles in 401 B.C. It completes the story of King Oedipus, closing with his apotheosis.

The extraordinary dramatic and poetic power of Sophocles' tragedies stems, in part, from certain technical innovations which he introduced into the Athenian theater. Unlike Aeschylus, whose dramatic trilogies provide plot continuity and share characters, Sophocles focuses on individual tragedies. Thus by limiting his narrative scope, Sophocles achieved a concentration of emotional intensity and action surpassing Aeschylus' efforts. In addition, Sophocles enhanced the usually bare Greek stage with *skenographia,* or scene painting, and more expressive tragic masks, thereby bringing greater realism to each scene. Perhaps his most important innovation was the introduction of the third actor. Traditionally, two actors (all roles were played by male actors) along with the chorus, participated in the *epeisodia,* or episodes, of the play. The addition of the third actor enabled Sophocles to construct a more complex dialogue, thus keeping the focus on the characters rather than on the chorus. Correspondingly, he increased the chorus from twelve to fifteen members and, while limiting its participation in the action, composed some of his most beautiful poetry for it. Many commentators have praised the imaginative form, striking imagery, and emotional power of Sophocles' choral songs, with particular attention to their poetical and philosophical content.

Sophocles' dramatic style is often described as a felicitous union of strength and control. The noted classicist Moses Hadas has written: "a sensitive hand passing over a Greek marble can feel its inexhaustible energy. Sophocles has the same perfect control; his work is at the furthest remove from the protruding and knotty muscles of an exuberant Romantic artist." In measured, simple, and piercingly direct language, Sophocles' dramas move swiftly, logically, and inexorably toward their seemingly inevitable conclusions. The most painful human situations—utter personal humiliation, the accidental murder of a loved one, a cataclysmic reversal of one's station in life—are presented in a manner which implies compassion for the suffering individual but also places personal misfortune in a universal, cosmic context.

The hallmark of Sophocles' style is his gift for portraying exceptional characters under stress. His dramas are built around a strong-willed, highly principled, and passionate character who encounters a seemingly insurmountable ethical or moral difficulty. Sophocles thus created characters of heroic proportions; but his plays also suggest, as critics have noted, that heroic qualities may lead to disaster. For instance, Ajax's pride is also vanity, Antigone's stoicism also intractability, Oedipus' intellectual acuity seems overreaching, and Electra's love for her father prompts her to plot matricide. Every character experiences both the benefits and the burden of his or her *daimon,* or personal spirit. Sophocles' characters, as critics have observed, were not imagined as models or ideals, but rather as embodiments of human types. Their steadfast, sometimes blind, adherence to high principles makes

them—depending on the circumstances—either more or less than human. Dominated by powerful emotions, Sophocles' heroes seem capable of extremes in both hatred and love. Critics have praised the depth and psychological soundness of Sophocles' characterization, noting, however, certain ambiguities which offer numerous possibilities of critical interpretations.

As scholars assert, perhaps Sophocles' most important achievement relative to characterization was his shift of focus from his human heroes' passive acceptance of divine actions to their struggle to understand and ultimately accept humankind's place in a universe that appears random and yet organized according to an unfathomable plan. All the recurring themes in Sophoclean drama—the mysterious workings of divine justice, the nature and purpose of human suffering, and the role of knowledge—are rooted in Sophocles' fascination with human potential. The relationship between gods and humanity is problematic because the divinities are distant and essentially unknowable. Though the extent of their participation in human affairs remains unclear, the gods are respected and feared in the world of Sophocles' plays: oracles are consulted and heeded. Sophoclean characters may strive to overcome the obstacles posed by the gods, but the dramatist's religiosity, which implies humankind's subordinate position in relation to the gods, remains profound and free of doubt. Commenting on the inscrutability of divine intentions, Jacqueline de Romilly has written, "it is as if a veil were lifted only halfway, and mortals were expected to guess what lay behind it. The partial disclosures of oracles add pathos to human weakness without in any way illuminating it." Nevertheless, Sophocles brilliantly depicts his characters' struggle to learn, implying that the quest for knowledge is praiseworthy irrespective of its final outcome. "Many are the wonders of the world, but none is more wonderful than man," he writes in *Antigone.* Ironically, as critics often point out, in Sophocles' greatest play, *Oedipus Rex,* the characteristically human thirst for knowledge is both celebrated and condemned as futile. Oedipus' belief that he has avoided his destiny and his ability to solve the Sphinx's riddle have the most tragic and pathetic consequences imaginable. Yet his insatiable curiosity and intellectual energy in a sense redeem his extreme and legendary suffering, and he is granted the status of a divinity at the conclusion of *Oedipus at Colonus.*

Sophocles' reputation as a dramatist has been secure ever since his own time, when he was held in such high regard that the Athenian government appointed officials to safeguard the purity of his texts. Aristotle in his *Poetics* argued that *Oedipus Rex* was a model tragedy, naming certain elements of Sophoclean tragedy, such as reversal and discovery, as the key concepts of his general theory of drama. Sophocles' subsequent impact on European literature has been tremendous. In the seventeenth century, his influence was felt in the works of John Milton, Pierre Corneille, and Jean Racine. François Marie Arouet Voltaire and John Dryden (with John Lee) wrote versions of the Oedipus story in the eighteenth century. Johann Wolfgang von Goethe extolled his dramatic genius. He was admired by the leading nineteenth-century thinkers and literary figures, including Georg Wilhelm Friedrich Hegel, Søren

Kierkegaard, Friedrich Nietzsche, Matthew Arnold, William Wordsworth, and George Eliot. In the twentieth century, Sophocles' works still elicit critical attention and respect. Commentary on the drama has taken a staggering number of directions, from modern versions of the plays to the psychoanalytic and anthropological interpretations of Sigmund Freud, Erich Fromm, and Rene Girard. Scholars still address questions concerning Sophocles' views on divine justice, the meaning of human existence, and other philosophical and religious questions.

Although debate persists over certain aspects of Sophocles' oeuvre, there is complete consensus that his contribution to drama is inestimable. Scholars observe that classical Greek tragedy, founded by Aeschylus, attained perfection at the hands of Sophocles. For his consummate technical skill as a dramatist, for his unforgettable characters, and for his haunting, perfectly plotted plays, he remains one of the greatest figures of world literature.

(For further information on Sophocles' life and career, see *Classical and Medieval Literature Criticism,* Vol. 2.)

PRINCIPAL WORKS

PLAYS

Aias   c. 450 B.C.
Antigonē   c. 442 B.C.
Ichneutai   c. 440 B.C.
Trakhiniai   c. 440-30 B.C.
Oedipous Tyrannos   c. 425 B.C.
Ēlektra   c. 425-10 B.C.
Philoktētēs   409 B.C.
Oedipous epi Kolōnōi   c. 405 B.C.

PRINCIPAL ENGLISH TRANSLATIONS

The Theban Plays   1947
The Oedipus Cycle   1949
The Complete Greek Tragedies: Sophocles   1954-57
Plays   1956
Complete Plays of Sophocles   1982
The Three Theban Plays: Antigone, Oedipus the King, Oedipus at Colonus   1984
Antigone   1989

OVERVIEWS AND GENERAL STUDIES

Johann Wolfgang Goethe and Johan Peter Eckermann (conversation date 1827)

[*One of the greatest figures in world literature, Goethe was a writer, scientist, and thinker of genius; he also had successful careers as a theater director and a court administrator. Goethe's impact on German literature is truly inestimable, and he shaped the major literary movements of the late eighteenth and early nineteenth centuries. His first novel, Die Leiden des jungen Werthers (1774; The Sorrows of Werter, 1779) epitomizes the Sturm und Drang or "storm and stress" movement; his dramas Iphigenie auf Tauris (1787; Iphigenia in Tauris, 1793) and Torquato Tasso (1790; translated 1827), and the poetry collection Römische Elegien (1795; Roman Elegies, 1876), exemplify the neoclassical approach to literature; and his drama Faust (1808-32; translated 1823-39) is ranked beside the masterpieces of Dante Alighieri and William Shakespeare. Eckermann was Goethe's companion and secretary between 1823 and 1832. In 1837 he published Gespräche mit Goethe in den letzten Jahren seines Lebens (Conversations with Goethe, 1850), an important source of information on Goethe's ideas in his last years. In the following excerpt from that work, the two men discuss, in a conversation which started on March 21, 1827 and continued a week later, various aspects of Sophocles' dramatic genius.*]

Wednesday, March 21, 1827. Goethe showed me a little book, by Hinrichs, on the nature of antique tragedy. "I have read it with great interest," said he. "Hinrichs has taken the *Œdipus* and *Antigone* of Sophocles as the foundation whereon to develop his views. It is very remarkable; and I will lend it to you that you may read it, and that we may be able to converse upon it. I am by no means of his opinion; but it is highly instructive to see how a man of such thoroughly philosophical culture regards a poetical work of art from the point of view peculiar to [Hegel's] school. I will say no more to-day, that I may not influence your opinion. Only read it, and you will find that it suggests all kinds of thoughts."

Wednesday, March 28, 1827. I brought back to Goethe the book by Hinrichs, which I had read attentively. I had also gone once more through all the plays of Sophocles, to be in complete possession of my subject.

"Now," said Goethe, "how did you like him? He attacks a matter well—does he not?"

"This book affected me very strangely," said I. "No other book has aroused so many thoughts in me as this; and yet there is none I have so often been disposed to contradict."

"That is exactly the point," said Goethe. "What we agree with leaves us inactive, but contradiction makes us productive."

"His intentions," said I, "appear to me in the highest degree laudable, and he by no means confines himself to the surface. But he so often loses himself in refinements and motives—and that in so subjective a manner—that he loses the true aspect of the subject in detail, as well as the survey of the whole; and in such a case it is necessary to do violence to both oneself and the theme to think as he does. Besides, I have often fancied that my organs were not fine enough to apprehend the unusual subtlety of his distinctions."

"If they were philosophically prepared like his," said Goethe, "it would be better. But, to speak frankly, I am sorry that a man of undoubted innate power from the northern coast of Germany, like Hinrichs, should be so spoilt by the philosophy of Hegel as to lose all unbiassed and natural observation and thought, and gradually to get into an artificial and heavy style, of both thought and expression; so that we find passages in his book where our understanding comes to a standstill, and we no longer know what we are reading."

"I have fared no better," said I. "Still I have rejoiced to meet with some passages that appeared perfectly clear and fitted for mankind in general; such, for instance, as his relation of the fable of Œdipus."

"Here," said Goethe, "he has been obliged to confine himself strictly to his subject. But there are in his book several passages in which the thought does not progress, but in which the obscure language constantly moves on the same spot and in the same circle, just like the 'Einmaleins' [multiplication table] of the witch in my *Faust*. Give me the book again. Of his sixth lecture upon the chorus, I scarcely understood anything. What do you say, for instance, to this passage, which occurs near the end:

" 'This realization [i.e. of popular life] is, as the true signification thereof, on this account alone its true realization; which, as a truth and certainty to itself, therefore constitutes the universally mental certainty; which certainly is at the same time the atoning certainty of the chorus; so that in this certainty alone, which has shown itself as the result of the combined movement of the tragic action, the chorus preserves its fitting relation to the universal popular consciousness, and in this capacity does not merely represent the people, but is that people according to its certainty.'

"I think we have had enough of this. What must the English and French think of the language of our philosophers, when we Germans do not understand them ourselves?" "And in spite of all this," said I, "we both agree that a noble purpose lies at the foundation of the book, and that it possesses the quality of awakening thoughts."

"His idea of the relation between family and state," said Goethe, "and the tragical conflicts that may arise from them, is certainly good and suggestive; yet I cannot allow that it is the only right one, or even the best for tragic art. We are indeed all members both of a family and of a state, and there does not often befall us a tragical fate that does not wound us in both capacities. Still, we might be very good tragical characters, if we were merely members of a family or merely members of a state. For, after all, the only point is to get a conflict that admits of no solution; and this may arise from an antagonistic position in any relation whatever—provided a person has a really natural foundation, and is himself really tragic. Thus Ajax falls a victim to the demon of wounded honour, and Hercules to the demon of jealousy. In neither of these cases is there the least conflict between family piety and political virtue; though this, according to Hinrichs, should be the element of Greek tragedy."

"Clearly," said I, "in this theory he merely had *Antigone* in his mind. He also appears to have had before him mere-

ly the character and mode of action of this heroine: as he makes the assertion that family piety appears most pure in woman, and especially a sister; and that a sister can love only a brother with perfect purity, and without sexual feeling."

"I should think," returned Goethe, "that the love of sister for sister was still more pure and unsexual. As if we did not know of numerous cases where the most sensual inclinations have existed between brother and sister, both knowingly and unknowingly!"

"You must have remarked generally," continued Goethe, "that Hinrichs, in considering Greek tragedy, sets out from the *idea;* and that he looks upon Sophocles as one who, in the invention and arrangement of his pieces, likewise set out from an idea, and regulated the sex and rank of his characters accordingly. But Sophocles, when he wrote his pieces, by no means started from an *idea;* he seized upon some ancient readymade popular tradition in which a good idea existed, and then only thought of adapting it in the best manner for the theatre. The Atrides will not allow Ajax to be buried; but as in *Antigone* the sister struggles for the brother, so in *Ajax* the brother struggles for the brother. That the sister takes charge of the unburied Polyneices, and the brother takes charge of the fallen Ajax, is a contingent circumstance, and does not belong to the invention of the poet; but to the tradition, which the poet followed and was obliged to follow."

"What he says about Creon's conduct," replied I, "appears to be equally untenable. He tries to prove that, in prohibiting the burial of Polyneices, Creon acts from pure political virtue; and, since Creon is not merely a man but also a prince, he lays down the proposition that, as a man represents the tragic power of the state, this man can be no other than he who is himself the personification of the state itself—namely, the prince; and that of all persons the man as prince must be just that person who displays the greatest political virtue."

"These are assertions nobody will believe," returned Goethe with a smile. "Besides, Creon by no means acts out of political virtue, but from hatred towards the dead. When Polyneices endeavoured to reconquer his paternal inheritance, from which he had been forcibly expelled, he did not commit such a monstrous crime against the state that his death was insufficient, and that further punishment of the innocent corpse was required.

"An action should never be placed in the category of political virtue which is opposed to virtue in general. When Creon forbids the burial of Polyneices, and not only taints the air with the decaying corpse, but also affords opportunity for dogs and birds of prey to drag about pieces torn from the dead body and thus to defile the altars—an action so offensive to both gods and men is not politically virtuous, but a political crime. Besides, he has everybody in the play against him. He has the elders of the state, who form the chorus, against him; he has the people at large against him; he has Teiresias against him; he has his own family against him: but he hears not, and obstinately persists in his impiety; until he has brought to ruin all who belong to him, and is himself at last nothing but a shadow."

"And still," said I, "when we hear him speak, we cannot help believing he is somewhat in the right."

"That is the very thing," said Goethe, "in which Sophocles is a master; and in which consists the very life of the dramatic in general. His characters all possess this gift of eloquence, and know how to explain the motives for their action so convincingly that the hearer is almost always on the side of the last speaker.

"Evidently, in his youth, he enjoyed an excellent rhetorical education, by which he became trained to look for all the reasons and seeming reasons of things. Still, his great talent in this respect betrayed him into faults: he sometimes went too far. There is a passage in **Antigone** which I always look upon as a blemish, and I would give a great deal for an apt philologist to prove that it is interpolated and spurious. After the heroine has explained the noble motives for her action, and displayed the elevated purity of her soul, she at last, when she is led to death, brings forward a motive that is quite unworthy and almost borders upon the comic. She says that, if she had been a mother, she would not have done, either for her dead children or for her dead husband, what she has done for her brother. 'For,' says she, 'if my husband died I could have had another, and if my children died I could have had others by my new husband. But with my brother, the case is different. I cannot have another brother; for, since my mother and father are dead, there is nobody to beget one.'

"This is, at least, the bare sense of this passage, which in my opinion, when placed in the mouth of a heroine going to her death, disturbs the tragic tone and appears to me very far-fetched—to savour too much of dialectical calculation."

We conversed further upon Sophocles, remarking that in his pieces he always less considered a moral tendency than an apt treatment of the subject, particularly with regard to theatrical effect.

"I do not object," said Goethe, "to a dramatic poet having a moral influence in view; but, when the point is to bring his subject clearly and effectively before his audience, his moral purpose proves of little use, and he needs much more a faculty for delineation and a familiarity with the stage to know what to do and what to leave undone. If there be a moral in the subject, it will appear, and the poet has nothing to consider but the effective and artistic treatment of his subject. If a poet has as high a soul as Sophocles, his influence will always be moral, let him do what he will. Besides, he knew the stage, and understood his craft thoroughly."

"How well he knew the theatre," answered I, "and how much he had in view a theatrical effect, we see in his **Philoctetes,** and the great resemblance this piece bears to **Œdipus in Colonos,** in both arrangement and course of action.

"In each piece we see a hero in a helpless condition; both are old and suffering from bodily infirmities. Œdipus has at his side his daughter as a guide and a prop; Philoctetes has his bow. The resemblance is carried still further. Both have been thrust aside in their afflictions; but, when the oracle declares that victory can be obtained with their aid alone, endeavour is made to get them back; Ulysses comes to Philoctetes, Creon to Œdipus. Both begin their discourse with cunning and honeyed words; but when these are of no avail they use violence, and we see Philoctetes deprived of his bow, and Œdipus of his daughter."

"Such acts of violence," said Goethe, "give an opportunity for excellent altercations, and such situations of helplessness excited the emotions of the audience; on which account the poet, whose object it was to produce an effect upon the public, liked to introduce them. In order to strengthen this effect in the **Œdipus,** Sophocles brings him in as a weak old man—whereas, according to all circumstances, he must have been a man still in the prime of life. But, at this vigorous age, the poet could not have used him for his play; he would have produced no effect, and he therefore made him a weak, helpless old man."

"The resemblance to **Philoctetes,**" continued I, "goes still further. The hero, in both pieces, does not act, but suffers. On the other hand, each of these passive heroes has two active characters against him. Œdipus has Creon and Polyneices, Philoctetes has Neoptolemus and Ulysses; two such opposing characters were necessary to discuss the subject on all sides, and to gain the necessary body and fulness for the piece."

"You might add," interposed Goethe, "that both pieces bear this further resemblance: we see in both the extremely effective situation of a happy change; since one hero, in his disconsolate situation, has his beloved daughter restored to him, and the other his no less beloved bow."

The happy conclusions of these two pieces are also similar; for both heroes are delivered from their sorrows: Œdipus is blissfully snatched away; and as for Philoctetes, we are forewarned by the oracle of his cure, before Troy, by Æsculapius. (pp. 174-80)

> *Johann Wolfgang Goethe and Johan Peter Eckermann, in a conversation in* Conversations of Goethe with Eckermann, *edited by J. K. Moorhead, translated by John Oxenford, J. M. Dent & Sons Ltd., 1946, pp. 174-80.*

Friedrich Nietzsche   (essay date 1872)

[*Considered one of the most important modern philosophers, Nietzsche is known for his condemnation of Christianity as the glorification of passivity, a charge that culminated in his announcement of the death of God. As a proponent of the view that man is the sole master of his destiny, Nietzsche is a forerunner of existentialism. His philosophy has profoundly affected numerous fields of intellectual inquiry, including psychology, history, esthetics, and literary theory. His best known works are* Die Geburt der Tragödie aus dem Geiste der Musik *(1872;* The Birth of Tragedy, *1909), a brilliant revision of the dominant scholarly conception of Greek artistic ideals, and* Also sprach Zarathustra *(1883-85;* Thus Spake Zarathustra, *1909), a poetic exposition of his controversial philosophy of the Superman. In the following excerpt from a translation of the first-named work, Nietzsche, who was a classicist by training, comments on the mythological and psychological complexities of the Sophoclean hero.*]

Everything that comes to the surface in the Apollinian part of Greek tragedy, in the dialogue, looks simple, transparent, and beautiful. In this sense, the dialogue is an image of the Hellene whose nature is revealed in the dance because in the dance the greatest strength remains only potential but betrays itself in the suppleness and wealth of movement. Thus the language of Sophocles' heroes amazes us by its Apollinian precision and lucidity, so we immediately have the feeling that we are looking into the innermost ground of their being, with some astonishment that the way to this ground should be so short. But suppose we disregard the character of the hero as it comes to the surface, visibly—after all, it is in the last analysis nothing but a bright image projected on a dark wall, which means appearance through and through; suppose we penetrate into the myth that projects itself in these lucid reflections: then we suddenly experience a phenomenon that is just the opposite of a familiar optical phenomenon. When after a forceful attempt to gaze on the sun we turn away blinded, we see dark-colored spots before our eyes, as a cure, as it were. Conversely, the bright image projections of the Sophoclean hero—in short, the Apollinian aspect of the mask—are necessary effects of a glance into the inside and terrors of nature; as it were, luminous spots to cure eyes damaged by gruesome night. Only in this sense may we believe that we properly comprehend the serious and important concept of "Greek cheerfulness." The misunderstanding of this concept as cheerfulness in a state of unendangered comfort is, of course, encountered everywhere today.

Sophocles understood the most sorrowful figure of the Greek stage, the unfortunate Oedipus, as the noble human being who, in spite of his wisdom, is destined to error and misery but who eventually, through his tremendous suffering, spreads a magical power of blessing that remains effective even beyond his decease. The noble human being does not sin, the profound poet wants to tell us: though every law, every natural order, even the moral world may perish through his actions, his actions also produce a higher magical circle of effects which found a new world on the ruins of the old one that has been overthrown. That is what the poet wants to say to us insofar as he is at the same time a religious thinker. As a poet he first shows us a marvelously tied knot of a trial, slowly unraveled by the judge, bit by bit, for his own undoing. The genuinely Hellenic delight at this dialectical solution is so great that it introduces a trait of superior cheerfulness into the whole work, everywhere softening the sharp points of the gruesome presuppositions of this process.

In *Oedipus at Colonus* we encounter the same cheerfulness, but elevated into an infinite transfiguration. The old man, struck by an excess of misery, abandoned solely to *suffer* whatever befalls him, is confronted by the supraterrestrial cheerfulness that descends from the divine sphere and suggests to us that the hero attains his highest activity, extending far beyond his life, through his purely passive posture, while his conscious deeds and desires, earlier in his life, merely led him into passivity. Thus the intricate legal knot of the Oedipus fable that no mortal eye could unravel is gradually disentangled—and the most profound human joy overcomes us at this divine counterpart of the dialectic.

If this explanation does justice to the poet one may yet ask whether it exhausts the contents of the myth—and then it becomes evident that the poet's whole conception is nothing but precisely that bright image which healing nature projects before us after a glance into the abyss. Oedipus, the murderer of his father, the husband of his mother, the solver of the riddle of the Sphinx! What does the mysterious triad of these fateful deeds tell us?

There is a tremendously old popular belief, especially in Persia, that a wise magus can be born only from incest. With the riddle-solving and mother-marrying Oedipus in mind, we must immediately interpret this to mean that where prophetic and magical powers have broken the spell of present and future, the rigid law of individuation, and the real magic of nature, some enormously unnatural event—such as incest—must have occurred earlier, as a cause. How else could one compel nature to surrender her secrets if not by triumphantly resisting her, that is, by means of something unnatural? It is this insight that I find expressed in that horrible triad of Oedipus' destinies: the same man who solves the riddle of nature—that Sphinx of two species—also must break the most sacred natural orders by murdering his father and marrying his mother. Indeed, the myth seems to wish to whisper to us that wisdom, and particularly Dionysian wisdom, is an unnatural abomination; that he who by means of his knowledge plunges nature into the abyss of destruction must also suffer the dissolution of nature in his own person. "The edge of wisdom turns against the wise: wisdom is a crime against nature": such horrible sentences are proclaimed to us by the myth; but the Hellenic poet touches the sublime and terrible Memnon's Column of myth like a sunbeam, so that it suddenly begins to sound—in Sophoclean melodies. (pp. 67-9)

> *Friedrich Nietzsche, "The Birth of Tragedy,"
> in the* Basic Writings of Nietzsche, *edited and
> translated by Walter Kaufmann, The Modern
> Library, 1968, pp. 3-146.*

Werner Jaeger   (essay date 1936)

[*Jaeger was a distinguished German educator and classicist whose writings include* Aristoteles: Grundlegung einer Geschichte seiner Entwicklung *(1923;* Aristotle: Fundamentals of the History of His Development, *1934) and* Paideia: die Formung des griechischen Menschen *(1934;* Paideia: The Ideals of Greek Culture, *1939-44). In the following excerpt from a translation of the 1936 German second edition of the latter work, Jaeger extols Sophocles as representative of the greatness of the classical Greek spirit. In particular, he attributes Sophocles' enormous success as a dramatist to his talent for characterization and his sense of beauty and proportion in all things.*]

In any account of the educational power of Attic tragedy, Sophocles and Aeschylus must be named together. Sophocles consciously assumed the position of successor to Aeschylus, and his contemporaries, while venerating Aeschylus as the master and inspirer of the Attic theatre, readily gave Sophocles the place next to him. This idea of tradition and inheritance is deeply rooted in the Greek conception of poetry, for the Greeks did not focus their attention principally on individual poets, but on poetry itself as an independent and self-perpetuating form of art, which, when bequeathed by one poet to another, continued to be a complete and authoritative standard. We can realize this by studying the history of tragedy. As soon as it reached maturity, its magnificence almost compelled artists and thinkers of the fifth and subsequent centuries to exert their highest powers in a noble rivalry.

The competitive element which was implicit in all forms of Greek poetic activity grew in proportion as art became the centre of public life and the expression of the whole political and intellectual outlook of the age. Accordingly, it reached its highest point in drama. That is the only possible explanation of the huge numbers of second- and third-rate poets who took part in the Dionysiac competitions. Nowadays we are always amazed to hear of the swarm of satellites and minor planets which accompanied during their lifetime the few great and eternal lights of Attic poetry. For all its prizes and organized festivals, the state did not stimulate the enthusiasm of the minor poets—it merely guided it and controlled it, although its very guidance was an encouragement. It was then inevitable (quite apart from the permanence of professional tradition in all art, and especially in Greek art) that the constant competition and comparison between tragedies as they were produced from year to year should create a continuous form of intellectual and social control over this new artistic type—a control which did not interfere with artistic freedom, but made public taste extraordinarily sensitive to any falling-off in the great tradition and to any diminution in the power and depth of the influence which tragedy exercised.

Hence there is some measure of justification for comparing three artists so dissimilar and in many respects so incapable of comparison as the great Attic tragedians. It is always unfair, if not actually foolish, to regard Sophocles and Euripides as successors of Aeschylus, for that view imposes standards upon them which are too high for the age in which they lived. The best successor of a great man is he who, having creative powers of his own, goes his own way unperturbed by previous greatness. The Greeks themselves were always willing to admire, not only the man who struck out a new form, but also, perhaps even more, the man who brought it to perfection. In fact, they considered the highest originality to lie not in the first but in the most perfect achievement in any field of art. But since every artist develops his own art within the form which he finds ready to hand, and is therefore in some degree indebted to it, he must recognize that the traditional form which he uses is a standard for himself, and must allow his work to be judged as maintaining, diminishing, or enhancing the significance of the form which he employs. It is obvious then that the development of Attic tragedy does not run from Aeschylus to Sophocles and from Sophocles to Euripides, but that the immediate successor of Aeschylus is Euripides, quite as much as Sophocles, who actually

outlived him. Both Sophocles and Euripides continued the work of their master, but there is good reason for the emphasis which modern scholars lay on the fact that there are far more points of contact between Euripides and Aeschylus than between Sophocles and either of the other two. Aristophanes and other contemporary critics were right in regarding Euripides as the corruptor, not of Sophoclean, but of Aeschylean tragedy; for he took up the tradition where Aeschylus had left it, although in fact he did not curtail but vastly increased the scope of tragedy. His achievement was to admit the questionings and criticisms of his own age, and to build tragedies round up-to-date problems rather than the religious doubts which had exercised Aeschylus. But despite all the violent contrasts between the two poets, they were akin in their fondness for discussing and dramatizing large spiritual problems.

From this point of view, Sophocles once appeared to be almost outside the main stream of development. He seemed to have none of the passionate intensity and depth of personal experience which enriched the work of his two great fellow-dramatists; scholars felt that there was, in view of his perfection of form and his lucid objectivity, some historical justification but also much unnecessary prejudice in the classicists' admiration for him as the greatest of the Greek dramatists. Thus they followed the modern psychological trend in rejecting him in favour of the powerful but uncouth archaism of Aeschylus and the sophisticated subjectivism of Euripides, both of whom had been too long neglected. When they at last endeavoured to give Sophocles his true place in the revised history of Greek drama, they were compelled to look elsewhere for the secret of his success. They found it either in his religious attitude or in his technical skill as a playwright; which was developed during his youth by the great rise of dramatic technique led by Aeschylus, and which aimed at one thing above all else—dramatic effect. But if Sophocles' art is nothing more than dramatic craftsmanship (however important that may be), we should be compelled to ask why he was judged not only by the classicist critics but by the ancients themselves to be the perfection of tragedy. And it would be extremely difficult to assign him a worthy place in a history of Greek culture like this book, which is not fundamentally concerned with the purely aesthetic aspect of poetry.

There is no doubt that he has no religious message so powerful as that of Aeschylus. There was a deep quiet devoutness in his character, but it was not expressed with marked emphasis in his plays. What was once called the impiety of Euripides strikes us as far more religious than the unshakable but placid piety of Sophocles. We must admit that modern scholars are right in saying that his real strength did not consist in dramatizing problems, although as the successor of Aeschylus he inherited the ideas and problems with which Aeschylus had dealt. We must start by considering the effect produced by his plays on the stage—and that effect, be it noted, was not created entirely by clever technique. Of course, he was bound to be technically superior to old Aeschylus, since he belonged to the second generation, the generation which always refines and subtilizes the work of the pioneer. Yet how can we explain the fact that all attempts to satisfy the changed taste of to-day by putting Aeschylus and Euripides on the modern stage have failed—apart from a few experimental productions before more or less specialized audiences—while Sophocles is the one Greek dramatist who keeps his place in the repertoire of the contemporary theatre? Certainly he owes his position nowadays to no classicist prejudice. The rigid undramatic effect of the choruses which dominate Aeschylus' tragedies cannot be counteracted by the depth of their thought and the richness of their language, when they stand still to speak their lines, and neither dance nor sing. The dialectic of Euripides does indeed strike a sympathetic note in troubled times like our own; but nothing is more transient than the problems of bourgeois society. We need only think how remote we are to-day from Ibsen or Zola (who are of course infinitely beneath Euripides) to realize that the great strength of Euripides in his own day is an insuperable weakness on the modern stage.

The ineffaceable impression which Sophocles makes on us today and his imperishable position in the literature of the world are both due to his character-drawing. If we ask which of the men and women of Greek tragedy have an independent life in the imagination apart from the stage and from the actual plot in which they appear, we must answer, 'those created by Sophocles, above all others'. He was much more than a technician: for characters which *live* cannot be created by mere excellence in dramatic technique, which has at best a temporary effect. Perhaps nothing is harder for us to understand than the quiet, unpretentious, natural wisdom of Sophocles, which makes us feel that his real flesh-and-blood men and women, with violent passions and tender emotions, proudly heroic but truly human, are like ourselves and yet noble with an incomparable dignity and remoteness. There is no sophistical subtlety, no artificial exaggeration about these characters. Later ages vainly tried to achieve monumental sublimity by violence, by colossal size and startling effects. Sophocles found sublimity in the effortless calm of true proportion: for it is always simple and even obvious. Its secret lies in the abandonment of everything inessential and accidental, so that nothing is left but the perfect clarity of that inner law which is hidden from the outward eye. The men created by Sophocles have none of the earthy compactness of Aeschylus' characters, who look impassive, even stiff, beside them; nor is their mobility spoilt by lack of balance, as in so many of Euripides' puppets—it is hard to call them characters, since they never grow beyond the two dimensions of the theatre, costume and declamation, and never round out into real physical presences. Sophocles stands midway between his predecessor and his successor: he surrounds himself effortlessly with the men and women he has made. Or rather, they surround him. For true characters are never created by mere caprice. They must be begotten upon life by necessity: neither by the empty universal type nor the uniquely detailed individual, but by essential law, which is opposed to the inessential accident.

Many writers have drawn parallels between poetry and sculpture, and compared each of the three tragedians with one stage in the development of plastic art. There is always something trivial about such parallels—all the more when they are pedantically elaborate. . . . But when we call

Sophocles the sculptor of tragedy, we mean that he possesses one quality unlike any other poet—a fact which makes it impossible to institute any comparison between the development of tragedy and that of sculpture. A poetic and a sculptural character both depend on the artist's knowledge of ultimate laws of proportion. And that is as far as the parallel will go; for the specific laws of spiritual life cannot be applied to the spatial structure of visual and tangible physical existence. Yet the highest aim of the sculptors of Sophocles' time was to depict men in such a way that the spirit shone through the physical form; and therein they seem to have caught a ray of light from the spiritual world which was first revealed in the poetry of Sophocles. The most moving reflection of that light shines from the memorials set up at that time on Attic graves. Although they are artistically far inferior to the richness of feeling and variety of expression which make up the work of Sophocles, yet the deep quiet humanity which breathes in them is enough to show that their art and his poetry were inspired by the same emotion. Serene and fearless, they image eternal humanity triumphant over suffering and death: and show thereby a deep and genuine religious feeling.

The tragedies of Sophocles and the sculptures of Phidias are the two imperishable monuments of the great age of the Athenian spirit. Together, they represent the art of the Periclean era. Looking backward from the work of Sophocles, one seems to see all the previous development of tragedy as merely leading up to this perfection. Even Aeschylus appears to be only a preparation for Sophocles; but Sophocles cannot be said to prepare the way for Euripides or the tragic *epigonoi* [followers] of the fourth century. Later poets are merely echoes of the greatness of the fifth century, and the true strength and promise of Euripides are most manifest when he leaves poetry and invades the new domain of philosophy. Therefore Sophocles is classical, inasmuch as he is the climax of the development of tragedy: in him tragedy 'had its nature', as Aristotle would say. But there is another unique sense in which he is classical: and here that description connotes more than perfection within one literary form. His position in the development of the spirit of Greece makes him classical—and in this book we are concerned with literature chiefly as the expression of that spirit and its transformations. The work of Sophocles is the climax of the development of Greek poetry, considered as the process by which the formation of human character is increasingly objectified. From this point of view alone can our earlier discussion of his tragic characters be fully understood and even gain additional significance. Their excellence is not in their form alone; it is a more deeply human excellence, for in it aesthetic and moral and religious elements interfuse and interact. Such a fusing of motives is not unique in Greek poetry. . . . But in Sophocles' tragedies form and norm are unified in a special sense, and they are unified above all in his characters. He himself said tersely but accurately that his characters were ideals, not ordinary men like those of Euripides. As a creator of men, Sophocles has a place in the history of human culture essentially unlike that of any other Greek poet. In his work the fully awakened sense of culture is made manifest for the first time. It is something totally different from the educational effect of Homer or the educated purpose of Aeschylus. It assumes the existence of a society whose highest ideal is *culture,* the formation of perfect human character; and such an assumption was impossible until, after one entire generation had struggled to discover the meaning of destiny, after the sore spiritual agonies of Aeschylus, humanity itself had become the centre of life. The character-drawing of Sophocles is consciously inspired by that ideal of human conduct which was the peculiar creation of Periclean society and civilization. He assimilated that ideal so fully that he humanized tragedy, and converted it into an imperishable pattern of human culture which was entirely in the inimitable spirit of the men who created it. Sophoclean tragedy could almost be called a purely cultural art and be compared (though in far less artificial conditions of time and outlook) to *Tasso* with its unique position in Goethe's effort to discover form in life and art, were it not that the word culture has so many different associations that it inevitably tends to grow vague and colourless. We must carefully avoid certain contrasts which have become clichés of literary criticism (such as that between 'original experience' and 'cultural experience') if we are to understand the true Greek meaning of culture. Culture was for the Greeks the original creation and original experience of a process of deliberate guidance and formation of human character. Understanding that, we shall also understand the power of such an ideal to inspire the imagination of a great poet. It was a moment unique in the history of the world when poetry and culture came together to create an ideal.

The unity of the Athenian nation and the Athenian state, overarched, as it were, by the spiritual cosmos of Aeschylean tragedy, and won with such toil in the Persian wars, prepared the ground for a new national culture transcending all enmities and contrasts between the aristocratic civilization and the life of the common people. The happiness of the generation which on that ground built up the Periclean state and Periclean culture is strangely imaged in the life of Sophocles. The general facts of his career are well known, but they are much more significant than the smaller personal details which careful researchers have brought to light. No doubt it is only a legend that in the flower of his youth and beauty he danced in the chorus which celebrated the victory of Salamis, where Aeschylus had fought as a soldier; but it is important to observe that his life did not really begin until the storm of war had ended. He stands, so to say, on the narrow and precipitous peak of glory from which Athens was so soon to fall. His art shines clear and bright with the cloudless, windless serenity, $ευδία$ and $γαλήνη$, of that incomparable noon which dawned on the morning of Salamis. And he died shortly before Aristophanes called upon the ghost of Aeschylus to return and redeem his city. He did not see the final catastrophe of Athens. After the last Athenian victory, at Arginusae, had once more awakened the hopes of his nation, he passed away; and now he lives beyond the grave—so Aristophanes described him soon after his death—in the same calm harmony with himself and with the world which he had maintained throughout his earthly existence. It is difficult to say how much of his *eudaimonia* sprang from the favoured age in which he lived, how much from his happy nature, and how much again from his own deliberate art, from the quiet mysterious wisdom which a more showy talent can neither equal nor appreciate, and must therefore dismiss with a gesture of embarrassment. True culture is produced only by these three forces acting together, and its generation is an eternal mystery. The marvel of it is that we cannot explain it, far less create it: we can only point to it, and say 'it is here'.

Even if we knew nothing else of Periclean Athens, we could tell from the life and character of Sophocles that in his time men were for the first time engaged in deliberately forming human character in accordance with a cultural ideal. Proud of the manners of their new society, they coined for them the word $αστεῖδ$, *urbane* or *polite.* Twenty years later it was current in all Attic prose writers, Xenophon, the orators, and Plato; and Aristotle described and analysed the ideal of free courteous social intercourse and cultivated behaviour which it connoted. That ideal was the basis of Athenian society in the age of Pericles. The grace of refined Attic culture—which, be it noted, was vastly different from the pedantic conception of culture—could not be more beautifully illustrated than in a witty anecdote told by a contemporary poet, Ion of Chios. It describes an actual event in the life of Sophocles. Serving as a fellow-*strategos* of Pericles, he was the guest of honour in a small Ionian city. At dinner he sat next to a local teacher of literature and suffered agonies of annoyance and boredom when his neighbour criticized the poetic colouring of Phrynichus' fine old line: 'There shines on crimson cheeks the light of love.' With the ease of true sophistication and a touch of genuine personal grace, he extricated himself from the painful situation amid general applause, by convicting the pedant of incompetence in the fine art of poetic exegesis; and at the same time he proved that he understood his compulsory profession of generalship by carrying out a cunning 'stratagem' against the handsome page-boy who offered him the winecup. The charm and delicacy reflected in this story are unforgettable elements in the character, not only of Sophocles, but of the whole Athenian society of his time. The spirit and outlook of the anecdote remind us irresistibly of the bust of Sophocles in the Lateran. Beside it we may well set the sculptor Cresilas' bust of Pericles, which shows the face neither of a statesman nor (despite the helmet) of a general. As Aeschylus was, in the eyes of posterity, the Marathon-warrior, the faithful Athenian citizen, so Sophocles and Pericles, as depicted in story and bust, are the highest ideal of the *kalos kagathos* [beautiful and good], the Athenian gentleman of the fifth century.

That ideal was inspired by a clear and delicate perception of correct and appropriate behaviour in every situation, which, despite its precise rules for speech and conduct and its perfect sense of proportion and control, was in effect a new spiritual freedom. Entirely without effort or affectation, it was an easy and unconstrained way of life, appreciated and admired by all—and, as Isocrates wrote some years later, imitable by none. It existed only in Athens. It meant an abandonment of the exaggerated violence of emotion and expression that characterized Aeschylus, for the miraculously natural poise and proportion which we feel and enjoy in the sculptured frieze of the Parthenon as well as in the language of the men and women of Sophocles. An open secret, it can only be described, not defined;

but at least it is not a matter of pure form. After all, it would be too extraordinary if the same phenomenon appeared at the same time in poetry and sculpture without being created by some suprapersonal feeling common to all the men who were most characteristic of their age. It is the radiance of a life that has found the final peace and final harmony with itself which are expressed in Aristophanes' description of Sophocles: a life which even the passage through death cannot affect, which remains both 'there' and 'here,' εὐχολος, content. It would be trivial and unworthy to interpret this way of life as purely aesthetic, a complex of elegant attitudes, or as purely psychological, a harmony of consonant spiritual powers, and thereby to mistake its symptoms for its essence. It was not only the accidents of personal character that made Sophocles the master of the rich central tones which Aeschylus could never sound successfully. In his work more than in that of any other poet, form is the immediate and appropriate expression, in fact the full revelation of being, and its metaphysical manifestation. To the question, 'What is the nature and meaning of this life?' Sophocles does not reply like Aeschylus with a theory of the universe, justifying the ways of God to man, but simply by the form of his speech and the characters of his men and women. This can hardly be understood by those who have never turned to Sophocles for guidance at moments when, in the chaos and unrest of life, all principle and all structure seem to dissolve away, and have never restored the balance of their own lives by contemplating the firm harmonious repose of his poetry. The effect of its sounds and rhythms is always one of balance and proportion; and balance and proportion are for him the principle of all existence, for they mean the reverent recognition of that justice which is implicit in everything and which can be realized only at the fulness of spiritual maturity. It is not for nothing that his choruses again and again describe disproportion as the root of all evil. The pre-established harmony of Sophocles' poetry and Phidias' sculpture is ultimately based on the quasi-religious acceptance of this law of harmony. In fact, the universal recognition of the law in fifth-century Greece is such a natural expression of the characteristically Greek quality of *sophrosyné* [moderation]—a quality whose metaphysical basis was the Greek view of the meaning of all life—that when Sophocles himself glorifies harmony and proportion, we seem to hear a manifold echo of his words in every region of the Hellenic world. It was not a new idea; but the historical influence and the absolute significance of an idea do not depend on its novelty, but on the depth and power with which men understand it and live it. Sophocles' tragedies are the climax of the development of the Greek idea that proportion is one of the highest values in human life. The process leads up to him, and in him it finds its classical poetic expression as the divine power which rules the world and human life.

There is another way to demonstrate the close connexion between culture and the sense of proportion in the mind of fifth-century Greece. In general we are compelled to draw inferences from the works of the Greek artists to the artistic theories which they held; their works are in fact the principal evidence for their beliefs. But in trying to understand the obscure and yet fundamental principles which assisted in the creation of works of art so many in number and so various in possible interpretations, we are justified in seeking contemporary evidence to guide us. In this context, then, we possess two remarks made by Sophocles himself—which indeed owe their ultimate historical authority only to the fact that they harmonize with our intuitive judgment of his art. We have already quoted one of them, in which Sophocles described his own characters as ideal figures in contrast to Euripidean realism. In the other he distinguished his own work from that of Aeschylus by saying that Aeschylus wrote correctly without knowing why: he denied him that deliberate intention to be *right* which seems an essential element in his own work. Both remarks taken together presuppose a very special awareness of standards to be followed: Sophocles guided his work by a standard and in it presented men 'as they ought to be'. Now, such awareness of the ideal standards of character is peculiar to the period when the sophistic movement was beginning. The problem of the nature of human areté [virtue] is now taken up with terrific intensity from the educational side. All the discussions of that age, and all the efforts of the sophists, were directed towards finding and producing man 'as he ought to be'. Until then, poetry alone had given reasons for the values in which men believed; but it could not remain unaffected by the new educational movement. Aeschylus and Solon had given their work far-reaching influence by making it reflect the struggles of their own souls to apprehend God and Fate. Now Sophocles, following the cultural trend of his age, turned to Man, and expressed his own moral standards in the characters he drew. The beginnings of this movement can be traced in the later plays of Aeschylus, where he enhances the tragic element by depicting a conflict between destiny and some strongly idealized figure like Eteocles, Prometheus, Agamemnon, Orestes. In that device Sophocles is his immediate successor: for his principal characters embody the highest areté as envisaged by the great educators of his own time. It is impossible, and for Sophocles needless, to decide whether the cultural ideal or the poetic creation came first. What is essential is that in his time poets and educators had the same great purpose in view.

The sense of beauty that produced the men and women of Sophocles arose from a vast new interest in the *souls* of tragic characters. It was a manifestation of the new ideal of areté, which for the first time emphasized the central importance of the *psyché,* the 'soul', in all culture. In the course of the fifth century the word psyché acquired a new overtone, a loftier significance, which reached its fulness in the teaching of Socrates. The soul was now objectively recognized as the centre of man's life. From the soul came all men's actions. Long before, sculptors had discovered the laws that shape and govern the body and had studied them with the greatest enthusiasm. In the 'harmony' of the body they had rediscovered the principle of cosmos apprehended by philosophers in the structure of the universe. With that principle in mind the Greeks now turned to the exploration of the soul. They did not see it as a chaotic flow of inner experience, but subjected it to a system of laws, as the only realm of being which had not yet incorporated the ideal of cosmos. Like the body, the soul obviously had rhythm and harmony. Thus the Greeks reached the idea of a soul-structure. One is tempted to find its first clear expression in Simonides' description of areté as 'built foursquare in hand and foot and mind'. But it was a long way from that inchoate idea of the life of the soul as analogous to the physical ideal of athletic perfection, to the theory of culture which Plato no doubt rightly ascribes to the sophist Protagoras. That theory was a completely logical development of the idea that the soul can be formed like the body—an idea which has ceased to be a poetic image and become an educational principle. Protagoras said that the soul can be educated into true *eurhythmia* and *euharmostia,* rhythm and concord. The right rhythm and harmony are to be produced in it by the influence of poetry embodying these standards. Even in this theory the ideal of forming the soul is approached from a physical point of view; but Protagoras conceives the process to resemble sculpture, the work of a plastic artist, rather than athletic training, as Simonides had done. The standards of eurhythmia and euharmostia are likewise borrowed from the world of visible physical existence. Only in classical Greece could the concept of culture have been inspired by the sculptor's art. Even Sophocles' ideal of human character clearly betrays its sculptural origin. At that period education, poetry, and sculpture affected one another deeply—none of them could have existed without the others. Educators and poets were inspired by the sculptor's effort to create an ideal figure, and took the same path towards the ιδέα of humanity; while the sculptor or painter was led by the example of education and poetry to look for the soul in every model he used. The focus of interest for all three was the higher value which now attached to humanity. The Athenian mind has now become anthropocentric; humanism has been born—not the emotion of love for all other members of society, called *philanthropia* by the Greeks, but intellectual search for and interest in the true nature of man. It is especially significant that now for the first time tragedy shows women as well as men, as worthy representatives of humanity. Apart from such subordinate feminine characters as Clytaemnestra, Ismene, and Chrysothemis, Sophocles' power of drawing strong noble human beings is seen at its highest in many of his tragic heroines—Antigone, Electra, Dejanira, Tecmessa, Jocasta. After the great discovery that man was the real object of tragedy, it was inevitable that woman also should be discovered.

We can now understand the changes which tragedy underwent when Sophocles took it over from Aeschylus. The most obvious external change is Sophocles' abandonment of the trilogy, which had been Aeschylus' regular dramatic form. It was now replaced by single dramas, centred on one principal actor. It was impossible for Aeschylus to give dramatic treatment to the connected development of one destiny on the epic scale, often covering the sufferings of several generations of the same family, in anything less than a trilogy of tragedies. His chief concern was the unbroken course of the fate of a family, because it alone formed a whole large enough to demonstrate the working-out of divine justice, which even religious faith and moral sentiment can hardly trace in the doom of one individual. In his plays, therefore, single characters are subordinated to the main theme, although they may serve to introduce the spectator to it; and the poet himself is compelled to assume a higher and less human-position, making his pup-

pets move and suffer as if he himself were the power which guides the universe. But in Sophocles the ideal of justifying God's ways to man which dominates religious thought from Solon to Theognis and Aeschylus falls into the background. The tragic element in his plays is the inevitability of suffering: the necessity of destiny, seen from the point of view of the individual sufferer. He has not, therefore, abandoned Aeschylus' religious view of the nature of the world, but has merely shifted the emphasis from universal to individual problems. This is particularly clear in an early work like **Antigone,** where his conception of the meaning of the world is still boldly marked.

Aeschylus had traced through several generations of the Labdacid house the destructive effects of the curse which the family had brought on itself by early guilt. In Sophocles too, the curse of guilt looms in the background as the final cause of all their woe. Antigone herself is its last victim, as Eteocles and Polynices are in **Seven against Thebes.** Sophocles actually makes Antigone and her opponent Creon assist the curse in its work by their own violent actions, and the chorus never ceases to lament their transgression of the proper limits of action and to warn them of their partial responsibility for their own misfortune. But although these motives could be considered to justify the cruelty of destiny in the Aeschylean manner, the spectator's whole attention is focussed not on the problem of destiny, but on the individual characters, so much so that he feels that they are the chief interest of the drama, and that their predominance needs no external justification. By her own nature Antigone is destined to suffer—we might almost say chosen to suffer (without introducing Christian ideas of predestinate suffering), for her deliberate acceptance of suffering becomes her own peculiar form of nobility. Her tragic destiny is apparent in the prologue, in her first conversation with her sister. Ismene's tender maidenly nature shrinks from making the deliberate choice of ruin and death, although her love for Antigone never falters, as is touchingly proved later when she falsely accuses herself before Creon and makes a despairing attempt to join her sister in death. Still, she is not a tragic figure. Her gentle character accentuates the strength of Antigone, and we must admit that Antigone has a deeper justification for rejecting Ismene's fond readiness to share her doom. Just as the tragedy of Eteocles in the **Seven** is enhanced by the heroism which he displays when he is innocently involved in the fate of his family, so here his sister Antigone surpasses all the heroic qualities of her noble race.

The second song of the chorus creates a universal background for the suffering of the heroine. It hymns the power of man, who has created all arts, mastered nature through the power of the mind, and learned the highest skill of all—the power of justice which builds the state. A contemporary of Sophocles, the sophist Protagoras, had worked out a similar theory of the origin of civilized society; it was the first attempt at a rational account of man's development; and the majestic rhythms of this song have much of its Promethean pride in human progress. But with Sophocles' peculiar tragic irony, at the very moment when the chorus has extolled the power of justice and the state, and has proclaimed the banishment of the lawbreaker from all human society, Antigone is led onto the stage in chains. By obeying the unwritten law and performing the simplest duty of a sister to her dead brother, she has deliberately come into conflict with the king's command: for he had pronounced a decree which exaggerated the power of the state to the point of tyranny, by forbidding under pain of death the burial of Antigone's brother, Polynices, killed fighting against his own country. Instantly, therefore, the spectator is shown another aspect of humanity: the proud hymn dies away in the sudden tragic realization of the weakness and vanity of man.

With great penetration Hegel saw that *Antigone* dealt with the tragic conflict of two moral principles: the law of the state, and the rights of the family. From this point of view, the severe though exaggerated logic of King Creon's devotion to the state makes his character easier for us to understand; while the agony and defiance of Antigone justify the eternal laws of family duty against the interference of the state, with the irresistible persuasiveness of true revolutionary passion. Still, the emphasis is not upon this general problem, though a poet in the age of the sophist might well choose to universalize the two principal characters into representatives of a conflict of ideas. And the discussions of hybris, unreason, and immoderation are not the centre of interest, as in Aeschylus, but provide the background for the tragedy. There is always an immediately intelligible reason for the sufferings of a Sophoclean hero: he is not condemned to suffer, as if by some supernatural judge, he is through his own noble nature a visible example of the inevitability of the doom into which the gods lead men. The irrationality of até [fate] had puzzled Solon and exercised the minds of all the serious thinkers of that age, but for Sophocles it is the basis, not the central problem, of tragedy. Aeschylus had tried to solve the problem of até: Sophocles admits its insolubility as a fact. Yet he does not passively accept the unavoidable suffering sent by God, which Greek lyric poets had from the earliest times lamented; and he has no sympathy whatever for the resignation of Simonides, who concluded that man must forfeit his areté when cast down by inescapable misfortune. By making his tragic characters greatest and noblest of mankind, Sophocles cries Yes to the fateful question which no mortal mind can solve. His characters are the first who, by suffering by the absolute abandonment of their earthly happiness or of their social and physical life, reach the truest greatness attainable by man.

In their agony Sophocles draws from these characters a marvelous and delicate variety of tragical music; and he enhances its searching beauty by every device of the dramatist's imagination. Compared with those of Aeschylus, his plays are an immeasurable advance in dramatic effect. Yet he did not achieve this by abandoning the fine old choric songs and dances and telling a story for its own sake with Shakespearean realism. No doubt that view of his technique might be supported by the super-realistic power with which the tale of Oedipus is unfolded, and might even be responsible for much of the modern interest in staging that play; but it could never help us to understand the astonishing structural complexity and balance of his dramas. They were constructed not in accordance with the external sequence of physical events, but by a higher artistic logic which, in a series of contrasting scenes, each more

powerful than the last, expresses the very soul of the chief character, displaying it from every possible point of view. The classical example of this device is *Electra.* With brilliant invention, Sophocles uses one bold artifice after another to retard and interrupt the simple plot, so that the heroine passes through the whole gamut of emotion until she reaches the final agony of despair. And yet, violently as the pendulum swings from one extreme to the other, its central equilibrium is maintained throughout. The finest scene of all from this point of view is that in which Electra and Orestes recognize each other once again. Orestes has returned in disguise to save his sister and redeem his family honour, but he is made to reveal himself with such torturing slowness that Electra suffers every agony between heaven and hell. Sophoclean drama is the drama of the emotions through which the soul of the chief actor must pass, following in its own rhythm the harmonious development of the plot. The source of his dramatic effect is the hero's character, to which, as to the highest and final point of interest, it always returns. Dramatic action is for Sophocles the process by which the true nature of a suffering human being is unfolded, by which he fulfils his destiny, and through it fulfils himself.

Like Aeschylus, Sophocles thinks of drama as the instrument through which men reach a sublime knowledge. But it is not $\tau\grave{o}$ $\phi\rho ov\epsilon\hat{\iota}v$, [thinking] which was the ultimate certainty and necessity in which Aeschylus found peace. It is rather a tragical self-knowledge, the Delphic $\gamma v\hat{\omega}\theta\iota$ $\sigma\epsilon av\tau\acute{o}v$ [know thyself] deepened and broadened into a comprehension of the shadowy nothingness of human strength and human happiness. To know oneself is thus for Sophocles to know man's powerlessness; but it is also to know the indestructible and conquering majesty of suffering humanity. The agony of every Sophoclean character is an essential element in his nature. The strange fusion of character and fate is nowhere more movingly and mysteriously expressed than in the greatest of his heroes, to whom he returned once again at the very close of his life. It is Oedipus, a blind old man begging his way through the world, led by his daughter Antigone—another of Sophocles' most beloved figures. Nothing reveals the essence of Sophoclean tragedy more deeply than the fact that the poet grew old, as it were, along with his characters. He never forgot what Oedipus was to become. From the first, the tragic king who was to bear the weight of the whole world's sufferings was an almost symbolic figure. He was suffering humanity personified. At the climax of his career Sophocles proudly exerted all his powers to show him staggering under the tempest of ruin. He presented him at the very moment when he calls down curses on himself and in despair wishes to destroy his own life, as he has destroyed the light of his eyes with his own hand. And he snapped the thread, as he did in *Electra,* at that climactic moment when the character of the hero was tragically complete.

It is therefore highly significant that shortly before his death Sophocles took up the tale of Oedipus once again. It would be a mistake to expect the second drama to solve the problem of the first. If we were to interpret old Oedipus' passionate self-defence, his repeated claim that he acted unwittingly, as an answer to the question *Why?* we should be misunderstanding Sophocles, treating him, in fact, as if he were Euripides. Neither destiny nor Oedipus is acquitted or condemned. Yet in the later play the poet seems to look on life from a greater height. ***Oedipus at Colonus*** is a last meeting with the restless old wanderer, just before he reaches his goal. Despite misfortune and age, his noble character is unbroken, its impetuous violence still unquenched. By knowing his own strength and nobility, he has been helped to bear his own agony, the inseparable companion of his long years of exile, clinging to him until the last. There is no place for sentimental pity in this harsh portrait. Yet Oedipus' agony has made him venerable. The chorus feels its terror, but its grandeur even more; and the king of Athens receives the blind beggar as an honoured and illustrious guest. An oracle has said that Oedipus will find his final repose in Attica. But his death is veiled in mystery: he goes away, without a guide, into the grove, and is never seen again. Strange and incomprehensible as the road of suffering along which the gods have led him, is the miracle of release which he finds at the end. 'The gods who struck you down now lift you up.' No mortal eye may see the mystery: only he who is consecrated by suffering may take part in it. Hallowed by pain, he is in some mysterious way brought near to divinity: his agonies have set him apart from other men. Now he rests on the hill of Colonus, in the poet's own dear homeland, in the eternally green grove of the Kind Spirits where the nightingale sings from the branches. No human foot may tread in that place, but from it there goes out a blessing over all the land of Attica. (pp. 268-85)

> *Werner Jaeger, "Sophocles and the Tragic Character," in his* Paideia: The Ideals of Greek Culture, Archaic Greece, The Mind of Athens, Vol. I, *translated by Gilbert Highet, second edition, Oxford University Press, Inc., 1945, pp. 268-85.*

Kenneth Rexroth   (essay date 1965)

[*A prominent American poet, critic, and translator, Rexroth explored such varied subjects as jazz, mythology, world literature, and the Cabala. As a translator, he focused on Japanese and Chinese classics. Rexroth's writings include* The Classics Revisited. *In the following excerpt from that work, which was first published in 1965, he discusses the main characteristics of Sophocles' dramatic art, observing that the "men and women in the tragedies of Sophocles are human as ourselves but purer, simpler, more beautiful—the inhabitants of a kind of Utopia."*]

Sophocles' life might have been lived by his statue in the Louvre—so wise, so calm, so marmoreal. The same exemplary image could well have written his tragedies. Sophocles sang and danced as a boy in the choir of thanksgiving for Athens' naval victory over the Persians at Salamis. He was the intimate of Pericles and the friend of Phidias and Thucydides. Speakers in Plato's dialogues remembered him as an aged man. He died before the capture of Athens by Sparta. That was all there was: just the long lifetime of one man, from 495 to 406 B.C.

In Renaissance Florence, T'ang China, or Elizabethan En-

gland, he would have been too good to be true. His was a time never to occur again, and he was superlatively true to it. The unique artistic experience of Attic tragedy was contemporary with the glory of Athenian power, between the wars with Persia and Sparta. It lasted less than three generations; its perfect expression, only one. Aeschylus speaks at the opening of the greatest generation in the experience of man; Sophocles, for its brief years of mature achievement. To understand the Periclean Age requires an effort like no other. We find about us no standards or experiences that warrant a belief that life was ever like that. If the societies of other times and places are the measure of humanness, the Athenians for a moment were superhuman. The men and women in the tragedies of Sophocles are human as ourselves but purer, simpler, more beautiful—the inhabitants of a kind of Utopia. With all its agonies, this is life as it should be lived.

Sophocles' dramatic world, like Periclean Athens itself, is self-contained. Its ultimate sanctions are immanent, not transcendent. The mythic beings of Aeschylus are supernatural references for a new system of values, otherworldly midwives of a new social order. In Sophocles, this order is operating. The dilemmas of the natural community are not solved by reference to a supernatural one. Aeschylus' sacred democracy is personalized by Sophocles. For him a person is the most concrete thing there is. Tragedy arises out of the flux of fate and oracular doom, but so arises from the acts of free persons. The age-long puzzle of fate and free will is solved by the dialectic of dramatic moral action.

From the style of Aeschylus one could construct a rhetoric of majesty. Sophocles, a few years younger, has already learned to avoid all appurtenances of sublimity. His style is simple, almost plain. Its majesty owes little to symbol, metaphor. His figures of speech arise from the ordinary linkages of direct communication—the opposite of the vast disjunctions and incongruous juxtapositions of Aeschylus. This is the optimum human of Aristotle's ethics speaking. The virtues of his style are grandeur, grace, control, dynamic balance, proportion, dialectic organization, the equipoise of strength and beauty. Nothing is mean; all is golden. His characters may be infatuated, but never ignoble. Their calamities are their own fault, but that fault is never base. Their sins are arrogance, rashness, overconfidence, presumption, contempt, cruelty, anger, lust, carelessness—the family of pride. Not even the soldiers, slaves, and messengers are guilty of gluttony, sloth, cowardice, venality.

The plays themselves form the transcendent community whose natural product is value. They are the etherealizing mirror of contemporary Athens. It is because there was majesty in the audience that the Sophoclean chorus can so directly "bridge the footlights." The chorus is us. As the dialectic of dramatic speech and situation unwinds with that inevitable order which Sophocles learned from the Sophists and which they had learned by an analysis of the talk of Athens, the audience is transported into a purified region of conflicting hypertrophied motives. The audience is not "purged of pity and terror," but those emotions themselves of their dross—fear, of cowardice and pity, of sentimentality. Caught up in the catastrophe of tragedy, the audience learns compassion and dread. Unfortunately, it was not possible for the later Greeks, faced with the dilemmas of their deteriorating secular society, to transfigure their situation by joining a Sophoclean play, as one might join a church or monastery. So the nobility of Sophocles becomes for future ages the private consolation of the mature and never again functions as a social paradigm.

A humanistic religion like Sophocles' demands less and seems more impregnable than transcendentalism. It answers the mystery of evil with the qualities of art and with tone of character. Men suffer unjustly and learn little from suffering except to answer unanswerable questions with a kind of ultimate courtesy, an Occidental Confucianism that never pretends to solution. The ages following Sophocles have learned from him the definition of nobility as an essential aristocratic irony which forms the intellect and sensibility.

Oedipus the King, Oedipus at Colonus, Antigone are not a trilogy. Their chronological order is not that in which they were written. *Antigone* is the play of a mature man; *Oedipus the King* of a middle-aged one; *Oedipus at Colonus* of a very old man; yet they are, in spite of minor anachronisms, interdependent. It is as if Sophocles had held within his mind from the beginning a general structure for the Theban Cycle. The acts of Antigone and Creon in *Antigone* are made plausible by their behavior in *Oedipus at Colonus,* written fifty years later. The central play, *Oedipus the King,* is first in dramatic order. It may be the most perfect play ever written, and since it is the primary subject of Aristotle's *Poetics,* it has been the model for most tragedies since. It is by far the most dialectic of all Greek plays. One situation leads to another with an inexorable necessity. Yet each is created by the interplay of the faulty motives and rash choices of the protagonists.

Oedipus discovers that he has murdered his wife's husband; that he was a foundling; that he has murdered his father and married his mother in a series of dialogues more inevitable in motion than those of the Platonic Socrates evoking the realization of truth amongst his fellows. Realization comes in a succession of blows, and each blow reshapes the character of Oedipus as hammers form a white-hot ingot on the anvil.

In *Oedipus at Colonus,* there is hardly a plot at all—only the contrast of the aged, dying, blinded Oedipus with his daughters; his sons; his successor on the throne of Thebes; Theseus, his Athenian host; and the common people of the chorus. Each character's contrast illuminates him with a growing glory until, as he walks away to die in the sacred grove of Colonus, he has become a sacred being, a *daimon.*

This apotheosis is totally convincing, though Oedipus has lost not one of the faults that led him to disaster in the first place. He is still a rash and angry old, old man. He has learned only wisdom, wisdom that is indefinable, a quality of soul that comprehends suffering and evil, without understanding. Aeschylus justifies the ways of God to man by placing the mystery in God. Sophocles justifies the ways of man to man by placing the mystery in man.

Antigone, although written first, is a fitting conclusion. It is a conflict of people who have learned nothing and forgotten nothing. Creon has forbidden the burial of Polyneices, killed as a traitor attacking Thebes. Antigone defies him, buries her brother, and is condemned to death. Creon's son, Haemon, affianced to Antigone, kills himself; last, his mother, Eurydice, commits suicide. We are back with Aeschylus in the conflict of state and family, male and female. The drama is human, not mythic; the protagonists not wiser; experience has been in vain; the burnt children still love the fire; but the characters are real, each an end in himself, concrete with an absolute concreteness. (pp. 35-8)

> Kenneth Rexroth, "Sophocles, 'The Theban Plays'," in his Classics Revisited, *New Directions, 1986, pp. 35-8.*

Siegfried Melchinger   (essay date 1966)

[*A German scholar, critic, and editor, Melchinger wrote widely on the theater. His books include* Sophokles *(1966;* Sophocles, *1974),* Euripides *(1967;* Euripides, *1973), and* Anton Tschechow *(1968;* Anton Chekhov, *1972). In the following excerpt from the first-named work, he analyzes Sophocles' dramatic art with particular emphasis on Athenian stagecraft and the technical aspect of theatrical production. Recapitulating Sophocles' oeuvre, Melchinger asserts that the dramatist, "one of the greatest poets of all time, allowed a ray of hope to fall on the tragic picture of human existence."*]

The Theater

In March and April of each year the Athenians celebrated the Greater Dionysia—one of the festivals of Dionysus. . . . This god of ecstasy and metamorphosis, this god of the theater, was also the god of wine, and the Greater Dionysia was probably held in celebration of the grape harvest, and Athenians generously sampled the new wine that flowed freely from the casks. It was at such a festival that Thespis, the reputed founder of tragic drama, is said to have driven his cart into the city from a nearby vineyard and made his first appearance on the stage. Before this there had been choruses of singers and dancers, and it was from such a chorus, thought to have been clad in goatskins, that we get the word tragedy—*trag-odia,* or goat's song. But the precise origin and development of the theater is clothed in obscurity.

It is known that the tyrant Pisistratus raised the simple festival of a folk god to the status of a national festival (like all tyrants, he sought the support of the people in the struggle against the aristocracy). The traditional date given for Thespis' first stage appearance is 534 B.C., which coincides with the reign of the tyrant. The festival survived the tyrants. When democracy was restored, the plays that climaxed the Dionysia were so popular that the Athenians felt compelled to find a better location for them. So they built the "old temple" on the south side of the Acropolis at the edge of an extensive grove of olive trees. The foundations of this temple were discovered by archeologists not far from the "new temple," built much later.

A grassy hollow in the slope of the Acropolis created a

The Theatre of Dionysus in Athens.

natural amphitheater that could accommodate thousands. Later, terraced seats were cut into the soil, and even later still, wooden benches were provided. It was apparently when these benches collapsed during a performance of a play by Aeschylus that the decision was made to build a more permanent structure. But even then the seats were constructed of wood; the stone spectator area, as well as all the other ruined sections that we can see today, dates from the postclassical era. Indeed, we have only a very vague idea of what the theater must have looked like in classical times. (By classical, we refer to that period between 472 B.C., first performance of Aeschylus' *The Persians,* and 401 B.C., when Sophocles' ***Oedipus at Colonus*** was first staged.) Based largely on conjecture, drawn from existing ruins, the value of this mental image is disputable.

Accommodating between 14,000 and 17,000 spectators, the Theater of Dionysus was huge even by today's standards. Though it was by no means large enough to contain the entire population, it was nonetheless definitely the theater of the polis. The multitude must have swelled with pride in their city. Behind the seated spectators rose the Acropolis. The architectural wonders admired by present-day tourists were built during this classical era of tragedy: the Parthenon (probably dedicated shortly after the first

performance of ***Antigone***), the Propylaea, the Erechtheum, and the Temple of Victory. Statues of unmatched beauty adorned the citadel—Phidias was the general supervisor of the artists who worked on the Acropolis. If we wish to picture for ourselves the actors and choruses of classical tragedy, we need only look at the figures of the gods and heroes, at the bas-reliefs of the battles and the processions in the pediments and metopes of these buildings; we need only look at those completed at the same time on the Zeus temple in Olympia, or at the bronze statue of Poseidon, which was recently found in the sea off Cape Artemision.

With their backs to the Acropolis, the Athenians could look upon the sea, which they considered their own. (The site had been chosen for this very reason.) The land of Attica is bare and not very fertile, and from earliest times the sea therefore had an attraction for this busy people. Sea and trade soon became the source of the power and the wealth of the polis. Everyone had traveled by ship, many had served in the navy, and some owned ships that transported goods (mostly arms and tools) into the wide world and brought back a variety of imports. During the classical period all theaters had this view of the sea. In many of the extant tragedies the sea plays a significant role—the heroes' ships lie at anchor in the harbor, or the people wait for their return from journeys or wars across the seas.

To the left and right of the sea rise mountains and hills, for the most part bare and gray. But just behind the theater there were groves and gardens stretching down to the sea. The "treasure of the land," the leafy olive trees, glimmered like silver in the green of the landscape. And above this green and silver, above the blue of the sea shimmering away into the distance, was the great vault of the blue sky, out of which the sun shone brighter than anywhere else in the world. Even in the springtime the sun was so hot that by noon the plays, which were begun in the early morning, had to be interrupted. The audience retired to the shade of the trees or returned to the city for their midday meal. Later on, long colonnaded halls were erected, and here the people were able to rest and take refreshment. On returning to the amphitheater in the afternoon, Athenians again saw the irresistible silver and green superimposed on the interminable blue.

The quality of the light in Greece is unforgettable. People speak of its crystal clarity, but even this description is inaccurate, for there seems to be nothing between the viewer and what he is looking at. As one recedes from an object, it scarcely seems to diminish in size, and even at great distances the eye can distinguish fantastic details. There is no blurring of the images such as we see in impressionist paintings. Even from the top of the Acropolis one can see the actors in the theater distinctly; it is almost as if the clearly cut figures of the friezes had come to life and were walking about. No matter where one sat in the amphitheater, at either side or at the back, one had a perfect frontseat view. Mere numbers cannot express this nearness any more adequately than mathematics can convey the magnificence of the Parthenon, in which for optical reasons the columns are out of mathematical symmetry. With such clarity of light, the actors were more immediate, more close to the audience than they were on any other stage in the world.

This sense of proximity was not only visual, but stemmed from the acoustics of the ancient theaters, which were nothing short of miraculous. The secret of these wonderful acoustics has never been fully explained. From the very last row one can hear every word of a normal conversation held on the stage. The delicate sound of a flute, of a whisper, can be heard throughout the whole amphitheater. A fourth dimension seems to be added to the three dimensions of sight. It is as though ancient statues were speaking. There is a nearness and a fullness in the scene that is so extraordinary as to be hardly natural. But such rich and full unity of sound and sight only occurs when the audience listens and watches with extreme concentration, totally cutting off all other sounds and sights. With complete silence and a complete lack of distraction, the play can begin.

It was not only the play to which the audience felt so closely linked. They also felt close to each other. Looking down onto the stage one was conscious of the many thousands of heads; since the plays took place in daylight, one was always aware that a performance was being given. Nobody could fall into a trance and confuse the action on the stage with reality. And yet the audience was always prepared to identify with the feelings, thoughts, and passions expressed before them; they were always prepared to empathize.

Since they almost always knew the outcome of the play, the spectators were more interested in *how* everything was done than in *what* was done. They were preoccupied with how the dramatist treated his material and how it was portrayed on the stage. Indeed, they saw the material and its presentation almost as one, since the dramatist himself usually directed his play and, in the early classical period, acted in it as well. We find no stage directions in the texts of extant plays.

Only with the actual production did the play reach its finished form. The dramatists considered music and dance as elements in their plays, and gave as much thought to them as to the mime of the actors. Language was only a part of a grand unified work of art. The different elements did not merge into one; they were not drowned in a Wagnerian sea of music. Instead, the plays resembled those of the great Asiatic theaters. The dramatist's mastery was demonstrated by the way he was able to combine the various elements, by the originality with which he composed his work.

The musical sections of the work—the orchestra with chorus, the complex choreography—were distinctly and logically separated from the spoken section. As there was no curtain, entrances and exits were an important part of the production. The critical audience concentrated on the structure of the play, since the action was well known to them, and the dramatists did their best to introduce novelties. This was often done by means of short scenes and the use of processions. The visual spectacle was every bit as important as the spoken word. The Greek word *théatron,* which was originally used simply for the spectator area, actually means "seeing place."

One further reason the audience was so interested in how the events were presented was that their critical judgement of the play was an important element of the occasion. The festival was really a contest (*agón*). The dramatists submitted their plays, and a jury selected certain of them for performance. It was the audience, however, that awarded the prizes. There were, of course, official critics, but their task was to ascertain the effect on the audience. On each of three days of the festival, a given dramatist would be represented by three plays, followed by a farcical epilogue in the form of a satyr play. The term "satyr play" is derived from the chorus of goat-footed satyrs in shaggy skins who took possession of the stage when the tragedians had left it. There are fragments of a satyr play by Sophocles extant, a sort of joke predominantly in dance form, entitled **The Trackers.**

Initially the three plays were in the form of a trilogy. Only one such example is extant: Aeschylus' *Oresteia*. Though Sophocles used this as a model, his three plays treated three different subjects and three different heroes, and were followed by the satyr play. The longest of the three plays was presented first, beginning at about eight in the morning and lasting about two and a half hours. The other two plays were about two hours. They were given in the afternoon with a short interval between them. Torches were probably lighted during the satyr play, and often during the final scenes of the preceding play.

After the third day, first-, second-, and third-place prizes were awarded. The names of the prize winners were engraved on marble tablets, some of which still exist today. Sophocles won the first prize on eighteen occasions. But his greatest play, **Oedipus the King**—perhaps the greatest tragedy of all time—was never popular with an audience. Of all the plays by Sophocles, none ends with quite such an air of hopelessness, none moves quite so inexorably toward its tragic conclusion.

One astonishing clause in the rules for the contest was that each author was compelled to submit totally new plays. None of the tragic writers ever saw a play of his performed a second time in the Theater of Dionysus. The new productions of Aeschylus' plays were allowed only after his death, and then, of course, they were not presented for competition.

The texts of prize-winning plays were recorded by the state; however, these plays were "revived" only by the-aters in other cities. Delegations from allied states and envoys from foreign powers always attended the festivals and shared the front rows of the theater with the archons, or holders of high office. But the imposing armchairs, which can still be seen in the Theater of Dionysus, are from a later date. It goes without saying that during the classical period no seat could be superior to another.

Although the costs of a production were always borne by a rich citizen of the city, the *choragús,* there was an admission charge. Pericles introduced a law whereby lower income groups were allowed free admission. The tokens given out for this purpose represent one of the earliest examples of a state subsidy for the theater.

The Chorus

Without doubt, it is the chorus that most obviously distinguishes classical tragedy from contemporary theater. (Our opera is more akin to classical tragedy than is modern drama. Indeed, opera emulates tragedy in its use of the chorus and in other respects, too.) Modern drama, with its emphasis on the spoken word, is a relatively late development. Even comedy, which developed in Athens somewhat later than the tragedy and had its own festival, used the chorus in its classical form, represented by Aristophanes.

It is true that the chorus gradually lost its initial importance. Sophocles stands more or less in the middle of this development. In his plays the chorus still has powers of expression, but it is usually shorter and less lyrical than in Aeschylus' dramas, for example. Euripides pushed the chorus further and further into the background, and the trend that led to Menander's comedies, which are mostly spoken—and spoken, moreover, by single voices—began to appear in outline.

The chorus was one of the original elements in the composition of the tragic "total theater." It remained in existence as an independent genre, separate from the theater. Great poets and musicians wrote in this form, and there were concert halls for choral presentations, such as the Odeon near the Dionysian Theater. Like tragedy, this form was included among the contests of the Greater Dionysia.

Originally, the chorus probably consisted of fifty singers standing in a circle in the midst of the audience. This circle remained the true center of the Theater of Dionysus, and is probably a fairly true indication of its original form. This central area is known as the orchestra and is almost enclosed by the amphitheater. "Drama" (meaning "action" in Greek) came into being when one of the singers stepped before the rest of the chorus as a leader or soloist in order to speak to them or answer their questions. The Greek word for actor really means "responder."

This solo voice has behind it a tradition that goes back to the reciter, or rhapsodist of the Homeric epic; it is also the source of the great art of lyric poetry (that of Sappho, for example). We should not equate the introduction of a solo voice with the origin of dialogue any more than we should consider the chorus as purely musical (as it is in our opera, for example). The soloist was from the very beginning both singer and speaker, and the chorus was never so "musical" that every single word could not be clearly distinguished.

There was one further element essential to the chorus as we find it in the tragedy. This element seems to have been of decisive importance, for from it, as we have seen, came the word tragedy itself. It is the dance performed in costume and masks. These dances were executed only by the performers, but there were, in addition, round dances in which the audience participated. Older than the masked dances, they continued to be performed after the newer form developed.

But it was only in the masked dances—and this quite early—that the mimical elements of transformation developed along two lines: sudden terror and jubilation, the demonic and the farcical. Both elements have become integral parts of the Greek theater. The fear that Aeschylus' demonic Erinyes inspired in the audience is documented. In the satyr play, however, the aim was to complement the tragedies by providing pure delight. (They had a function similar to that of the *kyogen* interludes in the Noh theater, and the intermezzos in the baroque theater.)

Even before the development of tragedy, mime had given rise to a separate theatrical form: the *mímos.* Jesters traveled through the country giving performances at the fairs and in the marketplaces. They performed conjuring tricks, played the buffoon, satirized current events, and travestied those in power. Writing at the same time as Aeschylus and Sophocles, two poets of the *mímos* form achieved great fame: Epicharmus and Sophron.

We know little about them, but we can say that neither the satyr play nor the comedy could have developed as they did without the influence of the mime. The genre persisted to the very end of classical Greece, and toward the close of the era even eclipsed the other forms of theater. The great mimes were as celebrated as modern film stars.

All this played its part in the performance that took place

on the circular song and dance area in the orchestra, where the chorus held sway. The musicians probably sat here; though few in number, owing to the incredible acoustics, they were as effective as a modern orchestra. . . . [The] musical theory of the ancients was based on the medical and scientific teaching of the effects of music. Each instrument was thought to have a particular emotional effect—the flute created delight, the lyre solemnity, as percussion instruments beat out the rhythm. But we have little idea of how this music actually sounded.

In Sophocles' tragedies there are two main types of choral song: the primary song and the antiphonal song. The primary song was sung by the members of the chorus in accompaniment to rhythmical dance steps. The choreography varied in mood from the restrained to the excited and even orgiastic.

It has been established that Sophocles raised the number of singers in the chorus from twelve to fifteen. This may point to the growing artistic interest in symmetry, since fifteen allows for an arrangement of two rows of seven and a chorus leader who may often have functioned as a solo voice in the dialogue sections. Moreover, seven was the principal of the mystical numbers (in which Pythagoras himself believed). In any case, we may be sure that the Greeks, for whom proportion played such an important role, were aware of the symmetrical and proportional possibilities of the numbers involved.

Sophocles' chorus always has a dramatic function, and it often interrupts the action. It usually has a definite and clearly defined character. Sometimes it represents the council of elders—the *Gerousía* of the early Greek states—voicing the opinion of the people and urging caution. Sometimes the chorus is composed of young girls, women, and soldiers and simply represents the people (the *polloî*), those who think and speak on a level different from that of the hero. Sophocles is the most objective of the tragic poets. We never hear his opinion through the individual speeches, but we sense it from the meaning behind the whole tragedy.

The chorus is neither the voice of the audience nor that of the dramatist. Psychologically it stands between the audience and the hero, a fact symbolically represented by its physical position in the orchestra. One of its main functions is to convey to the audience by means of emotional music the moods of the dramatic situation. In the same way, the often profound thoughts embedded in the words of the chorus are transmitted to the spectators for reflection. But the audience is never obliged by suggestion or persuasion simply to accept what is put before it. The chorus never formulates what the audience should think but simply sets the thought processes in motion—it engages the sympathy of the spectators.

In a similar fashion, the chorus prepares the audience for what is about to take place. A premonition of catastrophe or jubilation at the approach of some happy event is contained in the song or can be detected in the movements of the dance. At times the chorus serves to suspend time or to make it move faster.

Images and myths are conjured up as metaphors for what

is felt and thought—and feelings and thoughts are almost always linked. The fifteen members of the chorus did not express themselves as one unit, as our modern opera choruses do, nor did they move in the identical steps of a well-rehearsed corps de ballet. Each member had to allow the feeling or thought to develop spontaneously within him. He then bodily expressed it in what seemed to him to be a proper form. (We never come across the word "we" in the chorus; it is always "I.") Accordingly, the director or choreographer gave only the broadest outline of what he required from the chorus. To some extent he was able to let things take their course because the songs and dances were all based on traditional models and received the particular slant necessary only within the context of the dramatic situation.

Whether they expressed grief or joy, all gestures were based on those the individual might have used in real life. The director simply combined the varied, but basically similar actions. The effect must have been like that conveyed by the Parthenon friezes in which the men, women, and children representing the people all have individual traits and yet are still part of a rhythmically proportioned whole. The choral song was usually divided into sections, each containing a strophe and an antistrophe. Sophocles' great art as a poet can be seen from the way he refused to let the strophic form determine his content. He arranged for the content to rise to a climax that demands the strongest and clearest expression before a precipitous drop is introduced. This is precisely how the modern poet deals with the traditional forms he has inherited.

In spite of innovations, the choral song retained an archaic character right up to the last classical tragedies. It was written in the Doric dialect—unfamiliar to the Athenian ear and was therefore immediately distinguishable from the rest of the text by its timbre alone. The dialogue was in the Attic dialect and sounded more or less like normal conversation, though in metrical form. The choral song was clearly intended to be raised above everyday language.

As tragedy developed further and further away from its origins, the chorus too diminished in importance. But Sophocles was conscious of the fact that this dramatic device could be, and should be, an essential element of tragedy. For the traditional is always part of the present; the past never completely dies out, and not everything that is old is doomed to pass into obscurity. In Sophocles' day, Homer was still very much part of the present and Athens was filled with old statues and temples. The people still made pilgrimages to the graves of dear and illustrious ancestors in the cemetery just outside the city. The closer to his contemporaries the poet tried to bring the old myths, the more clearly he wished to demonstrate that the theater and tragedy could be relevant to contemporary life only so long as the people recognized the importance of preserving the beauty of the past. It was on a par with continuing to worship Apollo at Delphi, with congregating for the Panhellenic Games at Olympia.

Compared with those of Aeschylus, Sophocles' tragedies represent a tremendous innovation without detracting from the earlier dramatist's achievement. Such innovation shows only one thing; that the traditional, the old, only lives on if it is rejuvenated. Sophocles did not dispense with the old and set up something new in its place. He simply gave new form to what already existed. We know that this was the way his thoughts ran; we know, too, that he foresaw a time when the old would no longer have the same meaning for people that it did for him. The chorus of the Old Men of Thebes prophesies this time in *Oedipus the King:*

> If all this perishes, if such deeds are held in
>   honor,
> Why then should I honor the gods in song and
>   dance?
> —The gods are fading away.

The traditional characteristics of the choral song—which disappear when the chorus joins in the dialogue (in Attic dialect), or takes up a dramatic function—have given rise to the opinion, unfortunately still current today, that tragedy not only had its origin in cult, but is by its very nature cultic and must therefore be played in a ritualistic manner.

Obviously, the cultic was one of the elements contributing toward the rise of tragedy, which originated as part of the Dionysia. But this was only *one* of many contributory factors. Cult and theater had existed side by side from very early times and continued to do so in the classical age. The cult made use of theatrical elements, and the theater absorbed aspects of the cult.

Where cult and theater coincide is in the presentation of events by means of actors, and it is precisely here that we are able to make a clear distinction between them. The cultic was invariable.

An integral part of the ritual of the Eleusinian mysteries were the presentations of sacred episodes. They were always identical in content, just as the central episodes in the mystery plays of medieval times were always identical. Each performance might vary slightly in the form of presentation and in minor details (just as the music changes from one composer's mass to another's), but the events themselves remained invariable. Since the mystery was always the same it was well known to everyone from beginning to end. The events were sacred, and their presentation fixed by canon. The same cannot be said of tragedy.

We have already pointed out that the earliest tragedy we possess, Aeschylus' *The Persians,* treats of a contemporary event; the defeat of the Persians at Salamis. It is far removed from cultic sanctity if only because the setting of the play is among the Persians and their gods. There were many similar plays in earlier times. The stories of those plays based on the myths were certainly well known to the audience, but the theatergoers were not particularly interested in the mythological content. Their interest lay in the new presentation and new interpretation given the story by the dramatist, whose intention was to move them so that this new rendering of the old seemed a representation of their own lives.

There was no question of cult here. The audience was not exhorted to offer up pious prayers but to think. Each of Sophocles' tragedies leads the spectator to a slowly dawning new insight. If the tragedies given at the Dionysian festival had not all possessed some kind of novel value that would appeal to the critical faculties of the audience, there could have been no contest. Who can critically appraise a ritual?

Because there is much talk of the gods in Sophocles, his work has often been termed "religious theater." But if this were so, Goethe's *Faust* would also be a religious play. One might just as well call Sophocles' plays political theater, for they are as much concerned with the polis as with the gods. In point of fact, his tragedies are both religious and political, but, as we shall see, even this description does not convey their essence.

The Stage

Thespis, who is said to have invented dialogue when he stepped out of the chorus as soloist, may well have been responsible for a second innovation on the Greek stage. When performances were given in market-places, there was a need for a raised platform, so that the soloist could be seen over the heads of the chorus. It is quite possible that Thespis' cart served as an impromptu stage.

The Greek word for stage, *skené,* really means "tent." A tent may have been put up alongside or behind the cart to serve as a dressing room or storage area. Because of the word's meaning it was long assumed that the Theater of Dionysus originally had some sort of tentlike stage area, which continued to be called the *skené* when the structure later became more permanent. This idea is generally discredited today. One can easily see that the "tent" could have been erected *behind* the stage, thus remaining hidden from the audience. We can still see today how steeply the grove slopes down behind the stage, and it is generally accepted that any dressing rooms or storerooms were situated here during the days of classical drama.

It is almost certain that the stage was one or two steps higher than the orchestra. The positioning of this stage as a sort of tangent to the circular orchestra area resulted in two "wings" stretching out on either side. These wings had steps running the full length. This arrangement of the stage into the *skené* with its two *paraskénia,* or side wings, is by no means absolutely certain, but it seems more than probable.

At a relatively early time supporting walls must have been built at each end of the amphitheater's terraced seats. The gaps between these walls and each end of the stage was probably utilized as an entrance for all those actors who did not enter from the middle of the stage. The chorus, above all, must have entered through this aperture. The opening song of the chorus took its name from the Greek word for corridor: *párodos.*

Originally the orchestra was simply a circle stamped out in the earth. Later separated from the audience by a ditch into which rain could drain, it was paved with flagstones. (The marble paving that can be seen today dates from a later period.) The stage developed along similar lines. It was originally of wood. Just exactly when it was paved with breccia stone is a matter of some dispute, but it was probably before the end of the classical era.

In the fourth century, a marble pavement was laid over the stone foundation, and in the same period the stonework of the terraces was completed. A palacelike stone facade was constructed for the *skené,* and henceforth utilized in all plays. This facade had a large central portal and smaller portals in the two projecting side wings. If there had ever been a similar structure during the classical era, it was probably made of wood and served as a decoration that could be removed or changed whenever a particular play demanded it. That this must have been true may be seen from the last two plays by Sophocles, which both demand a *skené* with a particular view: *Philoctetes* calls for a cave in some rocks, and *Oedipus at Colonus* for an olive grove.

It is clear, therefore, that some sort of removable decor, some kind of scene change, was commonly used for tragedies in the classical era. The scenic devices were probably more practical and more realistic than is commonly supposed. Sophocles' earliest play, *Ajax,* requires an empty stage with a tent. There is no doubt that this was a commander's tent, which was moved to one side (probably on rollers) during the performance, for the last act is set in an open field "near the sea." *Antigone, Oedipus the King,* and *Electra* probably all made use of a palacelike facade and the *paraskénia,* a set that had been popular at least since Aeschylus' *Oresteía.* In *The Women of Trachis,* Heracles' house was simpler—he was an exile—and probably lacked the projecting side wings.

Documents are available to us testifying that the great artists of the day cooperated in the design of the sets. It is said that Sophocles greatly encouraged the use of painted scenery, and wooden screens were no doubt used for this purpose. The rocky cave of Philoctetes was probably done in this way, or the rock to which Prometheus was secured in Aeschylus' *Prometheus Bound.*

Painting was also used to depict rocks, and the palacelike facade was also decorated in this way. (We should note that the facade was really a very solid affair: people seated in the higher seats at the back of the amphitheater could look down on the roof.) *Oedipus at Colonus,* Sophocles' last play, seems to show a reversion to an earlier lack of decor. The stage was as empty as in the earliest plays by Aeschylus. The only decoration was one of nature's: the grove behind the *skené,* into which the hero vanished so mysteriously.

The tragic dramatists had only one spotlight—the sun. But they certainly knew how to use it. Its passage across the heavens played a large role in those plays given in the mornings, and those long drawn-out shadows that fell across the theater in the evenings were actually part of the dramatist's plans. We must also consider the effect of the sunlight when it shone toward the audience from behind the stage. In *Oedipus the King,* written for morning performance, the sun would have been directly behind the stage when the blinded Oedipus stepped from the door of the palace; the facade, like the figure of the hero himself, would have been in the shadow, but the whole scene would have an aura of light around it.

Aeschylus is thought to have favored mechanical stage devices, whereas Sophocles had little use for them. Some of Aeschylus' plays are unthinkable without the high cranes that lowered the gods to the stage. Athena in Sophocles' *Ajax* may well have stood next to the mortals on the stage, her invisibility being demonstrated by having the actors behave as if she were not there. But provision was made for divine visitations by providing a raised platform, the *theologeíon,* or the "gods' speaking place." It is therefore possible that the actor playing Athena mounted some stairs behind the tent decor in order to appear on the *theologeíon.* At the end of *Philoctetes* Heracles appears as a god: he probably stood on the *theologeíon* amid the jagged points of the rocks.

Another mechanical device, known as the *eccýclema,* was a small, square platform that could be pushed onto the open stage of rollers from the midst of the scenic structures. Sophocles probably used this device only in his earlier plays. The *eccýclema* was normally used to convey dead bodies out into the center of the stage after a battle, or some other bloody event, had taken place. By means of this contrivance, in *Ajax,* the bloodspattered but triumphant hero was brought onto the stage, surrounded by the dead cattle he had slaughtered in the mistaken idea that they were his enemies.

Later Sophocles dispensed with the use of the *eccýclema,* but he did not spare his audience such gruesome sights. Instead, he simply made them part of the dramatic action. In *Antigone,* for example, Creon carries his son, who has just committed suicide, onto the stage. In *The Women of Trachis,* Heracles, racked by dreadful pain because of the poison smeared on his robe, throws off all covering in order to reveal to the bystanders (and the audience) his poison-pitted body. In *Electra,* Orestes, after he has killed Clytemnestra, forces Aegisthus, her lover and her accomplice in the murder of Agamemnon, to lift the shroud and view the bloody corpse. Theater at this time shows a predilection for such powerful and unforgettable spectacles set against a background of rather bare and bleak scenery.

The Actors

These spectacles and the scenery depended, of course, on actors whose behavior was lifelike rather than ritualistic. But, one may well ask, how can the use of mask be reconciled with the notion of living people? It is, in fact, precisely this point that has given rise to a fundamental misunderstanding of the nature of Greek theater.

One usually thinks of the mask as being similar to those we often see used in modern productions of classical plays: made of metal or some such inflexible material; the hair a mere imitation, as rigidly fixed as the rest of the mask; the mouth torn open in a suitably tragic expression. Such masks have, of course, become the symbol of the theater. But, in dealing with Aeschylus, Sophocles, and Euripides we must forget this stereotyped mask. It was not introduced until much later, when tragedy itself had become a rigidly fixed and archaic form in which the characters were as lifeless as the masks themselves.

It is these later masks that are seen in museums, for not a single genuine mask from classical times has survived. The masks used in the early performance of classical tragedy were made of perishable material. Soft enough to be drawn over the face, they had wigs of real hair firmly fixed to them. The mask was painted—Aeschylus is said to have introduced this custom, the intention being to make the mask more natural. (Tradition has it that Thespis had worn white makeup; for this reason the fabric of the mask was originally left white.)

The function of the mask was to hide the actor's own features and substitute those suited to the role he was to play. But underneath the painted mask, one could still detect a distinctly human face. (We may draw a parallel here between the actors' masks and the figures of the gods and mortals sculpted by Phidias and his school: underlying the particular quality identifying the character or god, there was an individual human quality.) The "alienating" effect of the mask was only such as was required by the verse which was clearly more elevated than everyday language.

The mask, then, was not ritualistic, it was not a mere archaism, and it did not strive for idealization. Its function was a heightening of effect. By obscuring the features of the actor's own face, the mask enabled the actor to "grow into" the character represented by the mask and to become this character unequivocally and unmistakably. The clearcut delineation of character facilitated by the mask was an absolute necessity for one very practical reason. The thousands of spectators all had to be able to recognize clearly, even from the very back row, the role being portrayed.

The function of these clearly delineated masks becomes even more obvious when we realize that certain roles required several masks. Antigone, for example, had a second mask that she wore as she was led off to her underground prison. Its hair was cropped short. And when Oedipus returned from the palace after having blinded himself, he wore a mask in which two black holes had been burned, and drops of blood could be seen running down the cheeks.

Like the metal masks, the *cothurnus* was also a later invention. It was a kind of shoe reaching as high as the calf, and it had a sole eight inches or more thick. Wearing this shoe, the actor appeared larger than life. The significance of the *cothurnus* has also been misinterpreted. From contemporary vase paintings we can see that the shoes worn by actors during the classical period were scarcely raised at all. Where the sole had been adapted, it is no thicker than the soles of the shoes worn by modern actors who want to appear somewhat taller. It is possible that only those actors playing heroes wore such slightly raised shoes, since they were meant to appear taller than the people in the chorus or the actors of minor roles; however, it seems more likely that the heroes were simply played by actors who were actually somewhat taller.

Just as the mask had an intensifying effect, so also did the costumes of the principal characters raise them above the everyday. But here, too, Sophocles was responsible for a change of emphasis; costuming became dramatically determined and was used as a means of characterization. We therefore find Clytemnestra, the queen, dressing her daughter Electra as a slave. The fallen or damned heroes present a lamentable picture because of what they wear. Philoctetes, cast away on Lemnos because of the stench

from the wound in his foot, is covered with filthy rags. Oedipus, worn by his long years of pilgrimage and deprivation, is likewise in rags in **Oedipus at Colonus.** Theseus, on the other hand, resplendent in the hero's costume, is the very epitome of a ruler.

As can be seen in the vase paintings, costume was also important in communicating character and fate. Queens, for example, appeared in purple robes embroidered with gold and silver trappings of royalty.

Stage properties were of great importance: weapons above all, but also sacrificial offerings, ribbons and garlands, the royal scepter (a long staff), the bent staff of the seer or that of the wanderer. The wanderer was immediately recognized by his staff and wide-brimmed sun hat. He traditionally entered from the right, for the sea, which represented distant regions for the audience, lay to the right of the theater. An entry from the left signified that the character was arriving from the city, for that was, indeed, where Athens lay. Part of the audience could see anyone entering from this side for some distance, so it was intentionally arranged for the chorus to walk in a procession when making its entrances and exits. Moreover, it was not only the chorus that entered as a procession. There were in all plays larger and smaller processions consisting of major characters with supernumeraries—bodyguards, servants and maids, military escorts (the Greek term *pompé* survives in our own word "pomp").

The number of soloists was limited. Traditionally, there had been only one but Aeschylus had added a second. When Sophocles added yet a third, Aeschylus followed suit. Sophocles' later plays call for four actors, as do the dramas of Euripides. Though the number of actors remained at four, this did not mean that the number of characters was also limited to four. By changing their costumes or masks the actors were able to play other roles in the same play. Indeed, not even the main character was exempted from the duty of playing other roles. The actor who played the part of Antigone, for example, took over the role of Tiresias after Antigone's death. (We [know] that female roles were played by male actors, as was the case in Shakespeare's time and as is still done in the Japanese *Noh* theater.)

The use of stereotyped characters by dramatists began fairly early in Greece, just as it did in other national dramas whose development we can trace. It was paralleled by the introduction of stereotyped masks, costumes, and even a certain way of acting particular roles. Even in classical Greek tragedy we can detect the type underlying the character, but the type always takes on personal traits and becomes a definite individual marked by his fate.

In Sophocles, for example, there is not a single main character who does not show such human, individual qualities. Neither Antigone, nor Oedipus, nor Philoctetes is a mere type. But since we can usually distinguish the type behind the individual, it is helpful to examine the various types. We shall deal first with those directly concerned in the unfolding of the tragedy, and then with those lesser characters who are not directly concerned.

The "old man" is usually portrayed with a white wig, a

long robe, and a staff on which he supports himself. Tiresias has the attributes of the seer—a crooked staff and a garland—in both *Antigone* and *Oedipus the King.* In *Oedipus at Colonus,* Creon, the aging king of Thebes, wears the long, decorated robe of a monarch, and carries a scepter and a sword.

The "mature man" is usually bearded and still strong, very much like the Poseidon statue of Artemision. In time of war he carries a sword and wears a short tunic with thorax (or breastplate), greaves, braces, and helmet. Odysseus and the Atridae in *Ajax* were probably dressed in this way, as were Heracles in *The Women of Trachis,* Aegisthus in *Electra,* Odysseus in *Philoctetes,* and Theseus in *Oedipus at Colonus.* Oedipus himself, in *Oedipus at Colonus,* represents this type fallen on hard times—in beggar's garb, haggard, and fatally ill.

The "thirty-or forty-year-old man" is usually the beardless, the heroic type; as king he wears a suitably long robe and a crown; he carries a scepter. In war-time this type also wears a short tunic with thorax, greaves, braces, and helmet, and he carries a sword. Ajax and Oedipus as kings are examples of this type. Philoctetes is one of this type in decline—sick and in rags, he nevertheless has the bow of Heracles.

The "young man," between sixteen and twenty-five, is usually clad in a sort of tunic and carries a sword. Examples are: Teucer in *Ajax,* Haemon in *Antigone,* Hyllus in *The Women of Trachis,* Orestes and Pylades in *Electra,* Neoptolemus in *Philoctetes,* and Polynices in *Oedipus at Colonus.*

The "older woman," about fifty, wears a long robe. As a queen, she wears a splendidly decorated dress, with a kind of wrap over this. In addition she wears jewelry and a crown. Eurydice in *Antigone,* Jocasta in *Oedipus the King,* Deianira in *The Women of Trachis,* and Clytemnestra in *Electra* are examples of this type.

The "young lady," unmarried and in her twenties, appears in only one Sophocles play: Electra is dressed in a maidservant's garb and wears a mask showing careworn features.

The "mother" also appears but once in Sophocles, and then in the plain dress of a slave: Tecmessa in *Ajax.*

The "girl," under twenty, wears a long, sleeveless, bright-colored robe. Antigone and Ismene are such characters. In *Antigone* they are princesses with the attributes of royalty. In *Oedipus at Colonus,* Antigone is clothed in the tattered rags of a beggar girl, while Ismene wears the garb of a wanderer with the usual wide-brimmed hat. Another example of this type is Chrysothemis in *Electra;* the role of the mysterious and beautiful—and silent—Iole in *The Women of Trachis* also conforms to this pattern.

The types drawn from the ranks of the ordinary people have been given such individuality by Sophocles that they are scarcely recognizable as types any longer. The herald in *The Women of Trachis* is an officer with military bearing; he is virile, yet discreet. The guard in *Antigone,* who reappears at one point as the messenger, is full of confidence; he is a soldier and an intelligent representative of the people. The herdman and the Corinthian messenger

in *Oedipus the King* are both old men, but of totally different characters. The herdsman is somewhat timid, the messenger naively self-assured.

The servant in *Electra* who had been responsible for the upbringing of Orestes is an old man; intelligent and jolly, he is still somewhat conscious of his former position as instructor, and a little bit of a gossip. In *Philoctetes,* there is a soldier or sailor who, disguised as a shipowner, shows himself to be capable, eloquent, and intelligent. Then there are a few types who are a little less colorful, a little less convincing as individuals. Their significance as characters is exhausted once they have said their piece and left the stage. There are the messengers (soldiers or servants, for the most part) in *Ajax, Oedipus the King,* and *Oedipus at Colonus* and the priest in *Oedipus the King.* In all the extant plays there is but one female part drawn from the people. It is that of the nurse in *The Women of Trachis.* This is a brilliant role. She is very old; cleverer than many of the nobles, she is entrusted with the shattering news of the death of her mistress.

In Aeschylus' tragedies the hero is either the mature type (Agamemnon) or the young man (Orestes). In Sophocles' dramas, however, the picture is incomparably richer, since the types, as we have seen, are greater in number and more varied in character.

Ajax is nearest to the old man type. But Heracles, modeled on the hero in his fifties, has a definite stamp of his own. Antigone, the first female protagonist we know of, must have been a tremendous gamble: a young girl as the heroine! The ideal of heroic bravery, of the active hero, such as is incorporated in Ajax and Heracles, is transcended in Oedipus as king, for he is not only courageous but also has great intellectual stature and is a ruling monarch. Electra as a heroine is so complex a figure that she can be explained only in conjunction with Orestes.

Philoctetes, like some figures in Euripides' tragedies, represents the hero in decline. Still in his thirties, he is already haggard. True, he still bears the bow of Heracles and carries himself as a hero. The decline shown in Philoctetes is even greater in Oedipus, fallen in *Oedipus at Colonus* from his former glory. Though scarcely fifty, he looks upon himself as an old man, a living corpse, and staggers around on the arm of his daughter. But though he is far removed from his former glory, his spirit remains unbroken; his conduct is that of a great hero.

How much of this was cult or ritual? The traditional type could be distinguished behind the character, but mask, costume, and theatrical appearance in general combined to show the character of great individuals, as did the quality of the acting.

What the mask hid or could not express was conveyed by a gesture, an actor's gait or movement. This was intended to appear spontaneous, even though it was carefully rehearsed. We can only imagine the mimic expression from the words, and we can only get a vague idea of the acting from pictorial art, where the expression shown is not only motionless but also adapted to the overall composition of the picture.

Sophocles' text leaves no doubt that excitement was conveyed spontaneously by actions and gestures and that the actor had to concentrate on achieving this excitement by means of his imagination. Sudden fear, growing anxiety, the change from doubt to certainty, and outbreak of joy, the plunging to the depths of despair, raging anger, horror and lamentation—all this had to be acted out convincingly. The goal every dramatist aimed at was excitement. This was a theater of passion.

It has already been pointed out that there were conventional gestures of lamentation and joy. In the dramatic situations of Sophocles' dramas, emotional gestures may have been ritualized, but starting from the conventionally automatic the actor was able to direct his own emotions into the special situation of the character being depicted. The gesture developed from the conventional into the particular and individual. Since no stage directions were written in the text, we can only determine how things were by looking closely at the text itself. We shall accordingly examine the types of spoken verses in order to ascertain just how the actor must have played his particular role.

The mode of expression of tragedy was the dialogue, which consisted of speech and counterspeech. We shall deal first of all with the speech. In Sophocles' plays this is never a mere showpiece tirade, never rhetoric for rhetoric's sake. On the one occasion where we do find more rhetoric (in the report of Orestes' "death" in *Electra*), the speaker is being deliberately deceptive. The rhetorical is, however, an important element in tragedy and is usually included in the drama as a report (by a messenger, for example), declaration, accusation, or defense. The report has a definite structure, invariably beginning, in the case of Sophocles, with the expression of the emotion or mood of the messenger. What he says is "pathetic" in the true sense of the word, for he reports not so much as if he has merely witnessed everything, but as if he has actually experienced it. And when he has given his account, he concludes by repeating both the emotion and the report in the form of a reflection. This reflection, also pathetic in tone, requires a response.

Declarations are constructed in a similar way. An edict will be given in the language of the law, as an expression of a dominant will. The speaker then deals with the reasons behind, and the consequences of, the edict. He spares himself no effort, turns from one person to another commandingly or threateningly, and works himself up into such a passion that a reaction must ensure, whether it be only a soft murmuring from the chorus or an embarrassed silence.

The majority of the longer speeches are written in the style of parliamentary debate or legal process. Arguments are introduced and directed toward the rational proof of a thesis with which the speaker confronts both the characters on the stage and the audience. Such speeches are always directed toward the counterspeech. They are dialectic, so that we find the forensic speech of the constitutional state pitted against the will of the people as it emerges in a democracy. The speeches often tend toward the theoretical and touch upon the political, the moral, the philosophic

or the theological. Usually these addresses have gnomic endings, pithy summarizing sentences.

Sophocles never allows a dramatic incident to stand in total isolation. By virtue of its dialectic interpretation, every single aspect of the plot, every event, is very much a part of the world in which the characters live, whether it be the world represented on the stage or the contemporary world of the audience—for the dramatist was always conscious of writing for his time. Why, after all, should a play be performed unless it bore some relevance to the lives of the people watching it?

Whenever the chorus gave its opinion after a great speech or counterspeech (it did so with what we would consider uncomfortable directness), and summed up by saying that both sides had argued well, it was merely reflecting that objectivity which Sophocles considered essential to any dramatist. If the hero's opponents were not supplied with telling counterarguments which made sense to his partners on the stage, the chorus, and the audience, then the hero's arguments, too, would be considered worthless and without weight.

As was true in Aeschylus' dramas, the speech and counterspeech in Sophocles' tragedies were developed by logical steps until two equally justified views or attitudes are seen to be quite irreconcilably opposed. At such a point the tragic bind is revealed as a condition of human existence. The hero then stands before a choice which will plunge him into guilt no matter what his decision. It is an essential characteristic of the hero that he stands by his decision, even though he may be deserted or even damned by the gods.

By means of dramatic dialogue the dialectic shatters the contrasts and drives them to extremes. The way of doing this is inherent in the nature of the dialogue. Sophocles uses this method as one possibility of expressing a discussion between two—and in the later dramas, three—persons in a manner befitting the compelling truth of the situation and characters.

The long speeches and counterspeeches are often summarized in shorter sections of about ten lines each. But these sections can also stand alone in opposition to one another and without any imposing speeches preceding them. They usually signify that time is pressing. At other times, speeches may be no more than two-line units which continue for considerable periods, sometimes as a climax to more lengthy sections, sometimes as independent units. The dialogue is not always dialectical in such passages. The dramatist uses them to present information dramatically, as one character slowly extorts from the other that which the others on stage (and the audience) must know. Such dialogue is particularly well suited to an interrogation which sometimes takes on the character of a cross-examination.

In this scheme the dialogue is sometimes reduced to a single line immediately followed by a one-line rejoinder (*stichomythía*). This adds to the tension, and has a sharpening and heightening effect. A further possibility within this stylistic scheme is to break up the lines into mere phrases or even single words, which strike home like arrows.

A sharp observer of human nature, Sophocles uses dialogue to characterize the speaker. Obviously, the servant speaks differently from his master, and this is expressed stylistically by even including slang expressions. Significantly, a servant might even express sounder views than his more stubborn or narrow-minded master (the guard in the **Antigone** is such an example). The mood of the text indicates the correct way of portraying the role.

The way in which the voices of Oedipus, Jocasta, and a man of the people are played off one against the other is masterly! And how magnificently and suddenly the voice of the divine rings out as Heracles speaks from the tops of the rocks and resolves the acute tragic bind between the heroically tragic Philoctetes and the simple and honest young Neoptolemus! What a contrast there is between the harsh, blind beggar Oedipus and the candid, unostentatious regality of Theseus! We are offered a spectrum of human possibilities in the state, in society, or in the family.

In none of the extant plays are there any love scenes. True, there are lovers, but they do not speak to one another of their love. At most they might make an appeal to an unco-operative partner concerning a matter other than love, and even in such cases it is a wife or mother, rather than a lover, who makes the appeal. It seems as if there were no place for the intimate on the stage. The chorus might sing of Eros' power, but the hero shows no sign of *éros* and scarcely ever speaks of it. The great scenes which Sophocles wrote for lovers—Haemon's fruitless intervention on behalf of his intended bride, Antigone, and Deianira's hapless struggle for the heart of her husband (**The Women of Trachis**)—take place without one of the lovers on stage.

The language rises to great heights when it shows the same people in different situations. There is in Sophoclean tragedy none of the self-destruction which drives Shakespeare's heroes to the brink of ruin and even further. Neither is there any of the dissolution of the personality to the point of interchangeability such as we find in some modern dramatists. But within the frame of human existence his tragedy jerks the character out of his self-confidence and makes him realize that in extreme situations the human being is powerless.

Whoever compares Oedipus' speeches at the beginning of the drama with those at the end without reading what comes between will find it impossible to believe that this is the same person speaking. But whoever looks at the tragedy as a whole—remembering the hero as he appeared at the beginning—will notice that the possibilities of the end were already present in the very first speeches. Once, right at the beginning, Oedipus speaks of the sleepless nights of care. In other words, he is capable as a human being and a hero of feeling the incomprehensible (in this case the plague afflicting the city) and seeing the darkness which engulfs all existence. The great knower will blind himself because he has come up against the limits of this knowledge. The possibility of the outcome is inserted into the opening of the play like a thorn in the flesh whose nagging presence becomes increasingly obvious. It is suggest-

ed in the opening scenes and, through language, is quietly developed and grows from strength to strength in each speech the hero makes.

It is not only the change in the hero's self-confidence which is expressed by means of language. The stages marked by the deeds of the hero are also given expression in the text. For example, the rage and indignation which enable Antigone to act as she does are matched by the furious tone of her dialogue. Immediately after the deed, her speech reflects in its clarity and calm the almost superhuman determination of the perfect heroine, only to decline finally into mortal fear in the face of the reality of death.

Sophocles not only separates determination and passing mood, the rational and the irrational emotion and reason in his portrayal of man, but also frequently allows them to merge one into the other. Even where pure reason is emphasized, language is dependent on the state the person is in as well as on the character of this person. But the treatment makes it plain that just as one particular and momentary state cannot represent the true essence of a person, neither can a person's range of thinking be determined simply by one mood. When stressing a thought, the actor must always remain aware of the emotional state to which the situation is driving the character, so that at any time (as in a sudden recognition of the tragic bind he is in) the emotion can effectively erupt out of his dialectic. An example of this is Oedipus' "O city, city!"

T. S. Eliot was quite right to call the text which Sophocles put into the actors' hands a kind of "shorthand." There is, as it were, a perspective to the words: they always reveal something which cannot actually be expressed by words, but which can be depicted by an action, a gesture, by the movement or posture of the actor. The meaning behind the words, between the lines, is *shown* by the actor. Such meaning can be gathered from countless apparently insignificant turns of phrase, from pauses, from the sound of the words and the tempo of the verse. The possibilities of the dialogue are fulfilled only upon being completed by acting. Without it the poet would not have been able to complete his text. In a sense, the poet, who was his own director, directed the play in his imagination while writing it.

Nonetheless we should not forget that language was still primarily verse, rhythm, sound—in a word, it was poetry. The process followed in the combination of form and content is mysterious, but the results are undisputed. If language and art had not been combined perfectly through the genius of Sophocles, these tragedies would hardly have survived for twenty-four hundred years. Through art, truth achieves the form in which the two are welded into a lasting unity. The form is both developed and perpetuated by its content.

As long as the dramatist was writing tragedies for the theater, he was faced with a system which he could not disregard. The arrangement of the action taking place was as fixed as the possibilities of the dialogue—verse, speech, speech and counterspeech, *stichomythía*. Then there was the whole complex matter of the chorus, a sort of erratic block from another age, which had to be fitted into the new form. The combination of the chorus and dialogue put into action resulted in "theater."

The disparateness of the component parts of early tragedy is still obvious in the later dramas. But a poet like Sophocles made it his business, as it were, to reinvent the combination and not leave it to historical accident to determine the form for him. He allowed the combination to develop out of the inner necessity of the play in question. The chorus was coordinated with the dialogue and each in turn was adjusted to the presentation. Hence situations had to be invented in which the chorus seems to flow naturally out of the dialogue, always as reflection or as a spontaneous emotional response. In other cases the dialogue seems to be prefigured by the chorus.

Sometimes the dialogue could actually develop out of a choral passage, but such a transition then invariably presented a major problem combining the various formal details. The solution to this problem (from Aeschylus on) lay in antiphony. Antiphonal song was sung (and danced) by the chorus with one or two (sometimes three) soloists. It always has an instrumental accompaniment, and is often interrupted by spoken dialogue. The resulting combination is as artistically constructed as the choral songs themselves (with strophe, antistrophe and other proportionally arranged refinements). The chorus and soloists do not sing in unison, so that the essential quality of dialogue is preserved. The music, however, suggests that something in the dialogue has changed and shows a tendency towards the choral.

Sophocles, throughout his career, brought the art of antiphony to ever greater degrees of perfection. Only in the work of a Mozart or Verdi do we find a comparable synthesis of lyric flow and dramatic tension. The song always springs directly from the dialogue and it is impelled toward its climax. It is, in fact, a continuation of the dialogue through other means.

It usually begins when the dialectic exchange has concluded and the characters are overcome by emotion. The instruments strike up, the actor becomes a singer and the chorus responds with song. Rhythm and song (*mélos*) seek to attain greater expression through antiphonal song. Grief is poured out in a loud lament, and joy is expressed in rapturous hymns. When the action reaches an impasse, fear, confusion, or supplication can unleash the antiphonal song which might rise to a state of highest ecstasy, or break out into insane terror, before gradually subsiding into a more composed lamentation. But sometimes it takes only a spoken exchange recalling the terrible truth to unleash new cries of anguish, which, in their turn, are taken up by music and song in one unified rhythmic and strophic movement.

Just as, in moments of silence, a simple action can sometimes express the deepest tragedy, so, too, does music express in sound that which cannot be expressed in any other way. Art makes it possible to combine the choral song and the dialogue into a single entity which is part of a final composite form. Traditional theatrical form is thereby raised to a higher plane, for this combination is now seen from the point of view of the whole play, as part of a greater and planned unity.

Through the form, the world represented on the stage comes to represent the whole world. Reason (*lógos*) is given expression primarily in the dialogue; emotion in the choral song. But there are in each possibilities for transition to or reflection of the other. Together with the action on the stage, a kind of animated sculpture, these means of expression combine to form a view of life.

It is a tragic view of life. Each scene is simply one dimension of the whole of existence. The hero embodies human nature and reason (*physis* and *lógos*) in an unusual human situation. Whether, as with Oedipus, it is the spirit which raises him above all others, or whether, as with Antigone, it is love (*philía*—not sexual love) which is the distinguishing feature, or whether as with Heracles, it is the power of a great spirit, these heroes invariably are caught in extreme situations which cause them to founder.

It lies in the nature of tragedy, as we have said, to make man conscious of the possibility of foundering. The gods strike. They are beyond good and evil, and they make no distinction between right and wrong.

In foundering, in meeting his end, the tragic hero pits himself against both man and the gods. In the certain knowledge of his innocence he preserves his human dignity, even though he is doomed to death, reduced to rags, to a mere nothing.

At the end of his long life, Sophocles, one of the greatest poets of all time, allowed a ray of hope to fall on the tragic picture of human existence. Posterity offers the tragic hero who is destroyed by the world, or destroyed while the world looks on, the reward of immortality for his sufferings. The gods, too, are part of the drama, and hence we see a light from another world shedding its light around the dying Oedipus. (pp. 28-67)

> *Siegfried Melchinger, in his* Sophocles, *translated by David A. Scrase, Frederick Ungar Publishing Co., 1974, 184 p.*

Jacqueline de Romilly   (essay date 1980)

[*De Romilly is a distinguished French classicist whose writings include* Precis de litterature grecque *(1980;* A Short History of Greek Literature, *1985) and other works on various aspects of classical Greek literature and culture. In the following excerpt from the book cited above, she comments on Sophocles' themes and characters, concluding that the general mood of his plays, despite elements of pessimism, "is not one of despair, and [that] he is no more 'pessimistic about' man's worth than he is about the beauty of life."*]

The Vision of Sophocles: Gods and Men

[Two sets of themes can be identified in the tragedies of Aeschylus], those related to the city and those concerning the gods. The first group are of minor importance in the surviving plays of Sophocles. The second half of the ***Ajax,*** and more especially the ***Antigone,*** do include discussions of the problem of absolute authority. The ***Antigone*** also contains reflections on the subject of law, which have encouraged some scholars (Victor Ehrenberg, among others) to compare Sophocles' position with that of Pericles. But it must be acknowledged that what Sophocles emphasizes are religious obligations or very broad moral ones. The political life of the city-state remains in the background except as it impinges on religious duties.

The relation between men and gods is . . . a major theme in Sophocles. But it is nothing like the relation between men and gods as described by Aeschylus. In the first place, the gods are more distant. In the surviving plays, they almost never appear onstage (the sole exception is Athene, in the prologue to the *Ajax*). Likewise, their influence on human emotions is less immediate; and the principles by which they act are harder to discern.

Yet the gods make their presence known, most frequently by means of oracles. The plays of Sophocles often find their points of departure in prophecies; as the action unfolds, the characters look for the fulfilment of the various prophecies, weigh them against each other, and seek reassurance in them. Sometimes as many as three or four are cited in a single tragedy (e.g., in *The Women of Trachis,* in *Oedipus the King,* and in *Philoctetes*). Yet these oracles are not understood. Often they are enigmatic, as in Herodotus. Thus Heracles was told that he would be killed by a dead man (in fact, the drug which killed him was given to Deianira by the dying Centaur): how could he be expected to interpret this? Even when the oracles themselves are clear, their application may be deceptive; thus Oedipus mistook the identity of his father and mother. To put it another way, the mystery surrounding the gods' designs does not involve a principle; it is as if a veil were lifted only halfway, and mortals were expected to guess what lay behind it. The partial disclosures of oracles add pathos to human weakness without in any way illuminating it.

Indeed, the contrast between human fate and human ignorance is a source of profound irony. It is no accident that disaster strikes at the very moment when the protagonists are taking heart. Nor is it by accident that Sophocles so often puts words of double meaning into his characters' mouths—words whose full import the speakers themselves are unaware of. Oedipus curses the murderer of Laius without knowing that he is himself the murderer, and swears to act "as if the dead man were his own father"—which is in fact the case. To the ironies of fate Sophocles adds ironies in the structuring of scenes and in the choice of words. The gods almost seem to be laughing at mankind, just as Athene in the *Ajax* makes cruel sport of the pitiful, crazed hero.

Yet in Sophocles' world view there are no signs of revolt against this divine regime. He respects the gods; and in his plays only the arrogant who are about to be struck down dare to doubt the veracity of oracles. Instead of revolt or doubt we find an overwhelming sense of the distance between gods and men. Among men, everything passes, everything changes. Sophocles says so repeatedly, in choral odes of rare nobility and power. One such marks the opening of *The Women of Trachis:* "Never has the son of Cronus, the king who ordains all things, given to mortals portions without pain. Joys and pains come to all by turns,

circling, even as the stars of the Great Bear resolve. For men, nothing endures—not the starry night, not misfortunes, not riches" [lines 126-33]. The sphere of the gods, by contrast, is the sphere of the absolute, which nothing disturbs; in this respect Sophocles mirrors the beliefs of Pindar. As the chorus in the *Antigone* declares, nothing can diminish Zeus's power; "neither sleep, which charms all creatures, nor the divine and weariless months can ever conquer him." The chorus then addresses Zeus directly: "Untouched by age and time, you remain absolute master of Olympus and its dazzling light" [605-10].

The awareness of this gulf between two worlds accounts for two aspects of Sophocles' thought that at first glance might appear contradictory. First, it explains what may be called his pessimism. How can man hope, in such circumstances, to understand divine acts or escape their effects? Such acts are equally mysterious whether they are generous (*Oedipus at Colonus*) or cruel (*Oedipus the King*): a man's efforts to act rightly may be his own undoing. Or, like Oedipus, he may do wrong in spite of himself, without knowing or wishing it.

At the same time, whatever comes from the gods derives from them a sacred quality that outweighs every other consideration. A man cannot be too pious; he must put nothing before the divine ordinances. For Sophocles, the "unwritten laws" (respect for the gods, for parents, for suppliants, for the dead) are not the projections of a human consciousness or, indeed, of a Greek consciousness; they are divine laws. It is they that Antigone puts before the edict against burying her brother; and she is exhilarated at the thought that these laws partake of the permanence of the distant gods: "They are not of today or yesterday; no one knows the day they first appeared" [456-57]. In the same vein, the chorus of *Oedipus the King* prays that it may never neglect the "laws begotten in the clear air of heaven, / whose only father is Olympus;" "No mortal nature brought them to birth, / no forgetfulness shall lull them to sleep; / for God is great in them and grows not old" [867-72]. In Sophocles, the eminence of the gods makes man's fate seem more tragic by contrast; but at the same time it increases the brilliance of the human ideal.

This brings us to another all-important aspect of Sophocles' thought that sets him apart from Aeschylus. In the absence of any clear understanding of the divine will, attention is focused on man: will he find an honorable response to the fate that threatens him? Sophocles shows us Ajax, Oedipus, Heracles, Philoctetes, even Electra at the moment when each is destroyed and brought low, though none of them can be said really to deserve such a fall; but it is at that very moment that their heroism is revealed—in the way they face the trial.

Characteristics and Virtues of the Sophoclean Hero

A primary feature of Sophocles' characters is the variety of positions they take, positions that are often in direct conflict with one another. This implies clear and effective characterization. After Aeschylus, literary expression had grown less rigid, and dialogue had gained in importance relative to the lyrical portion of tragedy. At the same time, the individual had gained a greater independence in society. As a result, we see more nuanced characterization, and frequent confrontations of two contrasting personalities. [We have] the pairs of sisters (Antigone/Ismene, Electra/Chrysothemis) and the contrasts between husband and wife or master and captive woman (Heracles/Deianira, Ajax/Tecmessa). Elsewhere Neoptolemus's candor is contrasted with Odysseus's guile, Odysseus's prudence with Ajax's reckless passion, Odysseus's moderation with Agamemnon's harshness. All these characters are vividly portrayed, the individuality of each brought out by such contrasts.

Yet a qualification is in order: Sophocles' characterization does not always presuppose a psychological study that can satisfy our modern expectations. In a famous but unjust critique, Tycho von Wilamowitz (son of the well-known classical scholar) went so far as to claim that Sophocles neglected psychology to the point of implausibility when it suited his dramatic purpose. Some passages are certainly problematic. When Ajax, just before killing himself, claims to be reconciled to life, is he partly sincere and partly dishonest? Sophocles never makes it clear. Nor does he say or even imply to what extent Deianira is sincere when she claims to forgive her husband's infidelity. Equally inexplicable is Antigone's sudden shift from a bold acceptance of death to plaintive laments over her fate.

These gray areas imply no contradictions; they merely indicate that Sophocles did not care to make every link explicit in a character's motivation. For psychological investigation was not his major concern in creating characters. His characters have different mentalities because each embodies a different moral ideal, to which he or she adheres. Each knows the basis for his actions and defends his principles, making them his cause; each stands in contrast to those among whom he lives as one philosophy of life stands in contrast to others.

As a result, we come to feel that the debate on stage transcends the characters and concerns us as well. In the opposition between Ajax and Tecmessa we can see the contrast between an aristocratic ethic based on honor and a more humane ethic based on obligations to individuals. In the same play there is the debate between the Atreidae, who represent the claims of discipline, and Teucer and Odysseus, who urge respect for a dead man's former stature. The conflict between Antigone and Ismene, like that between Electra and Chrysothemis, is based on the opposite reactions of revolt and submission. The scenes in which these characters confront one another are clearly designed to weigh conflicting duties. Thus we have long speeches balancing one another, or debates in lines of crackling riposte in which antitheses—sometimes on the level of individual words or syllables—follow one another in rapid succession. Finally, each play as a whole is built from a sequence of such contrasting scenes. Antigone debates her act first with her sister and then with Creon; one is a timid ally, the other an antagonist. Later, Creon must debate *his* position with his own allies—his son and the prophet Teiresias—who find him at fault. In this series of confrontations, positions are affirmed, vindicated, and clarified; at the same time, tension builds.

Such close identification between a character and the ideal

in whose name he acts implies a rare lucidity on the part of the character; yet complexity is by no means excluded. As we have seen, the sudden reversals in some characters' positions can be surprising. Neoptolemus's change of heart—his decision to embrace the right cause—is the whole subject of the play. Seldom, however, can we label a character's moral position without misrepresenting it; bad and good are usually intertwined. Creon, in the *Antigone,* defends the rights of the city-state, and his arguments are impressive; but they are also inflexible, and he tends to confuse the state with himself. Haemon and Teiresias try, each in his own way, to convince Creon of this. The truth is complex and emerges only gradually, as scene follows scene. It can honestly be said that after twenty-five centuries we are still debating the precise meaning of the conflict between Antigone and Creon. When the philosopher Hegel claims that Antigone represents the family in conflict with the state, he is oversimplifying. At different periods it has been said that Antigone stands for humane feeling as opposed to intransigence, or for the right to rebel as opposed to any abuse of power; these too are oversimplifications. In Sophocles, as in Thucydides, we find a tendency to identify the particular with the general—without, however, distorting the particular. Sophocles does not simply choose an ideal to embody in Antigone; he puts a living Antigone before us. Yet at every juncture of the plot he manages to reveal in her a set of principles and an ideal of proper conduct that together make up her unique personality. An individual and a philosophy of life can be identified with one another in Sophocles because all his characters are passionately concerned to define and to defend their reasons for living.

Among these reasons, honor takes first place. It seems to a reader of the plays that the notion of honor evolves and increasingly asserts itself. Thus we move from the altogether external honor of Ajax, made up of acknowledged exploits and finding expression in public esteem, to the internalized honor of Neoptolemus, which requires only moral courage and finds expression only in a clear conscience (to the neglect, in Neoptolemus's case, of the glory he might win, and at the risk of being misjudged by the entire Greek army). Sophocles takes us, in other words, all the way from the world of Homer to that of Socrates. The plays in all their diversity retrace this movement toward ever purer and higher values. Transcending such contrasts and such progress, however, is a fundamental trait common to all of Sophocles' protagonists; each is prepared to sacrifice everything to his honor and to his values as he understands them. These are *heroic* characters. From a fierce warrior like Ajax to young women like Antigone or Electra, all share the same resolve, the same acceptance of death, the same refusal to be swayed.

The result is that the heroes are isolated from their intimates, who misunderstand them, try to restrain them, call them reckless and unrealistic. Their acts draw down the taunts of the powerful. Ajax dies alone, killing himself on enemy soil with a sword that was the gift of an enemy. Deianira dies misunderstood and cursed by her husband. She too withdraws to die alone, as do Eurydice in *Antigone* and Jocasta in *Oedipus the King.* Antigone is condemned to die in a subterranean vault, utterly alone; she is led away amid the sarcasms of the chorus ("They are laughing at me!"). Electra can count on no one but herself to act ("I am alone"). Philoctetes has spent years alone on his island, where the Greeks want to abandon him a second time. Finally, Oedipus, at the very height of his exaltation, is left alone to face a death only he may witness.

This solitude in fact corresponds to the greatness of the hero; he is condemned to it by his insistence on an absolute. At the same time, he finds in it a sort of obligation to rise above himself with renewed strength.

Even on this point, Sophocles leaves us with an antithesis. On the one hand are the heroes, in all their greatness; on the other, their more human intimates. Naturally the spotlight is on the heroes; the brilliance, the glory are theirs. But are those who try in vain to sway them necessarily wrong? Is Ajax right to kill himself, to abandon Tecmessa, his son, and the sailors of his fleet? Is the pliancy of the more tolerant Odysseus, who can forget injuries, less praiseworthy? And is Philoctetes right to refuse so obstinately to go to Troy? The heroes, in truth, are limiting cases, proof of the nobility that can coexist with the cruelest of trials. They are not models for our emulation, any more than Sophocles' plays are disembodied sermons. They are expressions of his faith in man.

The Beauties of Sophocles' World

For a pessimist, Sophocles radiates a rare confidence in everything beautiful. This side of him is often revealed in his choral odes. What I have said thus far about his arrangement of scenes, his lucid dialogue, and his forceful antitheses gives an idea of his dramatic art as expressed in the spoken parts of the plays. But I have given no hint of the beauty of his great odes, which are less directly related to the action than those of Aeschylus, yet for that very reason reveal more of the poet himself. Sophocles' odes are hardly divorced from the action; but in most cases they translate the themes of the preceding episode into more universal terms, reflecting Sophocles' propensity for combining the particular and the general. In **Antigone,** for example, after the announcement that Polyneices has been buried in spite of the royal edict, the chorus sings of the greatness of human accomplishments but recalls that men are bound to obey laws; when Antigone's guilt has been discovered, it sings of the ease with which disaster strikes; after the scene with Haemon, it describes the universal power of love; and when Antigone has gone to her death, it recalls the deaths of figures from mythology. In each case there is the same broadening of focus—the same echo, in a more serene key, of the preceding action.

In this way Sophocles' odes, though far shorter than those of Aeschylus, open up broad perspectives in which we can glimpse the poet's tastes and convictions. An example is the ode in the **Antigone** that begins, "Many are the wonders in this world, but none is greater than man" [332ff.]. There is no finer statement in Greek of man's preeminence, no greater praise for his discoveries and creative intelligence. In the spirit of his age, with its faith in progress, Sophocles evokes the whole series of human inventions, closing (in a vein more characteristic of his own thought)

with the warning that if man uses his intelligence for ill, or against the law, it becomes ruinous.

Even expressions of grief and pain testify indirectly to Sophocles' love of life. When he wrote the poignant ode in **Oedipus at Colonus** deploring old age, the poet was in his nineties (the play was produced posthumously); it is a bitter piece, claiming that early death is best, and is often cited as evidence of Sophocles' pessimism. But behind the bitterness we can glimpse a sorrow at the loss of what made life worth living. In describing old age as "loathsome, impotent, unsociable, friendless" [1235-37], the poet may be suggesting nostalgia for the company, friendships, and happy life he had enjoyed as a younger man.

In this last tragedy, Sophocles even finds room for praise of his native Athens or, more precisely, his Attica. Oedipus comes there to die, and Sophocles takes advantage of the opportunity to describe the beauties of the Attic countryside—birds, growing things, and streams—which, together with the beneficent presence of the gods, inspire a great sense of peace. "In this land of good horses, stranger, you have found the best retreat on earth. This is white Colonus, favorite haunt of the sweet nightingale; she loves to sing in our green vales, amid the dark ivy, inviolable bower of the gods, sheltered by its thick growth of leaves from the sun and from every storm wind" [668ff.]. If Sophocles is elsewhere the tragedian who most insistently recalls the fragility of human happiness and portrays heroism at its highest pitch, the Colonus ode gives us a glimpse of the happier man suggested by his biography. In the contrast he so consistently draws between man's vulnerability and his greatness, the abiding impression is that vulnerability is not paramount. The mood of Sophocles' plays is not one of despair, and he is no more "pessimistic" about man's worth than he is about the beauty of life. (pp. 69-75)

> *Jacqueline de Romilly, "Drama in the Second Half of the Fifth Century: Sophocles, Euripides, and Aristophanes," in her* A Short History of Greek Literature, *translated by Lillian Doherty, The University of Chicago Press, 1985, pp. 66-89.*

ANTIGONE

CRITICAL COMMENTARY

Albin Lesky   (essay date 1957-58)

[*Lesky was a distinguished Austrian classicist and educator whose works include* Geschichte der griechischen Literatur *(1957-58;* A History of Greek Literature, *1966),* Die griechische Tragödie *(1958;* Greek Tragedy, *1965), and* Die tragische Dichtung der Hellenen, *(1972;* Greek Tragic Poetry, *1983). In the following excerpt from the first-named work, he discusses the conflict between Creon and Antigone in Sophocles'* Antigone. *Criticizing the view that the dramatist represents "two opposing views of equal moral validity," Lesky asserts that Antigone "stands for the eternal, immutable divine law, which cannot be disturbed by any human pretensions to power."*]

There is no other play [than **Antigone**] in which Sophocles brings out the leading themes so forcibly. Equally there is no other that has been so long and so determinedly misunderstood. The cause was the authority of Hegel, who highly praised the play in his *Ästhetik* (II. 2.1) while interpreting Creon and Antigone as representing state and family respectively. These are two opposing worlds of equal moral validity, whose representatives must needs come into a conflict that destroys both. What Hegel sketches out is a tragic theme of great potentiality—one which was developed in philosophy by Schopenhauer and in literature by Hebbel, and which has played its part in modern discussions of tragedy. But as applied to the **Antigone** the theory of equal but opposed schemes of values is a misinterpretation.

Polynices, who has organized the expedition of the seven against his native city, has died before her walls, an enemy of his country. Burial in his native soil might justly be refused him according to Greek notions of law, provided he was laid to his last rest somewhere outside the confines. But Creon, who has become master of Thebes after the mutual killing of the brothers, goes far beyond this. He

sets guards over the corpse to ensure that it is torn by dogs and vultures and that the remains rot in the sun. The Athenians who heard this Creon speaking could not but recall the curse which a priest from the family of the Buzyges had pronounced among them on anyone who left a corpse unburied. Sophocles' Creon is not the spokesman of a state which knows its rights and also its limitations. He is driven on by that arrogance which only recognizes itself: a *hybris* which is doubly dangerous, doubly culpable when it claims to speak with the voice of authority. The **Antigone** is not a propaganda-play, but in the actions and sufferings of its characters the question is clearly posed whether the state can lay claim to ultimate validity and authority, or whether it has to obey laws which have their origin elsewhere and which remain always beyond its reach.

The play runs its course as a drama of developing resistance to Creon and his gradual condemnation on all hands. The resistance is led by Antigone, and the poet makes her perform two acts of rebellion. On the first occasion she contrives unnoticed to throw a light coating of dust over her brother's corpse; then when the guards have again uncovered the rotting body, she comes back and is caught while trying to renew this symbolic burial. The repetition of the theme serves the single purpose of making her rebellion against Creon appear as forcibly as the diffi-

A fourth-century B.C. vase painting of Antigone brought before Creon.

cult circumstances of the attempted burial permit. In addition we are allowed to see Antigone momentarily triumphant, before we share the sorrow of her defeat.

Scarcely has Creon pronounced sentence of death upon Antigone when the process begins which is to lead to his destruction. His son Haemon, who loves Antigone, is the first to reject him. After a long dispute, beginning with mild filial expostulation and ending with a cry of despair, Haemon leaves his father's presence. From his lips Creon has had to learn that the city is unanimous in condemning his judgment [verses 692, 733]; but he stands firmly on what he takes to be his and the state's rights. Creon is not a vulgar tyrant who knowingly does what is wrong. His belief that his own power and that of the state (he equates them in v. 738) has no limits so inextricably ensnares him that his progress from *hybris* to disaster is not merely a moral paradigm but a piece of true tragedy.

The gods also abandon Creon. They do so first through the mouth of the seer Tiresias, who speaks of the ominous signs which show that the city is polluted by the presence of the unburied corpse. By now Creon is full of rash and hasty thoughts; the gods have made him mad. He suspects that the seer has been suborned; in a last access of arrogance he declares that the dead man shall not be buried even if the eagles of Zeus carry the remnants of the corpse to the throne of the most high. But when Tiresias has gone after pronouncing a terrible curse, that Creon will pay in his own flesh and blood for his impiety against the dead, Creon's blindness, pride and folly suddenly collapse, and he determines to save what can yet be saved.

But the gods will not take his change of heart as expiation. In the underground chamber from which he resolves to free Antigone he finds her hanged. Haemon, after a wild outburst of hatred against his father, kills himself upon her body. A messenger reports the event to Eurydice, Creon's wife, who goes without a word into the palace, where she curses her husband and dies. Broken and abandoned, Creon remains, spared only to recognize his mistake too late.

The play is a drama of two characters. Without being able to lay stress on either one, we can speak of a tragedy of Antigone and a tragedy of Creon. Hegel's influence has caused long-lasting doubt whether we can speak of 'tragic guilt' in connection with Creon. Victor Ehrenberg's splendid book [*Sophocles and Pericles*] might have been designed to put an end once for all to this false interpretation. What Antigone stands for is made clear in the great scene of conflict with Creon. She stands for the eternal, immutable divine law, which cannot be disturbed by any human pretensions to power. The whole feeling of the passage tells us that she is expressing the poet's own convictions, and the feeling is supported by the unequivocal testimony of the *Oedipus Tyrannus* [865], where Sophocles praises the law of heaven, which has its origin with the gods and not in the nature of man.

Ehrenberg has shown that the common opinion which makes Sophocles and Pericles representatives of a basically unitary epoch at the summit of the classical period conceals in fact a very significant difference. The poet and the statesman were respectively representatives of a theonomic and an anthroponomic view of the world—not indeed in open conflict, but in a state of tension which foreshadowed the battle of giants which a later age fought concerning man and existence. Sophocles witnessed with deep anxiety the stormy developments of his age. In political life these developments displayed themselves in the beginnings of Athenian imperialism, in the spiritual world in the iconoclastic ideas of the sophists. That very period in which Sophocles wrote the *Antigone* seemed ready to break all bounds. Then it was that he penned that ode which we find as the first stasimon in the play, which has echoed as no other has over the centuries down to our own day. Man is a great and powerful, but also strange and uncanny creature (both senses are borne by δεινόs): he can bend nature to his will in all fields, and treads every path with the utmost boldness. But still the one decisive question remains: Does he know of the absolute to which the gods have made him subject, or does he despise the eternal order and bring himself and his society to destruction?

In the first draft of his *Empedocles* Hölderlin has a beautiful passage in which Rhea speaks of the questions that Athenian maidens are asking: which of them did Sophocles have in his mind when he created Antigone, the brave yet tender heroine. In recent interpretations the figure is often grotesquely travestied: Hölderlin here grasped it in all that complete humanity with which the poet endued it. This is the whole person who says [523]: 'My destiny was not mutual hate, but mutual love'. No effort has been spared by scholars to strip these words, the basic expression of western humanism, of their full and true meaning, and to exclude from them a notion of love which Sophocles has been thought incapable of entertaining. It has also occasioned surprise that on her way to her death Antigone weeps for the life which she is to lose. Yet the primary reason why this drama has retained its validity over the centuries is that Antigone is no superhuman figure, but one of us, with our hopes and desires, but also with the great courage to follow God's command against all contradictions. But the loving Antigone, like all Sophocles' great tragic figures, must tread her road in total isolation. At the beginning of the play she asks her sister Ismene to help her. It is in vain: with a contrast that recurs in Sophocles, the great soul of Antigone, inaccessible to fear and coercion, is displayed against the human type that is ready to compromise and to turn away from the moral law under the stress of hardship.

The chorus of Theban elders also refuses to help, and its attitude has been accordingly condemned. But if we read on and see how after the scene with Tiresias this same chorus condemns Creon right down to the impressive closing words, we shall easily see that in the first section the poet makes the chorus hold back so that he can present Antigone in complete isolation. Fear of Creon is a simple and satisfactory motivation.

In one passage we are out of sympathy with Antigone, as Goethe was [see overview dated 1827]. It is in her last speech [905], where she justifies her action by saying that she could make good the loss of husband or child, but, since her parents are dead, she cannot replace her only brother. This is the expression of a basic trait of Greek character: some intellectual reason has to be found for the feelings of the heart. At the same time the passage is an interesting demonstration of the poet's familiarity with Herodotus, who makes effective use of the same idea in the story of Intaphernes' wife.

After the foregoing observations it can hardly be necessary to defend the inner unity of the play against those who find that the third part of it is too much an independent tragedy of Creon. This is not to deny, of course, that the compactness of the composition is not—we might well say not yet—at the level of perfection which Sophocles reached in the plays of his maturity. (pp. 279-82)

> *Albin Lesky, "The Flowering of the Greek City State: Sophocles," in his* A History of Greek Literature, *translated by James Willis and Cornelis de Heer, Methuen & Co. Ltd., 1966, pp. 271-302.*

Ruth Scodel   (essay date 1984)

[*Scodel is an American classicist and educator whose writings include* Sophocles *(1984). In the following excerpt from that work, she analyzes the conflict between Antigone and Creon in* Antigone. *Noting the complexity of moral issues involved and realizing that either side can be defended, Scodel remarks that "Antigone's rightness is a deeply ironic phenomenon: the right course for the city is proclaimed by one who has no concern for the city."*]

The Central Conflict

Antigone is an easily approachable, though not an easy work. Its basic dramatic conflict involves two characters and two principles: Creon embodies the state and its authority, Antigone the family and its religious tradition. This conflict is expressed in two closely related issues, Creon's refusal of burial to Polynices and Antigone's refusal to obey his edict. There is no doubt which side is in the right. Our sympathy is with Antigone from the start, and by the end the gods have visibly proved her right. But to emphasize merely the rightness of Antigone and the folly of Creon is to sentimentalize a work that is in no way sentimental. The complexity of the play does not reside in any fair balance of moral right and wrong between the opposing sides. Rather the central conflict is only one element in a drama which explores, as much as any of Sophocles' tragedies, the ambiguities of divine will and human action, of reason and irrationality. The moral of the play is not that the dead should be buried; but the dispute over the burial is the motive force and the framework.

Polynices' crime, the attempt to sack his native city, is one of the worst imaginable for a Greek, and in the entry-song of the chorus the horror of his attack is vivid. He is a bloodthirsty eagle. Even Antigone never defends him. In Athenian law, a traitor could not be buried in Attic soil. The relatives of one executed for treason could, however, carry his body beyond the border and give it funeral rites. Creon's edict thus transgresses ordinary practice. Yet the final outcome also violates normal rules in that Polynices is buried within the borders of Thebes. Moreover, Greek

literature reveals complex attitudes to the rule that the dead must receive proper burial. While the *Iliad* ends with the episode of reconciliation in which Achilles, at divine urging, restores the body of his enemy Hector to his family for burial, Menelaus would have exposed the body of his brother's murderer had he been able, although in the epic Menelaus is a sympathetic character.

Antigone's claim is double. On the one hand, she asserts the simple right of the family and the claims of affection: her duty to bury a brother is a matter with which no one has a right to interfere. At the same time, she defends her act as demanded by "unwritten ordinances" [lines 450-55]:

> It was not Zeus who proclaimed this, nor does Justice who lives with the gods below establish such laws among men. I did not think your edicts were so strong that as a mortal you could override the secure, unwritten usages of the gods.

"Unwritten laws" appear to have been a topic of controversy in the second half of the fifth century. Thucydides has Pericles in the Funeral Oration speak of Athenian obedience to those laws "which, though unwritten, confer an acknowledged shame," while an orator quotes Pericles as using the term for a ritual law (Lysias). Xenophon shows Socrates and the sophist Hippias discussing unwritten, universal laws such as those which enjoin gratitude to benefactors or forbid incest and demand reverence for the gods. These laws are attributed to the gods, and serve as a bridge between *physis,* nature, and *nomos,* custom, which anthropological study and speculation had sharply divided. Antigone's appeal is probably not based on a recognized inclusion of the duty to bury the dead as an unwritten law. But it was a traditional obligation to offer at least symbolic burial to an exposed body; the guard compares the first burial to the dust thrown by a wayfarer who offers it to avoid a curse [256]. Such an obligation could easily be put among "unwritten laws" as a basic act of piety, and its definition as such a law has great emotional power. Linked in the figure of Antigone with the equally basic law of devotion to family, her claim persuasively evokes fundamental responses. An unburied corpse violates the natural and religious order, for the dead belong beneath the earth. A sister who protects her brother is to be admired (since he no longer threatens the community). The appeal to the unwritten ordinances is original, but convincing and moving.

The speech raises a fundamental problem of which Antigone is not necessarily aware. She is concerned for the immediate issue, and knows only that eternal, divine law supersedes human law just as it is more important to please the dead than the living. Her speech, however, has been preceded in the play by Creon's discussion of political principles and by the chorus's view of human progress in the "Ode on Man." The ode has celebrated mortal development. Man "taught himself" language, thought, civic life. Antigone appeals to rules whose origin is unknown [456]. Creon rightly says that only within the city can we make friends; individual life depends on the common good. Yet Antigone's devotion is to those "friends" whom we do not make for ourselves. Her act and her claim are a reminder that the city is formed of families, that human life is not a matter of pure choice; they continue the pondering of the chorus on the unsure direction of progress. "While he honors the law of the land and sworn justice of the gods, high is his city" [369-70]. No one doubts that well-being depends on reverence toward the gods and justice. But for Creon the city is the basis for judging justice and piety; the chorus is ambiguous; Antigone asserts that there is another standard, but she does not refer to any public, civic standard. If Antigone is right, her very refusal to consider civic interest is the position which benefits the city, and in the end she is proved right.

Her rightness, however, solves only the particular question and leaves the wider question open. Creon is put decisively in the wrong by his unwillingness to listen to good advice: the chorus which suggests divine concern, Haemon who warns of popular opinion, and Tiresias with his prophetic message. He also, in burying Antigone alive, repeats his violation of eternal law in a clearer form, inverting the proper places of living and dead. But the true relation of the different spheres is unresolved: the city, a human creation, but one whose survival is the basis of civilized life, and whose survival depends on obedience to its laws; the families who constitute the city and can yet conflict with it; the gods whose requirements are eternal, yet unwritten, and thus not codified or clear.

Antigone

ISMENE. Antigone is entirely right, and there are obvious problems in presenting a heroine whose actions embody justice. But this is not a story of innocent suffering or simple martyrdom. Antigone is not vindicated until late in the action, though she always has our sympathies. These, however, cannot be one-sided. Antigone is balanced against other characters and against wider forces. The most obvious foil character is Ismene, whose timidity defines Antigone's courage. Like Odysseus in the prologue of *Ajax,* she is a vehicle for turning audience sensibility: she believes that Antigone is right to insist that the burial is just, but considers Antigone foolish in attempting the impossible and exceeding a woman's position.

But the debate shows an Antigone whose loyalty to family can quickly become rejection. She uses terms of actual hatred to her sister [86, 93]. Her very refusal to acknowledge the mutual hatred so prominent in her family—she insists on equal care for brothers who killed each other—expresses itself in a division with her living sister. Her kindness to the dead is not matched in kindness to the living. Yet Ismene's last words in the prologue show her as still loving her sister. Antigone can be loved even by the sister whose love she rejects, while Ismene's lack of greatness allows a generosity her sister lacks. And when we next hear of Ismene, she is described as hysterical: Creon thinks this is a sign of guilt, but we recognize her pain and fear [488-92].

When she reappears [526], the conflict becomes more intense, for she now seeks to equal Antigone in what only shortly before she called "folly" and is folly to Creon now [562]. Ismene has now, in effect, accepted Antigone's

view. She asks what life is left for her, if her sister dies [548], just as Antigone had insisted that she did not object to death since her family had suffered so much. Yet Antigone replies [549] by telling her to ask Creon; she calls her sister "A friend who loves in words," as if a desire to share her death were not deed enough. Antigone performed her act alone, and she refuses to allow Ismene any share in it. Yet at 553 she becomes slightly more gentle: "Save yourself. I do not begrudge your escape." The line introduces an ambiguity into Antigone's motives: she rejects Ismene both out of justice, for she cannot allow her to share the credit for what she did not do, and because she does not wish her death. In her last words to Ismene [559-60], she sums up the difference in nature between them: "Have courage. You live, but my soul long ago / Died, so as to help the dead." Ismene can try to sacrifice herself for Antigone, but only an Antigone, already in some sense devoted, will sacrifice herself for the dead.

Ismene is concerned with the affections of life, and appropriately it is she who protests Creon's killing of his son's betrothed. As Antigone presses austerely on to death, Ismene links her with the world of the living. After her exit at 581, Ismene is mentioned only once. Haemon, the lover Ismene has first named, in the following scene provides a further connection between Antigone and the living world. And the final Antigone, who can lament her fate, has absorbed something of both her supporters. Ismene has fulfilled her function, humanizing her sister even when she seems least humane, and suggesting that actions like Antigone's are not merely the result of goodwill.

HAEMON. Haemon's love for Antigone is an important factor in the action, as the mechanism by which Creon's error returns against himself. But the two never meet on stage, and we see them together only in the messenger's speech describing the terrible events at the tomb. Antigone only once (even if she speaks 572) mentions him; that their love is mutual is certain only from Ismene's single remark at 570, when she answers Creon's claim that Haemon can produce his heir elsewhere—"The fields of others can be ploughed too"—with "But not as suited as for him and for her." Antigone dies in utter isolation; Haemon can join her only by joining in her death, as Ismene sought to do. Yet her love for him, though barely mentioned, is like her hint of concern for Ismene's survival: some attachment to the living is still present in the death-devoted maiden of the first part of the play.

The episode between Creon and Haemon is introduced by a choral announcement [626-30]. The chorus's question—does he come in grief at the loss of his bride?—defines *eros* as the theme of the scene. But when Creon in effect repeats this question, Haemon declares that no marriage means more to him than his father. Creon praises obedience. Not only should Haemon obey his father, but he should recognize that Antigone's disobedience proves her a bad woman and hence unattractive, "a cold embrace" [650]. Haemon speaks in purely rational terms, as one concerned only for his father's best interest. But Creon refuses to believe that his son has any motive but passion. When Haemon cries that Antigone's death will lead to another's [751], it is clearly the lover who speaks. Yet Haemon is no hypocrite.

Creon is apparently incapable of accepting the complexity of human motives, or of listening seriously to an argument which is made because the speaker is in love. For him, Haemon cannot love both Antigone and himself, or say something true for emotional reasons.

Haemon is a subsidiary character, but this episode reveals a complexity which is reiterated in the scene at the tomb. His love and his filial piety are in ultimate conflict. Although he threatened suicide earlier, his death is not directly motivated by grief for Antigone, but by anger at himself after his attack on his father, according to the messenger [1235-36]. The disaster for Creon requires that Haemon's loyalty to him be strong enough to cause his destructive and instant remorse.

At the same time, the final image of the dead lovers lying side by side is explicitly erotic: this death is the consummation of a marriage [1240-41]. Antigone in the second half of the play has lamented both in song and in spoken verse her virgin death. Her burial alive is a kind of living descent into the netherworld, where she will become the bride of Death. Her laments point two ways. On the one hand, her regret at dying without marriage or children affirms what the figures of Ismene and Haemon have suggested, that despite her apparent devotion to death, she is not without attachments in life: she has not sacrificed a life which had no worth. She too is a complex person. And despite Creon's fear that she seeks to usurp a male role, her lament echoes her concern with funeral ritual, an especially female role—what she misses is the normal woman's life. At the same time, she does not name her betrothed and sees herself as dying unlamented, though the audience has seen Ismene's love for her—Ismene she has rejected, and she never learns of Haemon's fidelity. On the other hand, her agony can be linked to a sense that the entombment does not simply join her with the dead [850-51]—she will belong to neither world. Antigone was able to abandon life in order to be united with the dead, but her peculiar fate deprives her even of this. Deeply drawn to both worlds, she is deprived of both. When, in her last speech, she speaks of her hope that she will be a dear arrival to her family [897-99], suicide may already be on her mind.

CREON. The tragedy ends with the laments of Creon, and his fate in some ways conforms better to a popular idea of tragedy. He is ruined through his own mistakes, though the punishment is excessive in proportion to the crime; he learns wisdom through suffering, and too late. Creon's fate is an object lesson, a moral tale; and in this way he is a brilliant foil to the central figure, Antigone, whose fate is caused by greater forces and is more ambiguous.

Creon makes two basic errors, which appear in all he does. First, he cannot apply his excellent rules to anyone but himself. He stresses the need to hold to the best plans and to speak the truth without fear, but we hear that the citizens are afraid to tell him what they think, and he rejects good advice from Haemon and the chorus. Condemning Antigone's loyalty to family ties, he expects absolute loyalty from Haemon [634]. He is obsessed with social definitions: the king should rule, the son obey, women be subordinate. Thus he applies one rule to each entity. He first receives advice when the prophet frightens him. At last he

turns to the chorus to ask what he should do [1099]. This moment at which he changes his mind unites two sudden recognitions—that others can be right as well as himself and that he too values his family, and so is vulnerable.

His second error is more interesting. The hierarchial world he imagines he lives in is also a rational world. The family, in his speech to Haemon, is a small model of the city, and the city and the army are analogous. People have only one motive for any action: Haemon is in love, and therefore his arguments can be disregarded. He assumes that anyone who would bury Polynices must be a political enemy, and that the guard was bribed. Later in the play, after he knows of Antigone's burial of Polynices, he can still accuse Tiresias of having been bribed. Money and power, "rational" goals, are what he understands, and any opposition to him must be the work either of those seeking to depose him or of victims of madness.

This overrationality applies also to the gods, where it is most dangerous. Creon is by no means impious; his opening words piously attribute the salvation of the city to the gods. But he assumes that the gods, whose concern for the city has been thus proved, reason as he does himself. Surely they cannot care for Polynices, who tried to burn their shrines [284-89]. The gods do not honor the wicked. He is confident that his distinctions are also theirs. Again, when Tiresias reports that the gods, offended by the carrion which pollutes their altars, refuse to accept his sacrifices, he insists that mortals cannot pollute the gods, even if the birds bring carrion to the throne of Zeus [1040-44]. That the gods could not be polluted was not a new or impious belief, though most people probably assumed otherwise. But he draws an overprecise conclusion: if the gods are not polluted by an unburied corpse, his refusal to bury Polynices cannot offend them. He does fear ritual pollution, and has Antigone entombed with a little food so that the city will avoid a curse in her death [773-76]. This is a technical evasion, normal in Greek religious thinking. But in burying Antigone alive he repeats the offense against divine and natural order he committed in denying burial to Polynices. He thinks legally and logically, but the gods seem to be allied rather with the simple human feeling which is repelled by an unburied corpse, carrion on an altar of the gods, or burial alive.

Appropriately, Creon is destroyed by his son's emotional conflict and his wife's grief and anger. His own family is governed by the basic emotions he has denied, and he is vulnerable because he also is human and loves his wife and son. Chance or the gods keep him from reaching the tomb in time; the world does not allow each intention to attain a fixed and matching result. Creon is forced to recognize the power of the irrational, and he admits his guilt in the deaths of Haemon and Eurydice. He is pathetic and demands sympathy, as he reveals how ruinous human folly can be. The chorus has claimed that "nothing great comes into the life of mortals without ruin" [613-14]. Creon has met forces beyond his power.

The Curse

Creon is not by nature akin to this accursed greatness, but Antigone is. The chorus delivers this claim in contemplating Antigone's clan, the Labdacids. For the chorus, Antigone's self-destructive act is merely the last in a long line of divinely ordained troubles: "Whose house is shaken by a god, nothing of disaster is omitted" [584-85]. The singers identify the curse with Antigone's *physis,* the nature she has inherited from her ancestors; she is the victim of "a bloody dust belonging to the nether gods, a folly of speech and a Fury in the mind" [601-3]. The elders call her "violent child of a violent father" [471]. The curse is an external reality, but works within Antigone herself. In the prologue, Ismene presented the griefs of the house as a reason for self-restraint, while for Antigone they are a reason to desire death. Her devotion to her family is inevitably a devotion to death, not only because so many have died, but because ruin and self-destruction are their characteristics.

The chorus joins thoughts of the curse with condemnation of Antigone in their Aeschylean lament [853-56]:

> Advancing to the farthest point of daring, you have had a great fall against the high throne of Justice: but you are expiating some ancestral ordeal.

Although Antigone has committed no injustice, it is not the accusation to which she responds in her part of the lament. Instead she laments her birth from an incestuous marriage and her brother's ill-fated wedding with an Argive princess. She calls herself a "curse-bearer" [867]; she fulfills the curse in herself and also spreads it to Creon's family. The chorus is clearly right in seeing the curse at work in the play. It would be a mistake, however, to modernize the curse into a mere familial capacity for self-destruction: the curse works both through Antigone and Creon and in the situation itself. Moreover, Antigone's action is morally right and demanded by the gods, even as it embodies their curse; and no offense of the Labdacids against the gods is cited to justify divine hatred.

Within the plain contest of right and wrong is a complex network of causality and of involved sympathy. We cannot but feel sympathetic understanding for Ismene, whom Antigone rejects. Antigone acts rightly, yet is driven by a curse. In the first part of the play she desires death, but her laments reveal her regret for life, for marriage and children. Creon is wrong, but he is not merely stupid, obstinate, or impious. He cannot believe that the gods defend their own enemies. Haemon cannot reconcile his sense of duty to his father with his anger at him or his love for Antigone.

Much of the choral moralizing in this play is highly ambiguous. The song about the curse of the Labdacids ends with a reminder of the awesome power of Zeus and the deception of human expectation. The victim of hope perceives nothing until his foot is in the fire [620-25]:

> Wisely did the famous saying appear, that evil seems good at some time to him whose mind a god leads to ruin. He is outside ruin only briefly.

The chorus has Antigone in mind, of course, and a god is indeed leading her to destruction. Yet the following scene is that between Creon and Haemon, and they too are on their way to destruction. Haemon is maddened by Eros according to the chorus [790]. Creon is insane according to his son [765]. And a god cooperates in their madness.

The Gods and the Two Burials

The gods do not intervene blatantly in the action until the entry of Tiresias, but there are hints of their presence, both in choral songs, and in the unusual dramatic technique. At the end of the prologue, Antigone goes out to bury her brother. In the middle of the first episode, the guard reports that the body has been lightly covered with dust. There is no sign of who could have performed the deed. The guard leaves under Creon's threats. When he returns after the choral ode, he has captured Antigone. The guards had uncovered the body and waited. A dust storm arose at noon, and when it ended Antigone was beside the corpse, carrying out burial rites. Polynices is thus buried twice.

The first burial was complete, for the guard says that the doer "performed the proper rites" [247]. The description of it has a note of the miraculous. Not only was there no trace of wagon, mattock, or footprint, but no animal came close to the body. Each item can be explained naturalistically. The guard stresses the lack of tools, since without his complicity a full-scale burial could hardly have been accomplished. The burial took place at night, when vultures do not hunt. Yet we are directed to see the event as wondrous. The chorus first responds by suggesting that the gods are responsible [278-79], and when Creon refutes this idea, they sing an ode about human cunning, and the burial is doubtless the inspiring example. The two responses render the burial problematic. As audience, we have seen Antigone go to bury her brother, and we can hardly fail to assume that the guard's report proves that she has succeeded. At the same time, the report shows her attempt as amazingly successful. Not only has she performed the burial without being captured, but the thin layer of dust has protected the corpse.

Why then does she return? If Creon intended to denude the body each time dust was placed on it, she would have no hope of keeping it covered forever; and she has said that she will give up when the task is beyond her ability [91]. And Creon does not even order the body uncovered; the guard does this on his own. She cannot expect to keep the corpse physically covered, the ritual has been satisfactorily accomplished, and it is not at all clear how she knows what has happened. The second burial is as uncanny as the first. Antigone is hidden from the guards by the whirlwind of dust until she is already beside the body; she has traveled to the body through a storm during which the guards were forced to close their eyes. This is an implicit miracle—just natural enough to explain Creon's failure to see the gods at work. And if Antigone is aided by miraculous help here, we may suspect she had it earlier. The first burial leaves no trace behind; the doer disappears. For the second, the doer appears as if from nowhere. In each case, divine help seems to enable Antigone to reach her goal.

The second burial is interrupted as she pours libations. In the second half of the play, the corpse of Polynices is as effectively exposed as it was effectively buried. The prophet announces that carrion birds and dogs have polluted all the altars of Thebes [1016-18]. Once the control of the body is truly Creon's, his decision to expose it to carrion animals is effectively carried out, and the consequences fulfill themselves with astonishing speed.

So both Antigone and Creon succeed. Antigone can claim to have buried Polynices [900-03], although Creon has caused the corpse to be devoured by animals. Polynices is buried twice, then effectively unburied until Creon finally gives him authoritative burial. Antigone's return to the body thus demands neither a psychological nor a ritual reason. It is part of the divine management, by which the gods participate in the human battle of wills. Like all divine actions, it is beyond mortal explanation, and not entirely rational. The gods help Antigone in her task. Yet the concealing dust disappears, and once Antigone is captured, it is no longer Antigone's will they fulfill, but Creon's. The double burial may be their message to Creon, which he rejects because, just as he cannot imagine Haemon as motivated both by love and by concern for himself, so he cannot see the element of the miraculous in an act performed by a human agent. But the gods do not speak directly. Nor do they protect those who are loyal to them, as Antigone complains [921-24]. They only make human intentions effectual, and thus lead both principals to destruction for reasons we cannot know.

The gods thus ensure that human actions have their widest consequences. They justify Antigone's action, but that is not the only reason the play invokes them, for the tragedy is not really about the right or wrong of Polynices' burial. The drama shows how a catastrophe overcomes the royal house of Thebes through a conjunction of causes; it depicts a world of moral complexity in which Creon's reliance on reason is as mad as his son's erotic passion. Antigone's rightness is a deeply ironic phenomenon: the right course for the city is proclaimed by one who has no concern for the city. The tragedy points to the pathetic fragility of human institutions. Reason, celebrated in the "Ode on Man," is not infallible; Antigone's attachment to instinctual family ties is the correct guide. But Creon's fear of anarchy is not to be mocked, and Haemon shows that the conflicts of family and love can be as ruinous as those of family and authority. There are no easy solutions. (pp. 46-57)

> *Ruth Scodel, in her* Sophocles, *Twayne Publishers, 1984, 155 p.*

OEDIPUS REX

CRITICAL COMMENTARY

Sigmund Freud   (essay date 1900)

> [*An Austrian neurologist and author, Freud is known as the father of psychoanalysis, a method seeking to understand the power of the unconscious over the conscious mind. Freud's writings, which have exerted an enormous*

An ancient plate portraying Oedipus listening to the riddle of the Sphinx.

> *influence on literary criticism and other fields of intellectual endeavor, include* Die Traumdeutung *(1900;* The Interpretation of Dreams, *1953),* Zur Psychopathologie des Alltagslebens *(1914;* Psychopathology of Everyday Life, *1960),* Das Unbenhagen in der Kultur *(1930;* Civilization and Its Discontents, *1961), and* Der Mann Moses und die monotheistische Religion *(1939;* Moses and Monotheism, *1960). In the following excerpt from an English translation of the first-named work, he demonstrates how Sophocles'* Oedipus Rex *supports his assumptions regarding the Oedipus complex, and emphasizes that Oedipus' "fate moves us because it might have been our own."*]

In my experience, which is already extensive, the chief part in the mental lives of all children who later become psychoneurotics is played by their parents. Being in love with the one parent and hating the other are among the essential constituents of the stock of physical impulses which is formed at that time and which is of such importance in determining the symptoms of the later neurosis. It is not my belief, however, that psychoneurotics differ sharply in this respect from other human beings who remain normal—that they are able, that is, to create something absolutely new and peculiar to themselves. It is far more probable—and this is confirmed by occasional observations on normal children—that they are only distinguished by exhibiting on a magnified scale feelings of love and hatred to their parents which occur less obviously and less intensely in the minds of most children.

This discovery is confirmed by a legend that has come down to us from classical antiquity: a legend whose profound and universal power to move can only be understood if the hypothesis I have put forward in regard to the psychology of children has an equally universal validity. What I have in mind is the legend of King Oedipus and Sophocles' drama which bears his name.

Oedipus, son of Laïus, King of Thebes, and of Jocasta, was exposed as an infant because an oracle had warned Laïus that the still unborn child would be his father's murderer. The child was rescued, and grew up as a prince in an alien court, until, in doubts as to his origin, he too questioned the oracle and was warned to avoid his home since he was destined to murder his father and take his mother in marriage. On the road leading away from what he believed was his home, he met King Laïus and slew him in a sudden quarrel. He came next to Thebes and solved the riddle set him by the Sphinx who barred his way. Out of gratitude the Thebans made him their king and gave him Jocasta's hand in marriage. He reigned long in peace and honour, and she who, unknown to him, was his mother bore him two sons and two daughters. Then at last a plague broke out and the Thebans made enquiry once more of the oracle. It is at this point that Sophocles' tragedy opens. The messengers bring back the reply that the plague will cease when the murderer of Laïus has been driven from the land.

> But he, where is he? Where shall now be read
> The fading record of this ancient guilt?

The action of the play consists in nothing other than the process of revealing, with cunning delays and ever-mounting excitement—a process that can be likened to the work of a psychoanalysis—that Oedipus himself is the murderer of Laïus, but further that he is the son of the murdered man and of Jocasta. Appalled at the abomination which he has unwittingly perpetrated, Oedipus blinds himself and forsakes his home. The oracle has been fulfilled.

Oedipus Rex is what is known as a tragedy of destiny. Its tragic effect is said to lie in the contrast between the supreme will of the gods and the vain attempts of mankind to escape the evil that threatens them. The lesson which, it is said, the deeply moved spectator should learn from the tragedy is submission to the divine will and realization of his own impotence. Modern dramatists have accordingly tried to achieve a similar tragic effect by weaving the same contrast into a plot invented by themselves. But the spectators have looked on unmoved while a curse or an oracle was fulfilled in spite of all the efforts of some innocent man: later tragedies of destiny have failed in their effect.

If *Oedipus Rex* moves a modern audience no less than it did the contemporary Greek one, the explanation can only be that its effect does not lie in the contrast between destiny and human will, but is to be looked for in the particular nature of the material on which that contrast is exemplified. There must be something which makes a voice within us ready to recognize the compelling force of destiny in the *Oedipus,* while we can dismiss as merely arbitrary such dispositions as are laid down in [Grillparzer's] *Die Ahnfrau* or other modern tragedies of destiny. And a factor of this kind is in fact involved in the story of King Oedipus. His destiny moves us only because it might have been ours—because the oracle laid the same curse upon us before our birth as upon him. It is the fate of all of us, perhaps, to direct our first sexual impulse towards our mother and our first hatred and our first murderous wish against our father. Our dreams convince us that that is so. King Oedipus, who slew his father Laïus and married his mother Jocasta, merely shows us the fulfilment of our own childhood wishes. But, more fortunate than he, we have meanwhile succeeded, in so far as we have not become psychoneurotics, in detaching our sexual impulses from our mothers and in forgetting our jealousy of our fathers. Here is one in whom these primaeval wishes of our childhood have been fulfilled, and we shrink back from him with the whole force of the repression by which those wishes have since that time been held down within us. While the poet, as he unravels the past, brings to light the guilt of Oedipus, he is at the same time compelling us to recognize our own inner minds, in which those same impulses, though suppressed, are still to be found. The contrast with which the closing Chorus leaves us confronted—

> . . . Fix on Oedipus your eyes,
> Who resolved the dark enigma, noblest champi-
>   on and most wise.
> Like a star his envied fortune mounted beaming
>   far and wide:
> Now he sinks in seas of anguish, whelmed be-
>   neath a raging tide . . .

—strikes as a warning at ourselves and our pride, at us who since our childhood have grown so wise and so mighty in our own eyes. Like Oedipus, we live in ignorance of these wishes, repugnant to morality, which have been forced upon us by Nature, and after their revelation we may all of us well seek to close our eyes to the scenes of our childhood.

There is an unmistakable indication in the text of Sophocles' tragedy itself that the legend of Oedipus sprang from some primaeval dream-material which had as its content the distressing disturbance of a child's relation to his parents owing to the first stirrings of sexuality. At a point when Oedipus, though he is not yet enlightened, has begun to feel troubled by his recollection of the oracle, Jocasta consoles him by referring to a dream which many people dream, though, as she thinks, it has no meaning:

> Many a man ere now in dreams hath lain
> With her who bare him. He hath least annoy
> Who with such omens troubleth not his mind.

To-day, just as then, many men dream of having sexual relations with their mothers, and speak of the fact with indignation and astonishment. It is clearly the key to the tragedy and the complement to the dream of the dreamer's father being dead. The story of Oedipus is the reaction of the imagination to these two typical dreams. And just as these dreams, when dreamt by adults, are accompanied by feelings of repulsion, so too the legend must include horror and self-punishment. (pp. 260-64)

Sigmund Freud, "The Material and Sources of Dreams," in his The Interpretation of Dreams, *edited and translated by James Strachey, Basic Books, Inc., Publishers, 1955, pp. 163-276.*

Michael Grant   (essay date 1962)

[*Grant is a distinguished classicist, translator, and editor known for his eminently readable studies of the classical world, especially Rome. His numerous writings, which encompass a large variety of topics, include* Myths of the Greeks and Romans *(1962),* The Ancient Mediterranean *(1969), and* The History of Rome *(1978). In the following excerpt from the first-named work, Grant attempts to place* Oedipus Rex *in the context of European literary, intellectual, and mythological traditions, underlining the fundamental differences between Greek religiosity and the spirit of Christianity.*]

Thebes, on the southern edge of the eastern plain of Boeotia, had been the chief Mycenaean city in central Greece, though the mention of only a subsidiary settlement in the Homeric catalogue suggests that there was an interlude in its prosperity during which the town had been laid waste. The Thebans possessed good wheat and horses, and were agricultural and self-contained, having no part in overseas expansion. Though producers of fine poetry, they were reputed to be slow of wit.

We know a little of Thebes, for it has been partly excavated, but we have also lost the whole of the Theban epic cycle in which the myths of the House of Oedipus were handed down. The cycle's two leading poems, the *Thebais* and *Oedipodia,* are conjecturally attributed to the eighth century B.C. The *Thebais* was early, though dubiously assigned to Homer, and was greatly admired. The *Oedipodia* was ascribed to a certain Cinaethon of Sparta.

Oedipus may have been a real person: whose story absorbed, among other fabulous elements, the classic folktale situation of those who try to avert an unpleasant prophecy and believe themselves safe, whereas the prediction is, in the end, fulfilled in an unexpected fashion. Or he may be wholly mythical. In any case he is different from the Homeric heroes, because he is superior in intelligence and not in physical might (even Odysseus had both); and because he is not the son or direct protégé of a god but the individual member of a family, participating in its greatness and its faults of violence and anger.

Oedipus lacked physical strength because when he was a baby his father Laius, abandoning him, had thrust a spike through his feet, presumably to disable the ghost. Hence his name, "swell-foot." Not only were exposed children a phenomenon of Greek life with which many were familiar, but the recurrent myths of their survival symbolize defiance of fate. These stories may be derived from the initiation tests of early societies; in psychopathology, as Jung points out, they stand for the imaginative transformation of personal inadequacies into great pretensions and powers. The Maori hero Massi was thrown into the sea as an infant, and Vainamoinen, the hero of the *Kalevala,* "floated above dark waves." In the Mediterranean tradition there are Moses and Romulus and Remus and many others, and as early as the third millennium BC King Sargon the Akkadian had told of his own exposure. Not only has the foundling myth become familiar as a success story in comedy, but Shakespeare, in his last plays, illustrates the tragic helpless character of human life by showing many of his heroes and heroines as orphans, at the mercy of the

storm. Like Oedipus, they are delivered from the danger, but their lonely upbringing sets them apart from our common destiny.

Oedipus won his throne by defeating a female incubus from the underworld, the Sphinx. Her name is usually explained as the "throttler" or the "choker," but more probably means the "tight-binder," the demon of death. Sphinxes originated in Egypt, but became known throughout the near east. In Greece—where they appear frequently on orientalizing seventh-century friezes and vases—they have changed from male to female, the female fear-animal of nightmare that Freud attributed to the incest prohibition.

The Sphinx had been sent by Hera to Thebes, and had devoured its people, until Oedipus got the better of the monster by solving the riddle which others had failed to solve. Riddles, which may perhaps be of separate origin from folktales but circulate no less freely, are common in many lands from Mongolia to central Africa. In Greece, which loved them, these conundrums were the descendants of the parables and hard sayings in Hesiod's *Works and Days.* In particular, riddles often reflected the misleading darkness of divine utterances, and of the human choices which depended upon them. The riddle of the Theban Sphinx was this:

> A thing there is whose voice is one,
> Whose feet are two and four and three.
> So mutable a thing is none
> That moves in earth or sky or sea.
> When on most feet this thing doth go
> Its strength is weakest and its pace most slow.

Oedipus recognized in this the three ages of man. Freud, however, conjectured that the question the riddle was really designed to answer related to the oldest and most burning question to the immature—the origin of babies. At all events, Oedipus solved the riddle and gained the throne of Thebes. Tennyson, in his *Tiresias* (1885), tells how

> the fierce beast found
> A wiser than herself, and dashed herself
> Dead in her rage.

Although hardly anything "happens" in Sophocles' *King Oedipus*—other than the arrival of people with news—the play moves with intense, remorseless speed. Every word counts in this marvellously flexible dialogue and breathtaking choral poetry, and the issues are not intellectual abstractions but stamp themselves upon our hearts. To us it might seem an extraordinary improbability that Oedipus had never before heard, or inquired, how his predecessor had met his end. But in the dramatic tension of the performance, as it rapidly unfolded in the conditions of an open-air theatre, this aspect would be ignored. Besides, it is the self-appointed task of Sophocles to face the implausibilities of the myths—and display how such things nevertheless could have happened.

When first performed (at a date which we cannot determine), the play did not win first prize. But Aristotle handed it down to posterity as the model tragedy. Its continual imagery of blindness, light and darkness leads to a dramatic, harrowing conclusion. Yet the audience knew who the culprit was; it remained for Voltaire, in the preface of his *Mérope,* to advocate the virtues of suspense in regard to a plot. By the audience of Sophocles, on the other hand, the events that ineluctably take place are expected. Since, therefore, we are all in the secret but only the actors are not, the whole progression of events is a cumulation of the tragic irony which is particularly associated with the name of Sophocles. In this process the chorus plays an essential part, for he is the dramatist who most closely integrates its utterances both with the action of his plays and with the emotions of the spectators. More than the poet's mouthpiece or a sympathetic onlooker, the chorus organizes and gives rhythm and background to Sophocles' version of the myth, and helps him to use the story as a concrete example of the harrowing hatreds and aspirations of life.

For it is in the myths, even the cruellest myths, that Sophocles sees the permanent human battleground, accepting their horrors with his dramatic (if not altogether with his moral) sense, and more than Aeschylus adhering to their traditional framework. Yet these stories would be nothing without the poetry, for there comes a point, and this is reached by Sophocles, where form is so nearly perfect as to achieve the autonomous originality of a new concept. This is also true of the contemporary Parthenon in which, likewise, the achievement depends not on lavish ornament but on a simplicity modified by subtle constructional and stylistic effects. These, like the effects of Sophocles, "triumphantly escape, but just escape, the prosaic."

The supreme moment of tension is the passage from ignorance to "recognition" and knowledge, from success to despair. Oedipus is the most famous of all mythical searchers for truth behind illusion, and tragedy's function—in which Racine alone has approached Sophocles—is to display, and link with all that has gone before, the unendurable moment of truth in which the king knows who he is and what he has done. Sophocles is less interested in morality than in the human personalities which it exhibits. Yet in the rapid movement of the stage, comparable to the vivid breadth of a sculptural relief, the boldly contrasted dramatic lines in which character is presented are drawn not so much by psychological study as by concentration upon the qualities which prompted their decisions. As Aristotle saw, it is at one remove from ordinary men that the characters of Sophocles in their stark strength work out these crucial dilemmas, determining—as, in an era of change and questioning, Sophocles and his contemporaries had to determine for themselves—what they owe to the gods, their state, their family, and their own minds and hearts.

Among these demonic and iron-willed, yet arrogant, obstinate, and fierce-tempered sufferers of Sophoclean drama, Oedipus stands out: the self-taught ruler who unaided, and through his noble qualities, has risen to mastery over adversaries believed insuperable before. Oedipus illustrates Aristotle's theory that, in tragedy, misfortune should fall on an eminent man not because he is vicious but because there is something wrong about him, an error (*hamartia*). It has been endlessly discussed whether this

meant, or should mean, a flaw, a moral fault or frailty; or the intellectual foolishness or error of judgement of one who like Deianira "erred, intending well" (she killed Heracles with a supposed love-philtre in Sophocles' *Women of Trachis*); or a hereditary quasi-physical curse or blight—seeing that guilt, intentional or otherwise, was still regarded as such an infection. If, on the other hand, a wholly virtuous man were brought from prosperity to adversity, there would be no material for a tragedy. Shakespeare's Richard III and Macbeth are wicked, but have the compensating *grandeur d'âme* which Corneille, too, required in a central tragic figure. The Aristotelian ideal hero, exemplified by Oedipus, presents a more subtle problem. He is not only a figure of this same general grandeur, but he also possesses many specific qualities far above the common level. True, in an age of fighting and killing he killed hot-headedly at the crossroads when provoked (though without knowing it was a kinsman that he killed), and he shows fits of *hubris* in his over-confident, rash handling of the present situation. Yet these things are not the main, or at least not the sole, cause of his disaster. He is also the fatal victim of an unfathomed blow, tainted by some alloy of which the painful refinement brings him to utter ruin—ruin incurred, moreover, in conducting an investigation which he believes a duty, and an unpleasant one at that.

What Aristotle is referring to as Oedipus' "terror" lies in his ignorance of material facts and circumstances: in his misconception that touches off the casually linked events which lead to catastrophe. This misconception may or may not be blameworthy; its relevance to the problem of undeserved suffering is cryptic. The catastrophe, besides being complete, is also, according to Aristotle, the sort most proper to tragedy, in that it proceeds from a "reversal" of the situation (*peripeteia*)—an outcome contrary to the main actor's intention—combined with a dramatic "recognition" (*anagnorisis*) when the nature of what has happened dawns on him.

Downfalls such as that of Oedipus are caused by the gods, to whom all things are easy. They come when the divine order has somehow been breached. But we cannot always detect the breaching, or see why the divine purpose works as it does, or how the ensuing destruction harmonizes with our own fragmentary view of human justice. As in Theognis, suffering often seems to exceed deserts. In his *Women of Trachis* telling of Heracles' end, Sophocles concludes with words that are more equivocal than any clearcut victory of right over wrong.

> You have seen a terrible death
> And agonies, many and strange, and there is
> Nothing here which is not Zeus.

Men such as Oedipus are vulnerable and flawed since they are victims of the unpredictability of events, which, by injudicious acts, they often involuntarily help to deal them wounds.

Critics in the seventeenth and eighteenth centuries liked to stress the poetic justice in Greek tragedy. But Joseph Addison rightly saw that the ancient dramatists "treated men as they are dealt with in the world, by making virtue sometimes happy and sometimes miserable" (1711). A tragedian's handling of the myths, therefore, may well challenge or outrage our moral sense. Indeed, perhaps it must, in order to be tragedy at all—the frustrations and futility of which were dwelt upon by Schopenhauer. There is, in life, a stubborn residue of evil which no moralizing can easily justify, and Sophocles accepted this non-rational element, this lack of correlation between sin and punishment, this tolerance or support of evil by the supreme power. He did not feel obliged to resort to Manichaean dualism; Greece lies outside the great region of the earth (from the Iranian plateau eastwards to North America) which is the usual home of such beliefs. Nor did he need the African doctrine that the kind Supreme Spirit is followed about by an idiot brother who spoils what he has done.

Christian doctrine also rejects dualism. But unlike Sophocles it assumes that God is just. For this reason it is difficult to conceive a truly Christian tragedy; in Racine's *Phèdre,* for example, Friedrich von Schlegel (1807) saw a discrepancy between the tragic spirit and Christian providence—although the fierce fatalism of the Jansenists goes less badly with tragedy than, say, Rousseauist perfectibility. There is a contrast, too, between the various failures of individual human beings in classical drama and the Biblical doctrine of the Fall, by which all men become leprous and unclean until Jesus Christ redeems them. For Christians see evil as the harbinger of blessing, as something which always permits of reconciliation and atonement, a relief from what Dostoevsky saw as our complete and terrifying freedom: "O happy fault that has won for us so loving, so mighty a Redeemer."

Sophocles, like other Greek tragedians, found evil (expressed in suffering) beneficial for another reason—because of its educative power. Before the gods, or the god as Sophocles also says, man is nothing, and he must humble himself before their will; his mistakes and illustrations are on a far lower plane than theirs. *He* is entitled to understanding and compassion, yet *they,* however dreadful and inexplicable their manifestations, cannot ever be unjustified or wrong. For they embody the natural order of events.

The poet's piety is tranquil beneath the storms of action, and imperishable; his imagination wholly accepts the apparent evil in the divine dispensation. Yet man, in his gallant, losing struggle with necessity, is raised to a stature larger than life. For this is not only a pious but a humanistic creed, which incorporates the dilemmas of an optimistic and ambitious generation. Oedipus has extraordinary powers to match his extraordinary fate—and Sophocles also suggests that the forces which tolerate misery create, or augment, moral grandeur in the man who stands against them. There is, in defeat, a splendid heroism, peculiar to mankind and indissociable from their self-destruction. Thus, even at the appalling end, Oedipus is not wholly broken, and Creon says to him:

> Do not seek to be master in everything,
> For the things you mastered did not follow
>   You throughout your life.

Oedipus is reduced to utter destitution, stripped of everything—like Edgar, naked from the storm, of whom Lear asks: "is man no more than this?" The doom, which he gradually and horribly recognizes, is fixed from the start, and it comes from the Delphic oracle—which *has* to be fulfilled. Aeschylus had stressed the ancestral curse and the Furies' pursuit; Sophocles transfers the working out of events to Apollo and his oracle, which he inexorably justifies—at a time when disbelief was in the air.

Accordingly, the *Oedipus* has been used more than any other play to support the view that Greek tragedy deals with puppets helpless in the grip of destiny. And indeed, since fate was believed to be as much part of a man's endowment at birth as his looks or his mental gifts, the odds are overwhelmingly against Oedipus, who is therefore a more helpless victim of destiny than his daughter Antigone. He committed parricide and incest in all innocence. Yet, as H. D. F. Kitto remarks, if you mistake potassium cyanide for sugar, innocence and ignorance will not save you. Oedipus keeps his responsibility, for fate is the way life works out for a man, and he has a say in its working out. But fate also comprises the terrors of sheer ill-luck, of which Oedipus has much, and Sophocles seems to ask whether chance, or law, is at the root of the universe; later Greeks decided in favour of chance. And so Nietzsche calls tragedy the dancing ground of divine, unfathomable accident. Inexplicably cruel things do happen, but this only means that our knowledge of the universe's laws is fragmentary. Meanwhile, it is folly to neglect those which we do know. Such neglect is also disobedience to the gods. But Oedipus disobeys them without knowing it, and thus supplies an ever more terrifying manifestation of the divine will—irrefutable, sometimes incomprehensible, often unbearable.

The resulting events are painful, as their participants pass through anguish and are destroyed by forces they can neither understand nor master. Yet the plays which tell of these desperate, demon-ridden themes have appealed irresistibly to many generations. It has always been asked why this is; and the answers have been many. Aristotle, thinking of Sophocles rather than Aeschylus (and not following Plato in his desire to stamp out tragic pity as poison for the soul), said that tragedy, by actions arousing pity and fear, purifies or purges the corresponding passions in ourselves (*catharsis*). It arouses and then allays our pity and fear—pity prompted by unmerited misfortune, and fear caused by seeing the misfortune of man who is like, or not too unlike, ourselves. We share the mythical heroes' attempts to escape their dooms, comparing our desires and aims with theirs and hoping to avoid their catastrophes, and we depart in an emotional balance and equilibrium, all passion spent.

Yet St Augustine was still perplexed that "this very sorrow is the spectator's pleasure," and some (like the Athenian comic dramatist Timocles) have thought of tragedy as a gloating over horrors, while others again have condemned it for justifying and commending sufferings. Or should we rather interpret Aristotle as postulating the *retention* in us of pity and fear, but the elimination from these feelings of what is impure and harmful, making of them *not* a selfish sort of gloating but sympathy for human sorrows? Yet probably that is to introduce too much morality into a question that is primarily aesthetic rather than moral. For it is only through the poetic words, into which the suffering is translated by the artist, that this is elevated and transfigured into what is pure and moving and stimulating and delightful.

Since immediacy is a necessary part of fear, and tragedy is less immediate than films and novels, it is harder today than it was to effect the transference of emotional conflicts through these plays. But some modern writers still see a function in tragedy. "By its symbolic re-enactment," said Giraudoux, "it satisfies collectively the need of the public to commit a crime . . . To witness a tragedy in the theatre is to diminish in the heart of the spectator whatever murderous intention he may have had." To Anouilh on the other hand, tragedy is, paradoxically, restful: because you know that there is no more hope, dirty sneaking hope, and that you are caught, caught at last like a rat in a trap. (pp. 194-202)

> *Michael Grant, "Oedipus," in his* Myths of the Greeks and Romans, *New American Library, 1962, pp. 190-210.*

———————

ELECTRA

CRITICAL COMMENTARY

Thomas Woodard   (essay date 1966)

[*In the following excerpt, Woodard analyzes Sophocles'* Electra, *arguing that the structure of the play "makes the heroine stand on stage in the midst of an initially alien world, that of the men's plot, and play out her drama in relation to this, merging with it toward the end."*]

The *Electra* turns around Electra, but in order to appreciate her we must appreciate her play. Therefore let us take the *Electra* as a whole for our point of departure. What place does Electra occupy in it? What is her role in the history and action that absorbs us from beginning to end?

We may approach an answer by realizing that Electra is curiously alienated from one level of action through most of the drama. For at the outset Orestes and his men set in motion a plot to overthrow Clytemnestra and Aegisthus which continues, unabated, more or less behind the scenes, until it reaches complete fruition; reminders of it occur indirectly in every episode, and quite overtly when the Paedagogus enters to tell his false tale. The myth of the *Electra,* indeed, virtually passes over the heroine; as Aeschylus did in his *Oresteia.* History is made, in other words, even when Electra is oblivious of it. She initiates little of this larger action, and participates in it enthusiastically only after rebuke, and only in the closing minutes. And we must admit that this myth of vengeance could have provided a thrilling play by itself, without the presence of Electra; that in fact it does create suspense

throughout the play as it stands, and dominates the finale. Electra's predicament is resolved, if at all, only in the resolution of the history of Orestes' return and revenge.

The structure of the *Electra* makes the heroine stand on stage in the midst of an initially alien world, that of the men's plot, and play out her drama in relation to this, merging with it toward the end. More exactly, she lives out her own history while the men are making history in another sense; the *Electra* develops two kinds of action simultaneously, one in counterpoint with the other. We may describe these two kinds of action, these two dramatic *genres,* in terms of the theater of the fifth century B.C. The men act in high melodrama, serious, suspenseful, noble, and successful; Electra lives in the *agones,* or conflicts and suffering, of the older tragedy.

If this duality informs the *Electra,* Electra's experience cannot be simple. She must find her place in a larger order, the play as a whole; she must come into relation with a contrasting order, the world of the men. And so she does, superbly. Unlike Aeschylus, Sophocles makes Electra the focal point; and she overpowers the men's plot with her own strength and passion. We almost cease to feel suspense about revenge in our concern for her. Her figure dwarfs all others. In short, her tragedy bursts out of the framework of the double plot, just as her form of heroic action seems incommensurable with the men's activities.

For Electra dominates the *Electra* excessively: her speaking part is one of the longest in Greek tragedy; she remains in full view nine-tenths of the time; she includes the heights and depths of emotion in her range; she chants more lyrics than any other Sophoclean protagonist. We must suspect that these excesses of speech, stamina, passion, and lyric express something essential to Sophocles' conception of his heroine. At the same time, we are struck by what would ordinarily be outright defects: her ignorance of Orestes' return and strategy; her physical inactivity; her wrangling and iteration; her mistaken opinions; her hate. Yet these too seem to contribute to her power in the theater; these too must be essential to her heroic character.

We begin to appreciate Electra's world when we realize how in all her traits she defines herself by antithesis to the men. They are laconic; move on and off the stage with facility; display little feeling; have no lyrics. They know what's afoot; and behave with restraint, prudence, reasonableness. In fact, the men's dramatic personalities oppose Electra's at every point. As in action and *genre,* the *Electra* combines two distinct kinds of character.

In the course of her history Electra changes. At the beginning she is poles apart from the men. But by the time Orestes rejoins her, she has developed toward him in certain respects, so that they can work as partners in the finale. The present interpretation sees a dialectical pattern in the initial separation and subsequent reunion of brother and sister, and sees dialectic throughout in Electra's struggles and debates, internal and external. But when all is said and done, Electra triumphs. Though paired with Orestes, she is incomparable; and all the antitheses in the play are similarly imbalanced.

The Prologue scene initiates the design of dialectic and im-balanced antithesis. It has one feature unique in the extant work of Sophocles: it is divided between characters who neither address one another nor occupy the stage together. The separation of brother and sister, and the astonishing differences between the feelings and thoughts expressed by each, present to our eyes and minds a number of funda-mental contrasts, built into the divided scene. And while the men's half of the Prologue prepares for the entrance of Electra, the intensity of our response to her presupposes a response to them, since she startles us out of a world that we have taken for granted. We enter Electra's world, then, through a door provided by the play, the men's world.

In the theater what we see and hear coalesce, or rather exist as one. The contrasts in the Prologue are all self-evident in the sense that they are present in what the char-acters do, say, evoke, and imply. The halving of the Pro-logue corresponds to a number of dualities, but most obvi-ous, perhaps, is that of the sexes. First three men occupy the stage, then Electra, who is soon joined by the chorus of women. Sophocles found this dramatic contrast close at hand, in the rigorous social differentiation of men and women in fifth-century Athens. Women tended the home while able-bodied men controlled all public affairs as well as trades.

We see the Paedagogus and Orestes confidently, rational-ly, briskly planning a course of action. And both conclude their opening speeches with references to *erga*, acts, deeds, exhorting one another to set to work. *Ergon* implies not only many specifically male livelihoods and their prod-ucts, but "job" or "industry," "possessions" in general, and "interest" in the economic sense. So also both men stress the *kairos*, which means "profit" as well as "the right time." Their avowed goal in fact is *kerdos*, gain, prof-it, and wealth; they are even willing to get it by theft if nec-essary. Orestes announces his readiness to use *dolos*, cun-ning, deception, specifically by means of speech, to gain his ends. He has no hesitation about lying for profit. The oracle of Apollo itself had urged *dolos*: deceitful means to a just end. Orestes proves himself full of craft by outlining a lie, a *mythos*, for the Paedagogus to tell.

Orestes' language weaves a network of other allusions to the public life of an Athenian man. He sees himself en-gaged in the masculine occupation of warfare and pictures himself in competition at the games. He is an adventurer, an exile seeking to recover his patrimony, and virtually a wandering merchant or soldier of fortune; but he is also a vigorous young worker, bread-winner, and man of af-fairs. His venture is just, we cannot doubt it as he speaks: it is as just as commerce, as just as a prayer for success heeded by gods, as just as battling to win back a homeland. Our favorable impressions of him make us acquiesce in his ethic: a good, gainful end justifies any necessary, sanc-tioned means.

Orestes' mentality has usually perplexed critics, since he seems without any sensibility at all. He seeks his goal with complete assurance and no scruples, doubts, or passion. We see him lucidly and coolly plotting a venture of life and death. The reason for these peculiarities of "personality" is now clear. Orestes symbolizes a mind that exists only in external action, only for external action, rational and realistic.

The speeches of Orestes and the Paedagogus define more precisely this mentality and the dramatic world inhabited by the men. It is a world of *ergon*—bodily activity, exter-nality, work—in which *logos*—utterance, thought, lan-guage—depends on *ergon*—the product, action, fact—for its validity. In these terms Orestes' set-speech contrasts two kinds of *logos*: valid, correlated with *ergon*; and spuri-ous, opposed to it or separated from it. For him and the Paedagogus, meaningful *logoi*, words, statements, further the deed or spring from actualities. *Logoi* of this sort are a prerequisite for effective action because they lead to clar-ity about the best plan: we see the men using speech in this way in their discussion. In this sense also *logoi* correspond to *erga* as a true proposition or conception corresponds to the way things really are. Such *logoi* can be an instrument of action as well: the essential feature of Orestes' plan is a *mythos* or story for the Paedagogus to tell. Thus *logos* can connote pretense, since it can conceal the true state of affairs though grounded in it. In this vein Orestes draws on the common Greek antithesis of false *logoi* and the *erga* of truth:

> Why should it grieve me, if I die in pretense
> (*logos*)
> But in reality (*erga*) stay safe . . .

In this way too, Orestes affirms *erga*, since they cannot possibly be inauthentic and since they define the truth and falsehood of *logoi*.

Orestes' language is discursive, orderly, logical; and *logos* for him means prose. He speaks well, but his rhetoric is conventional, that of the public assembly, military strate-gy, or princely directive.

Orestes' speech as a whole is itself a *logos* corresponding to an *ergon* outside it, the physical action of the drama. For both the speech and the play begin with the Paeda-gogus; both continue with planning. The phrase, "Let that be the story" [line 50], stands at the exact center of the speech; the Paedagogus' story appears at the exact center of the play. Then Orestes alludes to his reappearance with the urn, then to his "rebirth" to confound his enemies. And, finally, the speech ends, as the play, with the *ergon* of slaying and vengeance.

At the end of the speech the three men prepare to leave the stage. They exit in different directions: the Paedagogus will act by *logoi*, befitting his age or his profession; the younger men, physically. Discussion has served its pur-pose. The end of their colloquy is the beginning of ven-geance.

Through its atmosphere of intrigue and adventure, and by the sheer logic of its development, Orestes' exposition brings us to a full sense of impending action. The exchange between him and his Tutor, then, after a voice moans off-stage, springs from the opposition of *logos* to *ergon* that comes into being when preparations are finished. "Should we wait and listen to the lament?" asks Orestes. "By no means," answers his instructor, "nothing should be set be-fore the necessary actions that will lead us to victory in our task." The rejection here of *logoi* (in the form of *gooi*, cries), for the sake of *erga,* sums up their dramatic world.

When Electra steps from the palace and begins her dirge, we are struck immediately by two things. First, the shift to lyrics, to the free anapests of chanted lamentation, breaks abruptly with the iambics of the preceding dialogue. Second, at the center of the stage we see a lone young woman in place of three men of varying ages. We may now appreciate that these contrasts re-enforce a distinction between a masculine world of *erga,* in which *logoi* are mere servants, and a feminine world of *logoi,* here laments, which preclude physical effectiveness but have another power all their own.

If Orestes is free-ranging, conscienceless, professional, athletic, and businesslike, Electra is tied to the home, unambitious, poverty-stricken, despairing, and frenzied. She stayed behind when Orestes was taken abroad. She is miserable at home because she is treated like a slave. This is her economic condition by contrast to Orestes'. She refuses to seek to better her standard of living. She does not see herself engaged in any public life at all. The palace walls bound her world.

We first hear Electra's voice ringing inside the palace. The Paedagogus stresses its location. When she comes forth through the doors we soon realize that she embodies the interior of that terrible dwelling, her backdrop throughout the play.

Electra's woman's life indoors symbolizes her essential sphere: the internal world of idea, image, and emotion. She grieves in her own bed at night; she locates the source of the family's ills in lust. She is a sensibility laid bare: there is her pity, her hate, and her depression. Orestes plans and acts; Electra suffers and endures. The men confer with one another, within an explicit context of communication. Electra soliloquizes, or rather addresses herself to the elements. She laments: reiterates the memories that haunt her, and dwells on her sufferings. The explicit context of her lament is lamentation itself. A typical one is in progress, and she asserts her intention to repeat the liturgy as long as she lives. Threnody is Electra's occupation, her only mode of action in the sense that Orestes recognized speech as a mode of action. But lamentation is not effectively instrumental, nor does Electra make that claim for it. Viewed as to results, it at best exhorts the spirits of the dead and the nether gods to send Orestes. Her threnody reaches its climax in a cry for her brother. He is to her as he is to himself and the Paedagogus: the requisite avenger of Agamemnon's murder.

Electra's language moves beyond prose. Her threnody is not organized schematically; its imagery evokes unreflecting response. It replaces logic with imaginative *logos* in organic rhythms. Electra's inward universe obliterates distinctions of time and place, and transforms everything tangible into a creature of her own experience.

Whether mourning becomes Electra or not, it has become her life. The thrust toward the future and the suspense built up in us by the schemes of the men recede and vanish. Harmonious exchange of advice has been supplanted by

the echo of Electra's voice crying in public solitude, as she vows

> With continual wailing, before paternal doors,
> To utter a resounding cry for all to hear.

Electra's grieving is, in a sense, self-perpetuated; yet it flows from a perception of real horror and torment. Through her eyes we see the murder of Agamemnon, as well as the wretched life that she has led since. She draws us into the domestic torment and tension as we respond to her inwardness, and into her inner torment and tension as we respond to the domestic.

In forcing us to enter her private world, Electra lodges us in an atmosphere that will dominate the play. *Logos* and *ergon* have reversed their relationship, for Electra suffers under *erga,* rather than produces them. Her *logoi* express emotion, rather than plot deeds. Her power lies all in *logos;* physically she is impotent. We are already aware of the tension within *logos* between truth and falsehood. Now we begin to realize that *logos* is an absolute, and in part beyond this distinction.

The Parodos, significantly in the form of a lengthy *kommos* or liturgical lament, turns not on any doubts about the condemnation of the vicious Clytemnestra but on the Chorus' friendly criticism of Electra's excessive talk and mourning. "Why do you continually lament?" the Chorus ask. "Why do you desire to suffer?" The questions and objections of the Chorus concerning Electra's verbal activity evoke the greater part of what she chants. From the outset she accepts the character ascribed to her. She links herself with the fabled singer, the nightingale, and with the perpetually weeping Niobe. She too will persist in rage, frenzy, and "countless threnodies."

The Parodos achieves a remarkable dramatic result. Electra wins our closest sympathy and touchingly defends her stance; at the same time, she exhibits and avows shameful behavior, irrationality, and sheer, self-defeating stubbornness. She defends lament for its own sake, though she grants that it is self-lacerating and self-degrading. She is, by a kind of necessary, heroic obstinacy, at war with herself as well as with her environment. Lamentation and rebuke make up her *ethos,* and this is a habit-and-trait that she feels futile and, in one sense, immoral. She can fully affirm only the righting of a now doubly violated moral order; and this would require an act of vengeance. But, alone, she is able only to mourn and censure the moral disorder, thus further separating herself from the wholly valid. Electra acts under a necessity more profound than moral "principles"; enduring her own conflict while facing her environment manifests her peculiar moral intuition. Her heroism, in other words, as it claims our sympathy in the theater, must express itself in contradiction. We must identify *logos* with this paradoxical intuition.

In part, Electra endures the inherent duality of *logos:* a meaningful activity and a mere substitute for action. Her *logoi* spring from *erga* that have impinged on her, that oppress her now, over which she has no control, and against which her only weapon is speech. On the other hand, her *logoi* possess the autonomy and literally incalculable power of lyric and liturgy.

I am ashamed, ladies, if I seem to you
To grieve too much with many threnodies.
But violence forces me to do them.

Beginning her first set-speech in this vein, Electra assents
to the whole drift of the Chorus in the Parodos. She is
trapped in a woman's world of polemic and lament. In entering her world of *logoi,* we enter on a series of scenes
made up precisely of oratory, polemic, and lament. The
issues intrinsic to the distinction of *logos* and *ergon* are debated, implicitly and explicitly, in scenes that advance the
physical action, the external plot, hardly at all. These
scenes are equally portraits, trials, and punishments. But,
passing through these scenes, Electra advances, still within the dilemmas of isolated *logos,* to a recognition of the
necessity for external *ergon.* Then the final episodes in the
drama present effective action more than they debate issues; Electra becomes Orestes' colleague and subordinates
herself to the necessities of vengeance. Yet the heart of the
Electra remains Electra in isolation and *logos* divorced
from *ergon,* not only because of quantitative proportions
but because this tragic Electra moves us as the melodramatic Electra cannot. And we recognize that, in the central scenes, *logos* justifies itself in a way that survives the
apparent triumph of *ergon* in the finale. In spite of all our
preconceptions about the sanctity of literal truth and the
urgency of efficient action, in spite of Electra's own acceptance of the correlation of *logos* and *ergon* as Orestes expressed it in the Prologue, the ***Electra*** shows *logos* omnip-
otent in its character of faith, ideal, and imaginative language.

The ostensible issue in the first encounter of the two sisters
is how one should live, and what one should do, in evil circumstances. But these questions of action are turned into
questions about what one should say, believe, and rely on,
and the point of the scene virtually becomes Electra's oral
forcefulness. The persuasive force of her arguments contains her moral supremacy, as it comes across to us in the
theater; her directives as to what Chrysothemis should do
(and not do) finally prevail. Though Electra boasts of active resistance, we discover that her accomplishment remains wholly verbal. The ironical result of the scene is
that only poor Chrysothemis must actually run a risk, in
disobeying her mother and offering a substitute sacrifice
to her father.

In the first part of the scene, both sisters show much contempt for mere *logoi,* and both attempt to prove that the
other lives by *logos* rather than by *ergon.* Chrysothemis'
opening words challenge Electra's futile talk and futile
passion [lines 328-31]. Chrysothemis then charges that
Electra only *seems* to be doing something, while really she
harms no one, effects no result. Electra then claims that
she has been the one engaged in *erga* [l. 350]. Chrysothemis has hated their common enemies merely in speech,
or "in pretence," while "in reality," "in truth," living
comfortably with them (*men logo/ergo de,* ll. 357-58).

To Electra's brilliant dialectical defense of her mode of life
by contrast to her sister's, Chrysothemis makes no reply
whatsoever, but brushes the whole speech and all its arguments aside by saying to the Chorus: "I am quite used to
her talk (*muthon,* l. 373)." And she simply turns to anoth-

er topic, which proves to be the plan of Clytemnestra and
Aegisthus for silencing Electra's "great groans," *ton
makron goon* [l. 375], a phrase suggesting *hoi makroi logoi,*
"long or over-long speeches," which we shall hear more
than once in connection with Electra later in the play. The
antithesis of this latter phrase, in fact, occurs a few moments later, when Electra asks for a report of Clytemnestra's dream.

> CHRYSOTHEMIS: Do these night terrors make
> you hopeful?
>
> ELECTRA: If you told me the vision, then I might
> say.
>
> CHRYSOTHEMIS: But I know only very little to
> tell.
>
> ELECTRA: Then say *that.* A few words (*logoi*)
> have often
> Overthrown or re-established men.
>
> CHRYSOTHEMIS: The story is. . . . (The *logos*
> is. . . .)

These lines might be said to speak for themselves. Electra's gnomic pronouncement about the power of "a few
words," *smikroi logoi,* deserves amplification, however.
These *logoi* are at once instrumental, instructive, and potent in themselves. Her defense of *logoi* as autonomous
forces in human life coheres with her own reliance on the
ritual *logoi* of lament, the competitive *logoi* of persuasion
and self-defense, and the battling *logoi* of reproach and insult.

The debate ends with Chrysothemis persuaded to do as
Electra bids.

> CHRYSOTHEMIS: I will do it. It is not reasonable
> for two people
> To dispute what is just, but rather to hasten to
> do it.

She contrasts the fruitless *logoi* of dispute with daring action (*to dran* and *ton ergon*). Then she begs for silence, the
necessary companion of a successful venture. We shall
meet this corollary of the basic duality again later. We
may notice here that the colloquy between the sisters ends
with the commencement of a deed, as at the exit of the
three partners in the Prologue. The silence of the interlocutors thus has positive dramatic effect.

Clytemnestra enters with attendants bearing ritual offerings such as Chrysothemis had carried in the previous Episode. In their first words both mother and sister rebuke
Electra for again being outside the palace talking. In both
scenes Electra proves stronger; here she convicts her
mother of criminal guilt. For it is a case of murder; or,
rather, there are two murders, Iphigeneia's and Agamemnon's. Electra acts as prosecutor against her mother, and
as lawyer for the defense of her father. The language of the
interchange seats us in the law-courts. And the whole
scene ultimately turns not so much on questions of sub-
stantive justice as on an examination of the debating process and of the use of speech as a mode of action.

Were we not attuned to the issue of *logos* and *ergon,* it
would be hard to understand why the most violent ex-

change in this most violent scene uses such abstruse language.

> ELECTRA: Shameful deeds are taught by shameful deeds.
>
> CLYTEMNESTRA: O shameless creature, I and my words
> And my deeds make you say much too much.
>
> ELECTRA: You say it, not I. For you do
> The deed; and deeds find words for themselves.
>
> CLYTEMNESTRA: By Lady Artemis, you'll pay
> for this impudence . . .

Clytemnestra's pairing of words and deeds, implying the sum total of behavior, contrasts to Electra's sole activity, talk. The phrase, "make you say too much," *agan legein poei,* presents the central duality in miniature. Electra's paradoxical reply, "*You* say it," attempts to justify her talk by pleading the compulsion of deeds. "You do the deed," she says, *su gar poeis/tourgon,* implying not only that Clytemnestra is her antithesis (as *ergon versus* her *logos*), but that deeds or circumstances produce speech.

"Deeds find words for themselves": *ta d'erga tous logous heurisketai.* Electra's ultimate line of self-defense implies that words are subservient to deeds, as passive to active, or as effect to cause. Thus she expresses the ambiguous autonomy of *logos* and of her own character in the face of *erga.* The debate between mother and daughter quite literally consists of words sprung inevitably from foul deeds. The next scene presents words necessitated by a just enterprise. In a sense not intended by Electra, "deeds find words for themselves" implies that deeds require *logoi* as means, and hence that the deed afoot, Orestes', will call forth the *mythos* of the Paedagogus. Thus the proposition serves as a transition in the theater.

The Paedagogus' false account of Orestes' death (the longest set-speech in the extant work of Sophocles) complements Clytemnestra's self-convicting prayer, and, by eye-for-eye justice, gives her what she deserves. But the *mythos,* which we have been expecting since Orestes outlined its plot in the Prologue, also complements Electra's verbal virtuosity. Her character, with its essentially monochromatic reliance on verbal action, and its duality of pathos and power, leaps to accept the Paedagogus' story in its shattering ramifications. Her suffering is real, and affects us. But we realize at the same time that it is consonant with her character to be taken in by a verbal stratagem, by verbal seeming. Clytemnestra says that *she* will wait for the ashes, as proof of the story. But Electra interrupts and pushes away the Chorus' suggestions about hope for Orestes' life. The succeeding scene will show Electra rejecting even concrete evidence on the question of the alleged death, and able in her turn to give a plausible explanation (*logos*) for Chrysothemis' discoveries. Electra shows a stubborn refusal to doubt the worst; an immense capacity to endow thought with reality.

The Paedagogus' speech stands dead-center in the play. It is not without significance that both the plan of Orestes and the total action of the drama pivot on this unrivaled exhibition of verbal verisimilitude. For us as audience, the speech flows naturally as part of the original scheme. But now the story has another level of impact on us. It completes the pathos of Electra; the compulsion behind her suffering as she listens proves its noble strength. The *mythos* becomes an *ergon* tormenting her.

The Paedagogus' speech deploys the power in *logoi,* just as Electra had in persuasive colloquy with Chrysothemis or in her admirable prosecution of Clytemnestra. And, in the Paedagogus' speech shines again the double nature of *logos.* The speech is instrumental, valid, justified, and effective, in the strategy of revenge; it is deceiving, spurious, and grievous in its immediate effects. We marvel at the persuasiveness of a story which we know is false. We suffer with Electra though we know that she will eventually rejoice.

Because the lie completes Electra's pathos, her transformation begins. In despair she finds new determination. For the first time in the play she makes a decision to act physically. The second confrontation between the sisters contrasts at many points with the first, emphasizing Electra's new attitude. Before, she had succeeded in persuading Chrysothemis to do something, however minimal, by way of rebellion; here, she fails to persuade, but vows she stands ready to act alone. She abandons the effort at persuasion. But, at the end of the scene, Electra does not depart. Chrysothemis she sends away, remaining on stage during the second Stasimon. For after all, we reflect, Orestes will come, has come; and Electra will never do the deed.

There is, in fact, similar irony throughout the second meeting of the sisters. Electra defends the deed that she proposes by stressing the good repute, *logon eukleia,* that will accrue. Again and again she argues from what others will say, quoting finally an imaginary eulogy at length. These rather suspect forms of reputation, spun out into a fable with a happy ending, contrast with the honor, accompanied by lands and rule, which Orestes seeks. The scene as a whole impresses us once again with the schism in Electra's stance. She would venture on deeds in pursuit of kind words.

The same schism lies behind the dispute over the tokens. Electra presents herself to Chrysothemis as tough-minded, and claims to judge by the way things are rather than by private opinions. She accuses her sister of being deceived by words.

> ELECTRA: Alas! Who told you this story (*logos*)
> That you believe in all too fully?

Chrysothemis argues that her "hypothesis" is warranted by clear evidence.

> CHRYSOTHEMIS: I saw clear signs for myself,
> And do not believe another's story.

The irony of Electra's position in this interchange is patent. So it is also in her last exhibition of persuasive force, when she counters Chrysothemis' self-conscious deduction from the tokens to Orestes' presence (lines 907-15) with her own evidence, mere hearsay.

CHRYSOTHEMIS: Alas! Who told you these
   things?

ELECTRA: The man nearest when he died.

For us, the plausibility of her explanation of the tokens
hardly belies its pathetic spuriousness. However, while
Chrysothemis had shown a merely logical skill, Electra's
moral and emotional force carries the day. This dispute,
then, exposes the deceitfulness of *logoi* (words, arguments,
reasons) when divorced from *erga* (acts, facts, things), but
simultaneously exhibits the potency of autonomous *logos*
(conviction, imagination, inwardness). If Electra reaches
her largest heroic stature in this scene, it can only be because her force and her folly unite in her essential commitment to pure *logos,* and only because *logos* itself possesses
an authenticity beyond the judgment of reason and the
world. Here *logos* completely triumphs over logic.

Since Orestes and Electra are living emblems of the play's
basic conceptual duality, in the "recognition" scene visible
dramatic effects stand out, corresponding to their physical
reunion. Orestes enters carrying an urn. This urn, like a
third actor, dominates the stage until the final minute of
the dialogue. It is the reason given for the stranger's presence; Electra cries out at the sight of it, and, holding it in
her arms, addresses it in a long and moving lament; finally, Orestes tries to recover it from her, and his explanation
of who he is revolves around explaining what the urn is
not.

ORESTES: Give up this urn then, so you may
   learn all.

For the urn is a surrogate Orestes, an Orestes by sham, a
fiction posing as fact. What Electra and we alike "recognize" in the scene is a distinction between reality and supposition, between expectation and event, between true and
false evidence.

In fact, something similar happens to Orestes as well. He
suffers in seeing (and hearing) Electra's suffering, and alters his course of action. As he replaces concealment
through silence with revelatory speech, Electra replaces
her compelling though misdirected lamentation with joy.
From this mutual shift results the sweetness of the climactic moments: Electra releases the urn [line 1217], soon to
take Orestes himself in her arms [line 1225]. Orestes with
one hand shows Electra the ring that proves what the urn
that he holds in the other had only shammed. At the end
of the dialogue, the urn recedes from the level of personage
to that of mere object, and all our attention rests on the
living pair.

But speech plays a major role in this scene alongside the
urn. Electra's lament overpowers us; and it overpowers
Orestes. At its conclusion he finds himself at a loss for
words:

   Woe, woe, what shall I say? So perplexed,
   Where can I go in speech? I no longer have the
      strength to control my tongue.

For the first time in the play, Orestes suffers under the
force of evils from without. Thus he shares, at least momentarily, his sister's trait of compulsive speech and also
her relationship to *erga kaka* [bad deeds]. At their mo-

ment of reunion Orestes enters the world of Electra, just
as she had already gone far toward entering his in the preceding scene. For this reason, contrary to plan, Orestes admits his former lie, saying that the urn is "not Orestes, except tricked out in speech (logo)."

The mutual recognition of brother and sister, and their experience of self-recognition, achieve a fragile resolution of
conflict in this scene. But it lasts only a moment. We then
plunge back into tension between talk and the deed at
hand which pulls apart the newly joined couple.

The seeming duet between Electra and Orestes [lines
1232-87] actually shows no harmonizing at all. For Orestes does not join in; he has no lyric lines, only the rational
iambics of discourse. We see dramatized again, in fact, the
contrast so striking in the Prologue, between Electra's
threnody, here reversed to exaltation, and Orestes' controlled deliberations. Orestes' constant effort is to terminate this "duet." We have forced on us again an awareness
that a violent endeavor, demanding secrecy, is in progress,
and that talk may give everything away and bring disaster.

The scene between the song and the short third Stasimon
serves as a vital transition to the so-called Exodos, which
is the climax of the action. The transition involves a gradual alteration in the attitude of Electra; and a few more,
final touches in the education of Orestes, supplied by the
Paedagogus. The scene takes us closer to the means and
the end represented by the Paedagogus, and more fully
into his world of *ergon.*

At the beginning of the dialogue Orestes puts his attitude
toward Electra's melic interlude as vigorously and as
bluntly as possible: "Cease all superfluous speech" [line
1288]. In a coherent, concise statement, built around a
rhetorical opposition of *logos* to *ergon,* he requests Electra
not to waste precious time with a recapitulation of the
past. "For," he says, "talk (*logos*) would hinder the moment of opportunity (*kairos*)" [line 1292]. In a gracious
though roundabout reply, Electra agrees to cooperate, and
gives him the facts that he needs to know. She thus explicitly recognizes the urgent requirements of the situation.

The Paedagogus' outburst, as he reenters, puts more
strongly what we ourselves feel increasingly: the crucial
act can wait no longer. He denounces both brother and sister because they could have been overheard inside if he
had not been on guard. The conclusion of his speech sums
up the dramatic moment as we experience it in terms of
the necessity to put talk aside.

   Now cease your long speeches
   And your insatiate cries of joy.
   Go in: in these circumstances, delay
   Means ruin, but the time is right for success.

But there is more delay, as Electra recognizes the old man
and realizes that he had "killed her with lies (*logois*), while
knowing the sweetest truths (*erga*)." Then, with his last
words in the play, the Paedagogus calls on the concepts
crucial to his first speech in the Prologue, *kairos* and
ergon. From now to the end of the drama, he remains silent, because the action moves ahead on schedule. After
Orestes transmits a final directive to his partner,

We have no more need of long speeches,
But only of getting inside as quickly as possible,

the men perform the ritual reverences preparatory to the sanctified slaying, and leave the stage in silence. As her part in the venture, Electra offers a prayer to Apollo. It contains suggestions that this verbal ritual is her best aid.

In this transitional scene, therefore, Electra begins to share the men's view of speech as an accompaniment to silent endeavor. In the concluding minutes of the play, she will turn her formidable verbal powers into instruments of vengeance: by reporting what happens; by deceiving Aegisthus; and by crucial exhortations to action.

At the outset, the final scene gives us two surprises: Electra leaves the stage for the first time since she entered in the Prologue; and, in the *kommos,* she has no lyrics, but leaves them all to the Chorus. Her first words convey the change that has occurred:

> Dear ladies, now in a moment the men
> Will finish their work. Wait in silence.

This directive to the Chorus repeats almost word for word Orestes' first objection to her joyous song [line 1236]. Her alliance is now with *tourgon* and she realizes that it requires silence. She re-enters, she tells the Chorus, to serve as lookout: she is on stage to *do* something. Then Clytemnestra's death-cries bespeak the effectiveness of Orestes. Electra encourages him to strike again. Indeed, what we see and what we hear at the moment of matricide make Electra the dramatic agent of vengeance. It is as though her shouts were swords.

Next, Electra deals with Aegisthus, in a masterpiece of *double entendre,* telling the truth and deceiving at the same time. Previously we have seen Electra in the reverse position, the victim of a lie. At other times she was unable to distinguish between literal truth and literal falsity. Now that she knows how things stand, she employs her wit to keep us constantly aware that she knows, while lulling Aegisthus to ignorance of his danger.

> AEGISTHUS: Where might the strangers be? Tell
> me that.

> ELECTRA: Inside. They have reached a kind
> hostess.

Here Electra's verb, *katenusan,* means not only "they have reached the house," but "they have accomplished the murder" of their "hostess." In this way, Electra proves her talent for *dolos* of a sort even more highly refined than the men's. Similarly, in the next exchange,

> AEGISTHUS: And did they genuinely report his
> death?

> ELECTRA: No, they have brought himself, not
> news alone.

Evidence and hearsay, truth and falsity, Electra plays on these ground-themes while sustaining ambiguity perfectly.

Clytemnestra's body under the sheet plays the same part as Orestes' urn: both serve as pivots for a reversal from delusion to truth. "Alas, I understand your word. It is Orestes speaking to me" [lines 1479-80]; Aegisthus recognizes

Orestes by what he says. This transition from the dead mother to the living son, and from sight back to speech, shifts our attention to the dialogue itself and prepares us for the climax of the role of Electra, as she interrupts the desperate attempt of Aegisthus to stall for time:

> AEGISTHUS: Just let me say a little bit.

> ELECTRA: Don't let him say any more!
> By the gods, brother, do not prolong speeches.
> What profit can delay bring, when a man
> In the midst of trouble is about to die?

Her rejection of talk, of "long speeches," here, in favor of pressing speedily toward the deed and the profit, completes her evolution into an effective ally for Orestes in the vengeance.

Just as Electra alters in her relation to *logoi,* so she will no longer remain crushed by *erga.* Aegisthus' instant death will relieve her. Her final words in the play encourage her brother in the style of the Paedagogus (though Orestes needs little chiding), adding a bitter sense of intolerable *kaka* all her own. Only by full requital of the extreme *kaka* under which she has suffered can she find release; thus she demands the harshest treatment for Aegisthus' body.

Orestes pushes Aegisthus inside, the concluding exit-for-action of the drama, leaving us with a statement of his attitude toward requital. Illegal or foul deeds beget just deeds as punishment, even if these just deeds mean murder. He is still firm in his belief that by the appropriate *ergon* we can diminish *to panourgon,* evil-doing. To this end, in silence Orestes and Aegisthus enter the palace; Electra watches in silence.

Thus the ***Electra*** plays out the dialectic of *logos* and *ergon* and presents Electra first and foremost in her relationship to these two principles. Throughout the play her temper remains constant, as does her reliance on *logoi;* yet her final attitude, for all practical purposes, is equivalent to that of Orestes in the Prologue. But what is our final attitude toward her? The last utterances of Orestes and Electra each show fully their characteristic mentalities: his legalistic, simplistic efficiency; her passionate, urgent absolutism. "Kill all wrongdoers"; "Throw him to the fitting buriers." And so, despite her evolving determination to act, Electra remains essentially the same from beginning to end. And so also our response to her in the Exodos or finale remains as it has been throughout, divided between admiration and disquiet. Yet, like *logos* and *ergon* and the other antitheses of the play, admiration and disquiet are incommensurable in the theater: Electra carries us away beyond criticism. In the lament over the urn, in the *kommoi* and the songs of joy, she retains the power that encounters us in her opening *threnos.* This is the power of *logos.* It draws us to the end.

Since the essential autonomy of his protagonist lasts as long as the play, Sophocles affirms a necessity beyond the practical and "realistic" necessity for the coordination of *logos* and *ergon* that we see in the Exodos. This other, higher necessity is that implied by spiritual *logos* in isolation from worldliness. The schism we notice within Electra and within her world dramatizes the contrast between a *logos* more profound than logic and a *logos* defined wholly in terms of external *ergon*. It is this latter *logos* alone that Orestes uses. By the end of the play Electra has shown some capacity to include the calculating, "rational" *logos* within her primarily emotional, intuitive, and imaginative *logos.* Thus again we find her bursting beyond the balance of opposites into a more capacious wholeness.

Electra dominates the other characters and the drama as a whole because she commands a language moving beyond logic. We recognize her nobility and strength most fully during the very moments in which she fails most pathetically to grasp *ergon* (facts, evidence, material reality). When she is in error about the tokens, deceived by the Paedagogus' lie, or deluded about the urn, she surges forth, deciding to act alone, enduring the torments of despair, lyrically overwhelming us with noble grief. In this way, each scene from her threnody on shows Electra's spiritual *logos* in tension with the demands of fact and deed. But this state of tension too is imbalanced. Its constant ironical undertone cannot counteract our attachment to Electra's truth. The tension only serves to bring into the light the essence of her truth: paradox. The paradox of Electra informs each scene; she so transcends ordinary logic that she draws our sympathies most when least reasonable.

The opening and closing of our play both show the world of *ergon* ostensibly dominant; both present the men in control, and support their world conceptually as well as dramatically. The large center of the play criticizes the world of *logos;* its keystone is the great speech of the Paedagogus, at the exact middle. With this structure, the *Electra* asserts the practical and literal truth of *ergon,* but also, shattering this frame, the uncanny force of *logos.* In the center, speeches, lyrics, and faith prove more authoritative than deeds, and Electra holds sway in a rhythmic world of meaningful pathos, ritual, and chant.

Because the center shatters its frame, the finale does not simply balance the beginning in abstract symmetry. It is not the same unambiguous melodrama, but sardonic and tense. And, while validating the men's purpose, it vindicates an Electra who remains self-contradictory. Her vindication, even her redemption, leaves us with unresolved issues, permanent paradoxes: the role of her thrust toward infinity in a finite world, the fate of her ideals in the midst of actuality. Forever intersecting and separating, these incommensurables are somehow, beyond our understanding, related. The limits of our understanding, after all, are those of logic in the face of *logos.* That the incommensurables are truly related, however, the play proves in its own perfect union of deed and word, real and ideal.

Silence, as we have noticed, has a positive dramatic function in the *Electra.* From her entrance on, Electra stands silent during only three periods of any length: the first two Stasima and the *mythos* of the Paedagogus. We appreciate well the force of the Paedagogus' speech and its relevance to Electra's symbolic character. The two choral odes, in a similar way, also derive an important part of their force and significance from Electra. The Chorus not only speaks in her favor but hardly exists at all in this drama except as an adjunct to her; always subordinate, always a helpful

backdrop for her attitudes, merits, emotions, pathos. In the only two developed choral odes, then, I suggest that the Chorus remains an extension of Electra's character and continues to bring it out and augment it: the Chorus represents her participation in the communal *logoi* of ritual. Electra can willingly stand silent on stage during these odes because the Chorus acts out, in lyric and dance, her own dedication to the liturgical truths of tradition, inwardness, and faith. As at the very end of the drama, Electra's silence displays assent, communion, and assurance; justice will prevail, it implies; divinities are working invisible like words.

This essay can only suggest in conclusion that the *Electra,* like its heroine, takes on its most profound dimension by uniting *logos* and *mythos* (terms used interchangeably throughout). For the men the prime example of *mythos* or *logos* is no doubt the well-wrought scheme or lie. For Electra, however, the *logoi* or *mythoi* imitate and exemplify the ebb and flow of nature itself. The cycles of nature—nature's rituals—like the seasons, life and death, or night and day, form *logoi* or *mythoi* (meaningful patterns), just as they form the basis of human ritual and of the traditional myths. Electra symbolizes *physis,* nature, in her endurance, her attachment to blood, her repetitions, and her refusal to compromise. Electra's truth (and her meaning), like that of nature, is beyond appearances, the surface truths or *erga* apprehended by the senses or sensible intelligence. The appearances are indeed against her; but only the appearances.

Ergon vs. logos, appearance *vs. physis,* fact *vs.* faith: Sophocles captures these great *agones* or conflicts by dramatizing them in perpetual motion, by imitating them for all time in a ritual drama in which the *agonistoi* or competitors play out their war over and over, the struggle without end, the whole ordered and stable. He triumphs by integrating dramatic *erga* and *logoi,* realism, fiction, and rite. But *logoi* and *mythoi* themselves triumph, by expressing the essence of the drama. And our access, such as it is, to this drama is also through *logos* and *mythos:* imagination allowing us to participate in another world. (pp. 125-45)

> *Thomas Woodard, "The Electra of Sophocles," in* Sophocles: A Collection of Critical Essays, *edited by Thomas Woodard, Prentice-Hall, Inc., 1966, pp. 125-45.*

OEDIPUS AT COLONUS

CRITICAL COMMENTARY

Cedric H. Whitman   (essay date 1951)

[*Whitman is an eminent classicist whose writings include* Sophocles: A Study of Heroic Humanism *(1951),* Aristophanes and the Comic Hero *(1964), and* Euripides and the Full Circle of Myth *(1974). In the following excerpt from the first-named work, he identifies* Oedi-

An ancient marble bust of Sophocles in the Uffizi Gallery, Florence.

pus at Colonus *as the final statement of Sophocles' humanistic creed. Oedipus' death and transfiguration symbolize, according to Whitman, "man's special partaking of death and life, of the transient and the eternal."*]

The *Philoctetes* contains the key to Sophocles' late period and throws light backward to the *Electra* and forward to the *Oedipus at Colonus.* It is often said that Sophocles in his later years showed the influence of Euripides in that he began to stage beggared kings and heroes in rags as his protagonists. But the merely theatrical aspects explain little. What Sophocles saw in these crownless and shattered figures was the everlasting contradiction of inner and outer value. It is hard to see how the supremacy of man's inner divinity could have achieved fuller expression than in the shimmering vision of Heracles [in *Philoctetes*]. And yet, even there the poet had been forced to introduce a divine character who was, technically at least, outside the plot. He was still to some extent bound by the old form of bringing the gods to man, though his real meaning was to raise the god within man to the dignity of a legitimate and recognized universal.

In the *Oedipus at Colonus,* there is no *deus ex machina* in any sense. Everything appears through the man himself, and from the messenger who relates his last hour. The understanding of a certain heroic, albeit paradoxical, supremacy attainable within the scheme of time, and itself constituting a kind of victory over time, grew steadily in the *Philoctetes* from a dim intuitive force into clear religious knowledge. Oedipus, beginning with that knowl-

edge, now becomes a god—in the specifically fifth-century sense of a god such as man can become. His anguished burden of tragic courage has by its very weight prevented him from turning into the shadow the gods would make of him; for his tragic courage is as divine and inviolable as they. The gods are shattering truth, but they are also moral perception and inner law. Herein, therefore, in the transfiguration of Oedipus, "deep calleth unto deep," and the gods meet. It is with a strange ambivalence, in his enormous strength and utter helplessness, guided at once by his oracular soul and by a frail girl, that Oedipus comes once more upon the stage.

The *Oedipus at Colonus,* it has often been observed, lacks the daemonic *élan* of the other two Theban plays; it contains less obvious conflict, save what is concentrated in the scenes with Creon and Polyneices. But in Sophoclean tragedy, action may be defined as the functioning of the hero's will, in whatever form. Since all his heroes exercise will, it follows that there are no so-called "passive" protagonists. The *Oedipus at Colonus* does not lack action, for the will of Oedipus functions steadily with great power and effect; but there is one element of heroic action which is absent for the first time in the extant works of Sophocles. That is the element of self-destructiveness which hitherto inevitably accompanied the operation of the hero's will. Even in the late works, where self-preservation plays so important a part, the conditions of self-preservation are sufficiently rigorous so that, in order to preserve integrity, the hero may choose rather to destroy himself, as Philoctetes does at first, or risk almost inevitable death, as Electra does when she elects to slay the tyrants herself. But Oedipus is beyond all such choices and risks. He would not be what he is, the most exalted of Sophocles' heroes, if he still had to achieve his height by self-destruction; he has been destroyed enough, and his tlemosyne [endurance] is complete. If victory costs him little, that is because life has already cost him so much. Action, insofar as it means simply the functioning of the heroic will, is present in dynamic abundance. But the struggles which had been deadly in earlier works appear now in a diminutive and fine focus; their issues are settled before they take place. All is still passionately felt, but more through the distilled medium of the intellect than directly through experience—a fact in itself appropriate to Oedipus, who had put faith in the intellect from the first.

The *Oedipus at Colonus* is a folk tale, a mystery play, and a national festival piece, the essential elements of whose plot may have belonged to the mythology attached to the hero-cult, though certainly not to the oldest form of the myth. Aeschylus in the *Seven against Thebes* dramatized the consequences of the curse which caused the sons of Oedipus to "divide their inheritance with the sword," and the poets of the Theban cycle knew of the curse; but in both the *Iliad* and the *Odyssey,* Oedipus is supposed to have remained king of Thebes, even after his self-discovery, until he died. Sophocles' account of how he came to the Athenian suburb of Colonus as a wanderer, underwent deification, and subsequently was worshipped, seemed to Pausanias doubtful, since it conflicted with Homer's version. Therefore the great archaeologist made inquiries, and learned still another story, that the bones of

Oedipus had been brought to Colonus after his death. Yet Sophocles did not invent his story, for Euripides alludes to it in the *Phoenissae* of 409 in a way that would have been incomprehensible if the tradition were not common knowledge. And two years before, when the Athenians won a slight cavalry skirmish over the Thebans near Acharnae, which is not far from Colonus, the credit for the victory had been accorded to the deified Oedipus. Neither Euripides nor Sophocles therefore can be the source of the tale. What is perhaps likely, though quite hypothetical, is that during the fifth century the tide of Athenian nationalism found religious expression not only in the monuments of the new age which were rising on the Acropolis, but equally in a revival of interest in the chthonian cults of the old Attic heroes, of which the greatest was Theseus. His bones were recovered from the island of Scyros in 473 by Cimon. If, as Pausanias seems to have found out, there actually was a similar "recovery" of the bones of Oedipus, the growth of such a story as Sophocles tells would be an almost indispensable means for explaining Oedipus' otherwise feeble connections with Attica. In any case, there he was, sharing his shrine at Colonus with Theseus, Pirithous, and Adrastus.

The plot which Sophocles presents fits smoothly into the **Oedipus Rex.** Not all the intervening events are told, but it is significant that Oedipus is now in exile, not of his own free will, but because he has been ejected from Thebes by the new ruler Creon, while his two sons, Polyneices and Eteocles, did nothing to help him. When the first of his shock and fury was past, Oedipus had thought better of his wish for death or exile. Even in Thebes his extraordinary resilience had partially restored him to his belief in himself, so that he was content to live his life out among his children. Not until then had his masters decided to drive him out. Much time has passed; Oedipus is now old, and Antigone, who was a little girl in the **Oedipus Rex,** is fully grown and able to accompany her father's wanderings.

The prologue, like all Sophoclean prologues, introduces not only the matter but also the spirit of the play. As Deianeira's monologue [in **Women of Trachis**] suits her peculiar isolation, or the clean-limbed issues of the **Antigone** are first symbolized in the formal, balanced contrasts of the opening scene, so the last two plays [**Philoctetes** and **Oedipus at Colonus**], where quiet deliverance after pain and true insights of inner value are the aims, have prologues where people enter searching, either on an unfamiliar island or at the fringes of an unknown city. Oedipus enters searching for a world in which the value that he has set upon himself through years of suffering may be acknowledged as true. Alone at first with Antigone, he enters the outskirts of Athens and asks where he is. Not recognizing the place, Antigone gazes about her and says:

> Straight ahead
> I can perceive towers that crown a city:
> And it is safe to guess, this place is holy,
> Teeming with laurel, olive, and the vine;
> Within the grove itself, the nightingales
> In numbers sing.
>
> [ll. 14-18]

Shortly a stranger enters who, shocked to see that the old man has seated himself on a sacred stone, will answer no questions till Oedipus moves. He then tells them that they are in Athens, the realm of Theseus, and more specifically in the sacred grove of the Eumenides in the deme of Colonus. Oedipus wishes to see the king at once; he says he has come to perform a great service. But the stranger begs him to stay where he is until he can fetch some of his fellows to decide whether Oedipus is to be allowed to remain or not. Oedipus waits patiently, and prays meanwhile to the dread goddesses to pity "this wretched shadow of Oedipus." But he has already won a sign of respect. Before he leaves, the stranger remarks that he seems noble, "save for what the gods have done to him" [ll. 75-6].

The people of Colonus now enter as chorus and question the wanderer further. They note his blindness, grow increasingly suspicious, and finally wring from him that he is Oedipus. In horror they order him to leave at once, lest he bring his guilt and pollution on the city. Oedipus defends himself vigorously, and the chorus, pitying him, agrees that Theseus must decide. A woman is now seen approaching on horseback. Antigone recognizes her as her sister Ismene, who has come to warn Oedipus of his danger. The latter manifests no surprise when he hears that a war for the throne of Thebes has broken out between his two sons, Eteocles and Polyneices. The combatants have need of Oedipus, for they have heard a prophecy that whichever side is favored by Oedipus' presence will be victorious, and Eteocles, the present ruler of Thebes, is sending the ex-regent Creon to fetch Oedipus home. The Thebans, however, have no intention of risking the presence of a polluted parricide within their walls; they merely want him near by, where he can be useful; but he is not to be reinstated in his home. Oedipus listens grimly and then with bitter words swears that neither of his sons shall have help from him. He will remain at Athens.

A lyric scene follows, in which Oedipus makes his peace with the Eumenides for having trespassed in their grove, and presently Theseus enters. All action halts as the two great men confront each other. During the whole scene, Antigone is silent, and the chorus makes only one shy interruption. The king's address is notable for its broad humanism:

> I myself was reared in exile
> Like you, and the perils of a foreign land
> I bore in my own person on my head.
> Wherefore I should be loath to fail assisting
> An exile, like yourself, a nothingness.
> For being a man, I know I have no share
> Of tomorrow which is greater than your own.
>
> [ll. 562-68]

Oedipus comes immediately to the point. He craves burial in Attica and has brought his own body to Theseus as a gift. These lines are only comprehensible, of course, in the context of the heroic cults of the dead. In order to receive any benefit from a hero, one had to possess his bones. The dead man was thus a chthonian divinity whose remains, albeit buried, performed a lively service of protection throughout a relatively small region. Greece was full of such heroic graves. The chthonian religion connected with them was much older than the Olympian hierarchy, and it seems to have suffered no comparable loss of belief in the fifth century, or even much later. Tombs of nameless heroes were carefully tended in Greece long after the Parthenon became a museum. Oedipus was, therefore, offering Theseus a real blessing in the form of his corpse, for both are perfectly aware that Oedipus is a heroic personage. The only surprising thing is that Oedipus can consider himself a hero before he is dead. This fact only emphasizes Sophocles' concern with the heroic nature, and how it comes to be. The mere superstition about dead bones is not enough for him.

Oedipus now leads the conversation around to the approaching war, and here again Sophocles does a characteristic thing. He deliberately confuses the prophecy. Ismene has reported from Delphi that Oedipus will be useful in the war threatening between Eteocles and Polyneices; Oedipus now prophesies that his body will be useful in the coming war between Thebes and Athens. Theseus in some surprise asks what will cause war to break out with this friendly power, and Oedipus, in a splendid speech, lays the cause at the door of time:

> O dearest son of Aegeus, for the gods
> Alone it is to feel nor age nor death:
> All other things almighty time confounds.
> The strength of the earth wanes, the body wanes,
> Faith dies and falsehood blossoms in its place,
> And so in men the spirit does not rest
> The same, either in cities or in friends.
> For some today, for others not long after
> Sweet turns to bitter, and again to sweet,
> And if today the weather's fair twixt Thebes
> And you, no less does countless time in passage
> Breed on and on his countless nights and days,
> Wherein your present bonds of harmony
> Shall scatter at the spear's point, for a word:
> And there my sleeping and long-buried corpse
> Cold in the earth shall drink their hot blood
>   down,
> If Zeus be Zeus, and his Apollo true.
>
> [ll. 607-23]

Thus in his own person Oedipus prophesies; but his words tell only what his own action shall bring about. Like the gods, who "feel nor age nor death," he can already speak from outside time. This prophecy is, like all the others in Sophocles, symbolic, not causal, and of greater significance to the character of the hero than to the plot. Theseus is impressed at once by the authority of the old man's manner and promises him not only burial in Attica, but also full protection and citizenship. He may even come and live in Theseus' own house, so little does the prince fear ritual pollution. But Oedipus declines, saying he is now on the spot where he will conquer those who have exiled him. Theseus then, with a few last words of reassurance, retires, and the chorus brings the first great section of the play to a close with one of the most exquisite lyrics to be found in Greek tragedy, the famous ode on Athens.

From the first moment of his arrival, Oedipus has put down roots in Attica; he has begun to assert a spiritual authority over his environment. Blind and beggarly as he is, he is nevertheless irresistible. The next section, or act, of the play shows Oedipus' struggle to defend his new posi-

tion. First Creon arrives from Thebes and attempts to win Oedipus' support in the impending contest. He begins with a specious pretense of pity for Oedipus' sufferings and says he has come to take him home. Oedipus denounces him roundly. Creon then resorts to force, abducts both Ismene and Antigone and tries to drag away Oedipus himself. His attempt is balked by Theseus, however, who leads out his soldiers, rescues the girls, and sends Creon off with a lecture on manners. Creon's answer is a declaration of war, and he departs.

Polyneices, the elder son of Oedipus, is now reported near. Oedipus at first refuses to see him, but finally agrees to do so, on the intercession of Antigone. In a long and moving appeal, Polyneices confesses his negligence and begs forgiveness and assistance. He wears the look of a man blasted and going to his doom. Unquestionably sincere both in his need and his remorse, he has come to Oedipus as a last hope to avert the destruction he feels overhanging the seven champions who are to attack Thebes. Oedipus is silent for a long time; then his answer comes in the form of one of the most inspired and daemonic execrations ever pronounced. He curses not only Polyneices, but Eteocles also, and offers not the slightest word of comfort or farewell. Shattered, Polyneices takes a sorrowful leave of Antigone; she begs him to abandon the expedition, but he feels his duty as a leader and returns to his forces.

These two scenes have caused much difficulty. They seem somewhat extraneous and, in the eyes of many, give the work a quality of melodramatic pastiche. Creon's abduction of Antigone and Ismene, for instance, and their rescue by Theseus may seem more at home in a medieval chivalric romance than in an otherwise religious piece. Nevertheless, in the earliest and most austere monument of Attic drama, the *Suppliants* of Aeschylus, not two but possibly as many as fifty girls are barely saved, by the timely arrival of the king, from being herded off into captivity and enforced marriage. Such scenes, in which a Greek prince prevents the incidence of barbarian outrage, or an Athenian ruler thwarts the highhandedness of an oligarchic authoritarian, embodied serious ideational contrasts for the Athenians of the fifth century. They were not mere action and excitement; they were commentaries on what it was felt Greek civilization was and should be, providing important evidence for the self-consciousness and world-outlook of the Athenians.

When Polyneices has departed, a roll of thunder, the sign for which Oedipus had waited, finally comes. It comes like the Sanctus Bell between the Ordinary and the Canon of the Mass, and it introduces a comparable communion between God and man. Oedipus sends hastily for Theseus, to whom he announces the hour of his death and gives final instructions. It is now the blind man's turn to lead. The dramatic effect of this moment is deeply thrilling. Oedipus, whose physical blindness and helplessness have been so carefully established throughout the play, now rises to his feet and without guidance from anyone present, leads the others into the sacred grove of the Eumenides. The rest is told by a messenger, how he prepared himself, tarrying until a mysterious voice called him by name, then bade farewell to his daughters, and unaccompanied save by Theseus, went into the most holy part of the glade and there was translated, while Theseus remained standing, shading his eyes from the unbearable vision of godhead. The play ends with a lyric scene, full of bereavement and yearning, as Antigone and Ismene mourn the loss of their father, and ask safe conduct back to Thebes. Then the chorus moves off singing a mysterious line:

> Weep not; for altogether, these things have authority.

If the *Oedipus at Colonus* fails to exhibit the dramatic alacrity of earlier plays, it is for a good reason. The play presents the long slow reversal of the *Oedipus Rex.* Instead of the abrupt plunge down the precipice, the movement here is laboriously uphill, and endurance is the criterion. The gods who speak from the whirlwind imparted their lightning swiftness to the *Oedipus Rex.* Oedipus himself sets the tempo for the play in which, hated by the gods and abandoned, he finds his answer to them. The gods who destroyed him earlier make no further move, either for or against him, until they finally acknowledge his dignity with the affidavit of their heavenly thunder and bring to pass the moment in which he is complete. The timeless divinities are the lords of time, but Oedipus is the actor, and he looks to them for nothing save the continuation of their dread function. If time continues, endurance continues; but while time remains the same in essence, endurance grows greater, and so does knowledge. Given time, tlemosyne [endurance] must achieve its victory.

Almost in his first words, Oedipus lists time as one of the three great elements of his moral fibre:

> Who will receive today the wanderer
> Oedipus, with some scanty charities?
> Who begs but little, and of that little still
> Gets less, but finds that it suffices him:
> For sufferings, and length of time, my comrade,
> And third, nobility, teach me content.
>
> [ll. 3-8]

Previously, Oedipus had spoken of himself as the "brother of the months" [*Oedipus Rex,* ll. 1082-83]. He now has time as his constant companion. Once time had "found him out"; now it stands by him as a medium of greatness and even as a teacher [*Oedipus Rex,* 1. 1213]. Again, as in the *Electra,* there is a contrast between what Oedipus is expected to learn from time and what he actually does learn. In the scene with Creon, the latter, staggered by Oedipus' proud replies, says that an old man in such misery ought to have learned to be mild and acknowledge his own weakness. But time teaches every man what he really is, and in Oedipus' case it has rather confirmed his high spirit and strength. It has, in a way, brought the man to pass, as it brings all things to pass, especially the most unexpected. Itself a paradox, time fosters paradox, and turns things into their opposites; it is the inevitable condition of becoming, yet in the end it reveals Being, even as Oedipus implied to Theseus in the great speech already quoted. The gods are free of time, deathless and ageless. Yet in the world they govern, in the events wherein they manifest themselves, all things are inverted to their opposites, friend becomes enemy and enemy friend, faith dies, and falsehood blossoms. But the helpless and aged Oedipus,

the prey of time, will become a timeless blessing, a member of those heroic dead whose power represented to the Greek mind one of the most holy and inviolable forces in the world.

This speech of Oedipus is somewhat reminiscent of Ajax' "yielding" speech, save that when Ajax says that in time things become their opposites, it is clear that he is resolved to be no more a part of the shoddy flux, but to get out of time, seize Being at a blow and be himself forever. The inflexible standard of the old arete [virtue] compelled Ajax. But Oedipus' virtue was one of the intellect; like the Homeric Odysseus, he could accept time with its contradictions as the framework of man's existence in which through devious ways he comes to fulfillment. His inner law has made survival difficult, but necessary. For the same intellectual honesty and skill which drove him in the earlier play to find out who he was, and to boast that he could bear the knowledge, has given him both the will and the strength to achieve that boast.

Oedipus himself states clearly his moral independence of the gods in the scene with his daughter. Ismene has told him that the victory in the war depends on him, and Oedipus, half-aside, reflects on the strangeness of the news; Ismene tries to give a pious answer:

> ISMENE: They say their victory lies in your hands.
>
> OEDIPUS: When I am nothing, then am I a man?
>
> ISMENE: Yes, for the gods who smote now raise you up.
>
> OEDIPUS: Cheap gift, to raise an old man, who fell young!
>
> [ll. 392-95]

The rejection of Ismene's pietism is unmistakable. A little later, when Ismene reports the prophecy that if Oedipus dies hostile to the Thebans his tomb will be an affliction to them, the old man, in deep self-consciousness of his inward power, says drily: "A man might know that by his wits, without a god's help" [1. 403]. Indifferent to what the gods may seem to do, Oedipus trusts his intellect still; he does not really fancy the gods care about him at all. His exaltation cannot be interpreted as an act of grace, as Ismene suggests. It is a product from within, born of Oedipus' own equipment.

It has long since been recognized that Oedipus, in fundamental character, is still the same as ever. His mind, the quality which made him "small and great," has only been deepened, not discredited by time. No less his famous wrath is vigorous as of old, and perhaps even a little more savage, as the insight and authority which motivate it grow. Innocent sufferer though he may be, he shows none of the religious transfiguration or humble self-abnegation of the Christian martyr. Half of his exalted function is to bless Attica, but the other half is to have personal revenge on his enemies, and the terrible explosions which Creon and Polyneices endure show the ferocity of his hatred and anger; even Theseus gets a rather sharp answer. Christian sentiment may recoil from the sheer violence of these outbursts; but the hypocrisy which they rebuke need find no sympathy. Oedipus is more right than ever in his anger, for his honesty has only grown fiercer with the years. The compromise which all expected of a condemned and polluted exile has not been forthcoming.

For all that, it is never for a moment forgotten that Oedipus is polluted, that he is the man who slew his father and married his mother. Not only his character but also his external fate remains unchanged. To emphasize this point, Sophocles has symbolized it nicely in the first part of the play by making him once more stumble into defilement. The first thing he does is to step on the consecrated ground and sit on a sacred stone. Thus throughout the prologue, first chorus, and first episode, he is technically guilty of sacrilege against the Eumenides. Eventually he makes amends, or rather sends his daughter to make them; but he is in no hurry, and in the end, it is into the most sacred and forbidden part of the grove that he turns. By this light touch the poet recalls and reasserts the same old fate of Oedipus the king—his almost innate luck of touching things which are forbidden, without knowing it. He is the man who treads blindly and innocently upon taboos. Yet even as Oedipus had formerly committed sacrilege and survived in greater wisdom and strength, so now the revelation of his error does not cause him to start up in alarm; he only asks on what land he is trespassing:

> STRANGER: Here the dread
> Goddesses dwell, daughters of Earth and Darkness.
>
> OEDIPUS: Let me hear by what name I should
>   address them.
>
> STRANGER: The people of this land call them the
>   all-seeing
> Eumenides; elsewhere they've other names.
>
> OEDIPUS: Graciously let them take their suppliant
> For from this place I never shall depart.
>
> STRANGER: What does this mean?
>
> OEDIPUS: The token of my fate.
>
> [ll. 39-46]

The last line, like so many of Oedipus' remarks, is spoken as an aside and goes uncomprehended by the stranger, who at once changes the subject. But it is clear that Oedipus has passed beyond the phase where technical defilement matters. If it had been his fate alone of all men to defile what was most sacred and to suffer for it, his suffering has invested him with certain rights; for now he alone of all men may walk in the Athenian grove of the Furies and not suffer.

And what strange Furies these are, who receive their suppliant graciously—and such a suppliant—and whose grove echoes with the song of nightingales. These are purely Athenian Furies; only after the first consistory of the Areopagus were the Furies given nightingale voices, when an earlier exile, "hated of the gods," Orestes, found relief and dignity again in the equable air of Athens. Now Oedipus comes to Athens, and there is no yelping of "insatiable, bronze-footed bloodhounds," but only the music of the birds, as if all the past evil of the Theban house were transformed by the mysterious forces of time and suffering into a present of tranquil beauty and a prospect of hope. Quite after his own fashion, Sophocles has borrowed the gentle goddesses of pain from Aeschylus and spun them magically into his many-leveled, symbolic scheme of the heroic life. Here, in the grove of these paradoxically sweet dread goddesses, Oedipus could recognize a token of his fate; and Athens too could see herself once more, as at the trial of Orestes, the defender of the weak, mediator between the suppliant and justice, the restorer of the fallen— the great role she loved to play. With characteristic finish, Sophocles brings in these nightingales again in the great ode on Athens, so that the whole episode of Oedipus' coming and acceptance is rounded off with the music of nightingales.

Error and exaltation, pollution and the song of nightingales! No union of opposites could be more Sophoclean. Nothing is denied or remitted; all the old misery, the horror of the fate of Oedipus remains unchanged and unrationalized. Nothing has been invented to show that the gods really meant well. Within and without Oedipus is the same man, save that he has added a new dimension of fortitude and knowledge. He continues to act his role with ever increasing self-consciousness. He knows the "token of his fate," and therein creates a historical self. He is the blind man who knows; he is the "hated of God" who is innocent and noble. In this role he will win recognition.

Oedipus' battle for significance finds its core in the defense of his nobility. Those about him on the whole believe that no one could do the things which he did and yet be a good man. The lack of distinction which antiquity, until the time of Socrates, made between inner and outer values is well expressed in the famous *scolion* of Simonides:

> No man can help being bad
> Whom hopeless misfortune seizes;
> For every man who fares well is good,
> But if he fares ill, he is bad; and the best on the
>   whole
> Are those the gods love.

The gods had not loved Oedipus; he had been seized with hopeless misfortune. Hence the chorus is suspicious of him from the first. When they hear who he is, their reaction shows clearly how they have formulated their feelings about him. He must be guilty, for if his murder of Laius had been the moral equivalent of mere manslaughter in self-defense, the gods would not have punished him:

> No fated punishment comes to him
> Who avenges what he first has suffered.
>
> [ll. 228-29]

The gods afflict him, he must be evil; let him get out. Antigone attempts to correct this attitude by presenting her father in the light of one undeservingly oppressed by the gods' arbitrary will:

> Among all men you will not find
> One who, if a god leads on,
> Has power to escape.
>
> [ll. 252-54]

In these two views the fate of Oedipus is summarized respectively as a tragedy of fault and a tragedy of fate. Antigone's appeal is meant to lighten the burden of guilt, but only Oedipus himself understands fully his own innocence.

The *Oedipus Rex* can hardly have failed to stir ambiguous reactions in Athens. The passages just quoted illustrate the interpretations which his story prompts; indeed, it is even possible that between 429 and Sophocles' resumption of the myth, the much debated question of the guilt or innocence of Oedipus had already begun to divide readers into bristling camps. Sophocles may have wished to settle it once and for all by the heavy emphasis he lays in this play upon his hero's innocence. In his very opening speech, Oedipus mentions "suffering, time, and third, nobility" as the things which have given him his strength. The emphasis upon "nobility" is beyond question. Time and suffering will do nothing for the ignoble man, except make him bitter. Even as in the *Oedipus Rex,* when he faced the imminent revelation of his parricide and incest, he knew that no external fortune could destroy his soul, so now in his old age he maintains his basic excellence. Later, when Antigone's appeal has quieted the chorus, in a speech of formal defense, he states quite explicitly that his deeds were unwilled, and that his griefs are due to no evil in his nature:

> And will you then
> Uproot me from this seat and drive me forth,
> Fearing a name alone? You cannot fear
> Either my body or my deeds; for these
> My deeds were not committed; they were suf-
> fered,
> If, as you must, you mean my history,
> My father and my mother, for which tales
> You fear me. Ah, full well I know it is!
> And yet, how am I evil in my nature,
> I who, when struck, struck back, so that had I
> Even known my victim, I'd not be condemned.
>
> [ll. 263-72]

The legal claim that he killed in self-defense and ignorance is backed by the moral claim that even if he had known that his assailant was his father, he would not be morally guilty. It will be remembered that Laius had hit him over the head with an ox-goad, for no reason other than that he was in the way, a fact which perhaps lends weight to Oedipus' claim. Be that as it may, the real innocence rests, in his own eyes, upon his inward conviction of integrity. Later he says to Creon:

> For not in me, not in myself, could you
> Discover any stain of sin, whereby
> I sinned against myself and mine.
>
> [ll. 966-68]

Oedipus' rejection of the word "hamartia" [sin] here clearly has an inward reference, while his outer misdeeds are undeniable. In a similar spirit he can use the old figure of the "gift of the gods," always a dangerous thing to receive:

CHORUS:	You have done—
OEDIPUS:	I have not done.
CHORUS:	What then?
OEDIPUS:	I have received a gift . . .

> [ll. 539f.]

The gods and their gifts, the misery of his life; these are all externals, and ineluctable. But he is himself, and the gods can do nothing to break the strong moral good he wills. Oedipus is a landmark in Greek morality, for he presents the first really clear exposition of the independence of the inner life, that doctrine which in Socrates and his followers became the cornerstone of a whole new phase of civilization.

Yet for this moral independence to be significant—to be real, one might say—it had to be recognized. Herein the feelings of the fifth-century poet differed from the mysticism of Plato, the reality of whose inner world was prior and causal. For Sophocles, the hero must win in this world; whether in such a death as Antigone's or in such a life as Oedipus', the heroic victory had all its reference and significance in the purely human sphere. Hence the rising action of the *Oedipus at Colonus* shows the hero's triumph over person after person. He already has Antigone, in whom for the first time a Sophoclean protagonist has a real companion. Antigone is not a foil, she is a counterpart to Oedipus; Sophocles kept in mind the character he had given her almost forty years before and here endowed her with no little of her father's endurance. Ismene shares her position to some extent, so that in the three of them, in the scenes where the old man praises his daughters, one detects the nucleus of a world in which Oedipus is acceptable and honored. With them, Oedipus stands on his own terms, commanding and receiving freely their love and honor.

It is not long before the stranger of the prologue adopts a respectful tone. The chorus similarly, in spite of its misgivings, is forced "to feel awe at his pronouncements." But the climax of Oedipus' triumph over society appears in the scene with Theseus, who recognizes him at once as a superior being. It is the essentially Athenian interpretation of arete which underlies this scene and makes it moving. Theseus represents Athens; without hesitation he penetrates all the disguises of fortune and circumstance and arrives at the true man. Drawn in the aristocratic colors of a legendary king, he is none the less the embodiment of the most enlightened kind of democratic individualism. Mutual recognition of virtue, as in the case of Philoctetes and Neoptolemus, can bring the great man back to the world, or, more accurately, can bring the world back to the great man, whose ethos has remained unchanged. The value of the true man, whatever his state, attains a just estimate in the liberal air of Athens. Theseus comes and listens respectfully before Oedipus, and Oedipus acknowledges his excellence. Hero recognizes hero as a fellow stranger in this world, knowing its uncertainty, and basing standards of behavior on its immanent sorrow. Oedipus makes for himself a world of the souls that can respect him in his tribulations, and when he departs, he is no longer isolated, but prized.

Thus, like Philoctetes, Oedipus is set free to bestow the value of himself upon the world. But those who would avail themselves of his blessing must accept the blind beggar himself and not try to use his greatness without understanding him. So too, Philoctetes' magic bow could not be separated from its lame and offensive owner. The paradox of human value must be taken whole; there is no short way. Philoctetes and disease are one; Oedipus and pollution are one. The hero's external daimon and internal daimon, that is, the inner and outer divine forces of his life, are inextricably interwoven until the great moment comes when the external yields, and the hero's inwardness may burst out and become a reality. And this is not so much a mystic process as a social one. Theseus and the Athenians could perceive that reality through the shell. They are therefore a little like Oedipus, who is blind but full of true insight: "All he says has eyes." His murmured remark, "When I am nothing, then am I a man?" conveys the whole secret. His triumph is prepared within himself, almost in defiance of the very gods themselves, and the Athenians, when they accept his paradox, are made worthy to share in his triumph.

But his triumph does not come without a struggle. The two scenes in which Oedipus sets his face against Thebes forever have occasioned much criticism. Their relevance has either been missed altogether, or else explained merely in connection with the original saga, the *fabula sacra.* But part of the saga is not necessarily part of the play. For the Greek dramatist, there was no *fabula sacra;* he was as free as Homer to exclude whatever detail he felt to be irrelevant. As examples of Oedipus' growing heroic powers, wherewith he settles his accounts in the world, the episodes of Creon and Polyneices clearly contribute something to the character of the protagonist; but their significance is greater than that. The moral essence of these scenes is derived from the problem of the *Philoctetes,* where an individual of heroic proportions, rejected long since and cast away by his comrades, becomes once more the object of their specific personal concern.

Over and over again we are told that the Thebans, and Creon in particular, had exiled Oedipus long after the latter had ceased to feel that exile was necessary or appropriate to his misfortunes; up till that time they had kept him against his will. Precisely why is a question. Euripides, in the closing scene of the *Phoenissae,* makes the exile of Oedipus begin after the expedition of the Seven is over; it is therefore an act of the new king, Creon, who perhaps may be thought to have planned it in order to consolidate his power. In Sophocles' play, however, Oedipus was exiled while Creon was merely regent, during the minority of the princes. The latter, apparently, had been quite passive in the matter. In the absence of conclusive evidence, it is perhaps safe to assume that the disposal of Oedipus in some way affected the various claimants' interest in the throne. In any case, the very doubtfulness of the motivation suggests Sophocles' real intention: the Thebans had used the legally justifiable reason for exile, blood guilt, as a kind of political cover for more selfish motives. Oedipus himself seems to feel that he ought to be received into Thebes and buried there. Yet technically, as a parricide, Oedipus could not possibly return. The Thebans certainly had no intention of bringing him into the city, but only of keeping him near at hand. One might well ask how it had been possible for him to stay in the first place, and why he thought he might return at all, if ritual pollution had really such a solemn significance.

But the fact is, such pollution was open to flexible treatment, and the sons of Oedipus and Creon had made political capital of it. And now, like Odysseus in the *Philoctetes,* Creon and Polyneices both wish to use the great man's power without accepting the man himself. The oracle told them they would conquer if they could get him back, but there is yet some question of how a hero must be received. The great contrast with the pragmatic scheme of the Thebans is the frank and generous attitude of Theseus. Not only does he feel a personal respect and kinship for Oedipus; he gives him the full rights of a citizen and even offers to take him to his own house. With Theseus' example before them, even the choristers seem no longer to fear the pollution which attends the old man, and they defend him valiantly against Creon's attack. To be sure, the Athenians are to gain much from him, but they have not tried to achieve it by the half-and-half plan of Creon.

In the scene with Creon, the political substance of the play becomes most clear, and brings the elements of festival drama into the foreground. All that the Athenian mind felt to be politically good clashes openly with the spiritual blindness of Creon. Creon arrives in guile and departs in violence. He behaves like a tyrant—indeed, he calls himself one—and he carries off women, as tyrants are supposed to do. But he is also much subtler, and like most fifth-century stage tyrants, he possesses less in common with the economic dictators of history than with the clever, sophistically trained oligarchs of the war years. His obsequious carefulness before the Athenian choristers who, by a curious anachronism, are at once the subjects of Theseus and liberal exponents of democracy, includes not only respectful compliments, but even a passing intimation that he represents a majority vote. With deft political skill he answers the arraignment of Theseus by trying to use Athenian institutions and the famous piety of Athens to his own advantage: he says smoothly that he is sure that Athens would never receive an unholy incestuous parricide; the Areopagus would never allow it. Creon seems to know well the principle formulated later by Aristotle [in the *Rhetoric*], that "we should know the moral qualities characteristic of each form of government, for the special moral character of each is found to provide us with our most effective means of persuasion in dealing with it."

Aristotle further states that the end of tyranny is protection of the tyrant, while the end of aristocracy is the maintenance of education and national institutions. Clearly Creon is here a tyrant speaking in his own defense; but with great skill he uses as his principal argument the moral end of the aristocratic Theseus, namely the maintenance of Athenian piety and the court of the Areopagus. A definite political antinomy, therefore, is only thinly veiled in this scene. It appears even more clearly in Theseus' reproof, which enters almost unnecessarily into Theban manners. Creon, says Theseus, is not only unworthy of Athens, but unworthy of Thebes herself, and the Theban tradition of breeding gentlemen.

By contrast with Creon, the failed aristocrat, the mythic figure of Theseus, characterized both as the true aristocrat and the man of the polis, with its ideal of legality and true piety, points the religious question implicit in the political antinomy. Creon's well-planned references to Athenian piety miss fire. Theseus designs no answer, but Oedipus in towering wrath bursts out in one of his terrible cannonades. He defends himself from the scornful, personal taunts of Creon, strips the veil from his pretense of justice, and then says:

> How fine for you to flatter Theseus' name
> And Athens, calling her well administered!
> But in your commendations you miss much;
> If any land knows how to honor gods
> With reverence, this land leads all the rest.
> Wherefrom you, plundering these girls and me,
> The aged suppliant, try to drag us off!

[ll. 1003-09]

Creon's breach of the most holy right of the aged and the suppliant fits oddly with his otherwise scrupulous observance of religious forms in treating a parricide. He will bring Oedipus into the vicinity of Thebes as a useful object, but will not admit his technical pollution within the walls. The Thebans are thus represented as standing on the forms of piety without regarding their essence, while Athens "knows how to honor the gods with reverence," by receiving the suppliant generously with no reservations. Far from dallying over mere religious formalities, Theseus leaves a sacrifice half-finished in order to go to battle for his guests—the sort of religious enlightenment which Sparta, for instance, would not risk in the crucial year of Marathon.

These details are too closely allied to the play's principal action to be regarded as merely adventitious. The paradox of seeming and being, which informs the character of the hero, is here extended to include a commentary on the spirit and the letter, in the culture and political ethics of Greece herself. In this scene, even more fully than in the great ode on Athens, Sophocles has poured out his love for the city and his faith in her as the genuine polis, where not merely the nightingales sing and the sacred olives flourish, but where also the individual man, that irreducible minimum of political or any other kind of greatness, holds his place by arete alone, and "whatever good he may do the city."

Scholars have long since recognized references to the Peloponnesian War in this play. The shadow of bitter hatred between Athens and Thebes overhangs the whole, and with reason, for in the late years of the war, Thebes showed herself Athens' most implacable enemy, ransacking her outlying fields for anything movable, and clamoring later at the peace table for demolition of her walls and enslavement of her inhabitants. In the years just preceding Arginusae (406), when the *Oedipus at Colonus* was written, Athens was in desperate condition. The treasury was empty, the statues stripped of their gold; her leaders were incompetent, her population starving, every nerve was strained to the breaking point. If Thucydides, writing probably at about this same time, could call Athens "the education of Greece," because she represented the greatest opportunity for an individual to be self-sufficient and at his best, it is not so surprising that Sophocles too, with his profundity of poetic insight, should have been able to see his city historically and create a vision of her which would be as timeless as the heroism of the old Oedipus. When he speaks of Athens in the play, he never mentions her suffer-

ings. He speaks of her as if she were inviolable, as if the sacred olive trees were not burned stumps and the land ravaged and ruined. Athens herself in those days was a pattern of heroic tlemosyne [endurance]; and if Sophocles could see beyond the ruins and the stumps, it was because he saw whence Athens derived her almost incredible fortitude. The value of man was implicit in it all, and embodied in the figure of Oedipus. The man whose intellect has brought him to divine insight has come to the place where only the true counts. The ideal Athenian setting is more than a patriotic motif: in it Sophocles symbolizes the world of man's metaphysical value, the world which is the only home for Oedipus. The picture is, of course, confessedly and purposely idealized, but it is not fiction. It is myth, which is to say, it is history distilled into meaning.

The scene with Polyneices completes the picture of society's misguided attempt to regain the great individual for its own ends. Once more, as in the *Philoctetes,* the attempt through guile and force yields to the attempt through persuasion and appeal, and once more the same refusal follows. Polyneices is no mere politician like Creon; he is very sympathetically drawn. Even though he is perhaps still too self-involved to rise above his practical need of Oedipus into a full understanding of the old man's worth, nevertheless his full admission of guilt, and especially his recognition that has come too late, stamp him at once as a serious and wellnigh tragic character. Therefore the appalling execrations which the old man calls down on him are the more surprising. But Polyneices really is too late, and it is only out of empty hope that he can suggest how he may make up for his sins.

For Polyneices' faults are in his nature and in the nature of his will. He has put himself where he cannot turn back, but he has done so not because of any moral standard, but because he wanted the throne. He is therefore in a tragic situation, perhaps, but he is not a tragic character; however genuine his penitence may be, it implies little understanding and no real morality. Fundamentally he needs Oedipus for precisely the same reason as Creon does, and he would never have come otherwise. Oedipus' refusal of him rests on the same absolute standard he had always espoused. Since now Oedipus is himself all but a god, it may be said that his refusal rests on a divine standard.

The curse may seem another matter. Many scholars have argued that Oedipus was wrong to curse his son; others that the curse merely illustrates Oedipus' great exaltation. Still others have collected much juridical evidence to prove that Polyneices, as the very image of a bad son, by all contemporary standards deserved damnation. Yet in a play about inner and outer religious standards, Sophocles would hardly allow Polyneices to be condemned on merely legalistic grounds. Polyneices is undoubtedly a bad son; yet he is drawn in touchingly human colors: in his parting from Antigone, in his rather high conception of generalship, and in the loneliness of his sorrow as he bravely accepts his fate, he carries away a good deal of our sympathy. The simply bad son might be forgiven, one feels, if Antigone could intercede for him. If Sophocles meant us to remember only his past deeds, he should have made him appear more like them. But instead, he has deliberately given his cause some justice by making him the elder, instead of the younger brother.

It has been wisely noted that in the epic source the curse on the sons of Oedipus precedes and apparently causes their strife, but in Sophocles the strife came first, arising "from some god and their own sinful mind" [ll. 371ff.]. By the time Oedipus utters his curse, Polyneices is already on his way to the war, and is too fatally involved to turn back, as his words to Antigone show. So the curse, which once had a supernatural causative force, is here simply a statement of fact, though Polyneices still refers to the Furies as the ones who will bring it to pass, as one always speaks of a god in connection with what is true. Obviously it is Polyneices who will bring it to pass, for he is already doing it, and Sophocles has made it doubly pointed by letting Antigone beg him so movingly to desist. But Polyneices, whose name means the "man of the heavy curse," knows who he is. Quite aside from his past cruelty to his father and sister, and even apart from the fact that he is still only trying to use Oedipus, Polyneices deserves the curse because he is accursed, as Esau was accursed long before the actual denunciation came. Oedipus, like an oracle, has simply told the truth. Once more, the supernatural element enters in such a way that it can only be symbolic. Appropriately enough, the last of the three gods whom Oedipus invokes to destroy Polyneices is the War itself, the really destructive element "which has cast such heavy strife" [1. 1391] between the brothers.

The Creon and Polyneices scenes are not loosely or poorly integrated, from the moral point of view. From the mere standpoint of plot they revive and restate the conflicts of the **Philoctetes,** illustrating with infinitely subtle turns the world with which the great individual must deal, in his struggle for weight, dignity, and reality. Individualism in terms of such values means more than ordinary individualism; it is a norm of heroic being. And the basic difference between Oedipus and Polyneices is that Oedipus asserts his heroic right to be, while Polyneices asserts only his right to have. Therefore the one is oracular and blessed, the other accursed and pathetically confused in his humanity.

With the retreat of Polyneices, Oedipus' moral triumph is complete, and the mastery which he has shown throughout the play is now symbolized in the final scene of divine mastery. The last and most impressive of the supernatural happenings in Sophocles has this in common with all the others: the supernatural "cause" follows its effect. Oedipus officially "becomes a hero," with the power of blessing and cursing. But manifestly, the transformation which takes place in the depth of the sacred grove adds little in itself to the power of Oedipus. The blind and aged hero has already repulsed Creon and cursed Polyneices; before he leaves, he pronounces the eternal blessing upon Theseus and Attica. To the Greek, a person could become a hero only if he really was one, and Oedipus has already exercised his full prerogatives. Viewed in their simplest and most profound light, these prerogatives are no more than the ability to see through the veils of circumstance into essential fact. Oedipus' words all "have eyes." His insight attains its perfect symbol when he himself leads the

way into the grove, unguided except by what he calls "the present deity"; nor does he hesitate to identify himself subtly with that divine force. The inward man has at last come true.

It is a grave mistake to overlook the moral qualities which have made Oedipus a hero, and to regard his apotheosis as a simple act of grace on the part of the gods, or as amends made by them for the sufferings which he has endured. The choristers, indeed, interpret it thus:

> Out of the many woes that came
> Without cause, now the god in justice
> Would lift him up.
>
> [ll. 1565-67]

On the other hand, they have already prayed on their own behalf, when they heard the thunder and saw Oedipus' fate coming, to be delivered from any share in such "gainless grace." It is clear that they regard the gods as the actors here, and the whole process as fraught with danger, not only for Oedipus, but also for the passive spectators. These good Athenians, with their simple, human limitations and their sophrosyne [moderation], know that the gods can be almost as perilous friends as they are enemies, and they would prefer to stand apart and pray. Oedipus himself rejects any such interpretation, however. He uses the word "grace," but always of the blessing he himself is to bestow on Athens.

It will be remembered with what contempt he treated the suggestion of Ismene, in an earlier scene, when she remarked that the gods who formerly destroyed him were now about to reinstate him. Oedipus, with his customary brutal truthfulness, called it a cheap favor. Indeed, the gods did little for Oedipus; he had to prove himself every inch of the way, and it is no wonder that he omits all sanctimonious expressions of gratitude. He speaks seriously of the gods and the world at large only to Theseus, for the latter is the only other character of sufficiently heroic proportions to understand him in his own terms. By the same token, Theseus alone is permitted to witness the last hour of Oedipus. Only the large soul can fully understand how "the gods look well but late," how time penetrates all things, or how the noblest in man is rooted in his essential weakness and subjection to change. Others may grasp the words when they are spoken, but Theseus comprehends out of his own being. And Theseus, champion of the true Athenian religiosity, regards Oedipus himself as the grace-bringer, not the gods. There was no Messiah in Greek theology; if man was to come near to the divine, he must get there himself. How this can be achieved is known only to him who has in some sense already achieved it; the rest of the world will view it with limited, and doubtless frightened, eyes. As Hölderlin once wrote:

> Only those who themselves are
> Godlike ever believe in gods.

Oedipus brings us to a vision of godhead, whose content and significance are Oedipus himself. Sophocles says nothing of the gods who greet him, but he has shown all he could of the man who, after long sorrow, greeted the gods.

The end, therefore, is no great change, except that it releases Oedipus from the struggle of asserting himself and the suffering which pursued the moral activity of his soul. He had exalted himself by his endurance in that activity, and the final scene shows only the universal of which the play was the particular. That universal is all important, but one must not forget how it came about. It is the result of "time, suffering, and his own nobility." How perfectly his last words to his daughters sum up the trial of values by which he has triumphed:

> Children, it now behoves you leave this place,
> Enduring, in nobility of mind.
>
> [ll. 1640-41]

Endurance, nobility, mind: these are the laws of the human soul. So stated, they sound very simple, and in essence perhaps they are. But in action, which is life and the only context in which human beings can know them, they are the stuff of tragedy, the divine scheme or *ananke* [necessity], which binds the magnanimous man to himself and puzzles and outrages the philistine world, until it finally can ratify itself in a form that can no longer be denied.

To the audience which first witnessed the **Oedipus at Colonus** the conviction must have inevitably come that this was not the end of the hero, but his real beginning. The eye involuntarily follows him out of sight, and creates its own image of what happened thereafter. The simple fact that Oedipus became one of the lesser, though doubtless more revered, local deities can never account for Sophocles' having written this long complex work, with its keenly dramatized distinctions between inner and outer, and its iridescent interplay of godlike and manlike qualities in the central figure. Sophocles must seek what the process of becoming a hero included for Oedipus himself; how and why the fallen—for Oedipus is in this play, as much as before, Everyman—can still achieve an inch of significance and grow before our eyes, though the weight of the unyielding, and to ancient eyes, divine forces seemed forever pressing downward.

The **Oedipus at Colonus** ends with an apocalypse which, together with some other lines in Sophocles, illustrates to some extent the fifth century's outlook on both hero cults and death in general. There is, for instance, a passage in the **Electra,** where the chorus, attempting to console the heroine for her brother's supposed death, says:

> I know that the king Amphiaraus,
> Betrayed by the golden wiles of woman, lies buried;
> And now under the earth
> All-shade he rules.
>
> [ll. 836 ff.]

In this difficult passage, the reference to Amphiaraus is clear enough, but there is considerable question of its relevance. The famous warrior-prophet, who was betrayed into joining the Seven against Thebes by his wife Eriphyle, seems to have little to do with Orestes. And what does the last line mean—"All-shade he rules"? The word translated "all-shade" ($\pi\alpha\mu\psi\upsilon\chi o\delta$) occurs only here, and the scholiast, confused but generous, offers three explanations: "Either," he says, taking it as "all-soul" rather than "all-shade," "he rules over all the souls, which stand in

need of his prophetic art"—referring presumably to the souls of the living who consulted his oracle near Thebes; for the shades of the dead have little need of prophecy— "or, he is 'all-soul' because he saved his whole soul; or, because throughout everything he keeps his soul, which is immortal." The idea that famous heroes become rulers among the dead is as old as Homer; hence the scholiast's first suggestion is the one generally accepted. Although this does not seem quite right, still the general meaning of the lines is clear. It is a contrast between the fact of death and the fact of ruling. Death has not deprived Amphiaraus of his eminence, but has given him an eternal though shadowy royalty. Therefore, it is implied that, in a similar way, though Orestes is dead, his arete still holds its place in the world of the shades.

Does this imply the immortality of the soul? The scholiast barely suggested the idea, and few would care to defend it. Yet the juxtaposition of death and power implies something; the paradox is pregnant with faith in the indestructible value of human nobility. Added to the other passages in which the inner divinity of the protagonist shows itself, these lines form one more link in the chain of Sophoclean humanism which sees godhead operative in the moral being of man. The Niobe passages of Antigone and Electra, the latter's reference to the present deity in Orestes, Philoctetes' vision of his patron god, the passage on Amphiaraus, and old Oedipus' departure from the stage unguided save by "the present god"—all these, and perhaps more, point steadily in one direction: toward a verity in human life which is, or at least becomes, immutable—a particular which becomes general and attains to the authority of a historical truth.

And for this truth, in what was perhaps the last line of poetry he ever wrote, Sophocles used the word *kyros* ($\kappa\upsilon\rho o\delta$), which indicates a universally ratified authority: "Weep not, for altogether these things have authority [*kyros*]." That which is conceived to be at once authoritative and universal was to the Greeks divine: the gods were divine, law was divine; certain aspects of nature, even aside from conscious or developed animism, had their own divinity—the sea, the earth, the sun. Not superstition but religious intuition lies in such terminology, for it is almost a way of saying that these things really exist and are wonderful—even as the Ionian philosophers equated real being with "the divine" or "godhead." Therefore when Sophocles says that the fate of Oedipus has complete *kyros,* he means that he has passed into the realm of what is universal, true, and authoritative, and so divine. His inner divinity is forever ratified and preserved. For Electra and Antigone, the universal symbol was Niobe; for Philoctetes, Heracles; for Orestes, perhaps Amphiaraus, in a lesser way. The ancient classic example, or *paradeigma,* was thus extended into a religious token or symbol. In the **Ajax,** this technique was not yet developed, and in the **Trachiniae** the faith that impelled it was lost. But Oedipus, who even in the earlier play could call himself the brother of the months, in the end dwarfs all the earlier heroes by becoming his own symbol. It had taken Sophocles ninety years of spiritual struggle, probing the depths of human evil, to see man finally in such a light.

Without the aid of doctrine, dogma, or formal creed, and without the weighty deliberation of ecumenical councils, a poet is not apt to evolve a system. Sophocles did not. His work is the truer therefore; all the paradoxes remain; nothing is oversimplified, and equally, nothing is explained by the cathedral-like rationale of a static theology. Experience for the poet remains fluid and valid; it crystallizes, if at all, only into myth and poetry, both of which are imperishable but plastic. Wherever the experience of the individual soul becomes important, there the value of society's systems is called in question and eventually relegated to a position of merely formal, social importance, if not altogether overthrown. The Italian Renaissance, of course, is the perfect illustration, and the works of Sophocles, seen in the light of their spiritual and humanistic import, gain still a new degree of incandescence when set beside the emotional stirrings of the Renaissance. There again faith in the individual becomes heroic, experience becomes at once illuminated and mysterious, the state religion recedes coldly before the intuition of human beauty and excellence and only glows for the last time when a fair lady guides an intensely personal and sensuous poet through its labyrinthine levels.

It is never easy to say what exactly is the content of humanistic faith. It is as broad as human experience; its core is moral, and it becomes authoritative and universal. But it is hard to say more. In Sophocles' plays, various specific elements have presented themselves; but as a whole, the underlying humanistic faith is an emotional and poetic one, most akin to the intuitive passion of the Renaissance. And indeed it is not surprising, on the brink of a great Enlightenment, where the blankest superstition may stand side by side with utter skepticism, that the men who most fully embody the spirit of their age should give themselves to neither, but on their own behalf seek out and evolve, not cautious middle ground, but a truly perspicuous faith. It is more wonderful that so plastic a religious attitude, at once passionate and refined, should be able for a brief period to flood the interstices of early disintegration in a culture where the canons of a powerful and once-satisfying orthodoxy and the aspirations of the individual's destiny have begun to diverge. Perhaps the finest commentary available on the work of Sophocles, and on the victory of Oedipus in particular, is to be found in the famous work on the *Dignity of Man* by Pico, Count of Mirandola. It would be dangerous to assume a direct connection; but in 1423, Giovanni Aurispa sent the great Laurentian manuscript of Sophocles to Niccolo de' Niccoli, a famous Florentine bibliophile, and three quarters of a century later, Pico wrote:

> I created thee (God is speaking to man) a being neither heavenly nor earthly, neither mortal nor immortal only, that thou mightest be free to shape and to overcome thyself. Thou mightest sink into a beast, and be born anew to the divine likeness. The brutes bring from their mother's body what they will carry with them as long as they live; the higher spirits are from the beginning, or soon after, what they will be for ever. To thee alone is given a growth and a development depending on thine own free will. Thou bearest in thee the germs of a universal life.

It is the germ of this universal life which in *Oedipus at Colonus* has come to full flower. The status of the chthonian hero, the dead *numen* in the earth, aptly symbolizes, as doubtless it did from the beginning, man's special partaking of death and life, of the transient and eternal. (pp. 190-218)

> *Cedric H. Whitman, in his* Sophocles: A Study of Heroic Humanism, *Cambridge, Mass.: Harvard University Press, 1951, 292 p.*

FURTHER READING

OVERVIEWS AND GENERAL STUDIES

Adams, S. M. *Sophocles the Playwright.* Toronto: University of Toronto Press, 1957, 182 p.

An overview of Sophocles' dramatic achievement in the seven major plays, stressing that "to the people for whom [they] were composed, nothing in [the plays] was undramatic."

Bowra, C. M. *Sophoclean Tragedy.* Oxford: Clarendon Press, 1944, 334 p.

Discusses the themes, characterizations, and structure of Sophocles' plays. In Bowra's view, the tragedies "show that Sophocles built his tragic conflicts on the relations of men and gods, and therefore we must know what these relations are and mean."

Ehrenberg, Victor. *Sophocles and Pericles.* Oxford: Basil Blackwell, 1954, 187 p.

Focuses on Sophocles and his contemporary, the Athenian statesman Pericles, as representatives of the intellectual movements of their time.

Gassner, John. "Sophocles the Serene." In his *Masters of the Drama,* pp. 40-55. Rev. ed. New York: Dover Publications, 1954.

An overview of Sophocles' life and works.

Hadas, Moses. "Sophocles." In his *A History of Greek Literature,* pp. 84-91. New York: Columbia University Press, 1950.

A concise discussion of Sophocles' dramatic art. Commenting on the difficulty of identifying Sophocles' own views in his plays, Hadas characterizes him as "almost Shakespearean in eliminating himself from his work."

Jebb, Sir Richard C., ed. *Sophocles: The Plays and Fragments.* 7 volumes. Cambridge: Cambridge University Press, 1883-1900.

Provides translations, critical notes, commentary, and lengthy introductions to Sophocles' plays.

Jones, John. "Sophocles." In his *On Aristotle and Greek Tragedy,* pp. 141-238. New York: Oxford University Press, 1962.

Delineates Sophocles' use of myth in *Electra, Ajax, Antigone, Oedipus Rex,* and *Oedipus at Colonus.*

Kitto, H. D. F. *Sophocles: Dramatist and Philosopher.* London: Oxford University Press, 64 p.

A summary of the philosophical ideas inherent in Sophocles' plays. Kitto concludes that the basis of Sophocles' religious thinking was the belief that "*dike,* the regular order of things, may be contravened for a time, but in the end it must reassert itself."

Lefkowitz, Mary R. "Sophocles." In her *Lives of the Greek Poets,* pp. 75-87. London: Duckworth, 1981.
     Compiles all the known biographical information about Sophocles and includes, in an appendix, the "Life of Sophocles," the earliest biography of the dramatist.

Letters, F. H. J. *The Life and Work of Sophocles.* London: Sheed and Ward, 1953, 310 p.
     An overview of Sophocles' life, times, and style, with a chapter on each of the plays.

Lucas, D. W. "Sophocles." In his *The Greek Tragic Poets: Their Contribution to Western Life and Thought,* pp. 106-54. Boston: Beacon Press, 1952.
     Examines the role of Sophocles in the Greek "Age of Enlightenment." Includes a section on each play.

Nicoll, Allardyce. "The Glory of the Greek Theatre: Sophocles." In his *World Drama from Aeschylus to Anouilh,* pp. 51-68. New York: Harcourt Brace and Co., 1950?, 1000 p.
     Provides brief analyses of most of Sophocles' dramas and discusses his relation to the ancient and modern stage. Nicoll stresses that, though "his dramas may be bound by the strict conventions of the Greek stage, . . . no conventions, however strange, can conceal the essential humanity which breathes out of his lines."

Norwood, Gilbert. "The Works of Sophocles." In his *Greek Tragedy,* pp. 132-85. London: Methuen & Co., 1953.
     Traces Sophocles' handling of characterization, "intrigue," and irony in his dramas, as well as in many of his fragments. In assessing Sophocles' overall contributions to world literature, Norwood writes that the description of Oedipus' last moments is "the culmination in Greek of whatever miracles human language can encompass in exciting awe and delight."

O'Connor, Margaret Brown. *Religion in the Plays of Sophocles.* Menasha: George Banta Publishing Co., 1923, 151 p.
     Surveys the religious elements in Sophocles' dramas, focusing on such topics as his attitude toward various gods and his views regarding death and the afterlife.

Romilly, Jacqueline de. "Time in Sophocles." In her *Time in Greek Tragedy,* pp. 87-111. Ithaca: Cornell University Press, 1968.
     Posits that there was a shift in Greek understanding of time from the dramas of Aeschylus to those of Sophocles, in whose plays "the misery of man comes from the mutability of things, and his greatness from the way he answers it."

Seale, David. *Vision and Stagecraft in Sophocles.* Chicago: University of Chicago Press, 1982, 269 p.
     Traces various visual conventions and motifs in Sophocles' dramas.

Selincourt, Aubrey de. "Sophocles." In his *Six Great Playwrights: Sophocles, Shakespeare, Molière, Sheridan, Ibsen, Shaw,* pp. 11-40. London: Hamish Hamilton, 1962.
     An introduction to the life, times, and style of Sophocles.

Shorey, Paul. "Sophocles." In *Martin Classical Lectures,* Vol. I. Cambridge, Mass.: Harvard University Press, 1931, 181 p.

An overview of Sophocles' work. Shorey maintains that Sophocles "is the most truly Hellenic of the Greek tragedians" and that he embodies "a union of reasonableness and beauty . . . no other dramatist has achieved."

Thirlwall, Connop. "On the Irony of Sophocles." In his *Essays, Speeches and Sermons,* pp. 1-57. Edited by J. J. Stewart Perowne. London: Richard Bentley & Son, 1880.
     An influential essay in which Thirlwall contends that destiny in the plays of Sophocles became no longer "a mere brute force, a blind necessity working without consciousness of its means and ends. The power indeed still remained, and was still mysterious in its nature, inevitable and irresistible in its operations; but it [became perceived as] under the direction of a sovereign mind, acting according to the rules of unerring justice."

Vickers, Brian. "Sophocles: Suffering Integrity." In his *Towards Greek Tragedy: Drama, Myth, Society,* pp. 495-552. *Comparative Tragedy,* Vol. 1. London: Longmanm 1973.
     Maintains that "in Sophocles, although the main character's suffering does produce an answering compassion, the dramatic emphasis often seems to be less on the suffering-sympathy relationship than on the ideals or values for which the hero suffers. The major issue is his integrity rather than his pain."

Webster, T. B. L. *An Introduction to Sophocles.* Oxford: Clarendon Press, 1936, 202 p.
     Presents a general introduction to the life, time, and works of Sophocles, pointing out that "his primary concern was to show his Athenian public great personalities in surroundings where their greatness and their weakness could be displayed."

ANTIGONE

Else, Gerald F. *The Madness of Antigone.* Heidelberg: Carl Winter Universitatsverlag, 1976, 110 p.
     A very detailed textual analysis of *Antigone.* Else claims that the gist of the play is not a Hegelian clash of ideas, but rather "is basically a matter of *gods* and *blood.*"

Goheen, Robert F. *The Imagery of Sophocles' "Antigone": A Study of Poetic Language and Structure.* Princeton, N. J.: Princeton University Press, 1951, 171 p.
     An in-depth study of the imagery, image-patterns, and poetic structures employed by Sophocles in his *Antigone.*

Steiner, George. *Antigones.* Oxford: Clarendon Press, 1984, 316 p.
     Surveys the various uses writers have made of the story of Antigone from Sophocles' times to the present.

OEDIPUS REX

Cameron, Alister. *The Identity of Oedipus the King: Five Essays on the "Oedipus Tyrannus."* New York: New York University Press, 1968, 165 p.
     A close analysis of the drama based on "the assumption that the continued power of the play to attract lies in what Sophocles did with the subject."

Dodds, E. R. "On Misunderstanding the *Oedipus Rex.*" *Greece & Rome* 13 (1966): 37-49.
     Disputes the popular views of the play as a drama of re-

venge by the gods or a drama of destiny and proposes instead that "Oedipus is a kind of symbol of the human intelligence which cannot rest until it has solved all the riddles—even the last riddle, to which the answer is that human happiness is built on an illusion."

Fergusson, Francis. "Oedipus, According to Freud, Sophocles, and Cocteau." In his *Literary Landmarks: Essays on the Theory and Practice of Literature,* pp. 101-03. New Brunswick, N.J.: Rutgers University Press, 1975.

A study of the various ways in which the three authors treat the character of Oedipus in their writings.

Fromm, Erich. "The Oedipus Complex and the Oedipus Myth." In *The Family: Its Function and Destiny,* edited by Ruth Nanda Anshen, pp. 420-28. Science of Culture Series, Vol. V. New York: Harper Brothers, 1959.

Comments on Freud's analysis of the story of Oedipus and posits that "the theme running through Sophocles' [Theban] trilogy is to be understood as an attack against the victorious patriarchal order by the representatives of the defeated matriarchal system."

Knox, Bernard M. W. *Oedipus at Thebes.* New Haven, Conn.: Yale University Press, 1957, 280 p.

An acclaimed examination of Oedipus as "a representative figure who in his action and suffering presents to his own time the image of its victory and defeat."

O'Brien, Michael J., ed. *Twentieth Century Interpretations of "Oedipus Rex."* Englewood Cliffs, N.J.: Prentice-Hall, 1968, 119 p.

A collection of various essays on the play by such critics as Karl Reinhardt, G. M. Kirkwood, Bernard Knox, and Werner Jaeger.

Versenyi, Laszlo. "Oedipus: Tragedy of Self-Knowledge." *Arion* 1, No. 3 (Autumn 1962): 20-30.

Discusses *Oedipus Rex* as a tragedy of self-discovery, asserting that "it is not to the gods but to himself that Sophocles makes man responsible."

Thornton Wilder

1897-1975

The only author to receive Pulitzer Prizes for both drama and fiction, Wilder is best known for his award-winning plays *Our Town* and *The Skin of Our Teeth.* The values Wilder promoted in his work—Christian morality, community, the family, appreciation of everyday pleasures— are traditional, yet his theatrical methods were highly un- orthodox. Considered among the most innovative drama- tists of the early twentieth century, he rejected naturalism in favor of techniques that frankly acknowledged the arti- fice of the theater and linked the lives of his characters with such universal themes as mortality and the existence of God. While critical assessments of Wilder's optimistic and life-affirming dramas have varied, *Our Town* endures as a widely performed American classic.

Wilder was born in Madison, Wisconsin, the surviving member of a pair of twin boys. In 1906, his father, Amos Parker Wilder, relocated the family to Hong Kong after accepting a post in the United States foreign service, the first of many such moves. As a result, Wilder obtained his early formal education from a variety of institutions that included German schools in Hong Kong and Shanghai as well as the China Inland Mission School at Chefoo. In 1915, he graduated from high school in Berkeley, Califor- nia where he, with his mother and siblings, had ultimately settled while his father continued to work in the Far East. Wilder then entered Oberlin College at the insistence of his father, but after two years of study, the elder Wilder compelled him to withdraw and enter Yale. As a student, Wilder began writing short plays and essays for publica- tion in the *Yale Literary Review,* and hoped, upon obtain- ing his degree, to pursue writing as a career. However, his father, concerned that his son maintain a stable income for the family, secured him a teaching position at Lawrence- ville School, a select preparatory school for boys in Prince- ton, New Jersey.

During his early years at Lawrenceville, Wilder spent his summers chaperoning wealthy students on tours of Eu- rope, an experience that inspired his first novel, *The Caba- la.* Its publication in 1926 coincided with the first profes- sional production of one of his plays, *The Trumpet Shall Sound.* A thinly disguised allegory concerning God's mercy toward humanity, the play focuses upon a master who forgives his servants after learning that they have de- ceived him. Considered significantly less accomplished than his later dramas, *The Trumpet Shall Sound* received little notice and closed promptly. Wilder continued writ- ing, however, and in 1927 published his second novel, *The Bridge at San Luis Rey.* An extraordinary critical and popular success, this story of eighteenth-century Peru earned Wilder the Pulitzer Prize and afforded him the fi- nancial security to resign his position at Lawrenceville. He next published *The Angel That Troubled the Waters and Other Plays,* a collection of extremely short scenes, many of which he wrote as a student at Oberlin College. These

plays, which critics tend to regard as affected, have yet to be produced and are considered virtually impossible for the theater. For example, one stage direction reads: "Sud- denly the thirty pieces of silver are cast upward from the revolted hand of Judas. They hurtle through the skies, flinging their enormous shadows across the stars, and con- tinue falling forever through the vast funnel of space." Yet, this blatant disregard for the limitations of the stage prefigures the innovative techniques of *Our Town* and *The Skin of Our Teeth,* which are considered among Wilder's major contributions to the theater.

When Wilder's next novel, *The Woman of Andros,* ap- peared following the onset of the Great Depression, Mi- chael Gold, a leader of the proletarian school of criticism, condemned its story of young love in ancient Greece as es- capist and rebuked the author for not using his art to champion much needed social reform. Gold's scathing comments in part prompted Wilder to abandon historical settings and to focus upon elements of his own time and place. The plays collected in *The Long Christmas Dinner and Other Plays in One Act* reflect this shift while also re- vealing Wilder's growing interest in the experimental dra- mas of European playwrights such as Bertolt Brecht. Two plays of the collection, "Pullman Car Hiawatha" and "The Happy Journey to Trenton and Camden" integrate some of the original staging techniques that critics consider hallmarks of Wilder's work. Both plays feature a stage manager who speaks directly to the audience and who occasionally enters the drama as a minor character. Both are also devoid of scenery, using chairs as their only props. The title play, "The Long Christmas Dinner," prefigures the predominant theme of *Our Town*—that life is a brief yet significant interlude before death—through its unusual presentation of a single holiday feast spanning ninety years. In the play, family members enter and exit through two doors representing birth and death while their time onstage represents their entire lives.

During the 1930s, Wilder gained entry into New York theatrical circles through his friendship with Alexander Woollcott, the influential critic for the *New York Times* to whom he dedicated *Our Town,* his first original Broadway offering. In *Our Town,* the central role belongs to the omniscient Stage Manager, who narrates the action, jokes with the audience, and, through his philosophizing, explicitly connects the people of the small New Hampshire town of Grover's Corners with the universe as a whole. As with Wilder's earlier dramas, *Our Town* features minimal props and scenery while the characters function as symbols rather than fully developed individuals. In the first two acts, entitled "Daily Life" and "Love and Marriage," he traces the prosaic existence of the Webbs and the Gibbs, two families who are united by the marriage of their children, George and Emily. In the final act, "Death," Emily Webb, who has died giving birth, arrives at the town cemetery where other deceased members of the community sit quietly in chairs. Unlike the others, who have grown detached from earthly concerns, Emily longs to return to Grover's Corners, and so obtains the permission of the Stage Manager to relive her twelfth birthday. However, the experience becomes too painful when, knowing the future, she attempts to savor each trivial moment with her family but cannot because "it goes so fast. We barely have time to look at one another." Returning to the dead, Emily bids farewell to "new-ironed dresses and hot baths," before expressing the central moral of the play that human beings must "realize life while they live it."

While opening to an initially cool reception, *Our Town* eventually ran for 336 performances and earned Wilder his second Pulitzer Prize, thereby establishing his reputation as a major dramatist. Observers now consider it America's most produced play, and, while some regard it as sentimental, most critics praise *Our Town* as a moving allegory that transcends the requirements of realistic theater. Rex Burbank asserted: "The artistic problem basic to *Our Town* is that of showing that the events of life are at once not all they could be because they are taken for granted—but are priceless. Wilder meets this problem by repeating the quotidian scenes and viewing them and the central actions of each act . . . from different perspectives of time and space and different metaphysical vantage points. By relating the ordinary events in the lives of these ordinary people to a metaphysical framework that broadens with each act, he is able to portray life as being at once

significant and trivial, noble and absurd, miraculous and humdrum."

Wilder's reputation as a playwright also rests on two comedies, *The Matchmaker* and *The Skin of Our Teeth.* A slightly revised version of his play *The Merchant of Yonkers: A Farce in Four Acts, The Matchmaker* is Wilder's most conventionally staged long play. It is based on nineteenth-century Viennese playwright Johann Nestroy's farce *Einen Jux will er sich machen,* which in turn was adapted from John Oxenford's English comedy *A Day Well Spent.* The title character of *The Matchmaker* is Dolly Levi, a vivacious, worldly-wise widow who attempts to dissuade an uncharitable merchant from opposing the marriage of his niece to an impoverished artist. In the course of her endeavor, she woos the merchant for herself and convinces him that his wealth should not be saved but spent for the good of all. Most consider this comedy a work of light entertainment that shares with Wilder's other writings a celebratory attitude towards life and adventure. However, others concur with David Castronovo's assessment that "for a play that has earned a reputation as a trivial farce, [*The Matchmaker*] offers a clever assessment of life in a competitive society. . . . Bubbling out of this farcical evening is a series of observations about isolation, neurotic self-involvement, and the waste of human potential." In 1964, Michael Stewart and Jerry Herman adapted *The Matchmaker* as their popular musical *Hello, Dolly!*

In *The Skin of Our Teeth,* a significantly more ambitious work than *The Matchmaker,* Wilder focuses upon the Antrobuses, a 1940s family from Excelsior, New Jersey, who symbolize humanity through the ages. Together they endure such cataclysmic events as the Ice Age and the Great Flood, as well as the malicious actions of son Henry, whose name was changed from Cain after the "accidental" death of his brother. The humor of *The Skin of Our Teeth* arises from the unexpected juxtaposition of events—for example the Great Flood interrupts a convention of mammals in Atlantic City—as well as from surprising staging techniques that emphasize theatricality. Actors step in and out of their roles to share their "true feelings" with the audience, and the "stage crew" rehearses to fill in for performers who have supposedly taken ill. Through the Antrobuses' struggle to overcome natural disasters and invent such civilizing tools as the wheel and the alphabet, Wilder underscores the ability of the human will to endure and ultimately flourish. While *The Skin of Our Teeth* earned Wilder his third Pulitzer Prize, the play was briefly the subject of controversy when Joseph Campbell and Henry M. Robinson, in a series of articles that appeared in the *Saturday Review,* accused Wilder of plagiarizing James Joyce's *Finnegans Wake.* Retrospective opinion vindicated Wilder's literary borrowing, yet critical reaction to *The Skin of Our Teeth* continues to vary. While some commentators regard the play as a disjointed farce directed toward "middlebrow" sensibilities, others consider it a thoughtful, inventive examination of human frailty.

Wilder's dramatic work following *The Skin of Our Teeth* consisted primarily of revivals, revisions, and productions in foreign countries, particularly Germany, where his work remains very popular. German theater groups produced his drama *The Alcestiad*—based upon Euripides' *Alcestis*—in its original form, then as an opera with libretto by Wilder. His one-act pieces "The Wreck of the 5:25"—which centers upon a commuter's attempted suicide—and "Bernice"—the story of an embezzler and his estranged daughter—both premiered in Germany, as did his satyr play *The Drunken Sisters*. Wilder originally wrote "Bernice" as part of a proposed dramatic cycle entitled *The Seven Deadly Sins*. While he did not complete the series or its companion group *The Seven Ages of Man*, selections from both were performed in 1962, including "Someone from Assisi," "Infancy," and "Childhood." These plays, like many of Wilder's later theatrical offerings, elicited a generally unfavorable critical response. Although Wilder produced no further dramatic works, recognition for his achievements in the theater and other literary fields continued. In 1963, he received the United States Presidential Medal of Freedom and in 1965 was honored with the National Medal of Literature. He also garnered the National Book Award for his penultimate novel *The Eighth Day*. Upon his death in 1975, Wilder was recognized as an accomplished dramatist and man of letters whose innovative works remain integral to discussions of the American theater.

(For further information on Wilder's life and career, see *Contemporary Literary Criticism*, Vols. 1, 5, 6, 10, 15, 35; *Contemporary Authors*, Vols. 13-16, rev. ed., 61-64 [obituary]; and *Dictionary of Literary Biography*, Vols. 4, 7, 9.)

PRINCIPAL WORKS

PLAYS

The Trumpet Shall Sound 1926
The Angel That Troubled the Waters and Other Plays 1928
*The Long Christmas Dinner and Other Plays in One Act 1931
Our Town 1938
The Merchant of Yonkers: A Farce in Four Acts 1938; revised as *The Matchmaker*, 1955
The Skin of Our Teeth 1942
Our Century 1947
The Alcestiad 1955; produced as *A Life in the Sun* 1955
"Bernice" 1957
"The Wreck of the 5:25" 1957
†*Plays for Bleeker Street* 1962
The Drunken Sisters 1970

OTHER MAJOR WORKS

The Cabala (novel) 1926
The Bridge of San Luis Rey (novel) 1927
The Woman of Andros (novel) 1930
Heaven's My Destination (novel) 1934

The Ides of March (novel) 1948
The Eighth Day (novel) 1967
Theophilus North (novel) 1974
American Characteristics and Other Essays (nonfiction) 1979

*Contains "The Long Christmas Dinner," "Queens of France," "Pullman Car Hiawatha," "Love and How to Cure It," "Such Things Only Happen in Books," and "The Happy Journey to Trenton and Camden."

†Includes "Infancy," "Childhood," and "Someone from Assisi."

AUTHOR COMMENTARY

Preface to *Three Plays* (1957)

[*In the following essay, Wilder summarizes the theatrical techniques he employed in* Our Town, The Matchmaker, *and* The Skin of Our Teeth, *while addressing the various criticisms made concerning his work.*]

Toward the end of the twenties I began to lose pleasure in going to the theatre. I ceased to believe in the stories I saw presented there. When I did go it was to admire some secondary aspect of the play, the work of a great actor or director or designer. Yet at the same time the conviction was growing in me that the theatre was the greatest of all the arts. I felt that something had gone wrong with it in my time and that it was fulfilling only a small part of its potentialities. I was filled with admiration for presentations of classical works by Max Reinhardt and Louis Jouvet and the Old Vic, as I was by the best plays of my own time, like *Desire Under the Elms* and *The Front Page;* but it was with a grudging appreciation, for I didn't believe a word of them. I was like a schoolmaster grading a paper; to each of these offerings I gave an A+, but the condition of mind of one grading a paper is not that of one being overwhelmed by an artistic creation. The response we make when we "believe" a work of the imagination is that of saying: "This is the way things are. I have always known it without being fully aware that I knew it. Now in the presence of this play or novel or poem (or picture or piece of music) I know that I know it." It is this form of knowledge which Plato called "recollection." We have all murdered, in thought; and been murdered. We have all seen the ridiculous in estimable persons and in ourselves. We have all known terror as well as enchantment. Imaginative literature has nothing to say to those who do not recognize—who cannot be *reminded*—of such conditions. Of all the arts the theatre is best endowed to awaken this recollection within us—to believe is to say "yes"; but in the theatres of my time I did not feel myself prompted to any such grateful and self-forgetting acquiescence.

This dissatisfaction worried me. I was not ready to condemn myself as blasé and overfastidious, for I knew that I was still capable of belief. I believed every word of *Ulysses* and of Proust and of *The Magic Mountain*, as I did of hundreds of plays when I read them. It was on the stage that imaginative narration became false. Finally, my dissatisfaction passed into resentment. I began to feel that the theatre was not only inadequate, it was evasive; it did not wish to draw upon its deeper potentialities. I found the word for it: it aimed to be *soothing*. The tragic had no heat; the comic had no bite; the social criticism failed to indict us with responsibility. I began to search for the point where the theatre had run off the track, where it had chosen—and been permitted—to become a minor art and an inconsequential diversion.

The trouble began in the nineteenth century and was connected with the rise of the middle classes—they wanted their theatre soothing. There's nothing wrong with the middle classes in themselves. We know that now. The United States and Scandinavia and Germany are middle-class countries, so completely so that they have lost the very memory of their once despised and ludicrous inferiority (they had been inferior not only to the aristocracy but, in human dignity, to the peasantry). When a middle class is new, however, there is much that is wrong with it. When it is emerging from under the shadow of an aristocracy, from the myth and prestige of those well-born Higher-ups, it is alternately insecure and aggressively complacent. It must find its justification and reassurance in making money and displaying it. To this day, members of the middle classes in England, France, and Italy feel themselves to be a little ridiculous and humiliated. The prestige of aristocracies is based upon a dreary untruth that moral superiority and the qualifications for leadership are transmittable through the chromosomes, and the secondary lie, that the environment afforded by privilege and leisure tends to nurture the flowers of the spirit. An aristocracy, defending and fostering its lie, extracts from the arts only such elements as can further its interests, the aroma and not the sap, the grace and not the trenchancy. Equally harmful to culture is the newly arrived middle class. In the English-speaking world the middle classes came into power early in the nineteenth century and gained control over the theatre. They were pious, law-abiding, and industrious. They were assured of eternal life in the next world and, in this, they were squarely seated on Property and the privileges that accompany it. They were attended by devoted servants who knew their place. They were benevolent within certain limits, but chose to ignore wide tracts of injustice and stupidity in the world about them; and they shrank from contemplating those elements within themselves that were ridiculous, shallow, and harmful. They distrusted the passions and tried to deny them. Their questions about the nature of life seemed to be sufficiently answered by the demonstration of financial status and by conformity to some clearly established rules of decorum. These were precarious positions; abysses yawned on either side. The air was loud with questions that must not be asked. These audiences fashioned a theatre which could not disturb them. They thronged to melodrama (which deals with tragic possibilities in such a way that you know from the beginning that all will end happily) and to sentimental drama (which accords a total license to the supposition that the wish is father to the thought) and to comedies in which the characters were so represented that they always resembled someone else and not oneself. Between the plays that Sheridan wrote in his twenties and the first works of Wilde

and Shaw there was no play of even moderate interest written in the English language. (Unless you happen to admire and except Shelley's *The Cenci*.) These audiences, however, also thronged to Shakespeare. How did they shield themselves against his probing? How did they smother the theatre—and with such effect that it smothers us still? The box set was already there, the curtain, the proscenium, but not taken "seriously"—it was a convenience in view of the weather in northern countries. They took it seriously and emphasized and enhanced everything that thus removed, cut off, and boxed the action; they increasingly shut the play up into a museum showcase.

Let us examine why the box-set stage stifles the life in drama and why and how it militates against belief.

* * *

Every action which has ever taken place—every thought, every emotion—has taken place only once, at one moment in time and place. "I love you," "I rejoice," "I suffer," have been said and felt many billions of times, and never twice the same. Every person who has ever lived has lived an unbroken succession of unique occasions. Yet the more one is aware of this individuality in experience (innumerable! innumerable!) the more one becomes attentive to what these disparate moments have in common, to repetitive patterns. As an artist (or listener or beholder) which "truth" do you prefer—that of the isolated occasion, or that which includes and resumes the innumerable? Which truth is more worth telling? Every age differs in this. Is the Venus de Milo "one woman"? Is the play *Macbeth* the story of "one destiny"? The theatre is admirably fitted to tell both truths. It has one foot planted firmly in the particular, since each actor before us (even when he wears a mask!) is indubitably a living, breathing "one"; yet it tends and strains to exhibit a general truth since its relation to a specific "realistic" truth is confused and undermined by the fact that it is an accumulation of untruths, pretenses and fiction. The novel is pre-eminently the vehicle of the unique occasion, the theatre of the generalized one. It is through the theatre's power to raise the exhibited individual action into the realm of idea and type and universal that it is able to evoke our belief. But power is precisely what those nineteenth-century audiences did not—dared not—confront. They tamed it and drew its teeth; squeezed it into that removed showcase. They loaded the stage with specific objects, because every concrete object on the stage fixes and narrows the action to one moment in time and place. (Have you ever noticed that in the plays of Shakespeare no one—except occasionally a ruler—ever sits down? There were not even chairs on the English or Spanish stages in the time of Elizabeth I.) So it was by a jugglery with time that the middle classes devitalized the theatre. When you emphasize *place* in the theatre, you drag down and limit and harness time to it. You thrust the action back into past time, whereas it is precisely the glory of the stage that it is always "now" there. Under such production methods the characters are all dead before the action starts. You don't have to pay deeply from your heart's participation. No great age in the theatre ever attempted to capture the audiences' belief through this kind of specification and localization. I became dissatisfied with the theatre because I was unable to lend credence to such childish attempts to be "real."

* * *

I began writing one-act plays that tried to capture not verisimilitude but reality. In **"The Happy Journey to Trenton and Camden"** four kitchen chairs represent an automobile and a family travels seventy miles in twenty minutes. Ninety years go by in **"The Long Christmas Dinner."** In **"Pullman Car Hiawatha"** some more plain chairs serve as berths and we hear the very vital statistics of the towns and fields that passengers are traversing; we hear their thoughts; we even hear the planets over their heads. In Chinese drama a character, by straddling a stick, conveys to us that he is on horseback. In almost every No play of the Japanese an actor makes a tour of the stage and we know that he is making a long journey. Think of the ubiquity that Shakespeare's stage afforded for the battle scenes at the close of *Julius Caesar* and *Antony and Cleopatra*. As we see them today what a cutting and hacking of the text takes place—what condescension, what contempt for his dramaturgy.

Our Town is not offered as a picture of life in a New Hampshire village; or as a speculation about the conditions of life after death (that element I merely took from Dante's *Purgatory*). It is an attempt to find a value above all price for the smallest events in our daily life. I have made the claim as preposterous as possible, for I have set the village against the largest dimensions of time and place. The recurrent words in this play (few have noticed it) are "hundreds," "thousands," and "millions." Emily's joys and griefs, her algebra lessons and her birthday presents—what are they when we consider all the billions of girls who have lived, who are living, and who will live? Each individual's assertion to an absolute reality can only be inner, very inner. And here the method of staging finds its justification—in the first two acts there are at least a few chairs and tables; but when she revisits the earth and the kitchen to which she descended on her twelfth birthday, the very chairs and table are gone. Our claim, our hope, our despair are in the mind—not in things, not in "scenery." Molière said that for the theatre all he needed was a platform and a passion or two. The climax of this play needs only five square feet of boarding and the passion to know what life means to us.

The Matchmaker is an only slightly modified version of *The Merchant of Yonkers,* which I wrote in the year after I had written *Our Town.* One way to shake off the nonsense of the nineteenth-century staging is to make fun of it. This play parodies the stock-company plays that I used to see at Ye Liberty Theatre, Oakland, California, when I was a boy. I have already read small theses in German comparing it with the great Austrian original on which it is based. The scholars are very bewildered. There is most of the plot (except that our friend Dolly Levi is not in Nestroy's play); there are some of the tags; but it's all "about" quite different matters. My play is about the aspirations of the young (and not only of the young) for a fuller, freer participation in life. Imagine an Austrian pharmacist going to the shelf to draw from a bottle which he knows to contain a stinging corrosive liquid, guaranteed

to remove warts and wens; and imagine his surprise when he discovers that it has been filled overnight with very American birch-bark beer.

The Skin of Our Teeth begins, also, by making fun of old-fashioned playwriting; but the audience soon perceives that he is seeing "two times at once." The Antrobus family is living both in prehistoric times and in a New Jersey commuters' suburb today. Again, the events of our homely daily life—this time the family life—are depicted against the vast dimensions of time and place. It was written on the eve of our entrance into the war and under strong emotion and I think it mostly comes alive under conditions of crisis. It has been often charged with being a bookish fantasia about history, full of rather bloodless schoolmasterish jokes. But to have seen it in Germany soon after the war, in the shattered churches and beerhalls that were serving as theatres, with audiences whose price of admission meant the loss of a meal and for whom it was of absorbing interest that there was a "recipe for grass soup that did not cause the diarrhea," was an experience that was not so cool. I am very proud that this year it has received a first and overwhelming reception in Warsaw. The play is deeply indebted to James Joyce's *Finnegans Wake*. I should be very happy if, in the future, some author should feel similarly indebted to any work of mine. Literature has always more resembled a torch race than a furious dispute among heirs.

The theatre has lagged behind the other arts in finding the "new ways" to express how men and women think and feel in our time. I am not one of the new dramatists we are looking for. I wish I were. I hope I have played a part in preparing the way for them. I am not an innovator but a rediscoverer of forgotten goods and I hope a remover of obtrusive bric-a-brac. And as I view the work of my contemporaries I seem to feel that I am exceptional in one thing—I give (don't I?) the impression of having enormously enjoyed it. (pp. vii-xiv)

> *Thornton Wilder, in a preface to his* Three Plays, *1957. Reprint by Harper & Row, Publishers, 1985, pp. vii-xiv.*

OVERVIEWS AND GENERAL STUDIES

Francis Fergusson   (essay date 1957)

[*Fergusson is one of the most influential drama critics of the twentieth century. In his seminal study,* The Idea of a Theater *(1949), he claims that the fundamental truths present in all drama are defined exclusively by myth and ritual, and that the purpose of dramatic representation is, in essence, to confirm the "ritual expectancy" of the society in which the artist works. Fergusson's method has been described as a combination of the principles of Aristotle's* Poetics *and the principles of modern myth criticism. In the following excerpt from his critical study* The Human Image in Dramatic Literature *(1957), Fergusson compares Wilder's work to the plays of German expressionist Bertolt Brecht, and concludes that, unlike Brecht, Wilder transcends political categories to present a "religious Platonism" through his subtle use of allegory.*]

A number of contemporary playwrights, of whom Brecht, Wilder and Eliot are among the most accomplished, are now writing some form of allegory. They reject the tradition of modern realism, perhaps because little remains to be done with direct reflections of contemporary life: the pathos of the lost individual or the decaying suburb has been done to death since Chekhov. They do not seek some form of theater-poetry based on folk forms or myths or rituals, or on symbolism on the analogy of the *symboliste* poets, as so many theater artists did in the twenties. They seek to use the theater in the service of their consciously worked-out moral or philosophical ideas. They do not, however, write thesis plays à la Brieux, in which some scheme of social reform is openly debated and "proved" on the stage; nor do they write Shavian intellectual farces, in which the point is in the game of ideas itself. Their aim is not discussion in any sense, but teaching: they use the stage, the characters, and the story to demonstrate an idea which they take to be the undiscussible truth. The truths which Brecht, Wilder and Eliot propound are very different; but they all write allegory according to the literal definition in the Oxford Dictionary: "speaking otherwise than one seems to speak."

One must be very detached from the contemporary theater and its audiences in order to write allegory of this kind. Brecht, Wilder and Eliot do not expect their audiences to share their intimate perceptions, whether "realistic" or "poetic." Such detachment is the natural result of the failure of the art theaters of the twenties. After World War I much of the creative energy of the theater went into small theater groups which tried to build special audiences like those of ballet, chamber music or lyric poetry. Playwrights who worked for such groups tried to cultivate their art first and their audiences second; they were encouraged to embody their visions in the theater medium as directly as possible. In that context the thought-out indirectness of allegory seemed cumbersome and artificial. But the contemporary allegorists despair of the effort to recruit an audience of connoisseurs. They accept the commercial theater (especially Wilder and Eliot) as the only theater we can have; and the problem they set themselves is to use that non-conducting medium—necessarily *indirectly*—for their didactic purposes.

All three of these allegorists are extremely conscious of what they are doing. One can study their philosophies not only in their plays but in their theoretical writings, and all of them have written technical studies of playwriting which reveal the knowing methods they use in making their plays. But in other respects they are dissimilar and unrelated. Each of them has followed a lonely road to his achievement, and speaks through the stage as though he were alone with his undiscussible truth. For that reason it is something of a tour de force to consider them together, as though they were voices in a dialogue; as though they were devoting their thought and their art to some common enterprise in the modern theater.

Nevertheless they all seek with some success to address the mysterious modern crowd; their plays may run at the same time in the same city. And all of them are obliged to come to terms with the theater itself, stage, actors, and audience; and the art of handling those elements, though seldom studied in its full scope, is not unknown. Brecht, Wilder and Eliot seek to work out *new* theatrical forms, and Brecht owes much of his peculiar force to his direct defiance of the tradition. But one may patiently put them back into relation to the tradition by enquiring what they do with the inescapable elements of plot, characterization, language, and the conventions of make-believe. In this way one can, I think, find a basis for comparing them and for estimating the meaning of the present trend toward allegory. (pp. 41-3)

. . . . .

The philosophy which Thornton Wilder presents in his plays, especially the two most famous, *Our Town* and *The Skin of Our Teeth,* is at the opposite pole from Brecht's. Brecht is exclusively concerned (like Barth in his "Theology of Crisis") with his obsessive vision of the emergency of our time. His Marxism is in essence partisan, and his theater lives by conflict. Wilder on the other hand tries to take his stance above all parties; he preaches the timeless validity of certain great old traditional ideas, and his theater is almost devoid of conflict, wooing its audience gently. Wilder's philosophy—that of a most cultivated man—is more sophisticated than Brecht's and more subtly presented. But on the evidence of the plays I think one can call it a sort of religious Platonism: deistic, but not more Christian than Unitarianism or Ethical Culture.

Brecht has paid his respects with characteristic vigor to those writers who even in our time reiterate the eternal verities: "It is true," he writes in *Fünf Schwierigkeiten,* "that Germany is falling into barbarism, and that rain falls downward. Many poets write truths of this kind. They are like painters who decorate the walls of a sinking ship with still lifes." If he read Wilder's still lifes he would characterize them in just such scornful terms. And as one turns from Brecht to Wilder one must be struck with the sudden quiet, and wonder what relevance these plays have to the actual texture of our lives. Yet Wilder's plays succeed at least as well as Brecht's in holding a modern crowd for two hours in the theater, and Wilder's art is at least as knowing, forewarned and forearmed, as Brecht's.

A very early play of Wilder's, perhaps his first, was produced by the American Laboratory Theatre in 1926, and has, I think, never been printed. It is a heavy allegory about a householder (God) who goes away on a journey, leaving his servants in charge. When he returns he finds that they have been faithful or unfaithful in various ways, and rewards them accordingly. This play is appropriately entitled *The Trumpet Shall Sound,* and it reveals Wilder's philosophy and his allegorical art at a crude, early stage. The distance between it and *Our Town* measures his extraordinary growth as technician. We have some of the experiments and finger exercises he did in the next eight years: his short plays, his adaptation of *A Doll's House,* his translation of Obey's *Viol de Lucrèce,* and his valuable technical essay, "Notes on Playwriting." On the evidence of the plays it appears that Joyce, Gertrude Stein, Obey, and in general the literary and theatrical great of "Paris in the twenties" have been his masters. But his art has been very little studied: we marvel at his results, but have not investigated his stage magic. This essay can therefore be no more than a preliminary exploration.

Our Town is Wilder's masterpiece to date. His nostalgic evocation of Grover's Corners, New Hampshire, at the turn of the century, is fed, more than any of his other works, with the sources of poetry: old, digested memories and associations. The atmosphere of the little town convinces before all thought, as poetry does. But at the same time a New England village before World War I is a natural illustration of the faint religious humanism which Wilder wants to present allegorically. The Stage Manager-Lecturer directs our attention to the protagonist (the town) and the narrative sequence from the cradle to the grave. By the end of Act I it is evening, and we have heard *Blest Be the Tie That Binds* sung offstage by the Ladies' Choir and then whistled by Mr. Webb. George and Rebecca Gibbs, as children, are leaning out an upstairs window enjoying the moonlight:

> REBECCA: I never told you about that letter that Jane Crofut got from her minister when she was sick. . . . He wrote Jane a letter and on the envelope the address was like this: It said: Jane Crofut; The Crofut Farm; Grover's Corners; Sutton County; New Hampshire; United States of America.
>
> GEORGE: What's funny about that?
>
> REBECCA: But listen; it's not finished: The United States of America; Continent of North America; Western Hemisphere; The Earth; The Solar System; The Universe; The Mind of God—that's what it said on the envelope.

This passage was perhaps inspired by the very similar address which young Stephen Daedalus writes in his geography book [in James Joyce's *A Portrait of the Artist as a Young Man*]; but it works beautifully at this point in the play, and the moral—that we live, whether we realize it or not, in the Mind of God, emerges naturally from the context of old-fashioned village childhood. In Act II Wilder uses the terrors and sentimental tears of a long-past marriage to suggest the same idea more gently; and in Act III he uses Emily's funeral and her ghostly return to earth on her fourteenth birthday for the same purpose: to present Grover's Corners *sub specie aeternitatis*. In the whole play the homesick vision and the Platonic-religious teaching work harmoniously together.

Wilder's "Notes on Playwriting" show that, like Brecht, his art of allegory is completely knowing. Like Brecht again, he stresses the conventional, make-believe quality of the stage—in opposition to the realists' "illusion"—for the purposes of allegory. All theater "lives by convention," he writes, and "a convention is an agreed-upon falsehood, a permitted lie." . . . "The convention has two functions: (1) It provokes the collaborative activity of the spectator's imagination; and (2) It raises the action from the specific to the general. . . . The stage continually strains to tell this generalized truth and it is the element

of pretense that reinforces it." That is an excellent description of the way the theatrical conventions of *Our Town* work. The bare stage and the Stage Manager who directly addresses the audience or tells the actors what to do enlist the audience in make-believe: induce it to imagine the little town waking up, years ago, in the dark of early morning. At the same time the frank theatricality of these conventions warns us not to take the characters too seriously as people: they are presented only by make-believe, as half-playful illustrations of a "generalized truth." It is this "generalized truth"—that we exist in the Mind of God—which we are to watch for, and when we get it we shall have the whole point and message of the play.

Wilder maintains, in his "Notes," that all drama is essentially allegory, "A succession of events illustrating a general idea," as he puts it. "The myth, the parable, the fable are the fountainheads of all fiction," he writes, "and in them is seen most clearly the didactic, moralizing employment of a story. Modern taste shrinks from emphasizing the central idea behind the fiction, but it exists there nevertheless, supplying the unity to fantasizing, and offering a justification to what otherwise we would repudiate as mere arbitrary contrivance, pretentious lying, or individualistic emotional association-spinning." This radically Platonic view of poetry—that its only justification is that it may be a means of teaching moral truth—might be disputed at some length. But I suppose it must be the belief of all three of our contemporary allegorists; Brecht would certainly agree in principle, for his plays are very obviously constructed as "a succession of events illustrating a general idea." But it is worth noting that Brecht's "truth" is the opposite of Wilder's—which suggests that moralizing is no more immune than poetry to the human weakness for arbitrary contrivance, pretentious lying, and individualistic emotional association-spinning.

In the art of both Brecht and Wilder plotmaking is basic, for the plot, while presenting the story, must be at the same time a demonstration of the idea. Wilder relies on plotting even more than Brecht; by its means, he explains, the playwright controls stage, actors, director and designer for his purposes. "He learns to organize the play in such a way that its strength lies not in appearances beyond his control, but in the succession of events and in the unfolding of an idea, in narration." He accomplishes precisely this feat by means of the plot—the succession of events—in *Our Town.* It is primarily the narrative sequence from morning to night, from the cradle to the grave, through the marriage to the funeral, which carries the play; and it is this sequence also which continually leads to the *idea*. Brecht arranges his plots in such a way as to present onstage only struggles; he avoids all pathos on the ground that it would demoralize the audience which he is grooming for the Revolution. But Wilder, in the interest of his opposite philosophy, bases the three acts of his play precisely upon the pathos of the great commonplaces of human life, birth, marriage and death; and he shows no conflict at all.

The plot with its unfolding idea is so effective, in *Our Town,* that it almost makes the play go without reference to the individual lives of its people. But not quite: the stage is after all not the lecture platform; one must put something concrete upon it. "Because a play presupposes a crowd," Wilder writes, "the dramatist realizes that the group mind imposes upon him the necessity of treating material understandable by the greater number." It is apparently in accordance with this principle that he has selected the concrete materials of *Our Town:* the characters, which are clichés of small-town life rather than individuals; the language they speak, which (in spite of its authentic New England flavor) is distressingly close to that of plays written for high schools and Sunday schools, or to the soap operas of radio, or to vapid "family magazines." If one looks at a few passages from the play apart from the movement of the plot—George and Emily absorbing their cherry phosphates, or George having his tearful talks with his father-in-law to be—the effect is embarrassingly stale and pathetic. It is evident that Wilder himself is not much interested in George or Emily. He hardly imagines them as people, he rather invites the audience to accept them by plainly labeling them; as sentimental stereotypes of village folksiness. They are therefore understandable by the greater number, and they serve to present the story and illustrate the moral. But they betray, I think, the worst weakness of Wilder's type of allegory. The distance between the life onstage, which the audience accepts because it is so familiar in this sense, and the idea which the author has in mind is too great. The "greater number" blubbers at the platitudes of character and situation, while the author, manipulating his effects with kindly care, enjoys the improbable detachment of the Mind of God.

André Obey's *Noah* is akin to *Our Town* in several respects; I even think it possible that it may have given Wilder some of the clues for his play. *Our Town* is based on the "world" of small-town Protestantism at the turn of the century, and *Noah* upon the "world" of French peasant religion. Both plays therefore owe some of their appeal to nostalgia, and when *Noah* is played one can hardly "get" it without an effort of sympathy which may be called sentimental. But once we make-believe that vanished world, we get a vision of human life which is full of the weight of experience. The imagined characters are intensely alive; we see at every moment how Noah is groping and struggling. It is his experience which leads us to the idea—or rather the vision—which the play presents. At the end we are made to feel what Noah's faith has cost him, and therein lies the strength and the authority of the play. But the dreamy situation of *Our Town* does not cost anyone anything, and that, I think, is why the idea may strike us as sentimental and pretentious. The idea is clear; in a sense it is appropriately illustrated in the atmosphere and the customs of Grover's Corners. But it is not incarnate in the characters and the language which make up the actual texture of the play.

In spite of this weakness *Our Town* is a "natural" for Wilder and his philosophy: the basic inspiration is propitious, the remembered village and the idea to be taught do harmonize. But in *The Skin of Our Teeth* Wilder set himself an even more difficult problem: that of presenting his religious Platonism in an urban context, and at a time—the beginning of World War II—of general crisis. In that play

both the theatrical virtuosity and the weakness, or limitation, of Wilder's kind of allegory are very clear.

Wilder is reported to have received the inspiration for *Skin* at a performance of *Hellza'poppin,* an extravaganza in the corniest style of old-fashioned vaudeville. But Campbell and Robinson, who attended the opening of *Skin* just after they had completed their *Skeleton Key to Finnegans Wake,* demonstrated in two well-documented articles in *The Saturday Review* that the play is a simplified dramatization of Joyce's mysterious work [See review dated 19 December 1942 and Further Reading]. There is probably no one but Wilder with enough imagination and enough understanding both of Joyce and of vaudeville to combine the two. But now that the work is done we can see what a brilliant notion it was to translate Joyce's dreamlike and ironic meditation on the eternal recurrences of human history into the ancient jokes, irrational horseplay and shameless sentimentality of burlesque. Burlesque provides Wilder with his "material understandable to the greater number," an urban folksiness corresponding to the village folksiness of *Our Town;* and *Finnegans Wake* suggests a plot-scheme and an abstract cast of characters to give narrative and rational form to the whole.

The plot of *Skin* is closely analogous to that of *Our Town.* The protagonist is Humanity, which corresponds to Grover's Corners. The three major crises on which the three acts are based, the Ice Age, the Flood, and War, correspond to Our Town's Birth, Marriage and Death. Just as Birth, Marriage and Death must be suffered by all villagers, and recur in every generation, so the crises in *Skin* are felt as common, similar, and recurrent ordeals, which must be suffered in every generation. *Skin,* like *Our Town,* is essentially a pathos, with little conflict—and that little unconvincing. The moral of the tale is the same: we have our being within the eternal verities, or the Mind of God. Thus at the end of Act I, when the Antrobus household in Excelsior, New Jersey, is getting ready to survive the Ice Age, Antrobus insists on saving Moses, Homer and the nine Muses (who are bums on the streets of New York) "to keep up our spirits." Moses and Homer each quote a bit from their works, in Hebrew and Greek respectively; and then all join in singing *Tenting Tonight.* At the end of Act II the Flood provides a more sinister hint of the truth behind our heedless lives (like the marriage in *Our Town*); and at the end of Act III bits from Spinoza, Plato, Aristotle and Genesis are quoted by members of the backstage staff. The quotations proclaim the intellectual love of God, and are supposed to be thought of as hours of the night, from nine to midnight, passing over our heads like the stars: an effect very much like the one in *Our Town,* when George and Rebecca are seen in the moonlight, with stars beyond, and beyond that the Mind of God.

All of this works very well in the theater, when "the greater number" is there to guffaw at the scenery when it leans precariously, the wise cracks aimed at the peanut gallery, and the racial jokes in the cozy style of *Abie's Irish Rose;* or to grow still and dewy-eyed when the old familiar tunes are heard. But if one happens to be feeling a little morose—smothered perhaps by so thick an atmosphere of sheer warm-heartedness—or if one tries the experiment of reading the play in cold blood, the marriage of Plato and Groucho Marx may fail to appeal. It is too evident that the "material," the actual texture, of the play, is a pastiche. The language is a collection of clichés, the characters unfused collections of familiar labels. Antrobus, for instance, consists of old jokes about the suburban householder, the middle-aged philanderer, and the Shriner on a binge, but he is also labeled the inventor of all human culture. The combination has no imaginative or intellectual unity at all. It is amusing and good-natured to set Moses, Homer and the nine Muses to singing *Tenting Tonight*, but what does Wilder's "greater number" get out of this reassuring effect? The austerity of the Ten Commandments, or tearful associations with last summer's bonfire at Camp Tamiment?

A reading of **Our Town** and **The Skin of Our Teeth** suggests that Wilder's extraordinary freedom and virtuosity in the theater is gained through eluding rather than solving the problem which most playwrights feel as basic: that of embodying form and meaning in character and language. If he had addressed himself to that problem in **Skin,** Antrobus, as the father-pilot of the race, would have had to sound a little more like Spinoza and a little less like George F. Babbitt. But Wilder has seen how it is possible to leave the "greater number" in peace with the material understandable to it, and Plato in peace in the supratemporal realm of the Mind of God. He is thus able to be "for" Plato (as politicians of every persuasion are for Peace, Freedom and Prosperity), and at the same time devote his great gifts to entertaining the crowd or "group mind."

This type of allegory is perfectly in accord with the Platonic kind of philosophy which it is designed to teach. The great Ideas are timeless, above the history of the race and the history of actual individuals. Any bit of individual or racial history will do, therefore, to "illustrate" them; but history and individual lives lack all real being: they are only shadows on the cave wall. It may be part of Wilder's consciously intended meaning that the material understandable to the greater number—comic-supplement jokes, popular tunes—*is* junky and illusory. That would be one explanation of the bodiless and powerless effect of his theater, as compared, for instance, with Brecht's. Brecht's vision is narrow and myopic, but a sense of the reality (at however brutal a level) of individual experience is truly in it. Brecht's philosophy is, of course, a philosophy of history, and leads him naturally to sharpest embodiments in the temporal struggle. But Wilder's philosophy lacks the historic dimension, and its intellectual freedom is therefore in danger of irrelevancy, pretentiousness and sentimentality.

Wilder's art, as I pointed out above, has not yet been critically digested or expounded. Wilder occupies a unique position, between the Great Books and Parisian sophistication one way, and the entertainment industry the other way, and in our culture this region, though central, is a dark and almost uninhabited no man's land. Partly for that reason, his accomplishments must seem rather puzzling and paradoxical. The attempt which I have been making, to take him seriously as allegorizing moralist, may be much too solemn. His plays belong in the theater;

they have their proper life only there, like the tricks of a stage magician. When the man pulls the rabbit out of the hat, the glamour of the occasion suffices: it is inappropriate to enquire whether he has really materialized a new creature, or only hauled out, by the ears, the same old mild vegetarian pet. (pp. 50-60)

> *Francis Fergusson, "Five Contemporary Playwrights," in his* The Human Image in Dramatic Literature, *Doubleday & Company, Inc., 1957, pp. 41-97.*

Patricia R. Schroeder   (essay date 1989)

[*In the essay below, Schroeder examines Wilder's fluid concept of time and charts its evolution from his early one-act plays such as "The Long Christmas Dinner" through* Our Town *and* The Skin of Our Teeth. *In these later works, Schroeder observes, Wilder "stressed the importance of each present moment, each choice, in determining as yet unrecognizable historical patterns."*]

At first glance, Thornton Wilder's stage past may seem to have only a tenuous connection with that of other twentieth-century American playwrights. For O'Neill, Miller, and Williams, the past is present in the memories of the characters; exposition therefore assumes a major dramatic role in their plays. Yet Wilder's work does share his compatriots' concern with portraying time's passage on the

Amos Parker Wilder and his sons Amos (standing left) and Thornton (standing right), 1915.

stage, although his emphasis is somewhat different. On Wilder's stage, time's passing is most often obvious to us but unnoticed by the characters, even as it shapes their lives and changes the world they inhabit.

In a 1956 essay entitled "The Man Who Abolished Time" [see Further Reading], Malcolm Cowley pointed out Wilder's pervasive interest in the effects of time. According to Cowley, Wilder's guiding principle and recurring theme is that *"Everything that happened might happen anywhere and will happen again."* As a result of this principle, says Cowley, Wilder continually experiments with time in his novels and his plays, "foreshortening time" to emphasize the repeated patterns of history. Cowley's essay is a landmark, since it offers one of the first analyses of Wilder's perennial experiments with time. Yet Cowley's assessment . . . is somewhat misleading, suggesting that Wilder holds a "disregard for history" and even that he "denies the importance of time."

It would be more accurate to say that Wilder's *characters* deny the importance of time; they do their best to preserve inherited patterns—annual Christmas dinners, familiar wedding ceremonies—designed to stave off the changes that time inevitably, if imperceptibly, brings with it. Yet to the spectators of a Wilder play, time passes quickly and visibly: characters grow gray before our eyes, and the Ice Age is immediately followed by World War II. With the exception of some very early plays, time is rarely "abolished" on Wilder's stage; rather, it becomes an actual theatrical presence.

This difference between time as it passes and time as characters perceive it is at the heart of Wilder's dramatic experiments; one might even call it the central conflict of his plays. For Wilder was aware that time passes at different rates, depending on who is measuring the pace. For a geologist, centuries count as nothing; for an archeologist or a historian, time collapses; for a lover in the presence of the beloved, an hour can pass unnoticed, yet to one who must wait, that same hour can seem interminable. Rather than focusing his theatrical experiments on methods of exposition, then, Wilder concentrated on depicting the profound and inescapable effects of time as well as the many perspectives available to measure its passing.

Throughout his career Wilder devised, recovered, and adapted stage techniques that produce a double vision of past and present, that demonstrate the role of the individual moment in creating the repeated patterns of history. The playwright described his problem in this way [in his Preface to *Three Plays;* see Author Commentary]:

> Every person who has ever lived has lived an unbroken succession of unique occasions. Yet the more one is aware of individuality in experience (innumerable! innumerable!) the more one becomes attentive to what these disparate moments have in common, to repetitive patterns. As an artist (or listener or beholder) which "truth" do you prefer—that of the isolated occasion, or that which includes or resumes the innumerable? Which truth is more worth telling?

Wilder's plays suggest that he found *both* truths worth telling, and his dramatic experiments all contribute to his

expressing them simultaneously. He continually adjusted stage time to portray situations both as "disparate moments" and also as contributors to "repetitive patterns." By presenting, as he said of *The Skin of Our Teeth,* "two times at once" [*Three Plays*], he was able to proclaim the intrinsic significance of each moment and simultaneously to explore the place of the moment, once past, in shaping the unfolding patterns of history.

The Compression of Time

Wilder's very first published plays (*The Angel That Troubled the Waters,* 1928) suggest both his willingness to experiment with stage time and the early difficulties he faced in creating a temporally flexible dramatic form; many of these plays, in fact, do "abolish" time in just the way Cowley described. The form the young Wilder employed—and Wilder admits to having begun experimenting with these plays while still a high school student—was the three-minute play for three actors, a literary form that, according to the playwright's "Forward" to the volume, "satisfies my desire for compression." Despite the immaturity of the three-minute plays themselves, this impulse toward compression led the young Wilder to experiment with the telescoping of time, thereby allowing his three minutes of stage time to incorporate many of the general patterns of history. The three-minute form became an early proving ground for the playwright who would later collapse the past into the present to stage the life of an entire village, and who would include the Ice Age, the Deluge, and a world war in a single three-act play.

The majority of these three-minute plays explore competing visions of time through one simple technique: they divorce well-known characters from their usual environments and force them to function in different times or in unfamiliar contexts. In one play Mozart, worrying over his poverty and despairing of a commission, is interrupted in his practical considerations by a commission from Death. Here, the concerns of the earthly world and human time contrast with those of the spiritual world and eternity, implying their concurrent but conflicting demands for our attention. Another play presents the death of Childe Roland, whose dying prayer to the Blessed Virgin is answered not by the Queen of Heaven he addresses, but by three mystical queens in a mythic dark tower, entrance to the underworld of a time period and a system of beliefs different from those he invokes.

In another play from this collection, entitled **"Proserpina and the Devil,"** Wilder's instinct for compression takes on an added dimension as he first conflates the traditions of classical mythology with those of Christianity and then inserts them into a seventeenth-century Venetian marionette show. On this puppet stage, the Lake of Wrath serves as the River Styx, Noah's Ark as Charon's barge, Pluto as Satan, Hermes as the Archangel Gabriel, and "a handsome Italian matron" in stiff brocade as Demeter. Wilder's interest in the repeated cycles of time is apparent here in this interchanging of mythic and religious figures in the more recent—although still historical—context of seventeenth-century Italy. His abridgement of time also demonstrates the ways in which the details of a workaday routine—represented in the play by the difficulties of the puppeteers, or the "matter of pins and hooks-and-eyes" that prevents Proserpina's rescue—can obscure the interaction of larger contexts, which shape and are shaped by the event itself.

In one three-minute play, **"Fanny Otcott,"** Wilder explores with some success both his interest in competing perspectives and his concern for the interaction between historical patterns and particular moments. **"Fanny Otcott"** is structurally different from its companion pieces in two important ways. Unlike many of the other plays, which present only the static meditations of ready-made mythic or historic figures, **"Fanny Otcott"** contains an evolving plot. The climax occurs when Fanny recognizes the possibilities afforded by conflicting interpretations of events past and present. In addition, in **"Fanny Otcott"** Wilder focuses his inquiries on one character's view of her personal past and so emphasizes both individual perception and the particular moment with an immediacy unmatched in the volume.

Against the backdrop of an Arthurian tower—a reminder that Fanny's situation has often been repeated through history—the aging actress Fanny Otcott sorts out her souvenirs—"in short, her past." Enter George, her long-ago lover and now a bishop, whose memories of his former "association" with Fanny are very different from her own. What Fanny remembers with tenderness and delight—"It was like hawthorn-buds and meadow larks and Mr. Handel's Water-music"—George recalls as "a distressing spot on my conscience." The play ends as Fanny dismisses the illusory memory world she has so long inhabited and resolves to rejoice in present life rather than in recollections of the past.

This is the earliest clear-cut instance in Wilder's dramatic canon of a dilemma his later plays insist upon: Fanny cannot seize the day if she insists on burying it with memories, but neither can she recognize the ultimate importance of the present moment if she isolates it from its place in the developing patterns of her life. The validity of the concept by which she has lived—that is, her interpretation of her affair with George—is called into question by George's conflicting recollections, and the possibility that contradictory patterns can emerge from a single event becomes clear to her. Fanny now recognizes that her own perception of a single past episode has shaped her entire past, present, and future. Although this recognition affirms the intrinsic significance of both that defining moment and her unique perception of it, it simultaneously suggests that the importance of a particular moment is undiscoverable until that moment has been absorbed into a larger context. By the end of this short play Fanny achieves a new awareness, as she seizes the present moment of the play—her disappointing reunion with George—to alter both her understanding of the past and the development of her future. She learns that living in the past obscures the value of the present.

Fanny's final recognition that an individual's interpretation of the past is the past that matters most seems to parallel a growing awareness of Wilder's. Throughout his next ten years of technical exploration with the one-act form, Wilder would continue to examine the invasion of

the present by past decisions and the distance in time needed to see the effects of such decisions—the central dilemma that would inform all his formal experiments and culminate in the achievement of **Our Town.**

The Rediscovery of Forgotten Goods

The young Wilder's precocious creativity in presenting stage time as both flexible and variable is evident in his three-minute plays, but their obviously contrived form produced insoluble problems as well. The interesting devices Wilder was learning to employ in these plays most often have lyric rather than dramatic effects, and the brief moments of the plays usually remain static, lacking climax or direction. By abolishing time, these plays demonstrate the young Wilder's tendency to "experiment with form before he had troubled to think up an adequate plot" [Malcolm Goldstein, *The Art of Thornton Wilder* (1965)].

Wilder's youthful digressions from traditional dramatic form are easy to understand, however, in the light of the overly plotted, inflexible dramatic models available to an aspiring young playwright in 1920s America. . . . [The] American stage at that time (with a few notable exceptions) was deeply entrenched in a formal realism much too rigid to have supported the overlapping temporal perspectives that interested Wilder. Like Eugene O'Neill, Wilder lamented the reductive vision of time demanded by the proscenium stage. In Wilder's view, the playwrights and producers of the conventionally realistic theatre had "shut the play up into a museum showcase"; they had "loaded the stage with specific objects," each of which

> fixes and narrows the action to one moment in time and place. . . . When you emphasize *place* in the theatre, you drag down and limit and harness time to it. You thrust the action back into the past time, whereas it is precisely the glory of the stage that it is always "now" there [*Three Plays*].

By rejecting its pretenses, the drama had forfeited its ability to telescope time, remaining content to mirror events significant only at a certain moment. On the proscenium stage, where time was "harnessed" to place, the past could no longer collide with the present in diverse and unexpected ways.

The problems confronting the young Wilder were thus manifold: formal realism had atrophied contemporary dramatic form, and his own three-minute plays were structurally weak, in one sense even evading the issue of stage time. How, then, was he to develop a form suitable for embodying conflicting visions of time? In his classical education Wilder found a partial answer to this question; [in his *American Playwrights on Drama* (1965)] he discovered that

> the history of the theatre shows us that in its greatest ages the stage employed the greatest number of conventions. The stage is fundamental pretense and it thrives on the acceptance of that fact and in the multiplication of additional pretenses

If few twentieth-century American playwrights had been able to develop new conventions for expressing contemporary attitudes toward time's passing, at least some of the drama's old vitality could be restored by rejuvenating its old conventions. Wilder therefore turned to the drama of past centuries and foreign countries. If the dramatic models available to him were incompatible with his design, then he would find alternative models.

As William A. Scally has noted, Wilder borrowed techniques for presenting "cyclic history" from the British medieval mystery plays ["Modern Return to Medieval Drama," in *The Many Forms of Drama*, edited by Karelisa V. Hartigan]. Other eras and other places provided other models. In the works of the Elizabethans, Wilder discovered the freedom that antimimetic staging could produce; as he says of *Romeo and Juliet:*

> When the play is staged as Shakespeare intended it, the bareness of the stage releases the events from the particular and the experience of Juliet partakes of that of all girls in love, in every time, place, and language.

In the works of the Japanese Noh dramatists, in which an actor's circling the stage represents a long journey and the passage of much time, Wilder discovered a similar freedom. And like O'Neill, who had recognized in the works of the new German expressionist playwrights a method for depicting a subjective reality, Wilder found in the expressionists and particularly in Bertolt Brecht some contemporary methods for breaking down the outdated verisimilitude, with its linear relationship between past and present, of the proscenium stage.

Wilder's theatrical debt to Brecht has attracted much critical attention. Wilder's thematic interests are very different from Brecht's—"humanistic" rather than "Marxist," to borrow a pair of convenient, albeit reductive, labels— but his methods of staging and his exuberant theatricality partake heavily of Brecht's own. Like Brecht, who exaggerates theatrical gestures and emphasizes conventions to produce his notorious "alienation effect," Wilder frequently uses an intrusive Stage Manager, self-conscious characters, and a disregard for chronological time; like Brecht, Wilder insists on the reality of theatre as theatre. For Wilder, however, the separate reality of theatre does not necessarily impose distance between audience and character; rather, it establishes the equal validity of multiple temporal contexts. By combining Brechtian theatricality, Elizabethan flexibility of space, and expressionistic distortions of time and perspective, Wilder synthesized a form that permitted him to portray concurrent yet rival perspectives on the passage of time.

Despite his enormous creativity in adapting techniques and developing a plastic dramatic form, Wilder himself minimized his own importance in rejuvenating the American theatre. As he expressed it, his experiments with dramatic form were mere stepping-stones for more talented playwrights:

> The theatre has lagged behind the other arts in finding the "new ways" to express how men and women feel in our time. I am not one of the new dramatists we are looking for. I wish I were. I hope I have played a part in preparing the way for them. I am not an innovator but a redis-

coverer of forgotten goods and a remover of obtrusive bric-a-brac.

Here, Wilder seems to have underestimated the importance of his particular moment (or imagination) in both absorbing and shaping general historical patterns—in this case, the inherited pattern of dramatic form. He was, in fact, a consummate innovator, the novelty of his mature work apparent in his new uses and original syntheses of restored techniques.

Before Wilder could effectively "unharness" stage time in full-length plays, however, he experimented with rival visions of time in one-act plays. These plays demonstrate the variety of techniques he had recovered to depict both the impact of time's passage and the many ways of viewing it.

Somewhere Where Time Passes

Wilder returned from his 1928 lecture tour of Europe armed with an entire new arsenal of antimimetic techniques, prepared to attack the reductive vision of the realistic stage. He proposed to bombard that "abject realism" which he saw as "deeply in earnest, every detail is true, but the whole finally tumbles to the ground—true but without significance" [*American Characteristics* (1979)]. The variety of the experiments in *The Long Christmas Dinner and Other Plays in One Act* attests to the vigor of his attack.

The title play of the volume dramatizes the interaction between passing moments and repeated patterns; it also demonstrates Wilder's maturing techniques for depicting rather than merely repudiating stage time. **"The Long Christmas Dinner"** presents a single occasion—the Bayard family's annual Christmas dinner—that evolves into a larger pattern of inherited traditions as it is repeated yearly. The ninety years of annual Christmas dinners pass in a continuum, unbroken by act divisions, scenery changes, or other abrupt transitions of the formally realistic stage. Characters simply enter the dining room when they are born or marry into the family and exit when they move away or die. In effect, the ninety-year cycle of repeated ritual becomes, on the stage, only one event, with one setting, one action—in short, one long, unbroken Christmas dinner despite the gradual alterations in its component parts. In this way, the present includes the past, each dinner is all dinners, and the particular moment expands to encompass the entire historical pattern.

As time passes and the play progresses, however, the participants at the dinner change: the baby carriage that stands near the table is eventually replaced by an adult actor, who later expresses the passage of even more time by donning a gray wig. As each character matures, he or she inherits a new role within the family hierarchy and reshapes that role according to his or her individual responses to it. The passage of time is thus linked to the inevitability of change: although the reenactment of certain familial roles by successive characters implies continuity of the pattern, the joys and griefs of each character are immediate, unprecedented, and contribute in unique ways to the development of that pattern.

Within this cycle of evolution and repetition, some things

change and some endure. The circular structure of the play emphasizes repetition: **"The Long Christmas Dinner"** begins and ends with the reflections of an elderly woman—in each case called "Mother Bayard" by the members of her family—on enjoying her first Christmas dinner in her grown child's new home. Each woman's outlook on her Christmas dinner party is unique, however, and these differences in detail affirm each character's role in shaping the inherited rituals. The rituals themselves endure, but they change by retaining the imprint of each character who has enacted them.

In other instances this change is emphasized, as the patterns and beliefs of one generation are modified by the next. Charles' assertion that "time certainly goes by very fast in a great new country like this" is refuted by his impatient son Roderick, who claims: "Time passes so slowly here that it stands still, that's what's the trouble. . . . I'm going somewhere where time passes." Here, Roderick shares his father's confusion of time with place but disagrees about the rate at which it passes. And in a number of instances throughout the play, a single, familial role—mother, sister, cousin—is filled successively by characters from different generations and demonstrates explicitly the mutually shaping effects of repeated patterns and individual responses, of past history and present moments.

In **"The Long Christmas Dinner"** Wilder successfully dramatized the past as a shifting yet essential part of the present; the characters may modify the patterns they have inherited, but the patterns continue to direct their actions. The wonder felt by each character at a repeated, special event—the birth of a baby, a twig wrapped in ice ("You almost never see that," we are told on four separate occasions)—illustrates Wilder's vision of an event as both an individual experience and a part of a larger context, apparent only through time. And because the form of the play depicts the restructuring through time of a single, repeated event, the passage of time becomes a felt experience as well as a central theme. The play beautifully illustrates both the concern for the past Wilder shared with his compatriots and the differences from them engendered by his interest in competing temporal contexts.

Other plays in this volume explore the effects of time in quite different ways and demonstrate the real flexibility that Wilder was now bringing to the stage. While in **"The Long Christmas Dinner"** Wilder compressed nearly a century of Bayard family history into one half-hour of stage time and so provided a sweeping retrospective viewpoint, in **"Pullman Car Hiawatha"** he employed an opposite strategy. The play presents a total cross-section, from personal detail to cosmic context, of a single moment in time—the moment of Harriet's death. By halting time to focus on one event, Wilder is able to dramatize concurrent but conflicting temporal contexts.

The most obvious context is human time—the time of Harriet's life, which is now at an end. What life has meant to Harriet becomes clear in her farewell speech:

> Goodbye, 1312 Ridgewood Avenue, Oaksbury, Illinois. I hope I remember all its steps and doors and wallpapers forever. Goodbye, Emerson Grammar School on the corner of Forbush Ave-

nue and Wherry Street. Goodbye, Miss Walker and Miss Cramer who taught me English and Miss Matthewson who taught me Biology. Goodbye, First Congregational Church on the corner of Meyerson Avenue and Sixth Street and Dr. McReady and Mrs. McReady and Julia. Goodbye, Papa and Mama.

Seen from this unique, retrospective viewpoint, time passes imperceptibly in an accumulation of details with significance only for the person involved. And while Harriet's farewell speech is clearly meant to move us, Wilder nevertheless takes pains in this play to show that the perspective of memory is limited, and that other time frames impart different sorts of meaning.

This becomes apparent through the actions of the Stage Manager. At the moment of Harriet's death, the Stage Manager breaks into the action and abruptly enlarges the prevailing viewpoint:

> All right. So much for the inside of the car. That'll be enough of that for the present. Now for its position geographically, astronomically, theologically considered.
>
> Pullman Car Hiawatha, ten minutes of ten. December twenty-first, 1930. All ready.

This sudden shift from the living and dying inside the train to conditions exterior to it forces us to acknowledge alternative ways of viewing the action. The moving train passes through a variety of contexts as it travels through an ever-changing landscape and through numerous systems for measuring time. By shifting the focus away from Harriet, the Stage Manager forces us to accept the limits of a human perspective on time.

Despite the convergence of these general contexts at the moment of Harriet's death, however, life on the Pullman Car Hiawatha is given an emphasis equal, within the framework of this play, to that given the local geography, the weather, and the stars; Harriet's death is in no way trivialized. In fact, none of the larger systems for measuring time—astronomical, geological, meteorological, theological—imparted nearly so much meaning to Harriet's life as did the domestic details she remembers. The Stage Manager's final action underscores the importance of particular human vision in both generating and acknowledging systems for measuring time. Although his role as central intelligence has permitted him to view all time frames equally as they converge, in his final action he chooses a limited and local perspective from which to view events. He abandons his managerial role and closes out the play as the particularly clumsy passenger in Upper Berth Five.

Despite his implication in **"Pullman Car Hiawatha"** that the individual or the local point of view provides the best vantage point from which to assess the importance of events, in **"The Happy Journey from Trenton to Camden"** the playwright explores the perils of maintaining too limited a perspective. In technique, this play is similar to its companion pieces: as in **"The Long Christmas Dinner,"** time is compressed, and a three-hour car trip takes only about fifteen minutes of stage time; as in **"Pullman Car Hiawatha,"** the characters ride an imaginary vehicle moving through time and space, represented on the stage only by a few suggestive boards and four chairs. This play differs from the others, however, in that it offers no temporal perspective between the uniquely personal and the eternal. Lacking intermediary contexts—such as the repeated family roles of the Bayards or the "geographical, meteorological, and astronomical" considerations through which the Pullman Car Hiawatha passes on its way to eternity— the daily routines of the Kirbys seem petty and inconsequential.

Early in their journey, the Kirbys must stop to allow a funeral procession to pass, and when they reach their destination we learn that the convalescent daughter they have traveled to visit has lost a newborn child. The twin deaths in the play are thus set in relief against the details of Kirby family life, and their response to the deaths illustrates their single-mindedness: despite the mysteries of death and afterlife, life must continue, the chicken must be roasted for dinner, and the loss of Beulah's child must not interfere with the functioning of the family unit. As Ma Kirby tells her daughter, "God thought best. We don't understand why. We just go on, honey, doin' our business." Unlike **"The Long Christmas Dinner,"** which spans nearly a century, or **"Pullman Car Hiawatha,"** which includes representatives of the entire galaxy, the world presented in **"The Happy Journey"** is totally grounded in the present. By the end of the play Ma Kirby's habitual recitation of proverbial wisdom becomes a rather annoying drone, and the colossal backdrop of eternity against which the Kirbys continue their homely activities serves only to diminish their importance.

"The Happy Journey" thus presents a vision of the world that is almost as narrow as that of the realistic stage Wilder eschewed. Yet the unconventional staging— reminiscent of the Elizabethan methods that Wilder admired—does offer us a new way of observing the limitations of such an artificially confined perspective.

In recovering forgotten conventions to compose the plays in this volume, Wilder developed an impressive array of antimimetic techniques. When transferred to his fulllength plays, these techniques allowed Wilder to portray time as something that moves in diverse ways and the past as something always encapsulated in the present, despite the limited and varying vantage points from which it can be viewed.

The Life of the Village and the Life of the Stars

In an early preface to *Our Town* (written with the play in 1938, but not published until 1979), Wilder uses an intriguing metaphor to explain the play's multiple ways of viewing time. He had tried to present, as he said, "the life of the village against the life of the stars" [*American Characteristics*]. *Our Town* does present "the life of the village," with its cyclic, daily patterns and its locally shared assumptions, enacted in loving detail by the inhabitants of Grover's Corners. The larger eternal patterns represented by "the life of the stars" also play a significant part in the action, as questions about birth, death, and afterlife occasionally interrupt the diurnality of the action, especially when introduced directly to the audience by the Stage

Manager. As a result of these conflicting yet concurrent methods of portraying life on the stage, the audience is continually forced to select, from among several points in time, a place to stand and view the action.

The necessity of such a choice is dramatized in act 3, when Emily returns posthumously to Grover's Corners to relive her twelfth birthday. At this point Emily, now dead, is largely the product of all she has been; her parents, her girlhood relationship with George, her life as a farm wife have all combined to color her perceptions and form her identity. She cannot, therefore, be again what she once was, and her now mature reliving of her twelfth birthday demonstrates explicitly—both to her and to the audience—the impossibility of recovering the past or of unraveling the patterns of life once they have been woven. The value of a seemingly trivial moment (in this case, Emily's birthday) is thus seen from the twofold perspective of past and present: the first demonstrates the moment's importance in developing the pattern of a lifetime; the second proclaims its intrinsic worth as something fleeting and unrepeatable.

This twofold interpretation of a present moment is offered throughout the play by the Stage Manager, who operates within two worlds—that of the production and that of the play—at once. His very first speech demonstrates his ability to function in both contexts, as he introduces the cast of players and the inhabitants of Grover's Corners almost simultaneously. In his role as a theatrical device, the Stage Manager single-handedly runs the show: he acts as a living playbill, he describes and prepares the imaginary set, he directs the actors, and he often interrupts the play to comment on the future significance of an action just presented. By intruding in this way between the audience and the characters, he permits us to share his double vision of present and future (which Emily achieves only after her death in the third act) from the very beginning of the play.

Early in the play the Stage Manager offers us our first choice of time frames, and the response we must inevitably make directs our attention to the importance of the present moment. The Stage Manager allows us to eavesdrop on a conversation between the town's current paper boy, Joe Crowell, and Dr. Gibbs, as both go about their early morning routines:

> DR. GIBBS: Anything serious goin' on in the world since Wednesday?
>
> JOE CROWELL, JR: Yessir. My schoolteacher, Miss Foster, 's getting married to a fella over in Concord.

This brief interchange between neighbors establishes the importance of community events and also indicates the limited perspective of a Grover's Corners youth, to whom the marriage of a teacher has national significance. The Stage Manager, however, in an attempt to broaden the temporal viewpoint, stops the action to reveal Joe's future:

> Want to tell you something about that boy Joe Crowell there. Joe was awful bright—graduated from high school here, head of his class. So he got a scholarship to Massachusetts Tech. Graduated head of his class there, too. It was all wrote

up in the Boston paper at the time. Goin' to be a great engineer, Joe was. But the war broke out and he died in France.—All that education for nothing.

The Stage Manager clearly has the ability to foretell the future, but his balanced viewpoint offers only a part of the picture. Within the pattern of world war, Joe's education was, certainly, meaningless, but within the pattern of life in Grover's Corners, Joe's academic accomplishment stands out as a significant achievement in his short life and a model of success in his community. The Stage Manager's timeless perspective would rob Joe of his achievements, but attention to the actual moment of Joe's success would preserve them. Evidently much of the dignity and value of daily life depends on a limited temporal perspective, one that disregards the formation of larger patterns and focuses on the present moment.

The Stage Manager's awareness of the future does not always blind him to the benefits of attending to the present, however; in fact, he often shrinks his own extended frame of reference by presenting the immediate impact of a moment along with its historical significance. That he does value immediacy is clearly evident when he presents the drug store scene, in which George and Emily first recognize their love for one another. The Stage Manager introduces the event by interrupting George and Emily's wedding and placing the drug store scene within the general context of "Love and Marriage" (the title of the second act):

> Now I have to interrupt again here. You see, we want to know how all this began—this wedding, this plan to spend a lifetime together. I'm awfully interested in how big things like that begin. You know how it is: you're twenty-one or twenty-two and you make some decisions; then whissh! you're seventy: you've been a lawyer for fifty years, and that white-haired lady at your side has eaten over fifty thousand meals with you. How do such things begin?

After establishing the drug store incident as a "big thing" in forming the pattern of George and Emily's future, however, the Stage Manager reminds us in an unabashed appeal to our emotions of some of the special properties intrinsic to the moment itself, qualities that are immediate and understandable only from a short-term perspective:

> George and Emily are going to show you now the conversation that they had when they first knew that . . . that . . . as the saying goes . . . they were meant for each other. But before they do I want you to remember what it was like to have been very young. And particularly the days when you were first in love: when you were like a person sleepwalking, and you didn't quite see the street you were in, and didn't quite hear everything that was said to you. You're just a little bit crazy. Will you remember that, please?

The Stage Manager's direct commentary on the number of ways one can view this scene is not his most important contribution to it, however; he also emphasizes the moment by shifting it from its ordinary dramatic context. In a formally realistic play, this meeting between George and

Emily would have been a focal point in time, a traditional, second-act "recognition scene." By interrupting the present day of the action (that is, George and Emily's wedding day) to introduce the recognition scene in a flashback, out of temporal sequence, he stresses the magic of the moment itself, outside any larger pattern, isolated in time. Furthermore, by modifying standard three-act form and presenting incidents nonsequentially, he repeats a familiar pattern (here, traditional dramatic form) by altering one of its components (the formally realistic handling of stage time). In this way he recapitulates in a theatrical context the constant reevaluating of particular moments in terms of developing patterns that the characters enact in the alternative world of Grover's Corners.

But even this theatrical exemplification of the play's thematic patterns is not always specific enough to ensure our attention to the moment at hand. It demands the Stage Manager's continued presence in a world outside that of the action and so implies that present action cannot display its own worth. To counteract this suggestion and so emphasize even more completely the value of the moment in a world of multiple temporal frameworks, the Stage Manager occasionally renounces his ability to foresee the future and becomes, at least temporarily, an ordinary citizen of Grover's Corners. In the recognition scene he jumps from his role as Stage Manager to become, with the addition of a pair of spectacles, the proprietor of Morgan's drug store. George and Emily's discussion there is important not only for the pattern of future events and family and community relationships it initiates (and which the Stage Manager describes), but also for the excitement and emotional impact of the moment itself (which Mr. Morgan shares and cheerfully approves). By alternating his all-knowing theatrical role with that of a specific character, the Stage Manager is able to study historical patterns and also to participate in momentary events. In this way he embodies the tensions that continually inform *Our Town*.

The importance of a particular moment is demonstrated so compellingly in this recognition in part because of the groundwork laid for it in act 1. The real "action" of act 1 is extremely limited: we are shown a community of simple characters performing their daily, habitual tasks. The act builds up no conflict, no potential clash between antagonists. In fact, if act 1 has any relationship to traditional dramatic form it is in the repetition of details and the circularity of daily activities that, by suggesting perpetual reenactment, expose the past while depicting the present. The act moves placidly through the events of a typical Grover's Corners day: predawn newspaper deliveries and the children's breakfast give way to stringing beans and baseball practice, which in turn make way for the evening meal and the smell of heliotrope in a moonlit garden. The circularity of these events is underscored by direct references to the life cycle, including the babies born in the first few minutes of the act and the impending death of Simon Stimson (choir master and genteel town drunk) at the end.

This finely focused attention to repeated detail and specific moments characterizes both the first and second acts of *Our Town*. Act 3, however, reverses the emphasis of the first two acts, as the death of Emily forces us to notice the larger perspectives of life and death, with only occasional references to the routines of "Daily Life" or the inherited patterns of "Love and Marriage." Just as the value of the moment was challenged in the first two acts by intermittent references to the necessity of a historical perspective, so in this act the larger temporal perspective is challenged by the local, immediate point of view that preceded it. This contrast is emphasized in the Stage Manager's opening soliloquy, in which he says:

> Now, there are some things we all know, but we don't take'm out and look at'm very often. We all know that *something* is eternal, and that something has to do with human beings. All the greatest people ever lived have been telling us that for five thousand years and yet you'd be surprised how people are always losing hold of it. There's something way down deep that's eternal about every human being.

In this way, the Stage Manager directs our attention away from the individual moments of life to the eternal importance of every individual. This time, however, he includes the audience specifically in his analysis. In describing the changes in Grover's Corners since act 2, he points not to stage left or stage right (as he did in act 1), but directly into the audience to locate the scene of the action. From the mountaintop cemetery on which he now stands—implying the more distanced, perhaps more elevated perspective he commands—the members of the audience become the living citizens of Grover's Corners. Because of our previous attention to (and eventual inclusion in) the daily moments of Grover's Corners, we are now offered a richer and more immediate understanding of the universal and the timeless.

In accordance with this reversal of emphasis in act 3, the structure of the act is also somewhat different from that of the first two. The present action of act 3 is interrupted by an important scene presented out of sequence, out of its usual place in the context of chronological time, as was that of act 2; the return to Emily's twelfth birthday in act 3, however, is more than a mere flashback, since this time Emily shares our retrospective view. Instead of merely acting out a scene for us, conscious only of the present, in act 3 Emily is painfully aware of the future significance of the events she relives. The resultant dramatic irony allows her to acknowledge the value of each fleeting moment and to lament her current inability to recapture it. Her double perspective on her own life forces her tormented question, "Do human beings ever realize life while they live it?—every, every minute?"

The routines of daily life that began acts 1 and 2 are thus relegated to this past scene in act 3, since the routines of daily life are now merely a cherished memory for Emily, framed within the boundaries of eternity. As she enters the kitchen for breakfast on her birthday morning, Emily is immediately bombarded with details she had either forgotten or never even noticed. Her new awareness of her past obliviousness causes her great pain. "I can't look at everything hard enough," she cries as she observes that her mother had once been young and remembers a long-forgotten childhood gift from George. Her new double perspective permits her to see not only that each moment

of life is priceless, but also, as Simon Stimson tells her, that to be alive is to "move about in a cloud of ignorance; to go up and down trampling the feelings of those . . . of those about you. To spend and waste time as though you had a million years."

The value of memory thus seems both a blessing and a curse: it enables Emily finally to appreciate the defining details of her own ended life, but it also illuminates the human inability to recognize the important moments of life until they have passed. Emily's double perspective allows her to see the multiple time frames at work during her life, and to recognize that the most limited of these is the one for which she will grieve most. In an echo of Harriet's farewell to life in *Pullman Car Hiawatha,* Emily addresses time and enumerates the details that she now sees as having been most significant in defining her identity on earth:

> Good-by, Good-by, world. Good-by, Grover's Corners . . . Mama and Papa. Good-by to clocks ticking . . . and Mama's sunflowers. And food and coffee. And new-ironed dresses and hot baths . . . and sleeping and waking up. Oh, earth, you're too wonderful for anybody to realize you.

The ultimate value of a timeless perspective, it seems, is the insight it can afford into the value of the particular moment. Emily's return to the graveyard places the final emphasis on the importance of specific events and unrepeatable moments in a world crowded with competing temporal contexts, as she resumes her place within that peaceful void, the solitary context of eternity. There, the details of life gradually fade from the memories of the graveyard inhabitants (like Mrs. Gibbs, who can no longer remember the names of the stars), and the characters, cut off from the concerns and routines of daily living, drift away from life itself. As the Stage Manager tells us:

> You know as well as I do that the dead don't stay interested in us living people for very long. Gradually, gradually, they lose hold of the earth . . . and the ambitions they had . . . and the things they suffered . . . and the people they loved. They get weaned away from the earth. . . .

Life in *Our Town,* finally, consists of a multitude of interacting systems for evaluating time, from those of the village to those of the stars. The ones that most clearly define and enrich life, however, are those that distract, disorder, and confuse the inhabitants and so protect them from death's timeless void: the ones composed of each character's ambitions and sufferings and joys, of significant details, of a limited perspective, and of cherished, particular events. The unusual structure of the play successfully embodies Wilder's ambition to "represent the Act in Eternity"—that is, to depict the importance of each fleeting moment within the ever-expanding boundaries of time.

Circumstances Variously Reported

In *Our Town,* Wilder employed firsthand what he saw in the Elizabethans: that a simply staged play could universalize the particular without denying the impact of individual moments. But Wilder was also interested, as his early plays show, in the changes that time brings, in the patterns that time creates from seemingly isolated present moments. In *The Skin of Our Teeth* Wilder used an overt theatricalism akin to Brecht's to demonstrate the importance of passing moments in unfolding history, regardless of the limited perspective of an individual acting at a given time.

From the opening of *The Skin of Our Teeth,* the audience is bombarded with an array of conflicting details; we cannot locate the characters in a specific time or place because both keep changing. The curtain does not even rise as the play begins but rather becomes a projection screen for slides of the daily "News Events of the World." In this curious newscast, the scrubwomen who clean the theatre are pictured and introduced, allowing the world of the theatre and the production to intrude into the world of the performance before the action can even begin. Another news item advertises a wedding ring currently in the theatre's lost and found, inscribed "To Eva from Adam. Genesis II:18," and so invokes a wider set of contexts—historical, temporal, biblical. The ring will be returned to its owner only with proper identification, however, and so the world of legal documents and credentials encroaches upon the context of theatre, the contexts of love and marriage, and the contexts of time and religion. The limitations of all these perspectives are made clear by the next slide: a wall of ice that "has not yet been satisfactorily explained" is disrupting communication and pushing a cathedral—monument of human aspirations—from Montreal to Vermont.

Contexts continue to overlap at this unprecedented rate throughout the play. In this way, Wilder once again poses the question that Emily had asked in *Our Town:* how is it possible to assess the value of the present until it has become part of the past, part of a pattern recognizable only through time? In *The Skin of Our Teeth,* once again, Wilder suggests the near impossibility of doing so.

Wilder draws attention to this concern primarily by collapsing temporal distinctions: the Ice Age in act 1 turns into both the antediluvian world and the New Jersey boardwalk in act 2, only to become a twentieth-century postwar city in act 3. Within this multitemporal framework, repeated patterns are emphasized because everybody assumes multiple identities. Henry Antrobus is four thousand years old, but a little boy; Sabina is a scullery maid, boardwalk beauty queen, camp follower, and Sabine woman, all at the same time. George Antrobus has recently "discovered" the wheel, a detail that defines George as a prehistoric man, an inventor, an explorer, or perhaps all three; he lives in the suburbs (conveniently located near a church, a school, and an A & P), a context that locates him in modern New Jersey; he has been a gardener (Adam?) but left the position "under circumstances which have been variously reported"; and he is a veteran of foreign wars, symbol of the omnipresent human conflict inevitably produced by competing contexts. Like the Bayards in *The Long Christmas Dinner,* who enact repeated but changing familial roles, the Antrobus family of *The Skin of Our Teeth* demonstrate the continuity of all human experience, throughout all time.

Within this palimpsest of competing chronologies and perspectives, every action of the characters is in some undetermined way important and in some way influences the course of events or the evolution of human beings. No present action can be seen as trivial in a world where George's decision to put the family pets out overnight leads to the extinction of the mammoth and the dinosaur, and where the audience's passing their chairs up to the stage can help "save the human race." From the beginning of the play, then, we are faced, as are the characters, with a universe of overlapping time frames, in which any event or any decision can have undreamed-of repercussions, and in which the significance of each moment becomes clear only when that moment has been engulfed by the past.

A play enacting multiple eras and embodying competing temporal viewpoints is not, of course, reducible to any simple thematic coherence; no one interpretation of an event or a moment ever seems sufficient in *The Skin of Our Teeth.* This becomes abundantly clear during the rehearsal scene, when Mr. Fitzpatrick, the stage manager, interrupts the play to rehearse some last-minute understudies (supposedly the cleaning crew of the theatre) because several of the actors have become ill. This rehearsal scene obviously underscores the importance of time in the play, since the passing hours of evening are depicted as characters quoting philosophers' thoughts. While explaining the scene to the audience, Mr. Fitzpatrick mentions that the personification of time doesn't "mean anything. It's just a kind of poetic effect." The actress Miss Somerset, however, vehemently disagrees: "Not mean anything! Why, it certainly does. . . . I think it means that when people are asleep they have all those lovely thoughts, much better than when they're awake." And Ivy, Miss Somerset's maid, presents yet another analysis of the playwright's device:

> The author meant that—just like the hours and stars go over our heads at night, in the same way the ideas and thoughts of the great men are in the air around us all the time and they're working on us, even when we don't know it.

The irony of all these conflicts of interpretation is apparent in the passage from Spinoza (otherwise known as "Nine o'clock"), which asserts that "all the objects of my desire and fear were in themselves nothing good nor bad save insofar as the mind was affected by them." In short, the subject of the scene is that the meanings of things can be determined only from an individual point of view and in the fullness of time; the action of the scene and the disagreement between the characters serve principally to dramatize the alternative perspectives that passing time demands.

Competing time frames and perspectives are thus much more than virtuoso technical devices in *The Skin of Our Teeth;* they are an actual subject of the play. *The Skin of Our Teeth* offers us, finally, a glimpse at the unlimited (if sometimes unrecognized) possibilities inherent in a world of rival contexts. What makes those possibilities recognizable in the pluralistic world of the play is Wilder's telescoping of stage time: by providing retrospective and future viewpoints simultaneously with an immediate one, Wilder demonstrates the value of the moment in creating history.

The Act in Eternity

In Thornton Wilder's two major full-length plays as well as in a number of his shorter ones, he stressed the importance of each present moment, each choice, in determining as yet unrecognizable historical patterns. Whether his technique for expressing such a theme included the intermingling of historical eras, the achronological rendering of stage time, or the presentation of events on an unlocalized, unbounded stage, it always typified his "effort to find the dignity in the trivial of our daily life, against those preposterous stretches which seem to rob it of any dignity." One is always aware, when watching a Wilder play, that present moments play a starring role in determining what will become the past.

What I hope is clear by now is that Wilder's contributions to American drama are not so different from those of his more frequently studied compatriots. He shares their awareness of the past's multiple relationships with the present, and he shares their interest in developing conventions to explore those relationships. Like O'Neill, Wilder began his career by exploding the proscenium stage and ended by exploiting that explosion, inviting the audience to share the experiences of his characters. Like Miller, he asserts that each moment, each choice, is part of a larger pattern; the difference here is that Miller focuses on the specific pattern of causation, while Wilder refuses to limit his perspectives at all. And like Williams, Wilder experiments with dramatic conventions to portray "two times at once," even though Williams's interest in the double vision of remembered time and chronological time is narrower in scope than Wilder's collapsing of eras.

In the light of Wilder's constant attempts to reconcile the particular moment with the larger forces of history, it seems fitting that his own place in the American drama should be assessed not only by the specific events that are the plays themselves, but also by their place in creating modern dramatic form. In part because of Wilder's "rediscovery of forgotten goods" and his combination of diverse elements into a flexible vehicle for expressing contemporary concerns, the American drama has moved away from the confines of formal realism to become an arena of evolving possibilities. In short, the "disparate moment" that is Thornton Wilder's dramatic canon has forever altered the "repetitive pattern" of inherited dramatic form. (pp. 53-75)

> *Patricia R. Schroeder, "Thornton Wilder: Disparate Moments and Repetitive Patterns," in her* The Presence of the Past in Modern American Drama, *Associated University Presses, 1989, pp. 53-75.*

OUR TOWN

PRODUCTION REVIEWS

Mary McCarthy (review date April 1938)

[*An accomplished editor and novelist, McCarthy infused her critical work with the sophistication, wit, satire, and caustic frankness that characterizes much of her acclaimed fiction, including* The Company She Keeps *(1942) and* The Group *(1963). Her review of* Our Town, *written while McCarthy served as theater critic for the* Partisan Review *and later collected in her* Sights and Spectacles, 1937-1956 *(1956), praises Wilder's theatrical innovations and his lyric evocation of life's "tragic velocity." The debut production of* Our Town *opened in New York on 4 February 1938 and featured Frank Craven as the Stage Manager. It received 336 performances in its initial run.*]

Mr. Thornton Wilder's play, *Our Town,* at the Morosco, is the inverse of [Marc Blitzstein's] *The Cradle Will Rock.* Both plays are done without settings or props; both employ a commentator who serves as intermediary between actors and audience; both deal with an American town. But while Mr. Blitzstein is a sort of public prosecutor of Steeltown of 1937, Mr. Frank Craven, stage manager and spokesman for Mr. Wilder, appears as a kind of indulgent defense attorney for a certain small New England town of thirty years ago. Mr. Blitzstein evokes an industrial town which is abstract and odious; Mr. Craven and Mr. Wilder, a home town which is concrete and dear. *Our Town,* like *Ah, Wilderness,* is an exercise in memory, but it differs from the O'Neill work in that it is not a play in the accepted sense of the term. It is essentially lyric, not dramatic. The tragic velocity of life, the elusive nature of experience, which can never be stopped or even truly felt at any given point, are the themes of the play—themes familiar enough in lyric poetry, but never met, except incidentally, in drama. Mr. Wilder, in attempting to give these themes theatrical form, was obliged, paradoxically, to abandon almost all the conventions of the theatre.

In the first place, he has dismissed scenery and props as irrelevant to, and, indeed, incongruous with his purpose. In the second place, he has invented the character of the stage manager, an affable, homespun conjuror who holds the power of life and death over the other characters, a local citizen who is in the town and outside of it at the same time. In the third place, he has taken what is accessory to the ordinary play, that is, exposition, and made it the main substance of his. The greater part of the first two acts is devoted to the imparting of information, to situating the town in time, space, politics, sociology, economics, and geology. But where in the conventional play, such pieces of information are insinuated into the plot or sugared over with stage business, and repartee, in Mr. Wilder's play they are communicated directly; they take the place of plot, stage business, and repartee. Mr. Craven himself tells the biographies of the townspeople; he calls in an expert from the state college to give a scientific picture of the town, and the editor of the local newspaper to describe its social conditions. The action which is intermittently progressing on the stage merely illustrates Mr. Craven's talk.

The Stage Manager (Frank Craven) officiates at the wedding of George (John Craven) and Emily (Martha Scott) in the original production of Our Town.

Mr. Wilder's fourth innovation is the most striking. In order to dramatize his feelings about life he has literally raised the dead. At the opening of the third act a group of people are discovered sitting in rows on one side of the stage; some of the faces are familiar, some are new. They are speaking quite naturally and calmly, and it is not until one has listened to them for some minutes that one realizes that this is the cemetery and these are the dead. A young woman whom we have seen grow up and marry the boy next door has died in childbirth; a small shabby funeral procession is bringing her to join her relatives and neighbors. Only when she is actually buried does the play proper begin. She has not yet reached the serenity of the long dead, and she yearns to return to the world. With the permission of the stage manager and against the advice of the dead, she goes back—to a birthday of her childhood. Hardly a fraction of that day has passed, however, before she retreats gratefully to the cemetery, for she has perceived that the tragedy of life lies in the fragmentary and imperfect awareness of the living.

Mr. Wilder's play is, in a sense, a refutation of its own thesis. **Our Town** is purely and simply an act of awareness, a demonstration of the fact that in a work of art, at least, experience *can* be arrested, imprisoned, and preserved. The perspective of death, which Mr. Wilder has chosen, gives an extra poignancy and intensity to the small-town life whose essence he is trying so urgently to communicate. The little boy delivering papers, for example, becomes more touching, more meaningful and important, when

Mr. Craven announces casually that he is going to be killed in the War. The boy's morning round, for the spectator, is transfigured into an absorbing ritual; the unconsciousness of the character has heightened the consciousness of the audience. The perspective is, to be sure, hazardous: it invites bathos and sententiousness. Yet Mr. Wilder has used it honorably. He forbids the spectator to dote on that town of the past. He is concerned only with saying: this is how it was, though then we did not know it. Once in a while, of course, his memory fails him, for young love was never so baldly and tritely gauche as his scene in the soda fountain suggests. This is, however, a deficiency of imagination, not an error of taste; and except in the third act, where the dead give some rather imprecise and inapposite definitions of the nature of the afterlife, the play keeps its balance beautifully. In this feat of equilibrium Mr. Wilder has had the complete cooperation of Mr. Craven, the serene, inexorable matter-of-factness of whose performance acts as a discipline upon the audience. Mr. Craven makes one quite definitely homesick, but pulls one up sharp if one begins to blubber about it. (pp. 26-9)

> *Mary McCarthy, "Class Angles and a Wilder Classic," in her* Sights and Spectacles: 1937-1956, *Farrar, Straus and Cudahy, 1956, pp. 21-9.*

George Jean Nathan   (review date May 1938)

[Nathan has been called the most learned and influential drama critic the United States has yet produced.

During the early decades of the twentieth century, he was greatly responsible for shifting the emphasis of the American theater from light entertainment to serious drama and for introducing audiences and producers to the work of Eugene O'Neill, Henrik Ibsen, and Bernard Shaw, among others. Nathan was a contributing editor to H. L. Mencken's magazine the American Mercury *and coeditor of the* Smart Set. *With Mencken, Nathan belonged to an iconoclastic school of American critics who attacked the vulgarity of accepted ideas and sought to bring a new level of sophistication to American culture, which they found provincial and backward. In the following review, Nathan dismisses* Our Town *as a sentimental theatrical "stunt."]*

Granting that [in *Our Town*] there is a certain theatrical novelty in applying the age-old Chinese stage devices to a play about a small American town and that now and again the author manages to evoke the usual sentimental emotional response to a wistful recollection of the past, what does it offer on its behalf? It is obviously unfair to point out against it that in every last technical detail it is exactly like a staging of a rehearsal of one of D. W. Griffith's old silent motion pictures. Anyone who knows anything of such rococo matters will immediately recognize the play's complete identity with Griffith's method: his description to the players, all gathered in a bare room, of the scenes and settings, the acting with imaginary props, the skeletonized plot, the pantomime accompanied by spoken lines (it was a paradox that the silent-screen players always spoke the appropriately accompanying dialogue at rehearsals), the employment of chairs and ladders to represent everything from a war trench to a palace staircase, and so on.

But it is less unfair to point out that Mr. Wilder cheats in the use he makes of such skeletonized drama. While insisting that he abandons all scenery and props, he still compromises with his plan by employing them. He shows us no houses, but he brings out two flower-covered latticed doorways to trick the imagination into an acceptance of their presence. He shows us no drugstore, but he trots out a long panel to realize his soda-water counter. He uses almost as many lighting tricks as the late Belasco to assist his audience's imagination in the matter of his described sunsets, dawns, and sunrises. He asks us to fit into his imaginative scheme by conjuring up the picture of a garden or pasture or chicken patch and then pulls a vaudeville act by having someone in the wings moo like a cow or crow like a rooster. He concretely shows us no marriage altar, but he puts his actress into a white bridal costume and has the electrician throw a stereoptican slide of a stained-glass window above the spot where he has asked us to visualize it. He says, in metaphorical effect, "this is no theater you are in" and yet he has steps leading up to his stage, and an actor in an orchestra seat shouting out a question to another actor on the stage, and two other players on their way to the above-mentioned marriage altar brushing against the audience on their march up the aisles. In other words, he seeks to take us out of a theater while still insisting upon a theater. And in other words still, he asks the child that is in all of us to visualize in our fancies the nursery of life and then distractingly assists us by making a noise like a choo-choo, blowing on a bird

whistle, and giving an imitation of us sucking an ice-cream soda through a straw.

The merit of any play, apart from its theme, is plainly predicated on its characters, its dialogue, and its philosophy. In *Our Town* there is no single achievement of character drawing, no single memorable line of dialogue, and the philosophy of death which its last act expounds amounts in sum to the remarkable cerebration that while life is turbulent death is serene and that the dead wouldn't care to come back if they could, because they would be unhappy living in a world whose future they would know and could foresee. (How they would know it and could foresee it, Mr. Wilder carefully refrains from confiding to us.) The exhibit, in short, remains fundamentally a stunt. A much more literate stunt than most, to be sure, and a stunt here and there profiting from the spontaneous emotional combustion resident in its sentimental chemicals, but a stunt nonetheless. (pp. 65-6)

> *George Jean Nathan, in a review of "Our Town," in* Scribner's Magazine, *Vol. 103, No. 5, May, 1938, pp. 65-6.*

Grenville Vernon   (review date 3 June 1938)

[In the review below, Vernon, while faulting the last act of Our Town *as banal, praises the play's evocation of rural New England life.]*

Our Town is an exceedingly well-written play, and gives the atmosphere of a small New England town with keen and sympathetic fidelity. Its weakness lies in its stunt quality, and its lack of anything but an atmospheric unity. The mere fact that it is given without scenery, and that the action is largely in pantomime, does not mean in itself that it is truly original or an important contribution to dramatic art. On the contrary, some of the pantomime is distinctly annoying as it merely detracts attention from the ideas and the dialogue. Moreover, the last act, with the dead sitting round on chairs to express the idea that death isn't really so important after all, seems to me distinctly banal, a very Unitarian sort of heaven. It makes death as New England and prosaic as the life it pictures. But the dialogue, and especially the monologues, are delicately and truly written, and the characters in the first two acts justly and delicately conceived.

> *Grenville Vernon, in a review of "Our Town," in* The Commonweal, *Vol. XXXVIII, No. 6, June 3, 1938, p. 161.*

CRITICAL COMMENTARY

John Mason Brown   (essay date 1938)

[A highly respected drama critic and editor for the Saturday Review *during the 1940s, Brown authored several critical studies of the American theater, including* The Modern Theater in Revolt *(1929),* Two on the Aisle *(1938), and* Broadway Review *(1940). In the following assessment of* Our Town, *which was written in 1938 and later included in his* Dramatis Personae *(1963), Brown*

supports Wilder's rejection of contemporary political and social issues while lauding his portrayal of such fundamental human concerns as death, love, and the passage of time.]

> *No scenery is required for this play. Perhaps a few dusty flats may be seen leaning against the brick wall at the back of the stage. . . . The Stage Manager not only moves forward and withdraws the few properties that are required, but he reads from a typescript the lines of all the minor characters. He reads them clearly, but with little attempt at characterization, scarcely troubling himself to alter his voice, even when he responds in the person of a child or a woman. As the curtain rises the Stage Manager is leaning lazily against the proscenium pillar at the audience's left. He is smoking.*

The chances are that if, during the course of one of those parlor games which offer to hostesses and guests alike an ideal retreat from bridge and conversation, some playgoers were asked to identify the play for which these stage directions were intended, they would not guess *Julius Caesar* at the Mercury. Yet they might be sufficiently foolhardy, in this season of sceneryless scripts, to pick upon Mr. Blitzstein's *The Cradle Will Rock* or Mr. Wilder's *Our Town.* If they choose *Our Town,* because the demand for a Stage Manager, leaning against the proscenium and smoking a pipe, brought the genial Frank Craven, [the originator of the role], to their minds, they would at least be "getting warm," as the gamesters have it. Still they would be very far from being "hot." Although Mr. Wilder is the author of these stage directions, *Our Town* is not the play for which they were intended. They were written for a charming one-act of his called **"The Happy Journey to Trenton and Camden"** which was copyrighted in 1931 and which can be found not only in a volume of his short plays called **"The Long Christmas Dinner"** but also in Professor Alexander Woollcott's first *Reader.*

I go back to Mr. Wilder's earlier usage of this frankly presentational form only because some theatregoers have been tempted to talk and write about *Our Town* as if it were a production which found Mr. Wilder and Mr. Harris trying to climb upon the Mercury's band wagon. It is important to note that when Mr. Wilder sent the script of **"The Happy Journey"** to Washington seven years ago, all he was attempting to copyright was the use to which he put this particular form in this particular script, and not the form itself. What really matters in all art is this very thing. Forms and subjects are comparatively few. Yet they can be made as various as are the talents of the many artists who have repossessed them.

Playgoers with short memories have found Benrimo's popularization of the conventions of the Chinese stage in *The Yellow Jacket* a convenient means of pigeonholing the outward form of *Our Town.* They might just as readily have recalled Quince, drawing up a bill of properties for *Pyramus and Thisbe,* "such as our play wants." Or the Chorus in *Henry V* asking the audience to let their "imaginary forces work." Or Mei Lan-fang. Or Ruth Draper and Cornelia Otis Skinner. Or the *Lutterworth Christmas Play.* Or the *Quem Quaeritis* trope. The form Mr. Wilder has

used is as old as the theatre's ageless game of "let's pretend" and as new as the last time it has been employed effectively. The cooperation it asks an audience to contribute is at heart the very same cooperation which the most realistic and heavily documented productions invite playgoers to grant. The major difference is one of degree. Both types of production depend in the last analysis upon their audiences to supply that final belief which is the mandate under which all theatrical illusion operates. The form Mr. Wilder uses is franker, that is all. It does not attempt to hide the fact that it is make-believe. Instead it asks its audiences to do some of the work, to enter openly and gladly into the imaginative conspiracy known as the successful staging of a play.

What such a drama as Mr. Wilder's does, of course, is to strip theatrical illusion down to its essentials. Mr. Wilder has the best of good reasons for so doing. What he has done in *Our Town* is to strip life down to its essentials, too. There is nothing of the "stunt" about the old-new form he has employed. His form is the inevitable one his content demands. Indeed, so inevitable is it, and hence so right, that I, for one, must confess I lost all awareness of it merely as a form a few minutes after Mr. Craven had begun to set the stage by putting a few chairs in place. There have been those who have been bothered because the pantomime was not consistent, because real umbrellas were carried and no visible lawnmower was pushed, because naturalistic offstage sounds serve as echoes to the actions indicated on stage. I was not one of the bothered. I found myself surrendering, especially during the first two acts, to the spell of the beautiful and infinitely tender play Mr. Wilder has written.

John Anderson has likened *Our Town* to India's rope trick. He has pointed out it is the kind of play at which you either see the boy and the rope, or you don't. Although I refuse to admit there is anything of the fakir's touch in *Our Town,* I think I understand what Mr. Anderson means. Mr. Wilder's is, from the audience point of view, an exceptionally personal play. More than most plays, since by its sweet simplicity it seeks to get in contact with the inmost nerves of our living, it is the kind of drama which depends upon what we bring to it.

Mr. Wilder's play is concerned with the universal importance of those unimportant details which figure in the lives of men and women everywhere. His Grover's Corners is a New Hampshire town inhabited by decent New England people. The very averageness of these quiet, patient people is the point at which our lives and all living become a part of their experience. Yet Mr. Wilder's play involves more than a New England township. It burrows into the essence of the growing-up, the marrying, the living, and the dying of all of us who sit before it and are included by it. The task to which Mr. Wilder has set himself is one which Hardy had in mind in a far less human, more grandiose way, when he had the Chorus in *The Dynasts* say:

> We'll close up Time, as a bird its van,
> We'll traverse Space, as Spirits can,
> Link pulses severed by leagues and years,
> Bring cradles into touch with biers.

Mr. Wilder succeeds admirably in doing this. He shows

us the simple pattern behind all simple living. He permits us to share in the inevitable anguishes and joys, the hopes and cruel separations to which men have been heir since the smoke puffed up the chimneys in Greece.

To my surprise I have encountered the complaint that Mr. Wilder's Grover's Corners is not like Middletown, U.S.A. It lacks brothels, race riots, huge factories, front-page scandals, social workers, union problems, lynchings, agitators, and strikes. The ears of its citizens are more familiar with the song of the robin than they are with the sirens of hurrying police cars. Its young people are stimulated to courtship by moonlight rather than by moonshine. They drink soda water instead of gin. Their rendezvous are held in drug stores rather than in night clubs. Their parents are hard-working people. They are quiet, self-respecting, God-fearing Yankees who get up early to do their day's work and meet their responsibilities and their losses without whining. The church organist may tipple, and thereby cause some gossip. But he is a neighbor, and the only good-neighbor policy they care about begins at home.

They do not murder or steal, borrow or beg, blackmail or oppress. Furthermore, they face the rushing years without complaints as comparatively happy mortals. Therefore to certain realists they seem unreal. "No historian," one critic has written "has ever claimed that a town like Mr. Wilder's was ever so idyllic as to be free from intolerance and injustice." Mr. Wilder does not make this claim himself. His small-town editor admits Grover's Corners is "little better behaved than most towns." Neither is Mr. Wilder working as the ordinary historian works. His interests are totally different interests.

He is not concerned with social trends, with economic conditions, with pivotal events, or glittering personalities. He sings not of arms and the man, but of those small events which loom so large in the daily lives of each of us, and which are usually unsung. His interest is the unexceptional, the average, the personal. His preoccupation is what lies beneath the surface and the routine of our lives, and is common to all our hearts and all our experience. It is not so much of the streets of a New England Town he writes as of the clean white spire which rises above them.

There are hundreds of fat books written each year on complicated subjects by authors who are not writers at all. But the ageless achievement of the true writers has always been to bring a new illumination to the simplest facts of life. That illumination has ever been a precious talent given only to a few. It is because Mr. Wilder brings this illumination to his picture of Grover's Corners that I admire *Our Town*. New Hampshire is the state which can claim Mr. Wilder's village, but his vision of it has been large enough to include all of us, no matter where we may come from, among its inhabitants. Personally, I should as soon think of condemning the Twenty-third Psalm because it lacks the factual observation of Sinclair Lewis and the social point of view of Granville Hicks as I would of accusing *Our Town* of being too unrealistically observed.

Anyone who hears only the milk bottles clink when early morning has come once again to Grover's Corners has not

heard what Mr. Wilder wants them to hear. These milk bottles are merely the spokesmen of time, symbols for the bigness of little things. In terms of the Gibbses and the Webbs, Mr. Wilder gives the pattern of repetition of each small day's planning, each small life's fruition and decline. He makes us feel the swift passage of the years, our blindness in meeting their race, the sense that our lives go rushing past so quickly that we have scarcely time in which to hold our breaths.

Only once does he fail us seriously. This is in his scene in the bleak graveyard on the hill. Although he seeks there to create the image of the dead who have lost their interest in life, he has not been able to capture the true greatness of vision which finds them at last unfettered from the minutiae of existence. Both his phrasing and his thinking are inadequate here. He chills the living by removing his dead even from compassion.

Nonetheless Mr. Wilder's is a remarkable play, one of the sagest, warmest, and most deeply human scripts to have come out of our theatre. It is the kind of play which suspends us in time, making us weep for our own vanished youth at the same time we are sobbing for the short-lived pleasures and sufferings which we know await our children. Geographically *Our Town* can be found at an imaginary place known as "Grover's Corners, Sultan County, New Hampshire, United States of America, Continent of North America, Western Hemisphere, the Earth, the Solar System, the Universe, the Mind of God." Mr. Wilder's play is laid in no imaginary place. It becomes a reality in the human heart. (pp. 79-84)

> *John Mason Brown, "Wilder's 'Our Town'," in his* Dramatis Personae: A Retrospective Show, *The Viking Press, 1963, pp. 79-84.*

Winfield Townley Scott   (essay date 1953)

[*Scott was an American poet, editor, and critic. In the essay below, he describes* Our Town *as a "hymn" and examines how Wilder transformed aspects of ordinary life into universal symbols.*]

Ten minutes up the road from where I live in Connecticut there is a town called Brooklyn, and when I go there or while I read the play I always see it as the scene of Thornton Wilder's Grover's Corners in *Our Town.* Which of course it is not. And it is even a smaller town—there is no high school, no railroad—than Wilder's imaginary New Hampshire one. Further, unlike Grover's Corners, Brooklyn has been touched a little with remarkability: a huge equestrian statue of General Israel Putnam holds down his Revolutionary bones not far from the town's crossroads; in pre-Civil War days Prudence Crandall was jailed at Brooklyn for admitting Negro youngsters to her school over the hills in Canterbury, and until her death a surprisingly few years ago old Mrs. Theodore Roosevelt spent her summers in a square white house, now gone into tenements, alongside the Putnam monument. Wilder's point, on the contrary, is that Grover's Corners is not in the least exceptional: William Jennings Bryan once spoke from the Town Hall steps, the Stage Manager tells us, but very soon he assures us of his beloved place that "Nobody very remarkable ever come out of it, —s' far as we know."

Nevertheless, I "see" Brooklyn as Wilder's typical New England small town: its few stores, the clapboard houses set comfortably apart across lawns and under maples and elms, the schoolhouse with the flagpole in the yard near the crossroads and flanking the crossroads the village green, the Congregational, Baptist, Episcopal, and Catholic churches, the post office, the roofed town pump, the farms off from the outskirts, and over it all a simple air of living that is neither rich nor poor, neither distinguished nor negligible, neither large nor shallow.

This I believe is the associational power of reading which Gertrude Stein warred against: if she wrote "brook," she wanted it new, abstract, a Platonic "brook"; and she did not wish you to call up at her word a particular brook familiar to you. But how futile! This is merely the habit of the mind. It is not at all a narrowing sentimentality, it is one of the warmest responses to be got from reading. Again and again we do not construct, as the novelist is allegedly doing, an invented scene: as he constructs it he *reminds* us, reading, of something we know—and, hardly conscious of the process, we adapt our memory to his text at once.

It may be that we most generally do this over books which are themselves soaked with a sense of time and place: that is, not over the vastest things—the *King Lear,* the *War and Peace*—but over lesser literatures intensely regional and profoundly native; for example, *Tom Sawyer, Spoon River Anthology, Winesburg, Ohio.* These are some of the masterpieces in a genre which even in minor instances such as Whittier's *Snow-Bound,* Sarah Orne Jewett's *Country of the Pointed Firs,* and many more, is curiously evocative and durable. *Our Town* has in this genre a high position, perhaps among the highest. It is narrower, less colorful, and sweeter than the best of the books I have mentioned, but it is a more intelligently managed work of art than any of them; it is not lacking in the instinctiveness which makes those other books great primitives—that is to say, it is not lacking in poetry—though no doubt it is more self-conscious and literary; yet in the very skillful construction of the play is the secret of why *Our Town* does rank as one of the most moving and beautiful of American books.

This construction, or this method, comes to its apotheosis almost at the very end of *Our Town* with the shattering scene in which the dead Emily wills her own return to a day in her childhood; actually the double point of view, an intermeshing of past and present, runs throughout the play and accounts for its peculiar poignancy. It is as though the golden veil of nostalgia, not stretched across stage for us to see through, bisects the stage down center: it glows left and right upon past and present, and the players come and go through its shimmering summer haze, now this side of it, now that; but the audience sees both sides of it. And so too of course does that deus ex machina of the entire play, the Stage Manager (whom, I have heard, Mr. Wilder himself can act very well).

Perhaps the germination of *Our Town* is in the legend

Chrysis tells her young men in *The Woman of Andros,* that slender novel of the dying Grecian spirit which Wilder published eight years before his play. Chrysis tells of a dead hero for whom Zeus interceded with the King of the Dead and to whom it was permitted " 'to live over again that day in all the twenty-two thousand days of his lifetime that had been least eventful; but that it must be with a mind divided into two persons,—the participant and the onlooker: the participant who does the deeds and says the words of so many years before, and the onlooker who foresees the end. So the hero returned to the sunlight and to a certain day in his fifteenth year.

" 'My friends,' continued Chrysis, turning her eyes slowly from face to face, 'as he awoke in his boyhood's room, pain filled his heart,—not only because it had started beating again, but because he saw the walls of his home and knew that in a moment he would see his parents who lay long since in the earth of that country. He descended into the courtyard. His mother lifted her eyes from the loom and greeted him and went on with her work. His father passed through the court unseeing, for on that day his mind had been full of care. Suddenly the hero saw that the living too are dead and that we can only be said to be alive in those moments when our hearts are conscious of our treasure; for our hearts are not strong enough to love every moment. And not an hour had gone by before the hero *who was both watching life and living it* called on Zeus to release him from so terrible a dream. The gods heard him, but before he left he fell upon the ground and kissed the soil of the world that is too dear to be realized.' "

At *Our Town* the audience is the resurrected hero.

Birth; marriage; death: these are the respective keynotes of the three acts as they are of most lives. In Act I, birth is used only as a momentary tone and for its symbolic sake: Dr. Gibbs is on his way home at dawn from delivering, "easy as kittens," Mrs. Goruslawski's twins. Wilder extends the symbol of birth to compose an innocent picture of ordinary daily life, the seemingly unimportant trivia of the middleclass at school, at its jobs, at church, and in its homes in a New England small town. Here are a group of people and their relationships. He gives us, in Robert Hillyer's phrase, the "pattern of a day." It is not, on its obvious level, impinged upon by the great—and ordinary—ceremonies which mark Acts II and III.

It is a specific day. The Stage Manager sets it as he will continue to arrange and comment upon everything to follow. It is May 7, 1901. Nearly dawn. We are given the idea of what size and sort of town this is—"Nice town, y' know what I mean?"—and its rhythms begin. The 5:45 to Boston whistles through. Joe Crowell, Jr., starts his rounds delivering Editor Webb's newspaper. Howie Newsome's milk wagon appears—Mrs. Gibbs thinks Howie is a bit late today, which he is: "Somep'n went wrong with the separator." Both Mrs. Webb and Mrs. Gibbs are soon calling upstairs to their youngsters—Wally and Emily Webb, and George and Rebecca Gibbs—to get a move on, hurry to breakfast and to school: as, one is sure, Mrs. Webb and Mrs. Gibbs holler up every school day in the year. And Dr. Gibbs, as I say, is just coming in from delivering Mrs. Goruslawski's twins. With his appearance on stage the scheme of *Our Town* quietly clicks into action. The scheme is hinted, even revealed, a moment or so before; now it really begins.

As *Our Town* literally begins, Wilder sets in motion the little wheel of daily doings. This is the only wheel there is in most plays and fictions; it turns upon the events presented. So here, it spins with normal activities, the comings and goings and the conversations, weaving a special era and place and a particular people, (though by the way I think Mrs. Gibbs and Mrs. Webb should not be stringing beans in early May in New Hampshire); and on through a gentle afternoon to the great moonlighted night of that May 7 and the ladies strolling chattering home from choir practice.

This is the realism of the play and, superficially at least, it is very good. That is, these folk may not be deeply imagined but they are typically imagined; it is as types of Americana that they and their Grover's Corners interest us and touch us. They and the town are unremarkable: we are told so and we see that it is so; and this of course is the point. The youngsters with their twenty-five cents spending-money and love of strawberry phosphates and their schoolday affairs, the fathers absorbed in jobs and bringing up these young, the wives similarly absorbed though perhaps a little wistfully aware of larger worlds and startled at just this era that an old highboy might fetch $350 as an antique; yes, we are convinced that this must have been the way it was, and in most essentials still is fifty years later, in that kind of American town. For what the little wheel does in carrying these doings of realism is to give one a sense of changelessness from day to day, year to year: mothers and fathers waken early, they rouse children to breakfast and school, a Joe Crowell, Jr., always comes along with the newspaper and Howie Newsome with the milk; there is talk of weather which does change season to season but the changes are regular and assured. Far later in the play the Stage Manager remarks something we have known from the first, and known with an intimate feeling, and are not surprised as he said we would be—"on the whole, things don't change much at Grover's Corners."

Thus this little wheel gives us a sense of timeliness and also, oddly, of timelessness. We are transported back to May 7, 1901. At the same time we sense a certain universality about it; or we sense its *being* as a seemingly permanent thing. And this achievement is the one for which so much writing strives. Nevertheless, we are quickly aware of another dimension which begins to operate when Dr. Gibbs comes on.

We have learned a little earlier that though this is May 7, 1901, in Grover's Corners, New Hampshire, and though the townsman who appears to us as the Stage Manager is there presenting us with this scene and time, he is also existing in our time. He describes stores, streets, schools, churches in the present tense (and this forwards the feeling of changelessness within change as the newly discovered context is revealed), but he suddenly says, "First automobile's going to come along in about five years." And presently: "There's Doc Gibbs comin' down Main Street now. . . . Doc Gibbs died in 1930. The new hospital's

named after him. Mrs. Gibbs died first—long time ago in fact. She went out to visit her daughter, Rebecca, who married an insurance man in Canton, Ohio, and died there—pneumonia . . . " and so on. "In our town we like to know the facts about everybody," he sums up matter of factly; and then: "That's Doc Gibbs." And Dr. Gibbs gets into a little gab with Joe Crowell, Jr., just as Mrs. Gibbs is seen entering her kitchen to start breakfast.

The whole tone of *Our Town* is understatement. The colloquial run of the talk, its occasional dry wit, the unheroic folk, all contribute to this tone. So does the important admission that this *is* a play: we are not bid to suspend our disbelief in the usual way; and so does the bareboard, undecorated presentation. All is simple, modest, easy, plain. And so, in tone, the Stage Manager's revelation is utterly casual. But with it Wilder sets in counter-motion to the little wheel a big wheel; and as the little one spins the little doings, the big one begins slowly—slowly—for it is time itself, weighted with birth and marriage and death, with aging and with change. This is the great thing that *Our Town* accomplishes; simultaneously we are made aware of what is momentary and what is eternal. We are involved by the Stage Manager in these presented actions and yet like him we are also apart; we are doubly spectators, having a double vision. We are not asked, as in the presentation of some philosophical concept, to perceive an abstract intellectualism. This is a play—this is art. So we are involved sensually and emotionally. Out of shirt-sleeved methods that would seem to defy all magic, and because of them not in spite of them, Wilder's play soon throttles us with its pathos; convinces and moves us so that we cannot imagine its being done in any other way; assumes a radiant beauty. And indeed we are not taken out of ourselves, we are driven deeper into ourselves. This, we say, is life: apparently monotonous, interminable, safe; really all mutable, brief, and in danger. "My," sighs the dead Mrs. Soames in Act III, "wasn't life awful—and wonderful." For what Wilder's art has reminded us is that beauty is recognizable because of change and life is meaningful because of death.

Later in Act I the Stage Manager deliberately and directly accounts for several future happenings. And again he sums up: "So, friends, this was the way we were in our growing up and in our marrying and in our doctoring and in our living and in our dying." This is the simplest way—and Thornton Wilder can be artfully simple—of saying what *Our Town* is about. It suggests why he chose a spare, documentary style as appropriate to his purpose. But the poetry, so to speak, comes from the juxtaposition of the points of view, human and superhuman, which combine, of course, to a fourth dimension.

The combination admits stars and people, universe and small town, eternity and time, the sense of wonder and the commonplace. This is the music of the play. By the end of Act I its harmonies and its dissonances are interweaving with authoritative power. It beats with the great silence of the moonlight on the streets and gardens of Grover's Corners, on the ladies dispersing from choir practice, on the heliotrope as the doctor and Mrs. Gibbs walk in the yard before retiring, on the weaving progress of drunken Simon

Stimson and on Mr. Webb chatting with Constable Warren making his rounds. "Blessed be the tie that binds" is the hymn which, like the ring of the moon, encircles this people. Finally, wistful diminuendo and frank statement of the interwoven tones modulate the conversation of the Gibbs children in the upper window when Rebecca describes the address on a letter Jane Crofut got:

> "It said: Jane Crofut; The Crofut Farm; Grover's Corners; Sutton County; New Hampshire; United States of America . . . Continent of North America; Western Hemisphere; the Earth; the Solar System; the Universe; the Mind of God . . . —and the postman brought it just the same!"
> "What do you know!" George exclaims.

Thornton Wilder is often a literary writer in the derivative sense; it is his severest limitation and makes some of his work pallid and fussy, too much derived from other books. This blight is not upon *Our Town.* Resemblances are momentary. For instance, here is a passage from the much earlier book by James Joyce, *The Portrait of the Artist as a Young Man:*

> He turned to the flyleaf of the geography and read what he had written there: himself, his name and where he was.
>
> Stephen Dedalus
> Class of Elements
> Clongowes Wood College
> Sallins
> County Kildare
> Ireland
> Europe
> The World
> The Universe
>
> That was in his writing: and Fleming one night for a cod had written on the opposite page:
> Stephen Dedalus is my name,
> Ireland is my nation.
> Clongowes is my dwellingplace
> And heaven my destination.

John V. Kelleher, a Joyce scholar who has kindly done my research in this matter, adds that the passage is parodied in "Finnegans Wake" in one of Isobel's footnotes to the study chapter: "2. Kellywick, Longfellow's Lodgings, House of Comments III, Cake Walk, Amusing Avenue, Salt Hill, Co. Mahogany, Izalond, Terra Firma."

Mr. Kelleher says: "My hunch is that Wilder's use of the series is taken from Joyce—but why not, after all? Joyce is only using a couple of standard scrawls that I've often turned up on the flyleaves of secondhand books, especially in Ireland." The hunch may be further fortified by Wilder's avowed use of *Finnegans Wake* in his later play, *The Skin of Our Teeth,* and by the title of the delightful novel he published just before *Our Town—Heaven's My Destination.* Still, the titlepage of *Heaven's My Destination* gives an American Midwest version of the little rhyme and the address on Jane Crofut's letter, if it was suggested by the Joyce passage, may also independently arise from folksay older than memory. Such material is free to repeated

poaching—and indeed all this is no great matter except for the fun of comparison.

Where *Our Town* reminds one of other writers, also it is no matter whether with deliberate or accidental echoes, for the integration is perfect and the resemblances are in every instance consistent with the regional genre. Here are two or three:

In the final Act when Emily cries out with love that she cannot look hard enough at everything, one thinks of the rather less restrained poem by Edna St. Vincent Millay beginning "O world, I cannot hold thee close enough!" Or, a little earlier, when the Stage Manager is describing the Grover's Corners cemetery and says, "Yes, an awful lot of sorrow has sort of quieted down up here," one may recall Emily Dickinson's magnificent

> After a hundred years
> Nobody knows the place.
> Agony that enacted there,
> Motionless as peace.

Closer still is yet another New England poem, "To Earthward," (such tautology!) when the Stage Manager in Act II speaks of the difficulty of remembering what it's like to be young: "For some reason," he says, "it is very hard . . . those days when even the little things in life would be almost too exciting to bear. And particularly the days when you were first in love . . ." and so on. The pertinent lines by Robert Frost are:

> Love at the lips was touch
> As sweet as I could bear;
> And once that seemed too much; . . .
> I craved strong sweets, but those
> Seemed strong when I was young;
> The petal of the rose
> It was that stung. . . .

The resemblances are probably inadvertent. They are pleasant evidence of how a particular landscape will sound similar notes in the various minds expressing it. *Our Town* has in fact the quality of folk tale. The "folksiness" of husbands' and wives' conversation, of school kids' talk together, is in tune with the Stage Manager and his wry, affectionate exposition.

"Why sure," says George to Emily as their high school romance dawns on them both; "Why sure, I always thought about you as one of the chief people I thought about." And George's offer to leave his "gold watch" with druggist Morgan as guarantee of payment for the strawberry phosphates he has recklessly bought Emily and himself bears the same adolescent, awkward sweetness. One thinks of Booth Tarkington just as one may think, a little later when George and Emily are to be married, of the adolescent-parental relationship in Eugene O'Neill's *Ah! Wilderness.* Dr. Gibbs exclaims, "I tell you, Mrs. G., there's nothing so terrifying in the world as a son. The relation of a father to a son is the damnedest, awkwardest. . . . I always come away feeling like a soggy sponge of hypocrisy." But neither Tarkington in his general preoccupation with youth nor O'Neill in that thin, singular comedy come anywhere near the poetic power, to which this folk-feeling is a vital part, of *Our Town.*

The wit is Yankee laconic; sometimes so wry you may ask if it is wit. Noting that lights are on in the distant farmhouses while most of Grover's Corners itself is still dark at six o'clock in the morning, the Stage Manager says, "But town people sleep late." It is funny—but is it funny to the Stage Manager? We have no way of knowing that the Stage Manager does not feel that people who don't get up till six-thirty or seven are late sleepers. This is a part of the charm.

The charm does not evade the big and the ephemeral troubles of life, the tears of youth and of age, and the terminal fact of death. As *Our Town* develops, it is more and more incandescent with the charges of change and of ending. There is not in it any of the ugliness present in the small town books I have likened it to: the violence and murder in *Tom Sawyer,* the meannesses and frustrations in *Spoon River Anthology* and *Winesburg, Ohio.* Yet these books also glow with a nostalgic beauty. True, the drunken, disappointed organist would be at home either in Masters' Spoon River or in Robinson's Tilbury Town; and in Act II, at the time of George's wedding, there is the bawdiness of the baseball players which, significantly, the Stage Manager quickly hushes. Brief touches: not much. Nevertheless, I would defend *Our Town* against the instant, obvious question whether Wilder in excluding harsher facts indigenous to life has written a sentimental play, by insisting Wilder would have warped the shape of his plan by such introductions. He was out not to compose a complete small-town history nor, on the other hand, to expose a seamy-sided one; his evident purpose was to dramatize the common essentials of the lives of average people. There are other colors, no doubt more passionate, but they would have deranged this simple purpose which, as I see it, is valid and has been well-served.

I do not know whether a great deal has been written about this play; I happen to have seen only a retrospective note by John Mason Brown. That is chiefly a paean of praise for the durable loveliness of *Our Town,* but Mr. Brown feels that Act III—the death act—loses the universality of the other two by being too colloquial and by serving forth "small ideas." I think this critic, and he is a fine critic, has hit to one side of a target which is there. It is not that Act III has a small idea; it has a very large one—the theory of death which the Stage Manager announces:

"You know as well as I do," he says, "that the dead don't stay interested in us living people for very long. Gradually . . . " and so on: readying us for the indifferent attitude of the dead and for the newly dead Emily's bewildered approach to it. This I would say is neither small nor too colloquial but too easy; it is too major a premise in the play to be tossed in casually. It cannot in itself carry conviction. The colloquialism of Act III, meanwhile, is proper to the tone of all that has gone before. We accept it and, presently, the conception of the dead because of the emotional power of the play's final passages. They throb with an accumulative and transcending strength.

The crisscross of feelings over the wedding in Act II starts the beat of an emotional pulse: the fear and love of the parents, the fear and desire of Emily and George, shudder in terror and wonder. Here is the new adult experience, central to most lives: marriage. It has its humor, for it is common; its pathos, for it is doomed. "No love story," Ernest Hemingway has remarked, "has a happy ending." By a leap of nine years we are plunged directly in Act III to the remaining enormous fact, death: Emily's death a matter of moments, so it seems, after her wedding.

It is twelve years since the literal time of Act I; it is the summer of 1913, and now the play vibrates with its full magic. Once again the Stage Manager sets the scene. He is in the Grover's Corners cemetery, but he lets us know that horses are rarer in the town, Fords frequenter, the youngsters avid for the movies. "Everybody locks their doors now at night. . . . But you'd be surprised though—on the whole, things don't change much at Grover's Corners." We now have the sense of knowing this town and its people a long while. "Here's your friend, Mrs. Gibbs," the Stage Manager says, pacing among the dead on the hill. "Here is Mr. Stimson, organist at the Congregational Church. And over there's Mrs. Soames who enjoyed the wedding so—you remember? . . . And Editor Webb's boy, Wallace . . . " and so on.

Now the "eternal" theme, counterpointed still to the little wheel, is carried by the dead; though with rural chatter. They talk of the weather, of George's barn on his uncle's farm; we discover from mention of Mrs. Gibbs' "legacy" of $350 to George and Emily that she must have sold that highboy she talked about in 1901 and that after all she did not persuade the doctor to travel on the money to Paris, France. Yes, we know them intimately, these emotionless dead and the grieving living townspeople who soon will come bearing young Emily to her grave.

Emily appears, to take her place with the dead. Already she is distant from the mourners, but her discovery that she can "go back" to past time seduces her despite the warnings of the older dead. The ubiquitous Stage Manager, too, can talk with Emily, and what he says to her introduces the summation scene with the keynote of the entire play: "You not only live it," he says, "but you watch yourself living it." Now Emily, in the yet more poignant way of self-involvement, will achieve that double vision we have had all along; and now we shall be burdened also with her self-involvement.

"And as you watch it," the Stage Manager goes on, "you will see the thing that they—down there—never know. You see the future. You know what's going to happen afterwards."

Then perfectly in key comes Mrs. Gibbs' advice to Emily: "At least, choose an unimportant day. Choose the least important day in your life. It will be important enough." There sound the central chords of the play: the common day and the light of the future.

Emily chooses her twelfth birthday and the magic begins to mount to almost unbearable tension. Now the Stage Manager repeats his enriched gesture as he announces that it is February 11, 1899, and once again, as we saw him summon it in the same casual way so many years before, the town of Grover's Corners stirs, awakens; a winter morning—Constable Warren, Howie Newsome, Joe Crowell, Jr., making their appearances along Main Street,

Mrs. Webb firing the kitchen stove and calling Wally and Emily to breakfast. The little daily rhythms recur, now more touching for the big wheel has become vaster. Now *we* are taken back with Emily's double-awareness accenting our own. Though the then-living are unaware as always, now the golden veil shines everywhere, even all around us ourselves. It is a terrific triumph of dramatic method.

"Oh, that's the town I knew as a little girl. And, look, there is the old white fence that used to be around our house. Oh, I'd forgotten that! . . . I can't look at everything hard enough," Emily says. "There's Mr. Morgan's drugstore. And there's the High School, forever and ever, and ever." For her birthday young George Webb has left a postcard album on the doorstep: Emily had forgotten that.

The living cannot hear the dead Emily of fourteen years later, her whole lifetime later. Yet she cries out in the passion, which the play itself performs, to realize life while it is lived: "But, just for a moment now we're all together. Mama, just for a moment we're happy. Let's look at one another." And when offstage her father's voice is heard a second time calling, "Where's my girl? Where's my birthday girl?", Emily breaks. She flees back through the future, back to the patient and disinterested dead: "Oh," she says of life, "it goes so fast. We don't have time to look at one another."

Here if the play is to get its proper and merited response there is nothing further to say of it: one simply weeps.

It is thus, finally, that Emily can say farewell to the world—that is, to Grover's Corners. Night, now; the night after Emily's burial. The big wheel of the mutable universe turns almost alone. The Stage Manager notices starlight and its "millions of years," but time ticks eleven o'clock on his watch and the town, though there, is mostly asleep, as he dismisses us for "a good rest, too."

The aptest thing ever said about *Tom Sawyer* was said by the author himself and applies as nicely to *Our Town.* Mark Twain said his book was "a hymn." (pp. 103-17)

> *Winfield Townley Scott, " 'Our Town' and the Golden Veil," in* The Virginia Quarterly Review, *Vol. 29, No. 1, Winter, 1953, pp. 103-17.*

Arthur Miller (essay date 1956)

[*The author of* Death of a Salesman *(1949),* The Crucible *(1953), and numerous other dramatic works, Miller is ranked among the most important and influential American playwrights since World War II. Insisting that "the individual is doomed to frustration when once he gains a consciousness of his own identity," Miller employs social and psychological realism to depict the individual's search for identity within a society that inhibits such endeavors. In the following excerpt, Miller praises* Our Town *as a poetic work that effectively links daily life to "the generality of men which is our society and our world," but contends that the play ultimately suffers due to Wilder's intentional sacrifice of psychological characterization in his pursuit of cosmic themes.*]

We recognize now that a play can be poetic without verse, and it is in this middle area that the complexities of tracing the influence of the family and social elements upon the form [are] . . . more troublesome. *Our Town* by Thornton Wilder is such a play, and it is important not only for itself but because it is the progenitor of many other works.

This is a family play which deals with the traditional family figures, the father, mother, brother, sister. At the same time it uses this particular family as a prism through which is reflected the author's basic idea, his informing principle—which can be stated as the indestructibility, the everlastingness, of the family and the community, its rhythm of life, its rootedness in the essentially safe cosmos despite troubles, wracks, and seemingly disastrous, but essentially temporary, dislocations.

Technically it is not arbitrary in any detail. Instead of a family living room or a house, we are shown a bare stage on which actors set chairs, a table, a ladder to represent a staircase or an upper floor, and so on. A narrator is kept in the foreground as though to remind us that this is not so much "real life" as an abstraction of it—in other words, a stage. It is clearly a poetic rather than a realistic play. What makes it that? Well, let us first imagine what would make it more realistic.

Would a real set make it realistic? Not likely. A real set would only discomfit us by drawing attention to what would then appear to be a slightly unearthly quality about the characterizations. We should probably say, "People don't really act like that." In addition, the characterization of the whole town could not be accomplished with anything like its present vividness if the narrator were removed, as he would have to be from a realistic set, and if the entrances and exits of the environmental people, the townspeople, had to be justified with the usual motives and machinery of Realism.

The preoccupation of the entire play is quite what the title implies—the town, the society, and not primarily this particular family—and every stylistic means used is to the end that the family foreground be kept in its place, merely as a foreground for the larger context behind and around it. In my opinion, it is this larger context, the town and its enlarging, widening significance, that is the bridge to the poetic for this play. Cut out the town and you will cut out the poetry.

The play is worth examining further against the Ibsen form of Realism to which it is inevitably related if only in contrast. Unlike Ibsen, Wilder sees his characters in this play not primarily as personalities, as individuals, but as forces, and he individualizes them only enough to carry the freight, so to speak, of their roles as forces. I do not believe, for instance, that we can think of the brother in this play, or the sister or the mother, as having names other than Brother, Sister, Mother. They are not given that kind of particularity or interior life. They are characterized rather as social factors, in their roles of Brother, Sister, Mother, in Our Town. They are drawn, in other words, as forces to enliven and illuminate the author's symbolic vision and his theme, which is that of the family as a timeless, stable quantity which has not only survived all the turmoil of time but is, in addition, beyond the possibility of genuine destruction.

The play is important to any discussion of form because it has achieved a largeness of meaning and an abstraction of style that created that meaning, while at the same time it has moved its audiences subjectively—it has made them laugh and weep as abstract plays rarely if ever do. But it would seem to contradict my contention here. If it is true that the presentation of the family on the stage inevitably forces Realism upon the play, how did this family play manage to transcend Realism to achieve its symbolistic style?

Every form, every style, pays its price for its special advantages. The price paid by **Our Town** is psychological characterization forfeited in the cause of the symbol. I do not believe, as I have said, that the characters are identifiable in a psychological way, but only as figures in the family and social constellation, and this is not meant in criticism, but as a statement of the limits of this form. I would go further and say that it is not *necessary* for every kind of play to do every kind of thing. But if we are after ultimate reality we must make ultimate demands.

I think that had Wilder drawn his characters with a deeper configuration of detail and with a more remorseless quest for private motive and self-interest, for instance, the story as it stands now would have appeared oversentimental and even sweet. I think that if the play tested its own theme more remorselessly, the world it creates of a timeless family and a rhythm of existence beyond the disturbance of social wracks would not remain unshaken. The fact is that the juvenile delinquent is quite directly traced to the breakup of family life and, indeed, to the break in that ongoing, steady rhythm of community life which the play celebrates as indestructible.

I think, further, that the close contact which the play established with its audience was the result of its coincidence with the deep longing of the audience for such stability, a stability which in daylight out on the street does not truly exist. The great plays pursue the idea of loss and deprivation of an earlier state of bliss which the characters feel compelled to return to or to re-create. I think this play forgoes the loss and suffers thereby in its quest for reality, but that the audience supplies the sense of deprivation in its own life experience as it faces what in effect is an idyl of the past. To me, therefore, the play falls short of a form that will press into reality to the limits of reality, if only because it could not plumb the psychological interior lives of its characters and still keep its present form. It is a triumph in that it does open a way toward the dramatization of the larger truths of existence while using the common materials of life. It is a truly poetic play. (pp. 38-9)

> *Arthur Miller, "The Family in Modern Drama," in* The Atlantic Monthly, *Vol. 197, No. 4, April, 1956, pp. 35-41.*

David Castronovo   (essay date 1986)

[*In the following excerpt from his critical study* Thornton Wilder *(1986), Castronovo acknowledges that modern audiences may consider* Our Town *irrelevant to their own lives. He contends, however, that viewers must approach the play as they would folk art which, like* Our Town, *presents "a colored, two-dimensional rendering of living that emblemizes social and cosmic concerns."*]

After seeing a production of **Our Town** in 1969, a young girl from Harlem commented to a *New York Times* reporter that she was unable to identify with the characters and situations. Grover's Corners, New Hampshire, was a completely alien place and its people were in no way relevant to her concerns. Such a response is not singular or especially unsympathetic. From its first tryouts in Princeton prior to the original New York production in 1938, the play has met with significant critical and popular resistance. If it isn't the distance of the urban audience from Wilder's small-town setting and values, it is a matter of contemporary sensibility or fear of sentimentality, or unease about the play's obsession with mortality, or lack of familiarity with unconventional theatrical forms. New York audiences did not immediately take to a play with no scenery and a last act that was set in a graveyard. Mary McCarthy, writing for *Partisan Review,* was favorable in her reactions, but somewhat ashamed that she liked the play. "Could this mean that there was something the matter with me? Was I starting to sell out?" [see review dated April 1938]. Miss McCarthy's review was careful to take shots at the scene between Emily and George: "Young love was never so baldly and tritely gauche" as this. She also made sure that readers of *Partisan* knew that **Our Town** was "not a play in the accepted sense of the term. It is essentially lyric, not dramatic." With this comment she was able to set the play apart from great modern dramas of movement and characterization like *Six Characters in Search of an Author* or *Miss Julie:* she could like the play without acknowledging that it was fully a play. On an emotional level, Eleanor Roosevelt also responded ambivalently—"Yes, **Our Town** was original and interesting. No, it was not an enjoyable evening in the theatre." She was "moved" and "depressed" beyond words. Edmund Wilson's reaction was similarly complicated: Wilder remarks in a letter that Wilson was "so moved that you found yourself trying to make out a case against it ever since" (January 31, 1938). Wilson's later pronouncement (letter to Wilder, June 20, 1940) that **Our Town** was "certainly one of the few first-rate American plays" is far less revealing about his emotional reaction than the earlier response. Wilder's play, in short, had its difficulties with general Broadway audiences, with intellectuals, and with prominent people of taste and moral sensitivity. For every Brooks Atkinson who enthusiastically found "a profound, strange, unworldly significance" in the play, there was an uncomfortable Mary McCarthy.

The barriers that stand between us and **Our Town** are even more formidable than those of 1938. McCarthy of course was writing as a literary modern in sympathy with the anti-Stalinist left: the commitment to experiment of the *Partisan Review* might have drawn her toward the lyric innovation of Wilder's work, but behind her reaction was an uneasiness with Wilder's sentimental situations. Other progressives of 1938, perhaps even Mrs. Roosevelt, were struck by Wilder's essentially tragic view of human potential: despite what we aspire to, we are always unaware of life around us and of the value of our most simple moments. We must face death in order to see. Such an informing theme could only cause the liberal, progressive mind to recoil. After more than forty years, audiences have accumulated attitudes, convictions, tastes, and experiences that set them farther apart than ever. Distrust of WASP America's values, the sexual revolution, feminism, fear of America's complacency, the resistance of many Americans to marriage and family life, the distrust of group mentalities, the rise of ethnic literatures, the general loosening of restraints on language and conduct: such obstacles have wedged their way between us and Wilder's drama. As a scene unfolds—for example, Mrs. Gibbs being gently chastised by her husband for staying out so late at choir practice—the way we live now occupies the stage beside the players, mocking them and pointing up their limitations as fully developed men and women in the modern world.

Many of the roads that lead us to the drama of mid-century seem to be in better shape than the Wilder road: O'Neill and Williams deal with obsession, sexual passion, illness, and torment. Miller deals with broken American dreams. But Wilder employs the notations of an essentially stable and happy society. To reach his work, we must pay more attention to the situations and themes that he created for people such as ourselves: *Our Town* has our themes, our fears, our confusion; Wilder built the play so that every scene has something to reach us. Our problem has been that whereas other American playwrights have offered encounters with desolation and the tragic isolation of tormented people—the themes of the great modernists and indeed of Wilder himself in his first two novels—Wilder's 1938 play is about another area of our struggle: the essentially ordinary, uncomplicated, yet terrifying battle to realize fully our own ordinary existences. Such a subject obviously is more difficult to present than the more visceral situations that many great contemporary writers have dealt with; but Wilder's style and form are what force the concerns of the play to become familiar truths charged with new vision.

His style and the design in the play produce the effects of American folk art: in setting, dialogue, and structure, the play comes before the audience like a late nineteenth-century painting depicting the customs, colors, and destinies of ordinary lives. Whereas O'Neill and Williams give resonance to their characters by exploring hidden motivations and desires, Wilder directs us to the bright surface and the overall pattern of his people's existences. Essentially plotless, the three acts are rooted in theme rather than dramatic movement. We do not so much wait for events or develop curiosity about characters; instead we are made to stand away from the tableau and contemplate three large aspects of earthly existence: daily life, love and marriage, death. As many folk artists do, Wilder positions us at some distance from his subjects: the audience even needs a stage manager to take us into the town and back to 1901. Like the folk artist, Wilder does not care much about verisimilitude, accurate perspective in drawing characters, and shading: "reality" does not require subtlety or many-layered characters or ingenuity of plot. Quot-

ing Molière, Wilder said that for the theater all he needed "was a platform and a passion or two" [see Author Commentary].

This attitude toward his art can best be understood if we look at Wilder's plot ingredients and observe their affinities to folk art. Act I is packed with natural scenery, social usages, material things, and typical encounters. The sky lightens and the "morning star gets wonderful bright." The town is presented building by building, and then the Gibbses and Webbs are shown in the foreground. Like figures in a typical folk painting, however, the two families are not drawn with careful perspective, and they are no more or no less important than the life that surrounds them in Grover's Corners. They are in the midst of the town and the universe, absorbing and emblemizing social and cosmic concerns. The stage manager dismisses people with, "Thank you, ladies. Thank you very much" just as the folk painter avoids focusing: Wilder's manager switches our attention from Mrs. Gibbs and Mrs. Webb to Professor Willard and his discourse on the natural history of the town. Soon social life and politics are surveyed; the act closes with a cosmic framing of the material. Jane Crofut, Rebecca Webb's friend, received a letter from her minister: after the address the envelope reads—"The United States of America; Continent of North America; Western Hemisphere; The Earth; The Solar System; The Universe; The Mind of God." Rebecca marvels that the postman "brought it just the same." This closing line—with its reminder that the most ordinary address in an average town has a clear relationship to the cosmic order—is Wilder's way of practicing the folk-painter's craft: Grover's Corners lies flat before us, open to the hills and firmament. Every person, object, feeling, and idea takes its place in the tableau of existence. If Wilder had taken the route of probing Mr. Webb's psyche, he would have ruined the simple design of his composition. Act I, in its multifariousness and plenitude, stands as a kind of celebratory offering to the universe, a playwright's highly colored, two-dimensional rendering of living.

Act II is called "Love and Marriage" and takes place in 1904. Once again, it does not appeal to our desire for complex shading and perspective. Character motivation is very simply presented: Emily has always liked George, then has her doubts about him because he is self-centered, and finally feels his capacity for remorse and development. George's motivation for redirecting his life and staying in Grover's Corners after high school is equally direct and simple: "I think that once you've found a person that you're very fond of . . . I mean a person who's fond of you, too, and likes you enough to be interested in your character . . . well, I think that's just as important as college is, and even more so." This is all that Wilder uses to set the act in motion: no ambivalence, no social complications, no disturbances. The primary colors of human love, however, do not preclude the black terror that seizes George before his wedding. He cries out against the pressures and publicness of getting married. Emily's response to the wedding day is no less plaintive; why, she wonders, can't she remain as she is? This apparently awkward doubling of fears and sorrows is the kind of strategy that has made Wilder seem hopelessly out of touch with modern men and women. Indeed, if we are looking for what Yeats called "the fury and mire of human veins" we have come to the wrong playwright; it is not that Wilder's lovers have no passion. It is simply that their creator has risen above their individuality and sought to measure them against time and the universe. What counts in the historical and cosmic sense is that they are two more accepters of a destiny that connects them with most of humanity: "M . . . marries N . . . millions of them," the stage manager comments at the end of the act. Hardly a romantic, Wilder directs us to the complete unadorned design of the human sequence. "The cottage, the go-cart, the Sunday-afternoon drives in the Ford, the first rheumatism, the grandchildren, the second rheumatism, the deathbed, the reading of the will." There is no mist of feeling, no religious sentiment, no attempt to assign high significance to the procession of events: if audiences find Act II touching—and if some people are moved to tears—the cause is certainly not in any overwriting and pleading for response. Wilder's language is almost bone dry. The stage manager's comments set the mood. As a man who has married two hundred couples, he still has his doubts about one of Grover's Corners' most cherished institutions.

Act III is about death and has the form of a memorial folk painting: like many pictures from the nineteenth century that memorialized famous or obscure men and women, Wilder's act brings in scenes from a life—in this case Emily's is featured—and surrounds the central figure with the routines and rituals of ordinary, rather than extraordinary, existence. A typical "important" memorial piece—for instance, the death of George Washington—is filled with references to valor and public deeds; a more modest person's life has the notation of his simple good works. Emily's death, and by extension the deaths of Mrs. Gibbs and lesser characters, is placed in the context of the quotidian. Newly arrived in the graveyard on the hill, the young woman at first refuses to accept her fate and yearns to reexperience the texture of her life. Any day will do; but once she returns to earth on her twelfth birthday, the details of existence—people's voices, a parent's youthful appearance, food and coffee, the gift of a postcard album—are overpowering. Through a clever ironic twist that both prevents the scene from being conventionally sentimental and also forces insight on the audience, Wilder has Emily refusing to mourn or regret. Instead, she throws the burden of loss and blindness on the audience, on the living people who never "realize life while they live it." This very short scene is both birthday and funeral—actually a grim, hard look at the spectacle of human beings, adorned by Wilder with folk motifs: habitual comings and goings, Howie Newsome, the paperboy on his route, breakfast being served. These details have had the curious effect of making some audiences find *Our Town* a cozy vision of New Hampshire life. Looked at in relationship to their structural function—the building up of a dense, ordinary, casual, and unfelt reality to stand against the cosmic order—they are chilling. Like Ivan Ilyich's curtain-hanging (which brings on his fatal illness) or his tickets for the Sarah Bernhardt tragedy (which he can't attend because he is dying) [in Leo Tolstoy's "The Death of Ivan Ilyich"] the Wilder folk objects and motifs are frightening fixtures of our lives that once gave pleasure but can only

stand in Act III for all the blindness of human existence. After having presented us with this striking fusion of folk art and existential dread, Wilder regrettably mars the last scene with hokum about stars and human aspirations. While this does complete the pattern in Act I where the "Wonderful bright morning star" opens the first scene, it also insists on a kind of message that the experience of the play does not support: only the earth, among the planets and stars, "is straining away, straining away all the time to make something of itself."

This kind of didacticism is disconsonant with and unworthy of Wilder's most fully realized scenes. The fact is that Grover's Corners hardly strains for anything: it isn't very progressive or cultured or enlightened or interesting. Culturally, there is *Robinson Crusoe,* the Bible, Handel's *Largo,* and Whistler's Mother—"those are just about as far as we go." Mrs. Gibbs has cooked thousands of meals. George aspires no higher than—perhaps not as high as—his father. "Straining" to be civilized and to make oneself into something is singularly absent from the play's action. Wilder has instead built up something far less sententious in his three acts: rather than give us yet another American story of social aspiration and the love of democratic vistas, he has used American ordinariness to embody the ardors and terrors of human existence. Tolstoy said of his existential protagonist Ivan Ilyich, "Ivan's life was most simple and most ordinary and therefore most terrible." Wilder would only add "wonderful" in summing up his own characters' lives.

Wilder had a very definite sense that his play was being manhandled by its first director, Jed Harris: the flavoring and style of Wilder's brand of folk art were in danger of being reduced to the level of calendar art. Harris insisted that the language of certain scenes be simplified—that poetry be sacrificed in the interests of movement and stagecraft. Later on, other changes in the play—having children cutely corrected by ever-scolding, kindly parents—made the production look like the worst kind of ersatz Americana. Wilder was infuriated that his cosmic drama was being brought down to the level of Norman Rockwell's small-town scene painting. Never a provincial, he was disturbed to find that his artful use of folk motifs could be translated into such vulgar stage forms. The folk-art techniques that he worked with were actually quite different from the flood of pictures and stories produced by local-color artists offering Americans souvenirs of New England. Wilder, of course, was not a "genuine primitive" artist: an accomplished adapter of Proustian motifs in *The Cabala* and *The Bridge,* he couldn't ever hope to have the innocence of the natural storyteller. At the same time he was not the meretricious sort of artist who fed off folk motifs and invested nothing in them. *Our Town* is one of many modern works of literature that employ abstraction, flattening, and distortion: its technique is like that of Hemingway's careful building up of a design from very simple physical details; the emphasis is on reverence for objects in themselves and the sensations that come from perceiving them. Attention to startling aspects of surface—just as Hemingway or Woolf or Picasso attend to physicality—makes *Our Town* a modernist exploration of being rather than a tendentious old-fashioned work that seeks to explain away the mystery of human and nonhuman reality through analysis. Wilder's people in *Our Town* are rarely allowed to move out of their mysterious innocence and become hokey figures who are too sophisticated for their setting and the terms of their dramatic existence. Emily—the young girl who poses the greatest threat to the play by her speechmaking about blindness and the fact that we never "look at one another"—is not allowed to spoil the play. After Emily bursts into lines about what has happened to them as a family—her brother Wally's death, the changes in fourteen years, the fact that her mother is a grandmother—Mrs. Webb answers with the reality of the twelfth birthday on her mind. In the haunting style of **"The Long Christmas Dinner,"** Wilder makes Mrs. Webb offer the young girl an unnamed present in a yellow paper, "something" from the attic and the family past. The immediacy of life—how we experience it at the time, not how we muse about it—is Wilder's concern. The New Hampshire details are accessible bits of the palpable world that Wilder shapes into a cosmic design: he has little interest in them as quaint reminders of a lost world.

Most of his play was written in a small village in Switzerland, once again reminding us that he is the international artist like Joyce or Hemingway who stands at a distance from his subject, respects its patterns, carefully builds its particulars, but has little interest in creating a New England period piece. The irony, of course, is that a work with great generalizing powers can also be received as a portrait of a specific time and place. Wilder profited in the short run from this irony as audiences began to feel comfortable with the play that was supposedly about small-town American life. But after almost fifty years, the "American" localism is eroding his stature among his contemporaries.

If *Our Town* is to remain alive as an American drama, it must come before us as a play about sensations—about how we receive the concrete news of cold, heat, food, love, joy, and death. In a letter to Edmund Wilson, dated January 31, 1938, Wilder remarked that his play—with its "columns of perspective on the trivialities of Daily Life"—"must be some atavistic dynamite." Since the impact of the play is not obscured by the social problems that muddy many of O'Neill's or Miller's plays or the sexual concerns that are likely to make Williams inaccessible to audiences attuned to a different image of women, Wilder is likely to stand out as an artist with a timeless concern for "Mama's sunflowers. And food and coffee. And new ironed dresses and hot baths . . . and sleeping and waking up." Whether audiences will be engaged by Wilder's existential tableau or whether they will prefer fascinating new social and psychological issues is not as yet clear. But one thing is certain in the 1980s: Sam Shepard's *True West*—with its wild parody and disjointed presentation of crazed American dreams—is what occupies the minds of serious theatergoers while *Our Town* has been relegated to television and summer theater. Once said, this should not obscure the claims that the play is likely to have on future audiences. The world of the Gibbses and the Webbs is an antielitist vision of human existence that may appeal to audiences sickened by domination and brutality. Grover's Corners reminds us that affection and family loyalty ani-

mate human lives; competition and self-interest—the themes of American life in the 1980s—are overshadowed in *Our Town* by more generous recognitions. Young George's feelings of guilt come from not having helped his mother; Emily's speech about "blindness" proceeds from her own sense that willfulness and vanity have made life a painful memory. Mrs. Gibbs's small savings, which have been accumulated from the sale of an old piece of furniture, do not serve her or give Dr. Gibbs his vacation: yet unknown to Emily and George, the money gives the young couple their start in life. Wilder's interlocking world of feelings and interests is a version of life in a democratic culture to which we are so unused that it may soon become remarkable. (pp. 83-93)

David Castronovo, in his Thornton Wilder, *Ungar Publishing Co., 1986, 174 p.*

THE SKIN OF OUR TEETH

PRODUCTION REVIEWS

Joseph Campbell and Henry Morton Robinson (review date 19 December 1942)

[*A poet and novelist, Robinson served as senior editor for* Reader's Digest *during the 1940s, while Campbell authored numerous works on mythology and folklore that provoked considerable theological and philosophical debate. His best known work,* The Power of Myth *(1988), is a companion volume to a series of televised interviews he gave prior to his death in 1987. In the review below, written while Robinson and Campbell conducted research for* A Skeleton Key to "Finnegans Wake" *(1944), the authors assert that Wilder plagiarized* The Skin of Our Teeth *from James Joyce's acclaimed novel, a charge that came to dominate early critical reaction to the play.* The Skin of Our Teeth *opened on 18 November 1942 at the Plymouth Theatre, New York, and enjoyed a run of 355 performances.*]

While thousands cheer, no one has yet pointed out that Mr. Thornton Wilder's exciting play, *The Skin of Our Teeth,* is not an entirely original creation, but an Americanized re-creation, thinly disguised, of James Joyce's *Finnegans Wake.* Mr. Wilder himself goes out of his way to wink at the knowing one or two in the audience, by quoting from and actually naming some of his characters after the main figures of Joyce's masterpiece. Important plot elements, characters, devices of presentation, as well as major themes and many of the speeches, are directly and frankly imitated, with but the flimsiest veneer to lend an American touch to the original features.

The Skin of Our Teeth takes its circular form from *Finnegans Wake,* closing and opening with the cycle-renewing, river-running thought-stream of the chief female character. The main divisions of the play are closed by periodic catastrophes (ice-age, deluge, war), devices which are bor-

Mr. Antrobus (Frederick March) instructs his children Gladys (Frances Heflin) and Henry (Montgomery Clift) in a scene from the original 1942 production of The Skin of Our Teeth.

rowed from the cosmic dissolutions of *Finnegans Wake*. Furthermore, Mr. Antrobus, Thornton Wilder's hero, is strangely reminiscent of Joyce's protagonist, H. C. Ear-wicker, "that homogenius man," who has endured throughout all the ages of the world, though periodically overwhelmed by floods, wars, and other catastrophes. The activities, talents, and troubles of the two characters have significant resemblances. In both works they are Adam, All-Father of the world. They are tireless inventors and land-conquerors; both are constantly sending communiques back home; both run for election, broadcast to the world, and are seen in television. Moreover, their characters have been impugned. In each case the hero repudiates the charges against him, but the secret guilt which each seeks to hide is constantly betrayed by slips of the tongue. To add to the long list of similarities, both are seduced under extenuating circumstances by a couple of tempt-resses, and are forever "raping home" the women of the Sabines.

Sabine leads both authors to Sabina, the name of Mr. Wilder's housekeeper, who has been "raped home" by Mr. Antrobus from one of his war expeditions. Her prototype is the garrulous housekeeper of *Finnegans Wake*. "He

raped her home," says Joyce, "Sabrine asthore, in a para-keet's cage, by dredgerous lands and devious delts." To this delicious Joycean line Mr. Wilder is apparently indebted for his rape theme and the name of the Antrobus housekeeper.

The conversation between Mrs. Antrobus and Sabina in Act I carries the lilt of the Anna Livia Plurabelle chapter, and rehearses some of its themes, notably the patience of the wife while younger love beguiles her husband; and again, the little feminine attentions lavished on the man while he broods in melancholy.

The wonderful letter which the wife of Mr. Antrobus throws into the ocean at the close of Act II—that letter which would have told him all the secrets of her woman's heart and would have revealed to him the mystery of why the universe was set in motion—is precisely the puzzling missive of *Finnegans Wake,* tossed into the sea, buried in the soil, ever-awaited, ever half-found, ever reinterpreted, misinterpreted, multifariously over-and-under interpreted, which continually twinkles, with its life-riddle, through every page of Joyce's work.

In Mr. Wilder's play, the wife's name is Maggy—which

is one of her names in *Finnegans Wake*. She has borne innumerable children—again see *Finnegans Wake*. Her daughter aspires to powder and rouge and fancies herself in silks. The two sons, Cain and Abel, the abominated and the cherished, supply a fraticidal battle-theme that throbs through the entire play, precisely as it does in *Finnegans Wake*. Cain in both works is a peeping-tom and publisher of forbidden secrets. In Mr. Wilder's work he spies on and speaks out about the love-makings in the beach cabana. In Joyce's, he tattles the whole story of the love life of his parents.

The ingenious and very amusing scene at the close of Act I in which Tallulah Bankhead [Sabina] turns to the audience and begs for wood—chairs, bric-a-brac, anything at all—with which to feed the fire that will preserve humanity during the approaching ice-age, is a clever re-rendering of a passage in *Finnegans Wake*. In Joyce's work, when elemental catastrophe has almost annihilated mankind, the heroine goes about gathering into her knapsack various odds and ends, to be reanimated by the fire of life. As Joyce puts it: "She'll loan a vesta (*i.e.,* borrow a light) and hire some peat and sarch the shores her cockles to heat and she'll do all a turfwoman can . . . to puff the blaziness on." Mr. Wilder here follows Joyce's lead even to the point of having his actress borrow a light with which to ignite the preserving hearth.

There are, in fact, no end of meticulous unacknowledged copyings. At the entrance of Mr. Antrobus, for instance: his terrific banging at the door duplicates the fantastic thumpings of Joyce's hero at the gate of his own home where he is arrested for thus disturbing the peace of the whole community. The great swathing of scarfs and wrappings, which Mr. Antrobus removes when he comes in, follows the mode of Joyce's hero who is characteristically enveloped in no end of costumery. [In a famous passage from *Finnegans Wake*] . . . , HCE is seen in heaped-up attire: "caoutchouc kepi and great belt and hideinsacks and his blaufunx fustian and ironsides jackboots and Bhagafat gaiters and his rubberized inverness." Perhaps the chief difference between the protean HCE and the rigid Mr. Antrobus is revealed when the latter's wrappings are removed, leaving only a thin reminder of Joyce's grotesque folk-hero.

Throughout the work there are innumerable minor parallelisms. The razzing which Mr. Antrobus endures at the Shriners' Convention repeats the predicament of H. C. Earwicker throughout Book II, Chapter III. "The Royal Divorce" theme of *Finnegans Wake* reappears in the wish of Mr. Antrobus to be divorced from his wife. Neither of the heroes achieves his end; the wish itself being liquidated by catastrophe. The fortune-teller in Act II plays the role of Joyce's heroine, A. L. P. who assigns to all at the Masquerade the tokens of their fate. Later Mr. Wilder's gypsy coaches the seductress of Mr. Antrobus, just as "Grandma Grammar" in *Finnegans Wake* teaches Isabelle how to "decline and conjugate" young men. Trivia-wise, the key-word "commodius" occurs in the second line of *Finnegans Wake* and within the first two minutes of *The Skin of Our Teeth*. Finally, at the end of Mr. Wilder's play, the Hours pass across the stage intoning sublime instructions. This

is a device conspicuous both in *Ulysses* and in *Finnegans Wake*. Many further similarities could be cited.

It is a strange performance that Mr. Wilder has turned in. Is he hoaxing us? On the one hand, he gives no credit to his source, masking it with an Olsen and Johnson technique. On the other hand, he makes no attempt to conceal his borrowings, emphasizing them rather, sometimes even stressing details which with a minimum of ingenuity he could have suppressed or altered. But if puzzlement strikes us here, it grows when we consider the critics—those literary advisors who four years ago dismissed *Finnegans Wake* as a literary abortion not worth the modern reader's time, yet today hail with rave-notices its Broadway reaction. The banquet was rejected but the Hellzapoppin's scrap that fell from the table they clutch to their bosom. Writes Alexander Woollcott, "Thornton Wilder's dauntless and heartening comedy stands head and shoulders above anything ever written for our stage." And why not, since in inception and detail the work springs from that "dauntless and heartening" genius, James Joyce! (pp. 3-4)

> *Joseph Campbell and Henry Morton Robinson, "The Skin of Whose Teeth?" in* The Saturday Review of Literature, *Vol. XXV, No. 51, December 19, 1942, pp. 3-4.*

Edmund Wilson   (review date 30 January 1943)

[*Wilson, considered America's foremost man of letters in the twentieth century, wrote widely on cultural, historical, and literary matters. He is often credited with bringing an international perspective to American letters through his widely read discussions of European literature. While Wilson adhered to no specific critical school, his work nevertheless centers upon certain guiding motifs concerning the historical, moral, and psychological implications of literature. Perhaps his greatest contributions to American literature were his tireless promotion of writers of the 1920s, 30s, and 40s, and his essays introducing the best of modern literature to the general reader. In his review of* The Skin of Our Teeth, *Wilson refutes the claim of Robinson and Campbell, asserting that "Joyce is a great quarry . . . and Wilder is a poet with a form and imagination of his own who may find his themes where he pleases without incurring the charge of imitation."*]

The *Saturday Review of Literature* of December 19, 1942, published an article by Joseph Campbell and Henry Morton Robinson asserting that Thornton Wilder's play *The Skin of Our Teeth* derived from James Joyce's *Finnegans Wake* [see review above]. At the time this article appeared I had been concocting the following little parody, based on Book I, Chapter 6, of Joyce's book, which I was intending to send to Wilder. I did not send it because the *Saturday Review* article would have taken the edge off the joke; but since the assertions of Messrs. Campbell and Robinson have been rather widely questioned, I am producing it in corroboration:

"What pyorrheotechnical edent and end of the whirled in comet stirp (a) brings dionysaurus to Boredway yet manages to remain good bronx orpheus; (b) gave Jed harrors but made Mike meyerbold; (c) was voted a tallulahpalooza and triumpet allakazan by the waitups of the dramatical dimout; (d) stamps them bump, backs them bim, oils them in the bowels and rowels them in the aisles, causes them to beep buckups and sends them hope sobhappy; (e) adds a dash of the commedia dead-hearty and a flicker of Fleerandello to the whoopfs of hellzapiaffin; sidesteps coprofoolya but seminates heimatophilia; (g!) translimitates polyglint prosematics into plain symbol words of one syrupull; (h - - - !!) disinflects Anna Livia and amenicanizes H. C. Earwicker?

"Answer: Skfinnegone Sleek."

The Messrs. Campbell and Robinson are, of course, quite right in their contention that Wilder has been influenced by Joyce. *The Skin of Our Teeth* is based on *Finnegans Wake*—as Mr. Carl Ballett, Jr., another writer in the *Saturday Review,* has pointed out—in very much the same sort of way that *The Woman of Andros* was based on Terence's *Andria.* It would certainly have amused Joyce to know that a Broadway play inspired by *Finnegans Wake* had been praised by critics who were under the impression that his book was unintelligible gibberish. People like Mr. Wolcott Gibbs, who has ridiculed, in a skit in the *New Yorker* [see Further Reading], the discoveries of the Campbell-Robinson article, make a very naive mistake when they assume that situations presented in the straight English of Thornton Wilder's play can have nothing to do with situations presented in the "kinks english" of sleep in which *Finnegans Wake* is written. It is precisely the same mistake that they would make if they insisted that *The Woman of Andros* could have nothing to do with Terence because Terence wrote in Latin. In Mr. Gibbs's case, it is clear that he has looked at the first page of *Finnegans Wake,* one of the relatively few passages in the book which present a real appearance of opacity, and emitted a hoot of derision. That he has not explored Joyce for himself is proved by his invoking a passage which is not in *Finnegans Wake* at all but which was printed in an article by Robert McAlmon before Joyce had removed it from his manuscript.

Mr. Gibbs's readiness to scoff at the borrowings indicated by Campbell and Robinson is due to his not understanding the peculiar kind of close attention to phrases, words, and rhythms which the reader of *Finnegans Wake* must cultivate. Words and rhythms here have a different kind of value from their value in ordinary books: they do not merely describe, they *represent,* the characters and the elements of the plot; and any real addict of *Finnegans Wake* recognizes in Wilder's play—though these may sometimes have been brought over unconsciously—cadences and words to which Joyce has given a life of their own. The general indebtedness to Joyce in the conception and plan of the play is as plain as anything of the kind can be; and it must have been conscious on Wilder's part. He has written and lectured on *Finnegans Wake;* is one of the persons who has been most fascinated by it and who has most thoroughly studied its text.

This derivation would not necessarily affect one way or the other the merits of Wilder's play. Joyce is a great quarry, like Flaubert, out of which a variety of writers have been getting and will continue to get a variety of different things; and Wilder is a poet with a form and imagination of his own who may find his themes where he pleases without incurring the charge of imitation. I do not think that *The Skin of Our Teeth* is one of Wilder's very best things, but it is certainly an adroit and amusing play on a plane to which we have not been accustomed in the American theater lately, with some passages of Wilder's best. It deserves a good deal of the praise it has had and all of the success.

I do think, however—though what Wilder is trying to do is quite distinct from what Joyce is doing—that the state of saturation with Joyce in which the play was written has harmed it in certain ways: precisely in distracting Wilder from his own ideas and effects; and that it suffers, as a serious work, from the comparison suggested with Joyce.

In the first act you get, for example, the following line spoken by Sabina in her description of Mr. Antrobus: "Of course, every muscle goes tight every time he passes a policeman; but what I think is that there are certain charges that ought not to be made, and I think I may add, ought not to be allowed to be made; we're all human; who isn't?" This has obviously been caught over from the first book of *Finnegans Wake,* in which Earwicker, in his fallen role of Lucifer-Napoleon-Finnegan-Humpty Dumpty-Adam, is arrested for obscure offenses. But this theme, which is wonderfully developed by Joyce at a length of several chapters, gets no further attention from Wilder. Antrobus in the second act becomes self-important and careless, falls for the hussy Sabina and is ready to divorce his wife; but we do not hear anything about him which makes us see why he should fear the police. The promising scene in the third act between Antrobus and Cain falls flat because the father is not really made to share the guilt of the son. Again, the letter which, in the second act, Mrs. Antrobus throws into the sea is Wilder's echo of the letter which plays such an important part in Joyce. But this scene is rather pointless in the play because it is simply something caught over and has no connection with anything else; and rather irritating to readers of Joyce because the letter is one of the main themes of *Finnegans Wake,* in which it represents the mystery of life itself, whereas Wilder has merely exploited—and in a rather sentimental way—Mrs. Earwicker's version of it.

Again, the character of Sabina-Lilith seems conventional and even a little philistine in comparison with the corresponding characters both in *Finnegans Wake* and in Bernard Shaw's *Back to Methuselah,* another work which *The Skin of Our Teeth* resembles without, I imagine, owing anything to it. The Lilith of Joyce is Lily Kinsella, who plays the remote and minor role of a woman who is odious to Mrs. Earwicker for having once had designs on Earwicker; but the conception of the Woman as Seductress is impossible to identify with any of the individual women of either the Earwicker family or the dream-myth. You cannot put your finger on her or isolate her because she may under appropriate circumstances be incorporated in any one of them: by the wife in her younger days, by the daughter in her adolescence, by the niece who is known as the "prankquean." She is something that any woman may be at some period or moment of her life. The Lilith of Shaw is the principle of change who always breaks up the pattern and leads to something different and higher. But the Lilith of Wilder is a hussy: parlor-maid, gold-digger, camp-follower—a familiar comic type perhaps a little too close to Mrs. Antrobus's disapproving notion of her.

Finally, I believe that Wilder has been somewhat embarrassed and impeded by the model of the Earwicker family. He has taken over the Earwicker daughter—in *The Skin of Our Teeth,* Gladys—and done with her practically nothing; and he has tried to avoid taking over the twin Earwicker brothers, who give Joyce a Shaun as well as a Shem, an Abel as well as a Cain, and figure in their duality the conflict inside the personality of their father. Wilder has got rid of Abel by having him killed by Cain in the Ice Age phase of the Antrobuses before the play begins; and in the subsequent phases he does not show us or hardly shows us the people whom Cain attacks. Thus we never see Cain confronted, as Joyce's Shem always is, by his inevitable complementary opponent—with the result that there is no real dramatization of the "war in the members" in humanity. Even the scene between Cain and Antrobus, as I have said, fails to get this on the stage. The pages of *Finnegans Wake,* with their words that take on malign meanings, produce a queer effect of uncertainty. The Antrobuses are a little too cozy, even when ruined by war. (pp. 167-68)

> *Edmund Wilson, "The Antrobuses and the Earwickers," in* The Nation, *New York, Vol. 156, No. 5, January 30, 1943, pp. 167-68.*

Mary McCarthy (review date January-February 1943)

[*In the following review, first published in 1943 in the* Partisan Review *and later collected in her* Sights and Spectacles, 1937-1956 *(1956), McCarthy characterizes* The Skin of Our Teeth *as a childish work directed at "middlebrow" intellectuals.*]

Thornton Wilder's latest play, *The Skin of Our Teeth,* is a spoof on history. For all its air of experimentalism, its debt to Joyce, as yet unacknowledged, its debt to Olson and Johnson, paid in full, it belongs to a tradition familiar and dear to the Anglo-Saxon heart. That is the tradition of *The Road to Rome, Caesar and Cleopatra, Hamlet* in modern dress, *Julius Caesar* in uniforms. Its mainspring is the anachronistic joke, a joke both provincial and self-assertive, a joke which insists that the Roman in his toga is simply a bourgeois citizen wearing a sheet, and that Neanderthal man with his bear-skin and his club is at heart an insurance salesman at a fancy-dress ball. The joke has a double fascination which it exerts on the middle-class public and the middle-class playwright alike. In the first place, it is conservative: it affirms the eternity of capitalism, which it identifies with "human nature," and it consoles us for the flatness of the present by extending that flatness over the past, so that whatever our sufferings, we shall at least not be racked by envy, that most dangerous of human passions. In the second place, it is sacrilegious, for it denies time and history, and this, to the modern ear,

is the moral equivalent of hubris, of ancestor-desecration, of the sin against the Holy Ghost. Hence it is that such works as *The Skin of Our Teeth* almost invariably have an appearance of daring: the shock value of *The Private Life of Helen of Troy,* say, did not derive from its rather mild sexual impropriety. Moreover, art and culture generally find themselves within easy range of the blasphemer (and this is only logical, since culture is an historical phenomenon); you get Mark Twain or Mr. Wilder's third act where the philosophers appear as half-audible quotations from their works, quotations which can only be introduced after a great deal of apologetic discussion: "I don't suppose it means anything," says the stage-manager. "It's just a kind of poetic effect." Mr. Wilder, being a professor, wants to have it both ways: he wants to sponsor the philosophers, but at the same time he does not want the audience to think that he is an ass.

The plot and structure of *The Skin of Our Teeth* must by this time be in the public domain. Everybody knows that the play deals with three great crises in human history, the return of the Ice Age, the Flood, the War, any war at all or this war in particular. It is Mr. Wilder's fancy that all these events happened to a man named George Antrobus of 216 Cedar Street, Excelsior, New Jersey, father of two, President of the Ancient Order of Mammals, inventor, soldier and occasional philanderer. Man, then, enlightened ape, is seen as the eternal husband, whose destiny is an endless commuter's trip between the Home and the Office, the poles of the human sphere. The trip may not be broken on pain of flood, ice, fascism; a stopover with the Other Woman will result in a disaster of millenial proportions. "Oh, oh, oh! Six o'clock and the master not home yet," says the maid, opening the play. In other words, if George misses the five-fifteen, Chaos is come again. This is the moral of the piece. Man, says Mr. Wilder, from time to time gets puffed up with pride and prosperity, he grows envious, covetous, lecherous, forgets his conjugal duties, goes whoring after women; portents of disaster appear, but he is too blind to see them; in the end, with the help of the little woman, who has never taken any stock in either pleasure or wisdom, he escapes by the skin of his teeth. *Sicut erat in principio. . . .*

It is a curious view of life. It displays elements of Christian morality. Christ, however, was never so simple, but on the contrary allowed always for paradox (the woman taken in adultery, the story of Martha and Mary, "Consider the lilies of the field") and indeed regarded the family as an obstacle to salvation. No, it is not the Christian view, but a kind of bowdlerized version of it, such as might have been imparted to a class of taxpayer's children by a New England Sunday School teacher forty years ago. And here we find again Mr. Wilder's perennial nostalgia, a nostalgia not for the past but for an eternal childhood, for the bedrock of middle-class family life, for *"the old Sunday evenings at home with the tinkling piano our guide."* It is a nostalgia which found a pure and lyrical expression in *Our Town,* but which has made its way more furtively into *The Skin of Our Teeth* and lurks there as an impediment both to action and to thought, for at the end of each act the play hits the suburban family group, stumbles over it, and comes to a halt; the repetition is inevitable, but not dramatic: the only conflict is the conflict between the submerged idea and the form. The play in general suffers from a certain embarrassment and uneasiness, as if its author were ashamed of the seriousness with which he adheres to his theme. Surely Miss Bankhead's [Sabina's] asides to the audience and the whole conceit that the end of the world is only a play that some actors are putting on serve no other purpose than to relieve the author's sense of awkwardness. "I don't understand a word of this play," Miss Bankhead complains again and again, but actually there is not a word in the play which Miss Bankhead cannot and does not perfectly comprehend. All this aspect of the play is, to put it frankly, fraudulent, an illusionist's trick; an elaborate system of mystification has been, as it were, installed in the theatre in order to persuade the audience that it is witnessing a complex and difficult play, while what is really being shown on the stage is of a childish and almost painful naiveté. To some extent, the illusion is successful: middlebrow members of the audience are, as usual, readily induced to disregard the evidence of their own ears and consider the play either monstrously profound or monstrously bewildering. Simpler people, however, who have never heard of Aristotle, see nothing difficult about it. They accept the performance as a sort of lark, which at best it is, a bright children's pantomime, full of boldly costumed figures out of Bible history. As the daily drama critics have said, over and over, with all the relish of Lucifer admitting a new registrant into hell, Mr. Wilder has become a *real* man of the theatre. (pp. 53-6)

> *Mary McCarthy, "The Skin of Our Teeth," in her* Sights and Spectacles: 1937-1956, *Farrar, Straus and Cudahy, 1956, pp. 53-6.*

Alexander Woollcott (review date March 1943)

[*During his years as a critic for the* New York Times, New York Herald, *and the* Atlantic Monthly, *Woollcott became known as one of the United States' most eccentric wits and raconteurs, as well as an influential pioneer of modern drama criticism. With his gossipy approach to reviewing, a style that focused on personalities, trivia, and general impressions of the plays, Woollcott attained and wielded the power of determining the success or failure of Broadway's offerings. In the review below, Woollcott favorably discusses* The Skin of Our Teeth *and compares the play to other dramatic works such as Anton Chekov's* The Cherry Orchard.]

> Observe how Miyanoshita cracked in two
> And slid into the valley; he that stood
> Grinning with terror in the bamboo wood
> Saw the earth heave and thrust its bowels
>   through
> The hill, and his own kitchen slide from view,
> Spilling the warm bowl of his humble food
> Into the lap of horror; mark how lewd
> This cluttered gulf,—'twas here his paddy grew.
> Dread and dismay have not encompassed him;
> The calm sun sets; unhurried and aloof
> Into the riven village falls the rain;
> Days pass; the ashes cool; he builds again
> His paper house upon oblivion's brim,
> And plants the purple iris in its roof.

So reads the eighth in that series of eighteen sonnets which Edna St. Vincent Millay once chiseled into some perishable substance as an "Epitaph for the Race of Man." In the eighteenth, we are vouchsafed a last glimpse of her standing on a distant and empty shore, her witch-hair stirred by a wind of danger new and deep, in her hands a skull.

Alas, poor Man, a fellow of infinite jest! And courage, too! It had taken more than the eruption of Miyanoshita and its like to get *him* down. Ravening monsters, famine, cold unbearable, earthquake, flood—these had left him undaunted. And he was quite bright. After aeons of study, jarred by wars, he had got good marks in music and astronomy and things like that. But as a species, he had proved inferior in one respect to the termites, let us say. At the all-important art of survival, he was not so good. From the first there had been that in him which foredoomed him to be done in by his own kind. Therefore, long before the end, there would be no trace of him on this indifferent planet, itself impermanent, save one round skull, left behind among the sand and pebbles of the beach. Thus Miss Millay, lifting herself by her poetic bootstraps, as one must to get the long view.

In the new and apparently agitating play called **The Skin of Our Teeth,** which has been packing the Plymouth Theatre in New York since mid-November, another solicitous friend of Man contemplates the same odd creature's progress, surveying it from an eminence rather less dizzy but still lofty enough to induce symptoms of vertigo in some members of every startled audience. The result does not pretend to be so conclusive as an epitaph—or need to be so depressing. Rather call it a bulletin issued from the sickroom of a patient in whose health we are all pardonably interested, a bulletin signed by a physician named Thornton Wilder. In its matter that bulletin may conscientiously avoid anything which would encourage us to relax a bit, but there *is* something flagrantly optimistic in the good physician's manner. There is exultation in the very title as it testifies to those same tonic dangers in spite of which Man, to the confounding of all skeptics, has wonderfully got as far as he has. Indeed, if another writing fellow named William De Morgan had not stolen a march on him, Wilder might have called his play "Somehow Good." His prognosis in this case will be accepted with reservations by those who remember how dearly he loves the patient.

The Plymouth [Theatre] program might well have read:—

> PLACE: Home of George Antrobus (Everyman
>   to you)
> TIME: All eternity up to now and then some.

It did take a bit of doing to crowd into the two hours' traffic of the stage the invention of the wheel and the multiplication table and the alphabet, the killing off of the wistful old dinosaurs, one glacial period, one flood, and the end of some war or other. This one, perhaps. But here is a theatrical craftsman every bit as bold, as impatient, as ingenious, and as sovereign in his field as Frank Lloyd Wright is in the field of architecture. Therefore only a little muttered resistance is left in each audience when, at the end of Act One (the chill of the last Ice Age having reached

New Jersey), there is the sound of rending wood at the back of the auditorium and the ushers come down the aisles bringing torn-up seats for the Antrobus fireplace, thereby aiding the Antrobus hired girl in her natural and perhaps commendable effort to save the human race.

But long before this, even with the rise of the first curtain, there had been another rending noise, the sound of Mr. Wilder, with a lot to be accomplished, briskly shattering all those comfortably familiar conventions of the theater which would only be in his way. Small wonder that every now and again there rushes forth from the Plymouth an immovable body, loudly voicing to the Broadway night his proverbial distaste for all irresistible forces.

Mr. Wilder probably thinks of such weaklings as playing hooky. You see, he is, like Bernard Shaw, a pedagogue at heart, and just before the final curtain of his exhilarating comedy he does score a schoolmaster's triumph. In some twilit hour when he was daydreaming of power, there may well have popped into his head the notion that it would be fun sometime to take an average audience of flabby and itching Broadway playgoers and jolly well make them listen to the philosophers.

In *The Skin of Our Teeth,* in the very moment when a meeker playwright would be resigned to the sight of his patrons reaching for their hats—See how strict he is standing there, ruler in hand, all ready to crack down on a knuckle or so!—Mr. Wilder requires *his* boys and girls to sit still and listen hard to a few words from Spinoza, Plato, Aristotle, and the author of the Pentateuch. You may think of me as decently awe-struck when I report that they do listen—with all their ears and with all their might.

All this happens in a play of the stature, let us say, of *Cyrano de Bergerac* or *Peer Gynt* or *The Cherry Orchard* or *Heartbreak House.*

It is not easy to think of any other American play with so good a chance of being acted a hundred years from now. His own *Our Town,* perhaps. (pp. 121, 123)

> *Alexander Woollcott, "Mr. Wilder Urges Us On," in* The Atlantic Monthly, *Vol. 171, No. 3, March, 1943, pp. 121, 123.*

CRITICAL COMMENTARY

Malcolm Goldstein (essay date 1965)

[*In the following excerpt from his* The Art of Thornton Wilder *(1965), Goldstein characterizes* The Skin of Our Teeth *as a highly successful comedy that combines elements of vaudeville with multi-layered characterizations to convey the essential resiliency of the human race.*]

The title itself [of *The Skin of Our Teeth*] announces the theme, which is that no matter how hard pressed or frightened, the human race has power to survive its great adventure in a world where physical nature and its own internal conflicts pose endless threats. Beneath this is the idea which forms the core of all Wilder's major works. As the action proceeds it becomes clear that the playwright holds

man to be worth preserving for all his absurdity, and holds also that man's lot is worth the effort it costs him to sustain life, however great his misfortunes. For the purposes of this play, Wilder's vision of life is comic, and the action which supports the theme develops the comic possibilities of its disparate sources.

As he had done with *Our Town,* Wilder designed a presentational method which would permit the audience to be drawn toward the characters as individuals with private problems while recognizing that they also function in a broader sphere as the representatives of the entire race. This, however, is only part of a quite elaborate scheme. There is a deliberately old-fashioned, expressionistic vaudeville quality in much of the action which is reminiscent of John Howard Lawson's *Processional* of 1925 and similar plays by Lawson, Michael Gold, and John Dos Passos for the New Playwrights' Theatre of the late 1920's: plays which combine elements of the subliterary stage with the abstract characters of the contemporary expressionistic drama of Europe. It is this vaudevillesque aspect of *The Skin of Our Teeth* which led many reviewers to assert that Wilder had written his play under the influence of Ole Olsen and Chick Johnson's *Hellzapoppin,* a long-running extravaganza contrived from bits of burlesque and revue material, when in fact he had drawn nothing from it at all. On the other hand, George and Maggie Antrobus and their servant Sabina occasionally take part in low-comedy clowning of the vaudeville and Keystone Cops variety at the same time that they represent Adam, Eve, and Lillith and, as the name Antrobus indicates, All Mankind. Yet, because they stand for the entire race, they must have genuine human qualities as well. To stress the essentially human, Wilder frequently lets them drop their stage roles and appear as actors who have been engaged to appear in a play titled *The Skin of Our Teeth.* The development of characters on so many planes at once requires skill in balancing and adjusting dialogue in such a way as to avoid awkwardness in the transition from one level of personality to another. Present always is the danger of baffling the audience where the intention is to instruct. Wilder's success is evident in the intensity of feeling generated by the characters, which at the appropriate moments reaches the heights of *Our Town* without jarring against the comic elements. In observing that the audience sees double while watching the action, Wilder underestimated his achievement; the keenest members of the audience will see not merely two sorts of personality in each character, but three, four, or even five as the play unfolds.

Thus it is apparent that George Antrobus is Adam, since his family is the race itself. But he also is a burlesque comedian who greets his family with epithets bordering on the obscene, and in addition he is a go-getting American businessman, rejoicing in his invention of the wheel and the alphabet, having the time of his life at a convention (of mammals) in Atlantic City, planning impatiently to rebuild his home and his community after nature and warfare have demolished them. On the other hand, and more importantly, his inventions, his pride in the scholarly attainments, such as they are, of his children, and his overriding wish to preserve human knowledge and dignity in

Scene from the original production of The Skin of Our Teeth: *Tallulah Bankhead as Sabina, with Remo Buffano (left) and Andrew Ratousheff as the Antrobus family pets.*

the face of disaster establish him as a figure representing the intellectual side of man's nature. Maggie, his wife, is Eve, the eternal homemaker and mother, cherishing even her wicked son Henry (who was called Cain before he killed his brother), looking after the well-being of the race, discovering that the tomato is edible. "If you want to know anything more about Mrs. Antrobus," her servant says, "just go and look at a tigress, and look hard." The home of the Antrobuses stands on Cedar Street in Excelsior, New Jersey, but like the Gibbs and Webb homes it stands at the same time in the center of creation, as the focal point of a struggling but venturesome race to sustain itself.

The sensual quality in mankind is presented by the servant Sabina, raped home like the Sabines and looking after man's desires, as opposed to Maggie, who looks after his needs. A new hat, a dish of ice cream, and a ticket to the movies are all that she requires for happiness, as Maggie remarks in a simplification of the sensual pleasures sought by humanity. By making her a comic figure, Wilder demonstrates his boundless tolerance of this element in human nature. She is potentially dangerous in one moment of the second act when she attempts to seduce Antrobus, but the

scene passes too quickly to render her contemptible. Her anti-intellectualism is not confined to her roles as servant and temptress, but spills over into her personality as Miss Somerset, the hard-up actress who is taking the maid's part because no other is available. "I can't invent any words for this play," she says in desperation when Maggie fails to respond to the cue Sabina has fed her, "and I'm glad I can't. I hate this play and every word in it."

> As for me [she continues] I don't understand a single word of it, anyway,—all about the troubles the human race has gone through, there's a subject for you.
> Besides the author hasn't made up his silly mind as to whether we're all living back in caves or in New Jersey today, and that's the way it is all the way through.
> Oh—why can't we have plays like we used to have—*Peg o' My Heart,* and *Smilin' Thru,* and *The Bat,* good entertainment with a message you can take home with you?
> I took this hateful job because I had to. For two years I've sat up in my room living on a sandwich and a cup of tea a day, waiting for better times in the theater. And look at me now: I—I

who've played *Rain* and the *Barretts of Wimpole Street* and *First Lady*—God in Heaven!

That she interrupts the action to make this complaint is in keeping with her part, inasmuch as she moves the play in the direction of comedy and renders cherishable, as an aspect of humanity, the low-brow attitude which allows no time for presumably serious drama. If the plays she mentions have messages, so of course has *The Skin of Our Teeth,* and her deliberate stopping of the action underscores them.

Another of Sabina's functions is the enhancement of the mockery of domestic drama which enters the play in the first and last acts. As the curtain rises at the start, she is present with duster in hand, like the servant in a nineteenth-century play of middle-class household intrigue, to let the audience in on the manners and means of her employers. And as she cleans the room, the flats which form its walls flap, buckle, and fly out of sight in a merry parody of the box set, letting in a glimpse of the outside world. Typical of such a part is her fear that a dire accident has befallen her master, who has not yet come home across the Hudson River. Within moments, however, he makes his appearance, and the greater dimensions of the family as Adam and Eve and their household become evident.

With the interactions of these three characters and Henry, who as Cain represents the opposing self, Wilder spreads out his view of the human condition. As the various elements of the personality are frequently at war with one another within each human being, so do these characters quarrel and complain, only to discover that they cannot exist separately. To make the whole man, thought, love, and lust play parts, and troublesome as it is, the self-destructive impulse is always present. Wilder's thought is deistic, combining a belief that God made the world and left the running of it to man with a belief that human activity is psychologically determined. The play abounds in Biblical allusions and includes a re-enactment of Noah's flood, yet at no point makes the suggestion that the race has survived its catastrophes through divine intervention. It is only by chance and the playwright's careful calculation that a ship is present to save the Antrobuses from the flood, and that two of each kind of animal are also on hand, though the action which precedes the embarkation makes obvious references to the deadly sins.

Again as with *Our Town,* Wilder stresses those traits of personality which are especially appealing, thus cajoling us into accepting the characters as representatives of ourselves. Most serviceable for this purpose are the interruptions of the action, such as Sabina's quoted above. In the last act, which occurs after the conclusion of a horrendous war, Wilder finds two such opportunities. The first is a pause brought on by the sudden illness of actors engaged to play Spinoza, Plato, Aristotle, and the author of Genesis. They were to cross the stage at the end of the play, each bearing a sign for one of the hours of the night—"a poetic effect," as the company's stage manager calls it, borrowed from **"Pullman Car Hiawatha."** Since no other actors are available, the parts must be taken by the wardrobe mistress, a maid, the captain of the ushers, and Antrobus's dresser, all of whom are glad to serve. With this

device Wilder implies that the writing of the great philosophers takes effect upon the members of the race even without their awareness of it. He assigns the Negro maid the task of articulating the idea, hinting all the while that a sense of racial inferiority slows down her words and renders them tentative or apologetic:

> Excuse me, I think it means—excuse me, Mr. Fitzpatrick . . . Mr. Fitzpatrick, you let my father come to a rehearsal; and my father's a Baptist minister, and he said that the author meant that—just like the hours and stars go by over our heads at night, in the same way the ideas and thoughts of the great men are in the air around us all the time and they're working on us, even when we don't know it.

The speech not only serves to express a concept of the intellectual life, but serves also, through its halting diction, to make an oblique plea for tolerance by warming us to the girl who speaks it.

Later, when the actor playing Henry comes close to strangling the actor playing his father, comes another passage pulsing with Wilder's humanitarian instinct. Here the younger actor attempts to show that his part in the play as the wartime enemy has elicited a harrowing response from his own, not his stage-character's, personality:

> HENRY: Nobody can say *must* to me. All my life everybody's been crossing me,—everybody, everything, all of you. I'm going to be free, even if I have to kill half the world for it. Right now, too. Let me get my hands on his throat. I'll show him. (*He advances toward* ANTROBUS. *Suddenly,* SABINA *jumps between them and calls out in her own person:*)

> SABINA: Stop! Stop! Don't play this scene. You know what happened last night. Stop the play. (*The men fall back, panting.* HENRY *covers his face with his hands.*) Last night you almost strangled him. You became a regular savage. Stop it!

> HENRY: It's true. I'm sorry. I don't know what comes over me. I have nothing against him personally. I respect him very much . . . I . . . I admire him. But something comes over me. It's like I become fifteen years old again. I . . . I . . . listen: my own father used to whip me and lock me up every Saturday night. I never had enough to eat. He never let me have enough money to buy decent clothes. I was ashamed to go downtown. I never could go to the dances. My father and my uncle put rules in the way of everything I wanted to do. They tried to prevent my living at all.—I'm sorry. I'm sorry.

> MRS. ANTROBUS (*Quickly*): No, go on. Finish what you were saying. Say it all.

> HENRY: In this scene it's as though I were back in High School again. It's like I had some big emptiness inside me,—the emptiness of being hated and blocked at every turn. And the emptiness fills up with the one thought that you have to strike and fight and kill. Listen, it's as though you have to kill somebody else so as not to end up killing yourself.

Henry is getting at the basis of man's antisocial drives, but at the same time that he reveals the seriousness of the matter he offers through his familiar, boyish imagery a plea for sympathetic understanding. At such moments of the play intellectual stimulus and emotional appeal are in precise balance.

These scenes occur shortly before the conclusion of action that spans the ages from the descent of the glaciers over North America to the end of the most grotesque war in history—presumably Wilder's image of the Second World War. Of the calamities which nearly put an end to the Antrobus family, each has a different cause. The great wall of ice which brings the coldest day of the year in the middle of August is malevolent nature, with which man must do battle constantly. The family conquers it with the warmth provided by coffee, group-singing, and a fire made of beds, tables, and the seats in the theater even as the ice pushes at the walls of their house in Excelsior. In other words, common sense and heartiness are sufficient for overcoming disasters in the natural world. The overwhelming flood of the second act is described as a storm, but is not altogether a natural phenomenon; apparently it is also a form of retributive justice handed down by an unnamed power. Wilder's unwillingness to identify the power as God obscures his message for part of the act, but ultimately he makes it clear that man is about to be punished for his sinfulness. All the family are sinners. We see Henry in ungovernable wrath picking a fight with a Negro and thus, it would seem, initiating race hatred. Mrs. Antrobus, filled with pride that her husband is the presiding officer at the convention of mammals, insults the man who ran against him for the position. Antrobus's sin is lust; he has succumbed to the effort of Sabina, now a beauty-contest winner named Miss Fairweather, to seduce him in a beach cabana. When the storm warnings have reached their peak, the Antrobuses and Sabina, who have recovered from their wickedness, board a ship which happens to be waiting off shore and take with them the two delegates to the convention of every species of animal.

The last act, which carries the play into the present, is a stronger expression of ideas. It begins, not with the outbreak of war, but, for the happy conclusion necessary for comedy and the furtherance of the theme of survival, with the coming of peace. The enemy posited in this act is not nature or original sin in any of its specific forms, but the self-destructive instinct within the human spirit, as represented by Henry—the deep-rooted, malign force that can measure its own growth only by killing. To contend successfully with this enemy is the gravest problem of all. Mankind can at best forge an uneasy truce with it by closely analyzing the phenomena which created it, as the actor taking the part of Henry attempts to do. When Henry is pacified for the time being by the sensual Sabina, it is possible to go on with the business of living, as though nothing worse could possibly happen. But Wilder is not so unastute as to wish to urge upon the audience the notion that evil is absolutely to be abolished with the end of the war, for the accumulated evidence of the millions of years of human life gives such a notion the lie. The ending, then, is only tentative. After a blackout the lights come up on Sabina in the Excelsior living room, her feather duster in her hand—precisely her stance at the beginning of the play.

At first thought it is astonishing that a play so full of stops, starts, tricks, and dodges should lay a strong grip upon the emotions. It is saved from archness by Wilder's humanity, which expresses itself in this play as in all the others through ordinary speech, though it does so in the midst of many-layered, allusive dialogue and commensurately complex action. In this respect the play bears a resemblance to the most stageworthy of the works of Bertolt Brecht, which despite the songs, lantern slides, and printed messages intended to hold the audience at a distance, are capable of arousing great feeling. Especially in the confrontations of the members of the Antrobus family with one another is the simplicity of speech effective. Families are families, even when the members are figures in an allegory, as Wilder had previously demonstrated in *Our Town.* Wilder's only defensive reply to his critics to date on any score has come as a response to complaints that *The Skin of Our Teeth* is "a bookish fantasia about history, full of rather bloodless school-masterish jokes" [see Author Commentary]. This he believes is not its usual effect, and for substantiation he cites productions in postwar Germany at which he witnessed gratifyingly warm reactions in the audience. It is not, however, a foolproof play. The production demands are very heavy, not only in comparison to *Our Town* but to the majority of twentieth-century plays, both as to stage equipment and acting skill. This limitation became apparent in the American production of 1955, when the play dwindled into dullness as a result of the inept performances of George Abbott as Mr. Antrobus and Mary Martin as Sabina. But, production difficulties notwithstanding, as the world spins from crisis to crisis, the play continues to live. It is certain to remain in the repertory of the intellectual theater. In 1964 plans were announced for a musical version, with Betty Comden and Adolph Green as librettists and Leonard Bernstein as composer.

The strongest complaints against *The Skin of Our Teeth* have risen, not in discussions of its theatrical viability, but in remarks on its sources. In December 1942 a thunderous controversy was initiated with two articles written for the *Saturday Review of Literature* by Henry Morton Robinson and Joseph Campbell, the young scholars then at work on the book ultimately to be published as *A Skeleton Key to Finnegans Wake* [see review dated 19 December 1942]. Unable to discriminate between the legitimate assimilation of a source and downright theft, they accused Wilder of plagiarism and of the debasement of Joyce's work. Although they proceeded beyond reason in their charges, they were correct enough in pointing to the similarity of the play to the novel. It is evident in the structure itself, which like that of the novel is circular, repeating the lines of the opening at the close. It is evident also in the resemblance between the Antrobuses and the Earwickers of the *Wake,* and in the procedure of describing all history through the family's activity, the past mixed in with the present and the banal mixed in with the profound. One serious result of the controversy was the refusal of the members of the New York Drama Critics Circle to present their annual award to Wilder, despite the obvious superiority of his play to all others of the season. Partial compensation for this injustice came soon afterward with the bestowal of the Pulitzer Prize.

Although the charges of plagiarism still come up in introductions to the play for text anthologies and were renewed by Robinson as late as March 1957 in an article for *Esquire,* they are now largely, and properly, ignored. Equally unsound, and now dropped, is the charge that the play cheapens the novel. To reach the general audience, as opposed to the coterie audience of the academic theater, Wilder found it necessary to broaden the substance of the book in order to clarify it. Professorial adaptations of passages of the novel have come along in the years since, but they cannot survive outside the academic theater and even there make no great impact. Remaining silent through the heat of the controversy, Wilder appeared to be taking for granted that his public would recognize honest borrowing for what it was. At last in the preface to *Three Plays,* published in October 1957, he acknowledged his source: "The play is deeply indebted to James Joyce's *Finnegans Wake.* I should be very happy if, in the future, some author should feel similarly indebted to any work of mine. Literature has always more resembled a torch race than a furious dispute among heirs" [see Author Commentary]. Should Wilder make a practice of studying the writers of the so-called Theater of the Absurd, who rely on slapstick, allegory, and seeming non-sequiturs for their reports on the meaning of existence, he would see the debts mounting. (pp. 118-29)

> *Malcolm Goldstein, in his* The Art of Thornton Wilder, *University of Nebraska Press, 1965, 179 p.*

Gerald Rabkin   (essay date 1969)

[*Rabkin is an American educator and author of the critical study* Drama and Commitment: Politics in the American Theatre of the Thirties *(1964). In the following essay, Rabkin praises the theatrical innovations of* The Skin of Our Teeth, *yet ultimately asserts that Wilder had "been overly conscious of his role as mediator between highbrow sensibility and middlebrow taste," and that he "too strenuously adapted his intellectual proclivities to the demand of the bourgeois theatre's 'group mind'."*]

Wartime—*real* wartime, not the grim twilight zone of police actions and unratified escalation—is, for obvious reasons, rarely productive of serious drama. Drama is a public art and all too clearly must join in the general mobilization. That exhortation and escapism tend to become its major aims may be confirmed by a brief glance at the American theatrical record from 1941 to 1945. The years immediately preceding American entry into the war had produced such plays as *The Time of Your Life* and *The Little Foxes,* but the theatre of the war years gravitated between escapist concoctions of the *Junior Miss, My Sister Eileen, Over Twenty-One* variety and "serious" declarations of faith in our fighting men and our democratic principles such as *Winged Victory, The Eve of Saint Mark,* and *Tomorrow the World.* The social concerns of the Depression were absorbed in the universality of the war effort—a

generalized anti-fascism remained the prime dramatic legacy of the 1930s. After the war new voices articulated new concerns. The most significant dramatic events of the 1940s are clearly the emergence of Miller and Williams and, after a decade of silence, the reemergence of O'Neill with *The Iceman Cometh.*

One play from the war years, however, did succeed in speaking both to the public need of its time and beyond. Thornton Wilder's *The Skin of Our Teeth* was presented in 1942 at a moment in history when it seemed quite possible that all civilized values—indeed, all human existence—were endangered by a barbarism greater than any the world had ever known. We need only think of the fortuitous outcome of the desperate race for atomic power to surmise how close that dread night came to being reality. Wilder's parable of man's capacity for survival spoke directly to this fear by placing contemporary catastrophe in the perspective of all human history and by pointing out that however close his possible annihilation man has always come through by the skin of his teeth. Despite its articulation of a grim moment in our history, the play, unlike so many works reflective of a period of convulsive social change (one need only cite the dramatic record of the 30s), succeeds in transcending the events which inspired it. Indeed, its continued stage popularity, particularly in Europe, indicates that the need for reassurance which it expresses did not disappear with World War II.

It is for these reasons curious to look back at a controversy which attended the successful original production of the play, a controversy which, some claim, prevented the New York drama critics from awarding it their annual prize for Best Play (although the Pulitzer Prize committee was not so inhibited). In brief, the controversy involves the claim that Wilder plagarized *The Skin of Our Teeth* from Joyce's *Finnegans Wake* (which had been published in 1939), a work so profoundly different in both form and scope as to make comparison appear almost gratuitous. Shortly after the New York opening of Wilder's play on November 18, 1942 Joseph Campbell and Henry Morton Robinson, who had been working on a "skeleton key" to Joyce's complex work published an article in the *Saturday Review of Literature* entitled "The Skin of Whose Teeth?" in which they claimed that the play was "not an entirely original creation, but an Americanized re-creation, thinly disguised of James Joyce's *Finnegans Wake*" [see review dated 19 December 1942]. They pointed out quite clearly and irrefutably Wilder's indebtedness with regard to plot elements, characters, devices of presentation, and thematic motifs: that *The Skin of Our Teeth* borrows *Finnegans Wake's* circular form, opening and closing with the cycle-renewing, riverrunning thought stream of the chief female character; that the main divisions of the play are closed by periodic catastrophes, devices similar to the comic dissolution of *Finnegans Wake;* that the character of Antrobus is strongly reminiscent of H. C. Earwicker who has endured through all the ages of the world despite periodic confrontations with disaster; that other characters (Sabina, Henry) and incidents (the letter in the sea) clearly show Wilder to be an avid student of Joyce.

The resemblances pointed out by Campbell and Robinson

are undeniable, indeed quite helpful in revealing Wilder's dependence upon Joyce's complex experiment in myth-making. What strikes one as extremely curious, however, is the alternation of attitude by Campbell and Robinson between admiration for the skill with which Wilder assimilated Joyce's complexities and outrage similar to having caught a bright freshman with a plagiarized theme. In this and in a later article written after the publication of the play, the Joyceans acknowledge Wilder's immense skill in transmuting Joyce for his dramatic purposes; they admit that Wilder has adapted the four books of *Finnegans Wake* to the exigencies of a three-act play "skillfully and without essential dislocation." And they praise his "creative re-interpretation" of H. C. Earwicker's dream of a future ideal and its dissolution into workaday toil into Antrobus' determination to persevere. In short, they show that Wilder has used Joyce as many other dramatists have creatively used their sources. Why then the tone of accusation as though Wilder had cunningly counted upon the complexity of *Finnegans Wake* from ever revealing his shameful indebtedness? One has not to read far to sense the reason for their outrage. Joyce's work, which now has achieved the status of unchallengeable classic despite its obscurity, had been dismissed by many contemporary reviewers as a "literary abortion," needlessly and pedantically puzzling. Robinson and Campbell were obviously furious that the same kind of critics who had contemptuously derided Joyce "today hail with rave-notices its Broadway reaction. . . . The banquet was rejected," they lamented, "but the Hellzapoppin's scrap that fell from the table they clutch to their bosom."

The tone of condemnation born of the injustice of it all (which seems now, of course, ironic) inevitably bred reactions. Woolcott Gibbs, who had praised Wilder's play highly, responded with characteristic *New Yorker* tongue-in-cheek: "The truth of the matter is that, instead of being partially borrowed from Mr. Joyce's work, *The Skin of Our Teeth* was actually taken almost in toto from an early novel of my own, called *Nabisco*. It is, of course, obvious from this title and the name of Mr. Wilder's heroine, Sabina both stem anagrammatically from the root word 'basin,' a circumstance that I regard as suggestive to say the least." Gibbs went on to claim that his heroine, stolen by Wilder, was "sometimes Mrs. Roosevelt and sometimes Mae West but always Lilith."

Edmund Wilson in the *Nation* [see Commentary dated 30 January 1943] maintained that Gibbs was wrong to ridicule the possible indebtedness of Wilder to Joyce: it was so evident as to have been clearly conscious on Wilder's part. Wilson quoted from a letter he had intended sending to Wilder before the controversy erupted: "What pyorrheotechnical edent and end of the whirled in comet strip (a) brings dionysaurus to Boredway . . . translimitates polyglint prosematics into plain symbol words . . . disinflects Anna Livia and Americanizes H. C. Earwicker." No, Campbell and Robinson are right in their facts but wrong in their conclusions. Indeed, far from trying to put Joyce over to the middlebrow audience, "what Wilder is trying to do is quite distinct from what Joyce is doing." In fact, Joyce often gets in Wilder's way: ". . . the state of saturation with Joyce in which the play was written has harmed

it in certain ways, precisely in distracting Wilder from his own ideas and effects. . . ."

To demonstrate that literary wounds heal slowly, Mr. Robinson returned to the attack fifteen years later after the success of another Wilder play, *The Matchmaker.* In *Esquire* of March 1957 he notes how carefully Wilder has attributed the sources of his latest play to Johann Nestroy and John Oxenford. After close analysis which implies that apart from the character of Dolly Levi all the real humor in the play is taken from Nestroy's version, Robinson returns to the unattributed source of *The Skin of Our Teeth.* Despite the passage of time the injustice to Joyce still rankles. Wilder credited Terence and Menander in *The Woman of Andros,* Catullus and Suetonious in *The Ides of March,* Nestroy and Oxenford in *The Matchmaker,* Robinson notes, but for *Finnegans Wake* "he was content to take the cash and let the credit line go." Indeed, until such time as Wilder publicly speaks on this question his reputation will be "clouded by puzzlement, controversy and contempt." The fact is that although Wilder never engaged in public debate with his detractors he has on many occasions given voice to his debt to Joyce. In the Introduction to *Three Plays* (1957) he replied to the charges in his own manner, acknowledging that *The Skin of Our Teeth* "is deeply indebted to James Joyce's *Finnegans Wake.* I should be very happy if, in the future, some author should feel similarly indebted to any work of mine. Literature has always more resembled a torch race than a furious dispute among heirs" [See Author Commentary].

From the vantage point of time this controversy seems hardly to have raised questions as serious as those evoked by the awarding of the Bollingen prize to Ezra Pound later in the forties, and one cannot help feeling that Wilder was wise to remain above this particular battle. *The Skin of Our Teeth* may be discussed more meaningfully in relation to the rest of Wilder's plays than to *Finnegans Wake.* For Wilder's vision of the theatre has remained remarkably consistent, and the virtues and vices of *The Skin of Our Teeth* are, in large part, those of his entire canon. His unabashed theatricality, for example, is a source not only of strength but of weakness. Emerging as a playwright in a period in which social realism dominated the stage, Wilder correctly pointed out that realism is itself a convention and a relatively new one at that in dramatic history. The great periods of drama—ancient Greece, Elizabethan England, the Spanish Golden Age—never attempted to create the illusion of reality. On the contrary, they affirmed the theatrical basis of their art, exploiting the very nakedness of their stage environments rather than masking them. Had Wilder emerged dramatically a decade earlier during the period of the experiments of O'Neill, Lawson, and Rice he might not have had to assert his case so forcefully. Nor might he have been as tempted to have rested so much of his case on theatricality itself. In many of his plays—**"The Happy Journey to Trenton and Camden," "The Long Christmas Dinner," "Infancy," "Childhood"**—he seems to feel that theatrical innovation can itself carry the dramatic burden (cars created by chairs, ninety years in thirty minutes, babies played by adults, etc.).

Our Town is a case in point. Theatrical simplicity is basic to its dramatic intent: to abstract the universality of human life from the experiences of individuals in a microcosmic American town. That the style *is* the play can be seen from the disastrous film version which fleshed out the audience's imaginative participation naturalistically and consequently destroyed Wilder's metaphor. But surely the film's failure demonstrates *Our Town's* dependence upon the theatrical impact of the bareness of the stage and the absence of properties. In a letter to producer Sol Lesser, Wilder pointed out that "realistically done—your wedding scene won't be interesting enough, and . . . will reduce many of the surrounding scenes to ordinary-ness." Which raises the disturbing question: divested of stepladders and chairs and umbrellas and Pirandellian interjections from the audience does not *Our Town* reveal an ordinary-ness, a banality born of folksiness, which its theatricalism fails to obscure? Wilder assumes the audience's unfamiliarity with his technique and his play leans heavily on the evocation of delight in his cleverness. It is the obverse of such early naturalistic dramas as James A. Herne's *Shore Acres* in which commonplace events are made theatrically attractive by the *innovation* of the accretion of naturalistic detail; in *Our Town* the commonplace is supposed to be rendered interesting by the very absence of this detail.

The Skin of Our Teeth seems to me more effective as a play because its theatricality is not as self-sufficient. Indeed, so wedded is form to theme that it is impossible to conceive of a naturalistic version in any medium. Wilder is successful in assimilating a whole range of influences—Olsen and Johnson and German Expressionism as well as Joyce—and in subordinating them to his thematic affirmation of faith in man's ability to survive the disasters, natural and self-inflicted, which assail him. As Mary McCarthy pointed out in the *Partisan Review,* part of the theatrical enjoyment of the play derives from the familiar mainspring of the anachronistic joke, "a joke which insists . . . that Neanderthal man with his bearskin and his club is at heart an insurance salesman at a fancydress ball" [see review dated January-February 1943]. (The joke is still being exploited in such mass-art concoctions as *The Flintstones.*) But Wilder does not rely solely on this comic device. When Antrobus banishes his pet Dinosaur and Mammoth to the oncoming ice we enjoy the playwright's skill in reducing their biological extinction to a simple theatrical gesture; when Sabina cries to the audience to "Pass up your chairs, . . . Save the human race" at the end of Act I the breaking of the proscenium barrier creates direct involvement in the incipient disaster; when the pre-flood frivolities of mankind are equated with "Fun at the Beach" at Atlantic City we admire the skill with which Wilder infuses contemporary comedy with mythic apprehension.

Indeed, so numerous are the virtues of *The Skin of Our Teeth* that one is particularly disturbed by what seems a crucial failure of nerve on Wilder's part. At various times during the action he has the actors drop character and express their bewilderment or annoyance at what is going on. Sabina reveals herself as Miss Somerset, an actress who laments the economic necessity of appearing in obscure pieces like the present one. "Why can't we have plays like we used to have—*Peg O' My Heart,* and *Smilin' Through,* and *The Bat*—good entertainment with a message you can take home with you?" Undoubtedly Wilder is having fun at the expense of the tired businessman's taste in theatre, but one wonders if the interjection is not really meant to assuage this philistinism by anticipating—and hence undercutting—hostile objections to the play's unconventional style. Similarly, the intense confrontation scene in Act III between Antrobus and Henry, now the embodiment of fascist violence, is terminated by Sabina (Miss Somerset) because of its potential violence: "Stop! Don't play this scene. You know what happened last night. Stop the play!" But the scene is too important to be resolved in this manner; if violence is to be stopped it cannot be by theatrical fiat.

Now it may be argued that Wilder has added another level of complexity by revealing the actors beneath the roles, that he has increased the relevance of past to present by exploiting the dimension of stage time through the play-within-a-play. But *The Skin of Our Teeth* is neither a Pirandellian journey to the noman's land between reality and illusion nor a Brechtian parable of social exploitation. Whatever metaphors used to describe them, the catastrophes which confront man are real and the struggle of the Antrobuses through history demands empathic response not alienation. That the breakaways exist as concessions to middlebrow taste can be seen by the scene at the beginning of Act III in which it is revealed that the actors who are to play the hours at the end of the play are ill and that backstage help must therefore be pressed into double duty. The real point of the scene is that it enables Wilder to articulate unambiguously the thematic complexities of his finale wherein humanistic philosophical values are shown to prevail over desolation. When the stage manager fails to explain why the author wants to show the hours of the night appearing as philosophers, Wilder democratically has the Negro wardrobe mistress point the moral: "Just like the hours and stars go by over our heads at night, in the same way the ideas and thoughts of the great men are in the air around us all the time and they're working on us, even when we don't know it." And so when the hour/philosophers *do* appear at the end of the play the audience can sigh collectively because it knows *who* are being quoted—Aristotle, Plato, and Spinoza as we've been told—and what the scene is supposed to mean. One is reminded of Stan Laurel's comment on Red Skelton's tendency to drop character: "Just dreadful. I love his talent but I hate the thing he does with it when he does that deliberate breaking up."

Perhaps this is somewhat unfair to Wilder. Is it his fault he has had the dramatic sense to anticipate his audience's objections? The answer is that more than in any other art first-rate drama demands first-rate audiences. Perhaps Wilder has been overly conscious of his role as mediator between highbrow sensibility and middlebrow taste, perhaps he has too strenuously adapted his intellectual proclivities to the demand of the bourgeois theatre's "group mind." "A group mind," he has written, "presupposes, if not a lowering of standards, a broadening of the fields of interest." Unlike the other arts, the drama cannot "presuppose an audience of connoisseurs trained in leisure and capable of being interested in certain rarefied aspects of life." Note the qualifying clause in the first sentence. The greatest of modern dramatists enlarged audience taste precisely by not conceding to it. But Wilder in play after play feels compelled to underline the obvious or provide a graspable theme "nugget." Two instances will serve. The stage manager in *Our Town:* "There's something way down deep that's eternal about every human being"; Officer Avonzino in **"Infancy":** "Babies acting like growed-ups; growed-ups acting like babies." Wilder's almost maddening tendency to aphorize contradicts his avowed aim, articulated in the Introduction to **Three Plays,** to disturb middleclass complacency: the theatre he rejected was "not only inadequate, it was evasive . . . it aimed to be soothing." He is enmeshed rather in the snares of what Dwight MacDonald has termed "midcult," the submerging of complexities in the tepid ooze of a cozy universality and folksiness. Even **The Skin of Our Teeth** ends on a note of coy optimism at odds with the spirit of much of the play as Sabina counsels the audience, "This is where you came in. We have to go on for ages and ages yet. . . . Mr. and Mrs. Antrobus! Their heads are full of plans and they're as confident as the first day they began." One notes these tendencies with regret, for Wilder's dramatic instinct and theatrical inventiveness are undeniable. Most of his plays, particularly **The Skin of Our Teeth,** hold the stage despite their defects. One keeps wishing that he hadn't played it so safe and that along with Joyce's ideas he had been more influenced by the Irishman's artistic intransigence. (pp. 113-20)

> Gerald Rabkin, " 'The Skin of Our Teeth' and the Theatre of Thornton Wilder," in The Forties: Fiction, Poetry, Drama, *edited by Warren French, Everett/Edwards, Inc., 1969, pp. 113-20.*

M. C. Kuner   (essay date 1972)

[Kuner is an American educator and dramatist. In the following excerpt from her *Thornton Wilder: The Bright and the Dark* (1972), she individually analyzes each scene of *The Skin of Our Teeth* and concludes that the play does not achieve the transcendency of *Our Town* due to the fact that Wilder cannot portray humanity's failings as skillfully as he does its virtues.]

A year after Wilder finished **Our Town** Europe erupted into World War II; two years later America was also at war. As the cancer of Fascism spread, plunging once civilized and cultured nations into incredible acts of barbarism—the "wrong" people and the "wrong" books were burned indiscriminately—universal pessimism kept pace with it: the world seemed on the brink of a new Dark Age. Before he left America for service abroad, Wilder produced his answer to the holocaust: **The Skin of Our Teeth** (1942), a testament to his faith in the survival of Man. Its German title is perhaps even more apropos; it translates as *We've Come Through Once Again.*

Wilder himself has given us the best description of his play when contrasted with the earlier one: "*Our Town* is the life of a family seen from a telescope, five miles away. *The*

Skin of Our Teeth is the destiny of the whole human group seen from a telescope 1,000 miles away." The three acts treat of three different moments in the creation of the world; the four major characters represent the types most prevalent in any society. And the characters themselves in turn represent different levels of meaning: they are actors, whose personal stories filter through the lines they are reading; they are Everyman and Everywoman; and they are the members of a typical American family. The actual setting for Acts I and III is the Antrobus home in Excelsior, New Jersey; Act II takes place on the boardwalk in Atlantic City. But as events continue to erupt, it is clear that the actual location is anywhere and everywhere.

Act I begins as a lantern slide, projected on the curtain, announces the name of the theater, and this is followed by News Events of the World. It is interrupted halfway through by a statement that a wedding ring has been found by some cleaning-women in the theater (three of them, like The Fates?) with the inscription "To Eva from Adam. Genesis II:18." (The reference, of course, is to God's promise to give Man a Helpmate.) The news continues, concerning the excessive cold reported in Vermont and Montreal, then shifting to a picture of Mr. Antrobus' home. He is a celebrity who "invented the wheel." He comes of very old stock "and has made his way up from next to nothing. It is reported that he was once a gardener" (Wilder's view of Adam's occupation), but "left that situation under circumstances that have been variously reported." Another picture shows us Mrs. Antrobus holding her roses: she was the inventor of the apron. And the play is off . . .

The maid, Sabina, begins by addressing the audience in a parody of nineteenth-century dramas: "Oh, oh, oh! Six o'clock and the master not home yet. Pray God nothing serious has happened to him crossing the Hudson River." She laments the excessive cold and the general mess everything is in, and cannot understand why the house hasn't fallen down long ago. At this point a fragment of the right wall leans precariously over, as though to intrude the shakiness of the stage setting into the general shakiness of the human condition. Throughout the play Wilder will use these devices, presenting the action and then reminding us in various ways that it is only a play, not reality at all. But there will be times that the actors become so involved in the reality of what they are doing that they will forget their real identities and show antagonisms they are supposed to be feeling only as *dramatis personae.* Taking a further cue from Pirandello, Wilder gives the maid a few observations concerning the author, who "hasn't made up his silly mind as to whether we're all living back in caves or in New Jersey today, and that's the way it is all the way through." (The Director in Pirandello's *Six Characters in Search of an Author* complains that he is rehearsing a play by Pirandello called *Mixing It Up,* which nobody can understand.)

Sabina continues to feed the audience information, half in the parodic style she has been using and half to try to explain the situation. The Antrobus family (the Greek word for man is *anthropos*) consists of two children, Henry and Gladys, in addition to the parents. Henry is a "real, clean-cut American boy." But Henry, Sabina tells us, can hit anything when he has a stone in his hand. So the Henry of the play is also the Cain of the Bible.

Sabina goes on lamenting the state of the world, making reference to the fact that "a few years ago we came through the depression by the skin of our teeth! One more tight squeeze like that and where will we all be?" This is a line that needs a response from another actor, but when he doesn't give it Sabina speaks the line again, desperately waiting for the other actor to pick up his cue. Then she bursts into tears, denounces the play and the fate that has reduced her to acting in such trash, and bemoans the old days of *Smilin' Through* and *Peg o' My Heart,* when plays were nice and cheerful. She herself (her real name is Miss Somerset) has appeared in *The Barretts of Wimpole Street* and *Rain* (further references to theatrical carpentry rather than great drama) and begins her speech again.

She and Mrs. Antrobus understand each other. For Sabina (whose history goes back to the rape of the Sabine Women) is also the daughter of Lilith, the temptress of the Bible with whom Mr. Antrobus has once fallen in love. Eventually she lost her place in his home and was demoted to maid. The Eternal Feminine, she is a symbol of those who love only comfort and ease: they can be bought for the simplest luxuries. And Mrs. Antrobus sums her up: "Always throwing up the sponge, Sabina. . . . But give you a new hat—or a plate of ice cream—or a ticket to the movies, and you want to live forever." If Mrs. Antrobus knows the truth about Sabina, the reverse is also true. Sabina says of Mrs. Antrobus, "You don't care whether we live or die; all you care about is [your] children. If it would be any benefit to them you'd be glad to see us all stretched and dead." Sabina, or sensual pleasure, taunts Mrs. Antrobus with the knowledge that she, Sabina, inspired Mr. Antrobus to invent the alphabet, but Mrs. Antrobus is not impressed. Sabina was demoted because she let the fire go out; Mrs. Antrobus keeps the home fires burning.

In the midst of all this weaving back and forth into the past and present (with a quick eye on the future), using the threads of Biblical allusions, Roman history, and American sources, two creatures of the Ice Age, a Dinosaur and a Mammoth, try to come in, for they are very cold in the subzero temperature of August. (Wilder's admiration for André Obey's *Noé* is quite apparent here, for the French dramatist had made ample use of actors in animal costumes who were part of the story of Noah and the Flood.) In the middle of this intrusion, in turn, Sabina breaks off and remarks that she wishes it were eleven o'clock and the silly play over. Her major function in the comedy is to break the action on stage and to remind the spectator of its illusionary quality. Just before Mr. Antrobus returns home he sends a telegram announcing that he has discovered something new about numbers: "ten tens make hundred." Antrobus-Adam, Man, the source of knowledge, of language, of mathematics, advises his family by telegram to fight the cold and keep warm by burning everything—except Shakespeare. Mrs. Antrobus, Eve-Earth Goddess, knows better than that: "I'd burn ten Shakespeares to prevent a child of mine from having one cold in the head." She lends the Telegraph Boy a needle (over Sabina's protests, for there are only two left), so that his wife may sew

some warm clothes; and to comfort him because of his fear of the cold in August, she advises, "Just keep as warm as you can. And don't let your wife and children see that you're worried."

Throughout the play Mr. and Mrs. Antrobus worry about Henry, wondering whether he has hit someone seriously with a stone. He is constantly warned by his mother to keep the hair brushed over his forehead so that the scar on it may not be seen. As the first act concludes, the ice threatens to engulf the entire world, and when refugees knock at the door to seek protection Mrs. Antrobus does not want to take them in; her first instinct is to save her own family. But Mr. Antrobus recognizes his duty to mankind and gives them shelter. They are neighbors, but their names are Judge Moses, Homer, and the nine Miss Muses. Both religion and literature are thus saved, while Sabina calls out to the audience to pass up chairs from the auditorium and save the human race. The ushers move back and forth between the stage and the orchestra, this time turning illusion into reality.

The first act, or Ice Age, may be called the geological division. The disasters are physical ones caused largely by nature. The second act, on the boardwalk at Atlantic City, involves the Flood; since in this act Mr. Antrobus contemplates abandoning his wife for Sabina, who is now not a maid but a beauty-contest winner named Miss Fairweather (the name indicates she functions best when there are no problems), he has committed a moral transgression. The disaster has moved from external to internal causes. Interestingly enough, when he announces to Mrs. Antrobus that he is leaving her, she rejects the idea that he can forsake either her or his responsibilities to his fellows in this new crisis. And she makes what is probably Wilder's definitive remark about human obligations:

> I didn't marry you because you were perfect. I didn't even marry you because I loved you. I married you because you gave me a promise. [*She takes off her ring and looks at it.*] That promise made up for your faults. And the promise I gave you made up for mine. Two imperfect people got married and it was the promise that made the marriage. . . . And when our children were growing up, it wasn't a house that protected them; and it wasn't our love, that protected them—it was that promise.

And the breaking of the promise has shattering implications, for their daughter, Gladys, finding attraction in sin, though she is as yet guiltless, appears wearing a pair of scarlet stockings that symbolize the Fall. Her father's horror when he understands the bad example he has set is exceeded only by his reaction to the news over the loudspeaker that the Flood is rising higher and higher.

Recalled to his sense of duty, Antrobus renounces Sabina and self, and moves to rescue his family as the act concludes. Its theme has been echoed earlier by the gaudy Fortune Teller; preposterous fraud though she is, Wilder gives her some characteristic lines:

> You know as well as I do what's coming. Rain. Rain. Rain in floods. The deluge. But first you'll see shameful things—shameful things. Some of

you will be saying: "Let him drown. He's not worth saving. Give the whole thing up." I can see it in your faces. But you're wrong. Keep your doubts and despairs to yourself. Again there'll be the narrow escape. The survival of a handful. From destruction—total destruction.

The third act, in contrast again, is historical; this time the disasters have been caused by war, which has just ended when the act begins. The chaos of the world after such a calamity is reflected in the backstage difficulties: seven of the actors have fallen ill, presumably of food poisoning, and the wardrobe mistress and others working on the crew will have to substitute. As it turns out, the understudies have minor roles in terms of lines, but major roles in terms of ideas: Planets, Hours, the same symbols Wilder had used in **"Pullman Car Hiawatha,"** make their appearance. Spinoza, the Ninth Hour, warns man of the confusion in the world outside; Plato, the Tenth Hour, warns of the chaos within the human heart; Aristotle, the Eleventh Hour, praises the beauty of reason. And at twelve, the Book of Genesis begins. The elements that survive are books and faith, or humanism and theology. And it is fitting that Genesis should begin the new day, one second after midnight, marking the Alpha and Omega of the human story. It is also significant that the "regular" actors could not play their parts, yet the substitutes were easy to find, for *everyone* can perform such a function in time of need; it requires no special talents.

The major conflict, such as it exists in this play, is concentrated in the third act, when Henry suddenly emerges in all his evil. He has not only killed his brother (Mrs. Antrobus weeps when a stranger says he thought she had *two* sons), he is wickedness personified. Sabina is quick to realize that he is the enemy. And Henry proves his nature in committing acts that Wilder surely equated with the Nazism that was rampaging across the world. He says, "The first thing to do is burn up those old books [his father's]; it's the ideas he gets out of those old books that . . . makes the whole world so you can't live in it." Sabina urges him to be more lovable; but Henry rejects love (he is the opposite of all the people who found the answer to life in *The Bridge of San Luis Rey*), shouting that he doesn't want anyone to love him.

> Tear everything down. I don't care what you smash. . . . You don't have to think I'm any relation of yours. I haven't got any father or any mother, or brothers or sisters. And I don't want any. And what's more I haven't got anybody over me; and I never will have. I'm alone, and that's all I want to be: alone.

But his is not the loneliness of the perceptive, sensitive human being who recognizes the difficulty of communication; it is the loneliness of the mind that removes itself from the race. Dolly Levi of **The Matchmaker** finds her purpose by rejoining the world; Henry renounces it. And Henry tells his father how he will make the world of the future—by repression of others. This is his father's answer (and Wilder's):

> How can you make a world for people to live in, unless you've first put order in yourself? Mark my words: I shall continue fighting you until my

last breath as long as you mix up your idea of liberty with your idea of hogging everything for yourself. I shall have no pity on you. I shall pursue you to the far corners of the earth. You and I want the same thing; but until you think of it as something that everyone has a right to, you are my deadly enemy and I will destroy you.

As the anger builds between the two, Sabina interrupts and begs them not to play out the scene, reminding them of what happened the last time. And now, not Henry the character but Henry the actor recalls his hatred for his father and his own unhappy boyhood, which he has projected into his role. He remembers being hated by his classmates in high school and his feeling of emptiness. And he feels "it's as though you have to kill somebody else so as not to end up killing yourself." Antrobus responds to him now also in his own personality, as an actor on stage, and muses, "It's not wholly his [Henry's] fault . . . it's my fault, too. He wouldn't feel that way unless there were something in me that reminded him of all that." And Henry, grateful for this understanding, leaves the stage, promising not to forget himself too much in the role on future nights.

Sabina, though not wicked or evil, is greedy and self-serving. She tries to make a little profit out of a situation—anything for comfort. Her complaint:

> I didn't make this war. I didn't ask for it. And, in my opinion, after anybody's gone through what we've gone through, they have a right to grab what they can find. . . . Oh, the world's an awful place, and you know it is. I used to think something could be done about it: but I know better now. I hate it. I hate it.

Antrobus, though driven to despair himself and not really anxious to do anything about saving the world a third time (the Ice Age and the Flood were quite enough), knows that all the same he has to keep trying. He explains to his wife:

> Now I remember what three things always went together when I was able to see things most clearly: three things. Three things. The voice of the people in their confusion and their need. And the thought of you and the children and this house. . . . And . . . my books!

Books can rebuild the world, he believes:

> Oh, I've never forgotten for long at a time that living is struggle. I know that every good and excellent thing in the world stands moment by moment on the razor-edge of danger and must be fought for—whether it's a field, or a home, or a country. All I ask is the chance to build new worlds and God has always given us that. And has given us [*opening the book*] voices to guide us; and the memory of our mistakes to warn us. . . . We've come a long ways. We've learned. We're learning. And the steps of our journey are marked for us here [*he turns the leaves of the book*].

This is the Holy Trinity for Antrobus: memory (of past experiences), learning (humanism), and faith (in God, Nature, Universal Mind—in short, a Creator).

For the last scene of the play the Hours and the Book of Genesis guard the stage, while the figure of Henry broods in the background; then everything vanishes with the stroke of the bell and Sabina begins the same speech with which she started the play, interrupting herself to tell the audience they can go home now. "The end of this play isn't written yet. Mr. and Mrs. Antrobus! Their heads are full of plans and they're as confident as the first day they began."

The Skin of Our Teeth is a curious mixture of diverse elements. Though some critics have gone so far as to say Wilder plagiarized from *Finnegans Wake,* Joyce, after all, employed the circular theory of time after he, in turn, had taken it from the Italian philosopher Giambattista Vico. Édouard Dujardin in his novel *Le Rétour Éternel* ("The Eternal Return") had also portrayed the survival of humanity in the story of a family that had undergone terrible sacrifices at different ages of history. Rather than accusing Wilder of plagiarism, it would be more accurate to say that he had taken a great many elements from his earlier plays. Thus Mrs. Antrobus is certainly a development of Mrs. Kirby in **"The Happy Journey to Trenton and Camden"**—the Eternal Mother-Wife. The constant speeches to the audience by the characters coming down stage and facing front recall the technique of **The Matchmaker,** which also parodied the conventions of the old-fashioned box-shaped set. The idea of time itself and man moving in and out of it had already been demonstrated in **Our Town.** And Mr. Antrobus, in the end, is no H. C. Earwicker (the hero of *Finnegans Wake*): he is too incurably American, in his faith, his optimism, and his sense of mission to be anything but another version of George Brush. Moreover, like everything else Wilder wrote, **The Skin of Our Teeth** is highly objective. With such a disjointed and open technique as he uses the tone is usually highly subjective, introspective, full of free association, as in the plays of August Strindberg (or the films of Ingmar Bergman): such dramas always sound deeply personal and autobiographical. But Wilder's comedy, while it expresses his philosophy, has nothing personally revealing about it: we learn everything we have to know by what the characters tell each other and the audience candidly and boldly. There is no feeling of an interior monologue here, probably because Wilder is too intellectual in his approach to submerge his ideas in emotional outpourings.

The Skin of Our Teeth carries the author's primary message that humanity can, must, and will triumph over adversity. But in this play Wilder also goes one step further in his explorations and examines in greater detail than usual the nature of evil itself. From where did it come? And why? The second question has already been answered for us, if indirectly: Wilder seems to suggest that evil almost *has* to be present as an ingredient of life in order for mankind to conquer it. But the answer to the first question proves to be the weakest portion of the play.

Although **The Skin of Our Teeth** is both amusing and technically effective, although it divorces itself from the tired concept of drama as a series of confrontations between opposing forces (after all, Chekhov did not believe much in confrontations and he managed to be dramatic

enough) and is inventive about what is substituted, the play fails because it attempts to define the problem of evil in terms of the character of Henry. If he is Cain and the symbol of wickedness, who really created him: how did he—Evil—originate?

Mr. Antrobus seems to feel that Henry's wickedness stems from being misunderstood: there is no other explanation for the scene when Henry suddenly becomes an unhappy actor who was badly treated by his friends. We are told that Henry would be able to understand the alphabet, which his father invented, if it were a little simpler—but that, too, is a simplification. Moreover, it is not Henry's act but the coming of the Flood that is timed to accompany the sins of Mr. Antrobus: his wrongdoing consists of wishing to abandon his family—that is, his human responsibility—but his transgressions seem too petty for the deluge that will engulf everyone. And the Ice Age of the first act, for which no one is to blame, for no moral lapse has been witnessed—how is that explained? Wilder simply has not the kind of talent to make evil seem real, and consequently the "dark" side of his moon never seems very dark. He is more at home in chronicling "Man's spiral progress and his progression through trial and error." He understands the anthropological or the ethical man a good deal more than the political one. That is why **Our Town** is more successful than **The Skin of Our Teeth.** Wilder himself has noted that the latter play is most successful when the world looks gloomy—one reason perhaps for its extraordinary success in Germany after the war. Its first production in America baffled some audiences and charmed others; when it was revived recently, its technique was no longer as startling as it had been almost thirty years before, and its philosophy was considered a bit too cheerful. For whatever reason one chooses to supply, it has always been disliked by the French, who are perhaps cynics by profession. (pp. 146-60)

> *M. C. Kuner, in her* Thornton Wilder: The Bright and the Dark, *Thomas Y. Crowell Company, 1972, 226 p.*

FURTHER READING

AUTHOR COMMENTARY

Goldstone, Richard H. "Thornton Wilder." *The Paris Review,* No. 15 (Winter 1957): 37-57.

> Interview with Wilder, in which he discusses various aspects of his dramatic craft.

Wilder, Thornton. "Some Thoughts on Playwrighting." In *The Intent of the Artist,* edited by Augusto Centeno, pp. 83-98. Princeton, N. J.: Princeton University Press, 1941.

> Essay in which Wilder outlines what he perceives are the "four fundamental conditions of the drama [that] separate it from the other arts."

OVERVIEWS AND GENERAL STUDIES

Cowley, Malcolm. "The Man Who Abolished Time." *Saturday Review* XXXIX, No. 40 (6 October 1956): 13-14, 50-2.
Insightful article that traces the origins and summarizes the major aspects of Wilder's art.

Fulton, A. E. "Expressionism—Twenty Years After." *The Sewanee Review* LII, No. 3 (July-September 1944): 398-413.
Compares *Our Town* and *The Skin of Our Teeth* to other expressionistic dramas of their day, including Eugene O'Neill's *The Hairy Ape* and John Dos Passos' *The Moon Is a Gong.*

Goldstein, Malcolm. "Thornton Wilder." In *The American Theater Today,* edited by Alan S. Downer, pp. 60-72. New York: Basic Books, 1967.
Succinct summary of Wilder's career in the theater.

Gould, Jean. "Thornton Wilder." In his *Modern American Playwrights,* pp. 204-24. New York: Dodd, Mead & Company, 1966.
Biographical approach to Wilder's work and career.

Hewitt, Barnard. "Thornton Wilder Says 'Yes'." *The Tulane Drama Review* 4, No. 2 (December 1959): 110-20.
Evaluation of *Our Town, The Matchmaker,* and *The Skin of Our Teeth* that defends the plays against charges of sentimentality and pretentiousness.

OUR TOWN

Atkinson, Brooks and Hirshfeld, Albert. *"Our Town."* In their *The Lively Years: 1920-1973,* pp. 134-37. New York: Association Press, 1973.
Briefly traces the production history of *Our Town* and the varying critical reaction to the play over time.

Corrigan, Robert W. "Thornton Wilder and the Tragic Sense of Life." *Educational Theater Journal* XIII, No. 3 (October 1961): 167-73.
Argues that Wilder is aware "that 'human kind cannot bear very much reality,' but his plays fall short of tragedy because he takes the Platonic escape, he moves into a world that denies the reality and the nemesis of destiny."

D'Ambrosio, Michael A. "Is *Our Town* Really Our Town?" *The English Record* XXII, No. 1 (Fall 1971): 20-2.
Examines the universal aspects of *Our Town.*

Dean, Alexander. "Our Town on the Stage." *The Yale Review* XXVII, No. 4 (June 1938): 836-38.

Praises Wilder for ridding *Our Town* of theatrical conventions and allowing language to dominate the work.

Kohler, Dayton. "Thornton Wilder." *The English Journal* XXVII, No. 1 (January 1939): 1-11.
Relates Wilder's earlier dramas and novels to *Our Town.*

Porter, Thomas E. "A Green Corner of the Universe: *Our Town.*" In his *Myth and Modern American Drama,* pp. 200-24. Detroit: Wayne State University Press, 1969.
Argues that the theatrical achievement of *Our Town* lies in Wilder's ability to dissect and symbolically present American ideals.

Stephens, George D. "*Our Town*—Great American Tragedy?" *Modern Drama* 1, No. 4 (February 1959): 258-64.
Concludes that while *Our Town* evokes "a gentle sadness," it cannot be described as a tragedy.

THE SKIN OF OUR TEETH

Atkinson, Brooks and Hirshfeld, Albert. *"The Skin of Our Teeth."* In their *The Lively Years: 1920-1973,* pp. 167-70. New York: Association Press, 1973.
Briefly traces the production history *The Skin of Our Teeth* and the varying critical reaction to the play over time.

Campbell, Joseph and Robinson, Henry Morton. "The Skin of Whose Teeth?—Part II: The Intention Behind the Deed." *Saturday Review* XXVI, No. 7 (13 February 1943): 16, 18-19.
Second article in which Campbell and Robinson elaborate upon their claim that Wilder plagiarized *The Skin of Our Teeth* from James Joyce's *Finnegans Wake.* See review dated 19 December 1942 for the first part of this essay.

Gibbs, Wolcott. "Finnegan's Teeth." *The New Yorker* XVIII, No. 45 (26 December 1942): 32.
Parody of the Campbell and Robinson articles in which Gibbs claims that Wilder plagiarized *The Skin of Our Teeth* from his own "early novel" entitled "Nabisco."

Life 13, No. 22 (30 November 1942): 93-4, 96, 98, 100.
Short essay on the play valuable for its photographs from the original production of *The Skin of Our Teeth.*

Nichols, Lewis. "Gnashing Teeth." *The New York Times* (3 January 1943): Section 8, p. 1.
Playful summary of the early controversy surrounding the origins of *The Skin of Our Teeth.*

CUMULATIVE INDEXES

This Index Includes References
to Entries in These Gale Series

Contemporary Literary Criticism presents excerpts of criticism on the works of novelists, poets, dramatists, short story writers, scriptwriters, and other creative writers who are now living or who have died since 1960.

Twentieth-Century Literary Criticism contains critical excerpts by the most significant commentators on poets, novelists, short story writers, dramatists, and philosophers who died between 1900 and 1960.

Nineteenth-Century Literature Criticism offers significant passages from criticism on authors who died between 1800 and 1899.

Literature Criticism from 1400 to 1800 compiles significant passages from the most noteworthy criticism on authors of the fifteenth through eighteenth centuries.

Classical and Medieval Literature Criticism offers excerpts of criticism on the works of world authors from classical antiquity through the fourteenth century.

Short Story Criticism compiles excerpts of criticism on short fiction by writers of all eras and nationalities.

Poetry Criticism presents excerpts of criticism on the works of poets from all eras, movements, and nationalities.

Drama Criticism presents criticism of the works of dramatists of all eras, movements, and nationalities.

Children's Literature Review includes excerpts from reviews, criticism, and commentary on works of authors and illustrators who create books for children.

Contemporary Authors Series encompasses five related series. *Contemporary Authors* provides biographical and bibliographical information on more than 97,000 writers of fiction and nonfiction. *Contemporary Authors New Revision Series* provides completely updated information on authors covered in *CA*. *Contemporary Authors Permanent Series* consists of listings for deceased and inactive authors. *Contemporary Authors Autobiography Series* presents specially commissioned autobiographies by leading contemporary writers. *Contemporary Authors Bibliographical Series* contains primary and secondary bibliographies as well as analytical bibliographical essays by authorities on major modern authors.

Dictionary of Literary Biography encompasses four related series. *Dictionary of Literary Biography* furnishes illustrated overviews of authors' lives and works. *Dictionary of Literary Biography Documentary Series* illuminates the careers of major figures through a selection of literary documents, including letters, interviews, and photographs. *Dictionary of Literary Biography Yearbook* summarizes the past year's literary activity and includes updated entries on individual authors. *Concise Dictionary of American Literary Biography* comprises six volumes of revised and updated sketches on major American authors that were originally presented in *Dictionary of Literary Biography*.

Something about the Author Series encompasses three related series. *Something about the Author* contains well-illustrated biographical sketches on juvenile and young adult authors and illustrators from all eras. *Something about the Author Autobiography Series* presents specially commissioned autobiographies by prominent authors and illustrators of books for children and young adults. *Authors & Artists for Young Adults* provides high school and junior high school students with profiles of their favorite creative artists.

Yesterday's Authors of Books for Children contains heavily illustrated entries on children's writers who died before 1961. Complete in two volumes.

Literary Criticism Series
Cumulative Author Index

This index lists all author entries in the Gale Literary Criticism Series and includes cross-references to other Gale sources. References in the index are identified as follows:

Author Index

Blackburn, Paul 1926-1971 . . . . . . **CLC 9, 43**
See also CA 81-84; obituary CA 33-36R;
DLB 16; DLB-Y 81

Black Elk 1863-1950 . . . . **TCLC 33**

Blackmore, R(ichard) D(oddridge)
1825-1900 . . . . **TCLC 27**
See also CA 120; DLB 18

Blackmur, R(ichard) P(almer)
1904-1965 . . . . **CLC 2, 24**
See also CAP 1; CA 11-12;
obituary CA 25-28R; DLB 63

Blackwood, Algernon (Henry)
1869-1951 . . . . **TCLC 5**
See also CA 105

Blackwood, Caroline 1931- . . . . **CLC 6, 9**
See also CA 85-88; DLB 14

Blair, Eric Arthur 1903-1950
See Orwell, George
See also CA 104; SATA 29

Blais, Marie-Claire
1939- . . . . **CLC 2, 4, 6, 13, 22**
See also CAAS 4; CA 21-24R; DLB 53

Blaise, Clark 1940- . . . . **CLC 29**
See also CAAS 3; CANR 5; CA 53-56R;
DLB 53

Blake, Nicholas 1904-1972
See Day Lewis, C(ecil)

Blake, William 1757-1827 . . . . **NCLC 13**
See also SATA 30

Blasco Ibanez, Vicente
1867-1928 . . . . **TCLC 12**
See also CA 110

Blatty, William Peter 1928- . . . . **CLC 2**
See also CANR 9; CA 5-8R

Blessing, Lee 1949- . . . . **CLC 54**

Blish, James (Benjamin)
1921-1975 . . . . **CLC 14**
See also CANR 3; CA 1-4R;
obituary CA 57-60; DLB 8

Blixen, Karen (Christentze Dinesen)
1885-1962
See Dinesen, Isak
See also CAP 2; CA 25-28; SATA 44

Bloch, Robert (Albert) 1917- . . . . **CLC 33**
See also CANR 5; CA 5-8R; SATA 12;
DLB 44

Blok, Aleksandr (Aleksandrovich)
1880-1921 . . . . **TCLC 5**
See also CA 104

Bloom, Harold 1930- . . . . **CLC 24**
See also CA 13-16R; DLB 67

Blount, Roy (Alton), Jr. 1941- . . . . . **CLC 38**
See also CANR 10; CA 53-56

Bloy, Leon 1846-1917. . . . . **TCLC 22**
See also CA 121

Blume, Judy (Sussman Kitchens)
1938- . . . . **CLC 12, 30**
See also CLR 2, 15; CANR 13; CA 29-32R;
SATA 2, 31; DLB 52

Blunden, Edmund (Charles)
1896-1974 . . . . **CLC 2, 56**
See also CAP 2; CA 17-18;
obituary CA 45-48; DLB 20

Bly, Robert (Elwood)
1926- . . . . **CLC 1, 2, 5, 10, 15, 38**
See also CA 5-8R; DLB 5

Bochco, Steven 1944?- . . . . **CLC 35**

Bodker, Cecil 1927- . . . . **CLC 21**
See also CLR 23; CANR 13; CA 73-76;
SATA 14

Boell, Heinrich (Theodor) 1917-1985
See Boll, Heinrich
See also CANR 24; CA 21-24R;
obituary CA 116

Bogan, Louise 1897-1970. . . . . **CLC 4, 39, 46**
See also CA 73-76; obituary CA 25-28R;
DLB 45

Bogarde, Dirk 1921- . . . . **CLC 19**
See also Van Den Bogarde, Derek (Jules
Gaspard Ulric) Niven
See also DLB 14

Bogosian, Eric 1953- . . . . **CLC 45**

Bograd, Larry 1953- . . . . **CLC 35**
See also CA 93-96; SATA 33

Bohl de Faber, Cecilia 1796-1877
See Caballero, Fernan

Boiardo, Matteo Maria 1441-1494 . . . . **LC 6**

Boileau-Despreaux, Nicolas
1636-1711 . . . . **LC 3**

Boland, Eavan (Aisling) 1944- . . . . . . **CLC 40**
See also DLB 40

Boll, Heinrich (Theodor)
1917-1985 . . . **CLC 2, 3, 6, 9, 11, 15, 27,
39**
See also Boell, Heinrich (Theodor)
See also DLB 69; DLB-Y 85

Bolt, Robert (Oxton) 1924- . . . . **CLC 14**
See also CA 17-20R; DLB 13

Bond, Edward 1934- . . . . **CLC 4, 6, 13, 23**
See also CA 25-28R; DLB 13

Bonham, Frank 1914- . . . . **CLC 12**
See also CANR 4; CA 9-12R; SAAS 3;
SATA 1, 49

Bonnefoy, Yves 1923- . . . . **CLC 9, 15, 58**
See also CA 85-88

Bontemps, Arna (Wendell)
1902-1973 . . . . **CLC 1, 18**
See also CLR 6; CANR 4; CA 1-4R;
obituary CA 41-44R; SATA 2, 44;
obituary SATA 24; DLB 48, 51

Booth, Martin 1944- . . . . **CLC 13**
See also CAAS 2; CA 93-96

Booth, Philip 1925- . . . . **CLC 23**
See also CANR 5; CA 5-8R; DLB-Y 82

Booth, Wayne C(layson) 1921- . . . . . **CLC 24**
See also CAAS 5; CANR 3; CA 1-4R;
DLB 67

Borchert, Wolfgang 1921-1947 . . . . . **TCLC 5**
See also CA 104; DLB 69

Borges, Jorge Luis
1899-1986 . . . **CLC 1, 2, 3, 4, 6, 8, 9, 10,
13, 19, 44, 48; SSC 4**
See also CANR 19; CA 21-24R; DLB-Y 86

Borowski, Tadeusz 1922-1951 . . . . . . **TCLC 9**
See also CA 106

Borrow, George (Henry)
1803-1881 . . . . **NCLC 9**
See also DLB 21, 55

Bosschere, Jean de 1878-1953 . . . . . **TCLC 19**
See also CA 115

Boswell, James 1740-1795. . . . . **LC 4**

Bottoms, David 1949- . . . . **CLC 53**
See also CANR 22; CA 105; DLB-Y 83

Boucolon, Maryse 1937-
See Conde, Maryse
See also CA 110

Bourget, Paul (Charles Joseph)
1852-1935 . . . . **TCLC 12**
See also CA 107

Bourjaily, Vance (Nye) 1922- . . . . **CLC 8, 62**
See also CAAS 1; CANR 2; CA 1-4R;
DLB 2

Bourne, Randolph S(illiman)
1886-1918 . . . . **TCLC 16**
See also CA 117; DLB 63

Bova, Ben(jamin William) 1932- . . . . **CLC 45**
See also CLR 3; CANR 11; CA 5-8R;
SATA 6; DLB-Y 81

Bowen, Elizabeth (Dorothea Cole)
1899-1973 . . . . . **CLC 1, 3, 6, 11, 15, 22;
SSC 3**
See also CAP 2; CA 17-18;
obituary CA 41-44R; DLB 15

Bowering, George 1935- . . . . **CLC 15, 47**
See also CANR 10; CA 21-24R; DLB 53

Bowering, Marilyn R(uthe) 1949- . . . **CLC 32**
See also CA 101

Bowers, Edgar 1924- . . . . **CLC 9**
See also CANR 24; CA 5-8R; DLB 5

Bowie, David 1947- . . . . **CLC 17**
See also Jones, David Robert

Bowles, Jane (Sydney) 1917-1973. . . . **CLC 3**
See also CAP 2; CA 19-20;
obituary CA 41-44R

Bowles, Paul (Frederick)
1910- . . . . **CLC 1, 2, 19, 53; SSC 3**
See also CAAS 1; CANR 1, 19; CA 1-4R;
DLB 5, 6

Box, Edgar 1925-
See Vidal, Gore

Boyd, William 1952- . . . . **CLC 28, 53**
See also CA 114, 120

Boyle, Kay 1903- . . **CLC 1, 5, 19, 58; SSC 5**
See also CAAS 1; CA 13-16R; DLB 4, 9, 48

Boyle, Patrick 19??- . . . . **CLC 19**

Boyle, Thomas Coraghessan
1948- . . . . **CLC 36, 55**
See also CA 120; DLB-Y 86

Brackenridge, Hugh Henry
1748-1816 . . . . **NCLC 7**
See also DLB 11, 37

Bradbury, Edward P. 1939-
See Moorcock, Michael

Bradbury, Malcolm (Stanley)
1932- . . . . **CLC 32, 61**
See also CANR 1; CA 1-4R; DLB 14

Author Index

Crowley, John   1942-
See also CA 61-64; DLB-Y 82

Crumb, Robert   1943- . . . . **CLC 17**
See also CA 106

Cryer, Gretchen   1936?- . . . . **CLC 21**
See also CA 114, 123

Csath, Geza   1887-1919 . . . . **TCLC 13**
See also CA 111

Cudlip, David   1933- . . . . **CLC 34**

Cullen, Countee   1903-1946 . . . . . **TCLC 4, 37**
See also CA 108, 124; SATA 18; DLB 4,
48, 51; CDALB 1917-1929

Cummings, E(dward) E(stlin)
1894-1962 . . . . **CLC 1, 3, 8, 12, 15**
See also CA 73-76; DLB 4, 48

Cunha, Euclides (Rodrigues) da
1866-1909 . . . . **TCLC 24**
See also CA 123

Cunningham, J(ames) V(incent)
1911-1985 . . . . **CLC 3, 31**
See also CANR 1; CA 1-4R;
obituary CA 115; DLB 5

Cunningham, Julia (Woolfolk)
1916- . . . . **CLC 12**
See also CANR 4, 19; CA 9-12R; SAAS 2;
SATA 1, 26

Cunningham, Michael   1952- . . . . **CLC 34**

Currie, Ellen   19??- . . . . **CLC 44**

Dabrowska, Maria (Szumska)
1889-1965 . . . . **CLC 15**
See also CA 106

Dabydeen, David   1956?- . . . . **CLC 34**
See also CA 106

Dacey, Philip   1939- . . . . **CLC 51**
See also CANR 14; CA 37-40R

Dagerman, Stig (Halvard)
1923-1954 . . . . **TCLC 17**
See also CA 117

Dahl, Roald   1916- . . . . **CLC 1, 6, 18**
See also CLR 1, 7; CANR 6; CA 1-4R;
SATA 1, 26

Dahlberg, Edward   1900-1977 . . . **CLC 1, 7, 14**
See also CA 9-12R; obituary CA 69-72;
DLB 48

Daly, Elizabeth   1878-1967 . . . . **CLC 52**
See also CAP 2; CA 23-24;
obituary CA 25-28R

Daly, Maureen   1921- . . . . **CLC 17**
See also McGivern, Maureen Daly
See also SAAS 1; SATA 2

Daniken, Erich von   1935-
See Von Daniken, Erich

Dannay, Frederic   1905-1982
See Queen, Ellery
See also CANR 1; CA 1-4R;
obituary CA 107

D'Annunzio, Gabriele
1863-1938 . . . . **TCLC 6, 40**
See also CA 104

Dante (Alighieri)
See Alighieri, Dante

Danziger, Paula   1944- . . . . **CLC 21**
See also CLR 20; CA 112, 115; SATA 30,
36

Dario, Ruben   1867-1916 . . . . **TCLC 4**
See also Sarmiento, Felix Ruben Garcia
See also CA 104

Darley, George   1795-1846 . . . . **NCLC 2**

Daryush, Elizabeth   1887-1977 . . . . **CLC 6, 19**
See also CANR 3; CA 49-52; DLB 20

Daudet, (Louis Marie) Alphonse
1840-1897 . . . . **NCLC 1**

Daumal, Rene   1908-1944 . . . . **TCLC 14**
See also CA 114

Davenport, Guy (Mattison, Jr.)
1927- . . . . **CLC 6, 14, 38**
See also CANR 23; CA 33-36R

Davidson, Donald (Grady)
1893-1968 . . . . **CLC 2, 13, 19**
See also CANR 4; CA 5-8R;
obituary CA 25-28R; DLB 45

Davidson, John   1857-1909 . . . . **TCLC 24**
See also CA 118; DLB 19

Davidson, Sara   1943- . . . . **CLC 9**
See also CA 81-84

Davie, Donald (Alfred)
1922- . . . . **CLC 5, 8, 10, 31**
See also CAAS 3; CANR 1; CA 1-4R;
DLB 27

Davies, Ray(mond Douglas)   1944- . . **CLC 21**
See also CA 116

Davies, Rhys   1903-1978 . . . . **CLC 23**
See also CANR 4; CA 9-12R;
obituary CA 81-84

Davies, (William) Robertson
1913- . . . . **CLC 2, 7, 13, 25, 42**
See also CANR 17; CA 33-36R; DLB 68

Davies, W(illiam) H(enry)
1871-1940 . . . . **TCLC 5**
See also CA 104; DLB 19

Davis, H(arold) L(enoir)
1896-1960 . . . . **CLC 49**
See also obituary CA 89-92; DLB 9

Davis, Rebecca (Blaine) Harding
1831-1910 . . . . **TCLC 6**
See also CA 104; DLB 74

Davis, Richard Harding
1864-1916 . . . . **TCLC 24**
See also CA 114; DLB 12, 23

Davison, Frank Dalby   1893-1970 . . . **CLC 15**
See also obituary CA 116

Davison, Peter   1928- . . . . **CLC 28**
See also CAAS 4; CANR 3; CA 9-12R;
DLB 5

Davys, Mary   1674-1732 . . . . **LC 1**
See also DLB 39

Dawson, Fielding   1930- . . . . **CLC 6**
See also CA 85-88

Day, Clarence (Shepard, Jr.)
1874-1935 . . . . **TCLC 25**
See also CA 108; DLB 11

Day, Thomas   1748-1789 . . . . **LC 1**
See also YABC 1; DLB 39

Day Lewis, C(ecil)
1904-1972 . . . . **CLC 1, 6, 10**
See also CAP 1; CA 15-16;
obituary CA 33-36R; DLB 15, 20

Dazai Osamu   1909-1948 . . . . **TCLC 11**
See also Tsushima Shuji

De Crayencour, Marguerite   1903-1987
See Yourcenar, Marguerite

Deer, Sandra   1940- . . . . **CLC 45**

Defoe, Daniel   1660?-1731 . . . . **LC 1**
See also SATA 22; DLB 39

De Hartog, Jan   1914- . . . . **CLC 19**
See also CANR 1; CA 1-4R

Deighton, Len   1929- . . . . **CLC 4, 7, 22, 46**
See also Deighton, Leonard Cyril

Deighton, Leonard Cyril   1929-
See Deighton, Len
See also CANR 19; CA 9-12R

De la Mare, Walter (John)
1873-1956 . . . . **TCLC 4**
See also CLR 23; CA 110; SATA 16;
DLB 19

Delaney, Shelagh   1939- . . . . **CLC 29**
See also CA 17-20R; DLB 13

Delany, Mary (Granville Pendarves)
1700-1788 . . . . **LC 12**

Delany, Samuel R(ay, Jr.)
1942- . . . . **CLC 8, 14, 38**
See also CA 81-84; DLB 8, 33

De la Roche, Mazo   1885-1961 . . . . . **CLC 14**
See also CA 85-88; DLB 68

Delbanco, Nicholas (Franklin)
1942- . . . . **CLC 6, 13**
See also CAAS 2; CA 17-20R; DLB 6

del Castillo, Michel   1933- . . . . **CLC 38**
See also CA 109

Deledda, Grazia   1871-1936 . . . . **TCLC 23**
See also CA 123

Delibes (Setien), Miguel   1920- . . . **CLC 8, 18**
See also CANR 1; CA 45-48

DeLillo, Don
1936- . . . . **CLC 8, 10, 13, 27, 39, 54**
See also CANR 21; CA 81-84; DLB 6

De Lisser, H(erbert) G(eorge)
1878-1944 . . . . **TCLC 12**
See also CA 109

Deloria, Vine (Victor), Jr.   1933- . . . . **CLC 21**
See also CANR 5, 20; CA 53-56; SATA 21

Del Vecchio, John M(ichael)
1947- . . . . **CLC 29**
See also CA 110

de Man, Paul   1919-1983 . . . . **CLC 55**
See also obituary CA 111; DLB 67

De Marinis, Rick   1934- . . . . **CLC 54**
See also CANR 9, 25; CA 57-60

Demby, William   1922- . . . . **CLC 53**
See also CA 81-84; DLB 33

Denby, Edwin (Orr)   1903-1983 . . . . . **CLC 48**
See also obituary CA 110

Dennis, John   1657-1734 . . . . **LC 11**

Dennis, Nigel (Forbes)   1912- . . . . **CLC 8**
See also CA 25-28R; DLB 13, 15

De Palma, Brian   1940- . . . . **CLC 20**
See also CA 109

De Quincey, Thomas   1785-1859 . . . **NCLC 4**

Freeling, Nicolas 1927- .... CLC 38
See also CANR 1, 17; CA 49-52

Freeman, Douglas Southall
1886-1953 .... TCLC 11
See also CA 109; DLB 17

Freeman, Judith 1946- .... CLC 55

Freeman, Mary (Eleanor) Wilkins
1852-1930 .... TCLC 9; SSC 1
See also CA 106; DLB 12

Freeman, R(ichard) Austin
1862-1943 .... TCLC 21
See also CA 113; DLB 70

French, Marilyn 1929- ...... CLC 10, 18, 60
See also CANR 3; CA 69-72

Freneau, Philip Morin 1752-1832 .. NCLC 1
See also DLB 37, 43

Friedman, B(ernard) H(arper)
1926- .... CLC 7
See also CANR 3; CA 1-4R

Friedman, Bruce Jay 1930- .... CLC 3, 5, 56
See also CANR 25; CA 9-12R; DLB 2, 28

Friel, Brian 1929- .... CLC 5, 42, 59
See also CA 21-24R; DLB 13

Friis-Baastad, Babbis (Ellinor)
1921-1970 .... CLC 12
See also CA 17-20R; SATA 7

Frisch, Max (Rudolf)
1911- .... CLC 3, 9, 14, 18, 32, 44
See also CA 85-88; DLB 69

Fromentin, Eugene (Samuel Auguste)
1820-1876 .... NCLC 10

Frost, Robert (Lee)
1874-1963 ... CLC 1, 3, 4, 9, 10, 13, 15,
26, 34, 44; PC 1
See also CA 89-92; SATA 14; DLB 54;
DLB-DS 7; CDALB 1917-1929

Fry, Christopher 1907- .... CLC 2, 10, 14
See also CANR 9; CA 17-20R; DLB 13

Frye, (Herman) Northrop 1912- .... CLC 24
See also CANR 8; CA 5-8R

Fuchs, Daniel 1909- .... CLC 8, 22
See also CAAS 5; CA 81-84; DLB 9, 26, 28

Fuchs, Daniel 1934- .... CLC 34
See also CANR 14; CA 37-40R

Fuentes, Carlos
1928- ...... CLC 3, 8, 10, 13, 22, 41, 60
See also CANR 10; CA 69-72

Fugard, Athol 1932- ... CLC 5, 9, 14, 25, 40
See also CA 85-88

Fugard, Sheila 1932- .... CLC 48
See also CA 125

Fuller, Charles (H., Jr.)
1939- .... CLC 25; DC 1
See also CA 108, 112; DLB 38

Fuller, John (Leopold) 1937- .... CLC 62
See also CANR 9; CA 21-22R; DLB 40

Fuller, (Sarah) Margaret
1810-1850 .... NCLC 5
See also Ossoli, Sarah Margaret (Fuller
marchesa d')
See also DLB 1, 59, 73; CDALB 1640-1865

Fuller, Roy (Broadbent) 1912- .... CLC 4, 28
See also CA 5-8R; DLB 15, 20

Fulton, Alice 1952- .... CLC 52
See also CA 116

Furphy, Joseph 1843-1912 .... TCLC 25

Futrelle, Jacques 1875-1912 ..... TCLC 19
See also CA 113

Gaboriau, Emile 1835-1873 ...... NCLC 14

Gadda, Carlo Emilio 1893-1973 .... CLC 11
See also CA 89-92

Gaddis, William
1922- .... CLC 1, 3, 6, 8, 10, 19, 43
See also CAAS 4; CANR 21; CA 17-20R;
DLB 2

Gaines, Ernest J. 1933- ...... CLC 3, 11, 18
See also CANR 6, 24; CA 9-12R; DLB 2,
33; DLB-Y 80

Gale, Zona 1874-1938 .... TCLC 7
See also CA 105; DLB 9

Gallagher, Tess 1943- .... CLC 18, 63
See also CA 106

Gallant, Mavis
1922- .... CLC 7, 18, 38; SSC 5
See also CA 69-72; DLB 53

Gallant, Roy A(rthur) 1924- .... CLC 17
See also CANR 4; CA 5-8R; SATA 4

Gallico, Paul (William) 1897-1976 ... CLC 2
See also CA 5-8R; obituary CA 69-72;
SATA 13; DLB 9

Galsworthy, John 1867-1933 ...... TCLC 1
See also CA 104; DLB 10, 34

Galt, John 1779-1839 .... NCLC 1

Galvin, James 1951- .... CLC 38
See also CANR 26; CA 108

Gamboa, Frederico 1864-1939 ..... TCLC 36

Gann, Ernest K(ellogg) 1910- ...... CLC 23
See also CANR 1; CA 1-4R

Garcia Lorca, Federico
1899-1936 .... TCLC 1, 7
See also CA 104

Garcia Marquez, Gabriel (Jose)
1928- .... CLC 2, 3, 8, 10, 15, 27, 47, 55
See also CANR 10; CA 33-36R

Gardam, Jane 1928- .... CLC 43
See also CLR 12; CANR 2, 18; CA 49-52;
SATA 28, 39; DLB 14

Gardner, Herb 1934- .... CLC 44

Gardner, John (Champlin, Jr.)
1933-1982 .... CLC 2, 3, 5, 7, 8, 10, 18,
28, 34; SSC 7
See also CA 65-68; obituary CA 107;
obituary SATA 31, 40; DLB 2; DLB-Y 82

Gardner, John (Edmund) 1926- .... CLC 30
See also CANR 15; CA 103

Garfield, Leon 1921- .... CLC 12
See also CA 17-20R; SATA 1, 32

Garland, (Hannibal) Hamlin
1860-1940 .... TCLC 3
See also CA 104; DLB 12, 71

Garneau, Hector (de) Saint Denys
1912-1943 .... TCLC 13
See also CA 111

Garner, Alan 1935- .... CLC 17
See also CLR 20; CANR 15; CA 73-76;
SATA 18

Garner, Hugh 1913-1979 .... CLC 13
See also CA 69-72; DLB 68

Garnett, David 1892-1981 .... CLC 3
See also CANR 17; CA 5-8R;
obituary CA 103; DLB 34

Garrett, George (Palmer, Jr.)
1929- .... CLC 3, 11, 51
See also CAAS 5; CANR 1; CA 1-4R;
DLB 2, 5; DLB-Y 83

Garrick, David 1717-1779 .... LC 15
See also DLB 84

Garrigue, Jean 1914-1972 .... CLC 2, 8
See also CANR 20; CA 5-8R;
obituary CA 37-40R

Gary, Romain 1914-1980 .... CLC 25
See also Kacew, Romain

Gascar, Pierre 1916- .... CLC 11
See also Fournier, Pierre

Gascoyne, David (Emery) 1916- .... CLC 45
See also CANR 10; CA 65-68; DLB 20

Gaskell, Elizabeth Cleghorn
1810-1865 .... NCLC 5
See also DLB 21

Gass, William H(oward)
1924- .... CLC 1, 2, 8, 11, 15, 39
See also CA 17-20R; DLB 2

Gautier, Theophile 1811-1872 ..... NCLC 1

Gaye, Marvin (Pentz) 1939-1984 ... CLC 26
See also obituary CA 112

Gebler, Carlo (Ernest) 1954- .... CLC 39
See also CA 119

Gee, Maggie 19??- .... CLC 57

Gee, Maurice (Gough) 1931- .... CLC 29
See also CA 97-100; SATA 46

Gelbart, Larry 1923?- .... CLC 21, 61
See also CA 73-76

Gelber, Jack 1932- .... CLC 1, 6, 14, 60
See also CANR 2; CA 1-4R; DLB 7

Gellhorn, Martha (Ellis) 1908- .. CLC 14, 60
See also CA 77-80; DLB-Y 82

Genet, Jean
1910-1986 ... CLC 1, 2, 5, 10, 14, 44, 46
See also CANR 18; CA 13-16R; DLB 72;
DLB-Y 86

Gent, Peter 1942- .... CLC 29
See also CA 89-92; DLB 72; DLB-Y 82

George, Jean Craighead 1919- ...... CLC 35
See also CLR 1; CA 5-8R; SATA 2;
DLB 52

George, Stefan (Anton)
1868-1933 .... TCLC 2, 14
See also CA 104

Gerhardi, William (Alexander) 1895-1977
See Gerhardie, William (Alexander)

Gerhardie, William (Alexander)
1895-1977 .... CLC 5
See also CANR 18; CA 25-28R;
obituary CA 73-76; DLB 36

Gertler, T(rudy) 1946?- .... CLC 34
See also CA 116

Gessner, Friedrike Victoria 1910-1980
See Adamson, Joy(-Friederike Victoria)

Hugo, Richard F(ranklin)
1923-1982 . . . . **CLC 6, 18, 32**
See also CANR 3; CA 49-52;
obituary CA 108; DLB 5

Hugo, Victor Marie
1802-1885 . . . . **NCLC 3, 10, 21**
See also SATA 47

Huidobro, Vicente 1893-1948 . . . . . **TCLC 31**

Hulme, Keri 1947- . . . . **CLC 39**
See also CA 123

Hulme, T(homas) E(rnest)
1883-1917 . . . . **TCLC 21**
See also CA 117; DLB 19

Hume, David 1711-1776. . . . . **LC 7**

Humphrey, William 1924- . . . . **CLC 45**
See also CA 77-80; DLB 6

Humphreys, Emyr (Owen) 1919-. . . . **CLC 47**
See also CANR 3, 24; CA 5-8R; DLB 15

Humphreys, Josephine 1945-. . . . **CLC 34, 57**
See also CA 121, 127

Hunt, E(verette) Howard (Jr.)
1918- . . . . **CLC 3**
See also CANR 2; CA 45-48

Hunt, (James Henry) Leigh
1784-1859 . . . . **NCLC 1**

Hunter, Evan 1926- . . . . **CLC 11, 31**
See also CANR 5; CA 5-8R; SATA 25;
DLB-Y 82

Hunter, Kristin (Eggleston) 1931-. . . **CLC 35**
See also CLR 3; CANR 13; CA 13-16R;
SATA 12; DLB 33

Hunter, Mollie (Maureen McIlwraith)
1922- . . . . **CLC 21**
See also McIlwraith, Maureen Mollie
Hunter

Hunter, Robert ?-1734 . . . . **LC 7**

Hurston, Zora Neale
1891-1960 . . . . . . **CLC 7, 30, 61; SSC 4**
See also CA 85-88; DLB 51, 86

Huston, John (Marcellus)
1906-1987 . . . . **CLC 20**
See also CA 73-76; obituary CA 123;
DLB 26

Huxley, Aldous (Leonard)
1894-1963 . . **CLC 1, 3, 4, 5, 8, 11, 18, 35**
See also CA 85-88; DLB 36

Huysmans, Charles Marie Georges
1848-1907
See Huysmans, Joris-Karl
See also CA 104

Huysmans, Joris-Karl 1848-1907 . . . **TCLC 7**
See also Huysmans, Charles Marie Georges

Hwang, David Henry 1957-. . . . . . . **CLC 55**
See also CA 127

Hyde, Anthony 1946?- . . . . **CLC 42**

Hyde, Margaret O(ldroyd) 1917- . . . **CLC 21**
See also CLR 23; CANR 1; CA 1-4R;
SATA 1, 42

Ian, Janis 1951- . . . . **CLC 21**
See also CA 105

Ibarguengoitia, Jorge 1928-1983 . . . . **CLC 37**
See also obituary CA 113, 124

Ibsen, Henrik (Johan)
1828-1906 . . . . **TCLC 2, 8, 16, 37**
See also CA 104

Ibuse, Masuji 1898- . . . . **CLC 22**

Ichikawa, Kon 1915-. . . . . **CLC 20**
See also CA 121

Idle, Eric 1943-
See Monty Python
See also CA 116

Ignatow, David 1914- . . . . . . **CLC 4, 7, 14, 40**
See also CAAS 3; CA 9-12R; DLB 5

Ihimaera, Witi (Tame) 1944- . . . . **CLC 46**
See also CA 77-80

Ilf, Ilya 1897-1937 . . . . **TCLC 21**

Immermann, Karl (Lebrecht)
1796-1840 . . . . **NCLC 4**

Ingalls, Rachel 19??-. . . . . **CLC 42**
See also CA 123

Ingamells, Rex 1913-1955 . . . . **TCLC 35**

Inge, William (Motter)
1913-1973 . . . . **CLC 1, 8, 19**
See also CA 9-12R; DLB 7;
CDALB 1941-1968

Innaurato, Albert 1948- . . . . **CLC 21, 60**
See also CA 115, 122

Innes, Michael 1906-
See Stewart, J(ohn) I(nnes) M(ackintosh)

Ionesco, Eugene
1912- . . . . **CLC 1, 4, 6, 9, 11, 15, 41**
See also CA 9-12R; SATA 7

Iqbal, Muhammad 1877-1938 . . . . . **TCLC 28**

Irving, John (Winslow)
1942- . . . . **CLC 13, 23, 38**
See also CA 25-28R; DLB 6; DLB-Y 82

Irving, Washington
1783-1859 . . . . **NCLC 2, 19; SSC 2**
See also YABC 2; DLB 3, 11, 30, 59, 73,
74; CDALB 1640-1865

Isaacs, Susan 1943- . . . . **CLC 32**
See also CANR 20; CA 89-92

Isherwood, Christopher (William Bradshaw)
1904-1986 . . . . . . **CLC 1, 9, 11, 14, 44**
See also CA 13-16R; obituary CA 117;
DLB 15; DLB-Y 86

Ishiguro, Kazuo 1954- . . . . . . **CLC 27, 56, 59**
See also CA 120

Ishikawa Takuboku 1885-1912 . . . . **TCLC 15**
See also CA 113

Iskander, Fazil (Abdulovich)
1929- . . . . **CLC 47**
See also CA 102

Ivanov, Vyacheslav (Ivanovich)
1866-1949 . . . . **TCLC 33**
See also CA 122

Ivask, Ivar (Vidrik) 1927- . . . . **CLC 14**
See also CANR 24; CA 37-40R

Jackson, Jesse 1908-1983 . . . . **CLC 12**
See also CA 25-28R; obituary CA 109;
SATA 2, 29, 48

Jackson, Laura (Riding) 1901-
See Riding, Laura
See also CA 65-68; DLB 48

Jackson, Shirley 1919-1965 . . . . . **CLC 11, 60**
See also CANR 4; CA 1-4R;
obituary CA 25-28R; SATA 2; DLB 6;
CDALB 1941-1968

Jacob, (Cyprien) Max 1876-1944 . . . **TCLC 6**
See also CA 104

Jacob, Piers A(nthony) D(illingham) 1934-
See Anthony (Jacob), Piers
See also CA 21-24R

Jacobs, Jim 1942- and **Casey, Warren**
1942- . . . . **CLC 12**

Jacobs, Jim 1942-
See Jacobs, Jim and Casey, Warren
See also CA 97-100

Jacobs, W(illiam) W(ymark)
1863-1943 . . . . **TCLC 22**
See also CA 121

Jacobsen, Josephine 1908-. . . . . **CLC 48**
See also CANR 23; CA 33-36R

Jacobson, Dan 1929- . . . . **CLC 4, 14**
See also CANR 2, 25; CA 1-4R; DLB 14

Jagger, Mick 1944-. . . . . **CLC 17**

Jakes, John (William) 1932- . . . . . . **CLC 29**
See also CANR 10; CA 57-60; DLB-Y 83

James, C(yril) L(ionel) R(obert)
1901-1989 . . . . **CLC 33**
See also CA 117, 125

James, Daniel 1911-1988
See Santiago, Danny
See also obituary CA 125

James, Henry (Jr.)
1843-1916 . . . . **TCLC 2, 11, 24, 40**
See also CA 104, 132; DLB 12, 71, 74;
CDALB 1865-1917

James, M(ontague) R(hodes)
1862-1936 . . . . **TCLC 6**
See also CA 104

James, P(hyllis) D(orothy)
1920- . . . . **CLC 18, 46**
See also CANR 17; CA 21-24R

James, William 1842-1910 . . . . . **TCLC 15, 32**
See also CA 109

Jami, Nur al-Din 'Abd al-Rahman
1414-1492 . . . . **LC 9**

Jandl, Ernst 1925- . . . . **CLC 34**

Janowitz, Tama 1957- . . . . **CLC 43**
See also CA 106

Jarrell, Randall
1914-1965 . . . . **CLC 1, 2, 6, 9, 13, 49**
See also CLR 6; CANR 6; CA 5-8R;
obituary CA 25-28R; CABS 2; SATA 7;
DLB 48, 52; CDALB 1941-1968

Jarry, Alfred 1873-1907. . . . . . . **TCLC 2, 14**
See also CA 104

Jeake, Samuel, Jr. 1889-1973
See Aiken, Conrad

Jean Paul 1763-1825 . . . . **NCLC 7**

Jeffers, (John) Robinson
1887-1962 . . . . **CLC 2, 3, 11, 15, 54**
See also CA 85-88; DLB 45

Jefferson, Thomas 1743-1826 . . . . **NCLC 11**
See also DLB 31; CDALB 1640-1865

Jellicoe, (Patricia) Ann 1927- . . . . . . **CLC 27**
See also CA 85-88; DLB 13

Kaufman, Bob (Garnell)
　　1925-1986 .... **CLC 49**
　　See also CANR 22; CA 41-44R;
　　obituary CA 118; DLB 16, 41

Kaufman, George S(imon)
　　1889-1961 .... **CLC 38**
　　See also CA 108; obituary CA 93-96; DLB 7

Kaufman, Sue 1926-1977 .... **CLC 3, 8**
　　See also Barondess, Sue K(aufman)

Kavan, Anna 1904-1968 .... **CLC 5, 13**
　　See also Edmonds, Helen (Woods)
　　See also CANR 6; CA 5-8R

Kavanagh, Patrick (Joseph Gregory)
　　1905-1967 .... **CLC 22**
　　See also CA 123; obituary CA 25-28R;
　　DLB 15, 20

Kawabata, Yasunari
　　1899-1972 .... **CLC 2, 5, 9, 18**
　　See also CA 93-96; obituary CA 33-36R

Kaye, M(ary) M(argaret) 1909?- .... **CLC 28**
　　See also CANR 24; CA 89-92

Kaye, Mollie 1909?-
　　See Kaye, M(ary) M(argaret)

Kaye-Smith, Sheila 1887-1956..... **TCLC 20**
　　See also CA 118; DLB 36

Kazan, Elia 1909- .... **CLC 6, 16, 63**
　　See also CA 21-24R

Kazantzakis, Nikos
　　1885?-1957............. **TCLC 2, 5, 33**
　　See also CA 105

Kazin, Alfred 1915- .... **CLC 34, 38**
　　See also CAAS 7; CANR 1; CA 1-4R

Keane, Mary Nesta (Skrine) 1904-
　　See Keane, Molly
　　See also CA 108, 114

Keane, Molly 1904- .... **CLC 31**
　　See also Keane, Mary Nesta (Skrine)

Keates, Jonathan 19??-........... **CLC 34**

Keaton, Buster 1895-1966 .... **CLC 20**

Keaton, Joseph Francis 1895-1966
　　See Keaton, Buster

Keats, John 1795-1821..... **NCLC 8; PC 1**

Keene, Donald 1922- .... **CLC 34**
　　See also CANR 5; CA 1-4R

Keillor, Garrison 1942- .... **CLC 40**
　　See also Keillor, Gary (Edward)
　　See also CA 111; DLB 87

Keillor, Gary (Edward)
　　See Keillor, Garrison
　　See also CA 111, 117

Kell, Joseph 1917-
　　See Burgess (Wilson, John) Anthony

Keller, Gottfried 1819-1890 ...... **NCLC 2**

Kellerman, Jonathan (S.) 1949-..... **CLC 44**
　　See also CA 106

Kelley, William Melvin 1937-...... **CLC 22**
　　See also CA 77-80; DLB 33

Kellogg, Marjorie 1922-........... **CLC 2**
　　See also CA 81-84

Kelly, M. T. 1947- .... **CLC 55**
　　See also CANR 19; CA 97-100

Kelman, James 1946-............. **CLC 58**

Kemal, Yashar 1922- .... **CLC 14, 29**
　　See also CA 89-92

Kemble, Fanny 1809-1893 .... **NCLC 18**
　　See also DLB 32

Kemelman, Harry 1908-........... **CLC 2**
　　See also CANR 6; CA 9-12R; DLB 28

Kempe, Margery 1373?-1440? .... **LC 6**

Kempis, Thomas á 1380-1471 ...... **LC 11**

Kendall, Henry 1839-1882....... **NCLC 12**

Keneally, Thomas (Michael)
　　1935- ...... **CLC 5, 8, 10, 14, 19, 27, 43**
　　See also CANR 10; CA 85-88

Kennedy, John Pendleton
　　1795-1870 .... **NCLC 2**
　　See also DLB 3

Kennedy, Joseph Charles 1929-...... **CLC 8**
　　See also Kennedy, X. J.
　　See also CANR 4; CA 1-4R; SATA 14

Kennedy, William (Joseph)
　　1928-............**CLC 6, 28, 34, 53**
　　See also CANR 14; CA 85-88; DLB-Y 85;
　　AAYA 1

Kennedy, X. J. 1929- .... **CLC 8, 42**
　　See also Kennedy, Joseph Charles
　　See also DLB 5

Kerouac, Jack
　　1922-1969 .... **CLC 1, 2, 3, 5, 14, 29, 61**
　　See also Kerouac, Jean-Louis Lebris de
　　See also DLB 2, 16; DLB-DS 3;
　　CDALB 1941-1968

Kerouac, Jean-Louis Lebris de 1922-1969
　　See Kerouac, Jack
　　See also CA 5-8R; obituary CA 25-28R;
　　CDALB 1941-1968

Kerr, Jean 1923-................. **CLC 22**
　　See also CANR 7; CA 5-8R

Kerr, M. E. 1927-............. **CLC 12, 35**
　　See also Meaker, Marijane
　　See also SAAS 1

Kerr, Robert 1970?- .... **CLC 55, 59**

Kerrigan, (Thomas) Anthony
　　1918-...................... **CLC 4, 6**
　　See also CANR 4; CA 49-52

Kesey, Ken (Elton)
　　1935-........... **CLC 1, 3, 6, 11, 46**
　　See also CANR 22; CA 1-4R; DLB 2, 16

Kesselring, Joseph (Otto)
　　1902-1967 .... **CLC 45**

Kessler, Jascha (Frederick) 1929-.... **CLC 4**
　　See also CANR 8; CA 17-20R

Kettelkamp, Larry 1933-........... **CLC 12**
　　See also CANR 16; CA 29-32R; SAAS 3;
　　SATA 2

Kherdian, David 1931-........... **CLC 6, 9**
　　See also CAAS 2; CA 21-24R; SATA 16

Khlebnikov, Velimir (Vladimirovich)
　　1885-1922 .... **TCLC 20**
　　See also CA 117

Khodasevich, Vladislav (Felitsianovich)
　　1886-1939 .... **TCLC 15**
　　See also CA 115

Kielland, Alexander (Lange)
　　1849-1906 .... **TCLC 5**
　　See also CA 104

Kiely, Benedict 1919-.......... **CLC 23, 43**
　　See also CANR 2; CA 1-4R; DLB 15

Kienzle, William X(avier) 1928- .... **CLC 25**
　　See also CAAS 1; CANR 9; CA 93-96

Killens, John Oliver 1916-......... **CLC 10**
　　See also CAAS 2; CANR 26; CA 77-80,
　　123; DLB 33

Killigrew, Anne 1660-1685.......... **LC 4**

Kincaid, Jamaica 1949?- .... **CLC 43**
　　See also CA 125

King, Francis (Henry) 1923- ..... **CLC 8, 53**
　　See also CANR 1; CA 1-4R; DLB 15

King, Stephen (Edwin)
　　1947-............. **CLC 12, 26, 37, 61**
　　See also CANR 1; CA 61-64; SATA 9, 55;
　　DLB-Y 80

Kingman, (Mary) Lee 1919-........ **CLC 17**
　　See also Natti, (Mary) Lee
　　See also CA 5-8R; SAAS 3; SATA 1

Kingsley, Sidney 1906-............ **CLC 44**
　　See also CA 85-88; DLB 7

Kingsolver, Barbara 1955-......... **CLC 55**

Kingston, Maxine Hong
　　1940-............... **CLC 12, 19, 58**
　　See also CANR 13; CA 69-72; SATA 53;
　　DLB-Y 80

Kinnell, Galway
　　1927-........... **CLC 1, 2, 3, 5, 13, 29**
　　See also CANR 10; CA 9-12R; DLB 5;
　　DLB-Y 87

Kinsella, Thomas 1928-...... **CLC 4, 19, 43**
　　See also CANR 15; CA 17-20R; DLB 27

Kinsella, W(illiam) P(atrick)
　　1935-.................... **CLC 27, 43**
　　See also CAAS 7; CANR 21; CA 97-100

Kipling, (Joseph) Rudyard
　　1865-1936 .... **TCLC 8, 17; SSC 5**
　　See also YABC 2; CA 105, 120; DLB 19, 34

Kirkup, James 1918- .... **CLC 1**
　　See also CAAS 4; CANR 2; CA 1-4R;
　　SATA 12; DLB 27

Kirkwood, James 1930-1989 .... **CLC 9**
　　See also CANR 6; CA 1-4R

Kis, Danilo 1935-1989 .... **CLC 57**
　　See also CA 118, 129; brief entry CA 109

Kivi, Aleksis 1834-1872........ **NCLC 30**

Kizer, Carolyn (Ashley) 1925-... **CLC 15, 39**
　　See also CAAS 5; CANR 24; CA 65-68;
　　DLB 5

Klappert, Peter 1942-............. **CLC 57**
　　See also CA 33-36R; DLB 5

Klausner, Amos 1939-
　　See Oz, Amos

Klein, A(braham) M(oses)
　　1909-1972 .... **CLC 19**
　　See also CA 101; obituary CA 37-40R;
　　DLB 68

Klein, Norma 1938-1989 .... **CLC 30**
　　See also CLR 2; CANR 15; CA 41-44R;
　　SAAS 1; SATA 7

Klein, T.E.D. 19??-.............. **CLC 34**
　　See also CA 119

Kleist, Heinrich von 1777-1811.... **NCLC 2**

Klima, Ivan 1931-. . . . . CLC 56
See also CANR 17; CA 25-28R

Klimentev, Andrei Platonovich 1899-1951
See Platonov, Andrei (Platonovich)
See also CA 108

Klinger, Friedrich Maximilian von
1752-1831 . . . . NCLC 1

Klopstock, Friedrich Gottlieb
1724-1803 . . . . NCLC 11

Knebel, Fletcher 1911-. . . . . CLC 14
See also CAAS 3; CANR 1; CA 1-4R;
SATA 36

Knight, Etheridge 1931-. . . . . CLC 40
See also CANR 23; CA 21-24R; DLB 41

Knight, Sarah Kemble 1666-1727 . . . . . LC 7
See also DLB 24

Knowles, John 1926- . . . . . . CLC 1, 4, 10, 26
See also CA 17-20R; SATA 8; DLB 6

Koch, C(hristopher) J(ohn) 1932- . . . CLC 42

Koch, Kenneth 1925- . . . . CLC 5, 8, 44
See also CANR 6; CA 1-4R; DLB 5

Kochanowski, Jan 1530-1584. . . . . . . LC 10

Kock, Charles Paul de
1794-1871 . . . . NCLC 16

Koestler, Arthur
1905-1983 . . . . CLC 1, 3, 6, 8, 15, 33
See also CANR 1; CA 1-4R;
obituary CA 109; DLB-Y 83

Kohout, Pavel 1928-. . . . . CLC 13
See also CANR 3; CA 45-48

Kolmar, Gertrud 1894-1943. . . . . . TCLC 40

Konigsberg, Allen Stewart 1935-
See Allen, Woody

Konrad, Gyorgy 1933-. . . . . CLC 4, 10
See also CA 85-88

Konwicki, Tadeusz 1926-. . . . . CLC 8, 28, 54
See also CA 101

Kopit, Arthur (Lee) 1937- . . . . CLC 1, 18, 33
See also CA 81-84; DLB 7

Kops, Bernard 1926-. . . . . CLC 4
See also CA 5-8R; DLB 13

Kornbluth, C(yril) M. 1923-1958. . . . TCLC 8
See also CA 105; DLB 8

Korolenko, Vladimir (Galaktionovich)
1853-1921 . . . . TCLC 22
See also CA 121

Kosinski, Jerzy (Nikodem)
1933-. . . . . . . CLC 1, 2, 3, 6, 10, 15, 53
See also CANR 9; CA 17-20R; DLB 2;
DLB-Y 82

Kostelanetz, Richard (Cory) 1940- . . CLC 28
See also CA 13-16R

Kostrowitzki, Wilhelm Apollinaris de
1880-1918
See Apollinaire, Guillaume
See also CA 104

Kotlowitz, Robert 1924-. . . . . CLC 4
See also CA 33-36R

Kotzebue, August (Friedrich Ferdinand) von
1761-1819 . . . . NCLC 25

Kotzwinkle, William 1938- . . . CLC 5, 14, 35
See also CLR 6; CANR 3; CA 45-48;
SATA 24

Kozol, Jonathan 1936-. . . . . CLC 17
See also CANR 16; CA 61-64

Kozoll, Michael 1940?-. . . . . CLC 35

Kramer, Kathryn 19??-. . . . . CLC 34

Kramer, Larry 1935- . . . . CLC 42
See also CA 124, 126

Krasicki, Ignacy 1735-1801. . . . . NCLC 8

Krasinski, Zygmunt 1812-1859 . . . . NCLC 4

Kraus, Karl 1874-1936. . . . . TCLC 5
See also CA 104

Kreve, Vincas 1882-1954 . . . . TCLC 27

Kristofferson, Kris 1936-. . . . . CLC 26
See also CA 104

Krizanc, John 1956-. . . . . CLC 57

Krleza, Miroslav 1893-1981. . . . . CLC 8
See also CA 97-100; obituary CA 105

Kroetsch, Robert (Paul)
1927-. . . . . CLC 5, 23,57
See also CANR 8; CA 17-20R; DLB 53

Kroetz, Franz Xaver 1946- . . . . CLC 41

Kropotkin, Peter 1842-1921. . . . . . TCLC 36
See also CA 119

Krotkov, Yuri 1917-. . . . . CLC 19
See also CA 102

Krumgold, Joseph (Quincy)
1908-1980 . . . . CLC 12
See also CANR 7; CA 9-12R;
obituary CA 101; SATA 48;
obituary SATA 23

Krutch, Joseph Wood 1893-1970. . . . CLC 24
See also CANR 4; CA 1-4R;
obituary CA 25-28R; DLB 63

Krylov, Ivan Andreevich
1768?-1844. . . . . NCLC 1

Kubin, Alfred 1877-1959 . . . . TCLC 23
See also CA 112

Kubrick, Stanley 1928-. . . . . CLC 16
See also CA 81-84; DLB 26

Kumin, Maxine (Winokur)
1925-. . . . . CLC 5, 13, 28
See also CANR 1, 21; CA 1-4R; SATA 12;
DLB 5

Kundera, Milan 1929- . . . . . CLC 4, 9, 19, 32
See also CANR 19; CA 85-88

Kunitz, Stanley J(asspon)
1905-. . . . . CLC 6, 11, 14
See also CA 41-44R; DLB 48

Kunze, Reiner 1933-. . . . . CLC 10
See also CA 93-96; DLB 75

Kuprin, Aleksandr (Ivanovich)
1870-1938 . . . . TCLC 5
See also CA 104

Kurosawa, Akira 1910-. . . . . CLC 16
See also CA 101

Kuttner, Henry 1915-1958. . . . . . . TCLC 10
See also CA 107; DLB 8

Kuzma, Greg 1944-. . . . . CLC 7
See also CA 33-36R

Kuzmin, Mikhail 1872?-1936. . . . . TCLC 40

Labrunie, Gerard 1808-1855
See Nerval, Gerard de

Laclos, Pierre Ambroise Francois Choderlos
de 1741-1803 . . . . NCLC 4

La Fayette, Marie (Madelaine Pioche de la
Vergne, Comtesse) de
1634-1693 . . . . LC 2

Lafayette, Rene
See Hubbard, L(afayette) Ron(ald)

Laforgue, Jules 1860-1887. . . . . NCLC 5

Lagerkvist, Par (Fabian)
1891-1974 . . . . CLC 7, 10, 13, 54
See also CA 85-88; obituary CA 49-52

Lagerlof, Selma (Ottiliana Lovisa)
1858-1940 . . . . TCLC 4, 36
See also CLR 7; CA 108; SATA 15

La Guma, (Justin) Alex(ander)
1925-1985 . . . . CLC 19
See also CA 49-52; obituary CA 118

Lamartine, Alphonse (Marie Louis Prat) de
1790-1869 . . . . NCLC 11

Lamb, Charles 1775-1834. . . . . NCLC 10
See also SATA 17

Lamming, George (William)
1927-. CLC 2, 4
See also CANR 26; CA 85-88

LaMoore, Louis Dearborn 1908?-
See L'Amour, Louis (Dearborn)

L'Amour, Louis (Dearborn)
1908-1988 . . . . CLC 25, 55
See also CANR 3; CA 1-4R;
obituary CA 125; DLB-Y 80

Lampedusa, (Prince) Giuseppe (Maria
Fabrizio) Tomasi di
1896-1957 . . . . TCLC 13
See also CA 111

Lampman, Archibald 1861-1899 . . NCLC 25

Lancaster, Bruce 1896-1963. . . . . . . CLC 36
See also CAP 1; CA 9-12; SATA 9

Landis, John (David) 1950-. . . . . CLC 26
See also CA 112

Landolfi, Tommaso 1908-1979. . . CLC 11, 49
See also obituary CA 117

Landon, Letitia Elizabeth
1802-1838 . . . . NCLC 15

Landor, Walter Savage
1775-1864 . . . . NCLC 14

Landwirth, Heinz 1927-
See Lind, Jakov
See also CANR 7; CA 11-12R

Lane, Patrick 1939-. . . . . CLC 25
See also CA 97-100; DLB 53

Lang, Andrew 1844-1912. . . . . TCLC 16
See also CA 114; SATA 16

Lang, Fritz 1890-1976 . . . . CLC 20
See also CA 77-80; obituary CA 69-72

Langer, Elinor 1939- . . . . CLC 34
See also CA 121

Lanier, Sidney 1842-1881 . . . . NCLC 6
See also SATA 18; DLB 64

Lanyer, Aemilia 1569-1645 . . . . LC 10

Lapine, James 1949-. . . . . CLC 39

Larbaud, Valery 1881-1957 . . . . TCLC 9
See also CA 106

Lardner, Ring(gold Wilmer)
  1885-1933 . . . . TCLC **2, 14**
  See also CA 104; DLB 11, 25

Larkin, Philip (Arthur)
  1922-1985 . . . **CLC 3, 5, 8, 9, 13, 18, 33,**
                                                    39
  See also CA 5-8R; obituary CA 117;
  DLB 27

Larra (y Sanchez de Castro), Mariano Jose de
  1809-1837 . . . . NCLC **17**

Larsen, Eric   1941- . . . . CLC **55**

Larsen, Nella   1891-1964 . . . . CLC **37**
  See also CA 125; DLB 51

Larson, Charles R(aymond)   1938- . . . CLC **31**
  See also CANR 4; CA 53-56

Latham, Jean Lee   1902- . . . . CLC **12**
  See also CANR 7; CA 5-8R; SATA 2

Lathen, Emma . . . . CLC **2**
  See also Hennissart, Martha; Latsis, Mary
  J(ane)

Latsis, Mary J(ane)
  See Lathen, Emma
  See also CA 85-88

Lattimore, Richmond (Alexander)
  1906-1984 . . . . CLC **3**
  See also CANR 1; CA 1-4R;
  obituary CA 112

Laughlin, James   1914- . . . . CLC **49**
  See also CANR 9; CA 21-24R; DLB 48

Laurence, (Jean) Margaret (Wemyss)
  1926-1987 . . CLC **3, 6, 13, 50, 62;** SSC **7**
  See also CA 5-8R; obituary CA 121;
  SATA 50; DLB 53

Laurent, Antoine   1952- . . . . CLC **50**

Lautreamont, Comte de
  1846-1870 . . . . NCLC **12**

Lavin, Mary   1912- . . . . . . CLC **4, 18;** SSC **4**
  See also CA 9-12R; DLB 15

Lawler, Raymond (Evenor)   1922- . . . CLC **58**
  See also CA 103

Lawrence, D(avid) H(erbert)
  1885-1930 . . . . TCLC **2, 9, 16, 33;** SSC **4**
  See also CA 104, 121; DLB 10, 19, 36

Lawrence, T(homas) E(dward)
  1888-1935 . . . . TCLC **18**
  See also CA 115

Lawson, Henry (Archibald Hertzberg)
  1867-1922 . . . . TCLC **27**
  See also CA 120

Laxness, Halldor (Kiljan)   1902- . . . . CLC **25**
  See also Gudjonsson, Halldor Kiljan

Laye, Camara   1928-1980 . . . . CLC **4, 38**
  See also CA 85-88; obituary CA 97-100

Layton, Irving (Peter)   1912- . . . . . CLC **2, 15**
  See also CANR 2; CA 1-4R

Lazarus, Emma   1849-1887 . . . . NCLC **8**

Leacock, Stephen (Butler)
  1869-1944 . . . . TCLC **2**
  See also CA 104

Lear, Edward   1812-1888 . . . . NCLC **3**
  See also CLR 1; SATA 18; DLB 32

Lear, Norman (Milton)   1922- . . . . . . CLC **12**
  See also CA 73-76

Leavis, F(rank) R(aymond)
  1895-1978 . . . . CLC **24**
  See also CA 21-24R; obituary CA 77-80

Leavitt, David   1961?- . . . . CLC **34**
  See also CA 116, 122

Lebowitz, Fran(ces Ann)
  1951?- . . . . CLC **11, 36**
  See also CANR 14; CA 81-84

Le Carre, John   1931- . . . CLC **3, 5, 9, 15, 28**
  See also Cornwell, David (John Moore)

Le Clezio, J(ean) M(arie) G(ustave)
  1940- . . . . CLC **31**
  See also CA 116

Leconte de Lisle, Charles-Marie-Rene
  1818-1894 . . . . NCLC **29**

Leduc, Violette   1907-1972 . . . . CLC **22**
  See also CAP 1; CA 13-14;
  obituary CA 33-36R

Ledwidge, Francis   1887-1917 . . . . . . TCLC **23**
  See also CA 123; DLB 20

Lee, Andrea   1953- . . . . CLC **36**
  See also CA 125

Lee, Andrew   1917-
  See Auchincloss, Louis (Stanton)

Lee, Don L.   1942- . . . . CLC **2**
  See also Madhubuti, Haki R.
  See also CA 73-76

Lee, George Washington
  1894-1976 . . . . CLC **52**
  See also CA 125; DLB 51

Lee, (Nelle) Harper   1926- . . . . . . CLC **12, 60**
  See also CA 13-16R; SATA 11; DLB 6;
  CDALB 1941-1968

Lee, Lawrence   1903- . . . . CLC **34**
  See also CA 25-28R

Lee, Manfred B(ennington)   1905-1971
  See Queen, Ellery
  See also CANR 2; CA 1-4R, 11;
  obituary CA 29-32R

Lee, Stan   1922- . . . . CLC **17**
  See also CA 108, 111

Lee, Tanith   1947- . . . . CLC **46**
  See also CA 37-40R; SATA 8

Lee, Vernon   1856-1935 . . . . TCLC **5**
  See also Paget, Violet
  See also DLB 57

Lee-Hamilton, Eugene (Jacob)
  1845-1907 . . . . TCLC **22**

Leet, Judith   1935- . . . . CLC **11**

Le Fanu, Joseph Sheridan
  1814-1873 . . . . NCLC **9**
  See also DLB 21, 70

Leffland, Ella   1931- . . . . CLC **19**
  See also CA 29-32R; DLB-Y 84

Leger, (Marie-Rene) Alexis Saint-Leger
  1887-1975
  See Perse, St.-John
  See also CA 13-16R; obituary CA 61-64

Le Guin, Ursula K(roeber)
  1929- . . . . CLC **8, 13, 22, 45**
  See also CLR 3; CANR 9; CA 21-24R;
  SATA 4, 52; DLB 8, 52

Lehmann, Rosamond (Nina)   1901- . . . CLC **5**
  See also CANR 8; CA 77-80; DLB 15

Leiber, Fritz (Reuter, Jr.)   1910- . . . . CLC **25**
  See also CANR 2; CA 45-48; SATA 45;
  DLB 8

Leino, Eino   1878-1926 . . . . TCLC **24**

Leiris, Michel   1901- . . . . CLC **61**
  See also CA 119, 128

Leithauser, Brad   1953- . . . . CLC **27**
  See also CA 107

Lelchuk, Alan   1938- . . . . CLC **5**
  See also CANR 1; CA 45-48

Lem, Stanislaw   1921- . . . . CLC **8, 15, 40**
  See also CAAS 1; CA 105

Lemann, Nancy   1956- . . . . CLC **39**
  See also CA 118

Lemonnier, (Antoine Louis) Camille
  1844-1913 . . . . TCLC **22**

Lenau, Nikolaus   1802-1850 . . . . . . NCLC **16**

L'Engle, Madeleine   1918- . . . . CLC **12**
  See also CLR 1, 14; CANR 3, 21; CA 1-4R;
  SATA 1, 27; DLB 52

Lengyel, Jozsef   1896-1975 . . . . CLC **7**
  See also CA 85-88; obituary CA 57-60

Lennon, John (Ono)
  1940-1980 . . . . CLC **12, 35**
  See also CA 102

Lennon, John Winston   1940-1980
  See Lennon, John (Ono)

Lennox, Charlotte Ramsay   1729 or
  1730-1804 . . . . NCLC **23**
  See also DLB 39, 39

Lennox, Charlotte Ramsay
  1729?-1804 . . . . NCLC **23**
  See also DLB 39

Lentricchia, Frank (Jr.)   1940- . . . . . . CLC **34**
  See also CANR 19; CA 25-28R

Lenz, Siegfried   1926- . . . . CLC **27**
  See also CA 89-92; DLB 75

Leonard, Elmore   1925- . . . . CLC **28, 34**
  See also CANR 12; CA 81-84

Leonard, Hugh   1926- . . . . CLC **19**
  See also Byrne, John Keyes
  See also DLB 13

Leopardi, (Conte) Giacomo (Talegardo
  Francesco di Sales Saverio Pietro)
  1798-1837 . . . . NCLC **22**

Lerman, Eleanor   1952- . . . . CLC **9**
  See also CA 85-88

Lerman, Rhoda   1936- . . . . CLC **56**
  See also CA 49-52

Lermontov, Mikhail Yuryevich
  1814-1841 . . . . NCLC **5**

Leroux, Gaston   1868-1927 . . . . TCLC **25**
  See also CA 108

Lesage, Alain-Rene   1668-1747 . . . . . . LC **2**

Leskov, Nikolai (Semyonovich)
  1831-1895 . . . . NCLC **25**

Lessing, Doris (May)
  1919- . . . . CLC **1, 2, 3, 6, 10, 15, 22, 40;**
                                                   SSC **6**
  See also CA 9-12R; DLB 15; DLB-Y 85

Lessing, Gotthold Ephraim
  1729-1781 . . . . LC **8**

Lester, Richard   1932- . . . . CLC **20**

Lucas, George 1944- . . . . CLC 16
  See also CA 77-80

Lucas, Victoria 1932-1963
  See Plath, Sylvia

Ludlam, Charles 1943-1987 . . . . . CLC 46, 50
  See also CA 85-88; obituary CA 122

Ludlum, Robert 1927- . . . . CLC 22, 43
  See also CANR 25; CA 33-36R; DLB-Y 82

Ludwig, Ken 19??- . . . . CLC 60

Ludwig, Otto 1813-1865. . . . . NCLC 4

Lugones, Leopoldo 1874-1938 . . . . . TCLC 15
  See also CA 116

Lu Hsun 1881-1936 . . . . TCLC 3

Lukacs, Georg 1885-1971. . . . . CLC 24
  See also Lukacs, Gyorgy

Lukacs, Gyorgy 1885-1971
  See Lukacs, Georg
  See also CA 101; obituary CA 29-32R

Luke, Peter (Ambrose Cyprian)
  1919- . . . . CLC 38
  See also CA 81-84; DLB 13

Lurie (Bishop), Alison
  1926- . . . . CLC 4, 5, 18, 39
  See also CANR 2, 17; CA 1-4R; SATA 46;
  DLB 2

Lustig, Arnost 1926- . . . . CLC 56
  See also CA 69-72; SATA 56

Luther, Martin 1483-1546 . . . . LC 9

Luzi, Mario 1914- . . . . CLC 13
  See also CANR 9; CA 61-64

Lynn, Kenneth S(chuyler) 1923- . . . . CLC 50
  See also CANR 3; CA 1-4R

Lytle, Andrew (Nelson) 1902- . . . . . . CLC 22
  See also CA 9-12R; DLB 6

Lyttelton, George 1709-1773 . . . . LC 10

Lytton, Edward Bulwer 1803-1873
  See Bulwer-Lytton, (Lord) Edward (George
  Earle Lytton)
  See also SATA 23

Maas, Peter 1929- . . . . CLC 29
  See also CA 93-96

Macaulay, (Dame Emile) Rose
  1881-1958 . . . . TCLC 7
  See also CA 104; DLB 36

MacBeth, George (Mann)
  1932- . . . . CLC 2, 5, 9
  See also CA 25-28R; SATA 4; DLB 40

MacCaig, Norman (Alexander)
  1910- . . . . CLC 36
  See also CANR 3; CA 9-12R; DLB 27

MacCarthy, Desmond 1877-1952 . . TCLC 36

MacDermot, Thomas H. 1870-1933
  See Redcam, Tom

MacDiarmid, Hugh
  1892-1978 . . . . CLC 2, 4, 11, 19, 63
  See also Grieve, C(hristopher) M(urray)
  See also DLB 20

Macdonald, Cynthia 1928- . . . . . . CLC 13, 19
  See also CANR 4; CA 49-52

MacDonald, George 1824-1905 . . . . . TCLC 9
  See also CA 106; SATA 33; DLB 18

MacDonald, John D(ann)
  1916-1986 . . . . CLC 3, 27, 44
  See also CANR 1, 19; CA 1-4R;
  obituary CA 121; DLB 8; DLB-Y 86

Macdonald, (John) Ross
  1915-1983 . . . . . . CLC 1, 2, 3, 14, 34, 41
  See also Millar, Kenneth

MacEwen, Gwendolyn (Margaret)
  1941-1987 . . . . CLC 13, 55
  See also CANR 7, 22; CA 9-12R;
  obituary CA 124; SATA 50; DLB 53

Machado (y Ruiz), Antonio
  1875-1939 . . . . TCLC 3
  See also CA 104

Machado de Assis, (Joaquim Maria)
  1839-1908 . . . . TCLC 10
  See also CA 107

Machen, Arthur (Llewellyn Jones)
  1863-1947 . . . . TCLC 4
  See also CA 104; DLB 36

Machiavelli, Niccolo 1469-1527 . . . . . . LC 8

MacInnes, Colin 1914-1976 . . . . . CLC 4, 23
  See also CA 69-72; obituary CA 65-68;
  DLB 14

MacInnes, Helen (Clark)
  1907-1985 . . . . CLC 27, 39
  See also CANR 1; CA 1-4R;
  obituary CA 65-68, 117; SATA 22, 44

Macintosh, Elizabeth 1897-1952
  See Tey, Josephine
  See also CA 110

Mackenzie, (Edward Montague) Compton
  1883-1972 . . . . CLC 18
  See also CAP 2; CA 21-22;
  obituary CA 37-40R; DLB 34

Mac Laverty, Bernard 1942- . . . . CLC 31
  See also CA 116, 118

MacLean, Alistair (Stuart)
  1922-1987 . . . . CLC 3, 13, 50, 63
  See also CANR 28; CA 57-60;
  obituary CA 121; SATA 23, 50

MacLeish, Archibald
  1892-1982 . . . . CLC 3, 8, 14
  See also CA 9-12R; obituary CA 106;
  DLB 4, 7, 45; DLB-Y 82

MacLennan, (John) Hugh
  1907- . . . . CLC 2, 14
  See also CA 5-8R

MacLeod, Alistair 1936- . . . . CLC 56
  See also CA 123; DLB 60

Macleod, Fiona 1855-1905
  See Sharp, William

MacNeice, (Frederick) Louis
  1907-1963 . . . . CLC 1, 4, 10, 53
  See also CA 85-88; DLB 10, 20

Macpherson, (Jean) Jay 1931- . . . . . . CLC 14
  See also CA 5-8R; DLB 53

MacShane, Frank 1927- . . . . CLC 39
  See also CANR 3; CA 11-12R

Macumber, Mari 1896-1966
  See Sandoz, Mari (Susette)

Madach, Imre 1823-1864 . . . . NCLC 19

Madden, (Jerry) David 1933- . . . . CLC 5, 15
  See also CAAS 3; CANR 4; CA 1-4R;
  DLB 6

Madhubuti, Haki R. 1942- . . . . CLC 6
  See also Lee, Don L.
  See also CANR 24; CA 73-76; DLB 5, 41

Maeterlinck, Maurice 1862-1949 . . . TCLC 3
  See also CA 104

Mafouz, Naguib 1912-
  See Mahfuz, Najib

Maginn, William 1794-1842. . . . . . . NCLC 8

Mahapatra, Jayanta 1928- . . . . CLC 33
  See also CANR 15; CA 73-76

Mahfuz Najib 1912- . . . . CLC 52, 55
  See also DLB-Y 88

Mahon, Derek 1941- . . . . CLC 27
  See also CA 113; DLB 40

Mailer, Norman
  1923- . . . . . . CLC 1, 2, 3, 4, 5, 8, 11, 14,
                                        28, 39
  See also CA 9-12R; CABS 1; DLB 2, 16,
  28; DLB-Y 80, 83; DLB-DS 3

Maillet, Antonine 1929- . . . . CLC 54
  See also CA 115, 120; DLB 60

Mais, Roger 1905-1955 . . . . TCLC 8
  See also CA 105

Maitland, Sara (Louise) 1950- . . . . . CLC 49
  See also CANR 13; CA 69-72

Major, Clarence 1936- . . . . CLC 3, 19, 48
  See also CAAS 6; CANR 13; CA 21-24R;
  DLB 33

Major, Kevin 1949- . . . . CLC 26
  See also CLR 11; CANR 21; CA 97-100;
  SATA 32; DLB 60

Malamud, Bernard
  1914-1986 . . . . . CLC 1, 2, 3, 5, 8, 9, 11,
                                     18, 27, 44
  See also CA 5-8R; obituary CA 118;
  CABS 1; DLB 2, 28; DLB-Y 80, 86;
  CDALB 1941-1968

Malherbe, Francois de 1555-1628 . . . . . LC 5

Mallarme, Stephane 1842-1898 . . . . NCLC 4

Mallet-Joris, Francoise 1930- . . . . . . CLC 11
  See also CANR 17; CA 65-68

Maloff, Saul 1922- . . . . CLC 5
  See also CA 33-36R

Malone, Louis 1907-1963
  See MacNeice, (Frederick) Louis

Malone, Michael (Christopher)
  1942- . . . . CLC 43
  See also CANR 14; CA 77-80

Malory, (Sir) Thomas ?-1471 . . . . LC 11
  See also SATA 33

Malouf, David 1934- . . . . CLC 28

Malraux, (Georges-) Andre
  1901-1976 . . . . . . CLC 1, 4, 9, 13, 15, 57
  See also CAP 2; CA 21-24;
  obituary CA 69-72; DLB 72

Malzberg, Barry N. 1939- . . . . CLC 7
  See also CAAS 4; CANR 16; CA 61-64;
  DLB 8

Mamet, David (Alan)
  1947-1987 . . . . CLC 9, 15, 34, 46
  See also CANR 15; CA 81-84, 124; DLB 7

Mamoulian, Rouben 1898- . . . . CLC 16
  See also CA 25-28R

Mandelstam, Osip (Emilievich)
    1891?-1938?. . . . . TCLC **2, 6**
    See also CA 104

Mander, Jane 1877-1949 . . . . TCLC **31**

Mandiargues, Andre Pieyre de
    1909- . . . . CLC **41**
    See also CA 103

Mangan, James Clarence
    1803-1849 . . . . NCLC **27**

Manley, (Mary) Delariviere
    1672?-1724. . . . . LC **1**
    See also DLB 39

Mann, (Luiz) Heinrich 1871-1950. . . TCLC **9**
    See also CA 106; DLB 66

Mann, Thomas
    1875-1955 . . . . . . TCLC **2, 8, 14, 21, 35;**
                                         SSC **5**
    See also CA 104, 128; DLB 66

Manning, Frederic 1882-1935 . . . . . TCLC **25**

Manning, Olivia 1915-1980 . . . . . . CLC **5, 19**
    See also CA 5-8R; obituary CA 101

Mano, D. Keith 1942- . . . . CLC **2, 10**
    See also CAAS 6; CANR 26; CA 25-28R;
    DLB 6

Mansfield, Katherine
    1888-1923 . . . . TCLC **2, 8, 39**
    See also CA 104

Manso, Peter 1940- . . . . CLC **39**
    See also CA 29-32R

Manzoni, Alessandro 1785-1873 . . NCLC **29**

Mapu, Abraham (ben Jekutiel)
    1808-1867 . . . . NCLC **18**

Marat, Jean Paul 1743-1793 . . . . LC **10**

Marcel, Gabriel (Honore)
    1889-1973 . . . . CLC **15**
    See also CA 102; obituary CA 45-48

Marchbanks, Samuel 1913-
    See Davies, (William) Robertson

Marie de l'Incarnation 1599-1672. . . . LC **10**

Marinetti, F(ilippo) T(ommaso)
    1876-1944 . . . . TCLC **10**
    See also CA 107

Marivaux, Pierre Carlet de Chamblain de
    (1688-1763) . . . . LC **4**

Markandaya, Kamala 1924- . . . . . . CLC **8, 38**
    See also Taylor, Kamala (Purnaiya)

Markfield, Wallace (Arthur) 1926- . . . CLC **8**
    See also CAAS 3; CA 69-72; DLB 2, 28

Markham, Robert 1922-
    See Amis, Kingsley (William)

Marks, J. 1942-
    See Highwater, Jamake

Marley, Bob 1945-1981 . . . . CLC **17**
    See also Marley, Robert Nesta

Marley, Robert Nesta 1945-1981
    See Marley, Bob
    See also CA 107; obituary CA 103

Marlowe, Christopher 1564-1593 . . . . . . DC **1**
    See also DLB 62

Marmontel, Jean-Francois
    1723-1799 . . . . LC **2**

Marquand, John P(hillips)
    1893-1960 . . . . CLC **2, 10**
    See also CA 85-88; DLB 9

Marquez, Gabriel Garcia 1928-
    See Garcia Marquez, Gabriel

Marquis, Don(ald Robert Perry)
    1878-1937 . . . . TCLC **7**
    See also CA 104; DLB 11, 25

Marryat, Frederick 1792-1848 . . . . NCLC **3**
    See also DLB 21

Marsh, (Dame Edith) Ngaio
    1899-1982 . . . . CLC **7, 53**
    See also CANR 6; CA 9-12R; DLB 77

Marshall, Garry 1935?- . . . . CLC **17**
    See also CA 111

Marshall, Paule 1929- . . . . . CLC **27**; SSC **3**
    See also CANR 25; CA 77-80; DLB 33

Marsten, Richard 1926-
    See Hunter, Evan

Martin, Steve 1945?- . . . . CLC **30**
    See also CA 97-100

Martin du Gard, Roger
    1881-1958 . . . . TCLC **24**
    See also CA 118

Martineau, Harriet 1802-1876. . . . NCLC **26**
    See also YABC 2; DLB 21, 55

Martinez Ruiz, Jose 1874-1967
    See Azorin
    See also CA 93-96

Martinez Sierra, Gregorio
    1881-1947 . . . . TCLC **6**
    See also CA 104, 115

Martinez Sierra, Maria (de la O'LeJarraga)
    1880?-1974. . . . . TCLC **6**
    See also obituary CA 115

Martinson, Harry (Edmund)
    1904-1978 . . . . CLC **14**
    See also CA 77-80

Marvell, Andrew 1621-1678 . . . . LC **4**

Marx, Karl (Heinrich)
    1818-1883 . . . . NCLC **17**

Masaoka Shiki 1867-1902 . . . . TCLC **18**

Masefield, John (Edward)
    1878-1967 . . . . CLC **11, 47**
    See also CAP 2; CA 19-20;
    obituary CA 25-28R; SATA 19; DLB 10,
    19

Maso, Carole 19??- . . . . CLC **44**

Mason, Bobbie Ann
    1940- . . . . CLC **28, 43**; SSC **4**
    See also CANR 11; CA 53-56; SAAS 1;
    DLB-Y 87

Mason, Nick 1945- . . . . CLC **35**
    See also Pink Floyd

Mason, Tally 1909-1971
    See Derleth, August (William)

Masters, Edgar Lee
    1868?-1950. . . . . TCLC **2, 25**; PC **1**
    See also CA 104; DLB 54;
    CDALB 1865-1917

Masters, Hilary 1928- . . . . CLC **48**
    See also CANR 13; CA 25-28R

Mastrosimone, William 19??- . . . . . . CLC **36**

Matheson, Richard (Burton)
    1926- . . . . CLC **37**
    See also CA 97-100; DLB 8, 44

Mathews, Harry 1930- . . . . CLC **6, 52**
    See also CAAS 6; CANR 18; CA 21-24R

Mathias, Roland (Glyn) 1915- . . . . . . CLC **45**
    See also CANR 19; CA 97-100; DLB 27

Matthews, Greg 1949- . . . . CLC **45**

Matthews, William 1942- . . . . CLC **40**
    See also CANR 12; CA 29-32R; DLB 5

Matthias, John (Edward) 1941- . . . . . . CLC **9**
    See also CA 33-36R

Matthiessen, Peter 1927- . . . CLC **5, 7, 11, 32**
    See also CANR 21; CA 9-12R; SATA 27;
    DLB 6

Maturin, Charles Robert
    1780?-1824. . . . . NCLC **6**

Matute, Ana Maria 1925- . . . . CLC **11**
    See also CA 89-92

Maugham, W(illiam) Somerset
    1874-1965 . . . . CLC **1, 11, 15**
    See also CA 5-8R; obituary CA 25-28R;
    DLB 10, 36

Maupassant, (Henri Rene Albert) Guy de
    1850-1893 . . . . NCLC **1**; SSC **1**

Mauriac, Claude 1914- . . . . CLC **9**
    See also CA 89-92

Mauriac, Francois (Charles)
    1885-1970 . . . . CLC **4, 9, 56**
    See also CAP 2; CA 25-28; DLB 65

Mavor, Osborne Henry 1888-1951
    See Bridie, James
    See also CA 104

Maxwell, William (Keepers, Jr.)
    1908- . . . . CLC **19**
    See also CA 93-96; DLB-Y 80

May, Elaine 1932- . . . . CLC **16**
    See also CA 124; DLB 44

Mayakovsky, Vladimir (Vladimirovich)
    1893-1930 . . . . TCLC **4, 18**
    See also CA 104

Maynard, Joyce 1953- . . . . CLC **23**
    See also CA 111

Mayne, William (James Carter)
    1928- . . . . CLC **12**
    See also CA 9-12R; SATA 6

Mayo, Jim 1908?-
    See L'Amour, Louis (Dearborn)

Maysles, Albert 1926- and Maysles, David
    1926- . . . . CLC **16**

Maysles, Albert 1926-
    See Maysles, Albert and Maysles, David
    See also CA 29-32R

Maysles, David 1932-
    See Maysles, Albert and Maysles, David

Mazer, Norma Fox 1931- . . . . CLC **26**
    See also CLR 23; CANR 12; CA 69-72;
    SAAS 1; SATA 24

McAuley, James (Phillip)
    1917-1976 . . . . CLC **45**
    See also CA 97-100

McBain, Ed 1926-
    See Hunter, Evan

Author Index

Millay, Edna St. Vincent
1892-1950 .... TCLC **4**
See also CA 104; DLB 45

Miller, Arthur
1915- ...... CLC **1, 2, 6, 10, 15, 26, 47;**
DC **1**
See also CANR 2, 30; CA 1-4R; CABS 3;
DLB 7; CDALB 1941-1968

Miller, Henry (Valentine)
1891-1980 ...... CLC **1, 2, 4, 9, 14, 43**
See also CA 9-12R; obituary CA 97-100;
DLB 4, 9; DLB-Y 80

Miller, Jason 1939?-.............. CLC **2**
See also CA 73-76; DLB 7

Miller, Sue 19??-................. CLC **44**

Miller, Walter M(ichael), Jr.
1923-..................... CLC **4, 30**
See also CA 85-88; DLB 8

Millhauser, Steven 1943-....... CLC **21, 54**
See also CA 108, 110, 111; DLB 2

Millin, Sarah Gertrude 1889-1968 .. CLC **49**
See also CA 102; obituary CA 93-96

Milne, A(lan) A(lexander)
1882-1956 .... TCLC **6**
See also CLR 1; YABC 1; CA 104; DLB 10

Milner, Ron(ald) 1938-........... CLC **56**
See also CANR 24; CA 73-76; DLB 38

Milosz Czeslaw
1911-.......... CLC **5, 11, 22, 31, 56**
See also CANR 23; CA 81-84

Milton, John 1608-1674............ LC **9**

Miner, Valerie (Jane) 1947-....... CLC **40**
See also CA 97-100

Minot, Susan 1956- .... CLC **44**

Minus, Ed 1938-................. CLC **39**

Miro (Ferrer), Gabriel (Francisco Victor)
1879-1930 .... TCLC **5**
See also CA 104

Mishima, Yukio
1925-1970 .... CLC **2, 4, 6, 9, 27; DC 1;**
SSC **4**
See also Hiraoka, Kimitake

Mistral, Gabriela 1889-1957 .... TCLC **2**
See also CA 104

Mitchell, James Leslie 1901-1935
See Gibbon, Lewis Grassic
See also CA 104; DLB 15

Mitchell, Joni 1943-.............. CLC **12**
See also CA 112

Mitchell (Marsh), Margaret (Munnerlyn)
1900-1949 .... TCLC **11**
See also CA 109; DLB 9

Mitchell, S. Weir 1829-1914 ...... TCLC **36**

Mitchell, W(illiam) O(rmond)
1914-.................... CLC **25**
See also CANR 15; CA 77-80

Mitford, Mary Russell 1787-1855.. NCLC **4**

Mitford, Nancy 1904-1973........ CLC **44**
See also CA 9-12R

Miyamoto Yuriko 1899-1951...... TCLC **37**

Mo, Timothy 1950-.............. CLC **46**
See also CA 117

Modarressi, Taghi 1931- .... CLC **44**
See also CA 121

Modiano, Patrick (Jean) 1945-..... CLC **18**
See also CANR 17; CA 85-88

Mofolo, Thomas (Mokopu)
1876-1948 .... TCLC **22**
See also CA 121

Mohr, Nicholasa 1935-........... CLC **12**
See also CLR 22; CANR 1; CA 49-52;
SATA 8

Mojtabai, A(nn) G(race)
1938- .... CLC **5, 9, 15, 29**
See also CA 85-88

Moliere 1622-1673 .... LC **10**

Molnar, Ferenc 1878-1952........ TCLC **20**
See also CA 109

Momaday, N(avarre) Scott
1934- .... CLC **2, 19**
See also CANR 14; CA 25-28R; SATA 30,
48

Monroe, Harriet 1860-1936...... TCLC **12**
See also CA 109; DLB 54

Montagu, Elizabeth 1720-1800 .... NCLC **7**

Montagu, Lady Mary (Pierrepont) Wortley
1689-1762 .... LC **9**

Montague, John (Patrick)
1929-.................. CLC **13, 46**
See also CANR 9; CA 9-12R; DLB 40

Montaigne, Michel (Eyquem) de
1533-1592 .... LC **8**

Montale, Eugenio 1896-1981... CLC **7, 9, 18**
See also CA 17-20R; obituary CA 104

Montgomery, Marion (H., Jr.)
1925-..................... CLC **7**
See also CANR 3; CA 1-4R; DLB 6

Montgomery, Robert Bruce 1921-1978
See Crispin, Edmund
See also CA 104

Montherlant, Henri (Milon) de
1896-1972 .... CLC **8, 19**
See also CA 85-88; obituary CA 37-40R;
DLB 72

Montisquieu, Charles-Louis de Secondat
1689-1755 .... LC **7**

Monty Python................... CLC **21**

Moodie, Susanna (Strickland)
1803-1885 .... NCLC **14**

Mooney, Ted 1951-.............. CLC **25**

Moorcock, Michael (John)
1939-.................. CLC **5, 27, 58**
See also CAAS 5; CANR 2, 17; CA 45-48;
DLB 14

Moore, Brian
1921- .... CLC **1, 3, 5, 7, 8, 19, 32**
See also CANR 1; CA 1-4R

Moore, George (Augustus)
1852-1933 .... TCLC **7**
See also CA 104; DLB 10, 18, 57

Moore, Lorrie 1957-.......... CLC **39, 45**
See also Moore, Marie Lorena

Moore, Marianne (Craig)
1887-1972 ... CLC **1, 2, 4, 8, 10, 13, 19,**
47
See also CANR 3; CA 1-4R;
obituary CA 33-36R; SATA 20; DLB 45

Moore, Marie Lorena 1957-
See Moore, Lorrie
See also CA 116

Moore, Thomas 1779-1852....... NCLC **6**

Morand, Paul 1888-1976.......... CLC **41**
See also obituary CA 69-72; DLB 65

Morante, Elsa 1918-1985........ CLC **8, 47**
See also CA 85-88; obituary CA 117

Moravia, Alberto
1907-......... CLC **2, 7, 11, 18, 27, 46**
See also Pincherle, Alberto

More, Hannah 1745-1833 .... NCLC **27**

More, Henry 1614-1687............ LC **9**

More, (Sir) Thomas 1478-1535 ...... LC **10**

Moreas, Jean 1856-1910 .... TCLC **18**

Morgan, Berry 1919-............. CLC **6**
See also CA 49-52; DLB 6

Morgan, Edwin (George) 1920-..... CLC **31**
See also CANR 3; CA 7-8R; DLB 27

Morgan, (George) Frederick
1922-..................... CLC **23**
See also CANR 21; CA 17-20R

Morgan, Janet 1945- .... CLC **39**
See also CA 65-68

Morgan, Lady 1776?-1859....... NCLC **29**

Morgan, Robin 1941-............. CLC **2**
See also CA 69-72

Morgenstern, Christian (Otto Josef Wolfgang)
1871-1914 .... TCLC **8**
See also CA 105

Moricz, Zsigmond 1879-1942 ..... TCLC **33**

Morike, Eduard (Friedrich)
1804-1875 .... NCLC **10**

Mori Ogai 1862-1922............ TCLC **14**
See also Mori Rintaro

Mori Rintaro 1862-1922
See Mori Ogai
See also CA 110

Moritz, Karl Philipp 1756-1793 ...... LC **2**

Morris, Julian 1916-
See West, Morris L.

Morris, Steveland Judkins 1950-
See Wonder, Stevie
See also CA 111

Morris, William 1834-1896 .... NCLC **4**
See also DLB 18, 35, 57

Morris, Wright (Marion)
1910-............. CLC **1, 3, 7, 18, 37**
See also CA 9-12R; DLB 2; DLB-Y 81

Morrison, James Douglas 1943-1971
See Morrison, Jim
See also CA 73-76

Morrison, Jim 1943-1971.......... CLC **17**
See also Morrison, James Douglas

Morrison, Toni 1931-..... CLC **4, 10, 22, 55**
See also CA 29-32R; DLB 6, 33; DLB-Y 81;
AAYA 1

Ortiz, Simon J.   1941-. . . . .   CLC 45

Orton, Joe   1933?-1967. . . . . .   CLC 4, 13, 43
See also Orton, John Kingsley
See also DLB 13

Orton, John Kingsley   1933?-1967
See Orton, Joe
See also CA 85-88

Orwell, George
1903-1950 . . . .   TCLC 2, 6, 15, 31
See also Blair, Eric Arthur
See also DLB 15

Osborne, John (James)
1929- . . . .   CLC 1, 2, 5, 11, 45
See also CANR 21; CA 13-16R; DLB 13

Osborne, Lawrence   1958- . . . .   CLC 50

Osceola   1885-1962
See Dinesen, Isak; Blixen, Karen
(Christentze Dinesen)

Oshima, Nagisa   1932- . . . .   CLC 20
See also CA 116

Oskison, John M.   1874-1947. . . . .   TCLC 35

Ossoli, Sarah Margaret (Fuller marchesa d')
1810-1850
See Fuller, (Sarah) Margaret
See also SATA 25

Ostrovsky, Alexander
1823-1886 . . . .   NCLC 30

Otero, Blas de   1916- . . . .   CLC 11
See also CA 89-92

Ovid   43 B.C.-c. 18 A.D.
See also PC 2

Owen, Wilfred (Edward Salter)
1893-1918 . . . .   TCLC 5, 27
See also CA 104; DLB 20

Owens, Rochelle   1936-. . . . .   CLC 8
See also CAAS 2; CA 17-20R

Owl, Sebastian   1939-
See Thompson, Hunter S(tockton)

Oz, Amos   1939- . . .   CLC 5, 8, 11, 27, 33, 54
See also CA 53-56

Ozick, Cynthia   1928- . . . . . .   CLC 3, 7, 28, 62
See also CANR 28; CA 17-20R; DLB 28;
DLB-Y 82

Ozu, Yasujiro   1903-1963 . . . .   CLC 16
See also CA 112

Pa Chin   1904-. . . . .   CLC 18
See also Li Fei-kan

Pack, Robert   1929-. . . . .   CLC 13
See also CANR 3; CA 1-4R; DLB 5

Padgett, Lewis   1915-1958
See Kuttner, Henry

Padilla, Heberto   1932-. . . . .   CLC 38
See also CA 123

Page, Jimmy   1944-. . . . .   CLC 12

Page, Louise   1955-. . . . .   CLC 40

Page, P(atricia) K(athleen)
1916- . . . .   CLC 7, 18
See also CANR 4, 22; CA 53-56; DLB 68

Paget, Violet   1856-1935
See Lee, Vernon
See also CA 104

Palamas, Kostes   1859-1943 . . . .   TCLC 5
See also CA 105

Palazzeschi, Aldo   1885-1974 . . . . . .   CLC 11
See also CA 89-92; obituary CA 53-56

Paley, Grace   1922-. . . . .   CLC 4, 6, 37
See also CANR 13; CA 25-28R; DLB 28

Palin, Michael   1943- . . . .   CLC 21
See also Monty Python
See also CA 107

Palma, Ricardo   1833-1919. . . . . . .   TCLC 29
See also CANR 123

Pancake, Breece Dexter   1952-1979
See Pancake, Breece D'J

Pancake, Breece D'J   1952-1979 . . . .   CLC 29
See also obituary CA 109

Papadiamantis, Alexandros
1851-1911 . . . .   TCLC 29

Papini, Giovanni   1881-1956. . . . . .   TCLC 22
See also CA 121

Paracelsus   1493-1541. . . . .   LC 14

Parini, Jay (Lee)   1948- . . . .   CLC 54
See also CA 97-100

Parker, Dorothy (Rothschild)
1893-1967 . . . .   CLC 15; SSC 2
See also CAP 2; CA 19-20;
obituary CA 25-28R; DLB 11, 45

Parker, Robert B(rown)   1932-. . . . .   CLC 27
See also CANR 1, 26; CA 49-52

Parkin, Frank   1940-. . . . .   CLC 43

Parkman, Francis   1823-1893. . . . .   NCLC 12
See also DLB 1, 30

Parks, Gordon (Alexander Buchanan)
1912- . . . .   CLC 1, 16
See also CANR 26; CA 41-44R; SATA 8;
DLB 33

Parnell, Thomas   1679-1718 . . . .   LC 3

Parra, Nicanor   1914- . . . .   CLC 2
See also CA 85-88

Pasolini, Pier Paolo
1922-1975 . . . .   CLC 20, 37
See also CA 93-96; obituary CA 61-64

Pastan, Linda (Olenik)   1932- . . . . . .   CLC 27
See also CANR 18; CA 61-64; DLB 5

Pasternak, Boris
1890-1960 . . . .   CLC 7, 10, 18, 63
See also CA 127; obituary CA 116

Patchen, Kenneth   1911-1972. . .   CLC 1, 2, 18
See also CANR 3; CA 1-4R;
obituary CA 33-36R; DLB 16, 48

Pater, Walter (Horatio)
1839-1894 . . . .   NCLC 7
See also DLB 57

Paterson, Andrew Barton
1864-1941 . . . .   TCLC 32

Paterson, Katherine (Womeldorf)
1932- . . . .   CLC 12, 30
See also CLR 7; CA 21-24R; SATA 13, 53;
DLB 52

Patmore, Coventry Kersey Dighton
1823-1896 . . . .   NCLC 9
See also DLB 35

Paton, Alan (Stewart)
1903-1988 . . . .   CLC 4, 10, 25, 55
See also CANR 22; CAP 1; CA 15-16;
obituary CA 125; SATA 11

Paulding, James Kirke   1778-1860. .   NCLC 2
See also DLB 3, 59, 74

Paulin, Tom   1949- . . . .   CLC 37
See also CA 123; DLB 40

Paustovsky, Konstantin (Georgievich)
1892-1968 . . . .   CLC 40
See also CA 93-96; obituary CA 25-28R

Paustowsky, Konstantin (Georgievich)
1892-1968
See Paustovsky, Konstantin (Georgievich)

Pavese, Cesare   1908-1950 . . . .   TCLC 3
See also CA 104

Pavic, Milorad   1929- . . . .   CLC 60

Payne, Alan   1932-
See Jakes, John (William)

Paz, Octavio
1914- . . . . .   CLC 3, 4, 6, 10, 19, 51; PC 1
See also CA 73-76

Peacock, Molly   1947-. . . . .   CLC 60
See also CA 103

Peacock, Thomas Love
1785-1886 . . . .   NCLC 22

Peake, Mervyn   1911-1968. . . . . . .   CLC 7, 54
See also CANR 3; CA 5-8R;
obituary CA 25-28R; SATA 23; DLB 15

Pearce, (Ann) Philippa   1920-. . . . . . .   CLC 21
See also Christie, (Ann) Philippa
See also CLR 9; CA 5-8R; SATA 1

Pearl, Eric   1934-
See Elman, Richard

Pearson, T(homas) R(eid)   1956- . . . .   CLC 39
See also CA 120

Peck, John   1941- . . . .   CLC 3
See also CANR 3; CA 49-52

Peck, Richard   1934-. . . . .   CLC 21
See also CLR 15; CANR 19; CA 85-88;
SAAS 2; SATA 18

Peck, Robert Newton   1928-. . . . . . .   CLC 17
See also CA 81-84; SAAS 1; SATA 21

Peckinpah, (David) Sam(uel)
1925-1984 . . . .   CLC 20
See also CA 109; obituary CA 114

Pedersen, Knut   1859-1952
See Hamsun, Knut
See also CA 104, 109

Peguy, Charles (Pierre)
1873-1914 . . . .   TCLC 10
See also CA 107

Pepys, Samuel   1633-1703. . . . .   LC 11

Percy, Walker
1916-. . . . .   CLC 2, 3, 6, 8, 14, 18, 47
See also CANR 1; CA 1-4R; DLB 2;
DLB-Y 80

Perec, Georges   1936-1982 . . . .   CLC 56

Pereda, Jose Maria de
1833-1906 . . . .   TCLC 16

Perelman, S(idney) J(oseph)
1904-1979 . . .   CLC 3, 5, 9, 15, 23, 44, 49
See also CANR 18; CA 73-76;
obituary CA 89-92; DLB 11, 44

Peret, Benjamin   1899-1959 . . . .   TCLC 20
See also CA 117

Peretz, Isaac Leib   1852?-1915. . . . .   TCLC 16
See also CA 109

Perez, Galdos Benito 1853-1920 . . . **TCLC 27**
See also CA 125

Perrault, Charles 1628-1703 . . . . **LC 2**
See also SATA 25

Perse, St.-John 1887-1975 . . . . **CLC 4, 11, 46**
See also Leger, (Marie-Rene) Alexis
Saint-Leger

Pesetsky, Bette 1932- . . . . **CLC 28**

Peshkov, Alexei Maximovich 1868-1936
See Gorky, Maxim
See also CA 105

Pessoa, Fernando (Antonio Nogueira)
1888-1935 . . . . **TCLC 27**
See also CA 125

Peterkin, Julia (Mood) 1880-1961 . . . **CLC 31**
See also CA 102; DLB 9

Peters, Joan K. 1945- . . . . **CLC 39**

Peters, Robert L(ouis) 1924- . . . . **CLC 7**
See also CA 13-16R

Petofi, Sandor 1823-1849 . . . . **NCLC 21**

Petrakis, Harry Mark 1923- . . . . **CLC 3**
See also CANR 4; CA 9-12R

Petrov, Evgeny 1902-1942 . . . . **TCLC 21**

Petry, Ann (Lane) 1908- . . . . . . **CLC 1, 7, 18**
See also CLR 12; CAAS 6; CANR 4;
CA 5-8R; SATA 5

Petursson, Halligrimur 1614-1674 . . . . **LC 8**

Philipson, Morris (H.) 1926- . . . . **CLC 53**
See also CANR 4; CA 1-4R

Phillips, Jayne Anne 1952- . . . . . **CLC 15, 33**
See also CANR 24; CA 101; DLB-Y 80

Phillips, Robert (Schaeffer) 1938- . . . **CLC 28**
See also CANR 8; CA 17-20R

Pica, Peter 1925-
See Aldiss, Brian W(ilson)

Piccolo, Lucio 1901-1969 . . . . **CLC 13**
See also CA 97-100

Pickthall, Marjorie (Lowry Christie)
1883-1922 . . . . **TCLC 21**
See also CA 107

Pico della Mirandola, Giovanni
1463-1494 . . . . **LC 15**

Piercy, Marge
1936- . . . . **CLC 3, 6, 14, 18, 27, 62**
See also CAAS 1; CANR 13; CA 21-24R

Pilnyak, Boris 1894-1937? . . . . **TCLC 23**

Pincherle, Alberto 1907-
See Moravia, Alberto
See also CA 25-28R

Pineda, Cecile 1942- . . . . **CLC 39**
See also CA 118

Pinero, Miguel (Gomez)
1946-1988 . . . . **CLC 4, 55**
See also CA 61-64; obituary CA 125

Pinero, Sir Arthur Wing
1855-1934 . . . . **TCLC 32**
See also CA 110; DLB 10

Pinget, Robert 1919- . . . . . **CLC 7, 13, 37**
See also CA 85-88

Pink Floyd . . . . **CLC 35**

Pinkwater, D(aniel) M(anus)
1941- . . . . **CLC 35**
See also Pinkwater, Manus
See also CLR 4; CANR 12; CA 29-32R;
SAAS 3; SATA 46

Pinkwater, Manus 1941-
See Pinkwater, D(aniel) M(anus)
See also SATA 8

Pinsky, Robert 1940- . . . . **CLC 9, 19, 38**
See also CAAS 4; CA 29-32R; DLB-Y 82

Pinter, Harold
1930- . . . . . **CLC 1, 3, 6, 9, 11, 15, 27, 58**
See also CA 5-8R; DLB 13

Pirandello, Luigi 1867-1936 . . . . . **TCLC 4, 29**
See also CA 104

Pirsig, Robert M(aynard) 1928- . . . **CLC 4, 6**
See also CA 53-56; SATA 39

Pisarev, Dmitry Ivanovich
1840-1868 . . . . **NCLC 25**

Pix, Mary (Griffith) 1666-1709 . . . . . . **LC 8**

Plaidy, Jean 1906-
See Hibbert, Eleanor (Burford)

Plant, Robert 1948- . . . . **CLC 12**

Plante, David (Robert)
1940- . . . . **CLC 7, 23, 38**
See also CANR 12; CA 37-40R; DLB-Y 83

Plath, Sylvia
1932-1963 . . . . **CLC 1, 2, 3, 5, 9, 11, 14,
17, 50, 51, 62; PC 1**
See also CAP 2; CA 19-20; DLB 5, 6;
CDALB 1941-1968

Platonov, Andrei (Platonovich)
1899-1951 . . . . **TCLC 14**
See also Klimentov, Andrei Platonovich
See also CA 108

Platt, Kin 1911- . . . . **CLC 26**
See also CANR 11; CA 17-20R; SATA 21

Plimpton, George (Ames) 1927- . . . . . **CLC 36**
See also CA 21-24R; SATA 10

Plomer, William (Charles Franklin)
1903-1973 . . . . **CLC 4, 8**
See also CAP 2; CA 21-22; SATA 24;
DLB 20

Plumly, Stanley (Ross) 1939- . . . . . . **CLC 33**
See also CA 108, 110; DLB 5

Poe, Edgar Allan
1809-1849 . . . **NCLC 1, 16; PC 1; SSC 1**
See also SATA 23; DLB 3, 59, 73, 74;
CDALB 1640-1865

Pohl, Frederik 1919- . . . . **CLC 18**
See also CAAS 1; CANR 11; CA 61-64;
SATA 24; DLB 8

Poirier, Louis 1910-
See Gracq, Julien
See also CA 122, 126

Poitier, Sidney 1924?- . . . . **CLC 26**
See also CA 117

Polanski, Roman 1933- . . . . **CLC 16**
See also CA 77-80

Poliakoff, Stephen 1952- . . . . **CLC 38**
See also CA 106; DLB 13

Police, The . . . . **CLC 26**

Pollitt, Katha 1949- . . . . **CLC 28**
See also CA 120, 122

Pollock, Sharon 19??- . . . . **CLC 50**

Pomerance, Bernard 1940- . . . . **CLC 13**
See also CA 101

Ponge, Francis (Jean Gaston Alfred)
1899- . . . . **CLC 6, 18**
See also CA 85-88

Pontoppidan, Henrik 1857-1943 . . . **TCLC 29**
See also obituary CA 126

Poole, Josephine 1933- . . . . **CLC 17**
See also CANR 10; CA 21-24R; SAAS 2;
SATA 5

Popa, Vasko 1922- . . . . **CLC 19**
See also CA 112

Pope, Alexander 1688-1744 . . . . **LC 3**

Porter, Gene Stratton 1863-1924 . . **TCLC 21**
See also CA 112

Porter, Katherine Anne
1890-1980 . . . . . **CLC 1, 3, 7, 10, 13, 15,
27; SSC 4**
See also CANR 1; CA 1-4R;
obituary CA 101; obituary SATA 23, 39;
DLB 4, 9; DLB-Y 80

Porter, Peter (Neville Frederick)
1929- . . . . **CLC 5, 13, 33**
See also CA 85-88; DLB 40

Porter, William Sydney 1862-1910
See Henry, O.
See also YABC 2; CA 104; DLB 12;
CDALB 1865-1917

Post, Melville D. 1871-1930 . . . . . . **TCLC 39**
See also brief entry CA 110

Potok, Chaim 1929- . . . . **CLC 2, 7, 14, 26**
See also CANR 19; CA 17-20R; SATA 33;
DLB 28

Potter, Dennis (Christopher George)
1935- . . . . **CLC 58**
See also CA 107

Pound, Ezra (Loomis)
1885-1972 . . . . . **CLC 1, 2, 3, 4, 5, 7, 10,
13, 18, 34, 48, 50**
See also CA 5-8R; obituary CA 37-40R;
DLB 4, 45, 63

Povod, Reinaldo 1959- . . . . **CLC 44**

Powell, Anthony (Dymoke)
1905- . . . . **CLC 1, 3, 7, 9, 10, 31**
See also CANR 1; CA 1-4R; DLB 15

Powell, Padgett 1952- . . . . **CLC 34**
See also CA 126

Powers, J(ames) F(arl)
1917- . . . . **CLC 1, 4, 8, 57; SSC 4**
See also CANR 2; CA 1-4R

Pownall, David 1938- . . . . **CLC 10**
See also CA 89-92; DLB 14

Powys, John Cowper
1872-1963 . . . . **CLC 7, 9, 15, 46**
See also CA 85-88; DLB 15

Powys, T(heodore) F(rancis)
1875-1953 . . . . **TCLC 9**
See also CA 106; DLB 36

Prager, Emily 1952- . . . . **CLC 56**

Pratt, E(dwin) J(ohn) 1883-1964 . . . . **CLC 19**
See also obituary CA 93-96

Premchand 1880-1936 . . . . **TCLC 21**

Author Index

Author Index

Stephens, James 1882?-1950 . . . . TCLC 4
See also CA 104; DLB 19

Stephens, Reed
See Donaldson, Stephen R.

Steptoe, Lydia 1892-1982
See Barnes, Djuna

Sterling, George 1869-1926 . . . . . . TCLC 20
See also CA 117; DLB 54

Stern, Gerald 1925- . . . . CLC 40
See also CA 81-84

Stern, Richard G(ustave) 1928- . . . CLC 4, 39
See also CANR 1, 25; CA 1-4R

Sternberg, Jonas 1894-1969
See Sternberg, Josef von

Sternberg, Josef von 1894-1969. . . . . CLC 20
See also CA 81-84

Sterne, Laurence 1713-1768. . . . . LC 2
See also DLB 39

Sternheim, (William Adolf) Carl
1878-1942 . . . . TCLC 8
See also CA 105

Stevens, Mark 19??- . . . . CLC 34

Stevens, Wallace 1879-1955. . . . . TCLC 3, 12
See also CA 104, 124; DLB 54

Stevenson, Anne (Katharine)
1933- . . . . CLC 7, 33
See Elvin, Anne Katharine Stevenson
See also CANR 9; CA 17-18R; DLB 40

Stevenson, Robert Louis
1850-1894 . . . . NCLC 5, 14
See also CLR 10, 11; YABC 2; DLB 18, 57

Stewart, J(ohn) I(nnes) M(ackintosh)
1906- . . . . CLC 7, 14, 32
See also CAAS 3; CA 85-88

Stewart, Mary (Florence Elinor)
1916- . . . . CLC 7, 35
See also CANR 1; CA 1-4R; SATA 12

Stewart, Will 1908-
See Williamson, Jack
See also CANR 23; CA 17-18R

Still, James 1906- . . . . CLC 49
See also CANR 10; CA 65-68; SATA 29;
DLB 9

Sting 1951-
See The Police

Stitt, Milan 1941- . . . . CLC 29
See also CA 69-72

Stoker, Abraham
See Stoker, Bram
See also CA 105

Stoker, Bram 1847-1912 . . . . TCLC 8
See also Stoker, Abraham
See also SATA 29; DLB 36, 70

Stolz, Mary (Slattery) 1920- . . . . CLC 12
See also CANR 13; CA 5-8R; SAAS 3;
SATA 10

Stone, Irving 1903-1989. . . . . CLC 7
See also CAAS 3; CANR 1; CA 1-4R;
SATA 3

Stone, Robert (Anthony)
1937?- . . . . CLC 5, 23, 42
See also CANR 23; CA 85-88

Stoppard, Tom
1937- . . . CLC 1, 3, 4, 5, 8, 15, 29, 34, 63
See also CA 81-84; DLB 13; DLB-Y 85

Storey, David (Malcolm)
1933- . . . . CLC 2, 4, 5, 8
See also CA 81-84; DLB 13, 14

Storm, Hyemeyohsts 1935- . . . . CLC 3
See also CA 81-84

Storm, (Hans) Theodor (Woldsen)
1817-1888 . . . . NCLC 1

Storni, Alfonsina 1892-1938 . . . . . . TCLC 5
See also CA 104

Stout, Rex (Todhunter) 1886-1975 . . . CLC 3
See also CA 61-64

Stow, (Julian) Randolph 1935- . . CLC 23, 48
See also CA 13-16R

Stowe, Harriet (Elizabeth) Beecher
1811-1896 . . . . NCLC 3
See also YABC 1; DLB 1, 12, 42;
CDALB 1865-1917

Strachey, (Giles) Lytton
1880-1932 . . . . TCLC 12
See also CA 110

Strand, Mark 1934- . . . . CLC 6, 18, 41
See also CA 21-24R; SATA 41; DLB 5

Straub, Peter (Francis) 1943- . . . . . . CLC 28
See also CA 85-88; DLB-Y 84

Strauss, Botho 1944- . . . . CLC 22

Straussler, Tomas 1937-
See Stoppard, Tom

Streatfeild, (Mary) Noel 1897- . . . . . CLC 21
See also CA 81-84; obituary CA 120;
SATA 20, 48

Stribling, T(homas) S(igismund)
1881-1965 . . . . CLC 23
See also obituary CA 107; DLB 9

Strindberg, (Johan) August
1849-1912 . . . . TCLC 1, 8, 21
See also CA 104

Stringer, Arthur 1874-1950 . . . . . . TCLC 37
See also DLB 92

Strugatskii, Arkadii (Natanovich)
1925- . . . . CLC 27
See also CA 106

Strugatskii, Boris (Natanovich)
1933- . . . . CLC 27
See also CA 106

Strummer, Joe 1953?-
See The Clash

Stuart, (Hilton) Jesse
1906-1984 . . . . CLC 1, 8, 11, 14, 34
See also CA 5-8R; obituary CA 112;
SATA 2; obituary SATA 36; DLB 9, 48;
DLB-Y 84

Sturgeon, Theodore (Hamilton)
1918-1985 . . . . CLC 22, 39
See also CA 81-84; obituary CA 116;
DLB 8; DLB-Y 85

Styron, William
1925- . . . . CLC 1, 3, 5, 11, 15, 60
See also CANR 6; CA 5-8R; DLB 2;
DLB-Y 80; CDALB 1968-1987

Sudermann, Hermann 1857-1928 . . TCLC 15
See also CA 107

Sue, Eugene 1804-1857 . . . . NCLC 1

Sukenick, Ronald 1932- . . . . . CLC 3, 4, 6, 48
See also CA 25-28R; DLB-Y 81

Suknaski, Andrew 1942- . . . . CLC 19
See also CA 101; DLB 53

Sully Prudhomme, Rene
1839-1907 . . . . TCLC 31

Su Man-shu 1884-1918. . . . . TCLC 24
See also CA 123

Summers, Andrew James 1942-
See The Police

Summers, Andy 1942-
See The Police

Summers, Hollis (Spurgeon, Jr.)
1916- . . . . CLC 10
See also CANR 3; CA 5-8R; DLB 6

Summers, (Alphonsus Joseph-Mary Augustus)
Montague 1880-1948 . . . . TCLC 16
See also CA 118

Sumner, Gordon Matthew 1951-
See The Police

Surtees, Robert Smith
1805-1864 . . . . NCLC 14
See also DLB 21

Susann, Jacqueline 1921-1974 . . . . . . CLC 3
See also CA 65-68; obituary CA 53-56

Suskind, Patrick 1949- . . . . CLC 44

Sutcliff, Rosemary 1920- . . . . CLC 26
See also CLR 1; CA 5-8R; SATA 6, 44

Sutro, Alfred 1863-1933. . . . . TCLC 6
See also CA 105; DLB 10

Sutton, Henry 1935-
See Slavitt, David (R.)

Svevo, Italo 1861-1928. . . . . TCLC 2, 35
See also Schmitz, Ettore

Swados, Elizabeth 1951- . . . . CLC 12
See also CA 97-100

Swados, Harvey 1920-1972 . . . . CLC 5
See also CANR 6; CA 5-8R;
obituary CA 37-40R; DLB 2

Swarthout, Glendon (Fred) 1918- . . . CLC 35
See also CANR 1; CA 1-4R; SATA 26

Swenson, May 1919-1989. . . . . CLC 4, 14, 61
See also CA 5-8R; SATA 15; DLB 5

Swift, Graham 1949- . . . . CLC 41
See also CA 117, 122

Swift, Jonathan 1667-1745. . . . . LC 1
See also SATA 19; DLB 39

Swinburne, Algernon Charles
1837-1909 . . . . TCLC 8, 36
See also CA 105; DLB 35, 57

Swinfen, Ann 19??- . . . . CLC 34

Swinnerton, Frank (Arthur)
1884-1982 . . . . CLC 31
See also obituary CA 108; DLB 34

Symons, Arthur (William)
1865-1945 . . . . TCLC 11
See also CA 107; DLB 19, 57

Symons, Julian (Gustave)
1912- . . . . CLC 2, 14, 32
See also CAAS 3; CANR 3; CA 49-52

Van Doren, Mark 1894-1972..... **CLC 6, 10**
See also CANR 3; CA 1-4R;
obituary CA 37-40R; DLB 45

Van Druten, John (William)
1901-1957 .... **TCLC 2**
See also CA 104; DLB 10

Van Duyn, Mona 1921-...... **CLC 3, 7, 63**
See also CANR 7; CA 9-12R; DLB 5

Van Itallie, Jean-Claude 1936-...... **CLC 3**
See also CAAS 2; CANR 1; CA 45-48;
DLB 7

Van Ostaijen, Paul 1896-1928..... **TCLC 33**

Van Peebles, Melvin 1932-...... **CLC 2, 20**
See also CA 85-88

Vansittart, Peter 1920-........... **CLC 42**
See also CANR 3; CA 1-4R

Van Vechten, Carl 1880-1964 ...... **CLC 33**
See also obituary CA 89-92; DLB 4, 9, 51

Van Vogt, A(lfred) E(lton) 1912-..... **CLC 1**
See also CA 21-24R; SATA 14; DLB 8

Varda, Agnes 1928-.............. **CLC 16**
See also CA 116, 122

Vargas Llosa, (Jorge) Mario (Pedro)
1936-........ **CLC 3, 6, 9, 10, 15, 31, 42**
See also CANR 18; CA 73-76

Vassilikos, Vassilis 1933-........... **CLC 4, 8**
See also CA 81-84

Vaughn, Stephanie 19??- .... **CLC 62**

Vazov, Ivan 1850-1921........... **TCLC 25**
See also CA 121

Veblen, Thorstein Bunde
1857-1929 .... **TCLC 31**
See also CA 115

Verga, Giovanni 1840-1922 .... **TCLC 3**
See also CA 104, 123

Verhaeren, Emile (Adolphe Gustave)
1855-1916 .... **TCLC 12**
See also CA 109

Verlaine, Paul (Marie)
1844-1896 .... **NCLC 2; PC 2**

Verne, Jules (Gabriel) 1828-1905 ... **TCLC 6**
See also CA 110; SATA 21

Very, Jones 1813-1880........... **NCLC 9**
See also DLB 1

Vesaas, Tarjei 1897-1970......... **CLC 48**
See also obituary CA 29-32R

Vian, Boris 1920-1959......... **TCLC 9**
See also CA 106; DLB 72

Viaud, (Louis Marie) Julien 1850-1923
See Loti, Pierre
See also CA 107

Vicker, Angus 1916-
See Felsen, Henry Gregor

Vidal, Eugene Luther, Jr. 1925-
See Vidal, Gore

Vidal, Gore
1925-........ **CLC 2, 4, 6, 8, 10, 22, 33**
See also CANR 13; CA 5-8R; DLB 6

Viereck, Peter (Robert Edwin)
1916-........................ **CLC 4**
See also CANR 1; CA 1-4R; DLB 5

Vigny, Alfred (Victor) de
1797-1863 .... **NCLC 7**

Vilakazi, Benedict Wallet
1905-1947 .... **TCLC 37**

Villiers de l'Isle Adam, Jean Marie Mathias
Philippe Auguste, Comte de,
1838-1889 .... **NCLC 3**

Vinci, Leonardo da 1452-1519...... **LC 12**

Vine, Barbara 1930-............. **CLC 50**
See also Rendell, Ruth

Vinge, Joan (Carol) D(ennison)
1948-...................... **CLC 30**
See also CA 93-96; SATA 36

Visconti, Luchino 1906-1976....... **CLC 16**
See also CA 81-84; obituary CA 65-68

Vittorini, Elio 1908-1966...... **CLC 6, 9, 14**
See also obituary CA 25-28R

Vizinczey, Stephen 1933-.......... **CLC 40**

Vliet, R(ussell) G(ordon)
1929-1984 .... **CLC 22**
See also CANR 18; CA 37-40R;
obituary CA 112

Voight, Ellen Bryant 1943-........ **CLC 54**
See also CANR 11; CA 69-72

Voigt, Cynthia 1942-............. **CLC 30**
See also CANR 18; CA 106; SATA 33, 48

Voinovich, Vladimir (Nikolaevich)
1932-.................... **CLC 10, 49**
See also CA 81-84

Voltaire 1694-1778............... **LC 14**

Von Daeniken, Erich 1935-
See Von Daniken, Erich
See also CANR 17; CA 37-40R

Von Daniken, Erich 1935-........ **CLC 30**
See also Von Daeniken, Erich

Vonnegut, Kurt, Jr.
1922-...... **CLC 1, 2, 3, 4, 5, 8, 12, 22,**
40, 60
See also CANR 1; CA 1-4R; DLB 2, 8;
DLB-Y 80; DLB-DS 3;
CDALB 1968-1987

Vorster, Gordon 1924-............ **CLC 34**

Voznesensky, Andrei 1933-... **CLC 1, 15, 57**
See also CA 89-92

Waddington, Miriam 1917-........ **CLC 28**
See also CANR 12; CA 21-24R

Wagman, Fredrica 1937-........... **CLC 7**
See also CA 97-100

Wagner, Richard 1813-1883....... **NCLC 9**

Wagner-Martin, Linda 1936-....... **CLC 50**

Wagoner, David (Russell)
1926-.................... **CLC 3, 5, 15**
See also CAAS 3; CANR 2; CA 1-4R;
SATA 14; DLB 5

Wah, Fred(erick James) 1939-..... **CLC 44**
See also CA 107; DLB 60

Wahloo, Per 1926-1975 .... **CLC 7**
See also CA 61-64

Wahloo, Peter 1926-1975
See Wahloo, Per

Wain, John (Barrington)
1925-.............. **CLC 2, 11, 15, 46**
See also CAAS 4; CANR 23; CA 5-8R;
DLB 15, 27

Wajda, Andrzej 1926-............. **CLC 16**
See also CA 102

Wakefield, Dan 1932-............. **CLC 7**
See also CAAS 7; CA 21-24R

Wakoski, Diane
1937-........ **CLC 2, 4, 7, 9, 11, 40**
See also CAAS 1; CANR 9; CA 13-16R;
DLB 5

Walcott, Derek (Alton)
1930-.......... **CLC 2, 4, 9, 14, 25, 42**
See also CANR 26; CA 89-92; DLB-Y 81

Waldman, Anne 1945-............. **CLC 7**
See also CA 37-40R; DLB 16

Waldo, Edward Hamilton 1918-
See Sturgeon, Theodore (Hamilton)

Walker, Alice
1944-...... **CLC 5, 6, 9, 19, 27, 46, 58;**
SSC 5
See also CANR 9, 27; CA 37-40R;
SATA 31; DLB 6, 33; CDALB 1968-1988

Walker, David Harry 1911-........ **CLC 14**
See also CANR 1; CA 1-4R; SATA 8

Walker, Edward Joseph 1934-
See Walker, Ted
See also CANR 12; CA 21-24R

Walker, George F. 1947-....... **CLC 44, 61**
See also CANR 21; CA 103; DLB 60

Walker, Joseph A. 1935-.......... **CLC 19**
See also CANR 26; CA 89-92; DLB 38

Walker, Margaret (Abigail)
1915-.................... **CLC 1, 6**
See also CANR 26; CA 73-76; DLB 76

Walker, Ted 1934-............... **CLC 13**
See also Walker, Edward Joseph
See also DLB 40

Wallace, David Foster 1962-....... **CLC 50**

Wallace, Irving 1916-........... **CLC 7, 13**
See also CAAS 1; CANR 1; CA 1-4R

Wallant, Edward Lewis
1926-1962 .... **CLC 5, 10**
See also CANR 22; CA 1-4R; DLB 2, 28

Walpole, Horace 1717-1797......... **LC 2**
See also DLB 39

Walpole, (Sir) Hugh (Seymour)
1884-1941 .... **TCLC 5**
See also CA 104; DLB 34

Walser, Martin 1927-............. **CLC 27**
See also CANR 8; CA 57-60; DLB 75

Walser, Robert 1878-1956........ **TCLC 18**
See also CA 118; DLB 66

Walsh, Gillian Paton 1939-
See Walsh, Jill Paton
See also CA 37-40R; SATA 4

Walsh, Jill Paton 1939-........... **CLC 35**
See also CLR 2; SAAS 3

Wambaugh, Joseph (Aloysius, Jr.)
1937-.................... **CLC 3, 18**
See also CA 33-36R; DLB 6; DLB-Y 83

Ward, Arthur Henry Sarsfield 1883-1959
See Rohmer, Sax
See also CA 108

Ward, Douglas Turner 1930-....... **CLC 19**
See also CA 81-84; DLB 7, 38

Warhol, Andy 1928-1987 . . . . **CLC 20**
See also CA 89-92; obituary CA 121

Warner, Francis (Robert le Plastrier)
1937- . . . . **CLC 14**
See also CANR 11; CA 53-56

Warner, Marina 1946- . . . . **CLC 59**
See also CANR 21; CA 65-68

Warner, Rex (Ernest) 1905-1986 . . . . **CLC 45**
See also CA 89-92; obituary CA 119;
DLB 15

Warner, Sylvia Townsend
1893-1978 . . . . **CLC 7, 19**
See also CANR 16; CA 61-64;
obituary CA 77-80; DLB 34

Warren, Mercy Otis 1728-1814 . . . **NCLC 13**
See also DLB 31

Warren, Robert Penn
1905-1989 . . . **CLC 1, 4, 6, 8, 10, 13, 18,**
39, 53, 59; SSC 4
See also CANR 10; CA 13-16R. 129. 130;
SATA 46; DLB 2, 48; DLB-Y 80;
CDALB 1968-1987

Warton, Thomas 1728-1790 . . . . **LC 15**

Washington, Booker T(aliaferro)
1856-1915 . . . . **TCLC 10**
See also CA 114, 125; SATA 28

Wassermann, Jakob 1873-1934 . . . . . **TCLC 6**
See also CA 104; DLB 66

Wasserstein, Wendy 1950- . . . . . . **CLC 32, 59**
See also CA 121; CABS 3

Waterhouse, Keith (Spencer)
1929- . . . . **CLC 47**
See also CA 5-8R; DLB 13, 15

Waters, Roger 1944-
See Pink Floyd

Wa Thiong'o, Ngugi
1938- . . . . **CLC 3, 7, 13, 36**
See also Ngugi, James (Thiong'o); Ngugi wa
Thiong'o

Watkins, Paul 1964- . . . . **CLC 55**

Watkins, Vernon (Phillips)
1906-1967 . . . . **CLC 43**
See also CAP 1; CA 9-10;
obituary CA 25-28R; DLB 20

Waugh, Auberon (Alexander) 1939- . . **CLC 7**
See also CANR 6, 22; CA 45-48; DLB 14

Waugh, Evelyn (Arthur St. John)
1903-1966 . . . **CLC 1, 3, 8, 13, 19, 27, 44**
See also CANR 22; CA 85-88;
obituary CA 25-28R; DLB 15

Waugh, Harriet 1944- . . . . **CLC 6**
See also CANR 22; CA 85-88

Webb, Beatrice (Potter)
1858-1943 . . . . **TCLC 22**
See also CA 117

Webb, Charles (Richard) 1939- . . . . . . **CLC 7**
See also CA 25-28R

Webb, James H(enry), Jr. 1946- . . . . **CLC 22**
See also CA 81-84

Webb, Mary (Gladys Meredith)
1881-1927 . . . . **TCLC 24**
See also CA 123; DLB 34

Webb, Phyllis 1927- . . . . **CLC 18**
See also CANR 23; CA 104; DLB 53

Webb, Sidney (James)
1859-1947 . . . . **TCLC 22**
See also CA 117

Webber, Andrew Lloyd 1948- . . . . . . **CLC 21**

Weber, Lenora Mattingly
1895-1971 . . . . **CLC 12**
See also CAP 1; CA 19-20;
obituary CA 29-32R; SATA 2;
obituary SATA 26

Webster, Noah 1758-1843 . . . . **NCLC 30**
See also DLB 1, 37, 42, 43, 73

Wedekind, (Benjamin) Frank(lin)
1864-1918 . . . . **TCLC 7**
See also CA 104

Weidman, Jerome 1913- . . . . **CLC 7**
See also CANR 1; CA 1-4R; DLB 28

Weil, Simone 1909-1943 . . . . **TCLC 23**
See also CA 117

Weinstein, Nathan Wallenstein 1903?-1940
See West, Nathanael
See also CA 104

Weir, Peter 1944- . . . . **CLC 20**
See also CA 113, 123

Weiss, Peter (Ulrich)
1916-1982 . . . . **CLC 3, 15, 51**
See also CANR 3; CA 45-48;
obituary CA 106; DLB 69

Weiss, Theodore (Russell)
1916- . . . . **CLC 3, 8, 14**
See also CAAS 2; CA 9-12R; DLB 5

Welch, (Maurice) Denton
1915-1948 . . . . **TCLC 22**
See also CA 121

Welch, James 1940- . . . . **CLC 6, 14, 52**
See also CA 85-88

Weldon, Fay
1933- . . . . **CLC 6, 9, 11, 19, 36, 59**
See also CANR 16; CA 21-24R; DLB 14

Wellek, Rene 1903- . . . . **CLC 28**
See also CAAS 7; CANR 8; CA 5-8R;
DLB 63

Weller, Michael 1942- . . . . **CLC 10, 53**
See also CA 85-88

Weller, Paul 1958- . . . . **CLC 26**

Wellershoff, Dieter 1925- . . . . **CLC 46**
See also CANR 16; CA 89-92

Welles, (George) Orson
1915-1985 . . . . **CLC 20**
See also CA 93-96; obituary CA 117

Wellman, Manly Wade 1903-1986 . . **CLC 49**
See also CANR 6, 16; CA 1-4R;
obituary CA 118; SATA 6, 47

Wells, Carolyn 1862-1942 . . . . **TCLC 35**
See also CA 113; DLB 11

Wells, H(erbert) G(eorge)
1866-1946 . . . . . . **TCLC 6, 12, 19; SSC 6**
See also CA 110, 121; SATA 20; DLB 34,
70

Wells, Rosemary 1943- . . . . **CLC 12**
See also CLR 16; CA 85-88; SAAS 1;
SATA 18

Welty, Eudora (Alice)
1909- . . . . **CLC 1, 2, 5, 14, 22, 33; SSC 1**
See also CA 9-12R; CABS 1; DLB 2;
DLB-Y 87; CDALB 1941-1968

Wen I-to 1899-1946 . . . . **TCLC 28**

Werfel, Franz (V.) 1890-1945 . . . . . . **TCLC 8**
See also CA 104

Wergeland, Henrik Arnold
1808-1845 . . . . **NCLC 5**

Wersba, Barbara 1932- . . . . **CLC 30**
See also CLR 3; CANR 16; CA 29-32R;
SAAS 2; SATA 1; DLB 52

Wertmuller, Lina 1928- . . . . **CLC 16**
See also CA 97-100

Wescott, Glenway 1901-1987 . . . . **CLC 13**
See also CANR 23; CA 13-16R;
obituary CA 121; DLB 4, 9

Wesker, Arnold 1932- . . . . **CLC 3, 5, 42**
See also CAAS 7; CANR 1; CA 1-4R;
DLB 13

Wesley, Richard (Errol) 1945- . . . . **CLC 7**
See also CA 57-60; DLB 38

Wessel, Johan Herman 1742-1785 . . . . **LC 7**

West, Anthony (Panther)
1914-1987 . . . . **CLC 50**
See also CANR 3, 19; CA 45-48; DLB 15

West, Jessamyn 1907-1984 . . . . . . **CLC 7, 17**
See also CA 9-12R; obituary CA 112;
obituary SATA 37; DLB 6; DLB-Y 84

West, Morris L(anglo) 1916- . . . . . **CLC 6, 33**
See also CA 5-8R; obituary CA 124

West, Nathanael 1903?-1940 . . . . **TCLC 1, 14**
See also Weinstein, Nathan Wallenstein
See also CA 125; DLB 4, 9, 28

West, Paul 1930- . . . . **CLC 7, 14**
See also CAAS 7; CANR 22; CA 13-16R;
DLB 14

West, Rebecca 1892-1983 . . **CLC 7, 9, 31, 50**
See also CANR 19; CA 5-8R;
obituary CA 109; DLB 36; DLB-Y 83

Westall, Robert (Atkinson) 1929- . . . **CLC 17**
See also CLR 13; CANR 18; CA 69-72;
SAAS 2; SATA 23

Westlake, Donald E(dwin)
1933- . . . . **CLC 7, 33**
See also CANR 16; CA 17-20R

Westmacott, Mary 1890-1976
See Christie, (Dame) Agatha (Mary
Clarissa)

Whalen, Philip 1923- . . . . **CLC 6, 29**
See also CANR 5; CA 9-12R; DLB 16

Wharton, Edith (Newbold Jones)
1862-1937 . . . . **TCLC 3, 9, 27; SSC 6**
See also CA 104; DLB 4, 9, 12, 78;
CDALB 1865-1917

Wharton, William 1925- . . . . **CLC 18, 37**
See also CA 93-96; DLB-Y 80

Wheatley (Peters), Phillis
1753?-1784 . . . . **LC 3**
See also DLB 31, 50; CDALB 1640-1865

Wheelock, John Hall 1886-1978 . . . . **CLC 14**
See also CANR 14; CA 13-16R;
obituary CA 77-80; DLB 45

Whelan, John 1900-
See O'Faolain, Sean

Whitaker, Rodney 1925-
See Trevanian

DC Cumulative Nationality Index

DC Cumulative Title Index